BACKCOUNTRY ADVENTURES
UTAH

Printed in Korea.

Third Printing, 2006.

Publisher's Cataloging-in-Publication
Massey, Peter, 1951-
    Backcountry adventures : Utah : the ultimate guide to
    the Utah backcountry for anyone with a sport
    utility vehicle / Peter Massey and Jeanne Wilson.
    — 2nd ed.
      p. cm.
      Includes bibliographical references and index.
      ISBN: 1-930193-27-0

    1. Automobile travel—Utah—Guidebooks.
    2. Four-wheel drive vehicles. 3. Trails—Utah—
Guidebooks. 4. Ghost towns—Utah—Guidebooks.
6. Animals—Utah—Identification. 7. Utah—Guidebooks.
I. Wilson, Jeanne, 1960- II. Title.

GV1024.M37 2002   917.9204'34
           QB102-83

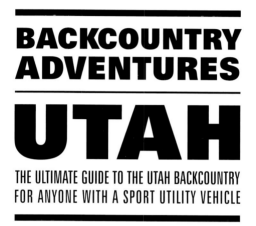

BACKCOUNTRY ADVENTURES
UTAH

THE ULTIMATE GUIDE TO THE UTAH BACKCOUNTRY
FOR ANYONE WITH A SPORT UTILITY VEHICLE

PETER MASSEY AND JEANNE WILSON

SWAGMAN
PUBLISHING

Acknowledgments

Many people and organizations have made major contributions to the research and production of this book. We owe them all special thanks for their assistance.

First, we would like to thank the following people who have played major roles in the production of this book and have been key to completing it in a timely fashion.

Senior Field Researchers:	**Donald McGann, Maggie Pinder**
Senior Researcher:	**Timothy Duggan**
Researchers:	**Scott Bloemendaal, Julie Jackson, Christopher Hall**
Editing and Proofreading:	**Jeff Campbell, Alice Levine**
Graphic Design and Maps:	**Deborah Rust**
Website Administration:	**Scott Bloemendaal**
Finance:	**Douglas Adams**
Office Administration:	**Peg Anderson**

We would also like to thank the many people at the Bureau of Land Management offices throughout Utah, who spent countless hours assisting us. In particular, we would like to thank Dennis Willis, outdoor recreational planner at the Price Field Office, Blaine Miller, archaeologist at the Price Field Office, and Jeanie Linn at the Hanksville Field Office

Staff at many offices of the National Forest Service also provided us with valuable assistance, particularly the offices in Price, Ferron, Teasdale, and Richfield.

We received a great deal of assistance from many other people and organizations. We would like to thank the Utah State Historical Society, the Denver Public Library Western History Department, Kari Murphy at the Moab to Monument Valley Film Commission, and the Moab Historical Society. Mrs. Betty Smith of Green River, Utah, was most helpful in providing information about Smith's Cabin.

The book includes over five hundred photos, and we are most thankful to the following organizations and people who have allowed us to publish so many of their wonderful photographs: Alan Barnett and Tara Thompson at the Utah State Historical Society, Jameson Weston at Utah's Hogle Zoo, Denver Botanical Gardens, Colorado Historical Society, Lori Swingle at the Denver Public Library Western History Collection, Lauren Livo and Steve Wilcox, Cornell Lab of Ornithology, the Huntington Library in San Marino, Joe Tucciarone, Doug Von Gausig, Don Baccus, Maggie Pinder, and Donald McGann. We also thank Mark Dreher at Werner's Mile High Camera in Denver for developing and transferring to Kodak PhotoDisc the thousands of photos we took while researching this book.

With a project of this size countless hours are spent researching and recording the trail information, and we would like to thank Carol and Gary Martin of the Virginian Motel in Moab for providing a base camp for our researchers and for their helpful trail suggestions.

For maintaining our vehicles, we would like to thank Dave Rager and George Nettles of Dave's European in Denver and Dave Johnson of TRI in Price.

We would also like to draw our readers' attention to the website (www.bushducks.com) of our senior researchers, the Bushducks–Donald McGann and Maggie Pinder. It provides information on current 4WD trail conditions and offers their valuable assistance to anyone who is planning a backcountry itinerary.

Publisher's Note: Every effort has been taken to ensure that the information in this book is accurate at press time. Please visit our website to advise us of any changes or corrections you find. We also welcome recommendations for new 4WD trails or other suggestions to improve the information in this book.

Adler Publishing Company, Inc.
Phone: 800-660-5107
www.4WDbooks.com

SWAGMAN
PUBLISHING

Contents

Introduction

With its spectacular variety of rugged terrain and exotic landscapes, Utah makes a more prominent spectacle of its geology than any other state in America. To the north the towering Rocky Mountains form a natural state border. Moving south across the vast Uinta Basin, you enter a world that looks peeled from the silver screen: the buttes, cliffs, canyons, contorted rock formations, sand, and sagebrush of the San Rafael Swell combine to make this the land of John Wayne Westerns. In the southeast two mighty rivers, the Green and the Colorado, have cut into the sedimentary rock laid down millions of years ago to create an endless maze of crumbling red canyons. In contrast, Utah's most famous natural feature, the Great Salt Lake, spent millions of years leveling out the miles of dead-smooth salt flats, mud flats, and wide, barren desert typical of western Utah's landscape.

Driving through Utah's thrilling backcountry, you cannot avoid thinking about the ancient Indian cultures who for thousands of years called the desert home, and of the heroic efforts of the Mormon pioneers who managed to cross and settle this vast and inhospitable land. Much of the landscape remains the same as it was in the late 19th century when riders of the Pony Express sped from station to station and daring young outlaws wreaked havoc on a multitude of newly established stage lines, railroads, and frontier towns. While early Utah settlers suffered Indian attacks, extreme weather conditions, and the scarcity of food and supplies, today all you have to do to experience Utah's remote grandeur is to pack your sport utility vehicle and head off the paved roads onto the hundreds of ancient Indian trails, old mining roads, abandoned railroad grades, superseded stagecoach networks, and stockways forged by early pioneers.

Four-wheel driving spells freedom and adventure. Yet most of the millions of four-wheel-drive (4WD) owners do not take advantage of the many opportunities their vehicles offer. If you are interested in taking your 4WD vehicle off the paved highways to explore the wilderness bypassed by main roads, then this book is for you.

We have selected 175 of the most spectacular 4WD trails that cross Utah's backcountry. All the trails are within the capabilities of stock sport utility vehicles, allowing you to escape into the remote wilderness in the same vehicle you use to drive to work or to pack the kids off to school. The trails range in difficulty from those suitable for drivers who have never been off-highway before to those that will offer a challenge to more-experienced four-wheel drivers. We have avoided the most difficult trails Utah offers—those that require modified vehicles and experts behind the wheel—so that anyone who has at least some off-highway experience can drive all of the trails in this book.

We are certain that as you head off into the backcountry you will discover the immense rewards of 4WD touring. We also hope that all our readers get the same enjoyment we have as they travel through the most scenic, awe-inspiring, and historic locations in Utah.

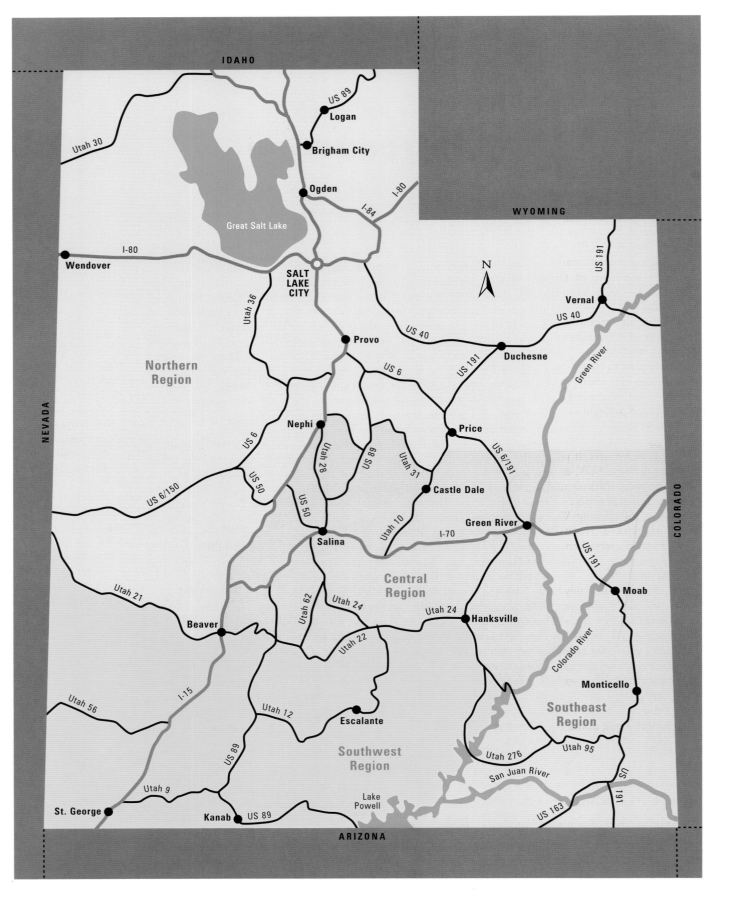

Before You Go

Why a 4WD Does It Better

The design and engineering of 4WD vehicles provide them with many advantages over normal cars when you head off the paved road:
- improved distribution of power to all four wheels;
- a transmission transfer case, which provides low-range gear selection for greater pulling power and for crawling over difficult terrain;
- high ground clearance;
- less overhang of the vehicle's body past the wheels, which provides better front- and rear-clearance when crossing gullies and ridges;
- large-lug, wide-tread tires;
- rugged construction (including underbody skid plates on many models).

If you plan to do off-highway touring, all of these considerations are important, whether you are evaluating the capabilities of your current 4WD or are looking to buy one; each is considered in detail in this chapter.

In order to explore the most difficult trails described in this book, you will need a 4WD vehicle that is well rated in each of the above features. If you own a 2WD sport utility vehicle, a lighter car-type SUV, or a pickup truck, your ability to explore the more difficult trails will depend on conditions and your level of experience.

A word of caution: Whatever type of 4WD vehicle you drive, understand that it is not invincible or indestructible. Nor can it go everywhere. A 4WD has a much higher center of gravity and weighs more than a car, and so has its own consequent limitations.

Experience is the only way to learn what your vehicle can and cannot do. Therefore, if you are inexperienced, we strongly recommend that you start with trails that have lower difficulty ratings. As you develop an understanding of your vehicle and of your own taste for adventure, you can safely tackle the more challenging trails.

One way to beef up your knowledge quickly, while avoiding the costly and sometimes dangerous lessons learned from on-the-road mistakes, is to undertake a 4WD course taught by a professional. Look in the Yellow Pages for courses in your area.

Using This Book

Route Planning

Regional maps at the beginning of each section provide a convenient overview of the trails in that portion of the state. Each 4WD trail is highlighted in color, as are major highways and towns, helping you to plan various routes by connecting a series of 4WD trails and paved roads.

As you plan your overall route, you will probably want to utilize as many 4WD trails as possible. However, check the difficulty rating and time required for each trail before finalizing your plans. You don't want to be stuck 50 miles from the highway—at sunset and without camping gear, since your trip was supposed to be over hours ago—when you discover that your vehicle can't handle a certain difficult passage.

You can calculate the distances between Utah towns by turning to the Utah Distance Chart at the end of this chapter.

Difficulty Ratings

We utilize a point system to rate the difficulty of each trail. Any such system is subjective, and your experience of the trails will vary depending on your skill and the road conditions at the time. Indeed any amount of rain may make the trails much more difficult, if not completely impassable.

We have rated the 4WD trails on a scale of 1 to 10—1 being passable for a normal passenger vehicle in good conditions and 10 requiring a heavily modified vehicle and an experienced driver who expects to encounter vehicle damage. Because this book is designed for owners of unmodified 4WD vehicles—who we assume do not want to damage their vehicles—most of the trails are rated 5 or lower. A few trails are included that rate as high as 7, while those rated 8 to 10 are beyond the scope of this book.

This is not to say that the moderate-rated trails are easy. We strongly recommend that inexperienced drivers not tackle trails rated at 4 or higher until they have undertaken a number of the lower-rated ones, so that they can gauge their skill level and prepare for the difficulty of the higher-rated trails.

In assessing the trails, we have always assumed good road conditions (dry road surface, good visibility, and so on). The factors influencing our ratings are as follows:
- obstacles such as rocks, mud, ruts, sand, slickrock, and stream crossings;
- the stability of the road surface;
- the width of the road and the vehicle clearance between trees or rocks;
- the steepness of the road;
- the margin for driver error (for example, a very high, open, shelf road would be rated more difficult even if it was not very steep and had a stable surface).

The following is a guide to the ratings.

Rating 1: The trail is graded dirt but suitable for a normal passenger vehicle. It usually has gentle grades, is fairly wide, and has very shallow water crossings (if any).

Rating 2: High-clearance vehicles are preferred, but not necessary. These trails are dirt roads, but they may have rocks, grades, water crossings, or ruts that make clearance a concern in a normal passenger vehicle. The trails are fairly wide, so that passing is possible at almost any point along the trail. Mud is not a concern under normal weather conditions.

Rating 3: High-clearance 4WDs are preferred, but any high-clearance vehicle is acceptable. Expect a rough road surface; mud and sand are possible but will be easily passable. You may encounter rocks up to 6 inches in diameter, a loose road surface, and shelf roads, though these will be wide enough for passing or will have adequate pull-offs.

Rating 4: High-clearance 4WDs are recommended, though most stock SUVs are acceptable. Expect a rough road surface with rocks larger than 6 inches, but there will be a reasonable driving line available. Patches of mud are possible but can be readily negotiated; sand may be deep and require lower tire pressures. There may be stream crossings up to 12 inches deep, substantial sections of single-lane shelf road, moderate grades, and sections of moderately loose road surface.

Rating 5: High-clearance 4WDs are required. These trails have either a rough, rutted surface, rocks up to 9 inches, mud and deep sand that may be impassable for inexperienced drivers, or stream crossings up to 18 inches deep. Certain sections may be steep enough to cause traction problems, and you may encounter very narrow shelf roads with steep drop-offs and tight clearance between rocks or trees.

Rating 6: These trails are for experienced four-wheel drivers only. They are potentially dangerous, with large rocks, ruts, or terraces that may need to be negotiated. They may also have stream crossings at least 18 inches deep, involve rapid currents, unstable stream bottoms, or difficult access; steep slopes, loose surfaces, and narrow clearances; or very narrow sections of shelf road with steep drop-offs and potentially challenging road surfaces.

Rating 7: Skilled, experienced four-wheel drivers only. These trails include very challenging sections with extremely steep grades, loose surfaces, large rocks, deep ruts, and/or tight clearances. Mud or sand may necessitate winching.

Rating 8 to 10: Stock vehicles are likely to be damaged and may find the trail impassable. Trails with these difficulty ratings are for highly skilled, experienced 4-wheel drivers only.

Scenic Ratings

If rating the degree of difficulty is subjective, rating scenic beauty is guaranteed to lead to arguments. Utah contains a spectacular variety of scenery— from its grand canyons and towering mountains and buttes to its seemingly endless desert country. We love the wide-open remoteness of many areas of Utah, but realize they are not to everyone's liking. Nonetheless, we have tried to provide some guide to the relative scenic quality of the various trails. The ratings are based on a scale of 1 to 10, with 10 being the most attractive.

Remoteness Ratings

Many trails in Utah are in remote country; sometimes the trails are seldom traveled, and the likelihood is low that another vehicle will appear within a reasonable time to assist you if you get stuck or break down. We have included a ranking

for remoteness of +0 through +2. Extreme summer temperatures can make a breakdown in the more remote areas a life-threatening experience. Prepare carefully before tackling the higher-rated, more remote trails (see "Special Preparations for Remote Travel," page 6). For trails with a high remoteness rating, consider traveling with a second vehicle.

Estimated Driving Times

In calculating driving times, we have not allowed for stops. Your actual driving time may be considerably longer depending on the number and duration of the stops you make. Add more time if you prefer to drive more slowly than good conditions allow.

Current Road Information

All the 4WD trails described in this book may become impassable in poor weather conditions. Storms can alter roads, remove tracks, and create impassable washes. Most of the trails described, even easy 2WD trails, can quickly become impassable even to 4WD vehicles after only a small amount of rain. For each trail, we have provided a phone number for obtaining current information about conditions.

Abbreviations

The route directions for the 4WD trails use a series of abbreviations as follows:

SO	CONTINUE STRAIGHT ON
TL	TURN LEFT
TR	TURN RIGHT
BL	BEAR LEFT
BR	BEAR RIGHT
UT	U-TURN

Using Route Directions

For every trail, we describe and pinpoint (by odometer reading) nearly every significant feature along the route—such as intersections, streams, washes, gates, cattle guards, and so on—and provide directions from these landmarks. Odometer readings will vary from vehicle to vehicle, so you should allow for slight variations. Be aware that trails can quickly change in the desert. A new trail may be cut around a washout, a faint trail can be graded by the county, or a well-used trail may fall into disuse. All these factors will affect the accuracy of the given directions.

If you diverge from the route, zero your trip meter upon your return and continue along the route, making the necessary adjustment to the point-to-point odometer readings. In the directions, we regularly reset the odometer readings—at significant landmarks or popular lookouts and spur trails—so that you won't have to recalculate for too long.

Most of the trails can be started from either end, and the route directions include both directions of travel; reverse directions are printed in blue below the main directions. When traveling in reverse, read from the bottom of the table and work up.

Route directions include cross-references whenever two 4WD trails included in this book connect; this allows for an easy change of route or destination.

Each trail includes periodic latitude and longitude readings to facilitate using a global positioning system (GPS) receiver. These readings may also assist you in finding your location on the maps. The GPS coordinates were taken using the NAD 1927 datum and are in the format dd°mm.mm′. To save time when loading coordinates into your GPS receiver, you may wish to include only one decimal place, since in Utah, the third decimal place equals about 2 yards and the second only about 20 yards.

Map References

We recommend that you supplement the information in this book with more-detailed maps. For each trail, we list the sheet maps and road atlases that provide the best detail for the area. Typically, the following references are given:

- Bureau of Land Management Maps,
- U.S. Forest Service Maps,
- Utah Travel Council Maps, Department of Geography, University of Utah—regions 1 through 5.
- *Utah Atlas & Gazetteer*, 1st ed. (Freeport, Maine: DeLorme Mapping, 1993)—Scale 1:250,000,
- Maptech-Terrain Navigator Topo Maps—Scale 1:100,000 and 1:24,000,
- *Trails Illustrated* Topo Maps; National Geographic Maps —Various scales, but all contain good detail,

We recommend the *Trails Illustrated* series of maps as the best for navigating these trails. They are reliable, easy to read, and printed on nearly indestructible plastic paper. However, this series covers only a few of the 4WD trails described in this book.

The DeLorme atlas is useful and has the advantage of providing you with maps of the entire state at a reasonable price. While its 4WD trail information doesn't go beyond what we provide, it is useful if you wish to explore the hundreds of side roads.

U.S. Forest Service maps lack the topographic detail of the other sheet maps and, in our experience, are occasionally out of date. They have the advantage of covering a broad area and are useful in identifying land use and travel restrictions. These maps are most useful for the longer trails.

Utah Travel Council maps cover Utah in five regions. They provide good overviews with a handful of 4WD trails, although with very little specific detail. Four of Utah's five regions are currently available: Southwestern #4, Southeastern #5, Northern #1, and Northeastern #3. Central map #2 has been out of print for several years and it is as yet undetermined when it will be available.

In our opinion, the best single option by far is the Terrain Navigator series of maps published on CD-ROM by Maptech. These CD-ROMs contain an amazing level of detail because they include the entire set of 1,524 U.S. Geological Survey topographical maps of Utah at the 1:24,000 scale and all 59 maps at the 1:100,000 scale. These maps offer many advantages over normal maps:

- GPS coordinates for any location can be found, which

can then be loaded into your GPS receiver. Conversely, if you have your GPS coordinates, your location on the map can be pinpointed instantly.

- Towns, rivers, passes, mountains, and many other sites are indexed by name so that they can be located quickly.
- 4WD trails can be marked and profiled for elevation changes and distances from point to point.
- Customized maps can be printed out.

Maptech uses seven CD-ROMs to cover the entire state of Utah, which can be purchased individually or as part of a two-state package at a heavily discounted price. The CD-ROMs can be used with a laptop computer and a GPS receiver in your vehicle to monitor your location on the map and navigate directly from the display.

All these maps should be available through good map stores. The Maptech CD-ROMs are available directly from the company (800-627-7236, or on the internet at www.maptech.com).

Backcountry Driving Rules and Permits

Four-wheel driving involves special driving techniques and road rules. This section is an introduction for 4WD beginners.

4WD Road Rules

To help ensure that these trails remain open and available for all four-wheel drivers to enjoy, it is important to minimize your impact on the environment and not be a safety risk to yourself or anyone else. Remember that the 4WD clubs in Utah fight a constant battle with the government and various lobby groups to retain the access that currently exists.

Although many vehicle manufacturer advertisements depict high-speed rally-style driving as proof of the automobile's off-highway abilities, these commercials are misleading—such driving techniques would only result in vehicle, occupant, and environmental damage. For all concerned, this style of driving is best left to professionals in controlled driving events. The fundamental rule when traversing the 4WD trails described in this book is to use common sense. In addition, special road rules for 4WD trails apply:

- Vehicles traveling uphill have the right of way.
- If you are moving more slowly than the vehicle behind you, pull over to let the other vehicle by.
- Park out of the way in a safe place. Blocking a track may restrict access for emergency vehicles as well as for other recreationalists. Set the parking brake—don't rely on leaving the transmission in park. Manual transmissions should be left in the lowest gear.

Tread Lightly!

Remember the rules of the Tread Lightly!® program:

- Be informed. Obtain maps, regulations, and other information from the forest service or from other public land agencies. Learn the rules and follow them.

■ Resist the urge to pioneer a new road or trail or to cut across a switchback. Stay on constructed tracks and avoid running over young trees, shrubs, and grasses, damaging or killing them. Don't drive across alpine tundra; this fragile environment can take years to recover.

■ Stay off soft, wet roads and 4WD trails readily torn up by vehicles. Repairing the damage is expensive, and quite often authorities find it easier to close the road rather than repair it.

■ Travel around meadows, steep hillsides, stream banks, and lakeshores that are easily scarred by churning wheels.

■ Stay away from wild animals that are rearing young or suffering from a food shortage. Do not camp close to the water sources of domestic or wild animals.

■ Obey gate closures and regulatory signs.

■ Preserve America's heritage by not disturbing old mining camps, ghost towns, or other historical features. Leave historic sites, Native American rock art, ruins, and artifacts in place and untouched.

■ Carry out all your trash, and even that of others.

■ Stay out of designated wilderness areas. They are closed to all vehicles. It is your responsibility to know where the boundaries are.

■ Get permission to cross private land. Leave livestock alone. Respect landowners' rights.

Report violations of these rules to help keep these 4WD trails open and to ensure that others will have the opportunity to visit these backcountry sites. Many groups are actively seeking to close these public lands to vehicles, thereby denying access to those who are unable, or perhaps merely unwilling, to hike long distances. This magnificent countryside is owned by, and should be available to, all Americans.

Remember that you are sharing the road with other users. It is courteous to slow down when you encounter travelers on foot, mountain bike, or horseback, and also sensible for safety reasons and to prevent a dust hazard. Pulling over and turning off your vehicle—whether it is a 4WD, ATV, or motor bike— is a simple gesture appreciated by those with horses. Offering water to people on foot or mountain bike is a small act of generosity that may be much valued by those engaged in physically demanding activities in remote locations.

Special Preparations for Remote Travel

Due to the remoteness of some areas in Utah and the very high summer temperatures, you should take some special precautions to ensure that you don't end up in a life-threatening situation:

■ When planning a trip into the desert, always inform someone as to where you are going, your route, and when you expect to return. Stick to your plan.

■ Carry and drink at least one gallon of water per person per day of your trip. (Plastic gallon jugs are handy and portable.)

■ Be sure your vehicle is in good condition with a sound battery, good hoses, spare tire, spare fan belts, necessary tools, and reserve gasoline and oil. Other spare parts and extra radiator water are also valuable. If traveling in pairs, share the common spares and carry a greater variety.

■ Keep an eye on the sky. Flash floods can occur in a wash any time you see "thunderheads"—even when it's not raining a drop where you are.

■ If you are caught in a dust storm while driving, get off the road and turn off your lights. Turn on the emergency flashers and back into the wind to reduce windshield pitting by sand particles.

■ Test trails on foot before driving through washes and sandy areas. One minute of walking may save hours of hard work getting your vehicle unstuck.

■ If your vehicle breaks down, stay near it. Your emergency supplies are there. Your car has many other items useful in an emergency. Raise your hood and trunk lid to denote "help needed." Remember, a vehicle can be seen for miles, but a person on foot is very difficult to spot from a distance.

■ When you're not moving, use available shade or erect shade from tarps, blankets, or seat covers—anything to reduce the direct rays of the sun.

■ Do not sit or lie directly on the ground. It may be 30 degrees hotter than the air.

Leave a disabled vehicle only if you are positive of the route and the distance to help. Leave a note for rescuers that gives the time you left and the direction you are taking.

■ If you must walk, rest for at least 10 minutes out of each hour. If you are not normally physically active, rest up to 30 minutes out of each hour. Find shade, sit down, and prop up your feet. Adjust your shoes and socks, but do not remove your shoes—you may not be able to get them back on swollen feet.

■ If you have water, drink it. Do not ration it.

■ If water is limited, keep your mouth closed. Do not talk, eat, smoke, drink alcohol, or take salt.

■ Keep your clothing on, despite the heat. It helps to keep your body temperature down and reduces your body's dehydration rate. Cover your head. If don't have a hat, improvise a head covering.

■ If you are stalled or lost, set signal fires. Set smoky fires in the daytime and bright ones at night. Three fires in a triangle denote "help needed."

■ A roadway is a sign of civilization. If you find a road, stay on it.

■ If hiking in the desert, equip each person, especially children, with a police-type whistle. It makes a distinctive noise with little effort. Three blasts denote "help needed."

■ To avoid poisonous creatures, put your hands or feet only where your eyes can see. One insect to be aware of in Utah is the Africanized honeybee. Though indistinguishable from its European counterpart, these bees are far more aggressive and can be a threat. They have been known to give chase for up to a mile and even wait for people who have escaped into the water to come up for air. The best thing to do if attacked is to cover your face and head with clothing and run to the nearest enclosed shelter. Keep an eye on your pet if you notice a number of bees in the area as many have been killed by these Africanized honeybees.

■ Avoid unnecessary contact with wildlife. Some mice in Utah carry the deadly Hanta virus, a pulmonary syndrome fatal in 60 to 70 percent of human cases. Fortunately the disease is very rare—only 41 cases have been reported in Utah and 283 nationwide—but caution is still advised. The area that first recorded instances of the virus was the Four Corners region that includes southeastern Utah.

Obtaining Permits

Backcountry permits, which usually cost a fee, are required for certain activities on public lands in Utah, whether the area is a national park, state park, national monument, Indian reservation, or BLM land.

Restrictions may require a permit for all overnight stays, which can include backpacking and 4WD or bicycle camping. Permits may also be required for day use by vehicles, horses, hikers, or bikes in some areas.

When possible, we include information about fees and permit requirements and where permits may be obtained, but these regulations change constantly. If in doubt, check with the most likely governing agency.

Assessing Your Vehicle's Off-Road Ability

Many issues come into play when evaluating your 4WD vehicle, though most of the 4WDs on the market are suitable for even the roughest trails described in this book. Engine power will be adequate in even the least powerful modern vehicle. However, some vehicles are less suited to off-highway driving than others, and some of the newest, carlike sport utility vehicles (SUVs) simply are not designed for off-highway touring. The following information should allow you to identify the good, the bad, and the ugly.

Differing 4WD Systems

All 4WD systems have one thing in common: the engine provides power to all four wheels rather than to only two, as is typical in most standard cars. However, there are a number of differences in the way power is applied to the wheels.

The other feature that distinguishes nearly all 4WDs from normal passenger vehicles is that the gearboxes have high and low ratios that effectively double the number of gears. The high range is comparable to the range on a passenger car. The low range provides lower speed and more power, which is useful when towing heavy loads, driving up steep hills, or crawling over rocks. When driving downhill, the 4WD's low range increases engine braking.

Various makes and models of SUVs offer different drive systems, but these differences center on two issues: the way power is applied to the other wheels if one or more wheels slip, and the ability to select between 2WD and 4WD.

Normal driving requires that all four wheels be able to turn at different speeds; this allows the vehicle to turn without scrubbing its tires. In a 2WD vehicle, the front wheels (or rear wheels in a front-wheel-drive vehicle) are not powered by the engine and thus are free to turn individually at any speed. The rear wheels, powered by the engine, are only able to turn at different speeds because of the differential,

which applies power to the faster-turning wheel.

This standard method of applying traction has certain weaknesses. First, when power is applied to only one set of wheels, the other set cannot help the vehicle gain traction. Second, when one powered wheel loses traction, it spins, but the other powered wheels don't turn. This happens because the differential applies all the engine power to the faster-turning wheel and no power to the other wheels, which still have traction. All 4WD systems are designed to overcome these two weaknesses. However, different 4WDs address this common objective in different ways.

Full-Time 4WD

In order for a vehicle to remain in 4WD all the time without scrubbing the tires, all the wheels must be able to rotate at different speeds. A full-time 4WD system allows this to happen by using three differentials. One is located between the rear wheels, as in a normal passenger car, to allow the rear wheels to rotate at different speeds. The second is located between the front wheels in exactly the same way. The third differential is located between the front and rear wheels to allow different rotational speeds between the front and rear sets of wheels. In nearly all vehicles with full-time 4WD, the center differential operates only in high range. In low range, it is completely locked. This is not a disadvantage because when using low range the additional traction is normally desired and the deterioration of steering response will be less noticeable due to the vehicle traveling at a slower speed.

Part-Time 4WD

A part-time 4WD system does not have the center differential located between the front and rear wheels. Consequently, the front and rear drive shafts are both driven at the same speed and with the same power at all times when in 4WD.

This system provides improved traction because when one or both of the front or rear wheels slips, the engine continues to provide power to the other set. However, because such a system doesn't allow a difference in speed between the front and rear sets of wheels, the tires scrub when turning, placing additional strain on the whole drive system. Therefore, such a system can be used only in slippery conditions; otherwise, the ability to steer the vehicle will deteriorate and the tires will quickly wear out.

Some vehicles, such as Jeeps with Selec-trac™ and Mitsubishi Monteros with Active Trac 4WD™, offer both full-time and part-time 4WD in high range.

Manual Systems to Switch Between 2WD and 4WD

There are three manual systems for switching between 2WD and 4WD. The most basic requires stopping and getting out of the vehicle to lock the front hubs manually before selecting 4WD. The second requires you to stop, but you change to 4WD by merely throwing a lever inside the vehicle (the hubs lock automatically). The third allows shifting between 2WD and 4WD high range while the vehicle is moving. Any 4WD that does not offer the option of driving in 2WD must have a full-time 4WD system.

Automated Switching Between 2WD and 4WD

Advances in technology are leading to greater automation in the selection of two- or four-wheel drive. When operating in high-range, these high-tech systems use sensors to monitor the rotation of each wheel. When any slippage is detected, the vehicle switches the proportion of power from the wheel(s) that is slipping to the wheels that retain grip. The proportion of power supplied to each wheel is therefore infinitely variable as opposed to the original systems where the vehicle was either in two-wheel drive or four-wheel drive.

In recent years, this process has been spurred on by many of the manufacturers of luxury vehicles entering the SUV market—Mercedes, BMW, Cadillac, Lincoln, and Lexus have joined Range Rover in this segment.

These higher-priced vehicles have led the way in introducing sophisticated computer-controlled 4WD systems. While each of the manufacturers has its own approach to this issue, all the systems automatically vary the allocation of power between the wheels within milliseconds of the sensors detecting wheel slippage.

Limiting Wheel Slippage

4WDs employ various systems to limit wheel slippage and transfer power to the wheels that still have traction. These systems may completely lock the differentials, or they may allow limited slippage before transferring power back to the wheels that retain traction.

Lockers completely eliminate the operation of one or more differentials. A locker on the center differential switches between full-time and part-time 4WD. Lockers on the front or rear differentials ensure that power remains equally applied to each set of wheels regardless of whether both have traction. Lockers may be controlled manually by a switch, a lever in the vehicle, or they may be automatic.

The Toyota Land Cruiser offers the option of having manual lockers on all three differentials, while other brands such as the Mitsubishi Montero offer manual lockers on the center and rear differential. Manual lockers are the most controllable and effective devices for ensuring that power is provided to the wheels with traction. However, because they allow absolutely no slippage, they must be used only on slippery surfaces.

An alternative method for getting power to the wheels that have traction is to allow limited wheel slippage. Systems that work this way may be called limited-slip differentials, posi-traction systems, or in the center differential, viscous couplings. The advantage of these systems is that the limited difference they allow in rotational speed between wheels enables such systems to be used when driving on a dry surface. All full-time 4WD systems allow limited slippage in the center differential.

For off-highway use, a manually locking differential is the best of the above systems, but it is the most expensive. Limited-slip differentials are the cheapest but also the least satisfactory, as they require one wheel to be slipping at 2 to 3 mph before power is transferred to the other wheel. For the center differential, the best system combines a locking differential and, to enable full-time use, a viscous coupling.

Tires

The tires that came with your 4WD vehicle may be satisfactory, but many 4WDs are fitted with passenger-car tires. These are unlikely to be the best choice because they are less rugged and more likely to puncture on rocky trails. They are particularly prone to sidewall damage as well. Passenger vehicle tires also have a less aggressive tread pattern than specialized 4WD tires, providing less traction in mud.

For information on purchasing tires better suited to off-highway conditions, see "Special 4WD Equipment" below.

Clearance

Road clearances vary considerably among different 4WD vehicles—from less than 7 inches to more than 10 inches. Special vehicles may have far greater clearance. For instance, the Hummer has a 16-inch ground clearance. High ground clearance is particularly advantageous on the rockier or more rutted 4WD trails in this book.

When evaluating the ground clearance of your vehicle, you need to take into account the clearance of the bodywork between the wheels on each side of the vehicle. This is particularly relevant for crawling over larger rocks. Vehicles with side-steps have significantly lower clearance than those without.

Another factor affecting clearance is the approach and departure angles of your vehicle—that is, the maximum angle the ground can slope without the front of the vehicle hitting the ridge on approach or the rear of the vehicle hitting on departure. Mounting a winch or tow hitch to your vehicle is likely to reduce your approach or departure angle.

If you do a lot of driving on rocky trails, you will inevitably hit the bottom of the vehicle sooner or later. When this happens, you will be far less likely to damage vulnerable areas such as the oil pan and gas tank if your vehicle is fitted with skid plates. Most manufacturers offer skid plates as an option. They are worth every penny.

Maneuverability

When you tackle tight switchbacks, you will quickly appreciate that maneuverability is an important criterion when assessing 4WD vehicles. Where a full-size vehicle may be forced to go back and forth a number of times to get around a sharp turn, a small 4WD might go straight around. This is not only easier, it's safer.

If you have a full-size vehicle, all is not lost. We have traveled many of the trails in this book in a Suburban. That is not to say that some of these trails wouldn't have been easier to negotiate in a smaller vehicle! We have noted in the route descriptions if a trail is not suitable for larger vehicles.

In Summary

Using the criteria above, you can evaluate how well your 4WD will handle off-road touring, and if you haven't yet purchased your vehicle, you can use these criteria to help select one. Choosing the best 4WD system is, at least partly, subjective. It is also a matter of your budget. However, for the type of off-highway driving covered in this book, we make the following recommendations:

■ Select a 4WD system that offers low range and, at a minimum, has some form of limited slip differential on the rear axle.

■ Use light truck, all-terrain tires as the standard tires on your vehicle. For sand and slickrock, these will be the ideal choice. If conditions are likely to be muddy, or traction will be improved by a tread pattern that will give more bite, consider an additional set of mud tires.

■ For maximum clearance, select a vehicle with 16-inch wheels, or at least choose the tallest tires that your vehicle can accommodate. Note that if you install tires with a diameter greater than standard, the odometer will undercalculate the distance you have traveled. Your engine braking and gear ratios will also be affected.

■ If you are going to try the rockier 4WD trails, don't install a sidestep or low hanging front bar. If you have the option, have underbody skid plates mounted.

■ Remember that many of the obstacles you encounter on backcountry trails are more difficult to navigate in a full-size vehicle than in a compact 4WD.

Four-Wheel Driving Techniques

Safe four-wheel driving requires that you observe certain golden rules:

■ Size up the situation in advance.

■ Be careful and take your time.

■ Maintain smooth, steady power and momentum.

■ Engage 4WD and low-range gears before you get into a tight situation.

■ Steer toward high spots, trying to put the wheel over large rocks.

■ Straddle ruts.

■ Use gears and not just the brakes to hold the vehicle when driving downhill. On very steep slopes, chock the wheels if you park your vehicle.

■ Watch for logging and mining trucks and smaller recreational vehicles, such as all-terrain vehicles (ATVs).

■ Wear your seat belt and secure all luggage, especially heavy items such as toolboxes or coolers. Heavy items should be secured by ratchet tie-down straps rather than elastic-type straps, which are not strong enough to hold heavy items if the vehicle rolls.

Utah's 4WD trails have a number of common obstacles, and the following provides an introduction to the techniques required to surmount them.

Rocks

Tire selection is important in negotiating rocks. Select a multiple-ply, tough sidewall, light truck tire with a large-lug tread.

As you approach a rocky stretch, get into 4WD low range to give maximum slow-speed control. Speed is rarely necessary, since traction on a rocky surface is usually good. Plan ahead and select the line you wish to take. If a rock appears to be larger than the clearance of your vehicle, don't try to straddle it. Check to see that it is not higher than the frame of your vehicle once you get a wheel over it. Put a wheel up on the rock and slowly climb it, then gently drop over the other side using the brake to ensure a smooth landing. Bouncing the car over rocks increases the likelihood of damage, as the body's clearance is reduced by the suspension compressing. Running boards also significantly reduce your clearance in this respect.

It is often helpful to use a "spotter" outside the vehicle to assist you with the best wheel placement.

Slickrock

When you encounter slickrock, first assess the correct direction of the trail. It is easy to lose sight of the trail on slickrock, as there are seldom any developed edges. Often the way is marked with small rock cairns, which are simply rocks stacked high enough to make a landmark.

All-terrain tires with tighter tread are more suited to slickrock than the more open, luggier type tires. As with rocks, a multiple-ply sidewall is important. In dry conditions, slickrock offers pavement-type grip. In rain or snow, you will soon learn how it got its name. Even the best tires may not get an adequate grip. Walk steep sections first; if you are slipping on foot, chances are your vehicle will slip too.

Slickrock is characterized by ledges and long sections of "pavement." Follow the guidelines for travel over rocks. Refrain from speeding over flat-looking sections, as you may hit an unexpected crevice or water pocket, and vehicles bend easier than slickrock! Turns and ledges can be tight, and vehicles with smaller overhangs and better maneuverability are at a distinct advantage—hence the popularity of the compacts in the slickrock mecca of Moab.

On the steepest sections, engage low range and pick a straight line up or down the slope. Do not attempt to traverse a steep slope sideways.

Steep Uphill Grades

Consider walking the trail to ensure that the steep hill before you is passable, especially if it is clear that backtracking is going to be a problem.

Select 4WD low range to ensure that you have adequate power to pull up the hill. If the wheels begin to lose traction, turn the steering wheel gently from side to side to give the wheels a chance to regain traction.

If you lose momentum, but the car is not in danger of sliding, use the foot brake, switch off the ignition, leave the vehicle in gear (if manual transmission) or park (if automatic), engage the parking brake, and get out to examine the situation. See if you can remove any obstacles, and figure out the line you need to take. Reversing a couple of yards and starting again may allow you to get better traction and momentum.

If, halfway up, you decide a stretch of road is impassably steep, back down the trail. Trying to turn the vehicle around on a steep hill is extremely dangerous; you will very likely cause it to roll over.

Steep Downhill Grades

Again, consider walking the trail to ensure that a steep downhill slope is passable, especially if it is clear that backtracking uphill is going to be a problem.

Select 4WD low range and use first gear to maximize braking assistance from the engine. If the surface is loose and you are losing traction, change up to second or third gear. Do not use the brakes if you can avoid it, but don't let the vehicle's speed get out of control. Feather (lightly pump) the brakes if you slip under braking. For vehicles fitted with ABS, apply even pressure if you start to slip; the ABS helps keep vehicles on line.

Travel very slowly over rock ledges or ruts. Attempt to tackle these diagonally, letting one wheel down at a time.

If the back of the vehicle begins to slide around, gently apply the throttle and correct the steering. If the rear of the vehicle starts to slide sideways, do not apply the brakes.

Stream Crossings

By crossing a stream that is too deep, drivers risk far more than water flowing in and ruining the interior of their vehicles. Water sucked into the engine's air intake will seriously damage the engine. Likewise, water that seeps into the air vent on the transmission or differential will mix with the lubricant and may lead to serious problems in due course.

Even worse, if the water is deep or fast flowing, it could easily carry your vehicle downstream, endangering the lives of everyone in the vehicle.

Some 4WD manuals tell you what fording depth the vehicle can negotiate safely. If your vehicle's owner's manual doesn't include this information, your local dealer may be able to assist. If you don't know, then avoid crossing through water that is more than a foot or so deep.

The first rule for crossing a stream is to know what you are getting into. You need to ascertain how deep the water is, whether there are any large rocks or holes, if the bottom is solid enough to avoid bogging down the vehicle, and whether the entry and exit points are negotiable. This may take some time and involve getting wet, but you take a great risk by crossing a stream without first properly assessing the situation.

The secret to water crossings is to keep moving, but not too fast. If you go too fast, you may drown the electrics, causing the vehicle to stall midstream. In shallow water (where the surface of the water is below the bumper), your primary concern is to safely negotiate the bottom of the stream, avoiding any rock damage and maintaining momentum if there is a danger of getting stuck or of slipping on the exit.

In deeper water (between 18 and 30 inches), the objective is to create a small bow wave in front of the moving vehicle. This requires a speed that is approximately walking pace. The bow wave reduces the depth of the water around the engine compartment. If the water's surface reaches your tailpipe, select a gear that will maintain moderate engine revs to avoid water backing up into the exhaust; and do not change gears midstream.

Crossing water deeper than 25 to 30 inches requires more extensive preparation of the vehicle and should be attempted only by experienced drivers.

Sand

As with most off-highway situations, your tires are the key to your ability to cross sand. It is difficult to tell how well a particular tire will handle in sand just by looking at it, so be guided by the manufacturer and your dealer.

The key to driving in soft sand is floatation, which is achieved by a combination of low tire pressure and momentum. Before crossing a stretch of sand, reduce your tire pressure to between 15 and 20 pounds. If necessary, you can safely go to as low as 12 pounds. As you cross, maintain momentum so that your vehicle rides on the top of the soft sand without digging in or stalling. This may require plenty of engine power. Avoid using the brakes if possible; removing your foot from the accelerator alone is normally enough to slow or stop. Using the brakes digs the vehicle deep in the sand.

Air the tires back up as soon as you are out of the sand to avoid damage to the tires and the rims. Airing back up requires a high-quality air compressor. Even then, it is a slow process.

In the backcountry of Utah, sandy conditions are commonplace. You will therefore find a good compressor most useful.

Mud

Muddy trails are easily damaged, so they should be avoided if possible. But if you must traverse a section of mud, your success will depend heavily on whether you have open-lugged mud tires or chains. Thick mud fills the tighter tread on normal tires, leaving the tire with no more grip than if it were bald. If the muddy stretch is only a few yards long, the momentum of your vehicle may allow you to get through regardless.

If the muddy track is very steep, uphill or downhill, or off camber, do not attempt it. Your vehicle is very likely to skid in such conditions, and you may roll or slip off the edge of the road. Also, check to see that the mud has a reasonably firm base. Tackling deep mud is definitely not recommended unless you have a vehicle-mounted winch—and even then, be cautious, because the winch may not get you out. Finally, check to see that no ruts are too deep for the ground clearance of your vehicle.

When you decide you can get through and have selected the best route, use the following techniques to cross through the mud:

■ Avoid making detours off existing tracks to minimize environmental damage.

■ Select 4WD low range and a suitable gear; momentum is the key to success, so use a high enough gear to build up sufficient speed.

■ Avoid accelerating heavily, so as to minimize wheel spinning and to provide maximum traction.

■ Follow existing wheel ruts, unless they are too deep for the clearance of your vehicle.

■ To correct slides, turn the steering wheel in the direction that the rear wheels are skidding, but don't be too aggressive or you'll overcorrect and lose control again.

■ If the vehicle comes to a stop, don't continue to accelerate, as you will only spin your wheels and dig yourself into a rut. Try backing out and having another go.

■ Be prepared to turn back before reaching the point of no return.

Snow

The trails in this book that receive heavy snowfall are closed in winter. Therefore, the snow conditions that you are most likely to encounter are an occasional snowdrift that has not yet melted or fresh snow from an unexpected storm. Getting through such conditions depends on the depth of the snow, its consistency, the stability of the underlying surface, and your vehicle.

If the snow is no deeper than about nine inches and there is solid ground beneath it, crossing the snow should not be a problem. In deeper snow that seems solid enough to support your vehicle, be extremely cautious: If you break through a drift, you are likely to be stuck, and if conditions are bad, you may have a long wait.

The tires you use for off-highway driving, with a wide tread pattern, are probably suitable for these snow conditions. Nonetheless, it is wise to carry chains (preferably for all four wheels), and if you have a vehicle-mounted winch, even better.

Vehicle Recovery Methods

If you do enough four-wheel driving, you are sure to get stuck sooner or later. The following techniques will help you get back on the go. The most suitable method will depend on the equipment available and the situation you are in—whether you are stuck in sand, mud, or snow, or are high-centered or unable to negotiate a hill.

Towing

Use a nylon yank strap of the type discussed in the "Special 4WD Equipment" section on page ??. This type of strap will stretch 15 to 25 percent, and the elasticity will assist in extracting the vehicle.

Attach the strap only to a frame-mounted tow point. Ensure that the driver of the stuck vehicle is ready, take up all but about 6 feet of slack, then move the towing vehicle away at a moderate speed (in most circumstances this means using 4WD low range in second gear) so that the elasticity of the strap is employed in the way it is meant to be. Don't take off like a bat out of hell or you risk breaking the strap or damaging a vehicle.

Never join two yank straps together with a shackle. If one strap breaks, the shackle will become a lethal missile aimed at one of the vehicles (and anyone inside). For the same reason, never attach a yank strap to the tow ball on either vehicle.

Jacking

Jacking the vehicle allows you to pack under the wheel (with rocks, dirt, or logs) or use your shovel to remove an obstacle. However, the standard vehicle jack is unlikely to be of as much assistance as a high-lift jack. We highly recommend purchasing a good high-lift jack as a basic accessory if you decide that you are going to do a lot of serious, off-highway four-wheel driving. Remember a high-lift jack is of limited use if your ve-

hicle does not have an appropriate jacking point. Some brush bars have two built-in forward jacking points.

Tire Chains

Tire chains can be of assistance in both mud and snow. Cable-type chains provide much less grip than link-type chains. There are also dedicated mud chains with larger, heavier links than on normal snow chains. It is best to have chains fitted to all four wheels.

Once you are bogged down is not the best time to try to fit the chains; if at all possible, try to predict their need and have them on the tires before trouble arises. An easy way to affix chains is to place two small cubes of wood under the center of the stretched-out chain. When you drive your tires up on the blocks of wood, it is easier to stretch the chains over the tires because the pressure is off.

Winching

Most recreational four-wheel drivers do not have a winch. But if you get serious about four-wheel driving, this is probably the first major accessory you should consider buying.

Under normal circumstances, a winch would be warranted only for the more difficult 4WD trails in this book. Having a winch is certainly comforting when you see a difficult section of road ahead and have to decide whether to risk it or turn back. Also, major obstacles can appear when you least expect them, even on trails that are otherwise easy.

Owning a winch is not a panacea to all your recovery problems. Winching depends on the availability of a good anchor point, and electric winches may not work if they are submerged in a stream. Despite these constraints, no accessory is more useful than a high-quality, powerful winch when you get into a difficult situation.

If you acquire a winch, learn to use it properly; take the time to study your owner's manual. Incorrect operation can be extremely dangerous and may cause damage to the winch or to your anchor points, which are usually trees.

Navigation by the Global Positioning System (GPS)

Although this book is designed so that each trail can be navigated simply by following the detailed directions provided, nothing makes navigation easier than a GPS receiver.

The global positioning system (GPS) consists of a network of 24 satellites, nearly 13,000 miles in space, in six different orbital paths. The satellites are constantly moving at about 8,500 miles per hour, making two complete orbits around the earth every 24 hours.

Each satellite is constantly transmitting data, including its identification number, its operational health, and the date and time. It also transmits its location and the location of every other satellite in the network.

By comparing the time the signal was transmitted to the time it is received, a GPS receiver calculates how far away each satellite is. With a sufficient number of signals, the receiver can then triangulate its location. With three or more satellites, the receiver can determine latitude and longitude coordinates.

With four or more, it can calculate altitude. By constantly making these calculations, it can determine speed and direction. To facilitate these calculations, the time data broadcast by GPS is accurate to within 40 billionths of a second.

The U.S. military uses the system to provide positions accurate to within half an inch. When the system was first established, civilian receivers were deliberately fed slightly erroneous information in order to effectively deny military applications to hostile countries or terrorists—a practice called selective availability (SA). However on May 1, 2000, in response to the growing importance of the system for civilian applications, the U.S. government stopped intentionally downgrading GPS data. The military gave their support to this change once new technology made it possible to selectively degrade the system within any defined geographical area on demand. This new feature of the system has made it safe to have higher-quality signals available for civilian use. Now, instead of the civilian-use signal having a margin of error being between 20 and 70 yards, it is only about one-tenth of that.

A GPS receiver offers the four-wheeler numerous benefits:

■ You can track to any point for which you know the longitude and latitude coordinates with no chance of heading in the wrong direction or getting lost. Most receivers provide an extremely easy-to-understand graphic display to keep you on track.

■ It works in all weather conditions.

■ It automatically records your route for easy backtracking.

■ You can record and name any location, so that you can relocate it with ease. This may include your campsite, a fishing spot, or even a gold mine you discover!

■ It displays your position, allowing you to pinpoint your location on a map.

■ By interfacing the GPS receiver directly to a portable computer, you can monitor and record your location as you travel (using the appropriate map software) or print the route you took.

However, remember that GPS units can fail, batteries can go flat, and tree cover and tight canyons can block the signals. Never rely entirely on GPS for navigation. Always carry a compass for backup.

Special 4WD Equipment

Tires

When 4WD touring, you will likely encounter a wide variety of terrain: rocks, mud, talus, slickrock, sand, gravel, dirt, and bitumen. The immense variety of tires on the market includes many specifically targeted at one or another of these types of terrain, as well as tires designed to adequately handle a range of terrain.

Every four-wheel driver seems to have his or her own preference when it comes to tire selection, but most people undertaking the 4WD trails in this book will need tires that can handle all of the above types of terrain adequately.

The first requirement is to select rugged, light-truck tires rather than passenger-vehicle tires. Check the size data on the sidewall: it should have "LT" rather than "P" before the number.

Among light-truck tires, you must choose between tires that are designated "all-terrain" and more-aggressive, wider-tread mud tires. Either type will be adequate, especially on rocks, gravel, talus, or dirt. Although mud tires have an advantage in muddy conditions and soft snow, all-terrain tires perform better on slickrock, in sand, and particularly on ice and paved roads.

When selecting tires, remember that they affect not just traction but also cornering ability, braking distances, fuel consumption, and noise levels. It pays to get good advice before making your decision.

Global Positioning System Receivers

GPS receivers have come down in price considerably in the past few years and are rapidly becoming indispensable navigational tools. Many higher-priced cars now offer integrated GPS receivers, and within the next few years, receivers will become available on most models.

Battery-powered, hand-held units that meet the needs of off-highway driving currently range from less than $100 to a little over $300 and continue to come down in price. Some high-end units feature maps that are incorporated in the display, either from a built-in database or from interchangeable memory cards. Currently, only a few of these maps include 4WD trails.

If you are considering purchasing a GPS unit, keep the following in mind:

■ Price. The very cheapest units are likely outdated and very limited in their display features. Expect to pay from $125 to $300.

■ The display. Compare the graphic display of one unit with another. Some are much easier to decipher or offer more alternative displays.

■ The controls. GPS receivers have many functions, and they need to have good, simple controls.

■ Vehicle mounting. To be useful, the unit needs to be placed where it can be read easily by both the driver and the navigator. Check that the unit can be conveniently located in your vehicle. Different units have different shapes and different mounting systems. If you are considering attaching a GPS unit to the dashboard of your vehicle be sure not to obstruct the safe deployment of air bags. A GPS unit could cause serious bodily harm to an occupant of the vehicle at the speed at which air bags deploy.

■ Map data. More and more units have map data built-in. Some have the ability to download maps from a computer. Such maps are normally sold on a CD-ROM. GPS units have a finite storage capacity and having the ability to download maps covering a narrower geographical region means that the amount of data relating to that specific region can be greater.

■ The number of routes and the number of sites (or "waypoints") per route that can be stored in memory. For off-highway use, it is important to be able to store plenty of waypoints so that you do not have to load coordinates into the machine as frequently. Having plenty of memory also ensures that you can automatically store your present location without fear that the memory is full.

■ Waypoint storage. The better units store up to 500 waypoints and 20 reversible routes of up to 30 waypoints each. Also consider the number of characters a GPS receiver allows you to use to name waypoints. When you try to recall a waypoint, you may have difficulty recognizing names restricted to only a few characters.

■ Automatic route storing. Most units automatically store your route as you go along and enable you to display it in reverse to make backtracking easy.

■ After you have selected a unit, a number of optional extras are also worth considering:

■ A cigarette lighter electrical adapter. Despite GPS units becoming more power efficient, protracted in-vehicle use still makes this accessory a necessity.

■ A vehicle-mounted antenna, which will improve reception under difficult conditions. (The GPS unit can only "see" through the windows of your vehicle; it cannot monitor satellites through a metal roof.) Having a vehicle-mounted antenna also means that you do not have to consider reception when locating the receiver in your vehicle.

■ An in-car mounting system. If you are going to do a lot of touring using the GPS, consider attaching a bracket on the dash rather than relying on a Velcro mount.

■ A computer-link cable and digital maps. Data from your GPS receiver can be downloaded to your PC; maps and waypoints can be downloaded from your PC; or if you have a laptop computer, you can monitor your route as you go along, using one of a number of inexpensive map software products on the market.

Yank Straps

Yank straps are industrial-strength versions of the flimsy tow straps carried by the local discount store. They are 20 to 30 feet long and 2 to 3 inches wide, made of heavy nylon, rated to at least 20,000 pounds, and have looped ends.

Do not use tow straps with metal hooks in the ends (the hooks can become missiles in the event the strap breaks free). Likewise, never join two yank straps together using a shackle.

CB Radios

If you are stuck, injured, or just want to know the conditions up ahead, a citizen's band (CB) radio can be invaluable.

CB radios are relatively inexpensive and do not require an FCC license. Their range is limited, especially in very hilly country, as their transmission patterns basically follow lines of sight. Range can be improved using single sideband (SSB) transmission, an option on more expensive units. Range is even better on vehicle-mounted units that have been professionally fitted to ensure that the antenna and cabling are matched appropriately.

Winches

There are three main options when it comes to winches: manual winches, removable electric winches, and vehicle-mounted electric winches.

If you have a full-size 4WD vehicle—which can weigh in excess of 7,000 pounds when loaded—a manual winch is of limited use without a lot of effort and considerable time. However, a manual winch is a very handy and inexpensive accessory if you have a small 4WD. Typically, manual winches are rated to pull about 5,500 pounds.

Electric winches can be mounted to your vehicle's trailer hitch to enable them to be removed, relocated to the front of your vehicle (if you have a hitch installed), or moved to another vehicle. Although this is a very useful feature, a winch is heavy, so relocating one can be a two-person job. Consider that 5,000-pound-rated winches weigh only about 55 pounds, while 12,000-pound-rated models weigh around 140 pounds. Therefore, the larger models are best permanently front-mounted. Unfortunately, this position limits their ability to winch the vehicle backward.

When choosing between electric winches, be aware that they are rated for their maximum capacity on the first wind of the cable around the drum. As layers of cable wind onto the drum, they increase its diameter and thus decrease the maximum load the winch can handle. This decrease is significant: a winch rated to pull 8,000 pounds on a bare drum may only handle 6,500 pounds on the second layer, 5,750 pounds on the third layer, and 5,000 pounds on the fourth. Electric winches also draw a high level of current and may necessitate upgrading the battery in your 4WD or adding a second battery.

There is a wide range of mounting options—from a simple, body-mounted frame that holds the winch to heavy-duty winch bars that replace the original bumper and incorporate brush bars and mounts for auxiliary lights.

If you buy a winch, either electric or manual, you will also need quite a range of additional equipment so that you can operate it correctly:

■ at least one choker chain with hooks on each end,
■ winch extension straps or cables,
■ shackles,
■ a receiver shackle,
■ a snatch block,
■ a tree protector,
■ gloves.

Grill/Brush Bars and Winch Bars

Brush bars protect the front of the vehicle from scratches and minor bumps; they also provide a solid mount for auxiliary lights and often high-lift jacking points. Additionally, they are an ideal place to fit a tall whip-antenna with a brightly colored flag atop, something that reduces safety concerns on trails with restricted visibility. The level of protection brush bars provide depends on how solid they are and whether they are securely mounted onto the frame of the vehicle. Lighter models attach in front of the standard bumper, but the more substantial units replace the bumper. Prices range from about $150 to $450.

Winch bars replace the bumper and usually integrate a solid brush bar with a heavy-duty winch mount. Some have the brush bar as an optional extra to the winch bar component. Manufacturers such as Warn, ARB, and TJM offer a wide range of integrated winch bars. These are significantly more expensive, starting at about $650.

Remember that installing heavy equipment on the front of the vehicle may necessitate increasing the front suspension rating to cope with the additional weight.

Portable Air Compressors

Most portable air compressors on the market are flimsy models that plug into the cigarette lighter and are sold at the local discount store. These are of very limited use for four-wheel driving. They are very slow to inflate the large tires of a 4WD vehicle; for instance, to reinflate from 15 to 35 pounds typically takes about 10 minutes for each tire. They are also unlikely to be rated for continuous use, which means that they will overheat and cut off before completing the job. If you're lucky, they will start up again when they have cooled down, but this means that you are unlikely to reinflate your tires in less than an hour.

The easiest way to identify a useful air compressor is by the price—good ones cost $200 and over. Many of the quality units feature a Thomas-brand pump and are built to last. Another good unit is sold by ARB. All these pumps draw between 15 and 20 amps and thus should not be plugged into the cigarette lighter socket but attached to the vehicle's battery with clips. The ARB unit can be permanently mounted under the hood. Quick-Air make a range of units including a 10-amp compressor that can be plugged into the cigarette lighter socket and performs well.

Auxiliary Driving Lights

There is a vast array of auxiliary lights on the market today, and selecting the best lights for your purpose can be a confusing process.

Auxiliary lights greatly improve visibility in adverse weather conditions. Driving lights provide a strong, moderately wide beam to supplement headlamp high beams, giving improved lighting in the distance and to the sides of the main beam. Fog lamps throw a wide-dispersion, flat beam; and spots provide a high-power, narrow beam to improve lighting range directly in front of the vehicle. Rear-mounted auxiliary lights provide greatly improved visibility for backing up.

For off-highway use, you will need quality lights with strong mounting brackets. Some high-powered off-highway lights are not approved by the Department of Transportation for use on public roads.

Roof Racks

Roof racks can be excellent for storing gear, as well as providing easy access for certain weatherproof items. However, they raise the center of gravity on the vehicle, which can substantially alter the rollover angle. A roof rack is best used for lightweight objects that are well strapped down. Heavy recovery gear and other bulky items should be packed low in the vehicle's interior to lower the center of gravity and stabilize the vehicle.

A roof rack should allow for safe and secure packing of items and be sturdy enough to withstand knocks.

Packing Checklist

Before embarking on any 4WD adventure, whether a lazy Sunday drive on an easy trail or a challenging climb over rugged terrain, be prepared. The following checklist will help you gather the items you need.

Essential

❑ Rain gear
❑ Small shovel or multipurpose ax, pick, shovel, and sledgehammer
❑ Heavy-duty yank strap
❑ Spare tire that matches the other tires on the vehicle
❑ Working jack and base plate for soft ground
❑ Maps
❑ Emergency medical kit, including sun protection and insect repellent
❑ Bottled water
❑ Blankets or space blankets
❑ Parka, gloves, and boots
❑ Spare vehicle key
❑ Jumper leads
❑ Heavy-duty flashlight
❑ Multipurpose tool, such as a Leatherman™
❑ Emergency food—high-energy bars or similar

Worth Considering

❑ Global Positioning System (GPS) receiver
❑ Cell phone
❑ A set of light-truck, off-highway tires and matching spare
❑ High-lift jack
❑ Additional tool kit
❑ CB radio
❑ Portable air compressor
❑ Tire gauge
❑ Tire-sealing kit
❑ Tire chains
❑ Handsaw and ax
❑ Binoculars
❑ Firearms
❑ Whistle
❑ Flares
❑ Vehicle fire extinguisher
❑ Gasoline, engine oil, and other vehicle fluids
❑ Portable hand winch
❑ Electric cooler

If Your Credit Cards Aren't Maxed Out

❑ Electric, vehicle-mounted winch and associated recovery straps, shackles, and snatch blocks
❑ Auxiliary lights
❑ Locking differential(s)

Utah Distance Chart

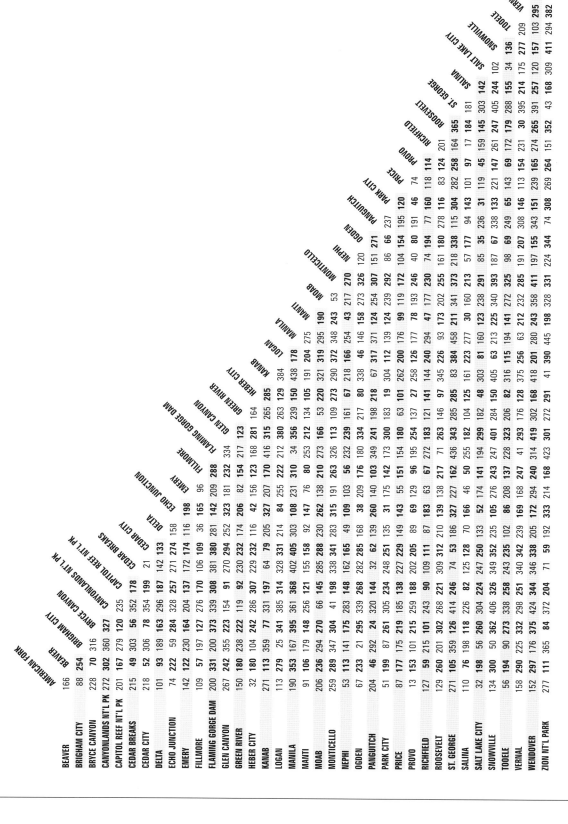

Distances are calculated using major highways.

Along the Trail

Towns, Ghost Towns, and Interesting Places

Adairville

Just north of the Arizona border, the ruins of Adairville sit in the same spot where the Domínguez-Escalante Expedition crossed the Paria River in 1776. Thomas Adair founded the town in 1872 after poor farming conditions upstream made survival there impossible. For the next few years, settlers built the town, worked the fields, and raised cattle, and Adairville became a supply stop for traveling prospectors. However, the droughts of the 1880s, creating very harsh living conditions, once again forced the people to relocate. As quickly as it was settled, the town of Adairville was abandoned. Today, there are only a few remains next to the Paria River just north of US 89.

Just southwest of the ruins of Adairville, a tin can full of gold coins is said to be buried. In 1886, Sam Clevenger, along with his wife, daughter, and two farm hands, John Johnson and Frank Wilson, were traveling through the area. Every night Mrs. Clevenger would bury their stash of coins near the camp. Then one evening Johnson and Wilson, the two hired hands, decided to steal the family fortune. They murdered the elder Clevengers with an ax. When they were unable to find the can of money, they instead made off with Jessie, the fifteen-year-old daughter. Eventually the bodies of the Clevengers were found and the murderers were brought to justice. However, the location of the tin baking powder can full of gold coins remains a mystery. It was said to have held $500 over a century ago. With the price of gold today, the can now holds a small fortune.

GPS COORDINATES: N 37°07.07' W 111°55.00'

Adventure

Several miles south of where Zion National Park is now located, Adventure was settled in 1860 by Phillip Klingensmith. The spot was chosen because it was beside the Virgin River, and the water could be diverted to the fertile soil on the banks.

For a few years, the small town grew steadily until flooding of the Virgin River washed away most of the settlement. Adventure was abandoned, and most of its residents moved one mile east, helping to establish the town of Rockville in 1862. At that time, settlers seeking safety from repeated floods and sporadic Indian Wars converged on this area from all along the Upper Virgin River.

For more on the history of Rockville, see pp. 41-42.

GPS COORDINATES: N 37°09.70' W 113°03.50' (approximately)

Aldridge (Aldredge)

By 1890, enough people had come to the area by the Fremont River, east of Capitol Reef National Park, to establish the town of Aldridge. About a dozen families, all members of the Church of Latter-day Saints, lived, raised fields, and even built a small schoolhouse here. Although they aspired to create a great and virtuous town, they were soon discouraged by the lack of water. By 1900 Aldridge was deserted. Since then, the town's buildings have been torn down and the materials used by others in the area, so little is left but memories at this quiet spot along Utah 24.

GPS COORDINATES: N 38°16.60' W 111°05.30' (approximately)

Alton

Alton, about 20 miles northeast of Glendale, was originally called Roundys Station, after Lorenzo Wesley Roundy, an early settler. Roundy built two log cabins here, but due to problems with the Indians, he was forced to abandon his site. He drowned in 1876 while crossing the Colorado River. Roundys Station was later renamed Graham, after Graham Duncan MacDonald, a bookkeeper of a nearby sawmill. MacDonald had helped haul lumber for the construction of the St. George Mormon temple. As time passed, various other names for the town were discussed, but in 1912 residents decided to hold a community drawing. A two-year-old child drew the name Alton from a hat, and that decided the matter. The name refers to the Alton Fjord in Norway and its surrounding mountains because the person who submitted the suggestion had just finished reading a book on the subject. Today Alton is a livestock and ranching community.

GPS COORDINATES: N 37°26.38' W 112°28.91'

Alunite

In 1912, Thomas Gillam, a prospector from Marysvale, first discovered the potash ore of alunite in Cottonwood Canyon. Mines were dug, and the town of Alunite was established to house the workers. Alunite's reduction plant, which extracted pure potash from the ore, eventually produced more potassium aluminum sulfate than any other plant in the country.

With the onset of World War I, the U.S. government became concerned that foreign sources of aluminum (a derivative of alunite) would dry up, and so they conducted experiments at the Alunite mines to extract aluminia. During these years, the town reached its highest population of just over a hundred people, and work in the mines was continuous. The town thrived; a post office, school, company store, church, and several homes were added. Though aluminum was successfully extracted from the ore, it proved to be excessively costly. By the late 1920s, potash extraction also became too expensive, so the mines closed down and the mill was demolished.

Some interest was regenerated in the alunite veins during World War II, and there was a local hope of reviving the town. But nothing substantial was produced, and the town was again abandoned.

GPS COORDINATES: N 38°22.84' W 112°14.61'

Black Rock

Black Rock gets its name from a nearby outcrop of black lava rock. A ranch was established here in 1876, and in 1893, a store was built nearby. As travelers and ranchers used the store, it developed a reputation as a stopping point, and Black Rock became a perfect station stop for the Los Angeles to Salt Lake City train line.

The town slowly grew around the activity of the train stop, and pumice quarries to the north attracted more settlers. Then in the 1930s the train line decided to bypass Black Rock in favor of bigger town stations. With the land becoming overgrazed, people began moving away, and today Black Rock is abandoned.
GPS COORDINATES: N 38°43.00' W 112°57.99'

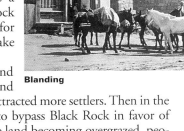
Blanding

Black Rock Station

Black Rock Station was a stop along the Pony Express and Overland Stage route. Located to the west of Dugway Pass, it was situated beside a black volcanic cone. A black volcanic stone cabin was erected there.

Black Rock Station was little more than a rest stop for weary travelers and a place where teams of horses were changed. The station did not offer meals or lodging.
GPS COORDINATES: N 39°52.68' W 113°16.24'

Blanding

Anasazi Indians occupied this area of southeast Utah as early as A.D. 600. Ute and Navajo also camped in the vicinity because of access to the local springs and seeps. When white settlers arrived, they referred to the area as White Mesa, and in 1897, Mormons Walter C. Lyman and his brother, Joseph, settled here. In an effort to make White Mesa habitable, they successfully dug a canal from Johnson Creek to camp. The town site was surveyed in 1905, and within three months, five other families had taken up residence. As the population grew, the name of the town was officially changed to Grayson, after Nellie Grayson Lyman, Joseph's wife. However, nearly a decade later, a wealthy easterner named Thomas Bicknell offered a 1,000-volume library to any town in Utah that would take his name. Grayson vied with Thurber, another town, to win the library, and they eventually settled on a compromise: Thurber took the name Bicknell in exchange for 500 volumes, and Grayson received the other half in exchange for taking the name Blanding, the maiden name of Bicknell's wife. It is reported that the people of Blanding, upon receiving the books, were somewhat disappointed to find they were of poor quality.

By 1909, telephone wires were strung connecting Blanding with Moab, and in 1916, residents constructed a reservoir whose distribution system consisted of wooden pipes. Electricity arrived on a part-time basis in 1918. A year later, Blanding's population reached 1,100 settlers, many of them returning Mormons who had fled to Mexico in the late 1800s to escape antipolygamy persecution.

In 1923, Blanding was the site of the Posey War, a clash in culture that pitted whites against the Ute and Paiute Indians. The war led to the establishment of the White Mesa Indian Reservation, 12 miles south of Bluff. (For more information on these events, see "Posey War," p. 79.)

Blanding's current population exceeds 3,200, and it is home to the San Juan campus of the College of Eastern Utah. The town borders some of southeastern Utah's most dramatic canyon country and receives many tourists and recreational visitors annually.
GPS COORDINATES: N 37°37.52' W 109°28.64'

Bluff

Bluff stands today as a testament to the determination and ingenuity of early Mormon settlers. In 1880, a group of 236 church members set out from southwest Utah to tame the rugged landscape of the state's southeastern corner. Under the leadership of Silas Stanford Smith, the Mormons took a direct route toward the Montezuma River. Traveling in this direction saved the pioneers more than 250 miles, but it presented them with a seemingly insurmountable obstacle: crossing the Colorado River down a deep, enormous gorge.

With no feasible way around the river, Smith decided to cross it; the spot would come to be known as the "Hole-in-the-Rock Pass." The Mormons built a series of roads along the sheer cliff edges and slowly made the gorge passable. After the long and arduous road construction, the expedition had to then ferry across the 300-foot-wide river. When they were done, the original six-week journey had taken over six months, and most of the pioneers were exhausted, without strength or will to carry on. However, they kept moving east, and eventually settled at the foot of the cliffs overlooking the San Juan River, calling their new town Bluff City.

Life continued to be difficult for the settlers. Their farms never really flourished and the water supply was inadequate. Though most settlers moved away, the town somehow managed to survive.

Bluff

Today it retains much of its old pioneer character. Bluff is home to some of the oldest Victorian houses in the area, as well as to an old cemetery and an ancient Indian pueblo.
GPS COORDINATES: N 37°17.05' W 109°33.12'

Bonneville Speedway

To most people—other than mining companies—the salt flats 7 miles northeast of Wendover in northwestern Utah might be considered a wasteland: a stark, white, flat slab of dry mud sparkling with salt crystals.

But in 1935, the British racing pioneer Sir Malcolm Campbell put the Bonneville Salt Flats on the map. Racing across the salt, he set a land speed record of 301.13 miles per hour and gave birth to the Bonneville Speedway.

Other racing pioneers have followed in Sir Malcolm's tire tracks. Craig Breedlove was first to break both the 400- and 500-mile-per-hour barriers, and in 1970, Gary Gabelich, utilizing a rocket-powered vehicle on wheels, reached 622.407 miles per hour to become the fastest man on land.

Bonneville Flats is not just for experts. It's world-renowned as an amateur proving ground, where regular folks from all walks of life can come in their souped-up cars and beat-up jalopies and let loose their desire to drive fast. The Southern California Timing Association and the Utah Salt Flats Racing Association are two organizations that arrange annual summer events where amateur racers compete to establish land speed records.

The area is a remnant of prehistoric Lake Bonneville, which left a massive deposit of rock-hard salt (when dry) that, it turns out, makes an ideal high-speed track. In winter months, the track remains submerged under shallow water.
GPS COORDINATES: N 40°45.75' W 113°53.00'

Bullion City

Established as a rough mining camp in the late 1860s, Bullion City produced gold and silver. It grew quickly, and by 1872, the town site had more than 50 buildings and a population in the hundreds. Seemingly destined for great things, Bullion City won the county seat of Piute County from Circleville.

Miners are a fickle breed, however. As new mining camps and rumors of big strikes sprung up in the region, Bullion City's population dissipated. Eager prospectors jumped from camp to camp, always chasing the richest gold lode they could find. Of the new camps, the richest was Snyder City, later renamed Kimberly.

By the end of the 1870s, Bullion City was virtually a ghost town, which presented Piute County with a unique problem: its county seat no longer had any residents. As a result, the privilege of being country seat was given to Marysvale.
GPS COORDINATES: N 38°24.70' W 112°20.00' (approximately)

Bullionville

In 1880, a group of miners formed the Carbonite Mining District. They established a settlement in the Uinta Mountains and called it Bullionville, anticipating an abundance of gold.

In 1887, L. P. Dyer, a cowboy and prospector, was looking for gold nearby and found little, but he did discover much good copper ore instead. He established a number of mines in the area, which collectively became known as the Dyer Group.

Bullionville, a rough little mining camp, was also known to see the likes of Butch Cassidy, Matt Warner, Elza Lay, and other members of the Wild Bunch, who would hide out there en route to nearby Brown's Park.

In 1899, a small mill and smelter were built to process ore from the mines rather than ship it to Wyoming on the Union Pacific Railroad. The town of Bullionville prospered until the copper veins played out in the early 1900s. Only a handful of workers stayed on, and in 1920 Bullionville shut down entirely.
GPS COORDINATES: N 40°42.05' W 109°34.36'

Caineville

In 1882, Mormon pioneers, responding to the directive of their church, tried to open this area of southern Utah to settlement. Elijah Cutler Behunin, the first man to take a wagon through Capitol Wash (which is now Capitol Reef Gorge in Capitol Reef National Park), established this settlement in the Fremont River valley and called it Caineville, after John T. Caine, the Utah Territory's representative to Congress.

Caineville residents planted crops, including fruit, corn, melons, and sorghum. A mill was built to process the sorghum, which was used as a sweetener as well as a potent liquor.

Caineville's post office was established in 1896, and the town prospered despite occasional flooding by the river. The friendly, social residents took special delight in their Saturday

Caineville

night dances. The socials were so popular and well attended that the hall could not accommodate all the attendees, so couples received numbers at the door when they arrived. Couples then had to wait until their numbers were called before they could take to the dance floor.

The whims and floods of the Fremont River eventually overwhelmed Caineville; after the turn of the century, the town suffered damage as often as every two or three years. Because of erosion of the soil, by 1910 the town was abandoned. Afterward, the area reverted to open range and ranch land. However, modern irrigation techniques have allowed the land to be cultivated once again. Today Caineville has a few residents, but most of the original townsite is derelict or gone.
GPS COORDINATES: N 38°20.06' W 111°01.40'

Callao

The story of Callao begins around 1859. Originally called Willow Springs, the town sits east of the Deep Creek Range in northwestern Utah. Mountain springs provided water to this otherwise inhospitable locale, so Willow Springs was deemed a suitable site for habitation and farming. In 1860, it functioned as a stop along the route of both the Overland Stage Line and the Pony Express.

Due to its remote location, Willow Springs was particularly vulnerable to attacks by Indians, who raided the stage company's horses. Nonetheless, with its station, store, and friendly locals, the town became an oasis for desert-weary travelers. One early visitor of Willow Springs was Mark Twain. He spent a night in an old log structure that became known as the "Mark Twain Cabin."

The Pony Express discontinued operations when the telegraph was completed in 1861, and the Overland Stage Line stopped coming to Willow Springs in 1869 with the advent of the transcontinental railroad. After that, the post office closed and the town slowly faded away.

Then in 1892, gold was found in the vicinity of nearby Gold Hill, and Willow Springs enjoyed a brief resurgence as a center for local activity. In 1895, a new post office was established, but because Willow Springs was such a common name throughout Utah, it was renamed Callao. The name may have been chosen by either an old prospector or a survey party who observed that Willow Springs bore a striking resemblance to the town of Callao, Peru. However, after only a short time, Callao faded once again, and its population dwindled as the town of Gold Hill developed to the north.

Today, Callao is home to a handful of people, and the streets are lined with trees and picturesque houses of yesteryear. Many of the homes are falling down, but some remain in good shape and are lived in. Though it never had a population of more than a few hundred, Callao has survived through the years as an oasis for travelers in the desert.

GPS COORDINATES: N 39°53.87' W 113°42.35'

Camp Floyd

In 1857, President James Buchanan, worried about rumors of a Mormon revolt and feeling that Brigham Young was abusing his powers as territorial governor, sent 3,000 troops into Utah under the leadership of Colonel Albert Sidney Johnston to quell any possible uprisings. Johnston marched his troops about 35 miles south of Salt Lake City and built a fort outside the small town of Fairfield. Named after U.S. Secretary of War John B. Floyd, the camp provided the army with a convenient place to watch over Salt Lake City and Provo without being so close as to further fuel tensions.

Camp Floyd was designated as an Overland Stage station in 1859 and a Pony Express stop in 1860. The troops protected against Indian attacks and kept the trail open for both businesses to operate. A local businessman named John Carson built a hotel, the Stagecoach Inn, for prominent visitors, and the inn became the stop for both the Overland Stage and the Pony Express.

Local Mormons came to see Camp Floyd as a mixed blessing. The army brought with it a great amount of money and jobs, and hired locals to do most of the building in camp. However, with the camp also came saloons, dance halls, and the many other vices that tend to follow young enlisted men. Fairfield grew to be the third largest city in Utah.

In 1860, as the Civil War approached, Secretary of War John B. Floyd was dismissed from his duties because of his Confederate sympathies, and Camp Floyd was renamed Fort Crittenden, after Kentucky senator, John Crittenden. Not long after, in May 1861, with the problems of the Civil War escalating, the troops were pulled out of Utah and the fort was quickly dismantled and closed for good. In its rush to leave, the army sold supplies worth $4 million for only $100,000 to the local Mormons. What the army did not sell, it destroyed.

What remains of Camp Floyd and the Stagecoach Inn is now a designated historical site and state park in Fairfield.

GPS COORDINATES: N 40°15.65' W 112°05.54'

Castle Dale

Castle Dale was established in 1877 as an agricultural and grazing community in response to Brigham Young's call for settlers to locate in Castle Valley. Though the town's name was slated to be Castle Vale, the post office listed it as Castle Dale, and it was never changed. For a time, there were two Castle Dales, Upper and Lower, about 3 miles apart; then Upper Castle Dale changed its name to Orangeville in honor of Bishop Orange Seely, an original settler.

Castle Dale grew steadily and the town expanded from the original plat beside Cottonwood Creek to the adjacent benchlands. A courthouse was built in 1892. Founded in 1889, Emery Stake Academy was the first high-school-level educational institution in southeastern Utah. The town was incorporated in 1900, and a number of commercial establishments, as well as a weekly newspaper, were set up.

Community growth evened off and then declined over subsequent decades. The main economic base was, and still is, farming, livestock, and some coal mining. From 1940 to 1970 the population declined from 953 to 541 people.

In mid-1970, the Utah Power and Light Company moved to the region and constructed two generating plants, one of which is the Hunter Plant 2 miles south of Castle Dale. Because it uses coal deposits from the region, the plant's economic impact on the town has been positive, and today Castle Dale is alive and well, with a population of about 1,700.

GPS COORDINATES: N 39°12.70' W 111°01.03'

Castle Gate

In the 1880s, the Pleasant Valley Coal Company, based at Winter Quarters, was looking to develop a new coal mine closer to the main line of the Denver & Rio Grande Western Railroad; it picked a rich vein in lower Price Canyon in central Utah. Castle Gate grew up around the mine and was named for the canyon's twin rock towers that stood where the highway entered the town.

A company store—the Wasatch Store, which also housed the coal company offices—is where Butch Cassidy and Elza Lay robbed the company payroll in April 1897. The pair escaped with $7,000 in gold coin, which was never recovered. It is rumored the gold may have been secreted in Buckhorn Draw, buried on what is now Sids Mountain.

Castle Gate, incorporated in April 1914, might still be thriving today except that McCulloch Oil (which eventually bought the property) decided the town was in the way of min-

Castle Gate, before road-widening eliminated one of the pillars of the "gate"

ing operations and moved it in 1974, making Castle Gate one of the most recent towns to become a ghost town. Though many homes were moved, the Wasatch Store was destroyed, despite a petition by residents to have it moved and transformed into a museum. Locals held a big farewell party to the town, complete with plenty of beer and musical bands.
GPS COORDINATES: N 39°44.12' W 110°52.22'

Castleton

Castleton was originally settled in the 1860s east of Moab on Castle Creek. It was established as a placer gold camp, but the placers did not produce for long. Then, when gold was found in the quartz of Miner's Basin in 1888, Castleton came back to life as a supply town for the mines. General stores, a post office, hotels, saloons, restaurants, assorted shops, and a physician's office quickly sprang up in town. Castleton had its own deputy sheriff, and at its peak in 1895, it had a larger population than Moab.

The local mining activity supported Castleton until about 1907, when the hardrock mines closed down. With no source of income, Castleton declined rapidly, and the town quietly evolved into an area where ranchers grazed their herds.
GPS COORDINATES: N 38°36.12' W 109°19.01'

Cisco

Cisco was founded in 1883 as a watering stop for the narrow-gauge Denver & Rio Grande Western Railroad. Water was pumped by a steam engine from the Colorado River to a reservoir 1 mile southeast of town.

Cisco became an important shipping point for livestock whose winter range was the Cisco Desert area and whose summer range was the Book Cliffs region. Nearby cattle ranchers and sheep herders used Cisco as a livestock and provisioning center. Numerous holding corrals were built for loading livestock onto trains. Stores, hotels, and restaurants sprang up to accommodate work crews and other travelers who came to Cisco. The post office was established in 1887.

When standard-gauge tracks were laid to replace the narrow gauge about 2 miles from town in 1890, the entire town relocated to stay on the railroad line. The construction activity benefited locals and brought a new influx of outsiders, pro-

viding increased ethnic and economic diversity. Cisco flourished and became noted for its wild, all-night parties.

The town's population jumped from 172 people in 1900 to 323 in 1910, only to decline to 95 by 1920. As in most towns, a core group of residents remained, while others came and went depending on the economy; Cisco in that era reflected the fortunes of the stock-raising industry. As the range deteriorated, and as sheep-shearing in particular declined, the population shrunk. Agriculture in the area was marginal at best; most of the many homestead applications in the first years of the century had failed by the third decade.

When I-70 came through and bypassed Cisco altogether, the final blow was dealt. Today, located off Utah 128, between exits 202 and 212 on I-70, the ghost town of Cisco has many boarded-up houses and maybe a dozen or so public buildings remaining.
GPS COORDINATES: N 38°58.18' W 109°19.05'

Clifton

In the 1850s, the mines around Clifton were known to have rich mineral deposits, and by 1858 prospectors had discovered veins of lead and silver ore, but conflicts with the Indians prevented steady working of the mines. By the 1870s, gold had been found, and mining picked up in earnest around Clifton. However, the nearest mill and smelter, built by General Patrick E. Connor, was 125 miles away across the Great Salt Lake Desert at Stockton. The large ore wagons that regularly traversed this distance were often robbed; eventually a small mill and smelter were built at Clifton in 1872. However, shortly after construction, the ore pockets stopped producing the anticipated quantities and quality of ore. When the smelter did not meet expectations, it was closed down, and the town died.

The road to Clifton is about 4 miles south of Gold Hill on the road to Callao. The ghost town is on private property.
GPS COORDINATES: N 40°06.27' W 113°49.06'

Colton

In 1883, when the Rio Grande Western was building a railroad from Soldier Summit toward Price, the town of Pleasant Valley Junction sprang up as a station stop. Soon after the construction of this line, another line was built from Pleasant Valley Junction to Scofield, to allow for easy shipment of the coal extracted from the mines around Scofield. Pleasant Valley Junction then became just what its name described, a junction between the two lines. It also provided trains approaching Sol-

Colton

dier Summit with helper engines, which they needed to climb the steep grade.

The town, essentially built by the rail company, included a depot, an 11-stall roundhouse, coal-loading facilities, and a water tower, as well as a few saloons and a hotel. By 1898, the name of the town had changed to Colton, in honor of William F. Colton, a Rio Grande Western official.

In 1940, Colton's population was 327, and the town was thriving as an important stop along the railroad—at least until diesel engines began to replace steam engines. Diesel-powered trains didn't need helper engines to climb to Soldier Summit, and Colton became obsolete. By the 1950s, the rail companies had taken anything they could use from Colton and relocated it to other stations.

During its lifetime, Colton burned down three times. Twice it was rebuilt, but after the final blaze no substantial efforts were made to reconstruct it, and Colton was left to sit as it was beside the tracks.

GPS COORDINATES: N 39°51.14' W 111°00.74'

Corinne

Corinne is unusual for a Utah ghost town, as it began as a railroad camp with visions of becoming a great city, big enough to rival Salt Lake City as the state's capital, and it was also non-Mormon, contrary to almost all the towns in Utah at the time.

The settlement was first referred to as Bear River (after the nearby river) or Connor (after the vocal anti-Mormon General Patrick E. Connor). However, for reasons that are now unclear, the name was soon changed to Corinne. Some say it was named after the daughter of General J. A. Williamson, one of the town's forefathers, while others say it was named for a popular actress who appeared at its opera house, Corinne LaVaunt.

In the late 1860s, the Union Pacific and the Central Pacific Railroads were coming closer and closer to their historic meeting at Promontory Summit, and in 1869 Corinne was strategically located along the route. The town was situated on the Bear River just north of its bay and about 6 miles west of Brigham City. Real estate speculators hoped that Corinne would be selected as the freight-transfer point between the railroad of the transcontinental line and the stagecoach of the Montana Trail.

Everyone was excited to get a piece of what was considered to be the last railroad boomtown, and in no time Corinne had more than a thousand permanent residents and nearly five times that many railroad workers, who found the town full of pleasant distractions. Being non-Mormon, Corinne had a number of saloons, liquor stores, dance halls, gambling dens, and hotels notorious for their ladies of ill-repute. Gunfights and murders were daily events.

One story of a Corinne gunfight begins north of Colorado Springs. George Tipton, Oscar Witherell, and Gene Wright held up a Colorado and Southern Express train to the tune of $105,000 in cash and $40,000 in jewels. They made it to Corinne and supposedly buried the bulk of the treasure about 4 miles upstream from town. Taking a few hundred dollars, they went into Corinne to celebrate. When they had spent the money, they tried to pawn some of the jewelry, but this aroused suspicions and a gunfight broke out. Wright and

Corinne's Main Street

Witherell were arrested and Tipton escaped with a bullet wound. He died soon after, supposedly never having dug up the treasure.

Corinne's rough reputation did not stop General Connor and the other town fathers from trying to persuade Washington, D.C., to make Corinne the state capital instead of Salt Lake City. They lobbied politicians back east by saying that the polygamy of Brigham Young was morally reprehensible. Connor and Young spent a couple years vying for the top spot in Utah, but it was in vain.

In 1871, Brigham Young ordered work to begin on the Utah Northern Railroad, which was to go north from Ogden to Franklin, Idaho. The railroad was completed in three years, and it bypassed Corinne along the way. Then in 1903, the Southern Pacific Railroad built a trestle across the Great Salt Lake, which rerouted the transcontinental line—once again bypassing Corinne.

These two bypasses sounded the death knell for Corinne as a major railroad junction and as the new state capital. Smaller today, its Wild West appearance and character completely gone, Corinne survives as a tame, rural farming community.

GPS COORDINATES: N 41°33.06' W 112°06.58'

Cove Fort

Just a few miles northwest of the junction of I-15 and I-70, Cove Fort stands near Cove Creek. This well-preserved fort was constructed in 1867 by Ira Nathaniel Hinckley under the orders of Brigham Young. Young saw the need for a guarded, permanent fort to be built in the area to give coach riders, freighters, and travelers a place where they could safely rest. It was also a pick-up and delivery station for the Pony Express and served to protect the newly constructed Desert Telegraph deep in Indian country.

Cove Fort is made up mostly of black volcanic rock and dark limestone. Its walls rise up to a height of 18 feet and run for 100 feet along the sides. Since the fort's construction, many different families have lived in it, but in 1988 it was donated back to the Church of Latter-day Saints. Cove Fort has undergone renovations in past years and stands today as a protected monument.

GPS COORDINATES: N 38°36.04' W 112°34.87'

Dalton

In 1864, John Dalton, his four wives, and a few other families came to southwest Utah. Several miles upstream from Virgin

City, the families settled and enjoyed prosperous farms. However, this good fortune would last for only a few years. By 1870, the Black Hawk War cleared out most of the settlers. By 1880, those who had stayed through the war were gone as well.

GPS COORDINATES: N 37°11.80' W 113°09.80' (approximately)

Dewey

Established in the 1880s on the Colorado River, Dewey was the site of a ferry operated by Samuel King, a farmer; in fact, the town was originally called Kings Ferry, and it served miners, farmers, and ranchers northeast of Moab.

The small community, settled by a few farmers and ranchers and located along the Old Spanish Trail, sat at one of the most favorable natural crossing points on the Colorado River. It was an active sheep-shearing locale in the first years of the century. A local school operated from 1902 to 1914. An accurate count of area residents seems never to have been made, but even at its height the town was merely the focal point for a few area families. Surely a few stores or businesses were established in Dewey, but they have not been chronicled.

A new ferry was constructed at Dewey in 1903 and operated by a law enforcement officer, Richard D. Westwood, until 1916. The Dewey Bridge was completed that same year, and Dewey was much in the news during the course of construction. Dewey then dropped from all but occasional mention. Grazing restrictions of the 1930s forced some residents from the area and gradually led to its status today, as a gathering of a few scattered farms and ranches.

GPS COORDINATES: N 38°48.82' W 109°18.13'

Dragon

In 1885, Sam Gilson discovered a black, solidified oil in northeast Utah; it was originally called uintaite, but it soon became known as gilsonite in honor of the man who did the most to promote it commercially. The Black Dragon Gilsonite Mine began production in 1888, but the camp didn't flourish until the Uintah Railway connected it to Mack, Colorado, in 1904. Dragon became an important town along the route, which went across Baxter Pass. The Uintah Railway's route over Baxter Pass made it the steepest railway in the world and a true feat of engineering: the narrow-gauge railroad had a 7.5 percent grade with 66-degree curves, and it crossed 75 bridges in 53 miles (see *4WD Adventures: Colorado* for more on this famous route).

Homesteaders and land developers began arriving in 1905 after the Uintah-Ouray Indian Reservation was opened to set-

Vernal-Dragon Stage

tlement, and the town flourished. For every train loaded with passengers to Dragon, there was a full shipment of gilsonite to return. At one time the population reached 750 people. Then in 1911, the train rails were extended another 10 miles beyond to a new camp named Watson. For the next decade, Dragon slowly dwindled in importance and population, and the Black Dragon Mine played itself out till there was no money to pay employees. By 1920, almost all the businesses in town had closed their doors permanently. Today, there are very few structures in evidence, as most have collapsed or been torn down.

GPS COORDINATES: N 39°47.14' W 109°04.37'

Duchesne

In 1776, the Domínguez-Escalante Expedition identified a site at the mouth of the Indian Basin, just above the junction of the Strawberry and Duchesne Rivers in northeastern Utah, that would make a good place for a town. However, it was not until 1905 that a town was actually founded there. A. M. Murdock, with permission from the U.S. government, set up a trading post at the spot, and others soon followed and settled in the area. Originally the town was called Dora after Murdock's daughter. The

Duchesne's Main Street

name was then changed to Theodore after the sitting president, but when a neighboring town took the name Roosevelt, Theodore's name was permanently changed to Duchesne.

Duchesne survives today as a small town that focuses on oil and farming.

GPS COORDINATES: N 40°09.80' W 110°24.03'

Duncan's Retreat

Chapman Duncan first settled this site in 1861, and several other families soon followed. But a year later the Virgin River flooded and destroyed most of the homes and farms, and almost everybody moved away, including Duncan. However, other settlers arrived, and for want of a better name, they called their tiny town Duncan's Retreat.

Within a year, Duncan's Retreat had grown to about 70 people, and in 1864, a post office, school, and meetinghouse were constructed. The settlers raised cotton, corn, wheat, and sorghum.

In 1866, the floods returned, and over the next few years high water from the Virgin River destroyed the fields and killed the town, which was completely deserted by 1891. All that remains of the town today is the grave of Nancy Ferguson Ott, who died here in 1863. Her grave marker is located on the north side of Utah 9, right off the highway.

GPS COORDINATES: N 37°11.00' W 113°08.00' (approximately)

Eagle City

High up in the Henry Mountains, Eagle City is perched near the head of Crescent Creek. Local legend has it that John Angrove was the one who first discovered gold in these mountains—and was murdered for it. This did little to deter others, and by the late 1880s, several rich lodes had been found, and Eagle City was the center for local mining speculations. It is said that some of the members of Butch Cassidy's Wild Bunch often stopped here, making this a true gun-slinging Wild West town.

The miners ran into trouble, though, when they dug deeper; water began to seep into the mines, and the tunnels

Eagle City, 1892

became flooded at 300 feet. A project to dig a drainage tunnel was halfway finished before funds ran out. Adding insult to injury, the town burned down in 1911, signaling the end of Eagle City. All that is left today are the remains of a log cabin, collapsed in a grove of aspens.

However, legend has it that the famous Lost Josephine Mine lies buried up in the Henry Mountains, some say near Eagle City. It is said to be rich with gold, but it was cursed by local Indians who were used as slaves by the Spanish. If you believe the tales, ruin and death are the only things people have found there since. For more on this well-known lost mine, see Southwest #48: Copper Ridge Trail.

GPS COORDINATES: N 38°04.41' W 110°44.70'

Escalante

Mormon cavalry discovered this area on the banks of the Escalante River during the Black Hawk War when they chased some Indians into the valley. The Mormons originally called it Potato Valley or Spud Valley after the wild potatoes that grew in the area, but mapmaker A. H. Thompson suggested that the settlement be called Escalante, even though the famous Spanish missionary and explorer had never been within 150 miles of the site. Still, by 1875, the name Escalante had stuck.

Escalante's old Main Street

For years Escalante was a Mormon outpost on the edge of the frontier. It was the last stop before the Hole-in-the-Rock Expedition set out to settle more of southeastern Utah.

Today, Escalante is still very much inhabited, and it serves as a great starting point for tourists who wish to explore the area.

GPS COORDINATES: N 37°46.23' W 111°36.54'

Fish Springs Station

Fish Springs Station, a main stop on the Pony Express route, got its name from the many springs dotting the area: some were boiling hot and others were ice cold and had fish swim-

ming in them. The main attraction, however, was that they were clean. The stage route passed a number of pools of water in this section of the western Utah desert, but most were stagnant and surrounded by black mud. Fish Springs was one of few places where travelers could have a drink and a swim to wash off the dust and grime of the long trail. Stagecoaches filled barrels with water here because it was such a dry journey to the next stop at either Boyd Station or Black Rock Station, depending on the direction of travel.

About 30 years later, a mining camp was established 15 miles to the west that also bore the name Fish Springs, but it was not related.

Fish Springs, on the southern edge of the salt flats, sits to the west of the border of what is now a national wildlife refuge, and it's still extremely hot and desolate in the summer. Even today, no matter which way you come from, you have to travel on at least 40 miles of dirt road to get there.

GPS COORDINATES: N 39°50.88' W 113°24.62'

Frisco

Like many Utah ghost towns, Frisco began as a mining camp, which was thrown up in haste after an enormous lode of silver was discovered in 1875 in this part of the San Francisco Mountains.

Frisco quickly developed into the commercial center for the local mining district and served as the terminus of the Utah Southern Railroad extension from Milford, which was located about 17 miles east. The town had a hospital, hotels, churches, a school, a newspaper, and many stores. Its preponderance of saloons, 23 by one estimate, also led to a preponderance of gunfights and killings, especially on pay day, and to its reputation as a haven for drunks, devils, and gamblers.

A large number of mines operated in the district, but the Horn Silver Mining Company was the main enterprise. In its first 10 years, the Horn Silver Mine produced $50 million in silver, making it one of the richest lodes anywhere, and to process the ore, the Frisco Mining and Smelting Company constructed a smelter with five beehive charcoal kilns. Then, one day in 1885, the entire open-pit Horn Silver Mine caved in—luckily during a shift change when no miners were in it—and the town never properly recovered. Most of the miners and residents moved away, although a new shaft was drilled and a handful of miners and families stayed on to work it, pulling out another $20 million over 20 years. Though the town was abandoned by 1920, sporadic work was done in the district until 1940.

Throughout its lifetime, Frisco remained a mining camp and never attained the status of an incorporated town. The charcoal kilns still stand, and in 1982 they were listed in the National Register of Historic Places. Frisco was once a popular stop for treasure hunters, but most of the old coins and trinkets have long since been dug up.

GPS COORDINATES: N 38°27.17' W 113°15.54'

Fruita

Though some had tried their luck in the area before, none had stayed until Niels (or Nels) Johnson made his home at the confluence of the Fremont River and Sand Creek in 1876.

Frisco, 1880

Johnson's home became a regular stopping point for people passing through the area, and for 15 years Johnson kept them supplied and provided overnight lodging.

The area had the potential to support many farms and orchards, and Johnson planted fruit trees. In the mid-1880s, other families came to live in the area, and the crops were expanded and proved to be very successful. The town, which the settlers called Junction, grew slowly. Around 1903, a post office was established, and due to the great number of other towns called Junction, the town's name was officially changed to Fruita.

The town never grew to be very large. A one-room schoolhouse was built in 1896 and was used until 1941. In 1955, the National Park Service bought the town and incorporated it into the expanding Capitol Reef National Park.

Currently, Fruita is home to a campground and the park's headquarters. The National Park Service has preserved a barn, a blacksmith shop, and the schoolhouse. Visitors can hear taped memories of some of the people who used to live and work in historic Fruita.

GPS COORDINATES: N 38°17.10' W 111°14.74'

Giles

The township of Giles, first established in 1883, was originally called Blue Valley, after the blue-gray barren clay hills in this desolate region. Founded by Mormons as an agricultural community, Blue Valley was divided by the Fremont River, which was used for irrigation, and the town's two halves were connected by a narrow wooden bridge. The Mormon church provided the town's

Old stagecoach roadhouse in Giles, 1941

social life and leadership. Originally it was a branch of the ward in the upper valley, but in 1885 a new ward was formed, which included Blue Valley and nearby Hanksville.

Most of the irrigated farming took place south of the Fremont River on the river flats. Nearly three thousand acres of corn, alfalfa, cabbages, and other fruits and vegetables were irrigated by canals and ditches that diverted water from the river.

In 1895, Blue Valley changed its name to Giles after a prominent resident, Bishop Henry Giles, who died in 1892. He is buried in the Giles cemetery.

The major reason for the formation of Giles also proved its undoing. In 1897, the Fremont River flooded, wiping out the bridge and most of the irrigation canals. The town of 200 people rallied to repair the damage, but in 1909 a second flood once again washed out their farms. The town never recovered and was officially disbanded in 1910.

GPS COORDINATES: N 38°22.13' W 110°50.64'

Gold Hill

Located on Gold Hill Wash, Gold Hill was a mining town with three lives: one of gold, one of copper, and one of arsenic. California gold prospectors first found riches here as early as 1858, and a smelter was built to process ore in 1871. It wasn't until 1892 that the town of Gold Hill was established, and it was mostly a tent city for miners. Other mines opened in the area to produce copper, silver, lead, tungsten, arsenic, and bismuth. At the turn of the century, the Gold Hill gold boom went bust, and the population exodus was such that about all that was left were dozens of mine shafts.

When World War I began, there was a great need for copper as well as for arsenic. Several Gold Hill mines were reopened around 1916. However, because the Western Pacific Railroad had bypassed Gold Hill 10 years earlier, Gold Hill miners had to use slow-moving stagecoaches and freight wagons to transport their products. When the Deep Creek Railroad arrived from Wendover in 1917, Gold Hill was given a much-welcomed helping hand, and the town boomed, its population reaching 3,000. Frame houses were built, as well as stores of all types, though the largest building was the pool hall, which doubled as a meetinghouse. Gold Hill was never particularly attractive, as miners—busy by day, in the saloon at night, and ready to move on to a better strike at any time—rarely bothered to maintain their property.

By the mid-1920s, the demand for copper, arsenic, and other products ceased. A few diehards stayed on, but the town eventually withered. The last train from Wendover left Gold Hill in 1938, and by 1940 the tracks were removed.

Thanks to World War II, Gold Hill was revived for a second time in the mid-1940s. There was again a great need for tungsten and arsenic. Idle mines reopened, buildings were repaired, new ones built (including a bowling alley), and electricity came to town for the first time. But the mines did their job too well, and within two years the government had all the arsenic it needed, and the mines were ordered to stop production. The population declined immediately, and by 1952, it was all but abandoned.

Today Gold Hill boasts a few hardy residents who live there at various times of the year. The town is one of Utah's most complete ghost towns; old mines and buildings dot the area if you take the time to find them. The old cemetery is on an adjacent hill, but looks as if it hasn't been visited in decades; there is no obvious path leading up to it. The most prominent ruins are the remains of an old general store at the main intersection.

GPS COORDINATES: N 40°09.98' W 113°49.81'

Grafton

Grafton was settled in 1859 by Nathan Tenney and other families on the south bank of the Virgin River. The river was the bane of the new settlement (for a short time known as Wheeler), and after many of the houses were washed away in 1862, the fledgling township was forced to relocate a mile upstream from the original

Green River ferry, 1898

site. The Indian Wars also troubled Grafton, forcing several families to leave the area; the graveyard contains a memorial to a family killed by Indians.

The Virgin River, which enabled Grafton to grow crops, was also the dividing point of the town. Residents would keep horses on both sides of the river—those on the far side for traveling north, those within the town for traveling over Grafton Mesa to the towns to the south. Thus, when the river flooded, they were not trapped in town.

By the mid-1880s, Grafton supported 28 families and was the first county seat for Kane County (Grafton is now part of Washington County). The adobe meetinghouse, the major building remaining today, was built in 1886 using timber imported from Mount Trumbull on the Arizona Strip, and it was

One-room Grafton schoolhouse

packed and rendered with local clay. This meeting hall was the focal point for the community, being used for dances, church meetings, funerals, and parties as well as religious worship. Residents also helped with the construction of the Hurricane Canal, an ambitious scheme to bring irrigation waters to the Hurricane Bench, which opened up the area for cultivation. In return for their work, these Grafton residents received parcels of land in Hurricane. For many, the temptation to dismantle their homes and rebuild in Hurricane, away from the Virgin River floodplain, was too great, and by the early 1920s, Grafton was nearing ghost town status. The final resident moved out in the early 1930s.

Grafton received a shot of notoriety when its photogenic, decaying buildings were used in scenes for the movie *Butch Cassidy and the Sundance Kid* (1969).

Today, Grafton is privately owned, and the remaining buildings are undergoing extensive renovations in conjunction with the Bureau of Land Management. In 2000, the adobe meeting hall was brought back from ruin; it has a new floor, patched adobe, and fresh paint. The oldest building in town, opposite the meeting hall, has been propped up and stabilized for safety, as have some of the other cabins.
GPS COORDINATES: N 37°09.93' W 113°04.88'

Green River

Settled in 1878, Green River is the town that grew up near the historic river crossing favored by Ute Indians for centuries and later by Spanish explorers—it was the only spot along a 200-mile stretch where the Green River could be forded. In fact, the town was first known as Ute Crossing, and in its early days, it served as a mail relay station between Salina, Utah, and Ouray, Colorado. This ended when the Denver & Rio Grande Western Railroad arrived four years later. Over its long history, the town has relied on many industries to survive, ranging from railroad and highway construction, uranium mining, and oil drilling to cattle and sheep ranching.

Green River is also famous for its production of luscious watermelon, cantaloupe, and honeydew melons; today, it celebrates this abundance with an annual Melon Days festival each September. Another big event in Green River is the Friendship Cruise, in which boaters make the trip down the Green River and up the Colorado River to Moab during Memorial Day weekend. Green River is also home to the John Wesley Powell Museum, located on the east bank of the Green River along Main Street. Recreation and tourism are the main sources of income for the town today.
GPS COORDINATES: N 38°59.72' W 110°09.87'

Hanksville

Sometime between 1869 and 1872, John Graves passed through the present-day site of Hanksville. Naming it Graves Valley, he kept going to Lake Powell. The area was still Graves Valley when, in the early 1880s, Ebenezer Hanks led a group of settlers to the valley. He and his cousin, Ephraim Hanks, were both notable pioneers in the area who most likely left Salt Lake City to escape the polygamy persecutions of the 1880s.

In 1885, Ebenezer Hanks died after suffering an injury while building a barn. Shortly thereafter, the town was renamed Hanksville. It soon became a regional supply depot for local miners and settlers.

One of the first men to work in the area was Charley Gibbons. He bought a store and a ranch. One of his cowhands at the time was the young Robert LeRoy Parker, later known as

Hanksville's Main Street

Butch Cassidy. Hanksville is actually the last stop before Robbers Roost Canyon, where Cassidy's gang would hide out. These outlaws were frequent visitors to Hanksville and to Gibbons's supply store. Over the years they paid hundreds in cash for supplies and Gibbons never had a problem with them.

Hanksville never grew too large, and it has remained a steady outpost for the past hundred years. Today the town is doing well with its traditional industries of mining and farming, and it also gets a boost from tourist traffic heading toward Lake Powell. Currently the old Wolverton Mill, relocated from the Henry Mountains, stands in Hanksville. The town also has a notable gas station and convenience store—built directly into the side of a sandstone cliff.

GPS COORDINATES: N 38°22.37' W 110°42.83'

Harper

Harper was part of a ranching community that developed with the settlement of Nine Mile Canyon. Ranchers and settlers were the first legal homesteaders who took up residence along the 40 miles of Nine Mile Canyon after the telegraph, which consisted of a single wire strung on iron poles to keep Indians from burning them, was constructed through the canyon.

Freight stops were established every 20 miles or so through the canyon and Harper was one of them. Located at the intersection of Argyle and Nine Mile Canyons, Harper grew into a town throughout the late 1800s. It was not until 1905, with the establishment of a school, that the town of Harper officially came into being. There was a log post office, a telegraph office, hotel, store, and saloon. By 1910, the town had grown to 130 in population. However, when the coach line fell through in the 1920s, the canyon fell victim to new railroads and Harper began to slowly fade away.

In 1902, prominent businessman and rancher Preston Nutter purchased the Brock Ranch in Nine Mile Canyon. He also acquired the saloon and hotel, which he converted into a bunkhouse for his cowboys. One of the most important ranchers in Utah, Nutter had property holdings in excess of 665,000 acres.

Today, a few abandoned buildings and scattered foundations can be found at the site of Harper.

GPS COORDINATES: N 39°48.03' W 110°22.08'

Heiner

Located about two miles north of Helper, Heiner was first settled in 1911. It was originally named Panther after the Panther Coal Mine. The little mining town then changed its name to Carbon and finally settled on Heiner in 1914 after U.S. Fuel Company vice president, Moroni Heiner.

The town grew in population and peaked at five or six hundred in the 1920s. However, in the 1950s coal prices fell, coal use decreased, and the local mines were running out. The town was soon obsolete and was abandoned.

GPS COORDINATES: N 39°42.49' W 110°51.93'

Helper

First settled in the 1880s by Teancum Pratt and his wives, Pratt's Landing began as any other mining town. However, soon after Pratt's arrival, the Denver & Rio Grande Western Railroad came into town and gave it a huge economic boost. The railroad needed a station at which it could change tracks from narrow to standard gauge and could provide "helper" engines for trains ascending the steep Soldier Summit. In 1891 the station was completed, and the

Helper's Main Street, circa 1910

town's name was officially changed to Helper.

As the railroad needed a large number of unskilled laborers to build the station, and since much of its unskilled labor force was composed of immigrants, Helper became a melting pot of many different nationalities; it was even once known as "the town of 57 varieties." Helper thrived throughout the early 1900s, and its position as a railroad hub even helped it weather the blow of the Great Depression. However, the second half of the century did not treat Helper as kindly. As the coal and train industries became less important, so did Helper.

Today the town holds some interesting features, one of which is the Western Mining and Railroad Museum. The museum houses many relics and pictures that trace the history of the town and its industry, and many of the old storefronts along Main Street have recently been converted to showcase paintings from the museum. Helper is currently the second largest town in Carbon County.

GPS COORDINATES: N 39°41.31' W 110°51.23'

Ibex

To confuse ghost town hunters, there are two ghost towns called Ibex, located fewer than 50 miles apart. The one traveled to in this book is the more southerly, lesser known of the two. It was an old mining and stockman's trading center that may have gained its name from local animals bred from desert bighorn sheep and domestic Indian goats. The resulting offspring had horns with a gradual curve, reminiscent of the ibex in Africa.

The settlement of Ibex consisted of homes, corrals, a post office, and a boardinghouse. It was a little community that lasted into the 1900s, but gradually dispersed when the miners and shepherds moved on.

Most of the buildings are gone, but a short hike reveals the remains of a dam wall across the mouth of a narrow canyon. Ruins of the now-collapsed corrals and several dumps of tin cans are all that remain of Ibex.

GPS COORDINATES: N 38°52.94' W 113°26.46'

Johnson

During the early 1870s, four brothers with the surname Johnson moved their families to the area known as Spring Canyon Ranch in southern Utah, and as you might guess, the area soon came to be known as Johnson. The community thrived on agriculture for a couple of decades. However, a drought set in toward the end of the century, and by 1910 the town was deserted.

Nearby Johnson Canyon has been used as a backdrop in several Western movies, as well as in the television series *Gunsmoke*. It is on private property and fenced.

GPS COORDINATES: N 37°0518' W 112°22.10'

Kanab

Mormons first arrived in this area in 1858, but for 12 years local Indians persistently attacked the settlers and thwarted their efforts to establish a town. However, in 1870, Mormon pioneers finally managed to build a secure fort. The area immediately became a center of activity for missionary work and functioned as a safe stopping point for travelers and traders. In April 1870, Brigham Young came to the fort to bless the land and its

Kanab, 1920

people. In 1871, the Deseret Telegraph Line came through town, and Kanab found itself connected to the outside world. From then on, it grew and prospered.

In 1912, Kanab was host to one of the country's more bizarre elections. A slate of nominees for the positions of mayor and for the town council was composed completely of women. Running unopposed, the women were all elected to office. Mary Elizabeth Wooley Chamberlain became the new mayor of Kanab. The story made national news and even prompted a visit from the prominent suffragist Susa Young Gates (Brigham Young's daughter). The women completed their terms and went back to their normal lives, but not before making many improvements in town, as well as making history.

Kanab is located between Bryce Canyon and the Grand Canyon, providing it with some truly breathtaking scenery. Hollywood discovered Kanab in the 1920s and began to film in and around the town, beginning with *Deadwood Coach* (1922), which was filmed in the surrounding Vermilion Cliffs. Since then hundreds of films and television series have used the area as a backdrop, including *Buffalo Bill* (1944), *The Arabian Nights* (1942), *The Rainmaker* (1956), and television episodes of *Lassie*. It is no wonder the area has earned the nickname "Little Hollywood."

With its natural attractions and its cinematic history, Kanab thrives on tourism. Every year many visitors come to see the movie sites, and others stop on their way to the canyons. No matter what the reason for coming, visitors of Kanab are treated to a small taste of the Old West.

GPS COORDINATES: N 37°02.88' W 112°31.66'

Kelton

Northwest of the Great Salt Lake, Kelton sits along the remnants of the original transcontinental railroad. During the construction of the original railroad, many residents lived in

tents, and there was a large population of immigrant Chinese workers. After the line began service, Kelton became an important junction between the east-west rails and the northern coach trails, as the large quantities of gold coming down from the Idaho and Montana mines had to pass through town on the way to Salt Lake City.

The constant traffic meant that Kelton prospered in the late 1800s, blossoming with hotels, a row of saloons, stores, and solid homes. However, its fate took a turn for the worse when the Lucin Cutoff was built in 1903. This bridge over the Great Salt Lake bypassed Kelton and dealt a serious blow to the town's economy.

In 1934, an intense earthquake rocked Kelton, damaging the school and many houses. Although many residents decided to leave town, Kelton remained viable until 1942, when the original railroad, which had been used as a back-up line, was taken up. With that, the town slowly faded for good. Today not much remains except for an old cemetery and some weathered headstones. The old railroad grade is still intact and can be driven on Northern #12: Transcontinental Railroad Trail.

GPS COORDINATES: N 41°44.78' W 113°06.39'

Kimberly

High up in the Tushar Mountains of the Fishlake National Forest, this gold-mining town was originally called Snyder City by the miners who struck it rich here in the 1890s. Then in 1899, Peter Kimberly, a businessman from Pennsylvania, bought the Bald Mountain Mine and changed the name to the Annie Laurie Mine. After the Annie Laurie reached a high-grade gold ore in the mountain, the town became known as Kimberly and developed into one of Utah's high-profile gold camps.

The town consisted of two parts: Upper Kimberly, which was mostly residential, and Lower Kimberly, which was home to the business district. As with many of the larger gold towns, Kimberly had a well-deserved reputation as a rough, wild place where the saloons and brothels were as busy as the jail, which was said to be the strongest for a hundred miles; it is currently on display at the Lagoon Amusement Park in northern Utah as a part of its reconstructed Wild West. It is said that Butch Cassidy and his Wild Bunch were often seen

Kimberly, 1917

in town, though they apparently never attempted to steal the local payroll during their stays in Kimberly.

A wealth of gold ore continued to flow from the mines; in 1905, the Annie Laurie was running three shifts a day, seven days a week. However, that same year Peter Kimberly died and a British company that knew nothing of gold mining took over. It began paying the workers in paper as opposed to gold currency, and many miners left the town in anger. By 1907, the mine found itself in debt and was forced to close. After the mine closure, the town became mostly deserted.

A new gold vein was found here in 1932. About 50 families worked the mine for the next six years until the ore played out. Today, ruins of the old Annie Laurie mill still haunt the abandoned Gold Mountain town, which has several houses and buildings standing silent and intact.

UPPER KIMBERLY GPS COORDINATES: N 38°29.12' W 112°23.80'
LOWER KIMBERLY GPS COORDINATES: N 38°29.50' W 112°23.41'

Latuda

Originally known as Liberty (after the Liberty Coal Company), this settlement opened its first coal mine in 1914 in the midst of other Spring Canyon coal-mining towns in Carbon County. A couple of years later, the town was renamed after the coal developer Frank Latuda.

Latuda was home to several mining innovations. An experimental mechanical loader was successfully tried here, as was an air-sand coal-cleaning plant. In the town's prime, about 300 to 400 people called Latuda home. But in 1927, a series of avalanches ravaged homes and killed some unfortunate miners. The town persevered through the ordeal for another 30 or 40 years, but as the nationwide coal industry declined in the 1950s, so did the town.

GPS COORDINATES: N 39°42.26' W 110°56.84'

Logan

Named for local trapper Ephraim Logan, who died here, the town of Logan sits at the mouth of Logan Canyon in northern Utah. In the summer of 1859, Brigham Young sent a small group of Mormons to survey and settle the region, and in less than a year, they had built a hundred homes and a schoolhouse.

Once the town was established, residents began construction of the Logan Tabernacle in 1865, which would take 25 years to complete because of stoppages for missionary expeditions. In 1877, they began building the Logan Temple, which was completed in 1884. These two buildings comprise the center of the Mormon faith and culture in Logan. In a strange twist of fate, the Shoshoni Indians, a tribe with whom the Logan settlers often came into conflict, actually helped to build the temple. They believed that the building would help preserve the sanctity of the land upon which they had performed sacred ceremonies for years.

Logan was, and still is, a center for higher education. In 1878, Brigham Young College was founded here, and 12 years later, the land-grant institution that would become Utah State University was founded. Today, Logan is a modern college town, and the state university is the largest employer.

Throughout the years, Logan has changed from an agricultural and mill-based community to one centered around man-

Logan's Main Street, 1896

ufacturing and research. However, the Logan Temple, which stands atop a hill overlooking downtown, still recalls the spirit of the early Mormon pioneers.

GPS COORDINATES: N 41°44.23' W 111°50.03'

Lucin

Lucin began as many towns did—along the tracks of the transcontinental railroad, first as a work camp, then as a railroad stop—though Lucin had the distinction of being the first stop in Utah for trains coming from the West. Once the line was completed, Lucin moved about 1.7 miles up the tracks to the east where it was equipped with a foreman's house and a section house for the laborers. The site where Lucin had once been later became known as Umbria Junction. Lucin remained a relatively successful town during the 1870s, finding some luck in the mines to the south and the southeast and as a supply depot for the Grouse Creek area.

In 1903, the construction began on the Lucin Cutoff, a 102-mile stretch of track between Ogden and Lucin that included a railroad bridge over the Great Salt Lake; this new route provided the lines with greater speed and efficiency, though many of the towns along the old route suffered and died because of it.

Driving the last pile in the Lucin Cutoff, October 26, 1903

Because of the cutoff, Lucin was forced to move once again. This time it relocated about a mile west along the tracks, to its present location. The move involved little more than moving the station a short ways down the line. Historic Lucin was renamed Grouse and was eventually dismantled in 1907 leaving hardly any indication of its existence. Today, the site of historic Lucin is marked by a sign along the old route of the transcontinental railroad.

Lucin received national attention in the 1970s as the location of Nancy Holt's *Sun Tunnels* and Robert Smithson's *Spiral Jetty*. These two pieces of modern art attempted to engage the landscape. Today, the works are gone, and there is little left of the old railroad town.

GPS COORDINATES: N 41°21.05' W 113°54.50'

Miners Basin

In 1888, gold was found high in the La Sal Mountains, and 10 years later the Miners Basin mining district was established. The town that developed had about 80 inhabitants during its peak years around the turn of the century. In 1907, hurt by economic panic, Miners Basin was all but abandoned.

However, one miner, Gordon Fowler, stayed on for the next 50 years keeping the town in order, convinced that more gold waited in the steep, hard rock of the mountains. He died without realizing his dream.

GPS COORDINATES: N 38°32.40' W 109°15.30'

Moab

Named for the biblical "land beyond Jordan," Moab sits on the banks of the Colorado River in southeastern Utah. Ute Indians lived here long before Mormons arrived to settle the area. In 1855, 41 Mormon men tried to establish the Elk Mountain Mission at the site of present-day Moab, but Indian attacks made life far too difficult and the project was abandoned.

It was not until the late 1870s that the Mormons were able to create a permanent settlement. By 1881, a railroad spur

The Moab ferry, put into operation in 1897 to replace a smaller one

connected the town with the Denver to Salt Lake City line. Soon after, a ferry system was set up across the Colorado River. By 1912, it was replaced with a bridge.

In its early years, Moab's economy depended on farming, ranching, and fruit orchards. Still, as early as 1906, local newspapers were promoting the area as a tourist spot; the first settlers were not blind to the natural beauty surrounding them.

In the 1950s, Moab experienced its largest economic boom—large quantities of uranium were discovered and a small oil bonanza hit the area, lasting into the 1960s. The population of Moab more than tripled. After uranium mining slowed down, potash mining (used in the manufacture of fertilizer) became an important industry.

As more people came to the area and saw the striking landscape, the tourism industry began to take off. After the establishment of Arches National Park to the north and Canyonlands National Park to southwest, Moab became a prime location for the exploration of southeastern Utah. For the past 25 years, with the marking of the slickrock trails, it has become a worldwide center for mountain biking.

Tourists were not the only ones flocking to this stunning countryside. Hollywood has arrived on a number of occasions. *Wagon Master* (1949), about the Hole-in-the-Rock journey,

was filmed in Moab, and such recent movies as *Indiana Jones and the Last Crusade* (1989), *Thelma and Louise* (1991), and *City Slickers II* (1994) have been filmed in and around Moab.

Moab and the surrounding area continue to grow in popularity as a tourist spot for amateur geologists, outdoor athletes, and people who just want to experience its primal landscape.

GPS COORDINATES: N 38°33.83' W 109°32.94'

Monticello

In the late 1880s, Francis A. Hammond, the Mormon stake president of San Juan County, ordered an exploration of the land on either side of Montezuma Canyon in southeast Utah. Though the land was used by a cattle and land company, its legal claims to it were somewhat dubious. Hammond had five men move to the northern mouth of the canyon to begin work on fields and a town site. The location was important because of the availability of water. The cowboys of the land company often came into conflict with the Mormon settlers, and both were sometimes attacked by local Indians, as the Ute made intermittent raids in an effort to scare off the pioneers.

In 1888, the town was finally dubbed Monticello after the estate of Thomas Jefferson. Monticello based its economy on agriculture. Just after the turn of the century, the Utah State Agricultural College experimented with dry-farming techniques in the area. Around the same time, the U.S. government made it possible to purchase large 320-acre plots for a relatively cheap price, thereby making the area very attractive to new settlers.

Throughout the 20th century, Monticello has remained a steady town in southeast Utah. Its well-groomed lawns and old houses make it stand out in stark contrast to the surrounding wilderness. Like Moab, Monticello has benefited from the recent boom in the southeastern Utah's tourism industry. This small town is a perfect place from which to explore the national parks and forests that surround it.

GPS COORDINATES: N 37°52.19' W 109°20.57'

Mutual

In the early 1900s, coal miners were working their way west from Helper in central Utah's Spring Canyon. The Mutual Coal Company developed a mine in the west end of the canyon, and in 1921, it built a town for its workers. The buildings were made out of stone and proved to be very strong; some still survive. A small suburb, called Little Standard, composed mainly of tents and shacks, even sprang up south of Mutual.

By 1938, the Mutual mines were pretty much played out, and people began leaving town. As the stone houses were vacated, people from Little Standard quickly moved in. However, once the coal mines closed, there was no other means of survival. Eventually, they too had to leave the area. Today there is little left of the mining region.

GPS COORDINATES: N 39°42.64' W 110°57.88'

Myton

Myton developed in the late 1800s as an Indian trading post in northeastern Utah. Located next to the only bridge across the Duchesne River, this loose grouping of buildings was originally known as "The Bridge."

Early view of Myton

In 1905, Congress opened up the Uintah-Ouray Reservation for settlement. Each married, adult Indian male received a 160-acre homestead; women and orphans received smaller plots. The rest of the land was opened to white settlers, and Myton was chosen as one of the towns to supervise the land rush. As new folks arrived in the area, the once-quiet Indian trading post became a growing supply town, and it was officially named after H. P. Myton, an Indian trader who had worked the post for some years.

For the next few decades, Myton grew and prospered. The town boasted many stores, a physician, an automobile dealership, and an opera house. Myton even fielded a baseball team that played against other small towns in the area.

However, the good times came to an end with the Great Depression. Banks and stores closed; and with them people left. Around the same time there were several suspicious fires in town that destroyed a good deal of property. This double blow proved very difficult to withstand, though the town was never deserted.

Even today, Myton claims a population of several hundred. Although many of these people live in farms outside of town, the sleepy downtown area is still used as a meeting place and supply stop.
GPS COORDINATES: N 40°11.74' W 110°03.75'

Newhouse
In 1900, a businessman named Samuel Newhouse bought the Cactus silver mine, made a success out of it, and a camp called Tent Town was established on the property. The name certainly seemed logical, as everyone lived in a canvas tent or covered wagon. In 1904 the mine was still producing big; a hospital, hotel, and many other permanent structures were built,

Newhouse, circa 1908

and the town was renamed Newhouse after the man who owned the land. An opera house and a large dance hall were erected, and in contrast to most other mining towns, the one saloon was located outside city limits. Sam Newhouse wanted a decent town, and he made sure he got one. The mining company even installed electricity and pumped water from Wah Wah Springs 5 miles away, and the Utah Southern Extension Railroad built a depot.

The Cactus Mine ran out just five years after the town was settled, and Newhouse's days were numbered. Other mines did not produce enough to keep the economy going. Some buildings were eventually relocated to Milford, and a cafe stayed open until 1921, but it has since burned down.
GPS COORDINATES: N 38°28.70' W 113°20.43'

Notom
In 1886, a little town named after Pleasant Creek was settled about 4 miles upstream from Aldridge in south-central Utah. The town was later called Pleasant Dale, but when its post office was established, neither name was acceptable to the government, since towns with both names already existed. The name Notom was then chosen, though it is unclear why. Without their own church or school, Notom residents went to the ones in Aldridge instead. The residents of the town, on the edge of a sand desert, struggled to grow crops—an ultimately fruitless effort as drifting dunes always covered the fields. Some townspeople found it more convenient to relocate to Aldridge, and others gave up and moved on. By 1900, Notom was deserted. The town site is now on a large, privately owned ranch.
GPS COORDINATES: N 38°13.94' W 111°06.99'

Osiris
Established in the 1910s on 80 acres of land on the east fork of the Sevier River in southwest Utah, this town was originally called Henderson, after William J. Henderson, who donated the land on which the town was built. In its early years, Henderson remained very small and could boast of little more than a building used for both church and school. When the town was granted a post office, the name was officially changed to Osiris.

In the 1920s, Widtsoe, a town located a few miles to the south, began to experience harsh droughts, and many people decided to move north and try their luck in Osiris. A man by the name of W. F. Holt became the town's chief benefactor, building a flour mill, creamery, reservoir, and telephone exchange. Farmland was cleared and canals dug to irrigate the crops.

However, the land around Osiris was no better than that around Widstoe; lack of water and early frosts killed many of the crops and people soon left the area. By the late 1930s, almost all the settlers had left. Osiris, named for the Egyptian god of the dead, eventually faded away into the desolate realm of its namesake.
GPS COORDINATES: N 38°01.32' W 111°57.65'

Paria (Pahreah)
Pahreah is the Piute Indian word meaning "muddy water." Pahreah (later spelled Paria) was established as an agricultural

community in 1870 by Peter Shirts, who led Mormon settlers from their original settlement at Rock House Cove 5 miles downstream on the Paria River. It is unclear whether Indians forced the settlers to flee from Rock House to Paria or if it had been a difficult location to grow and irrigate crops.

In Paria, settlers cultivated fruit and nut orchards, vineyards, and vegetable farms that flourished. They also ran cattle in the canyons. Paria became a popular and hospitable stopping place for river travelers, such as explorer John Wesley Powell, the "peacemaker" Jacob Hamblin, and various explorers, surveyors, and Indians trekking their way through the canyonlands.

The community of 47 families lived in both sandstone and log homes, and they built a church and a post office. However, the Paria River repeatedly flooded its banks and regularly wiped out both crops and housing. By 1892, only eight families remained; disheartened by their regular struggles, the other settlers had abandoned the town.

As many were leaving, the promise of gold attracted others, and in 1910 a small gold operation with modest production was established. This, too, was short lived, and floods wiped it out completely the following year. All the miners but one left for better pickings.

In the 1950s, movie-makers discovered the Paria Valley, and one or two miles from the ghost town is a Hollywood movie set with old-looking buildings, but this Paria is not truly historical. But even here, history repeats itself. In November 1999, a group of BLM employees and 85 volunteers dismantled the movie set from its original location next to the picnic ground because frequent floods were making the buildings unstable and unsafe. The original timbers were saved, and the BLM intends to reconstruct two of the buildings farther away from the creek, elsewhere on the backway, out of reach of floodwaters. Interpretive information will be added; the project is to be completed in 2000.

Today, remains of stone cabins and an old sluice from the mining operations can be seen on the far bank of the river, slightly downstream from where the road ends. The old town site was upstream from the trail end, but little remains.
GPS COORDINATES: N 37°15.04' W 111°57.29'

Peerless

Peerless was one of several coal-mining towns in Carbon County's Spring Canyon; it worked the same long vein as Mutual, Latuda, and Rains. Named after the Peerless Coal Company, the town supported nearly 300 residents from around 1917 to 1938. However, in the late 1930s, the vein started to play out, and many of the people decided to move to nearby Helper or Spring Glen.

World War II gave the town a little boost, but the mine and the school finally closed in the 1950s. Shortly thereafter, Peerless was mostly deserted.
GPS COORDINATES: N 39°41.29' W 110°54.04'

Pinto

Set along Pinto Creek in present-day Dixie National Forest, Pinto was first settled by Mormons in 1856. Located along the Old Spanish Trail, the site was a convenient place for travelers to stock up on supplies.

Pinto is also near the site of the Mountain Meadows Massacre—to this day, one of the bloodiest events in Utah history. In 1857, a wagon train led by Alexander Fancher passed through town on its way to California. The reception by local Mormons was less than cordial. President Buchanan had just ordered troops into Utah, and Mormons all over the territory were refusing to trade or sell supplies to gentile travelers. The wagon train left town under a cloud of animosity. It would only get about 10 miles farther when it was attacked by a band of renegade Mormons and Indians. More than 120 of the pioneers were slaughtered; only 17 young children were spared. It has never been completely clear who exactly was involved in the attack, but regardless, the tragedy lives on in the memories of people throughout Utah.

The town itself survived this dark spot in the region's past and continued to grow in the 1860s and 1870s, when a mail run and a telegraph line were set up in town. However, new settlers to town became fewer and fewer; the town slowly dwindled in importance until the Mormon church discontinued its ward in 1916. By 1920, many people from Pinto had moved about 10 miles north to the new town of Newcastle and left their old town deserted.
GPS COORDINATES: N 37°32.36' W 113°30.98'

Price

Price and Price River in northeast Utah are named for Bishop William Price, who explored the area in the summer of 1869. Although he did not settle here, he left his name.

The first permanent settlers faced a difficult life when they chose Price as their home in 1879. They had to carry water in barrels from the river in order to water their crops. It took over a year to dig an irrigation ditch to water their fields, but the canal is still in use today.

In 1883, the Denver & Rio Grande Western Railroad came through the Price River valley, and the isolated farming community opened up to become a commercial hub. The arrival of the railroad also expanded the potential of the local coal industry and brought workers to the mines.

Joe Walker, a legendary Wild Bunch member, lies in Price cemetery. Killed near Thompson in 1898 by a posse while he slept, Walker was believed to have partaken in the Castle Gate Pleasant Valley payroll robbery. A young cowboy named Johnny Herring lies beside Walker. Herring was killed by authorities because he matched the description of legendary outlaw

An early view of Price

Butch Cassidy. His funeral was widely attended because of the apparent celebrity status of the deceased. It was not until the following day that Herring's body was dug up and viewed by a Wyoming sheriff who knew Butch and was able to ascertain that the body was definitely not his. The young cowboy had been an innocent drifter in the wrong place at the wrong time.

Today, Price is a lively town with a variety of stores and businesses, recreational facilities, schools, and hospitals. Its natural resources include natural gas, oil, coal, sand, gravel, and lumber. Primary agricultural products are cattle, sheep, and animal feeds (alfalfa and hay). Tied to the coal industry, Price's economy has ridden the many good and bad times of the mines.

GPS COORDINATES: N 39°35.97' W 110°48.28'

Promontory

This famous site marks the meeting place between the Central Pacific and Union Pacific Railroad Companies, and the completion of the transcontinental railroad on May 10, 1869.

Promontory had its one shining moment when all the nation's eyes were upon it—which is a good bit more than most

Promontory, circa 1869

towns get—but it was otherwise a desolate place in a dry desert. Leading up to the great day and immediately thereafter, Promontory was more notorious than noted, filled with saloons and gambling tents and rough immigrant workers. Once the officials and the golden spike commemorating the great achievement left town, Promontory quickly faded away. Within a decade, the town was gone except for a lonely railroad station, and in 1904, the Promontory station was bypassed entirely with the completion of the Lucin Cutoff across the Great Salt Lake. Its only reason for existence gone, Promontory became nothing but a memory.

On May 10, 1969, a centennial celebration took place commemorating the "marriage of the rails." Today, Promontory is home to a national monument and museum dedicated to the country's most famous railroad.

GPS COORDINATES: N 41°37.00' W 112°33.05'

Funeral procession in Richfield, 1899

Rainbow

In northeast Utah, near the Colorado border, Rainbow served as the last point of the Uintah Railway after Watson. This tiny town was founded around 1900 solely to mine gilsonite; then oil was struck in 1920, and Rainbow experienced something of a boom. At its peak in 1931, 135 people resided in Rainbow, whose name origin remains a mystery.

Rainbow consisted of two rows of log cabins, a small church, and a one-room schoolhouse. The town's water had to be shipped in from a stream 35 miles away. As railroads gave way to newer and more efficient motor trucks, Rainbow's population diminished, the log cabins were sold to nearby Bonanza, and by 1939, all that remained was a ghost town.

GPS COORDINATES: N 39°50.58' W 109°10.97'

Rains

Named after L. F. Rains—who was a grand opera singer before breaking into the mining business—this small coal-mining town was similar to others in Carbon County's Spring Canyon, such as Peerless, Mutual, and Latuda. Rains opened this mine and the Carbon Fuel Company in 1914, and the company town prospered for over 30 years, pumping out a seemingly endless supply of coal. The typical town included the usual businesses and 60 houses.

Like other mines in the region, Rains declined as both demand for coal and its supply dwindled in the 1950s. Once the mines became idle, the town, too, was deserted.

GPS COORDINATES: N 39°42.63' W 110°57.53'

Richfield

This town was originally settled by the Mormons in January 1864 and known as Warm Springs, after the spring at the foot of the red hills to the west. The name was later changed to Omni in honor of a Mormon prophet, and then it was changed to Richfield after a good crop of wheat was produced in 1865.

That same year about a hundred more families arrived and the first schoolhouse was built. The families came from neighboring communities seeking safety from Black Hawk and his Indians, who had stolen 90 head of stock from Salina, killed two settlers, and had waged a savage attack on Glenwood. By 1874 there were 150 families living in Richfield and 117 children were attending school.

Richfield has continued to grow and develop economically, and today it is a shopping and cultural center of central Utah. It is also the county seat of Sevier County. Richfield's current population is about 6,000.

GPS COORDINATES: N 38°46.33' W 112°05.04'

Rockville

Rockville was first settled in 1862 in an attempt by the scattered settlers of the upper Virgin River to band together. The combination of the Indian Wars and repeated flooding made it difficult for individual pioneers to get ahead, so the people gathered and concentrated their efforts in Rockville. The township was originally called Adventure, but the name was changed to Rockville because of the rocky soils along the Virgin River. The town's single-lane steel bridge was built in 1926, providing a permanent route across the river and replacing the many shaky structures that were constantly having to be rebuilt after floods.

Rockville's pioneer meetinghouse and school were frame structures and succumbed to fire in 1932. Separate church and school buildings replaced the old buildings. Rockville's oldest existing pioneer structure is known as "The Rock House." Built by one of the Huber brothers as a residence, it is still in use as such; however, its most interesting feature is the frame building on the west end, which was one of the first telegraph offices in Utah.

Harry Longabaugh—aka the Sundance Kid—supposedly lived in Rockville in the early 1940s under the name Hiram BeBee with his common-law wife, Glame. According to Edward M. Kirby, Longabaugh's biographer, BeBee was a grouchy old man with his neighbors. Though most accounts say he died with Butch Cassidy in Bolivia, some believe the two staged their deaths so they could safely move back to the States.
GPS COORDINATES: N 37°09.66' W 113°02.23'

Round Valley

Located in northern Utah near the Idaho border, just south of Bear Lake, Round Valley, appropriately enough, sits in the heart of a round valley. In the early 1860s, the region was full of lush meadows and big game, and it was used by Indians in the summer. Mormon settlers arrived in the valley around this time and, much to the dismay of local Indians, built log cabins, barns, and a sawmill and even changed the flow of Big Creek by damming it up and digging canals.

In 1866, with the start of the Black Hawk War, the Mormon settlers in Round Valley began to have increasingly violent encounters with the Indians. Tensions grew; some settlers sold out and moved to Idaho, while others returned armed each fall to harvest their crops. New settlers who arrived in winter were sometimes forced out by returning Indians the next spring. Then, in 1870, the Indians arrived back from winter migrations prepared for a full-scale war. Brigham Young sent Stake President Charles C. Rich along with a bishop and interpreter to negotiate a settlement. Rich was successful and the Indians relocated to Wyoming.

The settlers of Round Valley were then left to work the land in peace, and for the next 30 years or so, they built up the town, establishing a school district and a church ward.

The town was prospering by 1906, but the following years saw a difficult period of drought, which forced many families to move away. Then, after the drought, a plague of locusts set upon the town. By chance or in answer to the Mormons' fervent prayers, a great wind blew up and swept the locusts into Bear Lake in time to salvage that year's crops.

Round Valley managed to recover from these trials, but never completely, and over the next 20 years, the population slowly dwindled. By the 1930s it was mostly deserted.

Today, the town may be empty, but the area is not. Bear Lake and its surrounding country are a center for tourism and recreational activities.
GPS COORDINATES: N 41°47.36' W 111°21.80'

Royal (Rolapp)

The town, originally called Bear Canyon, began as a camp at a coal mine in Price Canyon; it was established in 1913 by Frank Cameron, who also developed the Panther Canyon Mine and the town of Heiner a few miles south.

As the camp developed into a town, the name was changed to Cameron in honor of its founder. In 1917, Cameron sold his interest in the coal property to Henry Rolapp, and the 200 residents decided to change the town's name again—to Rolapp.

Then the Royal Coal Company bought the properties in the 1920s and the name changed for the final time—to Royal. Because it had been called Rolapp for such a long time, many people refused to call it by the new name. In 1930, Spring Canyon Coal bought out Royal Coal. The decline of the town was gradual, but by 1940 many people had left, even though the mine continued to produce coal. Many miners preferred to commute from Castle Gate and Helper.

As the demand for coal declined following World War II, so did the population. By the end of the 1950s, Royal was empty.
GPS COORDINATES: N 39°44.77' W 110°52.76'

Sand Wash (Desolation Canyon)

Sand Wash in Desolation Canyon, in northeast Utah, is where the Stewart family operated a ferry across the Green River in the 1920s. The ferry served as the only feasible crossing along the entire river from Green River, Wyoming, to Green River, Utah. The Stewarts ferried sheep and cattle for ranchers. The four-room log cabin still standing at the site was constructed elsewhere—possibly in Johnson, Utah—and was floated along the river to its current locale. The ferry was washed out in 1953 or 1954, and at that time the Stewarts ceased operations and moved on.
GPS COORDINATES: N 39°50.40' W 109°54.82'

Sand Wash ferry, circa 1945

Sego

In the early 1890s, Harry Ballard, a rancher living in Thompson Springs discovered coal in the area. He quietly bought the land surrounding his find and started operations on a small scale. The mining camp he established was called Ballard.

In 1911, Ballard sold the mine to a group of Salt Lake City investors. Production started with grand plans for a long and prosperous run of coal production. The new owners built a store, a

Silver Reef, 1880

boardinghouse, and other buildings, all with their own water supply. Nearly 500 people lived in town, bachelors in the main boardinghouse, and others in anything from attractive homes to the numerous dugouts in the canyon hillsides. The town was renamed Neslin, after Richard Neslin, general manager of the mine.

The Denver & Rio Grande Western Railroad built a subsidiary railroad, the Ballard and Thompson, from Thompson to the mines. This railroad was a boom to Neslin, as not only did it transport coal but it bought at least as much to fuel its own locomotives.

By 1915, various troubles plagued the mine. The water table had been dropping for some time, and the water supply was drying up. There had been several accidents and some financial mismanagement, and the investors were unhappy. Neslin was fired, but even after that, it was a year before all the miners were properly paid; instead they received company scrip, which enabled them to buy food and other necessities for their families. Wanting a new start, the town took the name Sego, in honor of the state flower. The miners must have become increasingly dissatisfied, for though they had rejected union organizers for years, in 1933 they agreed to become members of the United Mine Workers Union.

On November 1, 1947, the mine was closed and the property sold at an auction held in Moab. Today Sego is a true ghost town with a number of structures still intact and both pictographs and petroglyphs nearby.

GPS COORDINATES: N 39°02.03' W 109°42.16'

Shunesburg

In 1862, some Mormon settlers from Rockville moved farther east along the Virgin River and purchased land from Chief Shunes of the local Paiute tribe. The settlers couldn't pay much, so Shunes is reported to have lived among the pioneers, ostensibly waiting for the rest of his payment, and partaking in the benefits of their hard labor.

Within a few years, the pioneers were enjoying good cotton and corn harvests, and their fruit trees were producing, but flooding was a constant problem. Shunesburg was located where the East Fork of the Virgin River exits the deep, narrow Parunuweap Canyon. There were only two ways in and out of town: west over the floodplains or east up the canyon over what was known as the Wiggle Trail, a danger-

ous path up the cliffs to the canyon rim hundreds of feet above the canyon floor.

During the early 1870s, mail from St. George to Kanab was routed via Shunesburg. To avoid having to traverse the Wiggle Trail, the carrier from Kanab constructed a wire-and-winch system that dropped mail over the 1,500-foot cliff at the head of Parunuweap Canyon to the St. George carrier below, who passed up the mail to Kanab the same way. This short-cut saved a day of treacherous travel. It was not until the new century had dawned, however, that a wire-pulley apparatus was conceived to lumber over the cliffs by means of cables.

In 1872, the famous explorer Major John Wesley Powell based his survey team in Shunesburg while exploring Parunuweap Canyon during one of his Colorado River expeditions.

The severe, regular flooding of the Virgin River did all it could to make life miserable for the residents of Shunesburg, but it was a grasshopper plague later in the 1870s that finally brought the demise of the town. Millions of grasshoppers, or Mormon crickets, descended on the crops and fruit trees and devoured everything. Almost everyone moved away after that except for a few who stayed to raise livestock. Today the site is part of a private ranch.

GPS COORDINATES: N 37°09.52' W 112°58.78'

Silver Reef

The founding of Silver Reef is cloaked in legend, though it is generally agreed that a prospector named John Kemple was the first person to discover silver in the sandstone rock here, sometime between 1866 and 1870. At that time, it was thought impossible for silver to occur in sedimentary rock, such as sandstone, and certainly not in petrified wood, which littered this part of the desert—but both turned out to be possible, and the silver was of high quality and abundant.

William T. Barbee is credited with getting the silver mining going. In 1875 he had 22 claims here, ready to stake his money on what others had dismissed as folly (the Smithsonian Institution even called one sample of silver-encrusted petrified wood an "interesting fake"). Once underway, Silver Reef grew from mining camp to established town almost overnight. By 1876, there were 2,000 miners working 275 registered claims. Main street was over a mile long and lined with dozens of sturdy businesses, included several hotels, nine grocery stores, six saloons, a Wells Fargo office, a bank, a telegraph office, several restaurants, a hospital, a Catholic church, two dance halls, two newspapers, a bona fide Chinatown (with 250 Chinese laborers who elected their own mayor), and three cemeteries.

The boom times lasted through the 1870s, with larger operators buying up the small ones and everyone getting rich. A racetrack was even built near town, drawing horses from southern Utah and Nevada. However, a combination of events in 1881 brought most of the good times to a halt. The price of silver on the world market dropped suddenly, the mines were taking on water, and some of the best ore was getting played out. Miners' wages were cut nearly in half to make up for the drop in prices, and so the miners organized one of the first unions in the territory and immediately went on strike.

One by one, the mills and mines shut down, without the labor to operate and then no wages to pay. By 1884, the town had grown quiet, and the last mine shut down in 1891. In the end, almost $25 million in silver was extracted over nearly 15 years. Between 1891 and 1901, others moved in to Silver Reef and extracted another $250,000 of ore, and then many of the buildings were sold or moved.

Today, the old Wells Fargo Express office is on the National Historical Register and is a museum. The old bank is a gift shop. Some of the area has been preserved for its history and is worth visiting. However, note that Silver Reef has recently lost its ghost town status: people have moved into homes and housing developments in the areas surrounding the old town, and these are restricted to public access.

GPS COORDINATES: N 37°15.20' W 113°21.95'

Skutumpah

In the 1870s, John D. Lee settled a ranch about 15 miles up Johnson Canyon from Johnson. He named it for the Paiute Indian word *skutumpah*, meaning either "water where squirrels live" or "water where rabbit brush grows." Others moved in, many of whom were members of the Clark family. Because of their strong presence in the area, the town was also referred to as Clarksdale or Clarkston.

A sawmill was built in town to supply the settlers with the wood they needed, but the little town, which never had more than 10 families, was ultimately just too isolated to survive. Droughts hit the area in the late 1870s, and in 1879 the people abandoned Skutumpah. They disassembled and removed the sawmill, leaving little trace of civilization. The site of Skutumpah is now on private ranch property.

GPS COORDINATES: N 37°16.50' W 112°20.40' (approximately)

Soldier Summit

This old railroad town sits at the highest point (7,450 feet) along the original D&RGW railroad line. As legend has it, a group of soldiers left Camp Floyd in 1861 and were caught off guard by a powerful blizzard. Those who survived the storm buried the deceased at this site, which became known as Soldier Summit.

When the railroad was built over Soldier Summit, a small community of railroad employees lived here; then in 1919, the railroad moved the line's main division point here from the town of Helper. This made Soldier Summit the union point between the western branch based in Ogden and the eastern branch based in Grand Junction, Colorado, and the railroad company spent over a million dollars to build new rail facilities, including a passenger and freight depot, a hotel, a YMCA, and over 70 employee homes. Other businesses, such as stores, a restaurant, a billiard hall, a real estate office, and service stations, were also established. The town sprouted almost overnight.

By 1930, rail economics had changed, and the division point and much of the rail facilities were moved back to Helper. This essentially ended the town, and its 2,500 residents moved away. Today Soldier Summit has a service station and several occupied homes, whose residents can be seen shooing away the ghosts on cold, windy nights.

GPS COORDINATES: N 39°55.72' W 111°04.65'

Spring Canyon (Storrs)

In the early 1900s, various mines and mining towns were founded in Carbon County's Spring Canyon, which produced millions of tons of coal. They included Rains, Mutual, Peerless, Standardville, and Latuda, and their collective fortunes rose and fell with the coal industry.

The actual town of Spring Canyon was established in 1912 about a mile northeast of Standardville by prominent mining tycoon "Uncle" Jesse Knight. Aware that the land was rich in coal, Knight had purchased 1,600 acres of land west of Helper in order to operate his smelter in the Tintic Range. He established the Spring Canyon Coal Company and named the town Storrs, after his superintendent George A. Storrs, though the town name was changed to Spring Canyon when the post office arrived in 1924. Knight built 60 homes for mine workers and laid railroad tracks so he could transport coal to the station in Helper. A devout Mormon, he built a Mormon church and modern schoolhouse, which drew families from along the canyon, and he forbade saloons and gambling houses and even penalized his workers for too much carousing.

The town grew to around a thousand residents by 1920, and for the next 20 years it remained more or less the same. At its peak during World War II, the mine produced 2,000 tons of coal per day.

Spring Canyon's decline came soon after the war years, as the demand for coal slowly decreased. The Spring Canyon Coal Company steadily reduced its workforce, until by 1969 it had closed up altogether.

GPS COORDINATES: N 39°42.22' W 110°55.14'

Spring City

It took three attempts to permanently settle the area known today as Spring City in central Utah. The town was first called Allred's Settlement, after the Mormon explorer James Allred. He led the 1852 expedition to Sanpete County in which the town was first founded. However, because of Indian attacks during the Walker War in 1853–54, the settlers fled to neighboring forts and towns, while theirs was burned to the ground.

James Allred returned to this site in 1860 and created a new settlement, called Springtown, that lasted longer, but not much. In 1866, residents again fled from local Indians during the Black Hawk War. Finally, in 1867, there was resolution with the Indians, and Spring City was peacefully resettled by the Mormons.

With the settlers working cooperatively, the land was divided and common irrigation ditches were dug. This region was particularly fertile and the crops fared well. It was not long until the Denver & Rio Grande Western Railroad arrived in Spring City. This connection to the rest of Utah allowed the developing town to export its surplus agricultural products as well as its indigenous oolitic limestone (a stone used in the construction of fine buildings in the bigger cities to the north).

By the turn of the century, Spring City's population peaked at around 1,250, and many fine new buildings of stone or brick were erected, such as a tabernacle, a Victorian schoolhouse, the city hall, and many private residences. The town's population steadily declined throughout the 20th century, which meant the buildings were spared typical urban improvements. As such, present-day Spring City, which is still inhabited, has become one of the best places to see preserved examples of early pioneer architecture.

St. George, circa 1910

Historians and architecture enthusiasts began to realize Spring City's structural beauty in the 1970s. Since 1980, the town has been listed in the National Register of Historic Places. This historical preservation of Spring City has appropriately earned it the nickname "Williamsburg of the West."
GPS COORDINATES: N 39°28.69' W 111°29.72'

St. George

Though visited by the Domínguez-Escalante Expedition in 1776, St. George was not properly settled until after Brigham Young toured the region in 1861. About five years prior to this, experimental cotton farms had been set up in the area to investigate the land's potential to sustain the crop. With the Civil War looming on the horizon, Young wanted to develop a cotton district in Utah so as not to be heavily reliant on supplies from back east.

Once the land was deemed suitable for cotton, 309 families were relocated to the vicinity of St. George in what has been called the "Cotton Mission." The town was named after George A. Smith. Although not a settler himself, he had organized and directed much of the relocation. The settlers were successful in their mission, and the region was eventually dubbed "Utah's Dixie."

St. George had its beginnings in the cotton industry, but it is most noted for its early pioneer architecture, specifically the Mormon Tabernacle and Temple. Both buildings were finished in the 1870s, making them the first in Utah. The St. George Temple was dedicated by Brigham Young and was the only one he lived to see completed. Mormons living in the small towns of the Little Colorado River often made the trip to St. George to be married in its sacred temple. The route eventually earned the name the "Honeymoon Trail."

St. George has grown throughout the 20th century, but never more so than it has in recent years. In the 1960s, many senior citizens began retiring to or spending the winter in the area, and its location near Zion National Park and Dixie Na-

tional Forest makes St. George a perfect hub for tourism and recreational activities. Population statistics in the 1990s listed St. George as Utah's fastest growing town.
GPS COORDINATES:
N 37°06.39' W 113°34.95'

Standardville

Standardville was founded in 1912, about the same time as Spring Canyon, and it was one of the half dozen coal-mining towns that bloomed in the Carbon County Spring Canyon district. The town was named after the mine's owners, the Standard Coal Company, which made extensive efforts to spruce up its business district and residential areas. Homes were steam heated and had neat lawns; businesses and stores were attractive and well cared for; and the population grew to around 550.

Standardville's inevitable decline followed the same pattern as its neighboring towns. Although there was some labor unrest in the 1920s, the real blow to the coal industry came after World War II, when all the easiest mines were played out and demand for coal dropped precipitously. The mine closed in 1950, and by 1955 the town was completely abandoned. A few of the old stone buildings remain.
GPS COORDINATES: N 39°41.92' W 110°55.95'

Sunnyside (Upper Sunnyside)

In 1877, Jefferson Tidwell was called upon by the Mormon church to explore what is now Carbon, Emery, and Wayne Counties with a view to settling the region. In October 1879, Tidwell settled on the present-day town of Wellington. As the rest of the area was settled, many men claimed title to the rich coal mines it contained. The land changed hands many times between settlements, often with no claims filed and no formal land purchases.

Originally known as Verdi, Sunnyside was established in 1898 and named for the sunlit southern exposure of the Book Cliffs.

Sunnyside

Coal was transported to coke ovens in Castle Gate until 1902, when Sunnyside built its own—a total of 480 ovens. Hundreds more were built in subsequent years. Sunnyside was incorporated in 1916. At its peak, in 1929, there were 2,000 residents; afterward, the town declined steadily, falling to 424 residents by 1940. The area regenerated during World War II, and when the Geneva Steel plant arrived later in the 1940s, a new town emerged. Sunnyside is near East Carbon City, along Utah 123.

GPS COORDINATES: N 39°33.96' W 110°22.30'

Temple Mountain

Twice a ghost town, Temple Mountain, in Emery County, was first settled just before the turn of the 20th century when prospectors discovered uranium, radium, and vanadium ores in the area. By 1910, a small village had grown up around the mine. Most of the valuable minerals in the area were exported to France, and as legend has it, some of the radium ended up in the laboratory of Madame Curie, who performed her famous experiments on the minerals found at Temple Mountain.

The town and mine experienced a degree of prosperity until after World War I, when a cheaper source of uranium was found in Africa, making the mine at Temple Mountain obsolete. The town folded, and it was not until the uranium boom of the 1950s that people returned to the area. A more modern town quickly sprang up around the ruins of the old one. The latest machinery was used for mining, while the center of town was moved from the base of the mine to the junction of the mine road with nearby Utah 24.

When the uranium boom ended in the late 1960s, the town was once again deserted. In its years of operation, the Temple Mountain district produced more than 2.5 million tons of ore. Today, the ruins of the old town and mine are scattered throughout the area. However, the mine itself remains a health hazard, as it is still quite radioactive.

GPS COORDINATES: N 38°41.08' W 110°40.03'

Terrace

One of the largest of the Central Pacific Railroad's construction camps, Terrace thrived in the latter half of the 19th century. Terrace served the Salt Lake Division of the railroad company as a repair headquarters. Located 32 miles east of Nevada in Box Elder County, Terrace was one of the last towns to be built along the transcontinental railroad.

Equipped with an eight-track yard, a 16-stall roundhouse, and many maintenance shops, the railroad town grew quickly. Having no water of its own, Terrace piped in water from the Clear Creek Range. The town had a number of sizable shops and businesses, as well as the Athenium, a public bathhouse and library—for which the citizens of Terrace were taxed one dollar a year for its upkeep.

Between 6,000 to 12,000 Chinese laborers also called Terrace home during the construction of the railroad. Upon its completion in 1869, nearly a thousand of these laborers settled in Terrace. Chinatown, where they lived, boasted its own Buddhist Temple. It was also a center for opium production (which was sold legally in those days).

However, as the 20th century approached, Terrace's days were numbered. The Lucin Cutoff, built in 1903, bypassed

the town, and most of the shops and equipment were moved to other, more useful railroad stops. Terrace pretty much folded at that point, and the rails were finally taken up in 1942.

Today, aside from some old railroad ties, there are few remains of this once prosperous town. An old cemetery still exists, but in 1986 vandals stole many of the headstones.

GPS COORDINATES: N 41°30.23' W 113°30.96'

Thistle

Thistle, a ranching and farming area, received a railroad siding for the loading of food and livestock in the 1880s. In 1890, a railroad junction that came down through the Sanpete Valley was built in Thistle. The town eventually became an important stop along the north-south railroad from Salt Lake City to Marysvale.

By 1913, Thistle had its own roundhouse for the railroad station, and by 1917 about 600 residents called Thistle home. The town's fortunes would follow those of the railroad companies for the next 60 years. The depot was finally closed in 1972, and much of the town closed along with it, though a few residents remained along the still-used tracks.

The region was quiet until the fall and winter of 1982–83, when the area saw an unusually large amount of snow. When springtime came, the drenched earth slowly crept down into the valley—a 1.5-mile-long, 1,000-foot mudslide moving down into the Spanish Fork Canyon. In doing so, it created a 173-foot-high earthen dam that backed up the waters of the Spanish Fork River and its tributaries. Thistle Lake was soon formed behind the dam, with a high water mark of 165 feet and the decimated town of Thistle now resting at its bottom. Not only was Thistle lost, but the railroad was also sunk beneath the rising waters.

The Denver & Rio Grande Western Railroad Company lost no time and worked to reroute the tracks. It drilled a 3,000-foot tunnel through the Billies Mountain in an astonishing 81 days.

Eventually, the earthen dam was determined to be unstable, and the lake was drained. Upon completion of this enormous project, Thistle was once again on dry land, but many of its homes and buildings had been scattered throughout the region.

Locals still remember the Thistle Valley flood as one of the most destructive and costly natural disasters to have ever tak-

Railroad junction house at Thistle

en place. Today only the strongest of Thistle's remains are still visible, and it has become an abandoned ghost town. Instead, plants and wildlife have returned to the valley to reclaim what the mudslide destroyed.

GPS COORDINATES: N 39°59.52' W 111°29.85'

Thompson / Thompson Springs

Located along I-70 in southeastern Utah's Grand County, Thompson Springs (sometimes shortened to Thompson) was named for an early homesteader who settled in the area in 1883.

Thompson, 1909

The town sits at the mouth of Thompson Canyon near a natural spring. From an early date, the location was recognized as a favorable one, and the land was purchased by brothers Harry and Arthur P. Ballard (Harry later established Sego). They laid out and promoted the town, which with its water and later-discovered coal supplies became an important railroad stop—if not the most important, certainly one of the two or three most important in Grand County. The town was connected to the telegraph system in 1884; it was granted a post office in 1890.

With its remote nature and proximity to the rails, Thompson became a town through which many an outlaw passed. A few even met their deaths in and around the area, including Wild Bunch member Joe Walker (buried in Price) and the leader of the Hole-in-the-Wall Gang, Flat Nose George Curry.

Thompson did not grow very much through the years. Today it is home to a gas station, a tiny post office, a train depot, and a motel. Though the town is not widely known, its diner achieved a measure of fame, as it was used in the film *Thelma & Louise* (1991). Cult classic *Sundown* was also filmed in the area. With the rock art of Sego Canyon to the north and Arches National Park to the south, Thompson serves as a convenient and rustic stop along I-70.

GPS COORDINATES: N 38°58.29' W 109°42.84'

Tonaquint

In the mid-1850s, Mormon missionary Jacob Hamblin was sent to southern Utah to settle the area and convert the Indians. He and a few other families eventually settled at the confluence of the Virgin and Santa Clara Rivers. The town was named Tonaquint after a local band of Indians. The early settlers must have had a sense of humor, as the town also went by such names as Lick Skillet and Never Sweat.

Soon after they settled the area and established farms, Hamblin received some cotton seeds from a pioneer woman who brought them from the East. He planted the seeds, and by 1855 had a successful cotton harvest. As the impending Civil War threatened to cut off cotton supplies, Brigham Young was very excited at the prospect of turning the south-west portion of the state into Utah's Dixie. He sent about 300 families to the region, and in 1861, he visited it himself. It was here where he looked north and made his famous prophecy about the establishment of St. George: "There will yet be built, between those volcanic ridges, a city, with spires, towers, and steeples, with homes containing many inhabitants."

Although St. George would fulfill the prophecy and become a major city in southwest Utah for decades to come, Tonaquint was not so lucky. In 1862 a great storm flooded both rivers that ran by the town and completely destroyed it. Once was enough for these settlers, and no effort was made to rebuild the town. Instead they relocated to other settlements nearby.

GPS COORDINATES: N 37°04.36' W 113°34.87'

Tucker

Originally called Clear Creek, after the body of water that runs nearby, Tucker was established with the construction of the Denver & Rio Grande Western Railroad. It became an important loading point and construction camp that supported a population of about 500. Tucker housed helper engines that enabled eastbound trains to climb the steep gradient to Soldier Summit, 7 miles away.

Every day carloads of coal arrived from Pleasant Valley mines, and supplies and freight arrived from Salt Lake City,

Tucker

destined for Winter Quarters and railroad construction. Because there was much work to be found, numerous shanties, cabins, and houses were built in the small valley, as well as hotels, saloons, and boarding houses.

The name of the town was changed to Tucker, after James Tucker, possibly to differentiate the town from another named Clearcreek in Carbon County. However, in 1915 work was begun to reduce the gradient up to the summit. In the process, the town of Tucker was buried with fillwork.

Today, a roadside rest stop lies atop of what once was Tucker—leaving little, if any, trace of ruins.

GPS COORDINATES: N 39°56.13' W 111°11.90'

Verdure

In 1887, the Mormons sent a colonizing mission to the Blue Mountain region of San Juan County. A handful of families moved to a location just west of the Montezuma Creek and about 6 miles south of present-day Monticello. They named the spot South Montezuma, and some of the men rode up to the Monticello area to prepare the fields for farming. Local cattlemen and cowboys did not like this invasive presence on land they considered their own, and they threatened bloodshed if the farmers and fence-builders didn't leave. Instead of leaving, the settlers of South Montezuma called in soldiers from Fort Lewis for protection. The soldiers stayed for a year, and there was no more trouble from the less-than-cordial cowboys. The armed guards also helped repel some local Ute Indians, who had begun to carry out small raids on the town.

In the late 1880s, many settlers moved away to the more fertile soils of Monticello. Those who stayed saw a post office come into their town in 1893. Upon seeing the rich foliage of the area, the new postmaster changed the town's name to Verdure. However, the post office would only last for another decade or so, as almost everyone moved north to Monticello.

In the early part of the 20th century, the Utah State Agricultural College ran an experimental dry-farming station in Verdure. A six-week class was held during the winters to teach farmers the new techniques. The land upon which Verdure once existed is now part of a large, private ranch.

GPS COORDINATES: N 37°47.15' W 109°20.86'

Vernal

Tucked away in an area called the Bench in the northeast corner of the state, Vernal remains relatively isolated from the rest of Utah. Before the first settlers arrived in the 1870s, this wide and barren flat was a veritable no-man's land. When Brigham Young sent a scout to the region in the early 1860s, his report stated that the area was not worth the effort to settle it.

In 1861 President Lincoln gave the land to the south and west of Vernal to the Uintah Indians for a reservation. Captain Dodds, who was the agent sent to this reservation, ended up becoming the first settler of Vernal when he retired from his post in 1873. A few other families followed Dodds's lead and moved into the area. Vernal was a unique town for Utah, as it was one of the few not originally settled by Mormons.

Ironically, it was Colorado's Meeker Massacre in 1879 that

Uintah Avenue, Vernal, 1910

drew Vernal together as a unified town. After an Indian agent was killed by White River Utes in Colorado, the Utes tried to rally the Uintah Indians in Utah against all the white settlers in the region. The settlers in Vernal quickly built a fort and moved their families inside. Although the conflict in Colorado escalated into bloodshed by both whites and Indians, the violence did not spread across the state line. Vernal residents remained in their fort through the difficult winter, and by spring the tensions had settled.

Afterward, some moved back to their homesteads, while others stayed on in the fort, which became known as the Ash-ley Center. When a post office came to town, the town was officially renamed Vernal. The isolated town became self-sufficient by necessity, relying heavily on agriculture and ranching until 1948, when there was an oil boom. Since then, Vernal has had its economic ups and downs, but it has grown steadily; today it is Uintah County's largest city.

The Bank of Vernal, built in 1913, has a somewhat noteworthy construction story—all of its bricks were sent one by one through the mail. It seems that when the postal service increased its parcel post weight limit to 50 pounds, many citizens discovered that it was more economical to send their mail via train instead of stage freight. A brick company individually wrapped 13,700 bricks, a total of 35 tons, and mailed them to Vernal. This created such an uproar that the postal service changed its weight limits, but not before the Bank of Vernal became the first and only building to arrive by post.

Vernal today relies heavily on tourism to survive, which is not hard given the wealth of attractions nearby. About 20 miles east of Vernal, and extending into Colorado, is Dinosaur National Monument, which contains the largest quarry of Jurassic Period dinosaur bones ever found. Also nearby is Dinosaur Gardens, in which 14 life-size dinosaurs have been recreated. As a result, Vernal is now known as the dinosaur capital of the world. In addition, the Ashley National Forest and Flaming Gorge National Recreation Area are located not far to the north, and Vernal hosts the Outlaw Trail Festival every summer, during which the many outlaws who once passed through the city limits are remembered.

GPS COORDINATES: N 40°27.36' W 109°31.65'

Watercress

During the construction of the transcontinental railroad in the 1860s, Watercress served as an end-of-the-tracks railroad town. Located along the original line, Watercress's most distinctive feature was its large water tower. Water was scarce in this part of the desert, and so it was piped in from the springs to the north. As this area also had an abundance of watercress, the town soon found its name.

After the railroad was completed, Watercress lost many of its inhabitants. However, the stop remained important for the trains and their steam engines, which would replenish their water supply at the tower. Once the Lucin Cutoff was built in 1903, though, neither the tracks nor the water tower were of much use, and the town quickly faded away.

GPS COORDINATES: N 41°29.25' W 113°33.39'

Watson

Watson acquired its name from Wallace Watson, the engineer who laid the length of the Uintah Railway from Dragon to Watson, an 11-mile run. A railway terminus used primarily by area mines, Watson was an established small town by 1911.

Situated on a canyon floor surrounded by high cliffs, Watson boasted a general store, a warehouse, an array of houses and dugouts, and a small school. There were two hotels: one, owned by locals Joe Gurr and his wife, Jane Howarth, served as a resting place for miners and cattlemen; the other, the railway company-owned Savory Hotel, primarily attracted train passengers.

The Watson post office opened in 1913, and received its

Wendover, 1909

modern equivalent of 15 minutes of fame as the place where the Bank of Vernal bricks arrived. When the postal service increased its parcel post weight limit to 50 pounds, the Watson post office began seeing lots of odd, heavy items passing through their facility, but when 13,700 individually wrapped bricks addressed for Vernal began to stack up inside, outside, and down the street, the mail carriers decided they'd had enough, and they began to complain—loudly. Eventually, officials in Washington realized they had to do something, and they changed the regulations. But Vernal got its bank, one brick at a time.

However, when the Uintah Railroad closed in 1939, the post office, along with the rest of Watson, quickly closed shop. **GPS COORDINATES**: N 39°52.80' W 109°09.34'

Wellington

In 1877, Brigham Young sent Jefferson Tidwell to explore the Castle Valley region in central Utah in order to see if it was fit for settling. It was, and two years later Tidwell returned along with 14 other men to settle the northern section known as the Price River valley. However, the valley was not as welcoming as it first seemed, and it took Tidwell and his men three tries before they built a successful diversion dam to irrigate their fields.

The Price River valley attracted more and more settlers, and in 1889–90, the Mormon church set up a northern district in Spring Glen and a southern district in Wellington. With this, Wellington grew quickly as an agricultural and sheep-herding region.

Wellington, 6 miles southeast of Price, came to rely on its larger neighbor for many supplies and conveniences. However, in the 1910s, it also came into conflict with Price and the other coal-mining towns upstream when the Price River, which constituted Wellington's water supply, became insufficient and polluted. Wellington was the last town along the river and had to implement a canal system to deliver fresh water from farther upstream.

Since then, Wellington has grown and developed, but it remains a small country town. As it sits at the southern end of Nine Mile Canyon, it receives a steady stream of visitors and recreationalists. **GPS COORDINATES**: N 39°32.61' W 110°44.00'

Wendover

Sitting just west of the Bonneville Salt Flats along I-80, Wendover straddles the border between Utah and Nevada. The town was established in 1907 by the Western Pacific Railroad as a stop where trains could stock up on water. The origins of its name, however, are uncertain. Some say it was named after the railroad surveyor Charles Wendover, while others claim it comes from the fact that to get there requires "wending" over the desert.

Wendover became front-page news in 1914 when it was home to the completion of the transcontinental telephone line. Beginning in the 1930s, the Salt Flats also received a good deal of fame for the land-speed records being set in the area. During World War II, this was where the flight crew of the *Enola Gay* trained, whose mission was to drop the first atomic bomb on Japan.

In 1931, Nevada passed a wide-open gambling law. Ever since then, Wendover has been a popular gambling resort for the people of northern Utah who do not want to make the long drives to Reno or Las Vegas. Today, visitors to Wendover are greeted in true casino style by Wendover Will, a neon cowboy standing more than 50 feet tall. **GPS COORDINATES**: N 40°44.13' W 114°02.19'

White River (Ignatio)

White River served as a stage station around the time the Uintah railroad was constructed in 1905. The town housed mainly bridge tenders, guards, and maintenance workers, many of whom were employed by the Uintah Toll Road Company, a subsidiary of the Uintah Railway.

Several houses and a small store existed in the town, whose official railroad name was Ignatio, though most people still called it White River. When the toll bridge company closed due to expense problems in 1935, it took White River's function with it, and the town was abandoned. **GPS COORDINATES**: N 39°58.64' W 109°10.66'

Widtsoe

Issac Riddle was the first known settler of this area in southern Utah. He moved into Johns Valley in 1876 and settled on a ranch to the northeast of Bryce Canyon. Three years later, his home served as an important stop for the Hole-in-the-Rock Expedition on its way to southeastern Utah.

The area didn't began to resemble an early frontier town till Jedediah Adair bought and successfully ran Riddle's old ranch. He was able to grow wheat, oats, and barley on his land through the implementation of dry farming techniques. Adair's success enticed other settlers to move into the area, and by 1908 a small community of farmers had developed; they called their settlement Adairville (not to be confused with the Adairville in Kane County just above the Arizona border). In 1910, the land was opened to homesteading and attracted yet another influx of settlers. Adairville was renamed Houston in 1910 after the president of the Panguitch Stake of the Church of Latter-day Saints.

By this time, the townsite was becoming more permanent. When Julie Adair donated 40 acres of land to the town, its name was once again changed, this time to Winder, after another prominent man in southern Utah's Church of Latter-day Saints. A post office was established in 1912, and three years later, running water was piped in from a nearby spring. The town grew rapidly and soon had four stores, two hotels, and a population in excess of 300.

In 1917, the town's name was changed for the last time when postal authorities complained of the confusion caused by too many towns named Winder. Now called Widtsoe, after yet another prominent Mormon, the town reached its prime in the early twenties and grew to over a thousand people. Around this time, the forest service moved its district office (along with the first telephone) to Widtsoe, and an investor from California

Widtsoe, 1938

named W. F. Holt sank over $300,000 into the area. He built homes, constructed dams and irrigation systems, invested in telephone lines, and began raising high-altitude lettuce.

However, a severe drought that plagued southern Utah in the 1920s soon forced many settlers from the area. By 1935, about thirty families were given federal aid to resettle elsewhere; the Widtsoe Project, as it was called, cost the government over $80,000. The final families left the town in 1938, and Widtsoe was erased from the maps.

Today some buildings and ruins remain on the site of this old ghost town. After the government resettled its inhabitants, Widtsoe was split into thirds, with the federal government, the state government, and private landowners each claiming its share. If you happen to pass by Widtsoe, remember not to take any artifacts from the site, as it is a violation of both state and federal law.
GPS COORDINATES: N 37°49.93' W 112°00.11' (approximately)

Yellow Cat
Just east of Arches National Park, Yellow Cat was once a major mining area for uranium and vanadium ore. There was little cleanup after the mine was shut down, and as a result there was an abundance of leftover equipment, hazardous open mine shafts, old vehicles, and the likelihood of radioactive dust in the wind. There is a rock dugout bunkhouse built below one mine shaft that must have been occupied by a miner who knew too little to be wary of radioactive dust.
GPS COORDINATES: N 38°50.32' W 109°31.60' (approximately)

Historic Trails

Spanish Trail
American explorers coined the term the "Spanish Trail" because they believed that Spanish explorers were the first to open the route. In reality, the initial trailblazers were early Mexican trappers and traders in the late 18th century. The first documented expedition occurred in 1765 by Juan Maria de Rivera.

Not until 1829 did the trail become well traveled, after George Yount and William Wolfskill journeyed the entire length from Santa Fe, New Mexico, to Los Angeles, California. From 1830 to 1848, pack trains of a hundred or more Mexican traders, along with their woolen wares, made the annual trek to California.

Along the route trappers also captured Paiute Indian women and children for slave trading in California, a very marketable business at the time. After trading their goods, most often in exchange for horses, the groups would return to Mexico. The entire 1,120-mile trail usually took two and a half months to travel one way.

Utah contains the longest section of the trail, 460 miles, within any one state. Entering in the southeastern corner near the present-day town of Monticello, the trail travels through Castle Valley, the Wasatch Plateau, the Great Basin, the Sevier River valley, the Markagunt Plateau, the Parowan Valley, the Escalante Desert, Holt Canyon, the Santa Clara River, the Beaver Dam Mountains, and Utah Hill, then it enters the Mojave Desert of Nevada.

In 1853, Captain John Gunnison of the U.S. Corps of Topographical Engineers was the first to map part of the Spanish Trail. The explorer traveled from the Green River to the northern San Rafael Swell, the Wasatch Plateau, and the Sevier River.

In 1848, the fur trading business came to a close, and wagon trains became a more popular means of transportation. Narrow routes like the Spanish Trail gave way to larger roads constructed for wagon travel. Although the Mormons developed a section of the trail between Salt Lake City and California for wagon trains, the entire route would forever be known as the "Old" Spanish Trail. Today, most of the historic trail has been erased by modern highways.

Hole-in-the-Rock Trail
In 1879, Mormons in southwest Utah were called upon to blaze a trail across the southern portion of the state to the unexplored region to the east. Mormon leaders wanted to colonize this area as well as develop strong relations with the Indians. The route was scouted, and it was decided that, although it would be extremely difficult, they would take a direct route from Escalante to Montezuma Creek.

Under the leadership of Silas Stanford Smith, 236 people headed out; this route saved the pioneers over 250 miles, and at first travel went smoothly and they were in good spirits. Then they reached their most difficult obstacle, what would come to be known as the Hole-in-the-Rock Pass: a steep, 1,200-foot gorge down to the Colorado River. They arrived at the gorge in November 1879 and were faced with negotiating it in the freezing winter temperatures.

With no feasible way around it, Smith decided that the

gorge had to be crossed. The plan was to build a series of roads along the cliff edges that the settlers could descend to the river. The first drop-off was smoothed down by blasting away boulders, widening the crevice walls, and grading the path. Toward the bottom, other steep drops made passage impossible. Through an amazing feat of engineering, the men of the expedition tacked a road on to the face of the

An early view of the Hole-in-the-Rock

gorge. They chiseled holes into the rock and inserted log supports, creating a 50-foot wooden road.

The roads were still very steep, and many of the horses balked at the prospect of descent. Braking systems using ropes were designed to keep the wagons from rolling out of control.

After the long and arduous road construction, the expedition had to then ferry across the 300-foot-wide river. When they were done, most of the pioneers were exhausted, without strength or will to carry on. However, they kept moving east, and eventually settled at the foot of the cliffs overlooking the San Juan River, calling the town Bluff City. Others pushed on for another hundred or so miles across extremely rugged terrain. Upon arriving in southeast Utah, they were forced to tame the land, make peace with local Indians, and survive in whatever way they could. The journey, originally thought to take six weeks, had taken over six months. However, the successful expedition opened a crucial link across southern Utah.

Outlaw Trail

The phrase "Wild West" conjures images of rough-riding, gun-toting outlaws spurring horses out of dusty towns, their saddlebags laden with stolen money. Names such as Elza Lay, Harry Longabaugh (the Sundance Kid), and Butch Cassidy stand out in the early history of the Wild West. These and other outlaws, almost all of whom were cattle rustlers itching for excitement, distinguished themselves as master thieves. Along a trail that runs from northern Montana to the Mexican border, they robbed coaches, trains, ranches, and banks, using a network of hideouts and friendly ranchers, as well as an intimate knowledge of the land, to almost always to stay one step ahead of the law. This route became known as the Outlaw Trail

The outlaw period of the Wild West lasted about thirty years, from the 1880s to the beginning of the 20th century. Settlers of frontier cities, mining towns, and homesteads found themselves scratching their heads in wonder at the outlaws, who managed to make off with large amounts of money and avoid capture—all in broad daylight! After big heists, like the Telluride or Castle Gate robberies, the offenders would ride off into the untamed and often unexplored regions of the western desert, plains, and mountains. Following their immediate getaway, the outlaws would cover great distances, sleep-

ing by day and riding by night, until they reached one of their hideouts. These lengthy escapes were what earned the outlaws the nickname "long riders."

The land they covered was described in a March 4, 1898, issue of the *Denver News*:

> These men have a line of strongholds extending from Powder Springs, Wyoming, in a southwesterly direction across the entire state of Utah and down into Arizona, giving them easy access to Mexico.
>
> This strip of country is rugged and broken and almost impregnable by a stranger, and abounds in caves, deep gorges, and strongholds from which it is impossible to dislodge the outlaws who have trails unknown to any except themselves.

This passage makes clear that the Outlaw Trail was not, as its name suggests, a well-defined route but an ambiguous, difficult stretch of terrain. The criminals who rode it found safety for two reasons. First, only they knew many of the less-traveled sections, and second, as the newspaper article says, they had a series of "strongholds" along the way. The three main points of safety for any western outlaw were Hole-in-the-Wall in Wyoming and Brown's Hole and Robbers Roost in Utah.

Each of these places had unique geographical features, but what they had in common was that they were all naturally defensible and isolated from major towns and cities. These factors drew the outlaws and often frightened away the lawmen. Brown's Hole—located in the northeast corner of Utah and also called Brown's Park or Diamond Mountain—became

The Wild Bunch. From left: Harry Longabaugh (The Sundance Kid), Bill (News) Carver, Ben Kirkpatrick (The Tall Texan), Harvey Logan (Kid Curry), Robert LeRoy Parker (Butch Cassidy)

known early on as a safe haven from the law, as it was located near the boundaries of three states (Wyoming, Utah, and Colorado), and it was often difficult to figure out who had jurisdiction. This confusion allowed the outlaws to make a quick getaway into another state. However, pursuit often stopped at Brown's Hole in any case, since lawmen only entered the area when absolutely necessary. Such figures as Charlie Crouse and John Jarvie welcomed the outlaws and warned them if a posse was on their tail. The outlaws in turn were always very generous to their hosts in Brown's Hole (espe-

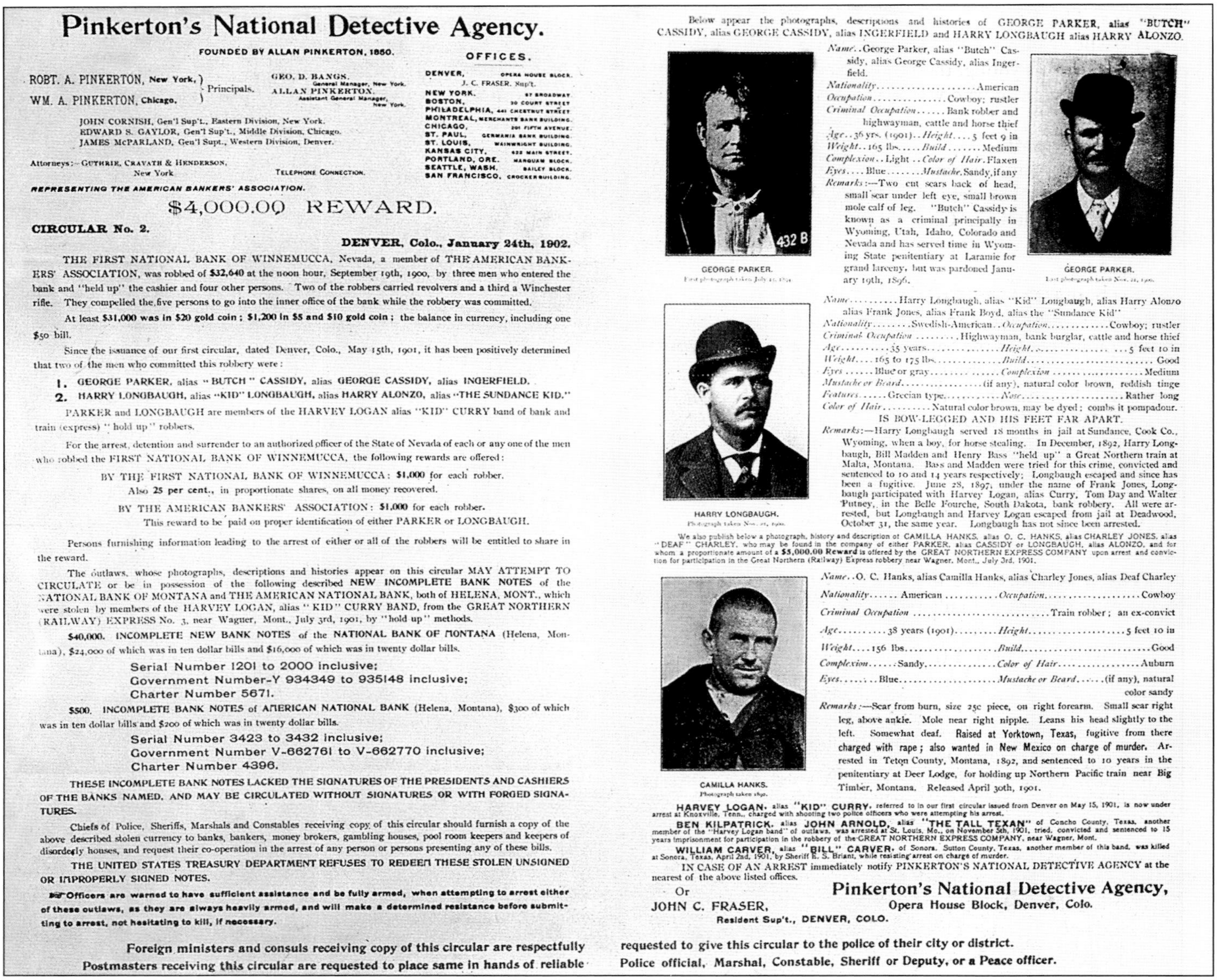

Pinkerton's National Detective Agency.

FOUNDED BY ALLAN PINKERTON, 1850.

ROBT. A. PINKERTON, New York, } Principals.
WM. A. PINKERTON, Chicago. }

GEO. D. BANGS, General Manager, New York.
ALLAN PINKERTON, Assistant General Manager, New York.

JOHN CORNISH, Gen'l Sup't., Eastern Division, New York.
EDWARD S. GAYLOR, Gen'l Sup't., Middle Division, Chicago.
JAMES McPARLAND, Gen'l Supt., Western Division, Denver.

Attorneys:—GUTHRIE, CRAVATH & HENDERSON, New York

TELEPHONE CONNECTION.

OFFICES.

DENVER, OPERA HOUSE BLOCK. J. C. FRASER, Sup't.
NEW YORK, 57 BROADWAY.
BOSTON, 30 COURT STREET.
PHILADELPHIA, 441 CHESTNUT STREET.
MONTREAL, MERCHANTS BANK BUILDING.
CHICAGO, 201 FIFTH AVENUE.
ST. PAUL, GERMANIA BANK BUILDING.
ST. LOUIS, WAINWRIGHT BUILDING.
KANSAS CITY, 622 MAIN STREET.
PORTLAND, ORE. MARQUAM BLOCK.
SEATTLE, WASH. BAILEY BLOCK.
SAN FRANCISCO, CROCKER BUILDING.

REPRESENTING THE AMERICAN BANKERS' ASSOCIATION.

$4,000.00 REWARD.

CIRCULAR No. 2.

DENVER, Colo., January 24th, 1902.

THE FIRST NATIONAL BANK OF WINNEMUCCA, Nevada, a member of THE AMERICAN BANKERS' ASSOCIATION, was robbed of **$32,640** at the noon hour, September 19th, 1900, by three men who entered the bank and "held up" the cashier and four other persons. Two of the robbers carried revolvers and a third a Winchester rifle. They compelled the five persons to go into the inner office of the bank while the robbery was committed.

At least **$31,000 was in $20 gold coin; $1,200 in $5 and $10 gold coin;** the balance in currency, including one $50 bill.

Since the issuance of our first circular, dated Denver, Colo., May 15th, 1901, it has been positively determined that two of the men who committed this robbery were:

1. GEORGE PARKER, alias "BUTCH" CASSIDY, alias GEORGE CASSIDY, alias INGERFIELD.
2. HARRY LONGBAUGH, alias "KID" LONGBAUGH, alias HARRY ALONZO, alias "THE SUNDANCE KID."

PARKER and LONGBAUGH are members of the HARVEY LOGAN alias "KID" CURRY band of bank and train (express) "hold up" robbers.

For the arrest, detention and surrender to an authorized officer of the State of Nevada of each or any one of the men who robbed the FIRST NATIONAL BANK OF WINNEMUCCA, the following rewards are offered:

BY THE FIRST NATIONAL BANK OF WINNEMUCCA: **$1,000** for each robber.
Also **25 per cent.**, in proportionate shares, on all money recovered.

BY THE AMERICAN BANKERS' ASSOCIATION: **$1,000** for each robber.
This reward to be paid on proper identification of either PARKER or LONGBAUGH.

Persons furnishing information leading to the arrest of either or all of the robbers will be entitled to share in the reward.

The outlaws, whose photographs, descriptions and histories appear on this circular MAY ATTEMPT TO CIRCULATE or be in possession of the following described **NEW INCOMPLETE BANK NOTES** of the NATIONAL BANK OF MONTANA and THE AMERICAN NATIONAL BANK, both of HELENA, MONT., which were stolen by members of the HARVEY LOGAN, alias "KID" CURRY BAND, from the GREAT NORTHERN (RAILWAY) EXPRESS No. 3, near Wagner, Mont., July 3rd, 1901, by "hold up" methods.

$40,000. INCOMPLETE NEW BANK NOTES of the **NATIONAL BANK OF MONTANA** (Helena, Montana), $24,000 of which was in ten dollar bills and $16,000 of which was in twenty dollar bills.

Serial Number 1201 to 2000 inclusive;
Government Number-Y 934349 to 935148 inclusive;
Charter Number 5671.

$500. INCOMPLETE BANK NOTES of **AMERICAN NATIONAL BANK** (Helena, Montana), $300 of which was in ten dollar bills and $200 of which was in twenty dollar bills.

Serial Number 3423 to 3432 inclusive;
Government Number V-662761 to V-662770 inclusive;
Charter Number 4396.

THESE INCOMPLETE BANK NOTES LACKED THE SIGNATURES OF THE PRESIDENTS AND CASHIERS OF THE BANKS NAMED, AND MAY BE CIRCULATED WITHOUT SIGNATURES OR WITH FORGED SIGNATURES.

Chiefs of Police, Sheriffs, Marshals and Constables receiving copy of this circular should furnish a copy of the above described stolen currency to banks, bankers, money brokers, gambling houses, pool room keepers and keepers of disorderly houses, and request their co-operation in the arrest of any person or persons presenting any of these bills.

THE UNITED STATES TREASURY DEPARTMENT REFUSES TO REDEEM THESE STOLEN UNSIGNED OR IMPROPERLY SIGNED NOTES.

Officers are warned to have sufficient assistance and be fully armed, when attempting to arrest either of these outlaws, as they are always heavily armed, and will make a determined resistance before submitting to arrest, not hesitating to kill, if necessary.

Below appear the photographs, descriptions and histories of GEORGE PARKER, alias "BUTCH" CASSIDY, alias GEORGE CASSIDY, alias INGERFIELD and HARRY LONGBAUGH alias HARRY ALONZO.

GEORGE PARKER.
First photograph taken July 15, 1894.

Name..George Parker, alias "Butch" Cassidy, alias George Cassidy, alias Ingerfield.
Nationality....................American
Occupation..............Cowboy; rustler
Criminal Occupation......Bank robber and highwayman, cattle and horse thief
Age..36 yrs. (1901)..*Height*....5 feet 9 in
Weight..165 lbs.....*Build*.......Medium
Complexion..Light..*Color of Hair*.Flaxen
Eyes....Blue.......*Mustache*.Sandy, if any
Remarks:—Two cut scars back of head, small scar under left eye, small brown mole calf of leg. "Butch" Cassidy is known as a criminal principally in Wyoming, Utah, Idaho, Colorado and Nevada and has served time in Wyoming State penitentiary at Laramie for grand larceny, but was pardoned January 19th, 1896.

GEORGE PARKER.
Last photograph taken Nov. 21, 1900.

HARRY LONGBAUGH.
Photograph taken Nov. 21, 1900.

Name..........Harry Longbaugh, alias "Kid" Longbaugh, alias Harry Alonzo alias Frank Jones, alias Frank Boyd, alias the "Sundance Kid"
Nationality........Swedish-American..*Occupation*............Cowboy; rustler
Criminal Occupation.........Highwayman, bank burglar, cattle and horse thief
Age..........35 years..............*Height*..................5 feet 10 in
Weight....165 to 175 lbs.............*Build*.......................... Good
Eyes......Blue or gray..............*Complexion*..................Medium
Mustache or Beard................(if any), natural color brown, reddish tinge
Features......Grecian type...........*Nose*......................Rather long
Color of Hair..........Natural color brown, may be dyed; combs it pompadour.
IS BOW-LEGGED AND HIS FEET FAR APART.
Remarks:—Harry Longbaugh served 18 months in jail at Sundance, Cook Co., Wyoming, when a boy, for horse stealing. In December, 1892, Harry Longbaugh, Bill Madden and Henry Bass "held up" a Great Northern train at Malta, Montana. Bass and Madden were tried for this crime, convicted and sentenced to 10 and 14 years respectively; Longbaugh escaped and since has been a fugitive. June 28, 1897, under the name of Frank Jones, Longbaugh participated with Harvey Logan, alias Curry, Tom Day and Walter Putney, in the Belle Fourche, South Dakota, bank robbery. All were arrested, but Longbaugh and Harvey Logan escaped from jail at Deadwood, October 31, the same year. Longbaugh has not since been arrested.

We also publish below a photograph, history and description of CAMILLA HANKS, alias O. C. HANKS, alias CHARLEY JONES, alias "DEAF" CHARLEY, who may be found in the company of either PARKER, alias CASSIDY or LONGBAUGH, alias ALONZO, and for whom a proportionate amount of a **$5,000.00 Reward** is offered by the GREAT NORTHERN EXPRESS COMPANY upon arrest and conviction for participation in the Great Northern (Railway) Express robbery near Wagner, Mont., July 3rd, 1901.

CAMILLA HANKS.
Photograph taken 1892.

Name..O. C. Hanks, alias Camilla Hanks, alias Charley Jones, alias Deaf Charley
Nationality...... American ....*Occupation*..................Cowboy
Criminal Occupation ....Train robber; an ex-convict
Age..........38 years (1901).........*Height*....................5 feet 10 in
Weight....156 lbs..................*Build*..........................Good
Complexion......Sandy..............*Color of Hair*................Auburn
Eyes........Blue...................*Mustache or Beard*......(if any), natural color sandy
Remarks:—Scar from burn, size 25c piece, on right forearm. Small scar right leg, above ankle. Mole near right nipple. Leans his head slightly to the left. Somewhat deaf. Raised at Yorktown, Texas, fugitive from there charged with rape; also wanted in New Mexico on charge of murder. Arrested in Teton County, Montana, 1892, and sentenced to 10 years in the penitentiary at Deer Lodge, for holding up Northern Pacific train near Big Timber, Montana. Released April 30th, 1901.

HARVEY LOGAN, alias **"KID" CURRY**, referred to in our first circular issued from Denver on May 15, 1901, is now under arrest at Knoxville, Tenn., charged with shooting two police officers who were attempting his arrest.

BEN KILPATRICK, alias **JOHN ARNOLD**, alias **"THE TALL TEXAN"** of Concho County, Texas, another member of the "Harvey Logan band" of outlaws, was arrested at St. Louis, Mo., on November 5th, 1901, tried, convicted and sentenced to 15 years imprisonment for participation in the robbery of the GREAT NORTHERN EXPRESS COMPANY, near Wagner, Mont.

WILLIAM CARVER, alias **"BILL" CARVER**, of Sonora, Sutton County, Texas, another member of this band, was killed at Sonora, Texas, April 2nd, 1901, by Sheriff E. S. Briant, while resisting arrest on charge of murder.

IN CASE OF AN ARREST immediately notify PINKERTON'S NATIONAL DETECTIVE AGENCY at the nearest of the above listed offices.

Or
JOHN C. FRASER,
Resident Sup't., DENVER, COLO.

Pinkerton's National Detective Agency,
Opera House Block, Denver, Colo.

Foreign ministers and consuls receiving copy of this circular are respectfully requested to give this circular to the police of their city or district.
Postmasters receiving this circular are requested to place same in hands of reliable Police official, Marshal, Constable, Sheriff or Deputy, or a Peace officer.

Wanted poster for Butch Cassidy and the Sundance Kid

cially if they had just robbed a bank) and never robbed them.

Another popular stopover southwest of Brown's Hole was an area known simply as the "Strip"; it was about 8 miles east of Roosevelt and 1.2 miles west of Gusher. In mapping the area, a surveyor missed this 700-acre triangular patch of land. Because of his mistake, there was no law in the region, and it became a wild hangout for the wandering outlaws, complete with a gambling hall and saloon. Gambling, prostitution, and drunken brawls were round-the-clock activities.

Unlike other waypoints on the Outlaw Trail, Robbers Roost was not a town. Located 300 miles south of Brown's Hole, Robbers Roost sits near the Dirty Devil River, west of Canyonlands National Park The outlaws set up their camps at a natural spring in this otherwise arid desert. This part of the Outlaw Trail in southeastern Utah was among the most treacherous, and the three trails leading into the Roost all had their own dangers. It was in the Roost that Cassidy and other outlaws laid low while posses searched for them. Even if the lawmen did make it into the outlaws' camp, they would find it very difficult and dangerous to apprehend the outlaws, who were using the terrain to their advantage. On an average salary of $500 a year, the normal, life-loving deputy just didn't find it was worth the risk.

Over the years, Butch Cassidy became the undisputed leader of the outlaws along the trail. His loosely held together group, known as the Wild Bunch, was responsible for rustling countless head of cattle. A smaller, more skilled and daring inner circle, called the Train Robbers' Syndicate, was known as the group of robbers who frequently made off with huge sums of cash at the major bank robberies, though the specific members of the gang changed for each job.

The Outlaw Trail, however, remained more or less the same, even as different routes were added and some were abandoned. Its legend runs throughout the settlement of the Wild West. In our modern age, when there is no uncharted "frontier" stretching vaguely west, it is difficult to imagine

Cassidy and his Bunch traversing the desert one step ahead of the law. The Outlaw Trail reminds us of these once wild days, when the law was young, the outlaws rode horses, and justice was often a matter of who was quicker on the draw.

Salt Lake Cutoff

Mormon military veterans constructed this route while returning home from battles in California in the late 1840s. The trail ran from Salt Lake City along present day I-15 to the Snowville vicinity near the Utah-Idaho border, then west into Nevada. Mormons encouraged the use of this route in order to gain the business of weary travelers on their way to California.

Between 1849 and 1857, approximately one-third of migrating pioneers used the Salt Lake Cutoff to reach their westbound destinations. Although the Utah War interrupted usage between 1857 and 1858, the trail continued to see frequent use until 1869. Many towns along the trail prospered during its popularity, including Bountiful, Ogden, Brigham City, Honeyville, Fielding, and Plymouth.

Railroads

Denver & Rio Grande Western Railroad

In the early days of the railroads, companies often came and went at a very rapid pace. The story of the Denver & Rio Grande Western Railroad (D&RGW) is one filled with legal maneuverings, near bankruptcies, and questionable buyouts. As the name indicates, the Denver & Rio Grande Western Railroad was a Colorado-based company. William Jackson Palmer, president of the company, originally intended to lay a north-south route along the eastern side of the Colorado Rockies down into Mexico. He had hoped to exploit the rich silver mines to the south, but he was beat out in 1878 by a rival company. As was commonplace at the time, the two railroad companies became involved in a heated legal battle, but the fighting did not stop in the courtroom. Both companies sent armed construction crews to secure strategic passes along the way. In the end, the courts upheld the Atchison, Topeka & Santa Fe (AT&SF) Railroad's right to build the line into Mexico. The confusing legal battle also allowed George Gould, son of railroad tycoon Jay Gould, the opportunity to buy into the D&RGW.

The bad blood escalated in Pueblo, Colorado, when the D&RGW went to reclaim some of its lines in the area. Both the AT&SF and the D&RGW accumulated munitions and hired gunmen in anticipation of conflict. Bat Masterson was one of the many gunmen hired by the AT&SF in its fight over the route to Leadville. Masterson led a takeover of the D&RGW roundhouse. It was only after a flurry of gunshots resulting in several deaths that Gould and Palmer were able to regain possession of their roundhouse and stations.

Appropriate to the general mood of railroad companies at the time, Gould pushed for rapid expansion of the railroad. He turned his attention westward toward Utah, hoping to form a connection between Denver and Salt Lake City. On July 21, 1881, the D&RGW became incorporated in the Territory of Utah, allowing the company to build in the region.

The next few years saw a lot of excitement in Utah at the prospect of breaking the Union Pacific's monopoly in the area. People saw the competition between the companies as very beneficial in that it would cut costs and allow for more commerce within the territory itself.

Gould and Palmer were busy in the early 1880s. The first tracks laid in Utah were the 50 miles between Salt Lake City and Springville. The Utah-based Denver & Rio Grande (D&RG), a subsidiary of the Colorado company, worked in conjunction with the D&RGW to lay the tracks that would connect Salt Lake City with Denver. Palmer and Gould also bought out some of Utah's smaller rail companies and worked quickly to connect Utah with western Colorado's coal mines. They began to diversify their interests, buying coal companies for fuel and buying trading companies to run the mining towns. They also purchased the Utah and Pleasant Valley Railway, allowing them greater access to the coal mines of Utah.

In 1883, the D&RGW finally completed the Salt Lake to Denver line. The tracks met at Deseret, near Green River, and a new route was opened. They also extended the line past Salt Lake City to Ogden in that year. However, the success of the D&RGW would not last for long. One sign of the coming troubles in Utah arrived with the first train to traverse the new tracks. The train arrived in Salt Lake City on a Sunday, much to the chagrin of devout Mormons.

With the track now in place, stockholders in the railroad company realized that they were not receiving their expected profits. Palmer and Gould had overextended themselves in the construction of the main line and their other financial endeavors. The next few years saw legal and financial battles between the Colorado-based D&RGW and the Utah-based D&RG. After both companies fell into receivership, the D&RG was sold at auction in 1886, though it continued operating more or less as it had been doing.

The D&RG began work on plans for a new standard-gauge line (56.5 inches wide) that would basically parallel the route of the narrow-gauge line (36 inches) established earlier by Palmer's company. Palmer was worried that the wider, stronger

D&RGW trains in the yards at Soldier Summit, 1926

railroad would spell disaster for the D&RGW. The company faced a period of restructuring and consolidation in 1889 and became known as the Rio Grande Western (RGW) Railway Company. It then began work on converting its narrow-gauge tracks to standard gauge, finally completing the job in 1890. Although the new line usually ran only a few hundred yards from the original one, it sometimes differed by a couple of miles. This meant that the towns along the original line either folded or, as in the case of Cisco, picked up and moved to the new line. The D&RGW also established the towns of Helper and Soldier Summit to serve as its main division points between Salt Lake City and Grand Junction, Colorado. In these early years, the location of the railroad would often make or break a town or region. In fact, the rails spurred much of the development in eastern Utah around towns such as Thompson and Crescent Junction.

Around the turn of the century, Gould began work on a line that would extend to the Pacific Coast. Although this line almost ruined him, Gould completed the 940 miles of track, which became known as the Western Pacific. Over the next few years, a number of mergers and administrative consolidations kept the railroads expanding throughout Utah. The restructured D&RG acquired the RGW in 1908 and reclaimed its original name. This merger gave the companies a measure of stability for a while. However, Gould defaulted in 1915. The federal government stepped in and took control of the railroad companies during the years of World War I, and after the war, business went back to normal. Once again, the companies were restructured, and a third and final D&RGW was chartered in the early 1920s.

This version of the company emerged as very strong. Though slowed by the Great Depression, it eventually re-linked Salt Lake City and Denver on a more direct line that went through Moffat Tunnel. After one final period of restructuring in the late 1940s, the D&RGW emerged with its feet on the ground, and it remained strong throughout the latter half of the 20th century. During the wild early years of railroad speculation, the D&RGW contributed greatly to the commerce and development of Utah by constantly pushing for rapid expansion. Although the company may have ruffled some Mormon feathers and disappointed some investors, the tracks of the Denver & Rio Grande Western Railroad remain as a backbone of transportation throughout Utah.

Transcontinental Railroad
Prior to May 10, 1869, there were only three options for individuals who wished to travel from one coast of the United States to the other. Travelers could journey six months via boat around the length of South America; they could walk, a grueling experience that took five to seven months; or they could take a very bumpy and expensive 24-day stagecoach ride. However, after the fateful day when two trains met in Promontory, Utah, travelers could buy a first-class ticket on the transcontinental railroad for $100 and make the journey in four comfortable days.

In 1862, Congress approved a venture to create the first coast-to-coast railroad in the United States. Two railroad companies were authorized for its construction: the Union Pacific Railroad (UP) in the east and the Central Pacific (CP) in the west. After delays due to disagreements over financing, Congress passed the Railroad Act of 1864, which allowed larger land grant offerings and 30-year loans to the companies. Pleased with the deal, the railroads began major construction in late 1865.

However, the Civil War was still winding down and the California gold rush was still on, and the railway companies were faced with a labor shortage, so they hired large numbers of immigrants to begin the work. UP hired over a thousand Irishmen and their animals, while CP shipped in 10,000 Chinese laborers to work for $30 per month. Once the Civil War ended, German and Italian immigrants as well as war veterans and ex-slaves became railroad employees.

Construction in the east began in Omaha, Nebraska, with UP workers laying an average of one mile of rail per day over the flat Nebraska plains. CP employees experienced a much different and taxing job of laying rail over the treacherous Sierra Nevada. Each company had the same goal in mind: to lay more rails in less time than its competitor.

With the approaching railroad growing closer every day, Mormon leader Brigham Young decided to face the inevitable head-on. In May 1868, Young negotiated a contract with Union Pacific in order to assure that his men would profit from the railroad construction. His workers graded, tunneled, and constructed bridges from Echo Canyon to the Great Salt Lake for an estimated cost of $2,125,000. Not only did the railway provide immediate employment for thousands of Mormons, the transportation would make travel for new immigrants much easier and safer. Although the railway would also transport many non-Mormon settlers into Utah, Young felt the pros outweighed the cons.

As the two railways grew closer, competition became even fiercer. Congress allowed the companies to send their respective graders up to 300 miles ahead of the end of the track. At one point, the UP and CP graders actually passed each other and proceeded to create parallel grades for 200 miles. Realizing the wastefulness, Congress ended this competition and set the official meeting place at Promontory Summit, Utah. Most of the parallel grades can still be observed today.

Joining of the rails ceremony at Promontory, 1869

In addition to the railroad, a second transcontinental telegraph was simultaneously constructed. This allowed workers to keep in constant communication with their headquarters during construction.

Near the end of the building, UP workers boasted to their competitors that they had completed an extraordinary 8 miles of rail in one day. Never to be outdone, the CP waited until the distance between the two was too short for UP to defeat them again and laid 10 miles and 56 feet in one incredible day. What makes this feat so remarkable is the fact that each 28-foot section of rail weighed approximately 522 pounds.

Union Pacific locomotive on the high trestle near Promontory, 1869

Although the railroad was actually completed on May 8, 1869, UP president Dr. Thomas Durant was unavoidably late, and the official ceremony at Promontory was delayed two days. Detained in Piedmont, Wyoming, by his own constructors, who had not been paid in four months, Durant was forced to have the outstanding money wired in from headquarters before he could leave.

Seven years after the railway's initial planning, a solid gold stake ceremoniously marked the completion of the first transcontinental railroad. Two trains, Central Pacific's *Jupiter* and Union Pacific's *119,* triumphantly came together, facing each other, joining two oceans and a world of individuals across what had previously been a daunting space. From that moment on, the Great West would no longer be such a mystery to the rest of the nation.

In early 1870, railroad officials agreed that Ogden served as a more favorable resting point for passengers than Promontory, and they closed the station there. Then in 1904, the Lucin Cutoff, a shorter route across the Great Salt Lake, replaced the entire Promontory branch of the railroad. The original rails were sold as scrap metal during World War II.

Engraved on the famous gold spike are the words, "May God continue the unity of our country as this Railroad unites the two great oceans of the world." The transcontinental railroad would not only unite two oceans but would change the lives of Americans forever.

Uintah Railway

Built at the dawn of the 20th century, the Uintah Railway ran the 68-mile stretch from Mack, Colorado to Watson, Utah. The Barbar Asphalt Paving Company began construction on the railway in 1903, and it was completed as far as Dragon by 1904. The asphalt company, which had been mining gilsonite in the region, built the railway as a quicker means of transporting the mineral out of the area.

The highly flammable material, originally called uintaite, gained its more popular name from Samuel H. Gilson, its first commercial producer. Gilsonite

Private car for the roadmaster of the Uintah Railway, 1918

was mined in vertical veins running from 2 to 12 feet wide and up to 2,000 feet deep. Many of the original mines can still be seen today.

At its most treacherous point over Baxter Pass (for route details of Baxter Pass, see *4WD Adventures: Colorado*), the Uintah Railway ran at a 7.5 percent incline with 66-degree curves. These factors made railroad maneuvering a very tricky prospect. However, the railway continued to be a popular means of transport for the mineral as well as for individuals. In 1911, Barbar extended the line 11 miles along Evacuation Creek into Watson and a few years later lengthened it 4 more miles to Rainbow.

Gilsonite mining continued in the area, but in 1939 motorized vehicles replaced the railroad as the quickest means of transportation, and the Uintah Railway closed. All of the materials were sold, and the scrap metal was used to create ammunition during World War II.

People

Explorers and Surveyors

Edward Beckwith

Edward Beckwith served as Captain John Gunnison's assistant commander during his expedition to survey a transcontinental railroad route to the Pacific. Following the massacre of Gunnison and seven of the men in his party, Beckwith retreated to Salt Lake City with the survivors for the winter of 1853–54.

In the spring of 1854, the government commissioned Beckwith to explore routes between the Salt Lake Valley and Fort Bridger. He successfully discovered two viable routes through the Weber and Timpanogos Canyons. Shortly after, the government again assigned Beckwith to explore routes through the Sierra Nevadas for the transcontinental railroad. Although the government dismissed Beckwith's suggestions because he was not an engineer, the first transcontinental railroad ran directly through his recommended route.

Captain Benjamin Louis Eulalie de Bonneville

Captain Bonneville arrived in Utah in 1831 on a fur trapping expedition while on leave from the army. Not a very talented trader, Bonneville met and partnered with mountain man Joseph Walker for several treks through the West.

In 1832, Bonneville constructed a trading post on the

Green River to which he would return for the Green River Rendezvous in 1833. During this event, the captain led a team to map the Great Salt Lake as well as to find its legendary outlet to the Pacific Ocean. Bonneville and his group soon realized this arm of the ocean, or "Rio Buenaventura," did not exist.

Captain Louis Eulalie de Bonneville

Other than mapping the Great Salt Lake, Bonneville's accomplishments were few. However, his friend and author Washington Irving immortalized Bonneville's explorations in his 1837 publication *Scenes and Adventures in the Rocky Mountains*. Today, the Bonneville Salt Flats bear the explorer's name.

Jim Bridger

In 1822, Jim Bridger answered an ad in the newspaper calling for adventurous young men who were seeking a new life in the West. Bridger and a hundred others, including Jedediah Smith, ventured to the Missouri River for their first assignment.

Bridger spent the summer of 1824 trapping in Cache Valley near present-day Cove, Utah. That winter, during a dispute over the course of the Bear River, the group elected Bridger to follow the river's course. In doing this, Bridger became the first non-Indian to behold the Great Salt Lake. However, when the explorer came upon the banks of the enormous body of water and tasted its saltiness, he believed it was part of the Pacific Ocean.

Jim Bridger

During the winter of 1825–26, the explorer spent his days trapping in Salt Lake Valley, where he returned for many winters in the years to come. In 1826, Bridger attended the Cache Valley Rendezvous on the Utah-Wyoming border, which was a popular event for trappers and traders. Bridger would return to these gatherings for the next several years.

Along with friend Louis Vasquez, Bridger organized the Rocky Mountain Fur Company in 1830. Unfortunately, the fur business was on the decline, and the venture closed after only four years. Around this time, Bridger and his business partner decided to pursue the trading industry and opened Fort Bridger on Black's Fork of the Green River.

Bridger first encountered Brigham Young and his Mormon followers soon after their arrival in Utah in 1847. On the one hand, Bridger enjoyed the new business of the settlers. Yet, in 1853, three years after Utah became a territory, a dispute arose between Bridger and the Mormons. They issued a warrant for his arrest, and the explorer left Utah for the east.

In 1855, Bridger returned to his fort only to sell it to the Mormons for $8,000. The structure stayed under their possession until army troops occupied it in 1857. The military controlled Fort Bridger until 1890, nine years after Bridger died.

Kit Carson

Kit Carson left his childhood home in Missouri at the age of 16 to pursue his dream of becoming a mountain man. He soon met up with a group of traders en route to the Rocky Mountains and ended up in Taos, New Mexico.

Although Taos would serve as Carson's home base for most of his life, the trapper could certainly have called the entire wilderness of the West his true home. In 1829, Carson met longtime trapper Ewing Young and stayed with his company for the next five years. During this time, Carson learned the ins and outs of the trapping business and became educated in several Indian languages. He married an Indian following the death of his first wife, who died in childbirth after giving Carson two children.

By 1840, the fur trading industry was rapidly declining, and many trappers and mountain men were leaving the area for other endeavors. Carson took his daughter to school in Missouri, where on a river boat he met John Frémont, who hired him as a route guide for the U.S. Topographical Engineers. This decision would transform the little-educated explorer into a figure of renowned popularity.

For the next several years, Carson led Frémont's excursions throughout the West. He married his third wife, Marie Josefa Jaramillo in 1842 and became brother-in-law to Charles Bent. The mountain-man-turned-guide led Frémont on his most important journey to the Great Salt Lake in 1843. Carson carved a cross on a rock on the summit of Fremont Island in Salt Lake during

Kit Carson

this expedition that can still be observed today. Kit Carson became a household name through Frémont's colorful novels about his western adventures.

From 1853 to 1861, Carson served as an Indian agent but resigned to became a colonel in the First New Mexico Volunteer Infantry. He received the breveted rank of brigadier general for taking part in the battle of Valverde, New Mexico. He would dutifully serve in the army until 1867, when he retired and moved to Boggsville, Colorado. Carson passed away at the age of 59, one month after the death of Marie Josefa. The couple is buried in Taos, New Mexico.

John Frémont

A native of Savannah, Georgia, John Frémont was born in 1813 to French and American parents. He grew up primarily in Charleston, South Carolina, where he attended the College of Charleston's Scientific Department before being expelled in 1831. After teaching math to midshipmen in the navy for a few years, Frémont joined the U.S. Corps of Topographical Engineers as second lieutenant.

It was during this time that Frémont met Missouri senator Thomas Hart Benton, a man who would have a great influence in the young explorer's life. Frémont also met and fell deeply in love with Benton's 16-year-old daughter, Jessie Benton. Despite the couple's 11-year age difference, they happily eloped and were married in October 1841.

Benton commissioned his new son-in-law to lead a "secret" expedition to explore the wagon routes to Oregon and to survey the Platte River. Frémont needed an experienced guide for his trip, so he hired Kit Carson for $100 a month. The two became life-long friends.

After each of Frémont's successful explorations, he would return home to his wife and energetically dictate his tales and findings while she wrote. These elaborate stories became best-sellers with the American public and even caught the attention of Congress. They were highly impressed by Frémont's scientific and topographical abilities. Later, even the Smithsonian Institute would recognize his accounts.

John Frémont

Nicknamed "The Pathfinder," Frémont crossed over the Great Salt Desert in 1845, again with Kit Carson leading the way. The group spent one month exploring the Utah Valley and Great Salt Lake, conducting scientific research on the area. The explorer was the first to accurately measure the elevation of the Great Salt Lake at 4,200 feet above sea level, as well as the first to map the region. Frémont's accounts of the Salt Lake region are credited with influencing Brigham Young's decision to settle his Mormon followers in the area.

Arriving in California during his 1845 expedition, Frémont became involved in the political upheaval between Mexico and United States. After refusing to side with the commander-in-chief of California, he was forced to leave and was court-martialed for his resistance. President Polk overturned the penalty, but Frémont resigned from the military.

Frémont led his fourth excursion in 1848 through the San Juan Mountains of Colorado in order to establish a central railroad route. One of Frémont's men perished during this trip, and many came close to death while caught in a snowstorm. Frémont led his last expedition in 1853, again to California on a railroad venture.

Between 1842 and 1853, John Frémont led five expeditions through the West. He is best remembered for completing the first comprehensive map of the West with accurate astronomical readings. Frémont attempted a political career later in life, serving briefly as a California senator and unsuccessfully running as the first Republican presidential candidate. As a result of several poor business ventures, Frémont died a virtual pauper in 1890.

John Gunnison

John Gunnison graduated second in his class of 50 from West Point in 1837. Shortly after, he was assigned to the U.S. Corps of Topographical Engineers. After spending three years in Florida, Gunnison married Martha Delony and moved to the Great Lakes to work on surveys in that region.

In the spring of 1849, the corps reassigned Gunnison to Howard Stansbury's expedition to survey the Great Salt Lake valley. En route to the region, Gunnison fell gravely ill and was forced to stay at Fort Bridger for several days while recovering. Gunnison spent the fall of that year surveying Utah Lake and the Jordan

John Gunnison

River. The following spring and summer the explorer dedicated his time to surveying and mapping the Great Salt Lake region.

Gunnison's first expedition proved so successful that the government assigned him to conduct a survey across central Colorado and Utah. Gunnison and his 37-man party departed on May 3, 1853, and after an uneventful journey arrived in Manti, on the Sevier River, in October.

Only days prior to Gunnison's arrival, white pioneers had killed several members of the local Paiute Indian tribe. The angry tribe sought revenge and massacred Gunnison along with seven of his men on the banks of the Sevier River on October 26, 1853. Although many easterners blamed the Mormons for instigating the attack, there is little proof to authenticate their accusation.

In 1862, a group of Mormon settlers named their community "Gunnison" in memory of the slain explorer. A monument lies 5 miles west of present-day Delta where Gunnison and his men are buried. Gunnison, who died at age 41, was the last official explorer before Colorado's gold rush period.

Ferdinand Hayden

Ferdinand Vandeveer Hayden was born in Westfield, Massachusetts, on September 7, 1828, and raised on a farm near Rochester, New York, before graduating in medicine from Albany Medical College in New York.

Hayden worked as a paleontologist and geologist throughout the Midwest and West. He collaborated on several survey expeditions to Missouri and the Dakotas during his early years as a member of the forerunner to the U.S. Geological Survey. After joining Governor K. Warren's expedition to Yellowstone, Hayden was recognized by Congress for his interest in preserving the area as a state park, which it became in 1872.

It was not until 1870 that the explorer found himself at Fort Bridger, near the Utah-Wyoming border. During this expedition, Hayden explored various rivers, including the Bear, Muddy, and Green, as well as the Uinta Mountains. More than for any geological surveys, this trip was significant because of the incredible photographs and paintings created by William Henry Jackson and Thomas Moran, who accompanied Hayden. These vivid portraits of the West allowed all Americans to experience the splendor of their country.

Hayden Survey party in Utah in 1870 (Hayden: seated in center)

Hayden was an initial appointee to the U.S. Geological Survey when it was established in 1879, but he was forced to retire due to ill health in 1886. He died the following year at age 59.

Clarence King

Yale graduate Clarence King personally originated the idea of a vast geological survey of the land that would be crossed by the Union Pacific and Central Pacific Railroads. At 25, King secured funding from the federal government that made him the first nonmilitary person to lead a U.S. geological expedition.

By July 1868, King and his party found themselves in the Salt Lake region. After exploring the entire area up to southern Idaho, the group reconvened in October of that year. Following a short break, King divided the party into three groups to explore different areas of Utah. One party explored the Provo River up through the Uinta Mountains; another group stayed and mapped the Great Salt Lake, which had grown by over 600 square miles since Stansbury's expedition almost 20 years earlier; and King's party explored the Echo Canyon region to the Bear River. On this journey, the engineer discovered hearty coal deposits along the Green River.

King was not only an educated surveyor but an avid adventurer. He was known to chase grizzly bears, climb steep mountains, bring outlaws to justice, and was even once struck by lightning. After 10 years of service, King was appointed director of the U.S. Geological Survey when it was first established in 1879.

John Macomb

In 1859, the U.S. Corps of Topographical Engineers assigned John Macomb to find additional wagon routes from New Mexico to Utah. Macomb's team, which included famed geologist John Newberry, was also supposed to survey and map the route, discover new minerals and geological specimens, and locate the junction of the Green and Colorado Rivers. Many believe the government's true motive for the expedition derived from the growing tension between the United States and the Mormons. This tension had just resulted in the bloodless Utah War of 1857–58 (see "Utah War").

Although Macomb and his group followed the Old Spanish Trail, they were unsuccessful in locating a direct route from Santa Fe to the junction of the rivers. Newberry, however, managed to find the first dinosaur bones ever to be discovered in Utah, and collected several geological samples (later acquired by the Smithsonian Institute). During a later expedition, Macomb was eventually able to locate the convergence of the two rivers.

Peter Ogden

Born in 1794, Peter Ogden was a British trapper who worked the northern and western parts of the country for the Hudson's Bay Company. In 1824, Ogden was leading the Snake River Country Expedition. The British at the time were trying to trap as much land as they could so as to discourage Americans from entering the region.

Ogden's trapping expedition traveled south into Utah along the Bear River. They trapped as far south as Mountain

Green (about 10 or 15 miles east of present-day Ogden). There they met two other groups of trappers: one led by French-Canadian Etienne Provost, and the other by American John Weber. With this many men in the area and a limited number of beavers, a conflict was inevitable.

When Provost and Weber heard that Ogden had been flying the Union Jack and treating the land as if it belonged to Great Britain, they became outraged. Joining forces, they decided to let Ogden know that he was trespassing in foreign territory. Although the situation remained nonviolent, a trapper from Provost's party named Johnson Gardner persuaded 23 men in Ogden's party to desert the British group. Ogden, realizing he was outnumbered, quickly withdrew from the area without ever stepping foot in the town that bears his name. It is interesting that while all of the groups claimed that their country was the rightful owner of the land, according to the Adams Onis Treaty of 1819, the land actually belonged to the Mexicans.

Peter Ogden

Ogden led another expedition into Utah in 1828. This time he went into the northwest corner of the state, where it is thought that he saw the Great Salt Lake. After trapping the area, he left Utah for good.

Throughout the first half of the 1800s, Ogden played a major role in the fur trade. He died in 1854, but his name lives on in northern Utah.

John Wesley Powell

John Wesley Powell was a Civil War veteran who lost his right arm at the Battle of Shiloh. This challenge did not dissuade Powell from becoming one of the most influential explorers in the history of the West. After the war, Powell served as a professor of geology at Wesleyan University in Illinois as well as a museum curator. However, after spending time with a Ute Indian tribe in 1869, Powell conceived of the idea of exploring the great rivers in the area by boat.

In May 1869, Powell led a group of 11 men down the Green River; they commenced in Green River, Wyoming, met the Colorado River, and traveled through the Grand Canyon. One man quit the expedition early, and three others refused to run the treacherous final rapids on the Colorado. Instead, they climbed out of the canyon walls only to be killed by Indians. Powell and the remaining men arrived safely at a Mormon settlement on August 30, 1869.

Impressed by the expedition, Congress agreed to give Powell $10,000 for a second trip in 1871. The explorer used this opportu-

John Wesley Powell on his horse

nity to conduct serious scientific research. Powell hired men to help map the region as well as to photograph the phenomenal scenery. This group eventually became the U.S. Geological and Geographical Survey, operating under the Smithsonian Institution.

During the 1870s, Powell focused much of his energy on researching the geography of the West and on studying the American Indians (which led to his classification of their languages). He presented his geological findings in the 1879 publication, "Reports on the Lands of the Arid Regions of the United States," and that same year, with the support of a $20,000 grant from the federal government, he founded the U.S. Bureau of Ethnology. Powell was the first director of the bureau, and in 1881 he was named director of the U.S. Geological Survey; he held both positions for the remainder of his life. The explorer died on September 23, 1892, and is buried at Arlington National Cemetery.

Antoine Robidoux

Antoine Robidoux was born on September 24, 1794, in Florissant, Missouri. His father, a fur trader, moved his family to St. Louis, where the family business flourished. It did not take long, however, until the young Antoine Robidoux ventured west to find his own fortune in the trading and trapping business.

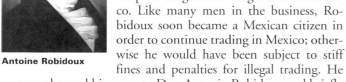

Antoine Robidoux

In 1825, Robidoux made his second trip to Santa Fe, where he established himself as a prominent trader and where, in 1828, he met and married Carmel Benevides, the adopted daughter of the governor of Mexico. Like many men in the business, Robidoux soon became a Mexican citizen in order to continue trading in Mexico; otherwise he would have been subject to stiff fines and penalties for illegal trading. He even changed his name to Don Antonio Robidoux and briefly served in the Mexican government.

That same year, Robidoux established the first of his trading posts near present-day Delta, Colorado. During Robidoux's time there, his nephew, William Reed, and friend Denis Julien left to locate a new post in northeastern Utah. The two traveled to the Uinta Basin, where they established the Reed Trading Post at the Whiterocks fork of the Uinta River (one mile south of present-day Whiterocks). In 1832, Robidoux purchased the Reed Trading Post, renamed it Fort Robidoux (sometimes called Fort Uinta), and expanded his business by bringing in trappers to hunt beavers in the streams of the Green and Uinta Rivers. There was intense competition from other posts, such as Fort Davy Crockett, and the fort enabled Robidoux to keep the upper hand in regional trading.

Fort Robidoux became the first permanent non-Indian settlement and business in Utah. In addition to trading with settlers, Robidoux also dabbled in trading horses, illegal guns, and liquor with the local Ute Indians. Often considered an unscrupulous businessman, Robidoux is rumored to have also sold Ute Indian women and children for prostitution and slavery. One account claims Robidoux even used the children for target practice.

However immoral Robidoux's business practices may have been, his trading endeavors thrived. In 1837, he ventured again into the Uinta Basin to build yet another trading post. An inscription on a rock in the basin, written in French, translates to read, "Antoine Robidoux passed here November 13, 1837, to establish a house of trade on the Green or Uinta River. However, some scholars disagree as to whether his French word indicates the Uinta or the White River, as there are trading posts (or the remains of buildings thought to have been trading posts) at both places.

Then, in 1844, Ute Indians attacked and burned both of Robidoux's Utah forts. The reason for these attacks is somewhat unclear, although historians suspect Robidoux's cheating of the Indians, his capture of Indian women and children for prostitution and slavery, and other unscrupulous deeds.

In declining health, Robidoux returned to his childhood home of St. Louis in 1857. Once described as "tall, slender, athletic and agile," Antoine Robidoux died there a blind, decrepit man on August 29, 1860.

James Hervey Simpson

James Simpson served on the U.S. Corps of Topographical Engineers in Texas and New Mexico prior to his appointment as chief topographical engineer in Utah in 1858. The army commissioned Simpson to rebuild the wagon route between Camp Floyd in Cedar Valley and Fort Bridger through Timpanogos Canyon.

After successfully completing this mission, Simpson was assigned to locate a new route from Camp Floyd through the Sierra Nevada. During the trek, the explorer discovered a viable natural spring perfect for watering and grazing livestock. This area, which was later used as a Pony Express stop, is now named Simpson Springs.

Simpson's third army expedition took him from Camp Floyd through the Colorado Rockies into Denver. In all, James Simpson covered more land on foot in 10 years than any other topographical engineer in history.

Jedediah Smith

Jedediah Smith was born on January 6, 1799, in New York State. A natural explorer, Smith answered an ad in the *St. Louis Gazette and Public Advertiser* in 1822 (the same ad that Jim Bridger responded to) calling for young men who wanted to explore the West. He soon became part of William Ashley's great fur trapping and exploration team.

On one of Smith's first expeditions, a grizzly bear attacked the young man, ripping off his scalp and one ear. His companions feared the worst, but Smith would not be defeated that easily. He ordered his friends to sew back his dangling parts and returned to the trail 10 days later.

In 1824, searching for the legendary "Buenaventura River," Smith became the first white man to cross overland into California. He crossed over the Continental Divide, "redis-

A sketch of Jedediah Smith made by a friend after Smith's death

covering" South Pass. These types of discoveries were not an unusual occurrence for Smith. The explorer was the first to cross the Great Basin, as well as to venture over the Sierra Nevadas from west to east.

Smith took part in the first recorded rendezvous on the banks of the Green River in Utah in 1825. These large annual gatherings allowed trappers and traders the chance to buy and sell goods after the winter hunts. Smith would return to almost the same spot the following year for his second and last rendezvous.

In 1827, Smith and his two-man party trekked across the Great Salt Desert, returning from California on their way to the Green River. The small group ran into trouble and almost did not survive; they even resorted to eating their horses to stay alive. They arrived late to the rendezvous and were greeted by suprised friends who had believed they were dead.

Smith, a highly religious man in a very secular trade, outwitted fate many times. A large number of his fellow explorers died at the hands of Indians, wild animals, or the elements. In 1831, Smith decided to retire, but he wanted to make one last journey along the Santa Fe Trail. While scouting for water on the Cimarron River, Jedediah Smith was slain by Comanche Indians. He was only 32 years old.

Howard Stansbury

Howard Stansbury joined the U.S. Topographical Bureau in October 1828 as a civil engineer. He would spend the following 21 years surveying regions such as the Atlantic Coast, the Great Lakes, and the Gulf of Mexico.

In 1849, Colonel John J. Abert commissioned Stansbury to lead an expedition to the Great Salt Lake Valley. Stansbury was asked to survey the Great Salt Lake and the Utah Lake; to explore wagon routes to the area; to determine whether or not the Mormon settlers (who had arrived two years before) were equipped to provide food to travelers; and to establish a military post in the Salt Lake region.

During his year in the area, Stansbury and his team of 14 men discovered a shorter route to Salt Lake through the Rocky Mountains; determined that the Great Basin was an ancient lake bed; recovered many Ute Indian artifacts; and successfully surveyed the lakes. Although first believing Cache Valley to be an ideal military post, the government abandoned the idea after Stansbury's survey deemed it unnecessary.

Howard Stansbury

Following his studies of the Mormon culture and after returning east, Stansbury published his report, which looked upon the settlers very favorably. In agreement with John Gunnison's publication, *The Mormons*, the two explorers determined the Salt Lake region an ideal area for establishing settlements.

There are two legacies to Captain Stansbury in Utah today. Adobe Rock, at the northwest point of the Oquirrh Mountains, is named after a small adobe home the explorer built during his expedition. Stansbury Park, a planned community just outside of Salt Lake City, was also named for the captain.

After the outbreak of the Civil War, Stansbury worked as a mustering officer in Columbus, Ohio. Later he was placed in charge of recruiting for the state of Wisconsin, where he died only forty-five days later of heart disease on April 13, 1863. Stansbury was 56 years old.

Edward Steptoe

Edward Steptoe was born in Virginia in 1816. After spending many years with the army in various locations, Steptoe was sent to Utah to investigate the murder of Captain John Gunnison and his seven men by Paiute Indians.

The lieutenant colonel spent the winter of 1854–55 in the Salt Lake region. Although not a member of the U.S. Corps of Engineers, Steptoe supervised the construction of a road on the Mormon Corridor. Many improvements were made between Cedar City and the head of the Santa Clara River, but funds ran out before the project was completed.

Early in 1855, President Franklin Pierce recommended the appointment of Steptoe as Utah Territory governor. Steptoe considered the offer but declined, believing the Mormons would only tolerate Brigham Young as their leader. He left Utah in April 1855 as tension grew between the Mormons and the federal government.

Joseph Reddeford Walker

Joseph Walker, a born mountain man and trapper who lived during the height of the trading business in the early 1800s, is best known for his partnership with Captain Benjamin Bonneville. Originally from Tennessee, Walker accompanied Bonneville on many expeditions through the West, including several to the Great Salt Lake region.

One of the great "trailblazers" of his time, Walker began as a surveyor on the Santa Fe Trail in 1826. In the early 1830s, the explorer joined Captain Bonneville on an expedition to find a route to California beginning at the Great Salt Lake. In 1833, Walker even constructed a trading post on the Green River, possibly the first in Utah.

Joseph Reddeford Walker

Throughout his many years in the West, Walker served as explorer, trader, trapper, horse herder, guide, and most importantly, a true pathfinder. He died in 1876 at the age of 78.

Mormon Leaders, Ranchers, Settlers, and Colorful Characters

William H. Ashley

William H. Ashley was a shrewd businessman and entrepreneur in the fur trading industry. A Virginia native, Ashley began the Rocky Mountain Fur Company in 1822 while living in St. Louis, Missouri. Ashley ran an advertisement in the St. Louis newspapers calling for "100 Enterprising Young Men," and the response was phenomenal; two of the young men who would go on to earn a measure of acclaim in Utah were Jim Bridger and Jedediah Smith.

Ashley's first two expeditions into the Utah wilderness

proved very unlucky: on the first his supply boat sank and all his men's gear was lost; and on the second, 14 men died during an Indian attack. After these disasters, Ashley opted to have his parties travel overland in smaller groups.

In 1825, Ashley personally traveled the Green River into the Uinta Basin with a group of his men. Constantly thinking in terms of business, Ashley realized the wastefulness of requiring his men to travel to St. Louis at the end of each season. Therefore, in 1825, the trader organized the first annual rendezvous on the Green River. This enormous gathering of trappers and traders allowed everyone to conduct business simultaneously, and Ashley reaped the benefits. After the first year, he brought over $50,000 worth of furs home with him to St. Louis. The rendezvous continued to be held in Utah for the following three years.

Jedediah Smith eventually purchased the Rocky Mountain Fur Company from Ashley in 1826. By this time, Ashley had made his fortune in the fur industry and returned to St. Louis to reestablish his political career.

John Moses Browning

In 1852, Jonathan Browning arrived in Ogden with his wives and children, including a young John Moses, and opened up a gun shop. When his father died, John Moses took control of the family's gunsmithing business and, along with his brothers, established the Browning Brothers Company.

John received the first of his 128 gun patents in October 1879. Two years later, production began on 25 .22-caliber single-shot rifles. During this time, he and his brothers labeled the store "The Largest Arms Factory Between Omaha and the Pacific." They sold the rifles for a net profit of $700. After producing a few hundred more, John and his brothers sold the patent to Winchester. Deciding to focus more on research and development, they contracted with other companies for the actual manufacturing of the guns.

Over the years, the Browning brothers patented such firearms as the Colt .45 semiautomatic pistol, the .30- and .50-caliber machine gun, and the Browning Automatic-5 shotgun. The Browning brothers designed the first automatic weapon, and by the turn of the century, 75 percent of America's sporting guns had been invented by John Moses Browning.

John Moses Browning

The family business continued after John's death in 1926. The scope of the company expanded to include all sorts of outdoor and sporting equipment. In 1977, the Browning Brothers Company was bought out by a Belgian company, though the headquarters remain in Mountain Green, Utah.

Today, Ogden is home to the Browning Firearms Museum, which houses many of the company's patented guns and traces the general evolution of firearms.

Ebenezer Bryce

At age 14, Ebenezer Bryce moved with his parents from Scotland to New Jersey. From there, Bryce decided to move out west, and somewhere along the way he became a member of the Mormon Church. Sometime in the 1870s, he eventually settled in the Paria Valley with his wife and 10 children. After water supplies dwindled, he relocated to a site upstream in the Henderson Valley.

Bryce and his friend Daniel Goulding began to work on the land by fencing in 200 acres. This would serve as a range for their cattle. They also built a 7-mile-long canal to irrigate their fields, planted fruit trees, and built a lumber road to a nearby wooded area. That road ended in a natural amphitheater formation, which was referred to by locals as Bryce's Canyon as early as 1876. Then Bryce and his family decided to move south to Arizona in 1880 because of his wife's weakening health.

Ebenezer Bryce

People soon began to appreciate the phenomenal landforms in the area, and in 1924, the land was set aside as a national park. When Bryce was asked what he thought of his old ranch, it is said that he replied, "It's a hell of a place to lose a cow."

Charlie Crouse

Charlie Crouse was born in Virginia in 1851. His father died shortly after his birth, and his mother soon remarried a man named James Frank Tolliver. Young Charlie hated his stepfather, and by age nine, he had left home.

Throughout the 1860s, Crouse traveled across the country. He served a brief time in the Union army during the Civil War, and upon leaving the service, he hauled freight across the Laramie Plains. During this time Crouse learned the customs and the languages of the Indian tribes with whom he dealt.

In the 1870s, Crouse arrived in Green River City. He settled in this untamed, northeastern Utah region and soon met Aaron Overholt and Billy Tittsworth. These three men became partners in many pioneer business ventures throughout the years, including land speculating and ranching.

Crouse soon opened up his own ranch around Brown's Park, calling it the Park Live Stock Company. Around 1886, a young man calling himself George Cassidy came to work on Crouse's ranch. Originally, his given name was Robert LeRoy Parker; however he would later become known throughout the West as Butch Cassidy. Besides fulfilling his duties as a ranch hand, Cassidy found success in racing Crouse's horses. Despite his achievements on horseback, Cassidy was a quiet and withdrawn young man.

In 1889, Cassidy, along with a few other men, robbed a bank in Telluride, Colorado. Returning to Brown's Park, the outlaws were welcomed back into Crouse's home. This pattern continued over the next few years, as George Cassidy became the Butch Cassidy we know today. Cassidy would leave town with some of his men and upon his return would be welcomed back by Charlie Crouse. Cassidy and his Wild Bunch turned out to be very welcome in Brown's Park. They would often share a dinner table with or give out gifts to the townspeople.

It is true that Crouse mixed with men of questionable character, and he himself often straddled both sides of the law. He was suspected in the mysterious disappearance of a few men. However, his public status and outlaw friends kept him beyond the reach of the law. In 1890, Crouse sold a part of the ranch and opened a saloon in Vernal. He also built and ran a toll bridge, charging people to cross the Green River.

After his wife, Mary, died in 1904 and his ranching interests were being run by his son, Crouse moved to Wyoming to live part of the year with his daughter Minnie. He sold most of his Brown's Park property in 1907, and died shortly thereafter in 1908. Charlie Crouse, with his love of drinking and gambling, his friendships with lawmen and outlaws, and his pioneering entrepreneurship, epitomizes to this day the spirit of the Wild West.

Jacob Hamblin

In 1819, Jacob Hamblin was born in Ashtabula County, Ohio. When he was around 17 years old, his family took up a homestead in the Wisconsin Territory. Two years later, his father wished him well and sent him off to work in galena mines about 100 miles to the west. After narrowly escaping a mining accident that killed a co-worker, Hamblin moved back to Wisconsin with an aversion to mining, took up his own homestead, and in 1939 married his first wife.

About three years later, Hamblin heard that Mormons were preaching in the area. After listening to their message, he felt called to the church and promptly joined in March 1842. Within a year he moved to Nauvoo, Illinois, which at that time was the Mormon Church's headquarters.

Hamblin immediately set out on his life as a missionary and faith healer among the Indians. He married again and moved his families to Utah during the Mormon's western exodus. In 1854 he was appointed to do missionary work in southern Utah. Along with his families, Hamblin moved south to Santa Clara to serve as the president of the southern Utah Indian Mission.

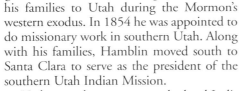
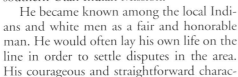
Jacob Hamblin

He became known among the local Indians and white men as a fair and honorable man. He would often lay his own life on the line in order to settle disputes in the area. His courageous and straightforward character earned Hamblin the nickname "peacemaker."

Unfortunately, he was not around to settle the dispute that resulted in the Mountain Meadows Massacre. On his way north to see Brigham Young, Hamblin met and directed the ill-fated, non-Mormon wagon train to the Mountain Meadows area as a good place to set up camp. He continued on his way to Salt Lake City, while the unfortunate pioneers headed to their deaths (for a description of this incident, see "John D. Lee," pp. 63-64). Upon hearing the news of the massacre, Hamblin expressed his disgust with those responsible for the atrocity.

Hamblin continued to work as a missionary in southern Utah for nearly the rest of his life. Due to his friendly relations with the Indians and his knowledge of the land, Hamblin also helped Major John Wesley Powell in his explorations. As guides and suppliers, Hamblin and his Indian friends con-

tributed greatly to the success of Powell's expeditions.

In 1882, with the passage of the Edmunds Act, Jacob Hamblin became an outlaw for the practice of polygamy. Though he separated from his first wife, this dedicated family man still had three others, as well as 24 children (not counting those he adopted). He moved his families to different parts of the southwest and Mexico. His final years were spent visiting his families and continuing his work as a missionary to the Indians. Jacob Hamblin died in August 1886.

William Henry Jackson

The famous photographer William Henry Jackson was born in 1843 in New York. He took up photography around the age of 15, and two years later, in 1860, he moved to Vermont to start his own studio. Jackson would keep moving, with only brief respites, for the rest of his life. He traveled cross-country to California in the mid-1860s, and on his way back, he settled in Omaha, Nebraska. From there he photographed the building of the transcontinental railroad.

William Henry Jackson

Through the 1870s Jackson worked as the official photographer of the Hayden Survey. Departing from Ogden, this expedition gained a great deal of attention because of its exploration and photography of the area that would become Yellowstone National Park. Specifically in Utah, the expedition visited such sites as Henry's Fork, Green River, and the Uinta Mountains.

In 1879, Jackson settled in Denver and built a studio, which served as a base for his work. For the next 20 years, he traveled and documented regions around the country and the world, from the mountains near his home to distant Siberia.

By the mid-1920s, Jackson moved to Washington, D.C., where he took up mural painting. He died at the age of 99 in New York, but not before leaving behind thousands of pictures of some of the world's wildest landscapes.

John Jarvie

Born in Scotland in 1844, John Jarvie began his working life in the Scottish mines. However, after a severe beating from his supervisor, he quit mining and headed for America to try his luck. In 1871, he moved to Rock Springs in the Wyoming Territory and opened up the Jarvie Saloon. He ran the saloon until 1880, when he met and married Nellie Barr. The couple, tired of the hectic pace of Rock Springs, moved south to Brown's Park, Utah.

At first they lived in a basic, two-room dugout, which became a storage cellar after they built their house. They also built a general store. The location—on the northern bank of the Green River—was perfect for Jarvie and for the settlers around Brown's Park, as his was the only store for 70 miles. It also sat at a natural river crossing that Indians and trappers had used for years. The store opened for business in 1881, and it soon included a post office and ferry service. Jarvie kept expanding over the years, adding a blacksmith shop, corrals, stables, and even a waterwheel to irrigate his fields.

Jarvie became a very popular figure in the Brown's Park area. He was an educated man who would readily lend books to his neighbors. He and his wife were musically talented and so were in demand for local gatherings. Travelers and settlers found a welcome rest stop at the Jarvie store—as did outlaws such as Butch Cassidy, Harry Longabaugh (the Sundance Kid), and Ann Bassett (Queen of Cattle Country).

For 28 years, Jarvie ran his general store. Though he lost some of his ferry business when Charlie Crouse built a toll bridge across the river, he gained it back when the bridge was washed out.

Finally, in 1909, by then a venerable, white-haired old man, John Jarvie was murdered while his store was being robbed by two transient workers from Wyoming. Instead of burying him, his friends put his body into a boat and shoved it down the Green River. About a week later it was found near the Gates of Lodore in eastern Brown's Park. He now lies buried in the Lodore cemetery.

The Jarvie homestead still exists and is preserved by the Bureau of Land Management.

Thomas Kane

A native of Philadelphia, Thomas Kane was born on January 27, 1822. At age 18, he went to Europe to recover from ill health. Seeing firsthand the controlling governments of the Old World, Kane began to appreciate the freedom of the United States. Upon his return, he put his convictions to work by helping with the Underground Railroad, which rescued blacks from slavery in the South.

In 1846, Kane was very taken by the address of Mormon Elder Jesse C. Little. While he did not convert, he did commit himself to aid the Mormon people in whatever way he could.

His first experience working on behalf of the Mormons  came later in 1846 when he went to Iowa to advise them on the creation of a Mormon Battalion. At the same time he helped them get official recognition from the federal government. Returning to Philadelphia in 1848, he continued to lobby for the rights of the Mormons. He also kept in contact with those Mormons who had recently arrived in Utah, advising them on various civic issues.

In the winter of 1858, Kane acted as intermediary between Brigham Young and territorial governor Alfred Cumming. The federal government, fearing a

Thomas Kane

supposed Mormon uprising, had just sent 3,000 men into Utah under Colonel Johnston, and a war seemed imminent. However, Kane arranged a meeting between Young and Cumming, and the resulting agreements prevented fighting and secured peace in Utah.

Needless to say, the outnumbered Mormons were very

thankful, and though Kane went back east, he kept up a very strong friendship with Brigham Young for years to come. He even went back in 1872 for a vacation in St. George.

Kane died in 1883, having earned a place in Mormon history, as well as their lasting respect and gratitude.

John D. Lee

Born in 1812 in the Illinois Territory, John D. Lee spent much of his life moving around the midwestern and southwestern parts of the country. He and his wife were first introduced to the Church of Latter-day Saints in the late 1830s. Strongly influenced by the Mormons, they moved to Missouri, where they met the Mormon prophet Joseph Smith. Smith baptized the young couple, who in turn dedicated their lives to the church.

After being kicked out of Missouri in 1838 by an "extermination order" from the governor, the Mormons resettled in Nauvoo, Illinois. Lee served at different times as a guard to Joseph Smith and a missionary to parts around the Midwest. After Smith's death, Lee captained one of the pioneer journeys to Utah, where he served with other Mormon elders on the venerable Council of Fifty.

John D. Lee

In 1850, Lee and his family were sent to the southwestern town of Parowan in Iron County as a part of the Iron Mission. Six years later, he was appointed to the position of Indian agent in Iron County.

In September 1857, Lee became involved in the Mountain Meadows Massacre. A wagon train of non-Mormon settlers was passing through the southwestern town of Pinto on its way to California. As President Buchanan had just ordered troops into Utah and tensions were high, the Mormons did not treat the wagon train well, and it left under a cloud of animosity. Ten miles outside of town, the wagon train was ambushed.

The pioneers endured five days of being shot at from all sides. Finally, under the flag of a truce, Mormons began to march the settlers out of the area. Then all at once, each "rescuer" turned and shot the man next to him. To this day it remains one of the bloodiest events in Utah history. More than 120 people died in the slaughter. The story of who was at fault is still not completely clear. Some say Indians. Others say Mormons.

Because Lee had supposedly served as negotiator between

The execution of John D. Lee (he is sitting on his coffin at the left, the firing squad is at the extreme right)

the Indians and the wagon train, he found it increasingly difficult to fulfill his role as a leader in the Church as more and more questions arose about Mormon involvement in the massacre. Lee found it increasingly difficult to fulfill his role as a leader in the Mormon Church.

In 1870, Brigham Young excommunicated Lee from the church for his role in the massacre. Seeking safety from the law, Lee left town in 1872 and founded Lee's Ferry on the Colorado River. However, authorities caught up with him two years later. Found guilty of murder, John D. Lee was taken to the site of the massacre and executed by a firing squad.

Preston Nutter

Born in Virginia, Preston Nutter was an opportunist who made his fortune in the Southwest. By 1886, he had become rich as part-owner of the Colorado Freight Company, but he sold his portion of the company and began looking for a way to get into the cattle industry.

He soon found the necessary land on the Uintah Indian Reservation in northeast Utah. In the 1890s, Nutter was successful in obtaining a five-year, summer-grazing lease from the

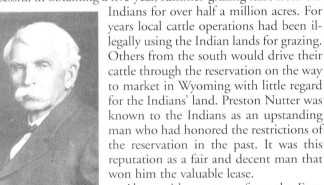

Indians for over half a million acres. For years local cattle operations had been illegally using the Indian lands for grazing. Others from the south would drive their cattle through the reservation on the way to market in Wyoming with little regard for the Indians' land. Preston Nutter was known to the Indians as an upstanding man who had honored the restrictions of the reservation in the past. It was this reputation as a fair and decent man that won him the valuable lease.

Along with a partner from the East, Nutter started the Strawberry Cattle Company. The land proved to be very good for the cattle. However, sheepherders soon moved their flocks into the area, much to the frustration of Nutter, who saw the sheep as a drain on the land.

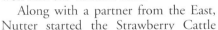
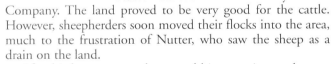
Preston Nutter

After his lease ran out, he moved his operation to the area around Nine Mile Canyon. In 1902, he bought the Brock Ranch near the old town of Harper and set up his headquarters. He converted the hotel into a bunkhouse for his cowboys. The previous owner of the ranch kept a peacock, and in the early part of the 20th century, a flock of peacocks was seen strutting around the ranch headquarters.

At its peak, Nutter's ranching operation extended through Colorado, Arizona, and Utah with more than 25,000 head of cattle. In addition, Nutter advised national politicians on grazing and ranching issues. He died in 1936, leaving the ranch and home to the care of his daughter, Virginia Nutter Price.

Orrin Porter Rockwell

In 1838, Missouri governor Lilburn W. Boggs issued an "extermination order" against the Mormons, who found themselves being driven out of the state. A peaceful group for the most part, the Mormons needed someone who would fight for them. They found such a man in Orrin Porter Rockwell.

Nicknamed the "Destroying Angel," Rockwell was associated with the militant Danites, a Mormon group not opposed to the use of violence in protecting themselves and their brethren. Rockwell was very angry at Governor Boggs, and in 1842 Rockwell was accused of attempting to assassinate him. He served some time in jail, but no official charges were brought and he was free to go later that year.

Rockwell then moved to the new Mormon settlement in Nauvoo, Illinois. There Joseph Smith revealed a prophecy about Rockwell, saying, "Cut not thy hair and no bullet or blade can harm thee." After Smith was killed while locked in jail, Rockwell took it upon himself to kill the man who had been in charge of protecting the revered Mormon leader.

Orrin Porter Rockwell

Once in Utah, Rockwell settled on a ranch in Tooele County and continued to fight for the Mormons. When President Buchanan decided to order troops into Utah, Rockwell (in the East at the time) was among those who heard of the plan. He hurried home to Utah to warn Brigham Young. When a group of soldiers attempted to reach the troops in Fort Bridger, Rockwell intervened and shot their leaders. He would be indicted 20 years later for the crime.

He also acted as a scout for Colonel P. E. Connor in an attack on the Shoshone Indians on the Bear River. Throughout his years with the Mormons, Rockwell was the man Young turned to when things got too hot. He was a noted frontiersman, marksman, and scout who was always ready to go into battle for his cause.

Rockwell lived an exaggerated life, and many stories about him have been exaggerated as well. The *Salt Lake Tribune* once reported that he killed over a hundred men. Although that is untrue, Rockwell did see his fair share of violence and bloodshed. Like many others of the Old West, it was often hard to tell if he was more lawman or outlaw. However, throughout his entire adult life, the "Destroying Angel" was most certainly on the side of the Mormons. Orrin Porter Rockwell died in June 1878.

Charlie Steen

Charles Steen was born in Caddo, Texas, in 1919. He studied geology at the Texas College of Mines and Metallurgy and received his degree in 1943. He worked in South America for the next couple of years before returning home, where he married and took a job with the Standard Oil Company. However, he was soon fired for insubordination and blacklisted throughout the industry.

In 1949, responding to a call for prospectors to find a uranium deposit on U.S. soil, Steen packed up his family and moved to the Colorado Plateau. Though mocked for his conviction that uranium could be collected in much the

Charlie Steen

same way as the oil, Steen explored many different claims throughout the region. Without the best equipment for the job, and not having any luck, Steen was about to give up when he struck it rich in the Lisbon Valley of southeastern Utah. Not only did his Mi Vida Mine make him a millionaire, it proved that uranium was plentiful in the region.

Steen, soon dubbed the "Uranium King," became rich overnight and decided to live accordingly. Besides establishing his own mining company, he built mansions near Moab and Reno, Nevada. But the surest sign of his new status was his weekly flights to Salt Lake City for rhumba lessons.

In 1958, Steen was elected to the Utah State Senate, but he resigned in 1961 to work on expanding his business interests. Unfortunately, he soon found himself in over his head and was bankrupt by 1968.

After his roller-coaster life had taken him full circle, Charles Steen moved to Colorado to work on his Cash Gold Mine, which represented the last of Steen's once astonishing fortune.

Albert "Speck" Williams

Born in West Virginia, Albert Williams made his way into the Brown's Park region of northeast Utah around 1893 or 1894. A black man with a speckled complexion, he quickly earned the nickname "Speck," in addition to other, less flattering

names. Williams didn't let the fact that he was one of only two or three black men in all of Brown's Park discourage him from settling in the area. Williams is quoted as saying, "If a black man wanted to survive in the West, he had to do good work and keep his mouth shut tight!"

Williams did just that. He became a jack-of-all-trades who worked many different jobs around Brown's Park. He was probably best known as the ferry operator at John Jarvie's store. However, he is thought to have also run errands for Butch Cassidy and the Wild Bunch.

Albert "Speck" Williams

Williams also worked for Charlie Crouse for a few years. Though Crouse was known to dislike black men, the two got along well as long as they were both sober. When the liquor flowed, the two men were known to have very violent tempers. One day, after they had been drinking, the two men began throwing punches. Crouse pulled out a knife, stabbed Williams in the stomach, and then left him to die. Mary Crouse heard about the fight and went out to rescue Williams, sewing him up and saving his life. Afterward, the two men remained good friends.

Williams lived in the Brown's Park area until the 1930s; some say he survived as a hermit. Eventually, he moved down to Vernal for the last few years of his life and died in 1934.

Brigham Young

Brigham Young, along with founder Joseph Smith, stands out in history as a true father of the Mormon faith. Where Smith was essentially a mystic who lived the ineffable life of a prophet—very innovative in his theology but with little time for earthly concerns—Young, who succeeded Smith as leader of the Mormons, proved very practical and down to earth. Young often shied away from bold theological declarations, but he was responsible for the Mormons' western exodus as well as their eventual colonization of Utah.

Brigham Young was born in 1801 into a strict frontier family in Vermont, and early on he showed little commitment to any particular faith. In 1830, Young and his wife were introduced to the Mormon Church. Attracted to the faith, Young was baptized on April 14, 1832. After meeting Smith, Young quickly rose to an influential position within the church and was appointed to the Council of the Twelve Apostles in

Brigham Young

1835. Three years later, when the Mormons were chased out of Missouri by an "extermination order," he led the church's migration to Nauvoo, Illinois.

In 1840, Young spent the year promoting the Mormon faith throughout England. When he returned the next year, he gave his complete loyalty to Joseph Smith and consummated his devotion by entering into the practice of polygamy (he would eventually have a great number of wives).

Joseph Smith was assassinated in 1844, and Brigham Young assumed the leadership of the Mormons. As the church was becoming very unpopular in Illinois, Young decided he needed to secure land for his people that would be conducive to their safety and worship. He organized a massive westward migration, and in 1846, the Mormons left Illinois, arriving in the Salt Lake Valley on July 24, 1847. They had reached their Zion!

Once the Mormons were settled in Utah, Young proved to be a very skilled leader and ardent promoter of the faith. He became the first territorial governor of Utah in 1850 and began colonizing areas throughout Utah and the West in the name of Mormonism. Back home in Salt Lake City, he was a practical businessman with personal investments in real estate, transportation, and manufacturing. Many of these side businesses helped Young to further promote his faith.

As time went on, the Mormons' polygamy greatly disturbed much of the country. Some militant Mormons had also been loosely connected with some mysterious deaths in Utah. In 1857, President Buchanan, fearing a Mormon uprising, decided to send 3,000 troops into Utah. This became known as the Utah War, though it was a bloodless invasion. Young stepped down as Utah's territorial governor during the crisis in order to avoid fighting, but he remained leader of the Mormons.

Young worked for the Mormon faith for the rest of his life. He tried to deal fairly with the local Indians as he spread his people throughout the state. A run-in with the law due to his multiple wives resulted in his being placed under house arrest for a brief spell.

When Brigham Young died in 1877, he was survived by 55

wives (some accounts say more, some less) and 57 children. In his lifetime, Young proved to be one of the great U.S. colonizers and one of the Mormons' greatest leaders.

Lawmen, Gunfighters, and Outlaws

Ann Bassett

Ann Bassett, commonly referred to as the Queen of Cattle Country, was born and spent the majority of her life in Brown's Hole. This northeastern corner of Utah was known for its successful ranchers and Bassett was no exception.

Upon her birth, Bassett received a cow and a calf as a gift from a family friend, a telltale sign of the girl's destiny. By the age of seven, Ann knew she wanted to be a cowboy, and she followed ranch hands around constantly in order to learn the trade. Unlike her sister and other girls her age, Ann donned buckskin suits instead of more proper dresses.

When Ann was a teenager, her father believed she should receive a proper education and sent her to a private ladies school in Boston. Ann, always excited for a new adventure, readily left for the East Coast. The cowgirl spent the next two years learning literature and "English" riding skills with the other girls, but she never seemed to fit in. Upon graduation, Ann happily returned to her true home in Brown's Hole.

Now an educated young woman, Ann became a prominent figure among the other ranchers in Brown's Hole. At one point, a large ranching company wanted to buy out all of the small, independent outfits in the area. Ann pulled the community together and rallied against the large company. From that time on, no one disputed the fact that Ann Bassett was a born leader of Brown's Hole.

Fellow ranchers saw Ann as an equal, a fact the woman cherished. She had no desire to involve herself romantically with any of the region's cowboys. However, one man traveling through the area as a cowhand did spark the Queen's interest. His name was Elza Lay, one of the famed members of the notorious Wild Bunch gang. Attracted to the educated outlaw, Ann saw Elza romantically for some time, but the roaming gang member never proposed.

Although Ann was never involved in outlaw excursions, she met her share of famed killers. Among the gang members who traveled through Ann's ranch were Butch Cassidy, Matt Warner, the McCarty brothers, Flat Nose George, and Black Jack Ketchum. Possibly through her connections with these wanted men, Ann herself was accused of cattle rustling around 1910. A large cattle outfit brought the Queen to trial over the ordeal, but the court acquitted her of any wrongdoing in 1913.

Soon afterward, Ann married Hi Bernard, the former manager of the cattle company that had accused her of rustling. The two lived happily until Bernard made the mistake of confessing to Ann that he had hired Tom Horn to murder Matt Rash and Isom Dart several years earlier. Ann, who had been friends of the two slain ranchers, could not forgive her husband and left him.

A few years later, after she had given up cattle ranching for sheepherding, Ann married Frank Willis. The two remained together for the rest of their lives. "Queen" Ann Basset died a happy, old woman in Leeds, Utah, in 1956.

Butch Cassidy (Robert LeRoy Parker)

Robert LeRoy Parker (sometimes referred to as George) was born on April 13, 1866, in Beaver, Utah. His parents, Ann and Maximilian Parker, were Mormon pioneers who moved their family to a ranch near Circleville, Utah, while Robert was still young. One of 10 children in the Parker family, he grew up without a formal education, learning the ins and outs of ranching instead.

It was in this setting that Robert met Mike Cassidy, a cowhand hired by Maximilian to help with the ranch. Among other skills, Mike taught Robert how to shoot his first gun, as well as the fine art of cattle rustling. "Rustling" involved the illegal practice of stealing unbranded calves from larger herds to sell to smaller ranchers. Throughout his career, Parker often made his illegal actions seem morally legitimate by looking out for those less fortunate.

Butch Cassidy

Under the influence of Mike Cassidy, it did not take long for Parker to have his first confrontation with the law. In 1884, at age 18, he was charged with stealing cattle and left home in order to save the family name. In this same spirit, Parker soon changed his last name to Cassidy, after his longtime mentor, to save his family from embarrassment. Accounts differ about how he eventually became "Butch," though the most likely is that it was the result of a brief stint in a butcher shop in Rock Springs, Wyoming.

After moving to Telluride, Colorado, Butch met future outlaw Matt Warner and began in the horse racing business. From Colorado, Butch moved quite frequently throughout the surrounding states of Wyoming, Utah, and South Dakota, usually obtaining "legitimate" work as a cowhand in order to take cover from his most recent outlaw endeavor; it was at this time, in 1886, that he first worked for Charlie Crouse at his Brown's Park ranch. During the next several years, Butch met his infamous Wild Bunch companions Harry Longabaugh (the Sundance Kid), Harvey Logan (Kid Curry), Ben Kilpatrick (the Tall Texan), and probably his closest friend, Elza Lay.

During the height of the gang's existence, it was responsible for the robberies of several banks and trains throughout the West. Ironically, the only jail time Butch ever served was from 1894 to 1896 for a cattle rustling incident in Wyoming. One of the outlaw's most infamous robberies took place on April 21, 1897, in Castle Gate, Utah. Along with Elza Lay and Joe Walker, Butch robbed the Pleasant Valley Coal Company payroll to the tune of $7,000. No one was shot during the course of the robbery.

One of the Wild Bunch's favorite hiding spots was located in southeast Utah. This extremely rocky terrain, known as Robbers Roost, had been a safe haven for outlaws many years before Butch's gang took up camp. The complicated and dangerous territory kept the Wild Bunch safe during the winter of 1896–97, shortly before the Castle Gate heist.

In 1899, the Wild Bunch robbed a train in Wilcox,

Wyoming, and netted $30,000. They fled to New Mexico, where they worked on a ranch for some time. It was there that Lay took part in a train robbery near Folsom and was imprisoned after a shootout. Cassidy tried to reform but his efforts were fruitless. His last documented holdup in the United States was in 1901; Cassidy, Longabaugh, and Logan held up a Great Northern train in Montana, netting $65,000 in easily traced bank notes.

Butch Cassidy and the Sundance Kid moved to a ranch in Argentina, and for several years they lived a normal life. However, the outlaws eventually took up their old ways, robbing banks and trains in Argentina and Bolivia. On November 6, 1908, after robbing a mule train in Bolivia, Cassidy and Sundance were tracked down in the town of San Vicente. The two gallantly attempted to fight off a large group of army officers, but to no avail. Sundance received a fatal gunshot wound, and the two found themselves trapped without escape. Instead of giving into the law, Cassidy shot his friend and, some believe, put a bullet into his own head—but we are left to speculate what really happened. Though it is fairly certain Sundance died as this story indicates, Cassidy's fate that day is not so clear. Some even attest that Butch and Sundance purposely staged their own deaths in order to return safely to the United States under aliases. Wherever the truth may lie, the legend of Butch Cassidy has remained steadfast.

Tom Horn

Tom Horn is remembered as one of the most ruthless, cold-blooded killers of the Old West. Ironically, he earned this chilling reputation while serving the majority of his career on the right side of the law, as an army scout and detective agent. It was only when he made a fateful mistake in his 40s that he became a fugitive and outlaw.

Growing up a farm boy in Missouri, young Horn favored almost any activity over schoolwork. After a severe beating from his father for skipping school, the 14-year-old Horn ran away to the charms of the West. Soon he became an Indian scout for the army, and in 1885 he replaced Al Sieber as the chief scout in the southwest.

Tom Horn

Horn functioned in this capacity for over a decade and served in the last Indian-American War, where he personally negotiated with Geronimo for his surrender. However, in the late 1880s, Horn left scouting for the ranching life, becoming a highly successful cattle roper.

In 1890, Horn joined the Pinkerton Detective Agency in Denver. As an agent, Horn discovered his true talent was hunting wanted men. During one occasion, Horn casually rode into Hole-in-the-Wall, Wyoming, and single-handedly captured the infamous Peg Leg Watson without even firing his gun. Throughout the next few years, Horn's gift for tracking and killing outlaws made his name legendary.

Tiring of the detective business, Horn found employment as a "horse breaker." However, his true source of income lay in the killing of known cattle rustlers for $500 each. For the next nine years, Horn's reputation spread fear through the outlaws in Colorado, Wyoming, and Utah. Horn brought down two rustlers in Brown's Hole, in the far northeastern corner of Utah, in 1900. The area, which had been infamous for outlaw activity for many years, quickly became a law-abiding region.

On July 18, 1901, Horn carelessly aimed and fired at his victim, Willie Nickell, shooting him several times until dead. However, the victim was not Mr. Nickell, but his 14-year-old son. The grave error would cost Horn his life. After running from the law for two years, Horn was finally caught and sentenced to death for the murder of the young boy. Tom Horn was hanged in Cheyenne, Wyoming, on November 28, 1903, at the age of 43.

Elza Lay

William Ellsworth Lay was born on November 25, 1868, in McArthur, Ohio. His parents, James and Mary Jane, moved to Wray, Colorado, while Elza (sometimes spelled Elzy) was still an infant. When Elza became a teenager, he grew hungry for a taste of cowboy life, and he and a childhood friend, William McGinnis, set out west on horseback, but McGinnis soon returned home.

Elza Lay

Elza never doubted his decision to roam the Wild West. He quickly went to work as a cowboy, and then a rustler, on a ranch in Wyoming. While working for a farmer in Ashley Valley, Utah, Elza met and fell in love with the farmer's daughter, Maude Davis. The two were married in a secret mountainside ceremony in 1896.

It was around this time that Elza began riding with Butch Cassidy and his Wild Bunch gang. Elza and Maude even spent their honeymoon in the rocky fortress hideaway known as Robbers Roost in southern Utah. Although many believe that Harry Longabaugh (the Sundance Kid) was Butch Cassidy's closest sidekick, in reality Elza was the famed outlaw's right-hand man.

An educated man, Elza is also believed to have been the ultimate mastermind behind many of the Wild Bunch's robberies. In 1897, Elza served as an accomplice to the infamous Pleasant Valley Coal Company burglary in Castle Gate, Utah. The two escaped unharmed with over $7,000 in payroll money. After the Castle Gate robbery, Elza returned home to his wife. When Maude pleaded to her husband to stop his outlaw ways, Elza refused, and the two divorced. Only a few months later their daughter, Marvel, was born. She would not have contact with her father until 1911.

Elza rejoined the Wild Bunch with his newfound freedom and aided the gang in the June 2, 1899, Union Pacific train robbery in Wyoming, in which they netted $30,000. They fled to New Mexico and worked on a ranch for some time. Against the advice of Cassidy, Elza joined Black Jack Ketchum and his band of outlaws to rob the Colorado and Southern train in Folsom, New Mexico. A gunbattle subsequently erupted and Elza was shot through the chest and shoulder. The bandit escaped for a while, but the law caught up with him a month later and sent Elza to the New Mexico Territorial Prison for life.

Elza was as successful a prisoner as he was an outlaw. He displayed superb conduct and once curbed a large potential riot; afterward, Governor Otero issued Elza a full pardon. He was released on January 10, 1906, after serving only seven years of his life sentence. Elza immediately returned to Baggs, Wyoming, where he met and married his second wife, Mary Calvert.

Elza unsuccessfully tried his hand at the oil business and moved his family to California when it failed. After a life of crime, Elza finally settled down with his wife and two new daughters. He got a job as head water master for the Imperial Valley Irrigation System and established a relationship with his first daughter, Marvel. Elza Lay died in 1934 at the age of 66 in Los Angeles.

Harvey Logan "Kid Curry"

Harvey Logan was born in Tama, Iowa, in 1865. When his mother died suddenly, he and his three brothers moved to Dobson, Missouri, to live with their Aunt Lee. Without much parental supervision, the Logan boys grew up free and wild. At 19, Harvey and his older brother, Henry, ventured into the Wild West for some excitement.

The two ended up in Landusky, Wyoming, where they made their living at cattle rustling. Beginning a life of crime, Harvey briefly joined the Red Sash gang, until their leader was killed and he was forced to return to rustling. However, Harvey did not escape scandal as a cowboy. After seducing the town founder's daughter, Elfia, Harvey found himself in trouble with her angry father, and he fled to Hole-in-the-Wall, Wyoming. This area would become a safe haven for Harvey during his many troubled times.

It was here, in January 1896, that Harvey met and befriended the old-timer and outlaw George "Flat Nose" Curry. Consequently, Harvey took his mentor's last name and added the infamous "Kid." Around this same time, Kid Curry met up with Butch Cassidy and his Wild Bunch gang. Curry was more than happy to become part of such a well-known and wanted group.

He joined the Wild Bunch on many train and bank robberies during 1896 and 1897, even hiding out with them at Robbers Roost. Unfortunately, Curry's enthusiasm for shooting to kill interfered with Cassidy's more even temperament. After several confrontations, Curry decided to leave the gang and set out on his own.

Harvey Logan "Kid Curry"

During this time, Curry joined Harry Longabaugh (the Sundance Kid), Tom O'Day, and Walt Putney for the June 28, 1897, bank robbery in Belle Fourche, South Dakota. The group was captured but managed to escape from prison on October 31, 1897.

Once again, Curry joined the Wild Bunch for the Union Pacific train robbery near Wilcox, Wyoming, on June 2, 1899. The gang successfully blew up the train car holding the loot, and when the engineer on board survived, Curry attempted to end his life. However, good-hearted Cassidy intervened and stopped Curry from shooting the innocent man. The outlaws escaped with $30,000.

In early 1900, Kid Curry was the third-most-wanted man in the West, just behind Butch Cassidy and the Sundance Kid. He moved on from Arizona to the Book Cliffs, near Thompson, Utah, always one step ahead of the law. On July 7, 1901, Curry would participate in his last robbery with the Wild Bunch. Cassidy, Longabaugh, and Logan held up a Great Northern train in Montana, netting $65,000 in easily traced bank notes and disbanded for a final time. Curry headed for Knoxville, Tennessee.

Rumors speculate that Curry tried to abandon his outlaw past after relocating to Knoxville. Some say that the mean-spirited killer even fell in love with a woman named Catherine Cross. But fate would have Kid Curry only as an outlaw. After a bar brawl, Curry shot and killed a policeman and was sentenced to a long prison term. Once again escaping from prison, Curry fled to his favorite hiding place, Hole-in-the-Wall.

On June 7, 1904, Kid Curry robbed a small train in Parachute, Colorado. Lowell Spence, a detective from Pinkerton, tracked down the outlaw, whom he had been trailing for a long time. During the struggle, Spence finally got the moment he had been waiting for and shot Curry through the arm and lungs. Knowing he was a dead man, Kid Curry drew his Colt .45 and put a bullet through his own head. The outlaw died on June 9, 1904.

Harry A. Longabaugh "The Sundance Kid"

Harry Alonzo Longabaugh, the youngest of five children, was born in the spring of 1867 in Mont Clare, Pennsylvania. In 1882, at the age of 15, Harry left his family in pursuit of adventure in the West. The young man found not only excitement but a life of crime.

Harry took up cattle rustling and horse thieving at several ranches in Colorado, Montana, Wyoming, and Utah. On February 27, 1887, Harry was caught and arrested for stealing a horse and sentenced to two years in the Sundance, Wyoming, jail. After serving his time, Harry was forever known as the "Sundance Kid."

In 1892, Sundance first encountered Butch Cassidy after an unsuccessful train robbery in Montana. The two would not meet again for several years. On June 28, 1897, Sundance, Kid Curry, and two other outlaws robbed a bank in Belle Fourche, South Dakota. Though they were captured and thrown in the Lawrence County jail, they managed to break free on October 31, 1897.

This second incarceration did not persuade Sundance to

abandon his criminal life. Instead, the outlaw met up with Cassidy and his Wild Bunch gang to rob a Union Pacific train near Wilcox, Wyoming, on June 2, 1899. Sundance slew a sheriff during the struggle but fled unharmed. A full-fledged member of the Wild Bunch, Sundance joined them in Nevada on September 19, 1900, for the Winnemucca National Bank robbery. On July 7, 1901, Longabaugh, Cassidy, and Logan held up a Great Northern train in Montana, netting $65,000 in bank notes.

Harry A. Longabaugh and Etta Place (taken in New York City in 1902)

Sundance and Butch Cassidy decided to head for Argentina, where they planned to live a normal life as ranchers, but before leaving they ventured to Fort Worth, Texas, for relaxation at Fannie Porter's well-known brothel. During this stay, Sundance reunited with his old companion Etta Place. The young woman, a bored housewife seeking adventure, accompanied the two outlaws to Buenos Aires on February 20, 1901.

Cassidy and Sundance settled uneventfully in Argentina for several years. Perhaps not finding the exciting life she had anticipated, Etta mysteriously returned to the United States in 1905. Shortly after her departure, the two outlaws began a crime spree throughout Argentina and Bolivia, and once again became wanted men.

The story of their fateful standoff with the Bolivian army on November 6, 1908, is the stuff of legend (see "Butch Cassidy," for a full description). Trapped and surrounded, Sundance was mortally wounded, and to avoid capture, Cassidy is said to have shot his friend and then killed himself. Whether or not this is really what happened is left to speculation. However, the Sundance Kid almost certainly met his final match with the law that day and died at the age of 41.

C. L. "Gunplay" Maxwell

"Gunplay" Maxwell was known throughout Utah as much for his outlaw mishaps as for any actual mischief he caused. The cattle rustler from Nine Mile Canyon desperately longed to be part of the Wild Bunch—or of any gang for that matter—but was never accepted.

A regular at the Robbers Roost hideaway in southern Utah, Maxwell tried to prove his worthiness by standing up to other outlaws. Unfortunately, he chose to pick on gang leaders such as Butch Cassidy, who quickly put Maxwell in his place. One attempt at a bank robbery in Provo went awry because members of his own gang warned the targeted bank beforehand.

Not knowing when to give up, Maxwell planned another bank holdup, this time in Springville, Utah. He, along with a fellow outlaw named Porter, successfully robbed the bank of $3,000 in gold. However, their getaway vehicle, a covered wagon, could not outrun the town's large posse. The two men were quickly discovered in some thick brush, but not before a townsman shot and killed Porter in self-defense.

Maxwell went to trial and was sentenced to 18 years in prison, of which he only served 2 years. Upon his release, Gunplay turned in his weapons for a job as a mine guard. However, lady luck jilted him even at this trade, as one night Maxwell was killed during a drunken fight with a fellow guard at the Castle Gate mine in central Utah.

Matt Warner

Matt Warner was born Willard Erastus Christianson in Ephraim, Utah, in 1864. His parents, German and Swedish immigrants, were among many of the Mormon pioneers of the day. Warner grew up in the small town of Levan, Utah. At the age of 14, during a dispute with friend Andrew Hendrickson over a mutual love interest, Matt hit the boy over the head with part of a picket fence. Believing he had killed Andrew, Matt saddled up a horse and left home for good.

Matt Warner

The young man ended up at Jim Warren's ranch in the northeast corner of Utah. Here, Matt spent the next couple of years learning the business both of stock raising and of cattle rustling, which was one of Jim Warren's side trades. It was at this point that Willard Christianson changed his name to Matt Warner.

After shooting a Mexican horse thief, Warner traveled to Arizona and Colorado, landing in Telluride, where he decided to try his hand at horse racing. After successfully beating a young man named Butch Cassidy, the two became good friends. They toured around the state for a while, earning their fair share at racing.

Always drifting, Warner soon moved on to Star Valley, Utah, with brother-in-law Tom McCarty. He settled into the comfortable society of Star Valley, where he met and married Rose Morgan. Soon after, the couple left Utah for a new life in Poudre, Oregon. Unfortunately, it did not take long for the law to track down Warner. The outlaw was forced to send his wife and newly born daughter, Mayda, to Salt Lake City, where Rose had family.

On May 7, 1896, Warner became involved in a dispute with three men over a mining prospect in Dry Fork Canyon, 20 miles from Vernal. The argument dissolved into a shootout, and Warner killed two men and wounded the third. Taking his chances with the court system, Warner turned himself in to the local sheriff and pleaded guilty. He was sentenced to five years in the Utah State Prison, a term of which he only served three years and four months. Warner was released on January 21, 1900, shortly after his wife, Rose, had died of cancer.

A reformed outlaw, Warner dedicated the rest of his life to the straight and narrow. He moved to Green River, Utah, where he took a job as justice of the peace and night marshal. Matt Warner died in 1938 at the age of 74.

American Indians in Utah

Evidence of human habitation in the Utah area dates back to around 10,000 B.C., though some archaeologists claim that humans may have arrived in the Southwest as long as 15,000 or even 35,000 years ago. Whenever they arrived, this Desert Archaic culture was composed primarily of nomadic tribes of extended family units that traveled throughout the Great Basin. They developed tools and weapons of stone, wood, and bone for use in both hunting and gathering. After the last ice age, their hunter-gatherer lifestyle slowly evolved to include primitive farming, first of corn and then of beans, squash, and cotton, and several new tools were added, such as baskets and the atlatl, a throwing spear; by A.D. 100, some groups were developing semipermanent villages.

By A.D. 400, the Desert Archaic culture had mostly faded away. Whether the people moved away or simply evolved into other cultures is not exactly clear. A few hundred years prior to this, Utah's next two major cultures emerged: the Fremont in northeastern Utah and the Anasazi in southeast Utah. The Fremont possessed similarities to the Desert Archaic culture, but they were more advanced; though the Fremont never completely abandoned their hunter-gatherer ways, they developed a horticultural system, ceremonial clay figures, and cliff dwellings. Evolving further still, and becoming even more sophisticated than the Fremont, were the Anasazi (the word is Navajo for "the ancient ones" or "enemy ancestor," and they are now sometimes referred to as "Ancestral Puebloans"). The Anasazi flourished into a vibrant, settled culture that relied on agriculture, developed pit-house granaries for communal food storage, constructed cliff dwellings and early masonry buildings, and created an evolved mythology that borrowed from Mesoamerican cultures.

Both the Fremont and the Anasazi cultures faded rapidly around 1200 or 1300, and within a hundred years or so they were almost completely gone from Utah. Why this happened is an enduring mystery. Most archaeologists believe a period of severe drought probably drove them away, though they were probably also absorbed into other, newer cultures. Competition with the Shoshonean peoples, who arrived around 1300, may have also played a role in the disappearance of the Fremont and Anasazi. The Shoshonean people eventually developed into the following groups: the Northern Shoshone, who settled in the northeast and resembled the culture of the Plains Indians; the Gosiute (also spelled Goshute) or "Digger Indians," who hunted and gathered across the wide western deserts; the Southern Paiute, who were a peaceful farming culture in the southwest; and the Ute, who inhabited a large portion of central and eastern Utah, and like the Northern Shoshone, bore a resemblance to the Plains Indians. When the Spanish introduced horses into Ute culture, the Ute became skilled at raiding neighboring tribes.

Around 1700, the Ute began to attack the Navajo, a new tribe that had recently arrived in Utah. Descendants of the Athapaskan tribes, the Navajo came up from the south and settled around the San Juan River valley. The Navajo suffered greatly at the hands of the Ute and were forced to leave their newfound settlement.

Until the mid-1800s and the arrival of the Mormons, Utah's Native American peoples saw very few Europeans or white settlers. However, although the local Indians were not especially pleased when Brigham Young settled the Salt Lake Valley, they basically accepted their new neighbors with few confrontations. This attitude changed as Young expanded the Mormon settlements throughout Utah, occupying land vital to the survival of the Utes. Facing starvation, the Indians fought back, many times raiding small exploring parties or early settlements. These skirmishes sometimes evolved into large-scale fighting, such as the Black Hawk War. As is known and documented all too well, this was a fight the Native Americans were doomed to lose (see "Events" for more on this period of history).

From 1861, when President Abraham Lincoln set aside the Uintah Valley Indian Reservation, through the rest of the 1800s, the federal government took more and more land from the Native Americans and forced them to move onto reservations. Sometimes even the reservation lands were taken away. For example, the Dawes Act broke up and sold much of the reserved land and opened it to incoming settlers.

The 20th century was a desperate time for Native Americans in Utah. Many tried to retain tribal ways of life in the face of poverty and the encroaching modern culture, but with little success. Many Indians were forced to find work outside of the reservations to survive. In the latter half of the century, some Native Americans received cash settlements for the land that was taken from them, but these ameliorative measures were largely too little, too late. Today, Native American communities continue the struggle to preserve their culture, not as an artifact but as a living entity, in the face of the enormous pressures of 21st-century America.

Anasazi

The Anasazi inhabited the Four Corners region of the southwest for about 1,500 years. Around A.D. 100, groups of Anasazi moved into the Colorado Plateau, including southeastern Utah. Their dependence on agriculture is probably a main reason they settled in a specific region. They also developed into expert basket makers; they used baskets to gather food and to store their surplus. The early Anasazi lived in pit houses—small, waist-deep pits with beams supporting a roof of poles,

Anasazi kiva

twigs, and mud—in small, family-based groupings.

By A.D. 700, the Anasazi began to make stylized pottery, cultivate beans in their crops, and use the bow and arrow. With these improvements, villages grew larger, and people moved out of pit houses, which were reserved for storage or for ceremonial purposes. Larger, aboveground structures served as living quarters. Researchers refer to this period of rapid development as the Developmental Pueblo period.

The Anasazi continued to improve their building techniques. They abandoned the adobe-and-pole structures in fa-

Anasazi cliff dwelling

vor of stone houses and buildings. These pueblos grew in size, and eventually each one contained in the center a small pit house for ceremonial use, known as a kiva. Their culture flourished from 950 to 1150, and toward the end of this time, the Anasazi began to build their houses into the base of cliffs. Some of these would have over a hundred rooms, and they were decorated with colorful designs, as was their pottery. Some villages developed irrigation systems to improve their agriculture. Religious ceremonies, using artistic jewelry and clothing, grew more involved and elaborate.

Then, at the height of their civilization, the Anasazi disappeared. No one can positively say why, though theories include displacement by other incoming tribes and a serious drought in the late 1200s. The latter is supported by evidence in tree rings, which show a serious drought from around 1270 to the beginning of the 14th century. Most likely, a combination of these threats put an end to the Anasazi civilization. By 1300, most of the larger communities in southeast Utah were abandoned. However, throughout the region, remnants of the Anasazi can be seen—from half-hidden cliff dwellings in canyon walls to ghostly petroglyphs—and undoubtedly more wait to be found.

Fremont

Rather than referring to a specific culture or tribe, "Fremont" is a collective name given to the scattered groups of Indians throughout the Great Basin and western Colorado who lived at the same time as the Anasazi. For this reason, the Fremont are not easily categorized, though one major similarity ties the disparate tribes together: at many of the Fremont excavation sites, a similar type of pottery has been found. Other than that, the groups that made up the Fremont varied in any number of ways.

The Fremont arrived in Utah around the same time as the Anasazi, around A.D. 100, and they were primarily nomadic hunter-gatherer tribes. The pottery of the Fremont is first dated to sometime around A.D. 500, and this is concurrent with their development and adoption of farming techniques, as they settled slowly in various ways into a more agrarian life. Around 750, there is evidence the Fremont lived in pit houses and other dwellings, further indicating an abandonment of

nomadic wanderings. Some of these houses were built into the sides of cliffs in very precarious positions. They also built camouflaged lookout towers high on top of bluffs in order to keep guard over their land. This defensive tendency of the Fremont indicates that they were generally a peaceful people prone to being attacked.

However, the most enduring legacy of the Fremont exists on many of the rocks and cliffs throughout Utah: their petroglyphs and pictographs depicting people and animals (see "Indian Rock Art" below). The pictures have a curious atheistic quality to them, which has intrigued anthropologists for years. Mostly they deal with hunting scenes in which varying numbers of people and animals are portrayed. Although this rock art can be seen in different places across Utah, the Nine Mile Canyon district is home to a large number of them.

The Fremont thrived until sometime after A.D. 1250. As with the Anasazi, scholars are uncertain as to the specific causes of their disappearance, though again, climatic changes and newly arriving groups of Indians are the likely culprits.

Gosiute

One of the Shoshonean-speaking Indian group, which slowly arrived in Utah from 1200 to 1500, the Gosiutes lived in what is now known as the Great Basin area, west to the Nevada border. In this desolate area, the Gosiutes developed a great understanding of agricultural cycles, the climate, and animal distribution patterns, and they lived in nuclear groups—families hunted and gathered with others that made up a village.

The harsh desert conditions and lack of cultural wealth helped isolate the Gosiutes from the white settlers until a fairly late date. According to his journal, Jedediah Smith encountered the Gosiutes in 1826, but it was only after the arrival of the Mormons in 1847 that the Gosiutes came into continual

Gosiute Indian woman

and prolonged contact with whites. By 1860, the Pony Express, the Overland Stage, and the transcontinental telegraph all ran through Gosiute territory, bringing numerous settlers—and with them came problems for the tribe's survival.

Ranchers and farmers moved into the region and took all the best lands with water and forage. Stock ate the grasses that the Gosiutes relied upon for seeds and fiber in the fragile desert environment. Water, always in short supply, was also taken by the Overland Stage operations and denied to the Gosiutes. They responded to these threats by attacking the stations and farms and killing inhabitants and livestock in a vain attempt to force them off their territory.

The government retaliated by attacking the Gosiutes, killing many and forcing them into a treaty to cease their hostile actions in 1863, thus allowing safe passage through their land. The treaty called for the Gosiutes to be paid $1,000 a year for 20 years to allow the construction of military posts and station houses, stage lines, telegraph lines, mining operations, and railways in their region.

After the treaty, the U.S. government tried to relocate the Gosiutes to other Indian reservations, including the Ute's reservation in the Uinta Basin, but these efforts weren't successful. In 1869, the government broke its treaty with the Indians by cutting off all annuities. Finally, early in the 20th century, the federal government established two reservations for the Gosiutes. One reservation is on the Utah-Nevada border at the base of the Deep Creek Mountains and the other is about fifty miles southwest of Salt Lake City in Skull Valley. Today they live in relatively small groups, somewhat isolated from their white neighbors.

Navajo

One of the Athapaskan tribes, the Navajo settled in southeast Utah sometime in the 1500s. It is possible there were still a few Anasazi living in the area when the Navajo arrived, since the latter seem to have learned certain farming techniques from the former. The Navajo also kept livestock such as sheep and goats for their survival.

Navajo weaver

The Navajo were known as efficient raiders; they would attack the Spanish to the south and the Utes and Mormons to the north. As the Mormons began to expand their settlements throughout Utah in the mid-1800s, these raids began to occur more frequently. The U.S. government decided that it had had enough and sent in the military. However, many of the military expeditions proved futile. Kit Carson was one of the men sent to deal with the problem, and instead of fighting the Navajo directly, he encouraged the Utes to step up their attacks on their southern neighbors. Carson also employed scorched earth tactics, burning the Navajo's fields. Between 1864 and 1866, about 8,000 Navajo (two-thirds of their population) surrendered and were sent to Fort Sumner in New Mexico. This 300-mile journey, entirely on foot, came to be known as the Long Walk.

Two years later, the Navajo were given a reservation, which was about a quarter of the size of the land they had previously used, and they returned from Fort Sumner. For the next 20 to 30 years, the Navajo, the Ute, and the Mormons all vied for land in southern Utah. However, the area continued to be settled by white men, and the Navajo struggled to maintain the valuable resources they needed for survival.

In the 1930s and 1940s, the Bureau of Indian Affairs decided to kill off thousands of sheep because of overgrazing and soil erosion. As the Navajo measured wealth in sheep, the federal government's slaughter of their herds spelled financial disaster for many families. Today, the Navajo still live on their reservation in southern Utah, where they have made some financial advances by exploiting their land's mineral and fuel resources.

Paiute

The Paiute Indians, one of the Shoshonean tribes, are thought to have arrived in southwest Utah around 1100 or 1200. Some settled along the banks of the Muddy and Virgin Rivers, while others went off to more arid desert climates; often living in wickiups like the one below. This peaceful group generally survived through hunting and gathering, using small-scale farming to supplement their diet. The Paiutes were loosely organized in small groups of families with no general leader. Although their family structures were somewhat traditional, a family unit would sometimes include more than one husband or wife.

When explorers made their way to the Paiute lands in the early 1800s, they found they could easily exploit this peaceful people. Once a route was laid across southwest Utah to California, the traveling emigrants and their livestock began destroying the land upon which the Paiutes depended. The neighboring Apache and Navajo tribes would also attack the Paiutes and take them prisoner, often selling their captives as slaves to the white men coming through.

However, it was the arrival of the Mormons that signaled the end of traditional Paiute life. The Mormon settlers took over most of the land's valuable resources, and the Indians were forced onto a reservation. The first Paiute reservation was established in 1891 near St. George, and over the years, other small lands have been returned to this native people.

One notable Paiute Indian, Wovoka (or Jack Wilson) from Nevada, is responsible for the founding of the Ghost Dance in 1888. This mystical religion uses chanting and dancing in a spiritual cleansing of self. It prophesies an end to the white man and his reign over the land and an eventual return of the Indians and the buffalo. The religion caught on with many other tribes throughout the West and has even excited the curiosity of mystics outside of Indian cultures.

Paiute wickiups

Shoshone

The Shoshonean peoples were a loosely organized group of tribes that arrived in Utah around the same time that the Fremont and Anasazi cultures were coming to an end. For the next few hundred years, the Shoshonean peoples spread throughout the state in relative peace. Those living in the northern Great Basin region in Utah have since become known as the Northern Shoshone.

Sometime in the late 1600s, the Northern Shoshone acquired horses from Spanish traders. With their newfound mobility, they became skilled raiders and hunters and adopted many of the same behaviors and customs of the Plains Indian cultures.

Shoshone men, late 1800s

As with all of the Native American cultures in Utah, the Northern Shoshone were forever changed by the coming of the Mormons in the mid-1800s. As Mormon expeditions began making their way north from Salt Lake City, the Indians watched as their land was taken and its resources depleted. First and hardest hit by this Mormon expansion was Cache Valley, which contained some of the most fertile of the Shoshone lands. As the Mormons arrived, the Shoshone were forced into the more barren desert region of western Utah. Under the leadership of Chief Bear Hunter, the Indians struck back at cattle herds, mining parties, stagecoaches, and Pony Express riders.

In 1863, after suffering a few months of attacks, Colonel Patrick Edward Connor led a counterattack on Bear Hunter's winter camp in Cache Valley. This four-hour siege on a cold January day resulted in the deaths of over 250 Shoshones, and it would become known as the Bear River Massacre (see "Events"). Chief Bear Hunter was killed, and in the summer of 1863, the Treaty of Box Elder was signed to bring peace to northern Utah.

After the Bear River Massacre, Utah officials tried to force the Indians onto the Fort Hall Reservation in Idaho. Although the Shoshone resisted at first, they saw it was their only option. The joining of the transcontinental railroad at Promontory in 1869 was bringing ever-greater numbers of white settlers entered into the region, and this influx forced the Shoshone off their land and out of Utah.

Ute—Northern

The northern Ute Indians were another Shoshonean tribe who moved into Utah during the twilight of the Anasazi and Fremont cultures. However, although the earlier groups had settled down and come to depend on agriculture, the northern Ute lived mostly as hunters and gatherers. Some Ute wandered the desert, while others lived high up in the mountains.

The Ute were in intermittent contact with their Spanish neighbors to the south and traded for horses in the late 1600s. Like the Northern Shoshone, the Ute evolved to use the horse in hunting and raiding expeditions, living in the manner of the Plains Indians.

The Ute soon became a very strong tribe and would gather slaves in their raids of other camps. They would then sell these slaves to the Spanish or to other tribes in the Great Basin.

As the Mormons entered Utah, the northern Ute came under the same hardships as the Shoshone. By the early 1850s, the Ute were unable to survive off the land as they had done in years past. In the summer of 1853, a Ute was killed by a Mormon during a trade gone wrong. When the Mormon was not brought to justice, Wakara, a leader of the northern Ute, led a series of raids against the Mormons that would come to be known as the Walker War. The raids, which proved to be much harder on the Indians than the Mormons, lasted for about ten months. In 1854, Brigham Young met with Wakara and although they could not settle on the exact terms of the Mormon occupation of Ute lands, presents were exchanged and both parties agreed to peace.

These raids did little more than aggravate the Mormons, who continued to settle the region. In 1861, President Lincoln set aside 2 million acres as the Uintah Valley Reservation for the Utes to live on. However, the Ute would not be so easily removed from their land, and in 1863, they began a new series of raids that served as a prelude to the Black Hawk War. Once again, they were frustrated by the retaliation of the Mor-

Uintah Ute warrior and his bride

mons, and in 1869, the Ute moved onto the reservation.

The Ute found life on the reservation to be very difficult. Their problems were then compounded when the federal government resettled the White River Utes and the Uncompahgre Utes on the expanded Uintah-Ouray Reservation. These bands of Indians did not always see eye to eye, and a number of small conflicts arose. These problems were again compounded when the government opened up the reservation for white settlement, first giving each Ute family its own 80- to 160-acre plot of land. By 1909, this and other land reductions had shrunk the reservation to about one-tenth of its original size. Although small outbreaks of violence erupted around the turn of the century, no organized revolt was ever successful.

Over the years, some of the northern Ute left the reservation for South Dakota. Others stayed on the reservation and fought a legal battle against the white men who took their lands. They won some sizable settlements, and today they continue to earn money by exploiting the oil and gas deposits on their land.

Ute—Southern

Scholars disagree as to the exact time when the southern Ute arrived in Utah. However a general agreement that they were established in the area by A.D. 1500 seems to prevail. In Utah, the most western band of the southern Ute known as the Weeminuche made its home between the Colorado and San Juan Rivers. The Weeminuche were often at odds with neighboring Navajo Indians, whom they would raid and sell as slaves to the Spanish. Although they would conduct peaceful business with their Spanish neighbors, tensions would sometimes escalate to a point where the two groups would find themselves enemies. In 1848, the United States took control of the Utah Territory in the aftermath of the Mexican War. It quickly found the southern Ute to be useful allies against the Navajo, who were relocated on the Long Walk to Fort Sumner, New Mexico, between 1864 and 1866.

In 1868, when the Navajo were returning from their displacement, the federal government gave both groups of Indians their respective reservations in western Colorado. However, the southern Utes did not feel much pressure to move from their land in southern Utah until the Mormons became interested in expansion through the area. The conflict between the advancing settlers and the Utes became serious, and they fought a number of small skirmishes throughout the 1880s. Ultimately, many of the Ute gave up the struggle and relocated to the reservation.

For the next 30 to 40 years, the conflict between the Ute and the white men occurred mostly on paper and in the courts. Many promises were made and broken by the government, including the establishment of a reservation near the southeastern town of Monticello. In 1887, the southern Ute agreed to move onto a new reservation in San Juan County. However federal politicians found one reason after another to delay the official establishment of the reservation. Tired of waiting, 1,100 Indians moved onto the land with their agent, David Day, only to be quickly removed and sent back to Colorado. One of the few violent skirmishes erupted in the early 1920s and came to be known as the Posey War (see "Events").

The southern Ute continued their legal battle with the federal government well into the 20th century. Although some accepted reservation life, others settled in Allen and Montezuma Canyons. Later, in the mid-1950s, a small Ute community began in White Mesa, south of Blanding. This community has grown through the years and serves as host to the annual spring festival known as the Bear Dance.

Indian Rock Art

Scholars still have many unanswered questions about the cultures of the early native Indians of Utah, such as the Desert Archaic tribes, the Fremont, and the Anasazi. One such puzzle adorns many of the state's cliffs and canyon walls. The rock art of eastern Utah has been studied by anthropologists for years, and yet we are still left wondering: what does it mean?

Early rock art dates back at least 2,000 years, when the Desert Archaic Indians inhabited the Great Basin. The presence of animals thought to be woolly mammoths in some rock art has scholars thinking that the earliest rock art may even go back as far as 10,000 years, though there is no conclusive evidence.

Fremont petroglyphs

The majority of the rock art throughout Utah has been attributed to the Fremont Indians, and it comes in two forms: petroglyphs, which are pictures etched into the rock, and pictographs, which are figures painted on the rock. Humans and animals are the typical subjects, and images of hunting parties are very common. A number of animals such as bighorn sheep, grizzly bears, snakes, and coyotes are represented. Often, the hunters of these animals are themselves dressed in the skins of these animals. Other rock art includes shapes and designs as well as unexplained symbols that are thought to be a form of picture writing. Some of the figures may relate to the heavens and act as some sort of calendar.

Unfortunately, we view these unique works of art outside of the culture that produced them. We will probably never be able to fully understand the significance of these figures as the Na-

Fremont pictographs

tive Americans themselves understood them. This won't stop scholars and delighted visitors from trying as they ponder the mysterious rock art at such places as Nine Mile and Horseshoe Canyons. Just remember, especially if you run across unprotected, unexpected petroglyphs in your desert hikes, this rock art is a historic treasure and should be left undisturbed.

Events

Bear River Massacre

In January 1863, a band of 450 Shoshones were living under the leadership of Chief Bear Hunter in its traditional winter village in Cache Valley, where Bear Creek meets Bear River. Since 1860, Mormon settlers had been taking over the Shoshone lands in the valley, and in three years there was little left for the Indians. Sporadic fighting had taken place during those years, but nothing like what happened on January 29.

That day, wanting to put an end to the Indian "problem," Colonel Patrick Edward Connor led a force of 200 men into the Shoshone village. They approached the camp at daybreak and were met with resistance from Chief Bear Hunter. However, the Shoshones were not well equipped for the attack, and after Connor's men had surrounded the village, they soon found themselves out of ammunition. Rather than taking prisoners, Connor's men drew their revolvers and proceeded to execute all the Indian men they could find.

After the fighting ended, Connor's men decided to go through the camp raping women and killing as they pleased. At the end of the day, about 250 Shoshones were dead, 90 of them women and children. Chief Bear Hunter had been killed, along with Lehi, the man next in line to be chief. Connor then ordered the village burned, and the invading force stole the Shoshone's horses. The bodies of the dead Indians were left unburied.

As it occurred during the Civil War, the Bear River Massacre did not receive a great deal of attention. However, it remains one of the most deadly Indian massacres in history, resulting in more victims than even the Battle of Wounded Knee in 1890.

Black Hawk War

The Black Hawk War officially took place between 1865 and 1868, though isolated raids and battles had gone on before the war and persisted after. The war started on April 9, 1865, when Ute Indians and Mormons met in Manti (in Sanpete County) to settle an argument. A Mormon insulted the band of Indians by pulling one from his horse. The Ute vowed revenge, and under the leadership of Black Hawk, they took it by stealing cattle and killing five Mormon settlers.

The incident made Black Hawk a hero in the eyes of many Ute, Paiute, and Navajo in the region, who were facing desperate times as white men pushed them out of their territory. For the next two years, Black Hawk and his loose organization of Indians raided many Mormon settlements, taking food and cattle and occasionally killing one of the settlers. The Mormons had little success in defending themselves from the Indians, and so they built forts around the frontier. The Mormons even mobilized as many as 2,500 men, but they were rendered helpless as they could never find Black Hawk or his men. The Native Americans knew the land far better than the pursuing Mormons, and they blended in among other Indian tribes who had no part in the raids.

For two years, there was open warfare between the two groups. The Mormons, whose polygamist practices had alienated them from the rest of the country, received little federal aid, and so Black Hawk's men were able to continue their raids without the interference of an established federal army.

However, in the summer of 1867, Black Hawk finally made peace with the white settlers after he had been wounded by a bullet. Without his dynamic leadership, the loosely structured Indian resistance fell apart, and a peace treaty was signed in 1868. Fighting continued sporadically until 1872, when the federal government finally intervened by sending 200 troops to pacify the region. By this time, the Black Hawk War and its aftermath had created some of the most hostile and uncertain times ever known in Utah's frontier.

Establishment of the Civilian Conservation Corps

Designed to provide financial relief from the Great Depression and to aid in a variety of conservation and public works projects, the Civilian Conservation Corps (CCC) arrived in Utah during President Roosevelt's New Deal era. In the nine years of its existence, the CCC had 116 camps in 27 of Utah's 29 coun-

ties. Various government agencies worked together with the U.S. Army to coordinate and direct the work of these camps, which were composed of young men mostly between the ages 18 to 23 as well as "local experienced men" who found themselves out of work. These skilled workers directed the young men, who were by and large without any particular skills.

Upon enlisting in the CCC, each man received a week's training in basic fire fighting. The years of the Depression happened to be extremely dry, and so the CCC was often called in to fight out-of-control forest fires. However, the bulk of the work included laying phone lines, controlling rodent and insect populations, and building roads, bridges, dams, dikes, cabins, and so on. Some of their larger projects in Utah included the bird refuges on Ogden Bay and Bear River as well as many loop roads in the Wasatch Range canyons. The men of the CCC were often noted for exceeding the call of duty. During harsh winter storms they would take convoys of food and dry wood to small towns otherwise cut off by the snow. They also worked in more urban areas to improve parks and other public facilities.

With the onset of World War II, the United States found itself once more in a growing economy, and like many New Deal programs, the CCC had run its course. In July 1942, the CCC came to an end, but its impact on Utah remains to this day in the many roads, bridges, utilities, and so on that were built. You can also still find the scattered remnants of old CCC camps tucked away throughout the state.

Age of the Dinosaurs

Millions of years ago, Utah belonged to the dinosaurs. What are now rocky, red cliffs were once covered with lush ferns and giant conifers. Enormous herbivores like the brontosaurus, stegosaurus, and diplodocus and carnivores such as the allosaurus (Utah's official state fossil) roamed Utah's primal climate.

The Age of the Dinosaurs spans the length of the Mesozoic Era, approximately 245 million to 65 million years ago. The Mesozoic Era is commonly broken down further into three time periods: the Triassic (245 to 208 million years ago), Jurassic (208 to 144 years ago), and Cretaceous (144 to 65 million years ago). Early on in the Mesozoic Era during the Triassic period,

Allosaurus, the official fossil of Utah

different classifications of dinosaurs were beginning to develop from an ancestral type of archosaur, or ruling reptile. Dinosaurs from this early time can be classified as either Saurischia, which are lizard-hipped, or Ornithischia, which are bird-hipped. Although there is little fossilized evidence of these early dinosaurs, their tracks can be found along with those of other Triassic reptiles in southern and northeastern Utah.

As dinosaurs continued to evolve throughout the Jurassic period, their numbers increased. Evidence of this proliferation comes in the numerous dinosaur tracksites throughout Utah in places thought to have once been oases in an otherwise arid climate. Later in the Jurassic period, Utah's desertlike climate was displaced as interior seaways made their way in from the north. As a result, marine fossils have been found in what is currently dry land. Deposits of Entrada sandstone in between these periods of marine climate are responsible for many of the dinosaur tracksites and natural arches in southern Utah. One in particular from this period is a 10-mile long "megatracksite" that runs along the Salt Valley Anticline north of Moab.

At the dawn of Utah's Cretaceous period, new types of dinosaurs, such as dromeosaurs, or running lizards, arrived on the scene. One such running dinosaur was a small, fierce predator called Utahraptor. The Cretaceous period also saw the development of some of the earliest "armored" dinosaurs. After another brief marine period, dinosaurs such as tyrannosaurus and triceratops are thought to have made their way into Utah.

Records of these ancient time periods have been preserved in rock formations throughout the Southwest. Ever since the Macomb Expedition of 1859 discovered the first dinosaur fossil in Utah, scientists have been able to learn more and more about these ancient animals. Today, the remains of these and other primitive creatures can be seen mainly in and among the rocks known as the Morrison Formation. This formation spreads throughout eastern Utah and Colorado and extends north to the Canadian border. It is known as one of the richest deposits of dinosaur fossils in the world.

Probably the most famous fossil quarry in Utah is Dinosaur National Monument. It is in this area that Earl Douglass first discovered the remains of an apatosaurus (a large herbivore similar to a brontosaurus or diplodocus). This fossil deposit has about 2,000 exposed bones in the quarry face for scientists to study and visitors to see. Utah's other major quarry is more centrally located near Cleveland. The Cleveland-Lloyd Dinosaur Quarry is a more remote site from which scientists actively remove fossils for further study. It is here where most of the allosaurus remains have been found. Besides these two main sites, smaller deposits of dinosaur fossils from the entire range of the Age of Dinosaurs can be found scattered throughout the eastern and southern parts of the state.

Domínguez–Escalante Expedition

In the summer of 1776, Spanish Franciscan missionaries Francisco Atanasio Domínguez and Silvestre Vélez de Escalante set out with cartographer Bernardo Miera y Pacheco to travel from Santa Fe, New Mexico, to Monterey, California.

Interestingly enough, if not for a delay in the original date of departure, the expedition would have begun on July 4, 1776. The men traveled, charted, and kept a precise journal of the different landforms, Indian tribes, plants, and animals they encountered.

They entered Utah from northwestern Colorado near Dinosaur National Monument and went west through Spanish Fork Canyon to Utah Lake. They never quite made it to the Great Salt Lake. The expedition then headed south to the area just north of present-day Cedar City. By this time it was late September, and the early mountain snows had become too great a threat to allow further travel west. Disappointed, the expedition decided to turn around and head back toward Santa Fe. They left Utah crossing south into Arizona. Although they didn't reach their final destination, their five-month, al-

most 2,000-mile journey provided the first glimpse of the Utah region to European settlers.

They disproved many common myths of the day, such as that there were cities of gold and countries of giants. However, they also set a few new ones in circulation, the greatest of which described the Utah and the Great Salt Lakes as one big lake and part of a westward drainage basin. This mapping error would affect the maps of the region for the better part of a century. Despite some inaccurate information, the exploration and its records blazed a trail for the westward expansion of future European and American settlers.

Donner-Reed Party

In July 1846, two parties left Fort Bridger, Utah, for California. One party elected to take the longer, well-known northern route. The other, lead by 62-year-old Jacob Donner of Illinois, risked the shorter and less-traveled southern route through the Great Salt Desert. The result of this infamous decision would prove fatal.

Donner, his wife, and their five children, along with fellow leader James Reed, chose to take the wagon trail recommended by Lansford Hastings. In his book, *The Emigrant's Guide to Oregon and California*, Hastings advised wagon trains to journey from Fort Bridger through the Wasatch Mountains, around the Great Salt Lake, and across the Great Salt Desert.

Hastings went ahead of the 87-member party, and when they reached Echo Canyon, the group found a note from their guide advising them to avoid Weber Canyon. Not knowing how to proceed, the party camped for five days while Reed left to consult with Hastings. Reed returned with detailed instructions on crossing the Wasatch Mountains, but without a guide.

After two and a half weeks of exhausting bushwhacking through the mountainous brush, the group finally made it to the Great Salt Lake. Tired, yet eager to continue on the next leg of the journey, the Donner-Reed party hurried past the lake region and headed straight into the Great Salt Desert on August 30, 1846.

Due to unusually soft ground, the typical two-day trip turned into a six-day nightmare. Afraid to lose any more time, the party drove on continuously, day in and day out, until they reached the Sierra Nevadas. Once again, luck would not favor the ill-fated party. In late October, the first snows made crossing the mountain range impossible, and the group was trapped for the winter.

Rescuers reached the survivors of the Donner-Reed party in early March 1847. However, half of the travelers had perished, and those who survived had been forced to commit cannibalism in order to live. Although no one traveled this dangerous route for many years following this incident, the trail the party cut through the Wasatch Mountains was used consistently in the following decade.

The Mormon Immigration

In 1820, 14-year-old Joseph Smith journeyed into the woods of upstate New York in order to find the answer to a lingering religious question and experienced the first in a series of spiritual epiphanies. An angel named Moroni appeared to him, telling him that he was a prophet and revealing hidden scriptures on golden tablets, which Smith translated from an unknown language. In 1830, Smith published these revealed writings as the *Book of Mormon*, and along with six other men, he formed the Church of Christ, later known as the Church of Jesus Christ of Latter-day Saints (LDS).

Due to religious opposition, Smith and his growing number of followers left New York for Kirtland, Ohio, a year later. Shortly after, in 1832, a young follower named Brigham Young was baptized into the faith and quickly moved up the ranks of the church.

The Mormons experienced increasing animosity from settlers in Ohio, so even as their church grew there, they established new settlements in Missouri. In 1835, Brigham Young was appointed to the Council of the Twelve Apostles, the highest governing group in the church.

In 1838, Missouri issued an "extermination order" against

The Hollywood version of the Mormon migration to Utah as seen in *Brigham Young: Frontiersman* **(1940)**

the Mormons. This animosity toward them came from exaggerated rumors of violence and the fear among original settlers that they would lose control of the area to the increasing number of Mormons. With harassment continuing in Ohio, the church moved to Nauvoo, Illinois, where things improved only temporarily. Here as well, non-Mormon settlers eventually began to persecute and even kill church members, mostly over their espousal of religious superiority and of polygamy. While jailed in Carthage, Illinois, in 1844, Joseph Smith and one of his followers were murdered by a furious mob.

Shortly before Smith's assassination, he had commissioned Young to lead an expedition west in order to find a place where the church could build a community free of persecution. He did this, and in April of 1847, Young, now the president of the Church of Latter-day Saints, led a large group of followers on a 111-day journey to find their new home. When Young arrived in the Salt Lake Valley near Emigrant Canyon on July 24, 1847, he declared to his people, "This is the right place."

Often referred to as one of the most significant colonizers in U.S. history, Brigham Young began his expansion in 1849 by moving 30 families south of the Salt Lake Valley. Young's idea was to establish communities along each of the eight major Utah streams. Any region that contained a water source was open for colonization.

During the next 20 years, over 80,000 Mormons emigrat-

ed to the Utah Territory, while approximately 6,000 perished along the way. Young endeavored to find places to live for arriving families as well as to establish livelihoods for his followers. Throughout this time, Young continually expanded the Mormon colonies to such areas as the Sanpete Valley and Little Salt Lake Valley in southern Utah.

In 1850, the Mormon leader helped found Parowan, the first iron enterprise of the LDS. Until this time, most Mormon colonies had been farming and livestock communities. Parowan began a trend of establishing mining towns based on natural resources, such as coal, silver, lead, and zinc.

The LDS under the leadership of Brigham Young devised two main types of colonization: direct and nondirect. The direct method was the most popular, and it consisted of establishing colonies with the full planning and guidance of the church. Religious leaders organized, formed, and financially backed the community, deciding which families would go, what their livelihood would be, and any other long-term goals of the town.

In contrast, nondirect settlements occurred when individual families ventured out in small groups to establish their own communities. They were not under the guidance of the LDS and did not receive any financial aid. However, the church encouraged nondirect settlements, especially for younger families.

When the transcontinental railroad was completed in 1869, it allowed for larger numbers of settlers to immigrate than ever before, and Young and the church welcomed this growth. However, in the early 1870s, overpopulation emerged as an obstacle for the Utah settlers. Consequently, many families began migrating to the outlying states of Nevada, Arizona, Colorado, Idaho, and Wyoming.

Perhaps as a result of this rapid growth, the U.S. government began to view the Mormons as a threat. In 1857, President James Buchanan sent 3,000 soldiers from Fort Leavenworth to infiltrate the Salt Lake Valley in what became known as the Utah War (see "Utah War"). There was no bloodshed during the "war," and the army ultimately succeeded in its mission—the removal of Brigham Young as leader of the territory and the appointment of a new, non-Mormon governor.

In the two decades spanning 1858 to 1877, the Mormons managed to establish 205 additional settlements. Areas such as Bear Lake, Cache Valley, Pahvant Valley, and the valleys along the Sevier, Virgin, and Muddy Rivers blossomed with Mormon communities. Despite the popularity of the LDS in Utah, the federal government continued to keep a tight hold on the territory. In 1887, Congress passed legislation that unincorporated the church, made voting for women illegal, and strongly enforced the law against polygamy. The new laws forced church leaders to renounce their doctrine encouraging plural marriages, which had been in effect since 1843.

During the early 1900s, very few regions in Utah did not have Mormon settlements, and church leaders changed their focus from colonization to building up previously established communities. The public view of the LDS has changed through the years from one of apprehension to that of acceptance. The growth of the church continues today in Utah as well as in many countries around the world.

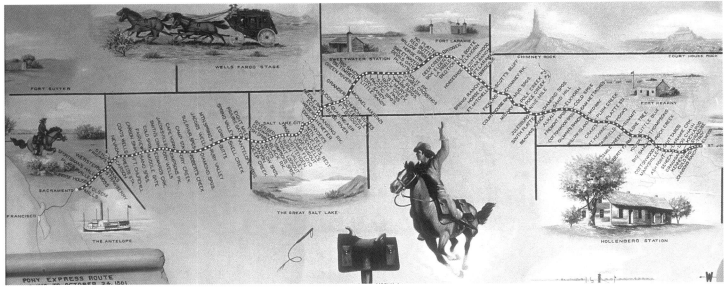

Map of the Pony Express route

Legend of Old Ephraim—the Last Grizzly Bear

The legend of Old Ephraim dates back to 1910. He is said to be the last, and some say the meanest, grizzly bear in Utah. As the story goes, Old Ephraim was 10 or 11 feet tall and very fond of the local cattle and sheep. For about 13 years he roamed the woods of Cache National Forest, killing a sheep from one ranch, a cow from another, but never taking from the same herd twice in a row. However, the bear met his match on August 22, 1923, in a battle with a local sheepherder named Frank Clark.

Clark moved to the region in 1911 and immediately set his sights on catching Old Ephraim. Over the years, Clark killed many bears, but he could rarely even get a glimpse of Old Ephraim, much less take a shot at him. Clark was only able to recognize the bear's presence in the area because of his distinctive tracks: Ephraim's left hind foot was missing its middle claw. Clark diligently set traps and one night was roused awake by an awful shrieking in the woods. Unable to fall back to sleep, Clark grabbed his gun and set out toward the sound. He actually walked past the bear, who could be heard rattling the chain in his trap. Since it was pitch dark, Clark climbed up the hillside and waited until morning to make his move. Then, at dawn, Clark approached the bear. Seeing the hunter, Ephraim raised up on his hind legs and charged. Clark shot off six rounds, but the bear kept coming. It was not until the seventh shot, which hit him in the head, that Old Ephraim fell back and died.

Local Boy Scouts erected a 10-foot monument on the site where Old Ephraim met his death. In 1966, the state built a larger monument to this legendary bear. His skull was sent to the Smithsonian and can now be found at the Bridgerland Travel Region Office in Logan.

Pony Express

On April 3, 1860, the first riders of the Pony Express set out across the West. Opened and run by the firm of Russell, Majors, and Waddell, the Pony Express lasted only a brief 19 months. Although the prospect of a mail system that could cross the country in 10 days excited the public (as opposed to an average of three weeks by stagecoach), lack of government subsidies and increasing debts forced the new postal system out of business. The establishment of a transcontinental telegraph line by Overland Telegraph in April 1861 also helped to make the Pony Express quickly obsolete. Twenty of the 190 stations that ran from St. Joseph, Missouri, to Sacramento, California, were established in Utah. The Pony Express brought news and supplies to the people of Utah and provided them with a means of communication to either side of the country.

The Pony Express only succeeded because of the extraordinary efforts of its riders, station masters, and work hands. Because the horses could efficiently carry only a relatively light load, riders had to keep to a weight of 120 pounds or less. They were equipped with a knife, revolver, horn, and some jerky. The land traversed by these men was some of the most desolate terrain in the country, and the riders would travel 100 to 125 miles daily (and nightly), braving Indian attacks and rough weather. It is said that Major Howard Egan, director of the Pony Express in Utah, even rode through a treacherous night of rain and sleet in which he and his horse fell off a bridge, carried on to cross the river, and eventually rode into Salt Lake City. All this so the mail would go through on schedule.

Due to weight restrictions, the Pony Express was extreme-

Deep Creek Pony Express station

ly expensive; one ounce of mail cost $5. As a result, much of the communication sent over the Pony Express was government or business related. Eventually, the expense of the operation outran income, and when no government subsidies came through, the Pony Express was forced to shut down with losses of about half a million dollars.

The Pony Express route entered eastern Utah from southwest Wyoming. Making its way to Salt Lake City, along what is now I-80, the trail then cut off to the south toward Fairfield and the Camp Floyd Station (west of the Utah Lake). This western portion of the trail, beginning around Fairfield, remains marked and passable. It heads southwest past Faust, Lookout Pass, and Simpson Springs, and then stretches out across the Flats to Callao and eventually Ibapah before finally crossing into Nevada.

Posey War

The Posey War was not actually a war but is the name for a moderately violent series of confrontations between white settlers and Native Americans around 1923 in San Juan County. Tensions began in the 1880s when arriving settlers began placing increasing demands on lands traditionally claimed by the Utes and Paiutes. By the turn of the century, the new ranchers and settlers had appropriated or destroyed most of the plants and animals that the Utes and Paiutes depended on, which led to much unrest between the whites and Indians.

In addition, white settlers would physically and verbally

Chief Posey

abuse the local Indians. They branded one man, a 60-year-old Paiute named Posey, as an arrogant troublemaker, and he became a symbol for their antagonism. As anti-Indian sentiment increased and the Indian food supplies decreased, the Utes and Paiutes began gathering harvests from a newly abundant source—the ranches of the settlers. Indians hunted and stole the flocks and herds of the ranchers. In 1923, Sheriff William Oliver arrested two young Utes for robbing a sheep camp, killing a calf, and burning a bridge. During their trial recess in Blanding, the two escaped with assistance from Posey. After Oliver failed to retrieve the pair, he returned to town and deputized a large number of local men to solve the "Indian problem"—that is, to shoot everything and anything that looked like an Indian. Oliver and his men, expecting a full-scale war, vowed to fight to the finish. Frightened by the aggressive whites, the Indians abandoned their homes and sought refuge in the countryside. But short of food and clothing and shivering in the harsh weather, the Ute and Paiute women and children quickly surrendered. The posse took 40 Indians as prisoners. First they were held in a school basement and then in a concentration camp of barbed wire in town. This action, however, was not without reaction from Posey and his men. During one of the many skirmishes between the parties, Posey

was fatally wounded and one young Indian escapee was killed.

In the wake of the "war," the federal government established an 8,360-acre reservation in Allen Canyon. Although the adults were confined to this land, most of their children were taken from them and forced to conform to white culture. Barbers cut their hair while local men restrained them; volunteers bathed and dressed boys in calico shirts and girls in dresses with gingham aprons. They were then sent to attend school in Tawaoc, Colorado.

Establishment of the Uintah-Ouray Indian Reservation

In 1861, due to an increasing number of white settlers arriving in Utah, Brigham Young agreed to a proposal that would set aside over 2 million acres of the Uinta Basin in northeastern Utah for use by tribes of the northern Ute. The same year, President Lincoln officially created the Uintah Valley Reservation. The northern Ute resisted the relocation at first, but within a decade most had moved to the reservation and become known collectively as the Uintah Ute.

Chief Ouray

Many bands of the northern Ute continued to live in Colorado, including Chief Ouray's tribe of Uncompahgre Ute. After uprisings by some of the tribes of the northern Ute, the federal government decided to relocate the Indians living in Colorado. Though they were a peaceful group, Chief Ouray's people were also relocated onto the newly formed Ouray Reservation. This 1.9-million-acre reservation was created in 1882 and located just south of the Uintah Valley Reservation. In 1886, the two reservations were merged into the Uintah-Ouray Indian Reservation.

The Ute were only in possession of the land for two years before the federal government began to take it back, slowly shaving off pieces of valuable land. Though it took a few years

Ute delegation to the opening of the Uintah-Ouray Reservation, 1905

to affect the people of the Uintah-Ouray Reservation, the government also began to break up Indian land according to the Dawes Act of 1887. Under the act, each Ute family on the reservation received an allotment of 80 to 160 acres while the rest of the land was opened to white settlers, who soon moved into the area. In 1905, the Uintah National Forest was created from 1.1 million acres of the reservation land. By 1909, the reservation had shrunk to about one-tenth its original size.

In following years, the U.S. government did return some of the reservation land to the Indians. However, it was not until a Supreme Court decision in 1986 that the people of the Uintah-Ouray Reservation were granted "legal jurisdiction" over 3 million acres of land that had been taken from them over the years. The case settled the issue of whether or not certain communities lay inside or outside the reservation's boundaries as well as returning certain lands to public domain.

Utah War

The so-called Utah War did not result in actual fighting, but that is not to say that it didn't come close. By 1857, the Mormon Church seemed threatening and/or abhorrent to many people across the country. Many considered its views on polygamy barbaric, and some hyperbolic officials in Washington, D.C., even equated it with the practice of slavery. Others feared the religious zeal of the Mormons, who considered other Christian denominations to be corrupt, and rumors spread throughout the nation that they would kill people based on religion.

That year, President Buchanan decided it was time to address the Mormon situation in Utah. Without further investigation, he sent Colonel Albert Sidney Johnston along with a force of 3,000 men to replace territorial governor Brigham Young with the non-Mormon Alfred Cumming. Many people, including Young, feared the worst.

Young swiftly mobilized Mormon forces and made efforts to delay the arrival of Johnston's men. Using guerrilla tactics, such as killing the army's livestock and burning supply trains, the Mormons managed to slow the approaching army. Young declared martial law in Utah and told his people to begin stockpiling supplies. He also called on Thomas Kane, an influential friend from the East, to come to Utah to help in negotiations. At the same time, Young prepared for a massive retreat to the south if peace could not be achieved through negotiations. As tensions rose, 30,000 people in Salt Lake City moved south to Provo and the surrounding areas.

When Kane arrived in February 1858, he accompanied Cumming into Salt Lake City to speak with Young. Young relinquished his position as territorial governor and tried to convince Cumming to withdraw the troops from Utah. Although the army remained, a peace settlement was struck. The army moved south and settled in Camp Floyd (near Fairfield), while the Mormons received amnesty for any past offenses. Johnston's forces then proceeded to march peacefully through the deserted Salt Lake City and continue south.

By summer 1858, the crisis was resolved, and the displaced Mormons moved back to Salt Lake City. Alfred Cumming turned out to be very friendly to the Mormons, and at the outbreak of the Civil War, the troops left Utah to fight in that conflict. With that, the Utah War, or "Buchanan's Blunder," was over.

Geography, Geology and Mining

Geological Timeline

The geological evolution of Utah stretches back over 3 billion years. The extreme, volcanic heat of the region's dynamic infancy characterized its first 2 billion years. The next 750 million years saw the development of warm, shallow seas that engulfed the land and laid sedimentary deposits up to 3 miles thick. As the seas slowly gave way, the next 150 million years brought the establishment of Sahara-like deserts on their shores. It was during this time that dinosaurs roamed the area that became the state. In time, their bones were embedded in the conglomerate shales and sandstones that were being formed during the period, and which have come to dominate much of Utah's present-day landscape.

About 100 million years ago, the North American continental plate collided with the Pacific continental plate off the coast of California. The reverberations of this massive geological event are thought to have triggered the formation of many of Utah's mountain ranges, a process that continued for the next 65 million years. During this time, the immense pressures deep under the earth's surface created the state's huge coal deposits. The culmination of this era was a period of extreme volcanic activity that lasted for another 20 million years and gave birth to the Henry and La Sal Mountains. Eventually, those mineral-bearing rocks just taking shape would provide the economic underpinnings for communities such as Alta and Park City.

The most recent phase in this timeline covers the last 15 million years and is characterized by the general uplift of western North America. In Utah, this caused glaciers and rivers to slice vast canyons into the surface of the land.

Today, Utah has an extraordinary geological diversity. Its landscape is composed of a wide variety of sedimentary, igneous, and metamorphic rocks, and geologists have catalogued nearly 600 different types of rocks and minerals scattered throughout the state.

Regions

Utah has an area of 84,916 square miles, making it the 13th largest state. It also has one of the greater elevation differentials in the nation: from Beaver Dam Wash at 2,350 feet to Kings Peak at 13,528 feet. Geologists generally divide this region into three major physiographic areas: the Basin and Range, the Colorado Plateau, and the Rocky Mountains provinces.

Basin and Range Province

The Basin and Range province stretches from the California-Nevada border to the western slope of the Wasatch Range. The northern area of this province is also known as the Great Basin, named by John C. Frémont in the 1840s.

The most conspicuous feature of the Great Basin in Utah is the remains of Lake Bonneville. As it disappeared, it left behind large salt and mud flats, easily spotted rings that were cut into surrounding foothills by waves along its shoreline, and the smooth alluvial deltas and beaches that have provided the flat land for most of Utah's urban development. Lake Bonneville is a relatively young geological feature; it started to form only about 25,000 years ago. At its peak 12,000 years ago, it was over 1,000 feet deep and covered 19,750 square miles of northwestern Utah before extending into Nevada and Idaho.

Large deltas were formed in the lake by the rivers flowing down from the Wasatch Mountains. As the level of Lake Bonneville dropped, these rivers cut deep canyons into the deltas and continued to flow further into the Great Basin. The level remains of these deltas, referred to as benches, provided suitable land for agricultural development and settlements along the Wasatch Front. Alluvial fans, created as the streams exited these canyons at lower elevations, eventually provided the sites for Salt Lake City, Provo, and many other settlements. Great expanses of undrained mud or salt-encrusted flats, which become large, shallow lakes during wet seasons, can be found at its lowest elevations. The Great Salt Lake, the largest remnant of Lake Bonneville, is about 1,500 square miles in area and has a maximum depth of only about 30 feet. It is the largest natural lake in the western United States and one of the saltiest lakes in the world. Over the years, table salt, potash, and magnesium have all been commercially produced from its waters.

Colorado Plateau Province

The Colorado Plateau province incorporates the eastern half and southern extremes of Utah, with all of its rivers and streams belonging to the Colorado River watershed. This semi-arid region contains a variety of landforms and can be divided into three sections: the High Plateaus, the Uinta Basin, and the Canyonlands. Dissected by the Sevier River, the High Plateaus form a strip about 200 miles long and 40 miles wide that extends from the southern end of the Wasatch Mountains south into Arizona. The highest point of the High Plateaus is Delano Peak, 12,173 feet, but the region also includes large tracts of gently rolling land above 10,000 feet. Heading south toward the Arizona border, the strata of the High Plateaus form successive lines of steep cliffs known as the Grand Staircase of Utah.

The Uinta Basin abuts the southern edge of the Uinta Range and extends south to the southern edge of the Roan Plateau and the Book Cliffs. It is drained by the Green River, which has cut a canyon deep into the sedimentary basin.

The striking Canyonlands encompass the southeastern corner of Utah. The general uplift of western North America during the last 15 million years has lifted Utah by as much as 5,000 feet. The increased gradient of the rivers and streams in the Canyonlands region greatly increased the rate at which they eroded the horizontal beds of layered, sedimentary rock. Despite their increased speed, these rivers maintained the meandering course established prior to the uplift, when they were flowing nearly at sea level. These deep, steep-sided canyons, gouged to reveal colorful layers of sedimentary rock, form the scenery typically associated with the Canyonlands area today.

This even pattern is only occasionally broken by pockets of volcanic activity, such as the La Sal and Henry Mountains, and by violently uplifted areas such as the San Rafael Swell and its jagged "reef" of uplifted sandstone, which rises 800 to 2,000 feet into the air.

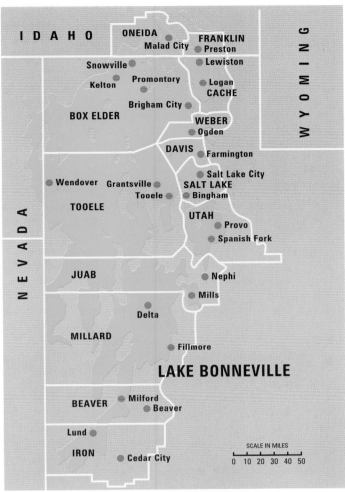

Map of Lake Bonneville, showing its relation to present cities, counties and towns in Utah, Idaho and Nevada.

The dramatic variety in the colors of the landscape throughout the Plateau region comes from the minor constituents of the rocks. Iron oxides create reds, pinks, and yellows; unoxidized iron particles create greens and blues; and manganese contributes lavender to the land's natural palette. The Colorado Plateau province is also rich in hydrocarbons, such as petroleum, oil shales, natural gas, and coal. Gilsonite (a type of solid asphalt), potash, uranium, and vanadium have been mined from the region as well.

Rocky Mountains Province

The Rocky Mountains province of Utah consists of two mountain ranges, the Wasatch and the Uintas. Both of these ranges have the unusual feature of being cut by rivers that pass straight across them. This geological anomaly occurred because the rivers preexisted the mountains and have been able to maintain their course as uplifts and erosion formed the ranges.

The Wasatch Mountains follow a north-south axis from Idaho to Nephi, a distance of about 200 miles. The highest peak is Mount Nebo at 11,877 feet. Since the Mormons arrived in Utah, most of Utah's population has chosen to settle along the western front of the Wasatch Mountains. The wide variety of rock types provided the granite to build the Mormon temple in Salt Lake City, and the silver, lead, and zinc deposits led to the establishment of towns like Alta and Park City in the late 1860s and 1870s.

The Uintas, the highest range in Utah, are unusual in the United States because they run from east to west. The highest point is Kings Peak, which rises to 13,528 feet. The Uintas receive about 30 inches of rain annually, which is nearly four times that received by the Uinta Basin below. During the past 2 million years the mountains have been extensively glaciated, resulting in the numerous glacial lakes that dot the Uintas today.

Mining in Utah

From the beginning, the Utah Territory was known for its vast mineral resources. However, though the Mormons were the first significant group of settlers on the scene, Brigham Young did not encourage his people to look for precious metals. Rather, he encouraged agriculture in order to create a more stable and enduring home. Young also did not want to see the new Mormon communities dissolve into a bunch of immoral boomtowns, which was the pattern everywhere gold and valuable minerals were found. Young could not ignore the resources that lay buried beneath their feet for long, though, and soon he and other church leaders became involved in the lucrative industry.

It turned out that Utah had wealthy deposits of gold, silver, lead, copper, and zinc, and most of these were south of Salt Lake City in Bingham Canyon, Park City, and the Tintic District. The early mining industry played a large role in the development of the state. Mining camps popped up and bloomed in all sorts of difficult terrain and unsettled regions, and they prompted railroad companies to expand throughout Utah, thereby linking many parts of the state. The biggest camps became sizable towns as they sprouted saloons, supply stores, hotels, gambling and dance halls, and all the other amenities, both legal and otherwise, the citizenry desired. The enormous mines themselves required large numbers of unskilled laborers, prompting a flood of immigrants.

In addition, in the early 1880s, Spring Canyon in Carbon County was discovered to have enormous deposits of coal. Coal mining took off quickly in Utah and lasted through World War I, after which demand for the fuel lessened, and the mines and the state suffered through poor economic times. Coal mining picked up again during and immediately after

Gilsonite mine in Utah

World War II, reaching its most productive point ever. However, coal was replaced with other fuel sources during the 1950s, and the ever-deepening mines were abandoned. With them, many old mining towns faded off the map, although coal is still produced today.

As coal mining was on its way out, the uranium boom quickly took its place. In 1952, Charles Steen hit it big when he discovered the precious mineral southeast of Moab. Uranium had been mined in earlier years, but never on the scale it was in the 1950s. Many prospectors rushed in to stake their claims, and mining in Utah was once again on the upswing.

Over the years, copper mining has been one of the state's most successful endeavors. Gilsonite, found in eastern Utah, and other hydrocarbons have been mined for use in paints and other building materials. Potash has also been successfully mined for use in fertilizers, and today Utah is the largest producer in North America.

All through its history, Utah has relied in some capacity on its mining industry. Despite leading to an inevitable boom-or-bust economic cycle, the extraction of valuable ores has contributed to the overall wealth of the state, to the development of the labor movement, and after the infamous Castle Gate robbery, to the personal wealth of one Mr. Butch Cassidy.

Animals

Mammals

Badger

Badgers measure about two feet long with short legs, clawed feet, and shaggy gray brown coats. They have a white stripe that reaches from midway on their pointy snouts back to their shoulders. They have bushy, short, yellowish tails. Found in open grasslands, sagebrush, and brushy areas, badgers use their powerful legs and front claws to dig out ground squirrels and other rodents. They are most active at night and make burrowed homes in the ground.

Badger

Beaver

Beavers are very large rodents with thick brown fur, chunky bodies, short legs, rounded heads, small rounded ears, yellowish-orange front incisors, webbed hind feet, and flat, hairless, paddle-shaped tails. Their weight ranges from 30 to 60 pounds. Beavers live in lakes, streams, ponds, and rivers where they eat bark and twigs. Because they do not hibernate, they collect large caches of twigs and branches to eat in their lodges during the winter. Beavers have thick layers of fat and waterproof fur, so icy waters don't bother them. They have skin

Beaver

flaps that close over their ears and nostrils when submerged and webbed feet for swimming. Their eyes have clear membrane covers that allow them to see in water and protect their eyes from floating debris. A beaver can remain submerged for up to 15 minutes before coming up for air. Beavers build dams of sticks and mud across streams and slow rivers. They gnaw down trees, strip them, cut them into small sections, and weave them into a dam, holding the logs in place with mud. They also build lodges with one or more entrances below water and the living chamber well above waterline. Beavers mate for life, which can be as long as 20 years. Furry beaver kits are born with their eyes open, in the lodges in spring.

The beaver population almost died out during the 19th century because of unregulated trapping for their fashionable fur (used primarily for hats), but the beaver population has been reestablished and is thriving.

Bison

The bison has an imposing appearance, with its dark brown, shaggy hair, woolly mane, massive head, high shoulders, short legs, and long tufted tail. Bison are the largest terrestrial animals in North America. Cows range in weight from 800 to 1,000 pounds, and bulls can weigh well over 2,000 pounds. Both sexes have short, black, sharply curved horns with pointy

Bison

tips. Bison are herd animals, grazing in groups of at least a dozen but also in massive herds; they feed mainly on grasses and shrubs. In winter, they clear snow from vegetation with their hooves and heads. Most active in early morning and late afternoon, they rest in the midday heat, chewing cud or dust-bathing. Bison are good swimmers, so buoyant that their heads, humps, and tails remain above water. When frightened, bison will stampede, galloping at high speeds. Males may battle each other in an attempt to mate with a cow. Fights can involve butting, horn locking, shoving, and hooking. When butting, males walk to within 20 feet of each other, raise their tails, and charge. Their foreheads collide with the force of freight trains, and without apparent injury, they continue charging until one animal gives up.

Once, the North American population of bison is estimated to have been 70 million. However, around 1830, the federal government encouraged a mass extermination in an attempt to subdue the Indians, and nearly all the bison were killed. Today's bison population is estimated at 30,000. You are unlikely to encounter bison on the open range as you travel the routes in this book. They are primarily found in national parks, refuges, game farms, and the like. Because they are unpredictable at all times, do not approach bison too closely for any reason.

Black Bear

Black bears can actually be black, brown, or cinnamon. Their bodies are powerful and densely furred, with slight shoulder humps, small rounded ears, small close-set eyes, and five dark,

Black bear

strongly curved front claws on each foot. Females range in weight from 120 to 200 pounds, and males range from 200 to 400 pounds. Nocturnal and solitary, black bears prefer forested habitats throughout the year, although they can sometimes be seen on open slopes searching for fresh greens. They usually make their dens in tree cavities, under logs, in brush piles, or under buildings, lining them with leaves or grass. Black bears are omnivorous; they eat both plants and animals. They feast on grasses, sedges, berries, fruits, tree bark, insects, honey, eggs, fish, rodents, and even miscellaneous garbage. In the fall they go into a feeding frenzy to gain as much weight as possible to get them through their winter hibernation, often adding a four-inch layer of fat to keep them warm and nourished. During hibernation, black bears crawl into their dens, and their bodies go dormant for the winter; they do not eat, drink, urinate, or defecate during their long sleep. Their kidneys continue to make urine, but it is reabsorbed into their bloodstream. They awaken by an internal clock in the spring and wander out in search of food. The black bear has a lumbering walk but can actually travel up to 30 miles per hour in a bounding trot. Black bears are powerful swimmers, able fishers, and agile tree climbers. Black bears breed in the summer; the females undergo a phenomenon in which the fertilized egg passes into the uterus but changes very little until late fall, when it implants and then begins to grow quickly. Females commonly give birth to a litter of one to five young in January or February.

Bobcat

Bobcats are a reddish tawny color, with dark spots on their body and legs. Their ears are slightly tufted. Their bellies are usually buff and spotted. They have short, stubby tails with three horizontal, dark stripes. Females range in weight from 15 to 25 pounds, and males range from 20 to 35 pounds. The most common wildcat, bobcats live in virtually every habitat below 10,000 feet—from dry, rocky mountainsides to forests and rocky or brushy arid lands. Because of their secretive nature, bobcats are seldom seen. Efficient predators, with keen eyes and ears to locate prey in poor light, bobcats feast mostly on rabbits, ground squirrels, mice, birds, insects, lizards, and frogs. They

Bobcat

stalk and move at blinding speed for short distances to pounce and make the kill. Solitary animals, they come together only for mating. Litters of two or three kittens are born in April and May in maternity dens, which are usually in hollow logs or under rock ledges or fallen trees and lined with dry leaves. The bobcat population is currently stable, although trapping by humans once nearly decimated the species.

Chipmunk

Several varieties of chipmunks share similar characteristics and are not easily discerned from one another. Ranging in color from chestnut to yellowish gray to light gray, chipmunks are

Chipmunk

small rodents with dark and light stripes on their faces. Dark stripes line their backs from the neck to the base of the tail, with white stripes running parallel on the back portion only. The palest chipmunks tend to be found in arid environments. They measure about three to six inches long, with three- to four-inch tails, and weigh a mere one to four ounces. Chipmunks are active during the day. Their diet includes a variety of vegetation, including seeds, leaves, fruits, flower components, and other plants. They have large, fur-lined internal cheek pouches used for carrying food. Chipmunks stow away a great deal of their food; instead of relying on stored body fat to sustain them during hibernation, they awaken periodically throughout winter and early spring to eat from their caches. They dig burrows and line them with grass underneath rocks, logs, and roots; these burrows become the nests where they have their young. Babies are born blind and naked after a gestation period of about 30 days.

Cottontail, Rabbit

One of the most abundant animals in nature, cottontails are very similar in appearance and behavior to hares (jackrabbits), except that they tend to be smaller and have shorter ears, smaller feet, and shorter hind legs. They do not turn white in winter. Of the several types in Utah, the buff brown desert cottontail is found in grasslands as well as creosote brush and desert areas. It will climb sloping trees and is known to use logs and stumps as lookout posts after dark. The mountain cottontail is grayish, with a white belly and black-tipped ears. It inhabits rocky wooded or brushy areas, often with sagebrush, throughout Utah. It uses either dense vegetation for shelter or, when not available, burrows and rocky crevices. Because of their

Cottontail

vulnerability at birth, cottontails are born in maternal nests, which the pregnant female finds and prepares about a week before giving birth. She locates a suitable spot where brush or high grass provides protection and makes a saucerlike depression in the ground, lining it with her own downy fur, soft grasses, and leaves. Adults may have three or four litters per year in a good habitat. Unlike hares, cottontails are born naked, with their eyes closed.

Cougar, Mountain Lion, Puma

Known by several names, these wildcats have brown fur that is shaded gray, yellow, or red, with buff areas on their bellies, necks, and faces. They are feline in appearance, with long heavy legs, padded feet, retractable claws, long black-tipped tails, small round heads, short muzzles, small rounded ears, and supple, strong bodies. The females range in weight from 80 to 150 pounds, and males range from 120 to 180 pounds. Cougars are good climbers and jumpers, able to leap more than 20 feet. Elusive and rarely seen, cougars are territorial loners that live in the wilderness throughout the mountains, foothills, and canyons. Carnivorous eaters, they thrive on large mammals such as deer and elk as well as on porcupine, mice, rabbits, and grouse. They locate prey, slink forward close to the ground, then spring onto their victims' backs, holding and biting the neck. They may bury the "leftovers" of a large kill and return one or more times to eat. Cougars breed in pairs, and females with young move together. Each cougar has its home range

Cougar

and rarely ventures outside it. Cougars breed every other year, and although there is no fixed breeding season, it often occurs in winter or early spring. Their maternity dens are lined with vegetation and may be located in caves, in thickets, under rock ledges, or in similarly concealed, protected places. Two to four spotted kittens are born in maternity dens from May to July.

Coyote

The coyote is grayish brown with rusty or tan fur on its legs, feet, and ears. Canine in appearance, with pointed muzzles and bushy tails, coyotes range in weight from 30 to 50 pounds. Their tracks appear much like those of a domestic dog but in a nearly straight line; hind feet usually come down in foreprints, with four toes per print. Coyotes rarely seek shelter and remain in dens only when they have pups. They are both carnivores and scavengers, and their opportunistic diet includes rabbits, mice, squirrels, birds, frogs, snakes, grasshoppers, fruits, berries, and sheep and other domestic livestock. In winter they often eat carrion from larger animals, especially deer, which is an important food source. They are vocal animals whose call is commonly heard at dusk or dawn, consisting of a series of barks and yelps, followed by a prolonged howl and short yaps. Coyotes howl as a means of communicating with one another; one call usually prompts other coyotes to join in, resulting in a chorus audible for significant distances. They are stealthy runners and can cruise at 25 to 35 miles

Coyote

per hour, making leaps as high as 14 feet. They hunt singly or in pairs, acting as a relay team to chase and tire their prey. Coyotes are monogamous and often mate for life. Their maternal dens are usually found or dug by the female under large boulders, in caves, on hillsides, or along river embankments. The openings, or mouths, of these dens usually measure several feet wide and are often marked by a mound of earth and tracks. A coyote might use the same den from year to year, unless it is disturbed. Coyotes breed in February, March, and April, and give birth to a litter of four or more pups by May.

The population of coyotes is flourishing, despite the popular demand for their fur in the 1970s and 1980s. Their main enemies are humans.

Desert Bighorn Sheep

Bighorn sheep are grayish brown with yellowish white rump patches and short brown tails. Some have whitish fur around their muzzles, eyes, bellies, and calves. They have muscular bodies and thick necks. Ewes weigh around 150 pounds, and rams range from 150 to 250 pounds. Both the male and female have horns that grow continually and never molt. The male's horns are massive and coil up and back around his ears in a C shape up to 40 inches long. The ewe's horns are thin and only slightly curved—no more than a half curl. Bighorn sheep are active by day, dwelling on cliffs, mountain slopes, and in canyons. They feed on a wide variety of grasses and shrubs. Rams challenge each other in butting contests in which they simultaneously charge each other.

Desert bighorn sheep

Their combined speed can be more than 40 miles per hour just before impact, and their foreheads meet with a crack that can be heard a mile away. These contests can last for as long as 20 hours. Horn size determines status among rams, but these ramming contests establish hierarchy among the rams with horns of similar size.

Many bighorns died in the 20th century from hunting, habitat fragmentation, and diseases contracted from domestic livestock. In the mid-1800s there were nearly 2 million bighorn sheep, but by 1975 their population had plummeted to about 10,000. Reintroduction programs and habitat protection has assisted in increasing their populations, but they are still endangered.

Elk

Native to Utah, the elk species flourishes today throughout most of the state, although it was practically eliminated by the early 1900s. Under careful wildlife management, elk were reestablished, and in 1971, Governor Calvin L. Rampton officially declared them Utah's state animal.

Elk are large, one-hoofed deer with brown bodies, tawny-colored rumps, thick necks, and sturdy legs. Cows range in weight from 500 to 600 pounds. Bulls range from 600 to 1,000 pounds and average about six feet in height. Only males have antlers, which they shed each year. Once widely ranged, elk are primarily mountain dwellers in the summer and valley dwellers in the winter. They remain in herds throughout the

year and feed on grasses, shrubs, and trees. In the late summer and early fall, bulls display mating behavior caused by their high levels of testosterone: They begin thrashing bushes and "bugling"—making a sound that begins as a bellow, changes to a shrill whistle or scream, and ends with a series of grunts. This vocalization broadcasts a bull's presence to other bulls and functions as a call of domination to the cows. Bulls become territorial and make great efforts to keep the cows together (a harem may consist of up to 60 cows), mating as they come into heat and keeping other bulls at a distance. Bulls often clash antlers

Elk

in mating jousts but are seldom hurt. Calves are born in the late spring after a gestation period of about nine months. Elk calves are primarily brown with light spots until the early fall of their first year.

Fox

Red foxes are rusty red in color, with white underparts, chins, and throats. Their tails are very bushy, long, and red, with white tips. Their lower legs and feet are black. The red fox weighs 8 to 12 pounds and measures about two feet long with a 15-inch tail. This animal is the most common fox in Utah, partly because of its adaptability to a wide variety of habitats. They are found everywhere from alpine tundra to farmland to forests. Red foxes are primarily nocturnal, elusive animals, making them difficult to spot. Their favorite foods are voles and mice, followed by almost anything that is available—including rabbits, birds, reptiles, fruits, berries, eggs, insects, and carrion from larger animals. An adult red fox can eat up to a hundred

Red fox

mice per week. Red foxes have keen hearing and can listen for burrowing or gnawing animals underground and then dig into the soil or snow to capture them. They continue to catch food even when they are full, burying the excess in the dirt or snow for later.

For years, unregulated trapping took a heavy toll on the red fox population, but the collapse of the fur industry has improved matters. With poultry farms being made nearly predator-proof, farmers also now kill fewer foxes. The red fox's range is expanding, although competition with the coyote may have a restraining effect.

Gray foxes are recognizable by their salt-and-pepper gray coats, with rust-colored legs and feet, white throat and belly, black-tipped tail, and a dark streak down the spine. The gray fox weighs 7 to 13 pounds and is about 22 to 30 inches long with a 10- to 15-inch tail. This animal prefers heavier cover and is more nocturnal than the red fox, so it is rarely seen. It lives in wooded and brushy slopes in the valleys. It is the only fox that commonly climbs trees and has been known to rest, hide, or escape into them. Gray foxes sometimes raise their young in large, hollow trees, some of which have entrance holes as high as 20 feet. More often, dens are located among rocks, in cliffsides, or in hollow trees or logs. Because the gray fox's pelt is undesirably bristly, it has never been heavily hunted or trapped for its fur. Like the other foxes, their worst enemies are humans.

Kit foxes, about the size of a house cat, are one of North America's smallest canids. These nocturnal animals have yellow eyes, buff yellow fur with grayish areas above, and white chins, throats, and bellies. Most have a black tip on their tails, and all have especially large ears. They inhabit sandy deserts, grasslands, arid shrublands, and juniper woodland areas in Utah. Well adapted to desert conditions, kit foxes avoid extremes of temperature and drought by hunting at night, using their extra-large eyes and ears to navigate through the darkness. The hot days are spent in a cool, humid, underground burrow. Kit foxes rarely drink water; instead they obtain dietary water from the food they consume. Their heavily furred paws give good traction on loose, dry, desert soils and insulate the pads from the hot ground. Their diet consists of nocturnally active rodents and includes kangaroo rats, jackrabbits, lizards, scorpions, and insects.

Hare, Jackrabbit

Hares are very similar in appearance to cottontails (rabbits), but they tend to be larger and have longer ears, bigger feet, and longer hind legs. It is suggested that hares got the name "jackrabbit" because their large ears resemble those of jackasses. Their fur is a mottled gray and brown in summer. It becomes almost pure white in northern areas of the state in winter, while in the south it gets paler but still holds tinges of brown and gray. Does (females) are larger than bucks, which is unusual in mammals. Their weight varies from 3 to 10 pounds. Utah's three

Snowshoe hare

species are the white-tailed jackrabbit, the black-tailed jackrabbit, and the snowshoe hare. In summer, jackrabbits eat mostly green plants, such as clover and flowers. In winter, they rely more on shrubs. Their huge ears are so sensitive that they can detect the muted sound of a coyote as its fur brushes against the grass. When threatened, they first freeze, laying their ears back to be less conspicuous, their coat assisting with the camouflage. If this fails, they can move from a hiding place like lightning, running at speeds up to 35 miles per hour and changing direction instantly. Unlike cottontails, young hares are born fully furred, with their eyes open. The female puts each young hare into an individual form, or depression, in the ground, thus decreasing a predator's chance of taking her entire litter. She keeps her distance by day and comes several times to nurse at night so that she attracts less attention.

Marmot

Brown to yellowish brown with yellowish bellies, marmots have heavy bodies with short legs, small ears, and bushy tails. Marmots range in weight from 5 to 10 pounds and measure one to two feet in length, with a five- to seven-inch tail. They feed on grass and plants. The largest ground-dwelling squirrels in the region, yellow-bellied marmots live in colonies throughout rocky areas. Habitats vary from talus slopes to pastures with large boulders. Sunbathing on rocks is a favored pastime; while the group enjoys the activity, at least one marmot stands guard to warn the others of danger. When danger encroaches, the sentry lets out high-pitched chirps so that the group can

Marmot

scurry to safety. These burrowing animals spend as much as eight months of the year underground and begin hibernation as early as September. In April and May, females give birth to three to six naked and blind young in grass-lined dens.

Moose

Moose are dark brownish-black overall, with a huge muzzle, beady eyes, long gangly legs, short neck, and big body. Cows range in weight from 600 to 800 pounds and bulls from 800 to 1,200 pounds. Only the males have antlers, which are massive, broad, and flat with prongs projecting from the borders; antlers are shed each year. Antler spread is usually four to five feet but can get as large as six and a half feet. Moose

Moose

live in forests, mountain meadows, river valleys, and swampy areas and are often seen in or near water. They feed on aquatic vegetation, shrubs, twigs, woody plants, and small saplings. Good swimmers, moose can move in the water at a speed of six miles per hour for a period of two hours, and they can stay submerged for three to four minutes at a time. Despite its ungainly appearance, they can run quietly through the forest at speeds up to 35 miles per hour. Moose rely heavily on their keen sense of smell and sharp hearing. Seldom heard, they vocalize by making a low mooing sound with an upward inflection at the end or a series of low grunts. In low population areas, both sexes may travel extensively in search of mates, whereas in highly populated areas, they may form breeding groups and the bulls may fight for the cows. The bulls do not get as violent as elk or deer, but the occasional shoving match can result. The young are usually born in May to June after a gestation period of about eight months.

Mountain Goat

Mountain goats have white shaggy hair all over their bodies, with longer hair under their chins to form beards. They have black eyes, nose, hooves, and horns. Their bodies are compact, and their legs are short. Nannies weigh around 150 pounds, and billies weigh from 200 to 325 pounds. Both females and males have smooth, backward-curving horns, although the male's are much larger. Because horns grow continuously throughout the animal's life-

Mountain goat

time and are never shed, the older males tend to have the largest horns. Mountain goats are found in the highest, most inhospitable, and remote places in Utah. They are hardy animals who live throughout the year on alpine cliffs and meadows, even when temperatures drop far below zero, winds gust up to 100 miles per hour, and blizzards rage. Mountain goats feed on grasses, sedges, and other green plants. Their hooves, with rubbery soles for traction, are well adapted for traversing rocky peaks. Their bodies are slender, so they can traverse narrow mountain ledges. Short legs and powerful shoulder muscles allow the goat to ascend steep, rugged terrain. Their shaggy outer layer of hair, with protective, long, hollow strands, insulates them from the extreme colds; their inner layer of hair is more like a thick woolen sweater. Mountain goats follow a social hierarchy. The older, stronger goats dominate, followed by aggressive adult females, followed by two-year-old males, two-year-old females, yearlings, and kids. Adult males are subordinate to other classes, except during rutting. In breeding season, rival billies threaten one another; but the threats do not always result in a fight.

Mountain goats were reintroduced to Lone Peak in the Wasatch Range in 1967. Additional populations are now established on Mount Timpanogos and in the Uinta and Tushar Mountains.

Mule Deer

Gray in winter, the mule deer's coat changes to reddish brown in summer. Some have a whitish throat and rump patch. Their tails are either black-tipped or black on top. Mule deer have large, mulelike ears that move almost constantly. They are medium-size deer with stocky bodies and long, slim, sturdy legs. Does range in weight from 100 to 180 pounds, and bucks range from 150 to 400 pounds. Only the buck has antlers; he sheds them in the winter and begins to grow another set in the spring. They spend the summers in mountain pastures, alpine meadows, and sometimes logged areas. The onset of winter snowstorms drives them to lower slopes, where food supplies are more abundant. The mule deer's summer

Mule deer buck

forage includes grasses, sagebrush, serviceberry, and chokecherry. In winter they browse on twigs, shrubs, and acorns. They are mostly active in the mornings and evenings, and on moonlit nights. A mule deer's social group generally consists of the doe and her fawn or twins, while the bucks often remain solitary. During the November breeding season, bucks become increasingly active and intolerant of one another, sometimes engaging in conflict or vigorous fights wherein each tries, with antlers enmeshed, to force down the other's head. Injuries are rare, and usually the loser withdraws. Mule deer breed in mid-November; fawns usually arrive in June, July, and August, with spotted coats for camouflage. A doe giving birth for the first time normally produces a single fawn, whereas an older doe tends to have twins.

Pika

These small rodents have short, dense, gray brown fur, round bodies, short legs, large heads, short rounded ears, and no visible tail. They are small and mouselike, about eight inches long and four to seven ounces in weight. Pikas live in colonies in rocky fields, talus slopes, and sub-

Pika

alpine meadows. They feed on a variety of grasses, sedges, and forbs, and spend their summers gathering huge quantities of vegetation and storing it for winter. They take bits back to rockpiles, where they spread it out to dry in the sun. If rain threatens before the stacks are cured, the pika carries its harvest one mouthful at a time to the shelter of a rocky burrow. It is not uncommon for one pika to store as much as four bushels. When not foraging, pikas like to find a safe perch near an escape route and keep an eye out for predators. Active during the day, they blend with the rocks, yet their characteristic squeak gives them away every time. You can often hear a pika before you see it, although it is usually difficult to tell the direction from which the sound comes. Uttered at the first sign of danger, the call is picked up by other pikas and echoed throughout the colony. Instead of hibernating for winter, the pika is active all year, moving around beneath the rocks in tunnels dug through the snow. It lives off the caches of food gathered in the summer. Pikas usually mate in the early spring, producing a litter in May or June; a second litter may be produced in late summer.

Porcupine

Porcupines are gray brown, with chunky bodies, high arching backs, and short legs. Yellowish hair covers long quills all over their backs, rumps, and tails. These rodents measure up to two feet in length, with an eight-inch tail, and range in weight from 10 to 28 pounds. Next to the beaver, they are the largest rodents in Utah. Found in nearly all forested areas throughout the state, porcupines are active year-round. Porcupines feast on green plants, grass, and leaves in summer and tree bark in winter. They are slow-moving animals with poor eyesight, yet they are equipped with thousands of barbed quills for protection against predators. Contrary to popular belief, porcupines do not throw their quills; quills are released from the porcupine's body and penetrate the attacker's skin. Not only are quills hard to pull out, they readily work themselves in further. This can produce painful and even fatal results. Porcupines are primarily nocturnal, but they can occasionally be seen resting in treetops during the day. They make their dens in logs or caves and use them for sleeping and birthing. Kits are born May and June, after a gestation period of seven months. They are born headfirst, with quills aimed backward.

Porcupine

Pronghorn Antelope

Pronghorns are pale or reddish tan in color on the upper body and outer legs, with two white bands across the throat, a white rump patch, white chest, white lower sides, and white inner legs. The buck has vertical black markings from eyes to snout and along the sides of the throat. Does range in weight from 75 to 110 pounds, and bulls range from 110 to 130 pounds. Both sexes have sets of horns; the doe's are seldom longer than three or four inches, but a buck's horns can grow as long as 20 inches, curving back and slightly inward. Horn sheaths are shed each year. Pronghorns are common and highly visible, preferring open rolling plains or grasslands. Active night and day, they alternate bits of sleep with watchful feeding. Pronghorns feed on grasses and forbs in summer and sagebrush and other shrubs in winter. They are the fastest animal in the Western Hemisphere and have been clocked at 80 miles per hour, although 45 miles per hour is more usual. Pronghorns run with their mouths open, not from exhaustion but to gasp extra oxygen. When it senses danger, a pronghorn snorts and erects the white hairs on its rump (twice as long as the body hairs), which creates a flash of white as it flees and warns other pronghorn of danger. If a surprise attack forces a pronghorn to fight rather than flee, it uses its sharp hooves, which can effectively drive off a coyote. Adult bucks establish territories in March and hold them through the September breeding season. Throughout the spring and summer, nonterritorial bucks gather into bachelor herds, while the does and fawns drift on and off the territories. By late September, territorial bucks try to hold groups of does and fawns on their territories for breeding and keep other bucks away. These territories are abandoned after the breeding season; horns are shed; and all ages and both sexes congregate on the winter range. The young are usually born in April, May, and June.

Pronghorn populations were reduced to less than 25,000 in

Pronghorn antelope

the mid-1920s due to the fencing of range land, which hampered migration and foraging (pronghorns cannot leap fences like deer—they crawl under them instead). With management and transplantation of herds by game departments, the pronghorn population is steadily increasing; current estimates are over 500,000.

Raccoon

Raccoons have salt-and-pepper coloring with black masks across their eyes and black-and-white ringed tails. Raccoons appear slightly hunchbacked. They are about two feet long, with a 10-inch tail. They range in weight from 10 to 25 pounds. Raccoons are found near water, living in dens in hollow trees, logs, rock crevices, or ground burrows. They feed mostly along streams, lakes, or ponds, and their favorite foods include fruits, nuts, grains, insects, eggs, and fish. They appear to wash their food before eating it, but they are actually feeling for the edible parts. Raccoons do not hibernate in winter, although they may sleep for several days during cold weather. Raccoons give birth in April and May to litters of between two and seven young. Naturalists estimate that there are 15 to 20 times as many raccoons now as there were in the 1930s.

Raccoon

River Otter

Dark brown in color, with silvery fur on their underparts, river otters have long, cylindrical bodies; small, rounded ears; large noses; small, beady eyes; long whiskers; and thick, furry tails. River otters are about three feet long, with ten- to eighteen-inch tails; they range in weight from ten to twenty-five pounds. River otters live in large rivers, streams, or beaver ponds and feed primarily on fish, frogs, and aquatic invertebrates. River otters can stay under water for two to three minutes because their pulse slows and skin flaps close over their ears and nostrils. They have powerful feet and webbed toes to propel them through the water. Stiff whiskers help them hunt by feel under water. Cold waters do not bother them because their dense fur and oily underfur does not allow water to reach their skin. River otters tend to use beaver and muskrat burrows as their own. They are very playful animals who spend much time frolicking and chasing each other. Pups are born in litters of one to four in March, April, and May—furry, blind, and helpless.

River otter

Squirrels

Several different types of squirrels inhabit Utah. Abert squirrels are found in Utah east of the Colorado River. Abert squirrels (also called tassel-eared squirrels) have grizzled gray, black, or reddish sides and backs, with white or black bellies. These tree squirrels live in ponderosa pine forests, feeding on the pine cones, bark, buds, and twigs of the trees. They build bulky nests of twigs high in the pines, where they sleep at night, court, mate, and raise their young. Abert squirrels do not hibernate; they remain in their nests during cold weather and venture out to recover stored food below. Mating chases last all day in late winter, during which males frantically chase the females around. A litter of about four young is usually born in April or May, after a gestation period of about 46 days.

Golden mantled ground squirrels resemble chipmunks, except chipmunks are smaller and have facial stripes. Their backs are brownish gray, with head and shoulders coppery red, forming the "golden mantle." Bellies are white or buff. They have one white stripe bordered by black stripes on each side. Also called copperheads, these little squirrels live throughout Utah in moist forests, in mountains to above timberline, and sometimes in sagebrush country or rocky meadows. They hibernate through winter, putting on a layer of fat in the fall. They have well-developed cheek pouches, where they carry food to their dens to be stored and eaten in spring when they awaken. Occasionally some individuals awaken to periodically feed. Diet consists of pinyon nuts, fruits, seeds, and fungi. They live in shallow burrows up to 100 feet long.

Abert squirrel

Red squirrels (also called pine squirrel or chickaree) have a flecked rust red coat in the summer that turns gray red in winter. These small tree squirrels are seven to eight inches long, with bushy four- to six-inch tails. Red squirrels enjoy opportunistic varieties of nuts, seeds, eggs, pine cones, and fungi. They often have a preference for a favorite feeding stump or branch, where you might find piles of cones or seed pods. In the fall, they stow large quantities of food in caches in the ground, in hollow trees, and in other spots. Red squirrels make nests of grass and shredded bark in tree cavities or branches. They do not hibernate in winter. Litters of young are born in April and May, after a gestation period of 35 days; sometimes mothers bear a second litter in August or September.

Rock squirrels are the largest of the ground squirrels. They are 17 to 21 inches, with a 6- to 10-inch tail. Coloring is mottled gray-brown in front and darker behind, with buff bellies. Tails are long and bushy with sprinklings of brown and buff edges. True to its name, the rock squirrel dwells in rocky locales throughout Utah—such as cliffs, canyon walls, talus slopes, and boulder piles—and digs its den in the ground below. They dine on berries, nuts, plants, or carrion and often collect food to transport and store back in their dens. Rock squirrels are often seen sitting on or running among rocks, but they are also good tree climbers. Vocalizations include an alarm call, which is short and followed by a lower-pitched trill. They have a sharp, sometimes quavering whistle. Females normally bear two litters during the year, one in late spring or early summer and the other in late summer or early fall.

Uinta ground squirrels are brownish to buff, with paler sides and a buff belly. The tail is buff mixed with black. They have cinnamon-colored heads and faces, with a grayish dab on top of the head and gray on the sides of the face and neck. Mainly found in north-central Utah, they live in dry sage and sage grass areas, including suburban lawns. This squirrel both estivates (goes dormant in summer) and hibernates. They begin estivation in July and all disappear by September. Directly from estivation, they enter hibernation. In spring, males emerge first, followed by the females in late March to early April; they remain active about three to four months before reentering the sleep cycle. They eat seeds and green vegetation. The badger is a major predator of the Uinta ground squirrel.

Utah Prairie Dog

Utah prairie dogs are fawny-colored, sprinkled with black on the back and sides, with whitish bellies, small ears, and white-tipped tails. They hibernate from fall to spring and live at higher elevations on plains in the south-central portion of Utah. Their pups are born in April, after a gestation period of about thirty days. They vacate their burrows in May and June, and the dens are taken over by other animals.

Utah prairie dog

White-Tailed Deer

White-tailed deer are grayish-brown in winter and reddish-brown in summer. Their tails are white below and brown above. They have small ears and a slim, graceful appearance. Does range in weight from 120 to 180 pounds, and bucks range from 150 to 400 pounds. Only the buck has antlers; he sheds them in the winter and begins to grow another set in the spring. White-tailed deer are occasionally found in farmlands, but they prefer a somewhat denser woodland habitat in riparian areas. These deer are adaptable to live near human communities, but are timid and elusive—primarily nocturnal. White-tailed deer forage on a variety of foods —including shrubs, trees, acorns, or grass —according to what is in season. They also enjoy garden vegetables (corn, peas, lettuce, apples, herbs) and other agricultural items. When nervous, the white-tailed deer snorts through its nose and stamps its hooves; when spooked, it raises its white tail, thus alerting other deer of danger. They are good swimmers, can run thirty to forty miles per hour, and can jump thirty feet horizontally and over eight feet vertically. White-tailed deer breed in much the same manner as mule deer, except that buck fighting is less common.

White-tailed deer buck

Reptiles

Desert Striped Whipsnake

A member of the racer family, the desert striped whipsnake has a yellow base color, with longitudinal dark stripes along the back and sides that fuse and fade toward the tail. It is a long,

Desert striped whipsnake

slender, active snake that reaches lengths of 4 to 5 feet. Found in all areas of Utah except the high mountains, desert whipsnakes have large eyes and are very quick-moving. It can cruise through sagebrush flats with its head in the air looking over tops of the brush. The snake is generally shy and will flee in response to human contact but will bite if it continues to feel insecure. They hibernate and emerge in spring. They feed on lizards, other snakes, small mammals, birds, and insects. In spring it may be found in large numbers warming in the sun near the opening of the den.

Desert Tortoise

Utah has four species of turtles: desert tortoise, spiny softshell turtle, painted turtle, and snapping turtle. These are all found in limited numbers, and only the desert tortoise is native to Utah. Desert tortoises have high-domed shells with stocky limbs that are covered with large conical scales. They are com-

pletely terrestrial, requiring firm ground for construction of burrows, adequate ground moisture for survival of their eggs, which females lay in holes they dig. Eggs hatch into fully formed young turtles. They frequent desert oases, riverbanks, washes, dunes, and

Desert tortoise

occasionally rocky slopes. Burrows have half-moon-shaped openings and may be 3 to 30 feet long, occupied by one to many individuals. Desert tortoises are a threatened species and take 15 to 20 years to reach maturity.

Garter Snake

The most abundant species of garter snake found in Utah is the western terrestrial, and it is distributed throughout the state. The moderately slender bodies of adults range from 24

Garter snake

to 42 inches in length. Their coloring is brown to gray, with a gray-and-tan checkerboard pattern that darkens and becomes obscure with age. They have light stripes down the sides of their bodies, which become less prominent with age. There is also a distinctive light stripe down the back of some individuals. Western terrestrial garter snakes feed on snails, slugs, earthworms, fish, various small

reptiles, and small rodents. When captured, they emit an unpleasant fluid from vent glands.

Gopher Snake

The Great Basin gopher snake is the most widely distributed snake found in the state; its habitats range from grassland, gravelly soil, coniferous forests, deciduous forests, riparian ar-

Gopher snake

eas, and agricultural areas to sagebrush and rabbit brush. It is a large snake, reaching over five and six feet in length. The head is oval and slightly flattened. Either yellow or cream colored, gopher snakes have smaller blotches found on the sides, with a prominent dark stripe across the top of the head that reaches from eye to eye. Gopher snakes can appear threatening—mimicking the coiling and hissing of a rattlesnake—yet the formidable-looking snake is harmless. They feed on rodents, small rabbits, birds and their eggs, and occasionally lizards.

Horned Lizard

The horned lizard is common throughout Utah. It has sharp-pointed "horns" along the back of its head and is often referred to as a horned toad. Its body is squat and somewhat flat. Horned lizards can be brown or bluish gray, with the color matching the local soil. Their sides and quite short tail are edged with whitish

Short-horned lizard

spines. Active by day between April and October, horned lizards prefer rocky to sandy open areas.

Milk Snake

Utah milk snakes have vivid buff, black, and red horizontal stripes around their bodies. Adults reach a maximum total length of about 36 inches. They are often confused with the Utah mountain king snake or the deadly coral snake, but the

Milk snake

coral snake does not live in Utah. Milk snakes are found in a wide range of habitats throughout most of the state, particularly in the foothills and mountain ranges. A constrictor, the milk snake kills its prey by squeezing. Milk snakes are frequently lured to farms, ghost towns, and abandoned buildings by their favorite food, rodents.

Rattlesnake

The rattlesnake is the only venomous snake in Utah. Seven kinds of rattlesnake live throughout the state, but the most common is the western rattlesnake. They are found in virtually every terrestrial habitat in Utah, from grasslands, sand hills, rocky areas, riparian vegetation, mountains, and semidesert shrublands to open coniferous forests; only perennially wet areas seem to be avoided. The western rattlesnake is typically greenish yellow with darker blotches (although individual colors will vary, depending on how long it has been since the last molt); it has a triangular head, narrow neck, and ranges from 15 to 65 inches, including the obvious rattle on the end of its tail. Western rat-

Western rattlesnake

tlesnakes live in prairie dog burrows or crevices during winter and emerge for spring-summer activities in May. In hot summer weather, they usually prowl at dusk and at night. Pores in their heads pick up scents and heat to help detect prey. The snake kills its prey by injecting it with venom through hollow fangs that snap downward and forward as it strikes.

To human beings, a western rattler's bite is painful and can cause infection and illness, but rarely death, although a few fatalities have been documented among bitten adults. They are not particularly aggressive snakes, although they usually rattle and assume a coiled, defensive posture when approached. If left alone, they normally crawl away and seek a hiding place. Exercise caution in tall grass, rocky areas, and around prairie dog towns, especially in the mornings and evenings and after summer thunderstorms.

Yellow-Headed Collard Lizard

These robust little lizards have bodies that measure three to five inches, with large heads, narrow necks, and long tails. In-

Yellow-headed collard lizard

cluding tails, collard lizards reach lengths of about 12 inches. The males have yellow heads and blue-green bodies with yellow spots. The females are typically gray or brown with creamy spots. They are found in rocky canyons, rocky ledges, and boulder-strewn areas; sun-warmed boulders serve as areas for basking and as lookout posts. They spring from boulders seizing lizard and insect prey with a rush. They are typically active from April through October. Collard lizards run from danger on their hind legs with tails in the air.

Birds

American Kestrel

A commonly seen bird of prey, this small falcon can often be spotted hovering in search of prey in open country and farmland. About 8 to 10 inches long, the American kestrel is similar to a robin in size but not temperament; it fiercely attacks small rodents and other birds as well as large insects. It has a loud voice, and

American Kestrel

when excited it lets out a shrill "killy, killy, killy." The American kestrel is identified by two distinctive facial stripes. The male is rusty on his back with blue-gray wings and crown. The female has a rusty back and wings. Both have long rusty tails. They make their nests in a natural cavity or the abandoned cavity of a northern flicker (see below).

Bald Eagle

Over a thousand of these fish-eating birds winter in Utah each year, arriving around November. The Rush Valley population is unique in that the eagles survive the winters by feeding on rabbits and deer carrion. Eagles are noted for their strength and keen vision. They have large, heavy, hooked bills and strong, sharp claws called talons. They are usually brown, black, or gray, sometimes with markings on the head, neck, wings, or tail. The bald

Bald eagle

eagle is not really bald; it was named for its white head. The rest of its plumage is brown, except for its white tail. They have very sharp eyesight and hunt while soaring high in the air or watching from a high perch, swooping down to make the kill with their powerful talons. The eagle makes its nest, or aerie, high in a tree or on a rocky ledge where it cannot be reached by other animals, since young eagles remain helpless for a long period. Each year the birds add new material to the same nest. The largest known nest ever measured was 20 feet deep and nearly 10 feet wide.

Black-Billed Magpie

A common bird throughout Utah, this bird's black-and-white coloration and long tail (one of the longest of any North American bird) make it easy to identify. It lives anywhere from cities to wilderness areas, and it eats almost anything, thriving by being adaptable. It is a big, flashy, boisterous, and loud bird, with a reputation for raiding the

Black-billed magpie

nests of other birds, picking sores of cattle, and attacking the eyes of injured animals. Their sturdy nests, made of mud and reeds, are used from year to year; they also mate with the same partners from year to year.

California Gull

The California gull is the official state bird of Utah and is protected under Utah statute. In 1848 it was credited with saving the crops of pioneers from complete decimation by a locust plague. Found in interior regions of Utah, the fully grown California gull reaches 18 to 23 inches in length. Cal-

California gull

ifornia gulls tend to nest on islands with very little cover because the open water keeps them safe from terrestrial predators. Nests are often on open beaches or shorelines on the ground in a shallow hole lined with plants, grass, feathers, and small sticks.

Canyon Wren

These small birds grow to about six inches and are brown and buff, with a long, down-curved bill. They are further identified by their flight pattern, in which they quickly raise and lower their hindquarters every few seconds. The agile canyon wren also has a slightly flattened body shape, which allows it to navigate through narrow crevices. They are usually found in open cliffs, canyons, and

Canyon wren

rocky slopes foraging for food, even throughout the hottest parts of the day, scanning ledges and crevices for insects and spiders. Canyon wrens nest on ledges, in crevices under rocks, or in caves, and they make cup-shaped nests of moss, twigs, and spider silk that are lined with fur and feathers.

Clark's Nutcracker

Identified by its light gray body, white tail feathers, and black wings, this gregarious and bold bird grows to 12 or 13 inches. It

Clark's nutcracker

was named for Captain William Clark, of the Lewis and Clark expedition, who collected the first specimen. He mistook the bird for a woodpecker because of its large, straight black bill. Despite the corrected name, this bird cracks more conifer cones than nuts. They hammer the cones with their bills and are known to store food for winter. They also eat insects. Clark's nutcrackers make their nests on horizontal limbs and construct a twig-and-stick platform lined with grass and strips of bark.

Cliff Swallow

These small birds grow to six inches. They have a square tail; blue-gray head and wings; cream-colored rump, forehead, and breast; and rusty cheeks, nape, and throat. Cliff swallows build gourd-shaped, all-mud nests on rocky cliffs, as well as under many low-elevation bridges.

Cliff swallow

Golden Eagle

Golden eagles are truly magnificent large birds, ranging in length from 30 to 40 inches with a wingspan of six to eight

Golden eagle

feet. The males and females are similar in appearance, with brown bodies that have a golden tint, especially on the neck and head. Their feet are yellow and their hooked bills are dark. While soaring above, golden eagles swoop down onto prey, which includes ground squirrels, marmots, and grouse. They are also capable of killing young goats, sheep, and deer. Normally they build nests of sticks, branches,

and roots atop a cliff that overlooks an open area with a reasonable population of small mammals.

Great Blue Heron

The great blue heron stands nearly five feet tall with blue gray feathers, a long curving neck, and a straight yellow bill. A wetland marsh bird, it is often mistaken for a crane because of its similar size, but cranes hold their necks outstretched in flight and herons fold their necks back on their shoulders. Found in all water habitats in Utah, these birds feed on aquatic fauna with a spearlike bill. Great blue herons nest in trees, creating flimsy to elaborate stick-and-twig platforms that are added to over the years. These nests can be up to four feet in diameter, and they accommodate the pair as they incubate their eggs.

Great blue heron

Great Horned Owl

The great horned owl has long ear tufts and yellow eyes. It is found throughout Utah in mixed forests, shrublands, riparian woodlands, and cottonwood groves below 10,000 feet. They are skilled hunters well equipped for killing their prey. They use their sharp talons to grip rabbits, weasels, squirrels, and birds in a deadly lock. At night you can sometimes hear their deep, resonating hoots. The owls have a wide range of vision: their necks can swivel nearly 180 degrees, and they can practically see in the dark. Shelter usually consists of the abandoned nests of red-tailed hawks, crows, ravens, eagles, or herons.

Great horned owl

Hummingbird

The name hummingbird originated from the noise the birds' wings make in flight. Hummingbirds, only a few inches long, are the smallest of all birds, and Utah contains a number of types, including black-chinned, broad-tailed, calliope, ruby-throated, and rufous. Hummingbirds feed on nectar, although they also regularly consume small insects. They obtain nectar by inserting their bills and tongues into a flower, thus accumulating pollen on their bills and heads; this pollen is then transferred from flower to flower. Hummingbirds are strong fliers and have exceptional flight characteristics for birds: they can hover and

Hummingbird

fly backward. The extremely rapid beating of their wings can reach 80 beats per second. Some hummingbirds save energy on cool nights by lowering their usually high body temperature until they become sluggish and unresponsive, a condition termed torpor. In contrast, during daylight hours hummingbirds are often very active and can be highly aggressive, sometimes attacking much larger potential predators, such as hawks and owls.

Mountain Bluebird

These beautiful, sky blue birds are primarily summer residents in Utah that arrive by mid-March. They normally take over nests abandoned by woodpeckers because their beaks are not strong enough to hollow out their own cavities. Their survival today is difficult, as the logging industry cuts down many standing dead trees that the birds would normally use as homes. They readily adapt to whatever homes they can find, including chipmunk burrows, abandoned car bumpers, and fence posts in open areas.

Mountain bluebird

Mountain Chickadee

The mountain chickadee is a small, energetic bird that sings its name: "Chick-a-dee-dee-dee." Identified by its black cap and bib, black eye line, white cheek, and gray underparts and tail, it grows to about five inches. Mountain chickadees must consume nearly their body weight in seeds and insects each day because of their amazingly fast heart rate of 500 beats per minute. During cold weather, it puffs out its feathers so it resembles a fluffy ball with a beak. Nests are usually in a natural cavity or abandoned woodpecker nest.

Mountain chickadee

Northern Flicker

The northern flicker, a type of woodpecker, can be identified in flight by a flash of salmon red under its wings and tail. Viewed at rest, the northern flicker has a brown crown, a brownish body, and a red streak behind its bill. Northern flickers are the most terrestrial of North American woodpeckers—they are sometimes seen hopping around in grassy meadows or forest clearings. They are occasionally spotted bathing in dusty depressions, as dust particles absorb oils and bacteria from their feathers. Northern flickers feed mostly on insects—particularly ants. They use their powerful beaks to create nesting holes in dead or dying deciduous trees and line the cavity with wood chips.

Northern Flicker

Northern Harrier

Northern harriers are slender hawks with long tails and wings. The male is gray with black wingtips; the female is larger and brown with a streaked underside. They both have white rump bands at the base of the tail and a dish-shaped ruff of feathers that give an owl-like face. This ruff of feathers serves as a sound-gathering system to assist in the pursuit of food. The northern harrier actively hunts, flying close to the ground, looking for motion and listening for the squeak

Male northern harrier

of mice and other small animals in the ground cover below. In fact, because of this behavior, the harrier may be the easiest hawk for novices to identify because no other hawk routinely flies so close to the ground. It cruises over fields and meadows, seemingly grazing the grasses with its belly. Northern harriers range from 16 to 24 inches in length and are found in almost any type of open country—including open fields, wet meadows, marshes, and alpine meadows. They nest on raised mounds on the ground in tall vegetation, with shelters made of grass and sticks.

Female northern harrier

Pinyon Jay

This bird is 9 to 11 inches long, with all gray-blue plumage, a long slender bill, and no crest on its head. Mainly found year-round in pinyon-juniper woodlands, this social bird is gregarious and loud. The pinyon jay forages in flocks of family members; jays roam the countryside for food while group members take turns being on the lookout for danger. The birds search mainly for pinyon or pine nuts and seeds, which they store in fall and consume during winter and spring. Alternative foods include insects and berries. Pinyon jays do not establish pair bonds until their third year, but afterward the pairs remain together year-round. Pinyon jays build bulky nests of sticks, twigs, and fibers in pinyons, junipers, and shrubs.

Pinyon jay

Prairie Falcon

Prairie falcons are medium-size birds with pale brown upperparts, a pale face, and creamy white and heavy brown spotting below. Their crown is streaked. Found in open, treeless desert country and prairies throughout Utah, prairie falcons are stealthy fliers and utilize a high-speed strike-and-kill method, swooping down on ground squirrels, chipmunks, waterfowl, grouse, songbirds, and other vertebrates. The young birds, when learning to fly, tend to make many attempts—with many crash landings. Prairie falcons typically seek shelter in rocky cliffs or outcrops and sometimes in trees, usually without nesting material.

Prairie falcon

Red-Winged Blackbird

These birds are about eight or nine inches long. Males are black with crimson shoulder patches bordered with yellow, while females are mottled brown, with heavily streaked underparts and a faint red shoulder patch. The red coloration serves as a flag during courtship and also for aggressive displays. During one scientific experiment, males whose red shoulders were painted

Red-winged blackbird

black soon lost their territories to rivals they had previously defeated. These birds inhabit marshes, wetlands, and open fields and make woven nests of dried grasses and soft materials among grasses or cattails. They migrate in late September to spend their winters in warmer areas, even as far south as Costa Rica.

Red-Tailed Hawk

This big, brown hawk with a reddish tail grows to 25 inches. The bird goes through several color phases, which can make  identification difficult. Generally the bird has dark upperparts, light underparts, and a red tail. Red-tailed hawks like open country, fields, and mixed woodlands. They perch in trees, overlooking open fields in a sit-and-wait technique, then swoop down on prey. They are also known to dive after prey while soaring. Diet ranges from small rodents to medium-size birds, amphibians, and reptiles. Red-tailed hawks normally nest in trees, constructing

Red-tailed hawk

bulky stick structures that are usually added to each year. Both parents incubate the egg, but only the female raises the young.

Sage Grouse

Ranging from 27 to 34 inches, the sage grouse is the largest grouse in North America. Males have white breasts, black bibs and bellies, mottled brown backs, and yellow combs. Females are mottled brown with black bellies. Sage grouse normally inhabit sagebrush flats in the plains, foothills, or intermountain valleys. They are noted for their spring courtship rituals, which are performed at ancestral dancing grounds —or "leks." During courtship, males dance to attract females and compete with other males.  These showmen flare their wings, raise their tails, and lower their heads till their bodies are nearly parallel to the ground. Then they stamp their feet rhythmically, gyrating like wind-up toys, and jump into the air while beating their wings. The females are very selective about getting the fittest and most experienced male; one attractive

Sage grouse

male may mate with up to 75 percent of the females. Diet consists mainly of sagebrush leaves, flowers, and terrestrial insects. Nests are built on the ground, usually under a sagebrush, in a shallow depression lined with leaves and grass.

Towhee

Spotted towhees are large sparrows, about seven or eight inches long. They have black heads, backs, wings, and tails; reddish-brown flanks; white spotting on the wings; and white bellies and undertails. Spotted towhees are found primarily in sagebrush, willows, streamsides, and brush thickets. They are most abundant in southern Utah and the Uinta Basin. Towhees scratch the ground vigorously for insects and seeds. They nest low in a bush, on the ground under

cover, or in a brushy pile in a cup nest with leaves, grass, and bark shreds. Another species likely to be seen is the green-tailed towhee. This towhee has green upperparts, a white throat and chest, and a red crown. These migratory visitors frequent dry brushy habitats, particularly in sagebrush.  They can be found throughout the state at nearly all elevations, from low to fairly high in the mountains.

Spotted towhee

Western Wood-Pewee

This five- or six-inch bird is a member of the flycatcher family. It is dark olive brown on the upperparts and has a lighter belly. It has a distinct voice; calls include a harsh, slightly descending "pee-yew," which it  calls persistently throughout the day. Found mainly in open woodlands, these birds perch on tree branches during the day and launch down to forage upon flying insects. Western wood-pewees build camouflaged nests of

Western wood-pewee

plant fibers that resemble a bump on a horizontal limb, which they defend fiercely, chasing away hawks, jays, and chipmunks.

White-Faced Ibis

This bird stands about two feet tall and has dark chestnut plumage, a long down-curved bill, and long dark or red legs. They are common in summer in the mudflats and farmlands along the Wasatch Front, where they feed on aquatic invertebrates, amphibians, and other small vertebrates. White-faced  ibis fly in long, wavering lines to and from their roosts, which are typically in bulrushes or other vegetation. They build deep nests of coarse materials lined with plant matter.

White-faced ibis

White-Throated Swift

The white-throated swift is a six- or seven-inch bird with a long, forked tail and a black upperpart with white below that tapers down the belly. These remarkable little birds spend most of their lifetime in flight; they feed, drink, bathe, and even mate while flying! One of the fastest birds in the world, the swift is estimated to reach speeds of nearly 200 miles per hour. White-throated swifts like open habitat, where they feed almost entirely on flying insects. They breed on cliffs and rocky outcroppings and build their nests in cracks or crevices of cliffs.

Wilson's Phalarope

Wilson's phalaropes have long thin bills, chestnut throats, bold blackish stripes on the face, and light gray underparts. They are unlike most bird species in that the female has bolder coloring and usually mates with several different males. This role reversal continues during breeding, since it is the male who incubates the eggs and the female who defends the nest. Nests are usually built near water, in a depression lined with grass and vegetation.

Wilson's phalarope

Plants

Wildflowers

Arrowleaf Balsamroot

This plant is a common wildflower found on foothills, open forest slopes, and in dry forest openings in early spring; it reaches peak blooms in May and June. The plant has clumps of arrow-shaped leaves with flowers on long, thick, woolly-haired stalks.

Arrowleaf Balsamroot

There are one or two small, narrow leaves about halfway up the stem. Single, brilliant yellow flowers measure about two or three inches across and foliage is pale silvery green, due to the numerous minute hairs on the surface. Native Americans derived a medicine for treating headaches and rheumatism by boiling the roots. The drug treatment caused profuse perspiration. The Native Americans also ground the seeds into a meal, which they ate for nourishment. Height: 12 to 24 inches.

Columbine

A member of the buttercup family, the Colorado columbine has five bluish lavender petals and five white ones. It is Colorado's state flower, with the blue symbolic of skies and the white representing snow. They are not important forage plants but sheep will feed on them in overgrazed ranges. Found

Columbine

at altitudes up to 6,500 feet, columbines bloom from early summer to midsummer. Height: 4 to 24 inches.

Daisy

These plants are members of the sunflower, or Erigeron, family. There are over 25 Utah species, and the types are somewhat difficult to distinguish. The showy daisy has stems up to 25 inches high and bears several one-and-a-half- to two-inch-diameter flower heads, each with 70 to 100 slim, purple, ray flowers. The centers are yellow orange. The Erigeron family is very similar to asters, but they flower earlier in the summer season and tend to have more purple flowers. Utah daisies are similar in size and appearance but have grayish-looking stems due to its short, stiff hairs. Withered leaves may be present at the base. Flower heads are just a half inch wide, and

Daisy

are solitary or in clusters with 10 to 40 bluish or white ray flowers surrounding a dense cluster of yellowish disk flowers. Height: to 25 inches.

Dogtooth Violet

This is actually a lily, not a violet, that is found in moist meadows, growing in large patches near melting snowdrifts. It has one or more yellow blossoms that curve backward from the stem. The flowers appear very early, sometimes even pushing up through the snowbanks. This plant is edible and serves as food to many mountain animals, including bears. Height: 6 to 18 inches.

Dogtooth violet

Elephanthead

A member of the figwort family, elephanthead has a dense spike of half-inch-long pink flowers that when closely examined resemble miniature elephant heads—with a curving trunk, big flappy ears, and a domed elephantlike forehead. The design of the plant actually aids in cross-pollination because the blossoms are perfectly shaped to accommodate nectar-seeking bumblebees. Inside, pollen dusts the bee's hairy body and the "trunk," which encloses the female flower parts, brushes the exact spot on the bee's back where pollen from other flowers has accumulated. Elephantheads bloom from June to August and are found on marshy mountain meadows, boggy areas, and stream banks at altitudes up to 10,000 feet. Height: 10 to 20 inches.

Elephanthead

Globemallow, Wild Hollyhock

Globemallows, with their bright scarlet- to peach-colored flowers, are members of the hollyhock family. The blossoms are shaped like miniature hollyhocks. The plants are covered with a dense, grayish, slightly sparkling coating of short hairs on the central stalk and three-lobed leaf blades. The hairs help the plant reflect sunlight and retain moisture. Globemallows are normally found from low deserts up to pinyon-juniper and ponderosa pine woodlands at altitudes to 8,000 feet. There are several species of globeflower, and

Globemallow

one of the eastern members was once used to make marshmallows. The white pith inside globemallow stems can be chewed like gum. Height: 2 to 18 inches.

Goldenrod, Yellowweed

Goldenrod is a genus in the sunflower family. It typically has a slender, unbranched stem with short-stalked or stalkless leaves and small, yellowish flower heads in complex clusters. It is one of the later-blooming plants, usually blooming around July to September. Height: 12 to 72 inches.

Goldenrod

Heartleaf Arnica

Heartleaf arnica

A member of the sunflower family, heartleaf arnica has a single yellow flower that measures two to three inches across on stems that have slightly hairy, heart-shaped, gray green leaves. They are found in Utah canyons, particularly in aspen and spruce-fir forests. Flowers bloom in early summer and develop seed heads with tufts. Various species of this plant are known to have medicinal value, and the flowers are most potent; however, in Utah, heartleaf arnica is considered a poisonous plant due to arnicin toxin in the leaves. Height: 8 to 13 inches.

Larkspur

Larkspur

Widely distributed throughout Utah, larkspur has dark purple or dark blue flowers with five sepals that resemble petals. Hummingbirds frequent these plants for their sweet nectar. American Indians and early settlers made blue dyes and ink from larkspur. Like lupines, these plants are toxic and should never be eaten by humans or livestock. Height: 1 to 2 feet (low larkspur); 3 to 6 feet (showy larkspur).

Lupine

Lupine

From the pea family, lupine in Latin means "wolfish," as they once were believed to destroy the soil. The opposite is in fact true; many members of the family actually improve soil fertility through nitrogen fixation. Lupines have blue, pink, white, or yellow flowers that grow in a cluster and are similar to garden sweet peas in shape. Seedpods are flatter and smaller than the garden pea, but unlike them, lupines are toxic and should never be eaten. Height: to 30 inches.

Marsh Marigold, Elk's Lips

Marsh marigold

Marsh marigolds each bear just one white flower one to two inches across, with many yellow stamens and heart-shaped leaves. Found in moist areas of the mountains, these early season bloomers sometimes push up through the melting snow. Within 48 hours they can blossom. Height: 3 to 10 inches.

Milkweed

Showy milkweeds have small but complex flowers in rounded clusters that vary from white or yellowish to red or purplish, with paired leaves and fruit pods filled with seeds. The sap has toxic properties that are destroyed by boiling; Native Americans used to cook and eat the shoots, leaves, buds, flowers, and seedpods. Monarch butterfly larvae con-

Milkweed

sume the toxic foliage, which makes them less vulnerable to predators. The seedpod down, which is five or six times more buoyant than cork, was used to stuff pillows and, during World War II, life jackets and flight suits. Milkweeds are commonly found in clumps beside streams, ditches, and roadsides. Height: 18 to 72 inches.

Moss Campion

Moss campion

Not truly a moss, this common mat-forming plant grows close to the ground and has many densely crowded, woody branches. Its many pink, rose, or white flowers do not bloom until the plant is about 10 years old. Distributed throughout the state, but most likely to be found in the Uinta Mountains, moss campion spreads like a blanket across rocky ridges and slopes in a tightly interwoven cushion. Height: less than 1 inch.

Paintbrush

Indian paintbrush

Indian paintbrush flowers are small, modified leaves called "bracts," which have colorful tips of fiery orange, pink, maroon, red, or yellow, giving the appearance of a dipped paintbrush at the end of the stems. The roots of these plants are semiparasitic and steal food from other plants. Native to slopes and meadows, this plant blooms from May to September. Height: 12 to 36 inches.

Parry Primrose

Parry primrose

The deep magenta flowers of this plant have yellow "eyes." They rest atop a vertical stem, with all the leaves sprouting from the base, rising nearly as tall as the flower and emitting an unpleasant odor. Found in rock crevices, meadows, bogs, and along streams and other moist areas, they bloom in June and July. Height: 10 to 24 inches.

Phlox

Carpet phlox

Carpet phlox are sweet-smelling, mat- or carpetlike plants with many little white, pink, blue, or lavender flowers. The spiny, stiff leaves are covered with long woolly hairs. They grow on open sites in sagebrush communities and shrubby slopes; several stems spread around and over rocks and gravel to form a deep rooting system. Desert phlox are similar but do not have woolly hairs on the leaves. Longleaf phlox, found in every county of the state, are again similar but are easily recognized because they are up to six inches taller, with softer, longer leaves. They bloom from May to July. Height: 6 to 12 inches.

Salsify, Goat Dandelion

This plant looks much like a tall, large dandelion after it goes to seed. Its yellow flowers bloom in the morning and close by noon. They are found in meadows, fields, and roadsides. Salsify was brought by European settlers to use as a garden vegetable; roots were soaked to remove the bitterness, then peeled and eaten raw or stewed. Their flavor is similar to that of oysters. Height: 12 to 18 inches.

Salsify

Scarlet Gilia, Skyrocket

These showy little wildflowers are members of the phlox family. It is primarily biennial, producing a small clump of leaves

Scarlet gilia

the first year, followed by flowering stems the next year. The bright red, trumpet-shaped flowers are three-quarters to one and a half inches long with a pointed, flaring lobe and yellow centers. Scarlet gilias are frequently visited by hummingbirds, which thrust their bills down the tube to reach the nectar at the base. The little bird's head becomes covered with pollen during this process, which it deposits at the next flower. Gilia plants may have a skunklike odor. Height: 12 to 40 inches.

Sego Lily

Governor William Spry named the sego lily as Utah's official state plant in 1911. It is often found on open grass and sage rangelands in the Great Basin during summer months. A member of the mariposa family, the sego lily has sepals, petals, and stamens in combinations of three; its ivory-colored petals may be tinted from yellow to pink. The bulbs were eaten by early Mormon settlers when food was scarce and by Native Americans before that. Today the plant serves as an important food source for many animals. Height: 6 to 8 inches.

Sego lily

Shooting Star, Birdbill

A member of the primrose family, the shooting star looks like a colorful rocket. It has backward-curving magenta petals with

Shooting star

a yellow circle in the center, pointing down to form the nose. There is a rosette of leaves around the base of the stalk. Elk, deer, and cattle graze on the young shoots, which grow in rich soil and partial shade along streams and in wet meadows during June and July. Height: 6 to 16 inches.

Sky Pilot, Skunkweed

When crushed, the leaves and stems of these plants emit a skunklike odor. The bluish purple flowers actually have a sweet, pleasant smell. Bell-shaped flowers grow in crowded clusters around the head, blooming from

Skypilot

June to August. They are often found growing in the Uinta Mountains on rocky slopes. Height: 4 to 12 inches.

Sulphur Buckwheat, Sulphur Flower

This highly variable species grows in a multitude of habitats throughout Utah, from sagebrush foothills to subalpine conifer communities. They are hearty plants that can survive

Sulphur buckwheat

in a rugged environment. Umbrella-like clusters of tiny yellow flowers appear in spring to midsummer, varying with elevation. As the flowers mature, they become red, then brown, and remain on the plant throughout winter. The base is woody, and from it spring leafless 10- to 14-inch stalks. Some leaves grow very near to the ground and eventually become part of the soil. Various species of birds and wildlife feed on the seeds, flowerheads, and leaves. Height: 10 to 14 inches.

Western Monkshood

This creamy white and bluish violet flower has two tiny petals under a hood. Monkshood contains poisonous alka-

Western monkshood

loids, especially in the roots, and it was once used as a medicine to lower fevers. It grows in meadows and other moist sites up to 9,000 feet in the major canyons. The species depends on bumblebees for pollination as smaller insects do not have the strength to push the floral parts aside to reach the nectar. It normally blooms in midsummer or late summer. Height: 24 to 72 inches.

Yarrow

A member of the sunflower family, yarrow is an aromatic herb with a strong but pleasant odor. The white flowers grow in flat clusters; the leaves are dissected into many fine segments, giving a feathery or fernlike appearance. Height: 6 to 10 inches.

Yarrow

Yellow Monkeyflower

These low, creeping plants have bright yellow blooms and grow in masses. Petals have tiny orange or reddish brown

Yellow monkeyflower

spots. Scarlet monkeyflowers are also common, and at least seven other species of the genus exist in Utah. This plant is also called wild lettuce because Native Americans and early settlers ate the bitter leaves. The blooming season is usually from June to August. Height: 4 to 18 inches.

Trees, Shrubs, Agaves, and Cacti

Aspen

Members of the poplar family, aspens are found in canyons and mountains at elevations from sea level to 10,000 feet. They have smooth, cream-colored bark with green, heart-shaped, deciduous leaves that turn brilliant gold in the fall. As-

Aspens with fall foliage

pens grow from 30 to 60 feet tall with a trunk diameter of 8 to 12 inches. These beautiful trees need only seven inches of water per year and tolerate a wide range of temperatures. The bark becomes black when scarred, and older trees are dark at the base. Groves of these trees allow sunlight to penetrate to the forest floor, thus encouraging diverse plant growth and providing food and shelter for numerous wildlife species.

Barrel Cactus

True to their name, barrel cacti are cylindrical or barrel-shaped and are among the largest cacti of the North American deserts. Members of this genus have prominent ribs and are armed with heavy spines. Most barrel cacti have one-and-a-half- to two-and-a-half-inch yellow-green or red flowers growing in a crown near the top of the plant. They grow to heights of up to

Barrel cactus

10 feet. Fruits become fleshy and often juicy when mature, but are not usually considered edible. Native Americans boiled young flowers in water to eat like cabbage and mashed boiled flowers for a drink. They also used the cactus as a cooking pot by cutting off the top, scooping out the pulp, and combining hot stones with food inside. In an emergency, the pulp of the stem can be chewed for its food and water content, but obvious care must be taken to avoid the spines. The pulp has been used to make cactus candy, a popular treat. Barrel cacti usually grow along desert washes, gravelly slopes, and beneath desert canyon walls. Most species bloom April through June, depending on local conditions.

Blue Spruce

The Picea pungens, blue spruce, was selected as Utah's state tree in 1933. It is found primarily in the Wasatch and Uinta Mountains at elevations between 6,000 and 11,000 feet. The pyramid-shaped tree ranges from 10

Blue spruce cones

to 100 feet tall with branches extending to the ground. The dark green or blue green needles are square shaped (roll them between your

Blue spruce

fingers), with a pointed tip, rising singly from the twig. Cones are two to three inches. Blue spruce bark is gray and is smooth in younger trees and lightly furrowed in older trees.

Bristlecone Pine

Bristlecone pines are evergreens with short, green, needlelike leaves that grow in bundles of five. They are crowded in a long, dense mass curved against the twig in a manner that resembles the tail of a fox. The stubby needles may be retained for 20 to 30 years before being replaced. The trees have a clear, sticky resin on the cones and needles that becomes white with age. Cones are dark brown, from two to four inches long, cylindrical, and covered in spiny scales. Bristlecone pine trees vary in height from 60 feet to a mere

Bristlecone pine

Bristlecone pine cone

3 feet at higher elevations. Bristlecones grow slowly and can take up to 3,000 years to reach their full height. Some bristlecone pines are among the oldest trees in the world.

Cholla

The silver cholla is a common cactus of the Utah deserts. It has yellowish flowers, and blooms between March and October. Silver cholla grows in well-drained sandy and gravelly soils in desert plant communities at lower elevations. It is very spiny, so take care as you walk in the desert—the spikes can penetrate through your shoe soles and are extremely painful to remove.

Silver cholla

Cottonwood

Cottonwoods are deciduous members of the poplar family, with smooth, grayish green bark that is often deeply furrowed on older trees. Their foliage is dark, shiny green above and paler below, turning dull yellow in the fall. Sometimes confused with

Cottonwood

aspen, the common cottonwood is distinguished by larger, coarser, more deeply toothed, heart-shaped leaves; cottonwoods are also larger than aspens and have coarser bark, except when young. Narrowleaf cottonwood leaves are pointed at the tip, almost willowlike, with a long oval shape. Cottonwoods like moist soils and are often found near mountain streams and in coniferous forests. This handsome hardwood usually reaches a height between 40 and 60 feet.

Creosote Bush

Creosote bush foliage is yellow, followed by white, fuzzy seedpods. The leaves are naturally varnished to slow evaporation and conserve water. Stems are gray and ringed with black. This abundant evergreen shrub is covered with aromatic resin (hence the name "creosote"). When older stems in the middle of the plant die off, new growth comes up around the edge. This process allows a plant, which is essentially a clone, to be a century or more old. It is believed that the creosote produces a toxic substance to prevent other plants from growing too close, thereby in essence dictating local water rights. Only when the soil below a creosote has been cleansed by rain will other plants grow for a brief time beneath them. The sweet, refreshing smell of the desert after a rain results partly from wet creosote bush foliage.

Creosote bush

Douglas Fir, Red Pine

The Pseudotsuga menziesii, Douglas fir, is a conical evergreen with flattened, needlelike leaves that are yellow green or blue green. Trees are pyramid-shaped when young, but the crown becomes irregular with age. The bark is dark red brown and smooth on young trees; it becomes thick, furrowed, and corky on older trees. At the end of the twigs there is usually one, though sometimes more than one, cone-shaped, sharp-pointed, red brown, oblong cone with three-pronged tongues sticking out between the cone scales. The cones are three to four inches long. Douglas fir are long-lived conifers that grow in vast forests in Utah, often in pure stands, in well-drained soil at elevations from 6,000 to 9,000 feet. They are also found in canyons below 6,000 feet. Among the world's most important timber trees, Douglas fir are often used for reforestation. Height ranges from 60 to 120 feet.

Douglas fir

Douglas fir cone

Engelmann Spruce

Picea engelmannii are straight, tall, and slender; vaguely shaped like church spires. They have horizontal branches that are often drooping. The dark or blue-green needles are square with a blunt tip, about one inch long, rising singly from the twig. The purplish red to russet red cones are found in the upper branches and are less than two inches long, with wedge-shaped scales. Engelmann spruces can grow from 60 to 160 feet, but at higher altitudes, the tree is dwarfed, straggling, and naked on the windward side. It is normally found above 9,000 feet.

Engelmann spruce cones

Engelmann spruce

Gambel Oak

This deciduous shrub or small tree grows in canyons and on sandy, gravelly, and rocky slopes, often in groves. When young, the leaves have hairs on both sides, gradually becoming greener and smoother on the top but remaining hairy below. Gambel oaks grow to 30 feet. They have egg-shaped acorns, which Native Americans used to grind into flour.

Gambel oak

Joshua Tree

The Joshua tree, the largest of the yuccas, is a member of the lily family. This picturesque, spike-leafed evergreen grows in dry soils on plains, slopes, and mesas, often in groves. They range from 15 to 40 feet in height with a diameter of one to three feet. Flowers are bell-shaped, one to one and a half inches long with six creamy, yellow-green sepals. The flowers are crowded into 12- to 18-inch, many-branched clusters with an unpleasant odor; they blossom mostly in the spring. Not all trees flower annually. Joshua tree fruit is elliptical, green brown, two to four inches long, and somewhat fleshy. It dries and falls soon after maturity in late spring, revealing many flat seeds. Joshua trees (and most other yuccas) rely on the female pronuba moth (also called the yucca moth) for pollination. No other animal visiting the blooms transfers the pollen from one flower to another. In fact, the female yucca moth has evolved special organs to collect and distribute the pollen onto the surface of the flower. She then lays her eggs in the flowers' ovaries, and when the larvae hatch,

Joshua tree

they feed on the yucca seeds. Without the moth's pollination, the Joshua tree could not reproduce, nor could the moth, whose larvae would have no seeds to eat. Although an old Joshua tree can sprout new plants from its roots, only the seeds produced in pollinated flowers can scatter far enough to establish a new stand.

Juniper—Utah

Utah junipers, Juniperus osteosperma, are primarily found in the foothills, canyons, and plateaus from 6,000 to 7,000 feet. They grow to about 8 to 20 feet tall with rounded crowns. These trees often have several branches as large as the main stem extending from ground level. The yellowish green foliage is pressed tightly to the twigs and is scale-shaped. Bark ranges from gray brown to gray and grows whiter as the tree ages. It is fibrous and tends to shred in long strips. The one-fourth- to one-third-inch diameter berries are bluish and turn whiter with age.

Utah juniper

Juniper—Rocky Mountain

Rocky Mountain junipers, Juniperus scopulrum, are also called mountain red cedars. They are stout, spreading, bushy trees with minute gray-green leaves that are blunt and grow close to the twig. The quarter-inch blue berries contain one or several seeds. Junipers range in height from 10 feet in exposed situations to as tall as 30 feet in sheltered canyons, where the limbs tend to droop like those of a weeping willow. Junipers are often found growing near pinyon trees (the forest service refers to the two together as P&J). The berries serve as an important food source to some birds and small wildlife.

Rocky Mountain juniper

Limber Pine

The pinus flexilis is appropriately named because its branches are so limber they can be bent over without breaking. Limber pines are narrow, pyramid-shaped trees often found on windswept ridges, slopes, and canyons from 7,000 to 10,000 feet. They grow 20 to 60 feet tall. Yellow green needles are one to three inches long, bound in clusters of five at the base with a

Limber pine

Limber pine cones

papery sheath. The cones are light brown and without prickles. Limber pines have smooth gray or silver bark when young, which turns scaly and dark brown to grayish with age. The seeds are an important food source for squirrels, chipmunks, pinyon jays, and magpies, while mule deer, elk, and moose eat the foliage.

Lodgepole Pine

Pinus contorta are found at elevations over 8,000 feet. They vary enormously in size from 30 to 80 feet, but they are smaller at higher elevations where winds twist them into gnarled, bent shapes. Taller trees typically have a narrow, conical, dense crown, while smaller ones can have a broad, rounded crown. When found in dense stands, trees have branch-

Lodgepole pine

Lodgepole pine cones

es only on their upper third, but in sparser stands trees have branches extending near their base. Bark on lodgepole pines ranges from orange brown to gray and is thin and loosely scaly. Needles are one to three inches long, yellow green, and grow two from a single point on a twig. The yellow-brown egg-shaped cones are resin-sealed and range from three-quarter to two inches long. They remain on the trees for many years; during a forest fire, the resin melts away and the cones open, distributing the seeds to regenerate the species. Taller trees can look like fields of evenly spaced telephone poles, with little separating them but fallen needles.

Mormon Tea Bush

Also called Indian tea bush, this erect shrub stands about three or four feet tall. The upright stems are parallel and smooth, with tiny scalelike leaves at the stem joints. They have an upside-down broomlike appearance. Both the male and female of this species develop cones up to three-eighths of an inch long. The tea bush grows at lower elevations in arid rocky areas on flats, slopes, or cliffs. Stems are

Mormon tea bush

sometimes grazed by cattle in the winter, and the branchlets can be steeped to make a noncaffeinated drink that's used to treat colds and congestion. This tea was brewed by the early pioneers, although Native Americans were first known to enjoy the beverage.

Pinyon Pine

Pinus edulis is a bushy evergreen with a short trunk and compact, rounded crown. The gray to red-brown bark is rough and scaly. Needles range from three-quarter to three inches long, usually two to a bundle, with blue-green foliage on the younger trees and dark, yellow-green foliage on more mature ones. Cones are one to two inches and have edible seeds, known as Indian nuts or pine

Pinyon pine

nuts, that can be eaten raw or roasted. Pinyon pines rarely grow taller than 30 feet. They are

Pinyon pine cones

usually found in open woodlands (often with juniper) at elevations under 8,000 feet.

Ponderosa Pine

Also called western yellow pine, the pinus ponderosa has long needles (5 to 11 inches) that grow in clusters of three from a single point. The bark of young trees is yellowish brown to cinnamon, while older trees develop orange, flaky bark. The spiky red-brown cones are about three to six inches long. Ponderosas can grow 60 to 130 feet tall and are usually found at altitudes of 6,000 to 8,500 feet.

Ponderosa pine cones

Ponderosa pine

Prickly Pear

This cactus has round pads with prickly spines, and it is covered with a thick layer of wax to prevent water evaporation. Its flowers may be red, purple, or yellow; the blooms appear from May to June and last only a few days. It has edible fruit, which is pear-shaped and spine-covered, with sweet flesh. It grows from 3 to 15 inches high.

Prickly pear

Rabbit Brush

Rabbit brush is an aromatic member of the sunflower family; the generic name means "golden bush." In the fall it becomes particularly conspicuous with its lovely golden colors. Rabbit brush ranges from two to six feet tall. The plant's branch ends have dense masses of yellow flower heads, which bloom from summer to fall. Stems are covered with hairy, cottonlike fibers, and leaves are linear. There are many subspecies of this plant, and since none have forage value, they tend to be common on overgrazed and overbrowsed ranges as the more palatable plants are overused and destroyed. Native Americans obtained a yellow dye from the flowers and a green dye from the inner bark. A tea is made from the leaves for easing the stomach. Rabbits use it for both food and as a favorite shelter.

Rabbit Brush

Rocky Mountain Maple, Dwarf Maple

This many-stemmed shrub grows in moist, deep soils of canyons and mountainsides at elevations between 5,000 to 10,500 feet. Its abundant leaves are typically maple-shaped with three lobes and coarsely toothed edges. Leaves are shiny green on top and paler green below, with reddish leaf stems. The seeds, called keys, are pairs of fruit with parchmentlike wings joining them together. When keys mature in the autumn, they drop from the tree to reforest their species. Leaves turn a pale yellow to orange red before they drop. Squirrels, chipmunks, and birds eat the seeds; moose, elk, and deer feed on the foliage.

Rocky Mountain maple

Sagebrush

Big sagebrush is the dominant shrub over vast areas of Utah, sometimes to the exclusion of almost all other plants. This aromatic shrub has a distinctive sagelike aroma and grows in arid basins, on mountain slopes, and overgrazed land—often with pinyons and junipers nearby. The evergreen leaves are gray green, hairy, and wedge-shaped, usually about three-quarters of an inch long. Flowering stems surpass the branches and contain numerous side branches bearing dense clusters of tiny, erect, spikelike, silvery green flowers. Height varies from two to seven feet. Sagebrush and culinary sage are not the same thing; sage used for seasoning is not obtained from these plants, but from members of the mint family. Sagebrush is a valuable and nutritious forage plant for wildlife, particularly during the winter and spring. It provides nesting habitats for sage grouse and various songbirds.

Sagebrush

Saltbush

Four-wing saltbush, also known as saltbrush, is a member of the goosefoot family. This shrubby bush ranges from two to five feet tall with small, gray green, densely branched stems. By the end of summer, its tiny yellow flowers produce conspicuous four-winged bracts, which are light green, papery, and distinctive. They become pale brown or nearly white when dry. The leaves are used as greens in salads or can be added to soups. The seeds can be ground and mixed with sugar and water to produce a drink called pinhole. Saltbush serves as an important food source for cattle, sheep, goats, deer, pronghorn, and rabbits, especially in the spring and winter when other forage is scarce. Some birds and animals also eat the seeds.

Saltbush

Shrubby Cinquefoil, Yellow Rose

These shrubs have yellow flowers that measure about one inch across, with five petals each. Cinquefoils keep their leaves in winter; big game animals eat them when food is scarce, although they don't enjoy the taste. Cinquefoils are found in open woods and meadows from June to August. Height ranges from one to three feet.

Shrubby cinquefoil

Subalpine Fir

Abies lasiocarpa is a spire-shaped tree found at elevations above 8,000 feet. They grow to 80 feet tall. The flat-shaped, blue green to dark green needles are less than one and a quarter inches long. The bark is smooth and chalky but furrowed and scaly on older trees. The purplish cones stand upright on the twigs and range from two and a quarter to four inches long.

Subalpine cones

Subalpine fir

Tamarisk, "Salt Cedar"

Often called "salt cedar" because the plant is fairly tolerant of saline soil and has foliage somewhat like that of junipers, tamarisk is found on riverbanks and moist sites in southeastern Utah. Classified as a shrub or moderate-size tree it has reddish bark, intricate feathery light green branches, and fragrant soft pink to nearly white blossoms in the spring. Dense thickets of tamarisk, a pioneer species, estab-

Tamarisk

lish themselves on surfaces devoid of other plants. Mature specimens produce millions of seeds annually, which are widely distributed by the wind. Tamarisk produce most of their seeds at the same time river levels drop from spring highs. Consequently, as rivers dwindle, they expose large areas of wet sand and silt, which are ideal seedbeds. Tamarisk were originally introduced from Eurasia in an effort to control soil erosion, but the plant has since escaped and now dominates water supplies needed for the survival of native plants and animals.

Winterfat

Winterfat is also called white sage, sweet sage, or winter sage, although it is not related to sage at all. The plant has many erect, woolly branches that arise from a woody base. It has flowering clusters that when gone to seed fluff out to look like

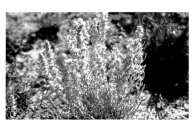
Winterfat

cottonballs. The plant has a fuzzy, white, and hairy appearance due to the densely woolly leaves that cover the entire plant. Leaves are dry in the fall but remain on the plant throughout winter. Winterfat serves as an important winter food source for wildlife and livestock.

Yucca

An agave, yuccas have a tall, dense cluster of creamy whitish or greenish globe-shaped flowers atop a stout, leafy stem. The numerous leaves grow from the base, up to two or three feet in length. Yuccas are members of the lily family and are pollinated by yucca moths. The moths cannot reproduce without yuccas; they lay eggs during pollination and their larvae feed upon the seeds. Yuccas grow in sandy, rocky places, in dry mesas, and on slopes. Native Americans ate the fruits, seeds, and flower buds—raw, roasted, or dried. They wove the fibrous leaves to make mats, sandals, baskets, and cloth.

Yucca

The Southeast Region

Trails in the Southeast Region

Central Region

GLEN CANYON
NATIONAL
RECREATION
AREA

MAP CONTINUES ON PAGE 106

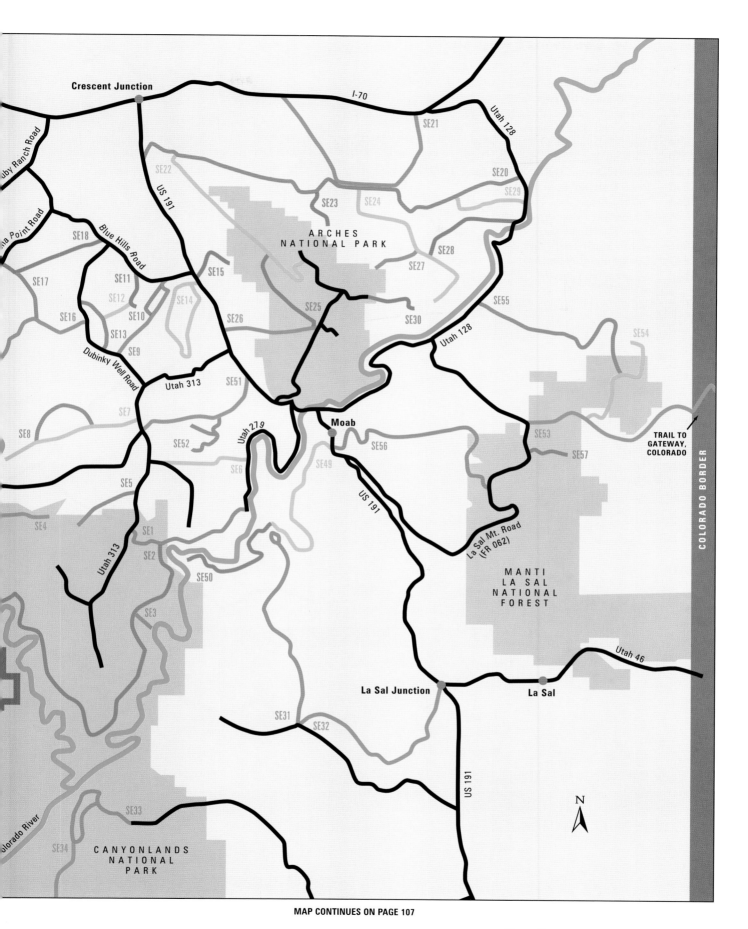

Crescent Junction

I-70

SE21

Utah 128

SE22

US 191

SE20

SE29

SE23

SE24

ARCHES
NATIONAL PARK

Ruby Ranch Road

SE18

Blue Hills Road

na Point Road

SE17

SE11

SE15

SE28

SE27

SE12

SE14

SE55

SE16

SE10

SE26

SE25

SE30

SE13

Dubinky Well Road

SE9

Utah 128

SE54

Utah 313

SE51

SE7

Utah 27.9

Moab

SE53

TRAIL TO
GATEWAY,
COLORADO

SE8

SE52

SE56

SE57

COLORADO BORDER

SE49

SE6

US 191

SE5

SE4

SE1

La Sal Mt. Road
(FR 062)

MANTI
LA SAL
NATIONAL
FOREST

SE2

Utah 313

SE50

SE3

Utah 46

La Sal Junction

La Sal

SE31

SE32

US 191

N

Colorado River

SE33

SE34

CANYONLANDS
NATIONAL
PARK

MAP CONTINUES ON PAGE 107

Trails in the Southeast Region

MAP CONTINUES ON PAGE 104

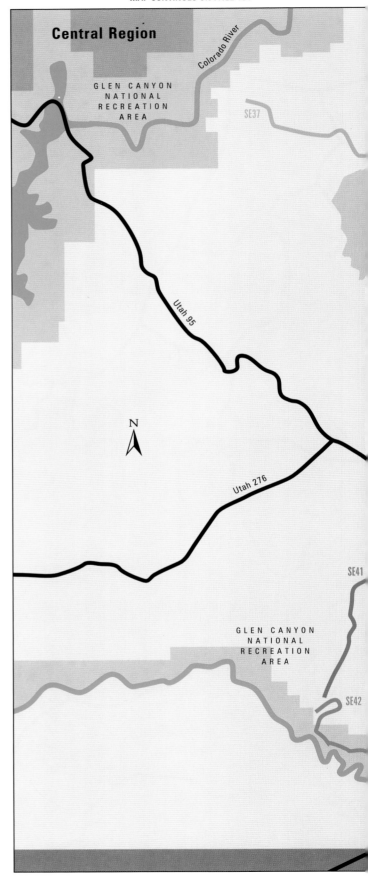

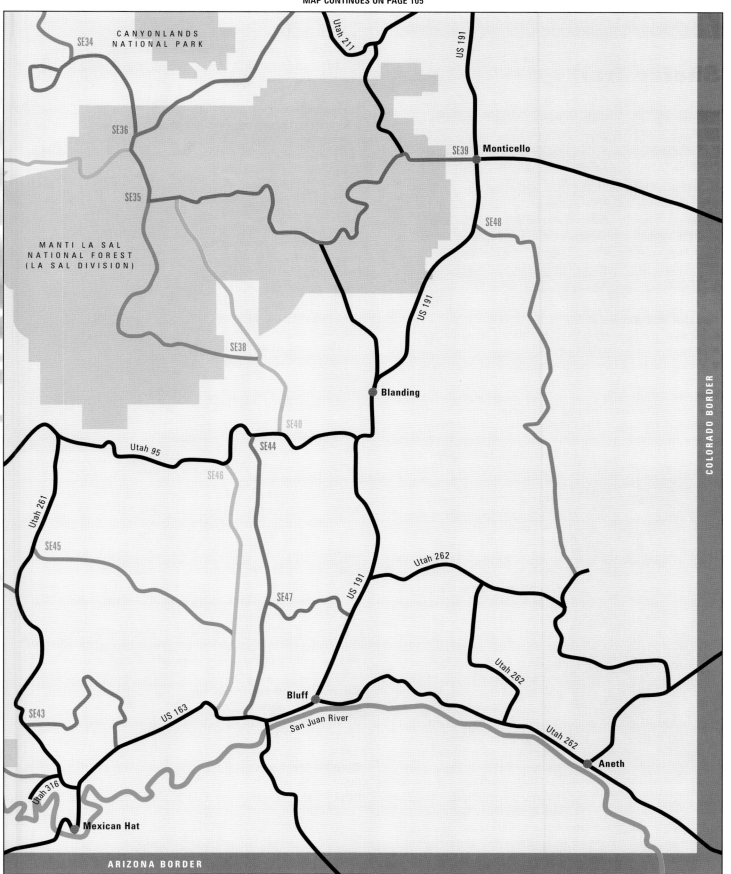

CANYONLANDS
NATIONAL PARK

SE34

SE36

SE35

MANTI LA SAL
NATIONAL FOREST
(LA SAL DIVISION)

SE38

Utah 211

US 191

SE39 **Monticello**

SE48

US 191

COLORADO BORDER

Blanding

SE40

Utah 95

SE44

SE46

Utah 261

SE45

SE47

US 191

Utah 262

Utah 262

Bluff

San Juan River

US 163

Utah 262

SE43

Utah 316

Aneth

Mexican Hat

Shafer Trail

Starting Point:	Island in the Sky Road (Utah 313) in Canyonlands National Park
Finishing Point:	Potash, at Utah 279
Total Mileage:	19 miles
Unpaved Mileage:	17 miles
Driving Time:	2 hours
Elevation Range:	3,900–5,900 feet
Usually Open:	Year-round
Difficulty Rating:	3
Scenic Rating:	10
Remoteness Rating:	+0

Special Attractions

- Island in the Sky region of Canyonlands National Park.
- Steep descent down tight switchbacks from rim.
- Views over the Colorado River and canyon country.

History

The Shafer Trail was named after Frank and John Shafer, ranchers in the area in 1914. Along with their family, they cut a steep stock trail into the cliffs of the canyon so they could

Looking down along the switchbacks of Shafer Trail

drive their cattle down from the top of the mesa to graze by the river in winter. In summer, cattle grazed on the mesa tops. In the 1950s during the uranium boom, the trail was widened to allow the ore trucks to drive to Moab, carrying ore from the uranium mines in Lathrop and Taylor Canyons.

Today, the Shafer Canyon area is often used by the movie industry. Many car commercials are filmed in the area, and the heroines in the movie *Thelma and Louise* took their famous final leap into Shafer Canyon from Fossil Point, now renamed Thelma and Louise Point.

At the base of the trail, there is an active potash mining operation. Utah is the nation's leading producer of phosphates, 95 percent of which are used in fertilizer. Solution mining replaced the more dangerous underground mining in 1972. The potash layer is leeched out in a salt solution and the resultant sludge is pumped to the surface into settling ponds, which can be seen beside the trail. The combined surface area of the ponds is over 400 acres. The vivid blue color of the ponds is actually a dye that is added to speed evaporation. As the water evaporates, the salt and potash remain. The by-product salt is not wasted; it is used for highway de-icing and industrial purposes.

Description

The ore trucks may be gone, but there is still plenty of traffic moving up and down the Shafer Trail. This incredible drive takes you from the Island in the Sky down to the potash works at the base of the trail in a very short time. The graded dirt road gradually descends as it leaves the canyon rim, wrapping back to the north, where it can be seen from the viewpoint opposite the visitor center. Almost immediately it turns into a shelf road, cut into the cliff on one side, with staggering drops on the other. It starts to switchback, and the grade increases, but it is still suitable for high-clearance vehicles with good tires in dry weather. The surface is mainly graded dirt, but because of its steepness, the trail does wash out. The lower end can be rough.

Top of Shafer Trail, looking down at the trail in the distance

There are a reasonable number of passing places for most of its length; remember that uphill vehicles have right of way.

After 4.3 miles, the switchbacks come to an end, and the trail undulates down to the potash works. The turnoff for Southeast #2: White Rim Trail is reached at 5.1 miles. The lower end of the trail follows the Colorado River for a short way, with views over the Goose Neck section. There are a couple of wide, sandy washes; look carefully for the trail leading out, as it is easy to miss.

From top to bottom, this trail offers magnificent views. The road may be closed at both the top and bottom in adverse weather, and the creeks may be impassable following heavy rain.

Current Road Information

Canyonlands National Park
Island Ranger District
(435) 259-4712

Map References

BLM La Sal, Moab
USGS 1:24,000 Musselman Arch, Shafer Basin, Gold Bar Canyon
1:100,000 La Sal, Moab
Maptech CD-ROM: Moab/Canyonlands
Trails Illustrated, #501; #210
Utah Atlas & Gazetteer, p. 30

SE #1: SHAFER TRAIL

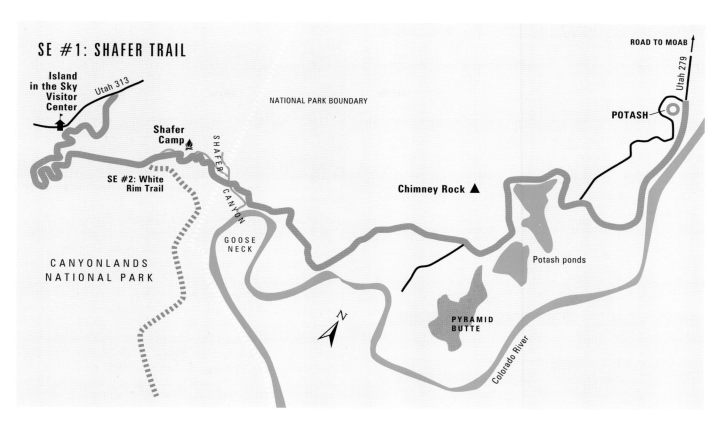

Utah Travel Council #5 (incomplete)
Other: Latitude 40—Moab West
      Canyon Country Off-Road Vehicle Trail Map—
      Island Area

Route Directions

▼ 0.0
Zero trip meter and turn south from Utah 313 onto the marked Shafer Trail.

    5.1 ▲
Trail ends at Utah 313. Turn right for Moab, left for the Island in the Sky Visitor Center.

GPS: N 38°28.29′ W 109°48.66′

▼ 0.1 SO
Park information board and trail closure gate. Trail descends along narrow shelf road with numerous switchbacks.

    5.0 ▲ SO
Park information board and trail closure gate.

▼ 4.3 SO
End of switchbacks.

    0.8 ▲ SO
Trail rises steeply and switchbacks along a narrow shelf road to the canyon rim.

▼ 5.1 TL
Trail closure gate, then sign, left for potash works, straight on for Southeast #2: White Rim Trail. Zero trip meter.

    0.0 ▲
Continue west on Shafer Trail.

GPS: N 38°27.57′ W 109°47.65′

▼ 0.0
Continue northeast on Shafer Trail.

    7.2 ▲ TR
Sign, left is Southeast #2: White Rim Trail, right is Island in the Sky Visitor Center. Trail closure gate. Zero trip meter at turn.

▼ 0.7 SO
Cross through creek.

    6.5 ▲ SO
Cross through creek.

▼ 1.0 SO
Shafer Camp on left, permit required.

    6.2 ▲ SO
Shafer Camp on right, permit required.

▼ 1.2 SO
Drop into creek bed.

    6.0 ▲ SO
Leave creek bed.

▼ 1.3 SO
Leave creek bed.

    5.9 ▲ SO
Drop into creek bed.

▼ 1.6 SO
Leave Canyonlands National Park, enter BLM land.

    5.6 ▲ SO
Leave BLM land, enter Canyonlands National Park. Fee area.

GPS: N 38°27.77′ W 109°46.19′

▼ 2.2 BR
View of Colorado River from rim. Do not follow creek bed; trail follows rim above the river.

    5.0 ▲ BL
Leaving Colorado River. Stay on graded track; do not follow creek bed.

▼ 2.4 SO
Goose Neck section of Colorado River, overlook on right.

    4.8 ▲ SO
Goose Neck section of Colorado River, overlook on left.

▼ 2.7 SO
Track on right.

    4.5 ▲ SO
Track on left.

▼ 4.2 SO
Colorado River viewpoint on right. Directly above is Dead Horse Point State Park, the far side of the river is Chicken Corners.

    3.0 ▲ SO
Colorado River viewpoint on left. Directly above is Dead Horse Point State Park, the far side of the river is Chicken Corners.

GPS: N 38°27.21′ W 109°43.94′

▼ 5.7 SO
Cross wash, track on right.

    1.5 ▲ SO
Track on left, cross wash.

▼ 5.8 SO
Track on left.

    1.4 ▲ SO
Track on right.

▼ 6.0 SO
Track on right, gate. Trail standard improves.

    1.2 ▲ SO
Trail becomes rougher at gate. Track on left.

▼ 6.6 SO
Chimney Rock on left, Pyramid Butte on right.

    0.6 ▲ SO
Chimney Rock on right, Pyramid Butte on left.

▼ 7.2 SO
Leave BLM lands through gate. Trail passes through private property, potash settling ponds on right. Zero trip meter.

    0.0 ▲
Continue into BLM land.

GPS: N 38°28.49' W 109°41.30'		
▼ 0.0		Continue toward potash works.
6.7 ▲	SO	Enter BLM lands through gate. Zero trip meter.
▼ 1.4	SO	Track on left.
5.3 ▲	SO	Track on right.
▼ 2.2	SO	Leave potash ponds.
4.5 ▲	SO	Potash settling ponds on the left.
▼ 3.1	SO	Stop sign, private roads right and left.
3.6 ▲	SO	Stop sign, private roads right and left.
▼ 3.2	BL	Numerous tracks on right and left. Remain on public road.
3.5 ▲	BR	Remain on public road.
▼ 5.2	SO	Boat launching area on Colorado River on right. Pavement begins.
1.5 ▲	SO	Pavement ends. Boat launching area on Colorado River on left. Numerous tracks on right and left, remain on public road.
▼ 6.7		Trail ends at the start of Utah 279. Continue straight on to Moab.
0.0 ▲		Trail begins at the potash works at end of Utah 279; sign reads, "Unimproved Road, next 10 miles." Zero trip meter and continue straight on.
GPS: N 38°31.43' W 109°39.20'		

The panoramic view from the hogback of White Rim Trail and Soda Springs Basin

SOUTHEAST REGION TRAIL #2

White Rim Trail

Starting Point:	**Canyonlands National Park, 5.1 miles along Southeast #1: Shafer Trail**
Finishing Point:	**Mineral Bottom**
Total Mileage:	**68.4 miles**
Unpaved Mileage:	**68.4 miles**
Driving Time:	**2 days**
Elevation Range:	**3,900–6,000 feet**
Usually Open:	**Year-round**
Difficulty Rating:	**4**
Scenic Rating:	**9**
Remoteness Rating:	**+1**

Special Attractions

■ Long two-day trail within Canyonlands National Park.
■ Access to hiking trails.
■ Wide variety of scenery and rock formations.

History

The White Rim came together as a trail using the network of uranium roads that were created during the boomtimes of the 1950s. It gained its name from the white sandstone rim that most of the trail follows.

Evidence of the region's earliest human inhabitants can be seen at Fort Bottom, accessed via a short hiking trail from the 4WD road. Moki Fort at the end of the hiking trail is an Anasazi rock structure dating back almost a millennium when the Anasazi farmed alongside the Colorado River.

Most of the later history of the trail relates to the ranchers and uranium miners, who pushed their way into the region and left their impressions of the territory in some of the names they gave to features along the trail. Hardscrabble Hill was the original rough, steep cow trail that wound its way down to Hardscrabble Bottom. The narrow shelf road is referred to as "Walker Cut," after Mark Walker who apparently blasted or cut the cow trail around the edge of the hill just after the turn of the 19th century. He also built a small cabin at Fort Bottom, often called "Outlaw Cabin," possibly because of the horse-thieving that happened in the region. (Just above Taylor Canyon is Horsethief Point.)

Musselman Arch, 3 miles into the trail, was named after Ross A. Musselman, who operated a rock shop and tour business in Moab. He also developed the Pack Creek Ranch, now a country inn, located 5 miles south of Moab. The arch was named by National Geographical Society writer Jack Breed in recognition of Musselman, who had assisted Breed in his research on the region.

Murphy Hogback was named after Otho, Jack, and Tom Murphy, the stockmen who built a trail over the ridge in the 1910s to facilitate the movement of cattle down to the White Rim.

The Murphys also named White Crack, where the present-day national park campsite is situated. Tom Murphy spotted a narrow "white crack" in the white sandstone, and in the 1910s the Murphys blasted a rough cow trail through the gap, opening up access to grazing areas in the south. In the 1950s it was widened with a bulldozer to work uranium mines down below. This trail is now closed to vehicle use.

Description

This extremely long trail can be completed in a single day, but that leaves no time to explore the side canyons or to appreciate the varied scenery. The trail is best completed over two days with an overnight camp. Campsites must be booked in advance with the National Park Service, and a backcountry permit is required. A special permit is not needed to drive the trail in one day, just the normal park entrance fee.

The White Rim Trail officially starts at the same point as Southeast #1: Shafer Trail. After descending the initial switchbacks into Shafer Basin, the White Rim Trail diverges and follows the edge of the Island in the Sky plateau to its southernmost point. You pass many points of interest along the way:

overlooks for the Colorado River Goose Neck, Musselman Arch (which is so large you can walk onto it), and views of Airport Butte and Washer Woman Arch (which, when seen side on, looks like a woman in a long skirt bending over a tub). You can see the turn for Southeast #3: Lathrop Canyon Trail, a spur trail leading to the Colorado River, as you proceed south around the rim. The trail then runs around the edge of Monument Basin, with its spurs, spires, and sandstone formations.

The western side of the trail is no less scenic. It passes through Soda Springs Basin and Holeman Spring Basin before dropping to travel above or alongside the Green River. The western side contains slightly more difficult sections of trail.

For the most part, the trail surface is a mix of broken rock and dirt. The trail is graded, but there are washouts and some moderately difficult sections over slickrock and loose broken rock. On the western side of the trail, there are some steep climbs and short sections of shelf road as the trail climbs around the rim and down along the Green River. Some of the surface is loose, but the trail is well within the capabilities of a high-clearance SUV. For the most part, the trail follows the White Rim, often running very close to the steep drop from the plateau. The entire trail has views to keep you glued to the window, but it's better still to get out frequently to peer into the canyons or to hike a tantalizing rise. The trail is nearly 70 miles of 4WD road, and from the end there are still 38 miles of dirt road and paved highway back to Moab.

The national park campsites are spread fairly evenly around the trail, roughly 10 miles apart. Sites are numbered, and visitors are required to select their campsite in advance. Perhaps the most popular is White Crack, which is roughly halfway around the trail. However, most of the sites are exposed, with little shade or shelter from the winds, which can spring up from nowhere. Some of the sites along the Green River have some shade. The visitor center at the Island in the Sky has photos of many of the campsites to help you choose, but be aware that at popular times of the year, typically late spring through early fall, you must book your site at least several weeks in advance. All of the campsites have pit toilets. To us, the best campsites are Murphy Campsite A (for its great view) and Potato Bottom Campsite A (for the cottonwoods and river).

The trail is open year-round, but snow or heavy rain can

temporarily close the trail. Information on trail conditions can be obtained from the Information Center in Moab or from the Island in the Sky Visitor Center. In particular, the exit from the trail up the Mineral Bottom Road switchbacks and along the dirt road out to Utah 313 can become impassable after rain. The trail is also popular with mountain bikers, who typically take three to four days to complete it.

Current Road Information
Canyonlands National Park
Island Ranger District
(435) 259-4712

Map References
BLM   La Sal, Hanksville, San Rafael Desert, Moab
USGS 1:24,000 Musselman Arch, Monument Basin, Turks Head, Upheaval Dome, Horsethief Canyon, Bowknot Bend, Mineral Canyon, The Knoll 1:100,000 La Sal, Hanksville, San Rafael Desert, Moab
Maptech CD-ROM: Moab/Canyonlands; Central/San Rafael
Trails Illustrated, #501; #210
Utah Atlas & Gazetteer, p. 30
Utah Travel Council #5
Other: Latitude 40—Moab West
Canyon Country Off-Road Vehicle Trail Map—Island Area

Route Directions

▼ 0.0		After descending switchbacks on Southeast #1: Shafer Trail for 5.1 miles, zero trip meter and proceed east along White Rim Trail.
10.8 ▲		End at intersection with Southeast #1: Shafer Trail. Right goes to potash works. Left travels 5.1 miles up switchbacks to Utah 313.
GPS: N 38°27.57' W 109°47.65'		
▼ 1.2	SO	Goose Neck Trail on left, 0.5-mile hike to Colorado River viewpoint.
9.6 ▲	SO	Goose Neck Trail on right, 0.5-mile hike to Colorado River viewpoint.
GPS: N 38°27.30' W 109°46.41'		
▼ 2.9	TR	Colorado River Overlook is straight on.
7.9 ▲	TL	Colorado River Overlook is to the right.
GPS: N 38°26.28' W 109°45.97'		
▼ 3.1	SO	Musselman Arch on left.
7.7 ▲	SO	Musselman Arch on right.
GPS: N 38°26.20' W 109°46.16'		
▼ 4.3	SO	Cross through wash. Musselman Canyon is on the left.
6.5 ▲	.SO	Musselman Canyon is on the right; cross through wash.
GPS: N 38°25.84' W 109°47.11'		
▼ 10.7	SO	Lathrop hiking trail is on the right.
0.1 ▲	SO	Lathrop hiking trail is on the left.
GPS: N 38°24.09' W 109°47.59'		
▼ 10.8	SO	Track on left is Southeast #3: Lathrop Canyon Trail to the Colorado River. Zero trip meter.
0.0 ▲		Continue around the White Rim.
GPS: N 38°24.02' W 109°47.62'		
▼ 0.0		Continue around the White Rim.
10.9 ▲	SO	Track on right is Southeast #3: Lathrop Canyon Trail to the Colorado River. Zero trip meter.

Monument Basin falls off to the side of White Rim Trail

SE #2: WHITE RIM TRAIL

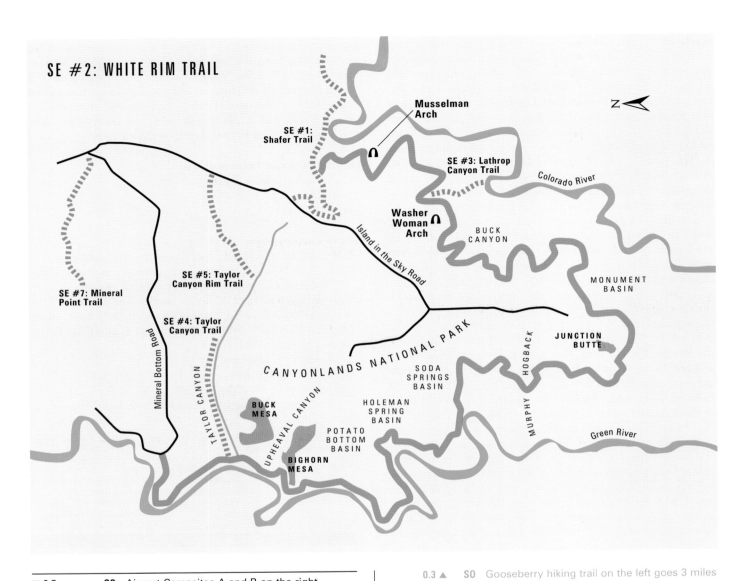

▼ 0.7	SO	Airport Campsites A and B on the right.	
10.2 ▲	SO	Airport Campsites A and B on the left.	
GPS: N 38°23.45' W 109°47.53'			
▼ 1.2	SO	Airport Campsites C and D on the right.	
9.7 ▲	SO	Airport Campsites C and D on the left.	
GPS: N 38°23.23' W 109°47.93'			
▼ 1.3	SO	Washer Woman Arch can be seen to the west.	
9.6 ▲	SO	Washer Woman Arch can be seen to the west.	
▼ 4.8	SO	Cross through wash at head of Buck Canyon.	
6.1 ▲	SO	Cross through wash at head of Buck Canyon.	
GPS: N 38°22.85' W 109°50.09'			
▼ 5.4	SO	Cross through wash.	
5.5 ▲	SO	Cross through wash.	
▼ 6.7	SO	Cross through wash.	
4.2 ▲	SO	Cross through wash.	
▼ 7.7	SO	Cross through wash on rock ledge; great views into Buck Canyon.	
3.2 ▲	SO	Cross through wash on rock ledge; great views into Buck Canyon.	
GPS: N 38°21.08' W 109°50.31'			
▼ 8.3	SO	Cross through wash.	
2.6 ▲	SO	Cross through wash.	
▼ 10.6	SO	Gooseberry hiking trail on the right goes 3 miles to the top of the rim.	

0.3 ▲	SO	Gooseberry hiking trail on the left goes 3 miles to the top of the rim.	
GPS: N 38°20.14' W 109°49.66'			
▼ 10.7	SO	Cross through rocky wash. Care needed to avoid scraping undercarriage.	
0.2 ▲	SO	Cross through rocky wash. Care needed to avoid scraping undercarriage.	
▼ 10.8	SO	Cross through wash, followed by Gooseberry Campsite A on the left.	
0.1 ▲	SO	Gooseberry Campsite A on the right, then cross through wash.	
▼ 10.9	SO	Track on right goes to Gooseberry Campsite B. Zero trip meter.	
0.0 ▲		Continue around the White Rim.	
GPS: N 38°19.80' W 109°49.59'			
▼ 0.0		Continue along the White Rim.	
7.7 ▲	SO	Track on left goes to Gooseberry Campsite B. Zero trip meter.	
▼ 0.4	SO	Cross through wash.	
7.3 ▲	SO	Cross through wash.	
▼ 3.6	SO	Edge of Monument Basin.	
4.1 ▲	SO	Leaving Monument Basin.	
▼ 4.4	SO	Cross through wash.	
3.3 ▲	SO	Cross through wash.	
▼ 4.7	SO	Cross through wash.	

3.0 ▲	SO	Cross through wash.
▼ 5.2	SO	Cross through wash.
2.5 ▲	SO	Cross through wash.
▼ 5.9	SO	Cross through wash.
1.8 ▲	SO	Cross through wash.
▼ 7.7	BR	Leaving Monument Basin. White Crack Campground on left. Zero trip meter.
0.0 ▲		Continue around the White Rim. Edge of Monument Basin.

GPS: N 38°16.46′ W 109°51.75′

▼ 0.0		Continue around the White Rim.
7.3 ▲	SO	White Crack Campground on right. Zero trip meter.
▼ 1.1	SO	Cross through wash many times in the next 5.1 miles.
6.2 ▲	SO	Cross through wash, end of wash crossings.
▼ 6.2	SO	Murphy hiking trail on right. End of wash crossings.
1.1 ▲	SO	Murphy hiking trail on left. Cross through wash many times in the next 5.1 miles.

GPS: N 38°19.15′ W 109°53.61′

▼ 6.9	SO	Start of narrow shelf road climbing to Murphy Hogback.
0.4 ▲	SO	End of descent from Murphy Hogback.
▼ 7.3	SO	Top of Murphy Hogback. Murphy Campsite A on left. Zero trip meter.
0.0 ▲		Continue around White Rim.

GPS: N 38°19.31′ W 109°54.36′

▼ 0.0		Continue around White Rim.
9.9 ▲	SO	Murphy Campsite A on right. Zero trip meter.
▼ 0.1	SO	Murphy Campsite B on right, then Murphy hiking trail on right.
9.8 ▲	SO	Murphy hiking trail on left, then Murphy Campsite B on left.

GPS: N 38°19.40′ W 109°54.40′

▼ 0.2	SO	Murphy Campsite C on left. Trail descends from Murphy Hogback into Soda Springs Basin with views to Candlestick Tower.
9.7 ▲	SO	Murphy Campsite C on right. Top of Murphy Hogback.
▼ 2.7	SO	Cross through wash. Many wash crossings in the next 10.5 miles as trail passes through Soda Springs Basin, then Holeman Spring Basin.
7.2 ▲	SO	Cross through wash.
▼ 9.9	SO	Boundary Campsite on right. Zero trip meter.
0.0 ▲		Continue around White Rim.

GPS: N 38°22.46′ W 109°57.87′

▼ 0.0		Continue along White Rim.
9.7 ▲	SO	Boundary Campsite on left. Zero trip meter.
▼ 3.3	SO	Cross through wash.
6.4 ▲	SO	Cross through wash. Many wash crossings in the next 10.5 miles as trail passes through Holeman Spring Basin, then Soda Springs Basin.
▼ 8.1	SO	Cross through wash. Trail runs close to Green River.
1.6 ▲	SO	Cross through wash.
▼ 9.0	SO	Cross through wash.
0.7 ▲	SO	Cross through wash.
▼ 9.3	SO	Cross through wash.
0.4 ▲	SO	Cross through wash.
▼ 9.7	SO	Potato Bottom Campsite A on left beside river. Zero trip meter.
0.0 ▲		Continue around White Rim.

GPS: N 38°25.30′ W 110°00.19′

▼ 0.0		Continue around White Rim.
4.1 ▲	SO	Potato Bottom Campsite A on right beside river. Zero trip meter.
▼ 0.6	SO	Potato Bottom Campsite B on left.
3.5 ▲	SO	Potato Bottom Campsite B on right.
▼ 0.7	SO	Potato Bottom Campsite C on left.
3.4 ▲	SO	Potato Bottom Campsite C on right.

GPS: N 38°25.84′ W 110°00.53′

▼ 0.9	SO	Cross through wash.
3.2 ▲	SO	Cross through wash.
▼ 1.7	SO	Start of narrow shelf road.
2.4 ▲	SO	Shelf road ends.
▼ 2.5	SO	Hiking trail on left goes to Fort Bottom. Views ahead to Hardscrabble Bottom.
1.6 ▲	SO	Hiking trail on right goes to Fort Bottom.

GPS: N 38°26.65′ W 110°01.02′

▼ 4.1	BR	End of shelf road, then track on left goes to Hardscrabble Bottom Campsite. Zero trip meter.
0.0 ▲		Continue along White Rim Trail.

GPS: N 38°27.20′ W 110°00.45′

▼ 0.0		Continue along White Rim Trail.
1.9 ▲	BL	Track on right goes to Hardscrabble Bottom Campsite. Start of narrow shelf road. Zero trip meter.
▼ 0.7	SO	Views ahead into Upheaval Bottom.
1.2 ▲	SO	Views ahead into Hardscrabble Bottom.
▼ 1.3	SO	Upheaval Dome Loop hiking trail on right, then cross through wash.
0.6 ▲	SO	Upheaval Dome Loop hiking trail on left, then cross through wash.

GPS: N 38°28.06′ W 109°59.90′

▼ 1.4	SO	Cross through wash.
0.5 ▲	SO	Cross through wash.
▼ 1.9	SO	Track on right is Southeast #4: Taylor Canyon Trail. Zero trip meter.
0.0 ▲		Continue along White Rim Trail.

GPS: N 38°28.52′ W 109°59.87′

▼ 0.0		Continue along White Rim Trail.
2.4 ▲	SO	Track on left is Southeast #4: Taylor Canyon Trail. Zero trip meter.
▼ 0.1	SO	Labyrinth Campsite B on left.
2.3 ▲	SO	Labyrinth Campsite B on right.
▼ 0.2	SO	Track on left goes to Labyrinth Campsite A.
2.2 ▲	SO	Track on right goes to Labyrinth Campsite A.

GPS: N 38°28.48′ W 110°00.01′

▼ 0.3	SO	Start of narrow shelf road.
2.1 ▲	SO	End of shelf road.
▼ 0.4	SO	End of shelf road.
2.0 ▲	SO	Start of narrow shelf road.
▼ 1.8	SO	Small corral in rock alcove on right.
0.6 ▲	SO	Small corral in rock alcove on left.
▼ 2.2	SO	Cross through wash.
0.2 ▲	SO	Cross through wash.
▼ 2.4	SO	Cattle guard. Leaving Canyonlands National Park. Zero trip meter.
0.0 ▲		Continue into national park.

GPS: N 38°30.01′ W 110°01.43′

▼ 0.0		Continue out of national park.
3.7 ▲	SO	Cattle guard. Entering Canyonlands National Park. Zero trip meter.
▼ 2.7	SO	Cattle guard.
1.0 ▲	SO	Cattle guard.
▼ 3.7		Trail ends at the intersection with Mineral Bottom Road. Turn left for spur trail to Mineral

Bottom, turn right for Utah 313 and Moab.

0.0 ▲ Trail starts at the intersection with the Mineral Bottom Road and the White Rim Trail. Turn west at the sign for Canyonlands National Park and zero trip meter.

GPS: N 38°31.03′ W 110°00.25′

SOUTHEAST REGION TRAIL #3

Lathrop Canyon Trail

Starting Point:	**Southeast #2: White Rim Trail**
Finishing Point:	**Colorado River**
Total Mileage:	**3.5 miles**
Unpaved Mileage:	**3.5 miles**
Driving Time:	**45 minutes (one-way)**
Elevation Range:	**3,900–4,400 feet**
Usually Open:	**Year-round**
Difficulty Rating:	**4**
Scenic Rating:	**8**
Remoteness Rating:	**+1**

Special Attractions

■ Sandy spur trail off the Southeast #2: White Rim Trail.
■ Access to the Colorado River.
■ Shady riverside picnicking.

History

Howard Lathrop, a sheepman from Colorado, built a trail from the canyon rim to the Colorado River in the 1940s. Today's trail was cut through in the early 1950s to gain river access in order to supply water for the uranium mine higher up in Lathrop Canyon, above the White Rim Trail. Today, the river access is used by river operators as a pickup point.

Description

This short spur trail drops 500 feet down Lathrop Canyon to finish at the Colorado River. It is the only place on the eastern side of Southeast #2: White Rim Trail where it is possible to

A tight fit beneath a tree along a detour of the Lathrop Canyon Trail

get down to the river, and if you have only a limited amount of time, driving the eastern side of the White Rim Trail, including the Shafer Trail switchbacks, as far as Lathrop Canyon makes a pleasant and popular day trip. This trek allows sufficient time to view the Goose Neck and Musselman Arch as well as have a riverside picnic in one day.

Any 4WD vehicle capable of accessing the top of the trail via

The Colorado River winds slowly past the end of Lathrop Canyon Trail

the White Rim will have no trouble negotiating the Lathrop Canyon Trail. The major difficulty on the trail is the loose, deep sand at the lower end of the canyon. There are a couple of large ledges that may be difficult to climb back up, but the worst one has a detour around the wash that avoids it. Tall vehicles will find the detour a problem though, as a tree limb hangs down far enough that it may catch a high roofline or roof rack.

The trail ends at a clearing in the tamarisks alongside the Colorado River. There are picnic tables in the shade and a pit toilet. You can see the river through a gap in the tamarisks. The site is for day use only; no camping is allowed.

Current Road Information

Canyonlands National Park
Island Ranger District
(435) 259-4712

Map References

BLM La Sal
USGS 1:24,000 Musselman Arch, Monument Basin
1:100,000 La Sal
Maptech CD-ROM: Moab/Canyonlands
Trails Illustrated, #501; #210
Utah Atlas & Gazetteer, p. 30
Utah Travel Council #5
Other: Latitude 40—Moab West

Route Directions

▼ 0.0 10.8 miles along Southeast #2: White Rim Trail from the junction with Southeast #1: Shafer Trail, turn southeast at the sign for Lathrop Canyon and zero trip meter. Trail immediately drops steeply.

GPS: N 38°24.02′ W 109°47.62′

▼ 0.2 SO Cross through wash. Trail follows wash and drops into tight canyon. There are many wash crossings to the end of the trail.

▼ 3.3 SO Picnic table on left underneath large cottonwoods.

GPS: N 38°22.28′ W 109°46.44′

▼ 3.4 SO Steep, soft sand as trail drops in and out of

SE #3: LATHROP CANYON TRAIL

Colorado River

LATHROP CANYON

SE #2: White Rim Trail

wash. A couple of ledges to watch. The trail forks a couple of times with the fork following the wash. These are alternate routes that rejoin the trail before the end.

▼ 3.5 Trail ends at clearing beside the Colorado River with three picnic tables and river access.

GPS: N 38°22.17' W 109°46.37'

SOUTHEAST REGION TRAIL #4

Taylor Canyon Trail

Starting Point:	**Southeast #2: White Rim Trail**
Finishing Point:	**Trailhead to Moses Rock and Taylor Canyon**
Total Mileage:	**4.8 miles**
Unpaved Mileage:	**4.8 miles**
Driving Time:	**30 minutes (one-way)**
Elevation Range:	**4,000–4,400 feet**
Usually Open:	**Year-round**
Difficulty Rating:	**2**
Scenic Rating:	**9**
Remoteness Rating:	**+1**

Special Attractions

- Interesting spur trail to complement Southeast #2: White Rim Trail.
- Moses and Zeus rocks.
- Access to hiking trails up Taylor Canyon.

History

Taylor Canyon is named after a prominent early cattleman in the area, Arth Taylor. Taylor arrived in Moab in the late 1800s and ran both cattle and sheep, whichever was the most profitable at the time. The Taylor family members were entrepreneurs who had several ventures over the years in and around Moab, including operating a rowboat ferry on the Colorado River, managing the first general store in Moab, and winning a contract for putting through the grade for the Denver & Rio Grande Railroad for part of the stretch between Grand Junction and Green River.

In the 1920s, Taylor Canyon was a good place to try to catch a burro. A prospector named Turner came here and then moved on, but he left his burros behind.

Description

This short spur trail from Southeast #2: White Rim Trail gives access to the Moses hiking trail and to trails up Taylor Canyon.

The Moses and Zeus rocks stand above the end of Taylor Canyon Trail

The Moses and Zeus rocks, large Entrada sandstone formations that are supposed to resemble stooping figures of the prophet and the god, are prominent at the end of the trail, high on the cliff to the north.

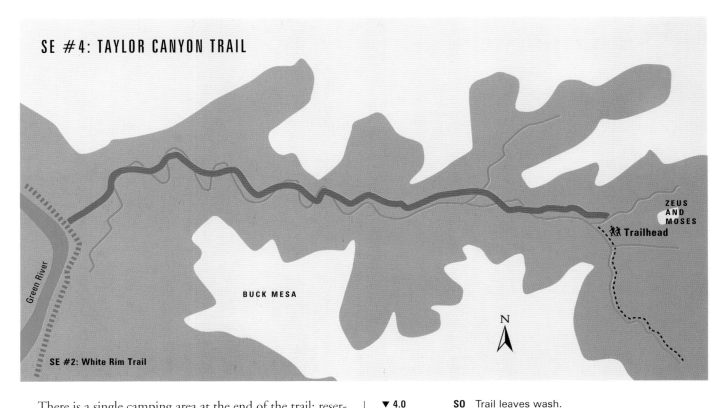

There is a single camping area at the end of the trail; reservations are required with the National Park Service.

The trail is generally easy as it follows along the wash in Taylor Canyon. It crosses the wash numerous times in the first 4 miles, at times running along the sandy wash. The trail has no real changes in gradient, and the wash bottom is firm. The trail is slightly sandy in dry weather.

Current Road Information
Canyonlands National Park
Island Ranger District
(435) 259-4712

Map References
BLM   La Sal (incomplete)
USGS 1:24,000 Upheaval Dome
          1:100,000 La Sal (incomplete)
Maptech CD-ROM: Moab/Canyonlands
Trails Illustrated, #210
Utah Atlas & Gazetteer, p. 30
Utah Travel Council #5
Other: Latitude 40—Moab West
       Canyon Country Off-Road Vehicle Trail Map—
       Island Area

Route Directions

▼ 0.0   From Southeast #2: White Rim Trail, close to the Labyrinth Campsites, turn east on the Taylor Canyon Trail at the sign and zero trip meter.

GPS: N 38°28.53' W 109°59.86'

▼ 0.5   SO   Trail enters wash. Many wash crossings or sections within the wash in the next 3.5 miles.

▼ 4.0   SO   Trail leaves wash.
▼ 4.6   SO   Taylor Campsite on right.

GPS: N 38°28.58' W 109°55.35'

▼ 4.8   Trail ends at trailhead for Moses hiking trail. Moses and Zeus rocks are ahead to the east.

GPS: N 38°28.57' W 109°55.20'

SOUTHEAST REGION TRAIL #5

Taylor Canyon Rim Trail

Starting Point:	**Island in the Sky Road (Utah 313)**
Finishing Point:	**Taylor Canyon Rim**
Total Mileage:	**4.8 miles**
Unpaved Mileage:	**4.8 miles**
Driving Time:	**45 minutes (one-way)**
Elevation Range:	**5,200–6,000 feet**
Usually Open:	**Year-round**
Difficulty Rating:	**3**
Scenic Rating:	**8**
Remoteness Rating:	**+0**

Special Attractions
- Beehive Butte and Whitbeck Rock.
- Short, easy hiking trail to rewarding viewpoint.
- Views over the Island in the Sky area of Canyonlands National Park.

Description

This short spur trail leads to a Taylor Canyon overlook in the Island in the Sky district of Canyonlands National Park. The trail starts at Island in the Sky Road, 2.4 miles south of Dead Horse Point Road. The trail, which is not signposted, leads to the south toward the large dome of Whitbeck Rock. To the right is prominent Beehive Butte, a large dome standing by itself on the plateau. The trail runs along a very loose, sandy plateau, on the western edge of Whitbeck Rock, and then gradually descends to run along an old seismic line toward the canyon rim. The drop down is very loose and sandy, with some deep sections of powder-fine sand. Vehicle marks show where vehicles have slid to the edge, unable to turn the corner in the sand. This section is more difficult in very dry weather. As the trail descends, you start to get views of the Island in the Sky district. On a clear day it is possible to see as far as the Henry Mountains to the west. The trail passes an unnamed butte and continues to the park boundary. Vehicle access stops at this point. Leave your vehicle and hike the 1.3 miles to the rim of Taylor Canyon. The viewpoint from the end is very rewarding—including Taylor, Rough, and Trail Canyons. You can see the wash and the remains of old vehicle tracks far below, the Green River Canyon to the right, and Upheaval Dome ahead. For those not wishing to hike as far, there is a nice viewpoint 0.4 miles from the end of the vehicle trail, looking east over Taylor and Rough Canyons.

This track provides access to some very quiet, little-used backcountry campsites. The best sites are after the drop-off to the point where juniper and pinyon trees provide some shade. The hardest part of the trail is the soft sand, although there are some deep washouts near the beginning. The soft sand makes this a brutal ride for mountain bikers.

Beehive Butte as seen from the trail

Current Road Information

BLM Moab Field Office
82 East Dogwood
Moab, UT 84532
(435) 259-2100

Map References

BLM Moab, La Sal
USGS 1:24,000 The Knoll, Musselman Arch, Upheaval Dome
  1:100,000 Moab, La Sal
Maptech CD-ROM: Moab/Canyonlands
Trails Illustrated, #501; #210

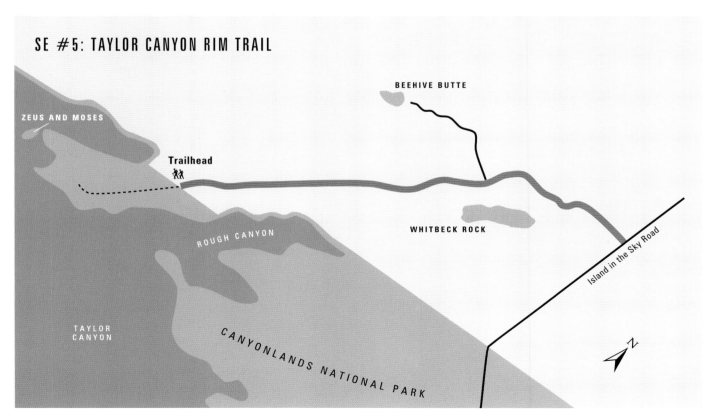

SE #5: TAYLOR CANYON RIM TRAIL

BEEHIVE BUTTE

ZEUS AND MOSES

Trailhead

ROUGH CANYON

WHITBECK ROCK

Island in the Sky Road

TAYLOR CANYON

CANYONLANDS NATIONAL PARK

Utah Atlas & Gazetteer, p. 30
Utah Travel Council #5
Other: Latitude 40—Moab West
　　　Canyon Country Off-Road Vehicle Trail Map—
　　　Island Area

Looking up the switchbacks of Long Canyon Trail

Route Directions

▼ 0.0		From the Island in the Sky Road, 2.4 miles south of Dead Horse Point Road, turn west on unmarked, ungraded sandy trail and zero trip meter.
	GPS: N 38°31.00′ W 109°48.02′	
▼ 0.4	BL	Track on right.
▼ 1.0	BL	Track on right goes to Beehive Butte. Whitbeck Rock is on the left.
	GPS: N 38°30.89′ W 109°49.17′	
▼ 1.1	SO	Track on left.
▼ 1.6	BL	Track on right.
▼ 2.0	BL	Track on right.
▼ 2.1	SO	Track on right rejoins. Trail descends.
▼ 2.2	SO	Two tracks on left and track on right. Second track on left goes to campsite with good views.
	GPS: N 38°30.33′ W 109°50.28′	
▼ 2.8	SO	Faint track on right opposite unnamed butte.
	GPS: N 38°30.12′ W 109°50.67′	
▼ 3.1	SO	Track on right before slickrock area and track on left. Keep going to the southwest.
▼ 3.4	SO	Track on left.
▼ 3.8	SO	Faint track on left.
▼ 4.8		Trail ends for vehicles at the boundary of Canyonlands National Park. Hike along the old vehicle trail 1.3 miles to Taylor Canyon Rim.
	GPS: N 38°28.98′ W 109°52.58′	

SOUTHEAST REGION TRAIL #6

Long Canyon Trail

Starting Point:	**Dead Horse Point Road (Utah 313)**
Finishing Point:	**Potash Road (Utah 279) at Jug Handle Arch**
Total Mileage:	**7.2 miles**
Unpaved Mileage:	**7.2 miles**
Driving Time:	**45 minutes**
Elevation Range:	**3,900–6,100 feet**
Usually Open:	**Year-round**
Difficulty Rating:	**3**
Scenic Rating:	**9**
Remoteness Rating:	**+0**

Special Attractions

■ Steep, narrow trail in tight red sandstone canyon.
■ Jug Handle Arch.
■ Views east to the La Sal Mountains and down into Long Canyon.

Description

The Long Canyon Trail (or as it is more popularly called, Pucker Pass) makes an exciting alternative way back to Moab from the Island in the Sky district. It was named Pucker Pass by some imaginative Jeepers back in the days when a drive down the canyon was a lot more hair-raising than it is now. The trail leaves Dead Horse Point Road and travels in a plumb line across Big Flat until it reaches the top of Long Canyon. From here it drops steeply down into the extremely narrow, sandstone-walled canyon.

After 3.3 miles, the trail goes underneath a huge slab of sandstone that fell down from the cliff face. The huge block has remained tilted at a precarious angle over the trail, luckily allowing vehicles to pass easily underneath. From here, the canyon opens up a bit, but it still switchbacks steeply down before joining Long Canyon Creek. For the last few miles, the trail crosses Long Creek several times before finishing on Potash Road (Utah 279) in the Jug Handle Arch parking area. True to its name, this unusual arch bends out from the cliff exactly like the jug handle. The area of cliffs bordering Potash Road is popular with rock climbers, and it is not unusual to see several groups swaying precariously from the cliff face.

A large, fallen rock creates a natural tunnel along the trail

The surface along this trail is generally pretty smooth. There are a few lumpy sections on the switchbacks, but normally nothing to catch an unwary undercarriage. There is a long section of narrow shelf road running down the canyon that's wide enough for a single vehicle, and it has a sufficient number of passing places.

The trail is normally open year-round, but heavy rains or

SE #6: LONG CANYON TRAIL

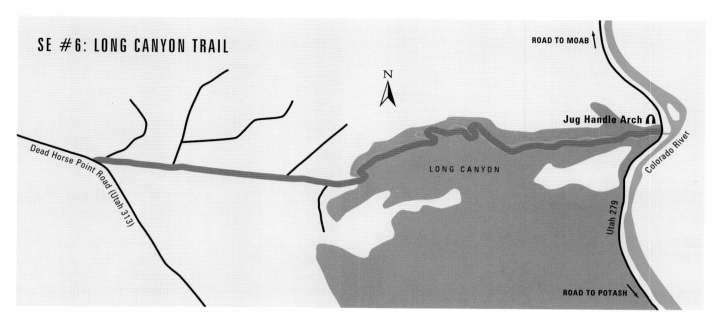

snow can make it impassable. Snow remains for a long time in the narrow canyon, which sees little sunlight in winter, and can become dangerously icy. Given the long drop if you slip, this is one trail to avoid in the snow. Camping is restricted in the upper canyon to protect the bighorn sheep habitat.

Current Road Information
BLM Moab Field Office
82 East Dogwood
Moab, UT 84532
(435) 259-2100

Map References
BLM Moab
USGS 1:24,000 Gold Bar Canyon, The Knoll
  1:100,000 Moab
Maptech CD-ROM: Moab/Canyonlands
Trails Illustrated, #501; #210
Utah Atlas & Gazetteer, p. 30
Utah Travel Council #5
Other: Latitude 40—Moab West
  Canyon Country Off-Road Vehicle Trail Map—
  Island Area

Route Directions

▼ 0.0			From Dead Horse Point Road (Utah 313), 1.5 miles from the junction with the Island in the Sky Road, turn east on the unmarked Long Canyon Road and zero trip meter.
	3.3 ▲		Trail finishes on Dead Horse Point Road, 1.5 miles from the junction with the Island in the Sky Road. Turn left to visit Dead Horse Point, turn right for the Island in the Sky and Moab.
GPS: N 38°32.71′ W 109°45.82′			
▼ 0.1		SO	Track on left.
	3.2 ▲	SO	Track on right.
▼ 0.5		SO	Track on right.
	2.8 ▲	SO	Track on left.
▼ 0.9		SO	Track on left.

	2.4 ▲	SO	Track on right.
GPS: N 38°32.62′ W 109°44.73′			
▼ 1.8		SO	Track on left.
	1.5 ▲	SO	Track on right.
▼ 2.0		SO	Track on left.
	1.3 ▲	SO	Track on right.
▼ 2.4		SO	Track on left.
	0.9 ▲	SO	Track on right.
▼ 2.5		SO	Track on right.
	0.8 ▲	SO	Track on left.
▼ 2.8		SO	Long Canyon on the right.
	0.5 ▲	SO	Leaving Long Canyon.
▼ 2.9		SO	Track on right. Trail starts to switchback down into Long Canyon.
	0.4 ▲	SO	Track on left. End of climb up Long Canyon.
GPS: N 38°32.50′ W 109°42.41′			
▼ 3.3		SO	Trail passes underneath huge fallen boulder tilted over the trail. Zero trip meter.
	0.0 ▲		Continue to climb up Long Canyon.
GPS: N 38°32.62′ W 109°42.36′			
▼ 0.0			Continue down Long Canyon.
	3.9 ▲	SO	Trail passes underneath huge fallen boulder tilted over the trail. Zero trip meter.
▼ 1.7		SO	Cross through wash.
	2.2 ▲	SO	Cross through wash.
▼ 1.8		SO	Cross through wash. End of descent.
	2.1 ▲	SO	Cross through wash. Start of climb.
▼ 2.1		SO	Cross over wash and track on right.
	1.8 ▲	SO	Cross over wash and track on left.
▼ 2.4		SO	Cross through Long Creek Wash.
	1.5 ▲	SO	Cross through Long Creek Wash.
▼ 2.7		SO	Cross through Long Creek Wash.
	1.2 ▲	SO	Cross through Long Creek Wash.
▼ 2.8		SO	Camping permitted past this point.
	1.1 ▲	SO	No camping past this point.
GPS: N 38°32.73′ W 109°40.12′			
▼ 3.0		SO	Cross over Long Creek.
	0.9 ▲	SO	Cross over Long Creek.
▼ 3.1		SO	Cross over Long Creek.
	0.8 ▲	SO	Cross over Long Creek.

▼ 3.5	SO	Track on left.
0.4 ▲	SO	Track on right.
▼ 3.8	SO	Trail enters the Jug Handle Arch parking area. The Jug Handle Arch is on the left.
0.1 ▲	SO	The Jug Handle Arch is on the right. Trail leaves out the back of the parking area.
▼ 3.9		Cross over railroad tracks, then trail finishes at Potash Road (Utah 279). Turn left to join US 191.
0.0 ▲		On Potash Road (Utah 279), 12.7 miles from US 191, turn into the Jug Handle parking area, cross railroad tracks and zero trip meter. There is no sign for the trail from Potash Road.

GPS: N 38°32.79' W 109°38.83'

The La Sal Mountains peek over the horizon as the trail forks along a flat stretch

SOUTHEAST REGION TRAIL #7

Mineral Point Trail

Starting Point:	**0.4 miles south of mile marker 11 on Utah 313**
Finishing Point:	**Mineral Point**
Total Mileage:	**11.6 miles**
Unpaved Mileage:	**11.6 miles**
Driving Time:	**45 minutes (one-way)**
Elevation Range:	**4,700–5,800 feet**
Usually Open:	**Year-round**
Difficulty Rating:	**2**
Scenic Rating:	**8**
Remoteness Rating:	**+0**

Special Attractions

■ Panoramic views from Mineral Point over the Green River.
■ Easy and scenic high-clearance road.
■ Provides access to a large network of interesting trails.

Description

This short spur trail runs out onto Mineral Point, one of the long ridges that overlooks the Green River. The trail is graded

View of Green River from the end of Mineral Point Trail

dirt along its entire length and is suitable in dry weather for high-clearance 2WDs. However, in wet weather the trail is often impassable to all vehicles because of the clinging red mud. The surface in dry weather is sandy with patches of southeast Utah's ubiquitous powder-fine sand traps. There are some minor rocky sections at the far end and a few small washes.

The main trail is easy to navigate and well defined, although there are no signs, and it connects to a maze of smaller tracks, some of which lead to other good viewpoints—Southeast #8: Hell Roaring Canyon Rim Trail is a loop spur off this route.

Mineral Point is a broad, gently sloping ridge that tapers down to the viewpoint over the Green River. The original tracks were put through for mineral exploration. As you descend gradually, there are views over the broad plateau and over to the Henry Mountains. At the end, the Green River is far below and the Maze district of Canyonlands National Park is visible on the far side.

Current Road Information

Canyonlands National Park
Island Ranger District
(435) 259-4712

Map References

BLM Moab
USGS 1:24,000 The Knoll, Mineral Canyon
      1:100,000 Moab
Maptech CD-ROM: Moab/Canyonlands
Trails Illustrated, #501; #210
Utah Atlas & Gazetteer, p. 30
Utah Travel Council #5
Other: Latitude 40—Moab West
      Canyon Country Off-Road Vehicle Trail Map—
      Island Area

Route Directions

▼ 0.0		Trail starts 0.4 miles south of mile marker 11 on Utah 313. Turn west on unmarked road and zero trip meter.

GPS: N 38°35.23' W 109°48.32'

▼ 0.3	SO	Track on left.
▼ 0.4	SO	Track on left.
▼ 0.5	SO	Track on left.

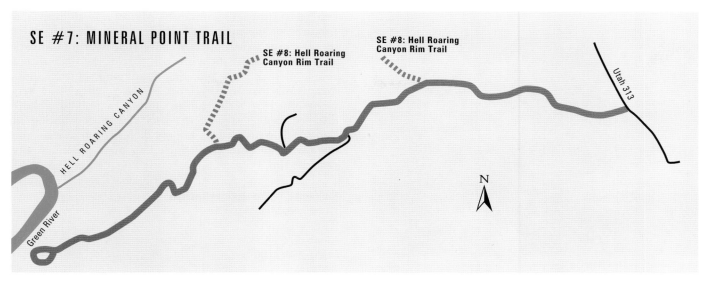

▼ 0.9	SO	Track on left.
▼ 1.1	SO	Track on left.
▼ 1.2	SO	Track on left.
▼ 1.6	SO	Two tracks on right, then track on left.
▼ 1.8	SO	Track on right.
▼ 1.9	SO	Track on right.

GPS: N 38°35.45' W 109°50.29'

▼ 2.2	SO	Old corral on right.
▼ 2.9	SO	Track on right.

GPS: N 38°35.51' W 109°51.30'

▼ 3.0	SO	Track on right.
▼ 3.3	SO	Track on left.
▼ 3.6	SO	Track on right toward ridge is Southeast #8: Hell Roaring Canyon Rim Trail, and track on left. Zero trip meter.

GPS: N 38°35.51' W 109°52.16'

▼ 0.0		Continue along trail.
▼ 0.1	SO	Cross through wash.
▼ 0.3	SO	Track on right.
▼ 0.8	SO	Cross through small wash.
▼ 3.0	SO	Track on right alongside butte, and track on left.

GPS: N 38°34.46' W 109°54.84'

▼ 3.6	SO	Cross through wash.
▼ 3.8	SO	Track on right.
▼ 4.3	SO	Track on right is end of Southeast #8: Hell Roaring Canyon Rim Trail. Zero trip meter.

GPS: N 38°34.45' W 109°56.08'

▼ 0.0		Continue toward Mineral Point.
▼ 0.8	SO	Track on left.
▼ 0.9	SO	Track on left.
▼ 1.0	SO	Cross through wash.
▼ 1.6	SO	Track on right.
▼ 2.4	BL	Track on right to oil drilling site.

GPS: N 38°33.21' W 109°58.06'

▼ 2.6	SO	Track on left.
▼ 2.8	SO	Tracks on right and left.
▼ 3.4	SO	Track on right.

GPS: N 38°32.89' W 109°59.15'

▼ 3.6	BL	Start of small loop at end of trail.
▼ 3.7		Trail ends at farthest point of loop on Mineral Point. Walk out onto the rocks for the best views of Green River and the Maze area of Canyonlands National Park.

GPS: N 38°32.83' W 109°59.44'

Hell Roaring Canyon Rim Trail

Starting Point:	Southeast #7: Mineral Point Trail, 3.6 miles from Utah 313
Finishing Point:	Southeast #7: Mineral Point Trail, 7.9 miles from Utah 313
Total Mileage:	5.7 miles
Unpaved Mileage:	5.7 miles
Driving Time:	1 hour
Elevation Range:	5,300–5,800 feet
Usually Open:	Year-round
Difficulty Rating:	4
Scenic Rating:	8
Remoteness Rating:	+0

Special Attractions

- Challenging trail that makes a spur loop off Southeast #7: Mineral Point Trail.
- Views into Hell Roaring Canyon.

Description

This short trail is picked up along Southeast #7: Mineral Point Trail; it starts and finishes on Mineral Point Road and makes a pleasant side trip. It travels on smaller, ungraded sandy and rocky tracks along a ridgetop on Mineral Point, offering wide-ranging views, before dropping to visit the edge of Hell Roaring Canyon.

There are many small, unmarked trails leading off from this trail, so pay close attention to the route to avoid getting lost. However, most of the side trails are dead ends or rejoin the route later, so it is hard to go too far wrong.

Looking down into Hell Roaring Canyon

small tracks to wrap around the edge of a small canyon, a tributary of the main Hell Roaring Canyon. It then descends to the bench directly above Hell Roaring Canyon. This descent is the most difficult part of the trail, with a couple of rock steps and some loose sand, but it is normally easily passable by most SUVs. You'll get the best viewpoints over Hell Roaring Canyon by walking a short distance to the edge of the rim. For those wanting to camp, this trail has better spots to pitch a tent than the main Mineral Point Trail, including some pleasant spots near the rim.

Current Road Information
BLM Moab Field Office
82 East Dogwood
Moab, UT 84532
(435) 259-2100

Map References
BLM   Moab
USGS   1:24,000   The Knoll, Mineral Canyon
          1:100,000 Moab
Maptech CD-ROM: Moab/Canyonlands
Trails Illustrated, #210
Utah Atlas & Gazetteer, p. 30

Within the first mile, this route climbs onto the ridge. Ahead are the Henry Mountains and the Maze district of Canyonlands National Park. The Needles, large buttes that are passed on Southeast #16: Spring Canyon Point Trail, are to the right and to the left are the La Sal Mountains and the Abajo, or Blue, Mountains near Monticello.

The trail leaves the ridge and drops through a maze of

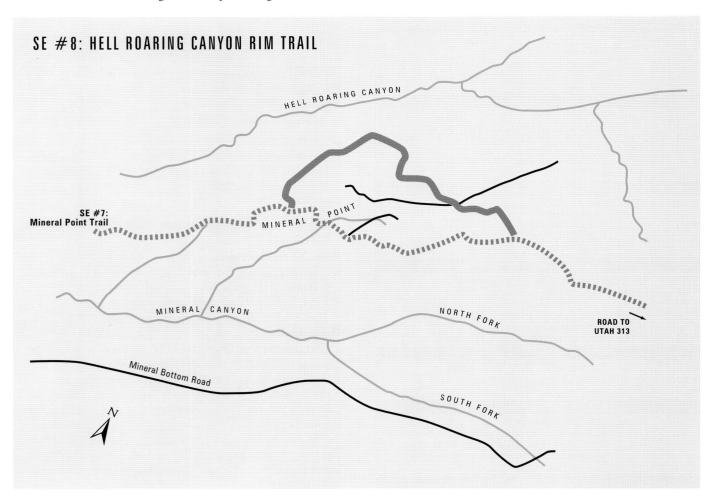

SE #8: HELL ROARING CANYON RIM TRAIL

HELL ROARING CANYON

SE #7:
Mineral Point Trail

MINERAL POINT

MINERAL CANYON

NORTH FORK

ROAD TO
UTAH 313

Mineral Bottom Road

SOUTH FORK

N

Utah Travel Council #5
Other: Latitude 40—Moab West
       Canyon Country Off-Road Vehicle Trail Map—
       Island Area

Route Directions

▼ 0.0		From Southeast #7: Mineral Point Trail, 3.6 miles from the start, turn northwest on an unmarked sandy track and zero trip meter.
5.7 ▲		Trail ends at the junction with Southeast #7: Mineral Point Trail. Turn left to exit to Utah 313, turn right to continue to Mineral Point.
GPS: N 38°35.51' W 109°52.16'		
▼ 0.5	TL	Turn onto unmarked track in front of rise.
5.2 ▲	TR	Turn onto unmarked track at the end of the rise.
GPS: N 38°35.74' W 109°52.80'		
▼ 0.6	TR	Track on left. Trail climbs onto ridge.
5.1 ▲	TL	Track on right. Trail leaves ridge.
▼ 1.1	SO	Track on left. Continue along ridge.
4.6 ▲	SO	Track on right. Continue along ridge.
GPS: N 38°35.51' W 109°53.33'		
▼ 1.3	TL	Turn left at T-intersection, track on right.
4.4 ▲	TR	Track straight ahead.
GPS: N 38°35.58' W 109°53.46'		
▼ 1.4	SO	Track on right.
4.3 ▲	SO	Track on left.
▼ 1.5	TR	Small intersection.
4.2 ▲	TL	Small intersection.
GPS: N 38°35.49' W 109°53.67'		
▼ 1.7	SO	Track on right.
4.0 ▲	SO	Track on left.
▼ 1.8	BL	Track on right.
3.9 ▲	BR	Track on left.
▼ 1.9	BL	Track on right.
3.8 ▲	BR	Track on left.
GPS: N 38°35.72' W 109°54.05'		
▼ 2.4	SO	Track on right.
3.3 ▲	SO	Track on left.
▼ 3.2	SO	Cross through wash.
2.5 ▲	SO	Cross through wash.
GPS: N 38°36.01' W 109°54.98'		
▼ 3.4	BL	Track on right goes to viewpoint over Hell Roaring Canyon.
2.3 ▲	BR	Track on left goes to viewpoint over Hell Roaring Canyon.
GPS: N 38°35.98' W 109°55.18'		
▼ 3.9	SO	Cross through slickrock wash.
1.8 ▲	SO	Cross through slickrock wash.
▼ 4.5	SO	Cross through wash.
1.2 ▲	SO	Cross through wash.
▼ 5.3	TL	Intersection. Follow more-used track to the left and pass to the south of the ridge.
0.4 ▲	TR	Pass to the south of the ridge, then intersection. Follow more-used track to the right.
GPS: N 38°34.68' W 109°56.36'		
▼ 5.7		Trail ends back on Southeast #7: Mineral Point Trail. Turn right to continue to Mineral Point, turn left to exit to Utah 313.
0.0 ▲		From Southeast #7: Mineral Point Trail, 7.9 miles from the start, turn northwest on an unmarked sandy track and zero trip meter.
GPS: N 38°34.45' W 109°56.08'		

Bartlett Wash Trail

Starting Point:	**Blue Hills Road, 2.2 miles west of US 191**
Finishing Point:	**Dubinky Well Road, 1.6 miles northeast of junction with Spring Canyon Road**
Total Mileage:	**7.3 miles**
Unpaved Mileage:	**7.3 miles**
Driving Time:	**1 hour**
Elevation Range:	**4,600–5,200 feet**
Usually Open:	**Year-round**
Difficulty Rating:	**3**
Scenic Rating:	**8**
Remoteness Rating:	**+0**

Special Attractions

- Easy to moderate trail along wide, sandy valley.
- Access to the mountain bike slickrock play area.
- Shady picnicking under large cottonwoods alongside the wash.

Description

Bartlett Wash Trail is a pleasant alternative to Southeast #10: Hidden Canyon Wash Trail for those not wanting to tackle the deep sand along Hidden Canyon. The trail is graded at the start and for much of its length, but it does have some moderately sandy sections, and toward the end where it joins Dubinky Well Road, there are some rocky ledges and slickrock sections.

The trail leaves Blue Hills Road at the same point as Southeast #10: Hidden Canyon Wash Trail, but it diverges within the first mile. Bartlett Wash Trail follows a smaller graded road and drops down into Bartlett Wash. The first section has some large cottonwoods in the wide part of the wash, which provide

Looking back across Bartlett Wash Trail

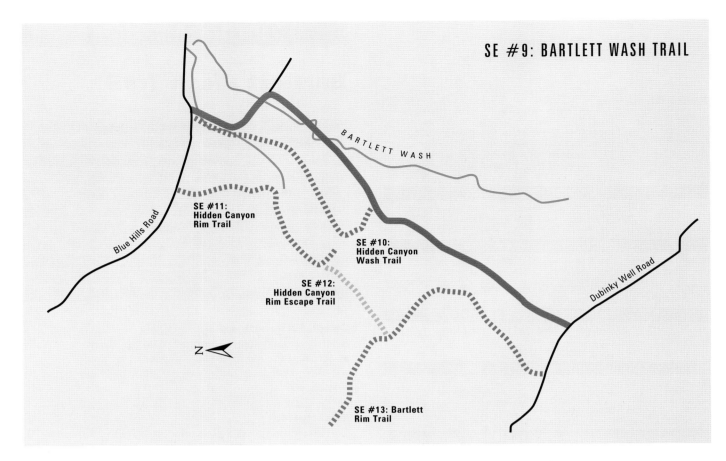

a pleasant place for a picnic, although there are no tables or facilities. People have camped here, but it is not advisable so close to the wash.

Once it enters the valley, the trail crosses the wash many times. There are several forks, and in a couple of places it is possible to follow along in the wash as an alternative to the trail. After 2.4 miles from the start of the trail, a mountain bike–only trail leaves the wash to the right and climbs onto the sandy ridges. This eventually gives access to the large slickrock domes between Bartlett Wash and Hidden Canyon. Mountain bikers can connect the two canyons in this way.

The valley gradually rises until it passes the far end of Southeast #10: Hidden Canyon Wash Trail. From here, the trail runs across the benches, past large sandstone buttes, until it gradually climbs to finish on Dubinky Well Road, 1.6 miles northwest of junction with Spring Canyon Road.

Current Road Information
BLM Moab Field Office
82 East Dogwood
Moab, UT 84532
(435) 259-2100

Map References
BLM Moab
USGS 1:24,000 Jug Rock
         1:100,000 Moab
Maptech CD-ROM: Moab/Canyonlands

Trails Illustrated, #501 (incomplete)
Utah Atlas & Gazetteer, p. 40
Other: Latitude 40—Moab West
       Canyon Country Off-Road Vehicle Trail Map—
       Island Area

Route Directions

▼ 0.0			Trail commences on Blue Hills Road, 2.2 miles from the junction with US 191. Turn south onto smaller, unmarked graded road and zero trip meter.
	1.4 ▲		Trail finishes at the junction with the graded dirt Blue Hills Road. Turn right to join US 191.
GPS: N 38°44.69' W 109°46.74'			
▼ 0.7		TL	Track straight on is Southeast #10: Hidden Canyon Wash Trail.
	0.7 ▲	TR	Track on left is Southeast #10: Hidden Canyon Wash Trail.
GPS: N 38°44.01' W 109°47.08'			
▼ 0.9		SO	Track on right.
	0.5 ▲	SO	Track on left.
▼ 1.1		SO	Cross through the wide, sandy Bartlett Wash.
	0.3 ▲	SO	Cross through the wide, sandy Bartlett Wash.
▼ 1.4		TR	Turn right onto unmarked roughly graded dirt trail and zero trip meter.
	0.0 ▲		Continue along wider road.
GPS: N 38°43.67' W 109°46.47'			
▼ 0.0			Continue to the southwest.
	2.3 ▲	TL	Turn left at T-intersection. Zero trip meter.
▼ 0.1		SO	Track on left.
	2.2 ▲	SO	Track on right.

▼ 0.3		SO	Track on left.
	2.0 ▲	SO	Track on right.
▼ 0.5		SO	Trail drops down and enters the Bartlett Wash valley; Bartlett Wash is on the right.
	1.8 ▲	SO	Trail leaves the Bartlett Wash valley.
▼ 0.9		SO	Cross through Bartlett Wash twice. Trail runs in or alongside the wash, crossing it many times.
	1.4 ▲	SO	Cross through Bartlett Wash for final time.
		GPS: N 38°43.05′ W 109°47.14′	
▼ 1.0		BL	Gate in wash then bear left out of wash. Remaining in wash at this point leads to the mountain bike trail which leaves up the sand ridge to the west.
	1.3 ▲	SO	Gate in wash. Turning left back up wash before the gate leads to the mountain bike trail which leaves up the sand ridge to the west.
		GPS: N 38°43.00′ W 109°47.19′	
▼ 1.4		BL	Fork in wash, follow graded track out of the main wash along smaller wash.
	0.9 ▲	SO	Join larger wash.
		GPS: N 38°42.71′ W 109°47.43′	
▼ 1.5		BR	Small track on left.
	0.8 ▲	BL	Small track on right.
		GPS: N 38°42.61′ W 109°47.51′	
▼ 1.7		SO	Track on right drops into wash.
	0.6 ▲	SO	Track on left drops into wash.
▼ 1.8		SO	Cross through small wash.
	0.5 ▲	SO	Cross through small wash.
▼ 2.0		SO	Old oil drilling marker on left.
	0.3 ▲	SO	Old oil drilling marker on right.
		GPS: N 38°42.41′ W 109°47.91′	
▼ 2.3		SO	Track on right is Southeast #10: Hidden Canyon Wash Trail. Zero trip meter.
	0.0 ▲		Continue to the north.
		GPS: N 38°42.33′ W 109°48.19′	
▼ 0.0			Continue to the south.
	3.6 ▲	SO	Track on left is Southeast #10: Hidden Canyon Wash Trail. Zero trip meter.
▼ 0.5		SO	Track on right goes to small viewpoint.
	3.1 ▲	BR	Track on left goes to a small viewpoint.
▼ 0.7		SO	Enter wash.
	2.9 ▲	SO	Exit wash.
▼ 0.8		SO	Exit wash.
	2.8 ▲	SO	Enter wash.
▼ 1.4		SO	Cross through wash.
	2.2 ▲	SO	Cross through wash.
▼ 1.8		SO	Cross through wash.
	1.8 ▲	SO	Cross through wash.
▼ 2.6		SO	Cross through wash.
	1.0 ▲	SO	Cross through wash.
		GPS: N 38°40.57′ W 109°49.71′	
▼ 3.0		SO	Cross through wash, then cross slickrock pavement.
	0.6 ▲	SO	Leave slickrock, then cross through wash.
▼ 3.2		SO	Leave slickrock.
	0.4 ▲	SO	Cross slickrock pavement.
▼ 3.6			Trail ends at the junction with Dubinky Well Road. Turn left to join Spring Canyon Road or Utah 313.
	0.0 ▲		Trail starts on the Dubinky Well Road, approximately 3 miles northwest of Utah 313, 1.6 miles northwest of the junction with the Spring Canyon Road. Zero trip meter and turn northeast on unmarked track.
		GPS: N 38°39.80′ W 109°50.30′	

Hidden Canyon Wash Trail

Starting Point:	Blue Hills Road, 2.2 miles west of US 191
Finishing Point:	Junction with Southeast #9: Bartlett Wash Trail
Total Mileage:	4.1 miles
Unpaved Mileage:	4.1 miles
Driving Time:	45 minutes
Elevation Range:	4,600–4,900 feet
Usually Open:	Year-round
Difficulty Rating:	5
Scenic Rating:	9
Remoteness Rating:	+0

Special Attractions

■ Multicolored sandstone domes of Hidden Canyon.
■ Fun, sandy trail to explore.
■ Very pretty canyon and creek wash.

Description

This short trail leads into the extremely scenic Hidden Canyon, with its walls of colored slickrock. The canyon is not particularly deep, and it has a wide, sandy valley floor. The trail starts off as a graded track, but the road standard quickly drops to a very loose sandy track. It follows the wash into the canyon before descending to run in the wash toward Southeast #9: Bartlett Wash Trail. The sand in the canyon is difficult to traverse, being very deep and loose. You will probably need to lower tire pressures to avoid bogging down.

After 3.2 miles, the trail turns left down the wash for the climb out, but you can continue ahead for a further 3.2 miles

Hidden Canyon Wash Trail from the viewpoint on Hidden Canyon Rim Trail

SE #10: HIDDEN CANYON WASH TRAIL

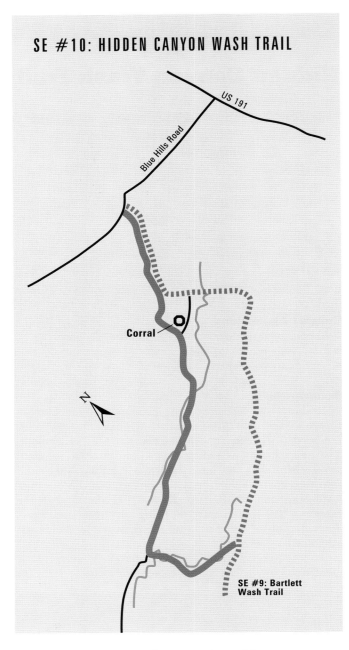

Corral

SE #9: Bartlett Wash Trail

Map References

BLM Moab (incomplete)
USGS 1:24,000 Jug Rock (incomplete)
1:100,000 Moab (incomplete)
Maptech CD-ROM: Moab/Canyonlands
Trails Illustrated, #501 (incomplete)
Utah Atlas & Gazetteer, p. 40
Other: Latitude 40—Moab West (doesn't show an exit from Hidden Canyon Wash)

Route Directions

▼ 0.0			Trail commences on Blue Hills Road, 2.2 miles from US 191. Turn south onto smaller, unmarked graded road and zero trip meter.
	3.2 ▲		Trail finishes at the junction with the graded dirt Blue Hills Road. Turn right to join US 191.
		GPS: N 38°44.69′ W 109°46.74′	
▼ 0.7		SO	Track on left is Southeast #9: Bartlett Wash Trail.
	2.5 ▲	SO	Track on right is Southeast #9: Bartlett Wash Trail.
		GPS: N 38°44.01′ W 109°47.08′	
▼ 0.9		SO	Track on right.
	2.3 ▲	SO	Track on left.
▼ 1.1		SO	Corral on left, then track on left.
	2.1 ▲	SO	Track on right, then corral on right.
		GPS: N 38°43.75′ W 109°47.21′	
▼ 1.5		BL	Two tracks on right.
	1.7 ▲	BR	Two tracks on left.
▼ 1.6		SO	Cross through wash.
	1.6 ▲	SO	Cross through wash.
▼ 1.8		SO	Cross through fence line.
	1.4 ▲	SO	Cross through fence line.
▼ 1.9		SO	Track on left.
	1.3 ▲	SO	Track on right.
		GPS: N 38°43.24′ W 109°47.71′	
▼ 2.0		SO	Cross through sandy wash.
	1.2 ▲	SO	Cross through sandy wash.
▼ 2.1		SO	Join Hidden Canyon Wash, entering through the wide mouth of Hidden Canyon.
	1.1 ▲	SO	Exit Hidden Canyon Wash, leaving through the wide mouth of Hidden Canyon.
▼ 2.3		SO	Exit wash.
	0.9 ▲	SO	Enter wash.
▼ 2.4		BR	Track on left.
	0.8 ▲	SO	Track on right.
▼ 2.5		SO	Cross through wash.
	0.7 ▲	SO	Cross through wash.
▼ 2.6		SO	Faint track on right.
	0.6 ▲	SO	Faint track on left.
▼ 2.8		SO	Cross through wash.
	0.4 ▲	SO	Cross though wash.
		GPS: N 38°42.78′ W 109°48.53′	
▼ 3.0		SO	Trail crests a loose and sandy rise, then drops down into Hidden Canyon.
	0.2 ▲	SO	Trail crests a loose and sandy rise.
▼ 3.2		TL	Turn left and drop into wash, heading southeast. Trail ahead at this point goes another 3.2 miles into Hidden Canyon before becoming too narrow for 4WD vehicles. Zero trip meter.
	0.0 ▲		Proceed to the northeast toward the mouth of Hidden Canyon.

into Hidden Canyon. At that point, the trail becomes too narrow for 4WDs, but some ATVs are able to travel a little farther. Both the head of the canyon and another short spur are worth investigating on foot.

The climb up to Southeast #9: Bartlett Wash Trail has the loosest and deepest sand; it's quite steep, but it's short. There are two alternative climbs, both visible when you get to the end of the canyon. At the time of writing, the left-hand climb is slightly easier, but this may not always be the case.

Current Road Information

BLM Moab Field Office
82 East Dogwood
Moab, UT 84532
(435) 259-2100

GPS: N 38°42.66' W 109°48.85'			
▼ 0.0			Proceed to the southeast and drop into the wash.
	0.9 ▲	TR	Trail exits wash. Trail to the left at this point goes another 3.2 miles into Hidden Canyon before becoming too narrow for 4WD vehicles. Zero trip meter.
▼ 0.4		SO	Trail enters narrow, sandy section of canyon.
	0.5 ▲	SO	Exit narrow section.
▼ 0.6		SO	Exit narrow section.
	0.3 ▲	SO	Trail enters narrow, sandy section of canyon.
GPS: N 38°42.35' W 109°48.49'			
▼ 0.7		SO	Track on left.
	0.2 ▲	SO	Track on right.
▼ 0.8		SO	Loose, sandy climb out of wash.
	0.1 ▲	SO	Loose, sandy descent into wash.
▼ 0.9			Trail finishes at the junction with Southeast #9: Bartlett Wash Trail. Turn left to return to Blue Hills Road, turn right to exit to Dubinky Well Road.
	0.0 ▲		Trail commences on Southeast #9: Bartlett Wash Trail, 3.7 miles from the junction with Blue Hills Road. Zero trip meter and turn west on unmarked sandy track.
GPS: N 38°42.33' W 109°48.19'			

SOUTHEAST REGION TRAIL #11

Hidden Canyon Rim Trail

Starting Point:	**Blue Hills Road, 3.9 miles west of US 191**
Finishing Point:	**Hidden Canyon Rim; connects to**
	Southeast #12: Hidden Canyon Rim
	Escape Trail
Total Mileage:	**4 miles**
Unpaved Mileage:	**4 miles**
Driving Time:	**1 hour**
Elevation Range:	**4,600–5,100 feet**
Usually Open:	**Year-round**
Difficulty Rating:	**4**
Scenic Rating:	**9**
Remoteness Rating:	**+0**

Special Attractions
- Moderate, rocky trail with extensive slickrock.
- Spectacular views into Hidden Canyon.
- Can be treated either as a spur trail or combined with Southeast #8: Hidden Canyon Rim Escape Trail to exit up to Bartlett Rim.

Description
This short trail travels out on the slickrock above a tributary of Hidden Canyon, swings around the head of the canyon, and drops down to end on a rock platform with a very pretty view. The first mile is easy going as you travel toward the edge of the first canyon; after that it is very slow going as you cross

lumpy slickrock. Navigation in this second part requires a keen eye—some of the trail is marked with small cairns and other sections with boulders. However, there are long sections where the only indications that you are still on the correct trail are occasional black tire marks on the slickrock or tire prints in the infrequent sandy sections. It is easy to miss the trail here, so the route directions include more than the usual number of GPS coordinates to aid navigation.

White chimney pot-like rocks can be found near the final viewpoint

The trail wraps around the head of the wash and then leaves the slickrock and follows a more defined sandy trail down to the viewpoint. It finishes on a rock platform right on the rim of Hidden Canyon. From here, you can also see multicolored slickrock domes around the edge and Southeast #10: Hidden Canyon Wash Trail along the bottom.

Either treat this trail like a spur and retrace your route to Blue Hills Road or follow Southeast #12: Hidden Canyon Rim Escape Trail, which connects with Southeast #13: Bartlett Rim Trail. The Escape trail is rated a 6 for difficulty, but it is the quickest and most exciting way out of the canyon.

Current Road Information
BLM Moab Field Office
82 East Dogwood
Moab, UT 84532
(435) 259-2100

Map References
BLM Moab (incomplete)
USGS 1:24,000 Jug Rock (incomplete)
1:100,000 Moab (incomplete)
Maptech CD-ROM: Moab/Canyonlands
Trails Illustrated, #501
Utah Atlas & Gazetteer, p. 40
Other: Latitude 40—Moab West
Canyon Country Off-Road Vehicle Trail Map—
Island Area

Route Directions
▼ 0.0			From Blue Hills Road, 3.9 miles west of US 191, zero trip meter and turn south on unmarked, graded dirt trail.
	1.2 ▲		Trail ends at intersection with Blue Hills Road. Turn right to exit to US 191.
GPS: N 38°44.84' W 109°48.05'			
▼ 0.3		TL	Intersection. Ahead goes to Exclosure; track

Driving along as the trail descends to Hidden Canyon viewpoint

on right is alternative exit to Blue Hills Road. Turn and immediately cross through wash.

0.9 ▲ TR Cross through wash, then intersection. Left goes to Exclosure; track ahead is alternative exit to Blue Hills Road.

GPS: N 38°44.61' W 109°48.19'

▼ 0.6 SO Cross through wash, then campsite on right.
0.6 ▲ SO Campsite on left, then cross through wash.

▼ 0.9 BR Track on left, then cattle guard, then track on right.
0.3 ▲ SO Track on left, then cattle guard, then track on right.

GPS: N 38°44.08' W 109°47.99'

▼ 1.0 SO Cattletank on left.
0.2 ▲ SO Cattletank on right.

GPS: N 38°44.01' W 109°48.06'

▼ 1.1 SO Brink Spring and tank on left. Trail is now ungraded and starts to climb.
0.1 ▲ SO Brink Spring and tank on right. Trail is now graded dirt.

GPS: N 38°43.90' W 109°48.10'

▼ 1.2 BL Track on right is dead end. Over the hill on left are the remains of some old cabins (not visible from the trail). Zero trip meter.

0.0 ▲ Continue toward Blue Hills Road.

GPS: N 38°43.88' W 109°48.17'

▼ 0.0 Continue toward Hidden Canyon.
2.8 ▲ BR Track on left is dead end. Over the hill on right are the remains of some old cabins (not visible from the trail). Zero trip meter.

▼ 0.2 SO Start to cross slickrock. Track on left leaves through wire gate. Keep right toward the hill and look for cairns to mark the way.
2.6 ▲ SO Follow around the hill, then track on right leaves through wire gate. End of slickrock.

GPS: N 38°43.71' W 109°48.03'

▼ 0.4 SO Tributary of Hidden Canyon is on the left. Follow trail along rim.
2.4 ▲ SO Trail follows the rim of a tributary of Hidden Canyon.

▼ 0.9 SO Track on right.
1.9 ▲ SO Track on left.

GPS: N 38°43.50' W 109°48.59'

▼ 1.4 BL Bear southeast and cross over head of wash on slickrock, then continue straight for approximately 100 yards before bearing south. Trail is difficult to follow.
1.4 ▲ BR Bear north before swinging left down to cross over head of wash on slickrock. Trail is difficult to follow.

GPS: N 38°43.38' W 109°49.00'

▼ 1.7 SO Trail is more defined across the sandy section. Bear southwest.
1.1 ▲ SO Trail leaves the defined sandy track and crosses slickrock. There are some cairns to mark the route.

GPS: N 38°43.17' W 109°49.20'

▼ 2.1 TL Track continues straight on. Turn left, descend soft sandy trail to wash crossing.
0.7 ▲ TR Cross through wash, then ascend sandy track and turn right at T-intersection.

GPS: N 38°42.98' W 109°49.57'

▼ 2.3 SO Cross through wash, then exit up small ridge.
0.5 ▲ SO Descend down small ridge and cross through wash.

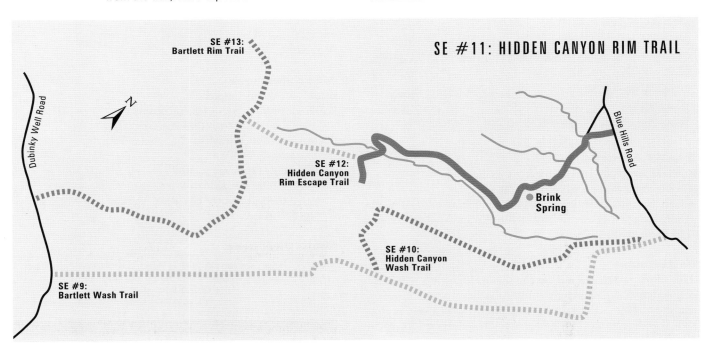

SE #13:
Bartlett Rim Trail

SE #11: HIDDEN CANYON RIM TRAIL

Dubinky Well Road

Blue Hills Road

SE #12:
Hidden Canyon
Rim Escape Trail

Brink Spring

SE #10:
Hidden Canyon
Wash Trail

SE #9:
Bartlett Wash Trail

		GPS: N 38°42.99' W 109°49.37'	
▼ 2.6	SO	Track on right is Southeast #12: Hidden Canyon Rim Escape Trail. Faint track on left.	
0.2 ▲	SO	Track on left is Southeast #12: Hidden Canyon Rim Escape Trail. Faint track on right.	
		GPS: N 38°42.78' W 109°49.44'	
▼ 2.8	BL	Hidden Canyon Rim is directly ahead. Trail swings northeast along the rim, then descends to end on the rock platform directly above Hidden Canyon.	
0.0 ▲		Return from Hidden Canyon overlook and exit either via Southeast #12: Hidden Canyon Rim Escape Trail or by retracing your steps.	
		GPS: N 38°42.68' W 109°49.19'	

SOUTHEAST REGION TRAIL #12

Hidden Canyon Rim Escape Trail

Starting Point:	**Southeast #11: Hidden Canyon Rim Trail**
Finishing Point:	**Southeast #13: Bartlett Rim Trail**
Total Mileage:	**1.5 miles**
Unpaved Mileage:	**1.5 miles**
Driving Time:	**30 minutes**
Elevation Range:	**5,000–5,400 feet**
Usually Open:	**Year-round**
Difficulty Rating:	**6**
Scenic Rating:	**9**
Remoteness Rating:	**+0**

Special Attractions

■ Short challenging trail that links Hidden Canyon Rim Trail and Bartlett Rim Trail.

Description

This short trail is a quick and exciting route from Southeast #11: Hidden Canyon Rim Trail up to Southeast #13: Bartlett Rim Trail. The trail begins by climbing up a section of slickrock marked by a cairn. After the first section, it swings around to the southwest and climbs a second very steep, smooth slickrock face. This climb looks a lot worse than it is; most stock vehicles are able to tackle it. There are normally a couple of small cairns to show the way, but the most reliable indications of the best route are the black tire marks on the slickrock. The trail then climbs a very steep dirt and rock slope, and this middle section presents the real challenge. There are two alternate ways up, both steep; the left-hand one is probably slightly less steep, although it has a couple of small rock ledges near the top. The routes rejoin to traverse a narrow ridge with a steep drop on both sides. This is not difficult, but it can be a bit nerve-wracking and should not be attempted in wet weather!

After the ridge, there is another short rocky climb which

Driving up a steep section of the slickrock climb

has an alternate route that is about the same difficulty. The trail is now on top of the plateau and runs south to join Bartlett Rim Trail. There are some rocky sections, but the most difficult part is behind you. The trail finishes at the junction with Bartlett Rim Trail.

The Moab Jeep Safari held each Easter incorporates this climb into its 3D trail.

Current Road Information

BLM Moab Field Office
82 East Dogwood
Moab, UT 84532
(435) 259-2100

Map References

BLM Moab (incomplete)
USGS 1:24,000 Jug Rock (incomplete)
1:100,000 Moab (incomplete)
Maptech CD-ROM: Moab/Canyonlands
Trails Illustrated, #501
Utah Atlas & Gazetteer, p. 40
Other: Latitude 40—Moab West

Route Directions

▼ 0.0		From Southeast #11: Hidden Canyon Rim Trail, 0.2 miles before the end of the trail, turn southwest onto an unmarked sandy trail and zero trip meter.	
1.5 ▲		Trail finishes at Southeast #11: Hidden Canyon Rim Trail. Turn right to go to viewpoint of Hidden Canyon, turn left to exit to Blue Hills Road.	
		GPS: N 38°42.78' W 109°49.44'	
▼ 0.4	BR	Faint track on left.	
1.1 ▲	SO	Faint track on right.	
		GPS: N 38°42.54' W 109°49.77'	
▼ 0.5	SO	Trail climbs first slickrock hump, then swings right and climbs second steep slickrock section.	
1.0 ▲	SO	Trail descends steep slickrock section, then swings left and descends last slickrock hump.	
		GPS: N 38°42.47' W 109°49.84'	

The final climb up to the top of the plateau

| ▼0.6 | | BL | Straight ahead is the steeper alternative. |
| 0.9 ▲ | | SO | Alternative route rejoins. |

GPS: N 38°42.44' W 109°49.85'

▼0.7		SO	Alternative route rejoins to cross ridge with steep drops on either side.
0.8 ▲		BR	Cross ridge with steep drops on either side, then alternative route forks. Right is the easier alternative.
▼0.8		BR	Track straight on is alternative route, which rejoins almost immediately.
0.7 ▲		SO	Track on right is alternative route, which rejoins almost immediately.

GPS: N 38°42.37' W 109°49.98'

| ▼0.9 | | SO | Trail is on top of the plateau. |
| 0.6 ▲ | | SO | Trail starts to descend from plateau. |

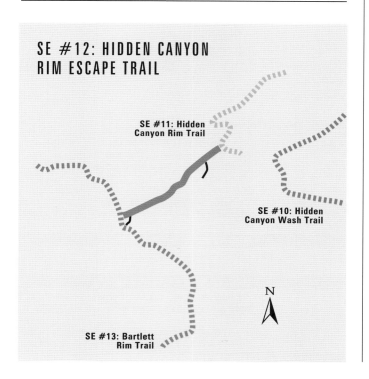

SE #12: HIDDEN CANYON RIM ESCAPE TRAIL

SE #11: Hidden Canyon Rim Trail

SE #10: Hidden Canyon Wash Trail

SE #13: Bartlett Rim Trail

N

GPS: N 38°42.33' W 109°50.02'

| ▼1.4 | | BR | Track on left also joins Southeast #13: Bartlett Rim Trail. |
| 0.1 ▲ | | BL | Track on right rejoins Southeast #13: Bartlett Rim Trail. |

GPS: N 38°42.15' W 109°50.49'

| ▼1.5 | | | Trail ends midway along Southeast #13: Bartlett Rim Trail. |
| 0.0 ▲ | | | Trail commences on Southeast #13: Bartlett Rim Trail, 3.7 miles from the northern end, 3.4 miles from the southern end. Turn northeast on unmarked trail and zero trip meter. |

GPS: N 38°42.24' W 109°50.55'

SOUTHEAST REGION TRAIL #13

Bartlett Rim Trail

Starting Point:	Dubinky Well Road, 2.5 miles from
	junction with Spring Canyon Road and
	approximately 4 miles from Utah 313
Finishing Point:	Dubinky Well Road, 1.2 miles north of
	Dubinky Well
Total Mileage:	7.1 miles
Unpaved Mileage:	7.1 miles
Driving Time:	1.25 hours
Elevation Range:	5,200–5,500 feet
Usually Open:	Year-round
Difficulty Rating:	4
Scenic Rating:	8
Remoteness Rating:	+0

Special Attractions
- Panoramic views over The Needles and the Book Cliffs.
- Views down into Bartlett Wash.
- Short, moderate trail with many viewpoints.

Description
This short trail runs around the edge of the Bartlett Wash valley and then into one of the fingers of Hidden Canyon. There are several spur trails leading from it that go to viewpoints over the canyons, and there are fantastic views from the trail itself, especially along the northern end.

The trail is an ungraded dirt track, soft and sandy for a couple of miles at either end. The middle section is rocky and there is one moderate pinch in the middle of the trail that looks worse than it is. The trail is difficult in wet weather and may not be passable.

The northern end of the trail descends along a rise, providing views in all directions. To the north, you can see the Book Cliffs. The Needles, a large butte passed on Southeast #16: Spring Canyon Point Trail, is to the south.

The trail ends back on the Dubinky Well Road, 3.7 miles to the north of where it started.

SE #13: BARTLETT RIM TRAIL

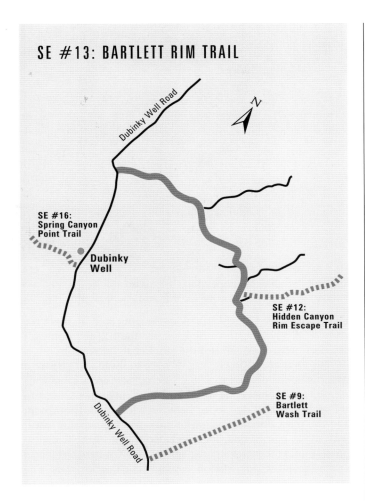

Current Road Information
BLM Moab Field Office
82 East Dogwood
Moab, UT 84532
(435) 259-2100

Map References
BLM Moab (incomplete)
USGS 1:24,000 Dubinky Wash, Jug Rock
1:100,000 Moab (incomplete)
Maptech CD-ROM: Moab/Canyonlands
Trails Illustrated, #501 (incomplete)
Utah Atlas & Gazetteer, p. 40
Other: Latitude 40—Moab West
    Canyon Country Off-Road Vehicle Trail Map—
    Island Area

Route Directions

▼ 0.0   From Dubinky Well Road, 2.5 miles northwest of the junction with Spring Canyon Road, zero trip meter and turn northeast on an unmarked, ungraded sandy track.

3.4 ▲   Trail finishes back on Dubinky Well Road, 3.7 miles south of the start of the trail. Turn left to exit to Utah 313.

GPS: N 38°40.13′ W 109°51.15′

▼ 0.2   SO   Pass through wire gate. Views to the right into Bartlett Wash.

3.2 ▲   SO   Views to the left into Bartlett Wash. Pass through wire gate.

GPS: N 38°40.30′ W 109°51.04′

▼ 1.1   SO   Track on right.

2.3 ▲   BR   Track on left.

GPS: N 38°40.81′ W 109°50.27′

▼ 1.6   SO   Cross short slickrock section.

1.8 ▲   SO   Cross short slickrock section.

▼ 1.7   SO   Faint track on right.

1.7 ▲   SO   Faint track on left.

▼ 1.9   SO   Views to the right into Bartlett Wash—walk up the rise for the best view.

1.5 ▲   SO   Views to the left into Bartlett Wash—walk up the rise for the best view.

GPS: N 38°41.34′ W 109°49.70′

▼ 2.4   SO   Steep rocky pinch.

1.0 ▲   SO   Steep rocky pinch.

GPS: N 38°41.56′ W 109°49.74′

▼ 2.5   SO   Track on right.

0.9 ▲   SO   Track on left.

GPS: N 38°41.74′ W 109°49.94′

▼ 2.6   SO   Track on right.

0.8 ▲   BR   Track on left.

▼ 2.7   SO   Faint track on left.

0.7 ▲   BL   Faint track on right.

▼ 3.3   SO   Large rock cairn on right with a post in it. Track on right joins Southeast #12: Hidden Canyon Rim Escape Trail. Also track on left.

0.1 ▲   SO   Large rock cairn on left with a post in it. Track on left joins Southeast #12: Hidden Canyon Rim Escape Trail. Also track on right.

GPS: N 38°42.13′ W 109°50.52′

▼ 3.4   SO   Track on right is Southeast #12: Hidden Canyon Rim Escape Trail. Zero trip meter.

0.0 ▲   Continue along Bartlett Rim.

GPS: N 38°42.24′ W 109°50.55′

▼ 0.0   Continue along Bartlett Rim.

3.7 ▲   BR   Track on left is Southeast #12: Hidden Canyon Rim Escape Trail. Zero trip meter.

▼ 0.1   SO   Track on right passes viewpoint.

3.6 ▲   SO   Track on left passes viewpoint.

GPS: N 38°42.30′ W 109°50.58′

▼ 0.2   SO   Track on left.

3.5 ▲   SO   Track on right.

Views of Bartlett Wash and the La Sal Mountains

▼ 0.4		SO	Faint track on left.
	3.3 ▲	SO	Faint track on right.
▼ 0.6		SO	Track on right, then faint track on left, then second track on right.
	3.1 ▲	SO	Track on left, then faint track on right, then second track on left.
	GPS: N 38°42.57' W 109°50.93'		
▼ 1.2		SO	Track on left and track on right.
	2.5 ▲	SO	Track on right and track on left.
	GPS: N 38°42.68' W 109°51.52'		
▼ 1.4		SO	Track on right goes to the pipeline and a great view.
	2.3 ▲	SO	Track on left goes to the pipeline and a great view.
▼ 1.5		SO	Track on right.
	2.2 ▲	BR	Track on left.
▼ 2.1		SO	Track on right.
	1.6 ▲	BR	Track on left.
	GPS: N 38°42.87' W 109°52.55'		
▼ 3.6		SO	Faint track on right.
	0.1 ▲	SO	Faint track on left.
▼ 3.7			Trail ends at the junction with Dubinky Well Road, 3.7 miles north of the start of the trail. Turn left to exit to Utah 313.
	0.0 ▲		Trail commences on Dubinky Well Road, 1.2 miles north of Dubinky Well. Zero trip meter and turn northeast on unsigned, ungraded dirt track beside a rocky outcrop.
	GPS: N 38°42.68' W 109°53.10'		

SOUTHEAST REGION TRAIL # 14

Monitor and Merrimac Trail

Starting Point:	**US 191, 0.2 miles north of mile marker 141**
Finishing Point:	**Same as starting point**
Total Mileage:	**12.1 miles**
Unpaved Mileage:	**12.1 miles**
Driving Time:	**2.5 hours**
Elevation Range:	**4,400–5,100 feet**
Usually Open:	**Year-round**
Difficulty Rating:	**5**
Scenic Rating:	**10**
Remoteness Rating:	**+0**

Special Attractions
- Monitor and Merrimac Buttes.
- Mill Canyon Dinosaur Trail.
- Historic sites of Mill Canyon Copper Mill and Halfway Stage Station.

History
The twin buttes of Monitor and Merrimac are both named after Civil War battleships.

The Halfway Stage Station near the end of the trail was also

Monitor stands on the right of the gap with Merrimac to the left

referred to as the Upper Courthouse Staging Station. It got the name Halfway Stage because it was at the halfway point for travelers between Moab and the railroad at Thompson.

The Denver & Rio Grande Western Railway was a boon to Moab when it opened in 1883, offering a more reliable connection with the outside world and attracting other settlers to the region. A trail developed between Moab and Thompson, and the most difficult section to cross was Courthouse Wash with its deep, soft sand. Heavily laden wagons were forced to go around to the west via the spring near Courthouse Rock, and a second staging station developed at this location. The trip took eight hours; stages with heavier loads needed two days to complete the journey.

Halfway Stage Station operated on a fairly primitive basis from the 1890s to 1903 until the grade around Courthouse Wash was improved, which eliminated the need to travel via Halfway. The Lower Courthouse Staging Station at the spring continued to operate until the 1920s. As the route gradually improved, and with the introduction of haulage trucks, the need for this staging station was also eliminated. The buildings of the Lower Courthouse Staging Station were demolished when the Potash Railroad was put through in the 1960s.

Copper mining began around the Courthouse Rock region about 1899, but the ore was of such poor quality that no milling process could make the mines profitable. The copper mill in Mill Canyon was abandoned not long after it started, possibly in 1902.

Description
This is a popular Moab area 4WD trail that is suitable for most high-clearance SUVs. It is a moderately challenging trail with a great variety of scenery and trail surfaces.

The trail leaves US 191 at the BLM sign for the Monitor and Merrimac Trail. It has signs sporadically along the route, so navigation should not be a problem. The BLM has posted a map and basic trail information at a parking area just off the highway.

The trail proper for 4WDs starts by going down the sandy Tusher Canyon Wash. It passes through a narrow section of canyon and then leaves the creek to swing around to the east and climb a sandy rise. After passing through a gap in the Entrada sandstone walls, it drops down and enters the equally sandy Courthouse Pasture. At this point, the trail passes right beside Determination Towers, large stand-alone buttes, and climbs steadily over slickrock pavements to their base. Just past the towers is the most difficult stretch of trail, a very short, steep pinch with some large boulders and deep gullies. Study the wheel placement before you start—the most obvious route will have larger vehicles tilting over toward a large rock on the left that could ding a panel.

After Determination Towers, the trail heads toward Monitor and Merrimac Buttes. You may want to take a short detour and follow the BLM sign to view the infamous Wipe Out Hill, which is 0.1 miles from the trail. This extremely difficult short hill, a vertical drop down into the wash bottom, is popular with the extreme Jeep crowd, who will spend hours getting their vehicles down, and occasionally up, the hill. This is only recommended for groups with heavily modified vehicles who are not fazed by the likely possibility of vehicle damage; but if you are lucky enough to see someone having a go at the hill, stay to watch and marvel at what a fearless driver can accomplish!

The trail then passes directly underneath Merrimac Butte on the north side. Before swinging north to cross Courthouse Pasture, take the short spur trail south to a slickrock platform between the two buttes. This platform has great views to the south over Sevenmile Canyon and makes a great place for lunch.

The sandy trail across Courthouse Pasture is easier going, and the trail then drops into Mill Canyon and crosses Mill Canyon Wash several times. Some of these crossings can be tricky depending on recent weather, and the lower end of Mill Canyon Wash can be muddy and soft. The sparse remains of the copper mill are on the right as you exit the creek, just before the parking area for the Mill Canyon Dinosaur Trail on the left. This self-guided, 0.25-mile trail passes by several petrified dinosaur bones embedded in the rock. This is a rare opportunity to see the bones as they were found. Trail brochures available at the start explain in detail where to look.

From the Dinosaur Trail, the surface is a good, graded dirt

A difficult 5-rated pinch along the Monitor and Merrimac Trail

road. A final detour at the end of the trail is down to the old Halfway Stage Stop, where there are substantial stone remains of the old station.

Current Road Information
BLM Moab Field Office
82 East Dogwood
Moab, UT 84532
(435) 259-2100

Map References
BLM Moab (incomplete)
USGS 1:24,000 Merrimac Butte, Jug Rock (incomplete)
1:100,000 Moab (incomplete)
Maptech CD-ROM: Moab/Canyonlands
Trails Illustrated, #211; #501
Utah Atlas & Gazetteer, p. 40
Other: Latitude 40—Moab West
Canyon Country Off-Road Vehicle Trail Map—Island Area

Route Directions

▼ 0.0		0.2 miles north of mile marker 141 on US 191, turn west on Mill Canyon Road, cross railroad and cattle guard and zero trip meter.
2.5 ▲		Trail finishes at intersection with US 191. Turn right for Moab, left for I-70.
GPS: N 38°43.66′ W 109°43.29′		
▼ 0.2	SO	Information board on right; then cross through Courthouse Wash.
2.3 ▲	SO	Cross through Courthouse Wash; information board on left.
▼ 0.5	SO	Track on right.
2.0 ▲	SO	Track on left.
▼ 0.6	BR	Track on left is end of Monitor and Merrimac Trail. Follow the sign for Tusher Canyon.
1.9 ▲	BL	Track on right is end of Monitor and Merrimac Trail.
GPS: N 38°43.55′ W 109°43.90′		
▼ 1.2	BL	Track on right follows power lines.
1.3 ▲	BR	Track on left follows power lines.
▼ 1.5	SO	Track on left.
1.0 ▲	SO	Track on right.
▼ 2.0	SO	Cross through wash.
0.5 ▲	SO	Cross through wash.
▼ 2.4	SO	Track on right; then enter Tusher Wash and bear left.
0.1 ▲	SO	Leave Tusher Wash; then track on left.
GPS: N 38°43.22′ W 109°45.63′		
▼ 2.5	TL	Remain in wash. Track on right leaves wash. Zero trip meter.
0.0 ▲		Continue along wash.
GPS: N 38°43.17′ W 109°45.71′		
▼ 0.0		Continue in wash along Tusher Canyon. Two small tracks to the right.
3.0 ▲	TR	Two faint tracks to the left, then track on left leaves wash. Zero trip meter.
▼ 0.7	SO	Track on right leaves wash; track on left. Remain in wash.
2.3 ▲	SO	Track on left leaves wash; track on right. Remain in wash.
GPS: N 38°42.68′ W 109°45.49′		

SE #14: MONITOR AND MERRIMAC TRAIL

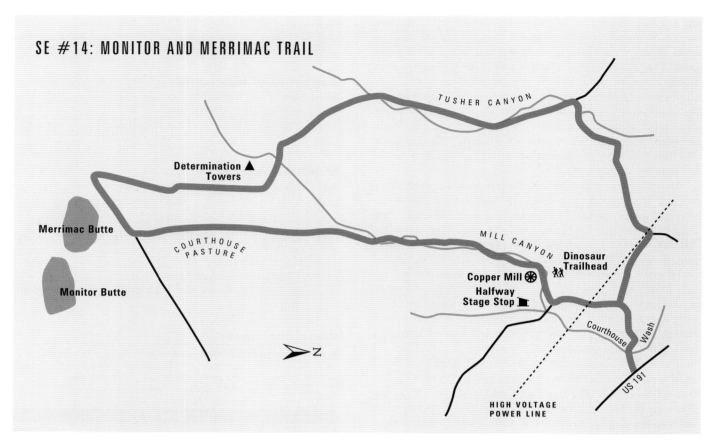

▼ 1.8	TL	Leave the wash, following sign for the Monitor and Merrimac Trail.
1.2 ▲	TR	Turn right and enter Tusher Canyon Wash.

GPS: N 38°41.78' W 109°45.79'

▼ 1.9	SO	Enter wash.
1.1 ▲	SO	Exit wash.

▼ 2.1	BL	Tracks on right; follow sign for the Monitor and Merrimac Trail.
0.9 ▲	BR	Tracks on left.

GPS: N 38°41.53' W 109°45.65'

▼ 2.4	SO	Exit wash.
0.6 ▲	SO	Enter wash.

▼ 2.6	SO	Pass through gap in cliffs. Determination Towers are ahead to the southeast.
0.4 ▲	SO	Pass through gap in cliffs. Tusher Canyon is ahead.

GPS: N 38°41.32' W 109°45.31'

▼ 2.8	TL	Turn left and cross through wash.
0.2 ▲	TR	Cross through wash and turn right.

GPS: N 38°41.18' W 109°45.17'

▼ 3.0	TR	Directly in front of Determination Towers, turn and climb up slickrock. Zero trip meter.
0.0 ▲		Continue toward Tusher Canyon. Trail heads generally north.

GPS: N 38°41.10' W 109°44.94'

▼ 0.0		Continue toward Determination Towers.
1.9 ▲	TL	T-intersection. Join sandy trail and zero trip meter.

▼ 0.2	SO	Pass beside Determination Towers. Trail crosses slickrock and heads generally south. Many smaller trails to the right and left; remain on main trail and go in the direction of Monitor and Merrimac Buttes.

1.7 ▲	SO	Many smaller trails to the left and right. Pass beside Determination Towers across slickrock. Trail leaves in a northerly direction.

GPS: N 38°40.96' W 109°44.94'

▼ 0.7	SO	Track on left.
1.2 ▲	SO	Track on right.

GPS: N 38°40.52' W 109°44.95'

▼ 0.8	SO	Short, steep, difficult uphill pinch.
1.1 ▲	SO	Short, steep, difficult downhill pinch.

GPS: N 38°40.43' W 109°44.90'

▼ 0.9	SO	Track on left.
1.0 ▲	SO	Track on right.

GPS: N 38°40.32' W 109°44.92'

▼ 1.2	SO	Cross through small wash.
0.7 ▲	SO	Cross through small wash.

▼ 1.4	TL	Track straight on goes to Wipe Out Hill. Continue along north face of Merrimac Butte.
0.5 ▲	TR	Track straight on goes to Wipe Out Hill.

GPS: N 38°39.90' W 109°45.06'

▼ 1.9	TL	Crossroads. Track on right is spur that goes 0.8 miles to a slickrock platform between Monitor and Merrimac Buttes. Zero trip meter.
0.0 ▲		Continue along north face of Merrimac Butte.

GPS: N 38°40.18' W 109°44.53'

▼ 0.0		Continue north across Courthouse Pasture.
3.0 ▲	TR	Crossroads. Straight ahead is a spur that goes 0.8 miles to a slickrock platform between Monitor and Merrimac Buttes. Zero trip meter.

▼ 0.5	SO	Track on right.
2.5 ▲	SO	Track on left.

▼ 0.8	SO	Track on left.
2.2 ▲	SO	Track on right.

GPS: N 38°40.95' W 109°44.58'			
▼ 1.0		SO	Track on left.
	2.0 ▲	SO	Track on right.
GPS: N 38°41.07' W 109°44.57'			
▼ 1.1		SO	Track on left.
	1.9 ▲	SO	Track on right.
GPS: N 38°41.25' W 109°44.56'			
▼ 1.9		BL	Track on right.
	1.1 ▲	BR	Track on left.
GPS: N 38°41.85' W 109°44.48'			
▼ 2.0		SO	Cross through Mill Canyon Wash.
	1.0 ▲	SO	Cross through Mill Canyon Wash.
▼ 2.1		SO	Cross through Mill Canyon Wash; track on right goes to campsite.
	0.9 ▲	SO	Track on left goes to campsite; cross through Mill Canyon Wash.
▼ 2.2		SO	Cross through Mill Canyon Wash.
	0.8 ▲	SO	Cross through Mill Canyon Wash.
GPS: N 38°42.13' W 109°44.43'			
▼ 2.5		SO	Enter Mill Canyon Wash.
	0.5 ▲	SO	Exit Mill Canyon Wash.
▼ 2.7		SO	Pass through gate.
	0.3 ▲	SO	Pass through gate.
GPS: N 38°42.56' W 109°44.41'			
▼ 2.9		SO	Leave Mill Canyon Wash. Remains of copper mill are up on the bank to the right just after the wash exit.
	0.1 ▲	SO	Remains of copper mill are up on the bank to the left; enter Mill Canyon Wash.
▼ 3.0		SO	Parking area for Mill Canyon Dinosaur Trail on the left. Zero trip meter.
	0.0 ▲		Continue down to Mill Canyon Wash.
GPS: N 38°42.75' W 109°44.32'			
▼ 0.0			Continue along graded dirt road.
	0.6 ▲	SO	Parking area for Mill Canyon Dinosaur Trail on the right. Zero trip meter.
▼ 0.1		SO	Cross through small wash.
	0.5 ▲	SO	Cross through small wash.
▼ 0.4		SO	Cross through small wash, then track on left.
	0.2 ▲	SO	Track on right, then cross through small wash.
▼ 0.6		BL	Track on right goes 0.3 miles to Halfway Stage Station. Zero trip meter.
	0.0 ▲		Continue on graded road.
GPS: N 38°43.07' W 109°43.89'			
▼ 0.0			Continue toward US 191.
	1.1 ▲	BR	Track on left goes 0.3 miles to Halfway Stage Station. Zero trip meter.
▼ 0.1		SO	Track on left.
	1.0 ▲	SO	Track on right.
▼ 0.5		TR	Track to the left is the start of the loop.
	0.6 ▲	TL	Track to the right is the finish of the loop.
GPS: N 38°43.55' W 109°43.90'			
▼ 0.6		SO	Track on left.
	0.5 ▲	SO	Track on right.
▼ 0.9		SO	Cross through Courthouse Wash; information board on left.
	0.2 ▲	SO	Information board on right; cross through Courthouse Wash.
▼ 1.1			Trail finishes at intersection with US 191. Turn right for Moab, left for I-70.
	0.0 ▲		0.2 miles north of mile marker 141 on US 191, turn west on Mill Canyon Road, cross railroad and cattle guard and zero trip meter.
GPS: N 38°43.66' W 109°43.29'			

Klondike Bluffs Trail

Starting Point:	**North of mile marker 142 on US 191**
Finishing Point:	**Klondike Bluffs**
Total Mileage:	**6.5 miles**
Unpaved Mileage:	**6.5 miles**
Driving Time:	**2.5 hours (one-way)**
Elevation Range:	**4,500–5,200 feet**
Usually Open:	**Year-round**
Difficulty Rating:	**5**
Scenic Rating:	**9**
Remoteness Rating:	**+0**

Special Attractions

- Moderately challenging 4WD trail, with the novelty of driving over expanses of slickrock.
- Far-ranging vistas to the west and south.
- Abandoned mine site and equipment.
- Dinosaur print.

Description

This interesting 4WD trail is perfect for those wanting a little driving excitement combined with fantastic scenery and historic interest. The Klondike Bluffs Trail is contained within BLM land to the east of US 191. The trail is used by mountain bikes as well as vehicles. The first 2.7 miles are graded dirt road suitable for most vehicles. After crossing a fence line, the trail becomes loose sand, wraps around the edge of Little Valley, and crosses a wide, sandy creek. The next 0.7 miles can be the trickiest, especially for large vehicles or those with side steps or low hanging brush bars, as the trail twists along a narrow canyon. A couple of spots call for careful wheel placement to avoid underbody damage.

After 4 miles, the trail heads steadily up a large slab of tilted slickrock. Boulders and white painted lines on the rock

Copper mine ruins can still be found near the end of Klondike Bluffs Trail

The trail traverses gullies and large expanses of slickrock.

show the direction, but keep your eyes open, as hidden gullies can catch the unwary.

Watch for the dinosaur print in the rocks, marked by informal rings of sticks or rocks. At the 5.4-mile mark, the trail reverts to dirt and rocks for the final section across the Klondike Bluffs plateau. A track on the right leads to the remains of a copper mine. The miners worked the poor-grade copper ore from the cliff behind and carried out the first stages of processing on the site. Hunt around to find the water source used—a hole drilled in solid sandstone reveals its location.

The trail is closed to vehicles shortly after the turn to the mine. Mountain bikes can continue on for another couple of hundred yards to the border of Arches National Park.

This trail becomes impassable for a day or two after light snow or heavy rain.

Current Road Information
BLM Moab Field Office
82 East Dogwood
Moab, UT 84532
(435) 259-2100

Map References
BLM Moab (incomplete)
USGS 1:24,000 Merrimac Butte, Klondike Bluffs
     1:100,000 Moab (incomplete)
Maptech CD-ROM: Moab/Canyonlands

Trails Illustrated, #211 (incomplete); #501
Utah Atlas & Gazetteer, p. 40
Utah Travel Council #5 (incomplete)
Other: Latitude 40—Moab West
     Canyon Country Off-Road Vehicle Trail Map—
     Arches Area

Route Directions

▼ 0.0		North of mile marker 142 on US 191, turn right through a gate. There is a small parking area, and a BLM sign points to Klondike Bluffs Trail.
	GPS: N 38°44.45′ W 109°43.97′	
▼ 0.9	SO	Track on right.
▼ 2.0	SO	Track on left.
▼ 2.4	BL	Road forks.
	GPS: N 38°46.24′ W 109°42.90′	
▼ 2.6	BL	Second leg of track enters on right.
▼ 2.7	SO	Cross through fence line. Trail standard turns to 4WD.
▼ 3.1	SO	Follow along the edge of Little Valley.
▼ 3.3	SO	Faint track on left, swing right and cross sandy wash.
▼ 3.4	TR	T-intersection. Follow route markers for Klondike Bluffs.
	GPS: N 38°46.98′ W 109°43.04′	
▼ 3.6	SO	Track on left into canyon. Couple of places need care with wheel placement.
▼ 4.1	SO	Start gradual climb over slickrock.
▼ 4.6	SO	Faint bike track on left. Follow white painted trail markers on rock.
▼ 4.7	SO	Cross crevasse in slickrock that has been filled with rocks.
▼ 4.8	SO	Dinosaur footprint marked by branches on right of trail.
	GPS: N 38°47.58′ W 109°42.34′	
▼ 5.4	SO	Leave slickrock pavement. Trail is now packed dirt and rock.
▼ 5.8	SO	Track on left.
▼ 5.9	TR	Follow brown trail markers.
	GPS: N 38°48.66′ W 109°42.22′	

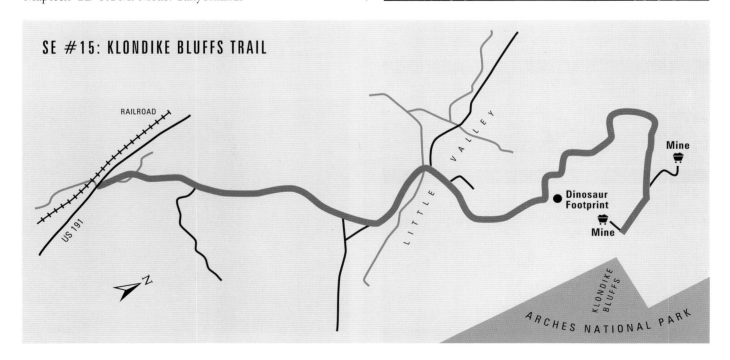

SE #15: KLONDIKE BLUFFS TRAIL

RAILROAD

US 191

N

LITTLE VALLEY

Dinosaur Footprint

Mine

Mine

KLONDIKE BLUFFS

ARCHES NATIONAL PARK

| ▼ 6.2 | BL | Track on right. |
| ▼ 6.5 | | Track on right goes to mining remains. Vehicle route ends here. Track continues and appears to climb bluff, but is blocked on first corner. National park boundary is 0.3 miles farther on. Foot travel only past this point. |

GPS: N 38°48.25′ W 109°41.85′

SOUTHEAST REGION TRAIL #16

Spring Canyon Point Trail

Starting Point:	Dubinky Well
Finishing Point:	Spring Canyon Point
Total Mileage:	12.9 miles
Unpaved Mileage:	12.9 miles
Driving Time:	1 hour (one-way)
Elevation Range:	4,100–5,300 feet
Usually Open:	Year-round
Difficulty Rating:	2
Scenic Rating:	8
Remoteness Rating:	+0

Special Attractions
■ Views over the Green River.
■ Access to a network of 4WD trails.

History
Dubinky Spring, at the start of this trail, is named after Dubinky Anderson, whose parents settled the area in the 1920s. The Anderson family used to live in Valley City, several miles north on US 191. Albert Anderson, Dubinky's father, was notorious for distilling illicit moonshine, and one time he was caught and did

six months in jail. A widely circulated tale tells of Dubinky seeing a ghost in an abandoned cabin in Valley City and taking flight barefoot. He was eventually found shivering and terrified many miles from Valley City at what is now called Dubinky Spring.

The well, named for the spring, was built in 1937 with the assistance of workers from the Dalton Wells Civilian Conservation Corps (located on US 191). In the ongoing battle between sheep herders and cattlemen, the sheep herders would damage the well when the cattlemen left the region in an attempt to get rid of the cattle. But cattle continued to be driven north to the railroad at Thompson and south to graze in the Island in the Sky region.

Rock cairn along the Spring Canyon Point

The Needles rise up behind the Spring Canyon wash crossing

Description
This easy and scenic trail leads along sandy, graded roads to finish on a narrow-necked promontory high above the Green River. The trail surface makes it suitable for high-clearance vehicles in dry weather. It is predominantly graded sandy road, with sections of deep, powder-fine sand. There are great views all along this trail: Early on there are rocky red buttes and glimpses into Spring Canyon to the southeast and, later, as you travel out onto the point, the Green River dominates the view far below.

The trail leaves Dubinky Well Road immediately south of the old windmill and spring. It crosses the very start of Spring Canyon Wash and then passes directly underneath The Needles. These large red rock buttes are also known as Tombstone Rock. Around their bases are a couple of pleasant campsites, which are the best on the trail—ones farther down tend to be very exposed.

Many trails that lead off from this road are worth exploring if you have time. The main trail ends on Spring Canyon Point. Scramble over the rocks at the end for views of the river; the trail below goes to Hey Joe Canyon.

Current Road Information
BLM Moab Field Office
82 East Dogwood
Moab, UT 84532
(435) 259-2100

Map References
BLM Moab, San Rafael Desert
USGS 1:24,000 Dubinky Wash, Tenmile Point, Bowknot Bend
1:100,000 Moab, San Rafael Desert
Maptech CD-ROM: Moab/Canyonlands; Central/San Rafael
Utah Atlas & Gazetteer, p. 40
Utah Travel Council #5 (incomplete)
Other: Latitude 40—Moab West
Canyon Country Off-Road Vehicle Trail Map—
Island Area

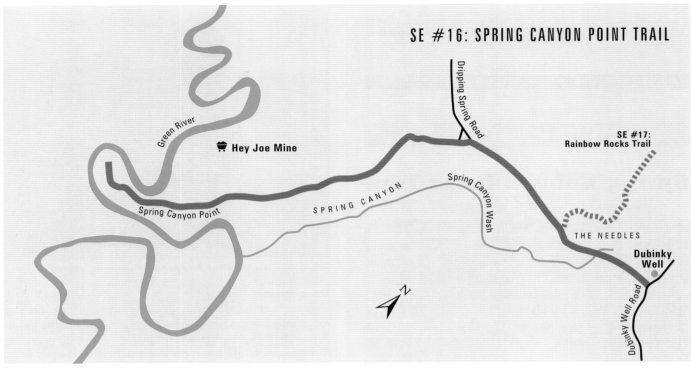

SE #16: SPRING CANYON POINT TRAIL

Route Directions

▼ 0.0		From Dubinky Well Road, 0.2 miles south of the windmill itself, zero trip meter and turn west onto unmarked graded sandy road.

GPS: N 38°41.45' W 109°52.87'

▼ 1.2	SO	Cross through wash; this is start of Spring Canyon Wash.
▼ 1.3	SO	Track on right.
▼ 1.4	SO	Cattle guard.
▼ 1.9	SO	Foot of The Needles. Small track on right, then track on left. Keep right around the base of The Needles. Continue to the northwest.

GPS: N 38°41.05' W 109°54.97'

▼ 2.0	SO	Cattle guard, then track on right.
▼ 2.1	BL	Track on right is Southeast #17: Rainbow Rocks Trail. Zero trip meter.

GPS: N 38°41.19' W 109°55.15'

▼ 0.0		Continue along main trail.
▼ 0.7	SO	Track on left.
▼ 1.0	SO	Track on right.
▼ 1.2	SO	Track on left.
▼ 1.3	BL	Track on right goes to Dripping Spring. Zero trip meter.

GPS: N 38°41.47' W 109°56.54'

▼ 0.0		Continue toward Spring Canyon Point.
▼ 0.1	SO	Second entrance to Dripping Spring road on right.
▼ 0.7	SO	Pass through fence line.
▼ 0.9	SO	Track on left.

GPS: N 38°41.33' W 109°57.54'

▼ 1.7	SO	Track on right.

GPS: N 38°41.13' W 109°58.28'

▼ 1.9	SO	Track on left, then track on right goes to cairn.
▼ 3.2	SO	Cross through rocky wash.
▼ 3.4	BR	Cross through fence line, then track on left.

GPS: N 38°40.07' W 109°59.09'

▼ 4.2	SO	Track on right.
▼ 4.5	SO	Track on right.

▼ 5.4	SO	Track on left. Main trail runs out along the narrow Spring Canyon Point.
▼ 5.8	SO	Cross through fence line.
▼ 5.9	SO	Viewpoint on left.
▼ 6.6	SO	Track on right.

GPS: N 38°37.77' W 110°01.30'

▼ 6.7	SO	Track on left.
▼ 7.0	SO	Track on left.
▼ 9.4	SO	Oil drilling hole on left.
▼ 9.5		Trail ends at overlook for the Green River. Large turnaround area on promontory, with river views on three sides.

GPS: N 38°36.91' W 110°03.67'

SOUTHEAST REGION TRAIL #17

Rainbow Rocks Trail

Starting Point:	**The Needles on Southeast #16: Spring Canyon Point Trail**
Finishing Point:	**Southeast #18: Levi Well Trail, 2.8 miles from western end**
Total Mileage:	**5.9 miles**
Unpaved Mileage:	**5.9 miles**
Driving Time:	**1 hour**
Elevation Range:	**4,400–5,200 feet**
Usually Open:	**Year-round**
Difficulty Rating:	**5**
Scenic Rating:	**9**
Remoteness Rating:	**+0**

Special Attractions
- Multihued sandstone rock cliffs.
- Interesting trail over a variety of surfaces.

Description
This short trail leaves immediately west of The Needles, the prominent Entrada sandstone butte near the start of Southeast #16: Spring Canyon Point Trail. Initially, the ungraded trail is soft and sandy as it runs near the western side of The Needles. Then after a fork, it parallels the cliff more closely, the sand gives way to rocks and slickrock, and it crosses a slickrock pavement marked by small cairns.

After 1.5 miles, the trail crosses through a wash with a short, steep slickrock exit. Once the trail drops down onto the plain of Freckle Flat, it becomes very sandy and is subject to frequent washouts. Some of these ruts can be very deep; negotiating them takes careful wheel placement. If any washouts are too deep, a few minutes' work with a shovel in the sand can often make them passable. As the trail passes along Freckle Flat, you can see the multihued sandstone rocks that give the trail its name. The Entrada sandstone domes are banded with colors from white to pale pink to the deepest reds. The trail ends on the equally sandy Southeast #18: Levi Well Trail—the shortest exit is to the left to Duma Point Road.

Climbing over a steep section of slickrock on the Rainbow Rocks Trail

For campers, the best place to pitch a tent is at the start of the trail, around the face of the Needles. Otherwise the trail does not offer much in the way of campsites.

Current Road Information
BLM Moab Field Office
82 East Dogwood
Moab, UT 84532
(435) 259-2100

Map References
BLM Moab (incomplete)
USGS 1:24,000 Dubinky Wash
1:100,000 Moab (incomplete)
Maptech CD-ROM: Moab/Canyonlands
Utah Atlas & Gazetteer, p. 40
Other: Latitude 40—Moab West
Canyon Country Off-Road Vehicle Trail Map—
Island Area

Route Directions

▼ 0.0 From Southeast #16: Spring Canyon Point Trail, 2.1 miles from the junction with Dubinky Well Road, turn north immediately past The Needles and zero trip meter.
5.9 ▲ Trail ends at the junction with Southeast #16: Spring Canyon Point Trail at The Needles. Turn right to continue to Spring Canyon Point; turn left to exit to Dubinky Well Road.

GPS: N 38°41.19' W 109°55.13'

▼ 0.2 BR Track on left.
5.7 ▲ SO Track on right.

▼ 1.0 SO Cross slickrock pavement; small cairns show the route.
4.9 ▲ SO Leave slickrock pavement.

▼ 1.5 SO Cross through wash with short, steep slickrock exit.
4.4 ▲ SO Cross through wash with short, steep slickrock exit. Trail now crosses slickrock; small cairns show the route.

▼ 2.2 BR Track on left.
3.7 ▲ BL Track on right.

GPS: N 38°42.37' W 109°54.66'

▼ 2.4 SO Cross through rocky wash. Trail is now very sandy.
3.5 ▲ SO Cross through rocky wash.

▼ 2.9 SO Cross through sandy wash.
3.0 ▲ SO Cross through sandy wash.

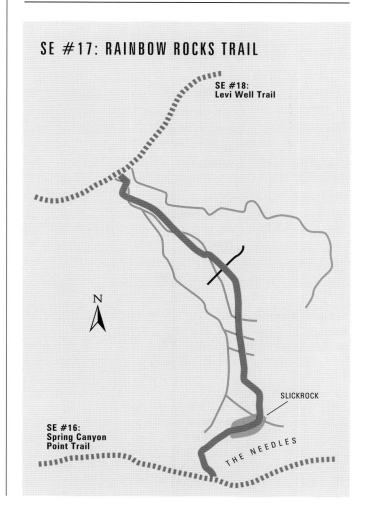

SE #17: RAINBOW ROCKS TRAIL

SE #18:
Levi Well Trail

N

SLICKROCK

SE #16:
Spring Canyon
Point Trail

THE NEEDLES

▼ 3.1		SO	Cross through wash.
	2.8 ▲	SO	Cross through wash.
▼ 3.8		SO	Tracks on right and left.
	2.1 ▲	SO	Tracks on right and left.
	GPS: N 38°43.79' W 109°55.01'		
▼ 5.0		SO	Enter wash.
	0.9 ▲	SO	Exit wash.
	GPS: N 38°44.40' W 109°55.93'		
▼ 5.3		BL	Exit wash up bank on left.
	0.6 ▲	BR	Enter wash.
	GPS: N 38°44.55' W 109°56.13'		
▼ 5.4		BL	Enter wash.
	0.5 ▲	BR	Exit wash on right.
▼ 5.5		SO	Exit wash on right.
	0.4 ▲	SO	Enter wash.
▼ 5.9			Trail ends at the junction with Southeast #18: Levi Well Trail. Turn left to exit via Duma Point Road; turn right to exit via Blue Hills Road.
	0.0 ▲		Trail starts at the junction with Southeast #18: Levi Well Trail, 0.1 miles east of a deep, sandy creek crossing and 2.8 miles from the western end of the trail. Zero trip meter and turn southeast on unmarked, small sandy track.
	GPS: N 38°44.94' W 109°56.63'		

SOUTHEAST REGION TRAIL #18

Levi Well Trail

Starting Point:	**Blue Hills Road, 0.2 miles north of Dubinky Well Road**
Finishing Point:	**Duma Point Road, 5.1 miles south of the junction with Blue Hills Road**
Total Mileage:	**8.8 miles**
Unpaved Mileage:	**8.8 miles**
Driving Time:	**1 hour**
Elevation Range:	**4,300–4,500 feet**
Usually Open:	**Year-round**
Difficulty Rating:	**4**
Scenic Rating:	**8**
Remoteness Rating:	**+0**

Special Attractions

- Beautiful Tenmile Canyon.
- Entrada buttes and the Blue Hills.
- Photo opportunities in the sand dunes.

Description

The difficulty with this trail is the loose, deep sand along most of its length, particularly the last 3 miles around Tenmile Canyon. The trail slants away from Blue Hills Road. The first section runs through the Blue Hills, close to the upper end of Tenmile Wash. This section can be extremely boggy when wet, as the remaining ruts testify. The trail passes out of the low Blue Hills and passes by Levi Well itself, which is just off the trail in a thicket of

Entering Tenmile Canyon along the Levi Well Trail

tamarisk. This is a free-flowing well that feeds a cattletank.

The trail rises slightly and runs along wide Tenmile Canyon. The surface is very loose in dry weather and, conversely, is often impassable in wet weather, as the deep sand traps turn to greasy mud! Just before the end of Southeast #17: Rainbow Rocks Trail, there are some very photogenic sand dunes off the trail to the north, set against the backdrop of the Entrada sandstone buttes. There are further small dunes a short way along Rainbow Rocks Trail. After you pass the end of the Rainbow Rocks Trail, the worst of the sand starts, as the trail immediately drops down to cross a sandy creek, a tributary of Tenmile Canyon. The crossing itself is easy, but the exit is up a steep, washed out, loose sandy slope that may give you trouble in drier weather.

The main Tenmile Canyon is crossed a mile farther on, and this is a very wide, flat-bottomed sandy canyon, with the loosest and deepest sand of all and a tricky exit. The creek flows pretty much year-round, reducing to a trickle in the drier months. This canyon is very pretty, with large cottonwoods in the wash around Dripping Spring, just off the trail to the left.

From Tenmile Canyon, there are a couple more wash crossings; then the trail proceeds to join the Duma Point Road.

Current Road Information

BLM Moab Field Office
82 East Dogwood
Moab, UT 84532
(435) 259-2100

Map References

BLM Moab
USGS 1:24,000 Valley City, Dee Pass, Dubinky Wash
1:100,000 Moab
Maptech CD-ROM: Moab/Canyonlands
Trails Illustrated, #501 (incomplete)
Utah Atlas & Gazetteer, p. 40
Other: Latitude 40—Moab West
Canyon Country Off-Road Vehicle Trail Map—
Island Area

Route Directions

▼ 0.0	From Blue Hills Road, 0.2 miles north of Dubinky Well Road, turn northwest onto

	1.6 ▲		unmarked track and zero trip meter. Trail ends at the junction with Blue Hills Road, 0.2 miles north of junction with Dubinky Well Road. Turn right to join Dubinky Well Road.

GPS: N 38°47.08' W 109°51.03'

▼ 0.5		SO	Track on left.
	1.1 ▲	SO	Track on right.
▼ 0.8		SO	Faint track on left.
	0.8 ▲	SO	Faint track on right.
▼ 1.0		SO	Pass through fence line.
	0.6 ▲	SO	Pass through fence line.

GPS: N 38°47.25' W 109°52.21'

▼ 1.3		SO	Cross through small wash, then track on left.
	0.3 ▲	SO	Track on right, then cross through small wash.
▼ 1.6		SO	Track on right goes to Levi Well, just off the trail. Also track on left. Zero trip meter.
	0.0 ▲		Continue to the east.

GPS: N 38°47.02' W 109°52.75'

▼ 0.0			Continue to the west.
	4.4 ▲	SO	Track on left goes to Levi Well, just off the trail. Also track on right. Zero trip meter.
▼ 0.1		SO	Cross through fence line.
	4.3 ▲	SO	Cross through fence line.
▼ 0.4		SO	Small track on right.
	4.0 ▲	SO	Small track on left.
▼ 1.1		BR	Track on left.
	3.3 ▲	BL	Track on right.

GPS: N 38°46.63' W 109°53.73'

▼ 2.5		SO	Track on left.
	1.9 ▲	SO	Track on left.
▼ 3.2		SO	Cross through wash.
	1.2 ▲	SO	Cross through wash.
▼ 3.7		SO	Sand dunes on right, just a short way from the track.
	0.7 ▲	SO	Sand dunes on left, just a short way from the track.
▼ 3.9		SO	Cattle guard.
	0.5 ▲	SO	Cattle guard.
▼ 4.2		SO	Cross through wide, sandy wash; entrance often washes out and may require a detour.

	0.2 ▲	SO	Cross through wide, sandy wash; exit often washes out and may require a detour.
▼ 4.4		SO	Track on left is start of Southeast #17: Rainbow Rocks Trail. Zero trip meter.
	0.0 ▲		Continue northeast.

GPS: N 38°44.94' W 109°56.63'

▼ 0.0			Continue southwest.
	2.8 ▲	SO	Track on right is start of Southeast #17: Rainbow Rocks Trail. Zero trip meter.
▼ 0.1		SO	Cross through sandy creek; washed out steep, sandy exit.
	2.7 ▲	SO	Cross through sandy creek; washed out steep, sandy entrance.
▼ 0.2		BR	Track on left, then track on right.
	2.6 ▲	SO	Track on left, then track on right.

GPS: N 38°44.84' W 109°56.76'

▼ 0.5		SO	Track on left, also track on right.
	2.3 ▲	BL	Track on right, also track on left.

GPS: N 38°44.73' W 109°57.09'

▼ 0.6		SO	Cross through slickrock wash.
	2.2 ▲	SO	Cross through slickrock wash.
▼ 0.8		SO	Cross through wash.
	2.0 ▲	SO	Cross through wash.
▼ 1.0		SO	Cross through wash, then track on left.
	1.8 ▲	SO	Track on right, then cross through wash.
▼ 1.1		SO	Faint track on left.
	1.7 ▲	SO	Faint track on right.
▼ 1.2		SO	Drop down to enter Tenmile Canyon.
	1.6 ▲	SO	Leaving Tenmile Canyon.
▼ 1.3		SO	Cross through Tenmile Canyon wash, then creek. Track on left along wash and corral on right in wash.
	1.5 ▲	SO	Cross through Tenmile Canyon creek, then wash. Track on right along wash and corral on left in wash.

GPS: N 38°44.75' W 109°57.92'

▼ 1.5		SO	Track on left.
	1.3 ▲	SO	Track on right.
▼ 1.6		BR	Track on left.
	1.2 ▲	BL	Track on right.

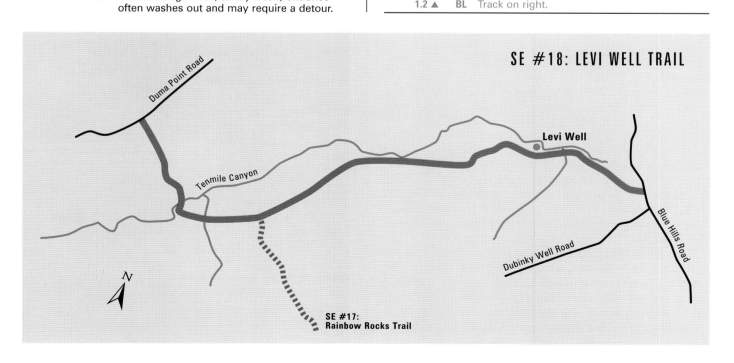

SE #18: LEVI WELL TRAIL

▼ 1.7	SO	Cross through wash.
1.1 ▲	SO	Cross through wash.
▼ 2.2	BR	Track on left.
0.6 ▲	SO	Track on right.

GPS: N 38°45.21' W 109°58.50'

| ▼ 2.8 | | Trail ends at intersection with the graded Duma Point Road. Turn right to exit via graded roads to US 191 and return to Moab. Turning right can also lead north to I-70. |
| 0.0 ▲ | | Trail starts at intersection with the graded Duma Point Road, 5.1 miles from the junction with Blue Hills Road. Turn southeast onto dirt track and zero trip meter. |

GPS: N 38°45.57' W 109°59.08'

SOUTHEAST REGION TRAIL #19

Crystal Geyser Trail

Starting Point:	Utah 6 (Old Highway)
Finishing Point:	Ruby Ranch Road
Total Mileage:	21.7 miles
Unpaved Mileage:	20.9 miles
Driving Time:	3 hours
Elevation Range:	4,000–4,400 feet
Usually Open:	Year-round
Difficulty Rating:	5
Scenic Rating:	8
Remoteness Rating:	+1

Special Attractions

■ The Crystal Geyser and colorful mineral deposits.
■ Views along the Green River.
■ Moderately challenging remote route between Green River and Moab.

History

Crystal Geyser and four other geysers in the region are the unexpected results of oil drilling. Directly underneath Crystal Geyser is the sloping rock strata of the San Rafael Swell. Water runs down the strata, and where Crystal Geyser is located, near the bottom, the water is under considerable pressure. Drillers searching for oil in the 1930s sunk a shaft that reached carbon dioxide pockets underneath the water. The geyser is the result of the gas pressure that builds until it shoots the water about 20 feet in the air at irregular intervals, roughly twice a day. These artificial geysers are the only cold water geysers on the continent.

The colorful deposits between the geyser and the Green River are calcite—calcium carbonate stained by various mineral impurities, creating hues from yellow and brown to vivid orange and rust red. The scalloped edges of the deposits act like tiny dams, and blue-green algae use them to immerse themselves in the mineral-rich waters. Tufa, the by-product of the algae's photosynthesis, gradually builds up over time,

adding to the colorful runoff from the geyser.

The geyser's water, brought up from the underlying rock strata, is highly mineralized. Crystal Geyser alone is responsible for adding 3,000 tons of salts each year to the Green River and hence also to the Colorado River. The salt has consequences for both the river ecosystem and for users of the water. In the mid-1970s, Mexico claimed that the waters it received from the Colorado River were too highly mineralized for domestic or even agricultural use. A desalinization plant was built near the Colorado River in southern California to render the water acceptable to Mexico.

Description

This trail leaves the town of Green River, visits the cold water Crystal Geyser, then travels farther along the Green River, crossing the desolate Morrison Formation on old mining trails, until it joins Salt Wash Road. The trail is moderately challenging—both for driving and route finding—but it is normally within the range of most stock high-clearance SUVs.

The route starts 4 miles east of the town of Green River along Utah 6, the Old Highway, which runs north of and parallel to I-70. For the first 5 miles to Crystal Geyser, the road is graded gravel. The geyser is particularly photogenic at sunset, when the setting sun intensifies the colors of the mineral deposits. From there, the trail parallels the Green River for a few more miles before bearing away on smaller, ungraded trails across the Morrison Formation. There are no route markings, so navigation can be tricky; this part of the trail is not on any map that we have seen. Therefore, we have provided additional GPS waypoints to help you navigate this difficult section. At times the correct trail is not the most used. There are a couple of short, steep sections with loose broken rock that will require careful wheel placement and maybe someone outside the vehicle to "spot," but most of the surface is easy going, with long sections of fairly smooth two-track. Interspersed with these are rougher rocky sections to

The trail winds along Green River with the San Rafael Reef in the distance

keep the driver's attention on the trail! Some of the wash crossings are ditchy, which may catch longer rear overhangs.

Once the trail joins Salt Wash it becomes a graded dirt road; it follows above the wash before finishing on the graded gravel Ruby Ranch Road.

Current Road Information
BLM Moab Field Office
82 East Dogwood
Moab, UT 84532
(435) 259-2100

Map References

BLM San Rafael Desert, Moab (incomplete)
USGS 1:24,000 Green River NE, Green River, Green River SE, Dee Pass (incomplete)
  1:100,000 San Rafael Desert, Moab (incomplete)
Maptech CD-ROM: Moab/Canyonlands; Central/San Rafael
Utah Atlas & Gazetteer, pp. 39, 40
Utah Travel Council #5 (incomplete)
Other: Canyon Country Off-Road Vehicle Trail Map— Island Area

Route Directions

▼ 0.0			From the Old Highway, 4 miles east of Green River, 0.3 miles east of where it passes underneath the railroad, turn south on unmarked single lane paved road and zero trip meter.
	4.8 ▲		Trail finishes on the Old Highway, 4 miles east of Green River. Turn left for Green River and I-70.
			GPS: N 38°58.52' W 110°04.61'
▼ 0.6		SO	Pass underneath I-70.
	4.2 ▲	SO	Pass underneath I-70.
▼ 0.7		SO	Cattle guard.
	4.1 ▲	SO	Cattle guard.
▼ 0.8		SO	Road is now graded gravel.
	4.0 ▲	SO	Road is now single lane and paved.
▼ 1.0		SO	Track on left.
	3.8 ▲	SO	Track on right.
▼ 1.4		SO	Pass underneath power lines, then intersection.
	3.4 ▲	SO	Intersection, then pass underneath power lines.
			GPS: N 38°57.39' W 110°05.23'
▼ 2.7		SO	Track on left.
	2.1 ▲	SO	Track on right.
▼ 3.0		SO	Track on left.
	1.8 ▲	SO	Track on right.
▼ 4.6		SO	Track on left.
	0.2 ▲	SO	Track on right.
▼ 4.8		BL	Track on right goes 0.5 miles to Crystal Geyser. After visiting the geyser, return to this junction and continue on the left fork. Zero trip meter.
	0.0 ▲		Continue toward I-70.
			GPS: N 38°56.08' W 110°07.72'
▼ 0.0			Continue south toward the Green River.
	2.9 ▲	SO	Track on left goes 0.5 miles to Crystal Geyser. After visiting the geyser, return to this junction and continue straight ahead. Zero trip meter.
▼ 0.5		SO	Track on left to corral, then second track on left at wash. Cross through Little Grand Wash.
	2.4 ▲	SO	Cross through Little Grand Wash. Track on right at wash, then second track on right to corral.
			GPS: N 38°55.69' W 110°07.69'
▼ 0.6		SO	Track on left. Main trail follows along the Green River.
	2.3 ▲	SO	Track on right.
▼ 1.4		SO	Gate.
	1.5 ▲	SO	Gate.
▼ 1.6		SO	Cross through wash.
	1.3 ▲	SO	Cross through wash.
▼ 2.2		SO	Track on right.
	0.7 ▲	SO	Track on left.

Difficult steep, rocky drop into the wash along the Crystal Geyser Trail

			GPS: N 38°55.19' W 110°09.48'
▼ 2.8		BL	Track on right, then cross through wash.
	0.1 ▲	SO	Cross through wash, then track on left.
			GPS: N 38°55.07' W 110°10.08'
▼ 2.9		BL	Track forks three ways; take left track. Middle track continues to river. Zero trip meter.
	0.0 ▲		Continue to the northeast.
			GPS: N 38°55.01' W 110°10.14'
▼ 0.0			Continue to the southwest.
	3.9 ▲	SO	Two tracks on left, continue straight ahead. First track on left goes to river.
▼ 0.1		SO	Track on left.
	3.8 ▲	SO	Track on right.
▼ 0.5		SO	Small ditchy wash crossing.
	3.4 ▲	SO	Small ditchy wash crossing.
▼ 0.7		SO	Track on right, then cross through fence line.
	3.2 ▲	SO	Cross through fence line, then track on left.
			GPS: N 38°54.35' W 110°10.11'
▼ 0.9		BL	Track on right, followed by second track on right, and very faint track on left.
	3.0 ▲	SO	Faint track on right, then track on left, followed by second track on left.
			GPS: N 38°54.23' W 110°10.01'
▼ 1.0		SO	Cross through wash.
	2.9 ▲	SO	Cross through wash.
▼ 1.3		SO	Cross through small wash.
	2.6 ▲	SO	Cross through small wash.
▼ 1.4		SO	Cross through small wash.
	2.5 ▲	SO	Cross through small wash.
▼ 2.3		TL	T-intersection. Track on right goes to viewpoint and continues. Turn left over ridge with views to both sides.
	1.6 ▲	TR	Track straight on goes to viewpoint and continues.
			GPS: N 38°53.87' W 110°08.92'
▼ 2.5		SO	Descend from ridge.
	1.4 ▲	SO	Top of ridge.
▼ 2.6		BL	At base of climb trail forks.

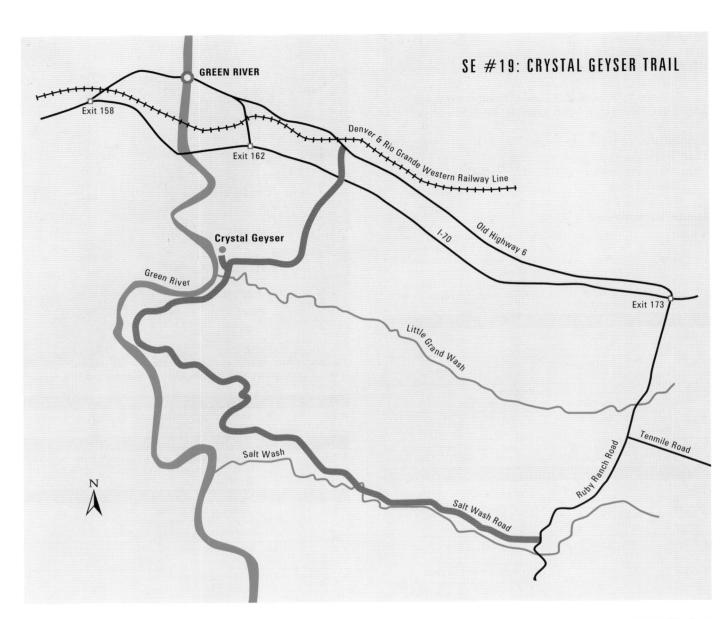

1.3 ▲	SO	Track on right. Trail climbs up ridge.	

▼ 3.0	SO	Cross wash.	
0.9 ▲	SO	Cross wash.	

GPS: N 38°53.78' W 110°08.19'

▼ 3.4	SO	Trail is wider and graded at this point.
0.5 ▲	SO	Trail is narrower and ungraded.

GPS: N 38°53.52' W 110°07.80'

▼ 3.9	TR	Turn right onto faint track; larger trail bears left here. Zero trip meter.
0.0 ▲		Continue on larger, graded trail.

GPS: N 38°53.56' W 110°07.22'

▼ 0.0		Continue on fainter trail.
7.8 ▲	TL	Track on right. Turn left onto wider graded trail. Zero trip meter.

▼ 0.1	TL	Intersection.
7.7 ▲	TR	Intersection.

GPS: N 38°53.46' W 110°07.34'

▼ 0.5	SO	Trail crosses rocky area; route is marked by small cairns. Then short drop into wash.
7.3 ▲	SO	Short, steep climb out of wash, then cross rocky area marked by small cairns.

GPS: N 38°53.17' W 110°07.19'

▼ 1.0	SO	Cross through fence line, then steep descent.
6.8 ▲	SO	Steep climb, then cross through fence line.

GPS: N 38°53.09' W 110°07.49'

▼ 1.3	SO	Enter wash.
6.5 ▲	SO	Exit wash.

GPS: N 38°52.88' W 110°07.68'

▼ 1.6	TL	T-intersection in small wash.
6.2 ▲	TR	Track on left in small wash.

GPS: N 38°52.68' W 110°07.92'

▼ 1.8	SO	Faint track on left.
6.0 ▲	SO	Faint track on right.

▼ 1.9	BL	Track on right.
5.9 ▲	SO	Track on left.

GPS: N 38°52.54' W 110°07.69'

▼ 2.0	TL	Track on right to viewpoint.
5.8 ▲	TR	Track on left to viewpoint.

GPS: N 38°52.50' W 110°07.62'

▼ 2.1	BR	Two faint tracks ahead, cairn on right. Swing right and descend onto bench.

5.7 ▲	BL	Leave bench and swing left, cairn on left and two faint tracks on right.

GPS: N 38°52.57' W 110°07.58'

▼ 2.2	SO	Cross gully, long vehicles watch rear.
5.6 ▲	SO	Cross gully, long vehicles watch rear.

GPS: N 38°52.59' W 110°07.42'

▼ 2.5	SO	Wire gate, cross through fence line.
5.3 ▲	SO	Wire gate, cross through fence line.

GPS: N 38°52.57' W 110°07.09'

▼ 2.7	SO	Cross through wash.
5.1 ▲	SO	Cross through wash.
▼ 2.9	SO	Track on right.
4.9 ▲	SO	Track on left.

GPS: N 38°52.48' W 110°06.68'

▼ 3.7	SO	Cross through wash.
4.1 ▲	SO	Cross through wash.

GPS: N 38°52.36' W 110°05.83'

▼ 3.8	SO	Tracks on left and right. Trail becomes easier.
4.0 ▲	SO	Tracks on left and right. Trail becomes rougher and narrower.

GPS: N 38°52.28' W 110°05.67'

▼ 3.9	SO	Track on left.
3.9 ▲	SO	Track on right.
▼ 4.7	BL	Track on right. Salt Wash is on the right.
3.1 ▲	BR	Track on left.

GPS: N 38°51.76' W 110°05.26'

▼ 5.1	SO	Track on right.
2.7 ▲	SO	Track on left.

GPS: N 38°51.58' W 110°04.82'

▼ 5.2	SO	Track on left.
2.6 ▲	SO	Track on right.
▼ 5.6	SO	Cross through wash.
2.2 ▲	SO	Cross through wash.
▼ 6.4	SO	Track on right.
1.4 ▲	SO	Track on left rejoins.

GPS: N 38°50.99' W 110°03.56'

▼ 6.6	SO	Track on right rejoins. Enter Salt Wash.
1.2 ▲	SO	Track on left. Exit wash.
▼ 6.8	SO	Leave wash.
1.0 ▲	SO	Enter Salt Wash.
▼ 6.9	SO	Two faint tracks on left.
0.9 ▲	SO	Two faint tracks on right.
▼ 7.6	SO	Cross through wash.
0.2 ▲	SO	Cross through wash.
▼ 7.8	TR	T-intersection. Join graded dirt road and zero trip meter.
0.0 ▲		Continue on smaller, ungraded road.

GPS: N 38°50.98' W 110°02.04'

▼ 0.0		Continue on graded road.
2.3 ▲	TL	Turn left onto smaller trail and zero trip meter.
▼ 1.0	SO	Corral against red rock on left.
1.3 ▲	SO	Corral against red rock on right.
▼ 2.1	SO	Cross though wash.
0.2 ▲	SO	Cross through wash.
▼ 2.2	SO	Cross through wash.
0.1 ▲	SO	Cross through wash.
▼ 2.3		Trail ends at junction with the graded gravel Ruby Ranch Road. Turn left for I-70.
0.0 ▲		Trail starts at the junction of the graded Ruby Ranch Road and Salt Wash Road, 3.1 miles south of Tenmile Road. Junction is unmarked. Zero trip meter and turn west on graded dirt Salt Wash Road.

GPS: N 38°50.19' W 109°59.68'

Yellow Cat Trail

Starting Point:	**US 191, 0.7 miles north of mile marker 152**
Finishing Point:	**Intersection with Utah 128**
Total Mileage:	**35.7 miles**
Unpaved Mileage:	**35.7 miles**
Driving Time:	**3.5 hours**
Elevation Range:	**4,200–5,200 feet**
Usually Open:	**Year-round**
Difficulty Rating:	**3**
Scenic Rating:	**8**
Remoteness Rating:	**+1**

Special Attractions

■ Uranium mining remains around The Poison Strip.
■ Longer, more remote version of Southeast #21: Yellow Cat Road.
■ Access to many remote 4WD trails.

History

Uranium deposits around the Moab area first attracted miners in the 1890s, but none of the mines paid off until the Atomic Energy Commission upped demand during the Cold War in the 1950s. Fortune hunters came out in droves, and there were many reasonably profitable mines located around Yellow Cat Flat and south of The Poison Strip. The area had quite a collection of miners, prospectors, and profiteers; as the old workings show, there were some large adits tunneled into the hillside. These mines were often abandoned as quickly as they sprung up, leaving workings, ore hoppers, cabins, vehicles, and other equipment to rust and rot.

One of the more famous miners to set up a base on Yellow

The Mollie Hogans rise above the dam along Yellow Cat Trail

A timber cabin beside the trail

Cat Flat, hoping to strike it rich, was Charlie Steen, who made his fortune when he founded the Mi Vida Mine down in the Lisbon Valley. The Steen family spent a winter in a small trailer on Yellow Cat Flat in the early 1950s, staking many small claims in the region.

Prior to uranium, Yellow Cat Flat yielded another find. A scientific expedition in the 1920s discovered two tons of dinosaur bones on the surface of Yellow Cat Flat.

The Poison Strip gained its name because of arsenic in the soil, which killed the sheep that grazed the area.

Description

This trail is the longer version of Southeast #21: Yellow Cat Road. It duplicates Yellow Cat Road for a short stretch along The Poison Strip, but it also includes some sections of

Timber supports line this adit near the eastern end of the trail

rougher trail at either end, and it passes by other mines and points of interest. In dry weather, this trail is suitable for a high-clearance vehicle, although some sections of the trail can be very loose and sandy in extremely dry weather, making 4WD preferable.

The trail leaves US 191 along the Thompson Cutoff Road and passes the north end of Southeast #22: Salt Valley Road; then it crosses the flat Little Valley and the desolate Yellow Cat Flat. After 15 miles, it turns onto a smaller, ungraded trail that winds through the once-busy uranium mining district. A multitude of side trails are worth exploring; many of them lead to mining remains, adits, and workings.

The trail joins Mine Draw and swings north. This is the start of Southeast #23: Salt Wash Overlook Trail, a short spur trail that passes more mining remains before finishing at an

overlook above Salt Valley. The main trail goes north to join graded Southeast #21: Yellow Cat Road, passing close to some of the more substantial uranium mine remains on the trail, the Parco Mines and the Little Eva Mines. These mines have tunnels so large you could drive a truck into them. It is possible, by cutting through the maze of smaller trails, to join Yellow Cat Road further to the east. A compass or GPS helps! These mines are private property and posted as the Lucky Strike, but they do not appear to be actively worked, and it is possible to see many of the old workings, adits, and old vehicles left abandoned. Remember that it is dangerous to enter adits or tunnels because of the buildup of deadly radon gas. Holes and diggings are also often unmarked, so exercise due care when exploring around the diggings.

The trail now joins the larger Yellow Cat Road, cuts through the gap of the blackstone incline, and then passes the substantial remains of an old ore hopper beside the trail. A maze of tracks to the right at this point leads back to the Parco Mines and the Little Eva Mines, and then you intersect the start of Southeast #24: Dome Plateau Trail.

Remaining on The Poison Strip, the trail continues east, just south of The Poison Strip ridge. The remains of the old Cactus Rat Mine are on both sides of the trail, but there is little here to see.

The trail leaves Yellow Cat Road 4.4 miles after joining it and continues along the plateau to the south. The trail standard drops to an ungraded dirt track again as it descends toward Owl Draw. This section has some of the prettiest scenery along the trail, as the multicolored sandstone domes appear. The surface is loose and sandy, and there can be washouts.

The trail, 7.6 miles after leaving Yellow Cat Road, passes two very solid log cabins built of railroad sleepers. There are mining remains and adits here, too, but the origin and the name of the mine are unknown.

The trail passes the northern end of Southeast #29: Wood Road, which is marked on some maps as being the end of Yellow Cat Trail. The main trail, however, runs along Owl Draw to finish on Utah 128.

Current Road Information

BLM Moab Field Office
82 East Dogwood
Moab, UT 84532
(435) 259-2100

Map References

BLM Moab
USGS 1:24,000 Crescent Junction, Thompson Springs, Klondike Bluffs, Mollie Hogans, Cisco SW, Dewey
1:100,000 Moab
Maptech CD-ROM: Moab/Canyonlands
Trails Illustrated, #501; #211
Utah Atlas & Gazetteer, pp. 40, 41
Utah Travel Council #5
Other: Latitude 40—Moab West
Latitude 40—Moab East
Canyon Country Off-Road Vehicle Trail Map—Arches Area

Route Directions

▼ 0.0			From US 191, 0.7 miles north of mile marker 152, turn northeast on graded dirt Thompson Cutoff Road. Turn is unsigned.
	1.2 ▲		Trail ends at intersection with US 191. Turn right to join I-70, turn left for Moab.

GPS: N 38°52.61′ W 109°48.69′

▼ 0.2		SO	Track on right.
	1.0 ▲	SO	Track on left.
▼ 1.1		SO	Cross over wash on bridge.
	0.1 ▲	SO	Cross over wash on bridge.
▼ 1.2		TR	Turn right onto unmarked, graded dirt road on right. Zero trip meter.
	0.0 ▲		Continue to the southwest.

GPS: N 38°53.55′ W 109°47.99′

▼ 0.0			Continue to the southeast.
	2.4 ▲	TL	Turn left onto graded dirt Thompson Cutoff Road. To the right goes to Thompson. Zero trip meter.
▼ 0.2		SO	Track on right.
	2.2 ▲	SO	Track on left.
▼ 1.4		SO	Pass through gate.
	1.0 ▲	SO	Pass through gate.
▼ 2.1		SO	Track on left.
	0.3 ▲	SO	Track on right.
▼ 2.2		SO	Cross through wash.
	0.2 ▲	SO	Cross through wash.
▼ 2.4		TL	T-intersection. Track to the right is Southeast #22: Salt Valley Road. Zero trip meter.
	0.0 ▲		Continue to the northwest.

GPS: N 38°52.87′ W 109°45.59′

▼ 0.0			Continue to the east.
	11.2 ▲	TR	Track on left is the Southeast #22: Salt Valley Road. Zero trip meter.
▼ 1.1		SO	Track on left.
	10.1 ▲	SO	Track on right.
▼ 1.4		SO	Track on right.
	9.8 ▲	SO	Track on left.
▼ 1.8		SO	Track on right.
	9.4 ▲	SO	Track on left.
▼ 3.3		SO	Track on right.
	7.9 ▲	SO	Track on left.
▼ 3.6		SO	Track on right.
	7.6 ▲	SO	Track on left.
▼ 4.4		SO	Track on right.
	6.8 ▲	SO	Track on left.
▼ 6.7		SO	Track on right.
	4.5 ▲	SO	Track on left.
▼ 7.7		SO	Track on right goes to brick ruin.
	3.5 ▲	SO	Track on left goes to brick ruin.

GPS: N 38°51.69′ W 109°36.98′

▼ 8.5		SO	Track on left.
	2.7 ▲	SO	Track on right.
▼ 9.3		BL	Track on right. Trail is now crossing Yellow Cat Flat.
	1.9 ▲	BR	Track on left.

GPS: N 38°50.90′ W 109°36.37′

▼ 10.8		SO	Cattle guard.
	0.4 ▲	SO	Cattle guard.
▼ 11.0		SO	Cross through wash.
	0.2 ▲	SO	Cross through wash.
▼ 11.1		SO	Cross through wash.
	0.1 ▲	SO	Cross through wash.
▼ 11.2		TR	Turn right onto smaller, ungraded track. Main

			track swings away to the left. Zero trip meter.
	0.0 ▲		Continue to the west across Yellow Cat Flat.

GPS: N 38°50.24′ W 109°34.29′

▼ 0.0			Continue to the east.
	2.2 ▲	TL	Turn left onto graded dirt road. Zero trip meter.
▼ 0.4		SO	Large dam on right.
	1.8 ▲	SO	Large dam on left.

GPS: N 38°50.25′ W 109°33.83′

▼ 0.5		SO	Track on left.
	1.7 ▲	SO	Track on right.
▼ 0.6		BL	Track on right.
	1.6 ▲	SO	Track on left.

GPS: N 38°50.11′ W 109°33.72′

▼ 0.7		SO	Track on right.
	1.5 ▲	SO	Track on left.
▼ 0.8		SO	Cross through wash.
	1.4 ▲	SO	Cross through wash.
▼ 1.1		SO	Track on right.
	1.1 ▲	SO	Track on left.

GPS: N 38°49.92′ W 109°33.26′

▼ 1.2		SO	Track on right.
	1.0 ▲	SO	Track on left.
▼ 1.4		SO	Cross through wide wash.
	0.8 ▲	SO	Cross through wide wash.
▼ 1.6		SO	Track on right.
	0.6 ▲	SO	Track on left.

GPS: N 38°50.04′ W 109°32.95′

▼ 1.7		SO	Cross through wash, then fenced seep on left underneath rock ledge.
	0.5 ▲	SO	Fenced seep on right underneath rock ledge, then cross through wash.

GPS: N 38°50.08′ W 109°32.83′

▼ 1.8		SO	Track on left at wash.
	0.4 ▲	SO	Track on right at wash.
▼ 1.9		SO	Mine workings on right.
	0.3 ▲	SO	Mine workings on left.
▼ 2.0		SO	Two tracks on right go to mine workings.
	0.2 ▲	SO	Two tracks on left go to mine workings.
▼ 2.1		SO	Cross through wash.
	0.1 ▲	SO	Cross through wash.
▼ 2.2		SO	Unmarked track on the right is the start of Southeast #23: Salt Wash Overlook Trail. Zero trip meter.
	0.0 ▲		Continue to the west leaving Mine Draw.

GPS: N 38°50.02′ W 109°32.35′

▼ 0.0			Continue on graded dirt road along Mine Draw.
	1.3 ▲	BR	Turn onto ungraded dirt road. Track straight ahead is the start of Southeast #23: Salt Wash Overlook Trail. Zero trip meter.
▼ 0.2		SO	Cross through wash. Many wash crossings along Mine Draw.
	1.1 ▲	SO	Cross through wash.
▼ 0.3		SO	Track on right goes to the Parco Mine remains, then cross through wash.
	1.0 ▲	SO	Cross through wash, then track on left goes to the Parco Mine remains.

GPS: N 38°50.21′ W 109°32.09′

▼ 0.6		SO	Mine workings on right.
	0.7 ▲	SO	Mine workings on left.
▼ 0.8		SO	Track on left, then track on right at wash.
	0.5 ▲	SO	Track on left at wash, then track on right.
▼ 1.0		SO	Leaving Mine Draw.

SE #20: YELLOW CAT TRAIL

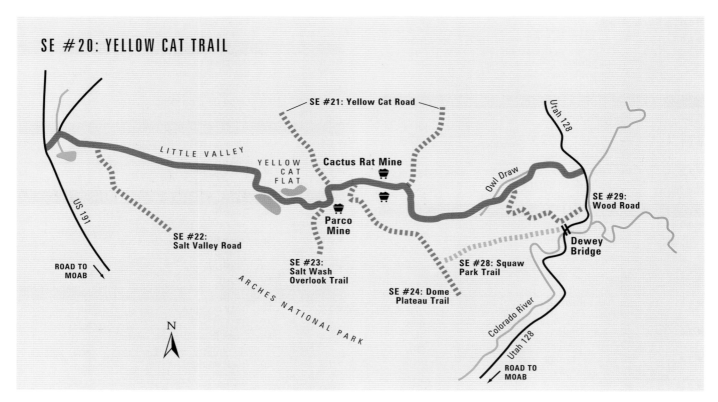

0.3 ▲	SO	Entering Mine Draw. Many wash crossings along the draw.	
▼ 1.3	BR	Yellow Cat Road comes in from the left. Turn right and join Southeast #21: Yellow Cat Road along The Poison Strip. Zero trip meter.	
0.0 ▲		Continue to the southwest.	

GPS: N 38°50.94' W 109°32.12'

▼ 0.0		Continue east toward The Poison Strip.	
1.4 ▲	BL	Track to the right is the continuation of Yellow Cat Road. Turn left, leaving Southeast #21: Yellow Cat Road. Zero trip meter.	
▼ 0.4	SO	Old ore hopper on left, then track on right goes to the remains of the Little Eva and Parco Mines.	
1.0 ▲	SO	Track on left goes to the remains of the Little Eva and Parco Mines, then old ore hopper on right.	

GPS: N 38°50.87' W 109°31.68'

▼ 1.4	SO	Graded road on right is Southeast #24: Dome Plateau Trail. Zero trip meter.	
0.0 ▲		Continue west along The Poison Strip.	

GPS: N 38°51.04' W 109°30.61'

▼ 0.0		Continue east along The Poison Strip.	
3.0 ▲	SO	Graded road on left is Southeast #24: Dome Plateau Trail. Zero trip meter.	
▼ 0.2	SO	Faint track on left climbs up on top of The Poison Strip.	
2.8 ▲	SO	Faint track on right climbs up on top of The Poison Strip.	
▼ 0.4	SO	Faint track on right.	
2.6 ▲	SO	Faint track on left.	
▼ 1.4	SO	Site of the Cactus Rat Mine on both sides of the trail.	
1.6 ▲	SO	Site of the Cactus Rat Mine on both sides of the trail.	

GPS: N 38°51.12' W 109°29.10'

▼ 1.6	SO	Track on right.	
1.4 ▲	SO	Track on left.	
▼ 1.7	SO	Track on left, then second entrance to same track on left.	
1.3 ▲	SO	Track on right, then second entrance to same track on right.	
▼ 2.1	SO	Dam on left.	
0.9 ▲	SO	Dam on right.	
▼ 2.3	SO	Cattle guard.	
0.7 ▲	SO	Cattle guard.	

GPS: N 38°50.87' W 109°28.29'

▼ 2.7	SO	Cross over natural gas pipeline.	
0.3 ▲	SO	Cross over natural gas pipeline.	
▼ 3.0	TR	T-intersection. Track on left is the continuation of Southeast #21: Yellow Cat Road. Zero trip meter.	
0.0 ▲		Continue west along The Poison Strip.	

GPS: N 38°50.90' W 109°27.47'

▼ 0.0		Continue south; track on right.	
3.6 ▲	TL	Track on left, then track ahead is Yellow Cat Road going to join I-70. Turn left and join Southeast #21: Yellow Cat Road along The Poison Strip.	
▼ 0.6	SO	Track on left.	
3.0 ▲	SO	Track on right.	
▼ 0.7	SO	Track on right.	
2.9 ▲	SO	Track on left.	
▼ 2.4	BL	Track on right connects to Southeast #24: Dome Plateau Trail.	
1.2 ▲	BR	Track on left connects to Southeast #24: Dome Plateau Trail.	

GPS: N 38°49.25' W 109°26.39'

▼ 2.6	SO	Track on left goes to collapsed wooden structure.	
1.0 ▲	SO	Track on right goes to collapsed wooden structure.	
▼ 2.7	SO	Track on left.	

0.9 ▲	SO	Track on right.

▼ 3.3	SO	Cattle guard.
0.3 ▲	SO	Cattle guard.

▼ 3.6	SO	Major graded track to the right goes to Auger Spring. Zero trip meter.
0.0 ▲		Continue on larger graded trail.

GPS: N 38°49.57' W 109°25.20'

▼ 0.0		Continue on smaller graded trail.
5.0 ▲	SO	Major graded track to the left goes to Auger Spring. Zero trip meter.

▼ 0.2	SO	Track on left.
4.8 ▲	SO	Track on right.

▼ 1.1	SO	Faint track on right.
3.9 ▲	SO	Faint track on left.

▼ 1.2	SO	Two tracks on left.
3.8 ▲	SO	Two tracks on right.

▼ 1.5	BR	Track on left. Trail starts to drop along escarpment.
3.5 ▲	SO	Track on right. Trail is now on top of escarpment.

GPS: N 38°49.83' W 109°23.58'

▼ 2.0	SO	Track on right.
3.0 ▲	SO	Track on left.

GPS: N 38°49.97' W 109°23.12'

▼ 2.8	BR	Track on left. Bear right and cross through Owl Draw.
2.2 ▲	BL	Cross through Owl Draw, then track on right.

GPS: N 38°50.35' W 109°22.34'

▼ 2.9	SO	Cross through small wash.
2.1 ▲	SO	Cross through small wash.

▼ 3.4	SO	Track on right, then second track on right.
1.6 ▲	SO	Track on left, then second track on left.

GPS: N 38°49.98' W 109°22.35'

▼ 3.9	SO	Track on left.
1.1 ▲	BL	Track on right.

▼ 4.0	SO	Two old timber cabins on left of trail, plus mining remains and adits.
1.0 ▲	SO	Two old timber cabins on right of trail, plus mining remains and adits.

GPS: N 38°50.33' W 109°21.93'

▼ 4.9	BR	Faint track on left down wash, then cross through wash.
0.1 ▲	SO	Cross through wash, then faint track on right down wash.

▼ 5.0	SO	Track on right is the start of Southeast #29: Wood Road. Zero trip meter.
0.0 ▲		Continue to the west.

GPS: N 38°50.95' W 109°21.31'

▼ 0.0		Continue to the northeast.
4.4 ▲	BR	Track on left is the start of Southeast #29: Wood Road. Zero trip meter.

▼ 0.1	SO	Faint track on left along draw. Trail drops down and follows along Owl Draw, crossing through it often.
4.3 ▲	SO	Faint track on right along draw. Trail leaves Owl Draw.

▼ 1.2	SO	Pass through wire gate in Owl Draw.
3.2 ▲	SO	Pass through wire gate in Owl Draw.

▼ 1.3	SO	Leave Owl Draw and climb up alongside of canyon.
3.1 ▲	SO	Descend to enter Owl Draw, crossing through it often.

▼ 1.5	SO	Track on left.
2.9 ▲	SO	Track on right.

GPS: N 38°51.76' W 109°20.18'

▼ 1.9	SO	Cross through Owl Draw.
2.5 ▲	SO	Cross through Owl Draw.

▼ 2.1	SO	Cattletank on left.
2.3 ▲	SO	Cattletank on right.

▼ 2.7	SO	Track on right.
1.7 ▲	SO	Track on left.

▼ 3.1	SO	Cross through wash.
1.3 ▲	SO	Cross through wash.

▼ 3.3	SO	Faint track on left.
1.1 ▲	SO	Faint track on right.

▼ 3.4	SO	Cross through wash.
1.0 ▲	SO	Cross through wash.

▼ 3.9	TL	Track on right is Kokopelli Trail for bikes and 4WDs.
0.5 ▲	TR	Track straight on is Kokopelli Trail for bikes and 4WDs.

GPS: N 38°51.28' W 109°18.00'

▼ 4.4		Trail ends on Utah 128 at corral. Turn right for Moab, left for I-70.
0.0 ▲		Trail commences on Utah 128, 0.2 miles north of mile marker 34. Turn southwest just before a corral on graded dirt road at the BLM sign for the Kokopelli Trail.

GPS: N 38°51.62' W 109°17.60'

Yellow Cat Road

Starting Point:	I-70, exit 190
Finishing Point:	I-70, exit 202
Total Mileage:	20.2 miles
Unpaved Mileage:	20.1 miles
Driving Time:	1 hour
Elevation Range:	4,350–5,000 feet
Usually Open:	Year-round
Difficulty Rating:	1
Scenic Rating:	8
Remoteness Rating:	+0

Special Attractions

■ Uranium mining remains around The Poison Strip.

■ Shorter, easier version of Southeast #20: Yellow Cat Trail.

■ Access to many remote area 4WD trails.

Description

This trail is a shorter, easier alternative to the full Southeast #20: Yellow Cat Trail, yet it passes the same major points of interest. This route is graded gravel or dirt the entire length, and in dry weather is suitable for passenger vehicles. It starts and ends at I-70, making access to the trail easy. However, the trail can quickly become impassable in wet weather.

From I-70, you cross Sagers Flat to the southeast. As you get away from the freeway, the scenery is suprisingly varied and hilly. Once you reach the uranium mining area, just south of The Poison Strip, the road swings to the east and becomes

The straight gravel road stretches from Yellow Cat Road back to I-70

graded dirt. Here it passes many sidetracks that lead to abandoned mines. The first is the Ringtail Mine; not too much remains there now, just some footings and tailings. A major track to the south is the longer Southeast #20: Yellow Cat Trail. There are many remains to be seen just down this road, which for the first couple of miles is a good standard of graded dirt and suitable for passenger cars in dry weather. See Southeast #20: Yellow Cat Trail for details.

As Yellow Cat Road continues, it cuts through the gap of the Blackstone incline and passes the substantial remains of an old ore hopper beside the trail. A maze of tracks to the right lead to the remains of what the topographical maps call the Parco Mines and the Little Eva Mines. These are private property and posted as the Lucky Strike, but they do not appear to be actively worked, and it is possible to see many of the old workings, adits, and old vehicles left abandoned. Remember that it is dangerous to enter adits or tunnels, because of the buildup of deadly radon gas. Holes and diggings are also often unmarked, so exercise due care when exploring around the diggings.

An old mining truck sits near an opening into the Parco Mines

Remaining on The Poison Strip, the trail continues to the east just south of The Poison Strip ridge. You pass the start of Southeast #24: Dome Plateau Trail and then the remains of the old Cactus Rat Mine on both sides of the trail, but there is little here to see. At a major fork in the road, the route bears left and follows the Pinto Draw road back to I-70. It winds through a gap in The Poison Strip, passing side trails to more adits and old workings. From here, the trail crosses back over Sagers Flats, Sagers Wash, and Pinto Draw before rejoining I-70, at the remains of the nearly ghost town of Cisco.

Current Road Information

BLM Moab Field Office
82 East Dogwood
Moab, UT 84532
(435) 259-2100

Map References

BLM Moab
USGS 1:24,000 Sagers Flat, Mollie Hogans, Cisco SW, White House
1:100,000 Moab
Maptech CD-ROM: Moab/Canyonlands
Trails Illustrated, #501
Utah Atlas & Gazetteer, pp. 40, 41
Utah Travel Council #5
Other: Latitude 40—Moab West
Latitude 40—Moab East
Canyon Country Off-Road Vehicle Trail Map—
Arches Area

Route Directions

▼ 0.0			From I-70, exit 190, turn south onto paved road. Zero trip meter at cattle guard.
	7.4 ▲		Trail ends at I-70 at exit 190. Turn west for Moab, east for Grand Junction, Colorado.
		GPS: N 38°56.46' W 109°36.84'	
▼ 0.1		SO	Road is now graded gravel.
	7.3 ▲	SO	Road is now paved.
▼ 0.5		SO	Track on left.
	6.9 ▲	SO	Track on right.
▼ 0.6		SO	Track on right.
	6.8 ▲	SO	Track on left.
▼ 1.6		SO	Corral on right.
	5.8 ▲	SO	Corral on left.
▼ 3.1		SO	Track on right.
	4.3 ▲	SO	Track on left.
▼ 3.3		SO	Track on left.
	4.1 ▲	SO	Track on right.
▼ 4.5		SO	Track on left and right.
	2.9 ▲	SO	Track on left and right.
▼ 5.7		SO	Track on left.
	1.7 ▲	SO	Track on right.
▼ 5.8		SO	Graded road on right joins Southeast #20: Yellow Cat Trail and gives access to the north end of Arches National Park.
	1.6 ▲	SO	Graded road on left joins Southeast #20: Yellow Cat Trail and gives access to the north end of Arches National Park.
		GPS: N 38°52.06' W 109°32.96'	
▼ 6.2		SO	Track on left.
	1.2 ▲	SO	Track on right.
▼ 6.3		SO	Cattle guard, then track on right.
	1.1 ▲	SO	Track on left, then cattle guard.
▼ 6.6		SO	Track on right.
	0.8 ▲	SO	Track on left.
▼ 7.3		SO	Track on right.
	0.1 ▲	SO	Track on left.
▼ 7.4		BL	Smaller track on right goes to the remains of the Ringtail Mine, then road forks. Right fork is Southeast #20: Yellow Cat Trail, which also goes to Southeast #23: Salt Wash Overlook Trail. Zero trip meter.
	0.0 ▲		Continue up Yellow Cat Road to the northwest.
		GPS: N 38°50.94' W 109°32.12'	
▼ 0.0			Continue east toward The Poison Strip.
	1.4 ▲	BR	First track to the left is Southeast #20: Yellow Cat Trail, which also goes to Southeast #23: Salt Wash Overlook Trail. Second smaller track

to the left goes to the remains of the Ringtail Mine.

▼ 0.4		SO	Old ore hopper on left, then track on right goes to the remains of the Little Eva and Parco Mines.
	1.0 ▲	SO	Track on left goes to the remains of the Little Eva and Parco Mines, then old ore hopper on right.

GPS: N 38°50.87' W 109°31.68'

▼ 1.4		SO	Graded road on right is Southeast #24: Dome Plateau Trail. Zero trip meter.
	0.0 ▲	SO	Continue west along The Poison Strip.

GPS: N 38°51.04' W 109°30.61'

▼ 0.0			Continue east along The Poison Strip.
	3.0 ▲	SO	Graded road on left is Southeast #24: Dome Plateau Trail. Zero trip meter.
▼ 0.2		SO	Faint track on left climbs up on top of The Poison Strip.
	2.8 ▲	SO	Faint track on right climbs up on top of The Poison Strip.
▼ 0.4		SO	Faint track on right.
	2.6 ▲	SO	Faint track on left.
▼ 1.4		SO	Site of the Cactus Rat Mine on both sides of the trail.
	1.6 ▲	SO	Site of the Cactus Rat Mine on both sides of the trail.

GPS: N 38°51.12' W 109°29.10'

▼ 1.6		SO	Track on right.
	1.4 ▲	SO	Track on left.
▼ 1.7		SO	Track on left, then second entrance to same track on left.
	1.3 ▲	SO	Track on right, then second entrance to same track on right.
▼ 2.1		SO	Dam on left.
	0.9 ▲	SO	Dam on right.
▼ 2.3		SO	Cattle guard.
	0.7 ▲	SO	Cattle guard.

GPS: N 38°50.87' W 109°28.29'

▼ 2.7		SO	Cross over natural gas pipeline.
	0.3 ▲	SO	Cross over natural gas pipeline.
▼ 3.0		TL	T-intersection. Track on right is Southeast #20: Yellow Cat Trail and goes to The Highlands. Zero trip meter.
	0.0 ▲		Continue west along The Poison Strip.

GPS: N 38°50.90' W 109°27.47'

▼ 0.0			Continue toward I-70.
	8.4 ▲	TR	Straight on is Southeast #20: Yellow Cat Trail to the Highlands. Zero trip meter.
▼ 0.2		SO	Track on right.
	8.2 ▲	SO	Track on left.
▼ 0.5		SO	Cross over natural gas pipeline and track on right along pipeline.
	7.9 ▲	SO	Cross over natural gas pipeline and track on left along pipeline.
▼ 0.7		SO	Track on right goes to diggings, then track on left to adits.
	7.7 ▲	SO	Track on right goes to adits, then track on left to diggings.

GPS: N 38°51.41' W 109°27.25'

▼ 0.8		SO	Track on left.
	7.6 ▲	SO	Track on right.
▼ 1.1		SO	Cross through wash.
	7.3 ▲	SO	Cross through wash.
▼ 1.3		SO	Cattle guard.
	7.1 ▲	SO	Cattle guard.
▼ 1.7		SO	Cross through wash.

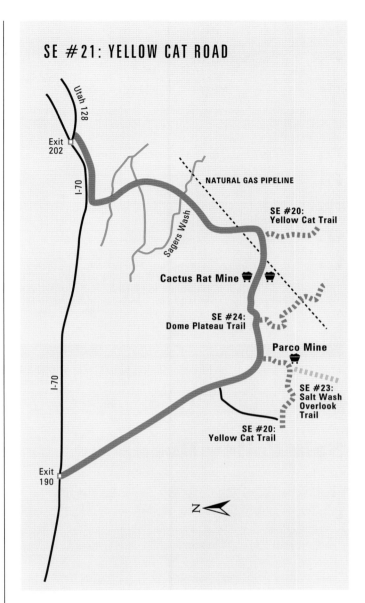

SE #21: YELLOW CAT ROAD

	6.7 ▲	SO	Cross through wash.
▼ 2.1		SO	Track on left goes to dam.
	6.3 ▲	SO	Track on right goes to dam.
▼ 2.9		SO	Cross through wash.
	5.5 ▲	SO	Cross through wash.
▼ 3.0		SO	Cross through wash.
	5.4 ▲	SO	Cross through wash.
▼ 3.1		SO	Track on right, then track on left.
	5.3 ▲	SO	Track on right, then track on left.
▼ 3.2		SO	Cross over Sagers Wash.
	5.2 ▲	SO	Cross over Sagers Wash.

GPS: N 38°53.18' W 109°25.98'

▼ 3.7		SO	Track on left goes to corral and track on right on top of the ridge.
	4.7 ▲	SO	Track on right goes to corral and track on left on top of the ridge.
▼ 4.6		SO	Cross through wash.
	3.8 ▲	SO	Cross through wash.
▼ 5.2		SO	Track on left.
	3.2 ▲	SO	Track on right.

▼ 5.5	SO	Cross through wash.
2.9 ▲	SO	Cross through wash.
▼ 5.6	SO	Track on left.
2.8 ▲	SO	Track on right.
▼ 6.5	TR	T-intersection. Turn right and follow alongside I-70.
1.9 ▲	TL	Turn south and leave I-70 frontage road.
▼ 6.9	SO	Track on right.
1.5 ▲	SO	Track on left.
▼ 7.3	SO	Cross through wash on concrete ford.
1.1 ▲	SO	Cross through wash on concrete ford.
▼ 7.4	SO	Cattle guard.
1.0 ▲	SO	Cattle guard.
▼ 7.8	SO	Cross through wash on concrete ford.
0.6 ▲	SO	Cross though wash on concrete ford.
▼ 8.3	SO	Track on right leaves through gravel pit.
0.1 ▲	SO	Track on left leaves through gravel pit.
▼ 8.4		Trail ends at the junction with I-70, at exit 202, and Utah 128. Turn right to go to Moab via Utah 128, turn left to join I-70.
0.0 ▲		Trail starts at exit 202 on I-70 at the junction with Utah 128. Turn south on Utah 128, then immediately turn west on unsigned frontage road and zero trip meter.

GPS: N 38°56.22' W 109°24.35'

SOUTHEAST REGION TRAIL #22

Salt Valley Road

Starting Point:	**Southeast #20: Yellow Cat Trail, 3.6 miles from US 191**
Finishing Point:	**Arches National Park**
Total Mileage:	**15 miles**
Unpaved Mileage:	**15 miles**
Driving Time:	**45 minutes**
Elevation Range:	**4,600–5,200 feet**
Usually Open:	**Year-round**
Difficulty Rating:	**2**
Scenic Rating:	**9**
Remoteness Rating:	**+0**

Special Attractions
■ Alternative entrance to Arches National Park.
■ Hiking trail to Tower Arch.
■ Easy trail along a long and scenic valley.

History
The small settlement of Valley City, located along US 191 and Thompson Road, was abandoned by 1930. In 1908, the settlement was flooded by a burst reservoir, which is accessible from the top of the trail, and continued flooding caused the demise of the town.

The reservoir was an important watering point for cattle driven from Dugout Ranch in the south up to the railroad at

Signpost along Salt Valley Road

Thompson. The town charged a fee per head of cattle—the Valley City Reservoir was the last watering point before the railroad, and often 2,000 to 3,000 head of cattle were driven along the stock route.

Albert and Dubinky Anderson (of Dubinky Well fame), lived here for a while, and Valley City was reputed to be one of the sites of a bootleg liquor operation, for which Albert did jail time.

Description
This easy trail leads down a long pretty valley into the north end of Arches National Park. It is best suited for high-clearance vehicles, because of the long stretches of deep sand traps that can quickly bog down a regular vehicle. In wet weather this road quickly becomes impassable to even 4WD vehicles, and the National Park Service may close it temporarily in wet conditions.

The trail travels quickly down Salt Valley. The northern end of the valley is fairly enclosed, but as the trail enters Arches National Park, it widens out to a wide, grassy valley. The preferable direction for travel is north to south, as this way gives great views into the park, the La Sal Mountains, Klondike Bluffs, and Devil's Garden. Farther down the trail, Skyline Arch comes into view to the east. This natural arch doubled in size in 1940 when a large chunk fell out of the window.

View of Skyline Arch from the trail

SE #22: SALT VALLEY ROAD

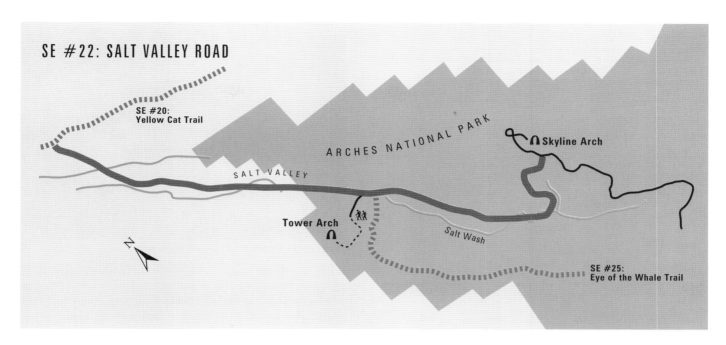

The trail within the park sees a lot more use than the northern end, and this part of the road is washboardy as a result. Many park visitors travel the trail to the north to access the hiking trailhead to Tower Arch, or to travel Southeast #25: Eye of the Whale Trail.

Camping within the national park is restricted to the Devil's Garden Campground, which can fill up by 10 A.M. during peak season.

Current Road Information
Arches National Park
PO Box 907
Moab, UT 84532
(435) 719-2299

BLM Moab Field Office
82 East Dogwood
Moab, UT 84532
(435) 259-2100

Map References
BLM   Moab
USGS   1:24,000   Crescent Junction, Valley City, Klondike Bluffs, Mollie Hogans, The Windows Section
1:100,000 Moab
Maptech CD-ROM: Moab/Canyonlands
Trails Illustrated, #211 (incomplete); #501
Utah Atlas & Gazetteer, p. 40
Utah Travel Council #5
Other: Latitude 40—Moab West
Canyon Country Off-Road Vehicle Trail Map—
Arches Area

Route Directions
▼ 0.0   From Southeast #20: Yellow Cat Trail, 3.6 miles from US 191, turn south on the unmarked, graded dirt Salt Valley Road and zero trip meter.

6.1 ▲   Trail ends at the junction with Southeast #20: Yellow Cat Trail. Turn left to exit to US 191, turn right to continue along the Yellow Cat Trail.

GPS: N 38°52.86′ W 109°45.59′		

▼ 0.4   SO Cattle guard.
5.7 ▲   SO Cattle guard.

▼ 0.6   SO Track on right.
5.5 ▲   SO Second entrance to track on left.

▼ 0.7   SO Second entrance to track on right.
5.4 ▲   SO Track on left.

GPS: N 38°52.28′ W 109°45.35′		

▼ 0.9   SO Track on left.
5.2 ▲   SO Track on right.

▼ 1.2   SO Track on left.
4.9 ▲   SO Track on right.

▼ 1.4   SO Track on left.
4.7 ▲   SO Track on right.

GPS: N 38°51.75′ W 109°44.89′		

▼ 1.7   SO Faint track on left.
4.4 ▲   SO Faint track on right.

▼ 6.0   SO Track on right.
0.1 ▲   SO Track on left.

▼ 6.1   SO Track on left and track on right, then entering Arches National Park over cattle guard (fee area). Zero trip meter.
0.0 ▲   Continue out of the park.

GPS: N 38°48.90′ W 109°41.08′		

▼ 0.0   Continue into Arches National Park. Klondike Bluffs are on the right.
2.0 ▲   SO Leaving Arches National Park over cattle guard, then track on left and track on right outside the park. Zero trip meter.

▼ 1.9   SO Track on right goes to the Tower Arch hiking trailhead.
0.1 ▲   SO Track on left goes to the Tower Arch hiking trailhead.

GPS: N 38°47.77′ W 109°39.48′		

▼ 2.0   SO Track on right is Southeast #25: Eye of the

		Whale Trail. Zero trip meter.
0.0 ▲		Continue north along Salt Valley.
GPS: N 38°47.70' W 109°39.42'		
▼ 0.0		Continue south along Salt Valley.
6.9 ▲	SO	Track on left is Southeast #25: Eye of the Whale Trail. Zero trip meter.
▼ 3.6	SO	Enter Salt Wash.
3.3 ▲	SO	Exit Salt Wash.
▼ 4.6	SO	Exit Salt Wash.
2.3 ▲	SO	Enter Salt Wash.
▼ 5.0	SO	Skyline Arch is directly in front.
1.9 ▲	SO	Skyline Arch is directly behind.
▼ 6.9		Closure gate, then trail ends at the junction with the paved road in Arches National Park. Turn right to exit the park, turn left for Devil's Garden Campground.
0.0 ▲		Trail starts on the paved Arches National Park Road, just before Skyline Arch. The trail is unmarked. Turn south on graded gravel road through closure gate and zero trip meter.
GPS: N 38°46.11' W 109°35.28'		

View over Salt Wash from the end of the trail

SOUTHEAST REGION TRAIL #23

Salt Wash Overlook Trail

Starting Point:	**Southeast #20: Yellow Cat Trail, 1.3 miles south of Southeast #21: Yellow Cat Road**
Finishing Point:	**Salt Wash Overlook**
Total Mileage:	**3.3 miles**
Unpaved Mileage:	**3.3 miles**
Driving Time:	**45 minutes (one-way)**
Elevation:	**4,500–4,700 feet**
Usually Open:	**Year-round**
Difficulty Rating:	**3**
Scenic Rating:	**10**
Remoteness Rating:	**+1**

Special Attractions
- Panoramic view over remote Salt Wash.
- Remains of the Black A uranium mine.

History
Moab Garage Company Stage ran the mail route in the 1920s when Moab was the only place in southeastern Utah with a bank. The company shipped deposits for merchants from all over the county to Moab. The following day, the stage would do the run in reverse, delivering receipts and change back to the merchants. It is interesting to speculate how the stage ended up at Yellow Bird Mine!

Description
This short, sandy spur trail leads past some very interesting uranium mining remains, and it ends on a slickrock platform above picturesque Salt Wash. Salt Wash is a little-known area; it has no vehicle access and sees very little human activity of any kind.

The spur trail is short, but confusing, with many turns, all unmarked. To add further confusion, the trail often washes out and detours are pushed through. However, finding the correct route is normally relatively easy. Although Southeast #21: Yellow Cat Road and Southeast #20: Yellow Cat Trail see some 4WD traffic, this spur trail is rarely traveled.

After 0.8 miles, a track to the left travels 0.3 miles to the remains of Black A Mine, located out of sight up on the mesa. The original trail leading up to it washed out and has been blocked by fallen boulders, so you will need to park at the base of the mesa and walk the short distance to the mine. The hike is well worth your while, as there are numerous large adits, the remains of a tramway, loading points, and a sturdy timber cabin that even has carpet on the floor!

The trail deteriorates shortly after the Black A, as it leaves Mine Draw and heads out toward the viewpoint. There are frequent washouts along this section and large ruts.

You pass the remains of Yellow Bird Mine after 2.5 miles, although the only things of note are the remains of the Moab Garage Compa-

A large opening to the Black A Mine reveals its timber supports

ny Stage vehicle, still with the writing on the side. Other than the stage, there are a few tailings piles and little else.

You reach the end of the trail 0.8 miles after the Yellow Bird, on the platform over Salt Wash. To your left is Cottonwood Wash, to the right is Mine Draw Canyon and Arches National Park. Salt Wash leads away in front of you, and the La Sal Mountains tower behind. Down in the bottom of Salt Wash, there is evidence of previous ranching activity if you look hard. Piles of timber are suggestive of old cattle troughs and fence lines.

There is a wonderful campsite near the end of the trail; although exposed, it has a breathtaking view.

SE #23: SALT WASH OVERLOOK TRAIL

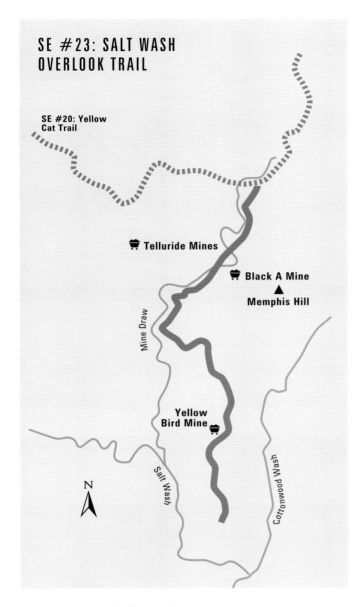

SE #20: Yellow Cat Trail

Telluride Mines

Black A Mine

Memphis Hill

Mine Draw

Yellow Bird Mine

Salt Wash

Cottonwood Wash

N

Current Road Information

Arches National Park
PO Box 907
Moab, UT 84532
(435) 719-2299

BLM Moab Field Office
82 East Dogwood
Moab, UT 84532
(435) 259-2100

Map References

BLM Moab
USGS 1:24,000 Mollie Hogans
1:100,000 Moab
Maptech CD-ROM: Moab/Canyonlands
Trails Illustrated, #211; #501
Utah Atlas & Gazetteer, p. 40
Other: Latitude 40—Moab East

Route Directions

▼ 0.0		Trail starts on Southeast #20: Yellow Cat Trail, 1.3 miles south of the western junction with Southeast #21: Yellow Cat Road. Zero trip meter, and turn southwest on the unmarked graded trail. Trail is following Mine Draw.
		GPS: N 38°50.02' W 109°32.35'
▼ 0.4	SO	Track on left.
▼ 0.8	SO	Track on left goes to the remains of the Black A Mine.
		GPS: N 38°49.48' W 109°32.73'
▼ 1.0	BL	Track on right continues in the wash.
		GPS: N 38°49.44' W 109°32.91'
▼ 1.1	BL	Trail detours around a major washout.
▼ 1.2	SO	Track on left at small wash, then track rejoins on the right.
▼ 1.5	BL	Track on right.
		GPS: N 38°49.15' W 109°33.09'
▼ 1.7	SO	View right into Mine Draw.
		GPS: N 38°49.03' W 109°32.93'
▼ 1.9	SO	Cross through wash twice, then climb up ridge.
▼ 2.1	BR	Track on left.
		GPS: N 38°48.89' W 109°32.65'
▼ 2.4	SO	Track on right.
▼ 2.5	SO	Track on left goes to campsite, then remains of the Yellow Bird Mine on the right.
		GPS: N 38°48.56' W 109°32.57'
▼ 3.1	SO	Best viewpoint ahead into Salt Wash.
▼ 3.2	SO	Campsite on left.
▼ 3.3		Trail ends on slickrock platform over Salt Wash.
		GPS: N 38°48.02' W 109°32.61'

SOUTHEAST REGION TRAIL #24

Dome Plateau Trail

Starting Point:	Southeast #21: Yellow Cat Road, 1.4	
	miles east of intersection with Southeast	
	#20: Yellow Cat Trail	
Finishing Point:	**Dome Plateau**	
Total Mileage:	**14.4 miles**	
Unpaved Mileage:	**14.4 miles**	
Driving Time:	**1.5 hours (including spur)**	
Elevation Range:	**4,700–5,800 feet**	
Usually Open:	**Year-round**	
Difficulty Rating:	**2**	
Scenic Rating:	**8**	
Remoteness Rating:	**+1**	

Special Attractions

- Natural arch near trail.
- Views over the Professor Valley and Arches National Park.
- Access to many spur trails and viewpoints.

The trail runs along the fence line on Dome Plateau

Description

The trail out to Dome Plateau is an easy trail that offers many vistas along its length. It leaves from Southeast #21: Yellow Cat Road to the south and crosses the undulating terrain known as The Highlands. The graded trail can be sandy and loose in sections, but it is normally passable by high-clearance vehicles. Like most trails around here, it is one to avoid when it is wet.

The trail passes the spur trails to Lost Springs Canyon and Southeast #27: Winter Camp Ridge Trail and gradually descends to Dome Plateau. The views are fantastic! To the west, you can see Arches National Park; to the north are the Book Cliffs and The Highlands. Ahead to the south are the La Sal Mountains. Once on Dome Plateau, tracks to the left lead to other viewpoints, including a smaller trail used by the Moab Jeep Safari. The main trail runs west along the edge of Dome Plateau, giving glimpses into Fisher Valley, Professor Valley, and Castle Valley. The trail ends at a turning circle, with views to the west of Arches National Park.

Current Road Information

BLM Moab Field Office
82 East Dogwood
Moab, UT 84532
(435) 259-2100

Map References

BLM   Moab
USGS   1:24,000   Mollie Hogans, Cisco SW, Big Bend
1:100,000 Moab
Maptech CD-ROM: Moab/Canyonlands
Trails Illustrated, #211 (incomplete); #501
Utah Atlas & Gazetteer, pp. 40, 41
Utah Travel Council #5 (incomplete)
Other: Latitude 40—Moab East
Canyon Country Off-Road Vehicle Trail Map—
Arches Area

Route Directions

▼ 0.0		Trail commences on Southeast #21: Yellow Cat Road, 1.4 miles east of the western junction of Yellow Cat Road and Southeast #20:

	2.5 ▲		Yellow Cat Trail. Turn south on unmarked graded dirt road and zero trip meter.
	2.5 ▲		Trail ends at intersection with Southeast #21: Yellow Cat Road, on The Poison Strip.
		GPS: N 38°51.03' W 109°30.60'	
▼ 0.6		SO	Track on right.
	1.9 ▲	SO	Track on left.
▼ 0.9		SO	Track on right.
	1.6 ▲	SO	Track on left.
▼ 1.3		SO	Track on left, then cross through wash.
	1.2 ▲	SO	Cross through wash, then track on right.
▼ 1.7		SO	Cross through wash.
	0.8 ▲	SO	Cross through wash.
▼ 2.1		SO	Cross through Cottonwood Wash.
	0.4 ▲	SO	Cross through Cottonwood Wash.
▼ 2.4		SO	Cross over natural gas pipeline.
	0.1 ▲	SO	Cross over natural gas pipeline.
▼ 2.5		BL	Track on right goes to Lost Spring Canyon. Zero trip meter.
	0.0 ▲		Continue toward Yellow Cat Road.
		GPS: N 38°49.44' W 109°29.74'	
▼ 0.0			Continue toward Dome Plateau.
	2.9 ▲	BR	Track on left goes to Lost Spring Canyon. Zero trip meter.
▼ 0.3		SO	Track on right.
	2.6 ▲	SO	Track on left.
▼ 0.4		BR	Track on left.
	2.5 ▲	SO	Track on right.
		GPS: N 38°49.31 W 109°29.35'	
▼ 1.0		SO	Gate.
	1.9 ▲	SO	Gate.
		GPS: N 38°49.05' W 109°28.87'	
▼ 1.5		SO	Track on left.
	1.4 ▲	BR	Track on right.
▼ 2.9		TR	Turn onto graded dirt road and zero trip meter.
	0.0 ▲		Continue toward Yellow Cat Road.
		GPS: N 38°48.53' W 109°26.90'	
▼ 0.0			Continue toward Dome Plateau.
	1.2 ▲	TL	T-intersection. Turn onto graded dirt road and zero trip meter.
▼ 0.1		SO	Cross through fence line.
	1.1 ▲	SO	Cross through fence line.
▼ 0.4		SO	Track on right.
	0.8 ▲	SO	Track on left.
▼ 0.7		SO	Cross through Fish Seep Draw.

View from atop Dome Plateau

SE #24: DOME PLATEAU TRAIL

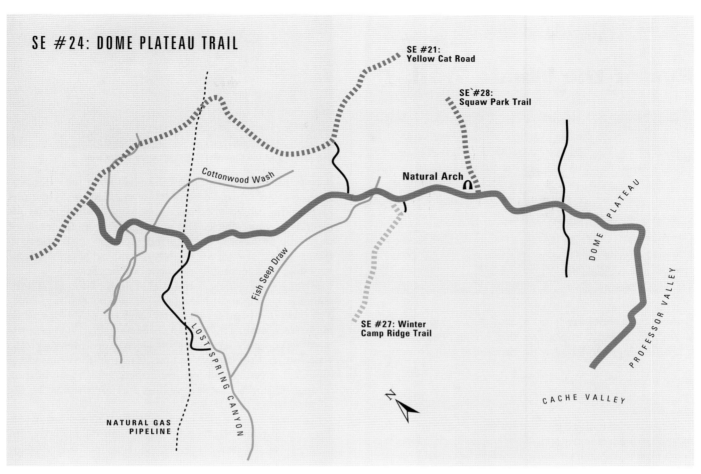

0.5 ▲	SO	Cross through Fish Seep Draw.	
▼ 1.2	SO	Track on right is Southeast #27: Winter Camp Ridge Trail. Zero trip meter.	
0.0 ▲		Continue toward Yellow Cat Road.	
		GPS: N 38°47.86' W 109°26.08'	
▼ 0.0		Continue toward Dome Plateau.	
1.4 ▲	SO	Track on left is Southeast #27: Winter Camp Ridge Trail. Zero trip meter.	
▼ 0.1	SO	Track on right joins Southeast #27: Winter Camp Ridge Trail.	
1.3 ▲	BR	Track on left joins Southeast #27: Winter Camp Ridge Trail.	
		GPS: N 38°47.83' W 109°25.89'	
▼ 0.3	SO	Track on left.	
1.1 ▲	SO	Track on right.	
▼ 0.7	SO	Track on left.	
0.7 ▲	SO	Track on right.	
		GPS: N 38°47.64' W 109°25.39'	
▼ 1.2	SO	Track on right.	
0.2 ▲	SO	Track on left.	
▼ 1.3	SO	Pass through gate, then track on right along fence, then track on left.	
0.1 ▲	BL	Track on right and track on left along fence, then pass through gate.	
		GPS: N 38°47.20' W 109°25.03'	
▼ 1.4	SO	Track on left is Southeast #28: Squaw Park Trail. A natural arch is just before the junction on the left. Zero trip meter.	
0.0 ▲		Continue toward Yellow Cat Road.	
		GPS: N 38°47.18' W 109°24.94'	

▼ 0.0		Continue toward Dome Plateau.	
▼ 0.2	SO	Track on left.	
▼ 0.4	SO	Faint track on left.	
▼ 0.6	BL	Track on right.	
		GPS: N 38°46.73' W 109°24.69'	
▼ 0.8	SO	Track on right.	
▼ 1.6	SO	Track on left and track on right.	
		GPS: N 38°46.31' W 109°23.86'	
▼ 1.7	BR	Track on left.	
▼ 2.0	BL	Fence line leaves trail on right.	
		GPS: N 38°46.01' W 109°23.87'	
▼ 2.4	SO	Cross through wash.	
▼ 2.7	BR	Track on left.	
		GPS: N 38°45.69' W 109°23.31'	
▼ 3.3	SO	Two tracks on left.	
		GPS: N 38°45.22' W 109°23.07'	
▼ 3.6	SO	Fence line. Track on left and track on right along fence, then second track on right after fence.	
		GPS: N 38°45.12' W 109°23.26'	
▼ 3.7	SO	Small track on right.	
▼ 3.8	SO	Cross through wash, then track on left goes to viewpoint.	
▼ 3.9	SO	Track on left.	
▼ 4.2	SO	Cross through wash.	
▼ 6.3	BR	Small track on right, then trail forks.	
		GPS: N 38°44.09' W 109°25.67'	
▼ 6.4		Trail ends at turning circle.	
		GPS: N 38°44.08' W 109°25.73'	

Eye of the Whale Trail

Starting Point:	**Southeast #22: Salt Valley Road, 6.9 miles**
	north of Arches National Park Road
Finishing Point:	**Willow Flats Road, Arches National Park**
Total Mileage:	**10.9 miles**
Unpaved Mileage:	**10.9 miles**
Driving Time:	**3 hours**
Elevation Range:	**4,600–5,200 feet**
Usually Open:	**Year-round**
Difficulty Rating:	**6**
Scenic Rating:	**10**
Remoteness Rating:	**+0**

Special Attractions

■ Only 4WD trail completely within Arches National Park.
■ Challenging 4WD trail with spectacular scenery along its length.
■ Eye of the Whale Arch.

Description

This spectacular trail is contained within Arches National Park near Moab. Exceptional scenery, a remote backcountry feel, and a challenging trail combine to make this an unforgettable driving experience. A parks permit is required to enter the park, although no special permit is required for the backcountry 4WD trail. The National Park Service recommended direction for travel to reduce environmental impact is counterclockwise, from north to south. In summer this is the only possible direction, so as to descend the long stretch of loose sand. The trail commences on Southeast #22: Salt Valley Road, 6.9 miles from the southern end. Turn west at the sign for the 4WD road to

A sandy section of the Eye of the Whale Trail

Salt Valley and the Klondike Bluffs sit beyond the sign

Balanced Rock. This first part of the trail is the most difficult; a very rocky climb and descent has several large rocks and ruts necessitating careful wheel placement to avoid scraping the underbody of your vehicle. The rocks show the scrape marks of those who were not so careful—use a spotter outside the vehicle to assist. The views north to the Marching Men and Klondike Bluffs ensure that cameras will be clicking.

After 1.7 miles, a dead-end trail heads for Klondike Bluffs, with a rewarding short hiking trail at the end to Tower Arch. The main trail becomes very sandy, and you travel for a while in the creek wash. This is still a challenging drive, as you cross many loose sandy sections, short steep drops over slickrock, washouts, and off-camber sections. The trail then runs along the valley, crossing and recrossing the creek and undulating through sagebrush to the parking area for the Eye of the Whale Arch.

The trail ends at the junction with Willow Flats Road. Turn left to rejoin the paved road through the park, or turn right to exit the park via the scenic Southeast #26: Willow Flats Road.

Current Road Information

Arches National Park
PO Box 907
Moab, UT 84532
(435) 719-2299

Map References

BLM Moab (incomplete)
USGS 1:24,000 Mollie Hogans, The Windows Section,
Klondike Bluffs, Merrimac Butte
1:100,000 Moab (incomplete)
Maptech CD-ROM: Moab/Canyonlands
Trails Illustrated, #211; #501
Utah Atlas & Gazetteer, p. 40
Utah Travel Council #5 (incomplete)
Other: Latitude 40—Moab West
Canyon Country Off-Road Vehicle Trail Map—
Arches Area

Route Directions

▼ 0.0		From Southeast #22: Salt Valley Road, zero trip meter and turn (at sign for Balanced Rock) onto trail heading southwest.
	GPS: N 38°47.70′ W 109°39.42′	
▼ 0.8	**SO**	Start of rocky climb, care with wheel placement needed. Marching Men formation is to the right.

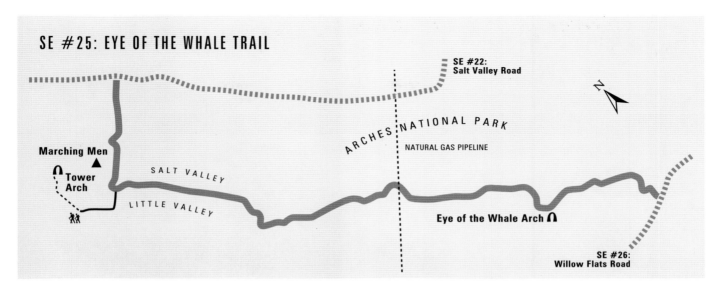

SE #25: EYE OF THE WHALE TRAIL

SE #22:
Salt Valley Road

ARCHES NATIONAL PARK

NATURAL GAS PIPELINE

Marching Men

Tower
Arch

SALT VALLEY

LITTLE VALLEY

Eye of the Whale Arch

SE #26:
Willow Flats Road

▼ 1.2	SO	Top of climb. Trail descends over rock ledges.
▼ 1.7	TL	Ahead leads to Tower Arch (1.3 miles). Trail is now predominately soft sand.
	GPS: N 38°46.74' W 109°40.63'	
▼ 3.4	SO	Tricky descent over slickrock into wash.
▼ 4.8	SO	Trail exits wash.
▼ 6.4	SO	Cross natural gas pipeline.
▼ 8.8	SO	Track is now predominantly dirt and rock base.
▼ 9.1	SO	Eye of the Whale Arch on right. Small parking area and hiking trail to arch.
	GPS: N 38°42.92' W 109°36.06'	
▼ 10.9		End at intersection with Southeast #26: Willow Flats Road. Turn left to return to main national park road. Turn right to exit park via Willow Flats Road.
	GPS: N 38°42.08' W 109°34.76'	

SOUTHEAST REGION TRAIL #26

Willow Flats Road

Starting Point:	Junction of Arches National Park Road and Willow Flats Road
Finishing Point:	US 191
Total Mileage:	8 miles
Unpaved Mileage:	8 miles
Driving Time:	1 hour
Elevation Range:	4,300–4,500 feet
Usually Open:	Year-round
Difficulty Rating:	4
Scenic Rating:	8
Remoteness Rating:	+0

Special Attractions

■ One of the few 4WD trails in Arches National Park.

■ Desert scenery and vegetation.

■ Moderately challenging alternative exit from Arches National Park.

Description

This less-traveled alternative route out of Arches National Park undulates through dry desert scenery and descends to cross several sandy washes and gullies before joining US 191. There are rewarding views east into Arches National Park and distant views of the La Sal Mountains to the southeast.

The trail begins at the Balanced Rock parking area in the national park and heads west. The trail surface at this stage is

View down the track of Willow Flats Road

graded gravel and dirt. After passing the southern end of Southeast #25: Eye of the Whale Trail, the surface becomes rougher and crosses a couple of rocky washes. After 4.2 miles the trail leaves the national park and enters public lands. It continues to undulate through junipers, yuccas, prickly pears, and shinnery oaks until it ends at US 191.

There are some interesting driving sections on this trail, mainly rocky or sandy washes and some fairly deep washouts that call for careful wheel placement. It should be easily managed by most stock high-clearance SUVs. The National Park Service may close this trail following light snow or heavy rain.

SE #26: WILLOW FLATS ROAD

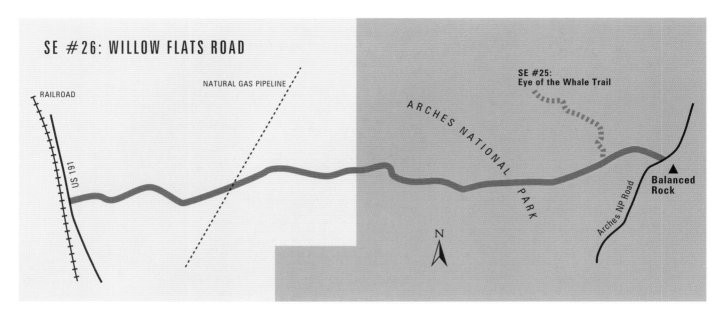

You must pay an entrance fee into Arches National Park, but no special backcountry driving permit is required. There is no camping allowed on Willow Flats Road within Arches National Park.

Current Road Information

Arches National Park
PO Box 907
Moab, UT 84532
(435) 719-2299

Map References

BLM   Moab (incomplete)
USGS   1:24,000   The Windows Section, Merrimac Butte
          1:100,000 Moab (incomplete)
Maptech CD-ROM: Moab/Canyonlands
Trails Illustrated, # 211; #501
Utah Atlas & Gazetteer, p. 40
Utah Travel Council #5
Other: Latitude 40—Moab West
          Canyon Country Off-Road Vehicle Trail Map—
          Arches Area

Route Directions

▼ 0.0   Turn west onto Willow Flats Road opposite the Balanced Rock parking area. Zero trip meter.

     8.0 ▲   Trail ends at the Balanced Rock parking area on the main Arches National Park road. Turn right for the park entrance.

GPS: N 38°42.12′ W 109°33.95′

| ▼ 0.1 | SO | Picnic tables and pit toilet. |
| 7.9 ▲ | SO | Picnic tables and pit toilet. |

| ▼ 0.2 | SO | Track on left to parks work area. |
| 7.8 ▲ | SO | Track on right to parks work area. |

| ▼ 0.8 | SO | Track on right to Southeast #25: Eye of the Whale Trail. Trail turns to dirt. |
| 7.2 ▲ | SO | Track on left to Southeast #25: Eye of the Whale Trail. Trail turns to gravel road. |

GPS: N 38°42.08′ W 109°34.76′

| ▼ 3.3 | SO | Trail crosses slickrock wash. |
| 4.7 ▲ | SO | Trail crosses slickrock wash. |

| ▼ 3.6 | SO | Trail dips into rocky wash. |
| 4.4 ▲ | SO | Views ahead to the La Sal Mountains. Trail dips into rocky wash. |

| ▼ 4.2 | SO | Leaving Arches National Park and entering state lands. |
| 3.8 ▲ | SO | Leaving state lands and entering Arches National Park (fee area). |

GPS: N 38°42.09′ W 109°38.06′

| ▼ 4.7 | SO | Gate. |
| 3.3 ▲ | SO | Gate. |

| ▼ 4.9 | SO | Fork. Trails meet up in 0.1 miles. Choose your route. |
| 3.1 ▲ | SO | Trails rejoin. |

| ▼ 5.0 | SO | Trails rejoin. |
| 3.0 ▲ | SO | Fork. Trails meet up in 0.1 miles. Choose your route. |

| ▼ 5.4 | SO | Track on right. |
| 2.6 ▲ | SO | Track on left. |

| ▼ 6.0 | SO | Cross natural gas pipeline, past hut for generator. Track on left. |
| 2.0 ▲ | SO | Track on right, then cross natural gas pipeline, past hut for generator. |

GPS: N 38°41.90′ W 109°39.81′

| ▼ 6.4 | SO | Cross small wash; care needed with wheel placement. Track on right. |
| 1.6 ▲ | SO | Track on left, then cross small wash, care needed with wheel placement. |

| ▼ 6.6 | SO | Cross wide sandy wash. |
| 1.4 ▲ | SO | Cross wide sandy wash. |

| ▼ 6.8 | TR | Turn right at T-intersection. |
| 1.2 ▲ | TL | Turn left. |

| ▼ 7.6 | SO | Track on left. |
| 0.4 ▲ | SO | Track on right. |

| ▼ 8.0 | | Exit through a gate onto US 191. Turn left for Moab. |
| 0.0 ▲ | | Trail commences 0.6 miles north of mile marker 138 on US 191. Turn east through a gate entering state lands and zero trip meter. |

GPS: N 38°41.80′ W 109°41.89′

Winter Camp Ridge Trail

Starting Point:	Southeast #24: Dome Plateau Trail, 6.6 miles south of Southeast #21: Yellow Cat Road
Finishing Point:	Boundary of Arches National Park
Total Mileage:	4.3 miles
Unpaved Mileage:	4.3 miles
Driving Time:	45 minutes (one-way)
Elevation Range:	4,900–5,300 feet
Usually Open:	Year-round
Difficulty Rating:	3
Scenic Rating:	9
Remoteness Rating:	+1

Special Attractions

■ Short spur trail can be done in conjunction with Southeast #24: Dome Plateau Trail.
■ Views into Arches National Park.
■ Sandy trail is fun to drive.

Description

This short trail is a spur leading off from Southeast #24: Dome Plateau Trail. It begins along an unmarked, roughly graded sandy trail that runs along the top of Winter Camp Ridge. The trail gradually descends the ridge top, offering some great views ahead into Arches National Park and south over Winter Camp Wash, Dome Plateau, and the La Sal Mountains. To the north you can see The Poison Strip, and farther to the north are the Book Cliffs. The difficulty factor of the trail comes from the very soft, deep, fine sand traps found along its entire length. There are no great grades to be negotiated; the trail gradually drops until it finishes at the boundary of Arches National Park. Directly ahead at the end of the trail is a jumble of red rocks that contains the distinctive Delicate Arch, although the arch itself is not visible. Behind them you can see the Windows Section of the park. There are a couple of nice campsites toward the end of the trail.

A hazy view over Arches National Park from Winter Camp Ridge Trail

Current Road Information

Arches National Park
PO Box 907
Moab, UT 84532
(435) 719-2299

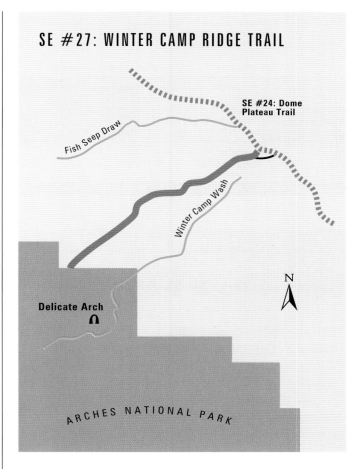

SE #27: WINTER CAMP RIDGE TRAIL

BLM Moab Field Office
82 East Dogwood
Moab, UT 84532
(435) 259-2100

Map References

BLM Moab
USGS 1:24,000 Cisco SW, Mollie Hogans
1:100,000 Moab
Maptech CD-ROM: Moab/Canyonlands
Trails Illustrated, #501; #211
Utah Atlas & Gazetteer, p. 40
Utah Travel Council #5
Other: Latitude 40—Moab East
Canyon Country Off-Road Vehicle Trail Map—
Arches Area

Route Directions

▼ 0.0		From Southeast #24: Dome Plateau Trail, 6.6 miles south of the junction with Southeast #21: Yellow Cat Road, turn west on an unmarked formed track and zero trip meter.
		GPS: N 38°47.86' W 109°26.08'
▼ 0.1	SO	Track on left is second entrance from Dome Plateau Trail.
▼ 1.4	BL	Track on right.
		GPS: N 38°47.35' W 109°27.37'
▼ 1.8	BR	Track on left.

GPS: N 38°47.17' W 109°27.79'		
▼ 2.1	SO	Track on left.
▼ 2.3	SO	Track on left.
▼ 2.8	SO	Cross through wash.
▼ 2.9	SO	Pass through gate, then faint track on left.
GPS: N 38°46.76' W 109°28.87'		
▼ 3.1	SO	Track on right.
▼ 3.4	BR	Track on left.
▼ 3.6	SO	Faint track on left.
GPS: N 38°46.33' W 109°29.29'		
▼ 4.3		Graded track ends at national park boundary. Trail swings right along fence line but does not continue.
GPS: N 38°45.66' W 109°29.47'		

SOUTHEAST REGION TRAIL #28

Squaw Park Trail

Starting Point:	Dewey Bridge on Utah 128
Finishing Point:	Junction with Southeast #24: Dome Plateau Trail
Total Mileage:	8.4 miles
Unpaved Mileage:	8.0 miles
Driving Time:	1 hour
Elevation Range:	4,200–5,200 feet
Usually Open:	Year-round
Difficulty Rating:	5
Scenic Rating:	9
Remoteness Rating:	+0

Special Attractions

■ Historic Dewey Bridge.
■ Moderately challenging trail through a beautiful open valley.
■ Access to a network of 4WD trails.

History

Dewey Bridge, at the start of this trail, has the distinction of being both the longest suspension bridge and the longest clear span bridge in the state of Utah. Built in 1916, it allowed the communities in southeast Utah to access the markets in western Colorado to sell their produce and buy supplies. The old bridge, now being restored through the use of grants and public donations, sits next to the modern concrete highway bridge, which was built in the 1980s.

There is some debate as to whether the name for the settlement of Dewey comes from a prospector who used to live in the area, Dewey Smith, or from a ferry that transported goods downriver, which in turn was named after Admiral Dewey. Samuel King set up a ferry here in the 1880s, and this in turn led to a small settlement that was referred to as Kings Ferry.

Yellow Jacket wash gets its name from the number of wasps in the area!

Description

You begin in the Rio Colorado subdivision immediately north of Dewey Bridge on Utah 128. Follow small BLM signs for the Kokopelli Trail through the subdivision to the start of the trail itself, which swiftly leaves the subdivision behind. The first mile of the ungraded sand and rock trail is the hardest, with a series of rock ledges leading up to the gate. There are great views from the gate back to Dewey Bridge and the Colorado River. From here, the trail is smoother as it runs alongside Yellow Jacket Canyon. This is a fun trail to drive, as the surface is firm and smooth, but there are several dips and off-camber sections to keep the driver watching the trail.

One of the more difficult sections of the Squaw Park Trail

After the junction where the Kokopelli Trail leaves to the right, there is a crossing of Yellow Jacket wash that is interesting to negotiate. There are two ways down to the wash, both steep and loose. One has some large ledges at the bottom that would be difficult to climb in the other direction. The rocky pour-off from the wash crossing has some pretty views into Yellow Jacket Canyon. From here, the trail is an easy and smooth drive as it crosses Squaw Park. It climbs a ridge, with Yellow Jacket Canyon on the right, and winds through the juniper trees to the junction with Southeast #24: Dome Plateau Trail. A natural arch is on the right at the end of the trail, though it is hard to see, as it is low down on the cliff face. Some of the smaller tracks to the right just before the trail ends lead down toward the arch.

Current Road Information

BLM Moab Field Office
82 East Dogwood
Moab, UT 84532
(435) 259-2100

Map References

BLM Moab (incomplete)
USGS 1:24,000 Dewey, Cisco SW (incomplete)
1:100,000 Moab (incomplete)
Maptech CD-ROM: Moab/Canyonlands
Trails Illustrated, #501
Utah Atlas & Gazetteer, p. 41
Other: Latitude 40—Moab East
Canyon Country Off-Road Vehicle Trail Map—
Arches Area

Route Directions

▼ 0.0		Immediately north of Dewey Bridge on Utah 128, turn west into the Rio Colorado subdivision and zero trip meter. Immediately turn right at the first intersection.

3.7 ▲		Turn left, then trail ends at the junction with Utah 128 at Dewey Bridge. Turn right for Moab, turn left for I-70.

GPS: N 38°48.82' W 109°18.13'

▼ 0.4	TR	Cross through concrete ford, then immediately turn right on ungraded dirt track.
3.3 ▲	TL	Turn onto paved road in the Rio Colorado subdivision and cross through concrete ford.

GPS: N 38°48.88' W 109°18.54'

▼ 0.7	SO	Cross through wash, then cross through second wash and track on left.
3.0 ▲	SO	Track on right and cross through wash, then cross through second wash.
▼ 1.0	SO	Pass through gate in old fence line.
2.7 ▲	SO	Pass through gate in old fence line.

GPS: N 38°48.80' W 109°19.01'

▼ 1.5	SO	Cross through wash.
2.2 ▲	SO	Cross through wash.
▼ 1.6	SO	Cross through wash.
2.1 ▲	SO	Cross through wash.
▼ 2.1	SO	Track on left.
1.6 ▲	SO	Track on right.

GPS: N 38°48.78' W 109°19.65'

▼ 2.3	SO	Cross through wash.
1.4 ▲	SO	Cross through wash.
▼ 2.7	SO	Track on right then cross through wash. Trail is traveling alongside Yellow Jacket Canyon.
1.0 ▲	SO	Cross through wash, then track on left.

GPS: N 38°48.98' W 109°20.26'

▼ 3.0	SO	Cross through wash.
0.7 ▲	SO	Cross through wash.
▼ 3.1	SO	Rock arch to the right, high up on the sandstone escarpment.
0.6 ▲	SO	Rock arch to the left, high up on the sandstone escarpment.

GPS: N 38°49.06' W 109°20.72'

▼ 3.7	TL	Turn left at T-intersection. There is a hard-to-spot arch on the right at the junction. Zero trip meter.
0.0 ▲		Continue to the east.

GPS: N 38°49.30' W 109°21.26'

▼ 0.0		Continue to the west.
4.7 ▲	TR	There is a hard-to-spot arch on the left at the junction. Zero trip meter.
▼ 0.1	BR	Trail divides and descends to cross Yellow Jacket wash. Both descents are steep; the right-hand one is usually easier.
4.6 ▲	BL	Trails rejoin.
▼ 0.2	SO	Cross through Yellow Jacket wash. Tracks rejoin.
4.5 ▲	SO	Cross through Yellow Jacket wash, then trail divides. Both ascents are steep; the left-hand one is usually easier.

GPS: N 38°49.29' W 109°21.46'

▼ 0.5	SO	Cross through wash. Trail crosses Squaw Park.
4.2 ▲	SO	Cross through wash.
▼ 1.5	SO	Cross through wash, then track on left.
3.2 ▲	SO	Track on right, then cross through wash.

GPS: N 38°48.82' W 109°22.76'

▼ 1.6	SO	Track on right and faint track on left.
3.1 ▲	SO	Track on left and faint track on right.

GPS: N 38°48.76' W 109°22.87'

▼ 1.8	SO	Cross through wash.
2.9 ▲	SO	Cross through wash.
▼ 1.9	SO	Cross through wash.
2.8 ▲	SO	Cross through wash.
▼ 2.1	SO	Cross through wash.
2.6 ▲	SO	Cross through wash.
▼ 2.2	SO	Cross through wash.
2.5 ▲	SO	Cross through wash.
▼ 2.3	SO	Cross through wash, then track on left is alternative route.

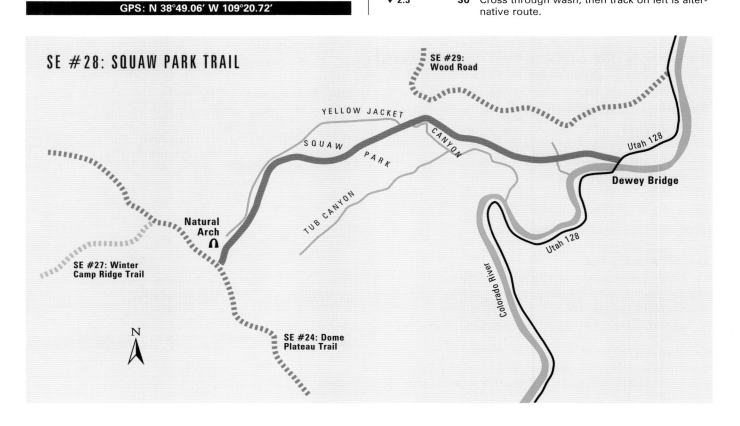

SE #28: SQUAW PARK TRAIL

SE #29: Wood Road

YELLOW JACKET

SQUAW PARK

CANYON

Utah 128

Dewey Bridge

TUB CANYON

Natural Arch

SE #27: Winter Camp Ridge Trail

Colorado River

Utah 128

N

SE #24: Dome Plateau Trail

2.4 ▲		SO	Alternative route rejoins to the right, then cross through wash. Trail crosses Squaw Park.
▼ 2.5		SO	Alternative route rejoins to the left.
2.2 ▲		BL	Track on right is alternative route.

GPS: N 38°48.78' W 109°23.69'

▼ 2.7		SO	Cross through wash.
2.0 ▲		SO	Cross through wash. Trail runs alongside Yellow Jacket Canyon.
▼ 4.1		SO	Crossroads.
0.6 ▲		SO	Crossroads.

GPS: N 38°47.68' W 109°24.62'

▼ 4.2		BL	Track on right, then second track on right.
0.5 ▲		SO	Track on left, then second track on left.
▼ 4.4		BL	Track on right.
0.3 ▲		SO	Track on left.

GPS: N 38°47.40' W 109°24.80'

▼ 4.6		SO	Track on right.
0.1 ▲		SO	Track on left.
▼ 4.7			Trail ends at the graded Southeast #24: Dome Plateau Trail. Faint trail continues on ahead. Turn left for Dome Plateau, turn right to exit 8 miles to Southeast #21: Yellow Cat Road. A natural arch is on the right at the junction.
0.0 ▲			Trail starts along Southeast #24: Dome Plateau Trail, 8 miles from Southeast #21: Yellow Cat Road. Turn northeast on ungraded dirt trail just east of a natural arch and zero trip meter.

GPS: N 38°47.18' W 109°24.94'

SOUTHEAST REGION TRAIL #29

Wood Road

Starting Point:	**Utah 128, 0.1 miles north of mile marker 32**
Finishing Point:	**Southeast #20: Yellow Cat Trail,**
	4.4 miles west of Utah 128
Total Mileage:	**6.4 miles**
Unpaved Mileage:	**6.4 miles**
Driving Time:	**1.25 hours**
Elevation Range:	**4,200–4,900 feet**
Usually Open:	**Year-round**
Difficulty Rating:	**4**
Scenic Rating:	**10**
Remoteness Rating:	**+0**

Special Attractions

- Interesting driving over a variety of trail surfaces.
- Fantastic views along the rim over Fisher and Professor Valleys and into Squaw Park.
- Connects with the Kokopelli Trail and other 4WD trails.

Description

This moderate trail climbs up on the rim over Squaw Park and gives great views to the south, first over Professor Valley and the La Sal Mountains, and then later over Fisher Valley and

Looking back at a short, steep descent along Wood Road

Fisher Towers. Directly below is Southeast #28: Squaw Park Trail running through Yellow Jacket Canyon.

The trail surface is predominantly rocky, with a couple of sections of slickrock pavement and some sand. The trail leaves Utah 128 north of Dewey Bridge and climbs up gradually to the rim overlooking Squaw Park. The major mountain bike trail, the Kokopelli Trail, follows the route for most of a mile before it diverges and continues down into Squaw Park. The trail crosses a section of sloping slickrock as it climbs to a small saddle and then swings sharp right and climbs a further steep section to the ridge. The best views are here at the top of the climb.

The final part of the trail is easier and sandy as it makes its way down to join Southeast #20: Yellow Cat Trail near Owl Draw. From here, the quickest way out is to follow the last couple of miles of the Yellow Cat Trail northeast to Utah 128.

This trail is shown on some maps as the eastern end of Yellow Cat Trail. However, this trail is considerably more difficult than Yellow Cat.

Current Road Information

BLM Moab Field Office
82 East Dogwood
Moab, UT 84532
(435) 259-2100

Map References

BLM Moab (incomplete)
USGS 1:24,000 Dewey
1:100,000 Moab (incomplete)
Maptech CD-ROM: Moab/Canyonlands
Trails Illustrated, #501
Utah Atlas & Gazetteer, p. 41
Other: Latitude 40—Moab East

Route Directions

▼ 0.0			From Utah 128, 0.1 miles north of mile marker 32, turn west off the highway at a turnout. The trail climbs up the embankment above the highway to the north, then swings around to the southwest. Zero trip meter.
3.3 ▲			Trail finishes at the junction with Utah 128. Turn right for Dewey Bridge and Moab, turn left for I-70.

GPS: N 38°49.96' W 109°17.20'

▼ 0.1		SO	Pass through wire gate.
3.2 ▲		SO	Pass through wire gate.
▼ 0.6		BL	Track on right.
2.7 ▲		SO	Track on left.

▼ 1.0		SO	Two tracks on left to viewpoints.
	2.3 ▲	SO	Two tracks on right to viewpoints.
▼ 1.2		SO	Track on right.
	2.1 ▲	SO	Track on left.
GPS: N 38°49.56′ W 109°18.24′			
▼ 1.3		SO	Track on left.
	2.0 ▲	SO	Track on right.
▼ 1.5		SO	Cross through wash.
	1.8 ▲	SO	Cross through wash.
▼ 1.6		SO	Cross through wash.
	1.7 ▲	SO	Cross through wash.
▼ 1.9		BR	Track on left.
	1.4 ▲	SO	Track on right.
GPS: N 38°49.33′ W 109°18.86′			
▼ 2.2		SO	Track on left and views to the south toward Ninemile Bottom.
	1.1 ▲	SO	Track on right and views to the south toward Ninemile Bottom.
▼ 2.3		SO	Track on right. Trail runs along the edge of the escarpment.
	1.0 ▲	SO	Track on left.
▼ 2.8		SO	Cross through wash.
	0.5 ▲	SO	Cross through wash.
▼ 3.0		SO	Walk to the edge for a great view into Squaw Park, Yellow Jacket Canyon, and the top end of the Professor Valley—no formal turnout.
	0.3 ▲	SO	Walk to the edge for a great view into Squaw Park, Yellow Jacket Canyon, and the top end of the Professor Valley—no formal turnout.

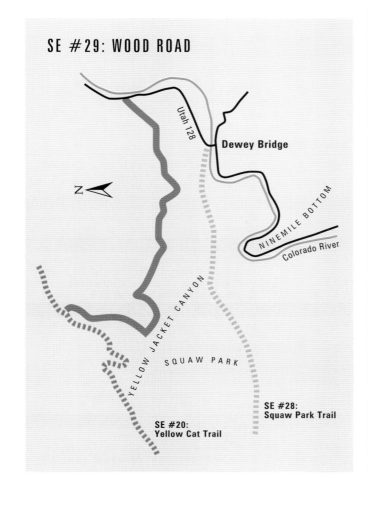

SE #29: WOOD ROAD

The landscape from a viewpoint along Wood Road

GPS: N 38°49.42′ W 109°20.15′			
▼ 3.3		BL	Track on right is the Kokopelli Trail, which joins the main trail at this point. Zero trip meter.
	0.0 ▲		Leave the Kokopelli Trail.
GPS: N 38°49.50′ W 109°20.33′			
▼ 0.0			Continue along the Kokopelli Trail.
	0.8 ▲	BR	Kokopelli Trail leaves to the left. Zero trip meter.
▼ 0.1		SO	Track on left goes to viewpoint.
	0.7 ▲	SO	Track on right goes to viewpoint.
▼ 0.4		TL	Follow the sign for the Kokopelli Trail to the left.
	0.4 ▲	TR	Follow the sign for the Kokopelli Trail to the right.
GPS: N 38°49.70′ W 109°20.65′			
▼ 0.5		SO	Trail crosses slickrock pavement and is marked with Kokopelli route markers.
	0.3 ▲	SO	End of slickrock section.
▼ 0.7		SO	End of slickrock section.
	0.1 ▲	SO	Trail crosses slickrock pavement and is marked with Kokopelli route markers.
▼ 0.8		SO	Intersection. Kokopelli Trail leaves to the left. Zero trip meter.
	0.0 ▲		Leave slickrock and continue straight.
GPS: N 38°49.83′ W 109°21.00′			
▼ 0.0			Trail crosses slickrock pavement. Keep to the right.
	2.3 ▲	SO	Intersection. Track to the right is the Kokopelli Trail, which joins the main trail at this point. Zero trip meter.
▼ 0.4		SO	Trail leaves slickrock and climbs to small saddle.
	1.9 ▲	SO	Trail crosses slickrock pavement. Keep to the left.
▼ 0.6		TR	Swing hard right at saddle and climb steep short pinch to top of ridge.
	1.7 ▲	TL	Swing hard left at saddle.
GPS: N 38°49.72′ W 109°21.70′			
▼ 0.7		SO	Top of ridge. Great views!
	1.6 ▲	SO	Descend steep short pinch to saddle.
▼ 1.5		BL	Track on right.
	0.8 ▲	SO	Track on left.
GPS: N 38°50.35′ W 109°21.41′			

| ▼ 1.7 | SO | Track on right. |
| 0.6 ▲ | SO | Track on left. |

GPS: N 38°50.45' W 109°21.42'

| ▼ 2.3 | | Cross through wash, then trail ends at intersection with Southeast #20: Yellow Cat Trail, 4.4 miles from Utah 128. |
| 0.0 ▲ | | Trail commences at Southeast #20: Yellow Cat Trail, 4.4 miles west from Utah 128. Zero trip meter, and turn south on unmarked, ungraded sandy trail. |

GPS: N 38°50.93' W 109°21.28'

SOUTHEAST REGION TRAIL #30

Cache Valley Trail

Starting Point:	Arches National Park
Finishing Point:	Cache Valley
Total Mileage:	3.6 miles
Unpaved Mileage:	3.6 miles
Driving Time:	45 minutes (one-way)
Elevation Range:	4,400–5,000 feet
Usually Open:	Year-round
Difficulty Rating:	4
Scenic Rating:	8
Remoteness Rating:	+0

Special Attractions
■ Views along the wide Cache Valley.
■ View of Delicate Arch.
■ Interesting side trail to add to a day in Arches National Park.

Description
This short spur trail is an enjoyable side trip to a day in Arches National Park. It leaves from the end of the paved road to Delicate Arch and descends to Cache Valley Wash running along Cache Valley. It runs along the wash, crossing it frequently. The trail then turns to the south and climbs toward Dry Mesa. This route finishes on a ridge with

Sandstone spires as the trail climbs the steep ridge toward Dry Mesa

Trail as it climbs away from Cache Valley Wash

a great view back along Cache Valley to Arches National Park. The trail does continue up onto the mesa, but it is very steep and because it is so difficult, it is well beyond the scope of this book.

It is possible to continue along the wash in Cache Valley for another mile before it becomes too narrow for vehicles.

Current Road Information
Arches National Park
PO Box 907
Moab, UT 84532
(435) 719-2299

Map References
BLM Moab
USGS 1:24,000 The Windows Section, Big Bend
   1:100,000 Moab
Maptech CD-ROM: Moab/Canyonlands
Trails Illustrated, #211; 501
Utah Atlas & Gazetteer, p. 40
Utah Travel Council #5 (incomplete)
Other: Latitude 40—Moab East

Route Directions

| ▼ 0.0 | | From the end of the paved road to Delicate Arch, zero trip meter and continue on the ungraded dirt Cache Valley Road. |

GPS: N 38°44.01' W 109°30.05'

| ▼ 0.1 | SO | Cross through small wash. View of Delicate Arch to the left. |

GPS: N 38°44.00' W 109°29.91'

| ▼ 0.4 | SO | Trail enters wash and runs alongside or in it, crossing it frequently, for the next 1.3 miles. |
| ▼ 0.6 | SO | Pass through gate, please keep closed. Boundary of Arches National Park. |

GPS: N 38°43.87' W 109°29.42'

▼ 1.7	SO	Leave wash and follow south side of Cache Valley.
▼ 2.1	SO	Cross through small tributary wash.
▼ 2.6	BL	Trail forks around washed-out section.
▼ 2.7	SO	Alternative routes rejoin.
▼ 2.9	SO	Track to the left continues along the wash for another mile before becoming too narrow for vehicles. Zero trip meter.

GPS: N 38°43.53' W 109°27.21'

| ▼ 0.0 | | Continue along Cache Valley. |
| ▼ 0.5 | BR | Enter wash and swing right, then swing left out of wash along trail. Some vehicles go straight across, which is harder. Look back to |

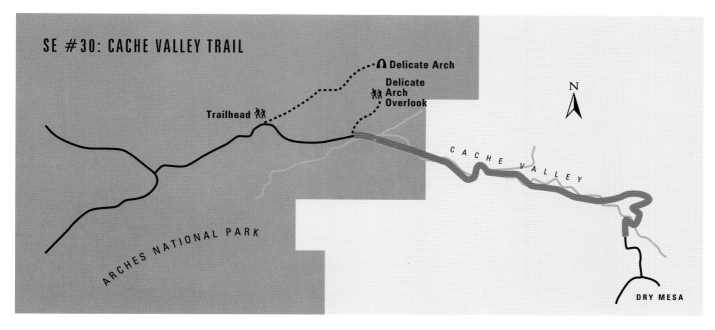

SE #30: CACHE VALLEY TRAIL

Delicate Arch

Delicate Arch Overlook

Trailhead

N

CACHE VALLEY

ARCHES NATIONAL PARK

DRY MESA

	see a cave or mine, with a short dead-end tunnel in the cliff.
▼ 0.7	Harder trail rejoins on left. Trail continues and climbs very steeply up to Dry Mesa. The extremely difficult climb has very large ledges and deep holes and gullies that take it beyond the scope of the book. Turn around at this viewpoint over Cache Valley and retrace your steps back to Delicate Arch.

GPS: N 38°43.26' W 109°27.27'

SOUTHEAST REGION TRAIL #31

Anticline Overlook Trail

Starting Point:	Needles Overlook Road (CR 133), 14.5 miles from US 191
Finishing Point:	Anticline Overlook
Total Mileage:	15.6 miles
Unpaved Mileage:	15.6 miles
Driving Time:	1 hour (one-way)
Elevation Range:	5,500–6,300 feet
Usually Open:	Year-round
Difficulty Rating:	1
Scenic Rating:	10
Remoteness Rating:	+0

Special Attractions

- Easy trail to spectacular viewpoint at the Anticline Overlook.
- Access to a number of 4WD trails and backcountry campsites.
- Wine Glass Arch.

History

In 1881, Alonzo Hatch settled near a spring in the northwest section of Dry Valley and gave his name to Hatch Point, Hatch Wash, and Hatch Rock. Hatch Wash was also known as Hudson Wash after a local character called Spud Hudson, who always carried a potato in his pocket!

The Dave Minor Overlook near the end of the trail was named by Fran Barnes after a recreation officer in the BLM.

Description

This easy trail follows a graded gravel road to the panoramic Anticline Overlook. The trail, which is suitable for passenger vehicles, gradually descends over the sagebrush benches of Hatch Point to the overlook. The views are not confined to the overlook at the end of the trail. From the start, you get glimpses into Lockhart Basin and of the Henry Mountains beyond; a couple of marked turnouts farther on have spectacular views of the deep Dripping Spring Canyon and the Col-

View from the Anticline Overlook includes Southeast #49: Hurrah Pass Trail in Kane Springs Canyon. The snowcapped La Sal Mountains are behind.

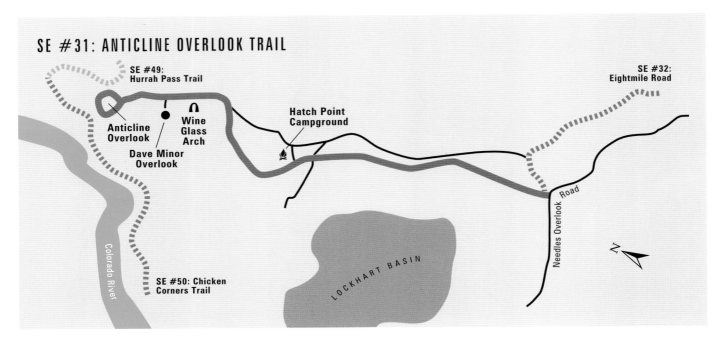

SE #31: ANTICLINE OVERLOOK TRAIL

orado River. To the north of the trail, the La Sal Mountains rise up in direct contrast to the jumbled boulders of the Behind The Rocks area.

Halfway along the trail is the BLM's Hatch Point Campground. This small campground has several sites scattered along an escarpment just off the trail. There is limited shade, but it is a pleasant place to camp (fee required).

The Anticline Overlook itself has some scattered picnic tables in the small juniper trees. A short scramble leads to the

The Wine Glass Arch

fenced overlook and its staggering views. To the west, you can see Southeast #50: Chicken Corners Trail far below, as well as the Colorado River with the Island in the Sky district of Canyonlands National Park and Dead Horse Point rising up behind. To the north, the view stretches over the lower reaches of Kane Springs Canyon through The Portal in the Moab Rim to Arches National Park. Moab can be glimpsed through The Portal. Southeast #49: Hurrah Pass Trail can clearly be seen. To the east is Kane Springs Canyon and the La Sal Mountains.

For an easily accessible, awe-inspiring viewpoint, this one is hard to beat!

Current Road Information
BLM Moab Field Office
82 East Dogwood
Moab, UT 84532
(435) 259-2100

Map References
BLM La Sal
USGS 1:24,000 Eightmile Rock, Shafer Basin, Trough Springs Canyon
1:100,000 La Sal
Maptech CD-ROM: Moab/Canyonlands
Trails Illustrated, #501 (incomplete)
Utah Atlas & Gazetteer, p. 30
Utah Travel Council #5
Other: Latitude 40—Moab West (incomplete)
Canyon Country Off-Road Vehicle Trail Map—
Canyon Rims & Needles Areas

Route Directions

▼ 0.0		From the Needles Overlook Road (CR 133), 14.5 miles from US 191, turn northwest onto graded gravel road and zero trip meter.
GPS: N 38°15.45' W 109°34.84'		
▼ 0.1	SO	Track on right is Southeast #32: Eightmile Road.
▼ 1.1	SO	Faint track on right.
▼ 2.3	SO	Track on left.
GPS: N 38°17.44' W 109°35.08'		
▼ 2.7	SO	Faint track on left.
▼ 2.8	SO	Faint track on left.
▼ 3.2	SO	Track on left.
▼ 3.5	SO	Track on left.
▼ 4.0	SO	Track on right goes to corral, then track on left.
▼ 4.5	SO	Cattle guard.
GPS: N 38°19.35' W 109°35.95'		
▼ 4.8	SO	Views on left into Lockhart Basin.
GPS: N 38°19.64' W 109°36.06'		
▼ 4.9	SO	Track on right.
▼ 5.7	SO	Track on right.
▼ 6.7	SO	Track on right.
▼ 7.8	SO	Track on right and track on left.
GPS: N 38°22.19' W 109°37.05'		
▼ 8.0	SO	Track on right goes to Hatch Point Campground (fee area). Zero trip meter.

		GPS: N 38°22.35' W 109°37.23'
▼ 0.0		Continue to the Anticline Overlook.
▼ 0.9	SO	Track on left, then track on right.
▼ 1.8	SO	Track on left.
▼ 2.8	SO	Track on left, then second gravel track on left goes to Dripping Spring Canyon overlook; potash works are on far side of Colorado River.
▼ 3.7	SO	Track on right is Trough Springs track.
		GPS: N 38°24.72' W 109°36.25'
▼ 3.9	SO	Cattle guard.
▼ 4.0	SO	Track on right.
▼ 4.7	SO	Track on right.
▼ 4.9	SO	Track on right.
▼ 5.2	SO	Track on right, then the Wine Glass Arch is on the left.
		GPS: N 38°25.93' W 109°36.50'
▼ 5.9	SO	Graded gravel road on left goes short distance to the Dave Minor Overlook. Zero trip meter.
		GPS: N 38°26.50' W 109°36.77'
▼ 0.0		Continue to Anticline Overlook.
▼ 1.4	SO	Cattle guard.
▼ 1.6	BR	Start of loop at end of overlook.
▼ 1.7		End of trail at start of hiking trail out to the overlook.
		GPS: N 38°27.91' W 109°37.60'

SOUTHEAST REGION TRAIL #32

Eightmile Road

Starting Point:	**CR 171, 0.1 miles along Southeast #31: Anticline Overlook Trail**
Finishing Point:	**US 191**
Total Mileage:	**16.5 miles**
Unpaved Mileage:	**16.5 miles**
Driving Time:	**1 hour**
Elevation Range:	**5,600–6,300 feet**
Usually Open:	**Year-round**
Difficulty Rating:	**2**
Scenic Rating:	**8**
Remoteness Rating:	**+0**

Special Attractions

■ Large arch in Looking Glass Rock.
■ Rock dwellings in Eightmile Rock and Hatch Rock.
■ Access to numerous 4WD spur trails over Hatch Wash.

History

Hatch Rock, like Hatch Point and Hatch Wash, was named for Alonzo Hatch, whose small ranch stood just west of Hatch Rock in the 1880s. The rock was also used as a navigation point by the Macomb Expedition of 1859.

As you approach the rock, it appears there are several "houses" set right up against it. As you get closer, however, you will see that the doors and windows are actually in the rock, which is

Looking along the face of dugout dwellings in Eightmile Rock

now home to a small alternative community called Rocklands Ranch, a group founded by Bob Foster in 1974. The inhabitants live in dwellings dug, tunneled, and dynamited into Hatch Rock. The government has granted the group a 50-year lease for dwelling purposes. The community has well water, propane for cooking, and solar units for heating.

Description

This trail follows county roads from the beginning of Southeast #31: Anticline Overlook Trail east to US 191. Eightmile Road first leaves the Anticline Overlook Trail and follows the graded dirt road (CR 171) to the northeast. After a mile, it passes Eightmile Rock. To the left at this point are some dwellings tunneled into the rock. One digging is used as a small cabin; the others are used as feed storage for cattle.

The road descends the bench, crossing many small washes. The surface is graded dirt, easily passable when dry by a high-clearance vehicle, but add moisture and the surface deteriorates to sticky mud and is often impassable. There are many spur trails as the road travels along Hatch Point; many leading northeast go to overlooks of Hatch Wash.

After 7.8 miles, the road (CR 132) swings east, where it meets another graded county road (CR 135) from the south. On the left is Hatch Rock and the community of Rocklands Ranch. The trail follows

View of the moon and adventurer through Looking Glass Rock

Wind Whistle Draw until it joins in with the larger Hatch Wash.

The next major feature on the trail is the large Looking Glass Rock, which has a large arch on the southeast corner. A short loop track takes you to the base of the arch, and it is an easy scramble over the slickrock to the window. There is a long drop on the far side! The trail finishes 1.8 miles farther on, at the junction with US 191.

Current Road Information

BLM Moab Field Office
82 East Dogwood
Moab, UT 84532
(435) 259-2100

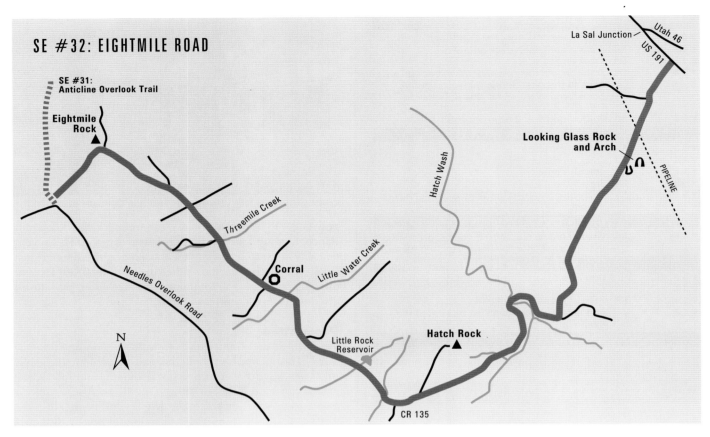

SE #32: EIGHTMILE ROAD

Map References

BLM La Sal

USGS 1:24,000 Eightmile Rock, Harts Point North, Hatch Rock, La Sal Junction
1:100,000 La Sal

Maptech CD-ROM: Moab/Canyonlands

Trails Illustrated, #501 (incomplete)

Utah Atlas & Gazetteer, pp. 30, 31

Utah Travel Council #5

Other: Latitude 40—Moab West (incomplete)
Latitude 40—Moab East (incomplete)
Canyon Country Off-Road Vehicle Trail Map—
Canyon Rims & Needles Area

Route Directions

▼ 0.0		0.1 miles from the start of Southeast #31: Anticline Overlook Trail, turn northeast on graded dirt road (CR 171), following the sign for Eightmile Rock, and zero trip meter.
7.8 ▲		Trail finishes 0.1 miles from the start of Southeast #31: Anticline Overlook Trail. Turn right to continue to the Anticline Overlook. Turn left on CR 133 to reach US 191.

		GPS: N 38°15.52′ W 109°34.92′
▼ 0.5	SO	Track on right.
7.3 ▲	SO	Track on left.
▼ 1.1	BR	Track on left at Eightmile Rock. Small cabin and farm sheds set into the rock itself, just up the track on the left.
6.7 ▲	SO	Track on right at Eightmile Rock. Small cabin and farm sheds set into the rock itself, just up the track on the left.

		GPS: N 38°16.29′ W 109°34.08′
▼ 1.6	SO	Track on right.
6.2 ▲	SO	Track on left.
▼ 2.4	SO	Track on left and faint track on right.
5.4 ▲	SO	Track on right and faint track on left.
▼ 2.6	SO	Track on left.
5.2 ▲	SO	Track on right.
▼ 2.8	SO	Track on right and track on left.
5.0 ▲	SO	Track on left and track on right.
▼ 3.6	SO	Track on right, then cross through Threemile Creek.
4.2 ▲	SO	Cross through Threemile Creek, then track on left.

		GPS: N 38°15.06′ W 109°31.75′
▼ 4.6	SO	Track on left.
3.2 ▲	SO	Track on right.
▼ 4.7	SO	Track on right and corral on left.
3.1 ▲	SO	Track on left and corral on right.

		GPS: N 38°14.43′ W 109°30.81′
▼ 5.1	SO	Cross over Little Water Creek.
2.7 ▲	SO	Cross over Little Water Creek.
▼ 5.9	SO	Track on left.
1.9 ▲	SO	Track on right.
▼ 6.8	SO	Track on left goes to Little Rock Reservoir.
1.0 ▲	SO	Track on right goes to Little Rock Reservoir.

		GPS: N 38°13.31′ W 109°29.14′
▼ 7.0	SO	Cattle guard.
0.8 ▲	SO	Cattle guard.
▼ 7.6	SO	Cross over creek.
0.2 ▲	SO	Cross over creek.
▼ 7.8	SO	Track on right is CR 135. Zero trip meter.
0.0 ▲		Continue toward Eightmile Rock.

		GPS: N 38°12.78′ W 109°28.32′
▼ 0.0		Continue toward Hatch Rock.

6.9 ▲	BR	Track on left is CR 135. Zero trip meter.	
▼ 0.3	SO	Track on left goes to Hatch Rock and Rocklands Ranch community.	
6.6 ▲	SO	Track on right goes to Hatch Rock and Rocklands Ranch community.	

GPS: N 38°12.91' W 109°27.98'

▼ 1.2	SO	Track on left.
5.7 ▲	SO	Track on right.
▼ 2.1	SO	Trail runs alongside Hatch Wash.
4.8 ▲	SO	Trail runs alongside Hatch Wash.
▼ 3.0	SO	Cross through wash.
3.9 ▲	SO	Cross through wash.
▼ 3.9	SO	Track on right. Trail is now CR 131.
3.0 ▲	SO	Track on left. Trail is now CR 132.

GPS: N 38°14.18' W 109°25.50'

▼ 6.6	SO	Cattle guard. Looking Glass Rock is on the right.
0.3 ▲	SO	Cattle guard. Looking Glass Rock is on the left.
▼ 6.8	SO	Track on right goes to base of Looking Glass Rock and arch.
0.1 ▲	SO	Track on left goes to base of Looking Glass Rock and arch.
▼ 6.9	SO	Graded track on right goes to Looking Glass Rock and arch. Zero trip meter.
0.0 ▲		Continue toward Hatch Rock.

GPS: N 38°16.59' W 109°24.38'

▼ 0.0		Continue toward US 191.
1.8 ▲	BR	Graded track on left goes to Looking Glass Rock and arch. Zero trip meter.
▼ 0.4	SO	Track on right, then cross pipeline.
1.4 ▲	SO	Cross pipeline, then track on left.
▼ 0.8	SO	Track on right.
1.0 ▲	SO	Track on left.
▼ 1.1	SO	Track on left through gate.
0.7 ▲	SO	Track on right through gate.
▼ 1.8		Cross cattle guard, then trail ends at intersection with US 191, 0.6 miles south of La Sal Junction.
0.0 ▲		From US 191, at the sign for Looking Glass Road, 0.6 miles south of La Sal Junction, turn southwest on graded CR 131 and zero trip meter.

GPS: N 38°18.11' W 109°23.67'

SOUTHEAST REGION TRAIL #33

Elephant Hill Loop

Starting Point:	**Elephant Hill Trailhead, Canyonlands National Park**
Finishing Point:	**Elephant Hill Trailhead, Canyonlands National Park**
Total Mileage:	**7.3 miles**
Unpaved Mileage:	**7.3 miles**
Driving Time:	**6 hours (entire loop)**
Elevation Range:	**5,000–5,400 feet**
Usually Open:	**Year-round**
Difficulty Rating:	**7**
Scenic Rating:	**9**
Remoteness Rating:	**+0**

Jeep trail sign at the top of Elephant Hill

Special Attractions

- Extremely challenging and technical trail.
- Canyonlands National Park.
- Spectacular red rock scenery along Devil's Lane.

History

Elephant Hill was originally a cattle trail forged to gain grazing access to Chesler Park and the Grabens. In the 1940s Al Scorup of the Dugout Ranch contracted a bulldozer to improve the cattle trail over Elephant Hill. The trail passes along "grabens," which are down-dropped sections between elevated fault lines. The trail took its name from the rounded formations on the many sides of the hill, which reminded the stockmen of the tops of elephant heads. The Silver Stairs farther along the trail were named because of the silvery color of the ledges in certain light.

The Moab Jeep Safari, held every Easter, has special permission from the National Park Service to include this trail in their program.

Description

This extremely challenging and difficult trail is nevertheless passable for an experienced driver in a high-clearance stock SUV with good tires. The trail is short, but it will still take the best part of a day to drive, especially if you take the side trail to the confluence of the Colorado and Green Rivers. Elephant Hill is one trail on which you want to have a camera or better still a video—most people will be amazed at what their vehicle can do!

The hills provide the challenge on this trail, and Elephant Hill itself is only the first. These hills are very steep and extremely rocky, with large rocks, ledges, and holes to negotiate. The National Park Service has filled in the worst of the trail with concrete so that park vehicles can get over it, but do not underestimate the trail—it is still extremely difficult. Although the NPS uses a

The Squeezeplay, the narrowest section of the Elephant Hill Loop

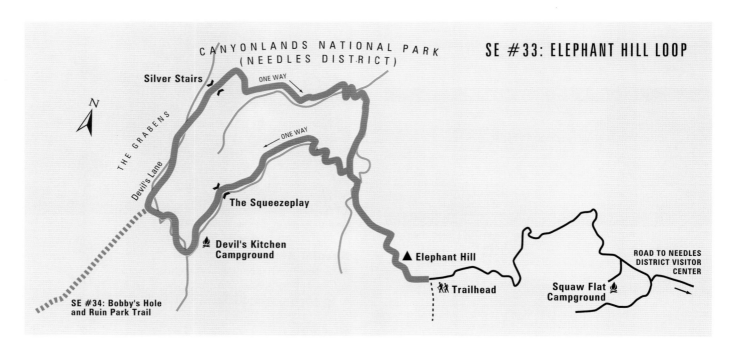

CANYONLANDS NATIONAL PARK
(NEEDLES DISTRICT)

SE #33: ELEPHANT HILL LOOP

Silver Stairs

ONE WAY

N

THE GRABENS

Devil's Lane

ONE WAY

The Squeezeplay

Devil's Kitchen Campground

SE #34: Bobby's Hole and Ruin Park Trail

▲ Elephant Hill

Trailhead

Squaw Flat Campground

ROAD TO NEEDLES DISTRICT VISITOR CENTER

modified Jeep Wrangler, most robust 4WDs will be able to handle it. However, extra clearance is a definite advantage; low-hanging winch bars or side steps will increase the difficulty. Careful wheel placement is needed all along this trail to avoid scraping the undercarriage. The "Squeezeplay," where the trail passes through an extremely narrow crevice in the rock for about 100 yards, is very tight for larger vehicles. We drove through in a Land Rover Discovery, but not before we had first measured the widest part of the vehicle against the width of the gap. We estimated the Land Rover needed 77 inches, not including mirrors, to fit through, and we only had a scant couple of inches to spare on each side. The narrowness is made worse by the fact that the trail is seriously off-camber in the gap, tilting a vehicle over and effectively increasing its width. There are no alternate routes around this or any of the obstacles along the trail.

The trail lets you know immediately what you are in for, as it leaves the Elephant Hill parking area and climbs steeply. The first switchback has been modified by the NPS into a flat concrete turning area, so the first turn is easy. Continue up the

Driving down Elephant Hill

hill. At the top of Elephant Hill, a small Jeep sign points the way down. The descent is far steeper, rockier, and more difficult than the ascent—and remember, you have to come back up it at the end! In fact, the ascent on the return trip is possibly the most difficult section on the entire trail. Stop at the top and take a look down before committing yourself. If you are unsure about your own or your vehicle's ability to return back up this hill, there is still time to turn around. The stretch to study is from the top down to the first "Pull Up and Back Down" sign. The park service says that towing fees for vehicles stranded here typically exceed $1,500! The "Pull In and Back Up" sign, at the halfway point, marks the notorious stretch where the switchback is too tight for a vehicle to make the turn. Vehicles are required to pull up and then back down for approximately 100 yards, then back up and continue on in the normal forward manner! Returning vehicles must make the same maneuver. Luckily the section of trail you have to back along is flatter, wider, and easier than the rest, but it's still an interesting challenge.

Once past Elephant Hill, the trail is easy and sandy as it runs along in spectacular country. It passes the end of the loop and becomes one-way only as it follows a small creek, crossing the creek bed a couple of times; there are plenty of interesting sections here but nothing terribly difficult until the next hill. This hill is again steep and has very large boulders that must be climbed and deep holes to be avoided. It is also extremely loose. At the top it passes underneath a rocky overhang before descending again.

All along the Elephant Hill Loop, previous drivers have stacked rocks to help ease their vehicles up or down the worst of the rock ledges. Most drivers will need to adjust these rocks to best fit the wheel placement of their vehicle—so having a passenger to "spot" for you and move some rocks around is a definite advantage! In between the obstacles there are some long sections of easy sand driving.

Half a mile after this second difficult hill, you reach the

Squeezeplay. Note that the far end is very off camber and can catch the unwary—wider vehicles will need to watch the roofline on the rock on the right.

Just past the Squeezeplay is the farthest point of the loop and the junction with Southeast #34: Bobby's Hole and Ruin Park Trail.

The return trip along the second half of the loop is a lot easier than the way out. The trail runs along Devil's Lane before squeezing through another narrow canyon in the rock, although this looks like a freeway after the Squeezeplay! The Silver Stairs is a wide descent over some rock ledges, but there is a good line and the ledges are small and should not cause anyone any trouble who has made it this far. Next you reach the junction with the Confluence Overlook Trail, a 3-mile spur trail that goes to an overlook at the confluence of the Green and Colorado Rivers. The return section of the loop follows in or alongside a sandy wash for most of its way; there is only one other hill that is tricky, and it appears just after the Confluence Overlook Trail. The trail descends over steep slickrock before wrapping around to descend a loose ledgy hill. Again, this hill is easier than the ones encountered so far.

At the end of the loop, turn left to retrace your path over Elephant Hill and back to the trailhead.

The National Park Service does not allow pets on the trail, even in a vehicle, and an overnight permit is required if you are planning to camp at the campground at Devil's Kitchen. The trail can be open year-round, but may be closed due to snow for short periods. If in doubt, check ahead.

Current Road Information
Canyonlands National Park
Needles Ranger District
(435) 259-4711

Map References
BLM   La Sal
USGS 1:24,000   The Loop
          1:100,000 La Sal
Maptech CD-ROM: Moab/Canyonlands
Trails Illustrated, #210
Utah Atlas & Gazetteer, p. 30
Utah Travel Council #5 (incomplete)
Other: Canyon Country Off-Road Vehicle Trail Map—
       Canyon Rims & Needles Areas

Route Directions

▼ 0.0   Follow the park signs for Elephant Hill from The Needles visitor center to Elephant Hill Trailhead and picnic area. Zero trip meter at the picnic area, and proceed to climb up the 4WD trail.

GPS: N 38°08.51' W 109°49.64'

▼ 0.1   BR   Sharp switchback with turning area straight ahead.
▼ 0.3   SO   Top of Elephant Hill. Trail is sandy dirt as it runs along the top.

GPS: N 38°08.52' W 109°49.75'

▼ 0.5   SO   Descent of Elephant Hill is marked by small Jeep marker.

GPS: N 38°08.66' W 109°49.98'

Looking down at Elephant Hill from the first switchback

▼ 0.6   SO   "Pull Up and Back Down" sign—pull forward and then reverse down the trail for approximately 100 yards.

GPS: N 38°08.72' W 109°50.00'

▼ 0.7   SO   "Pull In and Back Up" sign—drive forward from this point. If approaching, pull in and back up trail approximately 100 yards.

GPS: N 38°08.73' W 109°49.99'

▼ 0.8   SO   End of descent from Elephant Hill.

GPS: N 38°08.74' W 109°50.02'

▼ 1.1   SO   Cross through wash.
▼ 1.2   SO   Cross through wash.
▼ 1.4   SO   Track on right is end of loop. Trail is now one-way. Zero trip meter.

GPS: N 38°09.10' W 109°50.52'

▼ 0.0   Continue along trail to the northwest.
▼ 0.7   SO   Cross through wash.
▼ 1.1   SO   Start of second difficult hill climb.
▼ 1.7   SO   The Squeezeplay.

GPS: N 38°08.24' W 109°51.64'

▼ 1.8   TR   Track on left goes into Devil's Kitchen Campground, permit required. Trail is now two-way.

GPS: N 38°08.22' W 109°51.65'

▼ 2.4   TR   T-intersection with Devil's Lane. Track on left is Southeast #34: Bobby's Hole and Ruin Park Trail. Zero trip meter.

GPS: N 38°08.44' W 109°52.05'

▼ 0.0   Continue northeast along Devil's Lane.
▼ 0.7   SO   Enter narrow passage of sandstone.
▼ 0.8   SO   Exit narrow passage of sandstone.
▼ 1.3   SO   Top of the Silver Stairs.

GPS: N 38°09.40' W 109°51.81'

▼ 1.4   SO   Bottom of the Silver Stairs.
▼ 1.5   TR   Trail straight on is the Confluence Overlook Trail. Zero trip meter.

GPS: N 38°09.52' W 109°51.68'

▼ 0.0   Continue toward the end of the loop. Trail is now one-way.
▼ 0.2   SO   Descend rocky hill.
▼ 0.3   SO   End of descent. For the next 1.7 miles the trail crosses the wash many times.

GPS: N 38°09.38' W 109°51.51'

▼ 2.0   TL   End of loop, turn left to retrace your steps over Elephant Hill toward trailhead.

GPS: N 38°09.10' W 109°50.52'

Bobby's Hole and Ruin Park Trail

Starting Point:	Canyonlands National Park, Southeast #33: Elephant Hill Loop
Finishing Point:	Junction with Southeast #36: Beef Basin Trail
Total Mileage:	16.3 miles
Unpaved Mileage:	16.3 miles
Driving Time:	3 hours
Elevation Range:	5,200–6,600 feet
Usually Open:	May to November
Difficulty Rating:	7
Scenic Rating:	9
Remoteness Rating:	+1

Special Attractions

- 4WD trail within the Needles district of Canyonlands National Park.
- Ancient pictographs and Anasazi ruins in Ruin Park.
- Extremely challenging stretch of trail at Bobby's Hole.

History

Evidence of early Native Americans abounds on this trail. The handprint pictographs under the rock overhang near the start of the trail are from the Fremont Indians and are about two thousand years old. There are two sorts of prints, both dating from the same time period. In one, the hand was held against the rock and color was blown through a reed to make an outline of the hand. In the other, the hand was dipped in paint and pressed against the rock to make a solid print.

The lack of year-round water and the difficult access has kept the human presence in the region low. Along with those on nearby Elephant Hill, today's 4WD access routes were once cow trails used by cattle ranchers as early as the mid-1880s. Chesler Park, now within the national park, was used as winter pasture by settler Tom Trout, an ex-Texan then residing in nearby Indian Creek.

Various other settlers came, improved, and sold out until the main name in the region was the S&S Co., the Somerville and

The Bobby's Hole and Ruin Park Trail winds along the jagged terrain of Devil's Lane

A sandy wash crossing runs in front of the outcrops along Devil's Lane

Scorup Cattle Company. Under the direction of Al Scorup, the more difficult sections of the trails were bulldozed through in the 1940s. Chesler Park was apparently used as an airstrip for ease of access during the bulldozing operations.

The ancient Anasazi tower in Ruin Park, like others in the region, was sometimes referred to as a "castle" by the early European explorers. Whether the tower was used as a fort, an observation point, a granary, a ceremonial chamber, or for other purposes is not known. Those with sufficient time may like to explore the side trails in Ruin Park. Many of them lead to other Anasazi ruins.

Today, Bobby's Hole and Ruin Park are the winter pastures for cattle from Dugout Ranch, near Cottonwood Canyon.

Description

This trail provides a connection between Southeast #33: Elephant Hill Loop in the Needles district of Canyonlands National Park and Southeast #36: Beef Basin Trail, which leads to Southeast #35: Cottonwood Canyon Trail. However, although most of the trail is relatively easy, there is an extremely difficult, 7-rated climb out of Bobby's Hole into Ruin Park that may be impassable. If you wish, approach this spot from the moderate, 3-rated Beef Basin Trail. Though still difficult, the descent of the loose, steep hill into Bobby's Hole from Ruin Park should not cause too many problems. However, drivers who choose to come this way solve one problem only to confront another: they must be prepared to exit via the equally difficult, 7-rated Elephant Hill Loop, because they may find it impossible to turn around and climb back out of Bobby's Hole. See Southeast #33: Elephant Hill Loop for a description of and warnings about this extremely technical trail. Those who wish to visit Ruin Park without confronting the difficult driving at Bobby's Hole (from either direction) can approach via Southeast #36: Beef Basin Trail and then proceed along the Bobby's Hole and Ruin Park Trail, turning back before the descent into Bobby's Hole.

A final word of caution—the minimum towing charge in this region is in excess of $1,500, so it pays to know the limits of your driving and your vehicle's ability before you go.

Warnings aside, this is a lovely, scenic, historic trail. The trail starts at the farthest point of the Elephant Hill Loop in The Needles district of Canyonlands National Park. The sandy track runs along Devil's Lane, a row of jagged sandstone spires. Just before a difficult zigzag hill, there is a series of pictographs under an overhang to the right of the trail. These are mainly handprints, both solid and silhouette on the rock.

The trail crosses many sandy washes as it goes toward the park boundary. It passes by the primitive national park campgrounds at Bobby Jo and Horsehoof Arch and crosses Chesler Park. This section is mainly easy going, although there is one very nasty, axle-twisting, off-camber turn over large rocks and loose sand.

Bobby's Hole is reached 1.6 miles after leaving the national park. The difficult section can clearly be seen as you climb steeply out of the basin. It is advisable to walk it first to see firsthand the current condition of the trail. This climb has very loose, deep sand washouts, and a steep grade. Just when your vehicle will be bogging down and losing traction near the top, there are large rock ledges to negotiate, very loose rubble, and then a sharp turn to the left! If you still have forward motion at this point—relax, you've made it! At the top of the climb there is a sign warning vehicles traveling in the other direction about the difficulties of the trail. If you are traveling in the other direction, from Beef Basin Trail, and do not want to tackle Elephant Hill—this is your signal to turn back.

Once out of Bobby's Hole, the route is an easier 3-rated trail. It runs along open Ruin Park, where many tracks lead right and left to pleasant campsites and to numerous Anasazi ruins in the area. It is worth taking the time to explore some of these trails.

The well-known landmark of the Anasazi tower is to the right of the trail, at the edge of the trees. The trail gets easier until it finishes at the well-marked junction with the Beef Basin Trail. Travelers who have come through from Elephant Hill in wet weather should be aware that the exit through the Manti-La Sal National Forest travels over some graded dirt shelf road that is extremely greasy, if not impassable, after rain.

An alternative name for this trail on some maps is Hushaby Road, or CR 119.

Current Road Information
Canyonlands National Park
Needles Ranger District
(435) 259-4711

Map References
BLM La Sal, Blanding
USGS 1:24,000 House Park Butte, Druid Arch, Cross
Canyon, Spanish Bottom, The Loop
1:100,000 La Sal, Blanding
Maptech CD-ROM: Moab/Canyonlands
Trails Illustrated, #210
Utah Atlas & Gazetteer, p. 30
Other: Canyon Country Off-Road Vehicle Trail Map—
Canyon Rims & Needles Areas

Route Directions

▼ 0.0			At the farthest point of Southeast #33: Elephant Hill Loop, turn southwest along Devil's Lane, following the sign for Chesler Park. Zero trip meter.
	7.0 ▲		Trail ends at the farthest point along Southeast #33: Elephant Hill Loop. Continue straight ahead for the Elephant Hill Loop.
GPS: N 38°08.44' W 109°52.05'			
▼ 0.8		SO	Pull in to the right to view handprint pictographs under the overhang.
	6.2 ▲	SO	Pull in to the left to view handprint pictographs under the overhang.
GPS: N 38°07.72' W 109°52.52'			
▼ 0.9		SO	Short zigzag hill through gap. Vehicles may need to back up to turn.
	6.1 ▲	SO	Short zigzag hill through gap. Vehicles may need to back up to turn.
▼ 1.6		SO	Cross through wash. Many sandy wash crossings in the next 1.2 miles.
	5.4 ▲	SO	End of wash crossings.
▼ 2.5		SO	Devil's Kitchen hiking trail on left.
	4.5 ▲	SO	Devil's Kitchen hiking trail on right.
GPS: N 38°06.68' W 109°52.14'			
▼ 2.8		BR	Chesler Park hiking trail on left. Follow sign to Beef Basin and cross wash.
	4.2 ▲	BL	Cross wash, then Chesler Park hiking trail on right. Many sandy wash crossings in the next 1.2 miles.
GPS: N 38°06.52' W 109°52.26'			
▼ 3.5		SO	Difficult off-camber section.
	3.5 ▲	SO	Difficult off-camber section.
▼ 4.0		SO	Bobby Jo Campground on right.
	3.0 ▲	SO	Bobby Jo Campground on left.
GPS: N 38°05.56' W 109°52.82'			
▼ 4.1		SO	Horsehoof Arch hiking trail and campground on right.
	2.9 ▲	SO	Horsehoof Arch hiking trail and campground on left.
GPS: N 38°05.53' W 109°52.86'			
▼ 4.3		SO	Cross through wash.
	2.7 ▲	SO	Cross through wash.
▼ 5.7		SO	Cross through wash.
	1.3 ▲	SO	Cross through wash.
▼ 7.0		SO	Gate. Leaving Canyonlands National Park, entering BLM land. Zero trip meter.
	0.0 ▲		Continue into the national park.
GPS: N 38°03.69' W 109°54.99'			
▼ 0.0			Continue toward Bobby's Hole.
	6.6 ▲	SO	Gate. Entering Canyonlands National Park. Camping is restricted to campgrounds and requires a backcountry permit. Zero trip meter.
▼ 0.5		SO	Track on left goes to campsite.
	6.1 ▲	SO	Track on right goes to campsite.
▼ 1.1		SO	Corral on right. Entering Bobby's Hole.
	5.5 ▲	SO	Corral on left. Leaving Bobby's Hole.
▼ 1.2		SO	Track on right.
	5.4 ▲	SO	Track on left.
▼ 1.6		BL	Track on right. Trail swings left and climbs steeply out of Bobby's Hole. This climb may be impassable to 4WD vehicles.
	5.0 ▲	BR	End of descent. Track on left at bottom of hill.
GPS: N 38°02.59' W 109°56.22'			
▼ 1.8		SO	Top of climb.
	4.8 ▲	SO	Final warning sign and start of difficult descent into Bobby's Hole. Vehicles that continue past this point must be prepared to exit via Elephant Hill. See Southeast #33: Elephant Hill Loop.

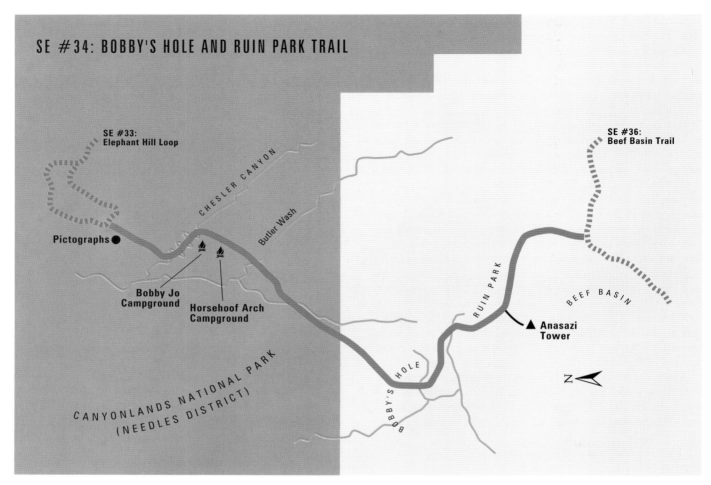

GPS: N 38°02.43' W 109°56.24'			
▼ 2.0		SO	Track on left.
	4.6 ▲	SO	Track on right.
▼ 2.5		SO	Campsite on right. Trail standard is now easier.
	4.1 ▲	SO	Campsite on left. Trail is getting harder. First warning sign about continuing on trail.
GPS: N 38°02.05' W 109°56.36'			
▼ 3.0		BR	Track on left.
	3.6 ▲	BL	Track on right.
GPS: N 38°02.14' W 109°55.85'			
▼ 3.2		SO	Entering Ruin Park.
	3.4 ▲	SO	Leaving Ruin Park.
▼ 3.4		SO	Cross through wash.
	3.2 ▲	SO	Cross through wash.
▼ 3.9		SO	Track on right goes to small ruin.
	2.7 ▲	SO	Track on left goes to small ruin.
▼ 4.5		SO	Cross through wash.
	2.1 ▲	SO	Cross through wash.
▼ 5.0		SO	Track on right goes to campsite.
	1.6 ▲	SO	Track on left goes to campsite.
GPS: N 38°01.14' W 109°54.74'			
▼ 5.6		SO	Track on right.
	1.0 ▲	SO	Track on left.
GPS: N 38°00.67' W 109°54.53'			
▼ 6.0		SO	Track on right.
	0.6 ▲	SO	Track on left.
▼ 6.6		SO	Track on right goes to Anasazi tower. Zero trip meter.

	0.0 ▲		Continue toward Bobby's Hole.
GPS: N 38°00.39' W 109°53.84'			
▼ 0.0			Continue toward Beef Basin.
	2.7 ▲	SO	Track on left goes to Anasazi tower. Zero trip meter.
▼ 0.7		SO	Track on left.
	2.0 ▲	SO	Track on right.
▼ 1.0		SO	Track on right.
	1.7 ▲	SO	Track on left.
▼ 1.2		SO	Two tracks on left.
	1.5 ▲	SO	Two tracks on right.
▼ 1.9		SO	Track on left.
	0.8 ▲	BL	Track on right.
GPS: N 37°59.52' W 109°52.26'			
▼ 2.1		SO	Faint track on left.
	0.6 ▲	SO	Faint track on right.
▼ 2.2		SO	Track on right.
	0.5 ▲	SO	Track on left.
▼ 2.6		SO	Track on right.
	0.1 ▲	SO	Track on left.
▼ 2.7			Trail ends at intersection with Southeast #36: Beef Basin Trail (CR 104). Turn right to continue around the Beef Basin Loop, turn left to exit via the Manti-La Sal National Forest.
	0.0 ▲		Trail starts at intersection with Southeast #36: Beef Basin Trail (CR 104). Turn north on graded dirt road (CR 119) following sign for Canyonlands National Park. Zero trip meter.
GPS: N 37°58.82' W 109°52.36'			

Cottonwood Canyon Trail

Starting Point:	Junction Utah 211 and CR 104
Finishing Point:	Junction of Southeast #38: North and South Elk Ridge Trail (FR 088) and Southeast #39: Blue Mountains Road (FR 095/CR 225)
Total Mileage:	29.6 miles
Unpaved Mileage:	29.6 miles
Driving Time:	3.5 hours
Elevation Range:	5,200–8,200 feet
Usually Open:	April to November
Difficulty Rating:	2
Scenic Rating:	8
Remoteness Rating:	+0

Special Attractions

■ Varied scenery from canyon floor to alpine forest.
■ Access to backcountry campsites.
■ Little-used backcountry road provides access to a number of 4WD trails.

Description

This long and highly scenic trail commences at the junction of Utah 211 and CR 104 (Beef Basin Road), 7.5 miles northwest of Newspaper Rock State Park. The first few miles pass through private property before the trail enters public land. It proceeds up a valley, with the jagged Bridger Jack Mesa to the west, crosses several small washes, and then runs alongside the deep-

View of Cottonwood Canyon Trail near Cathedral Butte

ening North Cottonwood Creek canyon before swinging away to run around the north side of Cathedral Butte.

The trail climbs out of the deep valley to enter the Manti-La Sal National Forest. The vegetation changes from the dry sagebrush and junipers of the valley floor to the ponderosa pines and aspens of the alpine life zone. The trail connects with Southeast #36: Beef Basin Trail, which leads to Beef Basin proper; then it connects with Southeast #37: North Long Point Trail and, after crossing grassy alpine meadows, finishes at Sego Flat at the junction with FR 095. This is an endpoint for both Southeast #38: North and South Elk Ridge Trail and Southeast #39: Blue Mountains Road.

There are good backcountry campsites along this road at all elevations.

The trail is a graded dirt road for its entire length. However, sections of it can be rough, requiring high clearance, and there can be washouts, especially in North Cottonwood Creek valley. This trail is suitable for high-clearance 2WD vehicles in dry weather, but after rain it can become impassable, even for 4WD vehicles, as the red soil turns to thick mud. It should be attempted in dry weather only to avoid track damage.

Dugout Ranch at the north end of the trail has been used as the location for many movies, but it is private property and cannot be visited.

Current Road Information

Canyonlands National Park
Needles Ranger District
(435) 259-4711

Manti-La Sal National Forest
Monticello Ranger District
496 East Central; PO Box 820
Monticello, UT 84535
(435) 587-2041

Map References

BLM La Sal, Blanding
USGS 1:24,000 Harts Point South, Shay Mt., Cathedral Butte, House Park Butte, Poison Canyon
1:100,000 La Sal, Blanding
Maptech CD-ROM: Moab/Canyonlands
Trails Illustrated, #703
Utah Atlas & Gazetteer, p. 30
Utah Travel Council #5
Other: Canyon Country Off-Road Vehicle Trail Map—
Canyon Rims & Needles Areas

Route Directions

▼ 0.0			From Utah 211, turn south on CR 104, following sign for Beef Basin Road, and zero trip meter. Cross cattle guard. Trail is crossing private property.
	16.5 ▲		End at intersection with Utah 211. Canyonlands National Park is to the left. Monticello and Moab are to the right.
		GPS: N 38°05.02′ W 109°34.08′	
▼ 0.2		SO	Mine dugout in rock on left, old building on right.
	16.3 ▲	SO	Mine dugout in rock on right, old building on left.
▼ 0.4		SO	Old wooden aqueduct on right.
	16.1 ▲	SO	Old wooden aqueduct on left.
▼ 0.5		SO	Cross Indian Creek on stony-bottomed ford.
	16.0 ▲	SO	Cross Indian Creek on stony-bottomed ford.

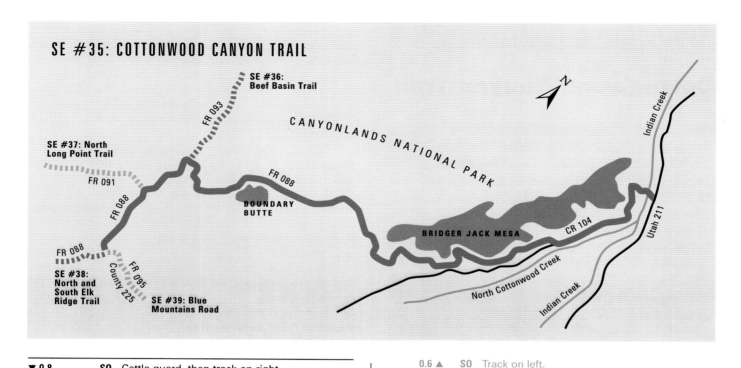

SE #35: COTTONWOOD CANYON TRAIL

▼ 0.8	SO	Cattle guard, then track on right.
15.7 ▲	SO	Track on left, then cattle guard.
▼ 1.4	SO	Track on left. Trail swings south up North Cottonwood Creek valley. Bridger Jack Mesa on right.
15.1 ▲	SO	Track on right.
▼ 4.1	SO	Cattle guard, then track on left. Entering public lands.
12.4 ▲	SO	Track on right, then cattle guard. Leaving public lands.
▼ 4.6	SO	CR 104A to the left. Continue on CR 104.
11.9 ▲	SO	CR 104A to the right. Continue on CR 104.
▼ 8.2	SO	Wire gate, please close.
8.3 ▲	SO	Wire gate, please close.

GPS: N 37°59.21' W 109°37.43'

| ▼ 8.8 | SO | Track on left. North Cottonwood Canyon is to the left. |
| 7.7 ▲ | SO | Track on right. North Cottonwood Canyon is to the right. |

GPS: N 37°58.92' W 109°36.99'

▼ 10.5	SO	Track on left to campsite.
6.0 ▲	SO	Track on right to campsite.
▼ 13.1	BR	Track on left. Continue on main trail. View of Cathedral Butte on left.
3.4 ▲	SO	Track on right. Continue on main trail. View of Cathedral Butte on right.
▼ 13.7	SO	Track on right.
2.8 ▲	SO	Track on left.
▼ 14.1	SO	Track on left.
2.4 ▲	SO	Track on right.
▼ 14.5	SO	Track on right.
2.0 ▲	SO	Track on left.
▼ 14.9	SO	Small track on right.
1.6 ▲	SO	Small track on left.
▼ 15.3	SO	Track on left to campsite overlooking Cathedral Butte.
1.2 ▲	SO	Track on right to campsite overlooking Cathedral Butte.
▼ 15.9	SO	Track on right.

0.6 ▲	SO	Track on left.
▼ 16.0	SO	Track on left.
0.5 ▲	SO	Track on right.
▼ 16.4	SO	Track on right to viewpoint over the eroded sandstone of East Fork Salt Creek.
0.1 ▲	SO	Track on left to viewpoint over the eroded sandstone of East Fork Salt Creek.
▼ 16.5	SO	Bright Angel hiking trailhead on right. Parking area and campsite with shade and views. Track on left to campsites. Zero trip meter.
0.0 ▲		Continue to the northeast.

GPS: N 37°57.01' W 109°42.25'

▼ 0.0	SO	Continue along trail, heading southwest.
7.5 ▲	SO	Track on right to campsites. Bright Angel hiking trailhead on left. Parking area and campsite with shade and views. Zero trip meter.
▼ 1.0	SO	Track on right and left. Many small tracks to campsites for the next 1.7 miles.
6.5 ▲	SO	Track on left and right.
▼ 1.3	SO	Fence line, views on left to Davis Canyon.
6.2 ▲	SO	Fence line, views on right to Davis Canyon.
▼ 2.7	SO	Entering Manti-La Sal National Forest over cattle guard, then track on right along fence line. Trail becomes FR 088, skirts Boundary Butte on left and Salt Creek Canyon on right.
4.8 ▲	SO	Track on left along fence line, then trail leaves Manti-La Sal National Forest and enters public land over cattle guard. Trail becomes CR 104. Many small tracks to campsites for the next 1.7 miles.

GPS: N 37°55.86' W 109°44.79'

▼ 4.6	BR	Track on left.
2.9 ▲	BL	Track on right.
▼ 5.5	SO	Salt Creek Canyon viewpoint on right, then hiking trail on left.
2.0 ▲	SO	Hiking trail on right, then Salt Creek Canyon viewpoint on left.
▼ 6.1	SO	Views back over Salt Creek Canyon and Boundary Butte.
1.4 ▲	SO	Views ahead over Salt Creek Canyon and Boundary Butte.
▼ 7.5	SO	Intersection with Southeast #36: Beef Basin Trail

0.0 ▲			(FR 093/CR 104) to the right. Zero trip meter. Continue along FR 088.

GPS: N 37°54.37' W 109°47.40'

▼ 0.0		SO	Continue south on FR 088.
	2.4 ▲	SO	Southeast #36: Beef Basin Trail (FR 093/CR 104) on left. Ahead is FR 088. Zero trip meter.
▼ 2.0		SO	ATV trail #423 on right.
	0.4 ▲	SO	ATV trail #423 on left.
▼ 2.4		SO	Track on right is FR 091 (CR 221), Southeast #37: North Long Point Trail. Zero trip meter.
	0.0 ▲		Continue straight, signed to Dugout Ranch and Beef Basin.

GPS: N 37°52.74' W 109°47.48'

▼ 0.0			Continue staight, signed to Gooseberry Guard Station.
	3.2 ▲	SO	Track on left is FR 091 (CR 221), Southeast #37: North Long Point Trail. Zero trip meter.
▼ 1.1		SO	Track on right to corral.
	2.1 ▲	SO	Track on left to corral.
▼ 1.3		SO	ATV trail #444 on left, followed by FR 144 on right.
	1.8 ▲	SO	FR 144 on left, followed by ATV trail #444 on right.
▼ 2.9		SO	Track on right.
	0.3 ▲	SO	Track on left.
▼ 3.2			End at intersection with FR 095 (CR 225). Right is Southeast #38: North and South Elk Ridge Trail and goes to Blanding; left is Southeast #39: Blue Mountains Road and goes to Monticello.
	0.0 ▲		From the junction of FR 095 (CR 225) and FR 088 (CR 104), zero trip meter and proceed north on FR 088 toward Beef Basin.

GPS: N 37°50.42' W 109°46.39'

SOUTHEAST REGION TRAIL #36

Beef Basin Trail

Starting Point:	**Junction of FR 088 and FR 093, along**
	Southeast #35: Cottonwood Canyon Trail
Finishing Point:	**Beef Basin**
Total Mileage:	**13.7 miles**
Unpaved Mileage:	**13.7 miles**
Driving Time:	**1 hour**
Elevation Range:	**6,100–8,200 feet**
Usually Open:	**May to November**
Difficulty Rating:	**3**
Scenic Rating:	**9**
Remoteness Rating:	**+0**

Special Attractions

- Many ruins and cliff dwellings in Beef Basin.
- Views over Butler Wash Wilderness Study Area.

History

The many ruins in Ruin Park, House Park, and Beef Basin date back to the time of the Anasazi. Some of the ancient buildings are unusual in that they were built out in the open

A driver repairs part of the Beef Basin Trail before passing through

instead of being tucked under a cliff face. Other dwellings and granaries are built under the cliff overhang.

The Somerville and Scorup Cattle Company, the largest in the area in the 1930s, held its cattle in the basin until the roundup was complete. It would then take seven to eight days to drive the cattle north across the Colorado River to the railroad at Thompson. Today, Beef Basin is the winter pasture for cattle from the Dugout Ranch, located on Utah 211.

Description

This route leads off Southeast #35: Cottonwood Canyon Trail and descends into the large bowl of Beef Basin. The trail is a mixture of sandy sections and rock, and conditions can change quickly depending on recent weather. The first section of the trail, where it leaves Southeast #35, is impassable when wet. We saw tire tracks that went straight through the mud, missing the bend, and into a tree. Snow in the Manti-La Sal National Forest restricts access to Beef Basin along this road from November to May. You can also approach this area from Canyonlands National Park, using Southeast #33: Elephant Hill Loop and Southeast #34: Bobby's Hole and Ruin Park Trail.

View of Beef Basin Trail

However, this route is extremely difficult; make sure you have the experience and the right vehicle to tackle the notorious Bobby's Hole and Elephant Hill.

The trail often washes out after heavy rains, and it can take weeks or even months for the county grader to reach the area and make the road passable again.

After the trail descends into the flat open area of House Park, there are many side trails leading to ancient ruins. The

SE #36: BEEF BASIN TRAIL

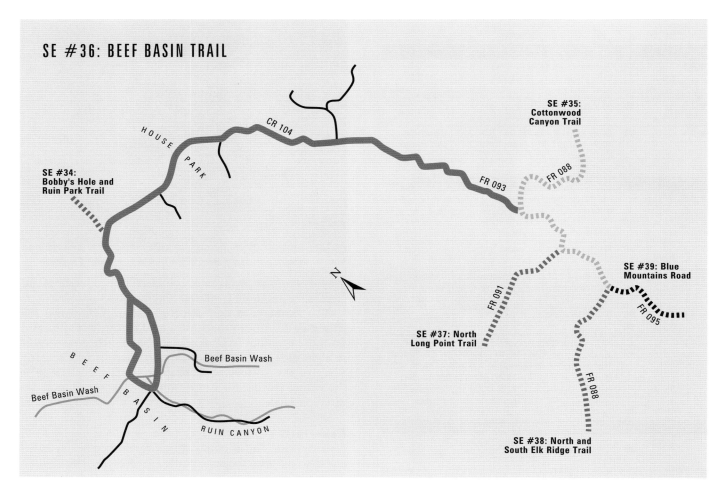

spur trail down Ruin Canyon is particularly good.

The short loop described goes through Beef Basin. If you have more time, a longer loop is possible, and sidetracks off both loops lead to numerous small ruins. Another option is to combine this route with the southern part of Southeast #34: Bobby's Hole and Ruin Park Trail to visit Ruin Park.

Current Road Information
Canyonlands National Park
Needles Ranger District
(435) 259-4711

Manti-La Sal National Forest
Monticello Ranger District
496 East Central; PO Box 820
Monticello, UT 84535
(435) 587-2041

Map References
BLM Blanding
USFS Manti-La Sal National Forest
USGS 1:24,000 House Park Butte, Fable Valley
1:100,000 Blanding
Maptech CD-ROM: Moab/Canyonlands
Trails Illustrated, #703; #210 (incomplete)
Utah Atlas & Gazetteer, p. 30

Utah Travel Council #5
Other: Canyon Country Off-Road Vehicle Trail Map—
Canyon Rims & Needles Areas

Route Directions

▼ 0.0   From Southeast #35: Cottonwood Canyon Trail, at junction of FR 088 and FR 093 (CR 104), turn north onto FR 093 and zero trip meter.

8.7 ▲   Trail ends at intersection with FR 088. Turn left to follow Southeast #35: Cottonwood Canyon Trail to Utah 211; turn right to follow Southeast #38: North and South Elk Ridge Trail to Blanding.

GPS: N 37°54.37' W 109°47.40'

▼ 0.8   **SO** Trail runs around shelf road as it descends to Beef Basin.

7.9 ▲   **SO** Shelf road ends.

▼ 2.6   **SO** Cattle guard, leaving Manti-La Sal National Forest, entering BLM land. Stay on established road, now CR 104.

6.1 ▲   **SO** Cattle guard, leaving BLM land, entering Manti-La Sal National Forest; road is now FR 093.

GPS: N 37°56.08' W 109°47.76'

▼ 3.1   **SO** Tracks on right and left.

5.6 ▲   **SO** Tracks on right and left.

▼ 3.8   **SO** Track on right.

4.9 ▲   **SO** Track on left.

▼ 4.5   **SO** Cross through rocky wash.

4.2 ▲   **SO** Cross through rocky wash.

▼ 5.3   **SO** Cattle guard.

3.4 ▲	SO	Cattle guard.	
▼ 5.7	SO	Campsite on right.	
3.0 ▲	SO	Campsite on left.	
▼ 5.9	BR	Track on left.	
2.8 ▲	SO	Track on right.	

GPS: N 37°58.35' W 109°49.61'

▼ 6.2	SO	Descending shelf road, with wilderness study area on right.
2.5 ▲	SO	End of shelf road.
▼ 6.7	SO	Entering House Park.
2.0 ▲	SO	Start of shelf road with wilderness study area on left. Leaving House Park.
▼ 7.4	SO	Track on left.
1.4 ▲	SO	Track on right.

GPS: N 37°58.55' W 109°50.95'

▼ 7.6	SO	Track on left.
1.1 ▲	SO	Track on right.
▼ 8.1	SO	Track on right.
0.6 ▲	SO	Track on left.
▼ 8.7	SO	Crossroads. Zero trip meter. To the right, Southeast #34: Bobby's Hole and Ruin Park Trail (CR 119) leads to Canyonlands National Park; track on left goes to campsite.
0.0 ▲		Continue toward the Manti-La Sal National Forest Boundary.

GPS: N 37°58.84' W 109°52.33'

▼ 0.0		Continue toward Beef Basin.
1.4 ▲	SO	Crossroads. Zero trip meter at intersection. To the left, Southeast #34: Bobby's Hole and Ruin Park Trail (CR 119) leads to Canyonlands National Park; track on right goes to campsite.
▼ 0.2	SO	Cross through sandy wash.
1.2 ▲	SO	Cross through sandy wash.
▼ 0.6	SO	Two campsite on left.
0.8 ▲	SO	Two campsites on right.
▼ 0.9	SO	Cattle guard, entering Beef Basin.
0.5 ▲	SO	Cattle guard, leaving Beef Basin.
▼ 1.4	SO	Track on right is end of short loop. Zero trip meter and commence the loop.

GPS: N 37°57.85' W 109°53.03'

▼ 0.0		Continue around short loop.
▼ 0.1	SO	Cross through wash.
▼ 0.2	SO	Cattle guard, then track on left.
▼ 0.4	SO	Water trough on right, then cattle guard.
▼ 0.5	BR	Track on left, then cross through Beef Basin Wash.

GPS: N 37°57.44' W 109°53.03'

▼ 0.6	SO	Cross through two washes.
▼ 0.7	SO	Cross through wash.
▼ 0.9	BR	Track on left goes to Calf Canyon.

GPS: N 38°57.15' W 109°53.44'

▼ 1.5	SO	Cross through Beef Basin Wash; this often washes out and may require a detour.
▼ 1.7	TR	Five-way junction. Take first right to continue around small loop. First left goes to small ruin. Second left goes to Ruin Canyon. Straight on is a longer loop around Beef Basin. Zero trip meter.

GPS: N 37°56.79' W 109°54.09'

▼ 0.0		Continue around small loop.
▼ 0.3	SO	Cross through Beef Basin Wash.
▼ 0.5	SO	Track on left, then campsite on right.
▼ 0.6	SO	Cross through fence line, then track on left.

GPS: N 37°57.25' W 109°54.00'

▼ 1.3	SO	Cross through fence line.
▼ 1.8	BR	Track on left.
▼ 1.9		End of loop. Turn left to exit Beef Basin.

GPS: N 37°57.86' W 109°53.02'

North Long Point Trail

Starting Point:	Junction of Southeast #35: Cottonwood Canyon Trail (FR 088) and FR 091
Finishing Point:	Middle Point, Dark Canyon Primitive Area
Total Mileage:	27.2 miles
Unpaved Mileage:	27.2 miles
Driving Time:	3 hours (one-way)
Elevation Range:	6,100–8,600 feet
Usually Open:	May to November
Difficulty Rating:	2
Scenic Rating:	8
Remoteness Rating:	+1

Special Attractions

- Diversity of life zones from alpine to arid desert plateau.
- Good selection of backcountry campsites.
- Very remote, little-traveled trail.

Description

This spur trail commences at the junctions of FR 088 and FR 091, near the south end of Southeast #35: Cottonwood Canyon Trail. The turnoff is well marked, and in dry weather the trail is accessible by high-clearance 2WDs as far as North Long Point. Snowfall is erratic in this region, so the trail may be open longer than the stated dates. This diverse trail winds down through the Manti-La Sal National Forest through stands of aspen and ponderosa pine. A couple of spur trails lead to natural springs in the area. After 6 miles, you reach North Long Point, with its far-reaching views over Dark Canyon Plateau and Canyonlands National Park.

The trail descends onto the arid Dark Canyon Plateau, where the vegetation changes to sagebrush, junipers, and pinyon pines. The surface is graded dirt and clay on the upper por-

Driving through standing water on the Dark Canyon Plateau

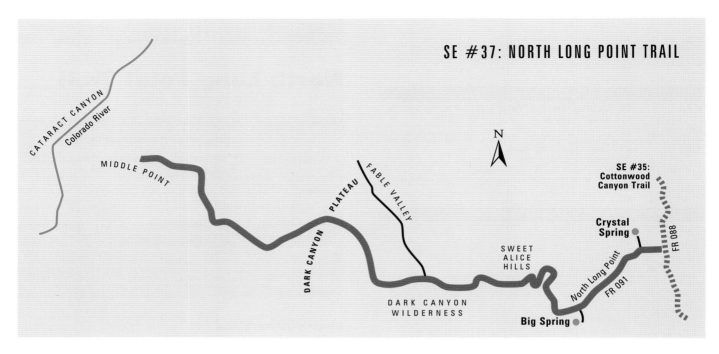

tions of track, while farther down on Dark Canyon Plateau it becomes predominantly sandy. This route is impassable to 4WDs in wet weather. After 11 miles, you reach the Sweet Alice Hills. A short spur goes 0.5 miles to the Sweet Alice Spring. The trail winds through increasingly arid land until it finishes on Middle Point in the Dark Canyon Primitive Area. Trails continue on from here, but they are mainly used by ATVs and are very narrow and twisty. The end of the trail has panoramic views over the Glen Canyon National Recreation Area and the Henry Mountains to the west and north toward Canyonlands National Park.

Current Road Information

Manti-La Sal National Forest
Monticello Ranger District
496 East Central; PO Box 820
Monticello, UT 84535
(435) 587-2041

Map References

BLM   Blanding, Hite Crossing
USFS   Manti-La Sal National Forest
USGS   1:24,000   House Park Butte, Poison Canyon, Warren Canyon, Fable Valley, Bowdie Canyon East, Bowdie Canyon West
1:100,000 Blanding, Hite Crossing
Maptech CD-ROM: Moab/Canyonlands
Trails Illustrated, #703
Utah Atlas & Gazetteer, p. 30
Utah Travel Council #5

Route Directions

▼ 0.0   At the intersection of FR 088 and FR 091, along Southeast #35: Cottonwood Canyon Trail, zero trip meter and turn west onto FR 091, North Long Point Road.

GPS: N 37°52.74′ W 109°47.48′		
▼ 0.6	SO	Cattle guard followed by track on left.
▼ 0.7	SO	Track on right to Crystal Spring. Main trail travels through semi-open areas of aspen and ponderosa pine. Numerous camps on right and left.
GPS: N 37°52.57′ W 109°48.66′		
▼ 3.1	SO	Track on right and campsite.
▼ 4.3	BR	Track on left to Big Spring. Views over Poison Canyon and the Dark Canyon Wilderness to the left.
▼ 5.7	SO	Track on right.
▼ 6.1	BR	North Long Point. Views of Dark Canyon Plateau and Sweet Alice Hills. Track starts to descend.
GPS: N 37°51.40′ W 109°52.38′		
▼ 7.5	SO	ATV trail #425 on right.
▼ 8.2	SO	Finish descent. Trail Canyon hiking trailhead on left at edge of Dark Canyon Wilderness.
▼ 8.3	SO	Leaving Manti-La Sal National Forest over cattle guard; entering Dark Canyon Primitive Area. Corral on right. Zero trip meter.
GPS: N 37°51.89′ W 109°52.80′		
▼ 0.0		Continue into primitive area.
▼ 1.9	SO	Sweet Alice Hills on right.
▼ 2.7	SO	Corral on left.
▼ 2.8	SO	CR 223 on right, immediately followed by CR 222 on right to Sweet Alice Spring. Faint track on left.
GPS: N 37°51.64′ W 109°55.44′		
▼ 5.4	SO	Trail follows the plateau, views ahead to the Henry Mountains, right over Fable Valley to Canyonlands National Park, and left over Dark Canyon.
▼ 6.0	SO	Fable Valley trail on right. Zero trip meter.
GPS: N 37°51.68′ W 109°58.74′		
▼ 0.0		Continue west.
▼ 0.2	SO	Little-used track on left.
▼ 1.0	SO	Fence line, followed by track on left. Trail runs over open plateau.
▼ 3.5	SO	Track on left, corral, and dam.

▼ 3.6	BL	Track on right.
▼ 8.1	BR	Faint track on left.

GPS: N 37°53.82' W 110°05.45'

▼ 10.1	SO	Track on right to campsite and view over Bowdie Canyon.
▼ 11.6	SO	Oil drill hole on left.
▼ 12.0	SO	End of county road maintenance. Track narrows and twists down through the small trees.
▼ 12.9		End at rocky area with180-degree views to Glen Canyon National Recreation Area and the Henry Mountains. Trail continues but is used mainly by ATVs.

GPS: N 37°55.98' W 110°08.61'

SOUTHEAST REGION TRAIL #38

North and South Elk Ridge Trail

Starting Point:	Junction Southeast #35: Cottonwood Canyon Trail (FR 088) and Southeast #39: Blue Mountains Road (FR 095)
Finishing Point:	Junction CR 228 and CR 227, midpoint Southeast #40: Cottonwood Wash Trail
Total Mileage:	26 miles
Unpaved Mileage:	26 miles
Driving Time:	2 hours
Elevation Range:	5,600–8,700 feet
Usually Open:	May to November
Difficulty Rating:	2
Scenic Rating:	8
Remoteness Rating:	+0

Special Attractions
■ Access to a network of 4WD trails.
■ The Notch Viewpoint.
■ Duck Lake.

Description
This wonderfully scenic drive in the Manti-La Sal National Forest also provides access to wilderness areas and some great viewpoints. This trail can be combined with either Southeast #35: Cottonwood Canyon Trail or Southeast #39: Blue Mountains Road and Southeast #40: Cottonwood Wash Trail to create a loop drive from Monticello.

The trail travels along the top of North Elk Ridge and is graded dirt its entire length. In dry weather, passenger cars can handle the drive without too much difficulty, although a high-clearance vehicle is preferred. In wet weather, the trail becomes very muddy and impassable even to 4WDs, as do most of the trails in the area.

The trail picks up at the end of Southeast #35: Cottonwood Canyon Trail, following FR 088 south from the junction with Southeast #39: Blue Mountains Road (FR 095) at

Sego Flats. For most of its length it travels through stands of ponderosa pines and aspens, interspersed with wide, grassy meadows. It passes by the Gooseberry Guard Station and, at the 2-mile mark, Duck Lake. This small natural lake is popular with waterfowl and offers some very pretty campsites along its shores.

After 6.4 miles, the trail runs around the rim of Dark Canyon, offering some spectacular views back to the northwest. Then it descends a series of tight switchbacks to the Notch, where there are views over Notch Canyon to the east as well as over the Dark Canyon Wilderness Area to the west. The best view, however, is slightly to the north of the actual Notch viewpoint—trees obscure the view west at the Notch itself.

After 12.5 miles, a vehicle trail to the northwest leads down into Kigalia Canyon, one of the rare vehicle trails that penetrates a wilderness area. The vehicle trail is a narrow corridor through the wilderness area.

At the 14-mile point, the trail passes through a logging area. Bark beetles have infested the trees in the Manti-La Sal National Forest, and the logging is part of an effort to contain the spread of the beetles, encouraging the healthy trees to grow, and salvaging the timber from the infested trees.

Tall aspens rise above both sides of North and South Elk Ridge Trail

The trail ends at the junction with the Cottonwood Wash Road (CR 227), midway along Southeast #40: Cottonwood Wash Trail. Head north to follow the Cottonwood Wash Trail back into the Manti-La Sal National Forest; continue straight to go to Blanding via Southeast #40: Cottonwood Wash Trail as it heads south before turning east onto Utah 95.

Current Road Information
Manti-La Sal National Forest
Monticello Ranger District
496 East Central; PO Box 820
Monticello, UT 84535
(435) 587-2041

Map References
BLM Blanding
USFS Manti-La Sal National Forest
USGS 1:24,000 Poison Canyon, Kigalia Point, Cream Pots
1:100,000 Blanding
Maptech CD-ROM: Moab/Canyonlands
Trails Illustrated, #703
Utah Atlas & Gazetteer, pp. 30, 22
Utah Travel Council #5

SE #38: NORTH AND SOUTH ELK RIDGE TRAIL

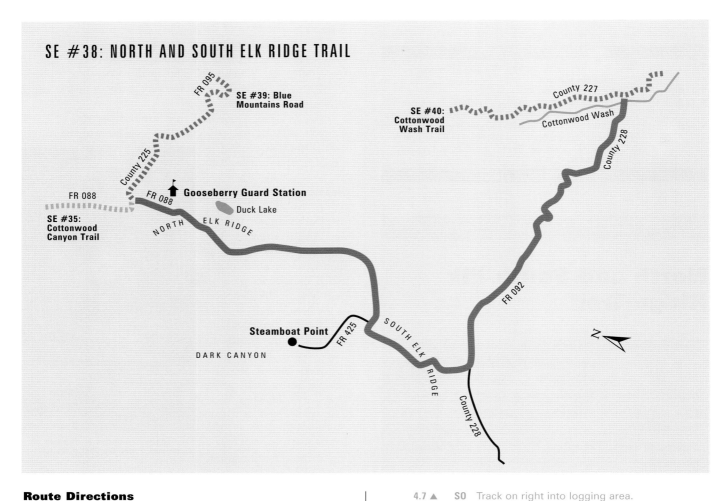

Route Directions

▼ 0.0			At the junction of Southeast #35: Cottonwood Canyon Trail (FR 088) and Southeast #39: Blue Mountains Road (FR 095/CR 225), zero trip meter and head south on FR 088 following the sign to Gooseberry Guard Station.
	7.1 ▲		End at the junction of Southeast #35: Cottonwood Canyon Trail (FR 088) and Southeast #39: Blue Mountains Road (FR 095/CR 225). Bear right for Monticello; turn left for Utah 211.
		GPS: N 37°50.41′ W 109°46.41′	
▼ 0.2		SO	Cattle guard.
	6.9 ▲	SO	Cattle guard.
▼ 0.6		SO	Tracks right and left are FR 048.
	6.5 ▲	SO	Tracks right and left are FR 048.
▼ 1.2		SO	Track on left to Gooseberry Guard Station.
	5.9 ▲	SO	Track on right to Gooseberry Guard Station.
		GPS: N 37°49.36′ W 109°46.36′	
▼ 1.3		SO	ATV trail #445 left.
	5.8 ▲	SO	ATV trail #445 right.
▼ 1.7		SO	Track on right and left.
	5.4 ▲	SO	Track on right and left.
▼ 1.9		SO	Cattle guard, then Duck Lake on left. Campsites at lake.
	5.2 ▲	SO	Duck Lake on right, then cattle guard. Campsites at lake.
▼ 2.1		SO	FR 178 on left to Deadman Point.
	5.0 ▲	SO	FR 178 on right to Deadman Point.
		GPS: N 37°48.69′ W 109°46.48′	
▼ 2.4		SO	Track on left into logging area.

	4.7 ▲	SO	Track on right into logging area.
▼ 2.7		SO	Track on left.
	4.4 ▲	SO	Track on right.
▼ 3.4		SO	FR 154 on right.
	3.7 ▲	SO	FR 154 on left.
▼ 3.6		SO	Track on right.
	3.5 ▲	SO	Track on left.
▼ 4.3		SO	Track on right.
	2.8 ▲	SO	Track on left.
▼ 4.6		SO	ATV trail #210 on right.
	2.5 ▲	SO	ATV trail #210 on left.
▼ 4.7		SO	Track on left.
	2.4 ▲	SO	Track on right. Sign to Gooseberry Creek ahead.
▼ 5.5		SO	Track on left.
	1.6 ▲	SO	Track on right.
▼ 5.7		SO	FR 168 on right to North Notch Spring.
	1.4 ▲	SO	FR 168 on left to North Notch Spring.
		GPS: N 37°45.84′ W 109°46.20′	
▼ 6.4		SO	Trail runs around the rim of Dark Canyon and starts to descend the shelf road switchbacks to the Notch.
	0.7 ▲	SO	Trail finishes switchbacks. End of shelf road.
▼ 7.1		SO	Sign, Big Notch. Zero trip meter.
	0.0 ▲		Continue north.
		GPS: N 37°45.09′ W 109°46.03′	
▼ 0.0			Continue southwest.
	5.4 ▲		Sign, Big Notch. Zero trip meter.
▼ 0.1		SO	Cattle guard followed by Big Notch trailhead.

	5.3 ▲	SO	Big Notch trailhead followed by cattle guard.
▼ 0.8		SO	End of shelf road, track on left.
	4.6 ▲	SO	Track on right, start of shelf road.
▼ 1.3		SO	FR 200 on left.
	4.1 ▲	SO	FR 200 on right.
▼ 1.7		SO	FR 208 on left.
	3.7 ▲	SO	FR 208 on right.
▼ 2.0		SO	Track on right.
	3.4 ▲	SO	Track on left.
▼ 3.0		SO	Cattle guard.
	2.4 ▲	SO	Cattle guard.
▼ 3.1		SO	Track on right.
	2.3 ▲	SO	Track on left.
▼ 3.3		SO	FR 425 on right to Steamboat Point.
	2.1 ▲	SO	FR 425 on left to Steamboat Point.

GPS: N 37°43.36' W 109°48.15'

▼ 3.4		SO	Track on right and left.
	2.0 ▲	SO	Track on right and left.
▼ 3.7		SO	Cattle guard.
	1.7 ▲	SO	Cattle guard.
▼ 4.6		SO	Track on left.
	0.8 ▲	SO	Track on right.
▼ 5.0		SO	Track on right.
	0.4 ▲	SO	Track on left.
▼ 5.4		SO	Little Notch. FR 089 on right (vehicle use) to Kigalia Canyon—wilderness access. Track on left to Hammond Canyon. Zero trip meter.
	0.0 ▲		Continue north on FR 088.

GPS: N 37°41.66' W 109°48.59'

▼ 0.0			Continue south on FR 088.
	1.9 ▲	SO	Little Notch. FR 089 on left (vehicle use) to Kigalia Canyon—wilderness access. Track on right to Hammond Canyon. Zero trip meter.
▼ 0.9		SO	FR 337 on right; followed by corral on left.
	1.0 ▲	SO	Corral on right; followed by FR 337 on left.
▼ 1.2		SO	Track on right.
	0.7 ▲	SO	Track on left.
▼ 1.5		SO	Track on right in logging area. Logged area has been infested by bark beetles.
	0.4 ▲	SO	Track on left in logging area. Logged area has been infested by bark beetles.
▼ 1.9		BL	Bear left on FR 092 (CR 228), follow signs for Blanding. Right on FR 088 (CR 228) leads to Natural Bridges National Monument. Zero trip meter.
	0.0 ▲		Continue northwest on FR 088.

GPS: N 37°40.57' W 109°47.82'

▼ 0.0			Continue northeast on FR 092, track on right.
	8.4 ▲	BR	Bear right onto FR 088 (CR 225) to Gooseberry Creek. Ahead, FR 088 (CR 228) leads to Natural Bridges National Monument. Zero trip meter.
▼ 0.1		SO	Track on left.
	8.3 ▲	SO	Track on right.
▼ 0.4		SO	FR 183 on right to Butts Point.
	8.0 ▲	SO	FR 183 on left to Butts Point.
▼ 0.7		SO	Track on right.
	7.7 ▲	SO	Track on left.
▼ 1.0		SO	Track on left.
	7.4 ▲	SO	Track on right.
▼ 1.6		SO	Cattle guard, then track on left to Hammond Canyon. Corral.
	6.8 ▲	SO	Track on right to Hammond Canyon, corral, and cattle guard.

GPS: N 37°40.83' W 109°46.06'

▼ 2.2		SO	FR 326 on left.
	6.2 ▲	SO	FR 326 on right.
▼ 2.3		SO	FR 182 (CR 262A) on right to Milk Ranch Point.
	6.1 ▲	SO	FR 182 (CR 262A) on left to Milk Ranch Point.
▼ 5.1		SO	Track on left, Hammond Canyon and Cream Pots Trail. Road is now gravel.
	3.3 ▲	SO	Track on right, Hammond Canyon and Cream Pots Trail. Road is now graded dirt.
▼ 5.9		SO	Track on right.
	2.5 ▲	SO	Track on left.
▼ 6.4		SO	Cattle guard.
	2.0 ▲	SO	Cattle guard.
▼ 8.4		SO	Leaving Manti-La Sal National Forest. Zero trip meter.
	0.0 ▲		Continue along gravel road.

GPS: N 37°39.43' W 109°40.57'

▼ 0.0			Continue along gravel road.
	3.2 ▲	SO	Entering Manti-La Sal National Forest. Zero trip meter.
▼ 2.1		SO	CR 229 on right.
	1.1 ▲	SO	CR 229 on left.
▼ 3.0		SO	Cross Cottonwood Wash.
	0.2 ▲	SO	Cross Cottonwood Wash.
▼ 3.2			End at the midpoint of Southeast #40: Cottonwood Wash Trail (CR 227). Continue straight on to Blanding; go left to Round Mountain.
	0.0 ▲		Begin at the junction of Southeast #40: Cottonwood Wash Trail (CR 227) and CR 228. Zero trip meter and continue west on CR 228.

GPS: N 37°38.99' W 109°37.57'

SOUTHEAST REGION TRAIL #39

Blue Mountains Road

Starting Point:	**US 191 in Monticello**
Finishing Point:	**Junction of Southeast #38: North and**
	South Elk Ridge Trail (FR 088) and
	Southeast #35: Cottonwood Canyon
	Trail (FR 088)
Total Mileage:	**44 miles**
Unpaved Mileage:	**38.9 miles**
Driving Time:	**3 hours**
Elevation Range:	**7,000–10,200 feet**
Usually Open:	**May to October**
Difficulty Rating:	**2**
Scenic Rating:	**9**
Remoteness Rating:	**+0**

Special Attractions

- Long trail with many varied views and brilliant scenery along its length.
- Natural features of Chippean Rocks and The Causeway.
- Access to a number of forest trails and backcountry camping areas.
- Aspen viewing in fall.

Description

This long and varied trail travels almost wholly within the Monticello Ranger District of the Manti-La Sal National Forest. It leaves from the center of Monticello, off US 191, two blocks south of the junction with US 666. A sign points to the national forest campgrounds at Dalton Spring, Buckboard, Monticello Lake, and the Blue Mountains ski area.

The pavement road enters the forest after 2 miles. After 4.5

miles, a gravel road heads south to the disused Blue Mountains ski area. The ski lifts remain but were closed in the early 1980s, and the runs are slowly revegetating.

After 5.1 miles, the route bears left onto the dirt FR 079 and starts to climb through some mature stands of aspen and ponderosa pine. At 6.3 miles the route enters the watershed area for the region, and camping is prohibited for the next 11.5 miles. If you plan on backcountry camping, there are a few sites, mainly on side

The Chippean Rocks rise above the trees along Blue Mountains Road

tracks before the watershed area is entered, and numerous sites after exiting from it.

The trail climbs steadily before emerging from the trees at North Creek Pass and the high point of the trail at 10,200 feet. The trail now starts to descend along a shelf road. Although fairly narrow, it has a good surface and grade and ample passing places.

After crossing Indian Creek, the trail starts to climb again over Jackson Ridge before swinging along the top of the plateau. At the halfway mark, the trail leaves FR 079 and turns onto

Looking down from North Creek Pass, the trail winds around Twin Peaks

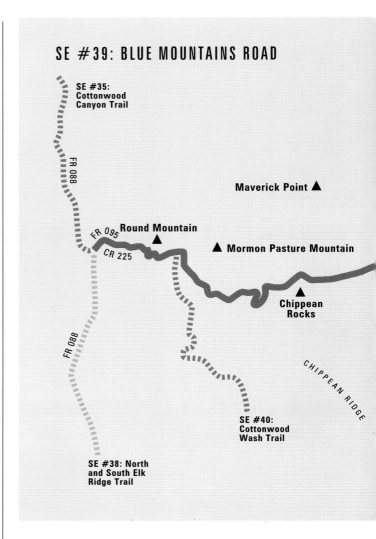

FR 095 toward Elk Ridge. This first part of the descent is not advised in wet or muddy conditions. The vegetation changes in this arid region to predominantly scrub oak and hardier plants. The trail then follows a long shelf road, with extensive views to the southwest over Cliffdwellers Pasture and Chippean Ridge, then north over Trough Canyon and Tuerto Canyon.

The Causeway, at the 31-mile mark, is a natural hogback ridge that separates the drainages of the Colorado River to the north and the San Juan River to the south. The Causeway itself is a narrow saddle with steep drops on either side.

The trail winds on, giving glimpses of the Chippean Rocks ahead. Just before the rocks is a grassy valley with some excellent campsites. About 3 miles before the campsites, the Maverick Point overlook gives sweeping views of the national forest, which is managed as a multiple use area: for recreation, grazing, protection of watershed and wildlife habitat, and logging.

Near the end, the trail connects with Southeast #40: Cottonwood Wash Trail, and it finishes at the junction of FR 088. From here, you can turn north and follow Southeast #35: Cottonwood Canyon Trail (leading to Utah 211), or turn south and follow Southeast #38: North and South Elk Ridge Trail (providing access to Blanding). A pleasant day's loop drive back to Monticello can be made by taking either of these trails.

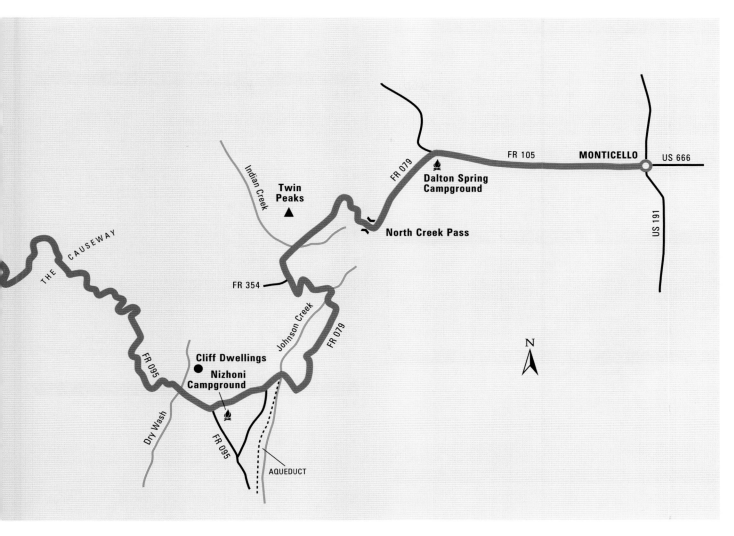

Current Road Information
Manti-La Sal National Forest
Monticello Ranger District
496 East Central; PO Box 820
Monticello, UT 84535
(435) 587-2041

Map References
BLM Blanding
USFS Manti-La Sal National Forest
USGS 1:24,000 Monticello South, Abajo Peak, Monticello
Lake, Mt. Linnaeus, Chippean Rocks, Poison Canyon
1:100,000 Blanding
Maptech CD-ROM: Moab/Canyonlands
Trails Illustrated, #703
Utah Atlas & Gazetteer, pp. 31, 30, 22
Utah Travel Council #5

Route Directions

▼ 0.0			From US 191 in Monticello (two blocks south of junction with US 666), zero trip meter and turn west onto FR 105 (North Creek Road). This intersection is marked with a sign for forest access.

	5.1 ▲		End in Monticello at intersection with US 191, two blocks south of US 666.
		GPS: N 37°52.19′ W 109°20.57′	
▼ 2.1		SO	Cattle guard, entering Manti-La Sal National Forest.
	3.0 ▲	SO	Cattle guard, leaving Manti-La Sal National Forest.
		GPS: N 37°52.16′ W 109°23.00′	
▼ 3.1		SO	Track on left, then track on right.
	2.0 ▲	SO	Track on left, then track on right.
▼ 3.5		SO	Cattle guard, leaving national forest into private property.
	1.6 ▲	SO	Cattle guard, reentering national forest.
▼ 4.2		SO	Cattle guard, reentering national forest.
	0.9 ▲	SO	Cattle guard, leaving national forest into private property.
▼ 4.5		SO	Gravel road on left to closed Blue Mountains ski area.
	0.6 ▲	SO	Gravel road on right to closed Blue Mountains ski area.
▼ 4.7		SO	Dalton Spring Campground on left.
	0.4 ▲	SO	Dalton Spring Campground on right.
▼ 4.9		SO	Exit from Dalton Spring Campground on left.
	0.2 ▲	SO	Exit from Dalton Spring Campground on right.
▼ 5.1		BL	Fork in road. Turn left onto dirt road (FR 079) and zero trip meter.
	0.0 ▲		Continue east on FR 105.

		GPS: N 37°52.54' W 109°26.34'	
▼ 0.0			Continue southwest along FR 079.
	8.1 ▲	TR	At intersection, turn right onto FR 105. Road is now pavement. Zero trip meter.
▼ 0.2		SO	Track on left then track on right. Trail is traveling though mature aspens.
	7.9 ▲	SO	Track on left, then track on right. Trail is traveling through mature aspens.
▼ 0.6		SO	Track on right.
	7.5 ▲	SO	Track on left.
▼ 0.9		SO	Track on left.
	7.2 ▲	SO	Track on right.
▼ 1.2		SO	Cattle guard, entering culinary watershed area; no camping beyond this point.
	6.9 ▲	SO	Cattle guard, leaving culinary watershed area; camping permitted beyond this point.
		GPS: N 37°52.06' W 109°26.98'	
▼ 2.9		SO	Track on right.
	5.2 ▲	SO	Track on left.
▼ 3.2		SO	Track on left.
	4.9 ▲	SO	Track on right.
▼ 4.4		BR	Track on left. North Creek Pass, trail starts to descend along shelf road.
	3.7 ▲	BL	Track on right. North Creek Pass, trail starts to descend.
		GPS: N 37°50.90' W 109°28.28'	
▼ 4.7		SO	Track on right.
	3.4 ▲	SO	Track on left.
▼ 5.0		SO	Hiking trails #020 and #159 on right.
	3.1 ▲	SO	Hiking trails #020 and #159 on left.
▼ 7.0		SO	End of shelf road and descent. Cross Indian Creek on shallow ford.
	1.1 ▲	SO	Cross Indian Creek on shallow ford, then ascend on shelf road to North Creek Pass.
		GPS: N 37°50.53' W 109°30.19'	
▼ 7.6		SO	Track on right, then Aspen Flat hiking trail #018 on right.
	0.5 ▲	SO	Aspen Flat hiking trail #018 on left, then track on left.
▼ 7.7		SO	Track on right.
	0.4 ▲	SO	Track on left.
▼ 8.1		SO	Track on right (FR 354) leads to Skyline Trail in 1.5 miles. Main trail ahead is signed to Blanding and is now marked as CR 285. Zero trip meter.
	0.0 ▲		Continue along FR 079.
		GPS: N 37°49.70' W 109°30.46'	
▼ 0.0			Start to descend on CR 285 (FR 079).
	8.6 ▲	SO	Track on left (FR 354) leads to Skyline Trailhead in 1.5 miles. Zero trip meter.
▼ 1.1		SO	Track on left.
	7.5 ▲	SO	Track on right.
▼ 1.3		SO	Aqueduct tunnel emerges from hillside on right.
	7.3 ▲	SO	Aqueduct tunnel emerges from hillside on left.
▼ 1.5		SO	Track on right.
	7.1 ▲	SO	Track on left.
▼ 2.3		SO	Cross Johnson Creek.
	6.3 ▲	SO	Cross Johnson Creek.
▼ 2.8		SO	Creek crossing.
	5.8 ▲	SO	Creek crossing.
▼ 2.9		SO	Track on right.
	5.7 ▲	SO	Track on left.
		GPS: N 37°49.01' W 109°29.24'	
▼ 3.2		SO	Track on left.
	5.4 ▲	SO	Track on right.

▼ 4.5		SO	Cattle guard, exiting culinary watershed area. Camping permitted.
	4.1 ▲	SO	Cattle guard, entering culinary watershed area. No camping beyond this point.
		GPS: N 37°48.04' W 109°29.98'	
▼ 4.8		SO	Track on right.
	3.8 ▲	SO	Track on left.
▼ 5.7		SO	Two tracks on left.
	2.9 ▲	SO	Two tracks on right.
▼ 6.3		SO	Track on left.
	2.3 ▲	SO	Track on right.
▼ 6.7		SO	Campsite, then cross creek. Track on right.
	1.9 ▲	SO	Track on left, then cross creek, then campsite.
▼ 6.8		SO	Track on left.
	1.8 ▲	SO	Track on right.
▼ 7.2		SO	FR 240 on left.
	1.4 ▲	SO	FR 240 on right.
▼ 7.3		SO	Track on left.
	1.3 ▲	SO	Track on right.
▼ 8.4		SO	Track on left into Nizhoni Campground, group and single sites. Track on right.
	0.2 ▲	SO	Track on right into Nizhoni Campground, group and single sites. Track on left.
▼ 8.6		TR	Turn right onto FR 095 (CR 225) to the Causeway and Elk Ridge. Straight on goes to Blanding. Zero trip meter.
	0.0 ▲		Continue along FR 079.
		GPS: N 37°46.82' W 109°32.55'	
▼ 0.0			Descend FR 095; keep off when muddy.
	9.2 ▲	TL	Turn left onto FR 079. The right turn goes to Blanding. Zero trip meter.
▼ 0.2		SO	Track on right.
	9.0 ▲	SO	Track on left.
▼ 0.9		SO	Cattle guard.
	8.3 ▲	SO	Cattle guard.
▼ 1.3		BL	Track on right up Dry Wash to cliff dwellings.
	7.9 ▲	BR	Track on left up Dry Wash to cliff dwellings.
		GPS: N 37°47.39' W 109°33.36'	
▼ 3.0		SO	Track on right.
	6.2 ▲	SO	Track on right.
▼ 3.1		SO	Track on left, then views over Chippean Ridge. Long wide shelf road gradually climbs through dense oak vegetation.
	6.1 ▲	SO	Track on right, shelf road finishes.
▼ 5.0		SO	Track on right, Allen Canyon on left.
	4.2 ▲	SO	Allen Canyon on right, track on left.
▼ 5.3		SO	Hiking Trail #013 on right.
	3.9 ▲	SO	Hiking Trail #013 on left.
▼ 8.0		SO	Track on left, followed by Skyline hiking trail on right. End of shelf road.
	1.2 ▲	SO	Skyline hiking trail on left, followed by track on right. Shelf road descends with views over Chippean Ridge.
		GPS: N 37°49.82' W 109°36.23'	
▼ 8.4		SO	Tuerto hiking trail on right.
	0.8 ▲	SO	Tuerto hiking trail on left.
▼ 9.2		SO	Cattle guard, then the Causeway viewpoint. Views left over Deep Canyon, right over Trough Canyon and Tuerto Canyon. Zero trip meter.
	0.0 ▲		Continue along FR 095.
		GPS: N 37°50.55' W 109°36.88'	
▼ 0.0			Continue over the Causeway.
	5.4 ▲	SO	The Causeway viewpoint. Views right over Deep Canyon, left over Trough Canyon and Tuerto Canyon. Zero trip meter at cattle guard.

▼ 0.6	SO	FR 349 on right.	
4.8 ▲	SO	FR 349 on left.	
▼ 1.2	SO	Maverick Point overlook.	
4.2 ▲	SO	Maverick Point overlook.	
▼ 1.7	SO	Track on left.	
3.7 ▲	SO	Track on right.	
▼ 3.9	SO	Track on left.	
1.5 ▲	SO	Track on right.	
▼ 4.1	SO	Track on right.	
1.3 ▲	SO	Track on left.	
▼ 4.5	SO	FR 164 on right and FR 206 on left. Wide grassy, shady area good for camping.	
0.9 ▲	SO	FR 164 on left and FR 206 on right. Wide grassy, shady area good for camping.	
▼ 5.4	BL	Fork, bear left to Chippean Ridge and Gooseberry. Right goes to Maverick Point. Zero trip meter.	
0.0 ▲		Continue along FR 095.	

GPS: N 37°49.70' W 109°41.00'

▼ 0.0		Continue toward Chippean Ridge.	
7.6 ▲	SO	Track on left to Maverick Point. Zero trip meter.	
▼ 1.4	SO	Track on left.	
6.2 ▲	SO	Track on right.	
▼ 2.3	SO	FR 096 right.	
5.3 ▲	BR	FR 096 left.	

GPS: N 37°49.56' W 109°42.20'

▼ 3.4	SO	Track on right to Mormon Pasture Mountain, then cattle guard. Start of shelf road, views over Southeast #40: Cottonwood Wash Trail on left.	
4.2 ▲	SO	Cattle guard, then track on left to Mormon Pasture Mountain. End of shelf road.	

GPS: N 37°49.51' W 109°43.20'

▼ 4.1	SO	Cattle guard.	
3.5 ▲	SO	Cattle guard.	
▼ 4.5	SO	End of shelf road.	
3.1 ▲	SO	Start of shelf road, views over Southeast #40: Cottonwood Wash Trail on right.	
▼ 4.8	BL	Fork in road. Continue left toward Gooseberry Guard Station. Mormon Pasture is to the right. View of Round Mountain directly ahead.	
2.8 ▲	BR	Fork in road. Continue right toward The Causeway. Mormon Pasture is on left.	

GPS: N 37°50.48' W 109°43.93'

▼ 4.9	SO	Left is FR 106, Southeast #40: Cottonwood Wash Trail to Blanding. Continue on FR 095 (CR 225).	
2.7 ▲	SO	Right is FR 106, Southeast #40: Cottonwood Wash Trail to Blanding. Follow the sign for Mormon Pasture to the next intersection.	

GPS: N 37°50.47' W 109°44.08'

▼ 6.0	SO	Cattle guard, then track on right.	
1.6 ▲	SO	Track on left, then cattle guard.	
▼ 7.6		Trail finishes at intersection with FR 088. Right begins Southeast #35: Cottonwood Canyon Trail, leading to Utah 211. Left begins Southeast #38: North and South Elk Ridge Trail. Gooseberry Guard Station is on left.	
0.0 ▲		At the junction of FR 088 (at the endpoints of Southeast #35: Cottonwood Canyon Trail and Southeast #38: North and South Elk Ridge Trail) and FR 095 (CR 225), zero trip meter and turn northeast onto FR 095.	

GPS: N 37°50.42' W 109°46.39'

Cottonwood Wash Trail

Starting Point:	**Junction of Southeast #39: Blue Mountains Road (FR 095) and FR 106/CR 227**
Finishing Point:	**Utah 95**
Total Mileage:	**24.4 miles**
Unpaved Mileage:	**23.2 miles**
Driving Time:	**2 hours**
Elevation Range:	**5,200–7,800 feet**
Usually Open:	**May to November**
Difficulty Rating:	**2**
Scenic Rating:	**7**
Remoteness Rating:	**+0**

Special Attractions

- Scenic descent from the Manti-La Sal National Forest to Cottonwood Wash.
- Can be combined with a choice of other forest roads to make a loop drive.

History

The southern end of Cottonwood Wash and its many tributaries is the site of one of the last battlegrounds between Native Americans and Utah settlers attempting to carve a living out of the harsh yet beautiful landscape.

Following the arrest of two Ute men near Blanding in 1923, Chief Posey helped them escape and led his people into a series of confrontations with the settlers, which led to further arrests and deaths. There were skirmishes on Murphy Point to the southeast and on the ridge above Butler Wash, just southwest of where one of the two Utes had been arrested. Comb Wash, just west of Cottonwood Canyon, was the site of a siege during which a large posse from Blanding attempted to capture the Utes. Although his people escaped, Chief Posey was injured

Crossing Cottonwood Wash

SE #40: COTTONWOOD WASH TRAIL

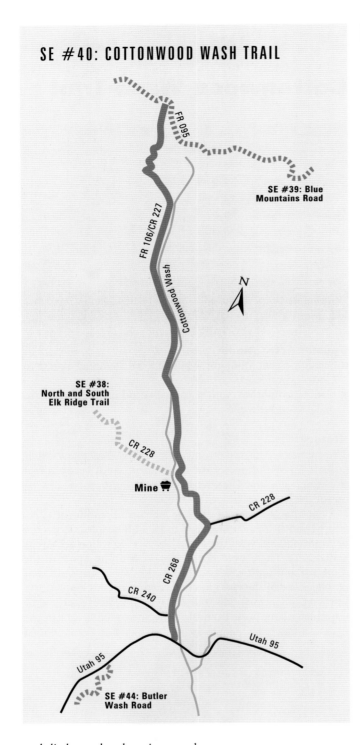

tice you are passing through Ute territory as you crisscross Cottonwood Wash. Time has passed; yet the Ute maintain a connection with the land.

Description

This trail commences at the junction of FR 106 and FR 095, near the west end of Southeast #39: Blue Mountains Road, and it heads south through pine forest toward Blanding. It winds through forest before descending to join Cottonwood Wash. There is a section of shelf road, but it is wide enough to allow two vehicles to pass fairly easily. The trail surface is good in dry weather, but should not be attempted in wet weather as it would be very hard for even good mud tires to get an adequate grip.

In the valley there are numerous crossings of the mainly dry Cottonwood Wash. These should not pose any problem for a high-clearance vehicle, since they are predominately wide and sandy. Cottonwood Wash runs in a wide red canyon and drops to leave the pine forest to enter the drier valley floor. The trail leaves the Manti-La Sal National Forest after 8.8 miles and then passes through sections of Ute land and sections of BLM land until it ends at Utah 95.

Current Road Information

Manti-La Sal National Forest
Monticello Ranger District
496 East Central; PO Box 820
Monticello, UT 84535
(435) 587-2041

Map References

BLM   Blanding
USFS Manti-La Sal National Forest
USGS 1:24,000 Chippean Rocks, Cream Pots, Mancos Jim
          Butte, Black Mesa Butte
          1:100,000 Blanding
Maptech CD-ROM: Moab/Canyonlands
Trails Illustrated, #703
Utah Atlas & Gazetteer, pp. 30, 22
Utah Travel Council #5 (incomplete)

Route Directions

▼ 0.0			At the junction of Southeast #39: Blue Mountains Road (FR 095) and FR 106/CR 227, zero trip meter and proceed south on FR 106/CR 227.
	8.8 ▲		Trail finishes at intersection with Southeast #39: Blue Mountains Road (FR 095) and FR 106. Turn right for Monticello via Southeast #39: Blue Mountains Road; turn left to meet Southeast #38: North and South Elk Ridge Trail and Southeast #35: Cottonwood Canyon Trail at FR 088.
GPS: N 37°50.47′ W 109°44.08′			
▼ 0.8		SO	Track on right.
	8.0 ▲	SO	Track on left.
▼ 0.9		SO	Cattle guard.
	7.9 ▲	SO	Cattle guard.
▼ 1.0		SO	ATV Trail #445 on right.
	7.8 ▲	SO	ATV Trail #445 on left.
▼ 2.8		SO	Cattle guard.
	6.0 ▲	SO	Cattle guard.
▼ 3.2		SO	Cottonwood Wash enters on right.

and died two days later in a nearby cave.

With their chief fallen, the Ute people surrendered and were taken into custody while the federal government decided their fate. A reservation was established for the adult Utes on 8,360 acres of land, where they received allotments for farming and grazing. Children were forced to take on Euro-American haircuts and clothing. In the 1940s and 1950s, the government moved the Utes again, this time to White Mesa, about 10 miles south of Blanding.

Though the signs may be old and weathered, you will no-

	5.6 ▲	SO	and runs alongside trail. Trail leaves Cottonwood Wash and starts to climb out of canyon.
▼ 5.1		SO	Track on left and remains of log cabin.
	3.7 ▲	SO	Track on right and remains of log cabin.
▼ 6.3		SO	Track on right to old mine tailings and tunnels; mining lease in effect.
	2.5 ▲	SO	Track on left to old mine tailings and tunnels; mining lease in effect.

GPS: N 37°46.34' W 109°41.95'

▼ 6.7		SO	Cross through creek, then track on right.
	2.1 ▲	SO	Track on left, then cross through creek.
▼ 7.0		SO	Track on right.
	1.8 ▲	SO	Track on left.
▼ 7.3		SO	Cross through creek.
	1.5 ▲	SO	Cross through creek.
▼ 7.6		SO	Track on right, then cross through creek.
	1.2 ▲	SO	Cross through creek, then track on left.
▼ 8.6		SO	Cross through creek.
	0.2 ▲	SO	Cross through creek.
▼ 8.7		SO	Cross through creek.
	0.1 ▲	SO	Cross through creek.
▼ 8.8		SO	Cattle guard, leaving Manti-La Sal National Forest; entering Ute land. Zero trip meter.
	0.0 ▲		Continue into Manti-La Sal National Forest.

GPS: N 37°44.52' W 109°41.29'

▼ 0.0			Continue on along Cottonwood Wash.
	7.9 ▲	SO	Cattle guard, leaving Ute land; entering Manti-La Sal National Forest. Zero trip meter.
▼ 1.6		SO	Two creek crossings.
	6.3 ▲	SO	Two creek crossings.
▼ 2.1		SO	Cross through creek.
	5.8 ▲	SO	Cross through creek.
▼ 2.5		SO	Corral on left, cattle guard, cross through creek.
	5.4 ▲	SO	Cross through creek, cattle guard, corral on right.
▼ 3.0		SO	Cross through creek.
	4.9 ▲	SO	Cross through creek.
▼ 3.6		SO	Cross through creek.
	4.3 ▲	SO	Cross through creek.
▼ 4.2		SO	Wide slickrock creek crossing.
	3.7 ▲	SO	Wide slickrock creek crossing.
▼ 4.9		SO	Track on left.
	3.0 ▲	SO	Track on right.
▼ 5.0		SO	Cross through creek.
	2.9 ▲	SO	Cross through creek.
▼ 5.3		SO	Track on right.
	2.6 ▲	SO	Track on left.
▼ 5.4		SO	Cross through creek.
	2.5 ▲	SO	Cross through creek.
▼ 5.8		SO	Leaving Ute land.
	2.1 ▲	SO	Entering Ute land.

GPS: N 37°40.52' W 109°38.53'

▼ 6.0		SO	Track on right.
	1.9 ▲	SO	Track on left.
▼ 6.1		SO	Track on right.
	1.8 ▲	SO	Track on left.
▼ 6.9		SO	Track on right.
	1.0 ▲	SO	Track on left.
▼ 7.0		SO	Track on right.
	0.9 ▲	SO	Track on left.
▼ 7.4		SO	Entering Ute land.
	0.5 ▲	SO	Leaving Ute land.
▼ 7.9		TL	Junction with CR 228. Turn left signed to

	0.0 ▲		Blanding. Right is Southeast #38: North and South Elk Ridge Trail. Zero trip meter. Continue along South Cottonwood Road.

GPS: N 37°38.98' W 109°37.55'

▼ 0.0			Continue along CR 228 toward Blanding.
	7.7 ▲	TR	Junction with CR 227. Turn right signed South Cottonwood Road. Ahead is CR 228, Southeast #38: North and South Elk Ridge Trail. Zero trip meter.
▼ 1.2		SO	Leaving Ute land.
	6.5 ▲	SO	Entering Ute land.
▼ 1.5		SO	Cattle guard.
	6.2 ▲	SO	Cattle guard.
▼ 2.1		SO	Track on right.
	5.6 ▲	SO	Track on left.
▼ 2.6		BR	Two tracks, left to corral and straight on for CR 228. Continue right on CR 268.
	5.1 ▲	BL	Track on right is second entrance to CR 228, second track goes straight to corral.
▼ 2.9		SO	Track on left, second entrance to CR 228.
	4.8 ▲	SO	CR 228 on right.
▼ 5.2		SO	Foundations of old mine works on left, followed by CR 274 on left and track on right.
	2.5 ▲	SO	CR 274 on right and track on left, followed by foundations of old mine works on right.
▼ 5.4		SO	Cross through creek.
	2.3 ▲	SO	Cross through creek.
▼ 5.7		SO	CR 274 on right.
	2.0 ▲	SO	CR 274 on left.
▼ 6.2		SO	Corral on left.
	1.5 ▲	SO	Corral on right.
▼ 6.7		SO	CR 240 on right. Road turns to pavement.
	1.0 ▲	SO	CR 240 on left. Road turns to graded dirt.
▼ 7.7			Cattle guard, then trail ends at intersection with Utah 95, 6 miles west of junction with US 191. Turn left for Blanding.
	0.0 ▲		Trail commences at intersection of CR 268 and Utah 95. Sign points to South Cottonwood Forest Access. Zero trip meter and proceed northwest on CR 268.

GPS: N 37°33.78' W 109°34.99'

Johns Canyon Overlook Trail

Starting Point:	0.1 miles north of mile marker 19 on Utah 261
Finishing Point:	Johns Canyon Overlook
Total Mileage:	12 miles
Unpaved Mileage:	12 miles
Driving Time:	1.25 hours (one-way)
Elevation Range:	5,900–6,600 feet
Usually Open:	March to December
Difficulty Rating:	4
Scenic Rating:	8
Remoteness Rating:	+0

View of Johns Canyon and Southeast #42: Johns Canyon Trail from overlook at end of trail

Special Attractions
- Overlook into Johns Canyon.
- Small cliff dwelling.
- Access to Grand Gulch hiking trails.

Description

This fairly short spur trail runs out onto Point Lookout and ends at a dizzying viewpoint over Johns Canyon. The trail starts off as graded dirt road and crosses over Polly Mesa. The grader stopped after 8 miles, however, and the trail becomes rougher and lumpier and crosses several slickrock sections. This section is a narrow winding two-track that threads through the cedars and junipers out to the rim of Johns Canyon. There are several pleasant campsites along the trail.

A small cliff dwelling, 9.7 miles from the start of the trail, sits underneath a rocky overhang in the wash. The dwelling is a single room and has incredibly precise stonework forming the door and walls. The Grand Gulch Primitive Area is rich in Anasazi ruins and cliff dwellings, and many other ruins are to be found here and in surrounding canyons. No vehicles are allowed in the primitive areas, so you will need to park and hike in to see them.

Current Road Information

BLM Monticello Field Office
435 North Main; PO Box 7
Monticello, UT 84535
(435) 587-1500

Map References

BLM Bluff, Navajo Mountain (incomplete)
USGS 1:24,000 Cedar Mesa North, Pollys Pasture, Cedar Mesa South, Slickhorn Canyon East
1:100,000 Bluff, Navajo Mountain (incomplete)
Maptech CD-ROM: Moab/Canyonlands
Trails Illustrated, #706
Utah Atlas & Gazetteer, p. 22
Utah Travel Council #5

Route Directions

▼ 0.0		0.1 miles north of mile marker 19 on Utah 261, turn west onto graded dirt road. Road is marked as CR 249. Zero trip meter.
		GPS: N 37°23.79' W 109°56.59'
▼ 0.3	SO	Pass through wire gate. Information board and fee station on the left after gate, also track on left.
▼ 0.4	SO	Track on left.
▼ 0.5	SO	Corral on left.
▼ 0.7	SO	Cross through wash.
▼ 0.9	BL	Track on right.
▼ 1.1	SO	Track on left.
▼ 2.4	BL	Track on right goes to Government Trail. Zero trip meter.
		GPS: N 37°24.45' W 109°58.82'
▼ 0.0		Proceed along graded dirt road.
▼ 1.6	SO	Track on right.
		GPS: N 37°23.49' W 110°00.08'
▼ 2.0	SO	Cross through wash.
▼ 2.6	SO	Track on left.
▼ 2.9	SO	Track on right.
▼ 4.2	SO	Track on right.
▼ 4.3	SO	Campsite on left, then drop down and cross through wash.
		GPS: N 37°21.17' W 109°59.59'
▼ 5.0	SO	Cattle guard.
▼ 5.3	SO	Cross through wash.
▼ 5.5	SO	Corral on right and track on right in cleared area. Zero trip meter.
		GPS: N 37°20.44' W 110°00.41'
▼ 0.0		Continue toward Johns Canyon.

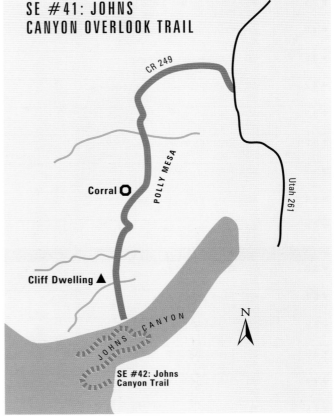

SE #41: JOHNS CANYON OVERLOOK TRAIL

CR 249
Corral
POLLY MESA
Utah 261
Cliff Dwelling
JOHNS CANYON
N
SE #42: Johns Canyon Trail

▼ 1.0	SO	Cross through wash.
▼ 1.3	SO	Trail becomes rockier.

GPS: N 37°19.18′ W 110°00.84′

▼ 1.6	BL	Track on right.

GPS: N 37°19.06′ W 110°00.81′

▼ 1.8	SO	Cross through wash. Small cliff dwelling is down the wash. To reach it, park and walk west along the wash for 0.1 miles downstream to where the wash feeds over a rocky pour-off into the lower canyon. The dwelling is immediately under this ledge. Walk to the south side of the canyon for the best view and access to the lower wash.

GPS: N 37°18.92′ W 110°00.71′

▼ 2.0	SO	Viewpoint over a tributary of Slickhorn Canyon.
▼ 2.1	BR	Small dam on right, then cross through slickrock wash.
▼ 2.4	SO	Cross through wash.
▼ 2.8	SO	Cross through wash.

GPS: N 37°18.19′ W 110°00.88′

▼ 3.8	BL	Track on right.
▼ 4.1		Trail passes an overlook over Johns Canyon and Southeast #42: Johns Canyon Trail below, before finishing at a second overlook.

GPS: N 37°17.17′ W 110°00.66′

SOUTHEAST REGION TRAIL #42

Johns Canyon Trail

Starting Point:	**0.4 miles along the San Juan Goosenecks Road (Utah 316) from Utah 261**
Finishing Point:	**Johns Canyon**
Total Mileage:	**17.3 miles**
Unpaved Mileage:	**17.3 miles**
Driving Time:	**1.5 hours (one-way)**
Elevation Range:	**4,700–5,400 feet**
Usually Open:	**Year-round**
Difficulty Rating:	**4**
Scenic Rating:	**9**
Remoteness Rating:	**+0**

Special Attractions

- Scenic Johns Canyon.
- The bluffs of Cedar Point and Muley Point.
- Indian petroglyphs.

History

Johns Canyon was formerly called Douglas Canyon after a prospector in the early 1900s, Jim Douglas, who found gold in the region. However, before he could return to work his find, the San Juan River rose and flooded his claim, and it remained underwater for the next 20 years. Disheartened, Jim jumped to his death into the San Juan River from the old wooden bridge at Mexican Hat. Douglas Mesa, across the river from Johns Canyon, still bears his name.

The name Johns Canyon comes from John Oliver, who ran cattle in the valley along with his brother, Bill. Their competition for the range was Jimmy Palmer, who was reputed to be a horse rustler and a murderer! Palmer killed John and crossed into Arizona in an attempt to evade the consequences of his crime. He was later captured and died in a Texas jail.

Muley Point

Description

This narrow trail leads into the Glen Canyon National Recreation Area and enters into Johns Canyon, a tributary of the main San Juan River. The trail is graded dirt road for most of its length; only the final part of the trail merits the 3 difficulty rating. The rest of the trail is suitable for high-clearance vehicles in dry weather.

The first part of the trail leaves the San Juan Goosenecks road (Utah 316) and heads west toward the steep face of Cedar Mesa. It enters the Glen Canyon National Recreation Area and passes underneath Cedar Point. The trail narrows as it winds around several deep canyons, containing tributaries of the San Juan River, just to the south. There are some sections of shelf road, but they are short and not especially narrow.

After passing through a gate on a narrow section of the trail, you can see two sets of petroglyphs. The first set is easier to spot on the return journey, as it is on a large southwest facing boulder. The second set is higher up above the trail. Both sets show several human and animal shapes chipped into the black desert varnish.

The trail passes underneath Muley Point before swinging around to enter Johns Canyon. The canyon is long, with several fingers at the north end. The trail crosses the rocky Johns Canyon creek with a pour-off and several pools below it on the left. Shortly after, the trail forks. The main trail goes left and becomes narrower and ungraded. There is one

Petroglyphs found along the trail

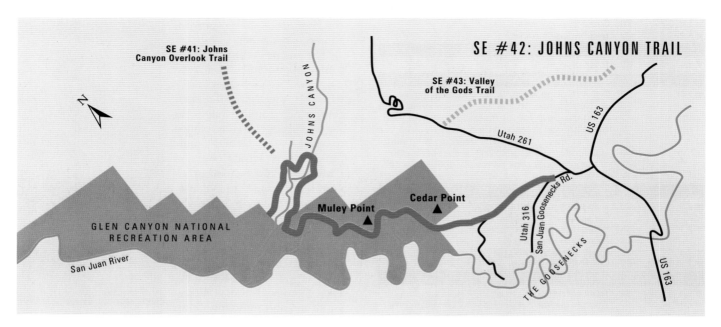

SE #41: Johns Canyon Overlook Trail

JOHNS CANYON

SE #42: JOHNS CANYON TRAIL

SE #43: Valley of the Gods Trail

Utah 261

US 163

Cedar Point ▲

Muley Point ▲

GLEN CANYON NATIONAL RECREATION AREA

San Juan River

Utah 316

San Juan Goosenecks Rd.

THE GOOSENECKS

US 163

section, 2 miles after the fork, that can wash out badly. This is also the narrowest section of the entire trail, with a steep drop-off into the canyon! It has been filled with rocks on several occasions but remains a low-traction climb with lots of rubble.

Although shown as continuing on most maps, the latter part of the trail enters an area now managed as wilderness by the Glen Canyon National Recreation Area, and no vehicles, including mountain bikes, are permitted.

The right fork after the Johns Canyon creek leads to a maze of tracks that head up Johns Canyon for another couple of miles. There is a nice campsite immediately after the turn. These sandy tracks often wash out, and there are several alternatives. If you keep to the right, you will pass the remains of a small dugout.

Current Road Information
BLM Monticello Field Office
435 North Main; PO Box 7
Monticello, UT 84535
(435) 587-1500

Map References
BLM   Bluff, Navajo Mountain (incomplete)
USGS 1:24,000   The Goosenecks, Goulding NE, Slickhorn
          Canyon East, Cedar Mesa South
          1:100,000 Bluff, Navajo Mountain (incomplete)
Maptech CD-ROM: Moab/Canyonlands
Trails Illustrated, #706
Utah Atlas & Gazetteer, p. 22
Utah Travel Council #5

Route Directions

▼ 0.0		Along San Juan Goosenecks road (Utah 316), 0.4 miles from Utah 261, turn northwest onto Johns Canyon Trail (CR 244), an unmarked graded dirt road, and zero trip meter.

		GPS: N 37°12.02′ W 109°53.23′
▼ 2.5	BR	Track on left.
		GPS: N 37°12.18′ W 109°55.97′
▼ 4.2	SO	Entering Glen Canyon National Recreation Area, followed by small track on right. Zero trip meter.
		GPS: N 37°12.77′ W 109°57.79′
▼ 0.0		Continue into the recreation area. Cedar Point is on the right, Muley Point is ahead.
▼ 0.8	SO	Small track on left.
▼ 1.0	SO	Turnout on left, with views down tributary canyon of the San Juan River.
▼ 2.3	SO	Gate. Please keep closed. Zero trip meter.
		GPS: N 37°14.17′ W 109°59.07′
▼ 0.0		Continue underneath the bluff.
▼ 0.3	SO	Petroglyphs to the right. Look back along the trail to see them.
▼ 0.9	SO	Passing underneath Muley Point.
▼ 1.6	SO	Petroglyphs to the right, slightly above the trail.
		GPS: N 37°14.26′ W 110°00.08′
▼ 3.2	SO	Cross through wash.
▼ 4.3	SO	Track on left goes 0.2 miles to viewpoint.
▼ 6.9	SO	Cross through wash.
▼ 7.1	SO	Two tracks on right.
		GPS: N 37°16.36′ W 110°00.03′
▼ 7.3	SO	Cross through Johns Canyon creek on rocky crossing. Series of small pouroffs below trail on left, followed by track to the right.
		GPS: N 37°16.46′ W 109°59.83′
▼ 7.5	BL	Track on right leads up Johns Canyon for approximately 3 miles, passing beside a small dugout. Zero trip meter.
		GPS: N 37°16.60′ W 109°59.84′
▼ 0.0		Continue around the rim of Johns Canyon.
▼ 0.9	SO	Cross through wash.
		GPS: N 37°16.78′ W 110°00.61′
▼ 2.0	SO	Narrow section of trail, often very washed out.
▼ 3.3		Trail ends for vehicle travel at the boundary of the wilderness area.
		GPS: N 37°15.95′ W 110°02.32′

Valley of the Gods Trail

Starting Point:	US 163, 4 miles east of Utah 261
Finishing Point:	Utah 261, at the bottom of the Moki
	Dugway
Total Mileage:	15.6 miles
Unpaved Mileage:	15.6 miles
Driving Time:	1.5 hours
Elevation Range:	4,400–5,200 feet
Usually Open:	Year-round
Difficulty Rating:	2
Scenic Rating:	9
Remoteness Rating:	+0

Special Attractions

■ Eroded rock formations along an easy valley trail.
■ The Setting Hen, the Rooster, Balanced Rock, and more rock formations.
■ Spectacular backcountry campsites.

Description

This graded dirt road winds through a valley of eroded rock formations not unlike the better-known Monument Valley, just over the border in Arizona. The trail passes such imaginatively named formations as the Setting Hen, Rooster Butte, and Rudolph and Santa Claus!

This well-used trail leaves from US 163, 4 miles east of the junction with Utah 261, and in dry weather it is easily traveled by passenger vehicles—though the trail can be washboardy with small sand traps. You immediately cross through Lime Creek, an easy creek crossing, and the trail then winds around the rock formations, with many turnouts to view and photograph the scene.

The trail approaches Setting Hen Rock on the right and Rooster Butte on the left

The floor of the valley is covered with sparse sagebrush, and the buttes and rock formations stand out well in the setting. The valley is rimmed by the white-topped cliffs of Cedar Mesa. There are a number of backcountry campsites, predominantly around Lime Creek near the beginning of the trail, although there are some spectacular ones around the midway point, at the base of the buttes along the ridge. These offer great views down Lime Creek and farther into the valley.

The trail passes many spectacular rock formations

The far end of the trail offers views back over the valley to Rooster Butte and the Setting Hen before the trail finishes at the base of the Moki Dugway, a graded gravel section of Utah 261 that drops abruptly down from Cedar Mesa in a series of switchbacks.

Current Road Information

BLM Monticello Field Office
435 North Main; PO Box 7
Monticello, UT 84535
(435) 587-1500

Map References

BLM Bluff
USGS 1:24,000 Mexican Hat, Cigarette Spring Cave, Cedar Mesa South
1:100,000 Bluff
Maptech CD-ROM: Moab/Canyonlands
Trails Illustrated, #706
Utah Atlas & Gazetteer, p. 22
Utah Travel Council #5

Route Directions

▼ 0.0			From US 163, 4 miles east of Utah 261, turn north on the graded dirt road at the sign for Valley of the Gods (CR 242) and zero trip meter.
	7.2 ▲		Trail ends at the junction with Utah 261. Turn right for Mexican Hat, turn left for Bluff.
		GPS: N 37°14.10′ W 109°48.82′	
▼ 0.1		SO	Cross through Lime Creek, followed by a track to the right along the creek.
	7.1 ▲	SO	Track on left along Lime Creek, then cross through the creek.
▼ 0.2		SO	Turnout on right.
	7.0 ▲	SO	Turnout on left.
▼ 0.3		SO	Track on right goes down to Lime Creek. Seven Sailors Rock is on the left.
	6.9 ▲	SO	Seven Sailors Rock is on the right. Track on left goes down to Lime Creek.
▼ 0.6		SO	Turnout on right gives views along Lime Creek.
	6.6 ▲	SO	Turnout on left gives views along Lime Creek.

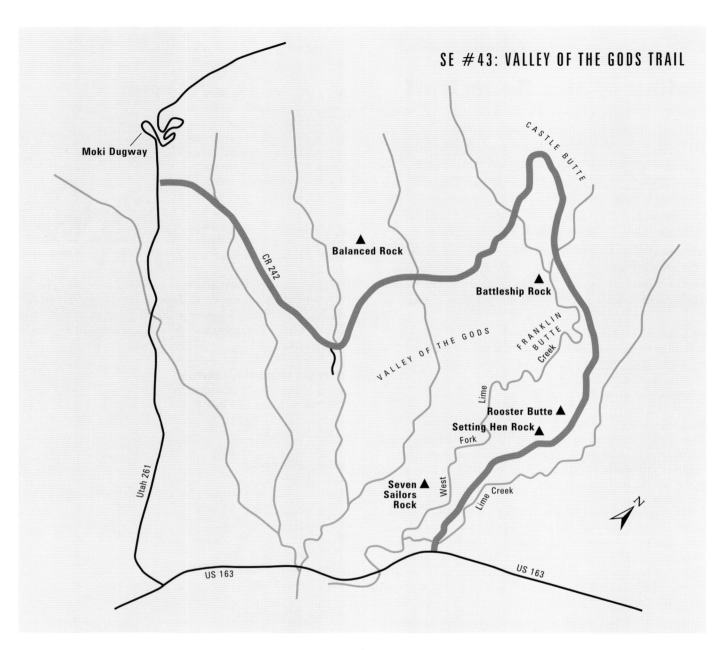

SE #43: VALLEY OF THE GODS TRAIL

▼ 0.8		SO	Track on left goes to West Fork Lime Creek. Setting Hen Rock is ahead, with Rooster Butte on the left.
	6.4 ▲	SO	Track on right goes to West Fork Lime Creek.
▼ 2.7		SO	Trail passes underneath Setting Hen Rock.
	4.5 ▲	SO	Trail passes underneath Setting Hen Rock.
▼ 3.5		SO	Track on left and track on right.
	3.7 ▲	SO	Track on left and track on right. Rooster Butte is ahead to the right, and Setting Hen Rock is slightly behind it.

GPS: N 37°16.94' W 109°48.52'

▼ 3.9		SO	Turnout on left gives view over Franklin Butte on the left.
	3.3 ▲	SO	Turnout on right gives view over Franklin Butte on the right.
▼ 4.0		SO	Track on right.
	3.2 ▲	SO	Track on left.
▼ 4.8		SO	Track on left alongside wash. Franklin Butte is

			due left; Battleship Rock is larger butte north of it.
	2.4 ▲	SO	Track on right alongside wash. Franklin Butte is due right, Battleship Rock is larger butte north of it.

GPS: N 37°17.75' W 109°49.34'

▼ 4.9		SO	Track on left.
	2.3 ▲	SO	Track on right.
▼ 5.5		SO	Cross through West Fork Wash.
	1.7 ▲	SO	Cross through West Fork Wash.

GPS: N 37°18.03' W 109°50.04'

▼ 6.2		SO	Track on right.
	1.0 ▲	SO	Track on left.
▼ 6.4		SO	Track on right.
	0.8 ▲	SO	Track on left.
▼ 6.9		SO	Track on right. The rock formation "De Gaulle and His Troops" on right.
	0.3 ▲	SO	Track on left. The rock formation

			"De Gaulle and His Troops" on left.
▼ 7.2		SO	Trail passes over a ridge underneath Castle Butte on the left. Track on right at top of the ridge goes to a campsite at the base of the butte. Zero trip meter at the top of the ridge.
	0.0 ▲		Continue along the graded trail.

GPS: N 37°18.95' W 109°51.31'

▼ 0.0		SO	Descend along wash.
	8.4 ▲	SO	Trail passes over a ridge underneath Castle Butte on the right. Track on left at the top of the ridge goes to a campsite at the base of the butte. Zero trip meter at the top of the ridge.
▼ 0.3		SO	Cross through wash. "Rudolph and Santa Claus" is ahead to the right of the trail.
	8.1 ▲	SO	Cross through wash.
▼ 0.9		SO	Cross through wash.
	7.5 ▲	SO	Cross through wash.
▼ 1.1		SO	Cross through wash.
	7.3 ▲	SO	Cross through wash. "Rudolph and Santa Claus" is ahead to the left of the trail.
▼ 1.5		SO	Cross through wash.
	6.9 ▲	SO	Cross through wash.
▼ 1.7		SO	Cross through wash.
	6.7 ▲	SO	Cross through wash.
▼ 2.2		SO	Rooster Butte and Setting Hen Rock are visible on the far side of the valley.
	6.2 ▲	SO	Rooster Butte and Setting Hen Rock are visible on the far side of the valley.

GPS: N 37°17.17' W 109°51.14'

▼ 2.8		SO	Turnout on left.
	5.6 ▲	SO	Turnout on right.
▼ 3.0		SO	Track on left.
	5.4 ▲	SO	Track on right.
▼ 3.1		SO	Cross through wash.
	5.3 ▲	SO	Cross through wash.
▼ 3.6		SO	Cross through wash.
	4.8 ▲	SO	Cross through wash.
▼ 3.7		SO	Track on right. Balanced Rock is ahead.
	4.7 ▲	SO	Track on left.
▼ 4.7		SO	Cross through wash.
	3.7 ▲	SO	Cross through wash.
▼ 4.9		SO	Cross through wash.
	3.5 ▲	SO	Cross through wash.
▼ 5.0		SO	Track on left.
	3.4 ▲	SO	Track on right.

GPS: N 37°15.43' W 109°52.32'

▼ 5.1		SO	Oil drilling post and Balanced Rock on right.
	3.3 ▲	SO	Oil drilling post and Balanced Rock on left.
▼ 5.6		SO	Track on left.
	2.8 ▲	SO	Track on right.
▼ 6.9		SO	Cross through wash.
	1.5 ▲	SO	Cross through wash.
▼ 7.9		SO	Cross through wash.
	0.5 ▲	SO	Cross through wash.
▼ 8.0		SO	Valley of the Gods B&B on the right.
	0.4 ▲	SO	Valley of the Gods B&B on the left.
▼ 8.4			Trail ends on Utah 261, at the bottom of the Moki Dugway. Turn right to ascend the dugway, turn left for Mexican Hat.
	0.0 ▲		Trail commences on Utah 261 at the bottom of the Moki Dugway. Turn east on the graded dirt road at the sign for Valley of the Gods (CR 242). Zero trip meter.

GPS: N 37°15.85' W 109°55.90'

Butler Wash Road

Starting Point:	US 163, 18.2 miles east of Mexican Hat or about 1.4 miles west of junction of US 163 and Utah 191
Finishing Point:	Utah 95, 9.4 miles west of US 191
Total Mileage:	20.2 miles
Unpaved Mileage:	20.2 miles
Driving Time:	1.5 hours
Elevation Range:	4,400–5,400 feet
Usually Open:	Year-round
Difficulty Rating:	1
Scenic Rating:	10
Remoteness Rating:	+0

Special Attractions

- Butler Wash Anasazi ruins near the north end of the trail.
- Anasazi cliff dwellings in the canyons of Comb Ridge.
- Views of the tilted slab of Comb Ridge.

Description

This graded county road follows along the tilted side of the Comb Ridge monocline and alongside Butler Wash. From the trail you can view the canyons cutting deeply into Comb Ridge, many of which contain very unspoiled Anasazi cliff dwellings. Hikes to explore these side canyons can reveal many surprises. However, because of the unspoiled nature of the ruins, the BLM has asked that exact locations and directions not be published.

The road starts on US 163, 18.2 miles east of Mexican Hat; look for the Butler Wash Road BLM sign. The large bulk of Tank Mesa is on the right; its red walls provide a contrast to the lighter stone of Comb Ridge. Many of the numerous side trails to the right and left lead to good, small

Cliff dwelling at the end of canyon hike

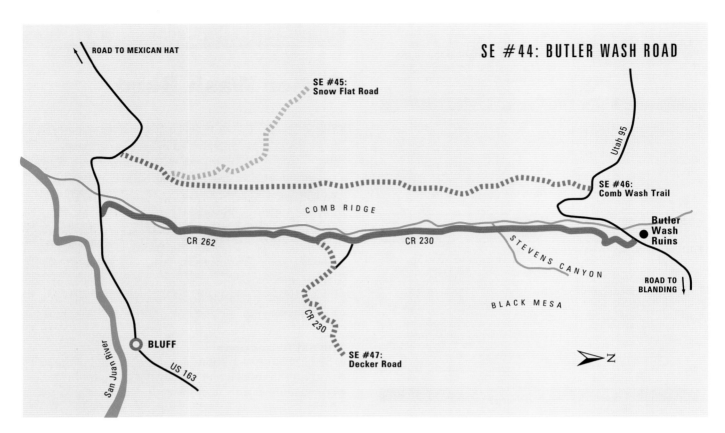

campsites. The northern end of the trail leaves Butler Wash and winds around Black Mesa and Black Mesa Butte through stands of juniper and cedar trees before joining Utah 95.

The road is graded for its full length and is suitable for year-round travel. Snow or heavy rain may temporarily make it impassable for short periods.

Current Road Information

BLM Monticello Field Office
435 North Main; PO Box 7
Monticello, UT 84535
(435) 587-1500

Map References

BLM Blanding, Bluff
USGS 1:24,000 Bluff SW, Bluff, No Mans Island, Bluff NW, Hotel Rock, Black Mesa Butte
1:100,000 Bluff, Blanding
Maptech CD-ROM: Moab/Canyonlands
Trails Illustrated, #706
Utah Atlas & Gazetteer, p. 22
Utah Travel Council #5

Route Directions

▼ 0.0			From US 163, 18.2 miles east of Mexican Hat, turn north onto the graded dirt road at the BLM sign for Butler Wash Road. Pass through gate and zero trip meter.
	7.9 ▲		Pass through gate, then trail ends at the junction with US 163. Turn left for Bluff, turn right for Mexican Hat.

			GPS: N 37°15.90' W 109°38.16'
▼ 0.3		BR	Track on left.
	7.6 ▲	SO	Track on right.
▼ 0.9		SO	Track on left, then cattle guard and information board.
	7.0 ▲	SO	Cattle guard and information board, then track on right.
			GPS: N 37°16.58' W 109°38.44'
▼ 1.7		BL	Track on right.
	6.2 ▲	SO	Track on left.
▼ 2.5		SO	Cross through wash.
	5.4 ▲	SO	Cross through wash.
▼ 3.0		SO	Cross through wash.
	4.9 ▲	SO	Cross through wash.
▼ 3.2		SO	Cross through wash.
	4.7 ▲	SO	Cross through wash.
▼ 3.3		SO	Track on left.
	4.6 ▲	SO	Track on right.
▼ 3.6		SO	Track on left.
	4.3 ▲	SO	Track on right.
			GPS: N 37°18.85' W 109°37.64'
▼ 3.8		SO	Track on right, then cross over creek.
	4.1 ▲	SO	Cross over creek, then track on left.
▼ 4.1		SO	Cross through wash.
	3.8 ▲	SO	Cross through wash.
▼ 4.4		SO	Cross through wash.
	3.5 ▲	SO	Cross through wash.
▼ 4.8		SO	Track on right.
	3.1 ▲	SO	Track on left.
▼ 5.1		SO	Track on left, then cross through wash.
	2.8 ▲	SO	Cross through wash, then track on right.
▼ 5.5		SO	Cross through wash.
	2.4 ▲	SO	Cross through wash.

▼ 5.9	SO	Track on left.
2.0 ▲	SO	Track on right.

GPS: N 37°20.81' W 109°37.61'

▼ 6.2	SO	Track on left.
1.7 ▲	SO	Track on right.
▼ 6.5	SO	Cross through wash.
1.4 ▲	SO	Cross through wash.
▼ 6.7	SO	Track on left.
1.2 ▲	SO	Track on right.

GPS: N 37°21.44' W 109°37.74'

▼ 6.8	SO	Track on left.
1.1 ▲	SO	Track on right.
▼ 7.1	SO	Track on left.
0.8 ▲	SO	Track on right.
▼ 7.9	BL	Cross through fence line, then track to the right is Southeast #47: Decker Road (CR 230). Zero trip meter.
0.0 ▲		Continue along Butler Wash Road (CR 262).

GPS: N 37°22.33' W 109°37.26'

▼ 0.0		Continue along Butler Wash Road (CR 262).
1.6 ▲	SO	Track to the left is Southeast #47: Decker Road (CR 230), then cross through fence line. Zero trip meter.
▼ 0.5	SO	Track on left.
1.1 ▲	SO	Track on right.
▼ 0.6	SO	Track on left.
1.0 ▲	SO	Track on right.

GPS: N 37°22.82' W 109°37.53'

▼ 1.2	SO	Track on left.
0.4 ▲	SO	Track on right.

GPS: N 37°23.35' W 109°39.43'

▼ 1.6	TL	T-intersection. Right and left is CR 230. Zero trip meter.
0.0 ▲		Continue along CR 262.

GPS: N 37°23.54' W 109°37.10'

▼ 0.0		Continue along CR 230 and immediately cross through wash.
10.7 ▲	TR	Cross through wash, then turn right onto CR 262. Zero trip meter.
▼ 0.4	SO	Cattle guard.
10.3 ▲	SO	Cattle guard.
▼ 0.6	SO	Two tracks on left.
10.1 ▲	SO	Two tracks on right.

GPS: N 37°24.02' W 109°37.39'

▼ 1.0	SO	Oil drilling post on left, then track on left.
9.7 ▲	SO	Track on right, then oil drilling post on right.

GPS: N 37°24.38' W 109°37.40'

▼ 1.2	SO	Cross through wash.
9.5 ▲	SO	Cross through wash.
▼ 1.3	SO	Track on left, then track on right.
9.4 ▲	SO	Track on left, then track on right.

GPS: N 37°24.58' W 109°37.49'

▼ 1.7	SO	Cross through wash.
9.0 ▲	SO	Cross through wash.
▼ 2.1	SO	Cross through wash.
8.6 ▲	SO	Cross through wash.
▼ 2.5	SO	Cross through wash, then track on right and track on left. Large cave in Comb Ridge on left.
8.2 ▲	SO	Track on right and track on left, then cross through wash. Large cave in Comb Ridge on right.

GPS: N 37°25.69' W 109°37.65'

▼ 2.6	SO	Track on left, then cross through fence line.
8.1 ▲	SO	Cross through fence line, then track on right.
▼ 3.0	SO	Cross through wash.

7.7 ▲	SO	Cross through wash.
▼ 3.3	SO	Cross through wash.
7.4 ▲	SO	Cross through wash.
▼ 3.8	SO	Faint track on right, then cross through wash.
6.9 ▲	SO	Cross through wash, then faint track on left.
▼ 4.8	SO	Cattle guard.
5.9 ▲	SO	Cattle guard.

GPS: N 37°27.71' W 109°37.81'

▼ 5.1	SO	Track on right.
5.6 ▲	SO	Track on left.
▼ 6.0	SO	Track on right.
4.7 ▲	SO	Track on left.

GPS: N 37°28.66' W 109°37.73'

▼ 6.5	SO	Track on right.
4.2 ▲	SO	Track on left.

GPS: N 37°29.09' W 109°37.67'

▼ 6.6	SO	Track on left.
4.1 ▲	SO	Track on right.
▼ 7.4	SO	Cross through fence line.
3.3 ▲	SO	Cross through fence line.
▼ 7.5	SO	Cross through wash.
3.2 ▲	SO	Cross through wash.
▼ 8.0	SO	Track on left, then cross through fence line.
2.7 ▲	SO	Cross through fence line, then track on right.
▼ 9.1	SO	Track on right, then cross through wash.
1.6 ▲	SO	Cross through wash, then track on left.
▼ 9.3	SO	Cross through wash.
1.4 ▲	SO	Cross through wash.
▼ 10.4	BL	Cross through wash, then track on right.
0.3 ▲	TR	Track on left, then cross through wash.

GPS: N 37°32.04' W 109°37.90'

▼ 10.5	SO	Information board for Cedar Mesa on left.
0.2 ▲	SO	Information board for Cedar Mesa on right.
▼ 10.7		Trail ends at the junction with Utah 95. Turn right for Blanding, left for Lake Powell.
0.0 ▲		Trail commences on Utah 95, 0.6 miles west of mile marker 113, 9.4 miles west of US 191. Turn east on unmarked graded dirt road and zero trip meter.

GPS: N 37°32.09' W 109°37.19'

SOUTHEAST REGION TRAIL #45

Snow Flat Road

Starting Point:	**Southeast #46: Comb Wash Trail, 2.2 miles north of US 163**
Finishing Point:	**Utah 261, 0.4 miles south of mile marker 23**
Total Mileage:	**21.4 miles**
Unpaved Mileage:	**21.4 miles**
Driving Time:	**1.5 hours**
Elevation Range:	**4,400–6,600 feet**
Usually Open:	**March to December**
Difficulty Rating:	**3**
Scenic Rating:	**8**
Remoteness Rating:	**+0**

Snow Flat Trail winds through rocky domes at the top of The Twist

Special Attractions
- Old Mormon Pioneer Trail.
- The Twist—a rocky climb up onto Cedar Mesa.
- Views of Cedar Mesa and Road Canyon.
- Snow Flat Spring Cave.

Description
Snow Flat Road follows part of the old Mormon Pioneer Trail that traveled west to the San Juan Mission. The trail leaves Southeast #46: Comb Wash Trail and for the first few miles runs along the west side of Comb Wash. This section is very sandy, with several deep, powder-fine sand traps. The trail climbs a slight ridge away from Comb Wash, offering spectacular views back to Comb Ridge, north to the Blue Mountains, and south into Road Canyon.

At The Twist, the trail climbs up through the slickrock onto Cedar Mesa. It is not particularly steep, but the surface changes to rock and is lumpy with a few ledges. This is possibly the best scenery of the whole trail, as the dark green of the cedar trees contrasts with the pink sandstone of The Twist. This section has many viewpoints and some of the best camping along the trail, in small sites looking east to Comb Ridge.

After The Twist, the trail reverts to a narrow, smooth, graded dirt road interspersed with short rocky sections. The turnoff to Snow Flat Spring Cave is not marked but is easy to find. The large shallow cave itself is a short hike down the

The canyon falls away below Snow Flat Spring

wash. At the back, under an overhang, two springs drip out of the rock wall into two wooden cowboy tanks. The moisture promotes the growth of ferns and mosses in hanging gardens on the wall above the spring.

After the turnoff to the cave, the trail is smoother graded dirt and not too sandy. There are several small, unmarked tracks to explore, and a hiking trail.

Snow can temporarily close the road in the winter months, as can heavy rain, but it is often passable the entire year. The trail finishes on Utah 261, north of the Moki Dugway.

There are a number of Indian relics in the vicinity of this trail, which are interesting to view, but please respect these sites and don't remove anything.

Current Road Information
BLM Monticello Field Office
435 North Main; PO Box 7
Monticello, UT 84535
(435) 587-1500

Map References
BLM Bluff
USGS 1:24,000   Bluff SW, Bluff NW, Snow Flat Spring
Cave, Cedar Mesa North
1:100,000 Bluff
Maptech CD-ROM: Moab/Canyonlands
Trails Illustrated, #706
Utah Atlas & Gazetteer, p. 22
Utah Travel Council #5

Route Directions

▼ 0.0			From Southeast #46: Comb Wash Trail, 2.2 miles north of the junction with US 163, turn north onto the graded dirt road, marked CR 237, and zero trip meter.
	2.5 ▲		Trail ends at the junction with Southeast #46: Comb Wash Trail. Turn right to exit to US 163, turn left to continue along Comb Wash Road.
		GPS: N 37°17.82' W 109°39.61'	
▼ 0.2		SO	Cross through wash.
	2.3 ▲	SO	Cross through wash.
▼ 2.0		SO	Cross through wash.
	0.5 ▲	SO	Cross through wash.
▼ 2.5		SO	Track on right and information board and fee station for Cedar Mesa. Zero trip meter.
	0.0 ▲		Continue along graded road.
		GPS: N 37°19.85' W 109°39.81'	
▼ 0.0			Continue along graded road.
	9.4 ▲	SO	Track on left and information board and fee station for Cedar Mesa. Zero trip meter.
▼ 0.2		SO	Cattle guard.
	9.2 ▲	SO	Cattle guard.
▼ 0.3		SO	Cross through wash.
	9.1 ▲	SO	Cross through wash.
▼ 1.3		SO	Track on left. Trail swings away from wash.
	8.1 ▲	SO	Track on right. Trail joins the wash.
▼ 2.2		SO	Track on left to campsite.
	7.2 ▲	SO	Track on right to campsite.
		GPS: N 37°20.88' W 109°41.34'	
▼ 4.3		SO	Track on left, then track on right. You are crossing the Mormon Trail.

5.1 ▲		SO	Track on left, then track on right.

GPS: N 37°22.03' W 109°43.01'

▼ 5.4		SO	Faint track on right, then climb The Twist.
	4.0 ▲	SO	Trail reaches bottom of The Twist, then faint track on left.
▼ 5.6		SO	Viewpoint and campsite on right.
	3.8 ▲	SO	Viewpoint and campsite on left.
▼ 5.8		SO	Viewpoint and campsite on right.
	3.6 ▲	SO	Viewpoint and campsite on left.
▼ 6.1		SO	Track on left goes to viewpoint and campsite.
	3.3 ▲	SO	Track on right goes to viewpoint and campsite.
▼ 6.7		SO	Viewpoint on right at oil drilling post.
	2.7 ▲	SO	Viewpoint on left at oil drilling post.

GPS: N 37°22.78' W 109°44.46'

▼ 6.8		SO	Pass through wire gate.
	2.6 ▲	SO	Pass through wire gate.
▼ 6.9		SO	Campsite on right.
	2.5 ▲	SO	Campsite on left.
▼ 8.7		SO	Track on right goes to viewpoint over the canyon and campsite. Snow Flat Spring Cave is visible from the viewpoint to the north, high on the cliff.
	0.7 ▲	SO	Track on left goes to viewpoint over the canyon and campsite. Snow Flat Spring Cave is visible from the viewpoint to the north, high on the cliff.

GPS: N 37°23.86' W 109°45.86'

▼ 8.9		SO	Track on right.
	0.5 ▲	SO	Track on left.
▼ 9.4		SO	Well-used, ungraded spur track on right goes to Snow Flat Spring and Cave. Zero trip meter.
	0.0 ▲		Continue along the graded trail.

GPS: N 37°24.11' W 109°46.57'

Spur to Snow Flat Spring Cave

▼ 0.0			Proceed along small well-used track.
▼ 0.4		TR	Cross through small wash, then turn right after wash.
▼ 0.6		UT	Trail ends for vehicles at turning circle.

GPS: N 37°24.32' W 109°46.07'

To reach the cave, walk south to join the wash and proceed southeast down the main wash, staying on the north side. After approximately 350 yards the wash goes over a big rocky pour-off. Look for the small trail that stays high on the north side of the wash, and follow this for approximately 175 yards to Snow Flat Spring Cave. There is a small stone ruin just before the cave against the cliff.

GPS AT THE CAVE: N 37°24.19' W 109°45.97'

Continuation of Main Trail

▼ 0.0			Continue along the graded trail.
	9.5 ▲	SO	Well-used, ungraded spur track on left goes to Snow Flat Spring and Cave. Zero trip meter.
▼ 1.2		SO	Cross through wash.
	8.3 ▲	SO	Cross through wash.
▼ 1.7		SO	Track on left and hiking trail to the right.
	7.8 ▲	SO	Track on right and hiking trail to the left.

GPS: N 37°25.05' W 109°47.94'

▼ 2.9		BR	Track on left.
	6.6 ▲	BL	Track on right.
▼ 3.0		SO	Track on left.
	6.5 ▲	SO	Track on right.
▼ 4.5		SO	Pass through fence line.
	5.0 ▲	SO	Pass through fence line.

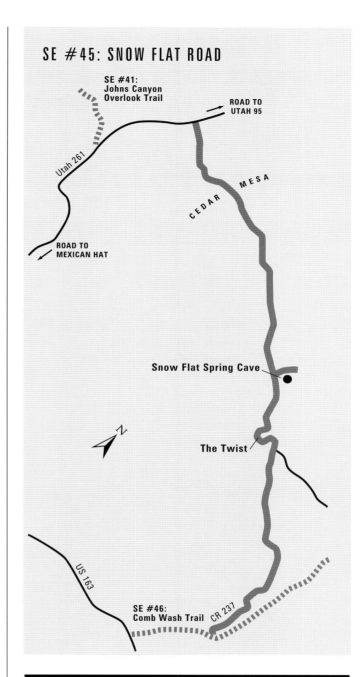

SE #45: SNOW FLAT ROAD

SE #41:
Johns Canyon
Overlook Trail

ROAD TO
UTAH 95

Utah 261

CEDAR MESA

ROAD TO
MEXICAN HAT

Snow Flat Spring Cave

The Twist

US 163

SE #46:
Comb Wash Trail

CR 237

GPS: N 37°26.05' W 109°50.48'

▼ 4.6		SO	Track on right goes to campsite.
	4.9 ▲	SO	Track on left goes to campsite.

GPS: N 37°26.09' W 109°50.60'

▼ 4.7		SO	Track on right.
	4.8 ▲	SO	Track on left.

GPS: N 37°26.08' W 109°50.73'

▼ 7.6		SO	Faint track on left.
	1.9 ▲	BL	Faint track on right.
▼ 8.6		SO	Information board and fee station for Cedar Mesa on left.
	0.9 ▲	SO	Information board and fee station for Cedar Mesa on right.

GPS: N 37°26.17' W 109°54.39'

▼ 9.0		SO	Track on left.
	0.5 ▲	SO	Track on right.

| ▼ 9.1 | SO | Large track on left, then second faint track on left. |
| 0.4 ▲ | BL | Faint track on right, then second large track on right. |

GPS: N 37°26.34' W 109°54.96'

| ▼ 9.3 | SO | Track on left. |
| 0.2 ▲ | BL | Track on right. |

| ▼ 9.5 | | Trail finishes at the junction with Utah 261. Turn right to join to Utah 95, turn left for Mexican Hat. |
| 0.0 ▲ | | Trail starts on Utah 261. Turn east on CR 237 and zero trip meter. BLM sign reads, "Impassable when wet." |

GPS: N 37°26.45' W 109°55.32'

SOUTHEAST REGION TRAIL #46

Comb Wash Trail

Starting Point:	Utah 95, 13.5 miles west of junction with US 191
Finishing Point:	US 163, 0.7 miles east of mile marker 37
Total Mileage:	17.4 miles
Unpaved Mileage:	17.4 miles
Driving Time:	1 hour
Elevation Range:	4,400–5,000 feet
Usually Open:	Year-round
Difficulty Rating:	2
Scenic Rating:	9
Remoteness Rating:	+0

Special Attractions
- Comb Ridge monocline.
- Anasazi cliff dwellings in the area.
- Significant section of the Mormon Hole-in-the-Rock Expedition.
- Cave Towers near the north end of the trail.

History
Comb Ridge is a long monocline running for almost 80 miles from Elk Ridge in the north down to Kayenta, Arizona. A monocline is the bending of the earth's crust in one direction only, and Comb Ridge has its sheer scarp face on the western side. Formed over 65 million years ago, Comb Wash is a major drainage for the area, with tributaries draining from Cedar Mesa to the west as well as down the face of the monocline. It takes its name from the scalloped appearance of the ridgetop, which resembles the comb of a rooster.

The earliest inhabitants of the region were the Anasazi, or

A small, wooden cabin sits at the foot of Comb Ridge

The trail moves past jumbled rocks below Comb Ridge

Ancient Puebloans, who have left many relics and signs behind them. Various dwellings and structures of stone and mud are found in nearby Mule Canyon and its surroundings (farther west on Utah 95). Some of the best examples are the Butler Wash Ruins (a couple of miles east along Utah 95). Here you can see a large cluster of dwellings high up under an overhang in the cliff, accessed by steep hand and footholds up the cliff wall. Most of the cliff dwellings are oriented toward the south, so that they could take full benefit of the low winter sun for warmth and light. The well-marked site includes a 0.5-mile walk to an overlook over the ruins. Another ruin is Cave Towers (near Mule Canyon Ruins on Utah 95, 0.3 miles west of mile marker 103), a cluster of seven towers in a tributary of Mule Canyon. A short, 0.6-mile, unsigned dirt road leads south from Utah 95; a very short hike at the end of the road leads down the wash to the three remaining towers on either side, above a series of large caves.

To the 1880 Mormon Hole-in-the-Rock Expedition, Comb Ridge appeared an impassable barrier as they descended from Cedar Mesa. They were forced to swing south and eventually succeeded in crossing Comb Ridge at San Juan Hill near where the San Juan River cuts through the ridge.

Description
This trail runs down the west side of Comb Ridge, one of the most prominent features of the region. The trail runs close to both Comb Wash and Comb Ridge for its full length. From this side, Comb Ridge is a series of cliff faces forming an impenetrable barrier to east-west travel.

The trail leaves Utah 95 on a graded dirt road, CR 235. There is no sign at the start other than the county road marker, but a BLM information board can be seen from the highway. The information board gives general information for camping, hiking, and exploring in the region. A large well-used informal camping area is nearby, situated under the cottonwoods alongside Comb Wash. This is a pleasant area, although it's rather close to the highway.

The trail leads south, crossing a few small sandy washes. Other tracks in the first few miles lead to camping areas; the most attractive campsites on the trail are at the northern end.

The trail, traveling almost due north to south, is graded for its full length, but it is loose and sandy with several patches of deep sand traps. It is suitable for high-clearance vehicles, but in dry weather 4WD may be necessary to successfully negotiate the sandy sections. The northern end of the trail is the sandiest; the southern end tends to be firmer, but the trail does cross the wide sandy Comb Wash at the lower end. This trail is impassable during wet weather.

The ever-changing Comb Ridge makes for fascinating scenery. To the west are views over Cedar Mesa. After 8.9 miles, an access track to Cedar Mesa is marked by a BLM information board. The BLM is using the area to try out a day-use fee system. Day hiking and overnight backpacking requires a permit, which can be obtained at the entry points using a self-pay system during winter months. Hikers at other times of the year require advance reservations. Car camping and traveling along the established county roads does not currently require a permit, although camping stays are limited to two nights and you are requested to use existing campsites.

The trail passes the eastern end of Southeast #45: Snow Flat Road before finishing at the junction of US 163.

Current Road Information
BLM Monticello Field Office
435 North Main; PO Box 7
Monticello, UT 84535
(435) 587-1500

Map References
BLM   Blanding, Bluff
USGS 1:24,000   Hotel Rock, Bluff NW, Bluff SW
          1:100,000 Blanding, Bluff
Maptech CD-ROM: Moab/Canyonlands
Trails Illustrated, #706
Utah Atlas & Gazetteer, p. 22
Utah Travel Council #5

Route Directions

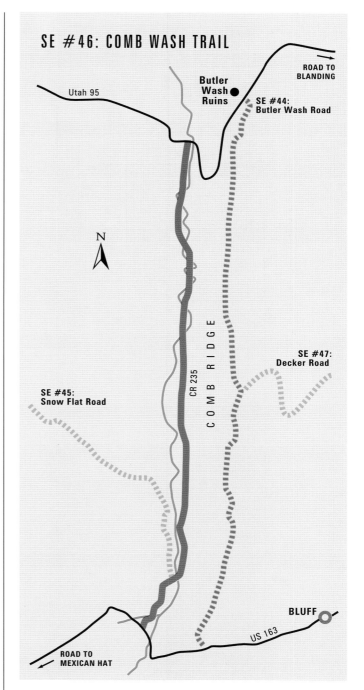

| ▼ 0.0 | | From Utah 95, 13.5 miles west of US 191, turn south on graded gravel road CR 235 and zero trip meter. Turn is approximately 1 mile west of where the highway crosses Comb Ridge. |
| 4.0 ▲ | | Trail ends on Utah 95 just west of Comb Ridge. Turn right for Blanding, left for Hite Crossing. |

GPS: N 37°30.67′ W 109°39.18′

▼ 0.1	SO	Information board and well-used large camping area under cottonwoods alongside Comb Wash. Multiple tracks to the right and left lead to camping areas for the next 0.5 miles.
3.9 ▲	SO	Information board and well-used large camping area under cottonwoods alongside Comb Wash.
▼ 0.6	SO	Cross through wash.
3.4 ▲	SO	Cross through wash. Multiple tracks to the right and left lead to camping areas for the next 0.5 miles.
▼ 1.0	SO	Track on right.
3.0 ▲	SO	Track on left.
▼ 1.4	SO	Cross through sandy wash.
2.6 ▲	SO	Cross through sandy wash.
▼ 2.7	SO	Cross through wash.
1.3 ▲	SO	Cross through wash.
▼ 3.1	SO	Cross through wash.
0.9 ▲	SO	Cross through wash.
▼ 3.7	SO	Track on right.
0.3 ▲	SO	Track on left.
▼ 4.0	SO	Pass through wire gate, then corral on right. Zero trip meter.
0.0 ▲		Continue along Comb Wash.

GPS: N 37°27.29′ W 109°39.18′

▼ 0.0		Continue along Comb Wash.
4.9 ▲	SO	Corral on left, then pass through wire gate. Zero trip meter.
▼ 1.1	SO	Track on right.

3.8 ▲	SO	Track on left.
▼ 1.8	SO	Track on right.
3.1 ▲	SO	Track on left.

GPS: N 37°25.79' W 109°39.16'

▼ 2.4	SO	Track on right.
2.5 ▲	SO	Track on left.
▼ 3.8	SO	Track on left.
1.1 ▲	SO	Track on right.

GPS: N 37°24.14' W 109°39.36'

▼ 4.5	SO	Track on right.
0.4 ▲	SO	Track on left.

GPS: N 37°23.47' W 109°39.37'

▼ 4.9	SO	Track on right goes to Cedar Mesa. Information board at intersection. Zero trip meter.
0.0 ▲		Continue along Comb Wash.

GPS: N 37°23.14' W 109°39.38°

▼ 0.0		Continue along Comb Wash.
6.3 ▲	SO	Track on left goes to Cedar Mesa. Information board at intersection. Zero trip meter.
▼ 0.2	SO	Cattle guard.
6.1 ▲	SO	Cattle guard.
▼ 0.3	SO	Track on left.
6.0 ▲	SO	Track on right.

GPS: N 37°22.91' W 109°39.41'

▼ 1.1	SO	Track on right goes to old cabin.
5.2 ▲	SO	Track on left goes to old cabin.
▼ 3.5	SO	Cattle guard.
2.8 ▲	SO	Cattle guard.

GPS: N 37°20.16' W 109°39.24'

▼ 3.6	BL	Track on right.
2.7 ▲	SO	Track on left.

GPS: N 37°20.06' W 109°39.28'

▼ 4.9	SO	Track on left.
1.4 ▲	SO	Track on right.
▼ 5.9	SO	Cross through Comb Wash.
0.4 ▲	SO	Cross through Comb Wash.
▼ 6.3	SO	Track on right is Southeast #45: Snow Flat Road (CR 237). Zero trip meter.
0.0 ▲		Continue toward Utah 95.

GPS: N 37°17.85' W 109°39.69'

▼ 0.0		Continue toward US 163.
2.2 ▲	BR	Track on left is Southeast #45: Snow Flat Road (CR 237). Zero trip meter.
▼ 0.9	SO	Track on left.
1.3 ▲	SO	Track on right.
▼ 1.0	SO	Track on left, then cross through wash.
1.2 ▲	SO	Cross through wash, then track on right.
▼ 1.7	SO	Cross through wash.
0.5 ▲	SO	Cross through wash.
▼ 1.8	SO	Cross through wash.
0.4 ▲	SO	Cross through wash.
▼ 2.0	SO	Faint track on right.
0.2 ▲	SO	Faint track on left.
▼ 2.1	SO	Information board on left.
0.1 ▲	SO	Information board on right.
▼ 2.2		Trail ends at the junction with US 163 just west of Comb Ridge. Turn left for Bluff, turn right for Mexican Hat.
0.0 ▲		Trail starts on US 163, 0.7 miles east of mile marker 37. Turn north on the graded dirt road and zero trip meter. Road is marked as CR 235.

GPS: N 37°16.41' W 109°40.62'

Decker Road

Starting Point:	**US 191, at mile marker 33**
Finishing Point:	**Junction with Southeast #44: Butler Wash Road, 7.9 miles north of US 163**
Total Mileage:	**9.3 miles**
Unpaved Mileage:	**9.3 miles**
Driving Time:	**45 minutes**
Elevation Range:	**4,600–5,100 feet**
Usually Open:	**Year-round**
Difficulty Rating:	**2**
Scenic Rating:	**7**
Remoteness Rating:	**+0**

Special Attractions

- Views across to the Comb Ridge monocline.
- Pretty Black Rock Canyon.
- Many graded county roads for easy exploration.

Description

There are many graded county roads in the vicinity of Southeast #44: Butler Wash Road, and these easy trails offer some varied, attractive scenery for driving and hiking. This trail covers some of these well-marked roads east of Butler Wash.

Decker Road leaves US 191, 14.3 miles south of the junction with Utah 95 and travels west across Cottonwood Wash. It passes through some private property around the wash; signs request that you remain on the county roads. The road travels around the south end of No-Mans Island, a large mesa that towers over the sagebrush bench, before dropping to cross through the pretty Black Rock Canyon. This shallow canyon winds north, and a county road runs alongside it for much of its length.

The road ends on the Butler Wash Road; entering from the west there is a good view of Comb Ridge and Butler Wash.

Decker Road winds along the crossing of the Black Rock Canyon Wash

SE #47: DECKER ROAD

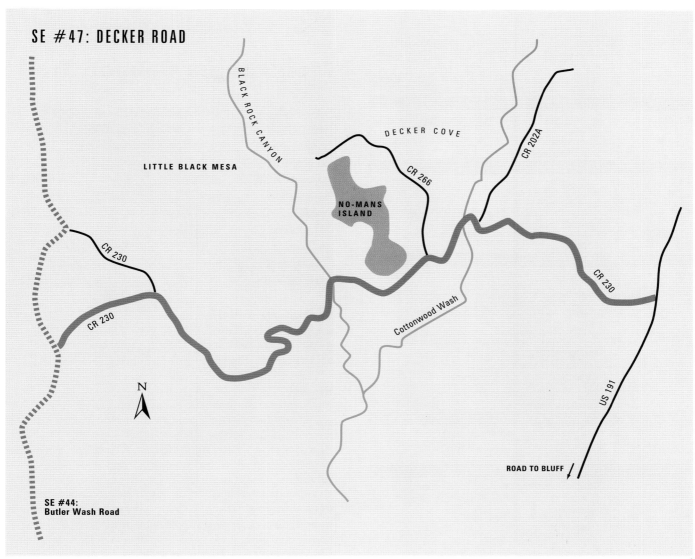

Current Road Information
BLM Monticello Field Office
435 North Main; PO Box 7
Monticello, UT 84535
(435) 587-1500

Map References
BLM   Bluff
USGS 1:24,000   No Mans Island, Bluff
          1:100,000 Bluff
Maptech CD-ROM: Moab/Canyonlands
Utah Atlas & Gazetteer, p. 22
Utah Travel Council #5

Route Directions

▼ 0.0			From US 191, opposite mile marker 33, turn southwest onto graded dirt road and cross over cattle guard. Sign for CR 230 is above cattle guard.
	2.5 ▲		Cross cattle guard, then the trail ends at the junction with US 191. Turn left for Blanding, turn right for Bluff.

			GPS: N 37°22.78' W 109°30.15'
▼ 0.8		SO	Cattle guard.
	1.7 ▲	SO	Cattle guard.
▼ 1.5		SO	Track on left.
	1.0 ▲	SO	Track on right.
			GPS: N 37°23.38' W 109°31.26'
▼ 1.8		SO	Entering private property. Remain on county road.
	0.7 ▲	SO	Leaving private property.
▼ 2.1		SO	Cabin on right.
	0.4 ▲	SO	Cabin on left.
▼ 2.2		SO	Corral on right, then cattle guard.
	0.3 ▲	SO	Cattle guard, then corral on left.
▼ 2.5		SO	Graded road on right is CR 202A. Zero trip meter.
	0.0 ▲		Continue along CR 230.
			GPS: N 37°23.53' W 109°32.23'
▼ 0.0			Continue along CR 230.
	3.8 ▲	SO	Graded road on left is CR 202A. Zero trip meter.
▼ 0.1		SO	Cross through Cottonwood Wash. Old Buick LeSabre on right before wash.

3.7 ▲	SO	Cross through Cottonwood Wash. Old Buick LeSabre on left after wash.
▼ 0.7	BR	Cattle guard, exiting private property. Faint track on left after cattle guard. No-Mans Island is directly ahead.
3.1 ▲	SO	Faint track on right, then cattle guard. Entering private property, remain on county road.

GPS: N 37°23.15' W 109°32.63'

▼ 0.9	BL	Graded road on right is CR 266, which goes to Decker Cove.
2.9 ▲	SO	Graded road on left is CR 266, which goes to Decker Cove.

GPS: N 37°23.21' W 109°32.77'

▼ 1.5	BR	Track on left.
2.3 ▲	SO	Track on right.
▼ 2.1	SO	Graded road on right goes up Black Rock Canyon.
1.7 ▲	SO	Graded road on left goes up Black Rock Canyon.

GPS: N 37°23.00' W 109°33.89'

▼ 2.4	SO	Cross through Black Rock Canyon Wash.
1.4 ▲	SO	Cross through Black Rock Canyon Wash.
▼ 2.9	SO	Cross through wash.
0.9 ▲	SO	Cross through wash. No-Mans Island is ahead.
▼ 3.1	SO	Cross through small creek, flowing from spring on right.
0.7 ▲	SO	Cross through small creek, flowing from spring on left.
▼ 3.3	SO	Cross through wash.
0.5 ▲	SO	Cross through wash.

GPS: N 37°22.43' W 109°34.66'

▼ 3.8	BR	Graded road to the left is CR 270. Zero trip meter.
0.0 ▲		Continue northeast.

GPS: N 37°22.15' W 109°34.70'

▼ 0.0		Continue southwest.
1.7 ▲	SO	Graded road to the right is CR 270. Zero trip meter.
▼ 0.4	SO	Track on left.
1.3 ▲	BL	Track on right.
▼ 0.6	SO	Cross through wash.
1.1 ▲	SO	Cross through wash.
▼ 0.8	SO	Cross through wash.
0.9 ▲	SO	Cross through wash.
▼ 1.4	SO	Track on left.
0.3 ▲	SO	Track on right.
▼ 1.6	SO	Cross through wash.
0.1 ▲	SO	Cross through wash.
▼ 1.7	TL	Turn onto unsigned graded dirt road and zero trip meter. Comb Ridge is now directly ahead.
0.0 ▲		Continue southeast along graded road.

GPS: N 37°22.91' W 109°36.08'

▼ 0.0		Continue toward Comb Ridge.
1.3 ▲	TR	T-intersection, turn right onto CR 230 (Decker Road) and zero trip meter.
▼ 1.3		Trail ends at the junction with Southeast #44: Butler Wash Road, 7.9 miles north of US 163. Turn left to exit to US 163 for Bluff or Mexican Hat. Turn right to continue along Butler Wash Road.
0.0 ▲		Trail commences on Southeast #44: Butler Wash Road, 7.9 miles north of US 163. Turn northeast onto graded dirt road, marked CR 230, and zero trip meter.

GPS: N 37°22.32' W 109°37.25'

Montezuma Canyon Trail

Starting Point:	Hatch Trading Post, junction of CR 212
	and CR 446
Finishing Point:	US 191
Total Mileage:	41.4 miles
Unpaved Mileage:	41.4 miles
Driving Time:	2.5 hours
Elevation Range:	4,700–6,900 feet
Usually Open:	Year-round
Difficulty Rating:	1
Scenic Rating:	9
Remoteness Rating:	+0

Special Attractions

■ Many small cliff dwellings and petroglyphs.
■ Ancient Anasazi ruins at Three Kiva Pueblo.
■ 11th-century Bradford Canyon Ruins.

History

The history of this trail stretches as far back as the Anasazi and extends to the uranium boom of the 1940s and 1950s. The most significant feature along the trail is possibly the Three Kiva Pueblo, 13 miles from the start. This 14-room Anasazi site experienced three building phases and three occupations between A.D. 1000 and 1300. It consists of three belowground kivas (ceremonial sites) and the remains of some aboveground stone rooms once used for living and storage areas. One area when excavated revealed a very high concentration of turkey bones, indicating that it was probably used as a turkey run, providing food and feathers for blankets.

The site is managed by the Bureau of Land Management, which has restored one of the three underground kivas. You can descend a ladder to view the kiva as it would have looked when used for the tribal ceremonies of the Anasazi. The floor of the kiva has a fire pit and a sipapu—a hole in the ground representing the opening through which the mythical tribal ancestors first emerged into the world. Benches surround the fire pit, and holes in the side allow fresh air into the chamber.

There are many small Anasazi cliff dwellings along the length of the drive. Those that are next to the trail are mentioned on the directions, but there are others to be found by

Opening of a small cliff dwelling

the keen of sight, notably near the junctions of Montezuma Creek and Monument Canyon as well as at Coal Bed Canyon, slightly off the trail.

At nearly the same time as the Anasazi, around 800 years ago, other inhabitants in the canyon constructed cliff dwellings at what is now called the Bradford Canyon Ruins, found near the junction of Bradford Creek and Montezuma Creek. These dwellings are low down on the cliff face and spread the length of a large crack in the cliff. A fence, erected in the 1960s, protects them from damage.

The Hatch Trading Post, at the southern end of the route, is an example of more recent Native American history. The trading post is one of several that came into existence between 1900 and 1930. The Shiprock Indian Agency was encouraging the development of arts, crafts, and agriculture, and the trading posts were set up to deal with the corresponding increase in two-way trade. Historically, barter has always been an important part of Native American economy, and the trading posts acted as focal points for the community as well as allowing the Ute and Navajo to trade their goods with the outside world. By the 1980s most trading posts had disappeared, as wages reduced the need for barter. Many traders were unable to compete and went out of business. Hatch, like many of the surviving trading posts, now sells mainly soft drinks and small goods to passing tourists.

The name Montezuma refers to the last Aztec ruler of Mexico, who, the story goes, escaped his captors and fled north. He supposedly eluded them for a while before being recaptured in this corner of Utah and executed. As a result, "Recapture" is a common name in this area, notably Recapture Creek and Reservoir near Blanding. There is no proof of the origin of this tale, but it makes for an unusual explanation nevertheless!

The recent history of Montezuma Creek includes some uranium mining—though a painted sign on a rock by the Utomic Corporation is pretty much the only visible remnant. The top end of the road into Montezuma Creek was built by the Civilian Conservation Corps in the late 1930s.

Description

This interest-packed route sees very few visitors. Its entire length is graded county road that poses no difficulties for passenger vehicles in dry weather. It travels mostly along the wide-bottomed floor of Montezuma Canyon; Montezuma Creek flows down the middle of it to join the San Juan River to the south. Montezuma Creek is dry for a large part of the year, but as with all creeks around this region, it has the capacity to be deep and fast flowing, and it's prone to flash floods. Extreme care should be taken if heavy rain is predicted, and if there is any doubt about the crossings, then do not cross. All of the creek crossings have a gentle approach and either a sandy or rocky bottom.

The route starts at the historic Hatch Trading Post and continues north along CR 446. There are a few tricky junctions but for the most part the major county road is correct.

The route passes through a mixture of private property and BLM land. There are some reasonable backcountry camping

Slickrock crossing of the Montezuma Creek ford

opportunities, but be sure you are not inadvertently trespassing on private property before making camp.

After 11 miles you come to the first cliff dwelling on the west side of the track. These dwellings can be difficult to spot, as they blend in so well with the surrounding cliffs. If you climb up to investigate the ruins, remember that it is illegal to remove, deface, or destroy any of the structures or artifacts within. Tread Lightly!™ The cliff dwellings along this route are for the most part very small, with only one or two rooms sandwiched into a crack in the cliff face. They are in original condition and unrenovated by the BLM.

At 13 miles, you reach the remains of the Three Kiva Pueblo on a meander in the creek. The BLM has provided a book to track visitor numbers, but there are no interpretive signs for the site.

At the northern end of the canyon there is a thriving community of market gardeners and even a vineyard. Local landowners use the natural caves in the base of the cliffs as sheds and storage areas to house a variety of things. Trailers, hay, farming equipment, and animals are all sheltered here.

The route finishes on US 191, 0.1 miles south of mile marker 67. Turn right for Monticello, left for Blanding.

Current Road Information

BLM Monticello Field Office
435 North Main; PO Box 7
Monticello, UT 84535
(435) 587-1500

Map References

BLM   Bluff, Blanding
USFS Manti-La Sal National Forest (incomplete)
USGS 1:24,000   Hatch Trading Post, Bug Canyon, Bradford Canyon, Devil Mesa, Monticello South
1:100,000 Bluff, Blanding
Maptech CD-ROM: Moab/Canyonlands
Utah Atlas & Gazetteer, p. 23
Utah Travel Council #5

Route Directions

▼ 0.0   Immediately northeast of the Hatch Trading Post at the fork in the road, zero trip meter and

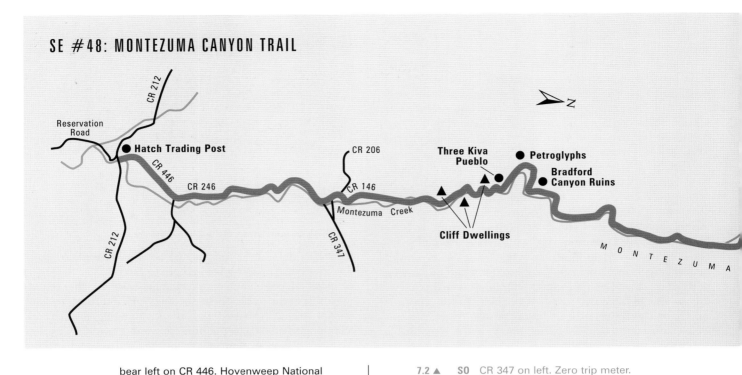

bear left on CR 446. Hovenweep National Monument is east along CR 212.

2.3 ▲   Trail ends at the Hatch Trading Post, just past the junction to Hovenweep National Monument. On CR 212, turn east to Hovenweep; straight on leads to US 191 and Blanding and Bluff.

GPS: N 37°23.51' W 109°13.55'

▼ 0.4	SO	Cattle guard.
1.9 ▲	SO	Cattle guard.
▼ 1.1	SO	Track on right.
1.2 ▲	SO	Track on left.
▼ 2.3	BL	Fork, good gravel road on right. Zero trip meter.
0.0 ▲		Continue on CR 446.

GPS: N 37°25.25' W 109°12.62'

▼ 0.0		Continue along CR 446.
6.1 ▲	SO	Good gravel road left. Zero trip meter.
▼ 0.8	SO	Cattle guard, road becomes CR 246 as the road surface deteriorates slightly.
5.3 ▲	SO	Cattle guard, road is now CR 446 as surface improves.
▼ 1.1	SO	Track on right.
5.0 ▲	SO	Track on left.
▼ 1.6	SO	CR 201A on left.
4.5 ▲	SO	CR 201A on right.
▼ 2.7	SO	Track on right.
3.4 ▲	SO	Track on left.
▼ 3.6	SO	Cattle guard.
2.5 ▲	SO	Cattle guard.
▼ 5.6	SO	Track on right.
0.5 ▲	SO	Track on left.
▼ 5.8	SO	CR 347 on right.
0.3 ▲	SO	Second turn onto CR 347 on left.

GPS: N 37°29.61' W 109°13.63'

▼ 6.1	SO	Second turn onto CR 347 on right. Zero trip meter.
0.0 ▲	SO	Continue straight.

GPS: N 37°29.77' W 109°13.87'

▼ 0.0		Continue straight ahead.

7.2 ▲	SO	CR 347 on left. Zero trip meter.
▼ 0.1	TR	Turn right onto CR 146 at gas pipeline tanks. Straight ahead is CR 206.
7.1 ▲	TL	Turn left at intersection onto CR 246 at gas pipeline tanks. Right is CR 206.
▼ 0.6	SO	Cattle guard. Road is graded dirt.
6.6 ▲	SO	Cattle guard. Road is gravel.
▼ 1.1	SO	Cattle guard.
6.1 ▲	SO	Cattle guard.
▼ 1.4	SO	Ranch sheds on left, small dam on right.
5.8 ▲	SO	Small dam on left, ranch sheds on right.
▼ 2.0	SO	Cattle guard.
5.2 ▲	SO	Cattle guard.
▼ 2.3	SO	Track on right, then cattle guard, then second track on right.
4.9 ▲	SO	Track on left, then cattle guard, then second track on left.
▼ 3.0	BL	Bear left at pipeline sheds.
4.2 ▲	SO	Track on left to pipeline sheds.
▼ 3.6	SO	Track on right, followed by track on left.
3.6 ▲	SO	Track on right, followed by track on left.
▼ 4.2	SO	Old corral on left.
3.0 ▲	SO	Old corral on right.
▼ 4.4	SO	Cross Montezuma Creek.
2.8 ▲	SO	Cross Montezuma Creek.

GPS: N 37°32.86' W 109°14.06'

▼ 4.8	SO	Immediately on left, a third of the way up the cliff is a small cliff dwelling.
2.4 ▲	SO	Immediately on right, a third of the way up the cliff is a small cliff dwelling.

GPS: N 37°33.01' W 109°14.36'

▼ 5.0	SO	Small cliff dwelling on right, halfway up cliff under overhang. On private land.
2.2 ▲	SO	Small cliff dwelling on left, halfway up cliff under overhang. On private land.

GPS: N 37°33.14' W 109°14.42'

▼ 5.1	SO	Track on right, then cattle guard.
2.1 ▲	SO	Cattle guard, then track on left.

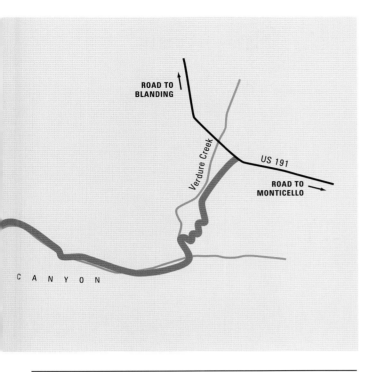

▼ 1.3		SO	Track on right.
19.7 ▲		SO	Track on left.
▼ 2.4		SO	Track on right.
18.6 ▲		SO	Track on left.
▼ 2.5		SO	CR 238A on left. Proceed straight ahead on CR 146 and cross Bradford Creek.
18.5 ▲		SO	Cross Bradford Creek, then CR 238A on right. Proceed straight ahead on CR 146.

GPS: 37°35.00' W 109°16.22'

▼ 2.6		SO	Bradford Canyon Ruins on left, protected by fence.
18.4 ▲		SO	Bradford Canyon Ruins on right, protected by fence.
▼ 3.4		SO	Remains of old mine hopper halfway up cliff on far side of creek on right.
17.6 ▲		SO	Remains of old mine hopper halfway up cliff on far side of creek on left.

GPS: N 37°35.10' W 109°15.61'

▼ 4.3		SO	Corral on left, then cattle guard.
16.7 ▲		SO	Cattle guard then, corral on right.
▼ 4.4		SO	Track on left.
16.6 ▲		SO	Track on right.
▼ 4.9		SO	Cross creek.
16.1 ▲		SO	Cross creek.
▼ 7.6		SO	Cattle guard, then private land left and right.
13.4 ▲		SO	Entering BLM land over cattle guard.
▼ 8.9		SO	Cattle guard.
12.1 ▲		SO	Cattle guard.
▼ 9.3		SO	Log cabin on left, then cattle guard.
11.7 ▲		SO	Cattle guard, then log cabin on right.
▼ 10.4		SO	Track on left and right. Road is now gravel.
10.6 ▲		SO	Track on left and right. Road is now graded dirt.
▼ 10.8		SO	Track on left to private property.
10.2 ▲		SO	Track on right to private property.
▼ 10.9		SO	Cattle guard.
10.1 ▲		SO	Cattle guard.
▼ 11.1		SO	Track on left. Canyon becomes narrower and steeper.
9.9 ▲		SO	Track on right. Canyon opens out.

GPS: N 37°39.80' W 109°14.91'

▼ 12.4		SO	Cattle guard.
8.6 ▲		SO	Cattle guard.
▼ 14.2		SO	Cattle guard, then grapevines on right.
6.8 ▲		SO	Cattle guard.
▼ 14.4		SO	Track on right.
6.6 ▲		SO	Track on left.
▼ 14.9		SO	Bridge.
6.1 ▲		SO	Bridge.
▼ 15.9		SO	Cattle guard.
5.1 ▲		SO	Cattle guard.
▼ 16.7		SO	Cattle guard.
4.3 ▲		SO	Cattle guard.
▼ 21.0		SO	Bridge. Leaving Montezuma Creek. Zero trip meter.
0.0 ▲			Continue along valley floor with Montezuma Creek on left.

GPS: N 37°46.92' W 109°16.52'

▼ 0.0			Climb out of valley with Verdure Creek on left.
4.8 ▲		SO	Bridge. Leaving Verdure Creek to run south along Montezuma Creek. Zero trip meter.
▼ 4.4		SO	Cattle guard, then road on right.
0.4 ▲		BR	Fork, then cross cattle guard on right-hand road.

GPS: N 37°47.59' W 109°20.19'

▼ 5.6		SO	Old painted sign on rock on right—Buckhorn Mine.
1.6 ▲		SO	Old painted sign on rock on left (look back slightly)—Buckhorn Mine
▼ 6.0		SO	Faint track on right up Tank Canyon.
1.2 ▲		SO	Faint track on left up Tank Canyon.
▼ 6.5		BR	Private track on left to pipeline works.
0.7 ▲		SO	Private track on right to pipeline works.
▼ 7.2		SO	Three Kiva Pueblo on left with small parking area. Zero trip meter.
0.0 ▲			Continue south on CR 146.

GPS: N 37°33.91' W 109°15.09'

▼ 0.0			Continue north on CR 146.
21.0 ▲		SO	Three Kiva Pueblo on right with small parking area. Zero trip meter.
▼ 0.5		SO	Track on right to campsite, then cross Montezuma Creek on rocky ford. Low-clearance vehicles beware of rock holes slightly on left of midline, bear slightly right.
20.5 ▲		SO	Cross Montezuma Creek on rocky ford. Low-clearance vehicles beware of rock holes slightly on right of midline, bear slightly left. Track on left to campsite after ford.
▼ 0.6		TL	Immediately after creek, turn left on small sandy track.
20.4 ▲		TR	Rejoin main track.
▼ 0.7		TR	Turn right before corral onto small sandy track. Small cliff dwelling immediately on left.
20.3 ▲		TL	Small cliff dwelling immediately on right before turn. Corral on right at turn.

GPS: N 37°34.23' W 109°15.31'

▼ 0.8		SO	Track on left.
20.2 ▲		SO	Track on right.
▼ 0.9		TL	Rejoin main track.
20.1 ▲		TR	Turn right onto small sandy track.
▼ 1.1		SO	Petroglyphs immediately beside track on left; look hard!
19.9 ▲		SO	Petroglyphs immediately beside track on right; look hard!

GPS: N 37°34.49' W 109°15.37'

▼ 4.8	Trail ends at intersefction with US 191. Turn right for Monticello, left for Blanding.
0.0 ▲	Begin trail at junction of US 191 and Montezuma Creek Road (CR 146), 0.1 miles south of mile marker 67. Turn southeast on Montezuma Creek Road and zero trip meter.

GPS: N 37°47.99' W 109°20.26'

SOUTHEAST REGION TRAIL #49

Hurrah Pass Trail

Starting Point:	**Junction of Main Street and Kane Creek Boulevard, Moab**
Finishing Point:	**Hurrah Pass**
Total Mileage:	**13.9 miles**
Unpaved Mileage:	**9.3 miles**
Driving Time:	**1 hour (one-way)**
Elevation	**3,900–4,780 feet**
Usually Open:	**Year-round**
Difficulty Rating:	**1 to Kane Creek Ford, 2 to Hurrah Pass**
Scenic Rating:	**9**
Remoteness Rating:	**+0**

Special Attractions
■ Ancient petroglyphs in Moonflower Canyon.
■ Colorado River access and views of the vista from Hurrah Pass.
■ Camping in Kane Springs Canyon.

History
Kane Springs Canyon has several rock art sites along its length. The easiest to find is the roadside cliff gallery at Moonflower Canyon, 2.9 miles from the start of the trail. The site is a panel of rock carvings of animals (plus a Barrier Canyon style figure) etched by ancient tribes into the sandstone cliffs. An interpretive sign at the site outlines the meaning of the most prominent figures. To the left of the panel are logs jammed in an apparently haphazard fashion into a large crack; these served as a ladder

Looking toward Hurrah Pass from an upper section of the track

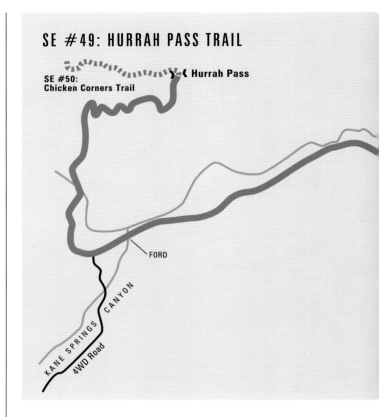

so the artists could access the higher portions of the cliff face. Unfortunately, this site has been vandalized in the past by graffiti and illegal moldings of the carvings.

Approximately 1.7 miles after the trail leaves the Colorado River, and some 80 feet below the trail, is Birthing Rock. This large boulder is covered with depictions of animals, stylized human figures, and a birth scene.

More recent history can be seen along this trail in the form of mining remains. The Climax and Climota uranium mines are set in the sheer-walled Kane Springs Canyon.

Kane Springs, to the southwest at the headwaters of Kane Creek, was a valuable watering place along the Old Spanish Trail, a trade route between New Mexico and present-day Los Angeles. This annual caravan of 200 horsemen crossed the Colorado River approximately 1.5 miles upstream from Moonflower Canyon. The timing of their trip was crucial—they had to leave Santa Fe in October before heavy rains made travel impossible, and the return trip had to depart California in April before the river fords were impassable following the spring snowmelt.

Since the 1940s, the Moab region has been featured in many movies and TV specials. In 1950, *Rio Grande*, starring John Wayne, was set in this region. Columbia Picture's 1983 movie *Spacehunter—Adventures in the Forbidden Zone* was partially filmed at Kane Creek. The 1997 film *The Perfect Getaway* included scenes at Hurrah Pass, and a 1998 SUV commercial depicts a vehicle riding along a subway, past "Moab Station" and emerging on the eastern side of Hurrah Pass.

Description
This trail, beginning in the center of Moab, is an excellent introduction to canyon country. It has a little bit of every-

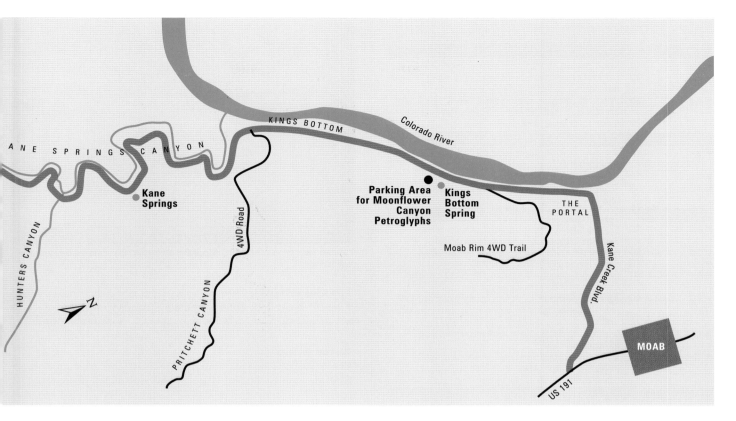

thing—stunning views in the canyon and from the plateau and the pass, ancient petroglyphs, the Colorado River, and access to hiking and 4WD trails.

The pavement road enters Kane Springs Canyon through The Portal, a gap in the Moab Rim, and it winds alongside the Colorado River through the canyon. The high Wingate sandstone walls are very popular with rock climbers. Camping in the Colorado Riverway area is restricted to designated sites, but there are plenty to choose from (a fee is charged).

From Moab, switchbacks descend toward Kane Creek

This trail is passable to passenger vehicles as far as Kane Creek ford in dry conditions. The ford is impassable at high water. Under normal conditions it is only a couple of inches deep, but it can change after a thunderstorm very quickly. Do not enter the ford if the water is deep or fast flowing. From the ford, the trail becomes rougher and a high-clearance vehicle is preferred. It winds underneath the Anticline Overlook to finish at Hurrah Pass (4,780 feet). From Hurrah Pass, there are views over the Colorado River to the potash evaporation ponds on the far side, Chimney Rock, and back down Kane Springs Canyon. Southeast #50: Chicken Corners Trail continues from this point.

Current Road Information

BLM Moab Field Office
82 East Dogwood
Moab, UT 84532
(435) 259-2100

Map References

BLM Moab, La Sal
USFS Manti-La Sal National Forest
USGS 1:24,000 Moab, Trough Springs Canyon
1:100,000 Moab, La Sal
Maptech CD-ROM: Moab/Canyonlands
Trails Illustrated, #501
Utah Atlas & Gazetteer, p. 30
Utah Travel Council #5 (incomplete)
Other: Latitude 40—Moab West
Canyon Country Off-Road Vehicle Trail Map—
Canyon Rims & Needles Areas

Route Directions

▼ 0.0		From Main Street in Moab, turn northwest onto Kane Creek Boulevard.
		GPS: N 38°33.83' W 109°32.94'
▼ 0.7	BL	Follow Kane Creek Boulevard, 500W road on right.
▼ 1.6	SO	Road follows Colorado River through The Portal into Kane Springs Canyon. Enter Colorado Riverway Recreation Area. Camping in designated sites only (fee area).
▼ 2.5	SO	Moab Rim, an extreme Jeep trail on left.
		GPS: N 38°33.54' W 109°34.94'
▼ 2.7	SO	Kings Bottom Recreation Site on right.

▼ 2.9	SO	Moonflower Canyon Petroglyphs, parking area on left.

GPS: N 38°33.24' W 109°35.20'

▼ 3.3	SO	Road on left.
▼ 3.6	SO	Dugouts used as work sheds in base of cliff on left.
▼ 4.3	SO	Pritchett Canyon, an extreme Jeep trail, leads off through campground on left. Pavement turns to graded dirt road.

GPS: N 38°33.24' W 109°35.20'

▼ 4.4	SO	Cattle guard. Road climbs away from Colorado River.
▼ 4.8	SO	Popular rock climbing area on left.
▼ 5.5	SO	Track on right is Amasa Back 4WD and mountain bike trail.

GPS: N 38°31.46' W 109°36.06'

▼ 6.5	SO	Spring Site Recreation Area on right. Kane Springs comes out of rock face on left.
▼ 7.4	SO	Hunters Canyon on left, walk-in camping.
▼ 7.6	SO	Echo Recreation Site on right.
▼ 8.1	SO	Leaving Colorado Riverway Recreation Area. Leave narrow part of canyon.
▼ 9.7	SO	As road passes through a rocky outcrop, look left to see remains of a mine high on canyon walls.
▼ 10.2	SO	Numerous tracks right and left, mainly to campsites.
▼ 10.5	SO	Kane Creek ford. Impassable in high water. Zero trip meter. After ford, this becomes a 2-rated track.

GPS: N 38°28.25' W 109°36.09'

▼ 0.0		Leave Kane Creek ford.
▼ 0.1	SO	Track on left to campsite.
▼ 0.4	SO	Track on left to campsite.
▼ 0.5	SO	Track on left, Kane Springs Canyon, difficult Jeep trail.
▼ 0.7	SO	Track on left.
▼ 1.8	SO	Road is smoother and wider.
▼ 2.6	SO	Track on right to overlook over Kane Springs Canyon.
▼ 3.2	SO	Track on right to overlook.
▼ 3.3	SO	Cattle guard.
▼ 3.4		Trail ends at Hurrah Pass, elevation 4,780 feet. Continue to Southeast #50: Chicken Corners Trail, or retrace your steps back to Moab.

GPS: N 38°28.92' W 109°37.46'

SOUTHEAST REGION TRAIL #50

Chicken Corners Trail

Starting Point:	**Hurrah Pass**
Finishing Point:	**Chicken Corners**
Total Mileage:	**11.2 miles**
Unpaved Mileage:	**11.2 miles**
Driving Time:	**2 hours (one-way)**
Elevation Range:	**3,700–4,780 feet**
Usually Open:	**Year-round**
Difficulty Rating:	**4**
Scenic Rating:	**10**
Remoteness Rating:	**+0**

Driving past the Chicken Rocks as the Colorado River flows through the valley below

Special Attractions
- Far-reaching views of Canyonlands area.
- Views of the Colorado River and potash evaporation ponds.

Description
The very popular spur trail to Chicken Corners continues from the top of Hurrah Pass, at the end of Southeast #49: Hurrah Pass Trail. It gradually descends along a rough shelf road, wrapping around gullies etched in the bluff to level off above the Colorado River. It winds along the river, at times coming very close to the edge. It continues on sandy tracks to the start of the Lockhart Basin Trail after 6.7 miles. Lockhart Basin trail takes two days to complete and has a very difficult, potentially vehicle-damaging section at its northernmost end. Route finding on the plateau above the Colorado River can be difficult in places as trails go off in all directions, but most of them either dead-end or rejoin the main trail later.

The trail wraps around the Chicken Rocks, at a point overlooking the Colorado River, and comes to a dead end a mile later. The trail used to continue on as a horse trail, but it would be a brave horse or foolhardy person who would continue around the outcrop on the old trail. Dead Horse Point State Park is almost directly opposite.

The name "Chicken Corners" comes from the local guides

The Colorado River slowly drifts past the end of the trail

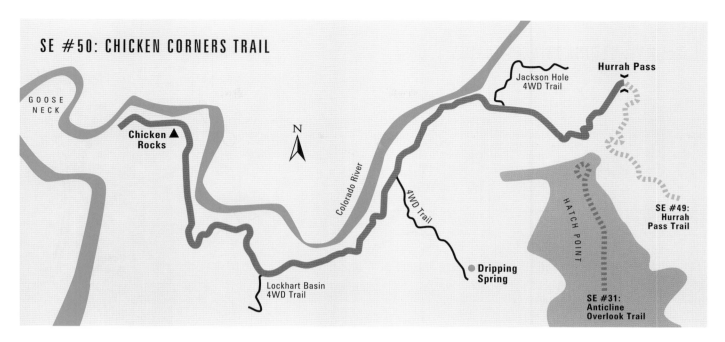

SE #50: CHICKEN CORNERS TRAIL

GOOSE NECK

Chicken ▲ Rocks

N

Colorado River

Jackson Hole 4WD Trail

Hurrah Pass

4WD Trail

HATCH POINT

SE #49: Hurrah Pass Trail

Dripping Spring

Lockhart Basin 4WD Trail

SE #31: Anticline Overlook Trail

who used to let the nervous passengers walk rather than ride the narrow trail around these rocks.

Current Road Information

BLM Moab Field Office
82 East Dogwood
Moab, UT 84532
(435) 259-2100

Map References

BLM   La Sal
USGS 1:24,000   Trough Springs Canyon, Shafer Basin
          1:100,000 La Sal
Maptech CD-ROM: Moab/Canyonlands
Trails Illustrated, #501
Utah Atlas & Gazetteer, p. 30
Utah Travel Council #5 (incomplete)
Other: Latitude 40—Moab West
       Canyon Country Off-Road Vehicle Trail Map—
       Canyon Rims & Needles Areas

Route Directions

▼ 0.0		Trail commences at the top of Hurrah Pass (4,780 feet) marked by a BLM sign, at the end of Southeast #49: Hurrah Pass Trail. Zero trip meter, bear left, proceed southwest over the pass, and continue down the shelf road.
	GPS: N 38°28.94' W 109°37.48'	
▼ 1.5	SO	Trail leaves the cliff edge and descends across plateau to Colorado River. Chimney Rock is directly ahead on the far side of the river.
▼ 2.4	SO	Track on right is Jackson Hole trail.
	GPS: N 38°28.29' W 109°38.95'	
▼ 2.5	BR	Leave creek wash and bear right up hill.
	GPS: N 38°28.22' W 109°39.08'	
▼ 2.7	SO	Colorado River overlook on right. Trail runs along edge of rim over river.

▼ 3.8	TR	Trail runs along wash. Track on left up wash.
▼ 4.1	SO	Track on left.
▼ 4.3	SO	Track on left to Dripping Spring. Sign to Lockhart Basin straight on.
	GPS: N 38°27.21' W 109°40.08'	
▼ 4.9	SO	Cross wash.
▼ 5.4	SO	Cross wash.
▼ 6.7	SO	Track on left down wash, sign to Lockhart Basin.
	GPS: N 38°25.76' W 109°41.34'	
▼ 9.7	BL	Trail passes around Chicken Rocks above the Colorado River.
	GPS: N 38°27.02' W 109°42.91'	
▼ 11.2		Trail ends, old horse trail continues, but unsafe for foot travel. Views north toward Dead Horse Point and the Goose Neck in the Colorado River.
	GPS: N 38°26.47' W 109°44.14'	

SOUTHEAST REGION TRAIL #51

Gemini Bridges Trail

Starting Point:	**US 191 and Gemini Bridges turnoff, north of Moab**
Finishing Point:	**Utah 313 and Gemini Bridges turnoff, north of Island in the Sky Visitors Center**
Total Mileage:	**12.7 miles**
Unpaved Mileage:	**12.7 miles**
Driving Time:	**2.5 hours**
Elevation Range:	**4,600–5,900 feet**
Usually Open:	**Year-round**
Difficulty Rating:	**5**
Scenic Rating:	**9**
Remoteness Rating:	**+0**

SE #51: GEMINI BRIDGES TRAIL

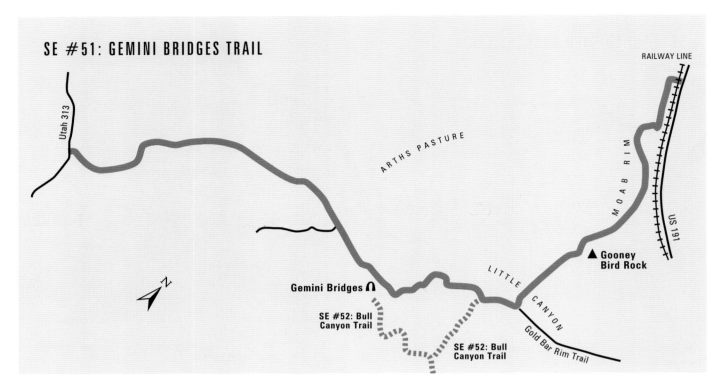

Special Attractions

■ Gemini Bridges double arch.
■ Moderately challenging 4WD trail in stunning desert scenery.
■ Connects with Southeast #52: Bull Canyon Trail.

Description

Gemini Bridges is a wonderful trail for a novice four-wheeler wanting a bit more of a challenge, yet not wanting to risk vehicle damage. The entire length of the trail is incredibly scenic, with red rock formations, sandstone cliffs, far-ranging views over to the La Sal Mountains, and the highlight of the trail, the twin arch of Gemini Bridges.

The trail leaves US 191 and winds along the northern end of the Moab Rim. Looking east you can see Arches National Park; on a clear day Balanced Rock is visible. The graded shelf road winds around through the gap into Little Canyon, crossing and recrossing a small creek as the canyon narrows. At the 4-mile mark, you pass by the aptly named Gooney Bird Rock immediately on your left.

Gooney Bird Rock overlooks the Gemini Bridges Trail

After passing the turnoffs for the difficult Gold Bar Rim Trail (not covered in this guide) and Southeast #52: Bull Canyon Trail, the trail becomes more challenging and earns its 5 rating. It travels over slickrock pavements and rocky ledges interspersed with sandy sections. A couple of sections call for careful wheel placement, but all high-clearance 4WDs should handle this with ease. It may be impassable following light snow or heavy rain.

After 7.3 miles, you come to the small parking area for Gemini Bridges. A short walk takes you out to the bridges; look down to see the 4WD trail in Bull Canyon far below.

From the bridges, the trail winds across the southernmost end of Arths Pasture. To the north is a flat sagebrush plain; to the south, the depression of Crips Hole. There are many short tracks leading to some good backcountry camping and viewpoints of Bull Canyon to the south and Monitor and Merrimac Buttes to the north.

The trail ends on Utah 313, a few miles north of the Island in the Sky Visitor Center.

Current Road Information

BLM Moab Field Office
82 East Dogwood
Moab, UT 84532
(435) 259-2100

Map References

BLM Moab
USGS 1:24,000 Merrimac Butte, Gold Bar Canyon, The Knoll
1:100,000 Moab
Maptech CD-ROM: Moab/Canyonlands

Trails Illustrated, #211; #501
Utah Atlas & Gazetteer, pp. 30, 40
Utah Travel Council #5
Other: Latitude 40—Moab West
     Canyon Country Off-Road Vehicle Trail Map—Is
     land Area

Route Directions

▼ 0.0			Turn west off US 191 onto Gemini Bridges Trail, 9.8 miles north of Moab. Cross a cattle guard, then the railroad tracks.
	5.1 ▲		Cross railroad tracks, then a cattle guard; the trail ends at US 191. Moab is 9.8 miles south.
		GPS: N 38°39.36′ W 109°40.58′	
▼ 1.2		SO	Trail climbs the face of Moab Rim.
	3.9 ▲	SO	Bottom of descent.
▼ 2.1		SO	Trail descends through gap into Little Canyon.
	3.0 ▲	SO	Trail ascends through the gap to run across face of Moab Rim.
▼ 2.5		BR	Track on left.
	2.6 ▲	BL	Track on right.
		GPS: N 38°37.69′ W 109°39.91′	
▼ 2.7		SO	Track on left.
	2.4 ▲	SO	Track on right.
▼ 2.8		SO	Track on left.
	2.3 ▲	SO	Track on right.
▼ 3.8		SO	Track on left.
	1.3 ▲	SO	Track on right.
▼ 4.0		SO	Gooney Bird Rock on immediate left at wash.
	1.1 ▲	SO	Gooney Bird Rock on immediate right at wash.
▼ 4.6		TR	Track on right, followed by T-intersection. Sign, Gemini Bridges on right, Gold Bar Rim on left.
	0.5 ▲	TL	Sign, US 191 left, Gold Bar Rim straight on. Followed by second track on left.
		GPS: N 38°36.02′ W 109°40.37′	
▼ 4.7		SO	Cattle guard.
	0.4 ▲	SO	Cattle guard.
▼ 5.0		SO	Track on left at crest.
	0.1 ▲	SO	Track on right at crest.
▼ 5.1		BR	Sign, Gemini Bridges on right, Southeast #52: Bull Canyon Trail on left.
	0.0 ▲		Continue west.
		GPS: N 38°35.80′ W 109°40.83′	
▼ 0.0			Continue northeast.
	2.2 ▲	SO	Sign, US 191 straight ahead, Southeast #52: Bull Canyon Trail on right.
▼ 0.2		SO	Faint track on right.
	2.0 ▲	SO	Faint track on left.
▼ 0.8		BL	Fork. Sign, Gemini Bridges on left. Trail travels over slickrock.
	1.4 ▲	SO	Track on left.
		GPS: N 38°35.78′ W 109°41.59′	
▼ 1.6		SO	Track on left.
	0.6 ▲	SO	Track on right.
▼ 2.0		TL	Sign, Gemini Bridges on left, followed by campsite.
	0.2 ▲	TR	Campsite, then turn right.
▼ 2.2		SO	Gemini Bridges parking area. Short walk to bridges. Zero trip meter.
	0.0 ▲		Turn east out of parking area; follow signs for US 191.
		GPS: N 38°35.33′ W 109°42.57′	
▼ 0.0			Turn north out of parking area; follow sign for Utah 313.
	5.4 ▲	SO	Gemini Bridges parking area. Short walk to bridges. Zero trip meter.
▼ 0.1		TL	T-intersection, immediately followed by track on right.
	5.3 ▲	TR	Track on left, then turn right.
▼ 0.9		TR	Four Arch Trail on left. Follow route marker and bear left; tracks on right are detour around rocky section.
	4.5 ▲	TL	Tracks on left are detour around rocky section, then turn left, Four Arch Trail is on right.
		GPS: N 38°35.51′ W 109°43.43′	
▼ 1.3		SO	Track on left.
	4.1 ▲	SO	Track on right.
▼ 1.6		TL	Intersection.
	3.8 ▲	TR	Intersection, follow sign for Gemini Bridges.
		GPS: N 38°35.75′ W 109°44.11′	
▼ 1.8		SO	Track on right. Graded road starts. Numerous side tracks between here and the highway lead to viewpoints and camping areas.
	3.6 ▲	SO	Track on left, trail becomes packed dirt.
▼ 5.4			Trail ends at intersection with Utah 313. Turn left for Island in the Sky Visitor Center, right for Moab.
	0.0 ▲		Trail starts on Utah 313, north of the Island in the Sky Visitor Center. Zero trip meter and turn east on graded dirt road at the sign for Gemini Bridges. For the first 3.6 miles numerous side tracks lead to viewpoints and camping areas.
		GPS: N 38°34.39′ W 109°47.52′	

SOUTHEAST REGION TRAIL #52

Bull Canyon Trail

Starting Point:	5.1 miles along Southeast #51: Gemini
	Bridges Trail
Finishing Point:	Bull Canyon
Total Mileage:	5.4 miles
Unpaved Mileage:	5.4 miles
Elevation Range:	4,600–5,000 feet
Driving Time:	2.5 hours (both canyons)
Usually Open:	Year-round
Difficulty Rating:	4 (Bull Canyon), 3 (Dry Fork Bull Canyon)
Scenic Rating:	8
Remoteness Rating:	+0

Special Attractions

■ Different perspective of the canyon country.
■ Unusual view of Gemini Bridges.
■ Towering red canyon walls and scenery.

Description

These two interesting side trips make a wonderful addition to Southeast #51: Gemini Bridges Trail. They add an enjoyable perspective of the canyons that few people see. They are generally much quieter than the popular Gemini Bridges Trail along the canyon rim.

SE #52: BULL CANYON TRAIL

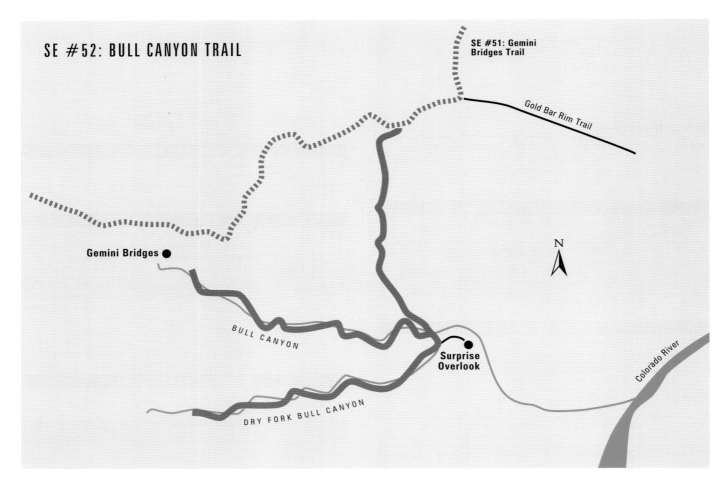

Bull Canyon dips down into a tight wash and twists between large boulders. It is wide enough for a full-size SUV, but this can be more difficult following heavy rain. The scenic route along the canyon floor, between towering red cliffs of Wingate sandstone, finishes directly below the twin arches of Gemini Bridges. In ranching days, Bull Canyon had a series of steps cut into the rock from the canyon rim to the floor, which allowed stock to descend precariously into the canyon to drink from a spring. Both trails follow a creek wash, dipping down to ride in the creek bed on occasion.

Dry Fork Bull Canyon twists through a narrow wash before opening out into a wider canyon with equally stunning scenery. An observant eye will spot the overgrown tailings piles left over from old mine workings—the reason for the existence of the trail. Though Dry Fork Bull Canyon continues for another 1.5 miles, it becomes very difficult to drive—beyond the difficulty rating of this guide—and is not suitable for large unmodified vehicles; it is extremely tight with large boulders and deep washouts making underbody damage likely.

An additional bonus is a short 0.2-mile spur trail in Dry Fork Bull Canyon that travels to Surprise Overlook. A short scramble up a sand dune reveals a panoramic vista: you can see into Day Canyon and over the rims to the La Sal Mountains.

Current Road Information

BLM Moab Field Office
82 East Dogwood
Moab, UT 84532
(435) 259-2100

Looking back down Bull Canyon from the end of the trail

Map References
BLM Moab
USGS 1:24,000 Gold Bar Canyon
1:100,000 Moab
Maptech CD-ROM: Moab/Canyonlands
Trails Illustrated, #211; #501
Utah Atlas & Gazetteer, p. 30
Other: Latitude 40—Moab West
Canyon Country Off-Road Vehicle Trail Map—
Island Area

Route Directions

▼ 0.0		5.1 miles from the east end of Southeast #51: Gemini Bridges Trail, zero trip meter and turn southwest onto graded dirt road, following sign to Bull Canyon.

GPS: N 38°35.80' W 109°40.82'

▼ 1.0	SO	Track on left. Small campsite on first bend.
▼ 1.3	SO	Cattle guard.
▼ 1.5	SO	Junction of Bull Canyon and Dry Fork Bull Canyon trails. Zero trip meter. Bear right to Bull Canyon, left to Dry Fork Bull Canyon.

GPS: N 38°34.69' W 109°40.62'

Bull Canyon

▼ 0.0		Bear right at intersection and descend down to sandy/stony wash.

GPS: N 38°34.69' W 109°40.62'

▼ 1.0	BR	Fork, continue along in wash.
▼ 1.5	SO	Track on left.
▼ 1.9	UT	Track on left. End of recommended vehicle trail. Park here and walk 300 yards to the base of Gemini Bridges on the left. To the right is an arch in the making—high on the cliff face. Vehicle tracks ahead and left are difficult to follow; there is risk of vehicle and environmental damage.

GPS: N 38°35.01' W 109°42.21'

Return to the junction of trails to Bull Canyon and Dry Fork Bull Canyon and zero your trip meter.

Dry Fork Bull Canyon

▼ 0.0		From junction of Bull Canyon and Dry Fork Bull Canyon trails, continue to the southeast.

GPS: N 38°34.69' W 109°40.62'

▼ 0.1	TR	Climb up rise out of creekbed. Left-hand trail goes 0.2 miles to Surprise Overlook.
▼ 0.6	SO	Small arch on right just after right-hand bend. Enter wash.
▼ 1.2	SO	Canyon opens out.
▼ 1.3	SO	Old stock tank on right.
▼ 1.5	SO	Dip down to cross creek, then look for small fragile arch high on sandstone column on right.
▼ 1.9	SO	Track on left.
▼ 2.0	UT	Old mining track on right, dried up dam on left. End of recommended vehicle trail. Ahead it is more difficult than our trail rating indicates and is not suitable for large unmodified vehicles. It is extremely tight with large boulders and deep washouts making underbody damage likely. You can hike another 1.5 miles to the trail end.

GPS: N 38°34.25' W 109°42.08'

Castleton-Gateway Road

Starting Point:	**Colorado 141, south of Gateway, Colorado**
Finishing Point:	**La Sal Mountain Road (FR 062), Utah**
Total Mileage:	**27.1 miles**
Unpaved Mileage:	**21.1 miles**
Driving Time:	**2 hours**
Elevation Range:	**5,000–8,500 feet**
Usually Open:	**Early June to Late October**
Difficulty Rating:	**2**
Scenic Rating:	**8**
Remoteness Rating:	**+0**

Special Attractions

- Spectacular canyon scenery around Gateway.
- Interstate trail providing alternative access to slickrock country.
- Far-ranging views across Beaver Creek and Fisher Valley in Utah.

History

The tiny settlement of Gateway, Colorado, lies along a route used by the Ute to reach the Uncompahgre Plateau, named after one of their chiefs. Gateway, set on the Dolores River, is a natural amphitheater. Overshadowed to the north by the Palisade, a gigantic sandstone monolith over 2,000 feet high, Gateway is surrounded by towering red sandstone buttes.

During the 1870s, gold was discovered in the beds of the Dolores and San Miguel Rivers. The gold boom didn't last long, and cattle ranching took over the valley's economy. The Washington Treaty signed in 1880 removed the Ute from the region by the following year, which was then settled by pioneers eager to claim their new ranches. Inevitably, with cattle ranching there were cattle rustlers. Sewemup Mesa to the south of John Brown Canyon is named after a band of rustlers that would cut the

Looking back down John Brown Canyon toward Gateway, Colorado

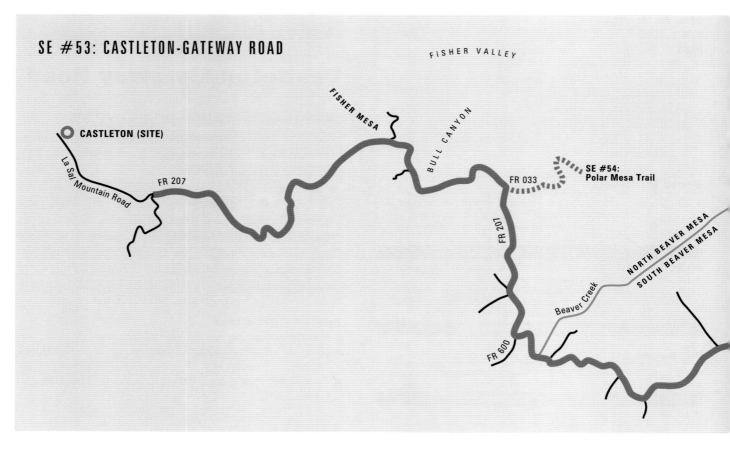

brands off the hide of the stolen cattle, sew 'em up again, and rebrand them with its own insignia.

Mining once again became the focus of the economy with the uranium boom in the 1950s. Carnotite, vanadium, and uranium ore were all mined around the Gateway and John Brown Canyon area.

At the western end of the route, in Utah, the trail wraps around the southern end of Castle Valley. The settlement of Castleton, named after the massive castlelike rock formation nearby, has today all but vanished. A supply town, built in the early 1890s, it had a hotel, saloons, a sheriff, a school, and stores. In its heyday, it competed with Moab to supply the mining camps and ranches in the area.

Today the Castleton-Gateway region is heavily used by recreationalists. A hut-to-hut mountain bike route from Telluride to Moab passes through here, rock climbers scale the sandstone towers in Castle Valley, and 4WD vehicles explore the many trails in the region.

Description
If you're driving from Colorado to Moab, this road provides an excellent scenic alternative to I-70. The route starts at Gateway, a small settlement set in a valley on the Dolores River, and follows the well-marked John Brown Canyon just south of town on Colorado 141. The road is subject to frequent washouts after heavy rain and can be rough. The surface is roughly graded packed dirt, with a high rock content. It switchbacks alongside the creek for the first few miles and then levels out on top of the mesa. Just before the Colorado-

Utah state line, a sign warns of the dangers of abandoned uranium mines. The state line is marked by an unofficial sign on a gatepost.

Once in Utah, the track quality drops as the trail undulates across open pasture into the La Sal Mountain State Forest. After heavy rain, this section becomes very difficult, turning into sloppy mud. The La Sal Mountain State Forest is used for cattle grazing in summer. There are some nice backcountry camping areas along this section, but there are sites with more spectacular views farther along near Castle Valley.

The vegetation ranges from sagebrush, prickly pear, small oaks, and pinyon pine in John Brown Canyon to stands of pine, rolling sagebrush, and the occasional stand of aspen on the plateau.

As the track continues, the views become more spectacular. First there are North and South Beaver Mesas and then, in the lower trail sections, the wide, red Fisher Valley, surrounded by towering sandstone cliffs, buttes, and outcrops. A couple of forest camping areas are along this stretch, plus many spur trails leading to quiet camping areas with great views. The route ends at the junction with La Sal Mountain Road (FR 062), 30 miles from Moab.

Current Road Information
BLM Moab Field Office
82 East Dogwood
Moab, UT 84532
(435) 259-2100

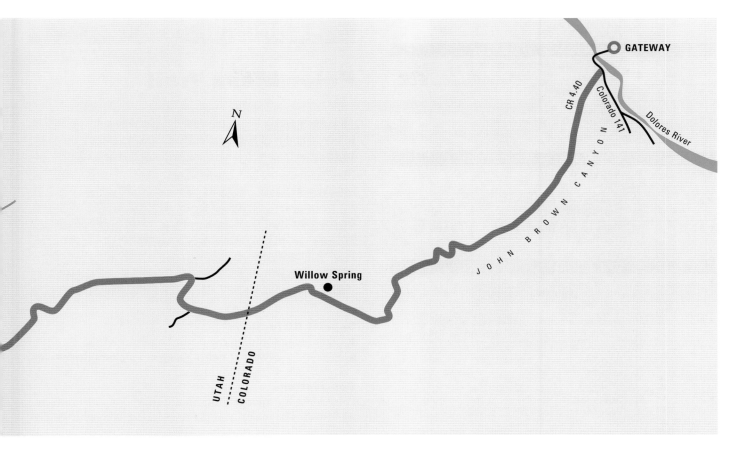

Manti-La Sal National Forest
Moab Ranger District
125 West 200 South
Moab, UT 84532
(435) 259-7155

Map References

BLM   Delta, CO; Moab, UT
USFS Manti-La Sal National Forest
USGS 1:24,000 Gateway, CO; Dolores Point North, CO;
          Dolores Point South, CO & UT; Mt. Waas, UT;
          Warner Lake, UT
          1:100,000 Delta, CO; Moab, UT
Maptech CD-ROM: Grand Junction/Western Slope, CO;
          Moab/Canyonlands, UT
Utah Atlas & Gazetteer, pp. 31, 41
Utah Travel Council #5 (incomplete)
Other: Latitude 40—Moab East

Route Directions

▼ 0.0   At the intersection of Colorado 141 and CR 4.40 (John Brown Canyon), south of Gateway and the Dolores River crossing, zero trip meter and turn west up CR 4.40.
    8.1 ▲   Route finishes at the intersection of Highway 141 and CR 4.40. Turn left for Gateway.

GPS: N 38°40.61' W 108°58.62'

▼ 0.5   **SO** Cattle guard, road turns to graded dirt. No winter maintenance from December to June from this point.

    7.6 ▲   **SO** Cattle guard, road turns to pavement.

▼ 5.1   **SO** Mine on right, on far side of canyon.
    3.0 ▲   **SO** Mine on left, on far side of canyon.

▼ 5.7   **SO** Track on left, CR Z2.40, unmarked.
    2.4 ▲   **SO** Track on right, CR Z2.40, unmarked.

GPS: N 38°36.84' W 109°01.24'

▼ 5.9   **SO** Track on left.
    2.2 ▲   **SO** Track on right.

▼ 6.6   **SO** Willow Spring on right.
    1.5 ▲   **SO** Willow Spring on left.

▼ 7.1   **BL** Track on right.
    1.0 ▲   **BR** Track on left.

▼ 8.1   **SO** Colorado-Utah state line at cattle guard. Zero trip meter.
    0.0 ▲   Continue into Colorado.

GPS: N 38°36.57' W 109°03.60'

▼ 0.0   Continue into Utah.
    9.2 ▲   **SO** Colorado-Utah state line at cattle guard. Zero trip meter.

▼ 0.8   **SO** Track on left into private property.
    8.4 ▲   **SO** Track on right into private property.

▼ 1.4   **BL** Track on right.
    7.8 ▲   **BR** Track on left.

▼ 4.1   **SO** Faint track on left.
    5.1 ▲   **SO** Faint track on right.

▼ 4.3   **SO** Track on right at small clearing.
    4.9 ▲   **SO** Track on left at small clearing.

▼ 4.7   **SO** Cattle guard.
    4.5 ▲   **SO** Cattle guard.

▼ 5.4   **SO** Entering La Sal Mountain State Forest. Road on left is Taylor Flat Road. View ahead to Mount Waas.

3.8 ▲	SO	Leaving La Sal Mountain State Forest. Road on right is Taylor Flat Road.	

GPS: N 38°34.00′ W 109°07.96′

▼ 5.7	SO	Cattle guard, old corral on left.
3.5 ▲	SO	Cattle guard, old corral on right.
▼ 6.5	SO	Track on left.
2.7 ▲	SO	Track on right.
▼ 7.0	SO	Track on left to 5 Bar A Ranch.
2.2 ▲	SO	Track on right to 5 Bar A Ranch, Gateway and Kirks Basin are signed straight on.

GPS: N 38°34.64′ W 109°09.20′

▼ 8.5	SO	Track on right.
0.7 ▲	SO	Track on left.
▼ 8.8	SO	Enter private property over cattle guard.
0.4 ▲	SO	Leave private property over cattle guard.
▼ 9.2	BR	Track on left, Beaver Basin trail, FR 600. Zero trip meter.
0.0 ▲		Continue along forest road.

GPS: N 38°34.83′ W 109°10.99′

▼ 0.0		Continue along forest road.
2.4 ▲	BL	Track on right, Beaver Basin trail, FR 600. Zero trip meter.
▼ 0.7	SO	Track on left, small stock pond on right.
1.7 ▲	SO	Track on right, small stock pond on left.
▼ 2.1	SO	Entering Manti-La Sal National Forest over cattle guard. Road is now FR 207.
0.3 ▲	SO	Leaving Manti-La Sal National Forest over cattle guard.
▼ 2.4	BL	Southeast #54: Polar Mesa Trail on right, FR 033. Zero trip meter.
0.0 ▲		Continue along FR 207.

GPS: N 38°36.70′ W 109°11.70′

▼ 0.0		Continue along FR 207.
7.4 ▲	BR	Southeast #54: Polar Mesa Trail on left, FR 033. Zero trip meter.
▼ 0.6	SO	Track on right to a small campsite.
6.8 ▲	SO	Track on left to a small campsite.
▼ 2.1	SO	Track on left at small dam, FR 622. Road wraps around Bull Canyon and Fisher Valley. Road turns to pavement.
5.3 ▲	SO	Track on right at small dam, FR 622. Road wraps around Bull Canyon and Fisher Valley. Road turns to graded dirt.
▼ 2.6	SO	Track on right.
4.8 ▲	SO	Track on left.
▼ 5.2	SO	Gravel road, FR 622, on right.
2.2 ▲	SO	Gravel road, FR 622, on left.
▼ 6.9	SO	Leaving Manti-La Sal National Forest.
0.5 ▲	SO	Entering Manti-La Sal National Forest.
▼ 7.4		Trail finishes at the junction with La Sal Mountain Road. Both direction lead to Moab, approximately 30 miles away.
0.0 ▲		Trail starts at the junction of La Sal Mountain Road (FR 062) and the Castleton-Gateway Road, approximately 30 miles from Moab. Zero trip meter and turn east on the Castleton-Gateway Road.

GPS: N 38°35.74′ W 109°17.38′

Polar Mesa Trail

Starting Point:	Junction FR 207 (Southeast #53: Castleton-Gateway Road) and FR 033
Finishing Point:	Polar Mesa, uranium mining ruins
Total Mileage:	9.7 miles
Unpaved Mileage:	9.7 miles
Driving Time:	1 hour (one-way)
Elevation Range:	7,000–8,200 feet
Usually Open:	May to November
Difficulty Rating:	3
Scenic Rating:	8
Remoteness Rating:	+0

Special Attractions

- Old uranium mining camp ruins on Polar Mesa.
- Spectacular views over Fisher Valley and Dolores River valley.

Description

Polar Mesa is a spur trail off Southeast #53: Castleton-Gateway Road. The majority of the road surface is roughly graded dirt; the final part traversing Polar Mesa is rockier and less maintained. It is suitable for a high-clearance vehicle in dry weather, but it should not be attempted in wet weather or immediately following a rainstorm, as the earliest sections turn treacherous and greasy.

The first part of the track winds around on a wide spur, with the upper reaches of Fisher Valley to the north and Beaver Creek canyon to the south. It climbs gradually to North Beaver Mesa and winds through scattered pine and open grassy areas. A couple of fairly well used tracks lead off toward Beaver Creek canyon.

The trail intersects with Southeast #55: Onion Creek and Thompson Canyon Trail, which is part of the Kokopelli Trail

A wide landscape spreads out behind the sign at the junction with Onion Creek and Thompson Canyon Trail

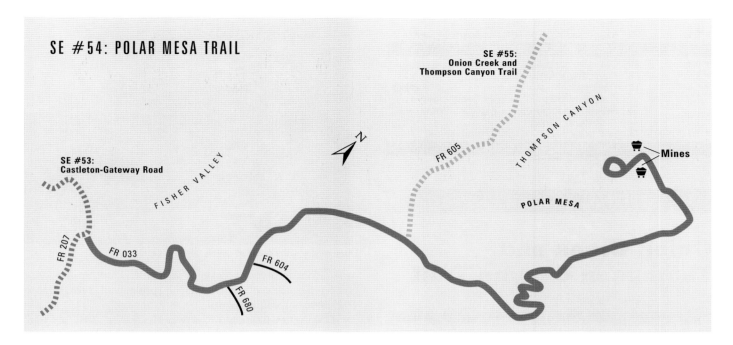

SE #54: POLAR MESA TRAIL

for mountain bikes, hikers, and in parts, 4WD vehicles.

As you approach the mining area, numerous trails appear to the right and left; most are little used and of a higher difficulty rating than the main trail. There are several old mining buildings to be found down these tracks, as well as tailings piles and mine tunnels and shafts. Polar Mesa in its heyday supplied extremely high quality uranium oxide—as much as 1.57 percent uranium. As with all ex-uranium mining areas, extreme care must be taken around the mine workings—tailings piles should be considered radioactive, and there is a danger of radon gas around the tunnels. Care with tire placement is needed, too—there are many old timbers, nails, tin, glass, and other hazards that may puncture a tire.

The track dead-ends at a small loop with a spectacular viewpoint.

Current Road Information

BLM Moab Field Office
82 East Dogwood
Moab, UT 84532
(435) 259-2100

Manti-La Sal National Forest
Moab Ranger District
125 West 200 South
Moab, Utah 84532
(435) 259-7155

Map References

BLM   Moab
USFS Manti-La Sal National Forest
USGS 1:24,000 Mt. Waas, Fisher Valley
          1:100,000 Moab
Maptech CD-ROM: Moab/Canyonlands
Trails Illustrated, #501
Utah Atlas & Gazetteer, p. 41

Utah Travel Council #5 (incomplete)
Other: Latitude 40—Moab East
       Canyon Country Off-Road Vehicle Map—
       La Sal Area

Route Directions

▼ 0.0   From FR 207 along Southeast #53: Castleton-Gateway Road, turn east on FR 033 (Polar Mesa Road), and zero trip meter. Follow sign to North Beaver Creek, Polar Mesa, and Fisher Valley.

GPS: N 38°36.73' W 109°11.67'

▼ 0.3   SO   Cross a small bridge over an irrigation ditch and continue past a corral on right. Views left over Fisher Valley and right over Beaver Creek. Road surface changes to red dirt.

▼ 1.8   SO   Sign reads "North Beaver Mesa."

▼ 1.9   SO   Track on right is FR 680.

GPS: N 38°37.29' W 109°10.32'

▼ 2.0   SO   Track on left.

▼ 2.4   SO   Track on right is FR 604

GPS: N 38°37.70' W 109°10.36'

▼ 3.0   SO   Cattle guard.

▼ 4.0   SO   Track on left is Southeast #55: Onion Creek and Thompson Canyon Trail (FR 605). Sign points left to Fisher Valley, straight on to Polar Mesa. A second BLM sign points left to the Kokopelli Trail. Continue over cattle guard.

GPS: N 38°38.68' W 109°09.44'

▼ 5.3   BL   Track on right. Continue over cattle guard and start to climb up mesa.

GPS: N 38°38.97' W 109°07.99'

▼ 6.2   SO   Cattle guard. Trail switchbacks up mesa.

▼ 6.8   SO   Track on right.

GPS: N 38°39.45' W 109°08.09'

▼ 7.4   SO   Leaving Manti-La Sal National Forest and entering private land.

▼ 7.9   SO   Track starts to descend, with views over the Dolores River valley.

▼ 8.3   SO   Track on right. There are now many faint tracks to the left and right; proceed straight

		ahead on the main track.
▼ 9.1	SO	More-used track on left goes to mining remains.
		GPS: N 38°40.51' W 109°08.50'
▼ 9.3	SO	Old mine shed on right.
▼ 9.5	BR	Start of final loop.
▼ 9.6	TL	Track on right, straight ahead track is blocked. A short walk straight ahead takes you to a tunnel and loading hopper. Wonderful view over Thompson Canyon.
▼ 9.7	TR	End of loop. Return the way you came.
		GPS: N 38°40.47' W 109°08.50'

SOUTHEAST REGION TRAIL #55

Onion Creek and Thompson Canyon Trail

Starting Point:	**Junction Utah 128 and Onion Creek Road**
Finishing Point:	**Junction of FR 605 and FR 033, at**
	Southeast #54: Polar Mesa Trail
Total Mileage:	**20.7 miles**
Unpaved Mileage:	**20.7 miles**
Driving Time:	**4.5 hours**
Elevation Range:	**4,200–7,600 feet**
Usually Open:	**April to November**
Difficulty Rating:	**3**
Scenic Rating:	**8**
Remoteness Rating:	**+0**

Special Attractions

■ Spectacular variety of scenery.

■ Numerous crossings of Onion Creek.

■ Backcountry camping opportunities.

■ Great one-day route from Moab when combined with Southeast #54: Polar Mesa Trail.

Description

This entire trail winds through a spectacular variety of scenery. The route commences 19.3 miles east along Utah 128 from the junction of US 191. Onion Creek Road is clearly marked. The first half of the trail is graded dirt until the start of the Thompson Canyon Trail. However, the numerous creek crossings mean it is best suited for a high-clearance 4WD vehicle. Do not attempt this route after heavy rain or if thunderstorms are threatening. Onion Creek often washes out, and flash flooding is possible. The second half of the trail is rougher, rocky, and sandy in places.

The first 7.2 miles of the trail are in the Colorado Riverway Recreation Area, and camping is restricted to designated sites. A portable toilet is required; these can be hired in Moab. There are many marked sites in the first 2.3 miles; they become less frequent as the trail winds tighter into the canyon.

The trail follows the canyon, either criss-crossing Onion Creek or on a shelf road above it. The red canyon walls and

One of the many fords of Onion Creek

weird rock formations make for an incredibly scenic drive. After 6 miles, the trail passes Stinking Spring, easily recognizable by the strong sulphur smell.

Leaving the Colorado Riverway Recreation Area, the trail winds up a ridge before descending into Fisher Valley. Onion Creek Road joins the Kokopelli Trail and turns north, winding up toward Thompson Canyon. It skirts right around Hideout Canyon before snaking onto a rocky ledge. A quiet BLM campsite here has picnic tables, a pit toilet, fire rings, plenty of shade, and good views. This is the most difficult part of the trail, with some rock ledges and large boulders, but all high-clearance 4WDs should have no problem. The top of this ridge provides expansive views over the Dolores River valley and later over Hideout Canyon and Polar Mesa.

The trail ends 4 miles from the start of Southeast #54: Polar Mesa Trail on FR 033. Turn right for Moab along Southwest #53: Castleton-Gateway Road, left to explore Polar Mesa.

Current Road Information

BLM Moab Field Office
82 East Dogwood
Moab, UT 84532
(435) 259-2100

Map References

BLM Moab

USFS Manti-La Sal National Forest (incomplete)

USGS 1:24,000 Fisher Towers, Fisher Valley
1:100,000 Moab

Maptech CD-ROM: Moab/Canyonlands

Utah Atlas & Gazetteer, p. 41

Utah Travel Council #5

Other: Latitude 40—Moab East
Canyon Country Off-Road Vehicle Map—La Sal Area

Route Directions

▼ 0.0		From Utah 128, turn south at sign for Onion Creek Road, and zero trip meter. Camp only in marked areas.
	9.3 ▲	Trail finishes at the junction with Utah 128. Turn right for Dewey Bridge, left for Moab.
		GPS: N 38°43.44' W 109°21.29'

▼ 0.6	SO	Track on left to campsite. Numerous tracks right and left to campsites.
8.7 ▲	SO	Track on right to final campsite before Utah 128.
▼ 0.7	SO	Parking area.
8.6 ▲	SO	Parking area.
▼ 0.9	SO	Cross Onion Creek. There are numerous creek crossings for the next 6 miles.
8.4 ▲	SO	Final creek crossing.
▼ 1.8	SO	Trail enters canyon.
7.5 ▲	SO	Trail exits canyon.
▼ 3.7	SO	Bridge over Onion Creek.
5.6 ▲	SO	Bridge over Onion Creek. Numerous tracks on right and left to campsites.
▼ 5.0	SO	Track on right.
4.3 ▲	SO	Track on left.

GPS: N 38°42.04' W 109°17.37'

▼ 5.9	SO	Stinking Spring on left.
3.4 ▲	SO	Stinking Spring on right.
▼ 7.2	SO	Leaving Colorado Riverway Recreation Area, end of designated site camping. Trail climbs away from Onion Creek toward the Fisher Valley.
2.1 ▲	SO	Entering Colorado Riverway Recreation Area, camping in designated sites only. Trail descends to run along Onion Creek. Numerous creek crossings for the next 6 miles.
▼ 8.6	SO	Gate followed by track on left.
0.7 ▲	SO	Track on right followed by gate. Trail leaves the Fisher Valley.
▼ 9.3	SO	Track on left is Kokopelli Trail. This leads up a very difficult 4WD trail to Entrada Bluffs Road. Zero trip meter.
0.0 ▲	SO	Continue on up sandy track.

GPS: N 38°41.32' W 109°13.19'

▼ 0.0	SO	Continue on down sandy track.
11.4 ▲	SO	Track on right is Kokopelli Trail. This leads up a very difficult 4WD trail to Entrada Bluffs Road. Zero trip meter.
▼ 0.4	SO	Gate, entering Fisher Valley Ranch (private property).
11.0 ▲	SO	Gate, leaving Fisher Valley Ranch, entering BLM land.
▼ 0.6	SO	Track on right to farm shed.
10.8 ▲	SO	Track on left to farm shed.
▼ 0.9	TL	Turn northeast; follow sign to North Beaver Mesa, La Sal Mountains, Thompson Canyon, and Kokopelli Trail.
10.5 ▲	TR	Turn northwest; follow sign to Utah 128, Moab, and Kokopelli Trail.

GPS: N 38°40.63' W 109°12.69'

▼ 1.6	SO	Gate at top of rise, entering BLM land. Descend to Hideout Canyon.
9.8 ▲	SO	Gate at top of rise, entering Fisher Valley Ranch (private property). Descend to Fisher Valley.
▼ 2.6	SO	Track on right to Hideout Campground. Remains of log cabin down track to campsite on left.
8.8 ▲	SO	Track on left to Hideout Campground. Remains of log cabin down track to campsite on left.

GPS: N 38°41.57' W 109°11.41'

▼ 2.9	SO	Small creek crossing.
8.5 ▲	SO	Small creek crossing.
▼ 3.2	SO	Views left over Cottonwood Canyon from ridge, and right to Cowhead Hill and Hideout Canyon.
8.2 ▲	SO	Views right to Cottonwood Canyon from ridge, and left over Cowhead Hill and Hideout Canyon.
▼ 3.8	SO	Rocky section of track.
7.6 ▲	SO	Rocky section of track.
▼ 4.5	SO	Track on right.
7.1 ▲	SO	Track on left.
▼ 4.9	SO	Track on left, expansive views over Dolores River valley.
6.7 ▲	SO	Track on right, expansive views over Dolores River valley.
▼ 7.6	BR	Old road on left. Bear right for views of Hideout Canyon and Onion Creek to the right, Thompson Canyon and Polar Mesa to the left.
3.8 ▲	BL	Old road reenters on right.

GPS: N 38°41.56' W 109°10.17'

▼ 8.4	BR	Old road reenters on left.
3.0 ▲	BL	Old road on right. Bear left for views of Hideout Canyon and Onion Creek to the left, Thompson Canyon and Polar Mesa to the right.
▼ 8.9	SO	Track on left.
2.5 ▲	SO	Track on right.
▼ 9.7	SO	Leaving BLM land, entering Manti-La Sal National Forest. Road becomes FR 605.
1.7 ▲	SO	Leaving Manti-La Sal National Forest, entering BLM land.

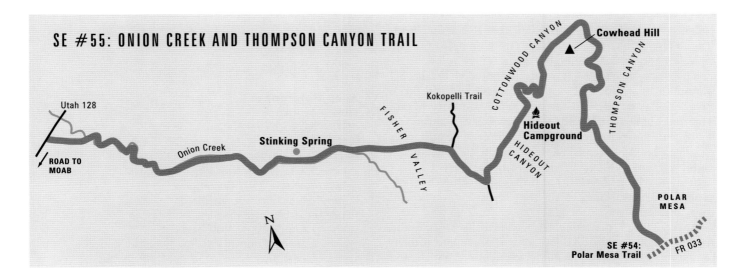

SE #55: ONION CREEK AND THOMPSON CANYON TRAIL

▼ 9.9	SO	Track on left.
1.5 ▲	SO	Track on right.
▼ 11.4		Trail ends at the intersection with FR 033, Southeast #54: Polar Mesa Trail. Turn right for Moab along Southeast #53: Castleton-Gateway Road, left to explore Polar Mesa.
0.0 ▲		Trail begins at the junction of FR 605 and FR 033, 4 miles from start of Southeast #54: Polar Mesa Trail. Zero trip meter and turn north onto FR 605; follow sign to Fisher Valley.

GPS: N 38°38.69' W 109°09.41'

SOUTHEAST REGION TRAIL #56

Sand Flats Road

Starting Point:	**Junction of La Sal Mountain Road (FR 062) and Sand Flats Road (FR 067)**
Finishing Point:	**Mill Creek Drive, Moab**
Total Mileage:	**18.7 miles**
Unpaved Mileage:	**16 miles**
Driving Time:	**1 hour**
Elevation Range:	**4,200–7,800 feet**
Usually Open:	**March to December**
Difficulty Rating:	**2**
Scenic Rating:	**9**
Remoteness Rating:	**+0**

Special Attractions

■ Access to mountain bike and 4WD trails.
■ Arid desert scenery and rock formations.
■ Sand Flats Recreation Area.

Description

Sand Flats Road is popular with mountain bikers and 4WD vehicles, as it provides access to a network of trails plus excellent camping in the Sand Flats Recreation Area. It is an alternative route into Moab to the more-used Castle Valley and La Sal Mountain Roads.

The start of the trail is at the junction of the La Sal Mountain Road (FR 062) and Sand Flats Road (FR 067); a sign directs travelers to the two major routes to Moab. The trail gradually descends with views over Spanish Valley to the Canyons Rims Recreation Area. The surface is rough and sandy in places, but should be passable to high-clearance vehicles in dry weather. Heavy rains or light snow may make this trail impassable. The scenery is varied and rewarding, with red sandstone cliffs and rugged desert vistas.

After 12 miles, the trail enters the Sand Flats Recreation Area at the mountain bike trailhead to Porcupine Rim. A camping and day-use fee is required for all hikers, 4WDs, and

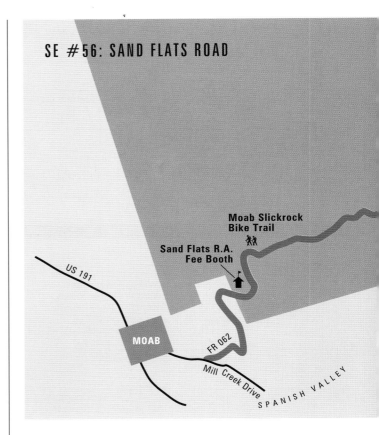

SE #56: SAND FLATS ROAD

mountain bikes, and camping is permitted in designated areas only. Further information on this area can be obtained at the entrance station or in Moab.

Sand Flats Road improves at this point to become a graded dirt road, although it is still subject to washouts and can be washboardy. It winds across the sandstone plateau between Negro Bill Canyon and the Mill Creek Wilderness Study Area, passing spectacular rock formations on the way. The final part of the trail passes by the Slickrock Bike Trail and the Alcove Recreation Site, before finishing in Moab at Mill Creek Drive.

Current Road Information

BLM Moab Field Office
82 East Dogwood
Moab, UT 84532
(435) 259-2100

Map References

BLM Moab
USFS Manti-La Sal National Forest
USGS 1:24,000 Warner Lake, Rill Creek, Moab
1:100,000 Moab
Maptech CD-ROM: Moab/Canyonlands
Trails Illustrated, #501 (incomplete)
Utah Atlas & Gazetteer, pp. 30, 31
Utah Travel Council #5
Other: Latitude 40—Moab East
Canyon Country Off-Road Vehicle Map—
La Sal Area

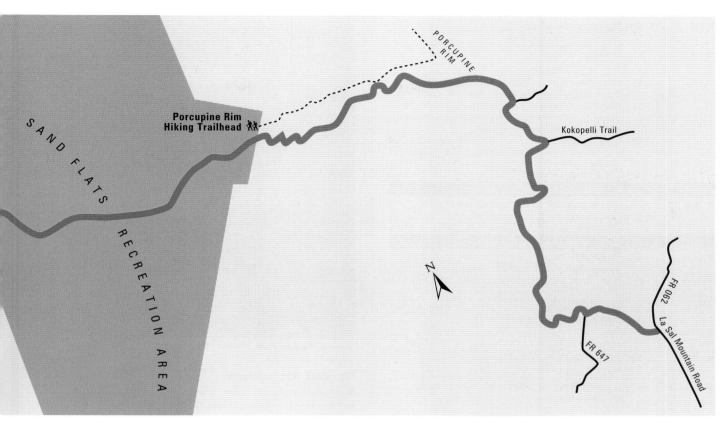

Route Directions

▼ 0.0		From La Sal Mountain Road (FR 062), turn northwest onto Sand Flats Roads (FR 067), and zero trip meter.
18.7 ▲		End at La Sal Mountain Road (FR 062). A sign-post directs you back to Moab.

GPS: N 38°31.34′ W 109°20.26′

▼ 1.1	SO	Track on left, FR 647, followed by cattle guard.
17.6 ▲	SO	Cross cattle guard, then track on right, FR 647.
▼ 2.0	SO	Views left over Spanish Valley and out to the Canyon Rims Recreation Area.
16.7 ▲	SO	Views right over Spanish Valley and out to the Canyon Rims Recreation Area.
▼ 2.9	SO	Track on left.
15.8 ▲	SO	Track on right.

GPS: N 38°32.51′ W 109°21.65′

▼ 3.1	SO	Track on right.
15.6 ▲	SO	Track on left.
▼ 3.4	SO	Cattle guard.
15.3 ▲	SO	Cattle guard.
▼ 4.0	SO	Track on right. Track becomes sandier with areas of slickrock pavement.
14.7 ▲	SO	Track on left.
▼ 4.4	SO	Cattle guard.
14.3 ▲	SO	Cattle guard.
▼ 4.6	SO	Track on left.
14.1 ▲	SO	Track on right.
▼ 4.9	SO	Track on left. Loose, sandy patch on trail.
13.8 ▲	SO	Track on right. Loose, sandy patch on trail.
▼ 5.2	SO	Kokopelli Trail enters on right over ledge.
13.5 ▲	SO	Kokopelli Trail enters on left over ledge.

GPS: N 38°33.84′ W 109°21.07′

▼ 5.8	BL	Two tracks on right. Crossing slickrock and sandy section.
12.9 ▲	BR	Crossing slickrock and sandy section. Two tracks on left.
▼ 6.2	BL	Track on right to Porcupine Rim camping area.
12.5 ▲	BR	Track on left to Porcupine Rim camping area.
▼ 6.5	SO	Leaving Manti-La Sal National Forest over cattle guard.
12.2 ▲	SO	Entering Manti-La Sal National Forest over cattle guard; road becomes FR 067.

GPS: N 38°34.71′ W 109°21.48′

▼ 7.1	SO	Track on left.
11.6 ▲	SO	Track on right.

Rock formations just off Sand Flats Road

▼ 8.3	SO	Tracks on left and right.
10.4 ▲	SO	Tracks on left and right.
▼ 8.4	BR	Track on left.
10.3 ▲	BL	Track on right.
▼ 10.3	SO	Porcupine Rim Trailhead. Entering Sand Flats Recreation Area (fee area). Past this point, the trail improves to graded dirt road. There are numerous tracks on sright and left to camping areas and 4WD trails.
8.4 ▲	SO	Leaving Sand Flats Recreation Area. Porcupine Rim Trailhead and parking area. Trail is now smaller with sandy areas interspersed with slickrock pavement.

GPS: N 38°34.90' W 109°24.94'

| ▼ 15.2 | SO | Gravel road left to Campsite Cluster E. |
| 3.5 ▲ | BL | Gravel road right to Campsite Cluster E. |

GPS: N 38°34.88' W 109°29.97'

▼ 16.0	SO	Pavement starts.
2.7 ▲	SO	Pavement turns to graded gravel road. Numerous tracks right and left to camping areas and 4WD trails (not listed here).
▼ 16.3	SO	Moab Slickrock Bike Trail on right, followed by parking area and toilets.
2.4 ▲	SO	Parking area and toilets followed by Moab Slickrock Bike Trail on left.
▼ 16.7	SO	Alcove Recreation Site on right.
2.0 ▲	SO	Alcove Recreation Site on left.
▼ 17.1	SO	Leaving Sand Flats Recreation Area, pass entrance booth.
1.6 ▲	SO	Entering Sand Flats Recreation Area (fee area).

GPS: N 38°34.51' W 109°31.37'

▼ 17.7	SO	"America's Most Scenic Dump" on left.
1.0 ▲	SO	"America's Most Scenic Dump" on right.
▼ 18.7		End at intersection with Mill Creek Drive in Moab.
0.0 ▲		Trail starts on Mill Creek Drive in Moab. Turn east onto paved Sand Flats Road and zero trip meter. The Grand Valley Cemetery is on the corner.

GPS: N 38°33.91' W 109°32.08'

Miners Basin Trail

Starting Point:	**Junction of La Sal Mountain Road (FR 062) and FR 065 (Miners Basin Trail)**
Finishing Point:	**Hiking trailhead for Miners Basin**
Total Mileage:	**2.7 miles**
Unpaved Mileage:	**2.7 miles**
Driving Time:	**30 minutes (one-way)**
Elevation Range:	**7,800–9,750 feet**
Usually Open:	**June to October**
Difficulty Rating:	**2**
Scenic Rating:	**8**
Remoteness Rating:	**+0**

View of the lake from the end of Miners Basin Trail

Special Attractions
- Access to Miners Basin hiking trails and cabins.
- Mountain vegetation and scenery, including aspen viewing in fall.
- Views over the Castle Valley.

History
Ten years after the discovery of gold-bearing gravel in 1888 on the upper reaches of Mount Waas, the town of Miners Basin was developed. Nestled at an elevation of 10,000 feet just above two scree faces, the town grew to a population approaching a hundred, serving several nearby gold, silver, and copper mines. "The Basin," as it became known, supported a hotel, a post office, and two saloons. In the northeastern part of the La Sal Mountains, Mount Waas, which is snow-capped throughout winter, is named after a Ute chief; another prominent peak farther south, Tukuhnikavats, is also named after a Ute and means "dirt seer." The La Sal Mountains, which mean Salt Mountains in Spanish, gained their name from the Domínguez-Escalante expedition, which passed this way in 1776. The mountains have unusual salty springs at their base.

Only 10 years after its establishment, The Basin began to fade as the surrounding mines ran out. Some mines only reached a depth of 150 feet. Today, little remains of the promising settlement except for a few log cabins constructed from the surrounding forests. Still intact, they are occasionally occupied and best treated as private property. Hauling the necessary mining and construction equipment to this elevation was quite a feat for the haulage contractors of the 19th century. Sturdy wagons and strong mules were a definite necessity. The present-day traveler can still appreciate the rocky ascent to Miners Basin; today's trail runs close to the original wagon and mule road.

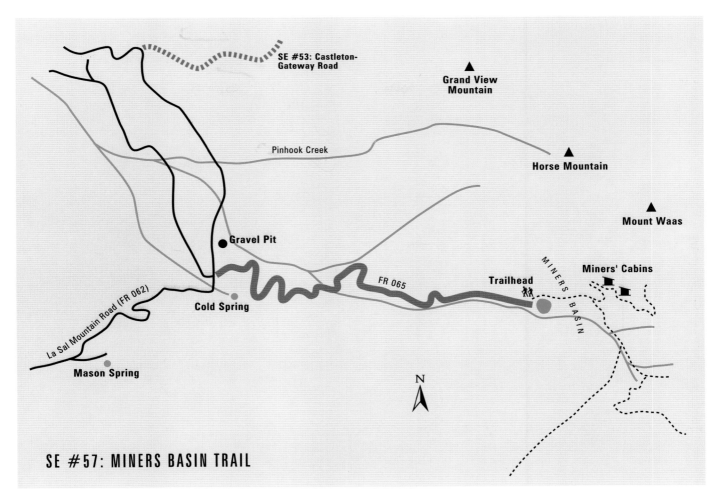

SE #57: MINERS BASIN TRAIL

Description

This short trail leaves La Sal Mountain Road (FR 062) and steadily switchbacks through pine and stands of aspen up to the hiking trailhead for Bachelors Basin and Miners Basin. The lower portions of the trail have spectacular views over Castle Valley. The second half of the trail crosses a couple of small talus slopes before finishing at a small reservoir at the hiking trailhead. From here, it is a gradual 0.75-mile hike to the cabins at Miners Basin.

The trail surface is mainly packed dirt and rock. It is graded, but there are a couple of loose rock sections at the lower end. Under normal conditions, it is suitable for high-clearance vehicles.

Current Road Information

Manti-La Sal National Forest
Moab Ranger District
125 West 200 South
Moab, UT 84532
(435) 259-7155

Map References

BLM Moab
USFS Manti-La Sal National Forest
USGS 1:24,000 Warner Lake

1:100,000 Moab
Maptech CD-ROM: Moab/Canyonlands
Trails Illustrated, #501
Utah Atlas & Gazetteer, p. 31
Utah Travel Council #5
Other: Latitude 40—Moab East
Canyon Country Off-Road Vehicle Map—
La Sal Area

Route Directions

▼ 0.0		From La Sal Mountain Road (FR 062), turn east onto FR 065. Coming from the north, the trail is just past, not immediately at, the signpost.
		GPS: N 38°32.82′ W 109°17.44′
▼ 1.1	SO	Gate.
▼ 2.6	SO	Cattle guard.
▼ 2.7		Trail ends at the hiking trailhead at a small lake. There is a pit toilet and trail information. Hiking trail 034 takes you to Bachelor Basins, trail 143 to Warner Lake Campground. It is approximately 0.75 miles to the cabins at Miners Basin.
		GPS: N 38°32.34′ W 109°15.65′

The Southwest Region

Trails in the Southwest Region

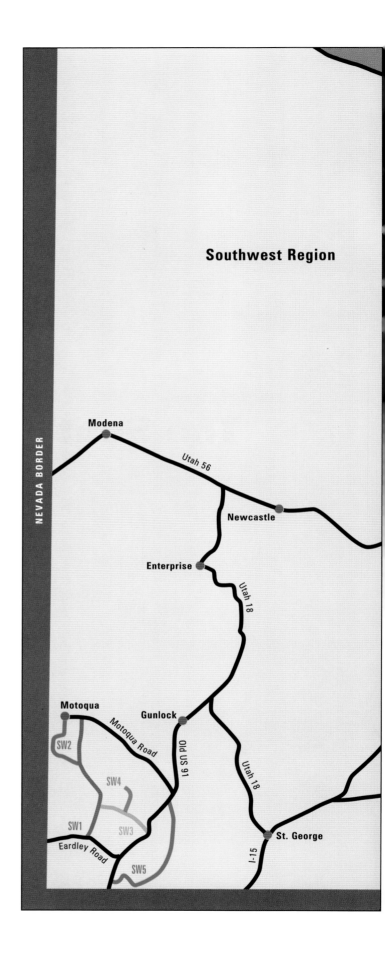

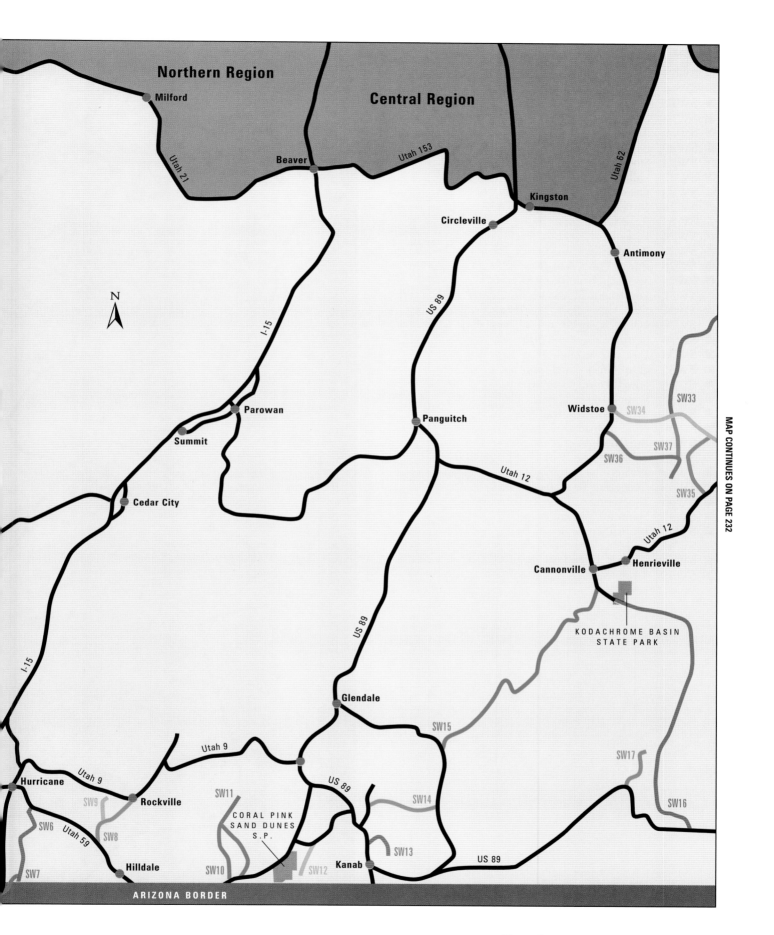

Northern Region

Central Region

Milford

Utah 21

Beaver

Utah 153

Kingston

Utah 62

Circleville

Antimony

US 89

N

I-15

Parowan

Panguitch

Widstoe

SW34

SW33

Summit

SW37

SW36

SW35

Cedar City

Utah 12

Utah 12

Cannonville

Henrieville

KODACHROME BASIN
STATE PARK

US 89

I-15

Glendale

SW15

SW17

Utah 9

US 89

SW14

Hurricane

Utah 9

SW16

SW9

Rockville

SW11

SW6

Utah 59

SW8

CORAL PINK
SAND DUNES
S.P.

SW13

SW7

Hilldale

SW10

SW12

Kanab

US 89

ARIZONA BORDER

MAP CONTINUES ON PAGE 232

Trails in the Southwest Region

MAP CONTINUES ON PAGE 104

MAP CONTINUES ON PAGE 231

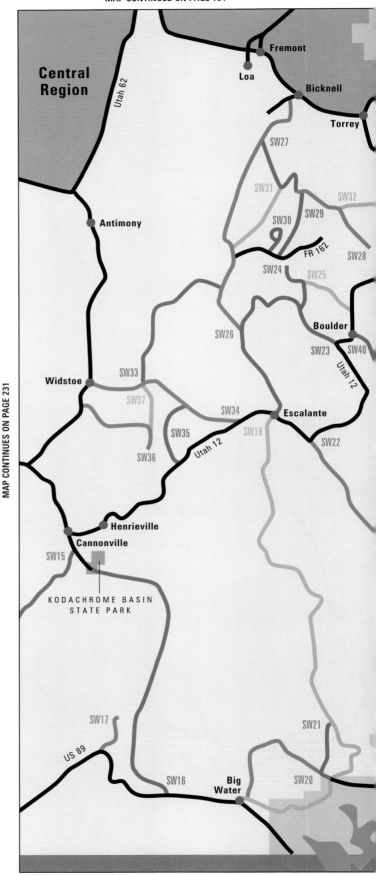

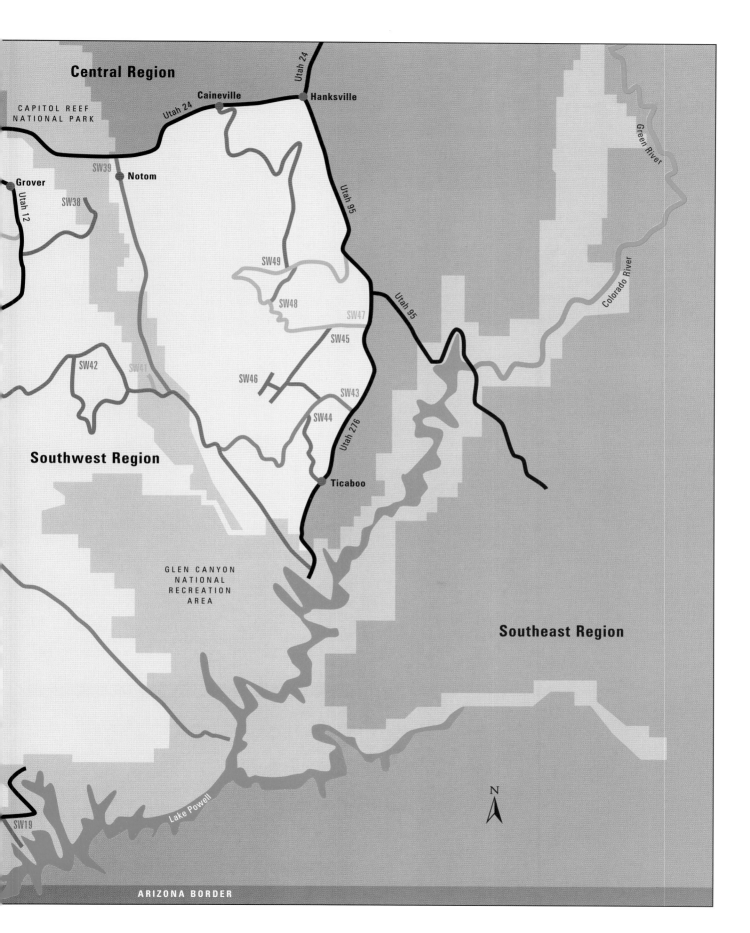

Central Region

CAPITOL REEF
NATIONAL PARK

Utah 24

Caineville

Utah 24

Hanksville

SW39

Notom

Grover

Utah 12

SW38

Utah 95

SW49

SW48

SW47

Utah 95

SW45

SW42

SW41

SW46

SW43

Southwest Region

SW44

Utah 276

Ticaboo

GLEN CANYON
NATIONAL
RECREATION
AREA

Green River

Colorado River

Southeast Region

N

Lake Powell

SW19

ARIZONA BORDER

Indian Spring Trail

Starting Point:	**Eardley Road**
Finishing Point:	**Motoqua Road, 14.4 miles west of Old US 91**
Total Mileage:	**17.4 miles**
Unpaved Mileage:	**17.4 miles**
Driving Time:	**1 hour**
Elevation Range:	**3,200–4,500 feet**
Usually Open:	**Year-round**
Difficulty Rating:	**2**
Scenic Rating:	**8**
Remoteness Rating:	**+1**

Special Attractions

■ Dense Joshua tree forest.
■ Far-ranging views across Beaver Dam Wash into Nevada.
■ Remote, lightly traveled trail along the western edge of the Beaver Dam Mountains.

Description

If you want to see Joshua trees and plenty of them in a rugged desert setting, then this is your trail! The meandering trail skirts the western edge of the Beaver Dam Mountains, running across the alluvial fan that slopes down to the Beaver Dam Wash.

To get to the start of the trail, turn west off Old US 91 down Eardley Road. The junction is marked by a sign for the High Desert Game Ranch, but has no directional sign. It leaves immediately south of Castle Cliff, 4.5 miles north of the Arizona state line. The start of Indian Spring Trail is 4.4 miles from this junction.

The trail undulates to the north, crossing many deep washes. Many trails lead off, mainly to springs used by ranchers, but a couple of longer ones such as Horse Canyon Trail lead partway up the eroded canyons in the Beaver Dam Mountains.

A large patch of Joshua trees along Indian Spring Trail

After 5.1 miles, Southwest #3: Hell Hole Pass Trail leads east over Hell Hole Pass to rejoin Old US 91. The Indian Spring Tank, which gives this trail its name, is at the junction.

The Joshua trees become more prolific the farther north you go; when you reach the turnoff for Southwest #2: Scarecrow Peak Trail, they are a dense forest of mature trees, interspersed with golden chollas. Joshua trees are a member of the lily family and are related to yuccas, which they somewhat resemble. Their upstretched arms reminded the Mormon pioneers, who named them, of the biblical Joshua, whose arms were upstretched to heaven.

Many animals and birds—including coyotes, mule deer, prairie falcons, golden eagles, rattlesnakes, and the endangered desert tortoise—make their home along the Beaver Dam Mountains, and if you are lucky, you will see some of them along this route.

The trail finishes on the graded dirt Motoqua Road, which is at the lower end of the Burnt Canyon ATV trail system, a popular network of trails suitable for ATVs, motorbikes, and 4WDs.

Current Road Information

BLM St. George Field Office
345 East Riverside Drive
St. George, UT 84790
(435) 688-3200

Map References

BLM St. George
USFS Dixie National Forest: Pine Valley Ranger District (incomplete)
USGS 1:24,000 Castle Cliff, West Mt. Peak, Motoqua
1:100,000 St. George
Maptech CD-ROM: Escalante/Dixie National Forest
Utah Atlas & Gazetteer, p. 16
Utah Travel Council #4

Route Directions

▼ 0.0			On Eardley Road, 4.4 miles from Old US 91, turn north on small graded dirt road, following sign for Motoqua Road, and zero trip meter. To find Eardley Road from Old US 91, look for intersection at Castle Cliff and follow sign for the High Desert Game Ranch.
	5.1 ▲		Trail ends at Eardley Road. Turn left for Old US 91.
		GPS: N 37°05.64' W 113°57.17'	
▼ 0.6		SO	Cross through wash.
	4.5 ▲	SO	Cross through wash.
▼ 1.0		SO	Faint track on left.
	4.1 ▲	SO	Faint track on right.
▼ 1.2		SO	Old corral on right—only the uprights remain.
	3.9 ▲	SO	Old corral on left—only the uprights remain.
▼ 1.4		SO	Cross through wash, with track on right up wash.
	3.7 ▲	SO	Cross through wash, with track on left up wash.
▼ 1.5		SO	Track on left to Middle Spring Pipeline and storage tank.
	3.6 ▲	SO	Track on right to Middle Spring Pipeline and storage tank.
		GPS: N 37°06.86' W 113°56.91'	
▼ 2.3		SO	Track on left.
	2.8 ▲	SO	Track on right.

▼ 2.5	SO	Cross through Reber Wash.
2.6 ▲	SO	Cross through Reber Wash.
▼ 2.6	BL	Track on right.
2.5 ▲	SO	Track on left.
▼ 2.8	SO	Two entrances to track on right.
2.3 ▲	SO	Two entrances to track on left.
▼ 3.1	SO	Faint track on right.
2.0 ▲	SO	Faint track on left.
▼ 3.5	SO	Track on right.
1.6 ▲	SO	Track on left.
▼ 3.6	SO	Track on right.
1.5 ▲	SO	Track on left.
▼ 3.8	SO	Track on right to tank.
1.3 ▲	BR	Track on left to tank.

GPS: N 37°08.22' W 113°56.10'

▼ 3.9	SO	Cross through wash, then track on left.
1.2 ▲	SO	Track on right, then cross through wash.
▼ 4.0	SO	Track on right.
1.1 ▲	SO	Track on left.
▼ 4.1	SO	Cross through wash.
1.0 ▲	SO	Cross through wash.
▼ 4.4	SO	Cross through wash.
0.7 ▲	SO	Cross through wash.
▼ 4.8	SO	Track on right.
0.3 ▲	SO	Track on left.

GPS: N 37°08.89' W 113°55.83'

▼ 4.9	SO	Cross through wash.
0.2 ▲	SO	Cross through wash.
▼ 5.1	SO	Track on left, followed by track on right; this is Southwest #3: Hell Hole Pass Trail. Zero trip meter.
0.0 ▲	BL	Continue south toward Eardley Road. Immediately bear left at fork following Hell Hole Pass Trail.
▼ 0.0		Continue north toward Motoqua, passing second entrance to Hell Hole Pass Trail.
2.5 ▲	SO	Two tracks to left are one end of Southwest #3: Hell Hole Pass Trail. Zero trip meter at the second.

GPS: N 37°09.17' W 113°55.75'

▼ 0.1	SO	Indian Spring tank is on the left, marked by sign. Washed out track on right.
2.4 ▲	SO	Indian Spring tank is on the right, marked by sign. Washed out track on left.
▼ 0.4	SO	Track on right.
2.1 ▲	SO	Track on left.
▼ 0.8	SO	Track on right.
1.7 ▲	SO	Track on left.
▼ 1.0	SO	Track on right.
1.5 ▲	SO	Track on left.
▼ 1.1	SO	Cross through wash.
1.4 ▲	SO	Cross through wash.
▼ 1.3	SO	Faint track on right.
1.2 ▲	SO	Faint track on left.
▼ 1.4	SO	Track on right and left, then cattle guard.
1.1 ▲	SO	Cattle guard, then track on right and left.
▼ 1.8	SO	Track on left.
0.7 ▲	SO	Track on right.
▼ 1.9	SO	Cross through wash.
0.6 ▲	SO	Cross through wash.

GPS: N 37°10.51' W 113°55.89'

| ▼ 2.5 | SO | Track on right is Horse Canyon Trail, marked by BLM sign, leading into the Beaver Dam Mountains. Also track on left. Zero trip meter. |

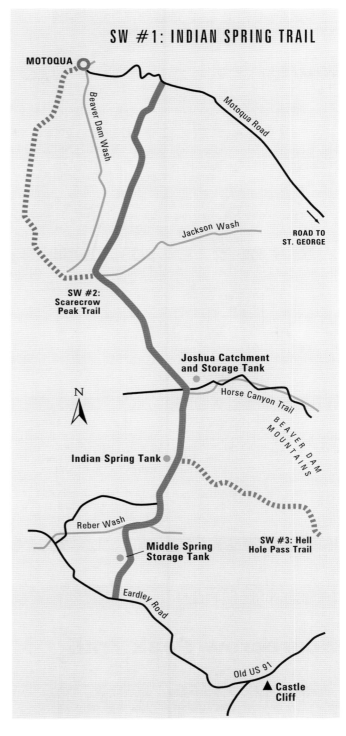

SW #1: INDIAN SPRING TRAIL

0.0 ▲		Continue toward Indian Spring.
▼ 0.0		Continue toward Motoqua Road.
3.8 ▲	SO	Track on left is Horse Canyon Trial, marked by BLM sign, leading into the Beaver Dam Mountains. Also track on right. Zero trip meter.

GPS: N 37°10.91' W 113°55.84'

| ▼ 0.1 | SO | Cattle guard, then Joshua catchment and storage tank on right, then track on right. |
| 3.7 ▲ | SO | Track on left, then Joshua catchment and storage tank on left, followed by cattle guard. |

	GPS: N 37°11.05' W 113°55.87'		
▼ 1.5		SO	Track on left to power lines.
2.3 ▲		SO	Track on right to power lines.
▼ 1.6		SO	Cross through wash.
2.2 ▲		SO	Cross through wash.
▼ 1.7		SO	Track on right at power lines, then cross over natural gas pipeline.
2.1 ▲		SO	Cross over natural gas pipeline, then track on left at power lines.
▼ 3.4		SO	Faint track on left, then cattle guard.
0.4 ▲		SO	Cattle guard, then faint track on right.
▼ 3.8		SO	Track on left is Southwest #2: Scarecrow Peak Trail, signed to Jackson Well. Zero trip meter.
0.0 ▲			Continue toward Indian Spring.
▼ 0.0			Continue toward Motoqua Road.
6.0 ▲		SO	Track on right is Southwest #2: Scarecrow Peak Trail, signed to Jackson Well. Zero trip meter.
	GPS: N 37°13.45' W 113°58.69'		
▼ 0.2		SO	Cross through Jackson Wash.
5.8 ▲		SO	Cross through Jackson Wash.
▼ 0.4		SO	Track on left.
5.6 ▲		SO	Track on right.
▼ 1.8		SO	Cross through wash, then climb ridge with views left to Beaver Dam Wash.
4.2 ▲		SO	Descend ridge with views right to Beaver Dam Wash, then cross through wash.
▼ 4.8		SO	Cattle guard, then track on right.
1.2 ▲		SO	Track on left, then cattle guard.
	GPS: N 37°17.42' W 113°57.94'		
▼ 4.9		SO	Track on left.
1.1 ▲		SO	Track on right.
▼ 6.0			End at intersection with the major graded dirt Motoqua Road. Turn left for the settlement of Motoqua, turn right for Old US 91 and St. George.
0.0 ▲			On Motoqua Road, 14.4 miles west of Old US 91, zero trip meter and turn southeast on the graded dirt road, following the sign for Indian Spring and Eardley Road.
	GPS: N 37°18.44' W 113°57.50'		

SOUTHWEST REGION TRAIL #2

Scarecrow Peak Trail

Starting Point:	**Motoqua**
Finishing Point:	**Southwest #1: Indian Spring Trail,**
	6 miles south of Motoqua Road
Total Mileage:	**13.1 miles**
Unpaved Mileage:	**13.1 miles**
Driving Time:	**1 hour**
Elevation Range:	**3,000–3,800 feet**
Usually Open:	**Year-round**
Difficulty Rating:	**2**
Scenic Rating:	**7**
Remoteness Rating:	**+1**

Special Attractions

- Joshua tree forests.
- Scarecrow Peak and Beaver Dam Wash.
- Views into two states—Utah and Nevada.

Description

This easy trail links the lower end of the Burnt Canyon ATV trail system with Southwest #1: Indian Spring Trail, passing through a remote, scenic area of the Mojave Desert as it does. The trail leaves from the small settlement of Motoqua; to get there, take Motoqua Road from Old US 91 in the Shivwits Indian Reservation. The trail immediately crosses Beaver Dam Wash, the lowest elevation in Utah, and climbs a ridge to the Nevada state line. The line is unmarked, except for a fence line, and the trail follows alongside it for nearly 3 miles, passing through large stands of mature Joshua trees.

Jackson Well

The trail then drops down a wash, winds around the bulk of Scarecrow Peak (4,398 feet), and then crosses the wide, sandy Beaver Dam Wash again. After passing Jackson Well, the trail finishes at Southeast #1: Indian Spring Trail, 6 miles south of Motoqua Road.

Current Road Information

BLM St. George Field Office
345 East Riverside Drive
St. George, UT 84790
(435) 688-3200

Map References

BLM St. George
USFS Dixie National Forest: Pine Valley Ranger District (incomplete)
USGS 1:24,000 West Mt. Peak, Scarecrow Peak, Dodge Spring, Motoqua
1:100,000 St. George
Maptech CD-ROM: Escalante/Dixie National Forest
Utah Atlas & Gazetteer, p. 16
Utah Travel Council #4

Route Directions

▼ 0.0		In Motoqua, at the junction before Beaver Dam Wash, zero trip meter and continue north along the graded dirt road following the sign to the Utah/Nevada state line. The settlement of Motoqua is to the right.
1.1 ▲		Trail ends at the settlement of Motoqua. Continue along Motoqua Road to reach Old US 91 and St. George.
	GPS: N 37°18.59' W 113°59.77'	

▼ 0.1		SO	Cross through Beaver Dam Wash.
	1.0 ▲	SO	Cross through Beaver Dam Wash.
▼ 0.2		SO	Corral on left.
	0.9 ▲	SO	Corral on right.
▼ 0.5		SO	Track on left.
	0.6 ▲	SO	Track on right.
▼ 0.6		SO	Cattle guard.
	0.5 ▲	SO	Cattle guard.
▼ 1.0		SO	Track on right is signed to Dodge Spring, then cross over wash.
	0.1 ▲	SO	Cross over wash, then track on left is signed to Dodge Spring.
▼ 1.1		TL	Turn left onto unmarked, smaller graded dirt road and zero trip meter.
	0.0 ▲		Continue toward Motoqua.

GPS: N 37°18.29′ W 114°00.48′

▼ 0.0			Continue toward the Nevada state line.
	4.0 ▲	TR	Turn right onto larger graded dirt road and zero trip meter.
▼ 0.1		SO	Cattle guard.
	3.9 ▲	SO	Cattle guard.
▼ 0.2		SO	Cross through wash, then track on left.
	3.8 ▲	SO	Track on right, then cross through wash.
▼ 0.8		SO	Cross through wash.
	3.2 ▲	SO	Cross through wash.
▼ 0.9		SO	Cross through wash.
	3.1 ▲	SO	Cross through wash.
▼ 1.0		SO	Track on right, then cross through wash.
	3.0 ▲	SO	Cross through wash, then track on left.
▼ 1.1		SO	Cross through wash.
	2.9 ▲	SO	Cross through wash.
▼ 1.4		SO	Cross through wash.
	2.6 ▲	SO	Cross through wash.
▼ 1.7		SO	Cross through smaller wash.
	2.3 ▲	SO	Cross through smaller wash.
▼ 1.8		BR	Track swings right, away from main wash.
	2.2 ▲	BL	Track swings left and joins main wash.

GPS: N 37°16.88′ W 114°01.13′

▼ 2.2		BL	Track on right.
	1.8 ▲	SO	Track on left.

GPS: N 37°17.07′ W 114°01.48′

▼ 2.9		SO	Track on left.
	1.1 ▲	SO	Track on right.
▼ 3.1		SO	Track on right, then cross through wash.
	0.9 ▲	SO	Cross through wash, then track on left.
▼ 3.6		SO	Track on right.
	0.4 ▲	SO	Track on left.

GPS: N 37°16.55′ W 114°02.70′

▼ 3.7		SO	Track on right, then cross through wash.
	0.3 ▲	SO	Cross through wash, then track on left.
▼ 4.0		TL	Nevada state line (unmarked). Turn left in front of cattle guard and follow along the fence line. Zero trip meter.
	0.0 ▲		Continue toward Motoqua.

GPS: N 37°16.38′ W 114°03.06′

▼ 0.0			Proceed south along state line.
	2.8 ▲	TR	Turn right at intersection and leave state line. Track on left crosses a cattle guard into Nevada. Zero trip meter.
▼ 2.8		TL	Turn sharp left, immediately in front of water tank and zero trip meter.
	0.0 ▲		The fence on left is Nevada state line. Proceed north along state line.

GPS: N 37°13.88′ W 114°02.73′

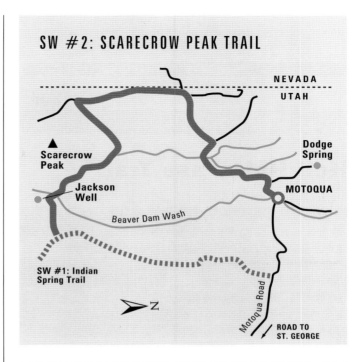

SW #2: SCARECROW PEAK TRAIL

▼ 0.0			Proceed away from state line.
	4.2 ▲	TR	Turn sharp right, immediately in front of water tank and zero trip meter.
▼ 0.6		SO	Track on right.
	3.6 ▲	SO	Track on left.
▼ 1.5		SO	Track on left, then trail drops toward wash.
	2.7 ▲	SO	Trail climbs away from wash, then track on right.

GPS: N 37°14.85′ W 114°01.53′

▼ 1.7		SO	Enter wash.
	2.5 ▲	SO	Exit wash.
▼ 1.9		TR	Track on left. Exit wash.
	2.3 ▲	BL	Enter wash. Track on right.
▼ 2.1		SO	Cross through wash.
	2.1 ▲	SO	Cross through wash.
▼ 2.2		SO	Trail drops to wash. Views south to Beaver Dam Mountains.
	2.0 ▲	SO	Trail climbs away from wash.
▼ 2.3		SO	Cross through wash.
	1.9 ▲	SO	Cross through wash.
▼ 3.8		SO	Edge of Beaver Dam Wash. Cross through wide wash.
	0.4 ▲	SO	Cross through Beaver Dam Wash.

GPS: N 37°13.58′ W 113°59.94′

▼ 4.2		TR	Pass through wire gate. Jackson Well windmill is on right next to the corral. Zero trip meter.
	0.0 ▲		Continue toward Nevada state line.

GPS: N 37°13.29′ W 113°59.80′

▼ 0.0			Continue toward Southwest #1: Indian Spring Trail, climbing away from wash.
	1.0 ▲	TL	Jackson Well windmill is on left next to the corral. Zero trip meter and turn sharp left through the wire gate next to corral.
▼ 0.2		SO	End of climb away from Beaver Dam Wash.
	0.8 ▲	SO	Trail descends to Beaver Dam Wash.
▼ 1.0			Trail ends at Southwest #1: Indian Spring Trail. Turn left to join Motoqua Road for St. George, turn right to continue along Indian Spring Trail to Old US 91.

0.0 ▲ On Southwest #1: Indian Spring Trail, 6 miles south of Motoqua Road, turn west on graded dirt road at the sign for Jackson Well and zero trip meter.

GPS: N 37°13.45′ W 113°58.69′

SOUTHWEST REGION TRAIL #3

Hell Hole Pass Trail

Starting Point:	**Old US 91, 0.9 miles south of Shivwits Indian Reservation**
Finishing Point:	**Southwest #1: Indian Spring Trail**
Total Mileage:	**7.9 miles**
Unpaved Mileage:	**7.9 miles**
Driving Time:	**45 minutes**
Elevation Range:	**4,400–6,300 feet**
Usually Open:	**Year-round**
Difficulty Rating:	**3**
Scenic Rating:	**7**
Remoteness Rating:	**+1**

Special Attractions
■ Extensive views west into Nevada.
■ Hell Hole Pass through the Beaver Dam Mountains.

Description
Hell Hole Pass is one of only a few small dirt roads that cross the Beaver Dam Mountains. The trail leaves Old US 91 south of the Shivwits Indian Reservation and immediately winds its way up toward the pass. The grade is moderately steep for the most part; the trail climbs a total of 1,900 feet from the highway to the pass. The surface is good, there are no large rocks, and although sections are loose, on the whole traction is good. There are some good views as the trail climbs—back to the east over St. George, the long Hurricane Cliffs escarpment, Sand Mountain, and as far as Zion National Park.

Leading off from the top of the pass is the challenging

Looking down through Indian Canyon

Southwest #4: TV Towers Jeep Trail, a steep, difficult spur trail that leads to stunning views. As Hell Hole Pass Trail descends into Indian Canyon, the trail standard drops somewhat, and the single-width ungraded trail becomes slightly sandy as it follows Indian Creek through the trees. There are a couple of small, sheltered campsites along the descent. The rockiest section is in the wash itself, as the trail rounds a point in a narrow valley—extra wide vehicles will find it tight but passable.

As Indian Spring spills out onto the sloping alluvial fan above the spring itself, the views spread out to the west into Nevada. The trail finishes at Indian Spring, which is marked by a large metal water tank; this north-south dirt road is Southwest #1: Indian Spring Trail. The original track is washed out, and the new route finishes just below the spring. A sign at the spring gives the distance south to Old US 91.

Current Road Information
BLM St. George Field Office
345 East Riverside Drive
St. George, UT 84790
(435) 688-3200

Map References
BLM St. George
USGS 1:24,000 Jarvis Peak, Shivwits, West Mt. Peak
1:100,000 St. George
Maptech CD-ROM: Escalante/Dixie National Forest
Utah Atlas & Gazetteer, p. 16
Utah Travel Council #4 (incomplete)

Route Directions

▼ 0.0			From Old US 91, 0.9 miles south of the Shivwits Indian Reservation, turn west on unmarked graded road, and zero trip meter. Cross cattle guard.
	4.1 ▲		Trail ends at Old US 91, immediately south of the Shivwits Indian Reservation. Turn left for St. George, turn right for Littlefield, Arizona.
			GPS: N 37°06.70′ W 113°49.27′
▼ 0.1		SO	Track on left.
	4.0 ▲	SO	Track on right.
▼ 0.2		SO	Track on left.
	3.9 ▲	SO	Track on right.
▼ 0.6		SO	Track on right opposite concrete foundations.
	3.5 ▲	SO	Track on left opposite concrete foundations.
			GPS: N 37°06.77′ W 113°49.92′
▼ 0.8		SO	Track on right.
	3.3 ▲	SO	Track on left.
▼ 1.1		SO	Faint track on left. Main trail climbs toward the pass.
	3.0 ▲	SO	Faint track on right.
▼ 2.1		SO	Tracks on left and right.
	2.0 ▲	SO	Tracks on left and right.
			GPS: N 37°07.48′ W 113°51.01′
▼ 2.8		SO	Faint track on left, then track on right.
	1.3 ▲	SO	Track on left, then faint track on right.
▼ 2.9		SO	Track on left to viewpoint.
	1.2 ▲	SO	Track on right to viewpoint.
▼ 3.4		SO	Cross through wash, then track on left.
	0.7 ▲	SO	Track on right, then cross through wash.

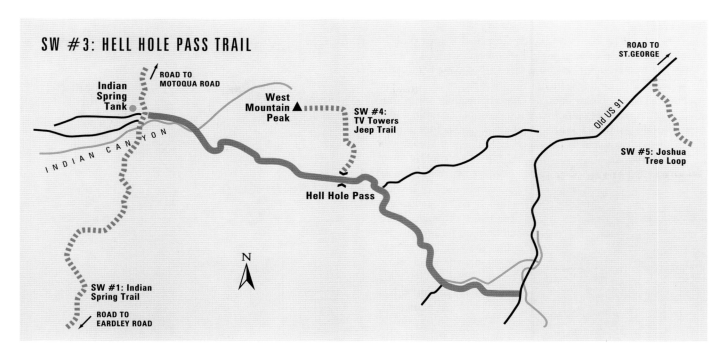

SW #3: HELL HOLE PASS TRAIL

▼ 3.7	SO	Cross over wash.
0.4 ▲	SO	Cross over wash.
▼ 4.1	BL	Saddle at Hell Hole Pass. Track on right is Southwest #4: TV Towers Jeep Trail. Also a small track on left. Zero trip meter.
0.0 ▲		Descend from saddle toward Old US 91.

GPS: N 37°08.27' W 113°52.24'

▼ 0.0		Descend from saddle, following sign for Indian Spring.
3.8 ▲	SO	Saddle at Hell Hole Pass. Track back to left is Southwest #4: TV Towers Jeep Trail. Also a small track on right. Zero trip meter.
▼ 0.6	SO	Cross through wash.
3.2 ▲	SO	Cross through wash.

GPS: N 37°08.39' W 113°52.92'

▼ 0.8	SO	Cross through Indian Creek Wash.
3.0 ▲	SO	Cross through Indian Creek Wash.
▼ 1.0	SO	Views ahead of West Mountain Peak.
2.8 ▲	SO	Views to left of West Mountain Peak.
▼ 1.4	SO	Track on left, then concrete tank on left.
2.4 ▲	SO	Concrete tank on right, then track on right.

GPS: N 37°08.51' W 113°53.64'

▼ 2.3	SO	Enter Indian Creek Wash.
1.5 ▲	SO	Exit Indian Creek Wash.
▼ 2.4	SO	Exit Indian Creek Wash.
1.4 ▲	SO	Enter Indian Creek Wash.
▼ 2.7	SO	Concrete tank on left.
1.1 ▲	SO	Concrete tank on right.
▼ 2.8	SO	Cross through wash.
1.0 ▲	SO	Cross through wash.
▼ 3.0	BL	Cross through wash, then track on right.
0.8 ▲	SO	Track on left, then cross through wash.

GPS: N 37°08.99' W 113°54.89'

▼ 3.1	SO	Track on right.
0.7 ▲	SO	Track on left.
▼ 3.6	BL	Two tracks on right.
0.2 ▲	SO	Two tracks on left.
▼ 3.8	BR	Track on left, then trail ends at T-intersection

with graded dirt Southwest #1: Indian Spring Trail, immediately south of Indian Spring tank. Turn right for Motoqua Road, turn left for Eardley Road.

0.0 ▲		On Southwest #1: Indian Spring Trail, 5.1 miles north of Eardley Road and just south of Indian Spring tank, zero trip meter and turn east on unmarked road. The original road is washed out and marked by a sign giving distances to Eardley Road and Old US 91.

GPS: N 37°09.13' W 113°55.74'

TV Towers Jeep Trail

Starting Point:	**Hell Hole Pass on Southwest #3: Hell Hole Pass Trail**
Finishing Point:	**TV Towers on West Mountain Peak**
Total Mileage:	**2.5 miles**
Unpaved Mileage:	**2.5 miles**
Driving Time:	**30 minutes (one-way)**
Elevation Range:	**6,100–7,600 feet**
Usually Open:	**March to December**
Difficulty Rating:	**6**
Scenic Rating:	**9**
Remoteness Rating:	**+1**

Special Attractions

- Panoramic views from West Mountain Peak into three states.
- Steep climb up exciting, rugged trail.

Description

Don't be fooled by the easy, graded start of this spur trail! It leaves from the top of Hell Hole Pass on Southwest #3: Hell Hole Pass Trail and climbs to the very top of West Mountain Peak, over a thousand feet higher than the pass.

The trail starts off easy enough, climbing steadily toward the TV towers. At the 1.9 mark though, it earns its Jeep trail status as it abruptly becomes a lot steeper, with some very loose rubble and rock. Most vehicles will spin wheels here as they try to

Rocky switchback near the top of TV Towers Jeep Trail

climb. The trail is shelf road for the remainder of the climb, most of it wide enough not to cause any concern, although there are limited passing places. After the first TV tower is reached, the trail runs briefly across a ridge with massive drops on either side. This looks particularly scary coming back down, when the steep descent aims your vehicle directly off the cliff edge.

However, the final climb to the tower makes it worthwhile. At the top, there are panoramic views stretching in all directions and into three states. Nevada is west, Arizona south, and Utah north and east. To the west, you can see the route down from Hell Hole Pass and the wide sandy Beaver Dam Wash, the lowest point in Utah at only 2,000 feet above sea level. Beyond that in Nevada are the Tule Springs Hills and the Mormon and the Meadow Dam Mountains. To the north, you can see Square Top Mountain, the cone-shaped Jackson Peak, and the Bull Valley Mountains. To the east is the sprawl of St. George in the valley, with Zion National Park, the Hurricane Cliffs, and the pink sands of Sand Mountain beyond. Pine Valley Mountain is northeast.

West Mountain Peak, at 7,746 feet, often has snow at the highest elevations in winter. It may be passable during dry winter months, but do not attempt this trail if there is snow on the ground, or in wet weather because of the steepness and looseness of the trail.

View from the telecommunications tower at the top of the trail

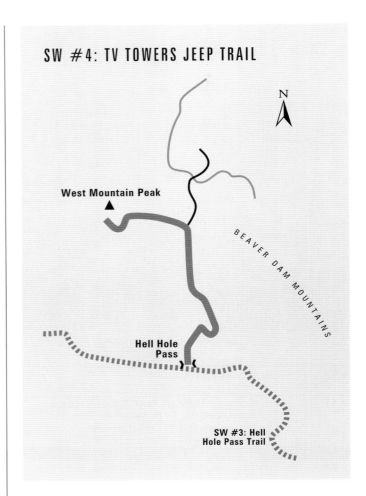

SW #4: TV TOWERS JEEP TRAIL

N

West Mountain Peak ▲

BEAVER DAM MOUNTAINS

Hell Hole Pass

SW #3: Hell Hole Pass Trail

Current Road Information

BLM St. George Field Office
345 East Riverside Drive
St. George, UT 84790
(435) 688-3200

Map References

BLM St. George (incomplete)
USGS 1:24,000 Shivwits, West Mt. Peak
1:100,000 St. George (incomplete)
Maptech CD-ROM: Escalante/Dixie National Forest
Utah Atlas & Gazetteer, p. 16

Route Directions

▼ 0.0		On Southwest #3: Hell Hole Pass Trail, from the saddle of Hell Hole Pass at the cattle guard, turn northwest on graded road following sign for TV Towers Jeep Trail and zero trip meter.
GPS: N 37°08.27' W 113°52.24'		
▼ 0.2	SO	Cross through small wash.
▼ 0.4	SO	Track on left.
▼ 0.9	SO	Saddle. TV towers are visible ahead.
GPS: N 37°09.24' W 113°52.34'		
▼ 1.4	SO	Track on right.
▼ 1.8	SO	Cross through wash.
▼ 1.9	SO	Track climbs steeply and is rougher and rockier.
▼ 2.2	SO	Pass first TV tower on left.

▼ 2.3	SO	Cross over narrow ridge with drops on either side.
▼ 2.4	BL	Start of loop around TV towers at end of trail.
▼ 2.5		End of loop; various viewpoints around loop.

GPS: N 37°09.33′ W 113°52.98′

The Beaver Dam Mountains provide a dramatic backdrop for this old corral

SOUTHWEST REGION TRAIL #5

Joshua Tree Loop

Starting Point:	Old US 91, 1 mile south of Motoqua Road, in Shivwits Indian Reservation
Finishing Point:	Old US 91, 1.8 miles north of the Arizona state line
Total Mileage:	17.9 miles
Unpaved Mileage:	17.1 miles
Driving Time:	1.5 hours
Elevation Range:	3,000–4,800 feet
Usually Open:	Year-round
Difficulty Rating:	2
Scenic Rating:	7
Remoteness Rating:	+0

Special Attractions

- Joshua tree forest.
- Views of the Beaver Dam Mountains.
- Mojave Desert vegetation and desert tortoise habitat.

History

The Apex Mine, situated along this trail, has been extracting copper since 1890. A smelter was built in St. George, on Diagonal Street, to process the metal after the mine was acquired by the Woolley, Lund and Judd Company. After World War I, the need for copper declined, and it remained low until World War II, when the Apex picked up production again.

The trail passes through the Woodbury Desert Study Area, a 3,040-acre area fenced off in 1977 to study the elusive desert tortoise, an endangered species. The area is named after Dr. Woodbury, who, along with Dr. Hardy, did pioneering research of the tortoise between 1936 and 1948. The fenced area allows the study of the plant and animal communities of this unusual region.

Description

This trail is shown on some atlases as the Joshua Tree Scenic Loop Drive, and the southern end of the road passes through large stands of Joshua trees; for a description of this member of the lily family, see p. 99 in "Along the Trail".

As well as Joshua trees, this trail offers many views of the Beaver Dam Mountains; this range marks the divide between the Mojave Desert and the Great Basin. Areas surrounding these mountains support plants and animals from both communities. Joshua trees, creosote bushes, and desert tortoises—all represen-

tatives of the Mojave Desert community—mingle with collared lizards and sagebrush. In addition, you are likely to see prairie falcons, golden eagles, rattlesnakes, Gambel's quails, and mule deer along this drive and the others in the region.

The trail leaves the highway south of Shivwits on the Indian reservation, and the first part of the trail crosses reservation land. Please respect the privacy of reservation residents by remaining on the major thoroughfare. The first section of the trail is a wide graded gravel road, as it is used by Apex Operations, which has a large plant near the start of the trail and a mine farther down, although the mine appears to be little used these days.

After leaving the Shivwits Reservation, the trail crosses into BLM land. Tracks to the left lead down to St. George via the open land of Blake's Lambing Grounds. To the west, Mount Jarvis rises up to 6,500 feet. Once you pass the turn to the Apex Mine (there's no public access to the workings), the trail gets narrower and slightly rougher as it travels through Mine Valley and Cedar Pockets before cresting Bulldog Pass. There is hiking access to the Beaver Dam Wilderness Area to the east.

The Joshua trees enter the landscape after Bulldog Pass, and the farther south you go the more abundant they be-

Joshua trees line this section of the Joshua Tree Loop. Southern Utah has the northernmost climate able to sustain this type of tree

come. They are densest after the trail passes through the Bulldog Gap at the mouth of Bulldog Canyon.

Unfortunately, a fire in 1999 destroyed many of the trees, especially in the upper areas of Bulldog Canyon. The trees are putting out new shoots, but it will be a while before they recover fully. The fire did not affect the lower areas of the trail or the Woodbury Desert Study Area, and the Joshua trees are especially prolific in the fenced area.

The trail finishes back on Old US 91, just north of the Arizona state line. In dry weather a carefully driven passenger car could make the trip, although high clearance is definitely preferable.

SW #5: JOSHUA TREE LOOP

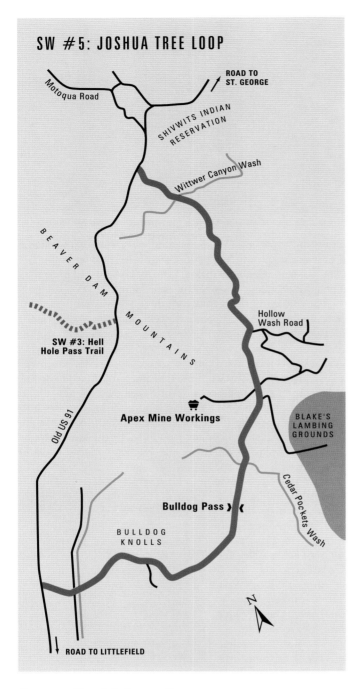

Current Road Information
BLM St. George Field Office
345 East Riverside Drive
St. George, UT 84790
(435) 688-3200

Map References
BLM St. George
USFS Dixie National Forest: Pine Valley Ranger District
(incomplete)
USGS 1:24,000 Shivwits, Jarvis Peak, Castle Cliff
1:100,000 St. George
Maptech CD-ROM: Escalante/Dixie National Forest

Utah Atlas & Gazetteer, p. 16
Utah Travel Council #4

Route Directions

▼ 0.0 From Old US 91 in the Shivwits Indian Reservation, 1 mile south of Motoqua Road, turn southeast on paved road at the large sign for Apex Operations and cross cattle guard. Zero trip meter.

7.2 ▲ Trail ends at Old US 91 in the Shivwits Indian Reservation. Turn right for St. George, turn left for Littlefield, Arizona.

GPS: N 37°09.76' W 113°47.01'

▼ 0.5 **SO** Apex Operations site on left.
6.7 ▲ **SO** Apex Operations site on right.

▼ 0.8 **SO** Road is now graded gravel. Beware of heavy mining trucks using the road.
6.4 ▲ **SO** Road is now paved.

▼ 2.6 **SO** Cross over Wittwer Canyon wash.
4.6 ▲ **SO** Cross over Wittwer Canyon wash.

▼ 3.0 **SO** Cattle guard. Leaving the Shivwits Indian Reservation (no sign).
4.2 ▲ **SO** Cattle guard. Entering the Shivwits Indian Reservation (no sign).

GPS: N 37°07.47' W 113°45.80'

▼ 5.2 **SO** Track on left.
2.0 ▲ **SO** Track on right.

▼ 5.3 **SO** Track on right, then track on left to corral.
1.9 ▲ **SO** Track on right to corral, then track on left.

▼ 5.4 **SO** Cattle guard, then track on left to corral.
1.8 ▲ **SO** Track on right to corral, then cattle guard.

GPS: N 37°05.67' W 113°45.98'

▼ 5.6 **SO** Track on right.
1.6 ▲ **SO** Track on left.

▼ 5.8 **SO** Track on left is Hollow Wash Road.
1.4 ▲ **SO** Track on right is Hollow Wash Road.

GPS: N 37°05.29' W 113°45.93'

▼ 7.2 **SO** Major graded road to the left; zero trip meter. Continue straight, following sign for Bulldog Canyon and Cedar Pockets Wash.
0.0 ▲ Continue toward Shivwits Indian Reservation.

GPS: N 37°04.18' W 113°46.30'

▼ 0.0 Continue toward Bulldog Canyon. Small track immediately on right.
0.8 ▲ **SO** Small track on left, then major graded road to the right; zero trip meter. Continue straight, following sign for Old US 91.

▼ 0.1 **SO** Cattle guard.
0.7 ▲ **SO** Cattle guard.

▼ 0.2 **BL** Large track on right to the Apex Mine workings (no access). Also small track on right. Main trail is now narrower and graded dirt.
0.6 ▲ **BR** Large track on left to the Apex Mine workings (no access). Also small track on left. Main trail is now wider and graded gravel road.

GPS: N 37°04.03' W 113°46.47'

▼ 0.6 **SO** Track on right.
0.2 ▲ **SO** Track on left.

▼ 0.8 **SO** Track on left to Blake's Lambing Grounds, signed to Bloomington. Zero trip meter.
0.0 ▲ Continue toward the Apex Mine.

GPS: N 37°03.59' W 113°46.56'

▼ 0.0 Continue toward Bulldog Pass.
9.0 ▲ **SO** Track on right to Blake's Lambing Grounds, signed to Bloomington. Zero trip meter.

▼ 0.1 **SO** Corral on right, then track on left.

8.9 ▲	SO	Track on right, then corral on left.
▼ 0.7	SO	Track on left.
8.3 ▲	SO	Track on left.
▼ 1.0	SO	Cattle guard on rise, then track on left.
8.0 ▲	SO	Track on right, then cattle guard on rise.

GPS: N 37°03.05′ W 113°47.38′

▼ 1.6	SO	Track on left.
7.4 ▲	SO	Track on right.

GPS: N 37°02.51′ W 113°47.53′

▼ 1.7	SO	Track on left.
7.3 ▲	SO	Track on right.
▼ 1.8	SO	Cross through Cedar Pockets Wash, then track on right.
7.2 ▲	SO	Track on left, then cross through Cedar Pockets Wash.
▼ 1.9	SO	Track on left.
7.1 ▲	SO	Track on right.
▼ 2.2	SO	Track on left.
6.8 ▲	SO	Track on right.
▼ 2.5	SO	Track on left.
6.5 ▲	SO	Track on right.

GPS: N 37°01.86′ W 113°48.08′

▼ 2.7	SO	Bulldog Pass. Trail descends into Bulldog Canyon. Joshua trees appear in increasing numbers.
6.3 ▲	SO	Bulldog Pass. Trail leaves Bulldog Canyon. Joshua trees decrease and stop.

GPS: N 37°01.71′ W 113°48.14′

▼ 3.5	SO	Cross through wash.
5.5 ▲	SO	Cross through wash.
▼ 3.6	SO	Track on left.
5.4 ▲	SO	Track on right.
▼ 3.9	SO	Faint track on right.
5.1 ▲	SO	Faint track on left.
▼ 4.0	SO	Track on left.
5.0 ▲	SO	Track on right.
▼ 4.1	SO	Cross through wash.
4.9 ▲	SO	Cross through wash.
▼ 4.2	SO	Track on left.
4.8 ▲	SO	Track on right.
▼ 4.3	SO	Cattle guard and cattletank on right.
4.7 ▲	SO	Cattle guard and cattletank on left.

GPS: N 37°00.78′ W 113°49.33′

▼ 4.5	SO	Cross through wash.
4.5 ▲	SO	Cross through wash.
▼ 4.6	SO	Faint track on left.
4.4 ▲	SO	Faint track on right.
▼ 5.2	SO	Track on left.
3.8 ▲	SO	Track on right.
▼ 5.6	SO	Track on right.
3.4 ▲	SO	Track on left.
▼ 5.9	SO	Track on left.
3.1 ▲	SO	Track on right.
▼ 6.4	SO	Cattle guard in Bulldog gap.
2.6 ▲	SO	Cattle guard in Bulldog gap.
▼ 6.6	SO	Cross through wash.
2.4 ▲	SO	Cross through wash.
▼ 6.8	SO	Track on left.
2.2 ▲	SO	Track on right.

GPS: N 37°01.25′ W 113°51.50′

▼ 6.9	SO	Cross through wash.
2.1 ▲	SO	Cross through wash.
▼ 7.2	SO	Track on right.
1.8 ▲	SO	Track on left.

▼ 7.5	SO	Track on right, then cross through wash, and second track on right to campsite.
1.5 ▲	SO	Track on left to campsite, then cross through wash and second track on left.
▼ 7.6	SO	Entering Woodbury Desert Study Area over cattle guard.
1.4 ▲	SO	Leaving Woodbury Desert Study Area over cattle guard.
▼ 8.5	SO	Cross through wash.
0.5 ▲	SO	Cross through wash.
▼ 8.9	SO	Cross through wash.
0.1 ▲	SO	Cross through wash.
▼ 9.0	SO	Camping area on right, then track on right, cattle guard, and track on left. Exiting Woodbury Desert Study Area. Information board at exit. Zero trip meter.
0.0 ▲		Continue toward Bulldog Gap.

GPS: N 37°01.09′ W 113°53.49′

▼ 0.0		Continue toward Old US 91.
0.9 ▲	SO	Track on right, then entering Woodbury Desert Study Area. Information board at entrance. Cattle guard, then camping area and track on left. Zero trip meter.
▼ 0.1	SO	Track on right.
0.8 ▲	SO	Track on left.
▼ 0.8	SO	Track on right.
0.1 ▲	SO	Track on left.
▼ 0.9		Trail ends at paved Old US 91. Turn left for Littlefield, Arizona; turn right for St. George.
0.0 ▲		On Old US 91, 1.8 miles north of the Arizona state line, turn southeast on graded dirt road at the sign for the Woodbury Desert Study Area, and zero trip meter.

GPS: N 37°01.60′ W 113°54.35′

SOUTHWEST REGION TRAIL # 6

The Divide Trail

Starting Point:	**Arizona–Utah state line**
Finishing Point:	**Utah 59, 3.2 miles east of Hurricane**
Total Mileage:	**11.6 miles**
Unpaved Mileage:	**11.6 miles**
Driving Time:	**1 hour**
Elevation Range:	**3,900–4,800 feet**
Usually Open:	**Year-round**
Difficulty Rating:	**1**
Scenic Rating:	**6**
Remoteness Rating:	**+1**

Special Attractions

■ Access point to the historic Honeymoon Trail.
■ Little Creek Mountain Mesa and the Divide.
■ Alternative route down to the Arizona Strip.

Description

This graded dirt road connects Utah 59 with the Arizona Strip district. In dry weather, it is an easy scenic drive that passes

A view of the trail with Little Creek Mountain on the right

Map References

BLM St. George
USGS 1:24,000 The Divide, Little Creek Mt., Virgin, Hurricane
1:100,000 St. George
Maptech CD-ROM: Escalante/Dixie National Forest
Utah Atlas & Gazetteer, p. 17
Utah Travel Council #4

Route Directions

▼ 0.0			Trail commences on the Arizona-Utah state line. In Arizona, the road is marked as BLM road #1015. Zero trip meter at the border fence and proceed north into Utah.
	8.6 ▲		Trail ends at the Arizona-Utah state line. Continuing on leads to the Arizona Strip.
		GPS: N 37°00.00' W 113°16.42'	
▼ 0.1		SO	Track on left is Southwest #7: Hurricane Cliffs Trail, part of the Honeymoon Trail.
	8.5 ▲	SO	Track on right is Southwest #7: Hurricane Cliffs Trail, part of the Honeymoon Trail.
		GPS: N 37°00.10 W 113°16.46'	
▼ 0.3		SO	Track on left joins the Honeymoon Trail and the Hurricane Cliffs Trail.
	8.3 ▲	SO	Track on right joins the Honeymoon Trail and the Hurricane Cliffs Trail.
▼ 0.4		SO	Track on right. Little Creek Mountain is large mesa ahead on right.
	8.2 ▲	SO	Track on left.
▼ 1.3		SO	Cattle guard, then major graded road on right.
	7.3 ▲	SO	Major graded road on left, then cattle guard.
		GPS: N 37°01.14' W 113°16.15'	
▼ 1.6		SO	Cross over wash.
	7.0 ▲	SO	Cross over wash.
▼ 1.8		SO	Track on right, then cross through wash.
	6.8 ▲	SO	Cross through wash, then track on left.
▼ 1.9		SO	Track on left.
	6.7 ▲	SO	Track on right.
▼ 2.6		SO	Track on left.
	6.0 ▲	SO	Track on right.
▼ 3.2		SO	Faint track on left. Trail passes through The Divide.
	5.4 ▲	SO	Trail passes through The Divide. Faint track on right.
		GPS: N 37°02.83' W 113°16.32'	
▼ 3.4		SO	Track on left.
	5.2 ▲	SO	Track on right.
▼ 3.8		SO	Old sign on left, "Ashby's Blvd."
	4.8 ▲	SO	Old sign on right," Ashby's Blvd."
▼ 3.9		SO	Track on left.
	4.7 ▲	SO	Track on right.
▼ 4.1		SO	Track on left, cattle guard, then track on right.
	4.5 ▲	SO	Track on left, cattle guard, then track on right.
▼ 4.6		SO	Cross over wash.
	4.0 ▲	SO	Cross over wash.
▼ 6.0		SO	Track on right. Gooseberry Mesa is directly ahead.
	2.6 ▲	SO	Track on left.
▼ 7.8		SO	Track on left.
	0.8 ▲	SO	Track on right.
▼ 8.3		SO	Track on left.
	0.3 ▲	SO	Track on right.
▼ 8.4		SO	Cattle guard.
	0.2 ▲	SO	Cattle guard.

through a wide-bottomed valley, with the Hurricane Cliffs on the west and Little Creek Mountain rising up to the east. It also provides access to the historic Honeymoon Trail, and adventurous drivers can make a loop from Hurricane by combining this easy trail with the 6-rated Southwest #7: Hurricane Cliffs Trail.

To reach the start of the trail, drive south on Utah 59 into Arizona (where it becomes Arizona 389), past Colorado City, to the junction with county highway 237. Turn right onto county highway 237 and proceed southwest to the junction with Navajo Trail Road. Turn right here and drive west to the junction with Arizona BLM road #1015. Turn right and head north toward Utah. The trail commences on the Arizona state line, where the Arizona BLM road #1015 crosses into Utah.

You reach the junction with the Hurricane Cliffs Trail, which is part of the long Honeymoon Trail, almost immediately. The Divide Trail heads north for most of its route, rising up to pass through the gap of the Divide. There are many small tracks to the left and right; most are short dead end trails that lead to a viewpoint or campsite, although a few loop around to rejoin the main trail later.

A sign post along the trail

After 8.6 miles, a major track to the right has a BLM sign for Little Creek Mountain. On maps, this climbs onto the mesa to the radio tower, but the track is washed out and impassable to vehicles. Access to Little Creek Mountain is via Apple Valley, farther east on Utah 59.

The trail finishes at Utah 59, 3.2 miles from Hurricane.

Current Road Information

BLM St. George Field Office
345 East Riverside Drive
St. George, UT 84790
(435) 688-3200

SW #6: THE DIVIDE TRAIL

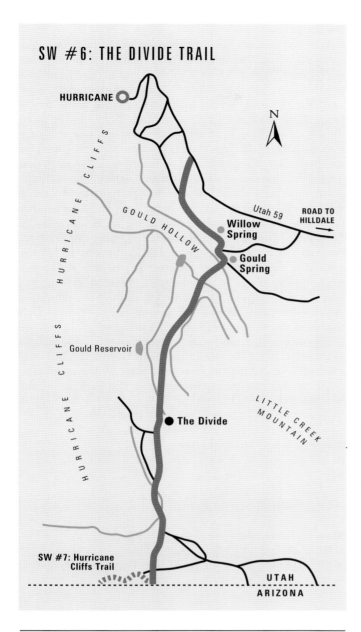

| ▼ 8.6 | SO | Track on right is signed to Little Creek Mountain, but road is washed out; no vehicle access. Zero trip meter at sign. |
| 0.0 ▲ | | Continue toward the Arizona state line. Little Creek Mountain is on left. |

GPS: N 37°07.03′ W 113°14.49′

▼ 0.0		Continue toward Utah 59.
3.0 ▲	SO	Track on left is signed to Little Creek Mountain, but road is washed out; no vehicle access. Zero trip meter at sign.
▼ 0.1	SO	Cross through Gould Wash.
2.9 ▲	SO	Cross through Gould Wash.
▼ 0.2	SO	Faint track on right.
2.8 ▲	SO	Faint track on left.
▼ 0.3	SO	Track on left.
2.7 ▲	SO	Track on right.
▼ 1.9	BR	Corral on right, two tracks on left.
1.1 ▲	SO	Corral on left, two tracks on right.

GPS: N 37°08.33′ W 113°15.68′

▼ 2.1	SO	Cattle guard.
0.9 ▲	SO	Cattle guard.
▼ 3.0		Trail ends on Utah 59, 0.1 miles southeast of mile marker 19. Turn left for Hurricane, turn right for Hilldale.
0.0 ▲		On Utah 59, 0.1 miles southeast of mile marker 19, 3.2 miles east of Hurricane, zero trip meter and turn south on unsigned, graded dirt road.

GPS: N 37°09.28′ W 113°15.45′

SOUTHWEST REGION TRAIL #7

Hurricane Cliffs Trail

Starting Point:	11 miles south of Hurricane Airport,
	0.4 miles south of Arizona state line
Finishing Point:	Southwest #6: The Divide Trail, at the
	Arizona state line
Total Mileage:	2.7 miles
Unpaved Mileage:	2.7 miles
Driving Time:	45 minutes
Elevation Range:	3,400–4,400 feet
Usually Open:	Year-round
Difficulty Rating:	6
Scenic Rating:	9
Remoteness Rating:	+1

Special Attractions

■ Section of the historic Honeymoon Trail.
■ Exciting, challenging climb up Hurricane Cliffs.
■ Desert cactus vegetation.

History

The Hurricane Cliffs lie along the north-south Hurricane fault line. Movement of this fault caused the lands east of the fault to lift by hundreds of feet, which left a basin to the west. The Hurricane Cliffs extend down into the Arizona Strip and present an almost unbroken face for more than 200 miles.

The Honeymoon Trail is an early Mormon route, con-

Looking back toward the mesas in Arizona from Hurricane Cliffs

Climbing the switchbacks along Hurricane Cliffs Trail

structed by John D. Lee, that led from the Mormon colonies along the Arizona Strip north to St. George. In the late 1800s, many Mormons were settling the remote areas of southwest Utah and the Arizona Strip district. Some were moving by choice, others at the direction of the Mormon Church, which was actively encouraging and directing pioneers into this remote region. Still others were quietly relocating there in an effort to evade the federal government in its crackdown on polygamists.

St. George Temple, the first Mormon temple built west of the Mississippi, was opened in 1877, a full 16 years before the better known temple in Salt Lake City. After St. George Temple opened, a steady stream of Mormons began to make the long trek from their settlements along the Arizona Strip to St. George to be married. They traveled in groups, and the route they traveled became known as the Honeymoon Trail. Most of this trail is still visible today and can be traveled in a 4WD.

This trail follows the section of the Honeymoon Trail that descends the Hurricane Cliffs, and it connects with the much easier Southwest #6: The Divide Trail to make a loop back to Hurricane.

Description

Getting to the start of this trail is a slight challenge in itself, as none of the roads are marked! From Utah 9, on the west side of Hurricane, turn south on the signed road to the airport. Follow this due south, then before entering the airport itself, swing right, then left. The graded road continues due south, closely following the base of the Hurricane Cliffs. After 11 miles from the airport entrance—past the subdivisions and just across the Arizona border (although there is no state line sign)—look for an upright wooden post carved with the words "Honeymoon Trail." The sign is to the left of the trail, where the trail drops down into a creek wash. This is the trail's original entrance, but it is washed out. Zero your trip meter here, and after another 0.1 miles, turn left onto an unmarked but well-used trail.

The trail climbs steeply almost immediately and becomes very steep in places, with low traction on loose rock. For the most part the trail follows an extremely narrow shelf road, where passing places are very limited. The most difficult section is near the top; a narrow, rocky, off-camber section tilts vehicles toward the drop. Those who do not like narrow shelf roads will rate this trail with a high fear factor!

As you climb, the views are stunning: over Sand Mountain to the west, along the face of the sheer Hurricane Cliffs, and south into Arizona over multicolored, banded buttes and mesas.

At the top, the trail is an easygoing two-track as it joins Southwest #6: The Divide Trail.

This trail should not be attempted in slippery conditions.

Current Road Information

BLM St. George Field Office
345 East Riverside Drive
St. George, UT 84790
(435) 688-3200

Map References

BLM Littlefield (AZ), St. George (UT)
USGS 1:24,000 Rock Canyon (AZ), The Divide (UT)

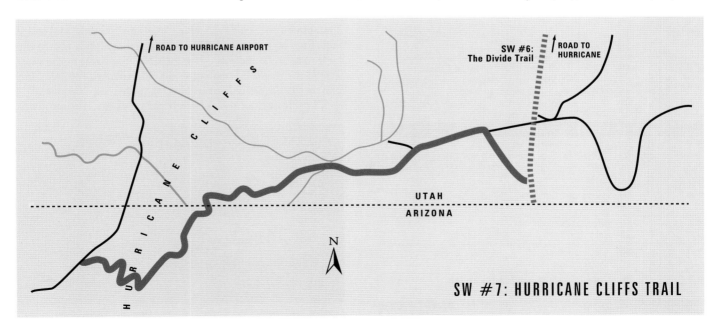

SW #7: HURRICANE CLIFFS TRAIL

1:100,000 Littlefield (AZ), St. George (UT)
Maptech CD-ROM: Grand Canyon (AZ); Escalante/Dixie
    National Forest (UT)
Utah Atlas & Gazetteer, p. 17

Route Directions

▼ 0.0		11 miles south of Hurricane Airport, on graded dirt road along the base of Hurricane Cliffs, zero trip meter in a wash, next to the Honeymoon Trail signpost. Continue south along graded road.
1.5 ▲		Trail ends at graded dirt road, in a wash, south of Hurricane. Continue north to return to Utah 9 via Hurricane Airport. Left leads into Arizona.
	GPS: N 36°59.73' W 113°18.54'	
▼ 0.1	TL	Turn left onto unmarked, narrow, ungraded, well-used dirt road.
1.4 ▲	TR	Turn right onto graded dirt road.
	GPS: N 36°59.69' W 113°18.60'	
▼ 0.3	SO	Track on left is the original washed-out trail. Trail climbs steeply along a narrow shelf road.
1.2 ▲	SO	Track on right is the original washed-out trail. End of steep descent.
▼ 0.8	SO	Cross through wash.
0.7 ▲	SO	Cross through wash.
	GPS: N 36°59.78' W 113°18.05'	
▼ 1.1	SO	Cross over wash.
0.4 ▲	SO	Cross over wash.
▼ 1.2	SO	Cross the Arizona state line (unmarked) at the 37° latitude line.
0.3 ▲	SO	Cross the Arizona state line (unmarked) at the 37° latitude line.
▼ 1.3	SO	Off-camber, loose, rocky short section.
0.2 ▲	SO	Off-camber, loose, rocky short section.
	GPS: N 37°00.03' W 113°17.84'	
▼ 1.5	TL	T-intersection at end of steep climb. Track on right goes 0.1 miles to viewpoint on the state line. Zero trip meter.
0.0 ▲		Proceed along trail, which quickly drops steeply along a narrow shelf road.
	GPS: N 37°00.05' W 113°17.65'	
▼ 0.0		Continue toward the Divide Trail and pass through wire gate.
1.2 ▲	TR	Pass through wire gate, then turn right. Track straight on goes 0.1 miles to viewpoint on the state line. Zero trip meter.
▼ 0.2	SO	Track on left to viewpoint.
1.0 ▲	SO	Track on right to viewpoint.
	GPS: N 37°00.14' W 113°17.45'	
▼ 0.7	SO	Track on left to dam.
0.5 ▲	BL	Track on right to dam.
▼ 0.9	BR	Track on left also joins the Divide Trail.
0.3 ▲	SO	Track on right rejoins the Divide Trail.
	GPS: N 37°00.28' W 113°16.71'	
▼ 1.2		Trail ends at the T-intersection with Southwest #6: The Divide Trail, just north of the Arizona state line. Turn left on the Divide Trail to Hurricane.
0.0 ▲		On Southwest #6: The Divide Trail, 0.1 miles north of the Arizona state line, turn northwest on dirt trail, marked with a Honeymoon Trail marker post and zero trip meter. The state line is marked with a cattle guard and a fence but no sign, although BLM road #1015 is marked on the Arizona side.
	GPS: N 37°00.10' W 113°16.46'	

Smithsonian Butte Trail

Starting Point:	Rockville
Finishing Point:	Utah 59 at Big Plain Junction, 0.1 miles north of mile marker 8
Total Mileage:	8.9 miles
Unpaved Mileage:	8.1 miles
Driving Time:	45 minutes
Elevation Range:	3,800–5,000 feet
Usually Open:	Year-round
Difficulty Rating:	2
Scenic Rating:	9
Remoteness Rating:	+0

Special Attractions
- Views over Zion National Park.
- Grafton ghost town.
- Designated national backcountry byway.

History
When the John Wesley Powell Expedition traveled through Zion, the expedition geologist, Edward Dutton, named Smithsonian Butte after the Smithsonian Institute, which was sponsoring the expedition. Dutton himself has a nearby pass named after him, Dutton Pass, which cuts through the Vermilion Cliffs to the southeast of Smithsonian Butte.

The town at the start of the trail, Rockville, was first settled in 1862 in an attempt by the scattered settlers of the upper Virgin River to band together. The combination of the Indian Wars and repeated flooding made it difficult for individual pioneers to get ahead, so the people gathered and concentrated their efforts in Rockville. The township was originally called Adventure, but the name was changed to Rockville because of the rocky soils along the Virgin River. The town's single-lane steel bridge was built in 1926, providing a permanent route across the river and replacing the many shaky structures that

Smithsonian Butte

were constantly having to be rebuilt after floods.

Across the river to the west, Grafton, now a ghost town, was settled in 1859 by folks from nearby Virgin, including Nathan Tenney. Here too the Virgin River was the bane of the new settlement (for a short time known as Wheeler), and after many of the houses were washed away in 1862, the fledgling township was forced to relocate a mile upstream from the original site. However, on January 8, 1862, with floodwaters still raging, Nathan Tenney's wife went into labor in the family's wagon box. The men of the town succeeded in lifting the wagon out of harm's way and later that night Mr. and Mrs. Tenney became the proud parents of a new son whom they appropriately named Marvelous Flood "Marv" Tenney. Besides repeated flooding of the unpredictable Virgin River, Indian Wars also troubled Grafton, forcing several families to leave the area; the graveyard contains a memorial to a family killed by Indians.

The Virgin River, which enabled Grafton to grow crops, was also the dividing point of the town. Residents would keep horses on both sides of the river—those on the far side for traveling north, those within the town for traveling over Grafton Mesa to the towns to the south. This way, when the river flooded, they were not trapped in town.

By the mid-1880s, Grafton supported 28 families and was the first county seat for Kane County (Grafton is now part of Washington County). The adobe meetinghouse, the major

The larger of the two roads approaching Wire Mesa

building remaining today, was built in 1886 using timber imported from Mount Trumbull on the Arizona Strip, and it was packed and rendered with local clay. This meeting hall, the focal point for the community, was used for dances, church meetings, funerals, and parties as well as religious worship. Residents also helped with the construction of the Hurricane Canal, an ambitious scheme to bring irrigation waters to the Hurricane Bench, which opened up the area for cultivation. In return for their work, these Grafton residents received parcels of land in Hurricane. For many, the temptation to dismantle their homes and rebuild in Hurricane, away from the Virgin River floodplain, was great, and by the early 1920s, Grafton was nearing ghost town status. The final resident moved out in the early 1930s.

Grafton had a brief resurgence when its decaying buildings

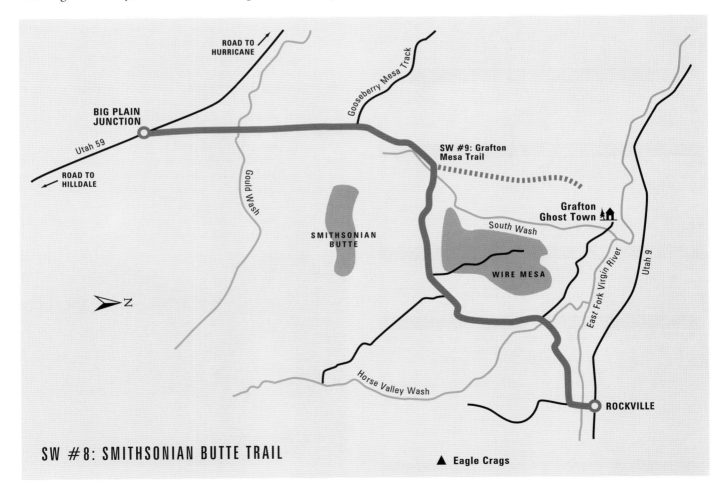

SW #8: SMITHSONIAN BUTTE TRAIL

were used in scenes for the movie *Butch Cassidy and the Sundance Kid* (1969).

Today, Grafton is privately owned, and the remaining buildings are undergoing extensive renovations in conjunction with the Bureau of Land Management. In 2000, the adobe meeting hall was brought back from ruin; it has a new floor, patched adobe, and fresh paint. The oldest building in town, opposite the meeting hall, has been propped up and stabilized for safety, as have some of the other cabins. Visitors are allowed to explore the area, but should not disturb the remains.

Description

Smithsonian Butte Road, a designated national backcountry byway, crosses over the Vermilion Cliffs between Utah 9 and Utah 59. The trail is short and graded road its entire length. It leaves the town of Rockville near the western edge of Zion National Park and immediately crosses the East Fork of the Virgin River on the historic steel girder bridge.

After 1.6 miles, you reach a T-intersection. Turn right to go 1.7 miles along a graded dirt road if you want to visit the ghost town of Grafton. You first pass the cemetery on the left, followed by the remains of the town itself.

The main trail follows Horse Valley Wash for a short distance before climbing steeply onto the mesa. This section can be a little rutty and washed out, but high-clearance 2WD vehicles will have no problems in dry weather. The prominent jagged peaks of Eagle Crags can be seen on the left.

Once on the mesa, you'll see the bulk of Smithsonian Butte ahead. The trail continues along the top, passing Southwest #9: Grafton Mesa Trail before dropping gradually down the south side of the Vermilion Cliffs.

The final part of the road crosses over farmland before reaching Utah 59 at Big Plain Junction. The junction appears on maps, but there are no signs for it on the road.

Current Road Information

BLM St. George Field Office
345 East Riverside Drive
St. George, UT 84790
(435) 688-3200

Map References

BLM St. George
USGS 1:24,000 Smithsonian Butte, Springdale West
1:100,000 St. George
Maptech CD-ROM: Escalante/Dixie National Forest
Trails Illustrated, #214 (incomplete)
Utah Atlas & Gazetteer, p. 17
Utah Travel Council #4

Route Directions

▼ 0.0			From Utah 9 at the east end of Rockville, turn south on Bridge Road (200 East Street) and zero trip meter.
	1.6 ▲		Trail ends at Utah 9 in Rockville. Turn right for Zion National Park, turn left for Hurricane.
		GPS: N 37°09.66′ W 113°02.23′	
▼ 0.1		SO	Cross over East Fork Virgin River on steel girder bridge.

	1.5 ▲	SO	Cross over East Fork Virgin River on steel girder bridge.
▼ 0.3		TR	Dirt road continues ahead. Follow the small sign for Grafton and Utah 59.
	1.3 ▲	TL	Road to the right.
▼ 0.8		SO	Road is now graded dirt.
	0.8 ▲	SO	Road is now paved.
▼ 0.9		SO	Cattle guard.
	0.7 ▲	SO	Cattle guard.
▼ 1.5		SO	Cattle guard.
	0.1 ▲	SO	Cattle guard.
▼ 1.6		TL	T-intersection. Right goes 1.7 miles to Grafton ghost town. Turn left and cross over Horse Valley Wash on bridge and zero trip meter.
	0.0 ▲		Continue toward Rockville.
		GPS: N 37°09.08′ W 113°03.52′	
▼ 0.0			Continue south.
	3.5 ▲	TR	Cross over Horse Valley Wash on bridge and zero trip meter. Continue straight to go 1.7 miles to Grafton ghost town.
▼ 0.3		SO	View of Eagle Crags on left.
	3.2 ▲	SO	View of Eagle Crags on right.
▼ 0.5		SO	Trail climbs to mesa.
	3.0 ▲	SO	End of descent.
▼ 1.2		SO	End of climb.
	2.3 ▲	SO	Descend to Virgin River.
▼ 1.4		SO	Track on right.
	2.1 ▲	SO	Track on left.
		GPS: N 37°08.04′ W 113°03.81′	
▼ 1.5		SO	Track on left.
	2.0 ▲	SO	Track on right.
▼ 1.6		SO	Track on left.
	1.9 ▲	SO	Track on right.
▼ 1.8		SO	Track on right goes out on Wire Mesa.
	1.7 ▲	SO	Track on left goes out on Wire Mesa.
		GPS: N 37°07.88′ W 113°04.13′	
▼ 3.3		SO	Cross over South Wash.
	0.2 ▲	SO	Cross over South Wash.
▼ 3.5		SO	Immediately before left-hand swing, track to right is Southwest #9: Grafton Mesa Trail. Parking area at the trailhead. Zero trip meter.
	0.0 ▲		Continue northeast.
		GPS: N 37°07.85′ W 113°05.83′	
▼ 0.0			Continue southwest.
	3.8 ▲	SO	Immediately after right-hand swing, track to left is Southwest #9: Grafton Mesa Trail. Parking area at the trailhead. Zero trip meter.
▼ 0.2		SO	Track on right. Smithsonian Butte is on left.
	3.6 ▲	SO	Track on left. Smithsonian Butte is on right.
▼ 0.4		SO	Major track on right.
	3.4 ▲	SO	Major track on left.
		GPS: N 37°07.55′ W 113°06.12′	
▼ 0.5		SO	Track on left.
	3.3 ▲	SO	Track on right.
▼ 0.7		SO	Track on left.
	3.1 ▲	SO	Track on right.
▼ 1.1		SO	Track on right is signed to Gooseberry Mesa. Main trail exits BLM land and crosses farmland.
	2.7 ▲	SO	Track on left is signed to Gooseberry Mesa. Main trail enters BLM land.
		GPS: N 37°07.00′ W 113°06.36′	
▼ 1.3		SO	Track on left.
	2.5 ▲	SO	Track on right.

▼ 2.3	SO	Track on left, then cattle guard.
1.5 ▲	SO	Cattle guard, then track on right.
▼ 2.6	SO	Cross over Gould Wash.
1.2 ▲	SO	Cross over Gould Wash.
▼ 3.3	SO	Corral on right.
0.5 ▲	SO	Corral on left.
▼ 3.8		Trail ends at Utah 59 at Big Plain Junction. Turn right for Hurricane, turn left for Hilldale.
0.0 ▲		On Utah 59 at Big Plain Junction, 0.1 miles north of mile marker 8, turn north on graded dirt road and zero trip meter.

GPS: N 37°04.55' W 113°06.36'

SOUTHWEST REGION TRAIL #9

Grafton Mesa Trail

Starting Point:	**Southwest #8: Smithsonian Butte Trail,**
	5.1 miles south of Utah 9
Finishing Point:	**Grafton Mesa**
Total Mileage:	**1.9 miles**
Unpaved Mileage:	**1.9 miles**
Driving Time:	**30 minutes (one-way)**
Elevation Range:	**4,300–4,800 feet**
Usually Open:	**Year-round**
Difficulty Rating:	**3**
Scenic Rating:	**8**
Remoteness Rating:	**+0**

Special Attractions

■ Views of Pastry Ridge and Mount Kinesava.
■ Accesses historic hiking trail into Grafton ghost town.

Description

This short spur leads off from Southwest #8: Smithsonian Butte Trail and runs out onto Grafton Mesa. The small trail is rocky and narrow, and the first part runs through the juniper and cedar trees that dot the top of the mesa. When the trees abate, there are wide-ranging views over the eroded Pastry Ridge, so named because of its resemblance to pie crust. The trail gradually descends, passing short spurs, one of which leads to a large pleasant campsite at an oil drilling post with views over Zion National Park.

The lower section of the trail gets narrower, rougher, and slightly brushy; wider vehicles who don't want to risk paint scratches should turn around just before the trail end. The trail

Hiking trail above the old town site of Grafton

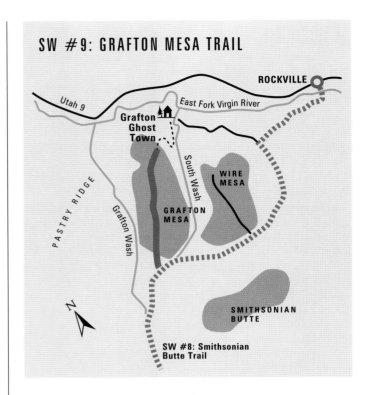

then finishes before a wash, with a rocky pour-off into South Wash far below. Immediately north of the wash, you can see the remains of a wagon road leading steeply down from the mesa. The road is well built up around the cliff face; timbers and rocks stabilize a narrow shelf. The start of the trail is washed out and impassable to vehicles, but it is possible to hike. It exits South Wash at the Grafton cemetery. The exact purpose of the trail is unknown, but it was likely a "wood road" for Grafton—a direct trail leading to the top of the mesa to obtain timber for firewood and building material. The Grafton cemetery is visible 700 feet below in the valley.

Current Road Information

BLM St. George Field Office
345 East Riverside Drive
St. George, UT 84790
(435) 688-3200

Map References

BLM St. George
USGS 1:24,000 Springdale West
1:100,000 St. George
Maptech CD-ROM: Escalante/Dixie National Forest
Trails Illustrated, #214
Utah Atlas & Gazetteer, p. 17

Route Directions

▼ 0.0	On Southwest #8: Smithsonian Butte Trail, 5.1 miles from Utah 9, zero trip meter and turn northeast on a small ungraded dirt road. Coming from Utah 9, turn is immediately before a left-hand bend and has a large parking area/campsite at the start.

GPS: N 37°07.85' W 113°05.83'

| ▼ 0.6 | SO | Views to the left over Pastry Ridge. |
| ▼ 0.8 | SO | Small campsite on right, then faint track on right. |

GPS: N 37°08.56' W 113°05.61'

▼ 1.1	SO	Turnout with view to the left.
▼ 1.4	SO	Faint track on right goes 0.1 miles to oil drilling post and large campsite with views over Zion National Park.
▼ 1.6	SO	Faint track on left.
▼ 1.8	SO	Turning point for wider vehicles who want to avoid brushy section of trail.

GPS: N 37°09.34' W 113°05.34'

| ▼ 1.9 | | Trail finishes just before a wash and rocky pour-off into South Wash. Old hiking trail continues to Grafton cemetery. |

GPS: N 37°09.42' W 113°05.30'

SOUTHWEST REGION TRAIL #10

Elephant Butte Trail

Starting Point:	**Coral Pink Sand Dunes Road, 4 miles south of state park entrance**
Finishing Point:	**Coral Pink Sand Dunes Road, 5.6 miles south of state park entrance**
Total Mileage:	**16.4 miles**
Unpaved Mileage:	**16.4 miles**
Driving Time:	**1.5 hours**
Elevation Range:	**5,600–6,300 feet**
Usually Open:	**Year-round**
Difficulty Rating:	**4 in main direction; 5 in reverse**
Scenic Rating:	**8**
Remoteness Rating:	**+1**

Special Attractions

- The Elephant Butte and Block Mesas.
- Views of Zion National Park.
- Fun, sandy trail.

History

North of Elephant Gap, the trail passes Harris Flat, with Harris Mountain visible to the northeast. Harris Ranch was one of the few prosperous ranches associated with nearby Shunesburg. The land was purchased from Chief Shunes of the local Paiute tribe in 1862. The town of Shunesburg was located to the northwest, deep in the Parunuweap Canyon on the East Fork Virgin River. This settlement was nearly impossible to access from Kanab. The only way was via the treacherous Shunes Creek Canyon, a route that became known as the Wiggle Trail. The Kanab mail carrier found an ingenious solution, lowering the mail over the edge of the 1,500-foot cliff in Parunuweap Canyon via wire cable and winch. The people from Shunesburg collected it at the foot of the cliff and continued with it to St. George.

Although crops were successful in Shunesburg, its location where the East Fork Virgin River exited the deep canyon

A beautiful view of Elephant Butte at sunset

meant flooding was a constant problem. The final straw was a grasshopper plague in the late 1870s, after which most people left the settlement. A few folk remained to ranch until the turn of the century, and today the site is part of a private ranch.

The famous one-armed geologist John Wesley Powell based his exploration team in Shunesburg while surveying the Parunuweap Canyon, which is now contained within Zion National Park.

Description

This formed trail is a lot of fun to drive—with its long, moderately challenging sandy sections—and it appears well used, although you are unlikely to see another vehicle except in hunting season, when the area is popular for its trophy deer (by permit only).

The trail passes through Elephant Gap, an opening in the series of buttes that make up the Block Mesas. The first major junction, a track to the right, leads to the Virgin River. On maps, this trail descends steeply down to the river. However, it is not recommended for vehicles.

After 8 miles, you reach the turnoff for Southwest #11: The Barracks Trail, and the main Elephant Butte Trail doubles back sharply on itself. For the next 3 miles, it follows the course of the wash through abundant sagebrush. This part of the trail can be a little brushy for wider vehicles.

The last few miles of the trail are the most difficult; a couple of deep sand descents have large holes made by vehicles coming up the trail. The easiest direction of travel is the main one described below; traveling around the loop in the reverse direction increases the difficulty rating to a 5.

The entire trail should not pose a problem for stock vehicles, although lower tire pressures are suggested. Note that many of the cattle guards have "sand mats" on either side of them to stop vehicles from wearing deep holes in the sand in front of the cattle guards. The entire trail has good views; the best are of Zion National Park as you approach the apex of the loop.

Current Road Information

BLM Kanab Field Office
318 North 100 East
Kanab, UT 84741
(435) 644-2672

Map References

BLM Kanab
USGS 1:24,000 Elephant Butte
1:100,000 Kanab
Maptech CD-ROM: Escalante/Dixie National Forest
Utah Atlas & Gazetteer, p. 18
Utah Travel Council #4

Route Directions

▼ 0.0			From Coral Pink Sand Dunes Road, 4 miles south of entrance to state park, zero trip meter and turn northwest on ungraded sandy trail. A small gravel parking area is at trailhead.
	3.3 ▲		End at Coral Pink Sand Dunes Road, 1.6 miles north of the starting point. Turn left for Coral Pink Sand Dunes State Park and US 89.
		GPS: N 37°01.46' W 112°48.13'	
▼ 1.0		SO	Track on right, then track on left, followed by second entrance to track on left.
	2.3 ▲	SO	Two entrances to track on right, then track on left.
▼ 1.1		SO	Track on left.
	2.2 ▲	SO	Track on right.
		GPS: N 37°02.48' W 112°47.95'	
▼ 2.2		SO	Track on left.
	1.1 ▲	SO	Track on right.
▼ 2.6		SO	Cross through small wash.
	0.7 ▲	SO	Cross through small wash.
▼ 2.9		SO	Cattle guard at the south side of Elephant Gap.
	0.4 ▲	SO	Cattle guard at the south side of Elephant Gap.
		GPS: N 37°03.95' W 112°48.08'	
▼ 3.2		SO	Track on left.
	0.1 ▲	SO	Track on right.
▼ 3.3		BL	Track on right goes to the Virgin River (recommended for ATVs only). Zero trip meter.
	0.0 ▲		Continue along main sandy trail.
		GPS: N 37°04.28' W 112°48.11'	
▼ 0.0			Continue along main sandy trail.
	4.7 ▲	SO	Track on left is second entrance to Virgin River trail. Zero trip meter.

A cattle guard and sand mats help you along past Elephant Gap

▼ 0.3		SO	Track on right is second entrance to Virgin River trail. Continue northwest toward the gap between two buttes. To the right are the Block Mesas and Harris Mountain.
	4.4 ▲	BR	Track on left goes to the Virgin River (recommended for ATVs only). To the left are the Block Mesas and Harris Mountain.
▼ 0.6		SO	Pass through gap in the buttes. Track on left and track on right at saddle. Views ahead to Zion National Park.
	4.1 ▲	SO	Pass through gap in the buttes. Track on left and track on right at saddle.
		GPS: N 37°04.78' W 112°48.44'	
▼ 0.7		SO	Pass through wire gate, then cattle guard.
	4.0 ▲	SO	Cattle guard, then pass through wire gate.
▼ 0.8		BR	Track on left. Sandstone Butte is on left.
	3.9 ▲	SO	Track on right. Sandstone Butte is on right.
		GPS: N 37°04.81' W 112°48.72'	
▼ 1.9		SO	Faint track on left.
	2.8 ▲	SO	Faint track on right.
▼ 2.0		SO	Track on right.
	2.7 ▲	SO	Track on left.
		GPS: N 37°05.42' W 112°49.80'	
▼ 3.4		SO	Track on right.
	1.3 ▲	SO	Track on left.
▼ 3.5		SO	Track on right, then pass through old fence line.
	1.2 ▲	SO	Pass through old fence line, then track on left.
▼ 4.1		BL	Track on right.
	0.6 ▲	SO	Track on left.
▼ 4.7		TL	Ahead is Southwest #11: The Barracks Trail. Turn sharp left in front of small area of white rock. Zero trip meter.
	0.0 ▲		Continue back southeast toward Sandstone Butte.
		GPS: N 37°07.24' W 112°51.09'	
▼ 0.0			Continue back southeast following the creek course. There is no defined wash, but abundant sagebrush makes trail narrow and brushy for next 3.2 miles.
	3.2 ▲	TR	Ahead is Southwest #11: The Barracks Trail. Turn sharp right and zero trip meter.
▼ 1.0		SO	Pass through fence line.
	2.2 ▲	SO	Pass through fence line.
		GPS: N 37°06.46' W 112°51.19'	
▼ 1.9		SO	Faint track on left.
	1.3 ▲	SO	Faint track on right.
▼ 2.1		SO	Exit creek course.
	1.1 ▲	SO	Enter creek course. There is no defined wash, but abundant sagebrush.
▼ 2.3		SO	Track on right.
	0.9 ▲	SO	Track on left.
		GPS: N 37°05.49' W 112°51.72'	
▼ 2.5		SO	Cross through wash.
	0.7 ▲	SO	Cross through wash.
▼ 3.2		SO	Track on left. Kane Spring and dam on the right. End of brushy section. Zero trip meter.
	0.0 ▲		Continue northwest.
		GPS: N 37°04.81' W 112°51.12'	
▼ 0.0			Continue south. Immediately pass second track on left.
	5.2 ▲	BL	Two tracks on right, Kane Spring and dam on the left. Views ahead to Zion National Park. The trail is narrow and brushy for the next 3.2 miles.
▼ 0.1		SO	Cross through wash.
	5.1 ▲	SO	Cross through wash.

SW #10: ELEPHANT BUTTE TRAIL

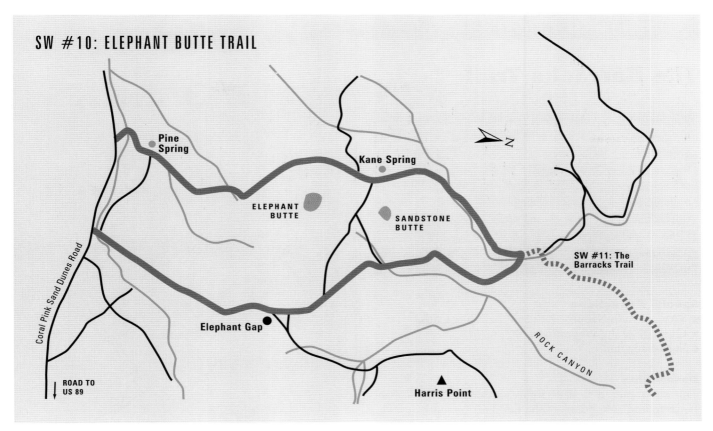

▼ 0.2	SO	Intersection. Elephant Butte is on left.	
5.0 ▲	SO	Intersection. Elephant Butte is on right.	

GPS: N 37°04.58' W 112°51.16'

▼ 0.5	SO	Track on right.
4.7 ▲	SO	Track on left.

GPS: N 37°04.31' W 112°51.18'

▼ 0.6	SO	Faint track on left.
4.6 ▲	SO	Faint track on right.

▼ 0.8	SO	Track on left.
4.4 ▲	SO	Track on right.

▼ 1.2	SO	Track on right.
4.0 ▲	SO	Track on left.

▼ 1.7	SO	Grassy campsite on left with views of Elephant Butte.
3.5 ▲	SO	Grassy campsite on right with views of Elephant Butte.

GPS: N 37°03.43' W 112°50.59'

▼ 1.8	SO	Faint track on right, then cross through slickrock wash.
3.4 ▲	SO	Cross through slickrock wash, then faint track on left.

▼ 2.3	SO	Steep, deep sandy descent.
2.9 ▲	SO	Top of ascent.

▼ 2.4	SO	Cross through wash, then track on left.
2.8 ▲	BL	Track on right, then cross through wash, followed by steep, deep sandy ascent.

GPS: N 37°03.17' W 112°49.95'

▼ 2.7	SO	Second loose descent to cross wash.
2.5 ▲	SO	Cross wash, then loose sandy ascent.

GPS: N 37°02.93' W 112°49.86'

▼ 2.8	SO	Track on left.
2.4 ▲	BL	Track on right.

GPS: N 37°02.89' W 112°49.83'

▼ 3.1	SO	Faint track on left, then cattle guard.
2.1 ▲	SO	Cattle guard, then faint track on right.

▼ 3.2	SO	Track on left.
2.0 ▲	BL	Track on right.

▼ 3.8	SO	Track on right and track on left.
1.4 ▲	SO	Track on right and track on left.

GPS: N 37°02.02' W 112°49.83'

▼ 4.2	SO	Track on left. Pine Spring in Rosy Canyon on the right.
1.0 ▲	SO	Track on right. Pine Spring in Rosy Canyon on the left.

GPS: N 37°01.73' W 112°49.89'

▼ 4.4	SO	Track on left.
0.8 ▲	SO	Track on right.

▼ 4.8	BL	Corral on right, then track on left.
0.4 ▲	SO	Track on right, then corral on left.

▼ 5.0	BL	Track on right.
0.2 ▲	BR	Track on left.

GPS: N 37°01.17' W 112°50.11'

▼ 5.1	BL	Track on right joins paved road.
0.1 ▲	SO	Track on left rejoins paved road.

▼ 5.2		End at paved Coral Pink Sand Dunes Road, 1.6 miles south of the starting point. Turn left for Coral Pink Sand Dunes State Park and US 89.
0.0 ▲		On Coral Pink Sand Dunes Road, 5.6 miles south of the state park entrance, zero trip meter and turn northwest on the unmarked, sandy trail, which briefly parallels paved road.

GPS: N 37°01.19' W 112°49.86'

The Barracks Trail

Starting Point:	**Southwest #10: Elephant Butte Trail**
Finishing Point:	**The Barracks**
Total Mileage:	**5.2 miles**
Unpaved Mileage:	**5.2 miles**
Driving Time:	**45 minutes (one-way)**
Elevation Range:	**5,100–6,200 feet**
Usually Open:	**Year-round**
Difficulty Rating:	**4**
Scenic Rating:	**8**
Remoteness Rating:	**+1**

Special Attractions

■ Views of Zion National Park and the White Cliffs.
■ Overlook of the Virgin River.
■ Fun, sandy trail.

Description

This short spur trail leads from Southwest #10: Elephant Butte Trail to an overlook of the East Fork Virgin River. The trail is sandy and ungraded, and it winds through scattered vegetation. After 3.3 miles, there is a spectacular, shaded campsite on the edge of the cliff, with views over Zion National Park and the White Cliffs.

After the campsite, a long, very sandy, loose descent leads to a slickrock wash crossing. Don't forget that you have to return this way, so if you are in doubt about your vehicle's ability to climb back up the loose sand, then the campsite makes a good place to stop. The trail descends for the next 1.9 miles to the final viewpoint on a narrow spur. You finish at a small turning circle and rock promontory high above the East Fork Virgin River.

The spur trail is remote, and you are unlikely to see anyone else out here. The BLM warns that it rarely visits the area, so travelers should be completely self-sufficient.

View of Zion National Park from a campsite along The Barracks Trail

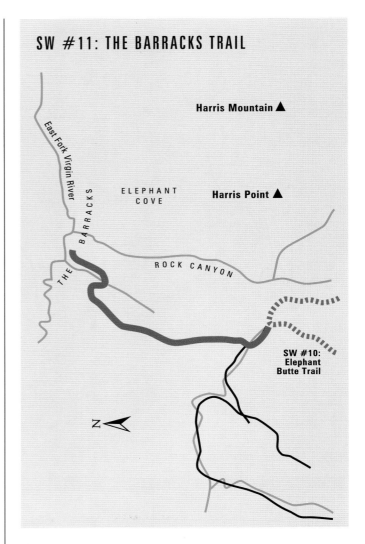

SW #11: THE BARRACKS TRAIL

Current Road Information

BLM Kanab Field Office
318 North First East
Kanab, UT 84741
(435) 644-4600

Map References

BLM Kanab
USGS 1:24,000 The Barracks, Elephant Butte
 1:100,000 Kanab
Maptech CD-ROM: Escalante/Dixie National Forest
Utah Atlas & Gazetteer, p. 18
Utah Travel Council #4

Route Directions

▼ 0.0		From Southwest #10: Elephant Butte Trail, at the farthest point of the loop, 8 miles from the start of the trail, turn northwest on unmarked trail and zero trip meter.
		GPS: N 37°07.24′ W 112°51.09′
▼ 0.3	BR	Track on left.
▼ 0.7	SO	Pass through wire gate.
		GPS: N 37°07.75′ W 112°51.18′

▼ 1.1	SO	Track on right.
	GPS: N 37°08.14' W 112°51.14'	
▼ 3.3	SO	Excellent campsite on left. Trail drops toward Rock Canyon.
	GPS: N 37°09.83' W 112°50.49'	
▼ 4.0	SO	Cross through wash.
	GPS: N 37°09.73' W 112°50.06'	
▼ 4.9	SO	Cross through rocky slickrock wash.
	GPS: N 37°10.06' W 112°50.06'	
▼ 5.2		Trail ends at viewpoint over the East Fork Virgin River.
	GPS: N 37°10.16' W 112°49.43	

SOUTHWEST REGION TRAIL #12

Moquith Mountains Trail

Starting Point:	Hancock Road, 5.5 miles southwest of US 89
Finishing Point:	Moquith Mountains
Total Mileage:	8 miles
Unpaved Mileage:	8 miles
Driving Time:	45 minutes (one-way)
Elevation Range:	6,000–7,000 feet
Usually Open:	Year-round
Difficulty Rating:	4
Scenic Rating:	8
Remoteness Rating:	+1

Special Attractions
■ Coral Pink Sand Dunes State Park.
■ Indian Canyon Pictographs Trail.
■ Fun, sandy trail with great views into Water Canyon.

Description
The dramatic pinkish red dunes of the Coral Pink Sand Dunes State Park are a major feature on this trail. Wind funnels through the Moccasin and Moquith Mountains, carrying particles of pink sand from the region's Navajo sandstone; as the air pressure drops, the grains fall to form the dunes. The dunes were one of the reasons that Kanab was once known as the most inaccessible town in the United States, and they have been the setting for their share of movies: *Arabian Nights* was filmed here in 1942, *Mackenna's Gold* in 1969, and *One Little Indian* in 1973. A conservation area within the dunes protects the coral pink beetle in its only known habitat.

The trail remains outside the boundary of the state park, but it provides a major access point into the dunes for dune buggies and sand bikes. There are also many quiet areas for hikers and photographers to enjoy the incredibly picturesque combination of vivid sands and vegetation.

From US 89, follow the signed Hancock Road for 5.5 miles to the start of the trail. An information board at the trail-

Some of southern Utah's unique wilderness found along the trail

head lists camping and off-road travel restrictions. Most of the Moquith Mountains are now within the boundaries of a wilderness study area, and vehicle travel is restricted to established roads. Those with sand vehicles can access the dunes themselves, but they are not suitable for 4WD vehicles, because of the extreme steepness and depth of the sand.

After 1.9 miles, you reach Sand Springs, the major camping area for the Moquith Mountains. The area is bare and open under large stands of pines. No campfires are allowed. The coral pink dunes rise abruptly on the right. Sand vehicles can use the designated access points to reach the dunes.

From Sand Springs, the formed track follows the dunes to the Moquith Mountains. The sand is deep and the road twisty as it winds through a mixture of tall pine trees, junipers, oaks, sagebrushes, and yuccas. Those with wide vehicles should exercise care to avoid scratching paintwork. The trail is used by ATVs as well as vehicles, and the sandy trail means you can expect fast-moving traffic in the opposite direction!

There are occasional patches of slickrock in the sand, but the first

Sand Springs and an old corral at the Coral Pink Sand Dunes State Park

part of the trail is easily traveled by stock vehicles, although you may need to deflate your tires.

After 5.2 miles, a track to the left leads to the hiking trailhead for the South Fork Indian Canyon Pictographs Trail. This narrow, twisty, 1.8-mile trail is fun to drive, but has several blind corners—watch for oncoming vehicles. At the end, hikers can follow a trail to descend into South Fork Canyon to view the pictographs.

From the turn to the hiking trail to the turnout at the end of the mapped trail, the views get better and better. The trail runs along a ridge, with views into the deep Water Canyon to the left and toward the Moccasin Mountains and Elephant Butte to the right.

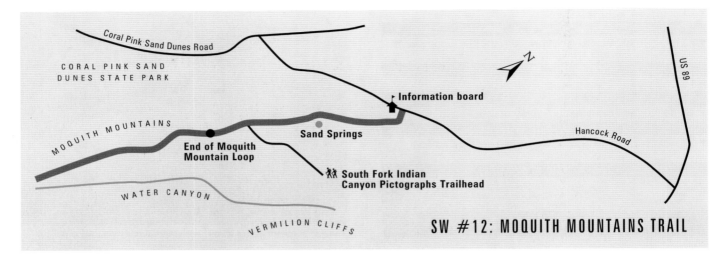

SW #12: MOQUITH MOUNTAINS TRAIL

The complete Moquith Mountains Trail is a loop trail that circles around the head of Water Canyon. However, sections of the loop beyond the final turnout involve obstacles that are beyond the reach of most stock vehicles and this book. There are very loose, steep, deep sand sections that may require winching, and there is a very difficult descent to Water Canyon over some slickrock ledges nearly 24 inches high embedded in deep sand. Vehicles should turn back at the turnout indicated.

Current Road Information
BLM Kanab Field Office
318 North First East
Kanab, UT 84741
(435) 644-4600

Map References
BLM Kanab
USGS 1:24,000 Yellow Jacket Canyon
1:100,000 Kanab
Maptech CD-ROM: Escalante/Dixie National Forest
Utah Atlas & Gazetteer, p. 18
Utah Travel Council #4

Route Directions

▼ 0.0   From Hancock Road, 5.5 miles southwest of US 89, turn southwest on graded dirt road at the information board and zero trip meter.

GPS: N 37°05.87' W 112°38.65'

▼ 0.1	SO	Information board for the dunes and Moquith Mountains.
▼ 0.2	SO	Track on left through gate. Sand dunes are now on right.
▼ 1.3	SO	Cattle guard.
▼ 1.4	SO	Faint track on left.
▼ 1.7	SO	Track on left, then main trail forks and rejoins at Sand Springs.

GPS: N 37°04.70' W 112°39.75'

▼ 1.9   SO   Tracks rejoin at Sand Springs. Old corral and spring on right. Many tracks lead off left to camping areas. Track on right is designated access to sand dunes for sand vehicles. Continue straight. Zero trip meter as you leave the open area on the track leading south.

GPS: N 37°04.54' W 112°39.87'

| ▼ 0.0 | | Continue south along the dunes. |
| ▼ 3.3 | SO | Track on left goes 1.8 miles to South Fork Indian Canyon Pictographs Trail. Zero trip meter. |

GPS: N 37°03.50' W 112°40.64'

| ▼ 0.0 | | Continue along main sandy trail. |
| ▼ 0.7 | SO | Track on left is the end of the Moquith Mountains Loop. |

GPS: N 37°02.93' W 112°40.88'

▼ 2.4   TL   Four-way junction, with large pine tree in the middle.

GPS: N 37°01.63' W 112°41.69'

▼ 2.8   UT   Views to the left into Water Canyon. Turnout on right. Main trail continues on, but becomes extremely difficult and is beyond the scope of this book. Retrace your steps to Hancock Road.

GPS: N 37°00.99' W 112°41.84'

SOUTHWEST REGION TRAIL #13

Hog Canyon Trail

Starting Point:	**US 89, 1.4 miles north of Kanab**
Finishing Point:	**Toms Canyon Overlook**
Total Mileage:	**3.9 miles**
Unpaved Mileage:	**3.9 miles**
Driving Time:	**45 minutes (one-way)**
Elevation Range:	**5,000–5,800 feet**
Usually Open:	**Year-round**
Difficulty Rating:	**6**
Scenic Rating:	**8**
Remoteness Rating:	**+0**

Special Attractions
■ Challenging, fun sandy climb out of Hog Canyon.
■ Views into Toms Canyon.
■ Short trail near to Kanab that can be completed in a couple of hours.

Description

The main feature of this trail is the challenging climb out of Hog Canyon—most vehicles will get a good workout.

The trail leaves US 89 just north of Kanab. The first mile or so along Hog Canyon on the roughly graded sandy track is easy going. At a four-way junction 1.6 miles into the trail, the fun starts. The trail climbs very steeply up a very loose and sandy section. The first part isn't too bad, but don't relax—the loosest and deepest sand is near the top. To add to the challenge, there are several deep holes in front of rock ledges. If you are going too fast at this stage, you risk undercarriage damage on the unexpected rocks. If you go too slowly, you will bog down and won't make it up! The best combination is a steady pace and low tire pressure.

An alternative route bypasses the large washout in Hog Canyon

Once you are at the top of the first climb, the worst is over, although the very loose, deep sand continues for most of the trail. There are good views over Wygaret Terrace, the White Cliffs, and down into the red-rocked Hog Canyon. After 3 miles, the trail forks. The right-hand spur takes you 0.5 miles to the radio towers on the bluff above Kanab; this trail has some good views and very challenging sandy sections. The radio towers are gated, so there is no access to the end of the spur.

Looking up the difficult, sandy climb out of Hog Canyon

The main trail goes left at the fork and continues for another mile before ending at a viewpoint overlooking Toms Canyon. Kanab can be glimpsed between the cliffs at the end of the canyon. The promontory to the east of the overlook is Savage Point.

The trail continues at this point, but it drops steeply down to run in a narrow wash with an extremely difficult exit. This part of the trail is used mainly by ATVs and is too narrow and brushy to be a pleasant experience for those in stock vehicles.

Although the trail is normally open year-round, the summer months can be extremely hot, and the first sand climb may well be impassable due to the loose sand.

Current Road Information

BLM Kanab Field Office
318 North First East
Kanab, UT 84741
(435) 644-4600

Map References

BLM Kanab
USGS 1:24,000 Kanab, Thompson Point
        1:100,000 Kanab
Maptech CD-ROM: Escalante/Dixie National Forest
Utah Atlas & Gazetteer, p. 18
Utah Travel Council #4

Route Directions

▼ 0.0		From US 89, 1.4 miles north of Kanab, 0.1 miles north of mile marker 67, zero trip meter and turn northeast on roughly graded sandy trail. Trail leaves through a parking area over a rise.
		GPS: N 37°04.74' W 112°32.27'
▼ 0.1	SO	Cattle guard. Entering Hog Canyon.
▼ 1.3	BL	North Fork Canyon enters on left, then small dead-end track on right.
▼ 1.6	TR	Four-way junction. Take second right; this well-used trail ascends a steep, sandy hill.
		GPS: N 37°05.32' W 112°30.81'
▼ 2.2	SO	Track on right. End of climb.
▼ 2.3	SO	Track on right.
▼ 2.8	BL	Track on right, then old, faded hiking trail sign on left and little-used hiking trail.
		GPS: N 37°04.44' W 112°30.68'

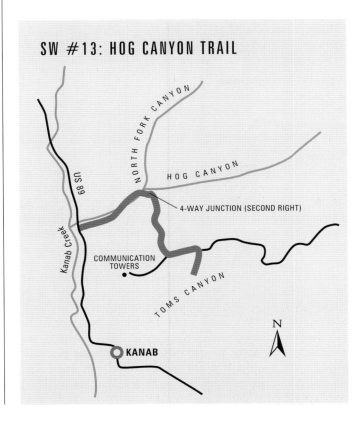

SW #13: HOG CANYON TRAIL

NORTH FORK CANYON

HOG CANYON

4-WAY JUNCTION (SECOND RIGHT)

US 89

Kanab Creek

COMMUNICATION TOWERS

TOMS CANYON

KANAB

N

▼ 3.0	BL	Track on right, then pass through fence line and bear left. The right fork goes 0.5 miles to the radio tower. Zero trip meter.
		GPS: N 37°04.33' W 112°30.55'
▼ 0.0		Continue northeast along fence line.
▼ 0.4	SO	Track on left passes through fence line.
		GPS: N 37°04.39' W 112°30.08'
▼ 0.5	BR	Track straight on continues along fence line.
▼ 0.6	SO	Track on left goes to viewpoint.
▼ 0.7	BR	Track on left drops into Toms Canyon and continues as ATV trail.
		GPS: N 37°04.30' W 112°29.94'
▼ 0.9		Trail ends at viewpoint over Toms Canyon and small turning circle and campsite.
		GPS: N 37°04.02' W 112°30.04'

SOUTHWEST REGION TRAIL #14

John R Flat Trail

Starting Point:	Kanab Creek Road, 2.7 miles from Utah 89
Finishing Point:	Johnson Canyon Road, 7.4 miles north of Utah 89
Total Mileage:	9.6 miles
Unpaved Mileage:	9.6 miles
Driving Time:	1.25 hours
Elevation Range:	5,200–5,800 feet
Usually Open:	Year-round
Difficulty Rating:	5 in main direction; 4 in reverse direction
Scenic Rating:	7
Remoteness Rating:	+0

Special Attractions
■ Kanab Creek Canyon.
■ Views over the White Cliffs and Cutler Point.
■ Fun, sandy trail.

History
The eastern end of this trail finishes in Johnson Canyon, a region of southwest Utah associated with tales of treasures and pioneer hardships. The canyon was settled in 1871 by the Johnson brothers, who had moved down the Virgin River to settle at the suggestion of Brigham Young. John D. Lee had become familiar with Johnson Canyon around this time, and he briefly settled in its upper reaches. He was keeping a low profile because of his association with the Mountain Meadows Massacre (in which, for reasons that are still unknown, Mormons killed more than a hundred non-Mormon pioneers), and one by one, his wives were deserting him. While there, he received word from nearby Kanab that government agents were tightening up on polygamists. As a precaution, he transferred his properties into the names of his remaining four wives. The church ordered him to move farther south, down to the confluence of the Paria and Colorado Rivers, and he ini-

tially took only one of his wives. His newest residence was to become the site of Lee's Ferry, once the only crossing point on the Colorado River in this region.

Farther down Johnson Canyon, a bit south of the end of the trail, is the ghost town of Johnson itself. Originally known as Spring Canyon Ranch, the settlement took on an air of permanence with the addition of a post office, schoolhouse, and stores. Orchards and vineyards prospered for a while before the settlers turned to ranching.

Johnson was the founding place of the United Order of Enoch in 1874. Under a socialistic ideal, all the townspeople agreed to contribute to the store and then receive dividends in return after five years of labor. However, when the time came for people to collect their rewards, there were no dividends to receive! As a result, people started drifting away, and by 1900 the town was completely deserted.

Johnson has become famous as a ghost town because the well-preserved buildings have been used as the setting for several movies, including *Deadwood Coach*, a silent western (1924), *Buffalo Bill* (1944), *Pony Express* (1953), and *Mackenna's Gold* (1969). The people of nearby Kanab pride themselves on being a "one-stop shop" for Hollywood. Every man, woman, and child in Kanab has a photo on file, and the town offers many movie locations. Hollywood can come to Kanab and pick the needed set, extras, and locations with little effort!

Johnson Canyon is also the scene of one of the more unusual and spooky treasure tales in Utah. In the 1500s Hernando Cortés led his Spanish army across Mexico, conquering the Aztec nation. It is widely believed that Montezuma secreted away fabulous Aztec riches to protect them from the invaders. Much of his treasure was transported north, away from the marauding armies, and hidden in what is now the American Southwest.

In 1914, a man named Freddy Crystal appeared in Kanab. He had with him a map he claimed would lead to the location of Montezuma's hidden treasure. Crystal spent a long time locating the petroglyphs in Johnson Canyon that would point him to the Aztec treasure. The map led

Difficult, sandy climb at the start of the John R Flat Trail

him to White Mountain. Crystal explored further and found ancient, hand-cut steps leading up the mountain to a concealed man-made shaft. The shaft was barricaded with granite blocks cemented into place. Both the blocks and the cement were of a stone unknown in the red sandstone country surrounding Johnson Canyon.

Realizing he needed help, Crystal approached the townsfolk of Kanab. Under their all-women council of the time, the townspeople flocked into Johnson Canyon, eager to find and share in the treasure. A tent city sprung up in the canyon, as people left their homes, farms, and businesses for the more exciting business of treasure hunting.

Eventually, access was gained to the tunnel. Inside, more granite walls and cement floors blocked passageways. A maze of tunnels penetrated into the mountain, and work was slow. The treasure hunters found the tunnels booby-trapped with large boulders poised to fall when disturbed.

After two years, the people of Kanab drifted back to their homes and occupations. The search for Montezuma's treasure was abandoned, with nothing ever being recovered. Freddy Crystal, too, gave up the search and drifted away.

But in 1989, the search for the treasure was on again! A man named Grant Childs discovered what he believed was an Aztec treasure site, not in Johnson Canyon but in a pond north of Kanab on US 89. A friend of his dove in the pond, following the treasure symbol, and located what appeared to be a man-made tunnel. Childs entered the tunnel, but became disorientated and felt a heavy current of water against him. He quickly returned to the surface. He tried again, this time with a line to help him keep his bearings and find his way out, but he was concerned when the line went limp and exited quickly. Back on the surface, his friend said the line had been taut all the time. Sonar showed that the tunnel was 100 feet long and ended in a large room.

In June, Childs returned with three professional divers, all of whom experienced disorientation and choking sensations in the tunnel. One of the divers dreamed that an Aztec warrior threw a spear at him. Every dive resulted in the same weird feelings of choking, and the divers left without ever accessing the room at the end of the tunnel.

Childs planned to drain the lake, but the lake turned out to be the only known habitat of the endangered Kanab amber snail. The property was fenced by the U.S. Fish and Wildlife Service, and all attempts to locate the treasure were halted.

Description

Like most of the trails around Kanab, the high difficulty rating for this trail is due to the extremely loose, deep sand. In this case, the most challenging section is the climb up to John R Flat from Kanab Creek.

From US 89, take Kanab Creek Road, signposted for Kanab Canyon. After 2.7 miles, the trail leaves Kanab Creek Road; it's initially a graded road, but immediately crosses over the creek. After 0.4 miles, the difficult section is reached, a short, very deep sandy climb. There are two ways up, neither one easier than the other. Both routes have large deep holes in the sand and rock ledges. Traveling from Kanab Creek to Johnson Canyon, the route has a difficulty rating of 5. In the reverse direction, the difficulty rating is a 4 as you descend the hardest section.

Once on John R Flat, the ungraded trail is easier going as it winds through junipers and across open areas. There are some good views to the north over the White Cliffs, especially of the prominent Cutler Point.

The east end of the trail descends into Johnson Canyon, crossing over Johnson Wash just before it joins the paved

First part of the trail at the crossing of Kanab Creek

Johnson Canyon Road. If you travel in the opposite direction, this ascent is far easier than the Kanab Creek end. However, it is still loose and sandy and may require lower tire pressures.

The trail is normally open all year, but the cooler months are the best time to travel because it is extremely hot in summer.

Current Road Information
BLM Kanab Field Office
318 North First East
Kanab, UT 84741
(435) 644-4600

Map References
BLM   Kanab
USGS   1:24,000   White Tower, Cutler Point
          1:100,000   Kanab
Maptech CD-ROM: Escalante/Dixie National Forest
Utah Atlas & Gazetteer, p. 18
Utah Travel Council #4

Route Directions

▼ 0.0			2.7 miles along Kanab Creek Road from US 89, turn east on unmarked, graded sandy road and zero trip meter.
	6.9 ▲		Trail ends at Kanab Creek Road. Turn left for US 89 and Kanab.
		GPS: N 37°08.71' W 112°32.41'	
▼ 0.1		SO	Cross over Kanab Creek, then proceed south along the creek.
	6.8 ▲	SO	Cross over Kanab Creek.
▼ 0.3		TL	Track continues straight ahead; turn left, then immediately bear left at fork.
	6.6 ▲	TR	Track on left, then T-intersection. Turn right at intersection.
		GPS: N 37°08.51' W 112°32.26'	
▼ 0.4		SO	Two alternate routes up very loose, steep sand and rock section.
	6.5 ▲	SO	Two alternate routes down very loose, steep sand and rock section.
		GPS: N 37°08.52' W 112°32.22'	
▼ 0.5		SO	Cattle guard, entering BLM land.
	6.4 ▲	SO	Cattle guard, entering private land.
▼ 0.6		BR	Track on left.
	6.3 ▲	SO	Track on right.

SW #14: JOHN R FLAT TRAIL

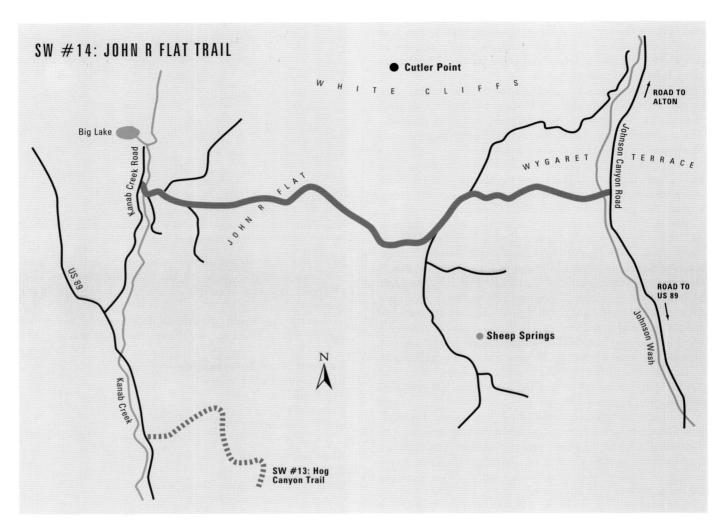

		GPS: N 37°08.59' W 112°32.09'	
▼ 0.8		SO	Track on left.
	6.1 ▲	BL	Track on right.
▼ 1.1		SO	Track on right.
	5.8 ▲	SO	Track on left.
		GPS: N 37°08.42' W 112°31.54'	
▼ 1.2		SO	Faint track on right.
	5.7 ▲	SO	Faint track on left.
▼ 1.8		SO	Track on left.
	5.1 ▲	SO	Track on right.
		GPS: N 37°08.36' W 112°30.81'	
▼ 2.5		SO	Cattle guard, then tracks on right and left.
	4.4 ▲	SO	Tracks on right and left, then cattle guard.
▼ 3.7		SO	Track on left.
	3.2 ▲	SO	Track on right.
		GPS: N 37°08.61' W 112°28.91'	
▼ 3.8		SO	Track on left to White Cliffs viewpoint. Main trail crosses Wygaret Terrace, a long, flat, sage-covered bench.
	3.1 ▲	BL	Trail crosses Wygaret Terrace, a long, flat, sage-covered bench. Track on right to White Cliffs viewpoint.
▼ 4.8		SO	Track on right.
	2.1 ▲	SO	Track on left.
		GPS: N 37°07.97' W 112°28.04'	
▼ 5.0		SO	Track on left.
	1.9 ▲	SO	Track on right.
▼ 5.4		SO	Track on right and track on left.
	1.5 ▲	SO	Track on right and track on left.
		GPS: N 37°07.79' W 112°27.38'	
▼ 5.6		SO	Track on right and track on left, then cattle guard.
	1.3 ▲	SO	Cattle guard, then track on right and track on left.
▼ 5.8		SO	Track on right.
	1.1 ▲	SO	Track on left.
▼ 5.9		SO	Track on right.
	1.0 ▲	SO	Track on left.
▼ 6.0		SO	Track on right, then track on left to two tanks, followed by second track on left.
	0.9 ▲	SO	Track on right, then second track on right to two tanks, followed by track on left.
		GPS: N 37°07.96' W 112°26.84'	
▼ 6.9		BR	Track on left; there is a rocky section at junction. Zero trip meter.
	0.0 ▲		Continue west.
		GPS: N 37°08.68' W 112°26.09'	
▼ 0.0			Continue southeast.
	2.7 ▲	SO	Track on right; there is a rocky section at junction. Zero trip meter.
▼ 0.8		SO	Track on right, then cattle guard.
	1.9 ▲	SO	Cattle guard, then track on left.
▼ 1.5		SO	Track on right and track on left.
	1.2 ▲	SO	Track on right and track on left.

▼ 2.1		SO	Three tracks on left and track on right.
	0.6 ▲	SO	Three tracks on right and track on left.

GPS: N 37°08.55' W 112°23.94'

▼ 2.3		SO	Bottom of descent from John R Flat. Trail divides in sandy section and rejoins almost immediately. The right fork passes a track to the right.
	0.4 ▲	SO	Trail divides in sandy section and rejoins almost immediately. The left fork passes a track to the left. Trail climbs to John R Flat.
▼ 2.5		SO	Cattle guard.
	0.2 ▲	SO	Cattle guard.
▼ 2.6		SO	Descend and cross Johnson Wash. Private track on left on exit.
	0.1 ▲	BL	Private track on right. Descend and cross Johnson Wash.
▼ 2.7			Trail ends at Johnson Canyon Road. Turn right to join US 89 and Kanab, left for Alton.
	0.0 ▲		From Johnson Canyon Road, 7.4 miles north of US 89, turn west on graded road and immediately cross cattle guard. There is a mailbox at the turn but no sign.

GPS: N 37°08.62' W 112°23.55'

SOUTHWEST REGION TRAIL #15

Skutumpah Road

Starting Point:	**Kodachrome Basin Road, 2.7 miles south of Cannonville**
Finishing Point:	**Johnson Canyon Road, 20 miles south of Alton**
Total Mileage:	**31.1 miles**
Unpaved Mileage:	**31.1 miles**
Driving Time:	**2.5 hours**
Elevation Range:	**5,800–6,800 feet**
Usually Open:	**March to December**
Difficulty Rating:	**1**
Scenic Rating:	**9**
Remoteness Rating:	**+0**

Special Attractions

- Historic Averett monument and grave.
- Canyon narrows of Bull Valley Gorge and Willis Canyons.
- Views of the Pink Cliffs.
- Long scenic road within the Grand Staircase–Escalante National Monument.

History

Indian Hollow and Averett Canyon along the Skutumpah Road are names reflecting the troubled times that existed between early pioneers and the Paiute Indians. In 1866, a party of Mormons from St. George was sent by Erastus Snow to Green River to assist the people there in the Black Hawk War. The party traveled up Johnson Canyon and over to what is now Cannonville. Some of the men fell sick, and a small par-

Heading up the ridge at the beginning of Skutumpah Road

ty of six was sent back. In what is now Averett Canyon, the disabled party was attacked by Paiute Indians. Elijah Averett was killed, and the rest of the party fled. Averett was buried where he died and the grave was marked by a sandstone slab with E. A. carved on it, but the shallow grave was disturbed by coyotes and the bones scattered. Local cowboys later reburied the body in the same location. The more permanent monument you see today was put in by the Boy Scouts from Tropic in 1937.

Bull Valley Gorge got its name from the grazing of cattle that took place upstream in Bull Valley. A simple wooden bridge was erected over the gorge in the 1940s, which opened up the route between Kanab and Cannonville. In 1954, a pickup slid off the road at the old bridge and became wedged in the narrow gorge, killing all three occupants. Although the bodies were recovered

Averett Canyon Monument

with great difficulty, the pickup was left. The wooden bridge was replaced with rubble and dirt wedged into the narrow crevasse, making a more solid and permanent bridge.

The name Skutumpah originates from various Paiute words that mean "an area where rabbitbrush grows and squirrels are found." John D. Lee gave this name to one of his many settlements, this one near present-day Alton. He lived in Skutumpah for approximately a year between 1870 and 1871.

Deer Springs Ranch, at the lower end of the road, was developed by the Ford brothers toward the end of the 19th century. The ranch alternated between cattle and sheep, following the market trends, and it was later taken over by the Johnson family. Today, it has several cabins that it rents out on a timeshare basis.

Description

This trail offers the opportunity to combine a very scenic, easy drive with some short, rewarding hikes into pretty canyon narrows. The graded road first travels along a ridge, giving good views over the Pink Cliffs in Bryce Canyon National Park, and then drops to cross several major creek drainages.

The first point of interest is Averett Canyon, where a short distance down the wash is the grave and memorial to Elijah Averett. To reach the site, park near the creek wash, and hike approximately a half mile southeast down the wash. Look for a slight bench studded with junipers that rises to the right of the creek. You can't see the memorial stone from the creek, but it is obvious once you climb up onto the bench. The GPS coordinates for the memorial are N 37°29.34' W 112°04.86'.

The next short hike is 1.4 miles farther along the main trail at Willis Creek. A hike downstream from here takes you into some spectacular canyon narrows in a very short time. The creek usually has water in it year-round.

The most exciting hike on this trail is into the Bull Valley Gorge Narrows, 1.8 miles after Willis Creek. These are the narrowest, deepest, and least accessible of the narrows on the trail. Park at the Bull Valley Gorge bridge and walk north through the hiker's gate on the east side of the bridge. The narrow trail runs along the rim of the gorge. After approximately one-half mile, you can scramble down into the gorge itself. To hike the full length of the narrows requires ropes and some climbing skill— the way is blocked by rubble and boulders in a couple of places. If you go as far as the Bull Valley Gorge bridge, it is just possible to see the remains of the pickup truck that became lodged in the crevasse above, although most of it is now covered by debris. Of course, do not attempt to enter any of the narrows if rain is forecast in the general region—there is little chance of escape in a flash flood.

A view of Bull Canyon where the road crosses

Much of the lower part of Skutumpah Road travels through private property. Deer Springs Ranch offers seasonal cabin accommodations (bookings recommended)— possibly the only accommodations within the Grand Staircase–Escalante National Monument. It also has a very small general store.

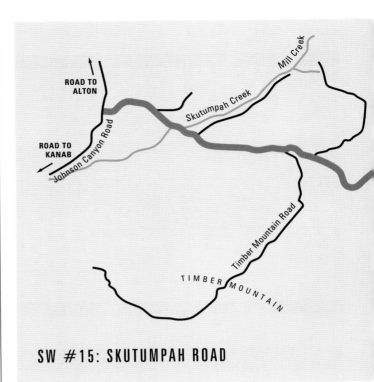

SW #15: SKUTUMPAH ROAD

The road is open year-round from the south as far up as Deer Springs Ranch. Above the ranch it is not maintained during the winter months, but it is often passable all year. The entire road is graded dirt or gravel and is suitable for passenger vehicles in dry weather.

The trail finishes on Johnson Canyon Road. If you turn left toward Kanab, Johnson Canyon Road passes close to the old ghost town of Johnson—a well-preserved movie set. Although privately owned, it is visible from the road. It also passes one end of Southwest #14: John R Flat Trail.

Please note that although currently no permits are required for camping within the Grand Staircase-Escalante National Monument, the management plan is still under development and this may change. Side trails mentioned in the route directions may or may not be open for vehicle travel and are included for reference purposes only. Some of the smaller trails are likely to be closed under the final management plan. Check with the Interagency Office in Escalante before planning to camp within the monument. The office is also extremely helpful with the latest information on road conditions.

Current Road Information

BLM Kanab Field Office
318 North First East
Kanab, UT 84741
(435) 644-4600

Grand Staircase–Escalante National
Monument Office
180 West 300 North
Kanab, UT 84741
(435) 644-4300

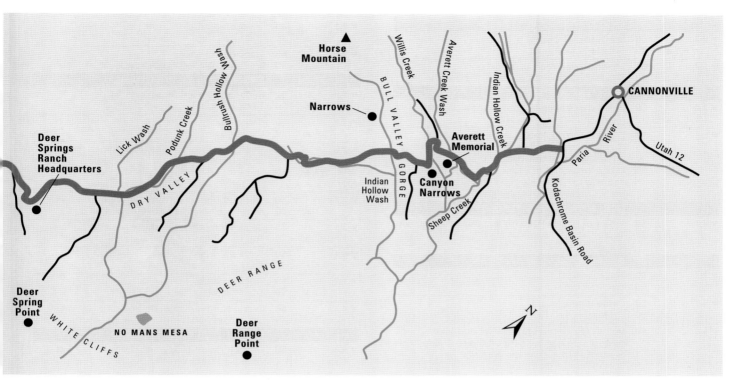

Escalante Interagency Office
755 West Main
Escalante, UT 84726
(435) 826-5499

Map References
BLM Panguitch, Kanab
USFS Dixie National Forest: Powell Ranger District (incomplete)
USGS 1:24,000 Cannonville, Bull Valley Gorge, Rainbow Point, Deer Spring Point, Skutumpah Creek, Bald Knoll
1:100,000 Panguitch, Kanab
Maptech CD-ROM: Escalante/Dixie National Forest
Utah Atlas & Gazetteer, pp. 18, 19
Utah Travel Council #4
Other: BLM Map of the Grand Staircase–Escalante National Monument

Route Directions

▼ 0.0   From Kodachrome Basin Road, 2.7 miles south of Cannonville, turn south on graded dirt road at sign for Bull Valley Gorge and Kanab and zero trip meter.

2.9 ▲   Trail ends at Kodachrome Basin Road, 2.7 miles south of Cannonville. Turn left for Cannonville and Utah 12, turn right to visit Kodachrome Basin State Park.

GPS: N 37°31.87' W 112°02.95'

▼ 0.1   **SO** Cross through wash.
2.8 ▲   **SO** Cross through wash.

▼ 0.2   **SO** Track on left to private property, then enter the Grand Staircase–Escalante National Monument.
2.7 ▲   **SO** Leaving Grand Staircase–Escalante National Monument, then track on right to private property.

GPS: N 37°31.72' W 112°03.10'

▼ 0.7   **SO** Track on left, then main trail climbs up sandy ridge.
2.2 ▲   **SO** Bottom of ridge, then track on right.

▼ 1.1   **SO** Top of ridge, turnouts on right and left.
1.8 ▲   **SO** Turnouts on right and left, then trail descends sandy ridge.

▼ 1.3   **SO** Track on right.
1.6 ▲   **SO** Track on left.

▼ 1.5   **SO** Cattle guard, then faint track on left.
1.4 ▲   **SO** Faint track on right, then cattle guard.

▼ 1.6   **SO** Track on left, then Indian Hollow Creek runs parallel to trail on right.
1.3 ▲   **SO** Track on right.

▼ 2.3   **SO** Track on left to corral.
0.6 ▲   **SO** Track on right to corral.

GPS: N 37°30.20' W 112°03.90'

▼ 2.7   **BR** Track on left. Continue and cross over old dam wall on Sheep Creek.
0.2 ▲   **BL** Track on right.

▼ 2.9   **SO** Cross over dam overflow and zero trip meter.
0.0 ▲   Continue and cross over old dam wall on Sheep Creek.

GPS: N 37°29.68' W 112°03.91'

▼ 0.0   Continue and cross over cattle guard.
8.6 ▲   **SO** Cattle guard, then cross over dam overflow and zero trip meter.

▼ 0.3   **SO** Cross through wash.
8.3 ▲   **SO** Cross through wash.

▼ 0.7   **SO** Track on left, then cattle guard, then track on right. Views ahead of the Pink Cliffs.
7.9 ▲   **SO** Track on left, then cattle guard, then track on right.

▼ 1.6   **SO** Cross through Averett Creek Wash. Park near the wash, and walk approximately 0.5 miles down the wash to the monument.
7.0 ▲   **SO** Cross through Averett Creek Wash. Park near the wash and walk approximately 0.5 miles down the wash to the monument.

		GPS: N 37°29.47′ W 112°05.24′	
▼ 2.2		SO	Small track on left.
	6.4 ▲	SO	Small track on right.
▼ 2.3		BL	Major graded road on right.
	6.3 ▲	SO	Second entrance to graded road on left.
		GPS: N 37°29.37′ W 112°05.71′	
▼ 2.4		SO	Second entrance to graded road on right.
	6.2 ▲	SO	Major graded road on left.
▼ 3.0		SO	Large camping area on right along Willis Creek, then cross through creek. The narrows are a short hike downstream.
	5.6 ▲	SO	Cross through Willis Creek, then large camping area on left along the creek. The narrows are a short hike downstream.
		GPS: N 37°28.99′ W 112°05.75′	
▼ 3.7		SO	Views of Powell Point on left, then track on left.
	4.9 ▲	SO	Track on right. Views of the Pink Cliffs to the left and of Powell Point ahead.
		GPS: N 37°28.61′ W 112°05.67′	
▼ 4.2		SO	Track on right.
	4.4 ▲	SO	Track on left.
▼ 4.7		SO	Cattle guard.
	3.9 ▲	SO	Cattle guard.
▼ 4.8		SO	Bull Valley Gorge bridge. Park and hike through the narrow gate on the east side of the bridge to access the narrows.
	3.8 ▲	SO	Bull Valley Gorge bridge. Park and hike through the narrow gate on the east side of the bridge to access the narrows.
		GPS: N 37°28.35′ W 112°06.57′	
▼ 5.7		SO	Cross through wash.
	2.9 ▲	SO	Cross through wash.
▼ 5.9		SO	Track on right.
	2.7 ▲	SO	Track on left.
▼ 6.7		SO	Cross through wash.
	1.9 ▲	SO	Cross through wash.
▼ 6.9		SO	Cross through Indian Hollow wash.
	1.7 ▲	SO	Cross through Indian Hollow wash.
▼ 7.4		SO	Cross through Indian Hollow wash.
	1.2 ▲	SO	Cross through Indian Hollow wash.
		GPS: N 37°26.53′ W 112°07.88′	
▼ 7.6		SO	Cross through Indian Hollow wash.
	1.0 ▲	SO	Cross through Indian Hollow wash.
▼ 8.0		SO	Cross through Indian Hollow wash.
	0.6 ▲	SO	Cross through Indian Hollow wash.
▼ 8.5		SO	Faint track on left and campsite on left.
	0.1 ▲	SO	Faint track on right and campsite on right.
▼ 8.6		BR	Cattle guard, then well-used track on left, then speed limit sign. Zero trip meter.
	0.0 ▲		Continue east.
		GPS: N 37°26.04′ W 112°08.67′	
▼ 0.0			Continue west.
	8.5 ▲	BL	Well-used track on right, then cattle guard, then speed limit sign. Zero trip meter.
▼ 1.2		SO	Faint track on left, then cattle guard.
	7.3 ▲	SO	Cattle guard, then faint track on right.
▼ 1.4		SO	Track on right to private property, then track on left.
	7.1 ▲	SO	Track on right, then track on left to private property.
▼ 1.9		SO	Cross through Bullrush Hollow wash, then track on right.
	6.6 ▲	SO	Track on left, then cross through Bullrush Hollow wash.
		GPS: N 37°25.06′ W 112°10.25′	
▼ 2.3		SO	Track on right.
	6.2 ▲	SO	Track on left.
▼ 2.8		BR	Track on left.
	5.7 ▲	SO	Second entrance to track on right.
		GPS: N 37°24.34′ W 112°10.45′	
▼ 2.9		BL	Second entrance to track on left.
	5.6 ▲	SO	Track on right.
▼ 3.1		SO	Cattle guard.
	5.4 ▲	SO	Cattle guard.
▼ 3.2		SO	Track on left to Swallow Park Ranch (private property).
	5.3 ▲	SO	Track on right to Swallow Park Ranch (private property).
▼ 3.4		SO	Track on right is private road.
	5.1 ▲	SO	Second entrance to private road on left.
▼ 3.5		SO	Second entrance to private road on right.
	5.0 ▲	SO	Track on left is private road.
▼ 4.1		SO	Track on right.
	4.4 ▲	SO	Track on left.
▼ 4.2		SO	Track on right.
	4.3 ▲	SO	Track on left.
▼ 4.3		SO	Corral and tank on right. Entering Dry Valley.
	4.2 ▲	SO	Corral and tank on left. Entering Dry Valley.
		GPS: N 37°23.13′ W 112°10.95′	
▼ 5.6		SO	Cross through Lick Wash. Track on right at wash and track on left.
	2.9 ▲	SO	Track on left at wash and track on right. Cross through Lick Wash.
▼ 5.7		SO	Cattle guard. Boundary of Deer Springs Ranch.
	2.8 ▲	SO	Cattle guard. Leaving Deer Springs Ranch.
		GPS: N 37°21.91′ W 112°11.37′	
▼ 6.6		SO	Track on left to Deer Spring Point.
	1.9 ▲	SO	Track on right to Deer Spring Point.
		GPS: N 37°21.40′ W 112°12.08′	
▼ 7.2		SO	Deer Springs Ranch on right.
	1.3 ▲	SO	Deer Springs Ranch on left.
▼ 7.3		SO	Track on left.
	1.2 ▲	SO	Track on right.
▼ 7.5		SO	Track on right.
	1.0 ▲	SO	Track on left.
▼ 7.8		SO	Cross over wash.
	0.7 ▲	SO	Cross over wash.
▼ 7.9		SO	Cattle guard, then tracks on right and left.
	0.6 ▲	SO	Tracks on left and right, then cattle guard.
▼ 8.5		SO	Intersection. Water tank on left. Road on left to Deer Springs Ranch headquarters. Road on right is private. Zero trip meter.
	0.0 ▲		Continue toward Cannonville.
		GPS: N 37°20.18′ W 112°13.36′	
▼ 0.0			Continue straight, following sign to Kanab.
	5.2 ▲	SO	Intersection. Water tank on right. Road on right to Deer Springs Ranch headquarters. Road on left is private. Zero trip meter.
▼ 0.2		SO	Track on left to Deer Springs Ranch. Cross cattle guard.
	5.0 ▲	SO	Track on right to Deer Springs Ranch. Cross cattle guard.
▼ 0.3		SO	Track on right is private.
	4.9 ▲	SO	Track on left is private.
▼ 0.7		SO	Track on right.
	4.5 ▲	SO	Track on left.
▼ 0.8		SO	Track on right, then cattle guard.
	4.4 ▲	SO	Cattle guard, then track on left.
▼ 0.9		SO	Track on left.

4.3 ▲		SO	Track on right.
GPS: N 37°20.13' W 112°14.35'			
▼ 1.7		SO	Track on right to private property.
	3.5 ▲	SO	Track on left to private property.
▼ 2.6		SO	Track on left.
	2.6 ▲	SO	Track on right.
GPS: N 37°19.07' W 112°15.03'			
▼ 3.5		SO	Faint track on left.
	1.7 ▲	SO	Faint track on right.
▼ 3.6		SO	Cattle guard, leaving Deer Springs Ranch.
	1.6 ▲	SO	Cattle guard, entering Deer Springs Ranch.
▼ 4.2		SO	Track on right, cross over creek, then second track on right.
	1.0 ▲	SO	Track on left, cross over creek, then second track on left.
▼ 5.2		SO	Track on left is Timber Mountain Road (a dead end). Zero trip meter at signpost.
	0.0 ▲		Continue toward Cannonville.
GPS: N 37°18.48' W 112°17.55'			
▼ 0.0			Continue toward Kanab.
	2.9 ▲	SO	Track on right is Timber Mountain Road (a dead end). Zero trip meter at signpost.
▼ 0.9		SO	Track on left.
	2.0 ▲	SO	Track on right.
▼ 1.2		SO	Track on right.
	1.7 ▲	SO	Track on left.
▼ 1.3		SO	Cattle guard.
	1.6 ▲	SO	Cattle guard.
▼ 2.6		SO	Track on left.
	0.3 ▲	SO	Track on right.
▼ 2.7		SO	Cattle guard.
	0.2 ▲	SO	Cattle guard.
▼ 2.9		SO	Track on right to Mill Creek. Zero trip meter.
	0.0 ▲		Continue straight, following sign for Deer Springs Ranch.
GPS: N 37°16.90' W 112°20.12'			
▼ 0.0			Continue toward Kanab.
	3.0 ▲	SO	Track on left to Mill Creek. Zero trip meter.
▼ 0.3		SO	Cattle guard.
	2.7 ▲	SO	Cattle guard.
▼ 0.5		SO	Cross over Skutumpah Creek.
	2.5 ▲	SO	Cross over Skutumpah Creek.
▼ 0.7		SO	Cattle guard.
	2.3 ▲	SO	Cattle guard.
▼ 1.3		SO	Track on right.
	1.7 ▲	SO	Track on left.
▼ 1.5		SO	Graded road on right, and small track on right. Smaller, ungraded track on left.
	1.5 ▲	SO	Graded road on left and small track on left. Smaller, ungraded track on right. Follow sign for Deer Springs Ranch.
GPS: N 37°16.57' W 112°21.81'			
▼ 1.8		SO	Track on right.
	1.2 ▲	SO	Track on left.
▼ 2.4		SO	Track on right, then track on left.
	0.6 ▲	SO	Track on right, then track on left.
▼ 2.8		SO	Cattle guard.
	0.2 ▲	SO	Cattle guard.
▼ 3.0			Trail ends at Johnson Canyon Road. Turn right for Alton, turn left for Kanab.
	0.0 ▲		On Johnson Canyon Road, 20 miles south of Alton, turn northeast on graded road, following the sign for Deer Springs Ranch and Cannonville.
GPS: N 37°15.55' W 112°22.70'			

Cottonwood Canyon Road

Starting Point:	Kodachrome Basin State Park
Finishing Point:	US 89, 0.7 miles west of mile marker 17
Total Mileage:	37.1 miles
Unpaved Mileage:	37.1 miles
Driving Time:	2.5 hours
Elevation Range:	4,600–6,500 feet
Usually Open:	Year-round
Difficulty Rating:	2
Scenic Rating:	10
Remoteness Rating:	+0

Special Attractions

- Kodachrome Basin State Park.
- Grosvenor Arch—a natural double arch.
- Butler Valley and Cottonwood Canyon Narrows.
- Views of the Paria River.

History

Kodachrome Basin, at the start of this trail, was originally called Thornys Pasture back in 1900, when Cannonville ranchers first used it for winter cattle grazing. In 1949, the National Geographic Society studied the area and named it after the brand of film it used. In 1962, the area was declared a state park, and for legal reasons was originally known as Chimney Rock State Park. Later, Kodak was happy to have its name associated with the area, and so the name Kodachrome Basin was reinstated.

At the southern end of the trail, the Paria River cuts a broad swath through the badlands scenery. The name comes from the Paiute word for "elk water" or "muddy water." Alongside the Paria River is Rock House Cove, the site of Peter Shirts's original settlement—he later settled the town of Paria, which was originally spelled Pahreah (located at the end of Southwest #17: Paria River Valley Trail). He moved to the Paria River region in 1865 with his family and established his smallholding in Rock House Cove. He built his stone house at the back of the cove along the cliff, using a natural cave in

Signpost at the south end of the trail

the cliff as the back of the dwelling. When the Black Hawk War erupted in 1866, Peter refused to leave, and he was successful in staving off the Indian attacks from his rock stronghold. However, by March 1866, he and his family de-

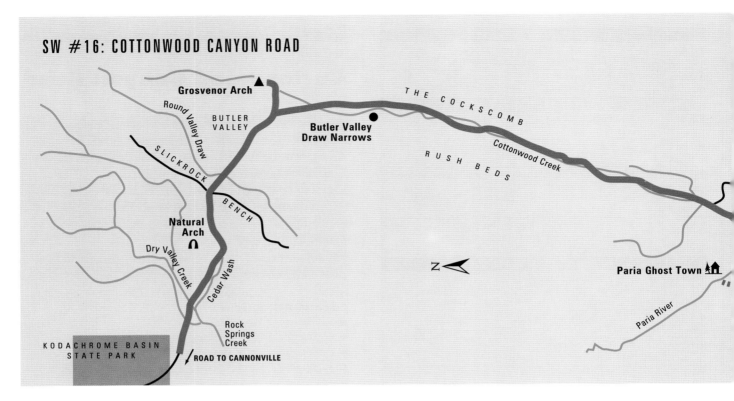

SW #16: COTTONWOOD CANYON ROAD

cided to relocate to Toquerville, eventually returning to settle what became the townsite of Paria.

Description

Cottonwood Canyon Road is a backcountry byway, one of the dirt roads that slant down through the Grand Staircase–Escalante National Monument. Unlike most of the other roads that cross the monument on the plateaus, this one runs alongside Cottonwood Wash for most of its length, traveling through the very scenic Cottonwood Canyon.

The trail commences at the entrance to the scenic Kodachrome Basin State Park, which has many-hued rock chimneys and scenery and is well worth a visit. The graded dirt road rises to cross Slickrock Bench, giving views to the distinctive pink and white cliffs of Powell Point. It then crosses Round Valley Draw and exits by winding around a

Driving through the valley along Cottonwood Wash Trail

large butte on a short, narrow shelf road.

After 9.2 miles, a short detour to the left goes to Grosvenor Arch, a very distinctive, rare double arch of pale sandstone. There is a day-use picnic area, and a wheelchair-accessible path that leads to the base of the arch.

About 3.4 miles after the turn to Grosvenor Arch, there is a very short, worthwhile hike into the Butler Valley Draw Narrows. Park alongside the trail near where it crosses over a side creek in a depression filled with red rock hoodoo spires. The way into the narrows is immediately west of the road. Immediately south of the drainage pipe under the road you will see a faint foot trail. Follow this west and scramble down into the main wash. Turn north (right) and immediately the canyon narrows. There is a short section of spectacular narrows, including a large tree trunk jammed in the canyon 20 feet up, washed down by flash floods. Turn south in the main wash to view the Cottonwood Canyon Narrows. Do not enter the narrows when there are any thunderstorm warnings or heavy rain in the forecast, or if there has been rain the preceding few days. To do so can be life threatening because of flash floods. In summer months, rattlesnakes like to hide in the relative coolness of the canyons, so be careful where you place hands and feet.

The main trail follows along the Cockscomb, a long, jagged ridge; the trail rises up to cross over it a couple of times. Like Comb Ridge to the east, Cockscomb is a monocline. To the west is Cottonwood Canyon, visible for most of the middle section of the trail. The lower end of the trail runs along a narrow ledge just over the Paria River, passes by Rock House Cove, and then swings up and away from the river through some badlands. It finishes at the junction with US 89, roughly midway between Kanab and Page, Arizona.

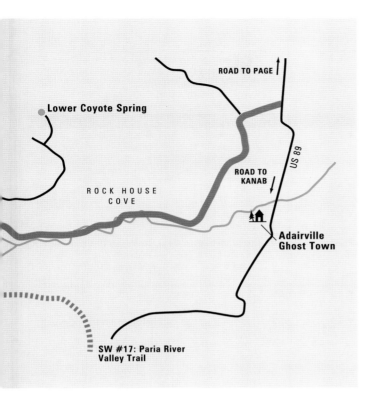

The trail is graded all the way. The section of trail that crosses over the Cockscomb travels across black shale, which gets very slippery after rain. The trail is normally open year-round, but may be temporarily impassable due to snow or heavy rain. There are many opportunities for backcountry camping along this route, especially along some of the side trails at the northern end. There are few sites within the canyon itself. Please note that although currently no permits are required for camping within the national monument, the management plan is still under development and this may change. Side trails mentioned in the route directions may or may not be open for vehicle travel and are included for reference purposes only. Some of the smaller trails are likely to be closed under the final management plan. Check with the Interagency Office in Escalante before planning to camp within the monument. The office is also extremely helpful with the latest information on road conditions.

Current Road Information
Grand Staircase–Escalante National Monument Office
180 West 300 North
Kanab, UT 84741
(435) 644-4300

BLM Escalante Field Office
PO Box 225
Escalante, UT 84726
(435) 826-5600

BLM Kanab Field Office
318 North First East
Kanab, UT 84741
(435) 644-4600

Escalante Interagency Office
755 West Main
Escalante, UT 84726
(435) 826-5499

Map References
BLM Panguitch, Escalante, Smoky Mt.
USGS 1:24,000 Henrieville, Slickrock Bench, Butler Valley, Horse Flat, Calico Peak, Fivemile Valley, West Clark Bench, Bridger Point
1:100,000 Panguitch, Escalante, Smoky Mt.
Maptech CD-ROM: Escalante/Dixie National Forest
Utah Atlas & Gazetteer, p. 19
Utah Travel Council #4
Other: BLM Map of the Grand Staircase–Escalante National Monument

Route Directions

▼ 0.0			At the entrance to Kodachrome Basin State Park, 6.5 miles south of Cannonville, zero trip meter and continue east on graded dirt road; follow sign for Grosvenor Arch.
	9.2 ▲		Trail finishes at the entrance to Kodachrome Basin State Park. Continue north for 6.5 miles on the paved road for Cannonville and Utah 12.
	GPS: N 37°30.09' W 111°59.56'		
▼ 0.7		SO	Track on right.
	8.5 ▲	SO	Track on left.
▼ 0.9		SO	Track on right, views north into Kodachrome Basin.
	8.3 ▲	SO	Track on left, views north into Kodachrome Basin.
▼ 1.1		SO	Track on left.
	8.1 ▲	SO	Track on right.
▼ 1.2		SO	Cross over wash.
	8.0 ▲	SO	Cross over wash.
▼ 1.4		SO	Track on left.
	7.8 ▲	SO	Track on right.
	GPS: N 37°29.73' W 111°58.01'		
▼ 1.7		SO	Track on left.
	7.5 ▲	SO	Track on right.
▼ 2.6		SO	Two entrances to track on left, which goes to campsite and continues into Big Dry Valley.
	6.6 ▲	SO	Two entrances to track on right, which goes to campsite and continues into Big Dry Valley.
	GPS: N 37°29.23' W 111°56.90'		
▼ 3.4		SO	Track on left.
	5.8 ▲	SO	Track on right.
▼ 4.4		SO	Track on left.
	4.8 ▲	SO	Track on right.
▼ 4.8		SO	Track on right.
	4.4 ▲	SO	Track on left.
▼ 5.2		SO	Faint track on left at base of short climb over Slickrock Bench.
	4.0 ▲	SO	Faint track on right at end of descent over Slickrock Bench.
	GPS: N 37°29.06' W 111°54.15'		
▼ 5.5		SO	Views from top of bench, including Powell Point to the north.
	3.7 ▲	SO	Views from top of bench, including

Powell Point to the north.

▼ 5.6		SO	Cattle guard, then tracks on left and right.
	3.6 ▲	SO	Tracks on left and right, then cattle guard.

GPS: N 37°29.05' W 111°53.79'

▼ 6.4		SO	Cross through Round Valley Draw.
	2.8 ▲	SO	Cross through Round Valley Draw.
▼ 6.5		BL	Track on right to Rush Beds, then trail climbs around the edge of a butte.
	2.7 ▲	SO	Trail descends down from butte, then track on left to Rush Beds.

GPS: N 37°28.62' W 111°53.21'

▼ 7.3		SO	Cattle guard, then enter Butler Valley.
	1.9 ▲	SO	Cattle guard, then leave Butler Valley.
▼ 8.1		SO	Cross underneath power lines.
	1.1 ▲	SO	Cross underneath power lines.
▼ 9.2		SO	Track on left to Grosvenor Arch (1 mile). Visit Grosvenor Arch, and zero trip meter on return.
	0.0 ▲		Continue along Cottonwood Canyon Road toward Kodachrome Basin State Park.

GPS: N 37°27.10' W 111°50.91'

▼ 0.0			Continue along Cottonwood Canyon Road toward US 89.
	7.7 ▲	SO	Track on right to Grosvenor Arch (1 mile). Visit Grosvenor Arch and zero trip meter on return.
▼ 0.2		SO	Two tracks on left.
	7.5 ▲	SO	Two tracks on right.
▼ 0.4		SO	Track on right.
	7.3 ▲	SO	Track on left.
▼ 0.7		SO	Track on left to corral.
	7.0 ▲	SO	Track on right to corral.
▼ 2.3		SO	Cattle guard, then track on right.
	5.4 ▲	SO	Track on left, then cattle guard.
▼ 3.4		SO	Butler Valley Draw narrows on right. Park where the road crosses over creek and hike down into the creek.
	4.3 ▲	SO	Butler Valley Draw narrows on left. Park where the road crosses over creek and hike down into the creek.

GPS: N 37°24.14' W 111°50.79'

▼ 4.6		SO	Track on right to campsites.
	3.1 ▲	SO	Track on left to campsites.
▼ 7.7		SO	Track on right is signposted to Pump Canyon Spring. Zero trip meter.
	0.0 ▲		Continue northeast.

GPS: N 37°20.60' W 111°52.19'

▼ 0.0			Continue southwest.
	8.7 ▲	SO	Track on left is signposted to Pump Canyon Spring. Zero trip meter.
▼ 0.3		SO	Cross through wash.
	8.4 ▲	SO	Cross through wash.
▼ 1.5		SO	Track on right to parking area.
	7.2 ▲	SO	Track on left to parking area.
▼ 2.4		BL	Track on right.
	6.3 ▲	SO	Track on left.
▼ 2.6		SO	Cross over wash.
	6.1 ▲	SO	Cross over wash.
▼ 6.4		SO	Cross through wash.
	2.3 ▲	SO	Cross through wash.

GPS: N 37°15.42' W 111°54.49'

▼ 6.6		SO	Track on left.
	2.1 ▲	SO	Track on right.

GPS: N 37°15.25' W 111°54.56'

▼ 6.7		SO	Cattle guard.
	2.0 ▲	SO	Cattle guard.

▼ 7.8		SO	Cattle guard.
	0.9 ▲	SO	Cattle guard.
▼ 8.7		SO	Track on right to confluence of Paria River and Cottonwood Creek. Main trail now follows the Paria River. Zero trip meter.
	0.0 ▲		Continue north along Cottonwood Canyon.

GPS: N 37°13.66' W 111°55.52'

▼ 0.0			Continue south along the Paria River.
	11.5 ▲	SO	Track on left to confluence of Paria River and Cottonwood Creek. Main trail now follows Cottonwood Creek. Zero trip meter.
▼ 0.2		SO	Track on right.
	11.3 ▲	SO	Track on left.
▼ 2.7		SO	Track on left to campsite.
	8.8 ▲	SO	Track on right to campsite.
▼ 3.4		SO	Cross through wash. Rock House Cove is on the left.
	8.1 ▲	SO	Cross through wash. Rock House Cove is on the right.
▼ 4.5		SO	Cross through wash.
	7.0 ▲	SO	Cross through wash.
▼ 5.0		SO	Track on right to campsite. Main trail leaves Paria River.
	6.5 ▲	SO	Track on left to campsite. Main trail now follows Paria River.
▼ 6.4		SO	Track on left, and track on right goes to viewpoint over Paria River.
	5.1 ▲	SO	Track on right, and track on left goes to viewpoint over Paria River.
▼ 6.5		SO	Cattle guard.
	5.0 ▲	SO	Cattle guard.

GPS: N 37°08.44' W 111°54.45'

▼ 6.8		SO	Cross through wash.
	4.7 ▲	SO	Cross through wash.
▼ 7.6		SO	Cross through wash.
	3.9 ▲	SO	Cross through wash.
▼ 10.0		SO	Track on left and track on right.
	1.5 ▲	SO	Track on right and track on left.

GPS: N 37°07.45' W 111°51.25'

▼ 10.2		SO	Leaving Grand Staircase–Escalante National Monument.
	1.3 ▲	SO	Entering Grand Staircase–Escalante National Monument.
▼ 10.4		SO	Track on left.
	1.1 ▲	SO	Track on right.
▼ 10.6		SO	Track on right, then cattle guard.
	0.9 ▲	SO	Cattle guard, then track on left.
▼ 11.0		SO	Track on left.
	0.5 ▲	SO	Track on right.
▼ 11.3		SO	Track on right.
	0.2 ▲	SO	Track on left.
▼ 11.4		SO	Cattle guard.
	0.1 ▲	SO	Cattle guard.
▼ 11.5			Trail ends at US 89, just west of the Grand Staircase–Escalante National Monument boundary. Turn left for Page, Arizona; turn right for Kanab.
	0.0 ▲		On US 89, just west of the Grand Staircase–Escalante National Monument boundary, 0.7 miles west of mile marker 17, turn north on graded dirt road at the sign for Cottonwood Canyon and Cannonville and zero trip meter.

GPS: N 37°06.32' W 111°50.77'

Paria River Valley Trail

Starting Point:	US 89, 0.7 miles west of mile marker 30
Finishing Point:	Ghost town of Paria
Total Mileage:	5.5 miles
Unpaved Mileage:	5.5 miles
Driving Time:	30 minutes (one-way)
Elevation Range:	4,800–5,300 feet
Usually Open:	Year-round
Difficulty Rating:	2
Scenic Rating:	8
Remoteness Rating:	+0

Special Attractions

- Old Paria movie set.
- Paria ghost town and cemetery.
- Views of the Paria River valley.

History

Paria (originally Pahreah) was founded in 1870 by Peter Shirts and his family after their original settlement at Rock House Cove (on Southwest #16: Cottonwood Canyon Road) was abandoned. The small settlement grew to include a general store, a post office, and some prosperous farmland. Like many pioneer settlements in the area, Paria suffered repeated flooding of the Paria River, which regularly wiped out both crops and housing. Disheartened by the cyclical struggle, the settlers abandoned their town.

As many people were leaving, the promise of gold attracted others, and some new buildings and a sluice gate were built. The gold rush, too, was short-lived, and by 1910 most miners had moved on to better pickings. One old miner's light lingered until 1929, but the floods and droughts won in the end and the settlement became a ghost town.

The trail overlooks the bentonite hills of the Paria River valley

In the 1950s, moviemakers discovered the Paria River valley and filmed several movies here—including *Cattle Drive* (1951), *Sergeants Three* (1963), and *Mackenna's Gold* (1969). The movie set for which the town is now best known was built for *Sergeants Three*.

However, history keeps repeating in Paria. In November 1999, a group of BLM employees and 85 volunteers dismantled the movie set from its original location next to the picnic ground. Frequent flooding from the creek was making the buildings unstable and unsafe. The original timbers were saved, and the BLM intends to reconstruct two of the buildings farther away from the creek, elsewhere on the backway, where they will be out of reach of floodwaters. Interpretive information will be added, and the project is to be completed in 2000.

Tucked away in the Paria River valley, the remains of an old cabin slowly fall victim to the elements

Today, you can see remains of stone cabins and an old sluice from the mining operations on the far bank of the river, slightly downstream from where the road ends. The town site was upstream from the trail end, but little remains.

Description

This is one of the designated scenic backways in this area; it's a short spur trail allowing vehicle access to the Paria River and to the ghost town of Paria. The trail is a well-maintained graded dirt road that, in dry weather, is suitable for passenger vehicles as far as the picnic ground. The sandy wash below the picnic area is more suited for high-clearance vehicles.

It is a pretty drive to the town site. The trail drops abruptly to the creek giving views into the Paria River valley and the red rock surroundings. The picnic area, set at the base of a red rock bluff on a slight rise, is a pleasant place for lunch. There is limited shade, however, and summers are very hot!

The trail passes the old Paria cemetery. It has only a solitary marker that lists the names of the 13 people buried in the cemetery. At the trail's end on the banks of the Paria River, you can walk across the river to view the remains of the town and the mining operations.

Current Road Information

BLM Kanab Field Office
318 North First East
Kanab, UT 84741
(435) 644-4600

Escalante Interagency Office
755 West Main
Escalante, UT 84726
(435) 826-5499

Map References

BLM Smoky Mt.
USGS 1:24,000 Five Mile Valley, Calico Peak
        1:100,000 Smoky Mt.
Maptech CD-ROM: Escalante/Dixie National Forest
Utah Atlas & Gazetteer, p. 19
Utah Travel Council #4
Other: BLM Map of the Grand Staircase–Escalante National
       Monument

Route Directions

0.0		From US 89, 0.7 miles west of mile marker 30, zero trip meter and turn northeast on graded dirt road. The road is unmarked, but there is a

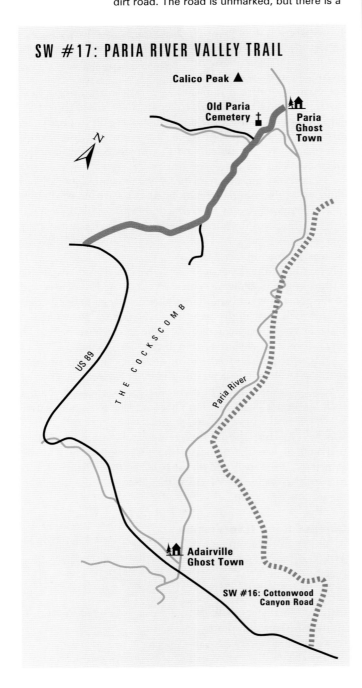

SW #17: PARIA RIVER VALLEY TRAIL

historical marker at the turn. Immediately cross cattle guard.

		**GPS: N 37°11.12′ W 111°59.71′**	
▼ 0.7	SO	Track on right.	
▼ 0.8	SO	Entering Grand Staircase–Escalante National Monument, then track on right.	
		GPS: N 37°11.75′ W 111°59.14′	
▼ 1.1	SO	Cross through wash.	
▼ 2.4	SO	Track on right, then cattle guard.	
▼ 4.4	SO	Cross through wash.	
▼ 4.5	SO	Picnic area and pit toilet on right, then cross through wash. This was the original location of the Paria movie set.	
		GPS: N 37°14.25′ W 111°57.42′	
▼ 4.6	SO	Cross through wash.	
▼ 4.7	SO	Track on right.	
▼ 4.8	BR	Cross through wash, then bear right after wash.	
▼ 4.9	SO	Track on left goes to Paria cemetery; fork rejoins almost immediately.	
		GPS: N 37°14.56′ W 111°57.39′	
▼ 5.3	BR	Track on left.	
▼ 5.4	SO	Cross through wash.	
▼ 5.5		Trail ends on the bank of the Paria River. To find the remains of Paria, walk a short distance south. The remains of one rock cabin and the sluice are on the far bank.	
		GPS: N 37°15.04′ W 111°57.29′	

SOUTHWEST REGION TRAIL #18

Smoky Mountain Road

Starting Point:	**US 89 at Big Water**
Finishing Point:	**Escalante**
Total Mileage:	**74.4 miles**
Unpaved Mileage:	**71.8 miles**
Driving Time:	**5 hours**
Elevation Range:	**3,900–7,000 feet**
Usually Open:	**March to December**
Difficulty Rating:	**2**
Scenic Rating:	**8**
Remoteness Rating:	**+1**

Special Attractions

- Grand Staircase–Escalante National Monument and Glen Canyon National Recreation Area.
- The switchbacks of Kelly Grade.
- Underground smoldering coal deposits.
- Long trail with varied scenery over the Kaiparowits Plateau.

History

When the pioneers and stockmen settled this region, they must have been intrigued by the wisps of smoke rising up from Smoky Mountain. Much of the mountain and the surrounding Kaiparowits Plateau have large deposits of underground coal, which are slowly smoldering and which give the mountain its name. As the coal underneath the topsoil burns,

Spectacular views from Kelly Grade

the topsoil collapses in on itself, causing slight depressions in the ground. On two occasions in the 1960s, the Bureau of Mines attempted to extinguish the fires by bulldozing vast tracts of land. Although the fires were put out wherever they were bulldozed, the burning ran underground to emerge elsewhere. For the most part now, they are left alone.

Early pioneers lent their names to many features along this trail. Alvey Wash and the Left Hand and Right Hand Collets are named after settlers who ran cattle and horses in the area.

The name for Wahweap Creek, at the southern end of the trail, comes from a Paiute Indian word that refers to the creek's brackish water. For a time the creek was known as Sentinel Creek. The bentonite clay hills at the south end of Smoky Mountain Road have been used as movie locations. They are featured in *Planet of the Apes* (1968) and *The Greatest Story Ever Told* (1965).

Description

The Smoky Mountain Road is the longest of the backcountry byways that cross through the Grand Staircase–Escalante National Monument. For the most part it crosses the Kaiparowits Plateau, providing good views of diverse scenery. Near Big Water, the trail runs across the steep Kelly Grade, an exciting drive of narrow switchbacks.

The trail commences in Big Water on US 89 (at the same starting point as Southwest #20: Nipple Creek and Tibbet Canyon Trail. The entrance from the highway is not marked except the sign for Ethan Allen Street, but the route is well signed from the first intersection in town. The road turns to graded gravel when it enters the Glen Canyon National Recreation Area, and it maintains a good standard as it winds along the face of Nipple Bench, underneath tall cliffs, and through a mix of badlands scenery.

Side roads lead farther into the Glen Canyon National Recreation Area; one such road is Recreation Road 230, which leads 4.1 miles to Southwest #19: Alstrom Point Trail and 27 miles to Grand Bench. Southwest #21: Smoky Hollow Trail then enters on the left, just as the main trail enters the Grand Staircase–Escalante National Monument.

As you drive toward Kelly Grade, it is difficult to envisage how you will manage to climb up the sheer cliff face. The first mile along a narrow shelf road is very steep, with one particularly tight switchback. As you climb, the views spread out to the south and west. Although the trail is narrow, it is well graded and two vehicles will be able to squeeze past each other at several places. The grader has created an earth barrier on the outside edge, but this is very soft and there is a sheer drop of 600 feet near the saddle. From the first saddle, the grade starts to level out, but the shelf road continues as it winds around the north side before climbing steeply again to the top. This north section can make Kelly Grade impassable in winter months, as snow and ice remain on the north face well after the snow has melted elsewhere. However, in a mild winter, Smoky Mountain Road can remain open all year. Heavy rainfall can also close Kelly Grade temporarily, as it is carved through mostly black Tropic shale, which quickly becomes impassable when wet. Southwest #21: Smoky Hollow Trail provides an alternate route around Kelly Grade that may be passable in wet conditions.

Once on top of Kelly Grade, Smoky Mountain Road starts its long run across the Kaiparowits Plateau to Escalante. The vegetation is mainly sagebrush, with scattered junipers and pinyon pines, which contrast well with the many-colored rocks along the plateau. As you travel across Smoky Mountain, look for wisps of smoke; these mark the naturally burning coal deposits that give the mountain its name. You can feel the heat of the smoldering coal by holding your hand above the earth. On the cliffs, look for the black charcoal that marks previously burnt areas.

Approaching Kelly Grade

On top of the plateau, the trail undulates, dropping slowly as it crosses several deep canyons—at Drip Tank Canyon, Last Chance Creek, and Dry Wash. Some of the climbs out of these, although not steep, can be a bit rougher and looser than the rest of the trail. The northern end of the trail travels through Alvey Wash Valley, a long, wide, flat-bottomed, sagebrush-covered valley, which gradually gets narrower until it becomes a high-walled rocky canyon. The trail crosses Alvey Wash many times; the wash has water in it most of the year.

The trail finishes in the center of Escalante.

There are many opportunities for backcountry camping along this route, especially along some of the side trails. Please note that although currently no permits are required for camping in the national monument, the management plan is still under development and this may change. Side trails mentioned in the route directions may or may not be open for ve-

Kelly Grade falls away toward the south end of Smoky Hollow

hicle travel and are included for reference purposes only. Some of the smaller trails are likely to be closed under the final management plan. Check with the Interagency Office in Escalante before planning to camp within the monument. The office is also extremely helpful with the latest information on road conditions.

Current Road Information

Grand Staircase–Escalante National Monument Office
180 West 300 North
Kanab, UT 84741
(435) 644-4300

BLM Escalante Field Office
PO Box 225
Escalante, UT 84726
(435) 826-5600

Escalante Interagency Office
755 West Main
Escalante, UT 84726
(435) 826-5499

Map References

BLM   Smoky Mt., Escalante
USFS Dixie National Forest: Escalante Ranger District
USGS 1:24,000 Escalante, Dave Canyon, Death Ridge, Carcass Canyon, Petes Cove, Ship Mt. Point, Needle Eye Point, Smoky Hollow, Warm Creek Bay, Lone Rock, Glen Canyon City
        1:100,000 Smoky Mt., Escalante
Maptech CD-ROM: Escalante/Dixie National Forest
Trails Illustrated, #213; #710 (incomplete)
Utah Atlas & Gazetteer, p. 19
Utah Travel Council #4
Other: BLM Map of the Grand Staircase–Escalante National Monument

Route Directions

▼ 0.0   On US 89 at Big Water, 0.3 miles west of mile marker 7, turn east on paved Ethan Allen Street at sign for the Lake Powell Village Resort Motel. Zero trip meter.
  2.0 ▲   Trail finishes on US 89 at Big Water. Turn right

for Kanab; turn left for Page, Arizona.

GPS: N 37°04.66' W 111°39.69'

▼ 0.3   TR   Intersection. Turn right, following sign for the Glen Canyon National Recreation Area and Utah 12. Ahead is Southwest #20: Nipple Creek and Tibbet Canyon Trail. Another road junction follows immediately; continue straight, following signs for Glen Canyon.
  1.7 ▲ TL   Continue straight at first road junction, then at intersection at the RV park, turn left and proceed through Big Water toward US 89. Road on right at the RV park is Southwest #20: Nipple Creek and Tibbet Canyon Trail.

GPS: N 37°04.90' W 111°39.66'

▼ 0.9   SO   Cross through Wahweap Creek on a gravel ford, then track on right.
  1.1 ▲ SO   Track on left, then cross through Wahweap Creek on a gravel ford.

▼ 2.0   SO   Entering Glen Canyon National Recreation Area. Road is now graded gravel. Zero trip meter.
  0.0 ▲   Continue toward Big Water.

GPS: N 37°04.58' W 111°37.87'

▼ 0.0   Continue into Glen Canyon National Recreation Area.
  6.8 ▲ SO   Leaving Glen Canyon National Recreation Area. Road is now paved. Zero trip meter.

▼ 0.9   SO   Cross over wash and pass around the end of Mustard Point.
  5.9 ▲ SO   Pass around the end of Mustard Point and cross over wash.

▼ 2.7   SO   Cross through Wiregrass Canyon Wash.
  4.1 ▲ SO   Cross through Wiregrass Canyon Wash.

▼ 4.8   SO   Pass around the head of Lone Rock Canyon.
  2.0 ▲ SO   Pass around the head of Lone Rock Canyon.

GPS: N 37°04.56' W 111°33.15'

▼ 6.8   SO   Track on right to Warm Creek Bay via Crosby Canyon Road. Zero trip meter at signpost.
  0.0 ▲   Continue toward Big Water.

GPS: N 37°05.40' W 111°31.31'

▼ 0.0   Continue through Crosby Canyon Wash.
  3.5 ▲ SO   Track on left to Warm Creek Bay via Crosby Canyon Road. Zero trip meter at signpost.

▼ 2.4   SO   Track on right.
  1.1 ▲ SO   Track on left.

GPS: N 37°06.82' W 111°29.50'

▼ 3.5   BR   Track to the left is Southwest #21: Smoky Hollow Trail. Bear right, following sign for Smoky Mountain Road and Grand Bench. Zero trip meter.
  0.0 ▲   Proceed toward Big Water.

GPS: N 37°07.80' W 111°29.66'

▼ 0.0   Proceed toward Smoky Mountain.
  1.0 ▲ SO   Track to the right is Southwest #21: Smoky Hollow Trail. Zero trip meter.

▼ 0.2   SO   Corral on left.
  0.8 ▲ SO   Corral on right.

▼ 0.4   SO   Cross through wash.
  0.6 ▲ SO   Cross through wash.

▼ 0.5   SO   Track on right.
  0.5 ▲ SO   Track on left.

▼ 1.0   SO   Track on right is Recreation Road 230 and goes to Southwest #19: Alstrom Point Trail (4.1 miles) and Grand Bench (27 miles). Smoky Mountain Road continues straight ahead; entering the Grand Staircase–Escalante National Monument. Zero trip meter.

0.0 ▲			Continue into Glen Canyon National Recreation Area.

GPS: N 37°08.13' W 111°28.89'

▼ 0.0			Continue into Grand Staircase–Escalante National Monument.
	12.6 ▲	SO	Track on left (Recreation Road 230) goes to Southwest #19: Alstrom Point Trail (4.1 miles) and Grand Bench (27 miles). Smoky Mountain Road continues straight ahead; entering Glen Canyon National Recreation Area. Zero trip meter.
▼ 0.1		SO	Track on left.
	12.5 ▲	SO	Track on right.
▼ 2.3		SO	Cross through wash.
	10.3 ▲	SO	Cross through wash.
▼ 2.6		SO	Cross through wash. Bottom of Kelly Grade.
	10.0 ▲	SO	Cross through wash. Bottom of Kelly Grade.

GPS: N 37°09.68' W 111°27.00'

▼ 3.6		SO	Saddle at top of first steep climb. Trail levels out but continues along narrow shelf road.
	9.0 ▲	SO	Saddle, then descend steepest section.
▼ 7.2		SO	Top of Kelly Grade. Track on left to Lookout Point.
	5.4 ▲	SO	Track on right to Lookout Point. Top of Kelly Grade.

GPS: N 37°11.29' W 111°27.03'

▼ 7.4		SO	Campsite on left, track on right.
	5.2 ▲	SO	Campsite on right, track on left.
▼ 8.5		SO	Track on left, then track on right.
	4.1 ▲	SO	Track on left, then track on right.
▼ 8.7		SO	Track on left.
	3.9 ▲	SO	Track on right.
▼ 9.5		SO	Track on right.
	3.1 ▲	SO	Track on left.
▼ 9.8		SO	Faint track on left.
	2.8 ▲	SO	Faint track on right.
▼ 10.1		SO	Faint track on right.
	2.5 ▲	SO	Faint track on left.
▼ 10.2		SO	Faint track on left.
	2.4 ▲	SO	Faint track on right.
▼ 11.3		SO	Track on left, then track on right.
	1.3 ▲	SO	Track on left, then track on right.
▼ 11.4		BR	Graded track on left.
	1.2 ▲	SO	Graded track on right.

GPS: N 37°14.62' W 111°29.25'

▼ 11.9		SO	Graded track on right.
	0.7 ▲	BL	Graded track on left.
▼ 12.3		SO	Track on left.
	0.3 ▲	SO	Track on right.
▼ 12.5		SO	Track on right.
	0.1 ▲	SO	Track on left.
▼ 12.6		SO	Graded track on left is Southwest #21: Smoky Hollow Trail. Signpost is just past the junction. Zero trip meter.
	0.0 ▲		Continue along Smoky Mountain Road.

GPS: N 37°15.43' W 111°29.80'

▼ 0.0			Continue along Smoky Mountain Road.
	2.5 ▲	SO	Graded track on right is Southwest #21: Smoky Hollow Trail. Zero trip meter.
▼ 1.5		SO	Track on left, then faint track on right.
	1.0 ▲	SO	Faint track on left, then track on right.
▼ 1.9		SO	Pilot Knoll is left of the trail.
	0.6 ▲	SO	Pilot Knoll is right of the trail.

GPS: N 37°16.82' W 111°31.13'

▼ 2.5		SO	Track to left is Heads of the Creek Road, which

joins Southwest #20: Nipple Creek and Tibbet Canyon Trail. Faint track on right. Zero trip meter. Signpost: "Escalante, 42 miles."

0.0 ▲			Continue toward Big Water.

GPS: N 37°17.32' W 111°31.39'

▼ 0.0			Continue toward Escalante.
	15.5 ▲	SO	Track on right is Heads of the Creek Road, which joins Southwest #20: Nipple Creek and Tibbet Canyon Trail. Faint track on left. Zero trip meter. Signpost: "Big Water, 30 miles."
▼ 0.3		SO	Cross through wash, then round the bottom of Pilot Rock at the end of Ship Mountain Point.
	15.2 ▲	SO	Round the bottom of Pilot Rock at the end of Ship Mountain Point, then cross through wash.
▼ 0.7		SO	Track on left to campsite.
	14.8 ▲	SO	Track on right to campsite.
▼ 1.1		SO	Cross through wash.
	14.4 ▲	SO	Cross through wash.
▼ 1.4		SO	Cattle guard.
	14.1 ▲	SO	Cattle guard.

GPS: N 37°18.38' W 111°31.61'

▼ 2.0		SO	Cross through wash.
	13.5 ▲	SO	Cross through wash.
▼ 2.7		SO	Cross through wash.
	12.8 ▲	SO	Cross through wash.
▼ 2.9		SO	Track on right.
	12.6 ▲	SO	Track on left.

GPS: N 37°19.37' W 111°31.95'

▼ 3.1		SO	Cross through Drip Tank Canyon wash.
	12.4 ▲	SO	Cross through Drip Tank Canyon wash.

GPS: N 37°19.41' W 111°32.12'

▼ 4.6		SO	Cross through wash.
	10.9 ▲	SO	Cross through wash.
▼ 5.7		SO	Faint track on right, then cattle guard.
	9.8 ▲	SO	Cattle guard, then faint track on left.
▼ 5.8		SO	Cross through Last Chance Creek.
	9.7 ▲	SO	Cross through Last Chance Creek.

GPS: N 37°20.79' W 111°31.54'

▼ 6.0		SO	Cross through wash; trail crosses Caine Bench.
	9.5 ▲	SO	Cross through wash; trail crosses Caine Bench.
▼ 7.3		SO	Cross through wash.
	8.2 ▲	SO	Cross through wash.
▼ 7.6		SO	Cross through rocky wash.
	7.9 ▲	SO	Cross through rocky wash.
▼ 8.6		SO	Two faint tracks on right.
	6.9 ▲	SO	Two faint tracks on left.
▼ 9.0		SO	Track on left, then cattle guard, then views on right into Dry Wash.
	6.5 ▲	SO	Views on left into Dry Wash. Cattle guard, then track on right.

GPS: N 37°23.25' W 111°30.85'

▼ 10.1		SO	Track on right.
	5.4 ▲	SO	Track on left.
▼ 12.2		SO	Cross through wash.
	3.3 ▲	SO	Cross through wash.
▼ 13.0		SO	Cattle guard.
	2.5 ▲	SO	Cattle guard.

GPS: N 37°26.13' W 111°31.83'

▼ 13.1		SO	Cross through wash.
	2.4 ▲	SO	Cross through wash.
▼ 13.7		SO	Faint tracks on left and right.
	1.8 ▲	SO	Faint tracks on left and right.

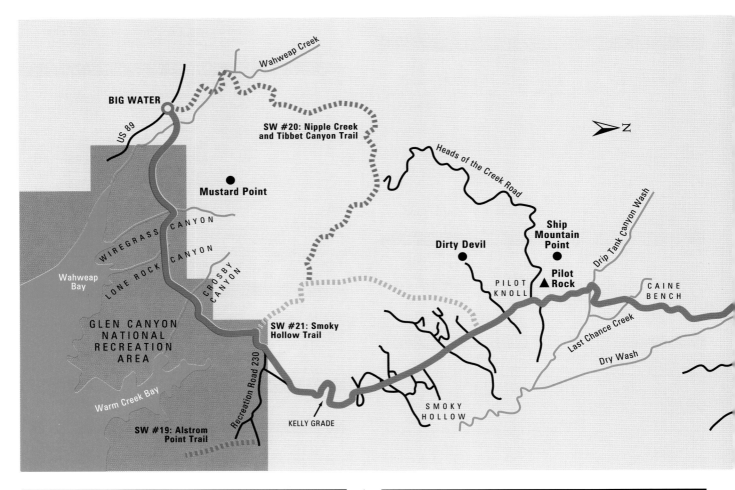

GPS: N 37°29.95' W 111°34.03'		
▼ 6.1	SO	Track on right.
15.6 ▲	SO	Track on left.
▼ 6.2	SO	Cattle guard.
15.5 ▲	SO	Cattle guard.
▼ 8.1	SO	Cross through wash.
13.6 ▲	SO	Cross through wash.
▼ 9.3	BL	Track on right, on top of ridge in clearing.
12.4 ▲	BR	Track on left, on top of ridge in clearing.
GPS: N 37°31.37' W 111°36.88'		
▼ 9.7	SO	Cattle guard.
12.0 ▲	SO	Cattle guard.
▼ 10.8	SO	Cross through wash.
10.9 ▲	SO	Cross through wash.
▼ 12.0	BL	Track on right. Bear left, then cross through Right Hand Collet Creek.
9.7 ▲	BR	Cross through Right Hand Collet Creek, then track on left.
GPS: N 37°32.51' W 111°38.38'		
▼ 12.1	BR	Track on left.
9.6 ▲	BL	Track on right.
▼ 12.7	SO	Track on right.
9.0 ▲	SO	Track on left.
▼ 13.4	SO	Cross over creek, then track on left.
8.3 ▲	SO	Track on right, then cross over creek.
▼ 14.1	SO	Cross through wash.
7.6 ▲	SO	Cross through wash.
▼ 15.5	SO	Cattle guard.

▼ 15.0	SO	Track on right.
0.5 ▲	SO	Track on left.
GPS: N 37°26.99' W 111°30.47'		
▼ 15.5	TL	Track on right is Left Hand Collet Canyon Trail. Large corral directly ahead. Zero trip meter.
0.0 ▲		Continue toward Big Water.
GPS: N 37°27.38' W 111°30.32'		
▼ 0.0		Continue toward Escalante.
21.7 ▲	TR	Track on left is Left Hand Collet Canyon Trail. Large corral on left. Zero trip meter.
▼ 0.1	SO	Two tracks on right.
21.6 ▲	SO	Two tracks on left.
▼ 0.8	SO	Cross over wash, then pass through fence line.
20.9 ▲	SO	Pass through fence line, then cross over wash.
▼ 2.8	SO	Cattle guard.
18.9 ▲	SO	Cattle guard.
GPS: N 37°28.25' W 111°32.52'		
▼ 2.9	SO	Cross through Left Hand Collet Canyon wash.
18.8 ▲	SO	Cross through Left Hand Collet Canyon wash.
▼ 3.5	SO	Faint track on left.
18.2 ▲	SO	Faint track on right.
▼ 3.6	SO	Track on right.
18.1 ▲	SO	Track on left.
▼ 4.3	SO	Two tracks on right.
17.4 ▲	SO	Two tracks on left.
▼ 4.6	SO	Cattle guard.
17.1 ▲	SO	Cattle guard.
▼ 5.6	SO	Track on right.
16.1 ▲	SO	Track on left.

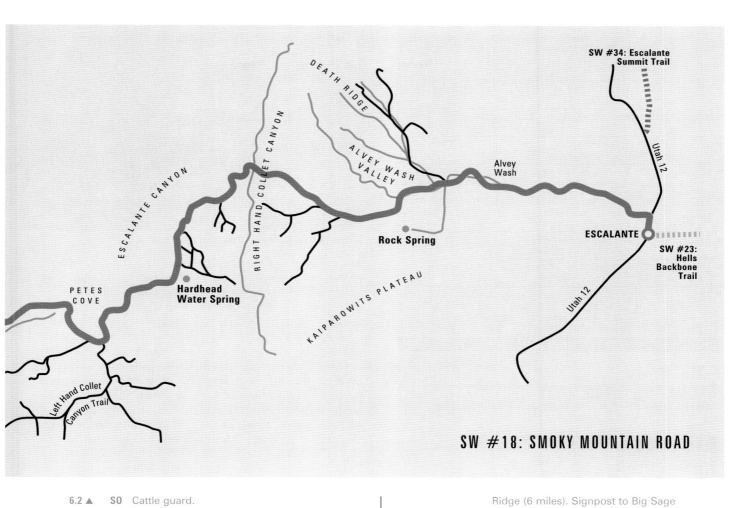

SW #18: SMOKY MOUNTAIN ROAD

6.2 ▲	SO	Cattle guard.	

GPS: N 37°34.69' W 111°36.95'

▼ 16.0		SO	Track on right. Main trail crosses Camp Flat.
	5.7 ▲	SO	Track on left. Main trail crosses Camp Flat.
▼ 16.2		SO	Track on right.
	5.5 ▲	SO	Track on left.
▼ 16.6		SO	Track on left.
	5.1 ▲	SO	Track on right.
▼ 16.8		SO	Track on right.
	4.9 ▲	SO	Track on left.
▼ 17.4		SO	Nice campsite in a stand of pines on right. Track on right and track on left.
	4.3 ▲	SO	Nice campsite in a stand of pines on left. Track on right and track on left.

GPS: N 37°36.11' W 111°36.18'

▼ 19.0		SO	Track on right. Trail enters Alvey Wash Valley.
	2.7 ▲	SO	Track on left. Trail leaves Alvey Wash Valley.
▼ 20.5		SO	Cattle guard.
	1.2 ▲	SO	Cattle guard.
▼ 21.3		SO	Track on right.
	0.4 ▲	SO	Track on left.
▼ 21.7		SO	Two entrances to track on left go to Death Ridge (6 miles). Signpost: "Escalante, 8 miles." Zero trip meter.
	0.0 ▲		Continue straight, following sign to Big Sage Junction.

GPS: N 37°39.38' W 111°37.94'

▼ 0.0			Continue toward Escalante.
	6.8 ▲	SO	Two entrances to track on right go to Death

Ridge (6 miles). Signpost to Big Sage Junction. Zero trip meter.

▼ 0.6		SO	Cross through Alvey Wash.
	6.2 ▲	SO	Cross through Alvey Wash.
▼ 1.0		SO	Track on left.
	5.8 ▲	SO	Track on right.
▼ 1.2		SO	Cross through Alvey Wash.
	5.6 ▲	SO	Cross through Alvey Wash.
▼ 1.6		SO	Faint track on left.
	5.2 ▲	SO	Faint track on right.
▼ 2.0		SO	Faint track on right. Trail crosses through Alvey Wash often in the next 4.8 miles.
	4.8 ▲	SO	Faint track on left.
▼ 4.4		SO	Track on right.
	2.4 ▲	SO	Track on left.

GPS: N 37°42.88' W 111°37.78'

▼ 5.6		SO	Cattle guard.
	1.2 ▲	SO	Cattle guard.
▼ 6.1		SO	Track on right.
	0.7 ▲	SO	Track on left.
▼ 6.7		SO	Faint track on left.
	0.1 ▲	SO	Faint track on right.
▼ 6.8		SO	Track on left. Leaving Grand Staircase–Escalante National Monument; cross over cattle guard into private land. Zero trip meter.
	0.0 ▲		Continue into Grand Staircase–Escalante National Monument. Trail crosses through Alvey Wash often in the next 4.8 miles.

GPS: N 37°44.76' W 111°37.47'

▼ 0.0			Continue into Escalante.
	2.0 ▲	SO	Leave private land over cattle guard and enter the Grand Staircase–Escalante National Monument, then track on right. Zero trip meter.
▼ 0.3		SO	Track on left.
	1.7 ▲	SO	Track on right.
▼ 0.6		SO	Escalante County Landfill on left.
	1.4 ▲	SO	Escalante County Landfill on right.
▼ 0.7		SO	Track on left.
	1.3 ▲	SO	Track on right.
▼ 1.0		SO	Two tracks on left, then cattle guard.
	1.0 ▲	SO	Cattle guard, then two tracks on right.
▼ 1.1		BR	Entering edge of Escalante. Remain on main road.
	0.9 ▲	SO	Leaving Escalante.
▼ 1.4		SO	Road is now paved.
	0.6 ▲	SO	Road is now graded gravel.
▼ 1.7		SO	Old County Fairgrounds on right.
	0.3 ▲	SO	Old County Fairgrounds on left.
▼ 2.0			Road ends at Utah 12 in Escalante.
	0.0 ▲		On Utah 12 in Escalante, turn south onto 500 West Street next to the Broken Bow RV Camp and zero trip meter.

GPS: N 37°46.23' W 111°36.54'

SOUTHWEST REGION TRAIL #19

Alstrom Point Trail

Starting Point:	Recreation Road 230, 4.1 miles east of Southwest #18: Smoky Mountain Road in Glen Canyon National Recreation Area
Finishing Point:	Alstrom Point
Total Mileage:	6.5 miles
Unpaved Mileage:	6.5 miles
Driving Time:	45 minutes (one-way)
Elevation Range:	4,300–4,600 feet
Usually Open:	Year-round
Difficulty Rating:	3
Scenic Rating:	10
Remoteness Rating:	+0

Special Attractions

■ Views of Gunsight Butte and Padre Bay and a high viewpoint over Lake Powell.

■ Excellent photography point.

■ Backcountry campsites.

Description

If you only have time to take in one trail with a view over Lake Powell, this is the one! The short spur in the Glen Canyon National Recreation Area travels on a sandy ungraded trail onto Alstrom Point, a mesa about 500 feet above Lake Powell. The sand can be soft, but it is not extremely deep and it is unlikely

Vehicle parked at the end of Alstrom Point Trail

you will need to drop tire pressures. The trail is often slightly washed out at the start, but as it travels along the point it becomes rockier and lumpier. There are a few tracks leading off the main trail—most of them lead quickly to viewpoints, though staying on the main trail leads past several great views.

The first viewpoint is 4.6 miles from the start; this spot is also popular for camping. It looks west over red Gunsight Butte rising out of the clear blue waters of Lake Powell. The notch in the rock immediately to the north of the butte is Gunsight Pass. In front of the butte is Gunsight Bay, and behind it is Padre Bay, which takes its name from the now flooded Padre Creek. It was at the mouth of this creek that the Domínguez-Escalante expedition managed to cross the Colorado River in 1776.

Low-clearance vehicles often turn back here, but high-clearance vehicles can continue along a rocky section of trail. A track to the right 1.5 miles later leads out for 0.4 miles onto the extremely narrow neck of land that connects Romana Mesa to Alstrom Point. There are no vehicle trails on Romana Mesa.

The main trail ends at a higher viewpoint that allows you to see Tower Butte and Wild Horse Mesa in the Navajo Nation to the south, Navajo Mountain, Gooseneck Point, and the pillar of Cookie Jar Butte behind Padre Bay, as well as the features in Gunsight Bay.

There is no shade along this trail, and it is extremely hot in summer.

Current Road Information

Glen Canyon National Recreation Area
1000 Highway 89
Page, AZ 86040
(928) 608-6404

Map References

BLM Smoky Mt.
USGS 1:24,000 Smoky Hollow, Warm Creek Bay
1:100,000 Smoky Mt.
Maptech CD-ROM: Escalante/Dixie National Forest
Trails Illustrated, #213
Utah Atlas & Gazetteer, p. 20
Utah Travel Council #5
Other: Glen Canyon National Recreation Area map

SW #19: ALSTROM POINT TRAIL

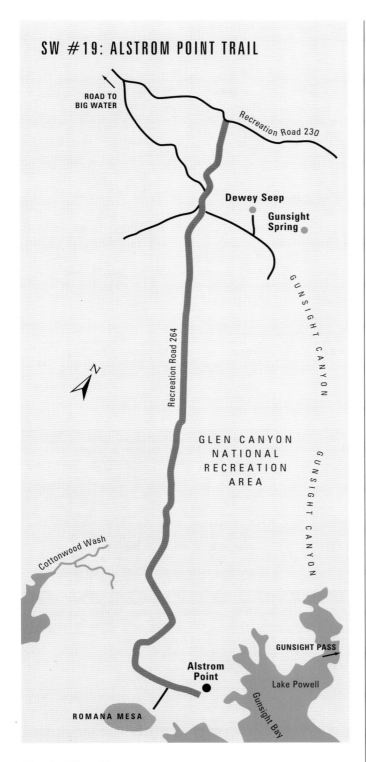

ROAD TO BIG WATER

Recreation Road 230

Dewey Seep

Gunsight Spring

Recreation Road 264

GLEN CANYON NATIONAL RECREATION AREA

GUNSIGHT CANYON

GUNSIGHT CANYON

Cottonwood Wash

GUNSIGHT PASS

Alstrom Point

Lake Powell

Gunsight Bay

ROMANA MESA

N

Route Directions

▼ 0.0		From Recreation Road 230, 4.1 miles east of Southwest #18: Smoky Mountain Road, on top of a small ridge, turn south on unmarked roughly graded small trail and zero trip meter.
	GPS: N 37°07.84′ W 111°24.80′	
▼ 0.6	SO	Track on right rejoins Recreation Road 230.
	GPS: N 37°07.33′ W 111°24.71′	
▼ 0.8	SO	Track on right, then track on left.

▼ 2.9	SO	Faint track on right goes short distance to drill hole.
▼ 4.0	SO	Well-used track on right goes 0.3 miles to a tank and viewpoint over Lake Powell. Zero trip meter.
	GPS: N 37°04.59′ W 111°23.06′	
▼ 0.0		Continue toward Alstrom Point.
▼ 0.6	SO	Viewpoint and campsite on left over Gunsight Bay, Gunsight Pass, and Gunsight Butte, with Padre Bay behind.
	GPS: N 37°04.15′ W 111°22.84′	
▼ 0.7	SO	Two alternate routes up small ridge.
▼ 1.6	BL	Track on right.
	GPS: N 37°03.51′ W 111°22.67′	
▼ 2.1	BL	Track on right goes 0.4 miles out on the neck of Romana Mesa.
	GPS: N 37°03.47′ W 111°22.21′	
▼ 2.2	SO	Faint track on right.
▼ 2.3	SO	Viewpoint on right looks over the lake to the Navajo Nation.
▼ 2.4	BR	Track on left goes 0.1 miles to slightly lower viewpoint and continues on.
	GPS: N 37°03.56′ W 111°21.84′	
▼ 2.5		Trail ends at panoramic viewpoint over Lake Powell.
	GPS: N 37°03.54′ W 111°21.80′	

Nipple Creek and Tibbet Canyon Trail

Starting Point:	Big Water on US 89	
Finishing Point:	Southwest #21: Smoky Hollow Trail,	
	3.4 miles from Southwest #18: Smoky	
	Mountain Road	
Total Mileage:	22.2 miles	
Unpaved Mileage:	21.9 miles	
Driving Time:	2 hours	
Elevation Range:	4,000–5,000 feet	
Usually Open:	Year-round	
Difficulty Rating:	3	
Scenic Rating:	8	
Remoteness Rating:	+1	

Special Attractions

- Varied scenery within the Grand Staircase–Escalante National Monument.
- Winding creek canyons of Nipple Creek and Tibbet Canyon.
- Nipple Butte.

Description

Most of this trail is contained within the Grand Staircase–Escalante National Monument. The winding trail runs up narrow

Sandy section of the trail along Wahweap Creek

Nipple Canyon, leaves it briefly to run through a very scenic area of badlands, and then climbs out the head of Nipple Canyon. It passes prominent Nipple Butte before descending back down wider Tibbet Canyon. There are a couple of backcountry campsites, but those looking to camp for the night will find better spots along Smoky Mountain Road.

The entire trail is graded dirt, but there are several rough spots that make it preferable to have a 4WD vehicle. One in particular is a short, low-traction, steep climb as the trail leaves Nipple Creek Canyon and ascends onto a bench. From the top of the bench, the trail passes through blue-gray shale before climbing around a narrow shelf road. This type of soil is extremely susceptible to damage, and vehicle tires can leave a visible scar on the landscape for a very long time. Please be extra careful to remain on the designated trail.

Back in Nipple Creek, the trail passes close to Nipple Spring and then exits to run alongside Nipple Butte. The cattle in the region often use the creek bed as their trail, churning it up and making it looser and sandier for vehicles.

The trail passes the start of the Heads of the Creek Road, which eventually joins Southwest #18: Smoky Mountain Road and then descends into Tibbet Canyon, where you can see some fair examples of the naturally occurring burnt coal deposits that are characteristic of Smoky Mountain.

The trail finishes at Southwest #21: Smoky Hollow Trail, 3.4 miles from its southern junction with Southwest #18: Smoky Mountain Road.

Nipple Spring

Current Road Information
BLM Kanab Field Office
318 North First East
Kanab, UT 84741
(435) 644-4600

Grand Staircase–Escalante National
Monument Office
180 West 300 North
Kanab, UT 84741
(435) 644-4300

Map References
BLM Smoky Mt.
USGS 1:24,000 Glen Canyon City, Nipple Butte, Tibbet
Bench
1:100,000 Smoky Mt.
Maptech CD-ROM: Escalante/Dixie National Forest
Utah Atlas & Gazetteer, p. 19
Utah Travel Council #5

Route Directions

▼ 0.0			Begin on US 89, 15 miles west of Page, Arizona, at Big Water, 0.3 miles west of mile marker 7. Turn east on paved Ethan Allen Street (at the sign for the Lake Powell Village Resort Motel) and zero trip meter.
	2.2 ▲		Trail finishes on US 89 at Big Water. Turn right for Kanab, turn left for Page, Arizona.
		GPS: N 37°04.66′ W 111°39.69′	
▼ 0.3		SO	Intersection. Southwest #18: Smoky Mountain Road is on right. Continue straight to the edge of town.
	1.9 ▲	SO	Intersection. Southwest #18: Smoky Mountain Road is on left. Continue straight through Big Water to US 89.
▼ 0.6		TL	T-intersection. Right goes to a gravel pit. Turn left and continue past the northern edge of Big Water. Road is now graded gravel.
	1.6 ▲	TR	Straight on goes to a gravel pit. Turn right onto paved road and continue through Big Water.
		GPS: N 37°05.16′ W 111°39.65′	
▼ 0.9		SO	Track on left. Gravel road on right to gravel pit.
	1.3 ▲	SO	Track on right. Gravel road on left to gravel pit.
▼ 1.3		SO	Gravel road on right to gravel pit.
	0.9 ▲	SO	Gravel road on left to gravel pit.
▼ 1.5		SO	Gravel road on right to gravel pit.
	0.7 ▲	SO	Gravel road on left to gravel pit.
▼ 2.2		BL	Fish hatchery (no sign) is directly ahead. Zero trip meter.
	0.0 ▲		Continue away from the fish hatchery.
		GPS: N 37°06.00′ W 111°40.41′	
▼ 0.0			Continue with the fish hatchery on your right.
	10.0 ▲	BR	Fish hatchery is on the left. Zero trip meter.
▼ 0.2		BL	Two tracks on right into fish hatchery.
	9.8 ▲	BR	Two tracks on left into fish hatchery.
▼ 0.6		TL	Intersection. Old water tank on right. Turn left onto sandy track and immediately bear right and follow along Wahweap Creek.
	9.4 ▲	TR	Bear left at faint track to the right, then intersection. Old water tank is ahead. Turn right onto larger track, then pass a fish hatchery (no sign) on left.

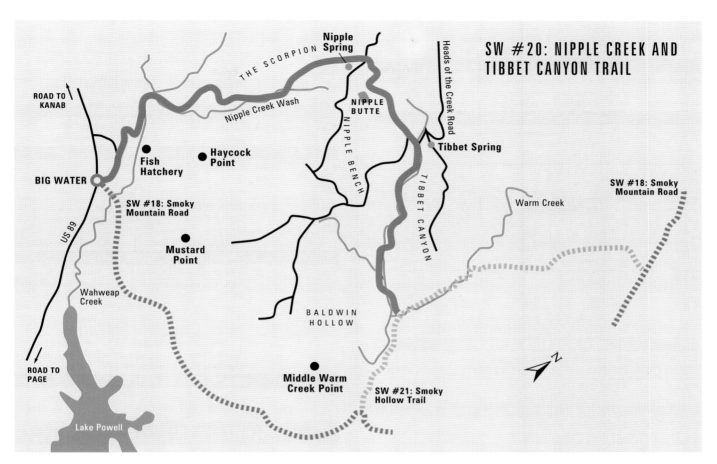

	GPS: N 37°06.35' W 111°40.97'		
▼ 0.9	SO	Cross through the wide, sandy Wahweap Creek, then follow along creek to the northwest on the far side.
9.1 ▲	SO	Cross through the wide, sandy Wahweap Creek, then follow along the creek to the southeast on the far side.

	GPS		
▼ 1.0	SO	Cross through small wash.
9.0 ▲	SO	Cross through small wash.

▼ 1.6	BR	Enter Nipple Creek Wash and bear right up wash. Trail crosses the wash often for the next 1.2 miles. Track on left crosses wash and continues.
8.4 ▲	BL	Bear left and exit Nipple Creek Wash. Track to the right leaves wash and continues.

	GPS: N 37°06.85' W 111°41.07'		
▼ 2.0	SO	Cross through wire gate. Entering the Grand Staircase–Escalante National Monument.
8.0 ▲	SO	Cross through wire gate. Leaving the Grand Staircase–Escalante National Monument.

	GPS: N 37°07.01' W 111°40.78'		
▼ 2.5	SO	Faint track on right. Remain in main creek wash.
7.5 ▲	SO	Faint track on left. Remain in main creek wash.

▼ 2.8	BL	Bear left out of creek wash.
7.2 ▲	BR	Enter Nipple Creek Wash and bear right down wash. Trail crosses wash often for the next 1.2 miles.

▼ 2.9	SO	Cross through wire gate; entering an area of blue-gray shale. Swing left and climb to top of bench.
7.1 ▲	SO	Bottom of descent from bench. Swing right and cross through wire gate.

	GPS: N 37°07.57' W 111°40.44'		
▼ 3.1	BR	Top of climb. Track on left.
6.9 ▲	BL	Track on right, then descend down from bench.

▼ 4.2	SO	Pass through wire gate.
5.8 ▲	SO	Pass through wire gate.

	GPS: N 37°08.32' W 111°40.45'		
▼ 4.6	SO	Cross through wash.
5.4 ▲	SO	Cross through wash.

▼ 5.0	SO	Cross through wash, then trail swings down to rejoin Nipple Creek Wash.
5.0 ▲	SO	Cross through wash.

▼ 5.7	SO	Enter Nipple Creek Wash. Area of naturally occurring burnt coal on left. Trail now follows alongside Nipple Creek Wash for the next 3.4 miles, crossing it frequently.
4.3 ▲	SO	Trail leaves Nipple Creek Wash. Area of naturally occurring burnt coal on right.

	GPS: N 37°09.01' W 111°39.82'		
▼ 6.6	SO	Track on right.
3.4 ▲	SO	Track on left.

▼ 7.1	SO	Mushroom-shaped rock in the wash on left.
2.9 ▲	SO	Mushroom-shaped rock in the wash on right.

▼ 9.1	SO	Trail leaves Nipple Creek Wash.
0.9 ▲	SO	Trail enters Nipple Creek Wash, crossing it often for the next 3.4 miles.

	GPS: N 37°11.25' W 111°39.84'		
▼ 9.6	TL	T-intersection. Turn left and pass through tall posts marking the fence line in the thick scrub. Track on right to Nipple Spring.
0.4 ▲	TR	Turn right just after two tall posts marking the

fence line in the thick scrub, just before a large cottonwood. Follow alongside Nipple Creek Wash. Track ahead to Nipple Spring.

	GPS: N 37°11.52′ W 111°39.68′		
▼ 10.0		BR	Track on left at the base of a large butte. Zero trip meter.
0.0 ▲			Descend toward Nipple Creek Wash.
	GPS: N 37°11.85′ W 111°39.64′		
▼ 0.0			Continue toward Nipple Butte.
3.3 ▲		BL	Track on right at the base of a large butte. Zero trip meter.
▼ 0.1		SO	Track on right.
3.2 ▲		SO	Track on left.
▼ 0.2		SO	Cross through wash, then large, fat pillar of rock immediately on the right.
3.1 ▲		SO	Large, fat pillar of rock immediately on the left, then cross through wash.
▼ 0.3		SO	Enter wash.
3.0 ▲		SO	Exit wash.
▼ 0.4		SO	Exit wash.
2.9 ▲		SO	Enter wash.
▼ 0.8		BR	Faint track on left. Bear right up the rise. Nipple Butte is directly ahead.
2.5 ▲		BL	Descend rise, then faint track on right.
	GPS: N 37°11.79′ W 111°38.86′		
▼ 1.5		SO	Pass through wire gate.
1.8 ▲		SO	Pass through wire gate. Nipple Butte is ahead.
▼ 2.2		SO	Cross through wash.
1.1 ▲		SO	Cross through wash.
▼ 2.3		SO	Cross through wash.
1.0 ▲		SO	Cross through wash.
▼ 2.4		SO	Cross through wash.
0.9 ▲		SO	Cross through wash.
▼ 2.5		SO	Enter wash.
0.8 ▲		SO	Exit wash.
▼ 2.7		SO	Exit wash.
0.6 ▲		SO	Enter wash.
▼ 2.8		SO	Cross through wash.
0.5 ▲		SO	Cross through wash.
▼ 2.9		BL	Graded track on right goes out on Nipple Bench.
0.4 ▲		BR	Graded track on left goes out on Nipple Bench.
	GPS: N 37°11.88′ W 111°37.10′		
▼ 3.0		SO	Enter wash.
0.3 ▲		SO	Exit wash.
▼ 3.2		SO	Pass through fence line.
0.1 ▲		SO	Pass through fence line.
▼ 3.3		BR	Exit wash, then graded track on left is Heads of the Creek Road, which goes to Southwest #18: Smoky Mountain Road. Zero trip meter.
0.0 ▲			Leave Tibbet Canyon, then enter wash and continue toward Nipple Butte.
	GPS: N 37°11.99′ W 111°36.73′		
▼ 0.0			Continue into Tibbet Canyon.
6.7 ▲		SO	Graded track on right is Heads of the Creek Road, which goes to Southwest #18: Smoky Mountain Road. Zero trip meter.
▼ 0.1		SO	Track on left joins Heads of the Creek Road.
6.6 ▲		BL	Track on right joins Heads of the Creek Road.
▼ 0.2		SO	Cross through Tibbet Canyon Wash. Trail crosses wash and enters it often for the next 6.2 miles.
6.5 ▲		SO	Cross through Tibbet Canyon Wash for the last time.

▼ 0.3		SO	Cross through fence line.
6.4 ▲		SO	Cross through fence line.
▼ 2.6		SO	Area of naturally occurring burnt coal on left of trail.
4.1 ▲		SO	Area of naturally occurring burnt coal on right of trail.
	GPS: N 37°10.94′ W 111°34.70′		
▼ 5.1		SO	Cattle guard, with rock pour-off on left.
1.6 ▲		SO	Cattle guard, with rock pour-off on right.
	GPS: N 37°09.84′ W 111°33.23′		
▼ 6.4		SO	Exit Tibbet Canyon Wash.
0.3 ▲		SO	Enter Tibbet Canyon Wash. Trail crosses wash and enters it often for the next 6.2 miles.
▼ 6.5		SO	Cross through wash at the confluence of Tibbet Canyon Wash and Warm Creek.
0.2 ▲		SO	Cross through wash at the confluence of Tibbet Canyon Wash and Warm Creek.
	GPS: N 37°09.71′ W 111°32.17′		
▼ 6.7			Trail ends at Southwest #21: Smoky Hollow Trail. Turn right to exit along Southwest #18: Smoky Mountain Road to US 89, turn left to ascend Smoky Hollow Trail.
0.0 ▲			On Southwest #21: Smoky Hollow Trail, 3.4 miles from the southern junction with Southwest #18: Smoky Mountain Road, zero trip meter and turn west on sandy, graded trail. Junction is unmarked.
	GPS: N 37°09.69′ W 111°32.00′		

Smoky Hollow Trail

Starting Point:	**Southwest #18: Smoky Mountain Road, 5.4 miles from the top of Kelly Grade**
Finishing Point:	**Southwest #18: Smoky Mountain Road, 12.3 miles west of Big Water**
Total Mileage:	**13.3 miles**
Unpaved Mileage:	**13.3 miles**
Driving Time:	**1 hour**
Elevation Range:	**4,000–5,400 feet**
Usually Open:	**Year-round**
Difficulty Rating:	**2**
Scenic Rating:	**7**
Remoteness Rating:	**+0**

Special Attractions

■ Easy, scenic trail winding through a pleasant canyon.

■ Naturally occurring slow-burning coal deposits.

■ Can be driven as a loop trail with the Kelly Grade portion of Southwest #18: Smoky Mountain Road.

Description

Smoky Hollow is a narrow canyon that is a tributary of the main Wesses Canyon, and the easy trail through it is accessed from Southwest #18: Smoky Mountain Road. In the canyon,

SW #21: SMOKY HOLLOW TRAIL

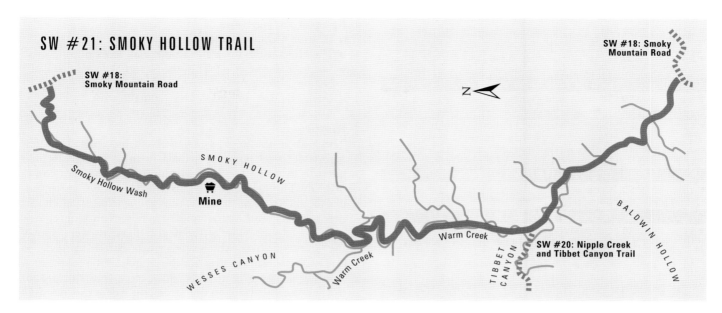

the trail passes some good examples of the naturally occurring slow-burning coal deposits that characterize the Smoky Mountain region. For the most part, the trail winds along in the wash, so sections can be slightly loose and sandy. The canyon is pretty, and at the lower end there are some good views down the larger Tibbet Canyon out into the Glen Canyon National Recreation Area.

This route is often passable in winter when there is snow on the Kelly Grade at the lower end of the Smoky Mountain Road, making the steep, narrow switchbacks on that route inadvisable for travel.

Current Road Information

BLM Kanab Field Office
318 North First East
Kanab, UT 84741
(435) 644-4600

Escalante Interagency Office
755 West Main
Escalante, UT 84726
(435) 826-5499

Middle part of Smoky Hollow

Map References

BLM Smoky Mt.
USGS 1:24,000 Smoky Hollow, Tibbet Bench, Ship Mt.
Point, Needle Eye Point
1:100,000 Smoky Mt.
Maptech CD ROM: Escalante/Dixie National Forest
Utah Atlas & Gazetteer, p. 19
Utah Travel Council # 5
Other: Glen Canyon National Recreation Area map
BLM Map of the Grand Staircase–Escalante National Monument

Route Directions

▼ 0.0		From Southwest #18: Smoky Mountain Road, 5.4 miles north of the top of Kelly Grade, turn west on the graded dirt road, following BLM sign for Smoky Hollow, and zero trip meter. Don't confuse the turn with the large graded road 1.2 miles south of it that goes to an airstrip.
9.9 ▲		Trail ends at Southwest #18: Smoky Mountain Road, north of the Kelly Grade. Turn right to descend the Kelly Grade to US 89, turn left to continue along Smoky Mountain Road to Escalante.
GPS: N 37°15.43' W 111°29.80'		
▼ 0.3	SO	Track on right, trail drops into Smoky Hollow.
9.6 ▲	SO	Track on left.
▼ 0.5	SO	Cattle guard.
9.4 ▲	SO	Cattle guard.
▼ 1.0	SO	Cross through wash.
8.9 ▲	SO	Cross through wash.
▼ 1.4	SO	Cross through wash, then Smoky Hollow Wash comes in from the right. Trail crosses the wash many times in the next 9 miles.
8.5 ▲	SO	Cross through wash, trail leaves Smoky Hollow Wash.
▼ 3.1	SO	Good example of naturally burnt coal deposits under the ledge to left of trail.
6.8 ▲	SO	Good example of naturally burnt coal deposits under the ledge to right of trail.
GPS: N 37°13.90' W 111°31.37'		

▼ 3.4		SO	Burnt coal deposits under ledges to right of trail.
	6.5 ▲	SO	Burnt coal deposits under ledges to left of trail.
▼ 3.6		SO	Large tailings piles of old mine to right of trail.
	6.3 ▲	SO	Large tailings piles of old mine to left of trail.
		GPS: N 37°13.47′ W 111°31.39′	
▼ 3.8		SO	Track on right to mine.
	6.1 ▲	SO	Track on left to mine.
▼ 6.6		SO	Small campsite and turnout on right. Smoky Hollow joins the main Wesses Canyon.
	3.3 ▲	SO	Small campsite and turnout on left. Smoky Hollow joins the main Wesses Canyon.
		GPS: N 37°11.67′ W 111°32.27′	
▼ 7.3		SO	Cattle guard.
	2.6 ▲	SO	Cattle guard.
		GPS: N 37°11.55′ W 111°32.03′	
▼ 9.9		SO	Graded road on right is Southwest #20: Nipple Creek and Tibbet Canyon Trail. Zero trip meter.
	0.0 ▲		Continue along to rejoin Smoky Mountain Road.
		GPS: N 37°09.69′ W 111°32.00′	
▼ 0.0			Continue along to rejoin Smoky Mountain Road.
	3.4 ▲	SO	Graded road on left is Southwest #20: Nipple Creek and Tibbet Canyon Trail. Zero trip meter.
▼ 0.5		SO	Exit wash for final time.
	2.9 ▲	SO	Enter wash. Trail crosses the wash many times in the next 9 miles.
▼ 2.2		SO	Cross through wash.
	1.2 ▲	SO	Cross through wash.
▼ 2.4		SO	Faint track on left.
	1.0 ▲	SO	Faint track on right.
▼ 2.7		SO	Cross through wash.
	0.7 ▲	SO	Cross through wash.
▼ 3.4			Trail ends at Southwest #18: Smoky Mountain Road. Turn west to exit to US 89. Turn east to ascend the Kelly Grade and continue along Smoky Mountain Road.
	0.0 ▲		On Southwest #18: Smoky Mountain Road, 12.3 miles from Big Water, turn northwest on the graded dirt road at sign for Smoky Hollow and zero trip meter.
		GPS: N 37°07.79′ W 111°29.68′	

SOUTHWEST REGION TRAIL #22

Hole-in-the-Rock Trail

Starting Point:	Utah 12, 3.6 miles east of Escalante
Finishing Point:	Hole-in-the-Rock
Total Mileage:	53.1 miles
Unpaved Mileage:	53.1 miles
Driving Time:	3 hours (one-way)
Elevation Range:	4,200–5,800 feet
Usually Open:	Year-round
Difficulty Rating:	1 for most of trail; 4 for last 5.3 miles
Scenic Rating:	10
Remoteness Rating:	+1

Special Attractions

- Historic Mormon Pioneer Trail.
- The Hole-in-the-Rock and Dance Hall Rock historic sites.
- Long interesting trail within the Grand Staircase–Escalante National Monument.
- Devils Garden, an outstanding natural feature.

History

The Hole-in-the-Rock, a remarkable achievement by a few hardy Mormon pioneers, enabled them to succeed in their quest to form the San Juan Mission in the southeast corner of Utah. Throughout the 1870s, the Mormon Church, under the direction of Brigham Young, was expanding into its new territory, and many families were sent to pioneer new regions in Utah. Most of the new settlements were west of the Colorado River, which was a major barrier to travel. In order to establish a footing for the church in the southeast, a scouting party was sent in 1879 to select a suitable site for the new colony. A site on the San Juan River at the mouth of Montezuma Creek was considered the best place, but there was no direct route to the proposed new San Juan Mission. The scouts had traveled a route of nearly 500 miles from Paragonah.

Two hundred men and women and 50 children traveling in 83 wagons, along with 200 horses and over a thousand head of cattle, gathered in Escalante in November 1879 and headed southeast. At first they made rapid progress, building a wagon road south toward the chosen shortcut, a narrow opening in the canyon rim, just downstream from the mouth of the Escalante River. The party moved to its new base camp at Forty-Mile Spring, and a group camped at the Hole-in-the-Rock to work at enlarging the opening.

The party at the base camp was in good spirits, and regular square dances were held at a large slickrock dome with a natural amphitheater on one side, which became known as Dance Hall Rock.

The work at the opening in

The Colorado River flows past a cutting from the Mormon Hole-in-the-Rock Expedition of 1879-80

the rim proved far harder than anyone had envisaged. The pioneers used mostly picks and shovels, and what little blasting powder they had was carefully used to the best effect. Men were lowered in barrels down the steep crack to manually hack away at the rocky sides of the passage. The drop to the river was nearly 2,000 feet, and the resulting grade was very steep, in some places as much as 45 degrees. In what seems an incredibly short time for the amount of work they had to do, the rough and steep passage was ready, and on January 26, 1880, the party made its way through. Wagons were lowered with the rear wheels tied, full brakes, and still a dozen men strained on ropes to stop them from plummeting to the river below.

Once down at the Colorado River, the expedition crossed on a

An old cabin and corral still remain along Hurricane Wash at Willow Tank

ferry built by Charles Hall, at what is now called Halls Crossing.

The Mormons found the trail on the far side of the Colorado very difficult, and it wasn't until May 1880 that the travelers established their new settlement in what is now Bluff, Utah. Bluff is a few miles away from the original site chosen by Silas S. Smith and his scouting party. The journey, originally estimated to take six weeks, took the expedition six months.

The Hole-in-the-Rock Road remained the primary link between the new San Juan Mission and the established settlements in the west for many years before it was abandoned.

Today, almost a third of the Hole-in-the-Rock is under the waters of Lake Powell. Many large boulders have fallen into the passageway, making it difficult to access Lake Powell through the gap. The original trail dropped 1,800 feet in less than a mile. Photographs of the Hole-in-the-Rock do not do it justice. It is difficult to imagine the enormity of the task the Mormon pioneers faced without seeing the difficult passage for yourself. If you plan on hiking down to the lake, allow at least an hour for the round trip. The Hole-in-the-Rock is listed on the National Register of Historic Places.

Description

This very long trail is mainly contained within the Grand Staircase–Escalante National Monument, with the final few miles traveling through the Glen Canyon National Recreation Area. The trail gently slopes down for most of its 53 miles, passing across several benches and flats. The graded dirt or gravel road can be very washboardy—it depends on how recently the last grader went down. There are a couple of sandy wash crossings and some slightly uneven road surfaces, particularly as you climb out of the wash crossings, but in dry weather all but the last 5.3 miles is suitable for a passenger vehicle. These last miles are for high-clearance 4WDs only—don't even think about attempting it in anything else!

The trail leaves Utah 12, 0.1 miles west of mile marker 65, 3.6 miles east of Escalante. The start of the trail is clearly marked to Hole-in-the-Rock. This modern-day route closely follows the original pioneer trail—wooden posts marked with a wagon symbol show the original route—and much of the original trail can still be seen. The trail descends across a series

of flats interspersed with wash crossings. The gently sloping flats are covered with sagebrush and scattered with juniper trees. To the west, Fiftymile Bench rises up above the flats. The trail crosses over the wide, sandy Tenmile Wash, then crosses Tenmile Flat and Seep Flat.

The first major track to the left goes 7 miles to the Harris Wash Trail, which offers several hiking opportunities in Upper Harris Wash, including some spectacular slot canyons in some of the side canyons. Another 1.5 miles along the main trail is the Devils Garden Picnic Area. This day-use area has pit toilets and several picnic tables set among extremely beautiful multicolored rock pillars and shapes. It makes a lovely place for a break and photo opportunity.

The main trail then passes the turnoffs for the Left Hand Collet Canyon Trail, a Jeep trail that climbs steeply onto Fiftymile Bench, and for the graded road that goes to Egypt, an area of sand dunes and interesting rock features. The trail then passes the well and corral at Cat Pasture, still used for cattle, and the left turn for the Dry Fork Trail, which provides access to several slot canyons off Dry Fork Wash.

After 35 miles, you reach Dance Hall Rock. You can clearly see the large bowl in the rock used for the early square dances. After another 2.5 miles, the trail dips to cross Carcass Wash. This is one of the lumpier, steeper exits—drivers of passenger vehicles may need to take extra care. A memorial in the wash marks the site of a truck accident in 1963 in which seven people died.

The trail is slightly rougher here as it winds through the picturesque slickrock domes of Sooner Rocks. Just before leaving the Grand Staircase–Escalante National Monument, the trail passes alongside Cave Point, which has many large cave-like hollows in the base of the rock. The trail then enters the Glen Canyon National Recreation Area.

Almost 4 miles after entering the recreation area, the road becomes rougher. A cattle guard marks this point. Passenger vehicles and low-clearance 4WDs will not be able to go much farther, and the flat area around the cattle guard has the easiest parking that does not block the trail for other users. Low-clearance vehicles should definitely stop before the first rocky slickrock section to avoid vehicle damage. From this point, the trail crosses several rough and ledgy sections of slickrock as it passes through a very scenic area of colorful slickrock

One of the more challenging 4WD sections of the Hole-in-the-Rock Trail

domes. There are some short, steep climbs, and careful wheel placement is needed in some sections to avoid underbody damage. Those driving vehicles with side steps or long front or rear overhangs will need to be extra careful—vehicles bend easier than slickrock does!

The trail ends at the Hole-in-the-Rock. A short scramble down to the hole soon shows the immensity of the work undertaken by the early pioneers. It is still possible to see scrapes from the wagons on the sides of the passage.

There are many opportunities for backcountry camping along this route, especially along some of the side trails. Please note that although currently no permits are required for camping in the national monument, the management plan is still under development and this may change. Side trails mentioned in the route directions may or may not be open for vehicle travel and are included for reference purposes only. Some of the smaller trails are likely to be closed under the final management plan. Check with the Interagency Office in Escalante before planning to camp within the monument. The office is also extremely helpful with the latest information on road conditions.

Current Road Information

Grand Staircase-Escalante National
Monument Office
180 West 300 North
Kanab, UT 84741
(435) 644-4300

BLM Escalante Field Office
PO Box 225
Escalante, UT 84726
(435) 826-5600

Escalante Interagency Office
755 West Main
Escalante, UT 84726
(435) 826-5499

Map References

BLM Escalante, Smoky Mt.
USGS 1:24,000 Escalante, Dave Canyon, Tenmile Flat, Seep Flat, Sunset Flat, Basin Canyon, Big Hollow Wash, Blackburn Canyon, Sooner Bench, Davis Gulch
1:100,000 Escalante, Smoky Mt.
Maptech CD-ROM: Escalante/Dixie National Forest
Trails Illustrated, #213; #710 (incomplete)
Utah Atlas & Gazetteer, pp. 19, 20
Utah Travel Council #5
Other: BLM Map of the Grand Staircase–Escalante National Monument

Route Directions

▼ 0.0		From Utah 12, 0.1 miles west of mile marker 65, 3.6 miles east of Escalante, turn southeast on the graded gravel road at the sign for Hole-in-the-Rock and zero trip meter.
GPS: N 37°43.65' W 111°31.84'		
▼ 0.2	SO	Track on right.
▼ 0.4	SO	Information board and mileage chart for the route.
▼ 1.0	SO	Track on right.
▼ 1.2	SO	Track on left.
▼ 2.1	SO	Track on right.
▼ 2.8	SO	Track on left.
▼ 3.2	SO	Track on right.
▼ 3.6	SO	Cattle guard.
▼ 4.0	SO	Cross over the wide channel of Tenmile Wash.
GPS: N 37°40.83' W 111°29.08'		
▼ 4.1	SO	Corral on right.
▼ 5.6	SO	Track on right.
▼ 7.0	SO	Track on right.
▼ 7.5	SO	Cattle guard.
▼ 7.7	SO	Track on right.
▼ 7.9	SO	Cross over Halfway Hollow wash.
▼ 8.5	SO	Track on right.
▼ 9.6	SO	Track on right.
▼ 10.0	SO	Track on left is signposted to Harris Wash (7 miles). Zero trip meter.
GPS: N 37°36.39' W 111°25.63'		

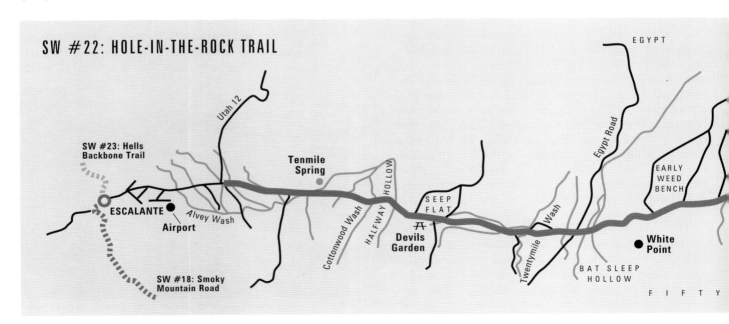

SW #22: HOLE-IN-THE-ROCK TRAIL

▼ 0.0		Continue southeast, crossing Seep Flat.
▼ 1.5	SO	Track on right goes 0.25 miles to Devils Garden Picnic Area.

GPS: N 37°35.28' W 111°24.57'

▼ 2.7	SO	Cross over wash.
▼ 3.0	SO	Track on right is Left Hand Collet Canyon Trail, signposted to Collet Top (11 miles).

GPS: N 37°34.15' W 111°23.69'

▼ 3.2	SO	Corral on left.
▼ 3.5	SO	Cross over Twentymile Wash, then cross cattle guard, followed by track on left to corral.
▼ 3.8	SO	Track on right.
▼ 5.6	SO	Track on left is Egypt Road and is signposted to Egypt (10 miles). Zero trip meter.

GPS: N 37°32.46' W 111°21.65'

▼ 0.0		Continue southeast, crossing Sunset Flat.
▼ 0.1	SO	Track on left joins Egypt Road, also track on right. Main trail now enters Kane County.
▼ 0.4	SO	Track on right.
▼ 0.6	SO	Cross through wash.
▼ 0.7	SO	Track on left and track on right.
▼ 1.0	SO	Track on left.
▼ 2.2	SO	Track on right. White Point is on the right.
▼ 2.7	SO	Track on right.
▼ 3.2	SO	Track on left and faint track on right.
▼ 4.7	SO	Track on left.
▼ 5.4	SO	Track on left.
▼ 5.9	SO	Track on left.
▼ 6.7	SO	Cross through wash. Trail enters Cat Pasture.

GPS: N 37°29.29' W 111°15.32'

▼ 6.8	SO	Track on left is signposted to Early Weed Bench (6 miles). Zero trip meter.

GPS: N 37°29.22' W 111°15.22'

▼ 0.0		Continue southeast.
▼ 0.1	SO	Corral on right, then cattle guard.
▼ 0.3	SO	Cattle guard.
▼ 1.2	SO	Track on right, views to the left into Dry Fork Wash.
▼ 2.2	SO	Track on right is dead-end road, then track on left is signposted to Dry Fork Trail (1.7 miles).

GPS: N 37°28.00' W 111°13.42'

▼ 2.3	SO	Track on right to Coyote Hole Spring.
▼ 4.2	SO	Track on right.
▼ 4.3	SO	Cattle guard.
▼ 4.9	SO	Cross through Big Hollow Wash.

GPS: N 37°26.33' W 111°11.13'

▼ 5.9	SO	Cross through small wash.
▼ 6.3	SO	Track on left.
▼ 6.7	SO	Track on left is signposted to Red Well Trail (1.5 miles). Also track on right.

GPS: N 37°25.27' W 111°09.69'

▼ 7.0	SO	Cattle guard, then track on left goes to private property.
▼ 8.8	SO	Track on left goes to Chimney Rock.

GPS: N 37°23.60' W 111°08.55'

▼ 9.4	SO	Cattle guard, then Willow Tank on the left, with old corral and cabin.
▼ 9.6	SO	Hurricane Wash 4WD Trail on the left, then cross over Hurricane Wash.

GPS: N 37°23.16' W 111°07.89'

▼ 9.9	SO	Track on right is signposted to Fiftymile Bench.

GPS: N 37°22.85' W 111°07.80'

▼ 10.6	SO	Cross through tributary of Hurricane Wash.
▼ 11.8	SO	Track on left is signposted to Fortymile Ridge Trail and runs out along the Fortymile Ridge. Dance Hall Rock can be seen immediately ahead.

GPS: N 37°21.73' W 111°06.84'

▼ 12.2	SO	Track on right.
▼ 12.5	SO	Dance Hall Rock on the left. Zero trip meter.

GPS: N 37°21.40' W 111°06.12'

▼ 0.0		Continue southeast.
▼ 0.2	SO	Track on left, then cattle guard.
▼ 0.6	SO	Cross through wash, then track on left to Fortymile Spring.

GPS: N 37°20.87' W 111°06.01'

▼ 1.6	SO	Cross through wash.
▼ 2.5	SO	Descend to cross Carcass Wash. Memorial marker on right at exit. Climb out of wash can be lumpy for passenger vehicles.

GPS: N 37°20.17' W 111°04.27'

▼ 2.7	SO	Track on right.
▼ 3.2	SO	Cross through wash.
▼ 3.5	SO	Faint track on right, then cross through Sooner Wash, followed by track on right after wash. The trail passes through the Sooner Rocks.

GPS: N 37°19.79' W 111°03.51'

▼ 3.7	SO	Track on right.

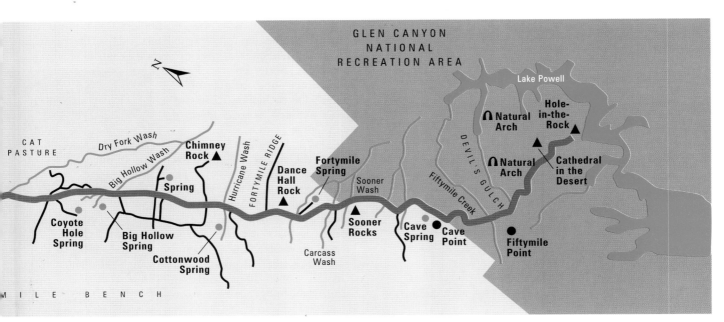

▼ 3.8	SO	Track on right.
▼ 3.9	SO	Track on right.
▼ 4.5	SO	Track on left.
▼ 5.0	SO	Cattle guard, then track on right and corral on right.
▼ 5.4	SO	Cross through wash.
▼ 5.9	SO	Cross through wash.
▼ 6.3	SO	Track on right is signposted to Fiftymile Bench. Zero trip meter.

GPS: N 37°18.25′ W 111°02.28′

▼ 0.0		Continue southeast.
▼ 0.8	SO	Cross through Willow Gulch Wash.
▼ 1.8	SO	Cattle guard.
▼ 2.1	SO	Track on right, then cross through wash. Cave Point is to the right.
▼ 2.3	SO	Cross through wash.
▼ 2.7	SO	Entering Glen Canyon National Recreation Area.

GPS: N 37°16.94′ W 111°01.07′

▼ 3.5	SO	Cross through wash.
▼ 3.8	SO	Track on left.
▼ 3.9	SO	Soda Spring on the right, then cross through wash.

GPS: N 37°16.32′ W 111°00.29′

▼ 4.3	SO	Cross through wash.
▼ 4.5	SO	Track on right.
▼ 5.4	SO	Cross through wash.
▼ 6.1	SO	Track on right.
▼ 6.2	SO	Track on right.
▼ 6.6	SO	Cattle guard. Passenger vehicles and low-clearance vehicles should not travel past this point. Difficulty rating is now a 4.

GPS: N 37°15.16′ W 110°58.58′

▼ 7.7	SO	Track on right.
▼ 7.9	SO	Plaque on the rock on the right for Hole-in-the-Rock Arch.

GPS: N 37°15.46′ W 110°57.54′

▼ 11.4	SO	Cross through wash.
▼ 11.9		Trail ends at the Hole-in-the-Rock. There is a small information board. The Hole-in-the-Rock is a short scramble over the slickrock.

GPS: N 37°15.41′ W 110°54.02′

SOUTHWEST REGION TRAIL #23

Hells Backbone Trail

Starting Point:	**Utah 12 in Escalante**
Finishing Point:	**Utah 12, 2.8 miles south of Boulder Town**
Total Mileage:	**36.6 miles**
Unpaved Mileage:	**33.3 miles**
Driving Time:	**2 hours**
Elevation Range:	**5,700–9,200 feet**
Usually Open:	**June to November**
Difficulty Rating:	**1**
Scenic Rating:	**8**
Remoteness Rating:	**+0**

Special Attractions

■ Historic Hells Backbone Bridge.
■ Panoramic views over the Box–Death Hollow Wilderness.
■ Aspen viewing in the fall.

Panoramic view over the rock pillars of Hells Backbone

History

The Hells Backbone Trail connects the towns of Escalante and Boulder Town. Escalante was first settled in 1876. The town was officially named on July 4 of that year, when with no American flag available, a Navajo blanket was raised on the flagpole. The town was named after Father Silvestre Vélez de Escalante, a Spanish priest who traversed this region with Father Francisco Domínguez in the late 1700s looking for a route from Santa Fe to California. Their expedition was the first to survey Utah.

Escalante was also the starting point for the Mormon Hole-in-the-Rock Expedition, which left there in 1879. For more on that incredible journey, see Southwest #22: Hole-in-the-Rock Trail. If you want to blend in with the locals, pronounce the name ES-ca-lant.

Boulder Town, at the northeastern end of this trail, was first settled in 1889 as a cattle and farming community. Prior to 1935, it had no automobile access, and it was the last town in the United States to receive its mail via mule. In winter, the mail was transported via the Old Boulder Road, but in the warmer summer months, the more intrepid mail carriers used the Boulder Mail Trail, which traversed Death Hollow. This route was shorter but much more dangerous—one origin of the name "Death Hollow" refers to a mule that fell to its death in the deep gorge.

The U.S. Forest Service connected the citizens of Boulder Town to the outside world in 1910. They strung galvanized wire from Escalante along the Boulder Mail Trail route, thus bringing telephone service to the isolated town. This line served the town as late as 1955.

During the Depression, the Civilian Conservation Corps constructed the bridge across the narrow chasm at Hells Backbone, which was

A twisted tree marks the spot where Hells Backbone starts its way across the wilderness

one of their many projects in southern Utah. The narrow, single-lane, precarious timber bridge made it possible to drive from Escalante to Boulder Town, but only in dry weather.

Today, Escalante and Boulder Town are established small towns offering services and recreation opportunities for the traveler.

Description

This easy trail provides a wonderful, relaxing drive through some incredibly scenic country, which culminates at the spectacular Hells Backbone Bridge. The long and winding trail is graded gravel for its entire length, making it passable for passenger cars in good weather. It leaves from the edge of Escalante and steadily climbs into the Dixie National Forest, winding around the edge of the Box–Death Hollow Wilderness area. The two main access points for hikers to enter the wilderness area depart from this route. The trail also connects to Southwest #26: Posey Lake Road.

After 10 miles, the focal point of the route is reached: Hells Backbone Bridge. Though now a sturdy concrete bridge, it is still only a single track, and it briefly crosses a dizzying gap in the ridge before reaching solid ground again. There are panoramic views from the bridge—to the north over Sand Creek and beyond to Burr Top and the Aquarius Plateau, and to the south over the Box–Death Hollow Wilderness area, with its sheer cliffs and deep chasms.

From the bridge, the trail descends gradually to Boulder Town. It passes Southwest #24: McGath Lake Trail and then winds past some private property to finish on Utah 12 just south of Boulder Town.

Current Road Information

Dixie National Forest
Escalante Ranger District
755 West Main
Escalante, UT 84726
(435) 826-5403

BLM Escalante Field Office
PO Box 225
Escalante, UT 84726
(435) 826-5600

Escalante Interagency Office
755 West Main
Escalante, UT 84726
(435) 826-5499

Map References

BLM Escalante
USFS Dixie National Forest: Escalante Ranger District
USGS 1:24,000 Escalante, Wide Hollow Reservoir, Posey Lake, Roger Peak, Boulder Town
      1:100,000 Escalante
Maptech CD-ROM: Escalante/Dixie National Forest
Trails Illustrated, #710
Utah Atlas & Gazetteer, pp. 19, 27, 28
Utah Travel Council #4
Other: BLM Map of the Grand Staircase–Escalante National Monument

Route Directions

▼ 0.0			From Utah 12 on the eastern edge of Escalante, turn north on 300E Road at the sign for Hells Backbone. Zero trip meter.
	6.7		Trail finishes at Utah 12 on the eastern edge of Escalante.
		GPS: N 37°46.17′ W 111°35.61′	
▼ 0.5		SO	Cross over Escalante River on bridge.
	6.2 ▲	SO	Cross over Escalante River on bridge.
▼ 0.6		TR	T-intersection.
	6.1 ▲	TL	Turn south toward Escalante.
		GPS: N 37°46.73′ W 111°35.51′	
▼ 2.0		SO	Cattle guard.
	4.7 ▲	SO	Cattle guard.
▼ 2.7		SO	Track on left.
	4.0 ▲	SO	Track on right.
▼ 3.1		SO	Cattle guard.
	3.6 ▲	SO	Cattle guard.
▼ 3.3		SO	Road surface turns to graded gravel.
	3.4 ▲	SO	Road surface turns to pavement.
▼ 3.4		SO	Track on left.
	3.3 ▲	SO	Track on right.
▼ 6.7		SO	Cattle guard, then enter Dixie National Forest, followed by Roundy hiking trail on right. Trail becomes FR 153. Zero trip meter at cattle guard.
	0.0 ▲		Continue toward Escalante.
		GPS: N 37°51.37′ W 111°38.02′	
▼ 0.0			Continue along FR 153.
	6.2 ▲	SO	Roundy hiking trail on left. Leave Dixie National Forest over cattle guard, and zero trip meter.
▼ 0.3		SO	Track on right is lower access to Box–Death Hollow Wilderness.
	5.9 ▲	SO	Track on left is lower access to Box–Death Hollow Wilderness.
▼ 0.9		SO	Cross through creek on concrete ford.
	5.3 ▲	SO	Cross through creek on concrete ford.
▼ 1.5		SO	Track on left.
	4.7 ▲	SO	Track on right.
▼ 3.0		SO	Track on left to shed.
	3.2 ▲	SO	Track on right to shed.
▼ 4.3		SO	Track on left.
	1.9 ▲	SO	Track on right.
▼ 6.2		TR	T-intersection. Track on left is Southwest #26: Posey Lake Road (FR 154) to Posey Lake and Bicknell. Zero trip meter.
	0.0 ▲		Continue south toward Escalante.
		GPS: N 37°55.53′ W 111°40.30′	
▼ 0.0			Continue toward Hells Backbone.
	4.3 ▲	TL	Track on right is Southwest #26: Posey Lake Road (FR 154) to Posey Lake and Bicknell. Zero trip meter.
▼ 0.4		SO	Cattle guard, then track on left.
	3.9 ▲	SO	Track on right, then cattle guard.
▼ 0.5		SO	Cross over Hungry Creek on culvert.
	3.8 ▲	SO	Cross over Hungry Creek on culvert.
▼ 1.1		SO	Cross over Deep Creek on culvert.
	3.2 ▲	SO	Cross over Deep Creek on culvert.
▼ 2.1		SO	Track on left.
	2.2 ▲	SO	Track on right.
		GPS: N 37°56.74′ W 111°39.50′	
▼ 2.5		BL	Five-way junction, stay on main gravel track.
	1.8 ▲	BR	Five-way junction, stay on main gravel track.
▼ 3.8		SO	Hiking trail on left on left-hand bend at Blue Spring Creek.

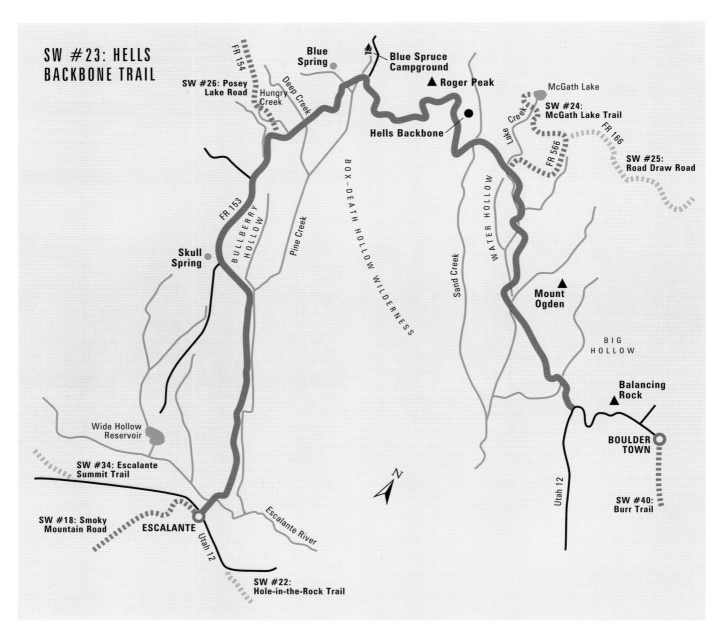

SW #23: HELLS BACKBONE TRAIL

FR 154
Blue Spring
Blue Spruce Campground
SW #26: Posey Lake Road
Hungry Creek
Deep Creek
▲ Roger Peak
McGath Lake
SW #24: McGath Lake Trail
FR 166
Hells Backbone
Lake Creek
FR 566
SW #25: Road Draw Road
FR 153
BULLBERRY HOLLOW
Pine Creek
BOX–DEATH HOLLOW WILDERNESS
WATER HOLLOW
Skull Spring
Sand Creek
Mount Ogden ▲
BIG HOLLOW
Balancing Rock ▲
Wide Hollow Reservoir
BOULDER TOWN
SW #34: Escalante Summit Trail
N
SW #18: Smoky Mountain Road
Utah 12
ESCALANTE
Escalante River
Utah 12
SW #40: Burr Trail
SW #22: Hole-in-the-Rock Trail

0.5 ▲	SO	Hiking trail on right on right-hand bend at Blue Spring Creek.	

GPS: N 37°57.70' W 111°39.25'

▼ 4.1	SO	Box–Death Hollow Wilderness, upper Box access hiking trail on right.	
0.2 ▲	SO	Box–Death Hollow Wilderness, upper Box access hiking trail on left.	
▼ 4.3	BR	Cross over Pine Creek on culvert, followed by track on left (FR 145) to Blue Spruce Campground. Zero trip meter.	
0.0 ▲		Continue on graded gravel road.	

GPS: N 37°58.00' W 111°39.10'

▼ 0.0		Continue toward Hells Backbone.	
6.0 ▲	BL	Track on right is FR 145 to Blue Spruce Campground, then cross over Pine Creek on culvert.	
▼ 1.4	SO	Track on left is FR 745. Views right over Pine Creek in the Box.	
4.6 ▲	SO	Track on right is FR 745. Views left over Pine	

		Creek in the Box.	
▼ 2.7	SO	Track on right, followed by track on left.	
3.3 ▲	SO	Track on right, followed by track on left.	

GPS: N 37°57.55' W 111°37.41'

▼ 3.1	SO	Track on right.	
2.9 ▲	SO	Track on left.	
▼ 4.2	SO	Box–Death Hollow Wilderness, Death Hollow access on right.	
1.8 ▲	SO	Box–Death Hollow Wilderness, Death Hollow access on left.	

GPS: N 37°58.34' W 111°37.01'

▼ 5.1	SO	Track on left to Sand Creek hiking trail. Track dead-ends at an oil drill hole and spectacular campsite.	
0.9 ▲	SO	Track on right to Sand Creek hiking trail. Track dead-ends at an oil drill hole and spectacular campsite.	

GPS: N 37°58.79' W 111°36.20'

▼ 5.2	SO	Cattle guard.	

0.8 ▲	SO	Cattle guard.	
▼ 6.0	SO	Cross over single-track Hells Backbone Bridge, then over a narrow ridge with views on both sides: Sand Creek to the left, Box–Death Hollow Wilderness to the right. Zero trip meter just after bridge.	
0.0 ▲		Continue to climb.	

GPS: N 37°58.22' W 111°35.91'

▼ 0.0		Descend from ridge.
4.7 ▲	SO	Trail runs over a narrow ridge with views on both sides: Sand Creek to the right, Box–Death Hollow Wilderness to the left. Then cross over single-track Hells Backbone Bridge. Zero trip meter just before bridge.
▼ 2.6	SO	Cross over Sand Creek on culvert, then track on left. Campsite on right.
2.1 ▲	SO	Track on right, campsite on left, then cross over Sand Creek on culvert.

GPS: N 37°58.27' W 111°34.88'

▼ 4.5	SO	Track on right to campsites.
0.2 ▲	SO	Track on left to campsites.
▼ 4.7	SO	Cross over Lake Creek on culvert, then Southwest #24: McGath Lake Trail (FR 566) on left. Zero trip meter.
0.0 ▲		Continue toward Hells Backbone.

GPS: N 37°57.86' W 111°33.19'

▼ 0.0		Continue toward Boulder Town.
8.7 ▲	SO	Track on right is Southwest #24: McGath Lake Trail (FR 566). Cross over Lake Creek on culvert, then zero trip meter.
▼ 0.1	SO	Track on right.
8.6 ▲	SO	Track on left.
▼ 0.5	SO	Track on right.
8.2 ▲	SO	Track on left.
▼ 0.7	SO	Track on right.
8.0 ▲	SO	Track on left.
▼ 1.1	SO	Track on left.
7.6 ▲	SO	Track on right.
▼ 1.8	SO	Track on right.
6.9 ▲	SO	Track on left.
▼ 3.7	SO	Entering private property on right and left.
5.0 ▲	SO	Leaving private property.
▼ 5.1	SO	Leaving private property.
3.6 ▲	SO	Entering private property on right and left.
▼ 5.7	SO	Track on left.
3.0 ▲	SO	Track on right.
▼ 6.0	SO	Track on right.
2.7 ▲	SO	Track on left.
▼ 6.2	SO	Track on right.
2.5 ▲	SO	Track on left.
▼ 8.0	SO	Track on right.
0.7 ▲	SO	Track on left.
▼ 8.3	SO	Track on left.
0.4 ▲	SO	Track on right.
▼ 8.4	SO	Leaving Dixie National Forest.
0.3 ▲	SO	Entering Dixie National Forest.
▼ 8.6	SO	Track on right.
0.1 ▲	SO	Track on left.
▼ 8.7		Trail finishes at Utah 12. Turn right for Escalante, left for Boulder Town.
0.0 ▲		On Utah 12, 2.8 miles south of Boulder Town, turn at sign for Hells Backbone and proceed northwest along graded gravel road.

GPS: N 37°53.31' W 111°27.45'

McGath Lake Trail

Starting Point:	**Southwest #23: Hells Backbone Trail (FR 153)**
Finishing Point:	**McGath Lake**
Total Mileage:	**5.5 miles**
Unpaved Mileage:	**5.5 miles**
Driving Time:	**1.5 hours (one-way)**
Elevation Range:	**8,300–9,400 feet**
Usually Open:	**June to October**
Difficulty Rating:	**6**
Scenic Rating:	**8**
Remoteness Rating:	**+0**

Special Attractions

- Challenging 4WD trail through spectacular scenery.
- Backcountry camping and fishing at McGath Lake.
- Aspen viewing in fall.

Description

This challenging trail has something for everyone: a technically difficult drive, panoramic views, and a secluded lake at the end.

The trail leaves Southwest #23: Hells Backbone Trail 8.7 miles from its eastern end, near Boulder Town. The first 2.6 miles are easy graded gravel as the trail winds along a wide shelf road. The trail then forks: the right-hand fork is Southwest #25: Road Draw Road, and the left-hand fork takes you to McGath Lake. The difficulty of the trail increases immediately. The next 1.5 miles alternates between slow crawls over large boulders and long drives across meadows that can be very muddy. There are many excellent backcountry campsites along the route, mainly tucked into the aspens at the edge of the meadows.

After 1.5 miles from the junction, the trail crosses Grimes

View of McGath Lake from a creek overflow

Creek. This can be a difficult crossing, especially after rain. There are two alternatives, both potentially difficult. The left-hand crossing traverses an area of boggy patches and then a large drainage pipe that the creek flows through. The right-hand crossing has less boggy spots, but fords the creek at a spot with a steep and greasy entrance and exit, both potentially difficult. Those not wanting to tackle the most difficult portion of the trail, which is still to come, are advised to park here and hike the remaining distance to the lake.

After Grimes Creek, the trail climbs a rocky section interspersed with loose shale, on which you can quickly lose traction. Drivers in wide or tall vehicles will need to watch their roofline on the trees in off-camber sections.

After 2.6 miles from the junction, you reach the most difficult section of the trail—a very steep, very loose climb with several large rock steps that need careful wheel placement. The difficulty is increased by the looseness of the surface, making it almost impossible to avoid spinning your wheels. At 2.8 miles, the track levels off, and apart from a couple of rocky sections, the worst is over. The final portion of the trail descends a hill to McGath Lake. This portion will cause no problems for an SUV unless it is wet. McGath Lake has a couple of beautiful campsites tucked into the trees at the water's edge. The lake provides good trout fishing, and it's a wonderful place to relax for a couple of hours before tackling the drive back.

Current Road Information
Dixie National Forest
Escalante Ranger District
755 West Main
Escalante, UT 84726
(435) 826-5403

Map References
BLM Escalante
USFS Dixie National Forest: Escalante Ranger District
USGS 1:24,000 Roger Peak
1:100,000 Escalante
Maptech CD-ROM: Escalante/Dixie National Forest
Trails Illustrated, #710 (incomplete)
Utah Atlas & Gazetteer, p. 27

Route Directions

▼ 0.0		On Southwest #23: Hells Backbone Trail, 8.7 miles from Boulder Town end, turn north on graded gravel FR 566, cross cattle guard, and zero trip meter.
2.6 ▲		Trail ends on Southwest #23: Hells Backbone Trail. Turn left for Boulder Town. Turn right for Escalante.
GPS: N 37°57.85' W 111°33.19'		
▼ 0.2	SO	Large camping area on left.
2.4 ▲	SO	Large camping area on right.
▼ 0.8	SO	Wide shelf road with views to the southeast.
1.8 ▲	SO	Wide shelf road with views to the southeast.
▼ 1.2	SO	End of shelf road.
1.4 ▲	SO	Start of shelf road.
▼ 1.6	SO	Campsite with good views on right.
1.0 ▲	SO	Campsite with good views on left.
▼ 2.1	BR	Track on left along fence line.

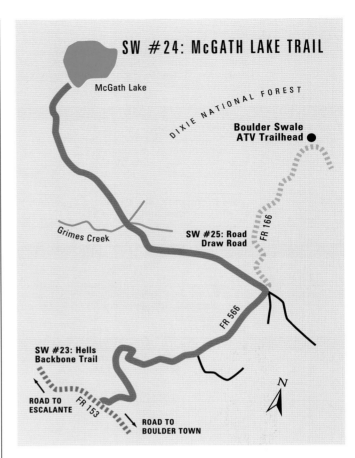

0.5 ▲	BL	Track on right along fence line.
GPS: N 37°58.51' W 111°32.41'		
▼ 2.4	SO	Campsite on left.
0.2 ▲	SO	Campsite on right.
▼ 2.6	BL	Bear left, following sign to McGath Lake. Right is Southwest #25: Road Draw Road (signed to Boulder Swale ATV trail). Trail standard drops to rough, ungraded dirt. Zero trip meter.
0.0 ▲		Intersection of Southwest #24: McGath Lake Trail and Southwest #25: Road Draw Road. Proceed south toward Southwest #23: Hells Backbone Trail.
GPS: N 37°58.90' W 111°32.20'		
▼ 0.0		Continue over ungraded track.
▼ 0.8	SO	Track on right.
GPS: N 37°59.09' W 111°33.00'		
▼ 1.2	SO	Faint track on right.
▼ 1.4	SO	Cattle guard.
▼ 1.5	BL	Cross Grimes Creek over pipe; crossing can be very muddy. Right fork fords through creek, but entry and exit can be difficult.
▼ 2.2	SO	Short, steep, rocky creek crossing.
GPS: N 37°59.45' W 111°34.12'		
▼ 2.5	BL	Bear left at fork; right is mainly ATV use.
GPS: N 37°59.56' W 111°34.24'		
▼ 2.6	SO	Loose, steep, washed-out climb.
▼ 2.8	BR	Slightly rutted descent to McGath Lake.
GPS: N 37°59.79' W 111°34.27'		
▼ 2.9		McGath Lake, end of trail. Campsite on left on lakeshore; trail on right continues over dam wall to second campsite.
GPS: N 37°59.86' W 111°34.18'		

Road Draw Road

Starting Point:	Southwest #24: McGath Lake Trail
Finishing Point:	Utah 12, 4.5 miles north of Boulder Town
Total Mileage:	10 miles
Unpaved Mileage:	10 miles
Driving Time:	1.5 hours
Elevation Range:	7,700–9,500 feet
Usually Open:	June to October
Difficulty Rating:	4
Scenic Rating:	8
Remoteness Rating:	+0

Special Attractions

- Moderately challenging 4WD trail.
- Access to ATV trails and backcountry campsites.
- Aspen viewing in the fall.

Description

This moderately challenging trail is easily handled by a high-clearance SUV in dry weather. The trail begins along Southwest #24: McGath Lake Trail, 2.6 miles from Southwest #23: Hells Backbone Trail and continues as a graded gravel road until the ATV unloading point for the Boulder Swale ATV trailhead. The routes over the divide are limited to ATVs from this point by a width restriction; there is ample parking at the trailhead. Just before the ATV trail, Road Draw Road heads east, becoming an ungraded, defined 4WD trail. The lumpy route descends through stands of aspens, twisting and turning as it crosses open meadows before reaching the graded road at Haws Pasture. The driving is not difficult; there are some moderately steep descents and rocky sections interspersed with long smooth sections across open meadow. However, use extra care when the road is

A lumpy section of the trail just after its intersection with the ATV trailhead

wet because those smooth meadow runs can become slow mud wallows. The trail is easiest downhill, from McGath Lake to Utah 12. Some of the climbs have a loose rocky surface that may cause loss of traction going uphill. There are several good backcountry campsites en route as well as large stands of aspens, whose colors are splendid in fall.

Current Road Information

Dixie National Forest
Escalante Ranger District
755 West Main
Escalante, UT 84726
(435) 826-5403

Map References

BLM Escalante
USFS Dixie National Forest: Escalante Ranger District
USGS 1:24,000 Roger Peak, Boulder Town
1:100,000 Escalante
Maptech CD-ROM: Escalante/Dixie National Forest
Utah Atlas & Gazetteer, pp. 27, 28

Route Directions

▼ 0.0   Begin from Southwest #24: McGath Lake Trail (FR 566), 2.6 miles from Southwest #23: Hells Backbone Trail. Zero trip meter and turn north onto FR 166, following signs to Boulder Swale ATV trailhead.

1.6 ▲   Trail ends at Southwest #24: McGath Lake Trail (FR 566). Turn left to join Southwest #23: Hells Backbone Trail, right to McGath Lake.

GPS: N 37°58.89' W 111°32.19'

▼ 0.2   SO   Track on right.
1.4 ▲   SO   Track on left.

▼ 0.6   SO   Gravel road turns to graded dirt.
1.0 ▲   SO   Graded dirt road turns to gravel.

▼ 1.6   TR   T-intersection. Follow sign right to Haws Pasture. Ahead goes to the Boulder Swale ATV trailhead. Zero trip meter.
0.0 ▲   Continue on graded dirt road.

GPS: N 38°00.03' W 111°31.68'

▼ 0.0   Continue on lesser standard 4WD track.
2.8 ▲   TL   Follow sign left to Hells Backbone. Right goes to the Boulder Swale ATV trailhead. Zero trip meter.

▼ 0.2   SO   Small waterhole on right.
2.6 ▲   SO   Small waterhole on left.

▼ 0.7   SO   Faint track on left.
2.1 ▲   SO   Faint track on right.

▼ 0.8   SO   Track on left, then cattle guard.
2.0 ▲   SO   Cattle guard, then track on right.

GPS: N 37°59.57' W 111°31.13'

▼ 0.9   BL   Left turn is fainter.
1.9 ▲   TR   T-intersection.

▼ 1.5   BL   Right track to campsite with great view.
1.3 ▲   TR   T-intersection. Left track to campsite with great view.

GPS: N 37°59.39' W 111°30.56'

▼ 1.7   BR   Cross through small creek; faint track on left. Cross small creek a second time.
1.1 ▲   BL   Cross through small creek; faint track on right. Cross small creek a second time.

▼ 1.9   SO   Views left toward Boulder Mountain.
0.9 ▲   SO   Views right toward Boulder Mountain.

▼ 2.0   BL   Fork.
0.8 ▲   TR   T-intersection.

GPS: N 37°59.26' W 111°30.14'

▼ 2.7   SO   Track on right.
0.1 ▲   SO   Track on left.

GPS: N 37°59.64' W 111°29.69'

SW #25: ROAD DRAW ROAD

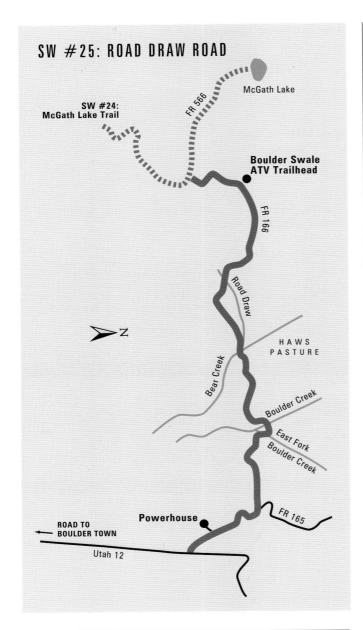

| ▼ 2.8 | TR | Cross through small creek, then turn right at T-intersection. Zero trip meter. |
| 0.0 ▲ | | Continue on lesser standard trail and cross through small creek. |

GPS: N 37°59.66' W 111°29.67'

▼ 0.0		Continue on graded gravel road.
5.6 ▲	TL	At junction, follow sign left to Boulder Swale ATV trailhead. Zero trip meter.
▼ 0.2	SO	Cattle guard, then cross over Bear Creek on culvert.
5.4 ▲	SO	Cross over Bear Creek on culvert, then cattle guard.
▼ 0.7	SO	Track on left.
4.9 ▲	SO	Track on right.
▼ 1.2	SO	Track on left.
4.4 ▲	SO	Track on right.

GPS: N 37°59.81' W 111°28.61'

| ▼ 2.2 | SO | Cross over Boulder Creek on culvert, then track on left. |
| 3.4 ▲ | SO | Track on right, then cross over Boulder Creek on culvert. |

▼ 2.4	SO	Cross over East Fork Boulder Creek on culvert.
3.2 ▲	SO	Cross over East Fork Boulder Creek on culvert.
▼ 2.9	SO	Pass through gate.
2.7 ▲	SO	Pass through gate.
▼ 3.0	SO	Track on right.
2.6 ▲	SO	Track on left.
▼ 3.1	SO	Track on left.
2.5 ▲	SO	Track on right.
▼ 3.9	BR	Track on left is FR 165 to Kings Pasture. Bear right, remaining on FR 166.
1.7 ▲	BL	Track on right is FR 165 to Kings Pasture. Remain on FR 166.

GPS: N 37°59.97' W 111°26.69'

▼ 4.7	SO	Cattle guard.
0.9 ▲	SO	Cattle guard.
▼ 4.8	SO	Track on left (private).
0.8 ▲	SO	Track on right (private).
▼ 5.2	SO	Track on right to powerhouse.
0.4 ▲	SO	Track on left to powerhouse.
▼ 5.6		Cross cattle guard; trail ends at Utah 12, 4.5 miles north of Boulder Town.
0.0 ▲		On Utah 12, 4.5 miles north of Boulder Town, turn west on FR 166, cross cattle guard, and zero trip meter.

GPS: N 37°58.94' W 111°25.78'

SOUTHWEST REGION TRAIL #26

Posey Lake Road

Starting Point:	**Utah 24 in Bicknell**
Finishing Point:	**Southwest #23: Hells Backbone**
	Trail (FR 153)
Total Mileage:	**34.1 miles**
Unpaved Mileage:	**32.4 miles**
Driving Time:	**2 hours**
Elevation Range:	**7,000–9,900 feet**
Usually Open:	**May to November**
Difficulty Rating:	**1**
Scenic Rating:	**8**
Remoteness Rating:	**+0**

Special Attractions

■ Long and scenic road for easy touring.
■ Fishing and camping opportunities at Posey Lake, Cyclone Lake, and others.
■ Access to a network of 4WD trails.

Description

This long, extremely scenic route crosses the Aquarius Plateau from north to south. The Aquarius Plateau is the highest timbered plateau in North America; it contains stands of spruces, pines, and aspens interspersed with large, natural grassy meadows. In the 1920s the plateau suffered an attack of spruce bark beetle, which decimated the mature

Roundy Reservoir

trees. Affected trees were harvested and the trees on the plateau now mainly date from after the infestation. Currently, there are no logging operations on the plateau.

The drive is suitable for a passenger car in dry weather; the entire trail is wide, graded gravel or dirt. From Bicknell, it climbs through BLM lands, crossing undulating plains of sagebrush where pronghorn antelope are frequently seen. After 8.2 miles, you pass Southwest #27: Boulder Tops Road.

After 16 miles, you enter the Dixie National Forest. The road meanders across open meadows, through stands of trees, and past many small lakes and reservoirs. Mule deer and elk live on the plateau in great numbers and are often seen. One likely area is around Big Lake, which is a wildlife area (established in 1957) where ponds and nesting islands have been constructed to improve the habitat for waterfowl. There are small numbers of black bear on the plateau; they can be a definite concern in the developed campgrounds in the summer months. On the plateau, this trail connects with Southwest #31: Dark Valley Trail and Southwest #33: Griffin Road.

Near the end of the trail is Posey Lake, which has a developed national forest campground and offers good fishing opportunities. There is a small boat launching area. The campground is popular in summer and has some pretty sites set back from the lake. From Posey Lake, the trail descends to join the spectacular Southwest #23: Hells Backbone Trail. The road is a popular snowmobile route in winter, though it is not groomed for such use.

Current Road Information

Dixie National Forest
Escalante Ranger District
755 West Main
Escalante, UT 84726
(435) 826-5403

BLM Escalante Field Office
PO Box 225
Escalante, UT 84726
(435) 826-5600

Escalante Interagency Office
755 West Main
Escalante, UT 84726
(435) 826-5499

Map References

BLM   Loa, Escalante
USFS   Dixie National Forest: Teasdale and Ecalante Ranger Districts (incomplete)
USGS   1:24,000 Bicknell, Smooth Knoll, Big Lake, Posey Lake
1:100,000 Escalante
Maptech CD-ROM: Escalante/Dixie National Forest
Trails Illustrated, #213; #710 (incomplete)
Utah Atlas & Gazetteer, p. 27
Utah Travel Council #4
Other: BLM Map of the Grand Staircase–Escalante National Monument (incomplete)

Route Directions

▼ 0.0		From Utah 24, on the western edge of Bicknell, turn south on paved 400 West Street at the scenic byway sign, and zero trip meter.
1.8 ▲		Trail ends at Utah 24, on the western edge of Bicknell.
	GPS: N 38°20.46' W 111°33.02'	
▼ 0.8	BR	Road swings right. Track on left.
1.0 ▲	TL	Track on right.
▼ 1.5	BL	Cross over Fremont River on bridge; swing left on the pavement road. Track on right.
0.3 ▲	BR	Track on left, then cross over Fremont River on bridge.
▼ 1.7	SO	Road turns to graded gravel.
0.1 ▲	SO	Road turns to pavement.
	GPS: N 38°19.65' W 111°34.03'	
▼ 1.8	BL	Unsigned fork, road on right. Zero trip meter.
0.0 ▲		Continue along graded gravel road.
	GPS: N 38°19.58' W 111°34.11'	
▼ 0.0		Continue along graded gravel road.
6.4 ▲	SO	Unsigned road on left. Zero trip meter.
▼ 0.2	BR	Fork. Bear right, following sign to Dixie National Forest.
6.2 ▲	SO	Continue toward Bicknell.
	GPS: N 38°19.45' W 111°34.18'	
▼ 3.4	TL	Turn left at intersection. Track ahead to the Flat Tops.
3.0 ▲	BR	Bear right at intersection. Track on left to the Flat Tops.
	GPS: N 38°17.89' W 111°36.98'	
▼ 4.1	SO	Bicknell Reservoir on left.
2.3 ▲	SO	Bicknell Reservoir on right.
▼ 5.0	SO	Track on left.
1.4 ▲	SO	Track on right.
▼ 5.2	SO	Gravel road on left.
1.2 ▲	BL	Fork; gravel road on right.
	GPS: N 38°16.23' W 111°36.97'	
▼ 5.7	BL	Fork. Road on right to Antelope Spring and Pollywog Lake.
0.7 ▲	SO	Road on left to Antelope Spring and Pollywog Lake.
	GPS: N 38°15.78' W 111°37.03'	
▼ 6.4	BR	Fork. Left is Southwest #27: Boulder Tops Road (FR 178), immediately followed by track on right and second entrance to Boulder Tops Road. Zero trip meter.
0.0 ▲		Continue toward Bicknell.
	GPS: N 38°15.19' W 111°37.32'	
▼ 0.0		Continue toward Escalante.
7.9 ▲	SO	Two entrances to Southwest #27: Boulder Tops Road on the right, and track on left. Zero trip meter.

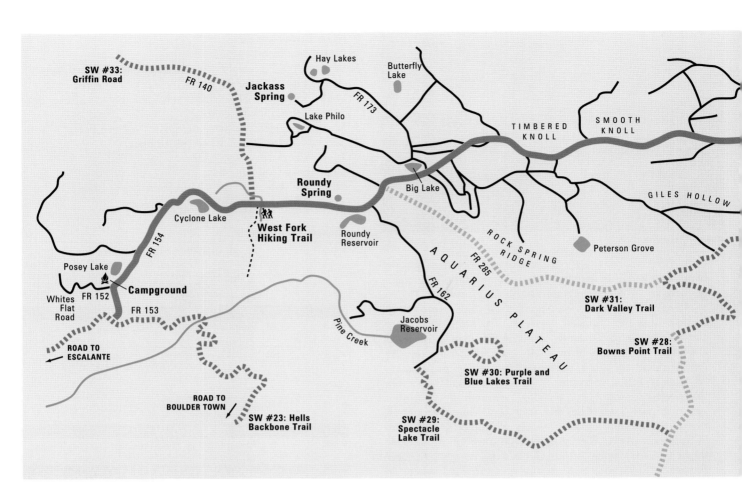

▼ 0.6		SO	Track on right.
	7.3 ▲	SO	Track on left.
▼ 1.4		SO	Track on left.
	6.5 ▲	SO	Track on right.
▼ 2.1		SO	Cattle guard. Views north over Thousand Lake Mountain.
	5.8 ▲	SO	Cattle guard. Views north over Thousand Lake Mountain.
▼ 2.9		SO	Track on left.
	5.0 ▲	SO	Track on right.
▼ 3.3		SO	Track on left.
	4.6 ▲	SO	Track on right.
▼ 3.6		SO	Track on right.
	4.3 ▲	SO	Track on left.
▼ 3.8		SO	Track on right, followed by track on left.
	4.1 ▲	SO	Track on right, followed by track on left.
▼ 6.0		SO	Tracks on right and left.
	1.9 ▲	SO	Tracks on left and right.
▼ 6.7		SO	Track on right.
	1.2 ▲	SO	Track on left.
▼ 7.9		SO	Entering Dixie National Forest over cattle guard. Road is now FR 154. Zero trip meter.
	0.0 ▲		Continue on graded gravel road.
GPS: N 38°08.56' W 111°40.21'			
▼ 0.0			Continue on graded dirt road.
	6.6 ▲	SO	Leaving Dixie National Forest over cattle guard and entering BLM lands. Zero trip meter.
▼ 0.1		SO	Track on right.
	6.5 ▲	SO	Track on left.

▼ 1.0		SO	Track on left to Peterson Grove.
	5.6 ▲	SO	Track on right to Peterson Grove.
GPS: N 38°07.73' W 111°40.57'			
▼ 1.8		BL	Track on right to Antelope Spring and Pollywog Lake. Dog Lake (dry) at intersection.
	4.8 ▲	SO	Track on left to Antelope Spring and Pollywog Lake. Dog Lake (dry) at intersection.
GPS: N 38°07.33' W 111°41.34'			
▼ 2.2		SO	Track on left.
	4.4 ▲	SO	Track on right.
▼ 2.4		SO	Track on right.
	4.2 ▲	SO	Track on left.
▼ 2.6		SO	Track on left.
	4.0 ▲	SO	Track on right.
▼ 2.8		SO	Track on right.
	3.8 ▲	SO	Track on left.
▼ 3.2		SO	Cattle guard.
	3.4 ▲	SO	Cattle guard.
▼ 3.6		SO	Track on left, then Big Lake Environmental Enclosure on right.
	3.0 ▲	SO	Big Lake Environmental Enclosure on left, then track on right.
GPS: N 38°05.79' W 111°41.48'			
▼ 4.5		SO	FR 173 on right to Hay Lakes and Lake Philo. Small track on left.
	2.1 ▲	SO	FR 173 on left to Hay Lakes and Lake Philo. Small track on right.
GPS: N 38°05.07' W 111°41.37'			
▼ 4.6		SO	Big Lake Wildlife Area on right.
	2.0 ▲	SO	Big Lake Wildlife Area on left.

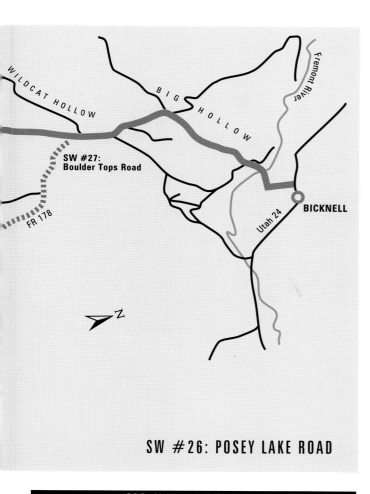

SW #26: POSEY LAKE ROAD

GPS: N 38°04.92' W 111°41.28'			
▼ 5.7		**SO**	FR 285 on left is Southwest #31: Dark Valley Trail.
	0.9 ▲	SO	FR 285 on right is Southwest #31: Dark Valley Trail.
GPS: N 38°03.94' W 111°41.45'			
▼ 5.9		**SO**	Track on right.
	0.7 ▲	SO	Track on left.
▼ 6.2		**SO**	Cattle guard.
	0.4 ▲	SO	Cattle guard.
▼ 6.6		**SO**	Track on left is FR 162 and leads to Southwest #30: Purple and Blue Lakes Trail, Southwest #29: Spectacle Lake Trail, and to Jacobs Valley. Zero trip meter.
	0.0 ▲		Continue toward Bicknell.
GPS: N 38°03.29' W 111°40.79'			
▼ 0.0			Continue toward Escalante.
	3.8 ▲	SO	Track on right is FR 162 and leads to Southwest #30: Purple and Blue Lakes Trail, Southwest #29: Spectacle Lake Trail, and to Jacobs Valley. Zero trip meter.
▼ 0.6		**SO**	Track on right.
	3.2 ▲	SO	Track on left.
▼ 0.7		**SO**	Roundy Reservoir on left.
	3.1 ▲	SO	Roundy Reservoir on right.
▼ 1.0		**SO**	Track on left.
	2.8 ▲	SO	Track on right.
GPS: N 38°02.44 W 111°41.10'			
▼ 1.5		**SO**	Great Western Trail, hiking access on left to Auger Hole Lake.
	2.3 ▲	SO	Great Western Trail, hiking access on right to Auger Hole Lake.

▼ 1.6		**SO**	Track on left.
	2.2 ▲	SO	Track on right.
▼ 2.1		**SO**	Campsite on left and track on right.
	1.7 ▲	SO	Track on left and campsite on right.
▼ 2.7		**SO**	Track on left.
	1.1 ▲	SO	Track on right.
▼ 3.1		**SO**	Track on right.
	0.7 ▲	SO	Track on left.
▼ 3.4		**SO**	West Fork hiking trail to Pine Creek on left.
	0.4 ▲	SO	West Fork hiking trail to Pine Creek on right.
▼ 3.8		**SO**	Track on right is Southwest #33: Griffin Road (FR 140) to Escalante Summit. Zero trip meter.
	0.0 ▲		Continue north.
GPS: N 38°00.20' W 111°42.40'			
▼ 0.0			Continue south.
	7.6 ▲	SO	Track on left is Southwest #33: Griffin Road (FR 140) to Escalante Summit. Zero trip meter.
▼ 0.9		**SO**	Track on right is FR 763.
	6.7 ▲	SO	Track on left is FR 763.
▼ 1.4		**SO**	Track on left to corral.
	6.2 ▲	SO	Track on right to corral.
▼ 1.6		**SO**	Track on right, trail runs alongside Cyclone Lake.
	6.0 ▲	SO	Track on left, main trail leaves Cyclone Lake.
▼ 1.8		**SO**	Track on right.
	5.8 ▲	SO	Track on left.
▼ 2.2		**SO**	Trail leaves Cyclone Lake.
	5.4 ▲	SO	Cyclone Lake on right.
▼ 2.9		**SO**	Track on right.
	4.7 ▲	SO	Track on left.
▼ 3.0		**SO**	Track on right to Velvet Lake.
	4.6 ▲	SO	Track on left to Velvet Lake.
GPS: N 37°58.10' W 111°43.34'			
▼ 4.0		**SO**	Cattle guard.
	3.6 ▲	SO	Cattle guard.
▼ 4.9		**SO**	Great Western Trail on right and left; right provides vehicle access to Barker Reservoir.
	2.7 ▲	SO	Great Western Trail on left and right; left provides vehicles access Barker Reservoir.
▼ 5.8		**SO**	Posey Lake on right.
	1.8 ▲	SO	Posey Lake on left.
▼ 5.9		**SO**	Posey Lake National Forest Campground on right (fee area).
	1.7 ▲	SO	Posey Lake National Forest Campground on left (fee area).
GPS: N 37°56.20' W 111°41.58'			
▼ 6.4		**SO**	Gravel road on right is Whites Flat Road (FR 152).
	1.2 ▲	SO	Gravel road on left is Whites Flat Road (FR 152).
GPS: N 37°55.86' W 111°41.47'			
▼ 6.7		**SO**	Small track on left.
	0.9 ▲	SO	Small track on right.
▼ 6.9		**SO**	Track on right over cattle guard and track on left.
	0.7 ▲	SO	Track on left over cattle guard and track on right.
GPS: N 37°55.79' W 111°40.93'			
▼ 7.4		**SO**	Track on right.
	0.2 ▲	SO	Track on left.
▼ 7.5		**SO**	Cattle guard.
	0.1 ▲	SO	Cattle guard.
▼ 7.6			Trail ends at Southwest #23: Hells Backbone Trail (FR 153). Turn left to continue over Hells Backbone to Boulder Town, turn right for Escalante.
	0.0 ▲		On Southwest #23: Hells Backbone Trail (FR 153), 13 miles from Escalante, turn northwest on FR 154 and zero trip meter.
GPS: N 37°55.53' W 111°40.32'			

Boulder Tops Road

Starting Point:	Southwest #26: Posey Lake Road (FR 154)
Finishing Point:	Southwest #28: Bowns Point Trail
Total Mileage:	12.5 miles
Unpaved Mileage:	12.5 miles
Driving Time:	1 hour
Elevation Range:	9,000–10,800 feet
Usually Open:	May to October
Difficulty Rating:	1
Scenic Rating:	7
Remoteness Rating:	+0

Special Attractions

■ Provides access to a network of more-difficult 4WD trails on Boulder Tops.

■ Access to three different lakes.

■ Scenic drive across undulating country in the Dixie National Forest.

History

This trail crosses the main part of the Aquarius Plateau, which was named by the Spanish explorer Silvestre Escalante. The plateau has many natural bodies of water, so he named it after the zodiac sign Aquarius, the water bearer. This plateau, with an elevation of over 10,000 feet, is the highest timbered plateau in the United States. Portions of Boulder Tops reach 11,300 feet. The area of Boulder Tops refers to the easternmost edge of the Aquarius Plateau as it abuts Boulder Mountain. This entire region forms part of the northwestern edge of the massive Colorado Plateau, a vast area spanning the Four Corners region of Colorado, Utah, New Mexico, and Arizona. Boulder Mountain is composed of sedimentary rocks topped with a cap of lava. The harder lava has protected the underlying formations from erosion. When this hard cap is eventually worn away, Boulder Mountain will become like the eroded buttes and canyons of the surrounding desert areas, such as Capitol Reef National Park. The height and spread of Boulder Mountain, and its northern neighbor Thousand Lake

Looking back toward Dark Valley from Boulder Tops Road

Mountain, support an alpine environment of spruce forests, wildflowers, aspens, and small natural lakes. As you travel on either of these mountains, you progress through a number of life zones, from the desert floor up to the alpine settings.

The names of these mountains are the result of an interesting blunder. When this region was mapped by the government survey team, it surveyed and named both Boulder and Thousand Lake Mountains, the area's two major mountains. The names were self-descriptive: Boulder Mountain has a proliferation of rocks on its summit, and Thousand Lake Mountain has many small natural lakes. However, somehow in the process from survey team to mapmakers to transcriber, the names of the mountains were switched. Boulder Mountain is really Thousand Lake Mountain, and vice versa.

Historically, the water rights to the small lakes on top of the plateau are owned by many of the ranchers miles away down in the valley. This fact does not affect fishing or recreation rights, however, and the Boulder Mountain lakes provide some of the best brook trout fishing in Utah!

The Great Western Trail passes along or crosses many of the roads in this area. The designation refers to a continuous recreation trail linking local trails in many regions to form a continuous trail from Mexico to Canada. Standards and permitted uses along the trail vary widely, from sedan car to hiking and horseback use only.

Description

This drive within the Dixie National Forest links Southwest #26: Posey Lake Road (FR 154) with the network of more difficult 4WD trails on Boulder Mountain. It is a beautiful drive in its own right, and it provides vehicle access to three small natural lakes. As you ascend Aquarius Plateau, you pass from the sagebrush and juniper of the lower benches up to the higher elevation alpine settings. There are few trees on the plateau itself, which is mainly open meadow with scattered stands of aspens, but as you ascend the western side, you pass through a mix of spruce and aspen forest.

The entire trail is graded dirt road, and it finishes at the 4WD/ATV trailhead on Boulder Tops, which includes Southwest #28: Bowns Point Trail. From here the standard immediately drops and recreationalists can choose from a variety of tracks with an equally diverse variety of standards.

After 2 miles, you reach the turn for Pine Creek Reservoir, just north of the Aquarius Ranger Station. This three-acre lake contains some large brook trout.

After 6.8 miles, you reach Southwest #31: Dark Valley Trail. A sign warns that the trails ahead on Boulder Tops are closed annually from November 1 to June 15 to protect wildlife and control erosion on the plateau. The second lake, Cook Lake, is another 3.8 miles farther on, and it's reached by a short, mile-long vehicle spur. This is also a popular trout fishing spot. About a mile farther on the main trail brings you to the vehicle access for Miller Lake, which can be seen down the valley to the south. Just after this turn is the closure gate to restrict vehicle access to Boulder Tops. The road then climbs for half a mile to the end of the trail, which is marked by an information board and motorized travel map for the Boulder Tops area.

SW #27: BOULDER TOPS ROAD

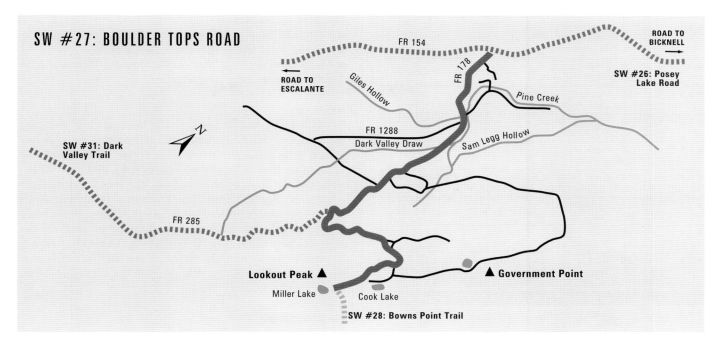

Current Road Information

Dixie National Forest
Teasdale Ranger District
PO Box 99
Teasdale, UT 84773
(435) 425-3702

Map References

BLM Loa
USFS Dixie National Forest: Teasdale Ranger District
USGS 1:24,000 Bicknell, Government Point
1:100,000 Loa
Maptech CD-ROM: Escalante/Dixie National Forest
Trails Illustrated, #707
Utah Atlas & Gazetteer, p. 27
Utah Travel Council #4

Route Directions

▼ 0.0			On Southwest #26: Posey Lake Road (FR 154), 8.2 miles from Bicknell, zero trip meter and turn southeast on FR 178; follow sign to Aquarius Ranger Station.
	5.2 ▲		Trail ends at Southwest #26: Posey Lake Road (FR 154). Turn right for Bicknell, left to continue along Posey Lake Road toward Escalante.
		GPS: N 38°15.21' W 111°37.33'	
▼ 0.3		SO	Track on left.
	4.9 ▲	SO	Track on right.
▼ 0.6		SO	Track on right.
	4.6 ▲	SO	Track on left.
▼ 1.0		SO	Track on left.
	4.2 ▲	SO	Track on right.
▼ 1.5		SO	Entering Dixie National Forest over cattle guard.
	3.7 ▲	SO	Leaving Dixie National Forest over cattle guard.
		GPS: N 38°14.22' W 111°36.36'	
▼ 1.8		SO	Giles Hollow Exclosure on right.
	3.4 ▲	SO	Giles Hollow Exclosure on left.

▼ 2.0		SO	Cross over Giles Hollow on culvert, then track on left.
	3.2 ▲	SO	Track on right, then cross over Giles Hollow on culvert.
▼ 2.1		SO	FR 1288 on right, followed by track on left through a wire gate, signed to Pine Creek.
	3.1 ▲	SO	Track on right through a wire gate to Pine Creek, followed by FR 1288 on left.
		GPS: N 38°14.05' W 111°35.78'	
▼ 2.8		SO	Cross over Dark Valley Draw on culvert.
	2.4 ▲	SO	Cross over Dark Valley Draw on culvert.
▼ 2.9		SO	Track on right.
	2.3 ▲	SO	Track on left.
▼ 4.4		SO	Track on left.
	0.8 ▲	SO	Track on right.
▼ 5.0		SO	Track on left to Pine Creek Reservoir. Trail crosses Allans Flat.
	0.2 ▲	SO	Track on left to Pine Creek Reservoir. Trail crosses Allans Flat.
		GPS: N 38°11.86' W 111°35.03'	
▼ 5.1		SO	Track on right.
	0.2 ▲	SO	Track on left.
▼ 5.2		BR	Bear right at fork; left goes to Aquarius Field Station. Zero trip meter.
	0.0 ▲		Continue along FR 178.
		GPS: N 38°11.63' W 111°34.90'	
▼ 0.0			Continue toward Boulder Tops.
	1.6 ▲	SO	Track on right to Aquarius Field Station. Zero trip meter.
▼ 0.8		BR	Two tracks on left; first is Great Western Trail.
	0.8 ▲	BL	Two tracks on right; second is Great Western Trail.
		GPS: N 38°10.96' W 111°34.72'	
▼ 1.4		SO	Potholes Exclosure, a protected wildlife area established in 1958, on left.
	0.2 ▲	SO	Potholes Exclosure, a protected wildlife area established in 1958, on right.
▼ 1.6		BL	Track on right is Southwest #31: Dark Valley Trail (FR 285/Great Western Trail). Zero trip meter.
	0.0 ▲		Continue across sagebrush benches.
		GPS: N 38°10.39' W 111°34.86'	

▼ 0.0			Climb toward Boulder Tops.
	5.7 ▲	TR	Track on left is Southwest #31: Dark Valley Trail (FR 285/Great Western Trail). Zero trip meter.
▼ 0.1		SO	Track on left.
	5.6 ▲	SO	Track on right.
▼ 0.3		SO	Views south over the Potholes.
	5.4 ▲	SO	Views south over the Potholes.
▼ 1.0		SO	Track on left.
	4.7 ▲	SO	Track on right.
▼ 1.1		SO	Track on right.
	4.6 ▲	SO	Track on left.
▼ 2.7		SO	Track on right, followed by track on left.
	3.0 ▲	SO	Track on right, followed by track on left.
▼ 2.9		SO	Track on left.
	2.8 ▲	SO	Track on right.
▼ 3.1		SO	Track on left.
	2.6 ▲	SO	Track on right.
▼ 3.8		SO	Track on right, followed by track on left to Cook Lake.
	1.9 ▲	SO	Track on right to Cook Lake, followed by track on left.
			GPS: N 38°11.02′ W 111°32.77′
▼ 4.2		SO	Track on right.
	1.5 ▲	SO	Track on left.
▼ 4.5		SO	Track on right.
	1.2 ▲	SO	Track on left.
▼ 4.6		SO	Track on left.
	1.1 ▲	SO	Track on right.
▼ 5.0		SO	Track on right to Miller Lake, then cattle guard.
	0.7 ▲	SO	Cattle guard, then track on left to Miller Lake.
			GPS: N 38°10.08′ W 111°32.59′
▼ 5.2		SO	Closure gate, followed by section of wide shelf road.
	0.5 ▲	SO	End of shelf road at closure gate.
▼ 5.7			Trail ends at information board at the start of Southwest #28: Bowns Point Trail.
	0.0 ▲		At information board at ATV/4WD trailhead, at endpoint of Southwest #28: Bowns Point Trail, zero trip meter and proceed on wide graded shelf road.
			GPS: N 38°09.75′ W 111°32.48′

SOUTHWEST REGION TRAIL #28

Bowns Point Trail

Starting Point:	**End of Southwest #27: Boulder Tops Road (FR 178)**
Finishing Point:	**Bowns Point**
Total Mileage:	**14.5 miles**
Unpaved Mileage:	**14.5 miles**
Driving Time:	**2 hours (one-way)**
Elevation Range:	**10,700–11,100 feet**
Usually Open:	**June 16 to October 31**
Difficulty Rating:	**4**
Scenic Rating:	**10**
Remoteness Rating:	**+0**

Special Attractions

- Panoramic viewpoint from Bowns Point.
- Moderately challenging trail for a stock SUV.
- Many small, natural lakes on the Boulder Tops that offer fishing and secluded camping.

History

Bowns Point takes its name from a local rancher who used to farm the Sandy Ranch, east of Boulder Tops. Sandy Ranch owned the water rights for Lower Bowns Reservoir and Upper Bowns Reservoir, now called Oak Creek Reservoir, and cattle from the ranch would spend the summer grazing on Boulder Tops. The quickest way up and down from the plateau was via what is now the Bowns Point Stock Driveway, which continues in a dizzying descent off the edge of the plateau from Bowns Point. The wide trail was originally put in by lumbermen in the 1950s, but is now used predominantly by cattle. Vehicle use is prohibited on the stock driveway.

Description

This meandering trail provides a moderately challenging drive, some beautiful scenery, the opportunity to relax by some tranquil mountain lakes, and finally a panoramic view east from Bowns Point.

The trail starts where the graded dirt Southwest #27: Boulder Tops Road ends, at the ATV/4WD trailhead on the western edge of Boulder Tops. There is a useful forest service information board that shows motorized travel routes. However, when surveyed, it was no longer strictly accurate; some routes had closed, and others had different uses to those shown.

The first few miles of the trail have been roughly graded, as they provide access to a number of ATV and

A view of Bowns Point Trail

4WD trails off to both sides. Navigation is easy along this stretch, since most trails have clearly posted forest route numbers. After 3.4 miles, you reach Elbow Lake and the connection with Southwest #29: Spectacle Lake Trail, and the trail becomes rougher.

Almost 3 miles past Elbow Lake is Southwest #32: Chokecherry Point Trail, a very rough and technically difficult 4WD trail. Continue on to Bowns Point, passing the very pretty Noon Lake on the right. The small lake is cradled in a scenic half circle of rock. Other tracks lead off from this trail to other Boulder Tops lakes, including Bess

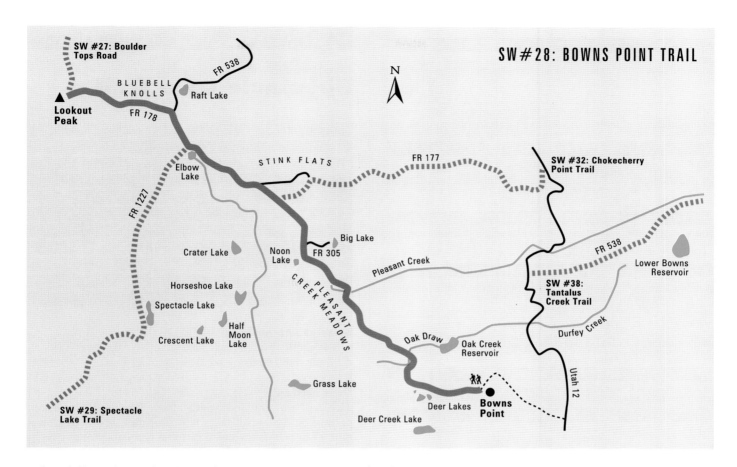

Lake, Skillet Lake, Raft Lake, and Big Lake; all have short trails leading to them, and most provide good trout fishing opportunities.

On the right of the trail, 5.5 miles past the turnoff for Chokecherry Point, is an old mill site. All that remains now is a well-constructed timber cabin and a large pile of sawdust. Loggers were responsible for many of the tracks on Boulder Tops. Once past the cabin, the trail standard drops again, and it traverses a large meadow as a faint two-track—take care not to become confused by the many faint tracks leading off from the main trail. If in doubt, take the one that's been most used. Deer Lakes are passed on the right, then the trail is indistinct again as it crosses the meadow. Follow in a southeasterly direction toward the trees.

The trail becomes lumpier, with many large boulders making for slow progress. Care is needed with wheel placement to avoid undercarriage damage, but the trail is suitable for most high-clearance SUVs with a careful driver. A mile past Deer Lakes, the trail finishes at Bowns Point. The Bowns Point Stock Driveway leads on from here, descending over the escarpment to Oak Creek Reservoir. This trail is for hiking and horse use only.

The view from Bowns Point is unparalleled: Capitol Reef National Park is northwest, and the Waterpocket Fold runs north to south parallel to the ridge. Directly below are Oak Creek Reservoir, Scout Lake, and Long Lake. Farther away is Lower Bowns Reservoir with the conical Wildcat Hill immediately to its south. On a clear day, you can see the Henry Mountains.

Current Road Information

Dixie National Forest
Teasdale Ranger District
PO Box 99
Teasdale, UT 84773
(435) 425-3702

Dixie National Forest
Escalante Ranger District
755 West Main
Escalante, UT 84726
(435) 826-5403

Map References

BLM   Loa
USFS Dixie National Forest: Teasdale Ranger District
USGS 1:24,000   Government Point, Blind Lake, Deer Creek
          Lake, Lower Bowns Reservoir
          1:100,000 Loa
Maptech CD-ROM: Escalante/Dixie National Forest
Trails Illustrated, #707
Utah Atlas & Gazetteer, pp. 27, 28
Utah Travel Council #4

Route Directions

▼ 0.0   From the information board at the southern end of Southwest #27: Boulder Tops Road, zero trip meter and proceed east on FR 178.

3.4 ▲   Trail ends at information board at the southern

			end of Southwest #27: Boulder Tops Road.
		GPS: N 38°09.75′ W 111°32.48′	
▼ 0.2		SO	Closed road to the left now gives hiking access to Government Point.
	3.2 ▲	SO	Closed road to the right now gives hiking access to Government Point.
▼ 0.8		SO	FR 541 on right to Chuck Lake and Surveyors Lake.
	2.6 ▲	SO	FR 541 on left to Chuck Lake and Surveyors Lake.
		GPS: N 38°09.60′ W 111°31.59′	
▼ 1.8		SO	Track on left.
	1.6 ▲	SO	Track on right.
▼ 2.5		BR	FR 538 on left to Raft Lake.
	0.9 ▲	BL	FR 538 on right to Raft Lake.
		GPS: N 38°09.38′ W 111°29.83′	
▼ 3.4		SO	Elbow Lake. FR 1277 on right is Southwest #29: Spectacle Lake Trail. Zero trip meter.
	0.0 ▲		Proceed northwest on FR 178.
		GPS: N 38°08.61′ W 111°29.40′	
▼ 0.0			Proceed southeast on FR 178. Trail is rougher.
	2.8 ▲	SO	Elbow Lake. FR 1277 on left is Southwest #29: Spectacle Lake Trail. Zero trip meter.
▼ 1.4		BL	FR 522 on right to Crater Lake, Horseshoe Lake, and Crescent Lake.
	1.4 ▲	BR	FR 522 on left to Crater Lake, Horseshoe Lake, and Crescent Lake.
		GPS: N 38°07.91′ W 111°28.21′	
▼ 2.1		BR	FR 424 on left to Bess Lake.
	0.7 ▲	BL	FR 424 on right to Bess Lake.
		GPS: N 38°07.73′ W 111°27.52′	
▼ 2.8		SO	Track on left is Southwest #32: Chokecherry Point Trail. Zero trip meter.
	0.0 ▲		Intersection of Southwest #28: Bowns Point Trail and Southwest #32: Chokecherry Point Trail. Proceed northwest toward Southwest #27: Boulder Tops Road (FR 178).
		GPS: N 38°07.42′ W 111°26.88′	
▼ 0.0			Continue to Bowns Point.
▼ 1.8		SO	FR 305 on left to Big Lake.
		GPS: N 38°06.11′ W 111°26.07′	
▼ 2.1		SO	Noon Lake on right.
		GPS: N 38°05.98′ W 111°25.88′	
▼ 2.8		SO	Descend into Pleasant Creek Meadows.
▼ 3.1		SO	Cross over Pleasant Creek.
▼ 5.5		SO	Old cabin and sawdust pile from old mill on right.
		GPS: N 38°04.13′ W 111°23.70′	
▼ 5.9		BR	Track on left, cross through Oak Draw.
▼ 6.1		SO	Cross through Oak Draw a second time, then track on left. Trail crosses meadow and is hard to follow. Watch carefully, and follow most-used track.
		GPS: N 38°03.94′ W 111°23.33′	
▼ 7.0		SO	Deer Lakes on right.
		GPS: N 38°03.41′ W 111°22.96′	
▼ 7.1		SO	Trail is again indistinct; head in a southeasterly direction to the trees.
▼ 7.5		SO	Trail enters trees.
		GPS: N 38°03.22′ W 111°22.34′	
▼ 8.1		BL	Bear left in clearing; correct exit is hard to follow.
		GPS: N 38°03.21′ W 111°21.73′	
▼ 8.3			Trail ends at Bowns Point. Gap in fence line is entrance to Bowns Point Stock Driveway (no vehicles). Great Western Trail goes left from this point to Behunin Point and Meeks Lake.
		GPS: N 38°03.36′ W 111°21.54′	

Spectacle Lake Trail

Starting Point:	**Southwest #28: Bowns Point Trail (FR 178) at Elbow Lake**
Finishing Point:	**Junction of FR 162 and FR 1277**
Total Mileage:	**11.4 miles**
Unpaved Mileage:	**11.4 miles**
Driving Time:	**1.5 hours**
Elevation Range:	**10,400–11,100 feet**
Usually Open:	**June 16 to October 31**
Difficulty Rating:	**3**
Scenic Rating:	**8**
Remoteness Rating:	**+0**

Special Attractions
- Bakeskillet and Spectacle Lakes.
- Scenic trail traversing the open Boulder Tops.

Description
This trail traverses the length of the Boulder Tops region, passing by two small lakes and providing access to several more. The trail is ungraded dirt and is suitable for any high-clearance SUV. Most of the surface across the tops is fairly smooth and easygoing, although it may be impassable after rain. The descent after Spectacle Lake is rocky and the road surface is lumpy, but there are no difficult sections that might cause any problems.

The trail begins at Elbow Lake from Southwest #28: Bowns Point Trail and heads southwest across the plateau. It undulates down to cross West Boulder Draw and then climbs to Spectacle Lake. The lake is a reservoir that is dammed at the south end. In summer, when it is partially dry, the lake separates into two ovals joined by a small channel of water—resembling spectacles. The water level in this lake is often low as it is used for irrigation storage. The lake provides some trout

A log cabin overlooks the south end of Spectacle Lake

SW #29: SPECTACLE LAKE TRAIL

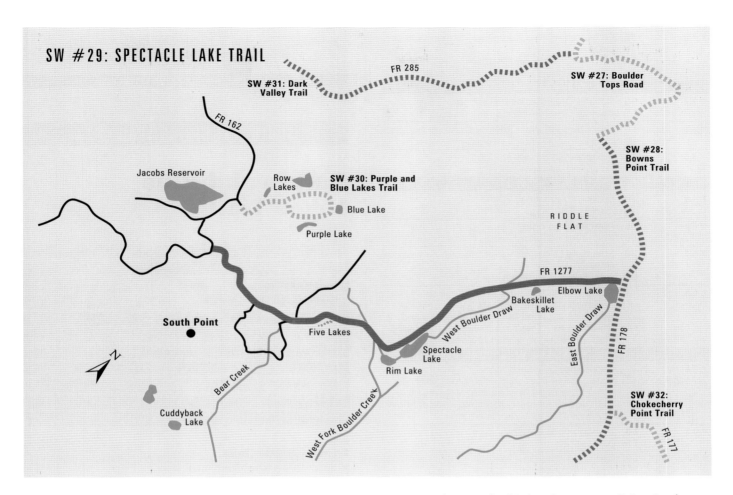

fishing opportunities, and there are some pleasant campsites around it, mainly at the southern end.

From the lake, the trail descends to join FR 162. It passes the small, natural depressions of Five Lakes, and 1.5 miles from the end of the trail you pass the seasonal closure sign—motorized travel is prohibited on the Boulder Tops between November 1 and June 15. However, when there is sufficient snow, snowmobiles can use the trail. FR 162 is about 6 miles from Spectacle Lake.

Current Road Information
Dixie National Forest
Teasdale Ranger District
PO Box 99
Teasdale, UT 84773
(435) 425-3702

Dixie National Forest
Escalante Ranger District
755 West Main
Escalante, UT 84726
(435) 826-5403

Map References
BLM Loa
USFS Dixie National Forest: Teasdale and Escalante Ranger Districts

USGS 1:24,000 Blind Lake, Government Point, Jacobs Reservoir
1:100,000 Loa
Maptech CD-ROM: Escalante/Dixie National Forest
Trails Illustrated, #707
Utah Atlas & Gazetteer, pp. 27, 28
Utah Travel Council #4 (incomplete)

Route Directions

▼ 0.0			From Southwest #28: Bowns Point Trail (FR 178) at Elbow Lake, zero trip meter and turn southwest on Spectacle Lake Trail (FR 1277).
	5.6 ▲		Trail finishes at Southwest #28: Bowns Point Trail (FR 178) at Elbow Lake. Turn right to continue to Bowns Point, left to exit the national forest via Southwest #27: Boulder Tops Road.
		GPS: N 38°08.60′ W 111°29.40′	
▼ 0.2		SO	Gravel pit on right.
	5.4 ▲	SO	Gravel pit on left.
▼ 1.0		SO	Track on left to Rain Lake.
	4.6 ▲	SO	Track on right to Rain Lake.
		GPS: N 38°07.93′ W 111°30.07′	
▼ 1.7		SO	Bakeskillet Lake on left.
	3.9 ▲	SO	Bakeskillet Lake on right.
		GPS: N 38°07.35′ W 111°30.36′	
▼ 1.9		SO	Oil drilling marker post on right.
	3.7 ▲	SO	Oil drilling marker post on left.
		GPS: N 38°07.27′ W 111°30.44′	

▼ 2.0		SO	FR 541 on right to Surveyors Lake and Chuck Lake.
	3.6 ▲	SO	FR 541 on left to Surveyors Lake and Chuck Lake.

GPS: N 38°07.19' W 111°30.54'

▼ 2.2		SO	Boulder Draw Exclosure on right.
	3.4 ▲	SO	Boulder Draw Exclosure on left.
▼ 2.3		SO	Cross through West Boulder Draw wash.
	3.3 ▲	SO	Cross through West Boulder Draw wash.
▼ 3.6		SO	Small lake in hollow on right.
	2.0 ▲	SO	Small lake in hollow on left.

GPS: N 38°05.96' W 111°30.94'

▼ 4.0		SO	Cross through small wash.
	1.6 ▲	SO	Cross through small wash.
▼ 4.6		BL	Faint track on right.
	1.0 ▲	SO	Faint track on left.
▼ 5.1		SO	Spectacle Lake; trail winds around the west side.
	0.5 ▲	SO	Trail leaves Spectacle Lake.
▼ 5.6		TR	South end of Spectacle Lake. Small cabin directly ahead. Track on left goes across dam wall to an exposed but pretty campsite and continues as a foot/pack trail. Zero trip meter.
	0.0 ▲		Continue along west side of Spectacle Lake.

GPS: N 38°04.68' W 111°30.45'

▼ 0.0			Leave Spectacle Lake.
	5.8 ▲	TL	South end of Spectacle Lake. Small cabin on right. Track on right goes across dam wall to an exposed but pretty campsite and continues as a foot/pack trail. Zero trip meter.
▼ 0.2		SO	Track on right.
	5.6 ▲	BR	Track on left.
▼ 0.3		SO	Track on left to Rim Lake.
	5.5 ▲	BL	Track on right to Rim Lake.

GPS: N 38°04.44' W 111°30.65'

▼ 0.9		SO	Cross through rocky wash.
	4.9 ▲	SO	Cross through rocky wash.
▼ 1.8		SO	Faint track on left.
	4.0 ▲	BL	Faint track on right.
▼ 2.1		SO	Trail passes alongside Five Lakes.
	3.7 ▲	SO	Trail leaves Five Lakes.

GPS: N 38°03.85' W 111°32.08'

▼ 2.4		SO	Trail leaves Five Lakes.
	3.4 ▲	SO	Trail passes alongside Five Lakes.
▼ 3.5		SO	Trail splits; both forks run parallel to each other.
	2.3 ▲	SO	Trails rejoin.
▼ 3.9		SO	Trails rejoin.
	1.9 ▲	SO	Trail splits; both forks run parallel to each other.
▼ 4.1		SO	Cattle guard.
	1.7 ▲	SO	Cattle guard.
▼ 4.2		SO	Leaving seasonal closure area on Boulder Tops.
	1.6 ▲	SO	Entering seasonal closure area for Boulder Tops.
▼ 5.4		SO	Track on left.
	0.4 ▲	BL	Track on right.
▼ 5.5		SO	Track on right.
	0.3 ▲	BR	Track on left.

GPS: N 38°02.96' W 111°34.33'

▼ 5.8			Trail finishes at FR 162. Turn right for Southwest #30: Purple and Blue Lakes Trail and also Southwest #26: Posey Lake Road which provides access to Escalante

and Bicknell.

	0.0 ▲		At intersection of FR 162 and FR 1277 (Spectacle Lake Road), zero trip meter and proceed northeast.

GPS: N 38°02.77' W 111°34.62'

Purple and Blue Lakes Trail

Starting Point:	**FR 162, 5.8 miles east of Southwest #26: Posey Lake Road**
Finishing Point:	**Blue Lake**
Total Mileage:	**4.1 miles**
Unpaved Mileage:	**4.1 miles**
Driving Time:	**1 hour**
Elevation Range:	**10,200–10,500 feet**
Usually Open:	**May to October**
Difficulty Rating:	**5**
Scenic Rating:	**8**
Remoteness Rating:	**+0**

Special Attractions

- Short trail passing four small lakes.
- Challenging 4WD trail in beautiful scenery.
- Fishing opportunities at Row, Blue, and Purple Lakes.

Description

This beautiful, scenic trail is a challenging drive for a high-clearance SUV. The trail leaves from FR 162, a graded gravel road that leads east from Southwest #26: Posey Lake Road. The trail standard is immediately rough, ungraded dirt; it winds around, crossing many boulder fields to the first of the two major Row Lakes. These are some of the many small natural lakes scattered around the lava cap rocks of the Boulder

Tall Conifers border the still waters of the Row Lakes

Tops plateau. The three Row Lakes are part of a chain of several small lakes. The largest is 30 acres and all are less than 10 feet deep. They are stocked annually with catchable rainbow trout.

From the first Row Lake, the trail continues toward an open meadow and then swings north into the trees. The trail here climbs steeply to Purple Lake. There are some medium-size boulders, a loose surface, and ruts to be negotiated as you approach the lake. Once at the lake the trail swings along the south shore. This section can be very muddy, and some of the mud wallows are deep.

Mud can become deep and lumpy as the Purple and Blue Lakes Trail crosses this open meadow

Purple Lake is probably the prettiest of the lakes on this trail, being set in a small tree-ringed depression. The lake is stocked with fingerling brook trout, and although many die when the lake freezes each winter, sufficient numbers survive each year to provide good fishing. There are limited backcountry campsites surrounding Purple Lake, but better sites are found around Blue and Row Lakes.

Half a mile farther is Blue Lake, which is set in a deep depression and is the smallest of the lakes along the trail. There are some good campsites on the east shore that are set among the trees. The lake is host to brook and cutthroat trout.

From Blue Lake, the trail descends back down to Row Lakes. This side is an easier slope than the climb to Purple Lake. The trail makes a loop past the second of the larger Row Lakes back to where you began the climb to Purple Lake. From here, retrace your steps back to FR 162.

Current Road Information

Dixie National Forest
Teasdale Ranger District
PO Box 99
Teasdale, UT 84773
(435) 425-3702

Dixie National Forest
Escalante Ranger District
755 West Main
Escalante, UT 84726
(435) 826-5403

Map References

BLM Loa
USFS Dixie National Forest: Escalante and Teasdale Ranger Districts
USGS 1:24,000 Jacobs Reservoir
1:100,000 Loa
Maptech CD-ROM: Escalante/Dixie National Forest
Trails Illustrated, #707
Utah Atlas & Gazetteer, p. 27

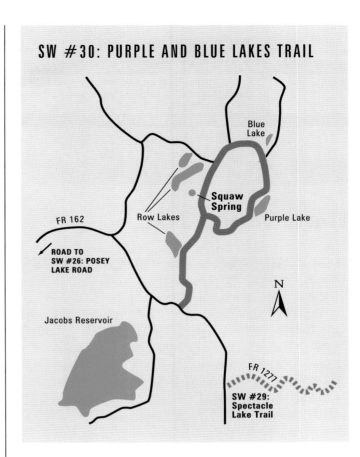

SW #30: PURPLE AND BLUE LAKES TRAIL

Route Directions

▼ 0.0		From FR 162, 5.8 miles east of Southwest #26: Posey Lake Road, turn northwest onto ungraded dirt trail, signed to Row Lakes. Zero trip meter.

GPS: N 38°03.50′ W 111°35.14′

▼ 0.6	SO	Track on left to Row Lakes and campsite.

GPS: N 38°03.94′ W 111°35.05′

▼ 0.7	SO	Track on left to lake and campsite.
▼ 0.8	SO	Cattle guard and sign for Great Western Trail. Trail leads across boulder-strewn meadow.
▼ 0.9	SO	Muddy section of track.
▼ 1.2	TR	Enter tall pines and spruce. Start of loop section. Track ahead is end of loop section. Turn right and zero trip meter.

GPS: N 38°04.35′ W 111°34.85′

▼ 0.0		Continue along lumpy track.
▼ 0.7	BL	Track on right. Purple Lake is directly in front. Continue along western shore.

GPS: N 38°04.40′ W 111°34.32′

▼ 0.8	SO	Muddy section along lakeshore.
▼ 1.0	SO	Trail leaves Purple Lake.
▼ 1.5	BL	Blue Lake directly ahead. Track on right to good campsites. Continue around southern shore.

GPS: N 38°04.93′ W 111°34.13′

▼ 1.6	SO	Campsite on right. Trail leaves Blue Lake.
▼ 2.2	TL	Zero trip meter. Great Western Trail goes to the right.

GPS: N 38°04.93′ W 111°34.69′

▼ 0.0		Continue along loop.
▼ 0.1	BL	Track on right to Row Lakes (second lake).
▼ 0.2	SO	Cross through old fence line.

| ▼ 0.5 | SO | Muddy section with large boulders; careful wheel placement needed. |
| ▼ 0.6 | SO | Faint track on right. |

GPS: N 38°04.46' W 111°34.92'

| ▼ 0.7 | | Abandoned vehicle on left, then track on left is start of loop to Purple and Blue Lakes. Retrace your steps to join FR 162. |

GPS: N 38°04.35' W 111°34.85'

SOUTHWEST REGION TRAIL #31

Dark Valley Trail

Starting Point:	**Southwest #26: Posey Lake Road (FR 154)**
Finishing Point:	**Southwest #27: Boulder Tops Road (FR 178)**
Total Mileage:	**12.2 miles**
Unpaved Mileage:	**12.2 miles**
Driving Time:	**1.5 hours**
Elevation Range:	**9,000–9,700 feet**
Usually Open:	**May to November**
Difficulty Rating:	**4**
Scenic Rating:	**8**
Remoteness Rating:	**+0**

Special Attractions

- Interesting and varied scenery on the Aquarius Plateau.
- Aspen viewing in the fall.
- ATV trail access and backcountry camping.

Description

This gentle, 12-mile route on the Aquarius Plateau contains a wide variety of scenery. The trail meanders along the wide valley of Rock Draw, passing through stands of aspen, spruce, and pine, and over rolling open meadows covered with sagebrush and grasslands. The road becomes tighter when it enters Dark Valley and passes between the rock cliffs of Rock Spring Ridge to the west and Dark Valley Shelf to the east. The Great Western Trail intersects the route.

After 8 miles, you reach the pretty Lava Spring, a natural spring near Birch Creek. There is private property at this

Wash crossing at Rock Spring Draw

A well-preserved log cabin stands at the foot of a tall pine in the Potholes

point, but the trail passes around the boundaries. After Birch Creek, the trail traverses the area known as the Potholes, which are deep depressions in the lava cap of the Aquarius Plateau. The open bowl north of the Potholes before the intersection with FR 178 has some excellent backcountry campsites, which are accessible even with a trailer from FR 178. Many people use this area as a base for hiking or further exploration via ATV or 4WD.

The ungraded trail surface is generally moderate going, although a couple of spots require greater concentration. The crossing over Birch Creek can be tricky as the area is muddy more often than not, and deep ruts have formed in the crossing. After rain, the section along Rock Draw can be difficult. In the trees there are a couple of rocky sections that need care with wheel placement, but this is a good trail for less experienced drivers in high-clearance SUVs who want to move to harder trails. The trail is used by snowmobiles in winter.

Aspens climb away from the water's edge in the Potholes

Current Road Information

Dixie National Forest
Teasdale Ranger District
PO Box 99
Teasdale, UT 84773
(435) 425-3702

Map References

BLM Loa
USFS Dixie National Forest: Teasdale Ranger District
USGS 1:24,000 Big Lake, Jacobs Reservoir, Government Point
1:100,000 Loa
Maptech CD-ROM: Escalante/Dixie National Forest
Trails Illustrated, #707 (incomplete)
Utah Atlas & Gazetteer, p. 27
Utah Travel Council #4

Route Directions

▼ 0.0			From Southwest #26: Posey Lake Road (FR 154), 21.8 miles from Bicknell, turn northeast on FR 285 at the sign for Rock Spring. Zero trip meter.
	9.0 ▲		Trail finishes at Southwest #26: Posey Lake Road (FR 154). Turn left for Escalante, right for Bicknell.

GPS: N 38°03.94' W 111°41.45'

▼ 1.3		SO	Cross through wash.
	7.7 ▲	SO	Cross through wash.

GPS: N 38°04.60' W 111°40.17'

▼ 1.5		SO	Rock Spring Pond on right.
	7.5 ▲	SO	Rock Spring Pond on left.

GPS: N 38°04.60' W 111°40.01'

▼ 1.6		SO	Cross through Rock Spring Draw. Trail enters trees, winding among stands of trees and open meadows.
	7.4 ▲	SO	Cross through Rock Spring Draw. Trail leaves trees and continues across the open valley.
▼ 4.3		SO	Exit trees and descend into Dark Valley.
	4.7 ▲	SO	Leave Dark Valley and enter trees, winding among stands of trees and open meadows.
▼ 5.4		SO	Small dam on right.
	3.6 ▲	SO	Small dam on left.
▼ 5.6		SO	Exclosure wildlife area on right.
	3.4 ▲	SO	Exclosure wildlife area on left.
▼ 6.2		SO	Track on right is ATV trail to Blue Lake. Great Western Trail now follows along the route.
	2.8 ▲	SO	Track on left is ATV trail to Blue Lake. Great Western Trail leaves the route and goes left.

GPS: N 38°06.25' W 111°35.96'

▼ 6.4		SO	Faint track on right.
	2.6 ▲	BR	Faint track on left.
▼ 7.1		BR	Faint track on left. Rock Spring Ridge is to the left, Dark Valley Shelf to the right.
	1.9 ▲	BL	Faint track on right. Rock Spring Ridge is to the right, Dark Valley Shelf to the left.
▼ 7.3		SO	Faint track on left.
	1.7 ▲	BL	Faint track on right.
▼ 7.6		SO	Faint track on right.
	1.4 ▲	SO	Faint track on left.

▼ 8.4		SO	Track on right, then cross through fence line.
	0.6 ▲	SO	Cross through fence line, then track on left.

GPS: N 38°07.69' W 111°35.52'

▼ 8.6		SO	Lava Spring on right.
	0.4 ▲	SO	Lava Spring on left.
▼ 8.7		SO	Cross over Birch Creek.
	0.3 ▲	SO	Cross over Birch Creek.

GPS: N 38°07.88' W 111°35.33'

▼ 9.0		SO	Pass through gate. Entrance to private property on left. Zero trip meter.
	0.0 ▲		Continue toward Dark Valley.

GPS: N 38°08.12' W 111°35.24'

▼ 0.0			Continue toward the Potholes.
	3.2 ▲	SO	Entrance to private property on right. Pass through gate and zero trip meter.
▼ 0.4		SO	Cross through creek. Entering the Potholes area.
	2.8 ▲	SO	Cross through creek. Leaving the Potholes area.
▼ 0.7		SO	Fork; tracks rejoin almost immediately.
	2.5 ▲	SO	Fork; tracks rejoin almost immediately.
▼ 1.0		SO	Small dam on right.
	2.2 ▲	SO	Small dam on left.
▼ 1.2		BR	Small lake on right, then track on left.
	2.0 ▲	SO	Track on right, then small lake on left.

GPS: N 38°08.86' W 111°34.94'

▼ 1.3		SO	Old log cabin in clearing in aspens.
	1.9 ▲	SO	Old log cabin in clearing in aspens.

GPS: N 38°08.93' W 111°34.85'

▼ 1.5		SO	Track on right.
	1.7 ▲	SO	Track on left.
▼ 2.7		SO	Track on left.
	0.5 ▲	SO	Track on right.

GPS: N 38°10.02' W 111°34.74'

▼ 3.0		SO	Track on left.
	0.2 ▲	SO	Track on right.
▼ 3.1		SO	Track on left.
	0.1 ▲	SO	Track on right.
▼ 3.2			Trail ends at Southwest #27: Boulder Tops Road (FR 178). Turn right to continue to

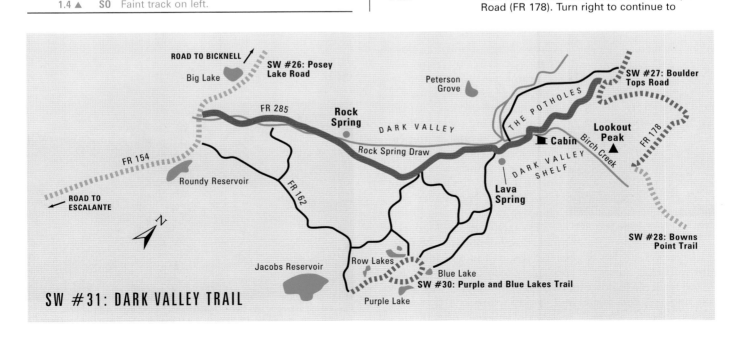

SW #31: DARK VALLEY TRAIL

Boulder Tops, turn left for Southwest #26: Posey Lake Road and Bicknell.

0.0 ▲   On Southwest #27: Boulder Tops Road (FR 178), turn south on FR 285 toward Dark Valley and zero trip meter. Trail enters the Potholes.

GPS: N 38°10.39′ W 111°34.86′

SOUTHWEST REGION TRAIL #32

Chokecherry Point Trail

Starting Point:	**Southwest #28: Bowns Point Trail (FR 178)**
Finishing Point:	**Utah 12**
Total Mileage:	**9.3 miles**
Unpaved Mileage:	**9.3 miles**
Driving Time:	**2.5 hours**
Elevation Range:	**8,700–11,000 feet**
Usually Open:	**June 16 to October 31**
Difficulty Rating:	**7**
Scenic Rating:	**8**
Remoteness Rating:	**+0**

Special Attractions

■ Extremely challenging 4WD trail.
■ One of the few through routes on the Boulder Tops.
■ Spectacular views as you descend down from Chokecherry Point.

Description

This difficult and technical 4WD trail should only be attempted by experienced drivers. It is passable with care by stock SUVs that have excellent clearance and good off-road tires. Additional lift is a definite advantage. The trail contains a long section of large boulders that twists tightly within the trees. However, the trail as far as Chokecherry Point is easier than the descent from that point to Utah 12. This steep descent has an extremely loose surface, making traction difficult. There are many rocky sections and some off-camber suspension-twisting ruts. It is easier to travel the trail from west to east, so that you descend from Chokecherry Point rather than climb up to it.

A steep section of loose rock near the top of the climb

The trail leaves Southwest #28: Bowns Point Trail 2.8 miles past Elbow Lake. For the first 2 miles, it is an ungraded, easy dirt road that crosses the appealingly named Stink Flats, followed by Beef Meadows and Willow Draw. After Willow Draw the track becomes fainter and hard to follow as it crosses the meadow. Follow the most well-used wheel ruts. After 3 miles, the trail enters the trees and gets progressively harder. This section is slow-going as it crawls over large boulders and rocks in the trees.

Just over 6 miles from the start, you reach Chokecherry Point. The actual point is north of the trail. The trail crosses through the logworm fence line and descends from Boulder Mountain. The first half mile is the steepest and loosest, and it is this section that will cause the most difficulties for vehicles traveling in the reverse direction. The trail continues to descend,

Looking back through the aspens at the lower end of Chokecherry Point Trail

crossing several hiking trails. The views are superb—on a clear day, you can see Mount Ellen and Mount Pennell in the Henry Mountains and even the La Sal Mountains. Closer by, you can see Lower Bowns Reservoir, the convolutions of the Waterpocket Fold in Capitol Reef National Park, and the stark, desolate Caineville Mesas. The lower you get, the easier the trail becomes. There are a couple of campsites tucked into the aspens on this section.

The trail receives no forest service maintenance. It is maintained as a 4WD trail by the Offroad Adventurers 4x4 Club from Richfield.

Motorized travel on the Boulder Tops is prohibited between November 1 and June 15, so the trail can only be traveled as a through route from June 16 to October 31.

Current Road Information

Dixie National Forest
Teasdale Ranger District
PO Box 99
Teasdale, UT 84773
(435) 425-3702

Panoramic views of the Henry Mountains, Lower Bowns Reservoir, and Capitol Reef unfold to the east as the trail descends from Chokecherry Point

Map References

BLM   Loa
USFS Dixie National Forest: Teasdale Ranger District
USGS 1:24,000 Deer Creek Lake, Blind Lake, Grover
          1:100,000 Loa

Maptech CD-ROM: Escalante/Dixie National Forest
Trails Illustrated, #707 (incomplete)
Utah Atlas & Gazetteer, p. 28
Utah Travel Council #4 (incomplete)

Route Directions

▼ 0.0   On Southwest #28: Bowns Point Trail (FR
                 178), 2.8 miles past Elbow Lake, turn east on
                 FR 177, following sign to Chokecherry Point.
                 Trail crosses Stink Flats.
   6.2 ▲   Trail finishes at Southwest #28: Bowns Point
                 Trail (FR 178). Turn left to continue to Bowns
                 Point, right to exit the Boulder Tops.

GPS: N 38°07.41' W 111°26.85'

▼ 1.2   SO   Trail leaves trees and crosses the edge of Beef
                 Meadows.
   5.0 ▲   SO   Beef Meadows on right.

▼ 1.6   SO   Great Western Trail enters on left.
   4.6 ▲   SO   Great Western Trail leaves on right.

GPS: N 38°07.80' W 111°25.49'

▼ 2.1   SO   Track on right to Meeks Draw.
   4.1 ▲   SO   Track on left to Meeks Draw.

GPS: N 38°07.77' W 111°25.05'

▼ 2.3   SO   Two small dams on left.
   3.9 ▲   SO   Two small dams on right.

▼ 2.5   BR   Fork at Willow Draw. Trail becomes fainter;
                 follow most well used wheel ruts.
   3.7 ▲   SO   Willow Draw. Trail is more defined.

GPS: N 38°08.01' W 111°24.63'

▼ 2.8   BR   Trail bears southeast.
   3.4 ▲   SO   Trail bears northwest.

GPS: N 38°08.09' W 111°24.33'

▼ 3.1   SO   Reenter trees; FR 177 sign on tree on right,
                 then track on right.
   3.1 ▲   SO   Track on left, then leave trees and cross
                 meadow.

GPS: N 38°07.96' W 111°24.09'

▼ 4.1   BL   Trail swings left.
   2.1 ▲   BR   Trail swings right.

GPS: N 38°08.21' W 111°23.14'

▼ 4.4   SO   Leave trees and bear slightly right to south-
                 east. Trail is faint across meadow.
   1.8 ▲   SO   Leave the meadow and enter the trees.

GPS: N 38°08.15' W 111°22.88'

▼ 4.6   SO   Small dam on left.
   1.6 ▲   SO   Small dam on right.

▼ 4.7   BL   Across meadow.
   1.5 ▲   BR   Across meadow.

GPS: N 38°08.26' W 111°22.30'

▼ 5.1   SO   Faint track on left.
   1.1 ▲   SO   Faint track on right.

▼ 6.2   SO   Chokecherry Point on left. Great Western Loop
                 Trail on right. Trail crosses fence line and
                 descends from Boulder Mountain. Zero trip
                 meter.
   0.0 ▲   Continue through the trees on lumpy trail.

GPS: N 38°08.15' W 111°21.12'

▼ 0.0   Descend from Boulder Mountain. Trail is steep
                 and loose.

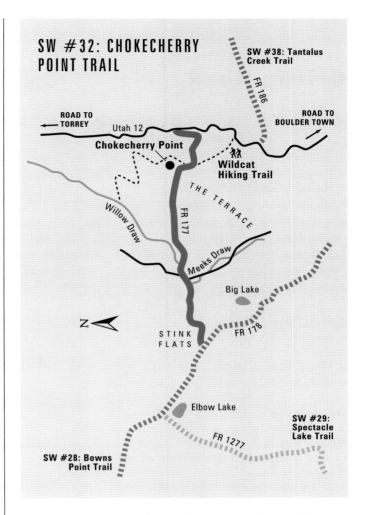

SW #32: CHOKECHERRY POINT TRAIL

   3.1 ▲   SO   End of climb. Chokecherry Point on right.
                 Great Western Loop Trail on left. Trail crosses
                 fence line. Zero trip meter.

▼ 0.4   SO   End of steepest part of descent.
   2.7 ▲   SO   Trail gets a lot steeper and is loose.

GPS: N 38°08.06' W 111°20.89'

▼ 0.6   SO   Wildcat Hiking Trail (#140) joins main trail
                 from the left.
   2.5 ▲   SO   Wildcat Hiking Trail (#140) leaves main trail to
                 the right.

GPS: N 38°07.80' W 111°20.85'

▼ 1.0   SO   Small saddle. Wildcat Hiking Trail (#140)
                 leaves main trail to the right.
   2.1 ▲   SO   Small saddle. Wildcat Hiking Trail (#140) joins
                 main trail from left.

GPS: N 38°07.70' W 111°20.81'

▼ 1.4   SO   Cross through fence line.
   1.7 ▲   SO   Cross through fence line.

▼ 1.7   SO   Cattletank on right in aspens.
   1.4 ▲   SO   Cattletank on left in aspens.

▼ 3.1   Trail finishes at Utah 12, 5.7 miles south of the
                 Dixie National Forest boundary. Turn left for
                 Torrey, turn right for Boulder Town.
   0.0 ▲   On Utah 12, 5.7 miles south of the Dixie
                 National Forest boundary, turn west at sign for
                 Chokecherry 4x4 Road and zero trip
                 meter.

GPS: N 38°08.09' W 111°19.66'

Griffin Road

Starting Point:	**Escalante Summit on Southwest #34:**
	Escalante Summit Trail
Finishing Point:	**Southwest #26: Posey Lake Road (FR 154)**
Total Mileage:	**21.1 miles**
Unpaved Mileage:	**21.1 miles**
Driving Time:	**1.5 hours**
Elevation Range:	**9,200–10,600 feet**
Usually Open:	**May to October**
Difficulty Rating:	**1**
Scenic Rating:	**8**
Remoteness Rating:	**+0**

Special Attractions

- Access to a network of 4WD tracks and backcountry campsites.
- Aspen viewing and fall colors.
- Wide-ranging scenic views and wildlife viewing.

Description

This beautiful drive crosses the high-altitude plateau of Griffin Top, with its long stretches of alpine meadows and wildlife viewing opportunities. The entire road surface is graded gravel and is suitable for a passenger car, but at the southern end some automobiles may find the grade steep.

The trail commences at Escalante Summit along Southwest #34: Escalante Summit Trail (FR 17), 13.8 miles from Utah 12. Turn north on FR 140 (Griffin Road), which immediately climbs steeply up a series of switchbacks around Horse Creek Top. As the road climbs, you get excellent views back down Main Canyon east of Escalante Summit.

The first couple miles are the steepest on the trail, which continues to climb until it reaches the plateau of Griffin Top, part of the Escalante Mountain Range. Johns Valley to the west is spread out below as the trail winds through stands of mature aspens. Horse Lake is 0.2 miles west of the trail near

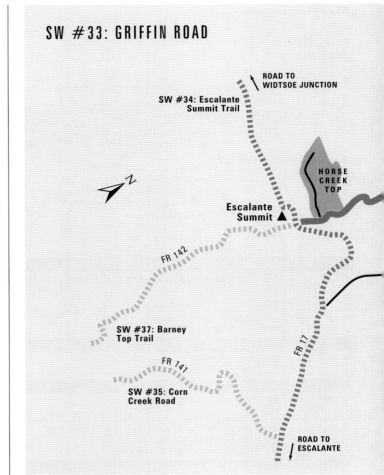

SW #33: GRIFFIN ROAD

the top of the climb. You can park and walk down to the small lake.

After 4.7 miles you reach Griffin Top, a large alpine meadow running predominantly north to south. As it crosses the meadow, the trail occasionally passes through stands of pine and aspen. You can often see mule deer and elk grazing in these high plateaus in summer. Cattle also graze here in summer, so take care on blind corners. You may also see wild turkeys, which have been introduced into the forest. There are plenty of good secluded campsites tucked into the trees on both sides of the meadow. A variety of trails leads off from this road. There are plenty of small trails, mainly dead ends, that are suitable for SUVs, and a network of 4WD trails leads northwest into the Poison Creek area of the Dixie National Forest. Many trails are suitable for ATV use or snowmobiles in the winter.

The trail continues to undulate across open meadows, finishing at Southwest #26: Posey Lake Road (FR 154).

Current Road Information

Dixie National Forest
Escalante Ranger District
755 West Main
Escalante, UT 84726
(435) 826-5403

A bend in Griffin Road reveals expansive views into Escalante Canyon

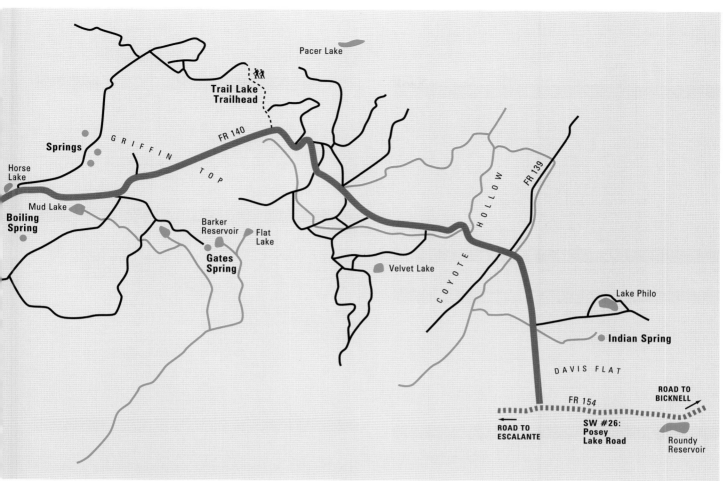

Escalante Interagency Office
755 West Main
Escalante, UT 84726
(435) 826-5499

Map References
BLM   Escalante, Loa
USFS Dixie National Forest: Escalante Ranger District
USGS 1:24,000 Sweetwater Creek, Griffin Point, Barker
      Reservoir
      1:100,000 Escalante, Loa
Maptech CD-ROM: Escalante/Dixie National Forest
Utah Atlas & Gazetteer, p. 27
Utah Travel Council #4
Other: BLM Map of the Grand Staircase–Escalante National
      Monument

Route Directions

▼ 0.0   At Escalante Summit on Southwest #34: Escalante Summit Trail (FR 17), turn north on Griffin Road (FR 140), following sign for Griffin Top. Zero trip meter.

4.7 ▲   Trail finishes at Escalante Summit on Southwest #34: Escalante Summit Trail (FR 17). Turn left for Escalante, right for Widtsoe Junction. Straight ahead is Southwest #37: Barney Top Trail (FR 142).

		GPS: N 37°49.53' W 111°52.89'	
▼ 0.8		**SO**	Track on left, then wide shelf road with excellent views down Main Canyon.
	3.9 ▲	**SO**	Track on right. End of shelf road.
▼ 1.1		**SO**	Track on left. End of shelf road.
	3.6 ▲	**SO**	Track on right, then wide shelf road with excellent views down Main Canyon.
▼ 1.6		**SO**	Great Western Trail on left to Sweetwater Road.
	3.1 ▲	**SO**	Great Western Trail on right to Sweetwater Road.
		GPS: N 37°50.64' W 111°52.69'	
▼ 1.7		**SO**	Track on right.
	3.0 ▲	**SO**	Track on left.
▼ 2.1		**SO**	Pull-in on left gives views west over Johns Valley.
	2.6 ▲	**SO**	Pull-in on right gives views west over Johns Valley.
▼ 2.5		**SO**	Small track on left.
	2.2 ▲	**SO**	Small track on right.
▼ 3.5		**SO**	Hiking trail on left leads to Horse Lake (0.2 miles).
	1.2 ▲	**SO**	Hiking trail on right leads to Horse Lake (0.2 miles).
		GPS: N 37°51.65' W 111°52.77'	
▼ 4.5		**SO**	Cattle guard.
	0.2 ▲	**SO**	Cattle guard.
▼ 4.6		**SO**	Small track on left.

0.1 ▲	SO	Small track on right; trail descends to Escalante Summit.
▼ 4.7	BL	Entering Griffin Top—large, open meadow. Two tracks on right, campsite on left. Zero trip meter.
0.0 ▲		Leave Griffin Top and enter trees.

GPS: N 37°52.52' W 111°52.30'

▼ 0.0		Continue along open meadow.
5.3 ▲	BR	Two tracks on left, campsite on right. Leave open meadow and zero trip meter.
▼ 0.9	SO	Track on right.
4.4 ▲	SO	Track on left.
▼ 1.0	SO	Track on right, then track on left.
4.3 ▲	SO	Track on right, then track on left.
▼ 1.3	SO	North Creek Lakes Trail on right.
4.0 ▲	SO	North Creek Lakes Trail on left.
▼ 2.1	SO	Track on left to Griffin Spring.
3.2 ▲	SO	Track on right to Griffin Spring.

GPS: N 37°54.35' W 111°52.08'

▼ 2.6	SO	Track on left goes past shallow lake.
2.7 ▲	SO	Track on right goes past shallow lake.

GPS: N 37°54.84 W 111°51.87'

▼ 3.2	SO	Track on left.
2.1 ▲	SO	Track on right.
▼ 3.9	SO	Track on left.
1.4 ▲	SO	Track on right.
▼ 4.4	SO	Track on right.
0.9 ▲	SO	Track on left.
▼ 5.3	SO	Cattle guard, then track on left is Trail Lake trailhead. Zero trip meter.
0.0 ▲		Continue along main trail.

GPS: N 37°57.26' W 111°51.86'

▼ 0.0		Continue along main trail.
7.3 ▲	SO	Track on right is Trail Lake trailhead. Zero trip meter at cattle guard.
▼ 1.2	SO	Track on left.
6.1 ▲	SO	Track on right.
▼ 2.0	SO	Track on right to the Sinkholes. Crossing the Salt Lake Meridian (longitude line).
5.3 ▲	SO	Track on left to the Sinkholes. Crossing the Salt Lake Meridian (longitude line).

GPS: N 37°57.73' W 111°50.53'

▼ 2.2	SO	Track on left.
5.1 ▲	SO	Track on right.
▼ 2.6	SO	Track on left gives access to Poison Creek. Also goes to snowmobile rest station.
4.7 ▲	SO	Track on right gives access to Poison Creek. Also goes to snowmobile rest station.

GPS: N 37°58.03' W 111°49.97'

▼ 3.0	SO	The Gap trailhead on right, Great Western Trail access point.
4.3 ▲	SO	The Gap trailhead on left, Great Western Trail access point.

GPS: N 37°58.18' W 111°49.59'

▼ 3.2	SO	Track on left.
4.1 ▲	SO	Track on right.
▼ 3.7	SO	Track on right to Velvet Lake.
3.6 ▲	SO	Track on left to Velvet Lake.

GPS: N 37°58.41' W 111°48.91'

▼ 3.9	SO	Intersection.
3.4 ▲	SO	Intersection.
▼ 4.5	SO	Track on left.
2.8 ▲	SO	Track on right.
▼ 6.1	SO	Cattle guard.

1.2 ▲	SO	Cattle guard.
▼ 7.1	SO	FR 465 on left to Coyote Hollow.
0.2 ▲	SO	FR 465 on right to Coyote Hollow.
▼ 7.3	SO	FR 139 on left to Pollywog Lake. Zero trip meter.
0.0 ▲		Continue along main trail.

GPS: N 38°00.82' W 111°46.52'

▼ 0.0		Continue on main trail.
3.8 ▲	SO	FR 139 on right to Pollywog Lake. Zero trip meter.
▼ 1.3	SO	Track on right.
2.5 ▲	SO	Track on left.
▼ 1.9	SO	Track on left to Lake Philo. Small dam on right is Indian Spring Reservoir.
1.9 ▲	SO	Track on right to Lake Philo. Small dam on left is Indian Spring Reservoir.

GPS: N 38°00.71' W 111°44.44'

▼ 2.8	SO	Track on right.
1.0 ▲	SO	Track on left.
▼ 3.0	SO	Cattle guard; trail crosses Davis Flat.
0.8 ▲	SO	Cattle guard; trail crosses Davis Flat.
▼ 3.3	SO	Track on left.
0.5 ▲	SO	Track on right.
▼ 3.5	SO	Corral on left.
0.3 ▲	SO	Corral on right.
▼ 3.8		Trail ends at Southwest #26: Posey Lake Road (FR 154). Turn right for Escalante, left for Bicknell.
0.0 ▲		On Southwest #26: Posey Lake Road (FR 154), 26.5 miles south of Bicknell, zero trip meter and turn northwest on FR 140, following sign for Escalante Summit.

GPS: N 38°00.20' W 111°42.42'

SOUTHWEST REGION TRAIL #34

Escalante Summit Trail

Starting Point:	**Utah 12, 4 miles west of Escalante**
Finishing Point:	**Widtsoe Junction on Utah 22**
Total Mileage:	**21.1 miles**
Unpaved Mileage:	**21.1 miles**
Driving Time:	**1.5 hours**
Elevation Range:	**6,100–9,500 feet**
Usually Open:	**May to October**
Difficulty Rating:	**1**
Scenic Rating:	**8**
Remoteness Rating:	**+0**

Special Attractions

- Access to a network of trails in the Dixie National Forest.
- Interesting drive down two different canyons.
- Backcountry camping opportunities.

Description

This trail runs through the Dixie National Forest and provides a more northern, backcountry alternative to the highway be-

Two small waterfalls punctuate the the course of the Escalante River

tween Escalante and Bryce Canyon National Park. It leaves Utah 12, 4 miles west of Escalante, at the sign for Main Canyon Road. The entire trail is a graded gravel road that is suitable for passenger vehicles. For the first few miles, the trail runs through Main Canyon following along Birch Creek. It gradually climbs until it reaches Escalante Summit, the high point of the trail at 9,302 feet. From here, Southwest #33: Griffin Road leads north and Southwest #37: Barney Top Trail leads south.

The trail continues down into Escalante Canyon. The first mile is a fairly steep descent along switchbacks; then the trail eases off to follow Sweetwater Creek through the canyon. A variety of backcountry campsites are scattered along here, and they offer better camping opportunities than the east end of the trail.

After the summit, you reach Widtsoe Junction and Utah 22 in 7.3 miles. There is little left of Widtsoe these days—just a few cabins and some more recent but still abandoned housing.

Current Road Information
Dixie National Forest
Escalante Ranger District
755 West Main
Escalante, UT 84726
(435) 826-5403

Escalante Interagency Office
755 West Main
Escalante, UT 84726
(435) 826-5499

Map References
BLM Escalante, Panguitch
USFS Dixie National Forest: Escalante Ranger District
USGS 1:24,000 Flake Mt. East, Sweetwater Creek, Griffin Point, Wide Hollow Reservoir
1:100,000 Panguitch, Escalante
Maptech CD-ROM: Escalante/Dixie National Forest
Utah Atlas & Gazetteer, pp. 19, 27
Utah Travel Council #4
Other: BLM Map of the Grand Staircase–Escalante National Monument

Route Directions

▼ 0.0		From Utah 12, 4 miles west of Escalante, turn west onto the graded gravel road at sign for Main Canyon Road and zero trip meter.
5.0 ▲		Trail ends at Utah 12. Turn left for Escalante, right for Bryce Canyon National Park.

GPS: N 37°45.91 W 111°40.93'

▼ 0.1	SO	Gravel road on right to Barker Reservoir.
4.9 ▲	SO	Gravel road on left to Barker Reservoir.
▼ 5.0	SO	Cattle guard, then enter Dixie National Forest and zero trip meter. The trail is now FR 17.
0.0 ▲		Continue along FR 17.

GPS: N 37°46.86' W 111°46.03'

▼ 0.0		Continue along FR 17.
1.6 ▲	SO	Leave Dixie National Forest, zero trip meter, and cross cattle guard.
▼ 1.2	SO	Faint track on left.

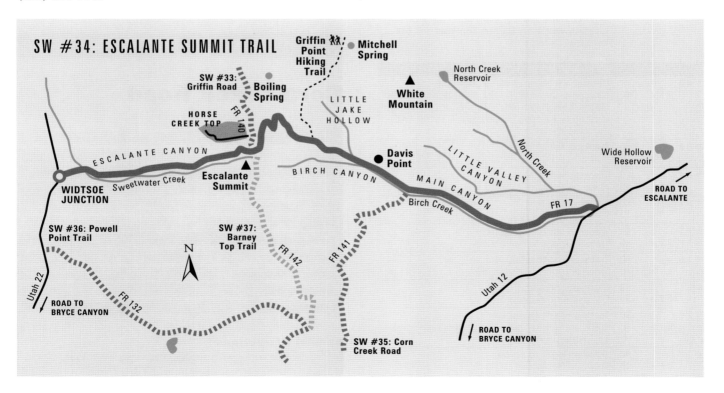

0.4 ▲		SO	Faint track on right.
▼ 1.6		SO	Gravel road on left is Southwest #35: Corn Creek Road (FR 141). Zero trip meter.
	0.0 ▲		Continue along FR 17.

GPS: N 37°47.56' W 111°47.65'

▼ 0.0			Continue along FR 17.
	7.2 ▲	SO	Gravel road on right is Southwest #35: Corn Creek Road (FR 141). Zero trip meter.
▼ 0.8		SO	Mill site on right.
	6.4 ▲	SO	Mill site on left.
▼ 0.9		SO	Small track on right.
	6.3 ▲	SO	Small track on left.
▼ 1.2		SO	Two old cabins on right of trail and one on left of trail.
	6.0 ▲	SO	Two old cabins on left of trail and one on right of trail.

GPS: N 37°48.27' W 111°48.66'

▼ 1.8		BL	Track on right.
	5.4 ▲	SO	Track on left.
▼ 2.5		SO	Track on right.
	4.7 ▲	SO	Track on left.
▼ 2.7		SO	Track on right.
	4.5 ▲	SO	Track on left.
▼ 3.4		SO	Griffin Point Hiking Trail on right to Barker Reservoir; also track on left.
	3.8 ▲	SO	Griffin Point Hiking Trail on left to Barker Reservoir; also track on right.

GPS: N 37°49.47' W 111°50.65'

▼ 4.2		SO	Track on left.
	3.0 ▲	SO	Track on right.
▼ 4.4		SO	Track on left.
	2.8 ▲	SO	Track on right.
▼ 5.3		SO	Track on right.
	1.9 ▲	SO	Track on left.
▼ 7.1		SO	Cattle guard.
	0.1 ▲	SO	Cattle guard.
▼ 7.2		SO	Escalante Summit. Track on right is Southwest #33: Griffin Road (FR 140), main track on left is Southwest #37: Barney Top Trail (FR 142). Zero trip meter.
	0.0 ▲		Continue toward Escalante.

GPS: N 37°49.51' W 111°52.90'

▼ 0.0			Continue toward Widtsoe Junction.
	7.3 ▲	SO	Escalante Summit. Track on left is Southwest #33: Griffin Road (FR 140), main track on right is Southwest #37: Barney Top Trail (FR 142). Zero trip meter.
▼ 0.3		SO	Track on left.
	7.0 ▲	SO	Track on right.
▼ 0.4		SO	Track on left.
	6.9 ▲	SO	Track on right.
▼ 0.7		SO	Track on right.
	6.6 ▲	SO	Track on left.
▼ 1.1		SO	Track on left to campsite.
	6.2 ▲	SO	Track on right to campsite.
▼ 1.6		SO	Track on left to campsite.
	5.7 ▲	SO	Track on right to campsite.
▼ 2.1		SO	Campsite on left.
	5.2 ▲	SO	Campsite on right.
▼ 2.2		SO	Track on left to campsite.
	5.1 ▲	SO	Track on right to campsite. Trail climbs toward Escalante Summit.
▼ 2.7		SO	Track on right to corral.
	4.6 ▲	SO	Track on left to corral.

▼ 3.0		SO	Track on left.
	4.3 ▲	SO	Track on right.
▼ 3.6		SO	Track on right.
	3.7 ▲	SO	Track on left.
▼ 3.8		SO	Track on right.
	3.5 ▲	SO	Track on left.
▼ 4.2		SO	Great Western Trail crosses. Road on right is a vehicle track that goes to Southwest #33: Griffin Road; then track on left.
	3.1 ▲	SO	Track on right. Road on left is a vehicle track that goes to Southwest #33: Griffin Road. Great Western Trail crosses.

GPS: N 37°49.61' W 111°56.74'

▼ 4.7		SO	Track on right.
	2.6 ▲	SO	Track on left.
▼ 4.9		SO	Track on right.
	2.4 ▲	SO	Track on left.
▼ 5.3		SO	Track on left.
	2.0 ▲	SO	Track on right.
▼ 5.7		SO	Leaving Dixie National Forest over cattle guard.
	1.6 ▲	SO	Entering Dixie National Forest over cattle guard. Road is now FR 17.
▼ 6.6		SO	Track on right.
	0.7 ▲	SO	Track on right.
▼ 6.8		SO	Track on left, then old cabins on left.
	0.5 ▲	SO	Old cabins on right, then track on right.
▼ 6.9		SO	Track on left to the remains of Widtsoe.
	0.4 ▲	SO	Track on right to the remains of Widtsoe.
▼ 7.1		SO	Track on left.
	0.2 ▲	SO	Track on right.
▼ 7.3			Trail finishes at Widtsoe Junction on Utah 22. Turn left for Bryce Canyon National Park.
	0.0 ▲		At Widtsoe Junction on Utah 22, turn east up FR 17 signed toward Escalante and zero trip meter.

GPS: N 37°50.03' W 112°00.11'

Corn Creek Road

Starting Point:	**Southwest #34: Escalante Summit Trail, 6.6 miles west of Utah 12**
Finishing Point:	**Utah 12, 12.3 miles west of Escalante**
Total Mileage:	**14.4 miles**
Unpaved Mileage:	**14.4 miles**
Driving Time:	**1.5 hours**
Elevation Range:	**7,100–8,700 feet**
Usually Open:	**May to November**
Difficulty Rating:	**1**
Scenic Rating:	**8**
Remoteness Rating:	**+0**

Special Attractions

- Easy, scenic route with spectacular views over Table Cliffs.
- Backcountry alternative route to Utah 12.

Description

This graded route leaves Southwest #34: Escalante Summit Trail (or FR 17, Main Canyon Road) 6.6 miles west of Utah 12. It winds south and rejoins Utah 12 about 12 miles west of Escalante. The trail runs along Corn Creek for 2 miles before climbing up along the eastern flank of the Escalante Mountains. There are striking views to the west of the red-and-white striated Table Cliffs, part of the promontory leading down to Powell Point.

Table Cliff Plateau towers above this stretch of Corn Creek Road

The trail then descends from the pine forest to enter the juniper and sagebrush sloping benches. A multitude of small tracks lead off from this section, and the graded road surface becomes rougher and slightly washed out. In wet weather, there can be muddy sections, but in dry weather the trail is suitable for passenger vehicles.

Current Road Information

Dixie National Forest
Escalante Ranger District
755 West Main
Escalante, UT 84726
(435) 826-5403

Map References

BLM   Escalante
USFS   Dixie National Forest: Escalante Ranger District
USGS   1:24,000   Griffin Point, Upper Valley
             1:100,000 Escalante
Maptech CD-ROM: Escalante/Dixie National Forest
Utah Atlas & Gazetteer, p. 19
Utah Travel Council #4 (incomplete)

Route Directions

▼ 0.0		From Southwest #34: Escalante Summit Trail (FR 17, Main Canyon Road), turn southwest onto graded gravel Corn Creek Road (FR 141) following the sign to Upper Valley Guard Station, and zero trip meter.
	7.5 ▲	Trail finishes at Southwest #34: Escalante Summit Trail (FR 17, Main Canyon Road). Turn right for Utah 12, left for Escalante Summit.

GPS: N 37°47.56' W 111°47.65'

▼ 0.1	SO	Old cabin on left.
7.4 ▲	SO	Old cabin on right.
▼ 2.2	BL	Fork, unsigned. Road is now graded dirt.
5.3 ▲	SO	Junction is unsigned. Road is now graded gravel.

GPS: N 37°47.02' W 111°49.95'

▼ 3.7	SO	Track on left.

3.8 ▲	SO	Track on right.
▼ 5.2	SO	Track on left.
2.3 ▲	SO	Track on right.
▼ 5.4	SO	Track on right.
2.1 ▲	SO	Track on left.
▼ 5.7	SO	Track on left. Continue around right-hand bend for striking view of Table Cliffs.
1.8 ▲	SO	Striking view back of Table Cliffs from left-hand bend, then track on right.

GPS: N 37°45.00' W 111°50.55'

▼ 5.9	SO	Cattle guard.
1.6 ▲	SO	Cattle guard.
▼ 7.5	TR	T-intersection. Turn right on FR 144 to Stump Spring; left is FR 147 to Utah 12. Zero trip meter.
0.0 ▲		Continue on Corn Creek Road (FR 141).

GPS: N 37°43.83' W 111°50.87'

▼ 0.0		Continue toward Stump Spring (FR 144).
3.0 ▲	TL	Ahead is FR 147 to Utah 12. Turn left onto FR 141, signed as Corn Creek Road.
▼ 0.9	SO	Track on left.
2.1 ▲	SO	Track on right.
▼ 1.0	SO	Track on left.

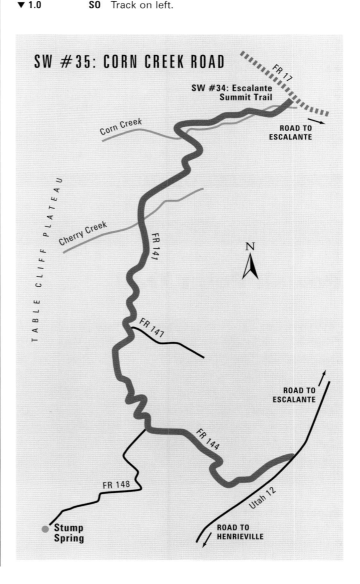

SW #35: CORN CREEK ROAD

2.0 ▲	SO	Track on right.	
▼ 1.2	SO	Track on left, then track on right.	
1.8 ▲	SO	Track on right, then track on left.	
▼ 1.4	SO	Track on right.	
1.6 ▲	SO	Track on left.	
▼ 2.1	SO	Track on left.	
0.9 ▲	SO	Track on right.	
▼ 3.0	TR	T-intersection, turn right. Zero trip meter.	
0.0 ▲		Continue northwest.	

GPS: N 37°42.40′ W 111°50.62′

▼ 0.0		Continue southeast.
3.9 ▲	TL	Turn left at intersection. Zero trip meter.
▼ 0.2	SO	Track on right is FR 148 to Stump Spring.
3.7 ▲	SO	Track on left is FR 148 to Stump Spring.

GPS: N 37°42.23′ W 111°50.55′

▼ 0.7	SO	Track on left.
3.2 ▲	SO	Track on right.
▼ 1.2	SO	Track on left.
2.7 ▲	SO	Track on right.
▼ 1.6	SO	Track on left.
2.3 ▲	SO	Track on right.
▼ 2.5	SO	Entering private property; remain on main track.
1.4 ▲	SO	Leaving private property into national forest.
▼ 3.2	SO	Old cabin on right is private property.
0.7 ▲	SO	Old cabin on left is private property.
▼ 3.8	BR	Track on left.
0.1 ▲	BL	Track on right.
▼ 3.9		Cross cattle guard, then trail ends at Utah 12. Turn left for Escalante, right for Henrieville.
0.0 ▲		From Utah 12, 12.3 miles west of Escalante, turn onto FR 144 signed toward Upper Valley Guard Station and Stump Spring. The first 1.4 miles cross private property; remain on main track.

GPS: N 37°41.72′ W 111°47.67′

SOUTHWEST REGION TRAIL #36

Powell Point Trail

Starting Point:	**Utah 22 (Johns Valley Road) and FR 132**
Finishing Point:	**Powell Point**
Total Mileage:	**14.4 miles**
Unpaved Mileage:	**14.4 miles**
Driving Time:	**1.5 hours**
Elevation Range:	**7,500–10,100 feet**
Usually Open:	**June to October**
Difficulty Rating:	**3**
Scenic Rating:	**9**
Remoteness Rating:	**+0**

Special Attractions

■ Powell Point lookout.
■ Pine Lake camping and fishing.
■ Access to ATV and hiking trails.

Pine Lake at sunset

History

Powell Point, named after American explorer John Wesley Powell, is a prominent bluff on the landscape. Its pink-tinged cliffs are visible for many miles. The point itself is the narrow end to the broad 10,000-foot summit of Table Cliffs.

The highly visible cliffs were used as a navigation reference point by Powell, who led the first exploratory trips down the Colorado River in 1869 and 1871. The expedition geologist, Clarence Dutton, described Powell Point as "the aspect of a vast acropolis crowned with a parthenon."

Description

This route commences in Johns Valley on FR 132, a graded gravel road that climbs gradually into Dixie National Forest. After 5 miles it passes by the popular camping and fishing spot of Pine Lake. The developed national forest campground here (fee required) has secluded sites set among tall pines; it's a short walk to the lake. After the campground, the trail standard becomes a rougher dirt road, which climbs up Pine Canyon and follows along Clay Creek. Many of the tributaries of Clay Creek can wash out quite severely, and the crossings through the wash can be very rough, since large boulders and quantities of rock often wash down. However, this part of the trail is normally suitable for a high-clearance vehicle. There are some sections of shelf road, but although rough, they are wide enough for a full-size vehicle and have ample passing places.

The Powell Point Trail winds through thick stands of aspen and pine

After 11 miles, you reach the turn for Powell Point; Southwest #37: Barney Top Trail also connects here from the north. The sign for Powell Point is very small and easily missed, and the start of the trail looks too narrow to be a proper vehicle trail. This first section is the narrowest, winding through dense pine and aspens. It is bumpy—not from rocks, but from tree roots growing across the track. This first section can also be mud-

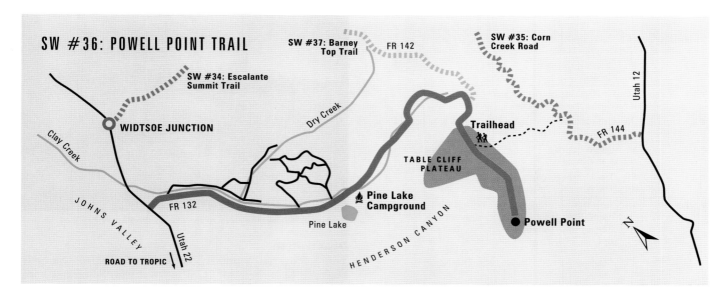

SW #36: POWELL POINT TRAIL

dy after rain, with several deep depressions, and you may want to avoid it then. The lack of traction from mud, combined with the tight clearance between the trees, might result in vehicle damage.

After a mile, the trail becomes less twisty, the trees sparser, and the trail surface rockier as it follows the eastern edge of Table Cliff Plateau, affording great views east. There are several campsites tucked into the trees along the edge of the escarpment. The trail ends at a turnaround. From here, you can hike just over half a mile to Powell Point proper at the end of the plateau.

Current Road Information

Dixie National Forest
Escalante Ranger District
755 West Main
Escalante, UT 84726
(435) 826-5403

Escalante Interagency Office
755 West Main
Escalante, UT 84726
(435) 826-5499

Map References

BLM Panguitch, Escalante
USFS Dixie National Forest: Escalante Ranger District
USGS: 1:24,000 Flake Mt. East, Sweetwater Creek, Pine Lake, Upper Valley
1:100,000 Panguitch, Escalante
Maptech CD-ROM: Escalante/Dixie National Forest
Utah Atlas & Gazetteer, pp. 27, 19
Utah Travel Council # 4 (incomplete)
Other: BLM Map of the Grand Staircase–Escalante National Monument (incomplete)

Route Directions

| ▼ 0.0 | | | On Utah 22 (Johns Valley Road), 2.5 miles south of Widtsoe Junction, turn east onto FR 132 (signed toward Pine Lake) and zero trip meter. |

	5.1 ▲		Trail finishes at Utah 22. Turn right for Widtsoe Junction, left for Tropic.
		GPS: N 37°47.84' W 112°01.20'	
▼ 0.4		SO	Enter Dixie National Forest over cattle guard.
	4.7 ▲	SO	Leaving Dixie National Forest over cattle guard.
		GPS: N 37°47.80' W 112°00.67'	
▼ 0.6		SO	Track on right.
	4.5 ▲	SO	Track on left.
▼ 1.0		SO	Track on left, then track on right.
	4.1 ▲	SO	Track on left, then track on right.
▼ 1.5		SO	Track on left, then faint track on right.
	3.6 ▲	SO	Faint track on left, then track on right.
▼ 2.3		SO	Track on left to campsite.
	2.8 ▲	SO	Track on right to campsite.
▼ 3.0		SO	Cattle guard.
	2.1 ▲	SO	Cattle guard.
▼ 4.6		SO	Cross over Clay Creek on culvert.
	0.5 ▲	SO	Cross over Clay Creek on culvert.
▼ 4.7		SO	Track on left.
	0.4 ▲	SO	Track on right.
▼ 5.0		SO	Track on right to Pine Lake (0.2 miles).
	0.1 ▲	SO	Track on left to Pine Lake (0.2 miles).
▼ 5.1		BL	Road on right to Pine Lake Campground. Zero trip meter.
	0.0 ▲		Continue along graded gravel road.
		GPS: N 37°44.78' W 111°57.13'	
▼ 0.0			Continue along rougher trail away from Pine Lake.
	5.8 ▲	TR	Road on left to Pine Lake Campground. Zero trip meter.
▼ 0.1		SO	Track on left is part of the Great Western Trail and goes to Sweetwater.
	5.7 ▲	SO	Track on right is part of the Great Western Trail and goes to Sweetwater.
▼ 0.4		SO	ATV staging area and trailhead on right.
	5.4 ▲	SO	ATV staging area and trailhead on left.
▼ 0.6		SO	Track on left, then track on right.
	5.2 ▲	SO	Track on left, then track on right.
		GPS: N 37°44.68' W 111°56.51'	
▼ 0.7		SO	Cross through rough stony wash.
	5.1 ▲	SO	Cross through rough stony wash.
▼ 0.8		SO	Track on right.

5.0 ▲	SO	Track on left.
▼ 1.0	SO	Track on right.
4.8 ▲	SO	Track on left.
▼ 1.3	SO	Cross through rough stony wash.
4.5 ▲	SO	Cross through rough stony wash.
▼ 1.6	SO	Cross through rough stony wash.
4.2 ▲	SO	Cross through rough stony wash.
▼ 1.8	SO	Cross through rough stony wash.
4.0 ▲	SO	Cross through rough stony wash.
▼ 2.2	SO	Cattle guard.
3.6 ▲	SO	Cattle guard.
▼ 3.1	SO	Track right to camping area.
2.7 ▲	SO	Track left to camping area.
▼ 5.8	TR	Turn right onto small trail signed for Powell Point. Straight ahead is Southwest #37: Barney Top Trail (FR 142). Zero trip meter.
0.0 ▲	TL	Return from Powell Point. Turn left for Pine Lake and Utah 22, turn right on FR 142 for Southwest #37: Barney Top Trail. Zero trip meter.

GPS: N 37°44.06' W 111°52.24'

▼ 0.0		Continue on small trail as it winds through the trees.
▼ 0.3	SO	Muddy section.
▼ 1.4	SO	Water Canyon hiking trail on left.

GPS: N 37°43.31' W 111°53.31'

▼ 1.8	SO	Trail runs on eastern edge of Table Cliff Plateau.
▼ 3.1	SO	Campsite with views on left. Many small campsites are on the edge tucked into the trees.
▼ 3.5	UT	End of vehicle trail. Scenic overlook is 3,000 feet along a hiking trail. Return to the junction of FR 132 and FR 142.

GPS: N 37°41.61' W 111°53.79'

SOUTHWEST REGION TRAIL #37

Barney Top Trail

Starting Point:	**Intersection of Southwest #33: Griffin Road and Southwest #34: Escalante Summit Trail**
Finishing Point:	**Southwest #36: Powell Point Trail (FR 132)**
Total Mileage:	**8.3 miles**
Unpaved Mileage:	**8.3 miles**
Driving Time:	**2 hours**
Elevation Range:	**9,000–10,700 feet**
Usually Open:	**June to October**
Difficulty Rating:	**5**
Scenic Rating:	**9**
Remoteness Rating:	**+0**

Special Attractions

■ Moderately challenging trail with a variety of driving conditions.

■ A wide range of backcountry campsites on Barney Top.

■ Panoramic views east over the Upper Valley.

A white cliff face falls away to the side of the Barney Top Trail

Description

This exciting trail connects Southwest #34: Escalante Summit Trail and Southwest #33: Griffin Road with Southwest #36: Powell Point Trail. The trail is a moderately difficult drive over a variety of surfaces and conditions, but in dry conditions it is suitable for most high-clearance 4WDs.

The trail starts from Southwest #34: Escalante Summit Trail (FR 17) at Escalante Summit, 7.3 miles east of Widtsoe Junction. The trail is marked as FR 142 on the ground; yet Dixie National Forest maps show it as FR 143. There are three alternatives at the junction; follow the sign for Barney Top, taking the middle trail south.

The narrow trail is only wide enough for a single vehicle, and it climbs almost immediately, winding around the eastern edge of the ridgetop. It can be very muddy if there has been recent rain and may be impassable. On a clear day, you can see east to the Henry Mountains. After 2.7 miles, the trail becomes harder, has larger rocks, and then there's a section of narrow shelf road that crosses a rocky scree slope. The shelf road climbs steeply and the surface can be loose—this is the most difficult part of the trail. Passing places are limited, and you may need to reverse to let on-coming vehicles pass. Passengers will enjoy the views east even if the driver doesn't! After 3 miles you reach Barney Top, and the trail becomes easier as it traverses open meadows and pine and aspen forest. There are ample backcountry campsites along this section.

After passing by the communications tower, the trail de-

View to the east through the rocky crags and small aspens of Barney Top

scends to join Southwest #36: Powell Point Trail. The descent is easier than the ascent, as the shelf road is wider and the surface offers better traction. The trail finishes where the Powell Point Trail turns toward the Powell Point spur.

Current Road Information
Dixie National Forest
Escalante Ranger District
755 West Main
Escalante, UT 84726
(435) 826-5403

Map References
BLM Escalante
USFS Dixie National Forest: Escalante Ranger District
USGS 1:24,000 Sweetwater Creek, Griffin Point, Upper Valley
1:100,000 Escalante
Maptech CD-ROM: Escalante/Dixie National Forest
Utah Atlas & Gazetteer, pp. 19, 27

Route Directions

▼ 0.0 On Southwest #34: Escalante Summit Trail (FR 17), 7.3 miles east of Widtsoe Junction, zero trip meter and turn south on FR 142, following sign to Barney Top.
5.7 ▲ Trail finishes at Escalante Summit and Southwest #34: Escalante Summit Trail (FR 17). Turn left for Widtsoe Junction, right for Escalante. Straight ahead is Southwest #33: Griffin Road.

GPS: N 37°49.51' W 111°52.90'

▼ 0.1 SO Campsite on left with good views. Trail starts to climb.
5.6 ▲ SO Campsite on right with good views.

▼ 1.0 SO Track on left.
4.7 ▲ SO Track on right.

GPS: N 37°48.75' W 111°53.01'

▼ 1.2 SO Track on right.
4.5 ▲ SO Track on left.

▼ 1.6 SO Viewpoint on left. Views east to the Henry Mountains.
4.1 ▲ SO Viewpoint on right. Views east to the Henry Mountains.

GPS: N 37°48.47' W 111°53.27'

▼ 2.0 SO Track on right at clearing.
3.7 ▲ SO Track on left at clearing.

▼ 2.3 SO Cross over small scree face.
3.4 ▲ SO Cross over small scree face.

▼ 2.7 SO Cross scree slope on narrow shelf road.
3.0 ▲ SO End of shelf road.

▼ 3.0 SO End of shelf road, trail levels out. Track on right.
2.7 ▲ SO Track on left. Cross scree slope on narrow shelf road; descend to Escalante Summit.

GPS: N 37°47.45' W 111°53.21'

▼ 3.5 SO Track on right crosses Barney Top (open meadow).
2.2 ▲ SO Track on left crosses Barney Top.

▼ 3.7 SO Track on right across meadow. Many backcountry campsites.
2.0 ▲ SO Track on left across meadow. Many backcountry campsites.

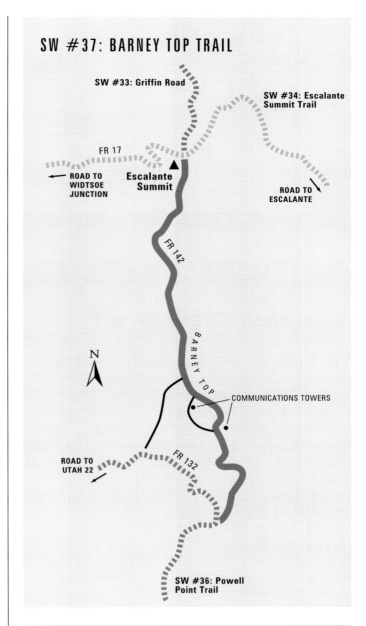

SW #37: BARNEY TOP TRAIL

▼ 4.5 BL Track on right into grassy area.
1.2 ▲ BR Track on left into grassy area.

▼ 4.9 SO Track on right.
0.8 ▲ BR Track on left.

▼ 5.7 SO Track on right, then communications tower immediately on left of trail. Zero trip meter at tower.
0.0 ▲ Continue north.

GPS: N 37°45.52' W 111°52.35'

▼ 0.0 Continue south.
2.6 ▲ SO Pass second communications tower immediately on right of trail and zero trip meter. Track on left after tower.

▼ 0.1 SO Track on right to second communications tower.
2.5 ▲ SO Track on left to communications tower.

▼ 0.5 SO Trail descends wide shelf road.
2.1 ▲ SO End of ascent.

▼ 0.9 SO Views right to Pine Lake. Trail standard is now easier.

1.7 ▲	SO	Views left to Pine Lake. Trail ascends wide shelf road; standard becomes harder.
▼ 1.3	SO	Track on right.
1.3 ▲	SO	Track on left.
▼ 1.8	SO	Track on left.
0.8 ▲	SO	Track on right.
▼ 2.5	SO	Campsite and views on left.
0.1 ▲	SO	Campsite and views on right.
▼ 2.6		Trail finishes at Southwest #36: Powell Point Trail (FR 132). Turn left to visit Powell Point, right for Pine Lake and Utah 22.
0.0 ▲		10.9 miles from the western end of Southwest #36: Powell Point Trail (FR 132) at the spur to Powell Point, zero trip meter and continue north on FR 142.

GPS: N 37°44.06′ W 111°52.24′

SOUTHWEST REGION TRAIL #38

Tantalus Creek Trail

Starting Point:	**Utah 12, 16.2 miles south of Utah 24**
Finishing Point:	**Capitol Reef National Park**
Total Mileage:	**17.8 miles**
Unpaved Mileage:	**17.8 miles**
Driving Time:	**2 hours**
Elevation Range:	**5,800–8,600 feet**
Usually Open:	**May to November**
Difficulty Rating:	**4**
Scenic Rating:	**10**
Remoteness Rating:	**+1**

Special Attractions

- Exciting trail partly within Capitol Reef National Park.
- Range of scenery from pine forest to red rock desert.
- Fishing and camping opportunities at Lower Bowns Reservoir.

Description

This trail sees surprisingly little use considering that it is partly within a popular national park. Moderately difficult, the trail encompasses a wide variety of scenery and trail surfaces. It starts from Utah 12, 16.2 miles south of its junction with Utah 24 near Torrey. Turn east on FR 186 (on *Delorme* it says 181 but on the Dixie NF it is 186), which begins as a graded gravel road and gradually descends through a shady pine forest toward Lower Bowns Reservoir. ATVs have their own trail, the Rosebud ATV trail, which takes a slightly more meandering route to the reservoir. Dispersed camping is permitted along the trail, and there are several pretty sites in pine clearings on the banks of a small creek. The trail passes the Wildcat Revegetation Program, an area cleared and then reseeded with grass and shrubbage to provide improved forage for deer and grazing livestock.

After 3 miles the trail forks, with the right-hand track going to Lower Bowns Reservoir. The reservoir has more lovely

camping areas (no facilities), some under the shade of large pines, but most in the open around its shores. The area is very popular in the summer for both camping and fishing. From the fork to the reservoir, the trail is smaller, with long stretches of a very fine, powdery surface. The grader stops at a large corral at the start of Jorgensen Flat. From there the trail is formed and narrower. There are some rocky sections as it drops further to cross Tantalus Creek, 2,000 feet lower than Utah 12.

Driving below the protruding rock formations along South Draw Wash

Jorgensen Flat is very pretty; the sagebrush benches are surrounded by red rocks and sandstone. Pleasant Creek cuts a deep canyon on the left-hand side of the trail. The approach to Tantalus Creek zigzags down a sandy gully, which can be washed out; it is also hard to climb back out—both in very dry and very wet weather!

From the creek, the trail gently climbs as it runs along Tantalus Flats. This section can be very muddy when wet. The trail then swings east and enters Capitol Reef National Park, 10 miles from the start of the trail. Dispersed camping is not permitted in the park, but there are some lovely sites at the end of the valley before the trail enters the park. The first part of the trail within the national park is the roughest section, as it climbs through a rocky gap toward the Waterpocket Fold and then drops to enter South Draw. Once in the draw, the trail follows the creekbed for the next 3.5 miles before crossing Pleasant Creek. After Pleasant Creek, the road returns to graded dirt until it finishes at the end of the paved scenic drive from Fruita and the park's information center. The portion of the trail within Capitol Reef National Park is subject to park fees.

Smooth section of the Tantalus Creek Trail overlooking Capitol Reef

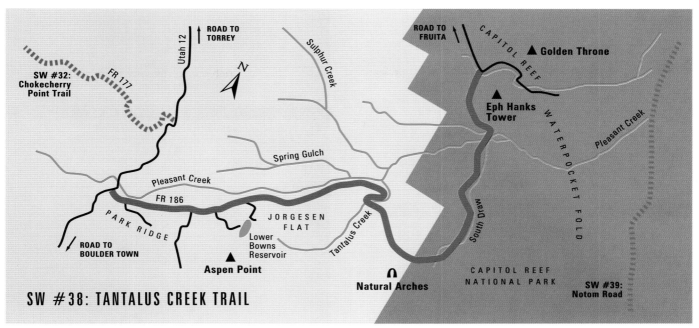

SW #38: TANTALUS CREEK TRAIL

Current Road Information
Capitol Reef National Park
HC-70 Box 15
Torrey, UT 84775
(435) 425-3791

Dixie National Forest
Teasdale Ranger District
PO Box 99
Teasdale, UT 84773
(435) 425-3702

Map References
BLM Loa
USFS Dixie National Forest: Teasdale Ranger District
USGS 1:24,000 Lower Bowns Reservoir, Grover, Golden
Throne, Bear Canyon
1:100,000 Loa
Maptech CD-ROM: Escalante/Dixie National Forest
Trails Illustrated, #707
Utah Atlas & Gazetteer, p. 28
Utah Travel Council #5
Other: Capitol Reef National Park map

Route Directions

▼ 0.0   From Utah 12, 16.2 miles south of Utah 24, turn southeast along the graded gravel FR 186, following sign to Lower Bowns Reservoir. Zero trip meter.

     3.0 ▲   Trail ends at Utah 12. Turn right for Torrey, left for Boulder Town.

GPS: N 38°06.01' W 111°20.22'

▼ 0.2   SO   Rosebud ATV trail on left. ATV unloading and parking at the trailhead. No ATVs on the graded road past this point.

     2.8 ▲   SO   Rosebud ATV trail on right. ATV unloading and parking at the trailhead.

GPS: N 38°05.86' W 111°20.10'

▼ 0.3   SO   Track on right to Park Ridge.

     2.7 ▲   SO   Track on left to Park Ridge.

GPS: N 38°05.82' W 111°20.04'

▼ 0.6   SO   Track on left.

     2.4 ▲   SO   Track on right.

▼ 0.9   SO   Track on right to campsite.

     2.1 ▲   SO   Track on left to campsite.

▼ 1.2   SO   Start of dispersed camping area alongside trail.

     1.8 ▲   SO   End of dispersed camping area.

▼ 2.2   SO   Cattle guard.

     0.8 ▲   SO   Cattle guard.

▼ 2.3   SO   Slickrock Trail (hiking, pack, and ATV only) enters on left and leaves on right.

     0.7 ▲   SO   Slickrock Trail (hiking, pack, and ATV only) enters on left and leaves on right.

GPS: N 38°06.28' W 111°17.85'

▼ 2.5   SO   Wildcat Revegetation Project on left.

     0.5 ▲   SO   Wildcat Revegetation Project on right.

▼ 3.0   BL   Track on right to Lower Bowns Reservoir. Proceed along FR 168 on left marked as Tantalus 4x4 Road. Zero trip meter.

     0.0 ▲   Continue toward Utah 12.

GPS: N 38°06.50' W 111°17.23'

▼ 0.0   Continue toward Jorgensen Flat.

     4.2 ▲   SO   Track on left to Lower Bowns Reservoir.

▼ 0.2   SO   Track on right is Rosebud ATV trail. ATVs are permitted on the main trail from this point.

     4.0 ▲   SO   Track on left is Rosebud ATV trail. ATVs are not permitted on the main trail from this point.

▼ 0.5   SO   Slaughter Flat. Track on left is Rosebud ATV trail.

     3.7 ▲   SO   Slaughter Flat. Track on right is Rosebud ATV trail.

GPS: N 38°06.84' W 111°16.81'

▼ 1.1   SO   Track on right to the north end of Lower Bowns Reservoir.

     3.1 ▲   SO   Track on left to the north end of Lower Bowns Reservoir.

GPS: N 38°07.12' W 111°16.34'

▼ 2.2		SO	Cattle guard, then corral on right. Trail is now ungraded.
	2.0 ▲	SO	Corral on left, then cattle guard. Trail is now graded.
▼ 2.4		SO	Track on left. Pleasant Creek is on left in a deep gorge.
	1.8 ▲	SO	Track on right.
▼ 3.7		SO	Faint track on left to campsites along the ridge overlooking Pleasant Creek.
	0.5 ▲	SO	Faint track on right to campsites along the ridge overlooking Pleasant Creek.
▼ 4.2		SO	Track on left is recommended only for vehicles fewer than 50 inches wide. Zero trip meter.
	0.0 ▲		Continue along Jorgensen Flat. Pleasant Creek is on right in a deep gorge.

GPS: N 38°08.65′ W 111°13.49′

▼ 0.0			Continue toward Capitol Reef National Park.
	3.0 ▲	SO	Track on right is recommended only for vehicles fewer than 50 inches wide. Zero trip meter.
▼ 0.1		SO	Cross through wash.
	2.9 ▲	SO	Cross through wash.
▼ 0.4		SO	Trail winds down to Tantalus Creek.
	2.6 ▲	SO	End of climb from Tantalus Creek.
▼ 0.5		SO	Track on right.
	2.5 ▲	SO	Track on left.
▼ 0.7		BL	Down at the creek, bear north alongside creek.
	2.3 ▲	BR	Sandy climb out of Tantalus Creek gully.

GPS: N 38°08.42′ W 111°13.17′

▼ 0.8		SO	Cross through Tantalus Creek. Small spring on right at exit flows out of a crack in the rock. Trail climbs out of creek gully.
	2.2 ▲	SO	Cross through Tantalus Creek. Small spring on left at entrance flows out of a crack in the rock. Trail follows south alongside creek.

GPS: N 38°08.39′ W 111°13.12′

▼ 0.9		SO	Cattle guard.
	2.1 ▲	SO	Cattle guard.
▼ 2.3		BL	Track on right.
	0.7 ▲	SO	Track on left.
▼ 2.6		BL	Track on right. Small arch on top of cliff on right.
	0.4 ▲	SO	Second entrance to track on left. Small arch on top of cliff on left.

GPS: N 38°07.42′ W 111°11.63′

▼ 2.7		SO	Second entrance to track on right, then cattle guard.
	0.3 ▲	BR	Cattle guard, then track on left.
▼ 3.0		SO	Entering Capitol Reef National Park. Zero trip meter.
	0.0 ▲		Continue toward Tantalus Creek.

GPS: N 38°07.54′ W 111°11.29′

▼ 0.0			Continue into Capitol Reef National Park.
	4.9 ▲	SO	Leaving Capitol Reef National Park. Zero trip meter.
▼ 1.4		SO	Cross through wash. Trail crosses wash numerous times and runs alongside or in the wash for the next 2.5 miles.
	3.5 ▲	SO	Trail leaves South Draw.
▼ 3.9		SO	Trail leaves South Draw.
	1.0 ▲	SO	Trail enters South Draw. Trail runs in or alongside the wash and crosses it numerous times for the next 2.5 miles.

GPS: N 38°10.04′ W 111°10.58′

▼ 4.2		SO	Cross through small, tight wash.
	0.7 ▲	SO	Cross through small, tight wash.
▼ 4.5		SO	Cross through South Draw.
	0.4 ▲	SO	Cross through South Draw.

▼ 4.6		SO	Enter wash.
	0.3 ▲	SO	Exit wash.
▼ 4.8		SO	Exit wash.
	0.1 ▲	SO	Enter wash.
▼ 4.9		SO	Cross through Pleasant Creek. Parking area and pit toilets on left. Zero trip meter.
	0.0 ▲		Continue on South Draw 4x4 Road.

GPS: N 38°10.81′ W 111°10.81′

▼ 0.0			Continue on graded dirt road.
	2.7 ▲	SO	Parking area and pit toilets on right. Zero trip meter and cross through Pleasant Creek.
▼ 0.1		SO	Track on left.
	2.6 ▲	SO	Track on right.
▼ 0.2		SO	Pass through stockyards and ranch buildings.
	2.5 ▲	SO	Pass through stockyards and ranch buildings.
▼ 0.4		SO	Track on right is for authorized vehicles only. Trail is now graded dirt.
	2.3 ▲	SO	Track on left is for authorized vehicles only. Trail is now ungraded dirt.
▼ 0.5		SO	Cross through wash.
	2.2 ▲	SO	Cross through wash.
▼ 0.6		SO	Cross through fence line. Track on right is for authorized vehicles only.
	2.1 ▲	SO	Track on left is for authorized vehicles only; then cross through fence line.
▼ 1.8		SO	Golden Throne viewpoint.
	0.9 ▲	SO	Golden Throne viewpoint.
▼ 1.9		SO	Cross through wash.
	0.8 ▲	SO	Cross through wash.
▼ 2.2		SO	Cross through wash.
	0.5 ▲	SO	Cross through wash.
▼ 2.6		SO	Cross through wash.
	0.1 ▲	SO	Cross through wash.
▼ 2.7			Trail ends at the paved scenic national park drive from Fruita. Turn left for Fruita and for park information center.
	0.0 ▲		At end of the paved scenic national park drive from Fruita and the Capitol Reef National Park information center, zero trip meter and turn south, following the sign for Pleasant Creek Road.

GPS: N 38°12.50′ W 111°11.66′

SOUTHWEST REGION TRAIL #39

Notom Road

Starting Point:	**Notom Road at Utah 24, eastern edge of Capitol Reef National Park**
Finishing Point:	**Southwest #40: Burr Trail**
Total Mileage:	**31 miles**
Unpaved Mileage:	**26.3 miles**
Driving Time:	**2 hours**
Elevation Range:	**5,000–5,700 feet**
Usually Open:	**Year-round**
Difficulty Rating:	**2**
Scenic Rating:	**9**
Remoteness Rating:	**+0**

Special Attractions
- Old town site of Notom.
- Views of the Waterpocket Fold and Oyster Shell Reef within Capitol Reef National Park.

History
Notom evolved from the settlement of Pleasant Creek, which was first settled in 1886 by Jorgen Christian Smith. When a post office was built, the state would not allow the name Pleasant Creek to be used, as there were already other settlements by that name. Smith suggested the name Notom for reasons unknown, and that is what the settlement came to be called.

Notom in the early days didn't amount to much, and many of the original families moved away. In 1904, an ex-cattleman, William Bowns, purchased land at Notom and farther to the south and built a large sheep property he named Sandy Ranch. The flocks, numbering an estimated 21,000 total animals, grazed on Boulder Mountain to the west and the Henry Mountains to the east and in the desert in between. The wool was taken to Salina for sale, while sheep for market were taken to the railroad in Green River or driven to Marysvale or Salina. Coyotes were a constant threat, but the state paid a bounty of six dollars per coyote skin, which helped to keep the problem in check. Following the Great Depression, sheep were deemed unprofitable, and the ranch slowly returned to cattle.

An old uranium mining truck in Notom

Another major ranching family around Notom was the Durfey family, which settled in the area in 1919. They, too, concentrated on sheep, but moved to cattle when the grazing rights for sheep were cut back by the forest service.

Sandy Ranch and Notom shared the water rights for Oak and Pleasant Creeks in an unusual arrangement. Notom had rights to the water from April 1 to October 30; the remainder of the year the water was diverted into Bowns Reservoir and used by Sandy Ranch.

In the 1950s the demand for uranium was so strong that a special use permit allowed mining within what was then the Capitol Reef National Monument. Notom Road saw a lot of traffic as Jeeps drove in and out of the park all day, and ore trucks passed by on their way to the processing plants at Moab and Marysvale.

Today, there is little to see in Notom; the town is mainly ranch property owned by the Durfey family.

Description
This easygoing route passes through the old town site of Notom and across the Sandy Creek Benches to travel along inside the Waterpocket Fold in Capitol Reef National Park. It is often suitable for passenger cars in dry weather, but loose sand, bulldust, and a couple of rough wash crossings make it

The well-maintained trail drops down onto Notom Bench

preferable to have a high-clearance vehicle.

Notom Road leaves Utah 24 on the eastern edge of Capitol Reef National Park. The first part of the trail is paved road as it crosses over Pleasant Creek and enters the settlement of Notom, now just a few private houses and ranch buildings. The trail crosses Notom Bench with spectacular and wide-ranging views east over Thompson Mesa to the Henry Mountains and west to the Waterpocket Fold in Capitol Reef National Park.

At Sandy Junction, a major trail leads east into the Henry Mountains and joins up with Southwest #47: Bull Creek Pass Trail. Notom Road continues south and enters Capitol Reef National Park. It goes through the Narrows and runs inside the Waterpocket Fold, with the Oyster Shell Reef to the west. The reef, named for the fossilized oyster shells found along its length, is a jagged yet delicate spine of rock that parallels the main Waterpocket Fold. The trail finishes at Southwest #40: Burr Trail, a few miles from the base of the Burr Trail switchbacks.

If you are planning to camp along this route, be aware that there is a lot of private property interspersed with the federal lands. There are some

Notom Road rolls over a succession of small hills along Waterpocket Fold

pleasant sites to be found on some of the side trails. Within the park, camping is restricted to the free Cedar Mesa Campground, which you pass 2 miles after entering the park.

Current Road Information
Capitol Reef National Park
HC-70 Box 15
Torrey, UT 84775
(435) 425-3791

Escalante Interagency Office
755 West Main
Escalante, UT 84726
(435) 826-5499

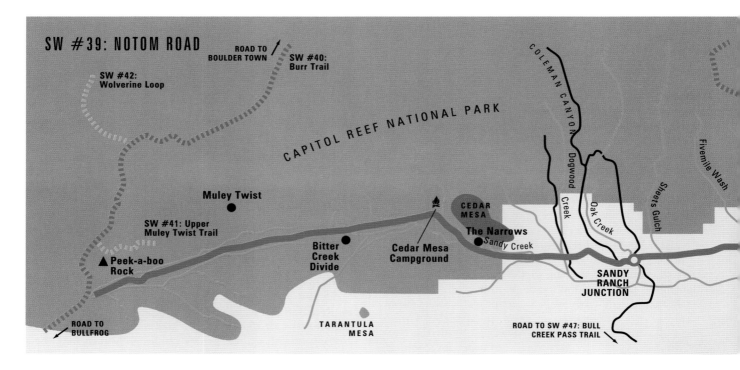

Map References

BLM Loa, Escalante

USGS 1:24,000 Fruita, Caineville, Notom, Sandy Creek
Benches, Bitter Creek Divide, Wagon Box Mesa
1:100,000 Loa, Escalante

Maptech CD-ROM: Escalante/Dixie National Forest

Trails Illustrated, #213

Utah Atlas & Gazetteer, p. 28

Utah Travel Council #5

Other: Capitol Reef National Park map
Recreation Map of the Henry Mountains Area
BLM Map of the Grand Staircase–Escalante National
Monument (incomplete)

Route Directions

| ▼ 0.0 | | | From Utah 24, turn south on paved Notom Road at the eastern edge of Capitol Reef National Park, following sign for Bullfrog. Zero trip meter. |
| 4.7 ▲ | | | Trail ends at Utah 24. Turn left for Capitol Reef National Park, turn right for Hanksville. |

GPS: N 38°17.01' W 111°07.66'

▼ 1.4		SO	Track on right.
3.3 ▲		SO	Track on left.
▼ 2.0		SO	Track on left, then cross over Pleasant Creek on bridge. Track on right after bridge.
2.7 ▲		SO	Track on left, then cross over Pleasant Creek on bridge. Track on right after bridge.

GPS: N 38°15.49' W 111°07.13'

▼ 2.1		SO	Track on left.
2.6 ▲		SO	Track on right.
▼ 3.0		SO	Track on left.
1.7 ▲		SO	Track on right.
▼ 3.4		SO	Notom. Track on left, then track on right.
1.3 ▲		SO	Notom. Track on left, then track on right.
▼ 3.7		SO	Track on right, then track on left.
1.0 ▲		SO	Track on right, then track on left.

▼ 4.6		SO	Track on right, then track on left.
0.1 ▲		SO	Track on right, then track on left.
▼ 4.7		SO	Road turns to graded gravel. Zero trip meter.
0.0 ▲		SO	Continue north.

GPS: N 38°13.13' W 111°06.67'

▼ 0.0		SO	Continue south.
8.1 ▲		SO	Road turns to pavement. Zero trip meter.
▼ 1.0		SO	Track on left.
7.1 ▲		SO	Track on right.
▼ 1.1		SO	Tracks on right and left.
7.0 ▲		SO	Tracks on right and left.
▼ 1.5		SO	Tracks on right and left.
6.6 ▲		SO	Tracks on right and left.
▼ 2.3		SO	Track on left.
5.8 ▲		SO	Track on right.
▼ 2.7		SO	Cross through Burro Wash.
5.4 ▲		SO	Cross through Burro Wash.

GPS: N 38°10.86' W 111°05.60'

▼ 3.8		SO	Cross through Cottonwood Wash, then track on right.
4.3 ▲		SO	Track on left, then cross through Cottonwood Wash.
▼ 4.7		SO	Cattle guard.
3.4 ▲		SO	Cattle guard.
▼ 4.8		SO	Cross through Fivemile Wash and enter Garfield County.
3.3 ▲		SO	Enter Wayne County and cross through Fivemile Wash.
▼ 5.6		SO	Cross through wash.
2.5 ▲		SO	Cross through wash.
▼ 5.9		SO	Cross through wash.
2.2 ▲		SO	Cross through wash.
▼ 7.4		SO	Cross through Sheets Gulch.
0.7 ▲		SO	Cross through Sheets Gulch.

GPS: N 38°06.85' W 111°04.20'

| ▼ 8.1 | | BR | Sandy Ranch Junction. Track on left to McMillan Springs Campground and Southwest |

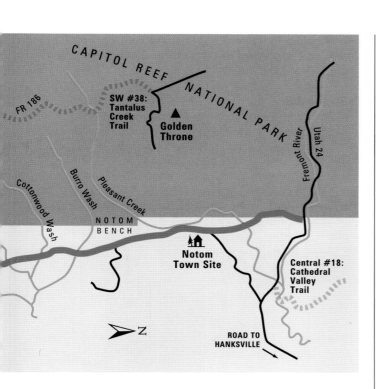

			#47: Bull Creek Pass Trail in the Henry Mountains. Zero trip meter.
	0.0 ▲		Continue north.

GPS: N 38°06.23′ W 111°04.12′

▼ 0.0			Continue south.
	5.4 ▲	SO	Sandy Ranch Junction. Track on right to McMillan Springs Campground and Southwest #47: Bull Creek Pass Trail in the Henry Mountains. Zero trip meter.
▼ 0.1		SO	Track on right to Oak Creek Canyon, then cross over Oak Creek on bridge.
	5.3 ▲	SO	Cross over Oak Creek on bridge, then track on left to Oak Creek Canyon.
▼ 0.3		SO	Track on left is private.
	5.1 ▲	SO	Track on right is private.
▼ 0.5		SO	Cattle guard.
	4.9 ▲	SO	Cattle guard.
▼ 0.8		SO	Track on right is private.
	4.6 ▲	SO	Track on left is private.
▼ 1.0		SO	Track on left is private.
	4.4 ▲	SO	Track on right is private.
▼ 1.7		SO	Tracks on right and left are private.
	3.7 ▲	SO	Tracks on right and left are private.
▼ 2.2		SO	Track on right is private.
	3.2 ▲	SO	Track on left is private.
▼ 2.8		SO	Track on left, then cattle guard, then track on right.
	2.6 ▲	SO	Track on left, then cattle guard, then track on right.

GPS: N 38°04.15′ W 111°03.86′

▼ 2.9		SO	Cross through Dogwood Creek.
	2.5 ▲	SO	Cross through Dogwood Creek.
▼ 3.9		SO	Cross through Sandy Creek.
	1.5 ▲	SO	Cross through Sandy Creek.
▼ 4.5		SO	Track on left.
	0.9 ▲	SO	Track on right.
▼ 5.4		SO	Entering Capitol Reef National Park over cattle guard. Zero trip meter.
	0.0 ▲		Continue toward Notom.

GPS: N 38°01.83′ W 111°03.88′

▼ 0.0			Continue into Capitol Reef National Park.
	12.8 ▲	SO	Leaving Capitol Reef National Park over cattle guard. Zero trip meter.
▼ 0.1		SO	Cross twice through Sandy Creek wash. Entering The Narrows.
	12.7 ▲	SO	Cross twice through Sandy Creek wash. Exit Narrows
▼ 0.5		SO	Track on left. Exit Narrows
	12.3 ▲	SO	Track on right. Entering The Narrows
▼ 0.6		SO	Cross through wash.
	12.2 ▲	SO	Cross through wash.
▼ 1.3		SO	Cross through wash.
	11.5 ▲	SO	Cross through wash.
▼ 1.4		SO	Cross through wash.
	11.4 ▲	SO	Cross through wash.
▼ 2.0		SO	Cedar Mesa Campground (free) on right.
	10.8 ▲	SO	Cedar Mesa Campground (free) on left.

GPS: N 38°00.42′ W 111°04.91′

▼ 3.0		SO	Cross through Sandy Creek.
	9.8 ▲	SO	Cross through Sandy Creek.
▼ 3.2		SO	Dam on left.
	9.6 ▲	SO	Dam on right.
▼ 4.9		SO	Dam on left.
	7.9 ▲	SO	Dam on right.
▼ 5.4		SO	Bitter Creek Divide.
	7.4 ▲	SO	Bitter Creek Divide.

GPS: N 37°57.51′ W 111°03.89′

▼ 12.7		SO	Cross through wash.
	0.1 ▲	SO	Cross through wash.
▼ 12.8			Trail ends at Southwest #40: Burr Trail. Turn left for Bullfrog, right to ascend the switchbacks and continue to Boulder Town.
	0.0 ▲		From Southwest #40: Burr Trail at the sign for Hanksville, 0.7 miles east of the Burr Trail switchbacks, zero trip meter and turn north on graded road.

GPS: N 37°51.32′ W 111°00.68′

SOUTHWEST REGION TRAIL #40

Burr Trail

Starting Point:	**Utah 276, 5 miles north of Bullfrog Marina**
Finishing Point:	**Boulder Town on Utah 12**
Total Mileage:	**62.6 miles**
Unpaved Mileage:	**16.8 miles**
Driving Time:	**2 hours**
Elevation Range:	**3,900–6,600 feet**
Usually Open:	**Year-round**
Difficulty Rating:	**1**
Scenic Rating:	**10**
Remoteness Rating:	**+0**

Special Attractions

- Long and historic pioneer route.
- Capitol Reef National Park.
- Wide variety of canyon and desert scenery.

History

The Burr Trail was created in the late 1800s as a cow path to move cattle to market and between summer and winter pastures. The trail is named after John Atlantic Burr, a rancher of Burrville, Utah, who was born on board the SS *Brooklyn* in the Atlantic Ocean.

The most striking feature along the route is the Waterpocket Fold, and the most prominent aspect of the trail itself are the Burr Trail switchbacks, which ascend some 1,500 feet in one mile up a cleft in the Waterpocket Fold. This section alone was the original Burr Trail, though today the entire road from Boulder Town to Bullfrog is known as the Burr Trail. The Waterpocket Fold, a hundred-mile long section of uplift in the earth's crust, was named by explorer John Wesley Powell. Powell observed many "pockets," or hollows, in the rock that retained water. The Waterpocket Fold is several miles wide and consists of weathered, exposed layers of sedimentary rock forming a jagged fin running from Thousand Lake Mountain in the north to Lake Powell in the south.

Just south of the switchbacks on the eastern side of Waterpocket Fold is the site of an old cabin and roundup corral known as "the Post." Nowadays nothing remains except the point of reference on maps.

For more than a hundred years, the Burr Trail was a dirt path. In the early 1990s the trail entered a new era, thanks to judicial courtrooms. Garfield County, in which the entire trail is contained, claimed that the trail was a highway under the Mining Act of 1866, and so it was entitled to improve the road for safety reasons. Despite strong opposition, all but 18 miles of the Burr Trail was paved. The only remaining dirt road section is within Capitol Reef National Park, plus a short section to the east.

Just past the southern end of the trail is Bullfrog and the western shore of Lake Powell across from Hall's Crossing. Charles Hall was an early pioneer in southern Utah. His first venture was to build the ferry that carried the Mormon pioneers across the river at the Hole-in-the-Rock in 1870. He operated his second Colorado River ferry from here in 1881. Hall's ferry ceased operation in 1884 when the Denver & Rio Grande Railroad crossed central Utah and reduced the need for the lower, more difficult route through the south. Hall's ranch in nearby Halls Creek was acquired by Eugene Baker at the turn of the century, but it was swallowed by the rising waters following the damming of Lake Powell.

Driving past Circle Cliffs at the eastern end of Long Canyon

Description

This long and easy route offers a great variety of scenery. Although it is now predominantly paved road, there are rough sections through Capitol Reef National Park on which low-slung vehicles will need to exercise care.

The trail commences 5 miles north of Bullfrog Marina and leads west, traveling within the Glen Canyon National Recreation Area. After crossing Bullfrog Creek, the road gradually climbs to travel along a ridgetop. You can see Lake Powell to the south, and there are views to the north over the deep Bullfrog Canyon to the Henry Mountains.

After 7 miles the trail leaves the Glen Canyon National Recreation Area. There are some small 4WD side trails that lead to impressive viewpoints over the deep Bullfrog Canyon. After 18.4 miles of paved road, the trail intersects with Southwest #43: Clay Point Road and becomes a good, graded gravel road that runs north parallel to Waterpocket Fold.

A series of switchbacks along the remote Burr Trail

The trail enters Capitol Reef National Park and passes by a point on maps named "the Post." After the junction with Southwest #39: Notom Road, the trail climbs up the infamous Burr Trail switchbacks. This is the only part of the trail likely to challenge a passenger car in dry weather. The switchbacks climb steeply up a notch in the Waterpocket Fold. The upper end is rough, and rocks in the track bear the marks of undercarriage scrapes from low-slung vehicles. Ideally, travelers should have high-clearance vehicles, but many passenger cars successfully traverse this section.

At the top of the switchbacks, there are a couple of very pleasant picnic areas. The Burr Trail passes by hiking trailheads and a short 4WD spur, Southwest #41: Upper Muley Twist Trail; then it exits Capitol Reef National Park and immediately enters the newly formed Grand Staircase–Escalante National Monument, which is managed by the BLM. The road becomes paved from here all the way to Boulder Town, and it first traverses the plateau, passing by the jagged range of the Studhorse Peaks and Southwest #42: Wolverine Loop, which leads to Wolverine Petrified Wood Area. Several tracks to the right and left access remote areas of the monument.

The Burr Trail passes by the northern end of Circle Cliffs, also named by John Wesley Powell, and then descends the narrow Long Canyon, enclosed on both sides by sheer cliffs of Wingate sandstone. The trail ends at the southern edge of Boulder Town at Utah 12.

Current Road Information

Capitol Reef National Park
HC-70 Box 15
Torrey, UT 84775
(435) 425-3791

Escalante Interagency Office
755 West Main
Escalante, UT 84726
(435) 826-5499

Map References

BLM   Hite Crossing, Escalante
USFS   Dixie National Forest: Escalante Ranger District (incomplete)
USGS   1:24,000   Bull Frog, Hall Mesa, Clay Point, Deer Point
      1:100,000 Hite Crossing, Escalante
Maptech CD-ROM: Moab/Canyonlands; Escalante/Dixie National Forest
Trails Illustrated, #213
Utah Atlas & Gazetteer, pp. 28, 20, 21
Utah Travel Council #5
Other: Recreation Map of the Henry Mountains Area (incomplete)
      BLM Map of the Grand Staircase–Escalante National Monument (incomplete)

Route Directions

▼ 0.0		Trail commences from Utah 276, 5 miles north of Bullfrog Marina. Zero trip meter and turn west on paved road.
18.4 ▲		Trail ends at Utah 276. Turn right for Bullfrog Marina, turn left for Hanksville.
	GPS: N 37°34.54' W 110°42.88'	
▼ 0.2	SO	Track on left and right.
18.2 ▲	SO	Track on right and left.
▼ 0.3	SO	Track on left.
18.1 ▲	SO	Track on right.
▼ 2.0	SO	Track on left to Bullfrog Bay South, primitive camping area (fee required).
16.4 ▲	SO	Track on right to Bullfrog Bay South, primitive camping area (fee required).
	GPS: N 37°34.66' W 110°44.75'	
▼ 2.1	SO	Cross over Bullfrog Canyon.
16.3 ▲	SO	Cross over Bullfrog Canyon.
▼ 3.4	SO	Track on left to Bullfrog Bay North, primitive camping area (fee required).
15.0 ▲	SO	Track on right to Bullfrog Bay North, primitive camping area (fee required).
	GPS: N 37°35.02' W 110°46.25'	
▼ 4.5	SO	Pedestal Alley hiking trail on right.
13.9 ▲	SO	Pedestal Alley hiking trail on left.
	GPS: N 37°35.89' W 110°46.67'	
▼ 4.8	SO	Enter Bullfrog Wash; wash is dirt and can be rough.
13.6 ▲	SO	Leave wash; road is paved again.

▼ 4.9	SO	Leave wash; road is paved again.
13.5 ▲	SO	Enter Bullfrog Wash; wash is dirt and can be rough.
▼ 7.1	SO	Cattle guard.
11.3 ▲	SO	Cattle guard.
▼ 7.3	SO	Leaving Glen Canyon National Recreation Area.
11.1 ▲	SO	Entering Glen Canyon National Recreation Area.
	GPS: N 37°37.73' W 110°48.02'	
▼ 9.3	SO	Track on left.
9.1 ▲	SO	Track on right.
▼ 9.9	SO	Track on right to campsite with view.
8.5 ▲	SO	Track on left to campsite with view.
▼ 11.4	SO	Track on right to campsite and Bullfrog Canyon Overlook.
7.0 ▲	SO	Track on left to campsite and Bullfrog Canyon Overlook.
	GPS: N 37°40.40' W 110°50.93'	
▼ 11.7	SO	Track on left.
6.7 ▲	SO	Track on right.
▼ 11.8	SO	Track on left.
6.6 ▲	SO	Track on right.
▼ 17.6	SO	Track on left to Halls Creek Overlook and trailhead.
0.8 ▲	SO	Track on right to Halls Creek Overlook and trailhead.
	GPS: N 37°44.78' W 110°54.52'	
▼ 18.4	TL	Track on right is Southwest #43: Clay Point Road. Zero trip meter.
0.0 ▲		Continue up paved road toward Bullfrog Basin.
	GPS: N 37°45.56' W 110°54.44'	
▼ 0.0		Continue along graded gravel road toward Capitol Reef National Park.
7.3 ▲	TR	Track ahead is Southwest #43: Clay Point Road. Zero trip meter.
▼ 1.5	SO	Track on left to flat area for primitive camping.
5.8 ▲	SO	Track on right to flat area for primitive camping.
▼ 3.2	SO	Track on left.
4.1 ▲	SO	Track on right.
▼ 5.1	SO	Track on right.
2.2 ▲	SO	Track on left.
▼ 7.3	SO	Entering Capitol Reef National Park. Zero trip meter.
0.0 ▲		Continue out of park.
	GPS: N 37°49.95' W 110°58.01'	
▼ 0.0		Continue into park. The Waterpocket Fold is on left.
3.0 ▲	SO	Leaving Capitol Reef National Park. Zero trip meter.
▼ 0.1	SO	Cross through wash.
2.9 ▲	SO	Cross through wash.
▼ 0.2	SO	Cross through wash.
2.8 ▲	SO	Cross through wash.
▼ 0.5	SO	Cross through wash, then cattle guard.
2.5 ▲	SO	Cattle guard, then cross through wash.
▼ 0.9	SO	Track on left to Lower Muley Twist hiking trail. Cross cattle guard.
2.1 ▲	SO	Cattle guard, then track on right to Lower Muley Twist hiking trail.
	GPS: N 37°50.00' W 110°58.85'	
▼ 1.4	SO	Surprise Canyon hikers area on left.

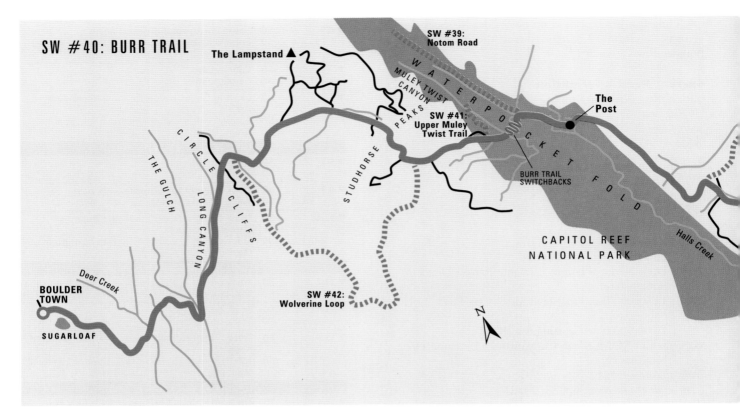

SW #40: BURR TRAIL

The Lampstand ▲

SW #39: Notom Road

WATERPOCKET

MULEY TWIST CANYON

STUDHORSE PEAKS

SW #41: Upper Muley Twist Trail

The Post

BURR TRAIL SWITCHBACKS

CIRCLE CLIFFS

THE GULCH

LONG CANYON

Deer Creek

BOULDER TOWN

SUGARLOAF

SW #42: Wolverine Loop

FOLD

CAPITOL REEF NATIONAL PARK

Halls Creek

N

1.6 ▲	SO	Surprise Canyon hikers area on right.	
▼ 3.0	BL	Right fork is Southwest #39: Notom Road to Utah 24. Zero trip meter.	
0.0 ▲		Continue south.	

GPS: N 37°51.29' W 111°00.65'

▼ 0.0		Continue west toward Burr Trail switchbacks.
2.9 ▲	BR	Left fork is Southwest #39: Notom Road to Utah 24. Zero trip meter.
▼ 0.1	SO	Cross through creek, then service road on right.
2.8 ▲	SO	Service road on left, then cross through creek.
▼ 0.2	SO	Enter gap in Waterpocket Fold; Burr Canyon Creek on right.
2.7 ▲	SO	Leave gap in Waterpocket Fold.
▼ 0.7	SO	Climb Burr Trail switchbacks. Trail is rougher; care needed for low-clearance vehicles.
2.2 ▲	SO	End of switchbacks.
▼ 1.9	SO	End of switchbacks. Track on left to picnic area.
1.0 ▲	SO	Track on right to picnic area. Descend Burr Trail switchbacks. Trail is rougher; care needed for low-clearance vehicles.

GPS: N 37°50.82' W 111°01.50'

▼ 2.0	SO	Lower Muley Twist Canyon hikers parking area on left.
0.9 ▲	SO	Lower Muley Twist Canyon hikers parking area on right.
▼ 2.1	SO	Cross through Muley Twist Wash.
0.8 ▲	SO	Cross through Muley Twist Wash.
▼ 2.4	SO	Track on left.
0.5 ▲	SO	Second entry to track on right.
▼ 2.6	SO	Second entry to track on left.
0.3 ▲	SO	Track on right.
▼ 2.9	SO	Track on right is Southwest #41: Upper Muley Twist Trail. Zero trip meter.

0.0 ▲		Continue east.

GPS: N 37°51.21' W 111°02.50'

▼ 0.0		Continue west.
2.0 ▲	SO	Track on left is Southwest #41: Upper Muley Twist Trail. Zero trip meter.
▼ 1.6	SO	Picnic area on right.
0.4 ▲	SO	Picnic area on left.
▼ 2.0	SO	Leaving Capitol Reef National Park. Road is now paved. Zero trip meter.
0.0 ▲		Continue on gravel road into Capitol Reef National Park.

GPS: N 37°51.79' W 111°04.60'

▼ 0.0		Continue on paved road.
1.6 ▲	SO	Entering Capitol Reef National Park. Road is now graded dirt. Zero trip meter.
▼ 0.1	SO	Entering Grand Staircase–Escalante National Monument.
1.5 ▲	SO	Leaving Grand Staircase–Escalante National Monument.
▼ 0.2	SO	Track on right to nice campsite with good views.
1.4 ▲	SO	Track on left to nice campsite with good views.
▼ 0.8	SO	Tracks on right and left.
0.8 ▲	SO	Tracks on left and right.
▼ 1.3	SO	Track on left.
0.3 ▲	SO	Track on right.
▼ 1.6	SO	Track on left is Southwest #42: Wolverine Loop. Zero trip meter.
0.0 ▲		Continue toward Capitol Reef National Park.

GPS: N 37°51.93' W 111°06.19'

▼ 0.0		Continue northwest.
9.9 ▲	SO	Track on right is Southwest #42: Wolverine Loop. Zero trip meter.

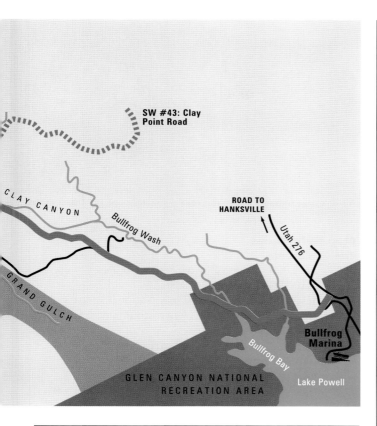

SW #43: Clay
Point Road

CLAY CANYON

Bullfrog Wash

GRAND GULCH

ROAD TO
HANKSVILLE

Utah 276

Bullfrog
Marina

Bullfrog Bay

Lake Powell

GLEN CANYON NATIONAL
RECREATION AREA

▼ 0.4		SO	Track left on right-hand bend goes to old dugouts and some pleasant campsites.
	9.5 ▲	SO	Track right on left-hand bend goes to old dugouts and some pleasant campsites.
▼ 0.8		SO	Dam on right. Road winds through the Studhorse Peaks.
	9.1 ▲	SO	Dam on left. Road winds through the Studhorse Peaks.
▼ 1.0		SO	Cattle guard.
	8.9 ▲	SO	Cattle guard.
▼ 2.0		SO	Track on right.
	7.9 ▲	SO	Track on left.
▼ 2.7		SO	Tracks on right and left.
	7.2 ▲	SO	Tracks on left and right.
▼ 3.4		SO	Track on left.
	6.5 ▲	SO	Track on right.
▼ 4.2		SO	Track on right.
	5.7 ▲	SO	Track on left.
▼ 4.4		SO	Track on right to the Lampstand.
	5.5 ▲	SO	Track on left to the Lampstand.
		GPS: N 37°55.04' W 111°07.90'	
▼ 4.7		SO	Dam, then track on left.
	5.2 ▲	SO	Track on right, then dam.
▼ 5.9		SO	Cattle guard.
	4.0 ▲	SO	Cattle guard.
▼ 6.7		SO	Track on left to the Lampstand.
	3.2 ▲	SO	Track on right to the Lampstand.
		GPS: N 37°55.77' W 111°10.36'	
▼ 8.6		SO	Track on right.
	1.3 ▲	SO	Track on left.
▼ 9.9		SO	Track on left is Southwest #42: Wolverine Loop. Zero trip meter.
	0.0 ▲		Continue east to Capitol Reef National Park.

		GPS: N 37°55.46' W 111°13.19'	
▼ 0.0			Continue west to Boulder Town.
	7.9 ▲	SO	Track on right is Southwest #42: Wolverine Loop. Zero trip meter.
▼ 0.3		SO	Track on right. Road passes through Circle Cliffs.
	7.6 ▲	SO	Track on left. Road passes through Circle Cliffs.
▼ 1.1		SO	Track on left.
	6.8 ▲	SO	Track on right.
▼ 1.6		SO	Cattle guard and turnout on left. Road descends Long Canyon.
	6.3 ▲	SO	Cattle guard and turnout on right. Top of Long Canyon.
		GPS: N 37°55.12' W 111°14.34'	
▼ 7.4		SO	Cross over The Gulch on bridge.
	0.5 ▲	SO	Cross over The Gulch on bridge. Road ascends Long Canyon.
▼ 7.9		SO	The Gulch hiking trail parking on right. Zero trip meter.
	0.0 ▲		Continue up Long Canyon.
		GPS: N 37°51.00' W 111°18.83'	
▼ 0.0			Continue toward Boulder Town.
	9.6 ▲	SO	The Gulch hiking trail parking on left. Zero trip meter.
▼ 0.7		SO	Top of The Gulch. Track on right.
	8.9 ▲	SO	Top of The Gulch. Second entrance to track on left.
▼ 0.8		SO	Second entrance to track on right.
	8.8 ▲	SO	Track on left.
▼ 1.4		SO	Cattle guard.
	8.2 ▲	SO	Cattle guard.
▼ 2.0		SO	Small track on right.
	7.6 ▲	SO	Small track on left.
▼ 2.3		SO	Small track on right.
	7.3 ▲	SO	Small track on left.
▼ 3.6		SO	Deer Creek Campground (fee area) on right, then cross over Deer Creek, followed by hiking trail on left.
	6.0 ▲	SO	Hiking trail on right, then cross over Deer Creek, followed by Deer Creek Campground (fee area) on left.
		GPS: N 37°51.29' W 111°21.28'	
▼ 6.1		SO	Small track on right.
	3.5 ▲	SO	Small track on left.
▼ 7.2		SO	Cattle guard.
	2.4 ▲	SO	Cattle guard.
▼ 7.7		SO	Road on right.
	1.9 ▲	SO	Road on left.
▼ 8.2		SO	Exiting Grand Staircase–Escalante National Monument.
	1.4 ▲	SO	Entering Grand Staircase–Escalante National Monument.
		GPS: N 37°53.49' W 111°24.25'	
▼ 8.8		SO	Boulder Pines Road on right.
	0.8 ▲	SO	Boulder Pines Road on left.
▼ 9.2		SO	Intersection on edge of Boulder Town.
	0.4 ▲	SO	Intersection on edge of Boulder Town. Follow sign for Circle Cliffs and Henry Mountains.
▼ 9.6			Trail ends at Utah 12 at the Burr Trail Trading Post. Information board at corner in Boulder Town.
	0.0 ▲		From Utah 12 at the Burr Trail Trading Post in Boulder Town, zero trip meter and turn east on the paved Burr Trail. Information board at corner.
		GPS: N 37°54.03' W 111°25.42'	

Upper Muley Twist Trail

Starting Point:	**Southwest #40: Burr Trail, 2.9 miles west of Southwest #39: Notom Road**
Finishing Point:	**Trailhead for the Strike Valley Overlook**
Total Mileage:	**2.7 miles**
Unpaved Mileage:	**2.7 miles**
Driving Time:	**45 minutes (one-way)**
Elevation Range:	**5,700–5,900 feet**
Usually Open:	**Year-round**
Difficulty Rating:	**3**
Scenic Rating:	**8**
Remoteness Rating:	**+0**

Special Attractions

- Moderate trail completely within Capitol Reef National Park.
- Strike Valley Overlook viewpoint.

Description

This interesting spur trail is contained within Capitol Reef National Park. It leads off from Southwest #40: Burr Trail, 2.9 miles west of Southwest #39: Notom Road. The start of the

Spectacular Double Arch

trail is signed for Upper Muley Twist. The first 0.4 miles can be used by passenger vehicles down to a small parking lot for the Muley Twist trail. From here, the trail becomes 4WD and enters the narrow, rocky wash. Caution is needed during flash flood seasons.

The next half mile of the trail, the lumpiest, has several large boulders. Drivers should place their wheels carefully. The trail follows along Muley Twist Creek wash, passing under Peek-a-boo Rock. There are several large arches up in the cliff walls, including the large Double Arch near the end of the trail.

The trail finishes at a small parking area, which is the trailhead for the Strike Valley Overlook. The hiking trail is a half-mile round-trip and provides outstanding views of the Waterpocket Fold and surrounding area.

Current Road Information

Capitol Reef National Park
HC-70 Box 15
Torrey, UT 84775
(435) 425-3791

A small cave tucked beneath this rock overhang along the Upper Muley Twist Trail

Map References

BLM   Escalante
USGS 1:24,000 Wagon Box Mesa, Bitter Creek Divide
         1:100,000 Escalante
Maptech CD-ROM: Escalante/Dixie National Forest
Other: Recreation Map of the Henry Mountains Area
       (incomplete)

Route Directions

▼ 0.0		From Southwest #40: Burr Trail, 2.9 miles west of Southwest #39: Notom Road, turn northeast onto signed road for Upper Muley Twist. Zero trip meter.
		GPS: N 37°51.21′ W 111°02.51′
▼ 0.2	SO	Cross through tight small wash.
▼ 0.4	SO	Passenger car parking area for hiking trail. Continue and enter narrow, rocky wash.
▼ 1.1	SO	Trail leaves wash.
▼ 1.2	SO	Trail rejoins wash; wash is wider with rising sandstone folds on either side.
▼ 1.5	SO	Cave under overhang under cliff on right.

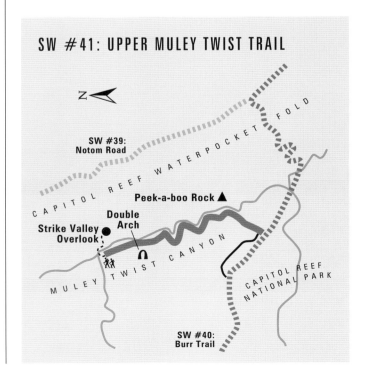

SW #41: UPPER MULEY TWIST TRAIL

		GPS: N 37°52.17' W 111°02.47'
▼ 1.8	SO	Trail re-enters narrows.
▼ 2.1	SO	Large double arch up on left.
		GPS: N 37°52.43' W 111°02.61'
▼ 2.2	SO	Large arch high up at top of cliff on left.
▼ 2.3	SO	Large double arch at top of cliff on left.
▼ 2.7		Trail ends at parking area for Strike Valley Overlook.
		GPS: N 37°52.88' W 111°02.74'

SOUTHWEST REGION TRAIL #42

Wolverine Loop

Starting Point:	**Southwest #40: Burr Trail, 3.6 miles west of Southwest #41: Upper Muley Twist Trail**
Finishing Point:	**Southwest #40: Burr Trail, 20 miles east of Boulder Town**
Total Mileage:	**20.9 miles**
Unpaved Mileage:	**20.9 miles**
Driving Time:	**2 hours**
Elevation Range:	**5,900–6,700 feet**
Usually Open:	**Year-round**
Difficulty Rating:	**3**
Scenic Rating:	**9**
Remoteness Rating:	**+1**

Special Attractions

- Wolverine Petrified Wood Natural Area.
- Slot canyons in Wolverine Canyon.
- Spectacular canyon scenery in the Grand Staircase–Escalante National Monument.

History

President Clinton, issuing a proclamation under the provisions of the Antiquities Act of 1906, established the Grand Staircase–Escalante National Monument on September 18, 1996. From the first, the designation of the national monument has been controversial. It encompasses about 1,870,800 acres of federal land in south-central Utah and is managed by the Bureau of Land Management. Created to protect a vast array of historic sites and natural resources, the monument has been vigorously protested by a variety of interested parties: local ranchers and miners who see their livelihood threatened, recreationalists who see their access restricted, and some people who feel that the creation of a formalized park will increase traffic to the area. The new monument is supported by the Sierra Club and a group called the Southern Utah Wilderness Alliance (SUWA). Opposition to SUWA is strong in the towns surrounding the monument.

Access to 4WD trails in the new monument has been somewhat restricted. Vehicles are required to remain on designated roads, though to date the trails that have been closed are predominantly dead-end trails that see little use. ATV use is

The Wolverine Loop climbs out of the wash along a loose, shaley surface

permitted on designated trails within the monument. It is hoped that responsible users will continue to be able to access trails in this area. A vehicle travel map is available from the BLM office in Escalante.

There has been some vandalism of the petrified wood along this trail. Please help keep access to this area open by not taking samples, especially of the less common crystal grottos in some of the logs.

Description

This loop trail, contained entirely within the Grand Staircase–Escalante National Monument, runs south of the Burr Trail, west of Capitol Reef National Park. For the most part, the route follows a loop trail that has been graded by the BLM. However, at the farthest end of the graded loop, the route breaks away from the graded trail in favor of a smaller ungraded sandy track that follows a small wash and runs briefly along a ridgetop offering excellent views.

The trail leaves from Southwest #40: Burr Trail 3.6 miles west of Southwest #41: Upper Muley Twist Trail at the BLM signpost for the Wolverine Petrified Wood Natural Area. For the first 2 miles it follows the BLM graded route and then turns off onto a rough, unmarked track heading southwest. It follows a small wash, which can be loose and sandy, for a couple of miles. A small section of ridgetop gives great views to the south and southwest toward the Circle Cliffs, Death Hollow, and Bitumen Mesa. A couple of secluded campsites in this section offer wide-ranging views but little shade.

The smaller trail crosses the wash repeatedly before rejoining the graded route 6.5 miles after leaving it. A small wash just before you rejoin the main road can wash out, which may cause longer vehicles to drag their rear bumpers. Drivers who do not wish to tackle this smaller trail may remain on the

Looking down into Wolverine Slot Canyon

Petrified logs along the trail

BLM graded road and continue around the loop.

After rejoining the BLM route, the trail winds down to Wolverine Canyon. After 10.7 miles, you will start to see petrified wood along the trail, even in the rocks thrown up by the grader! The long, sloping bench of rock to the east of the trail hides a secret world that's open to those willing to hike into it. Tributaries of Wolverine Creek have eroded deeply into the earth's surface, forming narrow, twisting slot canyons that are all but invisible from above. They can be difficult to enter, and once inside, you should expect to do a lot of scrambling and sloshing through mud and water. As always, do not enter slot canyons if there is any chance of rain or thunderstorms; there is little chance of escape in a flash flood.

The Wolverine Petrified Wood Natural Area is reached 3 miles after rejoining the main track. A hiking trail leads into the protected area, where you can find many examples of the ancient fossilized wood. Many millions of years ago, these trees were buried under soil, and over time the wood dissolved and was replaced with a silica material. Erosion has uncovered the resulting mineral wood.

From here, the trail climbs gradually to rejoin Southwest #40: Burr Trail. The graded road crosses many creeks, and washouts are common.

Current Road Information

Grand Staircase–Escalante National Monument Office
180 West 300 North
Kanab, UT 84741
(435) 644-4300

BLM Escalante Field Station
PO Box 225
Escalante, UT 84726
(435) 826-5600

Escalante Interagency Office
755 West Main
Escalante, UT 84726
(435) 826-5499

Map References

BLM Escalante
USFS Dixie National Forest: Escalante Ranger District

USGS 1:24,000   Lampstand, Pioneer Mesa, Wagon Box Mesa
      1:100,000 Escalante
Maptech CD-ROM: Escalante/Dixie National Forest
Trails Illustrated, #213
Utah Atlas & Gazetteer, p. 28
Utah Travel Council #5
Other: BLM Map of the Grand Staircase–Escalante National Monument

Route Directions

▼ 0.0			On Southwest #40: Burr Trail, 3.6 miles west of Southwest #41: Upper Muley Twist Trail, turn southeast at BLM sign for Wolverine Petrified Wood Area and zero trip meter.
	1.9 ▲		Trail finishes at Southwest #40: Burr Trail. Turn left for Boulder Town, right for Capitol Reef National Park.
		GPS: N 37°51.93' W 111°06.19'	
▼ 0.8		SO	Cross through wash.
	1.1 ▲	SO	Cross through wash.
▼ 0.9		SO	Cross through wash.
	1.0 ▲	SO	Cross through wash.
▼ 1.0		SO	Cross through wash.
	0.9 ▲	SO	Cross through wash.
▼ 1.8		SO	Cross through Death Hollow wash.
	0.1 ▲	SO	Cross through Death Hollow wash.
▼ 1.9		TR	Turn onto the small ungraded track and zero trip meter.
	0.0 ▲		Continue on main graded track.
		GPS: N 37°50.51' W 111°06.98'	
▼ 0.0			Continue on small track.
	6.5 ▲	TL	Rejoin the main graded route. Zero trip meter.
▼ 0.1		SO	Pass through wire gate, then cross through wash.
	6.4 ▲	SO	Cross through wash, then pass through wire gate.
▼ 0.2		SO	Enter wash.
	6.3 ▲	SO	Exit wash.
▼ 0.6		SO	Exit wash on right.
	5.9 ▲	SO	Enter wash.
		GPS: N 37°50.26' W 111°07.46'	
▼ 0.9		SO	Old dam on left, then cross through wash.
	5.6 ▲	SO	Cross through wash, then old dam on right.
▼ 1.2		SO	Track on right.
	5.3 ▲	SO	Track on left.
▼ 1.6		SO	Cross through wash.
	4.9 ▲	SO	Cross through wash.
▼ 1.8		SO	Cross through wash.
	4.7 ▲	SO	Cross through wash.
▼ 1.9		SO	Faint track on right.
	4.6 ▲	SO	Faint track on left.
▼ 2.0		SO	Trail crests rise; excellent views of Circle Cliffs and Death Hollow.
	4.5 ▲	SO	Trail crests rise; excellent views of Circle Cliffs and Death Hollow.
▼ 3.4		SO	Enter wash.
	3.1 ▲	SO	Exit wash.
▼ 4.0		BR	Leave wash up loose shale rise.
	2.5 ▲	BL	Descend loose shale to enter wash.
▼ 4.5		SO	Old track on right to old mine on mesa, then cross through wash.
	2.0 ▲	BR	Cross through wash, then old track on left to old mine on mesa.
		GPS: N 37°48.93' W 111°10.10'	

SW #42: WOLVERINE LOOP

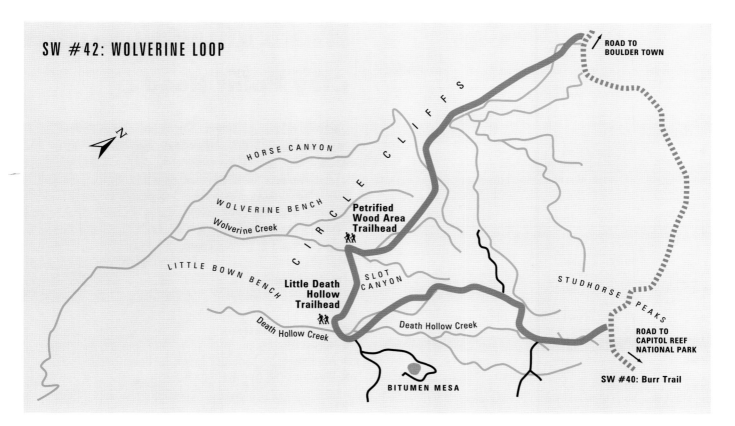

▼ 4.7		SO	Cross through wash.
	1.8 ▲	SO	Cross through wash.
▼ 5.0		SO	Cross through wash.
	1.5 ▲	SO	Cross through wash.
▼ 5.2		SO	Cross through wash.
	1.3 ▲	SO	Cross through wash.
▼ 5.6		SO	Track on left to dam.
	0.9 ▲	SO	Track on right to dam.
GPS: N 37°47.94′ W 111°10.26′			
▼ 6.1		SO	Cross through slightly washed out wash.
	0.4 ▲	SO	Cross through slightly washed out wash.
▼ 6.3		SO	Old dam on left.
	0.2 ▲	SO	Old dam on right.
▼ 6.4		SO	Slightly washed out wash crossing; longer vehicles should exercise care.
	0.1 ▲	SO	Slightly washed out wash crossing; longer vehicles should exercise care.
▼ 6.5		TR	T-intersection, rejoin BLM graded track and zero trip meter.
	0.0 ▲		Continue northeast.
GPS: N 37°47.26′ W 111°10.25′			
▼ 0.0			Continue along graded track.
	3.0 ▲	TL	Turn left onto unsigned small sandy trail.
▼ 0.3		SO	Track on left to campsite.
	2.7 ▲	SO	Track on right to campsite.
▼ 0.5		SO	Cross through sandy wash, then track on left goes past corral to Little Death Hollow hiking trail. Cross second wash. Little Bown Bench is directly ahead.
	2.5 ▲	SO	Cross through sandy wash, then track on right goes past corral to Little Death Hollow hiking trail. Cross second sandy wash. Little Bown Bench is directly behind.
GPS: N 37°47.06′ W 111°10.78′			

▼ 0.7		SO	Cross through wash.
	2.3 ▲	SO	Cross through wash.
▼ 1.2		SO	Track on left.
	1.8 ▲	SO	Track on right.
▼ 1.4		SO	Track on right.
	1.6 ▲	SO	Track on left.
▼ 1.5		SO	Cross through wash.
	1.5 ▲	SO	Cross through wash.
▼ 2.0		SO	Cross though wash, followed by track on left.
	1.0 ▲	SO	Track on right, then cross through wash.
▼ 2.3		SO	Large piece of petrified wood on right and other chunks scattered over the slab. Walk past large piece to look down into the slot canyons, tributaries of Wolverine Creek.
	0.7 ▲	SO	Large piece of petrified wood on left and other chunks scattered over the slab. Walk past large piece to look down into the slot canyons, tributaries of Wolverine Creek.
GPS: N 37°48.17′ W 111°11.65′			
▼ 2.4		SO	Track on left.
	0.6 ▲	SO	Track on right.
▼ 2.5		SO	Track on left, then cross through wash. Access slot canyon by scrambling down on foot following the wash to the right.
	0.5 ▲	SO	Cross through wash, followed by track on right. Access slot canyon by scrambling down on foot following the wash to the left.
▼ 3.0		TR	Track on left to Wolverine hiking trail and the major petrified wood area. Zero trip meter.
	0.0 ▲		Leave Wolverine Creek.
GPS: N 37°48.27′ W 111°12.31′			
▼ 0.0			Continue north along Wolverine Creek. Entrance to slot canyon on right. The wash can be loose and sandy.
	9.5 ▲	TL	Track on right to Wolverine hiking trail and the

			major petrified wood area. Entrance to slot canyon on the left. Zero trip meter.
▼ 0.5		SO	Leave wash.
	9.0 ▲	SO	Enter Wolverine Creek. The wash can be loose and sandy.
▼ 0.6		SO	Cross through wash.
	8.9 ▲	SO	Cross through wash.
▼ 0.8		SO	Cross through wash twice.
	8.7 ▲	SO	Cross through wash twice.
▼ 0.9		SO	Cross through wash.
	8.6 ▲	SO	Cross through wash.
▼ 1.3		SO	Cross through small, tight wash.
	8.2 ▲	SO	Cross through small, tight wash.
▼ 1.4		SO	Cross through small, tight wash.
	8.1 ▲	SO	Cross through small, tight wash.
▼ 1.8		SO	Cross through small, tight wash.
	7.7 ▲	SO	Cross through small, tight wash.
▼ 3.6		SO	Enter wash.
	5.9 ▲	SO	Leave wash.
▼ 3.7		SO	Cattle guard.
	5.8 ▲	SO	Cattle guard.
▼ 3.8		SO	Old mine remains up cliff on right.
	5.7 ▲	SO	Old mine remains up cliff on left.

GPS: N 37°50.93' W 111°12.94'

▼ 3.9		SO	Leave wash.
	5.6 ▲	SO	Enter wash.
▼ 4.0		SO	Enter wash.
	5.5 ▲	SO	Leave wash.
▼ 4.3		BR	Track swings right into larger wash.
	5.2 ▲	BL	Track swings left into smaller wash.

GPS: N 37°51.06' W 111°13.36'

▼ 4.5		SO	Track on left at fork in wash. There are multiple small splits in the wash for the next mile depending on the current washouts and the graded route. Select the best line.
	5.0 ▲	BL	Track on right at fork in wash.
▼ 5.5		SO	Exit wash.
	4.0 ▲	SO	Trail enters wash. There are multiple small splits in the wash for the next mile depending on the current washouts and the graded route. Select the best line.
▼ 6.8		SO	Track on left, then cross through small creek.
	2.7 ▲	SO	Cross through small creek, then track on right.
▼ 8.1		SO	Track on left is old mining track.
	1.4 ▲	SO	Track on right is old mining track.
▼ 8.4		SO	Track on left.
	1.1 ▲	SO	Track on right.
▼ 8.9		SO	Cross through small wash.
	0.6 ▲	SO	Cross through small wash.
▼ 9.0		SO	Cross through small wash.
	0.5 ▲	SO	Cross through small wash.
▼ 9.1		SO	Cross through small wash.
	0.4 ▲	SO	Cross through small wash.
▼ 9.2		SO	Cross through small wash.
	0.3 ▲	SO	Cross through small wash.
▼ 9.4		SO	Campsite area on right.
	0.1 ▲	SO	Campsite area on left.
▼ 9.5			Cross through wash, then trail ends at Southwest #40: Burr Trail. Turn right for Capitol Reef National Park, turn left for Boulder Town.
	0.0 ▲		On Southwest #40: Burr Trail, 20 miles east of Boulder Town, turn south at the BLM sign and zero trip meter.

GPS: N 37°55.46' W 111°13.18'

Clay Point Road

Starting Point:	Utah 276, 10 miles north of Ticaboo
Finishing Point:	Southwest #40: Burr Trail, 18.4 miles from Utah 276
Total Mileage:	24.9 miles
Unpaved Mileage:	24.9 miles
Driving Time:	1.5 hours
Elevation Range:	4,200–6,300 feet
Usually Open:	Year-round
Difficulty Rating:	2
Scenic Rating:	7
Remoteness Rating:	+0

Special Attractions

- Varied desert scenery.
- Alternative backcountry leg of the Burr Trail.
- Historic Starr Springs Ranch.

History

The Starr Ranch, which today is a National Forest Service recreation area, dates back to the 1880s. The ranch was owned by Al Starr, who eked out a living raising cattle. When miners started coming into the area to work the mines at Bromide Basin, Starr diversified and sold mules and horses to the miners.

He hired Franz Weber of Hanksville to build him a stone house and cellar, which you can see today just before the entrance to the campground. Franz Weber was an accomplished stone mason, who was responsible for several ranch buildings in the region as well as the stone church at Hanksville. However, before the house at Starr Ranch was finished, the mining operations at Bromide Basin wound down. Al Starr's livelihood disappeared, and Franz Weber had to stop working at

View along a small wash to the distant Dials Knob

Starr Ranch. The house was never finished and was abandoned. The stone cellar was completed; it is behind the house, built into the hillside.

Description

This trail provides an interesting alternative route to starting Southwest #40: Burr Trail on a paved road. The trail leaves Utah 276, 10 miles north of Ticaboo at the sign for the Starr Springs Recreation Area (fee required). The road is good graded gravel to the recreation site, which is at the start of the historic Starr Ranch. Camping and picnic areas are set in some shade, and you can view the remains of the stone cabin on the ranch.

A butte rises high above an old corral at the start of Coal Bed Mesa

From Starr Springs, the road becomes graded dirt and crosses the Copper Creek Benches. As it wraps around the base of Mount Hillers, the road surface has a higher rock content, but then it becomes clay as it heads toward Coal Bed Mesa. This section is fine for a passenger car, although after rain it is likely to be impassable. You pass connections to Southwest #45: Stanton Pass Trail and Southwest #44: Shootering Canyon Trail.

The route passes Coal Bed Mesa on the right as it wraps down to cross Hansen Creek in a deep V. The desert scenery is a mixture of steep-sided buttes and mesas to the north and gently sloping benches dropping to the south.

As the route descends toward Clay Point, it passes through badlands scenery composed of very soft blue shale. Water runoff has eroded the sides of the buttes into deep channels. The trail crosses through Saleratus Wash and Bullfrog Wash before finishing at Southwest #40: Burr Trail.

Current Road Information

BLM Henry Mountain Field Station
406 South 100 West
Hanksville, UT 84734
(435) 542-3461

Map References

BLM Hite Crossing
USGS 1:24,000 Copper Creek Benches, Ant Knoll, Clay
Point, The Post
1:100,000 Hite Crossing
Maptech CD-ROM: Moab/Canyonlands
Trails Illustrated, #213
Utah Atlas & Gazetteer, pp. 20, 21, 29
Utah Travel Council #5
Other: Recreation Map of the Henry Mountains Area

Route Directions

▼ 0.0			On Utah 276, 10 miles north of Ticaboo, turn northwest on Clay Point Road at the sign for Starr Springs Recreation Area and zero trip meter.
	3.1 ▲	SO	Trail ends at Utah 276. Turn left for Hanksville, right for Ticaboo.
		GPS: N 37°48.61' W 110°37.77'	
▼ 0.5		SO	Track on right.
	2.6 ▲	SO	Track on left.
▼ 1.9		SO	Track on left.
	1.2 ▲	SO	Track on right.
▼ 2.4		SO	Track on right.

	0.7 ▲	SO	Track on left.
▼ 3.1		SO	Track on right to Starr Springs Recreation Area (fee area), a National Forest Service campground and picnic area. Zero trip meter.
	0.0 ▲		Continue toward highway.
		GPS: N 37°50.73' W 110°39.56'	
▼ 0.0			Continue west.
	1.8 ▲	SO	Track on left to Starr Springs Recreation Area (fee area), a National Forest Service campground and picnic area. Zero trip meter.
▼ 0.1		SO	Track on left to cattletank.
	1.7 ▲	SO	Track on right to cattletank.
▼ 0.7		SO	Track on left.
	1.1 ▲	SO	Track on right.
▼ 1.0		SO	Track on left, then track on right.
	0.8 ▲	SO	Track on left, then track on right.
▼ 1.8		SO	Track on right is Southwest #45: Stanton Pass Trail. Zero trip meter.
	0.0 ▲		Continue east toward Starr Springs.
		GPS: N 37°50.35' W 110°41.30'	
▼ 0.0			Continue west.
	4.6 ▲	SO	Track on left is Southwest #45: Stanton Pass Trail. Zero trip meter.
▼ 2.3		SO	Track on left is Southwest #44: Shootering Canyon Trail.
	2.3 ▲	SO	Track on right is Southwest #44: Shootering Canyon Trail.
		GPS: N 37°48.88' W 110°43.12'	
▼ 2.4		SO	Track on right.
	2.2 ▲	SO	Track on left.
▼ 2.8		SO	Track on right to corral.
	1.8 ▲	SO	Track on left to corral.
▼ 4.3		SO	Cross through Copper Creek Wash, followed by small tracks on left and right.
	0.3 ▲	SO	Small tracks on left and right, then cross through Copper Creek Wash.
▼ 4.6		SO	Cross through Hansen Creek, followed by track on left to Shootering Canyon. Zero trip meter.
	0.0 ▲		Continue east.
		GPS: N 37°47.08' W 110°44.30'	
▼ 0.0			Continue west.
	5.5 ▲	SO	Track on right to Shootering Canyon, then cross through Hansen Creek. Zero trip meter.
▼ 0.4		SO	Cross through wash.
	5.1 ▲	SO	Cross through wash.
▼ 1.9		SO	Track on left.
	3.6 ▲	SO	Track on right.
▼ 2.3		SO	Cattle guard.
	3.2 ▲	SO	Cattle guard.
▼ 3.1		SO	Cross through wash.
	2.4 ▲	SO	Cross through wash.
▼ 3.4		SO	Track on right.
	2.1 ▲	SO	Track on left.
▼ 3.5		SO	Cross through wash.
	2.0 ▲	SO	Cross through wash.
▼ 4.1		SO	Cross through wash. Dials Knob on right.
	1.4 ▲	SO	Cross through wash. Dials Knob on left.
▼ 4.3		SO	Cross through wash.
	1.2 ▲	SO	Cross through wash.
▼ 4.8		SO	Track on left.
	0.7 ▲	SO	Track on right.
▼ 5.5		SO	Clay Point Road on left. Zero trip meter.
	0.0 ▲		Continue southeast.
		GPS: N 37°43.49' W 110°46.85'	

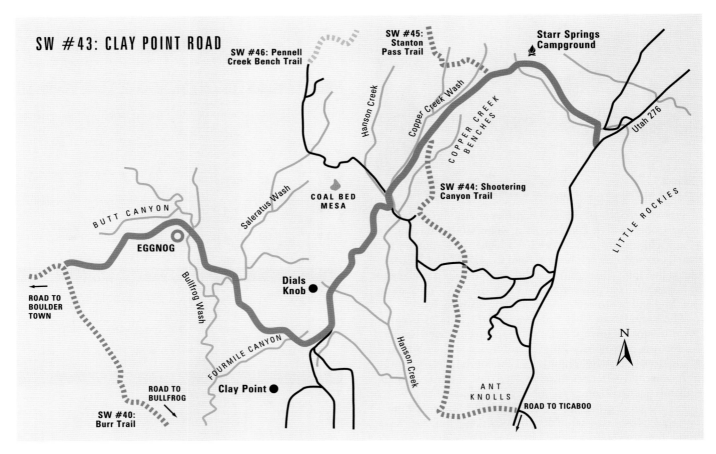

SW #43: CLAY POINT ROAD

SW #46: Pennell Creek Bench Trail

SW #45: Stanton Pass Trail

Starr Springs Campground

Hanson Creek

Copper Creek Wash

COPPER CREEK BENCHES

Utah 276

BUTT CANYON

Saleratus Wash

COAL BED MESA

SW #44: Shootering Canyon Trail

LITTLE ROCKIES

EGGNOG

Bullfrog Wash

Dials Knob

ROAD TO BOULDER TOWN

FOURMILE CANYON

Hanson Creek

N

ROAD TO BULLFROG

Clay Point

ANT KNOLLS

ROAD TO TICABOO

SW #40: Burr Trail

▼ 0.0			Continue northwest.
	5.9 ▲	SO	Clay Point Road on right. Zero trip meter.
▼ 0.8		SO	Cross through wash at head of Fourmile Canyon.
	5.1 ▲	SO	Cross through wash at head of Fourmile Canyon.
▼ 3.4		SO	Descend to cross through Saleratus Wash.
	2.5 ▲	SO	Descend to cross through Saleratus Wash.
▼ 5.7		TL	T-intersection. Swing sharply left. Track on right crosses through Bullfrog Wash and continues to the north.
	0.2 ▲	BR	Swing sharply away from Bullfrog Wash. Track ahead crosses through Bullfrog Wash again and continues to the north.
▼ 5.8		SO	Cross through Bullfrog Wash.
	0.1 ▲	SO	Cross through Bullfrog Wash.
▼ 5.9		BR	Track on left to Eggnog. Zero trip meter.
	0.0 ▲		Continue along main route.

GPS: N 37°46.37′ W 110°50.69′

▼ 0.0			Continue toward the Burr Trail.
	4.0 ▲	SO	Track on right to Eggnog. Zero trip meter.
▼ 0.1		SO	Track on right to corral in small canyon.
	3.9 ▲	SO	Track on left to corral in small canyon.
▼ 0.7		SO	Cattle guard.
	3.3 ▲	SO	Cattle guard.
▼ 1.6		SO	Track on left.
	2.4 ▲	SO	Track on right.
▼ 3.0		SO	Track on left on right-hand bend.
	1.0 ▲	SO	Track on right on left-hand bend.
▼ 3.5		SO	Track on left.
	0.5 ▲	SO	Track on right.

▼ 4.0			Trail finishes at Southwest #40: Burr Trail. Turn left for Bullfrog, right to continue along Burr Trail to Boulder Town.
	0.0 ▲		On Southwest #40: Burr Trail, 18.4 miles from Utah 276, zero trip meter and turn east toward Starr Spring.

GPS: N 37°45.58′ W 110°54.42′

Shootering Canyon Trail

Starting Point:	**Utah 276, 1.7 miles north of Ticaboo Gas Station**
Finishing Point:	**Southwest #43: Clay Point Road, 7.2 miles west of Utah 276**
Total Mileage:	**12.3 miles**
Unpaved Mileage:	**12.3 miles**
Driving Time:	**1.5 hours**
Elevation Range:	**4,200–5,200 feet**
Usually Open:	**Year-round**
Difficulty Rating:	**3**
Scenic Rating:	**8**
Remoteness Rating:	**+1**

Special Attractions

■ Tony M Mine and uranium mining relics.
■ Driving through a very narrow canyon.
■ Loose sandy track with many dry wash crossings.

History

Shootering Canyon has a long and colorful history, starting with early ranching days and continuing to its present-day mining operations. You may notice that the name of this canyon changes depending on who you talk to and which maps you read. It seems the original name, the one printed on the USGS maps, is Shitamaring Canyon. The local explanation for this name, one that has a "ring" of truth surrounding it, is that the water in the canyon has a laxative effect. The immediate results of this water on the cattle in the narrow, echoing canyon supplied the name!

The mill, however, goes by the name "Shootaring," while the BLM prefer the designation "Shootering." Whatever you call it, it's still the same canyon.

The mine in the canyon is recent compared to most uranium mines in the area. The construction of Shootaring Mill by Plateau Resources Limited was completed in 1979. Its purpose was to concentrate the ore for easier shipment. Ticaboo was established at that time as the company town. After three years of construction, the mill ran for only three months before being shut down. The price of uranium had dropped to

Shitamaring wash crossing

the point where it was uneconomical to produce. For 20 years, a skeleton crew has remained at the mine, waiting for the price of uranium to rise, and currently it is working toward opening the mine for production some time in 2000.

The mine in the canyon was originally called the Lucky Strike; today it goes by the name Tony M Mine.

Description

The trail leaves west from Utah 276 at an unmarked turn 1.7 miles north of Ticaboo Gas Station. After 0.8 miles, you can see the distinctive conical Ant Knolls to the north, and a little farther on, the Shootaring Uranium Mill stands out below the bluff. Passing by a corral, the trail descends to join the Shitamaring Creek wash. Both the descent and the trail along the wash can be very loose and sandy. You will need a 4WD and may need to deflate your tires slight-

An open uranium adit sits at the foot of a canyon wall

ly for better flotation in the deeper sand sections.

After 4.6 miles, the trail joins the graded gravel road that follows Lost Spring Wash. This good road does not last long, however; after passing the Tony M Mine 2.3 miles later, the standard drops again.

There are many uranium adits visible in the cliff faces on either side of the trail, plus piles of tailings and mining machinery. Care is needed around the workings.

The trail then enters the extremely narrow Shootering Canyon. There is just enough room for a vehicle to squeeze through between the towering rocky walls. After a mile, the trail leaves the canyon and climbs up to cross the Copper Creek Benches, finally joining Southwest #43: Clay Point Road. From here, turn left to head toward Southwest #40: Burr Trail or turn right to return to Utah 276.

Current Road Information

BLM Henry Mountain Field Station
406 South 100 West
Hanksville, UT 84734
(435) 542-3461

Map References

BLM Hite Crossing
USGS 1:24,000 Lost Spring, Copper Creek Benches
1:100,000 Hite Crossing
Maptech CD-ROM: Moab/Canyonlands
Trails Illustrated, #213 (incomplete)
Utah Atlas & Gazetteer, p. 28
Utah Travel Council #5
Other: Recreation Map of the Henry Mountains Area

Route Directions

▼ 0.0		On Utah 276, 1.7 miles north of Ticaboo Gas Station, turn west onto unmarked dirt track and zero trip meter.
	2.6 ▲	Trail ends at Utah 276, 1.7 miles north of Ticaboo. Turn right for Bullfrog Marina, left for Hanksville.
		GPS: N 37°41.65' W 110°40.36'
▼ 0.2	SO	Cross through small wash.
	2.4 ▲	SO Cross through small wash.
▼ 0.8	SO	The Ant Knolls, large conical domes, on right.
	1.8 ▲	SO The Ant Knolls, large conical domes, on left.
▼ 1.4	SO	Track on left. Shootaring Uranium Mill is visible on right.

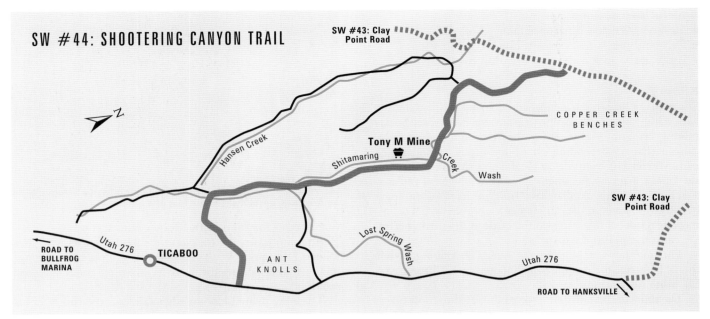

1.2 ▲	SO	Track on right. Shootaring Uranium Mill is visible on left.	
▼ 1.6	SO	Track on right at corral.	
1.0 ▲	SO	Track on left at corral.	

GPS: N 37°41.65' W 110°41.87'

▼ 1.7	SO	Track on right is second entrance to corral, followed by track on left. Trail descends to Shitamaring Creek wash.
0.9 ▲	SO	Track on right, followed by track on left to corral.
▼ 2.6	SO	Track on left to Hansen Creek. Zero trip meter.
0.0 ▲		Trail climbs out of Shitamaring Creek wash.

GPS: N 37°41.76' W 110°42.75'

▼ 0.0		Continue along Shitamaring Creek wash.
2.0 ▲	SO	Track on right to Hansen Creek. Zero trip meter.
▼ 0.1	SO	Cattle guard. Trail crosses though Shitamaring Creek wash nine times in the next 1.9 miles.
1.9 ▲	SO	Cattle guard.
▼ 2.0	SO	Join graded gravel road and zero trip meter.
0.0 ▲		Continue along sandy track. Trail crosses Shitamaring Creek wash nine times in the next 1.9 miles.

GPS: N 37°43.48' W 110°42.45'

▼ 0.0		Continue along gravel road.
4.1 ▲	BR	Turn onto small, unmarked sandy track and zero trip meter.
▼ 2.1	SO	Row of uranium adits halfway up cliff face on left.
2.0 ▲	SO	Row of uranium adits halfway up cliff face on right.
▼ 2.3	SO	Entrance to Tony M Mine on left.
1.8 ▲	SO	Entrance to Tony M Mine on right.

GPS: N 37°45.33' W 110°42.12'

▼ 2.5	SO	Cross over Shitamaring Creek wash on bridge, then pass through area of old mining activity, tailings piles, old machinery, and large mine adits in the cliff walls on both sides.
1.6 ▲	SO	Pass through area of old mining activity, tailings piles, old machinery, and large mine adits in the cliff walls on both sides, then cross over Shitamaring Creek wash on bridge.

▼ 2.8	SO	Cross through wash three times in the next 0.2 miles.
1.3 ▲	SO	Cross through wash a few times.
▼ 3.1	SO	Enter wash.
1.0 ▲	SO	Leave wash, then cross through wash three times in the next 0.2 miles.
▼ 3.2	BL	Faint track goes up Shitamaring Creek bed on right. Continue in main canyon and enter narrow part of canyon.
0.9 ▲	BR	Faint track goes up Shitamaring Creek bed on left. Continue in main canyon, narrow section ends.

GPS: N 37°45.89' W 110°42.10'

▼ 4.0	SO	Track climbs out of wash.
0.1 ▲	SO	Track descends into wash. Canyon becomes very narrow.

GPS: N 37°46.35' W 110°42.59'

▼ 4.1	TR	Unsigned T-intersection. Zero trip meter.
0.0 ▲		Continue down toward canyon.

GPS: N 37°46.36' W 110°42.62'

▼ 0.0		Continue northeast.
3.6 ▲	TL	Turn left on unsigned track and zero trip meter.
▼ 0.1	SO	Cross through wash, then track on right.
3.5 ▲	SO	Track on left, then cross through wash.
▼ 0.4	SO	Cross through wash.
3.2 ▲	SO	Cross through wash.
▼ 0.5	SO	Cross through wash.
3.1 ▲	SO	Cross through wash.
▼ 0.6	SO	Cross through wash. Mount Hillers is visible to the north.
3.0 ▲	SO	Cross through wash. Mount Hillers is visible to the north.
▼ 0.7	SO	Cross through wash.
2.9 ▲	SO	Cross through wash.
▼ 0.9	SO	Faint track on left. Trail rises up to Copper Creek Benches.
2.7 ▲	SO	Faint track on right.
▼ 1.2	BR	Fork.
2.4 ▲	SO	Track on right.

GPS: N 37°46.98' W 110°43.55'

▼ 2.2	SO	Track on right.

1.4 ▲	SO	Track on left.	
▼ 2.8	SO	Cross through wash.	
0.8 ▲	SO	Cross through wash.	
▼ 3.4	SO	Cross through wash.	
0.2 ▲	SO	Cross through wash.	
▼ 3.6		Trail ends at Southwest #43: Clay Point Road. Turn right for Utah 276, left to continue along Clay Point Road.	
0.0 ▲		On Southwest #43: Clay Point Road, 7.2 miles west of Utah 276, turn south at sign for Shooetring Canyon and zero trip meter.	

GPS: N 37°48.89' W 110°43.12'

SOUTHWEST REGION TRAIL #45

Stanton Pass Trail

Starting Point:	**Southwest #47: Bull Creek Pass Trail,**
	6 miles west of Utah 276
Finishing Point:	**Southwest #43: Clay Point Road,**
	4.9 miles from Utah 276
Total Mileage:	**14.3 miles**
Unpaved Mileage:	**14.3 miles**
Driving Time:	**2 hours**
Elevation Range:	**5,300–7,470 feet**
Usually Open:	**June to November**
Difficulty Rating:	**2**
Scenic Rating:	**8**
Remoteness Rating:	**+1**

Special Attractions

- Scenic pass with a range of backcountry scenery.
- Links two major 4WD roads, Southwest #47: Bull Creek Pass Trail and Southwest #43: Clay Point Road.

Description

This very pretty route links Southwest #47: Bull Creek Pass Trail in the north to Southwest #43: Clay Point Road in the south. It leaves Bull Creek Pass Trail 2.7 miles west of Trachyte Ranch and heads generally southwest, gradually ascending the benches alongside Benson Creek. There are panoramic views of Mount Hillers, Big Ridge, and the conical Cass Creek Peak to the southwest, of Mount Pennell to the west, and of Mount Ellen to the northwest.

Big Ridge stands off in the distance beyond an old corral

After 4 miles, the trail passes Quaking Aspen Spring on the right, which is fenced to prevent cattle from damaging the source; but you can see the spring trickling from under a rock ledge. A popular campsite is set under large oaks near the spring, a short way down a small track.

After 5 miles, the trail crests Stanton Pass, passing between Cass Creek Peak and Bulldog Peak, and then descends toward Clay Point Road. The descent through juniper vegetation is rough, but the graded trail should pose no difficulties to a high-clearance vehicle in dry weather. Good tires are an advantage; the rocks can be very sharp and can easily puncture a sidewall.

View of No Mans Mesa from the Stanton Pass Trail

After 9 miles, the trail winds across the top of Cow Flat, a long dry valley that marks the vegetation change from juniper and small pine to the sagebrush of the lower elevations. Southwest #46: Pennell Creek Bench Trail leads off from here.

The trail climbs briefly to run around the south flank of Mount Hillers, dominated by red rocky fins. On a clear day, you can see Lake Powell to the south as you descend through Copper Creek near the end of the trail, and you can always see the Little Rockies range, the southernmost peaks of the Henry Mountains: Mount Holmes and the higher Mount Ellsworth south of it, separated by Freds Ridge. This part of the trail is particularly lovely in early evening, as the light catches the Little Rockies and paints them red-purple.

The trail finishes on Southwest #43: Clay Point Road, 4.9 miles from its junction with Utah 276.

Current Road Information

BLM Henry Mountain Field Station
406 South 100 West
Hanksville, UT 84734
(435) 542-3461

Map References

BLM Hanksville, Hite Crossing
USGS 1:24,000 Cass Creek Peak, Copper Creek Benches, Ant Knoll
1:100,000 Hanksville, Hite Crossing
Maptech CD-ROM: Moab/Canyonlands
Trails Illustrated, #213
Utah Atlas & Gazetteer, pp. 28, 29
Utah Travel Council #5
Other: Recreation Map of the Henry Mountains Area

Route Directions

▼ 0.0		On Southwest #47: Bull Creek Pass Trail, 6 miles from Utah 276, zero trip meter and turn west toward Quaking Aspen Spring.
6.0 ▲		Trail finishes on Southwest #47: Bull Creek Pass Trail. Turn right to join Utah 276; turn left to return to Henry Mountains.

SW #45: STANTON PASS TRAIL

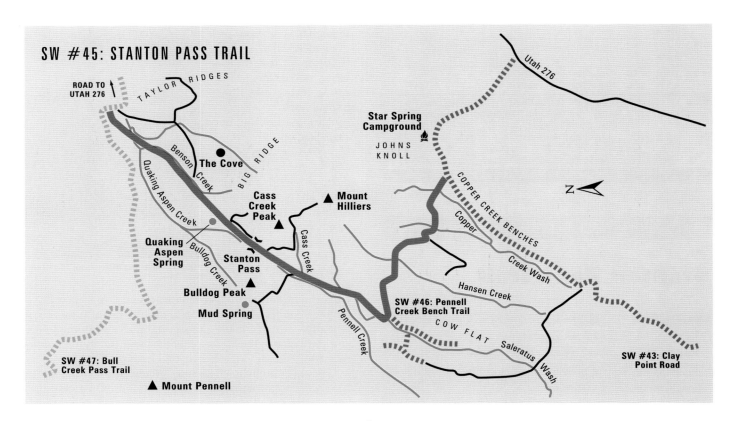

		GPS: N 37°57.88' W 110°39.61'	
▼ 0.1		SO	Second entrance from Bull Creek Pass Trail on right.
	5.9 ▲	SO	First exit to Bull Creek Pass Trail on left.
▼ 0.3		SO	Cross through creek. Track starts to climb.
	5.7 ▲	SO	End of descent from pass. Cross through creek.
▼ 1.0		SO	Old corral on left. Views ahead to Mount Hillers, Big Ridge, Cass Creek Peak, and Mount Pennell.
	5.0 ▲	SO	Old corral on right. Views back to Mount Hillers, Big Ridge, Cass Creek Peak, and Mount Pennell.
		GPS: N 37°57.25' W 110°40.20'	
▼ 1.7		SO	Cattle guard.
	4.3 ▲	SO	Cattle guard.
▼ 2.6		SO	Track on left.
	3.4 ▲	SO	Track on right.
		GPS: N 37°56.25' W 110°41.46'	
▼ 3.2		SO	Track on right.
	2.8 ▲	SO	Track on left.
▼ 3.9		SO	Track on left.
	2.1 ▲	SO	Track on right.
▼ 4.0		SO	Track on right to campsite under large oaks. Quaking Aspen Spring on right.
	2.0 ▲	SO	Quaking Aspen Spring on left, followed by track on left to campsite under large oaks.
		GPS: N 37°55.45' W 110°42.43'	
▼ 4.5		SO	Track on left.
	1.5 ▲	SO	Track on right.
▼ 4.8		SO	Old track on left.
	1.2 ▲	SO	Old track on right.
▼ 5.1		SO	Stanton Pass (7,470 feet). Bulldog Peak on the right, Cass Creek Peak on the left. Track descends.

	0.9 ▲	SO	Stanton Pass (7,470 feet). Bulldog Peak on the left, Cass Creek Peak on the right. Track descends.
		GPS: N 37°54.77' W 110°43.41'	
▼ 5.8		SO	Track on left.
	0.2 ▲	SO	Track on right.
▼ 6.0		SO	Track on right to Mud Spring and Southwest #47: Bull Creek Pass Trail. Zero trip meter.
	0.0 ▲		Continue climbing Stanton Pass.
		GPS: N 37°54.04' W 110°43.81'	
▼ 0.0			Continue descent from Stanton Pass.
	2.8 ▲	SO	Track on left to Mud Spring and the Horn. Zero trip meter.
▼ 0.8		SO	Track on left.
	2.0 ▲	SO	Track on right.
▼ 0.9		SO	Small dam on right.
	1.9 ▲	SO	Small dam on left.
▼ 2.5		SO	Cattle guard.
	0.3 ▲	SO	Cattle guard.
▼ 2.8		TL	Track on right is Southwest #46: Pennell Creek Bench Trail. Zero trip meter, then cross through Saleratus Wash.
	0.0 ▲		Continue toward Stanton Pass.
		GPS: N 37°51.99' W 110°45.25'	
▼ 0.0			Continue east.
	5.5 ▲	TR	Cross through Saleratus Wash, then track on left is Southwest #46: Pennell Creek Bench Trail. Zero trip meter.
▼ 0.7		SO	Track on right.
	4.8 ▲	BR	Track on left.
▼ 1.3		SO	Track on right.
	4.2 ▲	SO	Track on left.
▼ 2.3		SO	Views southeast over Mount Holmes, Freds Ridge, and Mount Ellsworth, and views south to Lake Powell and Waterpocket Fold.
	3.2 ▲	SO	Views southeast over Mount Holmes, Freds

Ridge, and Mount Ellsworth, and views south to Lake Powell and Waterpocket Fold.

▼ 3.1	SO	Track on right, followed by cattle guard.
2.4 ▲	SO	Cattle guard, followed by track on left.
▼ 4.5	SO	Track on left, then cross through Copper Creek Wash, followed by old stone ruin on left and campsite on right.
1.0 ▲	SO	Old stone ruin on right and campsite on left, cross through Copper Creek Wash, then track on right.
GPS: N 37°50.85′ W 110°42.00′		
▼ 4.8	SO	Track on left.
0.7 ▲	SO	Track on right.
▼ 5.5		Trail ends on Copper Creek Benches at Southwest #43: Clay Point Road. Turn right to continue along Clay Point Road, left to Utah 276.
0.0 ▲		On Southwest #43: Clay Point Road, 4.9 miles from Utah 276, zero trip meter and follow sign to Stanton Pass and the Horn.
GPS: N 37°50.35′ W 110°41.32′		

SOUTHWEST REGION TRAIL #46

Pennell Creek Bench Trail

Starting Point:	**Southwest #45: Stanton Pass Trail, 5.5 miles from southern end of trail**
Finishing Point:	**End of Pennell Creek Bench/Cow Flat**
Total Mileage:	**5.2 miles (all three legs)**
Unpaved Mileage:	**5.2 miles**
Driving Time:	**1.5 hours (all three legs)**
Elevation Range:	**5,700–5,800 feet**
Usually Open:	**April to December**
Difficulty Rating:	**3**
Scenic Rating:	**8**
Remoteness Rating:	**+2**

Special Attractions

■ Very remote, little-traveled spur tracks.
■ Stunning views over No Mans Mesa and Glen Canyon National Recreation Area.

Description

This short spur trail consists of three legs, each leading to a different viewpoint, and can be done in conjunction with Southwest #45: Stanton Pass Trail.

The trail starts 5.5 miles from the south end of Stanton Pass Trail, immediately west of Saleratus Wash. Turn south and follow the rough wheel tracks. There are no signs along the route, and tracks can be faint, so navigation can be very tricky. After 0.8 miles, fork right and cross through Saleratus Wash. This is normally dry, but can wash out quite badly, so care is needed on the crossing. Watch for other wheel tracks and pick your line carefully; there may be more than one option.

After the wash, there is a short climb onto Pennell Creek Bench, which is narrow and can have deep washouts. Once on

View of No Mans Mesa, Castle Rock, and the Pennell Creek Roughs from the overlook at the end of the trail's second leg

top of the bench, the trail winds through juniper bushes, passing the turn to the west leg and continuing south. It dead-ends at 2.5 miles with a panoramic view to the south and west over the Glen Canyon area, Waterpocket Fold, and back over the bench to the Henry Mountains.

Though the trail continues from this point, descending to cross the wash, at the time of research the climb up the far side had deep washouts and was beyond the scope of this book.

The west leg goes a short way to the edge of the Bench and gives unparalleled views over No Mans Mesa and the Pennell Creek Roughs badlands far below.

The third leg is the least dramatic of the three and continues down onto Cow Flat, past a fenced spring to stop at a rise.

Current Road Information

BLM Henry Mountain Field Station
406 South 100 West
Hanksville, UT 84734
(435) 542-3461

Map References

BLM   Hite Crossing (incomplete)
USGS   1:24,000   Ant Knoll
           1:100,000 Hite Crossing (incomplete)
Maptech CD-ROM: Moab/Canyonlands
Trails Illustrated, #213 (incomplete)
Utah Atlas & Gazetteer, p. 28
Other: Recreation Map of the Henry Mountains Area
           (incomplete)

Route Directions

▼ 0.0		5.5 miles from the south end of Southwest #45: Stanton Pass Trail, zero trip meter and turn south 0.1 miles west of Saleratus Wash. The turn is unmarked.
GPS: N 37°51.99′ W 110°45.25′		
▼ 0.2	SO	Track on left.
▼ 0.3	SO	Track on left. Trail now crosses the open Cow Flat and becomes ungraded dirt track.
▼ 0.8	TR	Turn is unmarked and faint. Look for the trail cutting up the bench on your right. Straight ahead is the start of the third leg (Cow Flat).

SW #46: PENNELL CREEK BENCH TRAIL

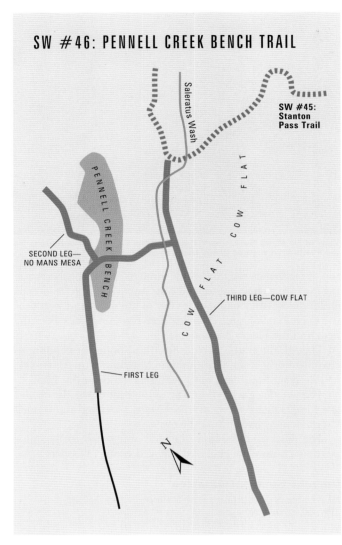

Roughs. Note the small castle-shaped rocky outcrop slightly to the south. Retrace your steps down from the mesa and return to the 0.8-mile mark on first leg.

GPS: N 37°52.06' W 110°46.36'

Third Leg: Cow Flat

▼ 0.0   At the 0.8-mile mark on first leg, zero trip meter and turn right (south) if coming from Pennell Creek Bench. Track on left (north) leads back to the start of the trail and Southwest #45: Stanton Pass Trail.

▼ 0.2   SO   Faint track on left.

▼ 0.7   SO   Faint track on right.

▼ 1.0   SO   Spring and corral below trail on left.

GPS: N 37°50.35' W 110°45.86'

▼ 1.5   SO   Cross through small wash.

GPS: N 37°50.02' W 110°46.14'

▼ 2.0   Trail finishes at point with view over Saleratus Wash directly below, Mount Hillers to the north, and Mount Holmes and Mount Ellsworth to the east.

GPS: N 37°49.64' W 110°46.23'

SOUTHWEST REGION TRAIL #47

Bull Creek Pass Trail

Starting Point:	**Utah 95, 21 miles south of Hanksville**
Finishing Point:	**Utah 276, 5 miles south of junction**
	with Utah 95
Total Mileage:	**52.3 miles**
Unpaved Mileage:	**52.3 miles**
Driving Time:	**7 hours**
Elevation Range:	**4,800–10,485 feet**
Usually Open:	**Early June to late November**
Difficulty Rating:	**2**
Scenic Rating:	**10**
Remoteness Rating:	**+2**

Special Attractions

■ Long, remote backcountry byway with varied scenery and elevation changes.

■ Bull Creek Pass at 10,485 feet.

■ Rare chance to see a wild bison herd.

History

The Henry Mountains are a geologic anomaly: frustrated volcanoes that were unable to reach the surface due to a thick, tough layer of sedimentary rock that prevented their erupting. The sedimentary layer bent upward instead, forming the domes of the Henry Mountains. The overlying sedimentary rock has eroded in places, exposing the igneous rock underneath. This geologic formation is called a stock. The Henry Mountains have five stocks: Mount Pennell, Mount Hillers, Mount Ellen, Mount Holmes, and Mount Ellsworth. In

GPS: N 37°51.33' W 110°45.69'

▼ 0.9   SO   Cross through small wash. Follow wheel tracks and pick your route carefully.

▼ 1.0   SO   Cross through Saleratus Wash and climb up to Pennell Bench.

▼ 1.3   SO   End of climb, trail undulates through junipers.

▼ 1.5   BL   Faint track on right; this is start of second leg of trail.

GPS: N 37°51.49' W 110°46.31'

▼ 1.9   BR   At cattletank and small dam, swing southwest. Tracks are faint.

GPS: N 37°51.21' W 110°46.52'

▼ 2.5   First leg ends as the trail runs out to a point. Trail continues but is badly washed out just past the wash. Retrace your steps to the 1.5-mile point.

GPS: N 37°50.77' W 110°46.85'

Second Leg: No Mans Mesa

▼ 0.0   At the 1.5-mile mark on first leg, zero trip meter and turn west.

▼ 0.2   SO   Cross through small wash.

▼ 0.4   SO   Cross through small wash.

▼ 0.7   SO   Trail finishes at a panoramic viewpoint over-looking No Mans Mesa and the Pennell Creek

1871, John Wesley Powell first named the mountain range after Joseph Henry, a professor at the Smithsonian Institute. However, it was not until 1875 that the Henry Mountains were first surveyed by geologist Grove Karl Gilbert. This late date of exploration stands as a testimony to the rugged remoteness of the Henry Mountains.

The history of the Henry Mountains region includes tales of lost mines, ghost towns, and more recently, wild buffalo. Human habitation dates back about eight thousand years to Archaic and Fremont Indian cultures, although there are few visible remains.

The Bull Creek Pass Trail passes the remains of Eagle City along Crescent Creek. All that is left now are the remains of a log cabin, collapsed in a grove of aspens, but Eagle City, founded in the 1890s, was once a thriving mining community, boasting cook houses, boarding houses, and saloons. The mines were located farther up Crescent Creek in Bromide Basin. When the mines ran dry, the people moved on to more profitable ventures. Eagle City dwindled, and by 1900 it was deserted.

Sandstone columns in the Little Egypt Geologic Site

A more recent introduction to the area is a herd of buffalo, one of the only free-roaming buffalo herds left in the United States. In 1941, 18 head of buffalo were transported from Yellowstone National Park to the Robbers Roost area, east of Utah 276, in order to safeguard the survival of the Yellowstone herd. The herd gradually migrated west of the highway over a period of a few years, first to the eastern slopes of the Henry Mountains and then to the western slopes, where it has remained. Best chances of seeing the buffalo are in the meadows surrounding the McMillan Springs Campground and south as far as Aeroplane Spring. The herd today numbers approximately 450 animals. Since 1950, there have been approximately 60 hunting permits granted annually, though exact numbers vary, and the season is broken into three hunts each fall. The permits are distributed via a lottery system and competition is fierce.

Trachyte Ranch, on the southeastern lowlands of this trail, dates back to 1913 when uranium was first discovered in the area. You can see a log cabin and associated buildings close to Trachyte Creek, and the ranch dam is just upstream. Mining adits can also be seen in the cliff walls surrounding Trachyte Creek.

Description

This trail is entirely on BLM land and is a designated scenic backcountry byway. The trail turns off Utah 95, 21 miles south of Hanksville. The turn is unsigned except for the small circular byway sign. It is graded dirt over the full 52.3 miles; the standard varies from a smooth surface suitable for a passenger

The remains of a stone miner's cabin near Crescent Creek

car to rough, rocky sections and washouts that require high clearance. Snow closes the higher portions of the trail any time from late October onward, but the lower parts are traversable most times of the year in dry conditions. Fall is a particularly beautiful time of year for the drive—the extreme summer heat has passed, the leaves are turning, and the weather is generally dry. Rain can render most of this trail impassable.

After 1.6 miles, the trail passes by the Little Egypt Geologic Site. Entrada sandstone columns banded with limestone form strange columnar formations that early settlers compared to the Sphinx of Egypt. The trail crosses Crescent Creek and winds through the lower elevations and badlands scenery. The vistas are desolate at this stage, with scrubby sage giving way to stunted juniper as the trail climbs. The sparse ruins of Eagle City are visible after 11.7 miles; an old log cabin is about all that remains. The trail then climbs up to the first of three passes, Wickiup Pass, and connects with Southwest #49: Town Wash and Bull Mountain Trail. There are stunning views east over the Burr Desert as the trail wraps around the hill.

Crescent Creek wash crossing

You reach Bull Creek Pass, the high point of the trail at 10,485 feet, after 18.2 miles. There are wide-ranging views to the northeast over the tributaries of the Dirty Devil River and Canyonlands National Park. On a clear day you can see the bulk of the La Sal Mountains east of Moab and the Abajo Mountains near Monticello. To the northwest are Waterpocket Fold, Circle Cliffs, and Boulder Mountain. The pass is the start of the hiking trail to the top of Mount Ellen, a 5-mile round-trip.

From the pass you will begin a long descent, past the intersection with Southwest #48: Copper Ridge Trail, to the de-

SW #47: BULL CREEK PASS TRAIL

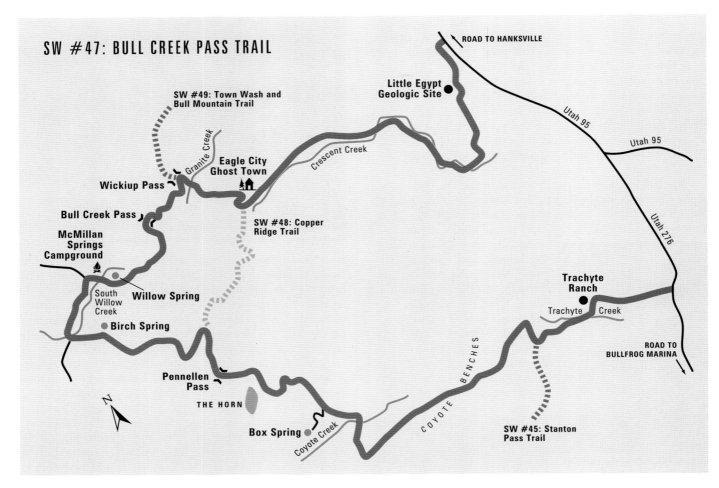

veloped campground at McMillan Springs. The wild bison herd that inhabits the Henry Mountains can often be seen grazing the grassy meadows just west of Bull Creek Pass. Remember that these are wild animals and can be aggressive if approached too closely. The trail then undulates down from the higher elevations, crossing Pennellen Pass, passing by the steep cliffs of the Horn, and traversing the sloping Coyote Benches before dropping back down into the arid badlands again. There are some good undeveloped campsites along this section at a variety of elevations, some sheltered in the shade of pines, others more open with good vistas. You get some of the best views of the entire trail while descending to Coyote Benches. To the east, distant views extend over the red rock of the Robbers Roost area to the Abajo Mountains. The distinctive shapes of Gunsight Butte and Sewing Machine Butte can be seen on a clear day.

After passing the connection with Southwest #45: Stanton Pass Trail and the remains of Trachyte Ranch, the trail finishes at Utah 276. With the exception of the starting and finishing points, this trail is well signed along its length. However, the region is very remote, and except during hunting season, you are unlikely to see any other vehicles. The BLM officials only occasionally travel the trails, so outside help should not be relied upon. Gas, accommodations, and limited supplies are available in Hanksville, Ticaboo, and Bullfrog Marina.

Current Road Information
BLM Henry Mountain Field Station
406 South 100 West
Hanksville, UT 84734
(435) 542-3461

Map References
BLM   Hanksville, Hite Crossing
USGS 1:24,000 Turkey Knob, Raggy Canyon, Mt. Ellen, Steele Butte, Mt. Pennell, Cass Creek Peak, Black Table
      1:100,000 Hanksville, Hite Crossing
Maptech CD-ROM: Moab/Canyonlands; Escalante/Dixie National Forest
Trails Illustrated, #213 (incomplete)
Utah Atlas & Gazetteer, pp. 28, 29
Utah Travel Council #5
Other: Recreation Map of the Henry Mountains Area

Route Directions

▼ 0.0		Turn west off Utah 95 onto unsigned, graded dirt road, 21 miles south of Hanksville, and zero trip meter.
3.5 ▲		Trail ends at Utah 95. Turn left for Hanksville, right for Bullfrog Marina.
GPS: N 38°05.84' W 110°37.28'		
▼ 0.2	BL	Follow main track left at sign to Little Egypt Geologic Site.

3.3 ▲		BR	Track on left.
▼ 1.6		SO	Little Egypt area on right; red Entrada columns banded with white limestone.
	1.9 ▲	SO	Little Egypt area on left; red Entrada columns banded with white limestone.
▼ 3.5		TR	Turn right at sign toward Sawmill Basin and the Horn, and zero trip meter.
	0.0 ▲		Continue toward Utah 95.

GPS: N 38°02.98′ W 110°37.87′

▼ 0.0			Continue toward Sawmill Basin.
	9.0 ▲	TL	Turn left at sign for Utah 95 and zero trip meter.
▼ 0.6		TR	Cross through Crescent Creek wash, normally dry.
	8.4 ▲	TL	Cross through Crescent Creek wash, normally dry.

GPS: N 38°02.76′ W 110°38.46′

▼ 0.7		SO	Cross through Crescent Creek wash; old crane on left of track.
	8.3 ▲	SO	Cross through Crescent Creek wash; old crane on right of track.
▼ 0.9		SO	Track on left. Trail follows Crescent Creek.
	8.1 ▲	SO	Track on right. Trail follows Crescent Creek.
▼ 1.4		SO	Track on right.
	7.6 ▲	SO	Track on left.
▼ 2.6		SO	Faint track on left.
	6.4 ▲	SO	Faint track on right.
▼ 3.0		SO	Track on left to active mine (Martinique Mining Co.).
	6.0 ▲	SO	Track on right to active mine (Martinique Mining Co.).

GPS: N 38°04.50′ W 110°39.62′

▼ 3.1		SO	Cross through Crescent Creek wash.
	5.9 ▲	SO	Cross through Crescent Creek wash.
▼ 3.3		SO	Single-room stone miner's cabin on right.
	5.7 ▲	SO	Single-room stone miner's cabin on left.

GPS: N 38°04.69′ W 110°39.69′

▼ 3.8		SO	Cattle guard.
	5.2 ▲	SO	Cattle guard.
▼ 4.0		SO	Timber miner's cabin on left under cotton-woods next to Crescent Creek.
	5.0 ▲	SO	Timber miner's cabin on right under cotton-woods next to Crescent Creek.

GPS: N 38°04.75′ W 110°40.40′

▼ 4.6		SO	Track on left is closed for mining reclamation. Entering juniper forest.
	4.4 ▲	SO	Track on right is closed for mining reclamation. Leaving juniper forest.
▼ 5.6		SO	Helipad on right, track on left.
	3.4 ▲	SO	Helipad on left, track on right.
▼ 6.2		SO	Track on right.
	2.8 ▲	SO	Track on left.

GPS: N 38°05.02′ W 110°42.60′

▼ 6.6		SO	Cattle guard, tracks on right and left along fence line.
	2.4 ▲	SO	Tracks on right and left along fence line, followed by cattle guard.
▼ 8.0		SO	Helipad on right, track on left.
	1.0 ▲	SO	Helipad on left, track on right.
▼ 8.1		BR	Track on left.
	0.9 ▲	BL	Track on right.

GPS: N 38°04.43′ W 110°44.58′

▼ 8.2		SO	Eagle City site—old log cabin on right.
	0.8 ▲	SO	Eagle City site—old log cabin on left.
▼ 8.4		SO	Cattle guard.
	0.6 ▲	SO	Cattle guard.
▼ 8.6		SO	Track on left is closed with wire.

	0.4 ▲	SO	Track on right is closed with wire.
▼ 9.0		TR	Sharp U-turn back; follow signs to Wickiup Pass and Sawmill Basin. Track on left is Southwest #48: Copper Ridge Trail. Zero trip meter.
	0.0 ▲		Continue east.

GPS: N 38°04.40′ W 110°45.61′

▼ 0.0			Climb up shelf road.
	3.1 ▲	TL	Sharp U-turn back to follow along Crescent Creek. Ahead is Southwest #48: Copper Ridge Trail. Zero trip meter.
▼ 2.2		SO	Cattle guard, sign "Granite Ridges" and track on left.
	0.9 ▲	SO	Cattle guard, sign "Granite Ridges" and track on right.
▼ 2.5		SO	Cross through Granite Creek.
	0.6 ▲	SO	Cross through Granite Creek.
▼ 3.1		SO	Wickiup Pass (9,360 feet). At intersection, go straight, bearing slightly left. The road on right is Southwest #49: Town Wash and Bull Mountain Trail to Utah 24 and Hanksville. Shady campsite at junction. Zero trip meter.
	0.0 ▲		Continue downhill.

GPS: N 38°05.70′ W 110°46.65′

▼ 0.0			Climb toward Bull Creek Pass.
	9.7 ▲	SO	Wickiup Pass (9,360 feet). At intersection, go straight, bearing slightly right. The road on left is Southwest #49: Town Wash and Bull Mountain Trail to Utah 24 and Hanksville. Shady campsite at junction. Zero trip meter.
▼ 2.6		SO	Bull Creek Pass (10,485 feet), high point of route. Hiking trail to the summit of Mount Ellen leads off to the north. Extensive views.
	7.1 ▲	SO	Bull Creek Pass (10,485 feet), high point of route. Hiking trail to the summit of Mount Ellen leads off to the north. Extensive views. End of climb from McMillan Springs Campground.

GPS: N 38°05.16′ W 110°48.11′

▼ 2.8		SO	Track on right to Burned Ridge.
	6.9 ▲	SO	Track on left to Burned Ridge.
▼ 4.6		BL	Track on right.
	5.1 ▲	BR	Track on left.
▼ 4.9		SO	Track on left joins Southwest #48: Copper Ridge Trail. Follow sign toward McMillan Springs Campground. Shady campsite in the aspens to the right.
	4.8 ▲	SO	Track on right joins Southwest #48: Copper Ridge Trail. Shady campsite in the aspens to the left.
▼ 5.5		SO	Track on right to campsite.
	4.2 ▲	SO	Track on left to campsite.
▼ 5.7		SO	Track on left to viewpoint on a rise.
	4.0 ▲	SO	Track on right to viewpoint on a rise.
▼ 6.9		BL	Track on right to log cabin; pass Willow Spring on right.
	2.8 ▲	BR	Pass Willow Spring on left, followed by a track on left to log cabin.
▼ 7.5		BL	Track on right to Dugout Creek and Cedar Creek. Entrance to McMillan Springs Campground on right (fee required).
	2.2 ▲	BR	Track on left to Dugout Creek and Cedar Creek. Entrance to McMillan Springs Campground on left (fee required). Leaving juniper and pinyon vegetation and entering ponderosa pines and aspens.

GPS: N 38°04.31′ W 110°50.84′

▼ 9.7		TL	Cross through South Willow Creek, then turn left, following signs for Birch Spring and the

Horn. Straight on goes to Southwest #39: Notom Road. End of descent from Bull Creek Pass. Zero trip meter.

0.0 ▲   Trail climbs to Bull Creek Pass

GPS: N 38°03.15' W 110°52.33'

▼ 0.0   Trail starts to climb.
6.3 ▲   TR   Turn right, following signs for Bull Creek Pass. Left goes to Southwest #39: Notom Road. Zero trip meter.

▼ 0.2   SO   Cattle guard.
6.1 ▲   SO   Cattle guard.

▼ 1.5   SO   Birch Spring on left of trail on a right-hand bend.
4.8 ▲   SO   Birch Spring on right of trail on a left-hand bend.

GPS: N 38°02.87' W 110°51.06'

▼ 2.7   SO   Cattle guard; trail undulates through junipers.
3.6 ▲   SO   Cattle guard.

▼ 3.9   SO   Track on right to viewpoint. Views southeast to the Horn.
2.4 ▲   SO   Track on left to viewpoint. Views southeast to the Horn.

▼ 6.3   TR   T-intersection. Track on left is Southwest #48: Copper Ridge Trail. Zero trip meter.
0.0 ▲   Continue north.

GPS: N 38°01.76' W 110°48.22'

▼ 0.0   Continue south toward the Horn.
9.3 ▲   TL   Turn left. Track ahead is Southwest #48: Copper Ridge Trail. Zero trip meter.

▼ 1.2   SO   Track on left to Box Spring.
8.1 ▲   SO   Track on right to Box Spring.

▼ 1.4   TL   T-intersection at Pennellen Pass (7,912 feet).
7.9 ▲   TR   Pennellen Pass (7,912 feet).

GPS: N 38°00.61' W 110°48.50'

▼ 2.0   SO   Trail passes the Horn.
7.3 ▲   SO   Trail passes the Horn.

▼ 3.0   SO   Campsite on left.
6.3 ▲   SO   Campsite on right.

▼ 4.5   SO   Track on right, then cattle guard. Views back to the Horn and left to Ragged Mountain.
4.8 ▲   SO   Cattle guard, then track on left. Views ahead to the Horn and right to Ragged Mountain.

GPS: N 37°59.67' W 110°46.52'

▼ 6.3   SO   Track on right to Willow Spring.
3.0 ▲   SO   Track on left to Willow Spring.

GPS: N 37°58.76' W 110°45.88'

▼ 6.4   SO   Camping areas on right and left, then corral on left.
2.9 ▲   SO   Corral on right, then camping areas on right and left.

▼ 7.7   BR   Track on left to campsite with view.
1.6 ▲   BL   Track on right to campsite with view.

▼ 8.8   SO   Turkey Haven undeveloped BLM campsite on left.
0.5 ▲   SO   Turkey Haven undeveloped BLM campsite on right.

GPS: N 37°57.61' W 110°45.43'

▼ 9.3   TL   T-intersection. Turn left, following sign to Coyote Benches and Trachyte Ranch. Track on right to Southwest #45: Stanton Pass Trail. Zero trip meter.
0.0 ▲   Continue north.

GPS: N 37°57.16' W 110°45.36'

▼ 0.0   Continue northeast.
5.4 ▲   TR   Turn right, following sign to the Horn. Track on left to Southwest #45: Stanton Pass Trail. Zero trip meter.

▼ 0.9   SO   Cattle guard. Spectacular views east.
4.5 ▲   SO   Cattle guard. Spectacular views east.

▼ 1.7   SO   Track on right to Coyote Benches. Views of Mount Hillers on right.
3.7 ▲   SO   Track on left to Coyote Benches. Views of Mount Hillers on left.

GPS: N 37°57.60' W 110°43.58'

▼ 4.7   SO   Cattle guard.
0.7 ▲   SO   Cattle guard.

▼ 4.9   SO   Track on left is signposted to North Wash, but is washed out after a couple of miles.
0.5 ▲   SO   Track on right is signposted to North Wash, but is washed out after a couple of miles.

GPS: N 37°57.85' W 110°40.31'

▼ 5.4   SO   Track on right is Southwest #45: Stanton Pass Trail to Quaking Aspen Spring. Zero trip meter.
0.0 ▲   Continue along main track.

GPS: N 37°57.88' W 110°39.61'

▼ 0.0   Continue along main track.
6.0 ▲   BR   Track on left is Southwest #45: Stanton Pass Trail to Quaking Aspen Spring. Continue toward Coyote Benches. Zero trip meter.

▼ 1.2   SO   Mine shaft visible on far side of creek.
4.8 ▲   SO   Mine shaft visible on far side of creek.

▼ 1.4   SO   Track on left to sheds—remains of Trachyte Ranch.
4.6 ▲   SO   Track on right to sheds—remains of Trachyte Ranch.

▼ 1.6   SO   Cross through creek.
4.4 ▲   SO   Cross through creek.

▼ 1.8   SO   Track on right.
4.2 ▲   BR   Track on left.

▼ 2.0   SO   Track on right.
4.0 ▲   SO   Track on left.

▼ 2.1   SO   Cross through creek.
3.9 ▲   SO   Cross through creek.

▼ 2.2   TL   Track on right to private property (Cat Ranch).
3.8 ▲   TR   Track ahead to private property (Cat Ranch).

GPS: N 37°57.88' W 110°37.78'

▼ 2.3   SO   Track on right.
3.7 ▲   SO   Track on left.

▼ 2.7   SO   Track on left to camping area and old log cabin, remains of Trachyte Ranch. Cross through Trachyte Creek, then track on right to camping area, wooden cabin, and remains of old truck.
3.3 ▲   SO   Track on left to camping area, wooden cabin, and remains of old truck. Cross through Trachyte Creek, then track on right to camping area and old log cabin, remains of Trachyte Ranch.

▼ 3.0   SO   Track on right.
3.0 ▲   SO   Track on left.

▼ 3.1   SO   Old corral on right, dam on left.
2.9 ▲   SO   Dam on right, old corral on left.

▼ 5.8   SO   Track on right.
0.2 ▲   SO   Track on left.

▼ 6.0   Trail ends at Utah 276, 4.4 miles south of the junction with Utah 95. Turn left for Hanksville, right for Bullfrog Marina.
0.0 ▲   On Utah 276, 4.4 miles south of junction with Utah 95, turn onto trail, following Scenic Backcountry Byway sign.

GPS: N 37°57.66' W 110°34.47'

Copper Ridge Trail

Starting Point:	Southwest #47: Bull Creek Pass Trail near Crescent Creek
Finishing Point:	Southwest #47: Bull Creek Pass Trail, 1.4 miles north of Pennellen Pass
Total Mileage:	6.3 miles
Unpaved Mileage:	6.3 miles
Driving Time:	1 hour
Elevation Range:	8,200–9,100 feet
Usually Open:	November to June
Difficulty Rating:	2
Scenic Rating:	8
Remoteness Rating:	+1

Special Attractions

- Spectacular views east over the Robbers Roost area.
- Long length of comfortable shelf road.
- Access to the higher elevation trails in Bromide Basin.

History

The Henry Mountains and Bromide Basin, in particular, have a long mining history. The most intriguing tale related to the mountains may have even occurred at Bromide Basin—though it may not have, depending on which version of the story you believe. Part truth, part legend, the tale of the Lost Mine of the Henry Mountains begins when the Spanish extensively explored this area as an offshoot of the Spanish Trail. According to the tale, they found an incredibly rich mine somewhere in the Henry Mountains and extracted the gold using the local Indians as slaves. One day, the Indians rebelled and a battle was fought with great loss of life on both sides. The Indians prevailed, and before they left the mine, they filled in the shaft and the medicine man placed a curse on the mine, so that all who attempted to work it would meet with disaster and death. The mine lay dormant for many years, its location known only to the Indians, who passed it down in their tales.

In 1853, John Frémont explored this area of Utah. He discovered steps cut into the wall at Spanish Bottoms that the Spanish had used to get their mules and men up to the Henry Mountains from the Colorado River. Along the old trail near the Henry Mountains, he found the bones of a pack mule with piles of gold ore on either side, spilled out from panniers long rotted away. Some of his men were very excited about the find, and some years later one of them, John Burke, returned to seek the lost mine. He was gone for several weeks, and then one day he staggered into the Desert Springs stage station with some ore samples he said came from an old Spanish mine. He said that Indians had stolen his horse and all of his gear and told him to leave the area.

The owner of the stage station, Ben Bowen, teamed up with him, and they hired a man named Blackburn to guide them and tend to the cooking and horses. En route to the mountains, they stopped at a ranch in Blue Valley for supplies. The rancher warned them against proceeding, saying that a hired Indian boy had told him that his grandfather had been forced to work in the mines and that there was a curse on anyone who went there. Undaunted, the three men proceeded, entering the Henry Mountains from the north and crossing the headwaters of Crescent Creek and Copper Creek before climbing up to what is now the Bromide Basin area. There they located the mine Burke had found before, a mine with the shafts filled in but much gold ore on the surface. They filled their sacks and began their return to the town of Pleasant Dale. In cutting across unknown desert terrain, they got hopelessly lost and against the advice of Blackburn, Burke and Bowen drank from a pool of stagnant water. They got very sick, but reached Pleasant Dale and recovered—only to die a few days later, after learning that the gold they had recovered had assayed out at over $6,000 a ton. Blackburn did go back to the mountain, but before he could locate the mine, a messenger caught up with him saying one of his children had died. He never went back.

Another possible victim of the Indian curse on the mine was Edgar Wolverton, who worked several smaller mines on Crescent Creek. He built a mill with a 18-feet-high waterwheel on the eastern flanks of Mount Pennell that took water from Straight Creek to help grind ore. This mill has been removed from the mountain for preservation and is now located next to the BLM office in Hanksville.

In 1911, his mines were flooded, leaving him with time on his hands to locate the lost Spanish mine. Wolverton spent 10 years searching for the mine and kept a detailed diary of his efforts. The entry for July 21, 1921, records that he "found the old Mexican mill

Looking east along Copper Ridge Trail late in the day

today whilst panning the hill south of camp." Shortly after that he had an accident with his horse—exact details vary—and was taken to Fruita, Colorado, for surgery. He survived the surgery, only to die a few days later. He is buried in the cemetery at Elgin, Utah. Wolverton's diary puts the location of the lost mine on the flanks of Mount Pennell rather than near Bromide Basin.

The area north of Copper Ridge was named Bromide Basin by early prospectors because it reminded them of bromide ore they had known in Colorado. In 1889, a small gold rush to Bromide Basin launched the growth of Eagle City, 2 miles below on Crescent Creek. The Bromide Mine was in full swing

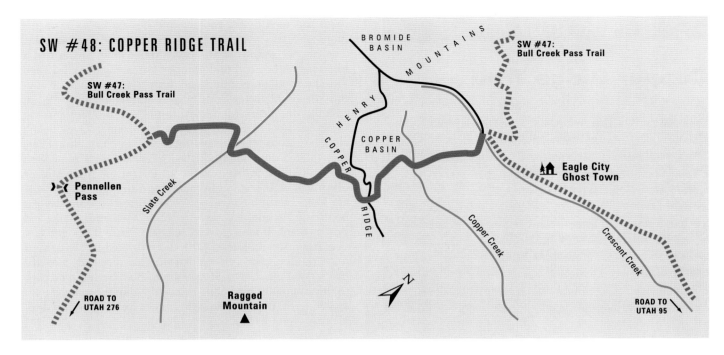

SW #48: COPPER RIDGE TRAIL

by 1891, and a five-stamp mill was constructed to process the ore. Between 1891 and 1893, $15,000 worth of gold was removed, and the Denver & Rio Grande Western Railroad was considering a branch line from the main line at Green River to Eagle City. However, the vein played out before any work could be started, and by 1900 both Eagle City and Bromide Basin were deserted.

There were sporadic attempts at mining after that, although nothing of great worth was ever found. The private lands up at Bromide Basin are now closed to the public.

Description

This short, easy trail offers an alternative to driving the complete Southwest #47: Bull Creek Pass Trail, as it cuts across and shaves 19 miles off the full loop. However, it is a worthwhile trail in its own right, as it provides unparalleled views east over the Robbers Roost area, Gunsight Butte, and Canyonlands National Park, as well as to the La Sal and Abajo Mountains.

The gradients are mild and the surface is graded dirt the entire way; in dry weather there should be no problems for high-clearance vehicles. In wet weather the trail, like most in this region, should be avoided.

The trail is shelf road for almost its entire length, but is a comfortable width for a full-size vehicle, and there are adequate passing places. It gives access up to the mining areas of Bromide Basin high on the flanks of Mount Ellen. Campsites are few along this trail, but there are good campsites at either end, particularly near Pennellen Pass.

Current Road Information

BLM Henry Mountain Field Station
406 South 100 West
Hanksville, UT 84734
(435) 542-3461

Map References

BLM   Hanksville
USGS 1:24,000 Mt. Ellen
            1:100,000 Hanksville
Maptech CD-ROM: Moab/Canyonlands; Escalante/Dixie
      National Forest
Trails Illustrated, #213
Utah Atlas & Gazetteer, p. 28
Utah Travel Council #5
Other: Recreation Map of the Henry Mountains Area

Route Directions

▼ 0.0			9 miles from the north end of Southwest #47: Bull Creek Pass Trail, zero trip meter and proceed southeast along the Copper Ridge Trail. Immediately cross through Crescent Creek, swing left and start to climb. Track on right is reclamation area; please stay out.
	2.2 ▲		Track on left is reclamation area; please stay out. Swing right and cross through Crescent Creek. Trail ends at Southwest #47: Bull Creek Pass Trail. Turn right for Utah 95.

GPS: N 38°04.40' W 110°45.61'

▼ 0.2		SO	Track on left.
	2.0 ▲	SO	Track on right.
▼ 0.9		SO	Track on left.
	1.3 ▲	SO	Track on right.
▼ 1.7		SO	Track on left to flat camping area with excellent views.
	0.5 ▲	SO	Track on right to flat camping area with excellent views.
▼ 2.2		SO	Intersection. Track on right to Bromide Basin; track on left runs out on Copper Ridge. Zero trip meter.
	0.0 ▲		Continue northeast as trail climbs.

GPS: N 38°03.02' W 110°45.85'

▼ 0.0			Continue southwest as trail descends.
	4.1 ▲	SO	Intersection. Track on left to Bromide Basin; track on right runs out on

			Copper Ridge. Zero trip meter.
▼ 0.1		SO	Views southwest to Mount Hillers, the Horn, Ragged Mountain, and Mount Pennell.
	4.0 ▲	SO	Views southwest to Mount Hillers, the Horn, Ragged Mountain, and Mount Pennell.
▼ 1.3		SO	Track on left.
	2.8 ▲	SO	Track on right.
▼ 2.6		SO	Cross through Slate Creek in grove of small aspens.
	1.5 ▲	SO	Cross through Slate Creek in grove of small aspens.
▼ 4.1			Trail finishes at Southwest #47: Bull Creek Pass Trail, 1.4 miles north of Pennellen Pass.
	0.0 ▲		On Southwest #47: Bull Creek Pass Trail, 1.4 miles north of Pennellen Pass, turn left onto Copper Ridge Trail and zero trip meter.

GPS: N 38°01.76′ W 110°48.22′

Cottonwoods grow near the dry Bull Creek Wash

SOUTHWEST REGION TRAIL #49

Town Wash and Bull Mountain Trail

Starting Point:	**Utah 24, 9 miles west of Hanksville**
Finishing Point:	**Southwest #47: Bull Creek Pass Trail**
	at Wickiup Pass
Total Mileage:	**35.9 miles**
Unpaved Mileage:	**35.9 miles**
Driving Time:	**3.5 hours**
Elevation Range:	**4,575– 9,300 feet**
Usually Open:	**May to November**
Difficulty Rating:	**3**
Scenic Rating:	**7**
Remoteness Rating:	**+1**

Special Attractions
■ Ghost town site of Giles.
■ Panoramic views of the Henry Mountains.
■ Remote, seldom traveled desert track.
■ Desolate badlands and moonscape scenery.

History
The township of Giles, near the start of this trail, was first established in 1883; it was originally called Blue Valley, after the blue-gray barren clay hills in this desolate region. Founded by Mormons as an agricultural community, Blue Valley was divided by the Fremont River, which was used for irrigation, and the two halves were connected by a narrow wooden bridge. The Mormon church provided the town's social life and leadership. Originally it was a branch of the ward in the upper valley, but in 1885 a new ward was formed, which included Blue Valley and nearby Hanksville.

Most of the irrigated farming took place south of the Fremont River on the river flats. Nearly three thousand acres of corn, alfalfa, cabbages, and other fruits and vegetables were irrigated by canals and ditches that diverted water from the river.

In 1895, Blue Valley changed its name to Giles after a prominent resident, Bishop Henry Giles, who died in 1892. He is buried in the Giles cemetery.

The major reason for the formation of Giles also proved its undoing. In 1897, the Fremont River flooded, wiping out the bridge and most of the irrigation canals. The town of 200 people rallied to repair the damage, but in 1909 a second flood once again washed out their farms. The town never recovered and was officially disbanded in 1910.

Fording the Fremont River

Today little remains of Giles. On the north side of the river, next to milepost 109, just east of the start of this trail, is a stone house that was originally the Abbot Cabin, a rest house for travelers. On the south side, just as the trail swings around Steamboat Point, there are some stone foundations in the undergrowth. The cemetery is found just off the trail to the east.

The Spanish Trail also came close to the Henry Mountains and early settlers established many mines in the area. An old folk legend places a supposed battle between the Spanish and the Indians at the north end of the mountain range. As the story goes, the site and graves were marked by a Latin cross dated 1777.

Description
This alternate route into the Henry Mountains from the north is little traveled; most visitors take the major dirt road leading directly south from Hanksville. The trail starts 9 miles west of Hanksville; turn south from Utah 24 on an unsigned dirt trail. You almost immediately cross a concrete ford through the Fremont River, which can be deep and fast flowing, and silt can

build up on the concrete, leading to a sticky trap for the unwary. If in doubt, walk the crossing first and engage 4WD. Do not attempt if the river is in flood stage.

The trail passes the ghost town of Giles set underneath Steamboat Point, a prominent butte that resembles a funneled steamship. Little is left of Giles these days; you can find the graveyard with a bit of hunting to the east of Steamboat Point—look for an old fence line.

The trail swings around Steamboat Point and heads south up Town Wash. It is narrow graded dirt, rough in places but traversable with a high-clearance vehicle in dry weather. Navigation along the trail is tricky; there are no signs, and junctions are often faint and easy to miss.

After 4 miles, the trail leaves Town Wash and climbs up onto the mesa, affording good views north over the wash and south toward the massive Henry Mountains, which rear up out of the flat land. The trail winds over the flat Blue Valley Benches, crossing many small washes and passing a myriad of small, unmarked two-track trails. There are some spectacular areas of badlands, a desolate moonscape with no vegetation, and patches of salt creeping up through the poor soil.

After almost 20 miles, the trail joins the graded road from Hanksville, and the worst of the difficult navigation is over, although the upper reaches of this road are rougher than anything encountered so far. The trail climbs steadily through large junipers and stunted pines toward Bull Mountain, visible east of the trail. The scenery changes dramatically as the trail climbs and winds around the slope of Bull Mountain and Bull Creek Wash. There is a small section of shelf road, but it is a comfortable width for a full-size vehicle, and there are adequate passing places.

You pass the picnic area of Dandelion Flat after 34 miles, where there are picnic tables set in a shady pine grove. The hiking trail to Log Flat and East Saddle starts here. Half a mile farther is the developed BLM campground of Lonesome Beaver (fee required). Many secluded campsites are set under tall pines and aspens.

The trail finishes on Wickiup Pass, where it intersects with Southwest #47: Bull Creek Pass Trail.

The trail runs along the canyon wall as it descends into Town Wash

Current Road Information
BLM Henry Mountain Field Station
406 South 100 West
Hanksville, UT 84734
(435) 542-3461

Map References
BLM Hanksville (incomplete)
USGS 1:24,000 Steamboat Point, Town Point, Hanksville, Bull Mt., Dry Lakes Peak, Mt. Ellen
1:100,000 Hanksville (incomplete)
Maptech CD-ROM: Moab/Canyonlands
Trails Illustrated, #213 (incomplete)
Utah Atlas & Gazetteer, pp. 28, 29
Utah Travel Council #5 (incomplete)
Other: Recreation Map of the Henry Mountains Area

Route Directions

▼ 0.0			On Utah 24, 9 miles west of Hanksville, turn south onto unmarked dirt road leading down through the tamarisks. Trail leads off just before a left-hand bend.
	9.6 ▲		Trail ends on Utah 24. Turn right for Hanksville, left for Capitol Reef National Park.
		GPS: N 38°21.56' W 110°52.39'	
▼ 0.1		SO	Cross through Fremont River on concrete ford.
	9.5 ▲	SO	Cross through Fremont River on concrete ford.
▼ 1.0		SO	Track on left.
	8.6 ▲	SO	Track on right.
▼ 1.5		SO	Track swings south around Steamboat Point and commences up Town Wash.
	8.1 ▲	SO	Track leaves Town Wash and swings west around Steamboat Point.
▼ 1.6		SO	Fence line in scrub on left marks Giles graveyard.
	8.0 ▲	SO	Fence line in scrub on right marks Giles graveyard.
▼ 2.6		SO	Cross through Town Wash.
	7.0 ▲	SO	Cross through Town Wash.
▼ 2.9		SO	Track on left.
	6.7 ▲	SO	Track on right.
		GPS: N 38°20.09' W 110°51.67'	
▼ 3.7		SO	Pass through wire gate in fence line.
	5.9 ▲	SO	Pass through wire gate in fence line.
▼ 3.8		SO	Drop down to enter Town Wash.
	5.8 ▲	SO	Trail leaves Town Wash.
▼ 4.1		SO	Trail leaves Town Wash and climbs mesa.
	5.5 ▲	SO	Enter Town Wash.
▼ 4.7		SO	Top of mesa, trail levels off.
	4.9 ▲	SO	Trail descends mesa to enter Town Wash. Views north over wash.
▼ 6.1		SO	Track on right.
	3.5 ▲	SO	Track on left.
		GPS: N 38°17.75' W 110°52.58'	
▼ 6.3		SO	Track on right.
	3.3 ▲	SO	Track on left.
▼ 6.9		SO	Pass through wire gate in fence line.
	2.7 ▲	SO	Pass through wire gate in fence line.
▼ 7.4		SO	Track on left to viewpoint over wash.
	2.2 ▲	SO	Track on right to viewpoint over wash.
▼ 7.6		SO	Track on left.
	2.0 ▲	BL	Track on right.

SW #49: TOWN WASH AND BULL MOUNTAIN TRAIL

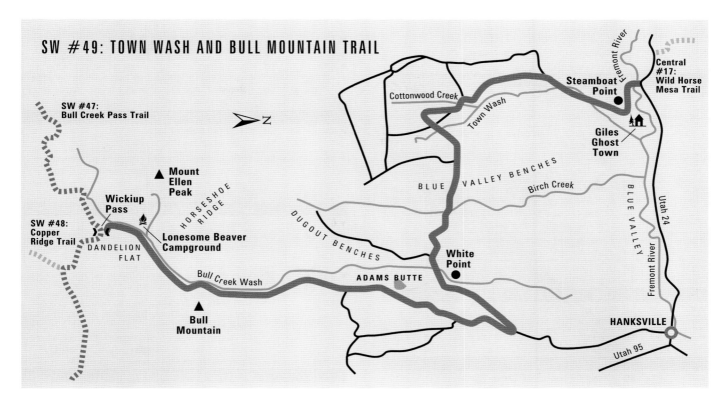

▼ 8.0		SO	Track on right.
	1.6 ▲	SO	Track on left.
▼ 8.1		SO	Cross through Cottonwood Creek.
	1.5 ▲	SO	Cross through Cottonwood Creek.
▼ 9.6		TL	T-intersection. Junction is unmarked. Zero trip meter.
	0.0 ▲		Continue north.
		GPS: N 38°15.11′ W 110°51.25′	
▼ 0.0			Continue northeast.
	6.3 ▲	TR	Junction is unmarked. Zero trip meter.
▼ 0.4		SO	Cross through Coaly Wash.
	5.9 ▲	SO	Cross through Coaly Wash.
▼ 0.6		SO	Track on right. Trail crosses Blue Valley Benches.
	5.7 ▲	SO	Track on left. Trail crosses Blue Valley Benches.
▼ 0.8		SO	Cross through small wash.
	5.5 ▲	SO	Cross through small wash.
▼ 1.9		SO	Small tracks on left and right.
	4.4 ▲	SO	Small tracks on left and right.
▼ 2.2		SO	Cattle guard, then descend to cross wash.
	4.1 ▲	SO	Cross wash, then cattle guard.
▼ 2.6		SO	Cross through small wash.
	3.7 ▲	SO	Cross through small wash.
▼ 2.7		SO	Track on left.
	3.6 ▲	SO	Second entrance to track on right.
▼ 2.8		SO	Second entrance to track on left.
	3.5 ▲	SO	Track on right.
▼ 3.9		SO	Cross through Birch Creek.
	2.4 ▲	SO	Cross through Birch Creek.
▼ 4.3		SO	Cattle guard.
	2.0 ▲	SO	Cattle guard.
▼ 4.5		SO	Trail runs down small wash.
	1.8 ▲	SO	Leave wash.
▼ 5.3		SO	Leave wash.

	1.0 ▲	SO	Trail runs along small wash.
▼ 6.3		SO	Major track on right to Dugout Benches and Birch Creek. Zero trip meter.
	0.0 ▲		Continue southeast.
		GPS: N 38°15.41′ W 110°45.66′	
▼ 0.0			Continue northwest.
	3.9 ▲	SO	Major track on left to Dugout Benches and Birch Creek. Zero trip meter.
▼ 0.5		SO	Cross through Bull Creek Wash, followed by track on right.
	3.4 ▲	SO	Track on left, then cross through Bull Creek Wash.
▼ 1.0		SO	White Point rocks on left.
	2.9 ▲	SO	White Point rocks on right.
▼ 2.5		SO	Small track on left.
	1.4 ▲	SO	Small track on right.
▼ 3.9		TR	T-intersection, follow sign to Lonesome Beaver Campground. Left goes to Hanksville. Trail standard improves to wider graded dirt. Zero trip meter.
	0.0 ▲		Continue southwest.
		GPS: N 38°17.65′ W 110°42.86′	
▼ 0.0			Continue south.
	5.7 ▲	TL	Turn onto unmarked dirt road. Trail standard drops. Straight on goes to Hanksville. Zero trip meter.
▼ 3.4		SO	Cattle guard.
	2.3 ▲	SO	Cattle guard.
▼ 4.0		SO	Adams Butte on right.
	1.7 ▲	SO	Adams Butte on left.
▼ 4.2		SO	Corral on left.
	1.5 ▲	SO	Corral on right.
▼ 4.3		SO	Cattle guard.
	1.4 ▲	SO	Cattle guard.
▼ 4.8		SO	Cattle guard.
	0.9 ▲	SO	Cattle guard.

▼ 5.7		SO	Track on left to Utah 95. Continue straight, following signs for Lonesome Beaver Campground. Zero trip meter.
	0.0 ▲		Continue north.

GPS: N 38°12.90' W 110°44.44'

▼ 0.0			Continue south.
	8.8 ▲	SO	Track on right to Utah 95. Continue straight, following signs for Hanksville. Zero trip meter.
▼ 1.1		SO	Track on right to private property.
	7.7 ▲	SO	Track on left to private property.
▼ 3.3		SO	Two tracks on right to campsites.
	5.5 ▲	SO	Two tracks on left to campsites.
▼ 4.6		SO	Some campsites on right as trail winds around Bull Mountain. Trail becomes rougher.
	4.2 ▲	SO	Some campsites on left as trail winds around Bull Mountain. Trail standard improves.
▼ 5.1		SO	Cattle guard, start of shelf road.
	3.7 ▲	SO	Cattle guard, end of shelf road.
▼ 5.5		SO	Track on left to viewpoint.
	3.3 ▲	BL	Track on right to viewpoint.

GPS: N 38°08.53' W 110°44.61'

▼ 6.0		SO	End of shelf road.
	2.8 ▲	SO	Start of shelf road.
▼ 7.4		SO	Trail drops to cross through Bull Creek Wash.
	1.4 ▲	SO	Cross through Bull Creek.

GPS: N 38°07.34' W 110°45.52'

▼ 7.7		SO	Cross through Bull Creek Wash.

	1.1 ▲	SO	Cross through Bull Creek Wash.
▼ 7.8		SO	Sign, "Entering Sawmill Basin."
	1.0 ▲	SO	Leaving Sawmill Basin.
▼ 8.4		SO	Dandelion Flat Picnic Area on right. Hiking trailhead to Log Flat and East Saddle on right.
	0.4 ▲	SO	Dandelion Flat Picnic Area on left. Hiking trailhead to Log Flat and East Saddle on left.

GPS: N 38°06.87' W 110°46.33'

▼ 8.6		SO	Small track on right.
	0.2 ▲	SO	Small track on left.
▼ 8.8		SO	Track on right is main entrance to Lonesome Beaver Campground (fee required). Zero trip meter.
	0.0 ▲		Continue north.

GPS: N 38°06.56' W 110°46.65'

▼ 0.0			Continue south.
	1.6 ▲	SO	Track on left is main entrance to Lonesome Beaver Campground (fee required). Zero trip meter.
▼ 0.1		SO	Side entrance to campground on right.
	1.5 ▲	SO	Side entrance to campground on left.
▼ 1.6			Trail ends at Wickiup Pass at Southwest #47: Bull Creek Pass Trail. Turn right to Bull Creek Pass, left to Utah 95.
	0.0 ▲		At Wickiup Pass on Southwest #47: Bull Creek Pass Trail, zero trip meter and turn north, downhill, from the pass.

GPS: N 38°05.70' W 110°46.65'

The Northern Region

Trails in the Northern Region

- **N1**   Hardware Ranch Road *(page 354)*
- **N2**   Millville Canyon Trail *(page 356)*
- **N3**   Left Hand Fork Canyon Trail *(page 359)*
- **N4**   Strawberry Valley Trail *(page 361)*
- **N5**   Temple Canyon Trail *(page 362)*
- **N6**   Old Ephraim Trail *(page 364)*
- **N7**   Peter Sinks Trail *(page 366)*
- **N8**   Idaho Loop *(page 367)*
- **N9**   Inspiration Point Trail *(page 369)*
- **N10**   Wendover to Lucin Trail *(page 371)*
- **N11**   Silver Island Mountains Loop *(page 374)*
- **N12**   Transcontinental Railroad Trail *(page 377)*
- **N13**   Pony Express Trail *(page 380)*
- **N14**   Clear Creek Ridge Trail *(page 385)*
- **N15**   Nine Mile Canyon Trail *(page 387)*
- **N16**   Argyle Canyon Trail *(page 391)*
- **N17**   Dry Canyon Trail *(page 392)*
- **N18**   Cottonwood Canyon Trail *(page 395)*
- **N19**   Green River Overlook Trail *(page 396)*
- **N20**   Twin Hollow Trail *(page 398)*
- **N21**   Franks Canyon & Sand Wash Trail *(page 399)*
- **N22**   Reservation Ridge Trail *(page 401)*
- **N23**   Tabbyune Creek Trail *(page 403)*
- **N24**   Timber Canyon Trail *(page 404)*
- **N25**   Brown's Park Trail *(page 407)*
- **N26**   Rainbow and Island Park Trail *(page 410)*
- **N27**   Echo Park & Yampa Bench Trail *(page 412)*
- **N28**   Rainbow & Watson Ghost Towns Trail *(page 416)*
- **N29**   Dragon Ghost Town Trail *(page 420)*
- **N30**   Sawtooth Mountain Trail *(page 423)*
- **N31**   Confusion Range Trail *(page 426)*
- **N32**   Frisco Peak Trail *(page 430)*
- **N33**   Frisco Ghost Town Trail *(page 432)*
- **N34**   Soldier Pass Trail *(page 434)*
- **N35**   Lincoln Mine Trail *(page 436)*

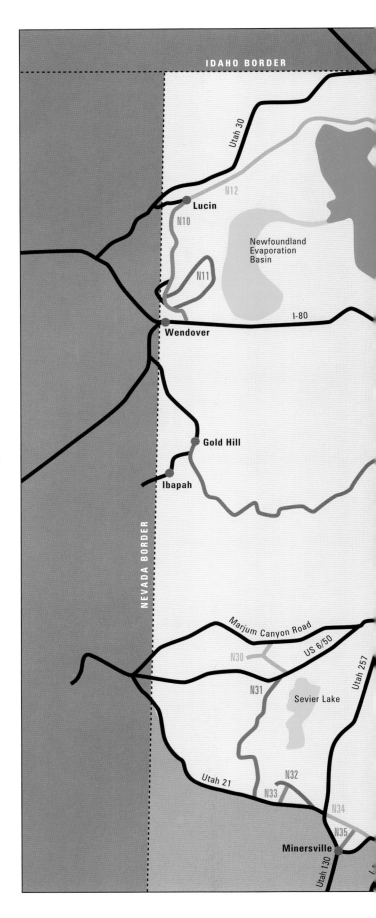

Hardware Ranch Road

Starting Point:	**Hyrum**
Finishing Point:	**US 89 and FR 055, west of Bear Lake**
Total Mileage:	**44 miles**
Unpaved Mileage:	**28.6 miles**
Driving Time:	**2 hours**
Elevation Range:	**4,800–8,700 feet**
Usually Open:	**May to October**
Difficulty Rating:	**2**
Scenic Rating:	**7**
Remoteness Rating:	**+0**

Special Attractions
■ Easy trail with varied scenery.
■ Access to many other 4WD trails.
■ Wildlife viewing, particularly elk.

History
Hardware Ranch was first homesteaded in 1868, and it was at one point owned by Alonzo Snow, a hardware dealer from Brigham City. Though his base of operations was at his store, Box Elder Hardware, he was known to deliver supplies to the loggers who lived near his ranch.

In 1945, the Utah Division of Wildlife Resources took over operations of the ranch, where biologists now feed and study over 700 elk (Utah's state mammal). Since then it has become one of the most popular winter wildlife viewing areas in the state. Sleigh rides to the ranch are currently offered in the winter if you want to see the animals up close. For more information and reservations, call Hardware Ranch at (435) 753-6168.

A view of the trail entering Saddle Creek Canyon

Saddle Creek Crossing

Description
To get to Hardware Ranch Road from Logan, head south along Main Street, then turn onto Utah 165 south, following signs to Providence and Hyrum. Hardware Ranch Road begins in Hyrum and heads east from town as a paved road.

After 7 miles, you reach Northern #3: Left Hand Fork Canyon Trail, and after 15.4 miles you reach the Hardware Ranch Visitors Center. From here to Danish Dugway, the road travels over imbedded rock along a rutted, bumpy surface; this section is by far the roughest part of Hardware Ranch Road. The trail here passes through grassland dotted with sagebrush, pinyon, and junipers and rolling hillsides with numerous stands of aspen and conifers.

After 21.6 miles, you come to Northern #4: Strawberry Valley Trail and Danish Dugway, where the road narrows and steeply descends for 1.1 miles. The surface is still corrugated and rocky, but should not cause any clearance problems.

The road levels out a bit after Danish Dugway, and half a mile later, you reach Northern #6: Old Ephraim Trail, a loop trail that returns you to Hardware Ranch Road 9.6 miles later. There are still a number of ruts and substantial mud holes along this section of the trail, and when wet, these otherwise benign road hazards can turn into formidable obstacles and make a high-clearance 4WD a must. It is the existence of the mud holes that warrants the 2 rating for this trail.

The road follows the course of Saddle Creek through a canyon, and as you continue along Hardware Ranch Road past the intersection with FR 211, the trail loops around a handful of beaver ponds and connects with Northern #5: Temple Canyon Trail.

The route progresses through Hells Hollow and Log Cabin Hollow, and then it passes the connection with the loop trail Northern #7: Peter Sinks Trail. The trail ends at US 89 near Bear Lake Summit. You must cross a number of dry washes in this last stretch of road, but they usually do not pose any great difficulty.

Current Road Information
Wasatch-Cache National Forest
Logan Ranger District
1500 East Highway 89
Logan, UT 84321
(435) 755-3620

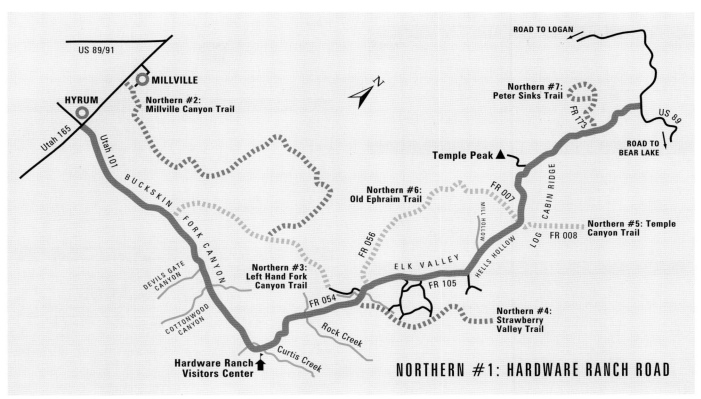

NORTHERN #1: HARDWARE RANCH ROAD

Map References

BLM Logan
USFS Wasatch-Cache: Logan Ranger District
USGS 1:24,000 Logan, Paradise, Porcupine Reservoir, Logan Peak, Hardware Ranch, Boulder Mt., Red Spur Mt., Meadowville, Garden City
1:100,000 Logan
Maptech CD-ROM: Upper Wasatch/Great Salt Lake
Utah Atlas & Gazetteer, pp. 60, 61, 63
Utah Travel Council #1

Route Directions

▼ 0.0   In Hyrum, at intersection of 800E (Utah 165) and Main Street (Utah 101), zero trip meter and turn east onto Utah 101.
7.0 ▲   Trail ends at intersection of 800E (Utah 165) and Main Street in Hyrum. Turn right for Logan and US 89/91.

GPS: N 41°38.03 W 111°49.90'

▼ 7.0   SO   Northern #3: Left Hand Fork Canyon Trail is on left. Zero trip meter.
0.0 ▲   Continue west.

GPS: N 41°37.91' W 111°42.41'

▼ 0.0   Continue east.
8.4 ▲   SO   Northern #3: Left Hand Fork Canyon Trail is on right. Zero trip meter.

▼ 8.1   SO   Hardware Ranch buildings. Marker on left and public toilets.
0.3 ▲   SO   Hardware Ranch buildings. Marker on right and public toilets.

GPS: N 41°36.12' W 111°33.95'

▼ 8.4   SO   Hardware Ranch Visitors Center driveway on right. Zero trip meter. End of Utah 101; begin FR 054.

0.0 ▲   Continue west along paved road.

GPS: N 41°36.22' W 111°33.56'

▼ 0.0   Continue east along unpaved road.
6.2 ▲   SO   Hardware Ranch Visitors Center driveway on left. Zero trip meter. Road becomes Utah 101.

▼ 2.3   SO   Cattle guard.
3.9 ▲   SO   Cattle guard.

▼ 3.3   BL   Road on right. Cross over Rock Creek.
2.9 ▲   BR   Cross over Rock Creek. Then road on left.

GPS: N 41°38.68' W 111°32.96'

▼ 5.4   SO   Cattle guard.
0.7 ▲   SO   Cattle guard.

▼ 6.2   BL   Danish Dugway; switchback down into valley. Track on right is Northern #4: Strawberry Valley Trail. Zero trip meter.
0.0 ▲   Continue along Hardware Ranch Road.

GPS: N 41°40.71' W 111°31.21'

▼ 0.0   Continue down switchback.
1.1 ▲   BR   End of Danish Dugway. Track on left is Northern #4: Strawberry Valley Trail. Zero trip meter.

▼ 0.4   SO   Cross over creek.
0.7 ▲   SO   Cross over creek.

▼ 1.1   SO/BR   Cross through Saddle Creek; end of Danish Dugway. Then trail on left leads into Left Hand Fork Canyon. Zero trip meter.
0.0 ▲   Continue along Hardware Ranch Road.

GPS: N 41°41.20' W 111°31.38'

▼ 0.0   Continue along Hardware Ranch Road.
0.5 ▲   BL/SO   Intersection; trail on right leads into Left Hand Fork Canyon. Cross through Saddle Creek. Start of Danish Dugway; switchback out of valley. Zero trip meter.

▼ 0.5   SO   Track on left is Northern #6: Old Ephraim Trail (FR 056). Zero trip meter. Main trail becomes FR 105.

0.0 ▲		Continue along Hardware Ranch Road.

GPS: N 41°41.54' W 111°31.26'

▼ 0.0			Continue along Hardware Ranch Road.
	2.9 ▲	SO	Track on right is Northern #6: Old Ephraim Trail (FR 056). Zero trip meter. Main trail becomes FR 054.
▼ 0.1		SO	Left is part of delta also leading to Northern #6: Old Ephraim Trail.
	2.8 ▲	SO	Right is part of delta leading to Northern #6: Old Ephraim Trail.

GPS: N 41°41.57' W 111°31.24'

▼ 0.6		SO	Cattle guard.
	2.3 ▲	SO	Cattle guard.
▼ 2.6		SO	Cattle guard.
	0.2 ▲	SO	Cattle guard.
▼ 2.9		SO	Road on right is an attractive connecting spur to Northern #4: Strawberry Valley Trail. Zero trip meter.
	0.0 ▲		Continue along Hardware Ranch Road.

GPS: N 41°43.42' W 111°29.51'

▼ 0.0			Continue along Hardware Ranch Road.
	6.5 ▲	SO	Road on left is an attractive connecting spur to Northern #4: Strawberry Valley Trail. Zero trip meter.
▼ 0.4		SO	Cattle guard.
	6.1 ▲	SO	Cattle guard.
▼ 1.1		BR	Track on left to Elk Valley.
	5.4 ▲	BL	Track on right to Elk Valley.

GPS: N 41°44.32' W 111°28.97'

▼ 1.6		SO	Cattle guard.
	4.9 ▲	SO	Cattle guard.
▼ 2.1		SO	Cross through wash.
	4.4 ▲	SO	Cross through wash.
▼ 2.4		BL	Cross through wash. Then FR 182 on right.
	4.1 ▲	BR	FR 182 on left. Then cross through wash.

GPS: N 41°45.02' W 111°28.05'

▼ 2.6		SO	Cross through creek.
	3.9 ▲	SO	Cross through creek.
▼ 3.4		SO	Cattle guard.
	3.1 ▲	SO	Cattle guard.
▼ 3.8		TR	FR 211 to Nebeker Spring and Mill Hollow on left. Then cross creek.
	2.7 ▲	TL	Cross creek. Then FR 211 to Nebeker Spring and Mill Hollow on right.

GPS: N 41°46.09' W 111°28.76'

▼ 5.6		SO	Government Spring on left.
	0.9 ▲	SO	Government Spring on right.
▼ 6.4		SO	Cattle guard.
	0.1 ▲	SO	Cattle guard.
▼ 6.5		TL	T-intersection. Northern #5: Temple Canyon Trail (FR 008) on right. Zero trip meter. Hardware Ranch Road becomes FR 055.
	0.0 ▲		Continue south.

GPS: N 41°48.17' W 111°28.07'

▼ 0.0			Continue north.
	0.2 ▲	TR	Northern #5: Temple Canyon Trail (FR 008) is straight. Turn right to follow Hardware Ranch Road, which becomes FR 105. Zero trip meter.
▼ 0.2		SO	Northern #6: Old Ephraim Trail (FR 007) on left. Zero trip meter.
	0.0 ▲		Continue along Hardware Ranch Road.

GPS: N 41°48.24' W 111°28.24'

▼ 0.0			Continue along Hardware Ranch Road.
	8.4 ▲	SO	Northern #6: Old Ephraim Trail (FR 007) on right. Zero trip meter.

▼ 0.4		BL	Track on right.
	8.0 ▲	BR	Track on left.
▼ 1.3		SO	Pond on left.
	7.1 ▲	SO	Pond on right.
▼ 3.7		SO	Track on left is FR 251 to Temple Peak.
	4.7 ▲	SO	Track on right is FR 251 to Temple Peak.

GPS: N 41°50.29' W 111°30.23'

▼ 4.3		SO	FR 253 (labeled FR 252 on forest map) on left.
	4.1 ▲	SO	FR 253 (labeled FR 252 on forest map) on right.
▼ 5.1		SO	Cattle guard. Then enter T. W. Daniel Experimental Forest.
	3.3 ▲	SO	Leave T. W. Daniel Experimental Forest. Cattle guard.
▼ 5.7		SO	Road on right.
	2.7 ▲	SO	Road on left.
▼ 5.9		SO	FR 175 on right.
	2.5 ▲	SO	FR 175 on left.

GPS: N 41°51.86' W 111°29.95'

▼ 7.0		SO	FR 238 on left.
	1.4 ▲	SO	FR 238 on right.
▼ 7.5		SO	FR 239 on right toward Cheny Creek Trail.
	0.9 ▲	SO	FR 239 on left toward Cheny Creek Trail.
▼ 7.8		SO	Leave T. W. Daniel Experimental Forest.
	0.6 ▲	SO	Enter T. W. Daniel Experimental Forest.
▼ 8.4		SO	Northern #7: Peter Sinks Trail (FR 173) on left. Zero trip meter.
	0.0 ▲		Continue along Hardware Ranch Road.

GPS: N 41°53.41' W 111°29.09'

▼ 0.0			Continue along Hardware Ranch Road.
	2.7 ▲	SO	Northern #7: Peter Sinks Trail (FR 173) on right. Zero trip meter.
▼ 0.3		SO	FR 240 on right.
	2.3 ▲	SO	FR 240 on left.
▼ 2.5		SO	Cattle guard.
	0.2 ▲	SO	Cattle guard.
▼ 2.7			Trail ends at stop sign at US 89. Turn right for Garden City and Bear Lake, left for Logan.
	0.0 ▲		On US 89, west of Bear Lake, zero trip meter and turn south on FR 055. This is also near the Limber Pine Nature Trail at the Cache County and Rich County lines.

GPS: N 41°55.55' W 111°28.39'

NORTHERN REGION TRAIL #2

Millville Canyon Trail

Starting Point:	**Utah 165 in Millville, south of Logan**
Finishing Point:	**Northern #3: Left Hand Fork Canyon Trail**
Total Mileage:	**23.2 miles**
Unpaved Mileage:	**21.6 miles**
Driving Time:	**3 hours**
Elevation Range:	**4,600–9,000 feet**
Usually Open:	**June to October**
Difficulty Rating:	**4**
Scenic Rating:	**9**
Remoteness Rating:	**+1**

A rutted section of the trail

Special Attractions
- Remote crossing of the Bear River Range through the dense Wasatch-Cache National Forest.
- Natural overlooks providing broad panoramic views.
- Numerous backcountry campsites.

History
In the 1850s, Brigham Young concentrated heavily on expanding Mormon settlements throughout Utah. Due to its proximity to Salt Lake City and abundance of natural resources, the Cache Valley quickly became a focal point in Young's plan of expansion.

In 1855, under the leadership of Bryant Stringham, a cattle company established Elkhorn Ranch about 3 miles southeast of present-day Logan. In the winter of 1856, Mormon settlers from the Elkhorn Ranch put cattle out to graze in Cache Valley. The cattle were soon overgrazing the land, which caused starvation among the local Shoshone. The Indians retaliated by killing the disruptive cows. These conflicts with the Indians, coupled with a particularly harsh winter, drove the Mormons off the land and back to Salt Lake City.

Elkhorn Ranch was eventually resettled in 1859, when the first sawmill in Cache Valley was built by Esias Edwards. Over the next 25 years, others followed suit—building a gristmill, broom mill, molasses mill, and distillery. The town's name was soon changed, appropriately enough, to Millville.

Description
From Utah 165, Millville Canyon Trail heads through the settlement of Millville toward the Millville Wildlife Management Area and the much larger Wasatch-Cache National Forest. From the game control fence at the 1.9-mile mark to the first cattle guard about a mile later, the road becomes quite rough with a large amount of imbedded rock. In some places, rocks up to eight inches in diameter make choosing the right line very important for the welfare of your vehicle's undercarriage. In the early stages, numerous side roads make navigation tricky, but the correct route tends to be straight ahead. Although it remains bumpy throughout, the road surface smooths out considerably after you pass the gate at the 2.8-mile point.

The narrow, slow-going trail continues through the canyon along the creek and passes by cottonwoods and tall scrub. The trees close in on the road in many places and make passing difficult for the first 3.5 miles.

After about 5.5 miles, the road begins to level off at the top of Millville Canyon. Besides aspens and conifers, low brush now lines the trail and can scratch the lower portion of your vehicle. The road along this portion of the trail is rutted in spots and impassable during the wet, early spring months. As you travel along the ridgeline, panoramic views of the surrounding countryside open up across the north.

At about the 10-mile point a short track takes you to an overlook at the edge of the Bear River Range. The ledge stands about 2,000 feet above a series of hollows and offers excellent views to the east.

After 18.3 miles, FR 147 leads east to Northern #6: Old Ephraim Trail, and then the road switchbacks through a large stand of aspens as it descends into Herd Hollow. The large, mature trees close in on the road and make for a spectacular autumn drive. In Herd Hollow, the aspens are replaced by cottonwoods. Millville Canyon Trail eventually ends at Northern #3: Left Hand Fork Canyon Trail.

Current Road Information
Wasatch-Cache National Forest
Logan Ranger District
1500 East Highway 89
Logan, UT 84321
(435) 755-3620

Map References
BLM Logan
USFS Wasatch-Cache: Logan Ranger District
USGS 1:24,000 Logan, Logan Peak, Boulder Mt.
1:100,000 Logan
Maptech CD-ROM: Upper Wasatch/Great Salt Lake
Utah Atlas & Gazetteer, pp. 60, 61

The stock troughs at Ferry Spring

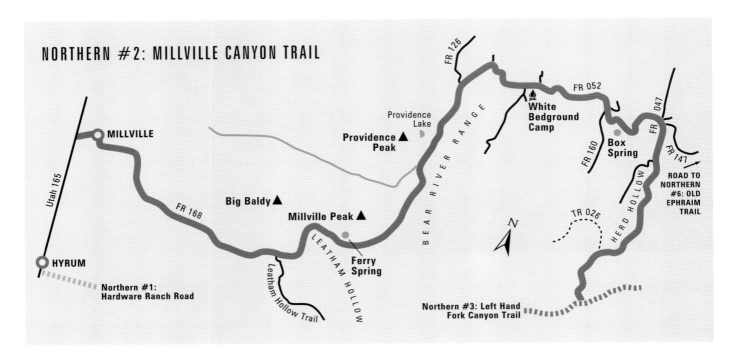

NORTHERN #2: MILLVILLE CANYON TRAIL

Route Directions

▼ 0.0   On Utah 165 in Millville, about 2.7 miles south of US 89/91, zero trip meter and turn onto Mill Road, signed for 238N.

     7.5 ▲   Trail ends at Utah 165. Turn right for Logan and US 89/91.

GPS: N 41°40.60' W 111°49.92'

▼ 0.4   **TR**   Turn right onto Main Street.

     7.1 ▲   TL   Turn left onto Mill Road.

▼ 0.5   **TL**   Turn left onto 300S.

     7.0 ▲   TR   Turn right onto Main Street.

▼ 1.3   **TR**   Turn right onto 500E.

     6.2 ▲   TL   Turn left onto 300S.

▼ 1.6   **BR**   Road forks and becomes gravel.

     5.9 ▲   SO   Continue toward Millville.

▼ 1.9   **SO**   Pass through big game control fence of Millville Wildlife Management Area. Tracks on left and right but proceed straight. Road becomes FR 168.

     5.6 ▲   SO   Pass through big game control fence of Millville Wildlife Management Area. Tracks on left and right but proceed straight. Road becomes 500E.

GPS: N 41°40.07' W 111°48.34'

▼ 2.8   **SO**   Cattle guard and gate.

     4.7 ▲   SO   Gate and cattle guard.

▼ 3.8   **BL**   Cross through creek. Then bear left.

     3.7 ▲   BR   Track on left. Then cross through creek.

GPS: N 41°39.53' W 111°46.32'

▼ 4.3   **BL**   Track on right is FR 023.

     3.2 ▲   BR   Track on left is FR 023.

GPS: N 41°39.44' W 111°45.83'

▼ 5.0   **BR**   Track on left rejoins main trail.

     2.5 ▲   SO   Track on right.

▼ 5.1   **BL**   Bear left at top of hill. Tracks on left and right but stay on main road, continuing to climb.

     2.4 ▲   SO   Tracks left and right. Follow main track downhill.

▼ 5.6   **SO/BL**   Small track on right, then bear left at fork in road; sign "Leatham Hollow Trail" on right.

     1.9 ▲   SO/BR   Track to Leatham Hollow enters on left; then small track on left.

GPS: N 41°39.50' W 111°44.69'

▼ 7.0   **SO**   Track on right and campsite.

     0.5 ▲   SO   Track on left and campsite.

▼ 7.3   **BR**   Fork in road.

     0.2 ▲   BL   Track enters on right.

▼ 7.5   **BR**   Water troughs. Zero trip meter.

     0.0 ▲   Continue downhill.

GPS: N 41°40.14' W 111°43.50'

▼ 0.0   Continue to climb.

     2.8 ▲   BL   Water troughs. Zero trip meter.

▼ 1.1   **SO**   Track on right. Then track on left.

     1.6 ▲   SO   Track on right. Then track on left.

GPS: N 41°40.39' W 111°42.41'

▼ 1.3   **SO**   Track on right.

     1.5 ▲   SO   Track on left.

▼ 2.6   **BL**   Track on right to overlook.

     0.2 ▲   BR   Track on left to overlook.

▼ 2.8   **TR**   T-intersection; turn right. Zero trip meter.

     0.0 ▲   Continue south.

GPS: N 41°41.73' W 111°42.10'

▼ 0.0   Continue north.

     8.0 ▲   TL   Turn left at intersection. Zero trip meter.

▼ 0.1   **BR**   Road forks.

     7.9 ▲   BL   Road on right.

▼ 0.4   **BR**   Road on left.

     7.5 ▲   BL   Road forks.

GPS: N 41°42.03' W 111°42.02'

▼ 1.1   **BR**   Road forks.

     6.9 ▲   TL   Road on left.

GPS: N 41°42.65' W 111°41.86'

▼ 2.0   **BR**   Road forks. FR 126 on left.

     5.9 ▲   BL   Road on right is FR 126.

GPS: N 41°43.34' W 111°41.65'

▼ 2.7	SO	Track on left and right and campsite on right.
5.3 ▲	SO	Campsite on left. Track on left and right.
▼ 2.8	SO	Steep downhill. Track on right rejoins main trail in 0.2 miles.
5.2 ▲	SO	Track on left rejoins.
▼ 3.0	SO	Track on right rejoins.
5.0 ▲	SO	Track on left rejoins main trail in 0.2 miles.
▼ 4.0	BL	Track on right and campsite. Road becomes FR 052.
4.0 ▲	BR	Track on left and campsite. Road becomes FR 168.

GPS: N 41°43.57' W 111°40.19'

▼ 4.0	SO	Track enters on right.
3.9 ▲	BR	Road forks.
▼ 4.2	SO	Track on left.
3.8 ▲	SO	Track on right.
▼ 4.9	BR	Track forks off on left.
3.0 ▲	SO	Track enters on right.

GPS: N 41°43.66' W 111°39.25'

▼ 6.1	SO	FR 160 on right.
1.8 ▲	SO	FR 160 on left.

GPS: N 41°43.56' W 111°38.22'

▼ 7.5	BR	Road forks and rejoins main trail.
0.4 ▲	SO	Road rejoins.
▼ 7.6	SO	Road rejoins.
0.3 ▲	BL	Road forks and rejoins main trail.
▼ 7.7	SO	Stock troughs and pond on left.
0.3 ▲	SO	Stock troughs and pond on right.
▼ 8.0	TR	Intersection with FR 047. Zero trip meter.
0.0 ▲		Continue west on FR 052.

GPS: N 41°43.58' W 111°36.98'

▼ 0.0		Continue south on FR 047.
4.8 ▲	TL	Intersection with FR 052. Zero trip meter.
▼ 0.1	SO	FR 147 on left leads east to Northern #6: Old Ephraim Trail.
4.7 ▲	SO	FR 147 on right leads east to Northern #6: Old Ephraim Trail.
▼ 0.3	SO	Cattle guard.
4.5 ▲	SO	Cattle guard.
▼ 0.4	SO	Track on left.
4.4 ▲	BL	Track on right.
▼ 0.7	SO	Track on right.
4.1 ▲	SO	Track on left.
▼ 1.0	SO	Track on right.
3.8 ▲	SO	Track on left.
▼ 3.6	SO/BL	Cattle guard, then bear left. Sheep Hollow Trail (TR 026) on right.
1.2 ▲	BR/SO	Bear right; Sheep Hollow Trail (TR 026) on left. Then cross cattle guard.

GPS: N 41°41.05' W 111°37.44'

▼ 3.9	SO	Cattle guard.
0.9 ▲	SO	Cattle guard.
▼ 4.8		Seasonal gate and trail ends at Northern #3: Left Hand Fork Canyon Trail. Turn right for Northern #1: Hardware Ranch Road, left for end of Left Hand Fork Canyon Trail.
0.0 ▲		On Northern #3: Left Hand Fork Canyon Trail, 5.7 miles from Northern #1: Hardware Ranch Road, zero trip meter and turn north onto FR 047.

GPS: N 41°40.04' W 111°37.58'

Left Hand Fork Canyon Trail

Starting Point:	**Northern #1: Hardware Ranch Road**
Finishing Point:	**Rock slide, 3.6 miles past Gray Cliff Spring**
Total Mileage:	**10.1 miles**
Unpaved Mileage:	**9.6 miles**
Driving Time:	**45 minutes (one-way)**
Elevation Range:	**5,200–6,200 feet**
Usually Open:	**Year-round**
Difficulty Rating:	**2**
Scenic Rating:	**8**
Remoteness Rating:	**+0**

Special Attractions

- Gray Cliff Spring.
- Spectacular fall scenery.
- Numerous backcountry camping sites along the stream that provide easy access to the area's many 4WD trails.

Description

The trail starts out on the paved FR 245 and then becomes an easy, 1-rated maintained road. Left Hand Fork Canyon has gently sloping walls dotted with pinyon and juniper as well as an unusually pretty floor. The trail follows along the stream past many cottonwoods and several scenic camping spots.

After you pass Northern #2: Millville Canyon Trail at the 5.7-mile mark, the canyon becomes narrower and the road deteriorates, becoming very bumpy as it passes over sections of low, imbedded rock. Passing may present a slight problem in some areas as the brush leaves only a sin-

A view of the trail

NORTHERN #3: LEFT HAND FORK CANYON TRAIL

gle lane. Navigation remains easy throughout, since there are few side roads.

Less than a mile later, Left Hand Fork Canyon Trail passes the very pretty Gray Cliff Spring, which cascades down the canyon wall on the left. The substantial flow of water feeds streams on either side of the trail, creating the unusual situation where the road becomes little more than a ribbon of dry land slicing between the two.

About 3.6 miles past Gray Cliff Spring there has been a substantial rock slide. Although this slide can be crossed by an expert in a suitable vehicle, we have ended the route at this point, since the difficulty of this section goes beyond the scope of this book. If you cross the rock slide, you'll find the road is extremely narrow as it forces its way through dense scrub. After 2 miles, the route rejoins Northern #1: Hardware Ranch Road.

Current Road Information

Wasatch-Cache National Forest
Logan Ranger District
1500 East Highway 89
Logan, UT 84321
(435) 755-3620

A view of one of the rock slides across the trail

Map References

BLM	Logan
USFS	Wasatch-Cache: Logan Ranger District
USGS	1:24,000 Logan Peak, Boulder Mt.
	1:100,000 Logan

Maptech CD-ROM: Upper Wasatch/Great Salt Lake
Utah Atlas & Gazetteer, p. 61
Utah Travel Council #1

Route Directions

▼ 0.0   On Northern #1: Hardware Ranch Road, 7.0 miles from Hyrum, zero trip meter and turn northeast on FR 245.

   5.7 ▲   Trail ends at Northern #1: Hardware Ranch Road. Turn right for Hyrum, left for US 89.

GPS: N 41°37.91' W 111°42.41'

▼ 0.2   SO   Cross bridge.
   5.4 ▲   SO   Cross bridge.

▼ 0.5   SO   Cattle guard.
   5.1 ▲   SO   Cattle guard.

▼ 0.7   SO   Seasonal gate.
   5.0 ▲   SO   Seasonal gate.

▼ 3.0   SO   Blacksmith Fork Guard Station on right.
   2.7 ▲   SO   Blacksmith Fork Guard Station on left.

GPS: N 41°39.57' W 111°40.41'

▼ 3.5   SO   Cache USFS Friendship Campground on right.
   2.2 ▲   SO   Cache USFS Friendship Campground on left.

▼ 4.1   SO   Cache USFS Spring Campground on right.
   1.6 ▲   SO   Cache USFS Spring Campground on left.

▼ 4.6   SO   Cattle guard.
   1.0 ▲   SO   Cattle guard.

▼ 5.7   SO   Left is Northern #2: Millville Canyon Trail (FR 047). Road becomes FR 231. Zero trip meter.
   0.0 ▲   SO   Road becomes FR 245.

GPS: N 41°40.04' W 111°37.58'

▼ 0.0   Continue along FR 231.
▼ 0.8   SO   Gray Cliff Spring waterfall on left directly beside road.

GPS: N 41°40.44' W 111°36.89'

▼ 1.5   SO   Cross through wash.
▼ 4.4   SO   Trail ends at rock slide, 3.6 miles past Gray Cliff Spring.

GPS: N 41°40.28' W 111°33.06'

Strawberry Valley Trail

Starting Point:	Northern #1: Hardware Ranch Road
Finishing Point:	Bear Lake and junction with Northern #5:
	Temple Canyon Trail
Total Mileage:	17.6 miles
Unpaved Mileage:	12.7 miles
Driving Time:	1 hour
Elevation Range:	6,000–7,200 feet
Usually Open:	May to October
Difficulty Rating:	1
Scenic Rating:	7
Remoteness Rating:	+0

Special Attractions

■ Bear Lake.
■ The town site of Round Valley.
■ A gentle, easy, and scenic canyon road.

History

When the Mormons arrived in Utah, the fertile area south of Bear Lake was a natural place to settle. Full of lush meadows and big game, Round Valley was not only a practical spot but a beautiful one. The only problem for the newly arrived settlers was that the region was already inhabited by local Indians. Competition for land and resources escalated and soon led to the brink of war. However, a settlement was reached in 1870, which brought about 30 years of peace and prosperity for the Mormons.

In the 1910s, drought and locusts crippled Round Valley's crops and signaled the slow demise of the town. By the 1930s Round Valley was almost completely deserted. (For more on Round Valley see p. 42.)

The old Round Valley cemetery is located off the main road on private property. A sign currently marks a walking path leading to the site.

Description

On Northern #1: Hardware Ranch Road, 21.6 miles from Hyrum, Strawberry Valley Trail heads northeast into a fairly shallow canyon. This relatively easy road follows beside a creek and travels through the scenic ranchland of Strawberry Valley. The trail enters Lodgepole Canyon and then crosses into Cottonwood Canyon before finally exiting onto the paved road to Laketown. Shortly after joining the paved road, the trail passes to the left of the old town site of Round Valley (and the walking track out to the old cemetery) as it travels through attractive, rolling ranchland.

The Strawberry Valley Trail comes to an end at the intersection of Main Street and Utah 30 in Laketown, on the southern shore of Bear Lake. To the left is the start of Northern #5: Temple Canyon Trail.

Current Road Information

Wasatch-Cache National Forest
Logan Ranger District
1500 East Highway 89
Logan, UT 84321
(435) 755-3620

Map References

BLM Logan
USFS Wasatch-Cache: Logan Ranger District
USGS 1:24,000 Boulder Mt., Red Spur Mt., Meadowville, Laketown
1:100,000 Logan
Maptech CD-ROM: Upper Wasatch/Great Salt Lake
Utah Atlas & Gazetteer, pp. 61, 63
Utah Travel Council #1

Route Directions

▼ 0.0			On Northern #1: Hardware Ranch Road, 21.6 miles from Hyrum, proceed northeast and zero trip meter.
	4.8 ▲		Trail ends at Northern #1: Hardware Ranch Road. Turn left for Hyrum, right for US 89.
		GPS: N 41°40.71′ W 111°31.21′	
▼ 0.9		SO	Track on right.
	3.9 ▲	SO	Track on left.
▼ 1.4		SO	Cross bridge.
	3.4 ▲	SO	Cross bridge.
▼ 4.1		BR	Road forks.
	0.7 ▲	SO	Track enters on right.
		GPS: N 41°42.36′ W 111°27.68′	
▼ 4.2		SO	Cross over creek.
	0.6 ▲	SO	Cross over creek.
▼ 4.7		SO	Track to corral on right.
	0.1 ▲	SO	Track to corral on left.
▼ 4.8		SO	Intersection. FR 058 to Bug Lake and Randolph on right. Zero trip meter. Pass corral and travel through Lodgepole Canyon.
	0.0 ▲		Continue along main road.
		GPS: N 41°42.93′ W 111°27.33′	
▼ 0.0			Continue along main road.
	7.8 ▲	SO	Pass corral, then intersection. FR 058 to Bug Lake and Randolph on left. Zero trip meter.
▼ 0.6		SO	Cattle guard.
	7.2 ▲	SO	Cattle guard.
▼ 0.8		SO	Track on left.
	7.0 ▲	SO	Track on right.
▼ 2.1		SO	Track on right.
	5.7 ▲	SO	Track on left.
▼ 2.3		SO	Track on left and right.
	5.5 ▲	SO	Track on right and left.
		GPS: N 41°43.61′ W 111°25.70′	
▼ 2.4		SO	Cattle guard. Leave Wasatch-Cache National Forest.
	5.4 ▲	SO	Enter Wasatch-Cache National Forest. Cattle guard.
▼ 4.4		SO	Cattle guard.
	3.4 ▲	SO	Cattle guard.
▼ 7.3		SO	Cattle guard.
	0.5 ▲	SO	Cattle guard.
▼ 7.8		TR	Cattle guard, then intersection with paved road. Zero trip meter.

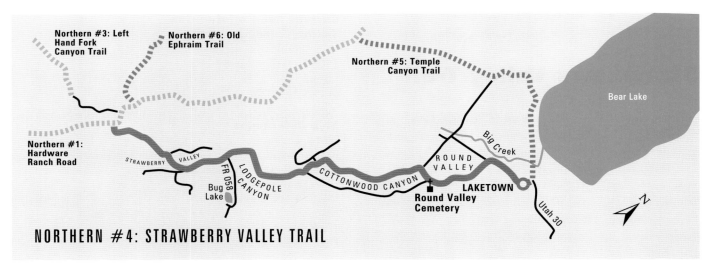

NORTHERN #4: STRAWBERRY VALLEY TRAIL

0.0 ▲			Proceed south through Cottonwood Canyon.
			GPS: N 41°47.39' W 111°22.44'
▼ 0.0			Proceed toward Laketown.
	4.9 ▲	TL	Intersection. Turn onto unpaved road, zero trip meter, then pass cattle guard.
▼ 0.6		SO	Round Valley cemetery on right.
	4.3 ▲	SO	Round Valley cemetery on left.
			GPS: N 41°47.36' W 111°21.80'
▼ 3.0		TR	Intersection.
	1.9 ▲	TL	Intersection.
▼ 4.5		TL	Laketown post office, then intersection at Old Rock Store. Turn left onto Main Street.
	0.4 ▲	TR	Intersection at Old Rock Store, then Laketown post office.
▼ 4.9			Trail ends at Bear Lake Boulevard (Utah 30) in Laketown. Turn left on Utah 30 for Northern #5: Temple Canyon Trail.
	0.0 ▲		At the intersection of Main Street and Bear Lake Boulevard (Utah 30) in Laketown, zero trip meter and proceed along Main Street.
			GPS: N 41°49.85' W 111°19.33'

Temple Canyon Trail

Starting Point:	**Laketown, end of Northern #4:**
	Strawberry Valley Trail
Finishing Point:	**Northern #1: Hardware Ranch Road**
Total Mileage:	**10.9 miles**
Unpaved Mileage:	**8 miles**
Driving Time:	**1 hour**
Elevation Range:	**5,900–7,600 feet**
Usually Open:	**May to October**
Difficulty Rating:	**1**
Scenic Rating:	**8**
Remoteness Rating:	**+0**

Special Attractions

- Bear Lake.
- Forms loop trail with Northern #4: Strawberry Valley Trail off Northern #1: Hardware Ranch Road.

Description

In Laketown, at the northern endpoint of Northern #4: Strawberry Valley Trail, Temple Canyon Trail heads northwest on Bear Lake Boulevard, which runs along the shore of Bear Lake. After the trail enters Temple Canyon, it runs along a wide shelf road with plenty of places to pass oncoming vehicles. Although the trail is only about 50 feet above the canyon floor, views over the aspen- and conifer-laden valley are quite pretty. After crossing a cattle guard at the 8.4-mile mark, the road enters a forest. From here, the road is bumpier as it proceeds over sections of imbedded rock. The trail comes to an end at Northern #1: Hardware Ranch Road.

Current Road Information

Wasatch-Cache National Forest
Logan Ranger District
1500 East Highway 89
Logan, UT 84321
(435) 755-3620

Map References

BLM Logan
USFS Wasatch-Cache: Logan Ranger District
USGS 1:24,000 Laketown, Meadowville
      1:100,000 Logan
Maptech CD-ROM: Upper Wasatch/Great Salt Lake
Utah Atlas & Gazetteer, p. 63
Utah Travel Council #1

Route Directions

▼ 0.0		At end of Northern #4: Strawberry Valley Trail, at intersection of Main Street and Bear Lake Boulevard (Utah 30) in Laketown, zero trip meter and proceed northwest along Bear Lake Boulevard.
	2.9 ▲	Trail ends at Main Street in Laketown. Turn

right on Main Street for Northern #4: Strawberry Valley Trail.

GPS: N 41°49.85' W 111°19.33'

▼ 2.7	SO	Rest stop and picnic area on right.
0.1 ▲	SO	Rest stop and picnic area on left.
▼ 2.9	TL	Turn left onto unpaved Meadowville Road, cross cattle guard, and zero trip meter.
0.0 ▲		Continue toward Laketown.

GPS: N 41°51.56' W 111°21.87'

▼ 0.0		Follow unpaved road.
8.0 ▲	TR	Turn right onto paved Bear Lake Boulevard (Utah 30). Zero trip meter.
▼ 1.1	SO	Track on right.
6.9 ▲	SO	Track on left.
▼ 1.6	SO	Cattle guard.
6.4 ▲	SO	Cattle guard.
▼ 2.0	BL	Cooks Road on right to Cooks Reservoir.
6.0 ▲	BL	Cooks Road on left to Cooks Reservoir.

GPS: N 41°51.20' W 111°23.54'

▼ 2.6	TR	Turn right onto dirt road.
5.3 ▲	TL	Turn left at intersection.
▼ 2.8	TL	Follow dirt road through Meadowville.
5.1 ▲	TR	Pass through Meadowville and turn right at intersection.
▼ 2.9	TR	Turn right onto road to Temple Canyon.
5.0 ▲	TL	Turn left toward Meadowville.
▼ 3.5	SO	Cattle guard.
4.5 ▲	SO	Cattle guard.
▼ 5.5	SO	Cattle guard and sign for Temple Canyon (FR 008).
2.5 ▲	SO	Cattle guard.
▼ 6.4	SO	Track on right.
1.6 ▲	SO	Track on left.

GPS: N 41°49.02' W 111°27.03'

▼ 6.6	BL	Track on right.
1.4 ▲	BR	Track on left.
▼ 6.7	SO	Track on left.
1.3 ▲	SO	Track on right and sign for Temple Canyon.

GPS: N 41°48.82' W 111°27.10'

A view of Bear Lake from the trail

▼ 7.1	SO	Follow sign for "Temple Flat, Blacksmith Fork, Sinks Road and Temple Fork" straight ahead. Then road on right.
0.9 ▲	SO	Road on left.
▼ 7.2	SO	Track on left is FR 181.
0.8 ▲	SO	Track on right is FR 181.

GPS: N 41°48.50' W 111°27.51'

▼ 8.0		Trail ends at Northern #1: Hardware Ranch Road. Turn right for US 89, left for Hyrum.
0.0 ▲		On Northern #1: Hardware Ranch Road, 11.3 miles from US 89, zero trip meter and turn east onto FR 008 toward Temple Flat.

GPS: N 41°48.17' W 111°28.07'

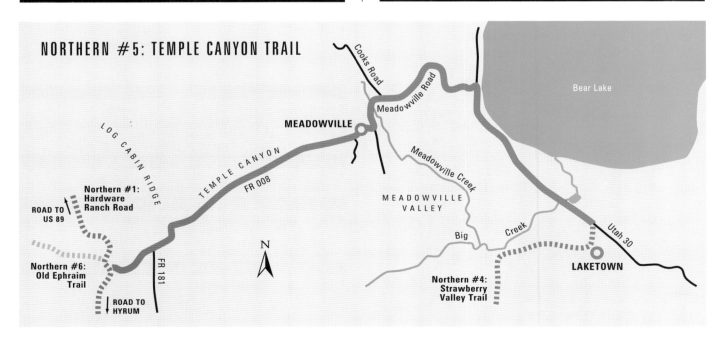

NORTHERN #5: TEMPLE CANYON TRAIL

Cooks Road

Meadowville Road

MEADOWVILLE

Bear Lake

Meadowville Creek

LOG CABIN RIDGE

TEMPLE CANYON FR 008

Northern #1: Hardware Ranch Road

ROAD TO US 89

FR 181

Northern #6: Old Ephraim Trail

ROAD TO HYRUM

MEADOWVILLE VALLEY

Big Creek

Utah 30

LAKETOWN

Northern #4: Strawberry Valley Trail

N

Old Ephraim Trail

Starting Point:	Northern #1: Hardware Ranch Road
Finishing Point:	Northern #1: Hardware Ranch Road
Total Mileage:	13.4 miles
Unpaved Mileage:	13.4 miles
Driving Time:	1.5 hours
Elevation Range:	6,400–7,900 feet
Usually Open:	June to October
Difficulty Rating:	4
Scenic Rating:	8
Remoteness Rating:	+1

Special Attractions

■ The story of, and monument to, Old Ephraim.
■ Aspen viewing in the fall.
■ Moderately challenging 4WD road.

History

The Old Ephraim Trail takes you to the gravesite of one of Cache Valley's most legendary figures. As far as anyone knows, Old Ephraim was the last grizzly bear to live in Utah. Before his death at the hands of Frank Clark on August 22, 1923, Old Ephraim was known to ranchers and sheepherders as an enormous, ghostlike predator who passed through the region snatching livestock without ever being seen by anyone. All the sheepherders like Clark knew about the bear were his hunting patterns and his distinctive footprint; Old Ephraim had a missing middle claw on his left hind foot.

Frank Clark lived in northern Utah for 12 years, and his sheep served as an occasional dinner for this clandestine grizzly bear. Clark was determined to catch him even though he'd never even glimpsed Old Ephraim. Through the years, the story of the legendary meeting between the two in the late summer of 1923 has become a mix of fact and pioneer folklore. For the full tale of the showdown between Clark and Old Ephraim, see "Legend of Old Ephraim," p. 78.

The monument erected by the local scouts to commemorate Old Ephraim

Description

The Old Ephraim Trail makes a loop off of Northern #1: Hardware Ranch Road, winding its way through a beautiful mountain forest. About 1.5 miles from the start, you come into a clearing with expansive views of the surrounding mountain landscape in all directions.

The trail runs in and out of the forest, which keeps a constant amount of moisture on the road's surface. This moisture has led to considerable erosion and rutting in the roads, making high clearance a must. In some of the more heavily rutted spots, choosing the right line often means brushing up against the bushes on the side of the road. The forest also closes in on the trail in spots, making the clearance between the trees tight.

Even though the road is quite often wet and boggy, imbedded rocks in the road's surface allow for good traction. This rough surface can be very helpful along some of the steeper sections of shelf road.

A little over halfway along the trail, at the 7.1-mile point, you come to the marker commemorating the death of Utah's last grizzly bear. The trail finishes through a few stands of aspen and returns you to Northern #1: Hardware Ranch Road.

Current Road Information

Wasatch-Cache National Forest
Logan Ranger District
1500 East Highway 89
Logan, UT 84321
(435) 755-3620

Map References

BLM Logan
USFS Wasatch-Cache: Logan Ranger District
USGS 1:24,000 Meadowville, Temple Peak, Boulder Mt.
1:100,000 Logan
Maptech CD-ROM: Upper Wasatch/Great Salt Lake
Utah Atlas & Gazetteer, pp. 61, 63
Utah Travel Council #1 (incomplete)

Route Directions

▼ 0.0			On Northern #1: Hardware Ranch Road, 11.1 miles south of US 89, zero trip meter and turn west onto FR 007.
	4.4 ▲		Trail ends at Northern #1: Hardware Ranch Road. Turn left for US 89, right for Hyrum.
		GPS: N 41°48.24′ W 111°28.24′	
▼ 0.5		SO	Cattle guard.
	3.8 ▲	SO	Cattle guard.
▼ 0.7		SO	Two tracks on left.
	3.7 ▲	SO	Two tracks on right.
		GPS: N 41°48.27′ W 111°29.08′	
▼ 1.6		SO	Track on left.
	2.7 ▲	SO	Track on right.
		GPS: N 41°48.19′ W 111°30.01′	
▼ 1.7		SO	Track on left (track on right seems deliberately blocked by rocks).
	2.6 ▲	SO	Track on right (track on left seems deliberately blocked by rocks).
		GPS: N 41°48.21′ W 111°30.17′	
▼ 2.1		SO	Cattle guard.
	2.3 ▲	SO	Cattle guard.
▼ 2.3		SO	FR 177 on left.
	2.1 ▲	SO	FR 177 on right.

▼ 4.4		TL	Turn left onto FR 056 and zero trip meter. FR 007 continues straight ahead.
	0.0 ▲		Continue along FR 007.

▼ 0.0			Continue along FR 056.
	2.7 ▲	TR	Intersection. Turn right onto FR 007. Zero trip meter.
▼ 2.5		SO	Cross over creek.
	0.1 ▲	SO	Cross over creek.
▼ 2.7		SO	Old Ephraim's grave marker on left. Zero trip meter.
	0.0 ▲		Continue along FR 056

▼ 0.0			Continue along FR 056.
	6.3 ▲	SO	Old Ephraim's grave marker on right. Zero trip meter.
▼ 1.4		SO	Dog Spring on left with trough.
	4.8 ▲	SO	Dog Spring on right with trough.
▼ 1.6		BL	FR 148 on right.
	4.7 ▲	BR	FR 148 on left.

▼ 1.7		SO	Steel Hollow hiking trail on right.
	4.6 ▲	SO	Steel Hollow hiking trail on left.
▼ 2.4		SO	FR 147 on right leads to Northern #2: Millville Canyon Trail.
	3.8 ▲	SO	FR 147 on left leads to Northern #2: Millville Canyon Trail.
▼ 5.4		SO	Track on right.
	0.9 ▲	SO	Track on left.
▼ 5.8		SO	Seasonal gate.
	0.4 ▲	SO	Seasonal gate.

A 4WD vehicle that slipped into a deep rut along one of the off-camber sections of the trail

▼ 6.2		BR	Fork in road is part of an intersection delta: left also goes to Hardware Ranch Road.
	0.1 ▲	SO	Track on right.
▼ 6.3			Trail ends at Northern #1: Hardware Ranch Road. Turn right for Hyrum, left for US 89.
	0.0 ▲		On Northern #1: Hardware Ranch Road, 23.2 miles from Hyrum, zero trip meter and turn northwest onto FR 056.

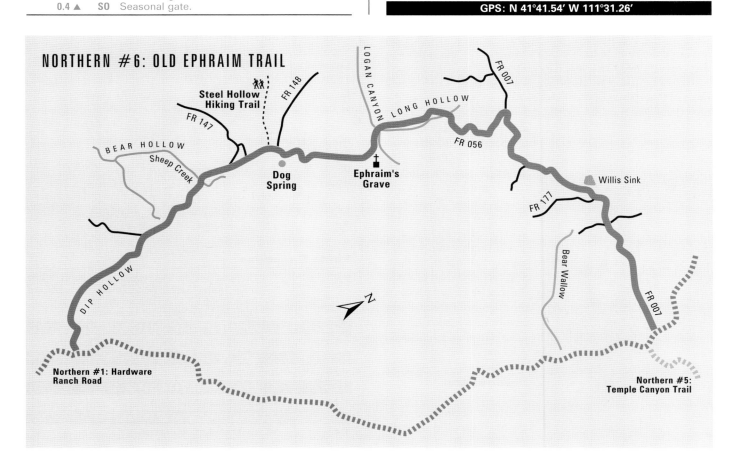

NORTHERN #6: OLD EPHRAIM TRAIL

Peter Sinks Trail

Starting Point:	Northern #1: Hardware Ranch Road
Finishing Point:	Northern #1: Hardware Ranch Road
Total Mileage:	7.6 miles
Unpaved Mileage:	7.6 miles
Driving Time:	1 hour (one-way)
Elevation Range:	8,000–8,600 feet
Usually Open:	June to October
Difficulty Rating:	3
Scenic Rating:	8
Remoteness Rating:	+1

Special Attractions

- Sinkholes in a remote alpine basin setting.
- Broad views across to Bear Lake.
- Fascinating side road from Northern #1: Hardware Ranch Road.

History

Peter Sinks Basin encompasses an area that is roughly 0.6 by 1.2 miles and about 600 to 700 feet lower than the surrounding terrain. The sinkholes in Peter Sinks were caused when underground water created caverns beneath the earth's surface. The caverns eventually collapsed and the ground caved in, leaving these deep holes. Do not try to explore the sinkholes; they are very deep and very dangerous.

Cold nighttime air also flows down into the lower elevations of Peter Sinks and collects in cold-air pools. Due to the high density of the cold air, the pools remain inside the basin and produce freezing cold temperatures. In the winter of 1985, Peter Sinks recorded the second lowest temperature in the continental United States —a frigid -56° Celsius (-69° Fahrenheit).

Currently, information gathered at the rural Peter Sinks is being used to study the nature of air pools in other more-urban basin environments such as Salt Lake City and Phoenix, Arizona.

Description

Peter Sinks Trail makes a loop that begins and ends at the same point on Northern #1: Hardware

A view of one of the sinks

Ranch Road. It travels through the Engelmann spruce and Douglas firs of the Wasatch-Cache National Forest. In areas where the landscape opens up, there are expansive views over Bear Lake. The trail also passes by the series of picturesque sinkholes that give the region its name.

The road itself is not very difficult, though you encounter the ruts, roots, and potholes that come hand in hand with forested trails. In spots, the trail becomes very narrow as it passes between the trees. There is little room to choose a line in these places because typically only one exists. The road is also usually damp and boggy, so high clearance and good tires are a big help in negotiating some of the more rock-rutted and slippery sections. After rains, the trail becomes very treacherous and is better left for another day.

The Great Western Hiking Trail crosses through the Peter Sinks Basin and offers an enjoyable walk through this unique region.

A section of the trail that squeezes through the trees before reaching the sinks

Current Road Information

Wasatch-Cache National Forest
Logan Ranger District
1500 East Highway 89
Logan, UT 84321
(435) 755-3620

Map References

BLM Logan
USFS Wasatch-Cache: Logan Ranger District
USGS 1:24,000 Garden City, Tony Grove Creek
1:100,000 Logan
Maptech CD-ROM: Upper Wasatch/Great Salt Lake
Utah Atlas & Gazetteer, p. 63

Route Directions

▼ 0.0		On Northern #1: Hardware Ranch Road, 2.7 miles from US 89, zero trip meter and proceed west along FR 173. Follow sign to "West Hodges, Little Bear and Peter Sinks."
	GPS: N 41°53.41' W 111°29.09'	
▼ 2.0	**TR**	Road on right is the beginning of loop trail.
	GPS: N 41°54.32' W 111°30.70'	
▼ 2.5	**TL**	Turn left.
	GPS: N 41°54.71' W 111°30.49'	
▼ 3.7	**SO**	Pass through gate.
	GPS: N 41°54.31' W 111°31.65'	
▼ 4.1	**SO**	Sinkhole beside the trail.
▼ 4.3	**TL**	Intersection; turn left.

NORTHERN #7: PETER SINKS TRAIL

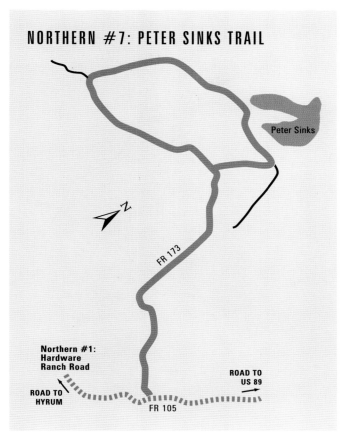

GPS: N 41°53.80' W 111°31.76'		
▼ 5.2	SO	Track on right.
GPS: N 41°54.13' W 111°30.99'		
▼ 5.4	SO	Pass through fence line.
▼ 5.6	SO	Track on left completes the loop.
GPS: N 41°54.32' W 111°30.70'		
▼ 7.6		Trail ends at Northern #1: Hardware Ranch Road. Turn left for US 89, right for Hyrum.
GPS: N 41°53.41' W 111°29.09'		

NORTHERN REGION TRAIL #8

Idaho Loop

Starting Point:	US 89, at CR 243
Finishing Point:	US 89, at FR 006
Total Mileage:	23.7 miles
Unpaved Mileage:	23 miles
Driving Time:	1.5 hours
Elevation Range:	6,600–8,500 feet
Usually Open:	June to October
Difficulty Rating:	2
Scenic Rating:	8
Remoteness Rating:	+1

Special Attractions

- Aspen viewing in the fall.
- Easy, pleasant 4WD trail with varied scenery.
- Numerous backcountry campsites with access to a network of 4WD roads to explore.

Description

The Idaho Loop trail, as its name implies, travels mainly through Idaho, making a loop off of US 89 in Utah. It begins beside Beaver Creek on a single-lane forest road. The road itself is only occasionally maintained and has been noticeably eroded in some spots. Stretches of imbedded rock can make this relatively easy road very rough in places.

For the first couple miles, the trail passes several camping spots as it winds through areas of aspen and conifer. Also, many beaver dams appear for mile after mile alongside the creek.

As you continue through Egan Basin toward Danish Pass, the trail can become slippery and muddy when wet. It is generally an easy road until the last couple miles, where it becomes rocky and considerably more rough.

As you come down from Danish Pass through the thick forest, turn onto FR 406 and head south back to Utah. On the return portion of the loop, the trail

The trail following beside Beaver Creek

travels through large, open meadows dotted with conifers and thick stands of aspen that offer wonderful fall viewing. About a mile and a half before the trail's ending point, beaver dams once again become prominent along the creek. Campsites, too, are prevalent throughout this final portion of the trail before it ends at US 89.

Current Road Information

Wasatch-Cache National Forest
Logan Ranger District
1500 East Highway 89
Logan, UT 84321
(435) 755-3620

Caribou-Targhee National Forest
Montpelier Ranger District
322 North Fourth
Montpelier, ID 83254
(208) 847-0375

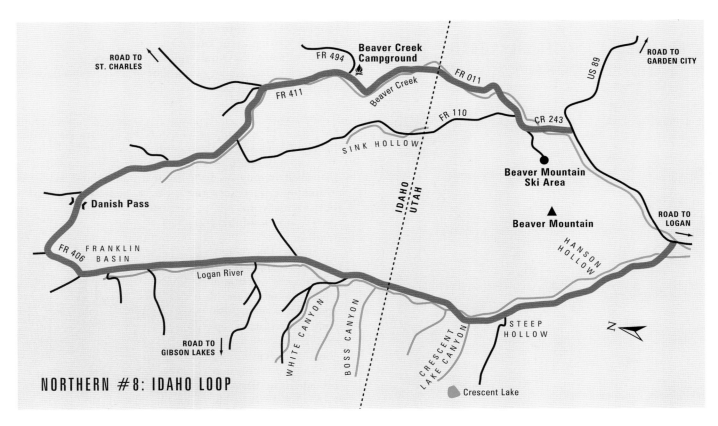

NORTHERN #8: IDAHO LOOP

Map References

BLM Logan (incomplete)
USFS Wasatch-Cache: Logan Ranger District (incomplete)
USGS 1:24,000 Tony Grove Creek (incomplete)
         1:100,000 Logan (incompete)
Maptech CD-ROM: Upper Wasatch/Great Salt Lake
Utah Atlas & Gazetteer, p. 63
Idaho Atlas & Gazetteer, p. 23
Utah Travel Council #1 (incomplete)

Route Directions

▼ 0.0   On US 89, zero trip meter and proceed north along CR 243 toward Beaver Mountain ski area.

     6.3 ▲   Trail ends at US 89. Turn right for Logan, left for Garden City and Bear Lake.

GPS: N 41°57.79' W 111°31.87'

▼ 0.7   **BR**   Bear right onto unpaved track (FR 011). Public toilets on right and Travel Management Area sign.

     5.6 ▲   **BL**   Bear left onto CR 243.

GPS: N 41°58.41' W 111°31.85'

▼ 0.9   **BR**   Track on left is FR 110 to Sink Hollow.

     5.4 ▲   **BL**   Track on right is FR 110 to Sink Hollow.

▼ 1.2   **SO**   Tracks to camping area on left.

     5.1 ▲   **BL**   Tracks to camping area on right.

▼ 1.5   **SO**   Cross over creek.

     4.8 ▲   **SO**   Cross over creek.

▼ 2.7   **SO**   Bridge over creek.

     3.6 ▲   **SO**   Bridge over creek.

▼ 2.8   **SO**   Idaho state line. Road is now FR 411.

     3.5 ▲   **SO**   Utah state line. Road is now FR 011.

GPS: N 41°59.94' W 111°31.09'

▼ 3.2   **SO**   Cross bridge over creek, then cattle guard.

     3.0 ▲   **SO**   Cattle guard, then cross bridge over creek.

▼ 3.4   **SO**   Track on right.

     2.8 ▲   **SO**   Track on left.

▼ 4.7   **SO**   USFS Beaver Creek Campground on right.

     1.6 ▲   **SO**   USFS Beaver Creek Campground on left.

▼ 4.8   **SO**   Track on right is FR 494.

     1.5 ▲   **SO**   Track on left is FR 494.

▼ 5.6   **SO**   Cross over creek. Then track on left.

     0.7 ▲   **SO**   Track on right. Then cross over creek.

GPS: N 42°01.99' W 111°31.96'

▼ 6.2   **SO**   Cross over creek.

     0.1 ▲   **SO**   Cross over creek.

▼ 6.3   **BL**   Road forks. Bear left to Egan Basin and US 89. Right goes to St. Charles. Zero trip meter.

     0.0 ▲   Continue along the trail.

GPS: N 42°02.57' W 111°32.20'

▼ 0.0   Continue along the trail.

     4.2 ▲   **BR**   Road to St. Charles enters on left. Zero trip meter.

▼ 0.5   **SO/SO**   Road on right. Then road on right to Pat Hollow Crash site.

     3.7 ▲ **SO/BR**   Road to Pat Hollow Crash site on left. Then bear right at fork in road.

▼ 0.8   **SO**   Corral on left.

     3.4 ▲   **SO**   Corral on right.

▼ 1.1   **SO**   Track on left to Gibson Basin.

     3.1 ▲   **SO**   Track on right to Gibson Basin.

GPS: N 42°02.74' W 111°33.46'

▼ 1.4   **SO**   Cattle guard.

     2.8 ▲   **SO**   Cattle guard.

▼ 2.1   **SO**   Track on left.

2.1 ▲	SO	Track on right.
▼ 2.5	SO	Track on right.
1.7 ▲	SO	Track on left.

GPS: N 42°03.74' W 111°34.23'

▼ 4.2	SO	Highline Trail crosses road. Then cattle guard and Danish Pass. Zero trip meter.
0.0 ▲		Continue along the trail.

GPS: N 42°04.93' W 111°35.28'

▼ 0.0		Descend from pass.
2.4 ▲	SO	Danish Pass. Then cattle guard and Highline Trail crosses road. Zero trip meter.
▼ 1.3	BL	Intersection.
1.1 ▲	BR	Intersection.

GPS: N 42°05.18' W 111°36.52'

▼ 2.3	BL	Intersection; bear left onto FR 406 to Franklin Basin.
0.1 ▲	BR	Intersection; bear right on road to Egan Basin.
▼ 2.4	SO	Road forks; track on right. Zero trip meter.
0.0 ▲		Continue along trail.

GPS: N 42°04.57' W 111°36.82'

▼ 0.0		Continue along FR 406.
10.8 ▲	BR	Track on left. Zero trip meter.
▼ 2.7	SO	Track on left.
8.0 ▲	SO	Track on right.
▼ 2.9	SO	Track on right to Gibson Lakes.
7.9 ▲	SO	Track on left to Gibson Lakes.

GPS: N 42°02.11' W 111°35.80'

▼ 3.5	SO	Track on left.
7.2 ▲	SO	Track on right.
▼ 4.5	SO	Track on right to White Canyon.
6.3 ▲	SO	Track on left to White Canyon.
▼ 5.2	SO	Cross Utah state line.
5.6 ▲	SO	Cross Idaho state line.

GPS: N 42°00.07' W 111°35.73'

▼ 6.6	SO	Cross bridge.
4.2 ▲	SO	Cross bridge.
▼ 7.4	SO	Track on right.
3.4 ▲	SO	Track on left.
▼ 7.5	SO	Track on right.
3.3 ▲	SO	Track on left.
▼ 7.6	SO	Track on right.
3.2 ▲	SO	Track on left.
▼ 7.9	SO	Tracks on left and right.
2.9 ▲	SO	Tracks on right and left.
▼ 9.0	SO	Track on left.
1.8 ▲	SO	Track on right.
▼ 9.3	SO	Track on right.
1.5 ▲	SO	Track on left.
▼ 9.5	SO	Cross creek.
1.3 ▲	SO	Cross creek.
▼ 10.4	SO	Track on right.
0.4 ▲	SO	Track on left.
▼ 10.5	SO	Cross bridge.
0.3 ▲	SO	Cross bridge.

GPS: N 41°56.02' W 111°33.95'

▼ 10.7	SO	Public toilets on right.
0.1 ▲	SO	Public toilets on left.
▼ 10.8		Trail ends at US 89. Turn right for Logan, left for Garden City and Bear Lake.
0.0 ▲		On US 89, zero trip meter and turn north onto Franklin Basin Road (FR 006).

GPS: N 41°55.88' W 111°33.67'

Inspiration Point Trail

Starting Point:	North Main Street in Mantua
Finishing Point:	Inspiration Point
Total Mileage:	13.7 miles
Unpaved Mileage:	11.6 miles
Driving Time:	1.5 hours (one-way)
Elevation Range:	5,200–9,422 feet
Usually Open:	May to October
Difficulty Rating:	3
Scenic Rating:	10
Remoteness Rating:	+0

Special Attractions

- Spectacular 360-degree view from the parking spot on the absolute summit.
- Scenic 4WD trail that offers a reasonable challenge for less-experienced four-wheelers.
- Easy access from Salt Lake City.
- Good backcountry camping.

History

In the mid-1800s Brigham Young's cousin, Willard Richards, served as one of his most trusted counselors. Although a medical man by trade, Richards also held many prominent positions in local government and in the Mormon Church. Before his death in 1854, he served as general church historian, postmaster of Salt Lake City, and editor of the *Deseret News*, the Mormon newspaper. He published its first issue.

The area east of Bear River Bay has since been named Willard Basin. In 1923, this area was the scene of one of Utah's worst floods. Over the years, overgrazing had stripped most of the vegetation in Willard Basin, and during the spring of 1923, runoff from melting snow began to cause serious erosion to the land. The Willard Basin was in a very precarious position, and many felt there was a catastrophe waiting to happen.

On the night of August 13, 1923, thunder struck and the

A view of the trail as it winds around Black Mountain

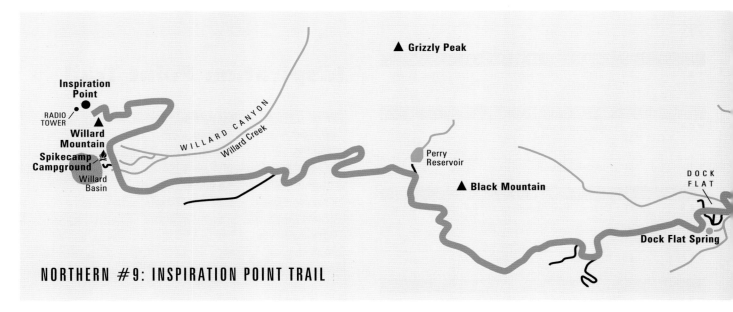

▲ Grizzly Peak

Inspiration Point

RADIO TOWER

Willard Mountain

Spikecamp Campground

Willard Basin

WILLARD CANYON

Willard Creek

Perry Reservoir

▲ Black Mountain

DOCK FLAT

Dock Flat Spring

NORTHERN #9: INSPIRATION POINT TRAIL

rains poured down. Flood waters soon followed causing multiple injuries, one death, and wiping out over 300 acres of prime agricultural land. Extensive damage was caused to many homes and barns. It took a crew of 250 men several weeks to clear the mud and rubble that had been deposited on the main road through the town of Willard. It took months of hard work and over $75,000 in relief funds for the town to recover from the flood.

However, the town still stood at risk for another flood. In the 1930s the federal government addressed the issue by establishing a Civilian Conservation Corps (CCC) camp in Willard Basin. The young men of the CCC constructed a dike and natural spillway to prevent further flooding. They also terraced the mountainside to further reduce the risk of flood in Willard Basin.

Description

The entire Inspiration Point Trail is very scenic, and it has a truly spectacular viewpoint at the end. The trail starts in Mantua in front of the municipal buildings (including the library and city offices) on North Main Street. After a couple of miles,

The view from Inspiration Point

the trail leaves paved roads behind and continues along a substantial, two-lane dirt road that offers a number of backcountry campsites.

At the 3.3-mile point, the road narrows as you begin to climb out of the valley. As you drive through the thick shrubbery of the Wasatch Range, you come across a number of side roads. However, they are noticeably minor tracks and navigation remains easy.

The trail then enters a coniferous forest on a steep shelf road that is closed in on either side by trees. At times, the trail passes along areas of less dense foliage that offer some remarkably expansive views. About 8 miles into the trail, the road climbs once again and becomes much more rough and narrow with sections of loose gravel. This half-mile stretch of road is about as difficult as the trail gets.

The trail eventually evens out near the Willard Point Overlook sign and continues along an open shelf road. This one-lane road has a number of places to pull off to allow someone to pass. From here, you loop around Willard Basin. The road is well below the ridgeline, which can make you feel as if you are driving through some kind of natural enclosure. There is a nice USFS campsite at the top of the basin.

The trail ends at Inspiration Point, where the top of the 9,422-foot peak offers views in every direction. To the east is Willard Basin. To the west is the Great Salt Lake, whose waters rest over 5,000 feet below in Willard Bay State Park. To the southeast, the Wasatch Range continues, with Ogden Valley to the east. The view from Inspiration Point is truly magnificent and worth savoring before heading back down the trail.

Current Road Information

Wasatch-Cache National Forest
Logan Ranger District
1500 East Highway 89
Logan, UT 84321
(435) 755-3620

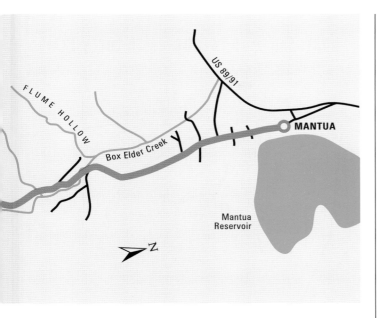

Map References
BLM   Ogden
USFS Wasatch-Cache: Ogden Ranger District
USGS 1:24,000 Mantua
       •1:100,000 Ogden
Maptech CD-ROM: Upper Wasatch/Great Salt Lake
Utah Atlas & Gazetteer, p. 60
Utah Travel Council #1 (incomplete)

Route Directions

▼ 0.0		On North Main Street in Mantua, between Fourth and Fifth Streets in front of the municipal buildings, zero trip meter and proceed south through town.
		GPS: N 41°30.21' W 111°56.55'
▼ 0.1	SO	Stop sign and fork in road. Keep right of church. Road becomes Willard Peak Road.
▼ 2.1	SO	Road becomes graded gravel.
▼ 3.3	BL	Numerous tracks left and right. Road narrows.
▼ 4.8	BR	Tracks on left.
		GPS: N 41°26.85' W 111°56.45'
▼ 5.1	SO	Tracks on left and right across road.
▼ 6.5	BR	Road forks.
▼ 7.0	SO	Track on right.
▼ 7.7	BL	Track on right goes downhill to a pond.
		GPS: N 41°25.65' W 111°57.71'
▼ 8.5	TR	Road forks. Follow switchback.
▼ 9.9	SO	Track on left, then zero trip meter at sign for Willard Basin and overlook. Numerous tracks left and right.
		GPS: N 41°24.67' W 111°58.13'
▼ 0.0		Proceed downhill to the south. The correct road is left of the sign.
▼ 0.8	SO	Track on left rejoins later.
▼ 1.6	SO	USFS Spikecamp Campground and public toilets.
		GPS: N 41°23.51' W 111°58.64'
▼ 1.8	SO	Cross through wash.
▼ 3.5	SO	Track on left.
▼ 3.7	BL	Track on right. Continue on switchback to left.
▼ 3.8		End at summit of Inspiration Point. An easy loop trail circles summit.
		GPS: N 41°23.46' W 111°59.12'

Wendover to Lucin Trail

Starting Point:	I-80, exit 4, just east of Wendover
Finishing Point:	Lucin, Northern #12: Transcontinental Railroad Trail
Total Mileage:	55.3 miles
Unpaved Mileage:	54.2 miles
Driving Time:	3 hours
Elevation Range:	4,200–5,200 feet
Usually Open:	Year-round
Difficulty Rating:	3
Scenic Rating:	8
Remoteness Rating:	+2

Special Attractions
- Remote trail through landscape of ancient Lake Bonneville.
- Provides access to two other historic trails.
- Access to Bonneville Speedway.

History
About 12,000 years ago, prehistoric Lake Bonneville began to shrink back to the current boundaries of the Great Salt Lake. As the lake's waters receded, they revealed the large, sprawling area known as the Bonneville Salt Flats. During most of the winter and spring months, the salt flats are submerged under shallow water. However, when dry, the salt flats that lie just northeast of Wendover are home to the Bonneville Speedway.

The speedway runs along natural terrain that remains consistently flat for many miles, and it has become the perfect area for both professional and amateur driving enthusiasts to attempt land speed records. Interest in the area as a natural speedway began in the early part of the 20th century when two drivers, W. D. Rishel and Ferg Johnson, promoted the area. In 1914, Terry Tetzlaff set the first unofficial land speed record at the Bonneville Speedway when he clocked in at 141 miles per hour. Then, in 1935, British racing pioneer Malcolm Campbell set an official record here of 301.13 miles per

Looking across the ancient salt flats of Lake Bonneville to the Silver Island Mountains from Patterson Pass

hour, and the speedway has been famous ever since. For more on the Bonneville Speedway, see p. 27.

This area was also home to some of Utah's earliest inhabitants. Evidence of the Desert Archaic culture, which dates back over 10,000 years, was discovered in the 1940s and 1950s during an excavation of Danger Cave. For more on the Desert Archaic culture, see p. 70. The cave got its name in 1941 when a large slab of rock fell down and just missed one of the archaeologists who was working at the dig site. All of the artifacts have been removed from the cave, and today it remains much the same as it was when the excavations were finished. Even though it is located in a state park, there is no visitor center and no exhibits to mark Danger Cave.

Another historical attraction along the Wendover to Lucin Trail is the old cabin of Eugene Munsee. Built in 1880, the dovetail-notched cabin stands today as a brilliant example of a traditional western homestead. Munsee homesteaded the area about 50 years ago and today lives in Wendover. The roof was restored in 1990 by the Crossroads chapter of the Oregon-California Trails Association. Munsee's old cabin is now part of the McKeller Ranch.

The Wendover to Lucin Trail connects with two other historic routes: Northern #11: Silver Island Mountains Loop and Northern #12: Transcontinental Railroad Trail. The Silver Island trail follows part of the route taken by the ill-fated Donner-Reed Party. The other historic route follows a portion of the original transcontinental railroad. This branch of the railroad became obsolete after the 1904 Lucin Cutoff rerouted the railroad over the Great Salt Lake, thus making the line faster and more efficient. Not wanting to become obsolete, the citizens of Lucin moved the town about a mile west of its original location along the old line to a new spot beside the Lucin Cutoff. Today, a marker along the original transcontinental railroad indicates the spot of historic Lucin.

Description

Before setting out on the Wendover to Lucin Trail, make sure to check the weather and call ahead for information on road conditions, since the trail can easily become flooded and impassable after rains or as the winter snows melt. You should also bring extra water, especially during the hot summer months, as well as plenty of fuel and supplies, since the area is remote and unforgiving.

The trail starts just east of Wendover at I-80, exit 4. Take the paved road toward the Bonneville Speedway for about a mile;

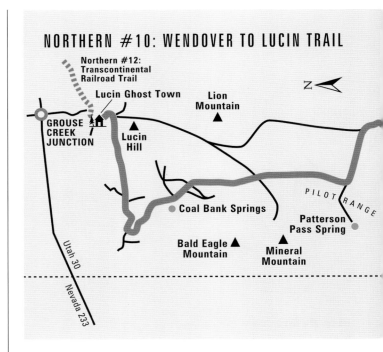

NORTHERN #10: WENDOVER TO LUCIN TRAIL

Crossing the mud flats with the Pilot Range ahead

the trail then turns onto an unpaved gravel road that leads over Leppy Pass to a three-way intersection. From here, right is Northern #11: Silver Island Mountains Loop, left is the main road to Lucin, and straight is the 4WD route described here. The trail proceeds across a wide area of mud flats toward the Pilot Range before ultimately reconnecting with the main Lucin road. Be careful as you drive along this section because trucks still use the road despite its being rather narrow. Also, if you find that the mud flats are impassable, you can backtrack to the three-way intersection and take the main Lucin road until you reach the Pilot Range, where the trail diverges again from the main road to follow a higher 4WD trail along the eastern side of the mountains. This section is not only more interesting than the main road but has better views of the salt and mud flats.

As you traverse this area, the mountains jut out from this prehistoric lake bottom to surround you. As you approach the Pilot Range, the Leppy Hills rise up to the south and the Silver Island Mountains stand to the east. As you pass the northern limit of the Silver Island Mountains, the view widens across the remains of Lake Bonneville. Eventually, the trail traverses the Pilot Range's eastern foot, and you move from the barren flats to desert shrub country.

At Patterson Pass turnoff, you turn off the main Lucin road onto a single-lane track and head toward Governors Spring. The trail eventually rises about 1,000 feet above the salt flats as it proceeds along the lower part of the Pilot Range through a grassy area dotted with saltbush and juniper. From here you can look across the flats for miles and imagine the days when the entire region was submerged beneath Lake Bonneville.

Once you are back on the main road, the trail runs along a rough pebble-and-gravel surface that, though bumpy, is an easy 1-rated level of difficulty. The main challenge along the earlier part of the trail is negotiating some potentially muddy areas, while the jagged rocks along this section can easily put a

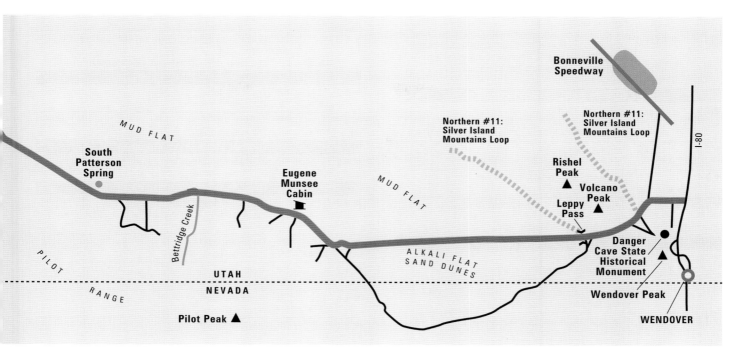

hole through your tires if you are not careful.

As you continue toward Coal Bank Springs, the single-lane trail narrows. Passing is difficult, but there is usually just enough room to pull over and allow another vehicle to get by. The character of the trail is quite different here, as you now must negotiate some deep and narrow washes. Depending on your vehicle's angles of entry and departure, crossing these washes can be tricky; take care when choosing the correct line to avoid getting hung up.

The trail eventually returns to the main road to Lucin; it continues past Lucin's railroad siding before coming to an end at the railroad tracks. This is the start of Northern #12: Transcontinental Railroad Trail. Head north for about 5 miles on the main road to get to Grouse Creek Junction and Utah 30.

If you are starting the trail from Lucin and driving south to Wendover, the intersection 5.8 miles from the railroad tracks at Lucin can be difficult to spot. It is sometimes marked with a white pole, but do not rely on the marker being there. Before you come to the turnoff, you pass a well-used track that leads to a radio tower.

Current Road Information

Wendover Area Chamber of Commerce
PO Box 2468
West Wendover, NV 89883
(775) 664-3414

BLM Salt Lake Field Office
2370 South 2300 West
Salt Lake City, UT 84119
(801) 977-4300

Map References

BLM Bonneville Salt Flats, Newfoundland Mt.
USGS 1:24,000 Silsbee, Tetzlaff Peak, Leppy Peak, Silver

Island Pass, Crater Island SW, Crater Island NW, Lucin
1:100,000 Bonneville Salt Flats, Newfoundland Mt.
Maptech CD-ROM: Lower Wasatch/Salt Lake City; Upper Wasatch/Great Salt Lake
Utah Atlas & Gazetteer, pp. 50, 58
Utah Travel Council #1

Route Directions

▼ 0.0		From I-80, exit 4, at the intersection of the exit/entry ramps and the overpass, zero trip meter and proceed north on paved road to Bonneville Speedway.
4.2 ▲		Trail ends at I-80, exit 4. Turn right for Wendover, left for Salt Lake City.
GPS: N 40°44.69' W 113°58.16'		
▼ 0.3	SO	Road on left to Danger Cave State Park.
3.9 ▲	SO	Road on right to Danger Cave State Park.
▼ 1.1	TL	Intersection. Turn left onto dirt road, following sign to Pilot Mountains and Silver Island Mountains. Straight goes to Bonneville Speedway.
3.1 ▲	TR	T-intersection.
GPS: N 40°45.70' W 113°58.14'		
▼ 1.7	SO	Road on right.
2.5 ▲	SO	Road on left.
▼ 1.9	BL	Fork in road. Follow sign to Leppy Pass. Right is end of Northern #11: Silver Island Mountains Loop.
2.3 ▲	BR	Track on left is end of Northern #11: Silver Island Mountains Loop.
GPS: N 40°46.17' W 113°58.76'		
▼ 2.7	SO	Track on left.
1.5 ▲	SO	Track on right.
▼ 3.3	SO	Track on left.
0.9 ▲	SO	Track on right.
▼ 4.1	BR	Track on left.
0.1 ▲	BL	Track on right.
GPS: N 40°47.81' W 114°00.07'		
▼ 4.2	SO	Three-way intersection at Leppy Pass. Track on

right is Northern #11: Silver Island Mountains Loop; track on left is main road to Lucin. Zero trip meter and proceed north (straight) on unmarked road. (Return to this intersection and take main Lucin road if mud flats are impassable.)

0.0 ▲   Continue south.

GPS: N 40°47.89' W 114°00.03'

▼ 0.0   Continue north.
11.1 ▲   SO   Leppy Pass. Track on left is Northern #11: Silver Island Mountains Loop. Zero trip meter.

▼ 0.3   SO   Trail crosses.
10.7 ▲   SO   Trail crosses.

▼ 2.4   SO   Stock trough on left.
8.6 ▲   SO   Stock trough on right.

▼ 11.1   TR   Intersection with main Lucin road. Zero trip meter.
0.0 ▲   Continue toward mud flats.

GPS: N 40°57.71' W 114°00.75'

▼ 0.0   Continue toward Lucin.
16.5 ▲   TL   Intersection. Zero trip meter and turn left. Main Lucin road continues straight. (Return to this intersection and take main Lucin road if mud flats are impassable.)

▼ 1.8   SO   Track on right along fence line.
14.6 ▲   SO   Track on left along fence line.

▼ 2.2   SO   Information board about Eugene Munsee cabin on right.
14.3 ▲   SO   Eugene Munsee cabin information board on left.

GPS: N 40°59.30' W 113°59.22'

▼ 16.5   TL   Track on left to Patterson Pass. Zero trip meter.
0.0 ▲   Continue toward salt flats.

GPS: N 41°11.05' W 113°54.92'

▼ 0.0   Continue west.
2.6 ▲   TR   Turn right onto larger, main Lucin road. Zero trip meter.

▼ 2.6   TR   Intersection. Patterson Pass straight ahead. Zero trip meter.
0.0 ▲   Continue east.

GPS: N 41°11.75' W 113°57.75'

▼ 0.0   Continue toward Governors Spring.
4.3 ▲   TL   Intersection. Zero trip meter.

▼ 0.2   SO   Track on left.
4.1 ▲   BR   Fork in road.

▼ 1.5   SO   Track on left.
2.7 ▲   SO   Track on right.

▼ 2.6   SO   Track on left.
1.7 ▲   SO   Track on right.

▼ 4.2   SO   Track on left.
0.1 ▲   SO   Track on right.

▼ 4.3   SO   Intersection. Tracks on left and right. Follow sign to Coal Bank Springs. Zero trip meter.
0.0 ▲   Continue south.

GPS: N 41°15.33' W 113°57.51'

▼ 0.0   Continue north toward Coal Bank Springs.
6.5 ▲   SO   Intersection. Track on right and left. Zero trip meter.

▼ 1.7   SO   Track on left.
4.9 ▲   SO   Track on right.

GPS: N 41°16.79' W 113°57.59'

▼ 2.9   BR   Fork in road. Left travels through wash.
3.6 ▲   SO   Road enters on right.

▼ 3.7   BL   Track on right, then Coal Bank Springs and stock trough. Follow track behind trough.
2.8 ▲   BR   Stock trough and Coal Bank Springs. Then track on left.

GPS: N 41°18.27' W 113°58.43'

▼ 5.0   SO   Corral and stock trough on left and track on right.
1.5 ▲   SO   Track on left. Corral and stock trough on right.

GPS: N 41°19.23' W 113°59.01'

▼ 5.7   BR   Track on left.
0.8 ▲   SO   Track on right.

▼ 6.3   BR   Track on left.
0.2 ▲   SO   Track on right.

GPS: N 41°19.89' W 114°00.14'

▼ 6.5   TR   Intersection. Zero trip meter.
0.0 ▲   Continue south.

GPS: N 41°20.09' W 114°00.13'

▼ 0.0   Continue east on larger road.
5.8 ▲   TL   Track on left. This can be hard to see. Zero trip meter.

▼ 1.1   SO   Track on right.
4.7 ▲   SO   Track on left.

▼ 1.2   SO   Track on right.
4.6 ▲   SO   Track on left.

▼ 1.3   SO   Track on right.
4.5 ▲   SO   Track on left.

▼ 2.1   SO   Track on right.
3.7 ▲   SO   Track on left.

▼ 5.1   TL   T-intersection with main Lucin Road.
0.7 ▲   TR   Road on right.

GPS: N 41°20.56' W 113°54.21'

▼ 5.3   SO   Travel through Lucin.
0.5 ▲   SO   Leave Lucin.

▼ 5.4   BL   Cattle guard. Then track on right.
0.4 ▲   BR   Track on left. Then cattle guard.

▼ 5.6   SO   Lucin railroad siding building.
0.2 ▲   SO   Lucin railroad siding building.

▼ 5.8   Trail ends at railroad tracks. This is start of Northern #12: Transcontinental Railroad Trail.
0.0 ▲   At railroad tracks near Lucin at the end of Northern #12: Transcontinental Railroad Trail, zero trip meter and proceed south. To get to the start of the trail from Utah 30, follow signs at Grouse Creek Junction south to Lucin.

GPS: N 41°21.05' W 113°54.50'

NORTHERN REGION TRAIL #11

Silver Island Mountains Loop

Starting Point:	**Northern #10: Wendover to Lucin Trail**
Finishing Point:	**Northern #10: Wendover to Lucin Trail**
Total Mileage:	**49.4 miles**
Unpaved Mileage:	**49.4 miles**
Driving Time:	**3 hours**
Elevation Range:	**4,200–4,800 feet**
Usually Open:	**Year-round**
Difficulty Rating:	**1**
Scenic Rating:	**8**
Remoteness Rating:	**+1**

Looking across to the Pilot Range from Donner-Reed Pass

Special Attractions
- Easy but remote trail along the old shoreline of Lake Bonneville.
- Wonderful, unusual scenery, from the dead-flat desert and mud flats that were once the bottom of Lake Bonneville to the mountains that jut 6,000 feet skyward.
- Dozens of side trails to explore.
- Historic route of the Donner-Reed Party.

History
About 200 million years ago, the Silver Island Mountains began to push themselves up from the bottom of Lake Bonneville. As the mountains uplifted, the surrounding salt flats were kept smooth under the weight of the lake. Millions of years later, after the ever-changing Lake Bonneville had receded and returned once again to flood most of northern Utah, the Silver Island Mountains rose out of the water as an island. A crease that has been eroded into the mountain's lower slope provides geologists with evidence of this ancient shoreline.

Over the years, igneous rock intrusions have forced their way into the Paleozoic rocks of the Silver Island Mountains. These intrusions created the many valuable deposits of minerals in the mountains, which have been extensively mined. The most abundant mineral has been tungsten, while smaller amounts of copper, gold, silver, and lead have also been extracted from the mountains.

There is little in the way of human history near the remote Silver Island Mountains. For the most part, people have just passed through on their way west. One infamous group of settlers to do so was the California-bound Donner-Reed Party in 1846. After experiencing many delays crossing the barren salt flats and Silver Island Mountains, the party was eventually caught in the early snowfall of the Sierra Nevadas near the California border. Most of the group died in the Sierras, and the survivors were forced to eat their dead or perish themselves. For more on the Donner-Reed Party, see p. 76.

Description
The Silver Island Mountains Loop begins and ends on Northern #10: Wendover to Lucin Trail. This 49.4-mile trail makes a clockwise loop around the Silver Island Mountains and through a desert environment. As you drive along the remote and barren trail, keep an eye out for the old shoreline of Lake Bonneville, which is marked by an eroded line along the side of the mountains where ancient waves once lapped.

The trail starts out along a wide, maintained gravel road that proceeds through saltbush and sparse grasses on the western side of the mountains with views across the mud flats. The flats are at an elevation of 4,200 feet and the distant Pilot Range rises up to 10,716 feet above sea level. After 8.6 miles, the road narrows but remains relatively flat and easy.

The trail is so flat, in fact, that you may be tempted to travel at speeds of 30 mph and up. However, appearances can be deceiving and very dangerous. A number of small wash crossings have dug narrow channels into the road. If you hit one of these dips too fast, it could do serious damage to the front end of your vehicle. Make sure to constantly scan the road ahead and keep your speed in check.

The Donner-Reed Pass marks the north end of the loop. Although it is not very high, the pass gives you a remarkably broad view of the Silver Island Mountains. As the trail winds around the east side of the mountains you can see Floating Island across the Great Salt Lake Desert. The appropriateness of the name will quickly become obvious as it seems to float above the shimmering desert flats.

Overall, the Silver Island Mountains Loop is rather easy, although after rains, some sections may become muddy and present some difficulty. There are also a number of side trails to explore along the way. The trail eventually makes its way back to Northern #10: Wendover to Lucin Trail, which provides access to Wendover and I-80.

Current Road Information
Wendover Area Chamber of Commerce
PO Box 2468
West Wendover, NV 89883
(775) 664-3414

BLM Salt Lake Field Office
2370 South 2300 West
Salt Lake City, UT 84119
(801) 977-4300

Map References
BLM Bonneville Salt Flats, Newfoundland Mt.
USGS 1:24,000 Tetzlaff Peak, Silver Island Pass, Graham Peak, Crater Island, Floating Island, Bonneville Racetrack
1:100,000 Bonneville Salt Flats, Newfoundland Mt.
Maptech CD-ROM: Lower Wasatch/Salt Lake City; Upper Wasatch/Great Salt Lake
Utah Atlas & Gazetteer, pp. 50, 58
Utah Travel Council #1

Looking across the salt and mud flats to Floating Island

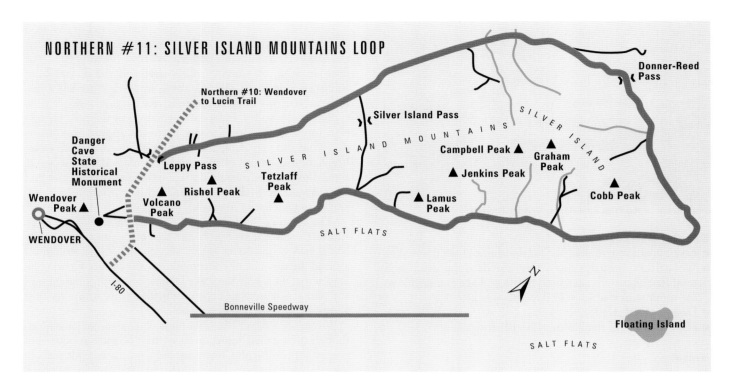

NORTHERN #11: SILVER ISLAND MOUNTAINS LOOP

Route Directions

▼ 0.0   On Northern #10: Wendover to Lucin Trail, 4.2 miles from I-80 at the three-way intersection, turn right on unmarked road and zero trip meter.

      8.6 ▲   Trail ends at Northern #10: Wendover to Lucin Trail. Go straight for I-80.

GPS: N 40°47.89' W 114°00.03'

▼ 0.1   SO   Track on right.
  8.5 ▲ SO   Track on left.

▼ 0.3   SO   Track on right.
  8.3 ▲ SO   Track on left.

▼ 0.4   SO   Tracks on right and left.
  8.2 ▲ SO   Tracks on left and right.

▼ 0.7   SO   Track on right.
  7.9 ▲ SO   Track on left.

▼ 2.1   SO   Track on left.
  6.5 ▲ SO   Track on right.

▼ 5.3   SO   Track on right.
  3.3 ▲ SO   Track on left.

▼ 8.6   SO   Track on right to Silver Island Pass. Connects with return loop of this trail. Zero trip meter.
  0.0 ▲   Continue southwest.

GPS: N 40°54.38° W 113°55.23'

▼ 0.0   Continue northeast.
 10.8 ▲   Track on left to Silver Island Pass. Zero trip meter.

▼ 0.9   SO   Track on right.
  9.8 ▲ SO   Track on left.

▼ 2.7   SO   Track on right.
  8.1 ▲ SO   Track on left.

▼ 4.2   SO   Track on right.
  6.6 ▲ SO   Track on left.

GPS: N 40°57.78' W 113°53.12'

▼ 7.1   SO   Sheep corral on left.
  3.7 ▲ SO   Sheep corral on right.

▼ 10.8   BR   Fork in road. Zero trip meter.
  0.0 ▲   Continue along main road.

GPS: N 41°00.65' W 113°46.92'

▼ 0.0   Continue along main road.
 11.1 ▲ BL   Road on right. Zero trip meter.

▼ 0.1   SO   Roads on left and right.
 11.0 ▲ SO   Roads on right and left.

▼ 0.3   SO   Donner-Reed Pass.
 10.8 ▲ SO   Donner-Reed Pass

GPS: N 41°00.59' W 113°46.54'

▼ 0.8   BL   Track on right.
 10.3 ▲ BR   Main road veers right. Track straight on.

▼ 2.3   SO   Track on right.
  8.8 ▲ SO   Track on left.

▼ 2.7   BL   Track on right.
  8.4 ▲ SO   Track on left.

GPS: N 40°59.60' W 113°44.25'

▼ 11.1   BR   Track on left to Floating Island. Zero trip meter.
  0.0 ▲   Continue straight ahead.

GPS: N 40°55.76' W 113°43.10'

▼ 0.0   Continue southwest.
  9.8 ▲ BL   Track on right to Floating Island. Zero trip meter.

▼ 3.0   SO   Track on right.
  6.7 ▲ SO   Track on left.

▼ 9.8   SO   Silver Island Pass road on right. Zero trip meter.
  0.0 ▲   Continue northeast.

GPS: N 40°51.72' W 113°52.53'

▼ 0.0   Continue southwest.
  9.1 ▲ SO   Silver Island Pass road on left. Connects with return loop of this trail. Zero trip meter.

▼ 1.1   SO   Track on right.
  8.0 ▲ SO   Track on left.

▼ 4.4   SO   Track on right.
  4.7 ▲ SO   Track on left.

▼ 5.7	SO	Track on right.
3.4 ▲	SO	Track on left.
▼ 6.0	SO	Track on right.
3.1 ▲	SO	Track on left.
▼ 6.2	SO	Track on right.
2.9 ▲	SO	Track on left.
▼ 6.5	SO	Track on right.
2.6 ▲	SO	Track on left.
▼ 8.5	SO	Track on right.
0.6 ▲	SO	Track on left.
▼ 8.6	SO	Track on right.
0.5 ▲	SO	Track on left.
▼ 8.9	BL	Track on right.
0.2 ▲	BR	Track on left.
▼ 9.1		Trail ends at Northern #10: Wendover to Lucin Trail. Turn right for Lucin, left for Bonneville Speedway and I-80.
0.0 ▲		On Northern #10: Wendover to Lucin Trail, 1.9 miles from I-80, zero trip meter and proceed northeast.

GPS: N 40°46.17′ W 113°58.76′

Transcontinental Railroad Trail

Starting Point:	**Lucin, end of Northern #10: Wendover to Lucin Trail**
Finishing Point:	**Golden Spike National Historic Site at Promontory Point**
Total Mileage:	**87.1 miles**
Unpaved Mileage:	**87.1 miles**
Driving Time:	**5 hours**
Elevation Range:	**4,200–4,800 feet**
Usually Open:	**Year-round**
Difficulty Rating:	**2**
Scenic Rating:	**8**
Remoteness Rating:	**+2**

Special Attractions

- Traveling a portion of the original transcontinental railroad.
- Visiting the town sites and cemeteries along the old railroad grade.
- Golden Spike National Historic Site at Promontory Point.

History

Much like the Pony Express, the transcontinental railroad has gone down in history as a testament to 19th-century America's determination to link East and West over the treacherous mountain region. Completed on May 10, 1869, at Promontory Summit, the transcontinental railroad shortened the once expensive and arduous cross-country journey to four days at the relatively cheap cost of $100.

Crossing one of the many trestle bridges along an arrow-straight section of the Transcontinental Railroad Trail

In 1902, officials of the Southern Pacific Railroad, which had taken over the Central Pacific, decided to shorten the route by crossing the Great Salt Lake, which meant laying an additional 102 miles of track between Ogden and Lucin, including 12 miles of trestle over the Great Salt Lake. The route was not only shortened by 44 miles, it made the railroad track more level, which saved in fuel costs.

The $8-million Lucin Cutoff took 3,000 men a year and a half to complete. When finished in 1904, it signaled the demise of the original line that ran around the northern rim of the lake, though this section was still used as an alternate route during bad weather. The original railroad tracks from Lucin to Corinne remained in place until 1942, when they were taken up and contributed as scrap metal to the war effort. A ceremonial pulling up of the "last spike" occurred in 1942 in much the same fashion as the ceremonies in May 1869.

While the faster route across Utah was welcomed by railroad officials and passengers, it meant the end for many towns along the original line. Two of the more prominent towns were Terrace and Kelton. Both were home to many settlers and permanent facilities before the Lucin Cutoff dealt the local economies their deathblow. Many other railroad camps and smaller settlements, such as Watercress, also died because of the bypass. One such camp was Rozel, which was the site of the Central Pacific's most productive day. In a race to lay more track than the Union Pacific, the Central Pacific set a record by putting down over 10 miles of track in a single day. To fully appreciate this feat, bear in mind that each 28-foot section of track weighed approximately 522 pounds—a total of 88 tons of rail!

Seven acres of land near Promontory, the meeting point of the original transcontinental line, was set aside in 1957 as a National Historic Site. That site was enlarged in 1965 to 2,176 acres and a road was put in to prepare for centennial celebrations in 1969. Finally, a visitors center was added in 1980, which has an exhibit on the history of the transcontinental railroad.

Description

From Lucin, the trail runs dead straight along a single-lane, elevated railroad bed. In most places it's only a few feet higher than the surrounding terrain, but along some stretches it can be as high as six or seven feet, which makes passing impossible. However, the road typically breaks away from the railroad bed at old trestles every quarter mile or so, and these allow for passing. The trestles are typically no more than four or five feet high and were used by the railroad to cross small washes. Beside the old trestles, you can see many old railroad ties and spikes strewn along this early part of the trail. Although they are interesting artifacts, they can also be hazards to your vehicle, and tire punctures are not at all uncommon.

There are no trees in this area and hardly any shrubs. The landscape is mostly desert grassland with some dotted saltbush. The vast plains seem to roll on for miles and miles as the tops of mountain ranges rise up in the distance.

The road remains easy and rates a difficulty level of 2 only because of occasional ruts and eroded areas. Although it is not what you would typically refer to as scenic, the Transcontinental Railroad Trail remains interesting because of its incredible history. Today, it is almost inconceivable to imagine thousands of men building the railroad by hand in this vast and remote setting.

The road proceeds toward Kelton through grassland and sagebrush along gentle rolling hills. In some areas, such as around Kelton, potholes become prevalent along the railbed. Keep your eye out for a side road about 20 or 30 yards north of the trail if you want a smoother ride along the same route.

As you continue along the Central Pacific grade, you can look to the right to see some of the Union Pacific grade. Due to the fierce competition between the two railroad companies to complete more of the route than the other, they ended up overshooting each other for about 200 miles. The Union Pacific's track was deemed superfluous and was eventually abandoned.

The trail passes signs for the BLM Transcontinental Railroad Backcountry Byway on its way to the Golden Spike National Historic Site. After passing the sign for Rozel, the trail ends at the information board and the junction with the West Grade Auto Tour, which runs up behind the board on a small road marked "one way." This seasonal auto tour runs along the old Central Pacific grade before coming to an end at the Golden Spike National Historic Site.

A headstone in Terrace Cemetery

Current Road Information

Golden Spike National Historic Site
PO Box 897
Brigham City, UT 84302
(435) 471-2209

BLM Salt Lake Field Office
2370 South 2300 West
Salt Lake City, UT 84119
(801) 977-4300

Map References

BLM Newfoundland Mt., Grouse Creek, Tremonton
USGS 1:24,000 Lucin, Lucin NE, Bovine, Terrace Mt. West, Prohibition Spring, Red Dome, Matlin, Hogup Bar, Peplin Flats, Crocodile Mt. NE, Kelton Pass SE, Locomotive Springs, Monument Point, Lake Ridge, Rozel
1:100,000 Newfoundland Mt., Grouse Creek, Tremonton
Maptech CD-ROM: Upper Wasatch/Great Salt Lake
Utah Atlas & Gazetteer, pp. 58, 59, 63
Utah Travel Council #1

Route Directions

▼ 0.0			At end of Northern #10: Wendover to Lucin Trail in Lucin, zero trip meter at railroad tracks and proceed north. Follow sign marked "Old Railroad Grade and Highway 30."
	22.5 ▲		Trail ends at railroad tracks at Lucin. This is start of Northern #10: Wendover to Lucin Trail. To get to the start of the trail from Utah 30, follow signs at Grouse Creek Junction south to Lucin.
		GPS: N 41°21.05′ W 113°54.50′	
▼ 0.8		TR	Intersection. Two tracks on right; take the first one along the old railroad grade.
	21.7 ▲	TL	Turn left toward Lucin.
		GPS: N 41°21.36′ W 113°53.74′	
▼ 1.3		SO	Lucin information board on left.
	21.2 ▲	SO	Lucin information board on right.
▼ 2.8		SO	Track crosses.
	19.7 ▲	SO	Track crosses.
▼ 6.9		SO	Cattle guard.
	15.6 ▲	SO	Cattle guard.
▼ 8.5		SO	Track crosses.
	14.0 ▲	SO	Track crosses.
▼ 12.1		SO	Bovine railroad siding.
	10.4 ▲	SO	Bovine railroad siding.
		GPS: N 41°26.01′ W 113°41.81′	
▼ 17.6		SO	Walden railroad siding.
	4.9 ▲	SO	Walden railroad siding.
		GPS: N 41°28.26′ W 113°35.98′	
▼ 20.0		BR	Intersection with road on left. Then cattle guard and old town of Watercress railroad siding.
	2.5 ▲	BL	Cattle guard and Watercress railroad siding. Road on right marked to Utah 30.
▼ 21.7		SO	Cross over trestle.
	0.8 ▲	SO	Cross over trestle.
		GPS: N 41°29.90′ W 113°31.78′	
▼ 22.0		SO	Cross through wash.
	0.5 ▲	SO	Cross through wash.
▼ 22.5		SO	Old town site of Terrace. Zero trip meter.
	0.0 ▲		Continue northeast.
		GPS: N 41°30.23′ W 113°30.96′	
▼ 0.0			Continue southwest.
	29.2 ▲	SO	Old town site of Terrace. Zero trip meter.
▼ 0.5		SO	Terrace cemetery on right.
	28.7 ▲	SO	Terrace cemetery on left.
		GPS: N 41°30.44′ W 113°30.39′	
▼ 1.4		SO	Old Terrace railroad siding.
	27.8 ▲	SO	Old Terrace railroad siding.
▼ 2.7		SO	Track on right.

NORTHERN #12: TRANSCONTINENTAL RAILROAD TRAIL

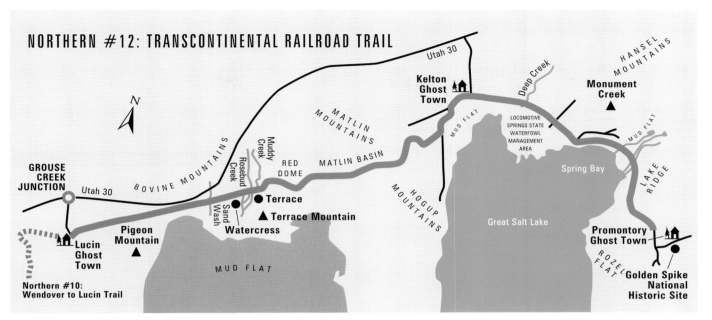

26.5 ▲	SO	Track on left.	
GPS: N 41°31.81′ W 113°29.11′			
▼ 2.8	SO	Track on left to Utah 30.	
26.4 ▲	SO	Track on right to Utah 30.	
▼ 6.0	SO	Red Dome railroad siding.	
23.2 ▲	SO	Red Dome railroad siding.	
▼ 6.9	SO	Track on left.	
22.3 ▲	SO	Track on right.	
▼ 10.2	SO	Matlin railroad siding.	
19.0 ▲	SO	Matlin railroad siding.	
GPS: N 41°33.55′ W 113°21.58′			
▼ 12.9	SO	Old corral on left.	
16.3 ▲	SO	Old corral on right.	
▼ 15.1	SO	Romola railroad siding.	
14.1 ▲	SO	Romola railroad siding.	
GPS: N 41°35.44′ W 113°16.54′			
▼ 17.7	SO	Intersection with CR 13. Right goes to Hogup Mountains.	
11.5 ▲	SO	Intersection with CR 13. Left goes to Hogup Mountains.	
GPS: N 41°36.32′ W 113°13.78′			
▼ 18.2	SO	Track on left.	
11.0 ▲	SO	Track on right.	
▼ 19.8	SO	Ombey railroad siding.	
9.4 ▲	SO	Ombey railroad siding.	
▼ 21.5	BR	Track on left	
7.7 ▲	BL	Track on right	
▼ 22.7	BR	Bear right onto side road to Kelton. Actual railroad grade continues straight.	
6.5 ▲	BL	Continue along railroad grade.	
GPS: N 41°38.85′ W 113°11.45′			
▼ 25.9	TL	T-intersection. Road on right.	
3.3 ▲	TR	Intersection.	
GPS: N 41°40.65′ W 113°09.16′			
▼ 27.2	SO	Track on left.	
2.0 ▲	SO	Track on right.	
▼ 27.4	SO	Old railroad grade crosses.	
1.8 ▲	SO	Old railroad grade crosses.	
GPS: N 41°41.93′ W 113°09.15′			
▼ 28.4	SO	Cattle guard.	

0.8 ▲	SO	Cattle guard.	
▼ 29.2	TR	T-intersection. Zero trip meter.	
0.0 ▲		Continue southwest.	
GPS: N 41°43.23′ W 113°08.58′			
▼ 0.0		Continue northeast.	
2.8 ▲	TL	Intersection. Road continues straight ahead. Turn left and zero trip meter.	
▼ 2.4	TR	Intersection.	
0.4 ▲	TL	Intersection. Follow sign to Terrace and Hogup Mountains.	
GPS: N 41°44.84′ W 113°06.68′			
▼ 2.5	SO	Two tracks on left. Kelton Boot Hill Cemetery on right.	
0.3 ▲	SO	Kelton Boot Hill Cemetery on left. Two tracks on right.	
▼ 2.6	BL	Bear left onto railroad grade.	
0.2 ▲	BR	Old railroad grade continues straight (closed to vehicles).	
▼ 2.7	SO	Track on right and two tracks on left. Follow diversion around trestle bridge.	
0.1 ▲	SO	Two tracks on right and one track on left. Follow diversion around trestle bridge.	
▼ 2.8	SO	Track on left. Information board on right. Old town site of Kelton (Indian Creek) railroad siding. Zero trip meter and continue past road on left to Utah 30.	
0.0 ▲		Continue southwest toward Kelton Cemetery.	
GPS: N 41°44.78′ W 113°06.39′			
▼ 0.0		Continue toward Promontory.	
10.1 ▲	SO	Road on right to Utah 30, then old town site of Kelton (Indian Creek) railroad siding. Information board on left. Track on right. Zero trip meter.	
▼ 0.1	SO	Wheeler Survey marker on left.	
10.0 ▲	SO	Wheeler Survey marker on right.	
▼ 2.6	SO	Trestle/cattle guard.	
7.5 ▲	SO	Cattle guard/trestle.	
GPS: N 41°45.04′ W 113°03.31′			
▼ 5.4	SO	Cross trestle.	
4.7 ▲	SO	Cross trestle.	
▼ 6.2	SO	Track crosses.	

3.9 ▲		SO	Track crosses.
▼ 8.8		SO	Seco railroad siding on left.
	1.3 ▲	SO	Seco railroad siding on right.
▼ 9.7		SO	Nella railroad siding on left.
	0.4 ▲	SO	Nella railroad siding on right.
▼ 10.1		SO	Road crosses. Right goes to Locomotive Springs. Left to Snowville. Zero trip meter.
	0.0 ▲		Continue southeast.

GPS: N 41°44.07' W 112°54.68'

▼ 0.0			Continue northwest.
	12.2 ▲	SO	Road crosses. Right goes to Snowville. Left to Locomotive Springs. Zero trip meter.
▼ 1.3		SO	Track crosses.
	10.9 ▲	SO	Track crosses.
▼ 2.1		SO	Track crosses.
	10.1 ▲	SO	Track crosses.
▼ 3.4		SO	Track crosses.
	8.8 ▲	SO	Track crosses.
▼ 3.5		BL	Bear left around gate, across cattle guard, to return to railway grade.
	8.7 ▲	BR	Gate across railroad grade. Bear right across cattle guard, then return to railroad grade.
▼ 3.7		SO	Track crosses.
	8.5 ▲	SO	Track crosses.
▼ 4.1		SO	Track crosses.
	8.1 ▲	SO	Track crosses.

GPS: N 41°42.18' W 112°50.56'

▼ 6.9		TL	Old concrete foundation. Railroad grade continues straight, but access closed to vehicles through Salt Wells Wildlife Habitat Area.
	5.3 ▲	TR	Turn right at old concrete foundation onto railroad grade.

GPS: N 41°42.95' W 112°47.44'

▼ 7.1		BR	Fork in road.
	5.1 ▲	BL	Road enters on right.
▼ 7.2		SO	Road enters on left.
	5.0 ▲	BL	Fork in road. Bear left to return to railroad grade.

GPS: N 41°43.17' W 112°47.36'

▼ 7.6		TR	Road on right.
	4.6 ▲	TL	T-intersection.

GPS: N 41°43.37' W 112°46.95'

▼ 7.7		SO	Cattle guard.
	4.5 ▲	SO	Cattle guard.
▼ 11.9		SO	Cattle guard.
	0.3 ▲	SO	Cattle guard.
▼ 12.2		TR	Road on right. Straight is alternative route to Golden Spike National Historic Site. Zero trip meter.
	0.0 ▲		Continue toward Kelton.

GPS: N 41°42.08' W 112°41.89'

▼ 0.0			Continue on railroad grade.
	10.3 ▲	TL	T-intersection. Right returns to Golden Spike National Historic Site. Follow sign to Kelton. Zero trip meter.
▼ 0.4		SO	Track on right.
	9.9 ▲	SO	Track on left.
▼ 1.4		SO	Track on left.
	8.9 ▲	SO	Track on right.
▼ 1.5		BL	Road enters on right.
	8.8 ▲	BR	Road forks. Old railroad grade bears left; closed to vehicles through Salt Wells Wildlife Habitat Area.

GPS: N 41°40.84' W 112°42.42'

▼ 4.9		SO	Cattle guard.
	5.4 ▲	SO	Cattle guard.
▼ 5.5		SO	Cattle guard.
	4.8 ▲	SO	Cattle guard.
▼ 6.0		SO	Cattle guard.
	4.3 ▲	SO	Cattle guard.
▼ 6.7		SO	Centre railroad siding.
	3.6 ▲	SO	Centre railroad siding.
▼ 7.7		SO	Road on right. Then cattle guard.
	2.6 ▲	SO	Cattle guard. Then road on left.

GPS: N 41°35.87' W 112°40.97'

▼ 8.8		SO	Track on left.
	1.5 ▲	SO	Track on right.
▼ 9.6		SO	Rozel railroad siding.
	0.7 ▲	SO	Rozel railroad siding.
▼ 9.8		SO	Cattle guard.
	0.5 ▲	SO	Cattle guard.
▼ 10.1		BR	Leave Central Pacific grade.
	0.2 ▲	BL	Join Central Pacific grade.
▼ 10.2		BL	Join Union Pacific grade.
	0.1 ▲	BR	Fork in road. Union Pacific grade bears left.
▼ 10.3			Pass the transcontinental railroad information board on right. Then trail ends at information board on left, which is also start of West Grade Auto Tour.
	0.0 ▲		Proceed west out of driveway of Golden Spike National Historic Site at Promontory Point. At start of West Grade Auto Tour (which turns off to the right), zero trip meter and continue west along county gravel road. Pass information boards for the transcontinental railroad on left.

GPS: N 41°34.92' W 112°38.24'

Pony Express Trail

Starting Point:	**Gold Hill**
Finishing Point:	**Camp Floyd/Stagecoach Inn State Park**
Total Mileage:	**129.7 miles**
Unpaved Mileage:	**110.6 miles**
Driving Time:	**5 hours**
Elevation Range:	**4,200–6,200 feet**
Usually Open:	**Year-round**
Difficulty Rating:	**1**
Scenic Rating:	**8**
Remoteness Rating:	**+2**

Special Attractions

■ Historic route used by the Pony Express and Overland Stage.

■ Extremely remote but easy route through desert terrain that has scarcely changed from the days of the Pony Express.

■ Desert scenery reflecting the impact of the ancient Great Salt Lake.

■ Rockhounding for geodes.

The makeshift stone fort at the Canyon Pony Express Station

History

During its brief life, the Pony Express delivered mail across 1,900 miles of America's frontier from St. Joseph, Missouri, to Sacramento, California. The original route entered Utah in the northeast from southwestern Wyoming and ran through Salt Lake City, across the western desert, and finally exited into Nevada near Ibapah. Although the Pony Express operated for only 19 months between 1860 and 1861, it has survived in American folklore as a testament to early pioneer ingenuity, fortitude, and determination. Even after the Pony Express went out of business, the trail was used as an Overland Stage route for cross-country travelers.

The portion of the trail that runs through western Utah crosses remote, desert terrain that looks much the same today as it did when the Pony Express was the fastest means of communication between East and West. Mark Twain once made the journey in 1861 and commented on the region's ruggedness in his book *Roughing It*. Upon reaching the way station at Callao, Twain wrote, "When we reached the station on the farther verge of the desert [Callao], we were glad, for the first time, that the dictionary was along, because we never could have found language to tell how glad we were, in any sort of dictionary but an unabridged one with pictures in it" (Twain, 95-98).

Northern #13: Pony Express Trail follows along most of the 133-mile-long Pony Express Trail National Backcountry Byway from Ibapah to Fairfield. The trail begins in the well-preserved mining town of Gold Hill, where gold, copper, arsenic, and tungsten were discovered in the region. During its life, the town suffered several boom-and-bust mining cycles as different ores came to prominence. In the early days, when gold was the town's main attraction, a young Jack Dempsey came to Gold Hill to find his fortune. As history shows, Dempsey made the right decision to leave the mines and search out his real fortune in the boxing ring.

As the trail continues across the desert floor, it passes the remains of many other way stations along the old Pony Express Trail. Although some have been restored, others are little more than markers maintained by the BLM. One of these is Canyon Station, which was the site of an Indian attack in July 1863. Both Pony Express riders and Overland Stage passengers faced the constant danger of being attacked by Gosiute Indians, through whose land they were crossing. The attack at Canyon Station resulted in the deaths of a stage driver and four soldiers. Afterward, the Gosiutes burned the station to the ground.

Other way stations along the route—such as Willow Springs, Fish Springs, and Simpson Springs—were known for their availability of fresh water. In the harsh desert, water was perhaps the most valuable resource. The 10,000-acre marsh near Fish Springs was acquired by the U.S. Fish and Wildlife Service in 1959. The nine impoundment pools that make up Fish Springs were completed in 1964. Today, Fish Springs is home to a large bird refuge that is visited by many species, including blue herons, snowy egrets, and Canadian geese.

Simpson Springs was named after Captain J. H. Simpson, the man who discovered the spring. The station was originally used as a stop along the old mail route before being used by the Pony Express. From 1939 to 1942, Simpson Springs was home to a Civilian Conservation Corps (CCC) camp. The young men of the CCC are responsible for many of the signs and markers along the Pony Express Trail, as well as the general improvement of the road.

Near Simpson Springs, the trail passes the Dugway Proving Grounds. Since the 1940s, there have been many questionable chemical and biological weapons tests at this base. In 1968, nerve gas was released and drifted beyond the base's boundaries, killing 6,000 sheep that were grazing nearby.

The trail winds to a close near Fairfield at the site of the historic Camp Floyd. It was here that Colonel Johnston's army camped during the so-called Utah War. In 1857, President Buchanan sent some 3,000 men into Utah in order to replace Brigham Young as territorial governor and quash a rumored Mormon uprising. Camp Floyd quickly became one of the largest non-Mormon settlements in Utah and was home to the state's first non-Mormon newspaper. The restored Stagecoach Inn was originally built in 1858 by John Carson to house officers and other influential visitors. Once the bloodless "war" was over in the summer of 1858, the camp was soon deserted as troops were sent back East to fight in the Civil War.

Description

To get to the start of the Pony Express Trail, take I-80 to Wendover, then turn onto Alt US 93 south for about 24 miles (crossing into Nevada) until it intersects with a paved

The Pony Express route snakes out of Overland Canyon

road to Ibapah. Turn left here and drive 15.2 miles until you come to the intersection with the unpaved Gold Hill Road. The trail starts at the abandoned general store in Gold Hill, 11.1 miles from the intersection of Gold Hill Road and the road to Ibapah. There are no facilities in Gold Hill, or at any point along the trail, so make sure you come prepared with plenty of gas, water, and food. The trail continues past a number of old Pony Express way stations and historical markers as it unfolds through miles of desert country and open range. Although the road has been well traveled and can be negotiated by a passenger car in good weather, the region is still no less remote than it was over a hundred years ago during the days of the Pony Express.

Leave the general store in Gold Hill on the road to Ibapah. After 5 miles the trail connects with the Pony Express Scenic Byway at the Overland Canyon turnoff. Turn left onto the by-way and continue along the well-maintained county road.

As happens frequently along this route, the scenic byway only approximates the original route used by the Pony Express and Overland Stage, which runs a little southwest of the sce-nic byway. To travel along a short section of the old route, con-tinue past the scenic byway along the road to Ibapah for three-quarters of a mile. From here, turn left onto a faint track. This is the actual route used by the Pony Express and Overland Stage and cuts the corner of the route now used by the main road. Almost immediately, the track splits in two, with the more defined track heading southwest toward the hill while the less-traveled Pony Express and Overland Stage route stays in the valley and heads southeast. After 2.2 miles along this faint trail, there is short dead-end track on the right that goes to a Pony Express commemorative pylon. The trail then re-connects with the scenic byway at the 2.1-mile mark. This 2.3-mile diversion trail along the unimproved stage road rates a 2 for difficulty because of a wash crossing and difficult nav-igation caused by the faintness of the trail.

Continuing along the scenic byway, you pass Canyon Sta-tion, Round Hill Station, and Willow Springs Station before reaching Callao. There are a number of original buildings from the Overland Stage era in Callao. Some are falling down,

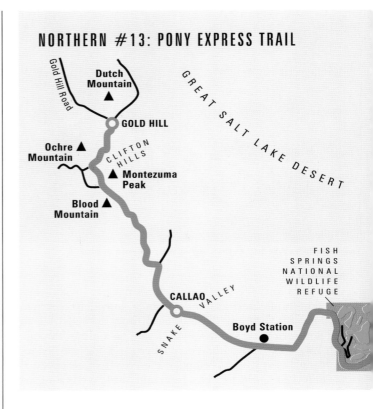

NORTHERN #13: PONY EXPRESS TRAIL

and others have remained in rather good shape and are still in-habited. However, note that all of Callao's buildings are on pri-vate property, so admire the structures from the trail, but do not go up to them.

The trail continues past Fish Springs, which is home to a large national bird sanctuary. Ornithologists and amateur bird watchers alike will find plenty to see in this unique desert oasis. After passing the Pony Express way station at Fish Springs, proceed past Black Rock Station to a road on the left signed to a geode field. At the field, you can hunt around for these bizarre rock formations. Although giving the appearance of plain rocks, geodes can be broken open to reveal hollowed-out centers that house fascinating crystal structures.

Because of the length of the trail, you may wish to take two days to drive it. If you need a place to camp overnight, there is fresh water and a campground at Simpson Springs Station. There are foundations of many old buildings at Simpson Springs as well as a restored Pony Express station and a historic marker. A few miles after the way station at Simpson Springs, you can look about 11 miles to the northwest to the Dugway Proving Grounds.

The trail ends at Camp Floyd/Stagecoach Inn State Park. Al-though not much is left of this military camp, you can still vis-it the cemetery, commissary, and the restored Stagecoach Inn.

Current Road Information
BLM Salt Lake Field Office
2370 South 2300 West
Salt Lake City, UT 84119
(801) 977-4300

Simpson Springs Pony Express Station

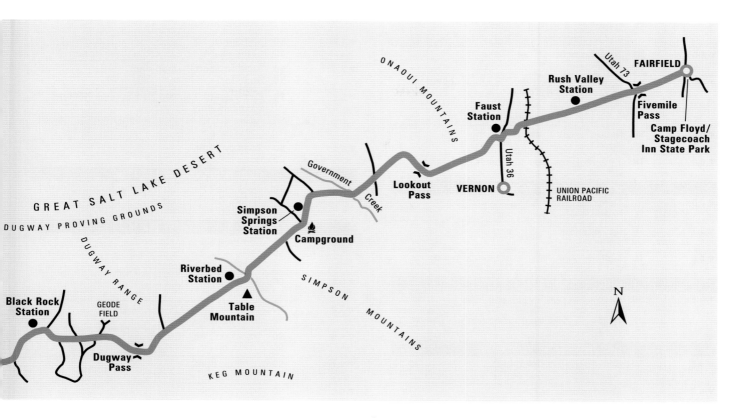

Map References

BLM   Wildcat Mt., Fish Springs, Lynndyl, Rush Valley

USGS   1:24,000 Gold Hill, Clifton, Goshute Canyon, Callao, Mud Lake Reservoir, Boyd Station, Fish Springs SW, Fish Springs NW, Fish Springs SE, Fish Springs NE, Dugway Range SW, Dugway Pass, Dugway Range NE, Table Mt., Coyote Springs, Simpson Springs, Indian Peaks, Onaqui Mt. South, Lookout Pass, Faust, Vernon NE, Fivemile Pass, Cedar Fort 1:100,000 Wildcat Mt., Fish Springs, Lynndyl, Rush Valley

Maptech CD-ROM: Lower Wasatch/Salt Lake City; Upper Wasatch/Great Salt Lake

Utah Atlas & Gazetteer, pp. 50, 42, 43, 52, 53

Utah Travel Council #1 (incomplete)

Route Directions

▼ 0.0			From Alt US 93 in Nevada, take paved road to Ibapah to Gold Hill Road. Take Gold Hill Road to Gold Hill; in front of abandoned general store on corner, turn south on the road to Ibapah and zero trip meter.
	5.0 ▲		Trail ends at intersection in Gold Hill. Left is Gold Hill Road, which leads to Alt US 93 and Wendover.
		GPS: N 40°09.98′ W 113°49.81′	
▼ 1.0		SO	Track on left.
	4.0 ▲	SO	Track on right
▼ 1.2		SO	Tracks on right.
	3.8 ▲	SO	Tracks on left.
▼ 2.4		SO	Track on left.
	2.5 ▲	SO	Track on right.
▼ 3.9		SO	Road on left, then track on right.

	1.1 ▲	SO	Track on left, then road on right.
▼ 4.1		SO	Road on left.
	0.8 ▲	SO	Road on right.
▼ 5.0		TL	Road on left and track on right. Straight goes 0.7 miles to a short section of original, unimproved Pony Express Trail (see description above). Zero trip meter and turn left.
	0.0 ▲		Continue toward Gold Hill.
		GPS: N 40°06.32′ W 113°51.88′	
▼ 0.0			Proceed southeast along Pony Express route.
	5.6 ▲	TR	Intersecton. Zero trip meter and turn right.
▼ 1.3		SO	Road on left.
	4.3 ▲	SO	Road on right.
▼ 2.1		SO	Track on right is a portion of actual, unimproved Pony Express route. 0.1 miles along that trail is a track on left that leads to an old, vandalized Pony Express marker.
	3.5 ▲	SO	Track on left is portion of actual, unimproved Pony Express route. 0.1 miles along that trail is a track on left that leads to an old, vandalized Pony Express marker (see description above).
▼ 2.2		SO	Old Pony Express marker on right (100 yards from road).
	3.4 ▲	SO	Old Pony Express marker on left (100 yards from road).
▼ 3.4		SO	Track on right.
	2.2 ▲	SO	Track on left.
▼ 3.8		SO	Track on left.
	1.8 ▲	SO	Track on right.
▼ 5.6		SO	Track on right to Pony Express Canyon Station and storyboards. Zero trip meter.
	0.0 ▲		Continue along main road.
		GPS: N 40°02.69′ W 113°48.20′	
▼ 0.0			Continue along main road.

8.0 ▲	SO	Track on left to Pony Express Canyon Station and storyboards. Zero trip meter.
▼ 4.8	SO	Track on right.
3.1 ▲	SO	Track on left.
▼ 6.8	SO	Six-mile Ranch on right. Springs behind ranch were used by the Pony Express.
1.1 ▲	SO	Six-mile Ranch on left. Springs behind ranch were used by the Pony Express.
▼ 6.9	BL	Road on right to ranch.
1.0 ▲	BR	Road forks.
▼ 8.0	TR	T-intersection. Zero trip meter.
0.0 ▲		Continue northwest.

GPS: N 39°57.49′ W 113°43.87′

▼ 0.0		Continue toward Callao.
14.0 ▲	TL	Road on left. Zero trip meter.
▼ 3.7	SO	Cattle guard.
10.3 ▲	SO	Cattle guard.
▼ 4.0	TL	T-intersection. Then cross cattle guard.
10.0 ▲	TR	Cattle guard, then intersection.

GPS: N 39°54.13′ W 113°43.45′

▼ 4.5	SO	Willow Springs Station and historic marker on left.
9.5 ▲	SO	Willow Springs Station and historic marker on right.

GPS: N 39°54.02′ W 113°42.81′

▼ 4.8	SO	Callao schoolhouse on left.
9.2 ▲	SO	Callao schoolhouse on right.
▼ 6.4	SO	Cattle guard.
7.6 ▲	SO	Cattle guard.
▼ 11.2	SO	Cattle guard.
2.7 ▲	SO	Cattle guard.
▼ 13.0	SO	Track on right.
1.0 ▲	SO	Track on left.
▼ 14.0	SO	Pull-off on left for Boyd Station. Road to Trout Creek and Partoun on right. Zero trip meter.
0.0 ▲		Continue toward Callao.

GPS: N 39°50.62′ W 113°33.17′

▼ 0.0		Continue toward Fish Springs.
12.7 ▲	SO	Pull-off on right for Boyd Station. Road to Trout Creek and Partoun on left. Zero trip meter.
▼ 0.1	SO	Road on right.
12.6 ▲	BR	Road forks.
▼ 3.2	SO	Track on right.
9.4 ▲	SO	Track on left.
▼ 4.4	SO	Track on right.
8.3 ▲	SO	Track on left.
▼ 4.7	SO	Track on right.
7.9 ▲	SO	Track on left.
▼ 9.5	SO	Cattle guard. Entering Fish Springs National Wildlife Refuge.
3.1 ▲	SO	Leaving Fish Springs National Wildlife Refuge. Cattle guard.
▼ 12.7	SO	Historic marker for Fish Springs Pony Express Station on left. Track on right. Zero trip meter.
0.0 ▲		Continue on main road.

GPS: N 39°50.88′ W 113°24.62′

▼ 0.0		Continue on main road.
10.1 ▲	SO	Historic marker for Fish Springs Pony Express Station on right. Track on left. Zero trip meter.
▼ 0.7	SO	Fish Springs National Wildlife Refuge headquarters on left.
9.4 ▲	SO	Fish Springs National Wildlife Refuge head-

		quarters on right.
▼ 1.7	SO	Cattle guard.
8.4 ▲	SO	Cattle guard.
▼ 2.0	SO	Road to Sand Pass on right.
8.1 ▲	SO	Road to Sand Pass on left.
▼ 6.2	SO	Cattle guard. Leaving Fish Springs National Wildlife Refuge.
4.0 ▲	SO	Entering Fish Springs National Wildlife Refuge. Cattle guard.
▼ 6.8	SO	Road on right.
3.3 ▲	SO	Road on left.

GPS: N 39°50.52′ W 113°18.84′

▼ 10.1	SO	Black Rock Pony Express Station monument on left. Zero trip meter.
0.0 ▲		Continue along main road.

GPS: N 39°52.68′ W 113°16.24′

▼ 0.0		Continue along main road.
14.7 ▲	SO	Black Rock Pony Express Station monument on right. Zero trip meter.
▼ 0.8	SO	Road on left.
13.9 ▲	SO	Road on right.
▼ 2.2	SO	Track on right.
12.5 ▲	SO	Track on left.
▼ 4.3	SO	Tracks on right and left.
10.4 ▲	SO	Tracks on left and right.
▼ 6.1	SO	Track on right.
8.6 ▲	SO	Track on left.
▼ 6.5	SO	Track on right.
8.2 ▲	SO	Track on left.
▼ 7.3	SO	Road to geode field on left.
7.4 ▲	SO	Road to geode field on right.

GPS: N 39°52.37′ W 113°08.27′

▼ 12.3	SO	Track on right.
2.4 ▲	SO	Track on left.
▼ 14.3	SO	Track on left.
0.4 ▲	SO	Track on right.
▼ 14.7	SO	Track on right. Zero trip meter.
0.0 ▲		Continue along main road.

GPS: N 39°53.08′ W 113°01.74′

▼ 0.0		Continue along main road.
8.6 ▲	SO	Track on left. Zero trip meter.
▼ 1.7	SO	Track on left.
6.9 ▲	SO	Track on right
▼ 7.4	SO	Track on right.
1.2 ▲	SO	Track on left.
▼ 7.6	SO	Track on right.
1.0 ▲	SO	Track on left.
▼ 8.6	SO	Track on left to Riverbed Pony Express Station historical marker. Zero trip meter.
0.0 ▲		Continue along main road.

GPS: N 39°57.58′ W 112°53.67′

▼ 0.0		Continue along main road.
7.7 ▲	SO	Track on right to Riverbed Pony Express Station historical marker. Zero trip meter.
▼ 0.2	SO	Tracks on right and left.
7.4 ▲	SO	Tracks on left and right.
▼ 5.4	SO	Track on right.
2.2 ▲	SO	Track on left.
▼ 7.7	SO	Simpson Springs Pony Express Station marker on left. Public toilets, campground, and recreation area on right. Several old structures. Zero trip meter at historic marker.
0.0 ▲		Continue along main road.

GPS: N 40°02.34′ W 112°47.19′

▼ 0.0		SO	Continue along main road.
	15.4 ▲	SO	Simpson Springs Pony Express Station marker on right. Public toilets, campground, and recreation area on left. Several old structures. Zero trip meter at historic marker.
▼ 3.2		SO	Track on left to Dugway Proving Grounds.
	12.2 ▲	SO	Track on right to Dugway Proving Grounds.
▼ 9.3		SO	Intersection. Right goes to Erickson Pass, left to Dugway.
	6.1 ▲	SO	Intersection. Left goes to Erickson Pass, right to Dugway.

GPS: N 40°06.17′ W 112°39.66′

▼ 12.6		BR	Road on left to Dugway Proving Grounds.
	2.8 ▲	BL	Intersection. Bear left toward Callao and Fish Springs, following Pony Express route.

GPS: N 40°08.29′ W 112°37.03′

▼ 13.8		BR	Road on left to Terra.
	1.5 ▲	BL	Road on right to Terra.
▼ 15.4		SO	Lookout Pass Pony Express Station historical marker. Zero trip meter.
	0.0 ▲		Continue along main road.

GPS: N 40°07.19′ W 112°34.56′

▼ 0.0			Continue toward Lookout Pass.
	9.5 ▲	SO	Lookout Pass Pony Express Station historical marker. Zero trip meter.
▼ 0.7		SO	Lookout Pass.
	8.8 ▲	SO	Lookout Pass.
▼ 1.5		BL	Fork in road. Right goes to Vernon.
	8.0 ▲	SO	Road enters on left.

GPS: N 40°06.74′ W 112°33.07′

▼ 7.1		SO	Road on left to scenic view.
	2.3 ▲	SO	Road on right to scenic view.
▼ 8.8		TL	T-intersection. Turn left onto Utah 36.
	0.6 ▲	TR	Turn onto gravel road.

GPS: N 40°09.92′ W 112°25.79′

▼ 9.5		TR	Faust Pony Express Station historical marker on left. Zero trip meter.
	0.0 ▲		Proceed south on Utah 36.

GPS: N 40°10.45′ W 112°25.58′

▼ 0.0			Proceed east on paved road opposite the historical marker.
	7.4 ▲	TL	Intersection with Utah 36. Cross road to Faust Pony Express Station historical marker. Zero trip meter.
▼ 2.0		SO	Cross railroad tracks.
	5.4 ▲	SO	Cross railroad tracks.
▼ 7.4		SO	Rush Valley Pony Express Station historical marker. Zero trip meter.
	0.0 ▲		Continue along main road.

GPS: N 40°12.39′ W 112°17.55′

▼ 0.0			Continue along paved road.
	11.0 ▲	SO	Rush Valley Pony Express Station historical marker. Zero trip meter.
▼ 5.9		TR	T-intersection with Utah 73.
	5.1 ▲	TL	Intersection.

GPS: N 40°13.85′ W 112°10.99′

▼ 10.9		TR	Turn right onto 1500 North toward the Stagecoach Museum.
	0.1 ▲	TL	Turn left onto Utah 73.
▼ 11.0			Trail ends at Camp Floyd/Stagecoach Inn State Park and Museum.
	0.0 ▲		In front of the Stagecoach Inn at Camp Floyd Pony Express Station marker, proceed west on paved road.

GPS: N 40°15.65′ W 112°05.54′

Clear Creek Ridge Trail

Starting Point:	**US 6, at the site of Tucker**
Finishing Point:	**Utah 31**
Total Mileage:	**27.6 miles**
Unpaved Mileage:	**27.6 miles**
Driving Time:	**1 hour**
Elevation Range:	**6,200–9,200 feet**
Usually Open:	**May to November**
Difficulty Rating:	**1**
Scenic Rating:	**8**
Remoteness Rating:	**+0**

Special Attractions

- Easy high-elevation scenic drive with good views.
- Wildflowers in spring and summer and wonderful fall colors.
- Many good backcountry campsites.

History

Although there is little evidence of the town now, the trail begins at Tucker, a once-important railroad town along the Denver & Rio Grande Western (D&RGW) Railroad. When the D&RGW decided to reroute the line in 1915 to avoid the steep grade up to Soldier Summit, Tucker was buried beneath large amounts of fillwork. All that remained of the once-booming town was a small station stop and a railroad siding. (For more on Tucker, see p. 47.) Over the years, Tucker cemetery, once located about a half mile from town along this trail, also vanished from the landscape.

Description

The Clear Creek Ridge Trail begins at the Tucker rest stop off US 6 and is one of the trails that makes up the popular route known as Skyline Drive. As you drive southwest from the Tucker rest stop, the trail climbs 3,000 feet along a 9-mile stretch of rough and bumpy road. Though some sections are rather narrow, the road is generally wide and easy to drive. The trail runs along an attractive, tree-lined forest road passing sev-

A stand of aspens along Clear Creek Ridge Trail

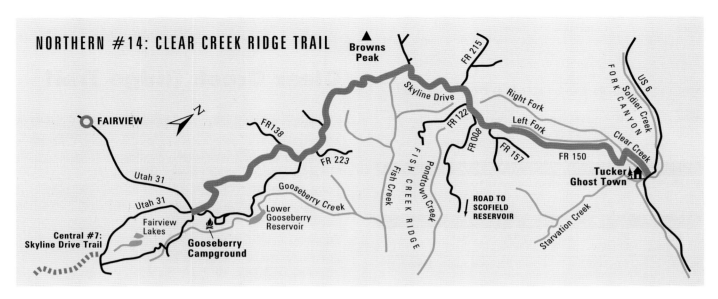

NORTHERN #14: CLEAR CREEK RIDGE TRAIL

eral stands of aspen around the 7-mile mark.

There are quite a few backcountry campsites along the way, especially in the first 10 miles. As the trail reaches the top of the plateau, the views open up over the countryside and extend into the distance. These expansive overlooks at the higher elevations of the Clear Creek Ridge Trail are well worth the trip.

For its entire length, the trail can be driven either by SUV or passenger car. To continue farther along Skyline Drive, take Utah 31 south for 4.8 miles and connect with the slightly more difficult, 3-rated Central #7: Skyline Drive Trail.

Current Road Information
Manti-La Sal National Forest
Sanpete Ranger District
540 North Main
Ephraim, UT 84627
(435) 283-4151

Map References
BLM Nephi
USFS Manti-La Sal National Forest: Sanpete & Price Ranger Districts
USGS 1:24,000 Tucker, Mill Fork, C Canyon, Fairview Lakes
      1:100,000 Nephi
Maptech CD-ROM: Central/San Rafael
Utah Atlas & Gazetteer, p. 46
Utah Travel Council #3

Route Directions

▼ 0.0		On US 6, several miles north of Soldier Summit, turn into the Tucker rest stop. Bear right past the picnic area on Skyline Drive and zero trip meter on the bridge over Clear Creek. This is CR 150.
9.6 ▲		Trail ends at bridge near site of Tucker. US 6 is straight ahead; turn right for Soldier Summit, left for Spanish Fork.
	GPS: N 39°56.13′ W 111°11.97′	
▼ 0.1	SO	Cattle guard.
9.5 ▲	SO	Cattle guard.
▼ 1.5	SO	Track on right.

8.1 ▲	SO	Track on left.
▼ 1.7	SO	Track on right. Cross bridge over Clear Creek.
7.9 ▲	SO	Cross bridge over Clear Creek. Track on left.
▼ 2.6	SO	Entering Manti-La Sal National Forest; road becomes FR 150. Track on left.
7.0 ▲	SO	Track on right. Leaving Manti-La Sal National Forest.
▼ 3.1	SO	Track on left.
6.5 ▲	SO	Track on right.
▼ 4.2	SO	Track on left.
5.4 ▲	SO	Track on right.
▼ 5.3	SO	Track on left.
4.3 ▲	SO	Track on right.
▼ 5.9	SO	Track on right to backcountry campsites.
3.7 ▲	SO	Track on left to backcountry campsites.
▼ 6.4-6.6	SO	Tracks on right to several campsites.
3.0-3.2 ▲	SO	Tracks on left to several campsites.
▼ 8.0	SO	Track on left.
1.6 ▲	SO	Track on right.
▼ 8.2	SO	Track on right. Then track on left.
1.4 ▲	SO	Track on left. Then track on right.
▼ 8.6	SO	Track on right.
1.0 ▲	SO	Track on left.
▼ 8.7	SO	FR 157 on left.
0.9 ▲	BL	FR 157 on right.
▼ 9.6	SO	FR 008 on left to Bear Ridge and Scofield Reservoir. Zero trip meter.
0.0 ▲		Continue north.
	GPS: N 39°51.35′ W 111°18.06′	
▼ 0.0		Continue south on Skyline Drive.
10.1 ▲	SO	FR 008 on right to Bear Ridge and Scofield Reservoir. Zero trip meter.
▼ 0.3	SO	FR 122 on left to Fish Creek Ridge and Scofield.
9.8 ▲	SO	FR 122 on right to Fish Creek Ridge and Scofield.
▼ 0.6	SO	Track on right.
9.5 ▲	SO	Track on left.
▼ 1.2	SO	FR 215 to Garret Ridge on right.
8.9 ▲	SO	FR 215 to Garret Ridge on left.
	GPS: N 39°51.34′ W 111°19.45′	
▼ 1.6	SO	Track to microwave towers on right.
8.5 ▲	SO	Track to microwave towers on left.
▼ 4.5	SO	Fish Creek National Recreation Trailhead on left.

5.6 ▲	SO	Fish Creek National Recreation Trailhead on right.
▼ 6.3	SO	Track on right. Then Trail #040 on right.
3.8 ▲	SO	Trail #040 on left. Then track on left.
▼ 10.1	SO	FR 223 on left. Zero trip meter.
0.0 ▲		Continue along main road.

GPS: N 39°45.68' W 111°19.36'

▼ 0.0		Continue along main road.
7.8 ▲	SO	FR 223 on right. Zero trip meter.
▼ 0.4	SO	FR 177 on right.
7.4 ▲	SO	FR 177 on left.
▼ 0.8	SO	Track on left.
6.9 ▲	SO	Track on right.
▼ 1.5	SO	Cabin Hollow track on left.
6.3 ▲	SO	Cabin Hollow track on right.
▼ 2.0	SO	FR 138 on right—Dry Creek Stock Driveway.
5.8 ▲	SO	FR 138 on left—Dry Creek Stock Driveway.
▼ 2.4	SO	Cattle guard.
5.3 ▲	SO	Cattle guard.
▼ 4.6	SO	FR 055 on right.
3.1 ▲	SO	FR 055 on left.
▼ 4.9	SO	Cattle guard.
2.8 ▲	SO	Cattle guard.
▼ 5.6-5.7	SO	Tracks on right.
2.1-2.2 ▲	SO	Tracks on left.
▼ 6.9	SO	Cattle guard.
0.9 ▲	SO	Cattle guard.
▼ 7.5	SO	Track on left to Mammoth Guard Station, Gooseberry Campground, and Lower Gooseberry Reservoir.
0.3 ▲	SO	Follow sign to US 6 and Skyline Drive. Track on right to Mammoth Guard Station, Gooseberry Campground, and Lower Gooseberry Reservoir.
▼ 7.6	SO	Intersection. Paved road on left.
0.2 ▲	BL	Bear left onto unpaved road.
▼ 7.8		Trail ends at Utah 31; turn right for Fairview, left for Huntington.
0.0 ▲		On Utah 31, 4.8 miles north of Central #7: Skyline Drive Trail and 9.5 miles northwest of Central #6: Upper Joe's Valley Trail, zero trip meter and turn north onto FR 150.

GPS: N 39°40.58' W 111°18.82'

Nine Mile Canyon Trail

Starting Point:	US 6/191, 1.9 miles east of Wellington
Finishing Point:	Northern #21: Franks Canyon and Sand Wash Trail
Total Mileage:	48.7 miles
Unpaved Mileage:	36.2 miles
Driving Time:	2 hours
Elevation Range:	5,200–7,600 feet
Usually Open:	Year-round
Difficulty Rating:	1
Scenic Rating:	9
Remoteness Rating:	+0

Special Attractions

- Easy, scenic route that connects with numerous other 4WD trails.
- The greatest concentration of petroglyphs in the United States.
- Numerous granaries and cliff dwellings built by the Fremont Indians.

History

One of the first things you notice as you drive along Nine Mile Canyon is that it is much longer than 9 miles. Over the years, several stories have arisen to explain how this 40-mile-long canyon got its name. One says it was because of the nine-member Miles family that lived in the area in the late 1800s. However, the most believable story says that it was named by

The petroglyphs at Balanced Rock

mapmaker Frank M. Bishop, on John Wesley Powell's 1869 survey expedition through the region. Some say Bishop used the name because he'd charted the canyon in a 9-mile triangulation drawing, while others say he found the creek that cuts through the canyon near his 9-mile marker. Whatever the case may be, Nine Mile Canyon is most assuredly about 30 miles longer than its name suggests.

Over a thousand years ago when the Fremont inhabited Nine Mile Canyon, they turned it into one of America's longest art galleries with a phenomenal amount of pictographs and petroglyphs. The Fremont were among the most prolific rock artists of Utah's early Indian inhabitants. The walls of Nine Mile Canyon reveal countless geometric patterns and images of humans and animals. As you drive by the images, remember to respect them as irreplaceable historic treasures.

Besides creating rock art, the Fremont also built a number of granaries into the canyon's cliffs. These storage shelters are typically camouflaged and located some distance up the cliffs, indicating that the Fremont felt they needed to go to great lengths to protect their food supply. It takes a keen eye to spot the remains of the small rock walls built into the horizontal indentations of the stratified cliffs.

In the 19th century, white men began traveling through the canyon. The first to blaze a footpath through the region were early explorers and trappers. In 1886, the path was upgraded to a federal highway by the U.S. Ninth Cavalry, which was composed of African Americans. A telegraph line was also run through the canyon to connect Fort Duchesne with Price and the rest of Utah.

Encouraged by the new road, the first permanent white settlers moved in and homesteaded this part of Duchesne County. A few scattered ranches and stopping points soon became the ranching community of Harper. In 1902, ranching tycoon Preston Nutter moved his headquarters into Nine Mile Canyon near Harper. Besides owning upward of 25,000 cattle all throughout the Southwest, this unique character had a flock of peacocks that could always be seen roaming about his headquarters. (For more on Nutter and Harper, see "Along the Trail.")

In 1990, with the completion of US 40 and US 191, the road through Nine Mile Canyon became a National Backcountry Byway and can now be enjoyed at a slow, leisurely pace.

Description

On US 6/191, 1.9 miles east of Wellington, turn northeast onto paved Soldier Creek Road, which is signed to Nine Mile Canyon. The first 12.5 miles of the trail are paved, after which the road turns to gravel. The trail remains wide and maintained throughout and can be driven in a passenger car.

As you proceed, keep an eye out for the now idle telegraph poles. Some are made of wood, but many are metal, built to withstand Indian attempts to destroy them. These old telegraph poles are particularly abundant between Harper and the area near the turnoff to Argyle Canyon.

To see the Fremont petroglyphs, pictographs, and granaries along the way, a set of binoculars is highly recommended. Although a number of them are pointed

A close-up of a Fremont granary (circled on the right in the photo above)

A close-up of a Fremont granary (circled on the left in the photo above)

A close-up of the granary (circled on the photo at left)

out below in the route directions, there are many more to be found at all levels up and down the cliff walls. Pay particular attention to the places where smaller canyons intersect with Nine Mile Canyon; rock art often becomes more prevalent in these areas. Granaries are often much more difficult to spot. Look for an impressed horizontal line that extends about halfway up the side of the canyon. The Fremont constructed their granaries into the cliff along these indentations and built up a pile of rocks and mud to close off the protective structures. Over the years, these protective front walls have crumbled away, though the bases of the walls have remained in some instances. It may take some looking, but these slightly out-of-place rock bases are in fact an indication of old Fremont granaries.

After about 42 miles, you reach the old town site of Harper, and about a mile past that is the intersection with Northern #16: Argyle Canyon Trail. Half a mile past this intersection is a precariously balanced rock near a set of petroglyphs. Over the years, the general consensus seems to be that the balanced rock looks similar to Porky Pig, though it's also named, quite simply, Balanced Rock. Shortly thereafter, you come to a stone building that was once home to Nine Mile Canyon's longtime resident and telegraph operator Ed Harmon.

Marking from the Argyle Canyon Trail intersection, you reach Northern #17: Dry Canyon Trail in 11.7 miles and Northern #18: Cottonwood Canyon Trail in 13.1 miles. In between these two trail intersections is the interesting Rasmussen's Cave. Besides having some wonderful pictographs, the cave was the site of early excavations that unearthed a number of Indian artifacts and mummies.

The latter portion of Nine Mile Canyon Trail becomes noticeably more narrow. While it continues as a 1-rated trail, you will now have to pull over to allow an oncoming vehicle to pass. The scenery also becomes more striking and dramatic as the rock walls close in and tower above the road. It is not uncommon to see deer and elk roaming through the canyon. About 1.7 miles after passing Cottonwood Canyon Trail, you pass a stone building and log cabin by the cliff; these buildings served as a telegraph relay station at the midway point between Price and the Fort Duchesne garrison. Past this, all the ranches and buildings along the trail are private property.

The trail ends at the locked gates to the old Nutter Ranch, where the trail connects with Northern #21: Franks Canyon and Sand Wash Trail.

Current Road Information

BLM Price Field Office
125 South 600 West
Price, UT 84501
(435) 636-3600

Map References

BLM   Price
USGS 1:24,000 Wellington, Deadman Canyon, Pine
      Canyon, Minnie Maud Creek East, Wood Canyon,
      Currant Canyon, Cowboy Bench
      1:100,000 Price
Maptech CD-ROM: Central/San Rafael
Utah Atlas & Gazetteer, p. 47
Utah Travel Council #3

Route Directions

▼ 0.0			On US 6/191, 1.9 miles east of the Wellington post office, turn northeast onto Soldier Creek Road and zero trip meter. The intersection is well marked and signed to Nine Mile Canyon.
	12.5 ▲		Trail ends at US 6/191; turn right for Wellington, left for Green River.
GPS: N 39°32.59′ W 110°41.22′			
▼ 5.6		BL	Road on right.
	6.9 ▲	BR	Road on left.
▼ 12.5		SO	Start of gravel road. Zero trip meter.
	0.0 ▲		Continue on main road.
GPS: N 39°42.18′ W 110°36.64′			
▼ 0.0			Continue on main road.
	18.1 ▲	SO	Pavement begins. Zero trip meter.
▼ 1.5		SO	Cross cattle guard.
	16.6 ▲	SO	Cross cattle guard.
▼ 2.1		SO	Dirt road on left.
	16.0 ▲	SO	Dirt road on right.
▼ 4.9		SO	Cross cattle guard.
	13.2 ▲	SO	Cross cattle guard.
▼ 6.0		SO	Old cabin on right.
	12.1 ▲	SO	Old cabin on left.
▼ 8.3		SO	Cross bridge over Minnie Maud Creek.
	9.8 ▲	SO	Cross bridge over Minnie Maud Creek.
▼ 8.5		SO	Old cabin on left.
	9.6 ▲	SO	Old cabin on right.
▼ 8.9		SO	Nine Mile Canyon BLM information board.
	9.2 ▲	SO	Nine Mile Canyon BLM information board.
▼ 9.8		SO	Old homestead on left. Cross cattle guard.
	8.2 ▲	SO	Cross cattle guard. Old homestead on right.
▼ 10.7		SO	Nine Mile Ranch B&B and Campground on right.
	7.4 ▲	SO	Nine Mile Ranch B&B and Campground on left.
▼ 12.3		SO	Cross cattle guard.
	5.8 ▲	SO	Cross cattle guard.
▼ 13.1		SO	Pictographs on left, pull-over area on right. Walk through entry in log fence for best viewing.
	4.9 ▲	SO	Pictographs on right, pull-over area on left.
GPS: N 39°46.79′ W 110°25.42′			
▼ 14.1		SO	Old cabin on right. Nine Mile Canyon Cottonwood Glen Picnic Area (day use only) on right.
	3.9 ▲	SO	Picnic area (day use only) on left. Old cabin on left.
▼ 14.7		SO	Old log structures left and right.
	3.3 ▲	SO	Old log structures left and right.
▼ 15.4		SO	Cross cattle guard.
	2.7 ▲	SO	Cross cattle guard.
▼ 17.2		SO	Site of Harper.
	0.9 ▲	SO	Site of Harper.
GPS: N 39°48.03′ W 110°22.08′			
▼ 18.1		SO	Cross creek. Northern #16: Argyle Canyon Trail on left. Zero trip meter at intersection.
	0.0 ▲		Continue west.
GPS: N 39°48.21′ W 110°21.11′			
▼ 0.0			Continue east.
	6.8 ▲	SO	Northern #16: Argyle Canyon Trail on right. Zero trip meter and cross creek.
▼ 0.6		SO	Balanced Rock and petroglyphs to right of rock, about 20 feet above ground.
	6.1 ▲	SO	Balanced Rock and petroglyphs to right of rock, about 20 feet above ground.
GPS: N 39°48.06′ W 110°20.49′			
▼ 0.9		SO	Wimer Ranch buildings.
	5.9 ▲	SO	Wimer Ranch buildings.
▼ 1.3		SO	Stone building on right was old telegraph office.
	5.5 ▲	SO	Stone building on left was old telegraph office.
GPS: N 39°48.58′ W 110°20.38′			
▼ 1.9		SO	Track on left. Then track to Harmon Canyon on right. Numerous petroglyphs on left, 20 feet above ground on patina rocks.
	4.9 ▲	SO	Track to Harmon Canyon on left. Numerous petroglyphs on right, 20 feet above ground. Track on right.
GPS: N 39°48.46′ W 110°19.83′			
▼ 3.5		SO	Stone ranch building on left.
	3.2 ▲	SO	Stone ranch building on right.
▼ 4.1		SO	Cross cattle guard.
	2.7 ▲	SO	Cross cattle guard.
▼ 6.3		SO	Historic Nutter's Ranch buildings.
	0.4 ▲	SO	Historic Nutter's Ranch buildings.
▼ 6.8		SO	Sign and intersection; zero trip meter. Straight for Prickly Pear Canyon, Dry Canyon, and Cottonwood Canyon. Myton via Gate Canyon to left.
	0.0 ▲		Continue along Nine Mile Canyon Road.
GPS: N 39°48.71′ W 110°15.09′			
▼ 0.0			Continue on Nine Mile Canyon Road.
	4.9 ▲	SO	Sign and intersection; zero trip meter. Straight for Wellington. Myton via Gate Canyon to right.
▼ 0.1		SO	Cross cattle guard; 15 feet after cattle guard on left is petroglyph about 6 feet above ground.
	4.8 ▲	SO	About 15 feet before cattle guard on right is petroglyph about 6 feet above ground. Cross cattle guard.
GPS: N 39°48.63′ W 110°14.88′			
▼ 0.4		SO	Very old corral in sage bushes on left, partly obscured.
	4.4 ▲	SO	Very old corral in sage bushes on right, partly obscured.
▼ 2.4		SO	Cross cattle guard. Granary on left (pictured).
	2.5 ▲	SO	Granary on right (pictured). Cross cattle guard.
GPS: N 39°47.76′ W 110°12.72′			
▼ 3.0		SO	Track to Prickly Pear Canyon on right.
	1.9 ▲	SO	Track to Prickly Pear Canyon on left.
▼ 4.8		SO	Cross cattle guard. Rock formation called "The Mummy" is ahead in the distance on right.

NORTHERN #15: NINE MILE CANYON TRAIL

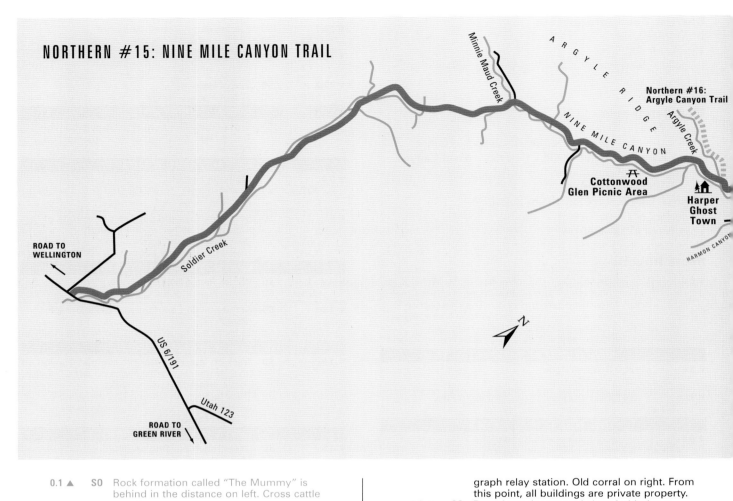

0.1 ▲	SO	Rock formation called "The Mummy" is behind in the distance on left. Cross cattle guard.	

▼ 4.9		SO	Track on right is Northern #17: Dry Canyon Trail. Zero trip meter.
	0.0 ▲		Continue along main trail.

GPS: N 39°47.06′ W 110°10.38′

▼ 0.0			Continue along main trail.
	1.4 ▲	SO	Track on left is Northern #17: Dry Canyon Trail. Zero trip meter.

▼ 0.4		SO	Rasmussen's Cave on left with pictographs. Pull-over area a little farther opposite corral. More pictographs on canyon wall between cave and corral.
	0.9 ▲	SO	Pictographs on canyon wall between cave and corral on right. A little farther is Rasmussen's Cave on right with pictographs.

GPS: N 39°47.14′ W 110°10.06′

▼ 1.4		BL	Fork in the road. Right is Northern #18: Cottonwood Canyon Trail. Zero trip meter.
	0.0 ▲		Continue along Nine Mile Canyon Road.

GPS: N 37°47.02′ W 110°09.01′

▼ 0.0			Continue along Nine Mile Canyon Road.
	5.0 ▲	BR	Track on left is Northern #18: Cottonwood Canyon Trail. Zero trip meter.

▼ 0.3		SO	Pass through gate.
	4.7 ▲	SO	Pass through gate.

▼ 0.7		SO	Cross cattle guard.
	4.3 ▲	SO	Cross cattle guard.

▼ 1.7		SO	Pass through gate and close behind you. Stone building and log cabin by cliff were tele-

graph relay station. Old corral on right. From this point, all buildings are private property.

3.3 ▲	SO	Pass through gate and close behind you. Stone building and log cabin by cliff were telegraph relay station.

GPS: N 39°47.13′ W 110°07.32′

▼ 2.2		SO	Several good petroglyphs on left, about 20 feet above ground.
	2.8 ▲	SO	Several good petroglyphs on right, about 20 feet above ground.

GPS: N 39°47.28′ W 110°06.91′

▼ 2.4		SO	Track on left.
	2.6 ▲	SO	Track on right.

▼ 2.5		SO	Pass through gate and close behind you. Corral on left.
	2.5 ▲	SO	Pass through gate and close behind you. Corral on right.

▼ 3.2		SO	Pass through gate and close behind you.
	1.8 ▲	SO	Pass through gate and close behind you.

▼ 3.7		SO	Old ranch buildings on left and right.
	1.3 ▲	SO	Old ranch buildings on left and right.

▼ 4.3		SO	Eye-level petroglyphs on a large rock directly beside road on right.
	0.7 ▲	SO	Eye-level petroglyphs on a large rock directly beside road on left.

▼ 4.5		SO	Track on left.
	0.5 ▲	SO	Track on right.

▼ 4.6		SO	Old stone buildings on left and a corral on right.
	0.4 ▲	SO	Old stone buildings on right and a corral on left.

GPS: N 39°48.00′ W 110°04.87′

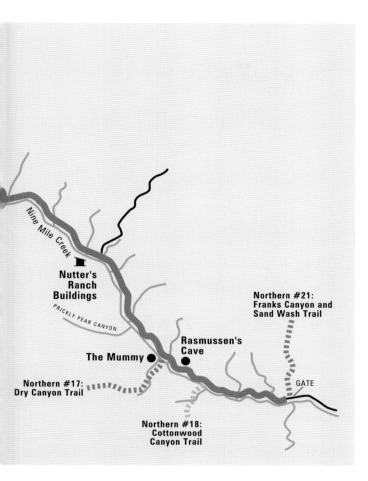

Special Attractions

■ Links Northern #15: Nine Mile Canyon Trail with Northern #22: Reservation Ridge Trail.

Description

According to the sign along US 191, the beginning of Argyle Canyon Trail is called Timber Lane. The maintained gravel road is used by logging trucks and is kept graded. The trail starts out through private forest land composed mainly of fir and aspen. Under normal circumstances, the road is not difficult; however, its clay-based surface can become slippery when wet.

As you drive farther into Argyle Canyon, fir and aspens give way to cottonwoods, pinyon, and sage. The canyon is generally broad and used as ranchland. Its walls are quite gentle and look more like hills than the cliff faces typical of most canyons in the region.

A view of the cottonwoods along the trail

The Argyle Canyon trail eventually comes to an end at Northern #15: Nine Mile Canyon Trail less than a mile from the old ghost town of Harper.

Current Road Information

BLM Price Field Office
125 South 600 West
Price, UT 84501
(435) 636-3600

Map References

BLM Price
USFS Ashley National Forest
USGS 1:24,000 Jones Hollow, Lance Canyon, Minnie Maud Creek East, Wood Canyon
1:100,000 Price
Maptech CD-ROM: Central/San Rafael
Utah Atlas & Gazetteer, p. 47
Utah Travel Council #3

Route Directions

▼ 0.0		On US 191 (0.9 miles from turnoff for Avintaquin Campground), turn northeast onto dirt road marked "Timberlane," and zero trip meter. Sign to Argyle Canyon and Nine Mile Canyon.
23.9 ▲		Trail ends at US 191; turn left for Northern #22: Reservation Ridge Trail, right for Duchesne.

GPS: N 39°53.02' W 110°44.82'

▼ 0.3	SO	Tracks on left and right.
23.6 ▲	SO	Tracks on left and right.

▼ 5.0	Trail ends at padlocked gate to old Nutter Ranch. Track on left is Northern #21: Franks Canyon and Sand Wash Trail.
0.0 ▲	At end of Northern #21: Franks Canyon and Sand Wash Trail, zero trip meter and turn right toward Nine Mile Canyon.

GPS: N 39°48.33' W 110°04.62'

NORTHERN REGION TRAIL #16

Argyle Canyon Trail

Starting Point:	US 191, near Northern #22: Reservation Ridge Trail
Finishing Point:	Northern #15: Nine Mile Canyon Trail
Total Mileage:	23.9 miles
Unpaved Mileage:	23.9 miles
Driving Time:	45 minutes
Elevation Range:	6,400–9,100 feet
Usually Open:	Year-round
Difficulty Rating:	1
Scenic Rating:	6
Remoteness Rating:	+0

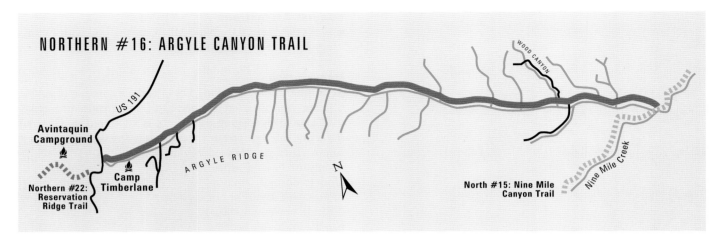

NORTHERN #16: ARGYLE CANYON TRAIL

▼ 1.5	SO	Camp Timberlane on right.
22.4 ▲	SO	Camp Timberlane on left.
▼ 4.8	SO	Pass through gate and close behind you. Private property along both sides of road.
19.1 ▲	SO	Pass through gate and close behind you.

GPS: N 39°53.35 W 110°39.93'

▼ 7.3	SO	Cattle guard.
16.6 ▲	SO	Cattle guard.
▼ 7.8	SO	Gate.
16.1 ▲	SO	Gate.
▼ 8.9	SO	Cattle guard.
15.0 ▲	SO	Cattle guard.
▼ 12.8	SO	Gate.
11.1 ▲	SO	Gate.
▼ 14.9	SO	Cattle guard.
9.0 ▲	SO	Cattle guard.
▼ 16.7	SO	Cattle guard.
7.2 ▲	SO	Cattle guard.
▼ 17.6	SO	Cattle guard.
6.3 ▲	SO	Cattle guard.
▼ 18.6	SO	Cattle guard.
5.3 ▲	SO	Cattle guard.
▼ 19.3	SO	Cattle guard.
4.6 ▲	SO	Cattle guard.
▼ 19.8	SO	Track to Wood Canyon on left.
4.0 ▲	SO	Track to Wood Canyon on right.
▼ 19.9	SO	Cattle guard.
4.0 ▲	SO	Cattle guard.
▼ 20.3	SO	Cattle guard.
3.6 ▲	SO	Cattle guard.
▼ 21.2	SO	Cattle guard.
2.6 ▲	SO	Cattle guard.
▼ 22.0	SO	Cattle guard.
1.9 ▲	SO	Cattle guard.
▼ 23.2	SO	Cattle guard.
0.7 ▲	SO	Cattle guard.
▼ 23.7	SO	Gate.
0.2 ▲	SO	Gate.
▼ 23.9		Trail ends at Northern #15: Nine Mile Canyon Trail. Turn right for US 6/191, left for Northern #21: Franks Canyon and Sand Wash Trail.
0.0 ▲		On Northern #15: Nine Mile Canyon Trail, 30.6 miles from US 6/191, zero trip meter and turn toward Argyle Canyon.

GPS: N 39°48.21' W 110°21.15'

Dry Canyon Trail

Starting Point:	Northern #15: Nine Mile Canyon Trail
Finishing Point:	US 6/191
Total Mileage:	39 miles
Unpaved Mileage:	26.4 miles
Driving Time:	3 hours
Elevation Range:	5,500–10,200 feet
Usually Open:	May to November
Difficulty Rating:	3
Scenic Rating:	9
Remoteness Rating:	+1

Special Attractions

- Moderate 4WD trail that crosses the high West Tavaputs Plateau with its high desert vegetation.
- Wonderful panoramic vistas from several viewpoints.
- Dry Canyon with its many cottonwoods, and Water Canyon with its stands of aspen.
- Fremont Indian petroglyphs and pictographs.

History

The histories of both East Carbon City and Sunnyside are inextricably intertwined with the history of coal mining in Carbon County. The coal-mining town of Sunnyside was officially settled in 1898, and within five years it had its own coke ovens. This enabled the town to begin on-site production of coke, a lighter fuel that burns at a higher temperature than coal; eventually the town had a total of 480 ovens. Sunnyside rode the highs and lows of the coal industry through the 20th century, which improved during World War II but then collapsed in the 1960s.

In 1973, East Carbon City incorporated the coal-producing towns of Dragerton and Columbia which, in 1899, had been the original eastern terminus for the Carbon County Railway. This railroad had one function only—to ship coal from the mines scattered throughout the region. Eventually the line was

The view from Bruin Point

extended farther south just west of the route followed by Utah 124.

Description

On Northern #15: Nine Mile Canyon Trail, toward the eastern end, head southwest along Dry Creek into the canyon. Dry Canyon has a lot in common with Cottonwood Canyon. Both are narrow and steep-walled and lined with cottonwoods and sagebrush. They are very attractive drives for viewing autumn colors. About 6 or 7 miles into the trail, aspens also become prevalent.

Like many other areas in this part of Utah, Dry Canyon can be extremely dusty (especially in the summer). Deep patches of powder-fine sand can slow down your vehicle at times and kick up thick clouds of dust.

The climb out of Dry Canyon follows a relatively gentle grade along a 3-mile stretch of broad, single-lane shelf road lined with trees. In some areas you may have to back up a short distance to allow someone to pass. There are many mature cottonwoods along this stretch of road and a good section of petroglyphs as well.

As you reach the top of the canyon, the scenery opens up and offers many good views from atop West Tavaputs Plateau. The trail continues to climb from here, ascending another 2,700 feet to the communication towers at Bruin Point.

On a clear day, you get a panoramic view from Bruin Point that stretches as far as 30 miles across the plains to the San Rafael Swell. Deer and elk are a common sight at the top of the plateau, as are golden eagles.

The descent south of Bruin Point runs along a much wider road than the northern approach. You will have no problem passing other vehicles along this graded, dirt road. About 3 miles from Bruin Point, the trail passes an old tramway with old cars still sitting on it.

Overall, the trail is not especially difficult. Navigation can become somewhat difficult on the plateau due to the number of side tracks. As you come down toward Sunnyside and East

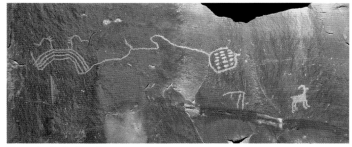
Petroglyphs in Dry Canyon

Carbon City, the gravel road is wide and maintained. As you reach Sunnyside, the trail passes a railroad spur and a mine entrance. A number of old, abandoned cottages remain in this once-thriving town.

The trail becomes paved 4.2 miles before the turnoff for Utah 124. Continue another 8.4 miles past this intersection along Utah 123 until the trail ends at US 6/191.

Current Road Information

BLM Price Field Office
125 South 600 West
Price, UT 84501
(435) 636-3600

Map References

BLM Price
USGS 1:24,000 Cowboy Bench, Twin Hollow, Bruin Point, Patmos Head, Sunnyside, Sunnyside Junction
1:100,000 Price
Maptech CD-ROM: Central/San Rafael
Utah Atlas & Gazetteer, p. 47
Utah Travel Council #3

Route Directions

▼ 0.0			On Northern #15: Nine Mile Canyon Trail, zero trip meter and turn south onto unmarked dirt track into Dry Canyon.
	6.5 ▲		Trail ends at Northern #15: Nine Mile Canyon Trail. Turn left for US 6/191, right for Northern #21: Franks Canyon and Sand Wash Trail.
		GPS: N 39°47.06′ W 110°10.38′	
▼ 0.1		SO	Cross through creek.
	6.4 ▲	SO	Cross through creek.
▼ 0.3		SO	Cattle guard.
	6.2 ▲	SO	Cattle guard.
▼ 0.4		SO	Track on left.
	6.1 ▲	SO	Track on right.
▼ 1.9		SO	Various petroglyphs on large patina rock outcropping 6 to 20 feet above ground on right.
	4.6 ▲	SO	Various petroglyphs on large patina rock outcropping 6 to 20 feet above ground on left.
		GPS: N 39°45.62′ W 110°10.25′	
▼ 3.0		SO	Petroglyphs to right of cave on right. Human figure with animal.
	3.5 ▲	SO	Petroglyphs to right of cave on left. Human figure with animal.
▼ 4.6		SO	Gate.
	1.9 ▲	SO	Gate.
▼ 5.6		SO	Oil tank on left.
	0.9 ▲	SO	Oil tank on right.
▼ 6.5		BL	Fork in road. Bear left to Bruin Point. Stone Cabin Canyon to right. Zero trip meter.
	0.0 ▲		Continue toward Nine Mile Canyon.
		GPS: N 39°44.49′ W 110°14.37′	
▼ 0.0			Continue southwest.
	9.8 ▲	BR	Track on left to Stone Cabin Canyon. Zero trip meter.
▼ 0.5		SO	Cross through creek (usually dry).
	9.3 ▲	SO	Cross through creek (usually dry).
▼ 0.8		SO	Cross through creek (usually dry).
	9.0 ▲	SO	Cross through creek (usually dry).
▼ 1.3		SO	Cross through creek (usually dry).

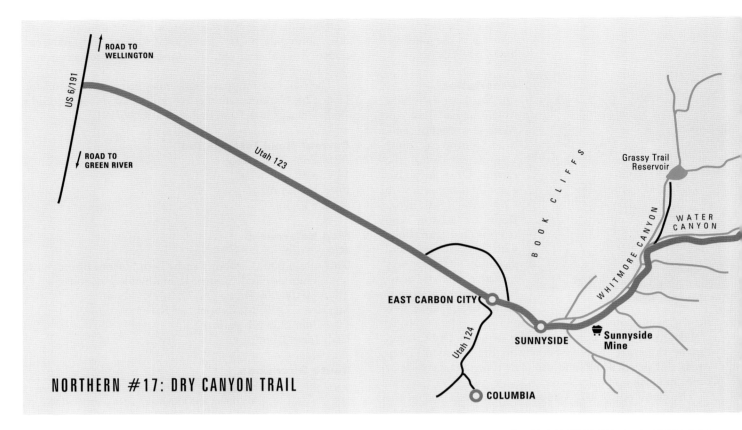

NORTHERN #17: DRY CANYON TRAIL

8.4 ▲	SO	Cross through creek (usually dry).
▼ 1.6	SO	Cross through creek (usually dry).
8.2 ▲	SO	Cross through creek (usually dry).
▼ 4.1	SO	Cross through creek.
5.7 ▲	SO	Cross through creek.
▼ 6.4	SO	Track on left.
3.3 ▲	SO	Track on right.
▼ 6.7	SO	Cross over creek.
3.1 ▲	SO	Cross over creek.
▼ 6.8	SO	Ascend out of canyon.
3.0 ▲	SO	Descend into canyon.
▼ 9.8	SO	Track on left. Zero trip meter.
0.0 ▲		Continue along trail.

GPS: N 39°40.33′ W 110°20.41′

▼ 0.0		Continue along trail.
3.1 ▲	SO	Track on right. Zero trip meter.
▼ 0.4	SO	Track on right.
2.7 ▲	SO	Track on left.
▼ 1.3	BL	Track on right. Then fork in road.
1.7 ▲	BR	Two tracks on left.

GPS: N 39°39.51′ W 110°21.25′

▼ 3.1	BR	Track on left. Zero trip meter.
0.0 ▲		Continue along trail.

GPS: N 39°38.64′ W 110°20.40′

▼ 0.0		Continue toward East Carbon City.
11.2 ▲	BL	Track on right. Zero trip meter.
▼ 0.1	SO	Cattle guard.
11.1 ▲	SO	Cattle guard.
▼ 0.2	SO	Bruin Point. Track on right to radio tower.
10.9 ▲	SO	Bruin Point. Track on left to radio tower.
▼ 0.4	SO	Track on right. Then track on left to radio tower.
10.8 ▲	SO	Track on right to radio tower. Then bear right at fork in road.

GPS: N 39°38.44′ W 110°20.74′

▼ 2.1	SO	Track on left.
9.1 ▲	SO	Track on right.
▼ 3.5	BR	Track on left.
7.7 ▲	BL	Track straight on.
▼ 5.0	SO	Track on right to private property.
6.2 ▲	SO	Track on left to private property.
▼ 5.6	SO	Cattle guard.
5.5 ▲	SO	Cattle guard.
▼ 5.7	SO	Track on right heads north into Whitmore Canyon.
5.4 ▲	SO	Track on left continues north in Whitmore Canyon.

GPS: N 39°35.98′ W 110°22.67′

▼ 5.9	SO	Track on right.
5.3 ▲	SO	Track on left.
▼ 6.3	SO	Track on left.
4.9 ▲	SO	Track on right.
▼ 7.0	SO	Track on left.
4.2 ▲	SO	Track on right.
▼ 8.5	SO	Sunnyside Mine (closed) on left.
2.7 ▲	SO	Sunnyside Mine (closed) on right.
▼ 11.2	SO	Utah 124 on left to Columbia. Zero trip meter.
0.0 ▲		Continue toward Sunnyside.

GPS: N 39°32.62′ W 110°24.82′

▼ 0.0		Continue toward US 6/191.
8.4 ▲	SO	Utah 124 on right to Columbia. Zero trip meter.
▼ 8.4		Trail ends at US 6/191. Turn right for Wellington, left for Green River.
0.0 ▲		On US 6/191, about 8 miles south of Wellington, zero trip meter and turn east on Utah 123 toward East Carbon City.

GPS: N 39°31.57′ W 110°34.38′

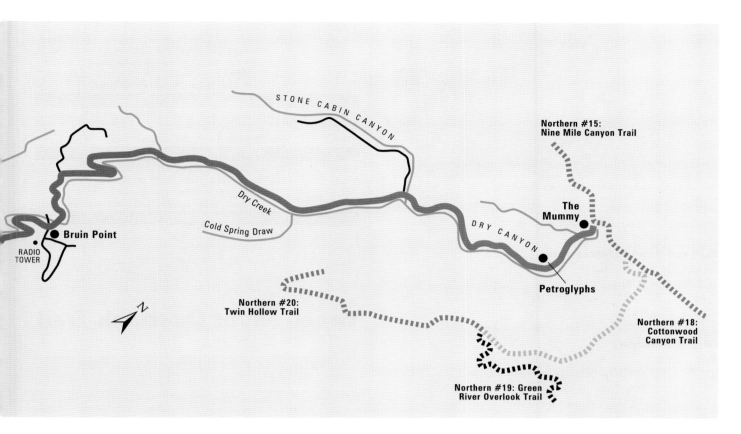

NORTHERN REGION TRAIL #18

Cottonwood Canyon Trail

Starting Point:	**Northern #15: Nine Mile Canyon Trail**
Finishing Point:	**Intersection of Northern #20: Twin**
	Hollow Trail and Northern #19: Green
	River Overlook Trail
Total Mileage:	**6.5 miles**
Unpaved Mileage:	**6.5 miles**
Driving Time:	**30 minutes (one-way)**
Elevation Range:	**5,400–7,200 feet**
Usually Open:	**Year-round**
Difficulty Rating:	**2**
Scenic Rating:	**8**
Remoteness Rating:	**+0**

Special Attractions

- Fremont Indian pictographs.
- Good view of Fremont granaries.
- Scenic canyon with high walls and cottonwoods along wash.
- Access to two spur trails onto West Tavaputs Plateau.

Description

Cottonwood Canyon Trail turns off of Northern #15: Nine Mile Canyon Trail and heads south through a deep, narrow canyon. In many ways, this short spur trail—with its many cottonwoods and some of the best pictographs in the region—is even more interesting than Nine Mile Canyon. The pictographs include a detailed hunting scene from the days of the Fremont Indians.

Besides the pictographs, remnants of ancient granaries indicate that the area around Cottonwood Canyon has been inhabited for well over a thousand years. Located back along the face of Nine Mile Canyon, but best viewed from Cottonwood Canyon, these granaries can be very difficult to see. Binoculars are often a great help in locating the remains of these hidden cliff structures.

The road is suitable for a passenger car in good weather, and navigation is easy. The trail ends at an intersection with

A view of the trail through Cottonwood Canyon

A close-up of the famous hunting scene petroglyph

two other spur trails, Northern #19: Green River Overlook Trail and Northern #20: Twin Hollow Trail.

Current Road Information
BLM Price Field Office
125 South 600 West
Price, UT 84501
(435) 636-3600

Map References
BLM   Price
USGS   1:24,000   Cowboy Bench, Twin Hollow
1:100,000 Price
Maptech CD-ROM: Central/San Rafael
Utah Atlas & Gazetteer, p. 47
Utah Travel Council #3

Route Directions
▼ 0.0   On Northern #15: Nine Mile Canyon Trail, 43.7 miles from US 6/191, zero trip meter and turn south into Cottonwood Canyon. Cross bridge over Nine Mile Creek.

GPS: N 39°47.02′ W 110°09.01′

▼ 0.2   SO   Cattle guard.
▼ 0.7   SO   Viewpoint for a Fremont granary looking back to the left to Nine Mile Canyon. Look on the green strata ledge between two large rocks.
▼ 1.2   SO   Pictographs (including hunting scene) on right on a rock outcropping beside road.

GPS: N 39°46.83′ W 110°03.05′

▼ 1.3   SO   Pictographs on right about 6 feet from ground.
▼ 1.7   SO   Cattle guard.
▼ 4.9   SO   Aqueduct across road overhead.

GPS: N 39°44.14′ W 110°08.67′

▼ 5.6   SO   Cattle guard.
▼ 6.5   Trail ends at gate. Track on right is Northern #20: Twin Hollow Trail. Straight ahead is Northern #19: Green River Overlook Trail.

GPS: N 39°43.59′ W 110°10.18′

Green River Overlook Trail

Starting Point:	**End of Northern #18: Cottonwood**
	Canyon Trail
Finishing Point:	**Overlook of the Green River**
Total Mileage:	**15.9 miles**
Unpaved Mileage:	**15.9 miles**
Driving Time:	**2 hours (one-way)**
Elevation Range:	**5,400–7,200 feet**
Usually Open:	**May to November**
Difficulty Rating:	**4**
Scenic Rating:	**10**
Remoteness Rating:	**+2**

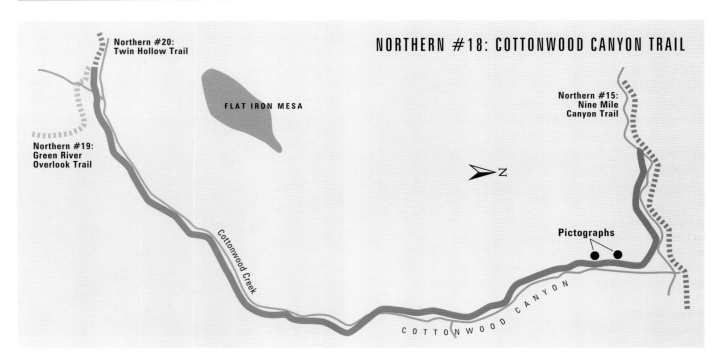

NORTHERN #18: COTTONWOOD CANYON TRAIL

Northern #20: Twin Hollow Trail

Northern #19: Green River Overlook Trail

FLAT IRON MESA

Northern #15: Nine Mile Canyon Trail

Pictographs

Cottonwood Creek

COTTONWOOD CANYON

N

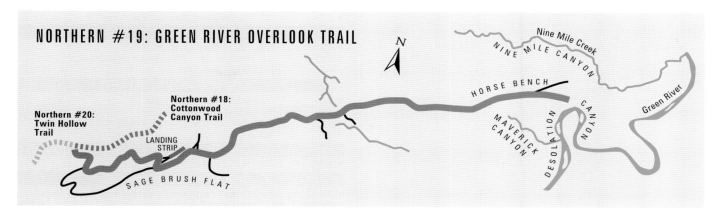

NORTHERN #19: GREEN RIVER OVERLOOK TRAIL

Special Attractions

- Extremely remote 4WD spur trail across the West Tavaputs Plateau.
- Spectacular Green River overlook.
- More challenging 4WD trail than most in the region.

Description

The Green River Overlook Trail is both extremely remote and wonderfully scenic. There are good views of Cottonwood Canyon as you ascend one of its walls, and the flat terrain of West Tavaputs Plateau leads you to a 1,000-foot cliff overlooking the Green River.

Beginning at the end of Northern #18: Cottonwood Canyon Trail, you immediately climb a steep stretch of fairly broad shelf road. Once out of Cottonwood Canyon, the trail crosses Sage Brush Flat past an old, graded airstrip before coming to another section of shelf road, which is narrow and off-camber. You then descend to a short, narrow ridgeline that extends across to Horse Bench. In spots, this section of the trail becomes narrow enough to make passing difficult without one vehicle reversing for a short distance. Erosion has collapsed the outside edge of the road in some places as well, thereby making the driving surface even more narrow and potentially intimidating.

The final portion of the trail runs across the perfectly flat landscape of West Tavaputs Plateau. Besides low open scrub, this area of flatland is dotted with pinyon and juniper. Although the last section of the trail is normally the easiest part, it becomes very boggy and impassable in wet weather.

The trail ends abruptly where the plateau falls away into the Green River. After enjoying this spectacular overlook, head back toward the trail's starting point in Cottonwood Canyon.

Current Road Information

BLM Price Field Office
125 South 600 West
Price, UT 84501
(435) 636-3600

Map References

BLM Price, Seep Ridge (incomplete)
USGS 1:24,000 Twin Hollow, Cedar Ridge Canyon, Pinnacle Canyon, Duches Hole
1:100,000 Price Seep Ridge (incomplete)

Maptech CD-ROM: Central/San Rafael; High Uinta/Flaming Gorge
Utah Atlas & Gazetteer, pp. 47, 48
Utah Travel Council #3

Route Directions

▼ 0.0		At the end of Northern #18: Cottonwood Canyon Trail, where it meets Northern #20: Twin Hollow Trail, zero trip meter and bear left onto shelf road, climbing out of canyon.
GPS: N 39°43.59' W 110°10.18'		
▼ 1.0	BL	Fork in track at top of plateau.
GPS: N 39°43.18' W 110°09.61'		
▼ 1.5	SO	Cross through gate.
▼ 2.2	SO	Mining operation on left.
▼ 2.6	SO	Abandoned buildings on left.
▼ 3.7	TL	Track on left. Zero trip meter.
GPS: N 39°43.81' W 110°07.45'		
▼ 0.0		Continue along trail.
▼ 0.1	TL	T-intersection.
▼ 0.8	SO	Airstrip on left beside road.
▼ 1.1	SO	Track enters on left.
▼ 1.5	SO	Track on right.

The view of the Green River from the end of the trail

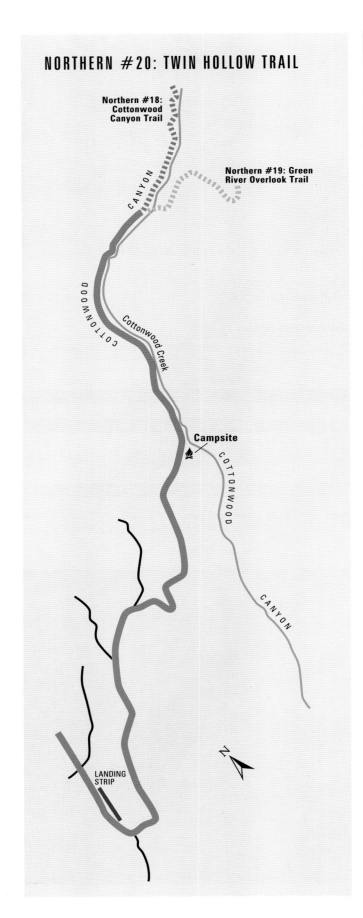

NORTHERN #20: TWIN HOLLOW TRAIL

Northern #18:
Cottonwood
Canyon Trail

Northern #19: Green
River Overlook Trail

COTTONWOOD CANYON

Cottonwood Creek

Campsite

COTTONWOOD CANYON

LANDING
STRIP

N

▼ 2.9	SO	Travel along spectacular ridgeline.
	GPS: N 39°45.18′ W 110°05.21′	
▼ 4.4	SO	Cross through gate.
▼ 4.8	BL	Fork in road. The right trail dead-ends. Zero trip meter.
	GPS: N 39°45.95′ W 110°03.31′	
▼ 0.0		Continue along route.
▼ 0.7	SO	Road on right.
▼ 1.1	SO	Various small tracks on left and right.
▼ 1.9	BR	Fork in road.
	GPS: N 39°46.75′ W 110°01.52′	
▼ 6.5	BR	Fork in road.
	GPS: N 39°48.11′ W 109°56.60′	
▼ 7.4		End at spectacular overlook of Green River.
	GPS: N 39°48.23′ W 109°55.62′	

NORTHERN REGION TRAIL #20

Twin Hollow Trail

Starting Point:	**At end of Northern #18: Cottonwood Canyon Trail**
Finishing Point:	**Scenic overlook**
Total Mileage:	**7.4 miles**
Unpaved Mileage:	**7.4 miles**
Driving Time:	**45 minutes (one-way)**
Elevation Range:	**6,400–8,300 feet**
Usually Open:	**May to November**
Difficulty Rating:	**4**
Scenic Rating:	**7**
Remoteness Rating:	**+1**

Special Attractions

- The top end of Cottonwood Canyon, which is less traveled and very scenic.
- A network of remote 4WD trails, popular in hunting season.
- The high desert country of the Tavaputs Plateau.
- Endless remote backcountry campsites well away from the crowds.

Description

The Twin Hollow Trail begins at the end of Northern #18: Cottonwood Canyon Trail, at the same starting point as Northern #19: Green River Overlook Trail. After a couple of miles, the trail climbs about 600 feet out of Cottonwood Canyon.

The trail becomes more difficult on the plateau, as it is noticeably rutted, rocky, and off-camber in spots. Tire damage is possible along this section of narrow road, which proceeds through tall pinyon pine and the occasional juniper. At the same time, be sure not to miss the spectacular, panoramic views that go on for miles.

After 6.2 miles, a short spur trail leads to the remains of what used to be an old landing strip off to the left. Though it certainly has not been used for many years, it appears to have

A crossing through the creek before the climb out of Cottonwood Canyon

at one time been graded. A little over a mile later, the trail dead-ends, and a short walk takes you to an overlook at the edge of Flat Iron Mesa.

Twin Hollow Trail is scenic, moderately challenging, and provides a pleasant change from the canyon floors traversed by many of the trails in the region.

Current Road Information
BLM Price Field Office
125 South 600 West
Price, UT 84501
(435) 636-3600

Map References
BLM Price
USGS 1:24,000 Twin Hollow, Bruin Point
1:100,000 Price
Maptech CD-ROM: Central/San Rafael
Utah Atlas & Gazetteer, p. 47
Utah Travel Council #3

Route Directions

▼ 0.0		At end of Northern #18: Cottonwood Canyon Trail, zero trip meter and bear right through a nongated fence line.
		GPS: N 39°43.59' W 110°10.18'
▼ 1.0	SO	Cross through Cottonwood Creek.
▼ 2.3	SO	Campsite on left at start of ascent from canyon.
▼ 4.8	SO	Track on right.
		GPS: N 39°42.09' W 110°13.87'
▼ 5.6	SO	Start of rutted uphill section.
▼ 6.2	BR	Fork in road. Left goes 0.25 miles to an overlook. Zero trip meter.
		GPS: N 39°41.25' W 110°14.97'
▼ 0.0		Proceed along trail.
▼ 0.2	SO	Track on left.
▼ 0.9	SO	Track on left.
▼ 1.2		Trail dead-ends. A short walk leads to views from Flat Iron Mesa.
		GPS: N 39°42.15' W 110°14.69'

Franks Canyon and Sand Wash Trail

Starting Point:	Northern #15: Nine Mile Canyon Trail
Finishing Point:	US 40, west of Myton
Total Mileage:	52.8 miles
Unpaved Mileage:	44.9 miles
Driving Time:	3 hours
Elevation Range:	4,600–6,500 feet
Usually Open:	Year-round
Difficulty Rating:	3
Scenic Rating:	9
Remoteness Rating:	+1

Special Attractions
■ Riverside access to the Green River.
■ Driving through Franks Canyon and along Sand Wash.
■ Access from the north to the eastern end of Northern #15: Nine Mile Canyon Trail.

History
Franks Canyon and Sand Wash Trail passes near two sites that both used to serve as river crossings in days gone by. The Sand Wash ferry was developed at the only feasible crossing of the Green River between the towns of Green River, Utah, and Green River, Wyoming. Owned and operated by the Stewart family in the 1920s, the ferry was in service until the mid-1950s, when it was washed out. The Stewarts' four-room log cabin still stands at the site.

Myton, originally known as "The Bridge," is located on what was once the only crossing of the Duchesne River, and it served as a gateway into the Uinta Basin in 1905 when the Uintah-Ouray Indian Reservation was opened up to white settlers. As settlers rushed to homestead the land, Myton became an important supply center in this otherwise remote region. The town grew and prospered for about 25 years, but the Great

Green River at the end of Sand Wash

The trail following along Sand Wash

Depression almost killed it. Today, Myton survives as a small supply center for the nearby farmers and ranchers of the Uinta Basin (for more on Myton, see pps. 38-39).

Description

At the east end of Northern #15: Nine Mile Canyon Trail, head north into Franks Canyon. The primitive trail runs along the stony surface of the canyon floor as it criss-crosses through the wash. The tall canyon walls seem to close in on you as you drive along this impressive section of narrow track. Make sure you check the weather before driving this trail, as the canyon floods after heavy rains.

After 15.3 miles, turn right onto a 3.4-mile spur trail to the Green River. The spur trail follows the bed of Sand Wash and ends near a ranger station on the riverbank. Easy access to the water's edge makes this a popular launching spot for river rafters.

Back on the main road, the landscape becomes a flat expanse of sagebrush that is remarkably different from the rocky walls of Franks Canyon. There is extensive oil drilling in the area, and a number of side tracks jump off the main road and lead to oil wells. Navigation is easy, though, since the service roads are all much smaller than the graded two-lane road to Myton.

This last section of the road is unexciting—it travels past more mining and oil drilling—and is described only because it provides access to Myton and US 40. As its name indicates, the trail's most interesting and scenic parts are in Franks Canyon and along Sand Wash to the Green River.

Current Road Information
BLM Price Field Office
125 South 600 West
Price, UT 84501
(435) 636-3600

BLM Vernal Field Office
170 South 500 East
Vernal, UT 84078
(435) 781-4400

Map References
BLM Price, Seep Ridge, Duchesne
USFS Ashley National Forest
USGS 1:24,000 Pinnacle Canyon, Duches Hole, Wilkin Ridge, Myton SE, Myton
    1:100,000 Price, Seep Ridge, Duchesne
Maptech CD-ROM: Central/San Rafael; High Uinta/Flaming Gorge
Utah Atlas & Gazetteer, pp. 47, 48
Utah Travel Council #3

Route Directions

▼ 0.0   At east end of Northern #15: Nine Mile Canyon Trail, zero trip meter at padlocked gate at end of canyon. Turn left onto unmarked track.

    5.0 ▲   Trail ends at east end of Northern #15: Nine Mile Canyon Trail.

GPS: N 39°48.33′ W 110°04.62′

▼ 0.9   **SO** Pass through gate.

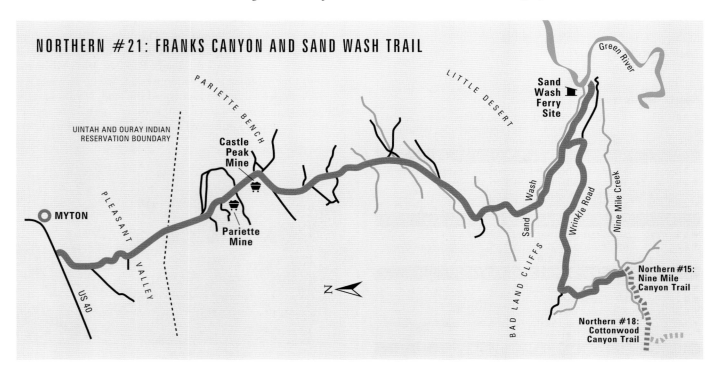

NORTHERN #21: FRANKS CANYON AND SAND WASH TRAIL

4.0 ▲		SO	Pass through gate.
▼ 4.9		BR	Fork in road. Pass BLM sign on left.
	0.1 ▲	BL	Track enters on right (part of a delta leading back to Wrinkle Road).

GPS: N 39°50.66' W 110°05.94'

▼ 5.0		TR	Intersection with Wrinkle Road. Left to Wellington-Myton Road. Zero trip meter.
	0.0 ▲		Continue into Franks Canyon.

GPS: N 39°50.83' W 110°05.94'

▼ 0.0			Proceed toward Sand Wash.
	10.3 ▲	TL	Intersection. Turn left to Franks Canyon and zero trip meter. Straight ahead leads to Wellington-Myton Road.
▼ 8.9		SO	Track on right.
	1.4 ▲	SO	Track on left.

GPS: N 39°50.27' W 109°57.76'

▼ 9.8		SO	Track on left.
	0.5 ▲	SO	Track on right.
▼ 10.1		TR	Intersection. Sign indicates Myton straight ahead. Turn right toward Sand Wash.
	0.2 ▲	TL	Intersection. Road on right is second entrance to Myton Road. Turn left toward Franks Canyon.
▼ 10.3		TR	Intersection. Left is continuation of main trail to Myton. Turn right on spur road to Sand Wash. You will return to this intersection after visiting the Green River. Zero trip meter.
	0.0 ▲		Continue along trail.

GPS: N 39°51.03' W 109°57.96'

Spur Trail to Sand Wash

▼ 0.0			Continue toward Sand Wash.
▼ 2.7		SO	Cattle guard.

GPS: N 39°50.36' W 109°55.33'

▼ 3.3		SO	Track on left to ranger station.
▼ 3.4		UT	Toilets on right. Ranger station and two cabins on left. Then end at Green River and site of old Sand Wash ferry. U-turn and return to the intersection where you zeroed before.

GPS: N 39°50.42' W 109°54.74'

▼ 6.8		SO	Intersection where you previously zeroed. Zero trip meter.

GPS: N 39°51.03' W 109°57.96'

Continuation of Main Trail

▼ 0.0			Continue toward Myton.
	12.0 ▲	SO	Track on right is continuation of main trail. Go straight on spur road to Sand Wash. You will return to this intersection after visiting the Green River. Zero trip meter.
▼ 0.3		SO	Intersection.
	11.7 ▲	SO	Right goes toward Franks Canyon.
▼ 0.6		SO	Cattle guard.
	11.4 ▲	SO	Cattle guard.
▼ 4.1		SO	Track on left.
	7.8 ▲	SO	Track on right.
▼ 4.5		SO	Track on right.
	7.4 ▲	SO	Track on left.
▼ 6.6		SO	Cattle guard and cross through wash.
	5.4 ▲	SO	Cross through wash; then cattle guard.
▼ 7.6		SO	Track on left.
	4.4 ▲	SO	Track on right.
▼ 8.3		SO	Track on left.
	3.7 ▲	SO	Track on right.
▼ 12.0		SO	Intersection. Zero trip meter.

0.0 ▲			Continue toward Sand Wash.

GPS: N 39°57.20' W 109°59.53'

▼ 0.0			Continue toward Myton.
	18.7 ▲	SO	Intersection. Zero trip meter.
▼ 1.1		SO	Intersection. Tracks on left and right.
	17.6 ▲	SO	Tracks on left and right. Follow signs to Sand Wash.

GPS: N 39°58.17' W 109°59.33'

▼ 1.6		SO	Tracks on left and right.
	17.1 ▲	SO	Tracks on left and right.
▼ 1.7		SO	Track on right.
	17.0 ▲	SO	Track on left.
▼ 3.7		SO	Track on left.
	15.0 ▲	SO	Track on right.
▼ 5.2		SO	Service road crosses right and left.
	13.5 ▲	SO	Service road crosses right and left.
▼ 6.4		SO	Track on right.
	12.3 ▲	SO	Track on left.
▼ 6.8		BR	Road on left.
	11.8 ▲	BL	Road on right.
▼ 7.7		TL	T-intersection.
	11.0 ▲	TR	Intersection.
▼ 9.1		SO	Road on left.
	9.6 ▲	SO	Road on right.

GPS: N 40°04.16' W 110°01.59'

▼ 12.1		SO	Road on right.
	6.6 ▲	SO	Road on left.
▼ 16.5		SO	Road on right.
	2.1 ▲	SO	Road on left.
▼ 18.7			Trail ends at US 40. Turn east for Myton.
	0.0 ▲		On US 40, about 1.7 miles west of the bridge over the Duchesne River in Myton, zero trip meter and proceed along 5550 West toward Pleasant Valley, Sand Wash, and Nine Mile Canyon.

GPS: N 40°11.17' W 110°05.66'

NORTHERN REGION TRAIL #22

Reservation Ridge Trail

Starting Point:	**US 191, 28 miles south of Duchesne**
Finishing Point:	**Northern #24: Timber Canyon Trail**
Total Mileage:	**17.8 miles**
Unpaved Mileage:	**17.8 miles**
Driving Time:	**1 hour**
Elevation Range:	**8,700–9,700 feet**
Usually Open:	**Mid-May to mid-November**
Difficulty Rating:	**2**
Scenic Rating:	**8**
Remoteness Rating:	**+0**

Special Attractions

■ Great views as you journey through the Ashley National Forest.

■ Access to a network of 4WD trails.

■ Aspen viewing in the fall.

History

Reservation Ridge follows along the old boundary line of the Uintah-Ouray Indian Reservation. Over the years, the reservation's boundaries have changed quite a lot, and much of the land originally set aside by Abraham Lincoln was quickly stripped away for use by white settlers. The east-west Reservation Ridge is located on West Tavaputs Plateau and lies south of the current reservation boundaries.

Description

Reservation Ridge Trail starts out along wide, maintained FR 147 and passes through the thick Engelmann, lodgepole, and aspen of Ashley National Forest. The start of the road is graded from time to time and could

A view of Reservation Ridge Trail

easily be driven by a 2WD car. Over the course of the next 4 miles it slowly deteriorates into a more typical forest road. The Avintaquin campground is located 1.1 miles into the trail on the right side and has limited facilities.

As you climb to the 6-mile point, the trail offers broad views to both the north and the south. Then the landscape gradually changes from forest to meadow and reveals more expansive views. By the time you reach the panoramic 270-degree overlook at Cat Peak, the trail is narrow and treeless.

Overall, the Reservation Ridge Trail is very scenic and has a number of excellent viewpoints. Short sections of wide shelf road look out over huge tracts of aspens that are breathtaking in autumn.

About 4 miles from the end, the trail intersects with the challenging spur Northern #23: Tabbyune Creek Trail, before coming to an end at Northern #24: Timber Canyon Trail.

Current Road Information

Ashley National Forest
Duchesne Ranger District
85 West Main
Duchesne, UT 84021
(435)738-2482

BLM Price Field Office
125 South 600 West
Price, UT 84501
(435) 636-3600

Map References

BLM Price
USFS Ashley National Forest: Duchesne Ranger District
USGS 1:24,000 Gray Head Peak, Matts Summit, Kyune, Flat Ridge
      1:100,000 Price
Maptech CD-ROM: Central/San Rafael
Trails Illustrated, #709 (incomplete)
Utah Atlas & Gazetteer, pp. 46, 47
Utah Travel Council #3

Route Directions

▼ 0.0			On US 191, 28 miles southwest of Duchesne, turn west onto FR 147 and zero trip meter. Follow sign to "Reservation Ridge Road and Avintaquin Campground."
	8.1 ▲		Trail ends at US 191. Turn left for Duchesne, right for Helper.
GPS: N 39°52.71' W 110°45.60'			
▼ 0.7		SO	Cross through seasonal gates.
	7.4 ▲	SO	Cross through seasonal gates.
▼ 0.8		SO	Track on left.
	7.3 ▲	SO	Track on right.
▼ 1.1		BL	Avintaquin Campground on right.
	7.0 ▲	BR	Avintaquin Campground on left.
▼ 1.3		SO	Track on right.
	6.7 ▲	SO	Track on left.
▼ 2.4		SO	Track on left.
	5.7 ▲	SO	Track on right.

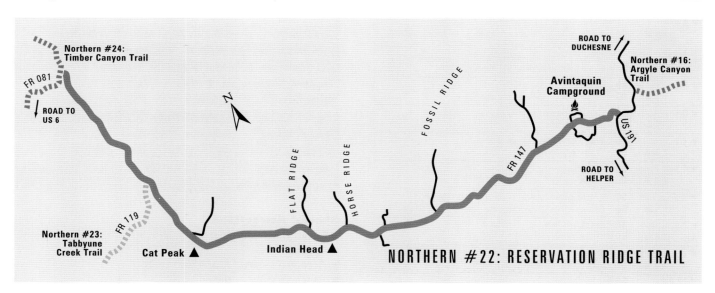

NORTHERN #22: RESERVATION RIDGE TRAIL

▼ 2.5		SO	Track on right.
	5.6 ▲	SO	Track on left.
▼ 2.7		SO	Cross cattle guard.
	5.4 ▲	SO	Cross cattle guard.
▼ 3.1		SO	Track on left.
	5.0 ▲	SO	Track on right.
▼ 5.7		SO	Track to Fossil Ridge on right.
	2.3 ▲	SO	Track to Fossil Ridge on left.

GPS: N 39°52.32' W 110°51.17'

▼ 6.0		SO	Track on left, then cross cattle guard.
	2.1 ▲	SO	Track on right, then cross cattle guard.
▼ 6.8		SO	Track on left.
	1.3 ▲	SO	Track on right.

GPS: N 39°52.44' W 110°52.27'

▼ 7.1		SO	Track on right.
	1.0 ▲	SO	Track on left.
▼ 8.1		SO	Track to Horse Ridge Canyon on right. Zero trip meter.
	0.0 ▲		Continue along main track.

GPS: N 39°52.84' W 110°53.52'

▼ 0.0			Proceed along main track.
	5.9 ▲	SO	Track to Horse Ridge Canyon on left. Zero trip meter.
▼ 0.3		SO	Cross cattle guard.
	5.6 ▲	SO	Cross cattle guard.
▼ 0.6		SO	Track on left.
	5.3 ▲	SO	Track on right.
▼ 1.1		SO	Track on right to Flat Ridge Trail.
	4.8 ▲	SO	Track on left to Flat Ridge Trail.
▼ 2.2		SO	Track on left.
	3.7 ▲	SO	Track on right.
▼ 2.4		SO	Track on right.
	3.5 ▲	SO	Track on left.
▼ 2.9		SO	Cross cattle guard.
	3.0 ▲	SO	Cross cattle guard.
▼ 4.2		SO	Track on left to Cat Peak.
	1.7 ▲	SO	Track on right to Cat Peak.

GPS: N 39°53.99' W 110°57.47'

▼ 4.3-4.9		SO	Good views on left, straight, and right of road as you travel along the ridge.
	1.0-1.6 ▲	SO	Good views as you travel along the ridge.
▼ 5.9		SO	Track on left is Northern #23: Tabbyune Creek Trail (FR 119). Track on right. Zero trip meter.
	0.0 ▲		Continue along main track.

GPS: N 39°55.46' W 110°57.95'

▼ 0.0			Continue along main track.
	3.8 ▲	SO	Track on left. Northern #23: Tabbyune Creek Trail (FR 119) on right. Zero trip meter.
▼ 1.1		SO	Track on right.
	2.7 ▲	SO	Track on left.
▼ 1.3		SO	Track on right.
	2.4 ▲	SO	Track on left.
▼ 1.9		SO	Track on right.
	1.9 ▲	SO	Track on left.
▼ 2.4		SO	Track on right.
	1.4 ▲	SO	Track on left.
▼ 3.4		SO	Track on right.
	0.4 ▲	SO	Track on left.
▼ 3.8			Trail ends at Northern #24: Timber Canyon Trail (FR 081). Continue straight for Timber Canyon, turn left for US 6.
	0.0 ▲		On Northern #24: Timber Canyon Trail (FR 081), 7.9 miles from US 6 at the top of Reservation Ridge, zero trip meter and turn right.

GPS: N 39°58.48' W 110°58.86'

Tabbyune Creek Trail

Starting Point:	**Northern #22: Reservation Ridge Trail**
Finishing Point:	**Uinta National Forest boundary**
Total Mileage:	**3.6 miles**
Unpaved Mileage:	**3.6 miles**
Driving Time:	**45 minutes (one-way)**
Elevation Range:	**7,600–9,000 feet**
Usually Open:	**Mid-May to mid-November**
Difficulty Rating:	**5**
Scenic Rating:	**7**
Remoteness Rating:	**+0**

Special Attractions

■ Challenging short spur trail.
■ Attractive fall colors.

Description

On Northern #22: Reservation Ridge Trail, 14 miles from US 191, turn southwest onto the narrow dirt FR 119. Initially, quite a few stands of overhanging aspens line the road, which then give way to conifers farther down the trail. At times, the trees crowd in on the road enough to make passing impossible without one vehicle backing up a short distance.

Over the years, the road has become very rutted, mainly because shade from the trees keeps the area muddy. High clearance is a must, as some sections of road seem to stay wet all the time. After heavy rains, the road becomes impassable and should be avoided.

Most of the trail runs downhill along a mild shelf road, which allows you to use your momentum to drive through any deeper sections of mud. However, driving the return back up to Northern #22: Reservation Ridge Trail can present much greater difficulty.

A rutted section of the trail crosses through a stand of aspen

Although the road continues to US 6 through private property, the trail proper ends at the boundary line of the Uinta National Forest. And remember, on this trail it's important to evaluate the road at all times: Don't go past any muddy sections that your vehicle may not be able to make it back up.

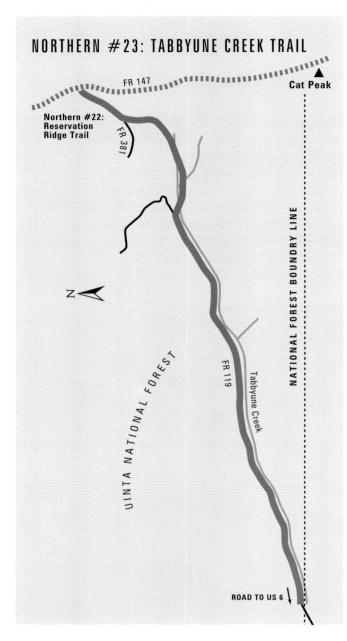

NORTHERN #23: TABBYUNE CREEK TRAIL

FR 147

Cat Peak

Northern #22:
Reservation
Ridge Trail

FR 381

N

UINTA NATIONAL FOREST

FR 119

Tabbyune Creek

NATIONAL FOREST BOUNDRY LINE

ROAD TO US 6

Current Road Information
Ashley National Forest
Duchesne Ranger District
85 West Main
Duchesne, UT 84021
(435)738-2482

Uinta National Forest
Heber Ranger District
2460 South Hwy 40
Heber, UT 84032
(801) 342-5200

BLM Price Field Office
125 South 600 West
Price, UT 84501
(435) 636-3600

Map References
BLM   Price, Nephi
USFS   Ashley National Forest: Duchesne Ranger District
USGS   1:24,000   Flat Ridge, Soldier Summit
        1:100,000 Price, Nephi
Maptech CD-ROM: Central/San Rafael
Trails Illustrated, #709
Utah Atlas & Gazetteer, p. 46
Utah Travel Council #3

Route Directions

▼ 0.0   On Northern #22: Reservation Ridge Trail (FR 147), 14 miles from US 191, zero trip meter and turn onto FR 119 (Tabbyune Canyon Road).

GPS: N 39°55.46' W 110°57.95'

▼ 0.3	SO	Track on right.
▼ 0.4	SO	FR 381 on right.
▼ 0.6	SO	Track on left.
▼ 1.5	SO	Cross through creek.
▼ 1.6	TL	T-intersection.

GPS: N 39°54.70' W 110°58.97'

▼ 3.6   Seasonal closure gate. End at forest boundary.

GPS: N 39°54.00' W 111°00.93'

NORTHERN REGION TRAIL #24

Timber Canyon Trail

Starting Point:	US 6, about 0.7 miles southeast of Soldier Summit
Finishing Point:	US 40, 7.8 miles west of Duchesne
Total Mileage:	42.1 miles
Unpaved Mileage:	37.3 miles
Driving Time:	2 hours
Elevation Range:	6,800–9,000 feet
Usually Open:	May to November
Difficulty Rating:	2
Scenic Rating:	8
Remoteness Rating:	+0

Special Attractions
■ Attractive scenery along Timber Canyon and Strawberry River and panoramic views.
■ Great fall colors.
■ A network of 4WD trails to explore.

History
Soldier Summit sits at the highest point along the Denver & Rio Grande Western Railroad through Utah. When the railroad's main division point moved in 1919 from Helper to Soldier Summit, the town was soon bustling with activity. At its peak, 2,500 people called Soldier Summit home. However, due to severe winters and the inefficient cost of basing opera-

Cottonwoods in Timber Canyon

tions in Soldier Summit, the division point was moved back to Helper in 1930. As the jobs left the area, so did the people, though there are still a few residents today. The town currently consists of little more than a gas station, a couple of modern houses, many deserted buildings, and a few foundations (for more on Soldier Summit, see p. 44).

Description
On US 6, about 0.7 miles southeast of Soldier Summit, head north on FR 081, a wide dirt road that runs along the Right Fork of the White River. For the first 5 miles or so, beaver dams can be seen on the river. The road passes by quite a few stands of aspen as it runs through sagebrush and willow bottoms.

For the first 6 miles, the road is considerably rutted and bumpy and can become boggy when wet. However once the trail crosses the creek, it becomes smoother, climbing up a broad section of shelf road and offering a pleasant view over the creek.

After 7.9 miles, you reach an intersection with Northern #22: Reservation Ridge Trail. The road to Timber Canyon smooths out and follows a level ridgeline with broad views to either side. About 8.4 miles after the trail intersection, there is a section of wide shelf road that runs along a 100-foot drop-off down into Timber Canyon.

The drive through Timber Canyon is very scenic and attractive. A number of old cottonwoods, willow bottoms, and oak trees line the Strawberry River. The trail also offers many gorgeous views that are at their most beautiful in the full color of autumn.

Toward the end, the road surface becomes maintained gravel and can be driven by car. Timber Canyon Trail ends at US 40, about 8 miles west of Duchesne.

Thick sagebrush along the approach to Timber Canyon

Current Road Information
Ashley National Forest
Duchesne Ranger District
85 West Main
Duchesne, UT 84021
(435)738-2482

BLM Price Field Office
125 South 600 West
Price, UT 84501
(435) 636-3600

Map References
BLM Nephi, Price, Duchesne
USFS Ashley National Forest: Duchesne Ranger District
USGS 1:24,000 Soldier Summit, Flat Ridge, Strawberry Peak, Avintaquin Canyon, Fruitland, Strawberry Pinnacles, Rabbit Gulch
  1:100,000 Nephi, Price, Duchesne
Maptech CD ROM: Central/San Rafael; High Uinta/ Flaming Gorge
Trails Illustrated, #709 (incomplete)
Utah Atlas & Gazetteer, pp. 46, 47
Utah Travel Council #3

Route Directions

▼ 0.0			On US 6, about 0.7 miles southeast of Soldier Summit, zero trip meter and turn onto unmarked dirt road (FR 081).
	7.9 ▲		Trail ends at US 6. Turn right for Soldier Summit, left for Price.
GPS: N 39°55.52′ W 111°04.16′			
▼ 0.2		BL	Cross cattle guard. Gated road on right.
	7.7 ▲	BR	Gated road on left. Cross cattle guard.
▼ 0.5		BR	Fork in road. Left goes to White River.
	7.4 ▲	BL	Road on right to White River.
▼ 0.6		SO	Track on left.
	7.3 ▲	SO	Track on right.
▼ 0.8		SO	Cross over Left Fork White River.
	7.1 ▲	SO	Cross over Left Fork White River.
▼ 1.8		SO	Track on right to riverside campsite.
	6.1 ▲	SO	Track on left to riverside campsite.
▼ 2.1		SO	Enter Uinta National Forest.
	5.8 ▲	SO	Leave Uinta National Forest.
▼ 3.0		SO	Johnson Fork.
	4.9 ▲	SO	Johnson Fork.
GPS: N 39°56.34′ W 111°01.47′			
▼ 4.3		SO	Track on left.
	3.6 ▲	SO	Track on right.
▼ 4.5		SO	Track on left. Cross bridge over Right Fork White River.
	3.4 ▲	SO	Cross bridge over Right Fork White River. Track on right.
▼ 5.4		SO	Track on left.
	2.5 ▲	SO	Track on right.
▼ 5.9		SO	Track on left.
	2.0 ▲	SO	Track on right.
GPS: N 39°58.04′ W 111°00.30′			
▼ 6.0		SO	Cross over creek.
	1.9 ▲	SO	Cross over creek.
▼ 7.1		BL	Fork in road. Continue to climb.

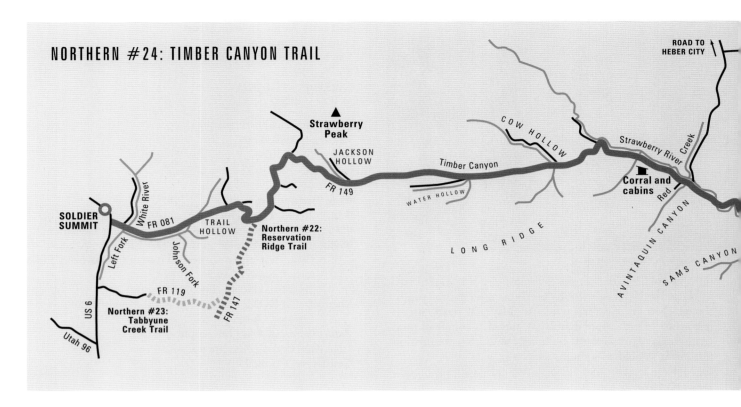

0.8 ▲	BR	Track on left.	

GPS: N 39°57.99' W 110°59.30'

▼ 7.9	TL	Intersection. Turn left toward Bumper Canyon, Timber Canyon, and Grassy Hollow. Zero trip meter. Right is Northern #22: Reservation Ridge Trail to US 191.
0.0 ▲		Continue toward US 6.

GPS: N 39°58.49' W 110°58.85'

▼ 0.0		Proceed toward Timber Canyon.
20.4 ▲	TR	Intersection. Turn right to US 6. Straight is Northern #22: Reservation Ridge Trail to US 191.
▼ 0.2	SO	Intersection. Long Ridge to the right.
20.2 ▲	SO	Track on left to Long Ridge.
▼ 0.3	BL	Fork in the road. Bumper Canyon and Rough Hollow to the right.
20.1 ▲	SO	Road enters on left.

GPS: N 39°58.77' W 110°58.87'

▼ 1.3	SO	Track on right.
19.1 ▲	SO	Track on left.
▼ 1.7	SO	Track on left.
18.7 ▲	SO	Track on right.
▼ 2.8	TR	Turn right at fork onto FR 149 toward Timber Canyon. Strawberry Peak is straight ahead.
17.5 ▲	TL	Intersection. Turn left onto FR 081 to Reservation Ridge. Strawberry Peak is to the right.

GPS: N 40°00.68' W 110°59.40'

▼ 3.6	SO	Track on left.
16.8 ▲	SO	Track on right.
▼ 6.1	SO	Track on left to Jackson Hollow.
14.3 ▲	SO	Track on right to Jackson Hollow.

GPS: N 40°01.39° W 110°56.19'

▼ 7.5	SO	Cross cattle guard. Track to Pine Hollow on left.
12.9 ▲	SO	Track to Pine Hollow on right. Cross cattle guard.
▼ 10.5	SO	Track to Water Hollow on right.
9.9 ▲	SO	Track to Water Hollow on left.
▼ 12.7	SO	Seasonal gate.

7.6 ▲	SO	Seasonal gate.

GPS: N 40°04.91' W 110°50.51'

▼ 12.8	SO	Cross cattle guard.
7.6 ▲	SO	Cross cattle guard.
▼ 13.5	SO	Cross over bridge.
6.8 ▲	SO	Cross over bridge.
▼ 13.6	SO	Track on left to Cow Hollow.
6.8 ▲	SO	Track on right to Cow Hollow.
▼ 13.8	SO	Track on right to Rough Hollow.
6.6 ▲	SO	Track on left to Rough Hollow.
▼ 14.4	SO	Cross over creek.
6.0 ▲	SO	Cross over creek.
▼ 14.5	SO	Cross over creek.
5.8 ▲	SO	Cross over creek.
▼ 14.7	SO	Cross over creek.
5.7 ▲	SO	Cross over creek.
▼ 14.8	SO	Cross cattle guard.
5.6 ▲	SO	Cross cattle guard.
▼ 15.3	SO	Cross over creek.
5.1 ▲	SO	Cross over creek.
▼ 15.6	SO	Cross over creek.
4.8 ▲	SO	Cross over creek.
▼ 15.7	SO	Cross bridge over Strawberry River. Road on left.
4.7 ▲	SO	Road on right. Cross bridge over Strawberry River.
▼ 15.8	BR	Intersection. Bear right toward Duchesne.
4.6 ▲	BL	Follow sign to Timber Canyon.

GPS: N 40°06.97' W 110°48.71'

▼ 18.1	SO	Corral and old cabins on right.
2.3 ▲	SO	Corral and old cabins on left.
▼ 19.7	SO	Track on left.
0.7 ▲	SO	Track on right.
▼ 20.1	SO	Road is now paved.
0.3 ▲	SO	Road is now unpaved.
▼ 20.2	SO	Avintaquin Canyon and Ashley to the right.

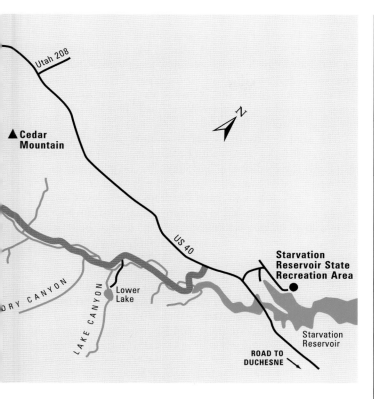

Brown's Park Trail

Starting Point:	Jones Hole Road
Finishing Point:	Jarvie Homestead
Total Mileage:	32.9 miles
Unpaved Mileage:	31.2 miles
Driving Time:	1.5 hours
Elevation Range:	5,300–7,800 feet
Usually Open:	Year-round
Difficulty Rating:	1
Scenic Rating:	8
Remoteness Rating:	+0

Special Attractions

- Historic location along the old Outlaw Trail.
- John Jarvie homestead.
- The swinging bridge across the Green River.
- Scenic Crouse Canyon.

History

As early as the 1820s Brown's Park, also known as Brown's Hole, was known to fur trappers from the United States and Canada. Brown's Park sits inside a circular ring of mountains where the borders of Utah, Colorado, and Wyoming all meet. Trappers such as William H. Ashley and Baptiste Brown were among the earliest white men to discover Brown's Park, and it is believed the region was named after the latter.

In 1837, a trading post called Fort Davy Crockett was established in the region for the many trappers who made Brown's Park their winter headquarters. However, as the beaver population soon began to dwindle, many left to search for the valuable pelts in other regions.

By 1868 there were still a few residents left when news came that a transcontinental railroad was to be built just south of Brown's Park. It would follow the relatively new route through the region that had been recently discovered by famed Utah trapper and trader Jim Bridger.

With the completion of the railroad, Brown's Park became a natural home and safe haven for outlaws, cattle rustlers, and men who lived their lives just around (and sometimes over) the limits of the law. While the

Tombstone in the cemetery at the Jarvie homestead

0.2 ▲	SO	Proceed straight toward Duchesne. Follow sign to Strawberry River and Timber Canyon.	
▼ 20.3	SO	Cross bridge over Red Creek.	
0.1 ▲	SO	Cross bridge over Red Creek.	
▼ 20.4	TR	Intersection. Zero trip meter.	
0.0 ▲		Continue along road.	

GPS: N 40°07.72' W 110°44.39°

▼ 0.0		Continue along unpaved road.
13.8 ▲	TL	Zero trip meter at intersection and follow signs to Camelot Resort.
▼ 3.3	SO	Cross bridge
10.5 ▲	SO	Cross bridge.
▼ 3.7	SO	Cross bridge over Strawberry River.
10.1 ▲	SO	Cross bridge over Strawberry River.
▼ 4.0	SO	Cross cattle guard.
9.8 ▲	SO	Cross cattle guard.
▼ 4.6	SO	Road on left.
9.2 ▲	SO	Road on right.
▼ 5.3	SO	Cross cattle guard.
8.4 ▲	SO	Cross cattle guard.
▼ 5.6	SO	Cross bridge over Strawberry River.
8.2 ▲	SO	Cross bridge over Strawberry River.
▼ 7.8	SO	Cross bridge over Strawberry River.
6.0 ▲	SO	Cross bridge over Strawberry River.
▼ 8.3	SO	Road on right.
5.4 ▲	SO	Road on left.
▼ 11.9	SO	Cross bridge over Strawberry River.
1.9 ▲	SO	Cross bridge over Strawberry River.
▼ 13.8		Trail ends at US 40. Turn right for Duchesne, left for Heber City.
0.0 ▲		On US 40, 7.8 miles west of Duchesne and US 191, zero trip meter and turn onto 29500 West Street.

GPS: N 40°10.38' W 110°32.88'

John Jarvie's cabin

railroad provided easy access to northeastern Utah, Brown's Park remained extremely isolated and naturally defensible, situated in 65 miles of mostly uncharted, mountainous terrain.

Notable local figures John Jarvie, who ran a general store and river ferry, and Charlie Crouse, a rancher and businessman, moved into Brown's Park in the 1870s and 1880s. Although not known as outlaws themselves, these men nonetheless provided food and shelter to such famed bank robbers as Butch Cassidy (who at one time worked for Crouse), Matt Warner, and Elza Lay. The bank robbers, in turn, generally treated their hosts with respect and generosity, and they became well liked by local townsfolk.

This trail passes by a number of historical landmarks in Brown's Park. In 1927, Stanley Crouse, Charlie's son, built a swinging bridge across the Green River. John Jarvie had been operating a ferry in the area since the early 1880s, but the bridge was only the second in the region to cross the Green River. The first bridge had been built just after the turn of the century by Charlie Crouse but lasted only a couple of years. The bridge proved very tenuous and collapsed less than a year later. Learning from his mistakes, the younger Crouse built a second bridge that lasted until 1950, when it again became irreparably damaged. In 1954 the BLM built a new swinging bridge with a load capacity equal to 400 sheep or a three-ton vehicle. This third swinging bridge is still in use today.

The swinging bridge across the Green River

The trail comes to an end at the old Jarvie homestead. From the 1880s until his death in 1909, Jarvie lived in Brown's Park and was a popular, well-liked character and a relatively well-educated man with a talent for music. For more on the region's historical figures, see Mormon Leaders, Ranchers, Settlers, and Colorful Characters (p. 60).

Description

To get to Brown's Park Trail from Vernal, follow the start of Northern #26: Rainbow and Island Park Trail. Leave Vernal on 500 North Street, which becomes Jones Hole Road. Rainbow and Island Park Trail turns off the paved Jones Hole Road at the 8.3-mile mark, but continue straight for another 17 miles until you reach Brown's Park Road. This intersection is the start of Brown's Park Trail.

The trail begins on a gravel country road that passes through rolling sagebrush with occasional pinyon and juniper. Although the road is easy and accessible by passenger car in dry weather, it becomes impassable in wet weather.

After 13.6 miles you reach the dramatic Crouse Canyon, which has a number of old cottonwoods and stunning rock formations. As you wind your way back and forth across the creek, the walls of the narrow canyon tower high above the trail.

After 17.3 miles, you enter Brown's Park National Wildlife Refuge and follow the Green River east into Colorado for a few miles until you reach the swinging suspension bridge. Just before the bridge, a side track branches off the main road and travels for 7 miles along the Green River before coming to an abrupt end at a gate, where it is closed to motorized vehicle traffic. Just before the gate, Hoy Draw (named for the Hoy family who lived in the area in the late 1800s) goes off to the right. Although it appears as a 4WD road on most maps, it is now closed to all motorized vehicles.

The Brown's Park Trail continues over the suspension bridge and turns back west into Utah, where it eventually comes to an end at the historic Jarvie Ranch.

To begin the trail from the Jarvie Ranch end, take US 191 to Minnies Gap just over the state line into Wyoming. From here, turn east onto Basin Road or Brown's Park Road Scenic Backway. Continue along this wide, country road through Jessie Ewing Canyon (named for yet another interesting figure in Brown's Park's history) until the turnoff for the John Jarvie Ranch. Turn right toward the ranch and the start of the trail.

Current Road Conditions

BLM Vernal Field Office
170 South 500 East
Vernal, UT 84078
(435) 781-4400

Map References

BLM   Dutch John
USGS 1:24,000   Crouse Reservoir, Hoy Mt., Swallow
           Canyon, Willow Creek Butte, Clay Basin
           1:100,000 Dutch John
Maptech CD-ROM: High Uinta/Flaming Gorge
Utah Atlas & Gazetteer, p. 57
Utah Travel Council #3 (incomplete)

Route Directions

▼ 0.0   On Jones Hole Road, 17 miles past the turnoff
               for Northern #26: Rainbow and Island Park
               Trail, zero trip meter and turn north onto
               Brown's Park Road. This is signed to Crouse

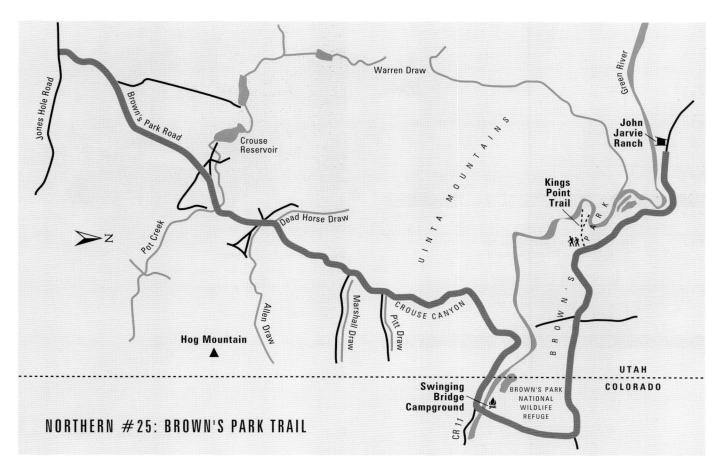

NORTHERN #25: BROWN'S PARK TRAIL

		Reservoir, Calder Reservoir, and Brown's Park. Then cross cattle guard.
5.5 ▲		Trail ends at Jones Hole Road. Turn right for Vernal and Northern #26: Rainbow and Island Park Trail.
GPS: N 40°39.25′ W 109°13.66′		
▼ 2.1	**BR**	Road forks. Crouse and Calder Reservoirs to the left.
3.4 ▲	BL	Crouse and Calder Reservoirs to the right.
GPS: N 40°40.77′ W 109°12.61′		
▼ 2.9	**SO**	Cattle guard.
2.6 ▲	SO	Cattle guard.
▼ 4.3	**SO**	Cattle guard.
1.2 ▲	SO	Cattle guard.
▼ 5.5	**SO**	Road to Crouse Reservoir on left. Zero trip meter.
0.0 ▲		Continue along main road.
GPS: N 40°42.77′ W 109°09.82′		
▼ 0.0		Continue straight.
10.9 ▲	SO	Road to Crouse Reservoir on right. Zero trip meter.
▼ 0.2	**SO**	Cattle guard.
10.7 ▲	SO	Cattle guard.
▼ 1.2	**SO**	Cross Pot Creek.
9.7 ▲	SO	Cross Pot Creek.
▼ 1.6	**SO**	Cattle guard.
9.3 ▲	SO	Cattle guard.
▼ 2.5	**SO**	Track on right to Allen Draw.
8.4 ▲	SO	Track on left to Allen Draw.
▼ 3.0	**BR**	Track on left to Dead Horse Draw.
7.8 ▲	BL	Track on right to Dead Horse Draw.
▼ 3.5	**SO**	Cattle guard.

7.4 ▲	SO	Cattle guard.
▼ 4.7	**SO**	Track on right.
6.2 ▲	SO	Track on left.
▼ 5.0	**SO**	Cattle guard.
5.8 ▲	SO	Cattle guard.
▼ 5.7	**SO**	Track on right to Marshall Draw.
5.2 ▲	SO	Track on left to Marshall Draw.
GPS: N 40°46.43′ W 109°06.36′		
▼ 6.7	**SO**	Track on right to Pitt Draw.
4.1 ▲	SO	Track on left to Pitt Draw.
▼ 8.1	**SO**	Cattle guard. Enter Crouse Canyon.
2.8 ▲	SO	Cattle guard. Exit Crouse Canyon.
GPS: N 40°48.23′ W 109°05.40′		
▼ 9.9	**SO**	Climb out of Crouse Canyon.
1.0 ▲	SO	Descend Crouse Canyon.
GPS: N 40°49.44′ W 109°05.63′		
▼ 10.9	**SO**	Track on left to Taylor Flat. Zero trip meter.
0.0 ▲		Continue north.
GPS: N 40°49.79′ W 109°04.75′		
▼ 0.0		Continue south.
3.5 ▲	SO	Track on right to Taylor Flat. Zero trip meter.
▼ 0.9	**SO**	Enter Brown's Park National Wildlife Refuge.
2.5 ▲	SO	Leave Brown's Park National Wildlife Refuge.
▼ 2.5	**SO**	Cattle guard.
1.0 ▲	SO	Cattle guard.
▼ 3.5	**BL**	Suspension bridge is on left; CR 11 is straight ahead. Zero trip meter at intersection.
0.0 ▲		Continue along trail.
GPS: N 40°49.60′ W 109°01.85′		
▼ 0.0		Continue over suspension bridge.

6.7 ▲	BR	Exit bridge. CR 11 on left. Zero trip meter at intersection.
▼ 0.1	SO	Swinging Bridge Campground on left.
6.6 ▲	SO	Swinging Bridge Campground on right. Cross the bridge.
▼ 0.3	SO	Track on right.
6.4 ▲	SO	Track on left.
▼ 1.3	SO	Cattle guard. Leave Brown's Park National Wildlife Refuge.
5.4 ▲	SO	Cattle guard. Enter Brown's Park National Wildlife Refuge.
▼ 2.8	TL	Cattle guard and intersection with paved road.
3.9 ▲	TR	Cattle guard and intersection with paved road.

GPS: N 40°51.96′ W 109°00.94′

▼ 4.5	SO	Cross cattle guard and Utah/Colorado state line.
2.2 ▲	SO	Cross Utah/Colorado state line and cattle guard.
▼ 6.2	SO	Cattle guard. Old log cabin on private property is in line with cattle guard on left.
0.5 ▲	SO	Cattle guard. Old log cabin on private property is in line with cattle guard on right.
▼ 6.7	SO	Track on left to Swallow Canyon (1.7 miles), which has small boat launch area with public toilets. Zero trip meter.
0.0 ▲		Continue along main road.

GPS: N 40°52.13′ W 109°05.36′

▼ 0.0		Continue toward Jarvie Ranch.
6.3 ▲	SO	Track on right to Swallow Canyon (1.7 miles), which has small boat launch area with public toilets. Zero trip meter.
▼ 2.0	SO	Kings Point Trail on left.
4.3 ▲	SO	Kings Point Trail on right.
▼ 4.7	TL	Track to Jarvie historic site on left.
1.6 ▲	TR	Turn right onto Brown's Park Road.
▼ 5.1	SO	David's Ranch on left.
1.2 ▲	SO	David's Ranch on right.
▼ 6.0	SO	Bridge Hollow Recreation Area to the left.
0.2 ▲	SO	Bridge Hollow Recreation Area to the right.
▼ 6.3		Trail ends at John Jarvie Ranch on left.
0.0 ▲		At historic John Jarvie Ranch, zero trip meter and proceed east toward Brown's Park Road.

GPS: N 40°53.97′ W 109°10.61′

NORTHERN REGION TRAIL #26

Rainbow and Island Park Trail

Starting Point:	Vernal
Finishing Point:	Green River in Island Park
Total Mileage:	29.4 miles
Unpaved Mileage:	19.7 miles
Driving Time:	1.25 hours (one-way)
Elevation Range:	5,000–5,800 feet
Usually Open:	Year-round
Difficulty Rating:	2
Scenic Rating:	8
Remoteness Rating:	+1

The old cabin at Ruple Ranch

Special Attractions

- McKee Spring petroglyphs.
- Green River overlooks.
- Ruple Ranch.
- Dinosaur National Monument.

History

The Rainbow and Island Park Trail runs through a part of northeastern Utah that was, millions of years ago, home to the dinosaurs, who lived in Utah throughout the Jurassic Period (for more on dinosaurs in Utah, see pp. 75-76). The first discovery of dinosaur fossils in Utah was made in 1909 by paleontologist Earl Douglass from the Carnegie Museum in Pittsburgh, Pennsylvania, who dug up the remains of an apatosaurus (known also as brontosaurus). Since then, his quarry has become one of the most important regions in the world for dinosaur research and excavation. In 1938, 200,000 acres in Utah and Colorado were set aside as Dinosaur National Monument. The park's visitor center, constructed in 1958, was built so that from inside you can see about two thousand exposed bones in the quarry's wall.

Petroglyphs just inside the boundary of the Dinosaur National Park

The McKee Spring petroglyphs located along the trail are evidence of the Fremont Indian culture, which lived in Utah from about A.D. 100 to 1250. No one knows its significance, but this rock art has endured for centuries. Please do not touch the art. McKee Spring gets its name from the large McKee family that lived near Rainbow and Island Park in the late 1800s. Much to father James McKee's chagrin, his eight boys were notorious thugs in the region, even going so far as to ride around killing bucks by clubbing them on the head and leaving them for dead. However, the McKees were among the first to run cattle on Diamond Mountain, north of Green River, and so have left their name attached to many of its landmarks.

Around the same time as the McKee boys were getting into mischief, Hank and May Ruple quietly made their home in

Island Park. The Ruple Ranch, established in 1883, is home to a large cottonwood tree that is thought to be the largest of its kind in the western United States. The Ruples used it to hang up saddles, bridles, and harnesses, and they enjoyed its peaceful shade. The cottonwood remains today as a distinctive landmark in Island Park.

In the late 19th century, Vernal became an important stop along the Outlaw Trail. The remote Brown's Park, in the very northeastern corner of the state, served as one of the Wild Bunch's main hideouts. When members of the Wild Bunch would come into "sudden riches," it was not uncommon to see them in Vernal celebrating, stocking up on supplies, and repaying old debts.

Description

Starting out on Main Street in Vernal, the Rainbow and Island Park Trail leaves town on paved roads before turning onto a well-maintained country gravel road. Once you cross into Dinosaur National Monument, the trail becomes a sandy and red, but easy, graded dirt road.

This trail enters the national monument from the north after 19.6 miles and is very interesting, providing wonderful views over the Green River. You reach the wall of Fremont Indian petroglyphs about three-quarters of a mile after you enter the monument.

Traveling mostly through sage with scattered pinyon and juniper, you eventually come upon the Ruple Ranch buildings and the enormous cottonwood. From this point, the trail becomes somewhat more difficult and follows a single-lane, sandy track out to an overlook of the Green River Valley and the old Ruple ranchlands.

Current Road Information

BLM Vernal Field Office
170 South 500 East
Vernal, UT 84078
(435) 781-4400

Dinosaur National Monument
4545 E. Highway 40
Dinosaur, CO 81610
(970) 374-3000

Map References

BLM   Vernal, Dutch John
USGS 1:24,000   Vernal NE, Naples, Donkey Flat, Dinosaur Quarry, Jensen Ridge, Island Park, Split Mt., Jones Hole
      1:100,000 Vernal, Dutch John
Maptech CD-ROM: High Uinta/Flaming Gorge
Trails Illustrated, #220 (incomplete)
Utah Atlas & Gazetteer, p. 57
Utah Travel Council #3

Route Directions

▼ 0.0		In Vernal, on Main Street (US 40), turn north on Vernal Avenue and zero trip meter.

GPS: N 40°27.36′ W 109°31.65′

▼ 0.4	SO	Ashley National Forest Office on left.
▼ 0.5	TR	Turn right onto 500 North Street.
▼ 3.4	BL	Bear left; road becomes Jones Hole Road. Road on right is Brush Creek Road.
▼ 8.3	TR	Turn right onto unmarked road and zero trip meter.

GPS: N 40°30.52′ W 109°24.11′

▼ 0.0		Proceed east.
▼ 0.7	TR	Intersection.
▼ 1.4	SO	Trail is now gravel road.
▼ 1.8	BL	Fork in road.
▼ 1.9	SO	Cross cattle guard.
▼ 2.1	SO	Track on right.
▼ 4.9	SO	Cattle guard.
▼ 5.9	SO	Track on left.
▼ 6.4	SO	Track on left.
▼ 7.0	SO	Cross over Stone Bridge Draw.
▼ 8.8	SO	Cross over Stone Bridge Draw. Then track on right.
▼ 9.4	SO	Cross through wash.
▼ 9.9	SO	Track on left.
▼ 10.1	SO	Cross through wash.
▼ 11.2	SO	Cross through wash.
▼ 11.3	SO	Cattle guard. Enter Dinosaur National Monument. Zero trip meter.

GPS: N 40°30.49′ W 109°12.63′

▼ 0.0		Proceed east.
▼ 0.7	SO	Several panels of petroglyphs on left; look at dark parts of rock face. You can pull off trail before crossing wash.

GPS: N 40°30.49′ W 109°11.88′

▼ 1.8	BR	Cross over Gorge Draw. Fork in road. Bear right on spur to Green River. Main trail continues left to Island Park. You will return to this intersection after spur to Green River.

GPS: N 40°30.32′ W 109°10.73′

▼ 2.0	SO	Cross over Gorge Draw.
▼ 2.6	UT	Picnic area with public restrooms and parking. Road dead-ends at Green River boat ramp. Return to previous intersection.

GPS: N 40°29.73′ W 109°10.41′

▼ 3.4	TR	Turn right at intersection and zero trip meter.

GPS: N 40°30.32′ W 109°10.73′

▼ 0.0		Continue along trail toward Island Park.
▼ 1.5	BR	Intersection with loop road to overlook with spectacular view of Green River and beyond.

GPS: N 40°31.14′ W 109°09.86′

▼ 1.7	BR	Bear right onto Island Park Road.
▼ 2.6	SO	Track on left.
▼ 3.4	SO	Cattle guard.

A view of the Green River from the Island Park overlook

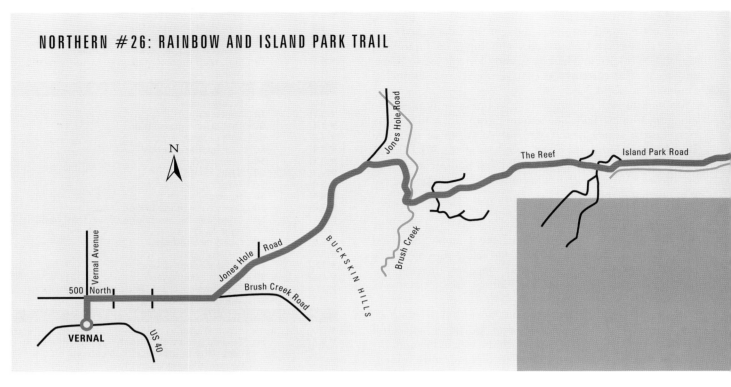

▼ 4.4	SO	Two tracks on right are 1.4-mile, 4WD loop road to the Green River. Zero trip meter.

GPS: N 40°31.74' W 109°08.95'

▼ 0.0		Continue past private track on left.
▼ 0.4	SO	Cross over wash.
▼ 0.7	SO	Gate into Ruple Ranch. Then track on left, which makes a 1.8-mile loop.
▼ 0.8	SO	Corral on left and cabin on right. The Ruples' enormous cottonwood tree is beside road.
▼ 2.0		End of trail.

GPS: N 40°30.84' W 109°07.35'

NORTHERN REGION TRAIL #27

Echo Park and Yampa Bench Trail

Starting Point:	US 40 in Utah, 12.3 miles east of Jensen
Finishing Point:	US 40 in Colorado, 28.5 miles east of
	Utah state line
Total Mileage:	81.4 miles
Unpaved Mileage:	68.2 miles
Driving Time:	4 hours
Elevation Range:	5,200–8,100 feet
Usually Open:	May to November
Difficulty Rating:	2
Scenic Rating:	10
Remoteness Rating:	+1

Special Attractions

- Travel through part of Dinosaur National Monument.
- Petroglyphs by the Fremont Indians.
- Spectacular views overlooking the Yampa River.
- Sand Canyon and Echo Park.
- Chew Ranch and Baker cabin.

History

The earliest known white men to pass through Echo Park were fur trappers (William H. Ashley, for example, came through in the 19th century) but the rock art displayed along the canyon walls shows that the region was inhabited by Indians at least 600 years earlier. Echo Park was named during John Wesley Powell's 1869 expedition of the Colorado Plateau, and in 1883, Patrick Lynch was the first man to homestead in the canyon.

Baker Cabin

Just before the trail passes the panel of petroglyphs, it comes to the remains of the old Chew Ranch. Born in England, Jack Chew moved to America with his family and grew up in southern Utah. Around the age of 12, Chew ran away from home and met up with the McCarty gang. A band of notorious outlaws and cattle rustlers, the McCarty gang demonstrated an unexpected soft side when they allowed Jack to live with them for the next 10 years, during which Jack learned about horses, cattle, and life in the Utah wilderness. He eventually started his own family and settled down in north-

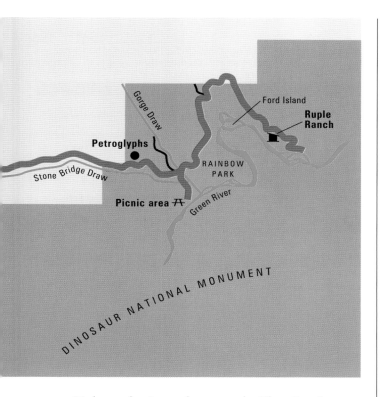

eastern Utah on what is now known as the Chew Ranch.

By 1912, the Chews had left their ranch and moved across to Pats Hole in Colorado. Pats Hole sits at the meeting of the Yampa and Green Rivers. In the days of the Outlaw Trail, members of the Wild Bunch found this place to be the best river crossing on their way in and out of Brown's Park to the north.

The Baker cabin is another historic site along the trail and is located about 150 yards off the main trail along a disused vehicle track. The cabin, stables, and corral were built in 1918 and abandoned in the 1930s.

Description

On US 40, about 12 miles east of Jensen and 1.2 miles east of Utah 45, turn north onto CR 16S (Blue Mountain Road) and head toward Dinosaur National Monument. The first section of the trail follows a graded county road that soon turns east and travels through dense pinyon and juniper about a mile south of the 2,000-foot cliffs that rise up to the Yampa Plateau. The trail then briefly crosses into Colorado, returns to Utah, and then returns to Colorado for the rest of the trail.

After 11.7 miles, you reach the national monument information center; turn north here onto paved Harpers Corner Drive. About 7.4 miles along Harpers Corner Drive, Canyon Overlook is to the right. The land here drops away quickly along the faultline between the Yampa and Red Rocks continental plates. Over millions of years, one of the Weber sandstone plates fell away from the other and was then carved out even further by the Yampa River. The result is this narrow river canyon 2,600 feet below the overlook.

About 5.5 miles farther up the road there is an overlook into the valley where three faults come together. Shortly thereafter, turn east onto Echo Park Road and begin the descent into the iron-red valley. Originally used by the Chew family, this

steep road had no switchbacks, forcing the homesteaders to hitch horses to the rear of their wagons to act as brakes. The road is not as difficult to negotiate these days and can be driven by passenger cars as well as SUVs; however, it should not be driven by large vehicles or ones towing trailers. Avoid the road when it is wet; the red clay becomes thick and greasy and is impassable.

About 5 miles from the turn onto Echo Park Road, the red scenery gives way to buff-colored sandstone as you enter Sand Canyon. The road surface in the canyon becomes sandy, but remains easy to drive. After 7.4 miles along Echo Park Road, a 3.8-mile spur trail leads down another beautiful sandstone canyon to the 800-foot Steamboat Rock at the confluence of the Green and Yampa Rivers. This Echo Park landmark stands at the old outlaw river crossing known as Pats Hole.

Along the spur to Pats Hole and Echo Park is the Chew Ranch and the Fremont Indian petroglyphs. At the end, there is a developed campground and a boat launch for white-water rafting on the Green River. Fees and noncommercial river permits are required for rafting; for information, call (970) 374-2468.

After returning to the main trail, you begin a 1,000-foot ascent onto Yampa Bench, which winds through a number of canyons and draws. Even though the road here is periodically graded, it does have a few washouts and occasional rough spots. This section of the route is more remote, and the scenery, though somewhat varied, consists mostly of sagebrush, pinyon, and juniper. The highlights along the Yampa Bench are the high overlooks above the twisting canyons of the Yampa River. The old Baker cabin sits about 150 yards off the main road up an old, abandoned vehicle track that still serves as a walking path.

Although the drive along the Echo Park and Yampa Bench Trail takes about four hours nonstop, you could easily spend a few days exploring the side canyons, camping along the river, and relaxing at some of the many overlooks. The trail eventually ends at US 40 in Colorado.

Current Road Information
Dinosaur National Monument
4545 E. Highway 40
Dinosaur, CO 81610-9724
(970) 374-3000

Steamboat Rock at Echo Park

Map References

BLM Vernal, Rangely, Dutch John, Canyon of Lodore
USGS 1:24,000 Cliff Ridge, Snake John Reef, Plug Hat Rock, Hells Canyon, Stuntz Reservoir, Jones Hole, Tanks Peak, Haystack Rock, Skull Creek
1:100,000 Vernal, Rangely, Dutch John, Canyon of Lodore
Maptech CD ROM: Craig/Meeker/Northwest Colorado (CO)
Trails Illustrated, #220 (incompete)
Utah Atlas & Gazetteer, p. 57

Route Directions

▼ 0.0		On US 40, about 12.3 miles east of Jensen, zero trip meter and turn north onto CR 16S (Blue Mountain Road).
11.7 ▲		Trail ends at US 40; turn right for Jensen, left for Colorado.

GPS: N 40°17.25′ W 109°08.40′

▼ 1.0	SO	Track on right. Then cross over Cliff Creek.
10.7 ▲	SO	Cross over Cliff Creek. Then track on left.
▼ 1.7	SO	Track on left.
10.0 ▲	SO	Track on right.
▼ 4.0	SO	Corral on left. Then cross Miners Draw.
7.7 ▲	SO	Cross Miners Draw. Then corral on right.
▼ 7.3	SO	Cattle guard.
4.4 ▲	SO	Cattle guard.
▼ 11.7	TL	Cattle guard, then turn left onto paved Harpers Corner Drive and zero trip meter. Dinosaur National Monument information center is to the left.
0.0 ▲		Continue along unpaved road.

GPS: N 40°21.76′ W 108°58.97′

▼ 0.0		Continue along paved road.
13.2 ▲	TR	Turn right onto CR 16S (Blue Mountain Road). Zero trip meter.
▼ 0.6	SO	Cattle guard.
12.6 ▲	SO	Cattle guard.
▼ 0.7	SO	Seasonal gate.
12.5 ▲	SO	Seasonal gate.
▼ 2.0	SO	Marker #12 for Wolf Creek Fault.
11.2 ▲	SO	Marker #12 for Wolf Creek Fault.
▼ 2.3	SO	Marker for good wildlife viewing area.
10.9 ▲	SO	Marker for good wildlife viewing area.
▼ 4.2	SO	Marker #14 notes that this is highest point along Harpers Corner Drive.
9.0 ▲	SO	Marker #14 notes that this is highest point along Harpers Corner Drive.
▼ 4.6	SO	Cattle guard.
8.6 ▲	SO	Cattle guard.
▼ 7.4	SO	Canyon Overlook on right. Picnic area and nature trail.
5.8 ▲	SO	Canyon Overlook on left. Picnic area and nature trail.
▼ 9.3	SO	Cross state line into Utah.
3.9 ▲	SO	Cross state line into Colorado.
▼ 11.7	SO	View right of Douglas Mountain and Zenobia Peak (9,006 feet)
1.5 ▲	SO	View left of Douglas Mountain and Zenobia Peak (9,006 feet).
▼ 12.0	SO	Corral on left; used in spring and fall for cattle and sheep.
1.2 ▲	SO	Corral on right; used in spring and fall for cattle and sheep.
▼ 12.9	SO	Marker notes meeting point of Yampa, Red Rock, and Mitten Park Faults. From overlook

		you can see Echo Park Road.
0.3 ▲	SO	Parking area and view back onto Echo Park Road.
▼ 13.2	TR	Turn right onto Echo Park Road. Then cross cattle guard. Zero trip meter.
0.0 ▲		Continue along main road.

GPS: N 40°28.62′ W 109°05.84′

▼ 0.0		Descend into canyon.
7.4 ▲	TL	Turn left onto paved Harpers Corner Drive. Zero trip meter.
▼ 3.2	SO	Cross cattle guard.
4.2 ▲	SO	Cross cattle guard.
▼ 4.9	SO	Entering Sand Canyon.
2.5 ▲	SO	Leaving Sand Canyon.
▼ 7.4	SO	Straight is spur trail to Pats Hole and Echo Park. Main trail continues right on Yampa Bench Road. Zero trip meter. You will return to this intersection.
0.0 ▲		Continue along route.

GPS: N 40°29.38′ W 108°59.37′

Spur Trail to Pats Hole

▼ 0.0		Proceed north toward Pats Hole.
7.6 ▲	SO	At intersection of Yampa Bench Road and Echo Park Road, zero trip meter and continue straight ahead.
▼ 1.2	SO	Chew Ranch buildings on right and left.
6.4 ▲	SO	Chew Ranch buildings on right and left.

GPS: N 40°29.97′ W 109°00.47′

▼ 1.3	SO	Cross Pool Creek ford.
6.2 ▲	SO	Cross Pool Creek ford.
▼ 1.7	SO	Log structure on left.
5.9 ▲	SO	Log structure on right.
▼ 2.7	SO	Ford.
4.9 ▲	SO	Ford.

GPS: N 40°30.68′ W 108°59.33′

▼ 2.8	SO	Petroglyphs about 35 feet above creek on left. Pullover area on right.
4.8 ▲	SO	Petroglyphs about 35 feet above creek on right. Pullover area on left.
▼ 3.2	SO	Whispering Cave on right.
4.4 ▲	SO	Whispering Cave on left.
▼ 3.3	SO	Ford.
4.2 ▲	SO	Ford.
▼ 3.4	SO	Ford.
4.2 ▲	SO	Ford.
▼ 3.6	SO	Road on left.
4.0 ▲	SO	Road on right.
▼ 3.7	SO	Ford.
3.9 ▲	SO	Ford.
▼ 3.8	UT	Pats Hole and Echo Park. Boat launch area, public toilets, and camping. Return to previous intersection where you zeroed trip meter.
3.8 ▲	UT	Pats Hole and Echo Park. Boat launch area, public toilets, and camping. Return to previous intersection where you zeroed trip meter.

GPS: N 40°31.19′ W 108°59.39′

▼ 7.6	TL	At intersection of Yampa Bench Road and Echo Park Road, zero trip meter and turn left onto Yampa Bench Road (CR 14N).
0.0 ▲		Continue toward Pats Hole.

GPS: N 40°29.38′ W 108°59.37′

Continuation of Main Trail

▼ 0.0		Continue along Yampa Bench Road.
6.4 ▲	TR	Turn right for spur trail to Pats Hole and Echo

Park. Main trail continues left on Echo Park Road. Zero trip meter. You will return to this intersection.

▼ 1.0		SO	Cross through wash.
	5.4 ▲	SO	Cross through wash.
▼ 2.7		SO	Cattle guard.
	3.7 ▲	SO	Cattle guard.
▼ 3.8		SO	Track on right.
	2.6 ▲	SO	Track on left.
▼ 5.7		SO	Cross through wash.
	0.7 ▲	SO	Cross through wash.
▼ 5.9		SO	Cross through wash.
	0.5 ▲	SO	Cross through wash.

GPS: N 40°28.13' W 108°54.62'

▼ 6.3		SO	Cross through wash.
	0.1 ▲	SO	Cross through wash.
▼ 6.4		SO	Castle Park Overlook on left. Zero trip meter.
	0.0 ▲		Continue toward Echo Park Road.

GPS: N 40°28.01' W 108°54.13'

▼ 0.0			Continue along Yampa Bench Road.
	2.7 ▲	SO	Castle Park Overlook on right. Zero trip meter.
▼ 0.9		SO	Cattle guard.
	1.8 ▲	SO	Cattle guard.
▼ 1.1		BR	Road forks. Left is private road to Mantle Ranch. Then cross through wash.
	1.6 ▲	BL	Cross through wash. Then road forks. Right is private road to Mantle Ranch.

GPS: N 40°27.50' W 108°53.33'

▼ 2.7		SO	Track on left to Harding Hole Overlook. Zero trip meter.
	0.0 ▲		Continue along main trail.

GPS: N 40°27.73' W 108°51.73'

▼ 0.0			Continue along main trail.
	1.2 ▲	SO	Track on right to Harding Hole Overlook. Zero trip meter.
▼ 1.2		SO	Wagon Wheel Point Overlook on left. For best views, walk about 250 yards. Zero trip meter.
	0.0 ▲		Continue along main trail.

GPS: N 40°27.59' W 108°50.64'

▼ 0.0			Continue along main trail.
	15.2 ▲	SO	Wagon Wheel Point Overlook on right. For best views, walk about 250 yards. Zero trip meter.
▼ 1.6		SO	Cross through wash.
	13.6 ▲	SO	Cross through wash.
▼ 4.5		SO	Closed track on right to Baker cabin, stables, and corrals.
	10.7 ▲	SO	Closed track on left to Baker cabin, stables, and corrals.

GPS: N 40°27.04' W 108°47.60'

▼ 7.2		SO	Track on left.
	8.0 ▲	SO	Track on right.
▼ 8.5		SO	Track on left.
	6.7 ▲	SO	Track on right.
▼ 12.1		SO	Cattle guard.
	3.1 ▲	SO	Cattle guard.
▼ 15.2		SO	Cattle guard. Leave Dinosaur National Monument. Zero trip meter.
	0.0 ▲		Continue along main trail.

GPS: N 40°25.69' W 108°39.36'

▼ 0.0			Continue along main trail.
	15.9 ▲	SO	Enter Dinosaur National Monument and cross cattle guard. Zero trip meter.

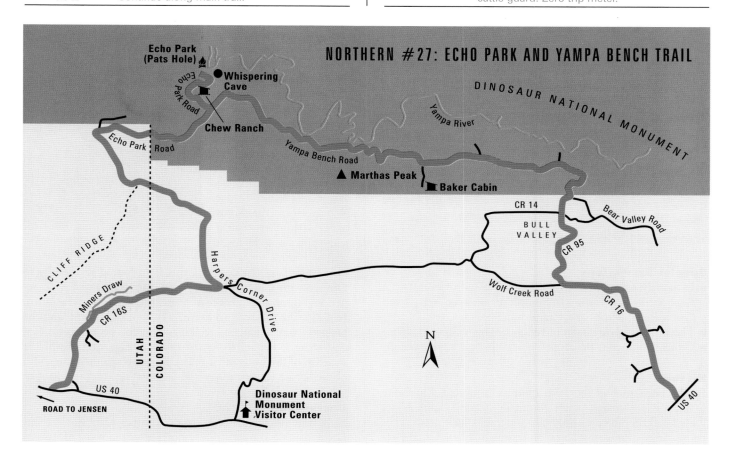

NORTHERN #27: ECHO PARK AND YAMPA BENCH TRAIL

▼ 0.1		BR	Bear right onto CR 95. CR 14N continues straight.
	15.8 ▲	BL	Bear left onto CR 14N.

GPS: N 40°25.65' W 108°39.30'

▼ 1.2		TR	T-intersection.
	14.7 ▲	TL	Road on left.

GPS: N 40°24.87' W 108°39.73'

▼ 1.3		BL	Road on right is CR 14. Continue on CR 95.
	14.6 ▲	BR	Road on left is CR 14. Continue along CR 95.
▼ 6.3		SO	Cattle guard.
	9.6 ▲	SO	Cattle guard.
▼ 6.5		TL	Turn left onto CR 16, Wolf Creek Road.
	9.4 ▲	TR	Turn right onto CR 95.

GPS: N 40°21.65' W 108°40.06'

▼ 6.7		SO	Cattle guard.
	9.2 ▲	SO	Cattle guard.
▼ 9.8		SO	Road on left.
	6.1 ▲	SO	Road on right.
▼ 15.9			Cattle guard. Trail ends at US 40. Turn right for Utah and Jensen.
	0.0 ▲		On US 40, about 28.5 miles east of the Utah/Colorado state line, zero trip meter and turn north onto CR 16.

GPS: N 40°16.67' W 108°33.54'

Rainbow and Watson Ghost Towns Trail

Starting Point:	**Central #25: Book Cliffs Loop**
Finishing Point:	**Utah 45, the American Gilsonite**
	Company, Bonanza Mines
Total Mileage:	**60.5 miles**
Unpaved Mileage:	**55.8 miles**
Driving Time:	**3 hours**
Elevation Range:	**5,000–8,400 feet**
Usually Open:	**Year-round**
Difficulty Rating:	**2**
Scenic Rating:	**8**
Remoteness Rating:	**+1**

Special Attractions

■ Extremely remote trail that when linked with Central #25: Book Cliffs Loop forms a connection between Vernal and Green River, Moab, and Grand Junction.

■ The historic ghost towns of Rainbow and Watson.

■ Gilsonite mines at Rainbow.

History

By the beginning of the 20th century, commercial gilsonite (which is almost exclusively found in eastern Utah's Uinta Basin) had become an important mineral in such products as paints, inks, storage batteries, and asphalt. However, the re-

One of the structures remaining at Watson Ghost Town

gion's gilsonite mines were soon producing more of the mineral than could be shipped out of this remote desert area.

The most efficient way to ship large amounts of gilsonite was by rail. The mining companies attempted to contract with the Union Pacific and the Rio Grande Western to build a rail line from Mack, Colorado, to the mines in Utah, but both companies refused. As a result, the Barber Asphalt Company decided to build the Uintah Railway itself.

Originally, the line extended only as far as Dragon, but when the mining operations began to move north, the railway followed. First it was extended to Watson and then an additional few miles to Rainbow (for more on these towns, see "Along the Trail"). All three towns relied almost completely on gilsonite and the Uintah Railway for their survival.

The gilsonite vein at Rainbow Ghost Town

Another ghost town that appears along the trail is White River, which has also been known as White River Crossing and Ignatio. This small settlement was established after the cost of extending the railroad to Vernal was deemed prohibitive. The railroad built a toll road instead, with a ferry crossing the Green River and a bridge over the White River. At the bridge, White River functioned as a little more than a stage stop along the route and as a home for workers and guards. The cost of a trip from Vernal all the way to Dragon with freight wagons varied from $2.50 to $3.50, depending upon the number of teams and wagons in the outfit. In 1935, the toll-road company went out of business and the property was transferred to the county for maintenance. Today, there is not much left of this old stage stop except the skeleton of the bridge that many years ago spanned the width of the White River.

Description

This trail heads northeast from Central #25: Book Cliffs Loop, passing through the remote desert country of eastern

Utah's Uintah County. Keep your eye out for deer and elk, animals common to the area. Driving through the thick pinyon and juniper of the region's desert landscape, it is hard to imagine how such towns as Rainbow and Watson once thrived along the Uintah Railway.

The trail proceeds through a number of gas fields along a broad, maintained dirt road. Most of the side trails that branch off from the main road lead to natural gas wells. The drive itself is not very difficult except for areas of thick, powder-fine sand. In some patches, the sand can be up to 8 to 10 inches deep and vehicles can kick up blinding clouds of dust. After rains, the trail is often impassable, as the entire region can become boggy and full of mud holes.

After 42 miles, you reach a short spur trail to the ghost town of Rainbow. Before it was played out, a major gilsonite vein ran through town; the channel looks like someone took a slice out of the ridge. For a nice view of the area, take a side road about 0.1 miles past downtown Rainbow to the communications tower. From here you can see old, wooden mining structures in the gilsonite vein as well as many other buildings and foundations. If you take the short road opposite the one to the communications tower, you reach a crest that offers another good view of the old gilsonite vein.

After Rainbow, the ruins of Watson sit 3.7 miles up the road. The site is heavily overgrown. However, a quick search reveals collapsing buildings and foundations that date back to Watson's heyday as a terminus along the Uintah Railway.

After another 5 miles, the trail intersects with Northern #29: Dragon Ghost Town Trail, which heads south back to Central #25: Book Cliffs Loop. The remains of the White River stage stop are another 5.5 miles past the trail intersection.

Just a couple of miles past White River, the trail proper finishes in front of the Bonanza Mines Office of the American Gilsonite Company. There are no services in Bonanza, so do not count on refueling there. However, you can reach Vernal quickly if you continue north on paved Utah 45.

Current Road Information

BLM Moab Field Office
82 East Dogwood
Moab, UT 84532
(435) 259-2100

BLM Vernal Field Office
170 South 500 East
Vernal, UT 84078
(435) 781-4400

Map References

BLM Vernal, Seep Ridge, Westwater
USGS 1:24,000 Bonanza, Southam Canyon, Weaver Ridge, Rainbow, Archy Bench SE, Cooper Canyon, Bates Knolls, Pine Spring Canyon, Seep Canyon, PR Spring
1:100,000 Vernal, Seep Ridge, Westwater
Maptech CD-ROM: High Uinta/Flaming Gorge
Utah Atlas & Gazetteer, p. 49
Utah Travel Council #3

Route Directions

▼ 0.0		On Central #25: Book Cliffs Loop, 38.6 miles from I-70, zero trip meter and proceed toward Seep Ridge Road, PR Junction, Indian Ridge, Pine Springs, and Ouray.
11.7 ▲		Trail ends about halfway along Central #25: Book Cliffs Loop; either direction leads to I-70.

GPS: N 39°27.14' W 109°16.43'

▼ 0.4	SO	Corral on right. Track on right to PR Spring.
11.3 ▲	SO	Track on left to PR Spring. Corral on left.
▼ 1.5	SO	Enter Uintah County.
10.2 ▲	SO	Enter Grand County.
▼ 2.4	SO	Track on left.
9.3 ▲	SO	Track on right.
▼ 3.7	SO	Cattle guard and corral. Track on right to Monument Ridge. Then track on left.
7.9 ▲	SO	Then track on left to Monument Ridge. Cross cattle guard with corral on left.

GPS: N 39°29.31' W 109°19.18'

▼ 5.9	SO	Track on left.
5.8 ▲	SO	Track on right.
▼ 7.1	SO	Track on left.
4.6 ▲	SO	Track on right.
▼ 8.0	SO	Track crosses road.
3.7 ▲	SO	Track crosses road.
▼ 11.3	SO	Track on right.
0.4 ▲	SO	Track on left.
▼ 11.6	SO	Corral on left. Track on right.
0.1 ▲	SO	Track on left. Corral on right.
▼ 11.7	SO	Intersection. Road on left to Pine Spring Canyon and Main Canyon. Stock pond on left. Zero trip meter.
0.0 ▲		Continue along main road.

GPS: N 39°34.55' W 109°24.06'

▼ 0.0		Continue along main road.
2.5 ▲	SO	Intersection. Road on right to Pine Spring Canyon and Main Canyon. Stock pond on right. Follow sign to Book Cliff Divide. Zero trip meter.
▼ 0.5	SO	Track on left.
1.9 ▲	SO	Track on right.
▼ 1.2	SO	Track on left.
1.3 ▲	SO	Track on right.
▼ 1.3	SO	Cross cattle guard. Corral on right.
1.2 ▲	SO	Corral on left. Cross cattle guard.
▼ 2.5	SO	Intersection. Right to Indian Ridge Road and McCook Ridge. Zero trip meter.
0.0 ▲		Continue toward PR Spring.

GPS: N 39°36.55' W 109°25.29'

▼ 0.0		Continue toward Ouray.

Some of the cabins at Watson Ghost Town

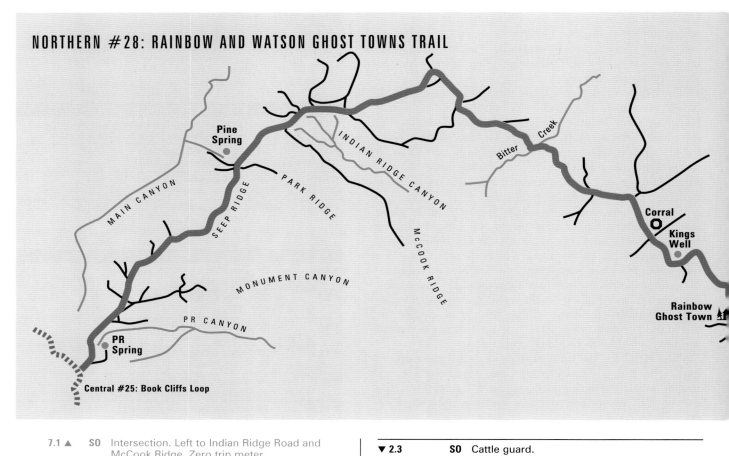

7.1 ▲	SO	Intersection. Left to Indian Ridge Road and McCook Ridge. Zero trip meter.	
▼ 1.0	SO	Track on right. Then road to Crow Roost Canyon on left.	
6.1 ▲	SO	Road to Crow Roost Canyon on right. Then track on left.	
▼ 1.4	SO	Track to Wood Canyon and Willow Creek on left.	
5.6 ▲	SO	Track to Wood Canyon and Willow Creek on right.	

GPS: N 39°37.73' W 109°25.85'

▼ 2.0	SO	Track on right.
5.1 ▲	SO	Track on left.
▼ 2.7	SO	Corral on left at intersection.
4.4 ▲	SO	Corral on right at intersection.

GPS: N 39°38.71' W 109°25.26'

▼ 4.3	SO	Track on right.
2.7 ▲	SO	Track on left.
▼ 4.8	SO	Track on left.
2.3 ▲	SO	Track on right.
▼ 6.7	SO	Intersection.
0.3 ▲	SO	Intersection.
▼ 7.1	TR	Turn right toward Kings Well and Bonanza. Zero trip meter.
0.0 ▲		Continue toward Book Cliffs.

GPS: N 39°42.05' W 109°26.38'

▼ 0.0		Continue toward Bonanza.
10.8 ▲	TL	Intersection. Zero trip meter.
▼ 0.3	SO	Track on right.
10.5 ▲	BR	Track on left.
▼ 0.7	BL	Track on right.
10.0 ▲	BR	Track on left.

▼ 2.3	SO	Cattle guard.
8.5 ▲	SO	Cattle guard.
▼ 7.3	SO	Cross over Bitter Creek.
3.5 ▲	SO	Cross over Bitter Creek.

GPS: N 39°45.22' W 109°21.28'

▼ 8.4	BL	Track on right.
2.3 ▲	BR	Track on left.
▼ 10.8	SO	Tracks on left and right. Zero trip meter.
0.0 ▲		Continue on main road.

GPS: N 39°46.62' W 109°18.41'

▼ 0.0		Continue on main road.
10.0 ▲	SO	Tracks on right and left. Zero trip meter.
▼ 0.8	SO	Track on right.
9.2 ▲	SO	Track on left.
▼ 1.0	SO	Track on left.
9.0 ▲	SO	Track on right.
▼ 1.5	BR	Track on left to West Asphalt and Bitter Creek. Bear right toward Rainbow and Bonanza.
8.5 ▲	SO	Track enters on right.

GPS: N 39°47.80' W 109°17.76'

▼ 1.6	SO	Track on left.
8.4 ▲	BL	Road forks. Right goes to West Asphalt and Bitter Creek. Bear left toward Seep Ridge Road.
▼ 1.7	SO	Track on right.
8.3 ▲	SO	Track on left.
▼ 1.8	SO	Track on right.
8.2 ▲	SO	Track on left.
▼ 2.1	SO	Track on right.
7.9 ▲	SO	Track on left.
▼ 3.2	SO	Track on right.
6.8 ▲	SO	Track on left.

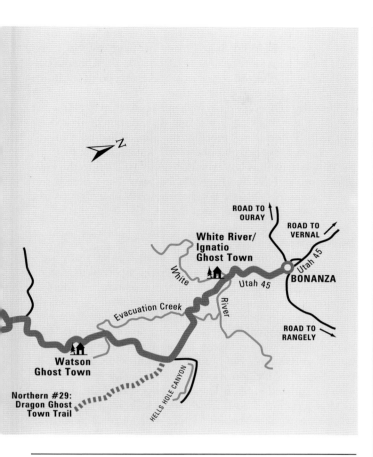

Continuation of Main Trail

▼ 0.0			Continue along main road.
	8.6 ▲	TL	Intersection. Turn left on spur trail to Rainbow. Zero trip meter. You will return to this intersection. Main trail continues straight.
▼ 0.5		SO	Track to Asphalt Wash on left.
	8.1 ▲	BL	Asphalt Wash road on right. Bear left on main road toward Rainbow and Kings Well.
▼ 3.7		SO	Town site of Watson. Ruins are in the overgrowth. Park along a short track on left.
	4.9 ▲	SO	Town site of Watson. Ruins are in the overgrowth. Park along a short track on right.

GPS: N 39°52.80' W 109°09.34'

▼ 3.8		SO	Cross through Evacuation Creek, which can be deep.
	4.8 ▲	SO	Cross through Evacuation Creek, which can be deep.
▼ 3.9		SO	Short track on right to various log and stone structures, part of Watson.
	4.7 ▲	SO	Short track on left to various log and stone structures, part of Watson.
▼ 6.5		SO	Track on right.
	2.1 ▲	SO	Track on left.
▼ 8.6		SO	Intersection. Right is Northern #29: Dragon Ghost Town Trail; road also leads to Baxter Pass, Colorado. Zero trip meter.
	0.0 ▲		Continue along main route.

GPS: N 39°55.69' W 109°07.43'

▼ 0.0			Continue along main route.
	3.7 ▲	SO	Intersection. Left is Northern #29: Dragon Ghost Town Trail; road also leads to Baxter Pass, Colorado. Zero trip meter.
▼ 0.1		SO	Corral on right.
	3.6 ▲	SO	Corral on left.
▼ 0.2		SO	Track on right to Hells Hole Canyon and Weaver Ridge.
	3.5 ▲	SO	Track on left to Hells Hole Canon and Weaver Ridge.
▼ 3.0		SO	Cross bridge over Evacuation Creek.
	0.7 ▲	SO	Cross bridge over Evacuation Creek.
▼ 3.4		SO	Track on right.
	0.3 ▲	SO	Track on left.
▼ 3.7		TR	Intersection with Utah 45. Southam Canyon and Asphalt Wash to the left. Zero trip meter.
	0.0 ▲		Continue along road.

GPS: N 39°57.54' W 109°09.74'

▼ 0.0			Continue on paved Utah 45.
	4.7 ▲	TL	Turn left onto unpaved road toward Book Cliffs, Rainbow Junction, and Baxter Pass. Zero trip meter.
▼ 1.4		SO	Track to White River (Ignatio) on left.
	3.3 ▲	SO	Track to White River (Ignatio) on right.

GPS: N 39°58.53' W 109°10.37'

▼ 1.8		SO	Cross bridge over the White River. Site of White River (Ignatio) stage stop is on left.
	2.9 ▲	SO	Cross bridge over the White River. Site of White River (Ignatio) stage stop is on right.
▼ 4.4		SO	Intersection. Rangely to the right and Ouray to the left.
	0.3 ▲	SO	Intersection. Rangely to the left and Ouray to the right.

GPS: N 40°00.82' W 109°10.20'

▼ 4.7			Trail ends at the American Gilsonite Company, Bonanza Mines Office, on Utah 45. Continue north on Utah 45 to reach Vernal.
	0.0 ▲		On Utah 45 in Bonanza, zero trip meter at American Gilsonite Company and head south.

GPS: N 40°01.13' W 109°10.33'

▼ 3.3		SO	Corral on left. Tracks on left and right.
	6.7	SO	Tracks on left and right. Corral on right.

GPS: N 39°48.11' W 109°15.80'

▼ 3.8		SO	Track on right.
	6.2 ▲	SO	Track on left.
▼ 4.2		SO	Track on left.
	5.8 ▲	SO	Track on right.
▼ 5.3		SO	Kings Well.
	4.7 ▲	SO	Kings Well.

GPS: N 39°48.70' W 109°13.96'

▼ 5.7		SO	Track on right.
	4.3 ▲	SO	Track on left.
▼ 9.5		SO	Gas well on right.
	0.5 ▲	SO	Gas well on left.
▼ 10.0		TR	Intersection. Turn right on spur road to Rainbow. Zero trip meter. You will return to this intersection. Main trail continues straight.
	0.0 ▲		Continue along main road.

GPS: N 39°50.87' W 109°11.28'

Spur Trail to Rainbow

▼ 0.0			Proceed toward Rainbow.
▼ 0.5		SO	Rainbow town site. Gilsonite mining structure on right.
▼ 0.6		SO	Road on right to radio tower and overlook of gilsonite mine and vein. Road on left to a crest where a deep gilsonite vein can be viewed clearly across the valley.
▼ 0.7		UT	Old dugout dwelling on the right. Turn around at the cattle guard and return to main road.

GPS: N 39°50.58' W 109°10.97

▼ 1.4		TR	Intersection with the main road. Zero trip meter.

GPS: N 39°50.87' W 109°11.28'

Dragon Ghost Town Trail

Starting Point:	**Northern #28: Rainbow and Watson Ghost Towns Trail**
Finishing Point:	**Central #25: Book Cliffs Loop**
Total Mileage:	**64.4 miles**
Unpaved Mileage:	**64.4 miles**
Driving Time:	**3 hours**
Elevation Range:	**5,500–8,600 feet**
Usually Open:	**Year-round**
Difficulty Rating:	**2**
Scenic Rating:	**8**
Remoteness Rating:	**+1**

Special Attractions

- Extremely remote region.
- Dragon, a historic gilsonite mining and railroad site.
- Connects with Northern #28: Rainbow and Watson Ghost Towns Trail and Central #25: Book Cliffs Loop to form a route from Vernal to Green River and Moab.

History

In 1885, Sam Gilson discovered a pocket of a black, oil-based mineral in Uintah County in what appeared to be the shape of a black dragon. The mineral came to be called gilsonite in honor of the man who both found it and promoted it as a commercially usable material. The mine where the ore was discovered soon became known as the Black Dragon Mine. Though it was established in the late 1800s, the Black Dragon Mine only became a major producer of gilsonite after 1904, when the Uintah Railway connected it to Mack, Colorado.

The mining town of Dragon quickly grew as more and more people were needed to work in the mine and the railyard. During its brief life span, Dragon was home to one of the Uinta Basin's finest hotels, a public school, and a public li-

The vein of gilsonite in Dragon Canyon

brary. Though it did not have a reputation as a lawless town, outlaws from the Wild Bunch made frequent stops in Dragon. Due to its remoteness (especially before the Uintah Railway was built), Dragon served as a safe resting point for Butch Cassidy, Elza Lay, and other outlaws.

However, Dragon's days were numbered. In 1908, a fire started in the Black Dragon Mine that supposedly lasted for two years. By this time, much of the mining had been moved north to such towns as Rainbow and Watson. Then, in 1911, the railway terminus was extended north 10 miles to the town of Watson, and slowly Dragon faded away. For a time it survived as a supply depot on the way to Vernal, but by the 1920s, it was pretty much abandoned.

Description

Although the remote Dragon Ghost Town Trail has many interesting attractions, one of its most appealing aspects is its location in the middle of nowhere. With the exception of a limited amount of mining in the region, the terrain through which the trail proceeds seems void of human influence or interference.

The trail begins along the north end of Northern #28: Rainbow and Watson Ghost Towns Trail, 10 miles after the turnoff to Rainbow, and heads south. The wide, dusty, maintained road to Dragon moves through grassy terrain dotted with pinyon and juniper. The trail's biggest obstacle, in fact, is its large amount of dust, which when kicked up by a passing vehicle can form a blinding cloud. When wet, these areas of powder-fine sand turn into mud holes, and if the area has just seen rain or melting snow, you should save this trail for another day, as it can become impassable.

After 8.6 miles, you come to a spur trail leading to the town site of Dragon, which has a number of old buildings still standing and foundations lying beneath the brush. From here, an interesting side road extends west from the town into Dragon Canyon. This canyon road winds through narrow gaps between shaley, sagebrush-covered hills. About 0.9 miles up Dragon Canyon on the left, you can look across the creek to a bluff where the old Dragon cemetery was located. About 0.1 miles later, look to the right to see the very conspicuous trench where a reef of gilsonite has been mined. About 3.5 miles up Dragon Canyon there is a gate where the trail peters out. Turn around and head back past Dragon to the main road.

From here, the main trail follows along sections of road that seem to have been dug into the ground. At times it feels like driving through a pipeline, as dense brush on either side rises above ground, seeming to wall you in. Make sure to stay alert through these areas because at times there can be considerable traffic associated with the mines.

About 10.4 miles after the turnoff to Dragon, you traverse Atchee Ridge and the desert shrub country becomes thick with pinyon and juniper. The road deteriorates along this section and becomes rougher and more narrow. This is more of a forest road than the mining road earlier in the trail.

Around Rat Hole Ridge and Canyon, 12 to 15 miles farther, the trail passes through significant stands of aspen that are somewhat uncharacteristic of the region. As you descend into Bitter Creek Canyon from Rat Hole Ridge, there are sections of narrow shelf road with rocky patches. Bitter Creek

Powder-fine dust billows up behind vehicles along the road

Canyon is a long narrow valley with a reasonably flat bottom and steep sides. This coniferous valley lined with aspens provides quite a nice change of scenery from the previous desert country. Deer and elk inhabit the valley and use Bitter Creek as a life-sustaining water source.

Near the south end of the trail, you drive along County Line Ridge and Overlook Ridge, which provide spectacular views southeast over the plains from the top of the Book Cliffs. The trail ends at Central #25: Book Cliffs Loop.

Current Road Information
BLM Moab Field Office
82 East Dogwood
Moab, UT 84532
(435) 259-2100

BLM Vernal Field Office
170 South 500 East
Vernal, UT 84078
(435) 781-4400

Map References
BLM   Seep Ridge, Westwater
USGS 1:24,000 Weaver Ridge, Dragon, Rainbow, Burnt Timber Canyon, Davis Canyon, Rat Hole Ridge, San Arroyo Ridge
        1:100,000 Seep Ridge, Westwater
Maptech CD-ROM: High Uinta/Flaming Gorge
Utah Atlas & Gazetteer, p. 49
Utah Travel Council #3 (incomplete)

Route Directions

0.0			On Northern #28: Rainbow and Watson Ghost Towns Trail, 3.7 miles from Utah 45, zero trip meter and turn south onto road toward Baxter Pass.
	8.6 ▲		Trail ends at Northern #28: Rainbow and Watson Ghost Towns Trail. Turn north for Utah 45, south for Central #25: Book Cliffs Loop.

GPS: N 39°55.69' W 109°07.43'

▼ 3.3		SO	Track on left.
	5.3 ▲	SO	Track on right.
▼ 3.6		SO	Track on left is mining operation.
	5.0 ▲	SO	Track on right is mining operation.
▼ 4.4		SO	Track on left to Rabbit Mountain.
	4.2 ▲	SO	Track on right to Rabbit Mountain.

GPS: N 39°52.19' W 109°06.34'

▼ 5.3		SO	Track on left.
	3.3 ▲	SO	Track on right.
▼ 6.9		SO	Track on left to Park Canyon. Then cross cattle guard.
	1.7 ▲	SO	Cross cattle guard. Then track on right to Park Canyon.

GPS: N 39°50.40' W 109°07.60'

▼ 7.2		SO	Cross bridge over Evacuation Creek.
	1.3 ▲	SO	Cross bridge over Evacuation Creek.
▼ 7.8		SO	Track on right. Then cross through wash.
	0.8 ▲	SO	Cross through wash. Track on left.
▼ 8.6		SO	Continue straight on spur trail to Dragon. Track on right is continuation of main trail to Three Mile Canyon and Atchee Ridge. After visiting Dragon the route will return to this intersection. Zero trip meter.
	0.0 ▲		Continue along route.

GPS: N 39°49.47' W 109°06.29'

Spur Trail to Dragon

▼ 0.0			Continue toward Dragon.
▼ 2.2		SO	Pass Mid-American Pipeline Company Dragon Station on left. Track on left to Missouri Creek.
▼ 3.3		UT	Site of Dragon. Tracks on left and right. Right track goes 3.5 miles up Dragon Canyon. Return to main trail after exploring canyon.

GPS: N 39°47.14' W 109°04.37'

▼ 6.6			Turn toward Atchee Ridge and Three Mile Canyon, zero trip meter.

GPS: N 39°49.47' W 109°06.29'

Continuation of Main Trail

▼ 0.0			Continue along route.
	10.4 ▲	TR	Intersection. Zero trip meter. Turn right on spur trail to Dragon. Straight is continuation of main trail. After visiting Dragon the route will return to this intersection.
▼ 4.4		BL	Fork in road. Bear left toward Boulevard Ridge and Rat Hole Ridge. Rainbow and Bonanza are to the right.
	6.0 ▲	SO	Track enters on left.

GPS: N 39°47.40' W 109°09.16'

▼ 4.5		BL	Road on right.
	5.9 ▲	TR	Straight continues to Rainbow and Bonanza. Turn right toward Three Mile Canyon and Evacuation Creek.
▼ 7.0		SO	Cattle guard.
	3.4 ▲	SO	Cattle guard.
▼ 7.4		SO	Tracks on right.
	3.0 ▲	SO	Tracks on left.

GPS: N 39°45.09' W 109°08.42'

▼ 8.8		SO	Track on right.
	1.5 ▲	SO	Track on left.
▼ 10.1		SO	Track on right.
	0.3 ▲	SO	Track on left.
▼ 10.4		SO	Track on right to Big Park, Cooper Canyon, and McCook Ridge Junction. Zero trip meter.
	0.0 ▲		Continue toward Three Mile Canyon.

GPS: N 39°42.48' W 109°08.54'

▼ 0.0			Continue toward Atchee Ridge.
	11.8 ▲	SO	Track on left to Big Park, Cooper Canyon, and McCook Ridge Junction. Zero trip meter.
▼ 0.5		SO	Track on left.
	11.3 ▲	SO	Track on right.
▼ 0.9		SO	Track on left.

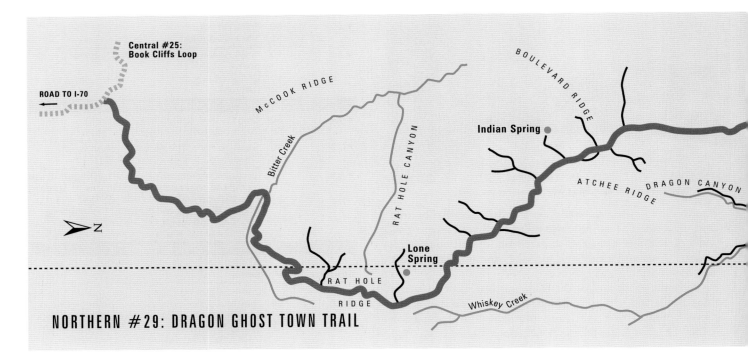

NORTHERN #29: DRAGON GHOST TOWN TRAIL

10.9 ▲	SO	Track on right.	
▼ 1.3	SO	Boulevard Ridge to the right.	
10.5 ▲	SO	Boulevard Ridge to the left.	
GPS: N 39°41.64' W 109°07.79'			
▼ 1.4	SO	Cross cattle guard.	
10.4 ▲	SO	Cross cattle guard.	
▼ 3.4	SO	Track on right to Indian Spring.	
8.4 ▲	SO	Track on left to Indian Spring.	
▼ 3.6	SO	Track on left and right. Right goes to Augusi Ridge.	
8.2 ▲	SO	Track on left and right. Left goes to Augusi Ridge.	
▼ 4.6	SO	Track on left.	
7.2 ▲	SO	Track on right.	
▼ 5.8	SO	Track to Moonshine Ridge on right. Then cross cattle guard.	
6.0 ▲	SO	Cross cattle guard. Track to Moonshine Ridge on left.	
GPS: N 39°38.99' W 109°04.90'			
▼ 6.2	SO	Track on right to Moonshine Ridge.	
5.6 ▲	SO	Track on left to Moonshine Ridge.	
▼ 6.4	SO	Track on left.	
5.4 ▲	SO	Track on right.	
▼ 9.7	SO	Cross cattle guard.	
2.1 ▲	SO	Cross cattle guard.	
▼ 10.0	SO	Track on left.	
1.8 ▲	SO	Track on right.	
▼ 10.3	SO	Track on left to Whiskey Creek Canyon.	
1.5 ▲	SO	Track on right to Whiskey Creek Canyon.	
▼ 11.6	SO	Old building on right.	
0.2 ▲	SO	Old building on left.	
▼ 11.8	SO	Track on left to Cripple Cowboy Ranch. Track on right to Lone Spring. Zero trip meter.	
0.0 ▲		Continue along main road.	
GPS: N 39°35.40' W 109°01.34'			
▼ 0.0		Proceed toward McCook Ridge and Bitter Creek.	
19.9 ▲	SO	Track on left to Lone Spring. Cripple Cowboy Ranch on right. Zero trip meter.	
▼ 0.5	BL	Road forks. Rat Hole Canyon to the right.	
19.3 ▲	BR	Road to Rat Hole Canyon on left.	

▼ 1.9	SO	Track on left.	
18.0 ▲	SO	Track on right.	
▼ 2.3	SO	Track on right.	
17.6 ▲	SO	Track on left.	
▼ 3.1	SO	Track on right to Rat Hole Ridge.	
16.7 ▲	SO	Track on left to Rat Hole Ridge.	
▼ 3.4	SO	Track on left.	
16.4 ▲	SO	Track on right.	
▼ 5.6	SO	Cross state line into Utah.	
14.3 ▲	SO	Cross state line into Colorado.	
GPS: N 39°32.25' W 109°03.03'			
▼ 7.7	SO	Cattle guard.	
12.1 ▲	SO	Cattle guard.	
▼ 7.9	SO	Track on left to Cripple Cowboy Ranch.	
12.0 ▲	SO	Track on right to Cripple Cowboy Ranch.	
▼ 9.1	SO	Track on right.	
10.8 ▲	SO	Track on left.	
▼ 9.3	SO	Cross over Bitter Creek.	
10.6 ▲	SO	Cross over Bitter Creek.	
GPS: N 39°31.51' W 109°05.95'			
▼ 9.4	SO	Cross cattle guard.	
10.5 ▲	SO	Cross cattle guard.	
▼ 13.3	SO	Cross cattle guard.	
6.6 ▲	SO	Cross cattle guard.	
▼ 13.5	SO	Track on left.	
6.3 ▲	SO	Track on right.	
▼ 19.7	TL	Cross cattle guard. Then turn left at intersection toward Divide and Ouray. McCook Ridge is to the right.	
0.2 ▲	TR	Proceed toward Overlook Ridge, Bitter Creek, Fatty Canyon, and Atchee Ridge. Cross cattle guard.	
▼ 19.9		Trail ends about halfway along Central #25: Book Cliffs Loop; either direction leads to I-70.	
0.0 ▲		On Central #25: Book Cliffs Loop, about 31.5 miles from I-70, turn north, following signs to Atchee Ridge and McCook Ridge.	
GPS: N 39°26.59' W 109°09.84'			

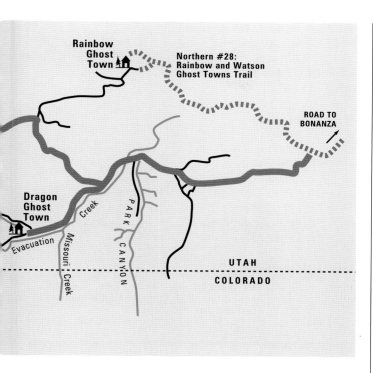

Rainbow Ghost Town

Northern #28: Rainbow and Watson Ghost Towns Trail

ROAD TO BONANZA

Dragon Ghost Town

Creek

Evacuation

Missouri Creek

PARK CANYON

UTAH

COLORADO

Sawtooth Mountain Trail

Starting Point:	**US 50, 0.6 miles west of mile marker 53**
Finishing Point:	**Marjum Canyon Road, 25.1 miles west**
	of US 50
Total Mileage:	**27.1 miles**
Unpaved Mileage:	**27.1 miles**
Driving Time:	**4 hours**
Elevation Range:	**4,500–8,000 feet**
Usually Open:	**Year-round**
Difficulty Rating:	**3**
Scenic Rating:	**7**
Remoteness Rating:	**+2**

Special Attractions
■ Mining remains in North Canyon.
■ Chance to travel some remote, little-used desert tracks.
■ Views of Lake Sevier, the House Range, and Tule Valley.

History
One of the major features on this trail is Sevier Lake, presently the third largest body of water in Utah. Sevier Lake is part of the ancient inland sea of Lake Bonneville, which covered 20,000 square miles of the Great Basin. Sevier Lake is situated on a southern tongue of the old lake. Until recently, the lake was slowly diminishing in size, but with higher than usual runoff in the past few years, it has expanded and become a permanent year-round body of water. Under normal condi-

tions, the lake is dry for part of each year. The lake is the drainage for the Sevier River, and both the lake and the river have no outlet to the sea, ending as they do in the Great Basin.

The lake has undergone several name changes. Originally it was named Laguna de Miera after a cartographer with the 1776 Domínguez-Escalante Expedition. Then it was known as Ashley Lake, after William Ashley, a fur trapper in the region in the 1820s. Next it became Nicollet Lake, after Joseph Nicollet, a French geologist who surveyed the region with Captain J. H. Simpson in the 1850s. Finally, it became known as Sevier Lake, after the river that drains into it.

The Sevier River takes its name not from American general John Sevier, but is a corruption of the Spanish word *severo*, which means "severe." The Spanish, the first non-Indian visitors to the region, called the river "Rio Severo" because of its dangerous passages.

The trail hugs the eastern flank of the House Range and then ascends into the range itself along a spur trail into North Canyon. The House Range was named in 1856 by Captain J. H. Simpson while he was surveying the western desert for the government. While still many miles away, he noted, "The range of mountains [is] quite remarkable on account of its well-defined stratification and the resemblance of portions of its outline to domes, minarets, houses, and other structures...I call it the House Range."

The Spanish mined the House Range extensively; in North Canyon, later miners found hand tools in an old tunnel, and another tunnel led to a series of rooms interconnected with ladders, where they found leather ore buckets and more hand tools for digging. This site is now caved in.

The range contains some of the oldest known animal fossils in Utah, and there are several sites that will be of interest to rock hounds. You can collect trilobites and remnants of ancient sponge reefs. The Warm Springs Resource Area map (see below) notes several sites as well as sites for collecting gemstones and minerals.

Description
This trail follows some very little used tracks in extremely remote desert country within the Warm Springs Resource Area. You are unlikely to see other travelers, and if you break down,

View from the saddle between North Canyon and Amasa Valley

help will be a long time coming. Local ranchers use these trails to varying degrees, and the part of the trail that runs up North Canyon is better traveled, but travelers should be well prepared and self-sufficient; carry additional fuel, food, and water. A detailed regional map is strongly recommended. You can obtain a free map of the Warm Springs Resource Area, which shows the area's major tracks, from the Fillmore BLM office.

The trail passes along the southern end of the House Range, which has striking, rugged escarpments and towering peaks 4,000 feet above the Tule Valley. The trail starts in the grassy plains, where harsh conditions and alkaline soil allow only a few salt-tolerant plants to survive. As the trail ascends, you pass through scattered pinyon, juniper, and sagebrush, and at the top, there are even small stands of aspens.

Navigation is difficult—there are no signs and many small tracks. A GPS is invaluable in this terrain, as vehicle tracks can quickly become overgrown or new ones pushed through, rendering the directions hard to follow.

The trail leaves US 50 approximately 30 miles west of Delta

View of Sawtooth Mountain from the trail

and begins as a small graded dirt road; you eventually loop back to US 50 on Marjum Canyon Road. Over the first 7 miles, the route makes several turns onto unmarked dirt roads, which get smaller and narrower until, at its least-used point, the trail is a narrow two-track with grass growing in the middle. A wise safety precaution is to check your vehicle's undercarriage at regular intervals to ensure that seeds and dry material are not collecting underneath, where they could be ignited by the heat from your exhaust.

The trail travels partway into Candland Canyon, and then it connects with a graded gravel spur trail up North Canyon. On the spur trail, once you cross North Canyon Creek, the trail standard becomes rougher with a short, moderately steep ledgy climb up the canyon. At the placer mines, there are many small tracks leading off among the remains. There are some interesting old buildings and vehicles lying derelict in the grass, and the original open pit mine is being revegetated and restored to a natural state. It is worth exploring some of the dead-end tracks leading off from the mines and into the Amasa Valley toward Pine Peak. The spur trail ends at a panoramic viewpoint of Sevier Lake and Miller Canyon. Sevier Lake is particularly beautiful from here on a clear day. The striking blue color of the lake and still conditions can make perfect mirror images in the shallow water. The trail continues, but it is steep and appears mainly to be used by ATVs.

From the viewpoint, retrace your path down North Canyon and continue northeast on the main trail to Marjum Canyon Road. This major gravel road will quickly take you back to US 50.

Although open year-round, snow or heavy rain can close the trail on occasion.

Current Road Information

BLM Fillmore Field Office
35 East 500 North
Fillmore, UT 84631
(435) 743-6811

Map References

BLM   Tule Valley
USGS 1:24,000 Long Ridge SW, Long Ridge Reservoir, Miller Cove, Notch Peak
          1:100,000 Tule Valley
Maptech CD-ROM: King Canyon/Fillmore
Utah Atlas & Gazetteer, p. 35
Other: BLM Recreation and Vehicle Guide to Warm Springs Resource Area

Route Directions

▼ 0.0   On US 50, 0.6 miles west of mile marker 53, turn northwest on unmarked small graded dirt road and zero trip meter.
   4.2 ▲   Trail ends at US 50. Turn left for Delta, right for Ely, Nevada.

GPS: N 39°06.35′ W 113°08.67′

▼ 1.2   SO   Cross through fence line on rise.
   3.0 ▲   SO   Cross through fence line on rise.

▼ 4.2   TR   Unsigned T-intersection. Zero trip meter.
   0.0 ▲   Continue toward US 50.

GPS: N 39°07.86′ W 113°12.93′

▼ 0.0   Continue north.
   3.7 ▲   TL   Unsigned junction; zero trip meter.

▼ 0.2   SO   Exclosure on left.
   3.5 ▲   SO   Exclosure on right.

▼ 0.3   TL   Turn left onto unmarked, ungraded, less-used small two-track.
   3.4 ▲   TR   Turn right onto unmarked larger track.

GPS: N 39°08.11′ W 113°12.87′

▼ 1.7   BL   Fork.
   2.0 ▲   SO   Fork.

GPS: N 39°08.47′ W 113°14.36′

▼ 3.1   SO   Cross through wash.
   0.6 ▲   SO   Cross through wash.

▼ 3.7   TR   Intersection. Turn right onto unmarked, ungraded two-track and zero trip meter.
   0.0 ▲   Continue east.

GPS: N 39°08.69′ W 113°16.68′

▼ 0.0   Continue north.
   2.9 ▲   TL   Intersection. Turn left onto unmarked, ungraded two-track and zero trip meter.

▼ 0.2   SO   Cross through small wash.
   2.7 ▲   SO   Cross through small wash.

▼ 0.5   SO   Cross through small wash.
   2.4 ▲   SO   Cross through small wash.

▼ 0.6   SO   Enclosure on left.
   2.3 ▲   SO   Enclosure on right.

▼ 1.4   SO   Enter creek wash.
   1.5 ▲   SO   Exit creek wash.

▼ 1.5   SO   Exit creek wash to the right.
   1.4 ▲   SO   Enter creek wash.

▼ 1.9   TR   Unmarked T-intersection.
   1.0 ▲   TL   Unmarked junction.

GPS: N 39°09.87′ W 113°17.68′

▼ 2.1   SO   Enter creek wash.

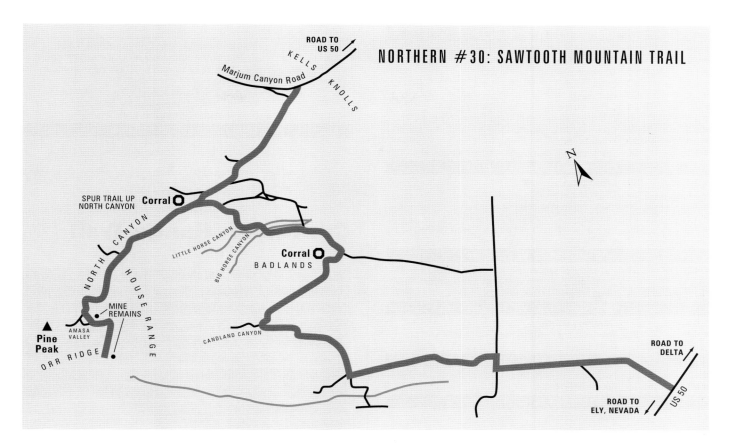

0.8 ▲	SO	Exit creek wash.	
▼ 2.3	SO	Exit creek wash.	
0.6 ▲	SO	Enter creek wash.	
▼ 2.5	SO	Cross through wash.	
0.4 ▲	SO	Cross through wash.	
▼ 2.9	TR	T-intersection. Left goes up Candland Canyon and dead-ends. Zero trip meter.	
0.0 ▲		Continue southeast on lesser-used trail.	

GPS: N 39°10.31' W 113°18.49'

▼ 0.0		Continue up slightly better used trail.	
2.7 ▲	TL	Straight goes up Candland Canyon and dead-ends. Zero trip meter.	
▼ 0.3	SO	Track on left, then cross through wash.	
2.4 ▲	SO	Cross through wash, then track on right.	
▼ 1.5	SO	Cross through small wash.	
1.2 ▲	SO	Cross through small wash.	
▼ 2.0	SO	Cross through small wash.	
0.7 ▲	SO	Cross through small wash.	
▼ 2.2	TR	Corral on left.	
0.5 ▲	TL	Turn left before corral.	

GPS: N 39°11.17' W 113°16.31'

▼ 2.4	SO	Cross through wash.	
0.3 ▲	SO	Cross through wash.	
▼ 2.5	SO	Cross through wash.	
0.2 ▲	SO	Cross through wash.	
▼ 2.7	TL	Unmarked T-intersection. Zero trip meter.	
0.0 ▲		Continue southwest.	

GPS: N 39°11.29' W 113°15.84'

▼ 0.0		Continue northwest.	
4.0 ▲	TR	Unmarked junction. Zero trip meter.	
▼ 0.3	SO	Cross through two small washes.	
3.7 ▲	SO	Cross through two small washes.	

▼ 1.0	SO	Track on left and track on right.	
3.0 ▲	SO	Track on left and track on right.	

GPS: N 39°11.94' W 113°16.56'

▼ 1.3	SO	Cross through wash.	
2.7 ▲	SO	Cross through wash.	
▼ 1.8	SO	Cross through wash.	
2.2 ▲	SO	Cross through wash.	
▼ 1.9	BR	Track on left goes up Big Horse Canyon.	
2.1 ▲	BL	Track on right goes up Big Horse Canyon.	

GPS: N 39°12.12' W 113°17.56'

▼ 2.2	SO	Cross through small wash.	
1.8 ▲	SO	Cross through small wash.	
▼ 2.7	BR	Track on left goes up Little Horse Canyon.	
1.3 ▲	BL	Track on right goes up Little Horse Canyon.	

GPS: N 39°12.43' W 113°18.21'

▼ 3.3	SO	Cross through wash.	
0.7 ▲	SO	Cross through wash.	
▼ 3.4	SO	Track on right.	
0.6 ▲	BR	Track on left.	

GPS: N 39°13.00' W 113°18.58'

▼ 3.8	SO	Track on right.	
0.2 ▲	SO	Track on left.	
▼ 4.0	TL	Unmarked T-intersection. Turn left onto spur trail up North Canyon and zero trip meter. You will return to this intersection after completing the spur trail.	
0.0 ▲		From end of North Canyon spur trail, bear right (southeast) at unmarked junction to continue along main trail toward US 50.	

GPS: N 39°13.12' W 113°19.20'

Spur Trail Up North Canyon

▼ 0.0		Continue on graded gravel road up North Canyon.	

	GPS: N 39°13.12' W 113°19.20'		
▼ 0.6	SO	Cross through wash.	
▼ 0.8	SO	Track on left.	
▼ 1.0	SO	Track on right.	
▼ 1.1	SO	Enter wash.	
▼ 1.8	SO	Exit wash.	
▼ 2.2	SO	Cattle guard.	
▼ 2.5	SO	Cross through wash, then track on right.	
▼ 2.6	SO	Cross through wash.	
▼ 3.0	SO	Track on left.	
▼ 3.1	SO	Track on left, campsite, and small corral.	
	GPS: N 39°11.93' W 113°22.08'		
▼ 3.3	SO	Cross through wash.	
▼ 3.5	SO	Old mine workings on right.	
▼ 3.6	SO	Enter wash and start to climb.	
▼ 3.8	SO	Leave wash; rough rocky climb.	
▼ 4.1	BL	Fork at saddle. Pine Peak is ahead to the southwest.	
	GPS: N 39°11.69' W 113°22.84'		
▼ 4.2	SO	Remains of placer mines: cabins, trucks, and diggings. Zero trip meter at intersection. More remains are on left.	
	GPS: N 39°11.60' W 113°22.84'		
▼ 0.0		Continue south.	
▼ 0.1	BL	Track on right, then bear left at fork and cross over creek.	
	GPS: N 39°11.53' W 113°22.84'		
▼ 0.2	BL	Fork.	
▼ 0.3	TL	Faint crossroads.	
	GPS: N 39°11.36' W 113°22.78'		
▼ 0.4	SO	Track on left.	
▼ 0.5	SO	Track on right and left.	
▼ 0.9	BR	Fork.	
	GPS: N 39°11.23' W 113°22.27'		
▼ 1.2	SO	Track on left.	
▼ 1.3	SO	Old mine workings on left.	
	GPS: N 39°10.92' W 113°22.45'		
▼ 1.4	SO	Track on left.	
▼ 1.5	UT	Spur trail ends at viewpoint over Miller Canyon and Lake Sevier. Trail continues, but used mainly by ATVs. From here, return to main trail and continue.	
	GPS: N 39°10.79' W 113°22.45'		

Continuation of Main Trail

▼ 0.0			From end of North Canyon spur trail, bear left (northeast) at unmarked junction to continue along main trail.
	3.9 ▲	TR	Unmarked junction. Turn right onto spur trail up North Canyon and zero trip meter. You will return to this intersection after completing the spur trail.
▼ 0.2		SO	Track on right.
	3.7 ▲	SO	Track on left.
▼ 0.9		SO	Cross through wash.
	3.0 ▲	SO	Cross through wash.
▼ 1.1		SO	Cross through wash.
	2.8 ▲	SO	Cross through wash.
▼ 1.2		SO	Cross through wash.
	2.7 ▲	SO	Cross through wash.
▼ 1.3		SO	Corral on left.
	2.6 ▲	SO	Corral on right.
	GPS: N 39°13.61' W 113°17.79'		
▼ 1.5		SO	Track on left.
	2.4 ▲	SO	Track on right.
▼ 3.3		SO	Cross through wash.

	0.6 ▲	SO	Cross through wash.
▼ 3.9			Trail ends at Marjum Canyon Road. Kells Knolls, small round hillocks, are on right and left. Turn right to rejoin US 50, near Delta, in 25 miles.
	0.0 ▲		On Marjum Canyon Road, 25.1 miles west of US 50, turn left immediately after Kells Knolls. Intersection is unmarked.
	GPS: N 39°14.90' W 113°15.40°		

Confusion Range Trail

Starting Point:	**US 50, 47 miles west of Delta**
Finishing Point:	**Utah 21, 25 miles west of Milford**
Total Mileage:	**49.1 miles**
Unpaved Mileage:	**49.1 miles**
Driving Time:	**3.5 hours**
Elevation Range:	**4,600–6,000 feet**
Usually Open:	**Year-round**
Difficulty Rating:	**3**
Scenic Rating:	**9**
Remoteness Rating:	**+2**

Special Attractions

- Ghost town of Ibex.
- Rockhounding for trilobites at Fossil Mountain.
- Rockhounding at zebra stone quarry.
- Desert scenery around Sevier Lake and the Confusion Range.

History

With its enclosed valleys, jagged peaks, and haphazard and rugged topography, the Confusion Range is well named. Blind Valley, so-named because of its isolated, enclosed geography, is a major valley bordered on the east by the Barn Hills and on the west by the Confusion Range. The Barn Hills contain a natural, deep valley that is completely enclosed. Jack Watson, who grazed his cattle there around 1910, named the Barn Hills—since he reckoned that when contained in this depression, his cattle were so safe they might as well be in a barn! The valley is called The Barn on topographic maps, and originally the Barn Hills were called the Ibex Hills.

The Wah Wah Mountains to the south take their name from the springs of the same name, located near Wallace Peak on the eastern edge of the range. *Wah wah* is an Indian word meaning good clear water. The springs were owned by Lydia and Edwin Squire, who sold them to Samuel Newhouse to supply his mining town on the far side of the valley, located below San Francisco Peak. In the Wah Wah Valley, the Wah Wah hardpan is created by water from the springs draining and drying out across the valley each year.

To confuse ghost town hunters, there are two ghost towns

called Ibex located less than 50 miles apart. The Ibex ghost town on this trail is the more southerly of the two (the more well-known one is north in the Drum Mountains). Ibex was an old mining and stockman's trading center. It may have gained its name from local animals that were bred from desert bighorn sheep and the Indian's captive goats; their horns were gradually curved like the African ibex. There are also petroglyphs in the area that seem to depict such animals. Ibex had housing, corrals, a post office, and a boardinghouse. The settlement lasted into the 1900s, but it gradually declined as the miners and sheepherders moved on. Most of the buildings are gone now; the most enduring remains are those of the stone dam walls built by settlers across the mouth of a narrow canyon to conserve precious water to the best advantage. The dams are a short hike up the small canyon. There are also remains of collapsed corrals and several dumps of tin cans.

The Confusion Range, too, has its tales of lost gold and missed opportunity. In 1870, a geologist, Frank Lane, was prospecting around the Confusion Range when he lost his way. In his desperate search for water, he came across some small holes in the rocks filled with stagnant puddles. The water saved his life, and as he drank the holes dry, he saw in the bottoms small nuggets of gold. He collected nearly 30 pounds of gold before thirst forced him out of the range; he headed across the Sevier Desert to Cove Fort near the present intersection of I-15 and I-70. A few months later he tried to return to the site of his find, but in three years of hunting he was never able to locate it.

Today, the BLM collects sagebrush seeds there each fall and uses them to revegetate portions of the Utah landscape damaged by fires or erosion.

Description

This long and varied trail travels over a mixture of maintained graded roads and little-used two-track roads to penetrate some of the valleys in the Confusion Range. The entire region is very remote, and travelers should be self-sufficient; carry extra food, water, and clothing. In addition, make sure you have a detailed regional map, since navigation can be tricky, especially over the latter part of the trail around Middle Park and Lawson Cove. The BLM at Fillmore provides a free vehicle travel map of the Warm Springs Recreation Area, which includes all the tracks on this route.

Fossil embedded in a rock at Fossil Mountain

Just prior to the start of the trail, fossil hunters may enjoy a stop at Skull Rock Pass on US 50 (GPS: N 39°01.93' W 113°20.48'). Where the highway has been cut through on the pass, Ordovician period fossils can be found in the shale on both sides of the road.

The trail proper starts 47 miles west of Delta, 0.8 miles west of mile marker 39. The trail leaves US 50 and follows the easygoing, graded Blackham Canyon Road for the first few miles. Then you reach the long, north-south Blind Valley, with its wide, flat sandy bottom, in the

Barn Hills in the foreground at the start of Blind Valley

Confusion Range. After 11.5 miles from the start, a left-hand, half-mile spur takes you to the remains of Ibex. There is little left of the ghost town these days, just the old series of dams, some foundations, fencing, and old tins. The site is pretty, set in a rock alcove, and there are some pleasant campsites.

Just after the turnoff for Ibex is the turnoff for a fossil-littered canyon on the north side of Fossil Mountain. If you drive a short distance to the mouth of the canyon and walk around the opening, you can find many marine invertebrate fossils in the rocks and slate. This site contains 13 fossil groups and a great variety of specimens. To the uninitiated, many of them look like clam shells and wood lice! Before you enter the canyon, there are some very pleasant vehicle campsites on the trail, that have soft sand for your tent and limited shade.

Continuing south, you pass Warm Point and head across the arid Tule Valley. The distinctive white Crystal Peak, another favorite rockhounding area, is visible to the north. The trail gets smaller and less defined as it approaches Middle Pass, a gentle grassy saddle in the Gray Hills. About 9.7 miles after the Crystal Peak turnoff, the trail drops to enter Lawson Cove, where rock hounds will find a bonus—just west of the trail is a vein of the distinctive Utah zebra rock, with its alternate bands of black and white.

From Lawson Cove, the trail is better defined as it heads southeast to join the graded gravel road leading past the Wah Wah hardpan (normally dry). It passes through the yards at Wah Wah Ranch to finish on Utah 21, 25 miles west of Milford.

Current Road Information

BLM Fillmore Field Office
35 East 500 North
Fillmore, UT 84631
(435) 743-6811

Map References

BLM   Tule Valley, Wah Wah Mountains North, Wah Wah Mountains South

USGS   1:24,000 Hell 'n Moriah Canyon, The Barn, Warm Point, Fifteenmile Point, Grassy Cove, Wah Wah Cove, Wallaces Peak
1:100,000 Tule Valley, Wah Wah Mountains North, Wah Wah Mountains South

NORTHERN #31: CONFUSION RANGE TRAIL

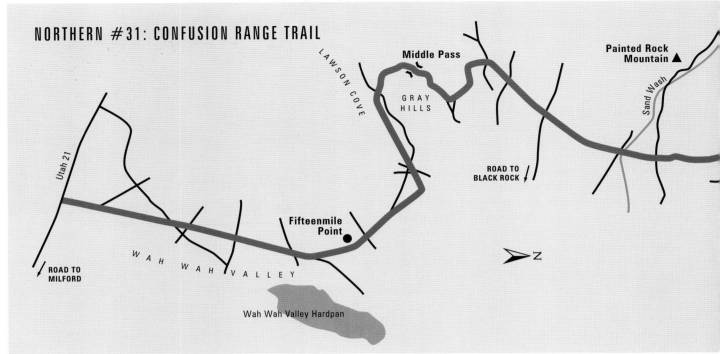

Maptech CD-ROM: King Canyon/Fillmore
Utah Atlas & Gazetteer, pp. 35, 25
Utah Travel Council #4 (incomplete)
Other: BLM Recreation and Vehicle Guide to Warm Springs
Resource Area

Route Directions

▼ 0.0			On US 50, 0.8 miles west of mile marker 39, turn southwest onto the graded dirt road, following sign to Blind Valley. Zero trip meter.
	3.9 ▲		Trail ends at US 50. Turn right for Delta, left for Ely, Nevada.
		GPS: N 39°01.73' W 113°22.70'	
▼ 0.4		SO	Intersection.
	3.5 ▲	SO	Intersection.
▼ 0.8		BL	Track on right.
	2.7 ▲	SO	Track on left.
		GPS: N 39°01.15' W 113°23.33'	
▼ 1.4		SO	Track on left.
	2.5 ▲	SO	Track on right.
▼ 2.1		TR	Intersection at north end of Barn Hills.
	1.8 ▲	TL	Intersection at north end of Barn Hills.
		GPS: N 39°00.18' W 113°24.02'	
▼ 3.4		SO	Track on left. Politician Point on right.
	0.5 ▲	SO	Track on right. Politician Point on left.
		GPS: N 38°59.65' W 113°25.42'	
▼ 3.9		SO	Track on right to Blackham Canyon. Zero trip meter.
	0.0 ▲		Continue toward US 50.
		GPS: N 38°59.42' W 113°25.96'	
▼ 0.0			Continue toward Blind Valley.
	7.6 ▲	SO	Track on left to Blackham Canyon. Zero trip meter.
▼ 0.2		SO	Cross through two washes.
	7.4 ▲	SO	Cross through two washes.
▼ 0.6		SO	Track on left.

7.0 ▲		SO	Track on right.
▼ 1.0		SO	Cross through wash.
	6.6 ▲	SO	Cross through wash.
▼ 1.4		SO	Cross over wash, followed by track on right to Bonny Stairs Canyon. Trail crosses wash many times in next 2.3 miles.
	6.2 ▲	SO	Track on left to Bonny Stairs Canyon, then cross over wash.
		GPS: N 38°58.52' W 113°27.09'	
▼ 3.7		SO	Entering Blind Valley.
	3.9 ▲	SO	Leaving Blind Valley. Trail crosses over wash many times in next 2.3 miles.
		GPS: N 38°56.60' W 113°27.90'	
▼ 4.4		SO	Track on right; then second faint track on right.
	3.2 ▲	SO	Faint track on left; then second track on left.
▼ 4.6		SO	Track on left.
	3.0 ▲	SO	Track on right.
		GPS: N 38°55.81' W 113°27.53'	
▼ 7.6		BR	Fork, directly in front of conical hillock. Fossil Mountain is prominent on right. Track on left to Ibex ghost town (0.5 miles). Zero trip meter.
	0.0 ▲		Continue north along Blind Valley.
		GPS: N 38°53.12' W 113°27.05'	
▼ 0.0			Continue toward Fossil Mountain.
	4.4 ▲	SO	Track on right to Ibex ghost town (0.5 miles). Zero trip meter.
▼ 0.1		BL	Right fork goes short distance into canyon north of Fossil Mountain. Fossils can be found around mouth of canyon.
	4.3 ▲	SO	Track on left goes short distance into canyon north of Fossil Mountain. Fossils can be found around mouth of canyon.
		GPS: N 38°53.10' W 113°27.08'	
▼ 0.5		SO	Cross through wash. Fossil Mountain is directly right.
	3.9 ▲	SO	Cross through wash. Fossil Mountain is directly left.

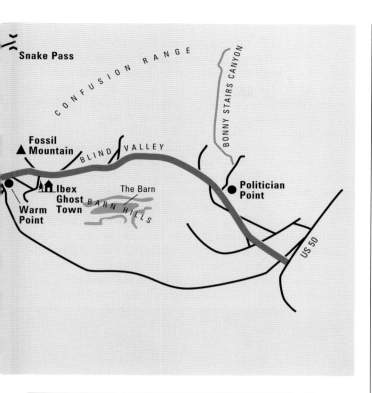

Snake Pass

CONFUSION RANGE

BONNY STAIRS CANYON

Fossil
Mountain

BLIND VALLEY

Ibex
Ghost
Town

BARN HILLS

The Barn

Warm
Point

Politician
Point

US 50

▼ 1.2		SO	Track on right.
	3.2 ▲	SO	Track on left.
▼ 1.4		SO	Track on left to Ibex ghost town. Warm Point on left.
	3.0 ▲	SO	Track on right to Ibex ghost town. Warm Point on right.
		GPS: N 38°51.94' W 113°26.95'	
▼ 1.6		SO	Intersection. Road on left to Tule Valley.
	2.8 ▲	SO	Intersection. Road on right to Tule Valley.
		GPS: N 38°51.82' W 113°26.90'	
▼ 1.7		SO	Track on left.
	2.7 ▲	SO	Track on right.
▼ 2.5		SO	Track on right.
	1.9 ▲	SO	Track on left.
▼ 4.4		SO	Major intersection. Road on left to Tule Valley, right to Snake Pass. Zero trip meter.
	0.0 ▲		Continue north.
		GPS: N 38°49.34' W 113°27.07'	
▼ 0.0			Continue south.
	4.6 ▲	SO	Major intersection. Road on right to Tule Valley, left to Snake Pass. Zero trip meter.
▼ 1.4		SO	Track on right.
	3.2 ▲	SO	Track on left.
▼ 1.5		SO	Cross through Sand Wash.
	3.1 ▲	SO	Cross through Sand Wash.
▼ 4.5		SO	Track on right. Crystal Mountain is visible on right.
	0.1 ▲	SO	Track on left. Crystal Mountain is visible on left.
		GPS: N 38°45.59' W 113°28.83'	
▼ 4.6		SO	Major intersection. Road on left to Black Rock, right to Crystal Peak. Zero trip meter.
	0.0 ▲		Continue north on more-used trail.
		GPS: N 38°45.46' W 113°28.98'	
▼ 0.0			Continue south on less-used trail.
	3.8 ▲	SO	Major intersection. Road on right to Black Rock, left to Crystal Peak. Zero trip meter.

▼ 0.1		SO	Cross through deep wash.
	3.7 ▲	SO	Cross through deep wash.
▼ 1.4		SO	Cross through deep wash.
	2.4 ▲	SO	Cross through deep wash.
▼ 1.7		SO	Cross through deep wash.
	2.1 ▲	SO	Cross through deep wash.
▼ 3.0		SO	Cross through wash.
	0.8 ▲	SO	Cross through wash.
▼ 3.4		SO	Cross through wash.
	0.4 ▲	SO	Cross through wash.
▼ 3.8		TL	Unmarked small intersection. Zero trip meter.
	0.0 ▲		Continue north.
		GPS: N 38°42.85' W 113°31.50'	
▼ 0.0			Continue east.
	5.9 ▲	TR	Unmarked small junction. Zero trip meter.
▼ 0.8		SO	Cross through wash.
	5.1 ▲	SO	Cross through wash.
▼ 1.4		SO	Cross through wash.
	4.5 ▲	SO	Cross through wash.
▼ 1.5		BR	Main track goes left. Bear right on lesser-used faint trail.
	4.4 ▲	BL	Track on right. Trail is now slightly better used.
▼ 2.0		TR	Track on left. Join more-used track.
	3.9 ▲	TL	Turn left on lesser-used faint trail.
		GPS: N 38°42.08' W 113°30.05'	
▼ 3.0		SO	Track on left. Trail follows wash. Gray Hills are on left.
	2.9 ▲	SO	Track on right. Trail follows wash. Gray Hills are on right.
		GPS: N 38°41.48' W 113°30.85'	
▼ 4.2		SO	Slight grassy rise is Middle Pass. Trail descends to Lawson Cove.
	1.7 ▲	SO	Slight grassy rise is Middle Pass. Trail descends.
		GPS: N 38°40.67' W 113°31.53'	
▼ 4.8		SO	Track on left.
	1.1 ▲	SO	Track on right.
▼ 5.0		BL	Track on right, then cross through wash.
	0.9 ▲	BR	Cross through wash, then track on left.
		GPS: N 38°39.93' W 113°31.24'	
▼ 5.3		SO	Cross through fence line.
	0.6 ▲	SO	Cross through fence line.
▼ 5.9		TL	Unmarked T-intersection. Immediately on right are diggings in a vein of zebra rock. Turn left onto larger, graded dirt road and zero trip meter.
	0.0 ▲		Continue northwest.
		GPS: N 38°39.59' W 113°30.37'	
▼ 0.0			Continue east.
	4.2 ▲	TR	Unmarked junction. Immediately ahead are diggings in a vein of zebra rock. Turn right onto smaller ungraded trail and zero trip meter.
▼ 3.3		SO	Faint tracks on right and left.
	0.9 ▲	SO	Faint tracks on right and left.
▼ 4.2		TR	Unmarked intersection. Zero trip meter.
	0.0 ▲		Continue on graded dirt road.
		GPS: N 38°41.19' W 113°25.93'	
▼ 0.0			Continue on good, graded dirt road.
	5.3 ▲	TL	Unmarked intersection. Zero trip meter.
▼ 2.8		SO	Track on right.
	2.5 ▲	SO	Track on left.
▼ 3.3		SO	Track on right.
	2.0 ▲	SO	Track on left.

▼ 4.4		SO	Cattle guard. Wah Wah Valley hardpan on left.
	0.9 ▲	SO	Cattle guard. Wah Wah Valley hardpan on right.
▼ 5.3		TR	Join graded gravel road. Road on left to Wah Wah Well. Zero trip meter.
	0.0 ▲		Continue on smaller gravel road.

GPS: N 38°37.05' W 113°22.96'

▼ 0.0			Continue on larger gravel road.
	9.4 ▲	BL	Straight on to Wah Wah Well. Turn left at sign for Lawson Cove and zero trip meter.
▼ 0.5		SO	Track on right.
	8.9 ▲	SO	Track on left.
▼ 1.0		SO	Cattle guard, then track on left along fence line.
	8.4 ▲	SO	Track on right along fence line, then cattle guard.
▼ 2.7		SO	Track on right.
	6.7 ▲	SO	Track on left.
▼ 4.0		SO	Tracks on right and left.
	5.4 ▲	SO	Tracks on right and left.
▼ 4.4		SO	Track on right.
	5.0 ▲	SO	Track on left.
▼ 4.6		SO	Tracks on right and left.
	4.8 ▲	SO	Tracks on right and left.

GPS: N 38°32.95' W 113°24.43'

▼ 8.2		SO	Cattle guard.
	1.2 ▲	SO	Cattle guard.
▼ 8.9		SO	Pass through Wah Wah Ranch property and yards.
	0.5 ▲	SO	Pass through Wah Wah Ranch property and yards.
▼ 9.4			Trail ends at Utah 21. Turn left for Milford.
	0.0 ▲		On Utah 21, 25 miles west of Milford, turn north onto graded gravel road at sign for Wah Wah Ranch and zero trip meter.

GPS: N 38°28.76' W 113°25.90'

NORTHERN REGION TRAIL #32

Frisco Peak Trail

Starting Point:	**Utah 21, 7.8 miles west of Milford**
Finishing Point:	**Frisco Peak**
Total Mileage:	**11.8 miles**
Unpaved Mileage:	**11.8 miles**
Driving Time:	**45 minutes (one-way)**
Elevation Range:	**5,100–9,600 feet**
Usually Open:	**May to November**
Difficulty Rating:	**5**
Scenic Rating:	**9**
Remoteness Rating:	**+0**

Special Attractions

■ Narrow, moderately difficult 4WD spur trail.
■ Panoramic views from Frisco Peak.

History

From the top of Frisco Peak, you can see the remains and tailings of the ghost town of Newhouse. Newhouse sprang into existence in 1900 when Samuel Newhouse purchased the Cactus Mine. He established a model city for his workers, building them houses, a café, a store, and a dance hall. Newhouse was as sober as nearby Frisco was rowdy. The only saloon was deliberately built one mile outside of town, so that it didn't exert any undue influence on the good citizens of Newhouse. When the railroad arrived, that too had to stop south of town. Samuel Newhouse died before his dream city could be completed, but his brother Matt continued in his shoes until 1910, when the ore in the mines ran out.

The mines at Newhouse dug up a total of $3.5 million worth of gold, silver, and copper. The Cactus Mill in town processed the ore, which was then shipped by railroad to market. The town survived for a short time after the ore ran out. The Cactus Café and boardinghouse served sheepherders and ranchers, and there was a shearing shed there until the 1930s.

A switchback as the trail ascends toward Frisco Peak

The railroad disappeared shortly after, because there was no more wool to collect. The Cactus Mill was purchased in 1914 for salvage, and many of the homes were moved to Milford in the 1920s. In 1922, Newhouse achieved a modicum of notoriety when it provided the setting for the silent movie *The Covered Wagon.*

En route to Frisco Peak, the trail crosses Moorehouse Canyon, at the head of which is Moorehouse Springs. The springs and canyon are named after Charles Moorehouse, who carted water from the springs to sell to the miners at Frisco. The trail then travels along Sawmill Canyon. In the 1870s, a sawmill was built there to provide timber for mines in the region, including the nearby Golden Reef and the mines of Frisco.

Description

This spur trail climbs steadily to one of the highest points in the region, Frisco Peak at 9,660 feet in the San Francisco Range. From Utah 21, the trail begins as an unmarked, graded dirt road, and it quickly crosses the sagebrush benches on the eastern side of the San Francisco Range. After 6.2 miles, you reach the intersection with Northern #33: Frisco Ghost

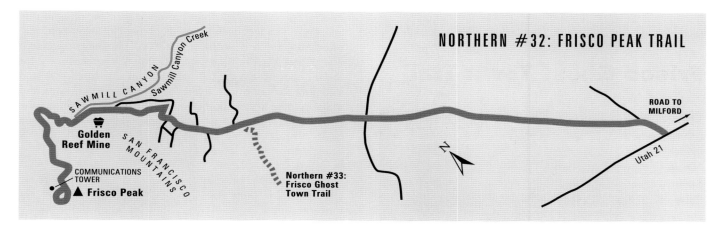

NORTHERN #32: FRISCO PEAK TRAIL

Town Trail, and after 8.7 miles, you pass the tailings piles of the Golden Reef Mine as the trail climbs up Sawmill Canyon. From the mine, the trail climbs steeply. The surface is loose and lumpy, but is generally fairly good. The most difficult section is the switchbacks that snake up toward the ridge. The trail is narrow, and the highest portions are mostly shelf roads. There are adequate passing places, but you should be prepared to back up if you meet an oncoming vehicle. The road is suitable for any high-clearance SUV.

As the trail climbs, it passes out of the juniper and sagebrush and encounters larger pines. The views get better the farther up you go. From the peak, there is a 360-degree view. To the north is the San Francisco Range, the Wah Wah Valley, the Wah Wah Hardpan, and Lake Sevier. To the northwest is the Confusion Range and the Wah Wah Mountains, which extend to the south. To the south are the Blue Mountains. Looking down from the peak to the southwest, you can see the remains of Newhouse.

At the peak there are communications towers and two hang glider launch sites (Level IV skills required). The visitors book for the launch area seems to have more entries from four-wheelers than from hang gliders.

Current Road Information
BLM Cedar City Field Office
176 East D.L. Sargent Drive
Cedar City, UT 84720
(435) 586-2401

Maps References
BLM Wah Wah Mountains South, Wah Wah Mountains North
USGS 1:24,000 Milford NW, High Rock, Frisco Peak
1:100,000 Wah Wah Mountains South, Wah Wah Mountains North
Maptech CD-ROM: King Canyon/Fillmore
Utah Atlas & Gazetteer, p. 25
Utah Travel Council #4

Route Directions
▼ 0.0   On Utah 21, 7.8 miles west of Milford, turn northwest on unmarked graded dirt road and zero trip meter.

		GPS: N 38°26.36' W 113°09.16'
▼ 0.1	SO	Cross through wash.
▼ 0.3	BL	Track on right.
▼ 4.4	SO	Tracks on right and left.
▼ 6.2	SO	Track on left is Northern #33: Frisco Ghost Town Trail.
		GPS: N 38°30.23' W 113°14.27'
▼ 6.5	SO	Track on right.
▼ 6.6	SO	Track on right.
▼ 7.0	SO	Track on left.
▼ 7.3	SO	Tracks on right and left.
▼ 8.0	SO	Track on left.
▼ 8.7	SO	Tailings pile of Golden Reef Mine on left. Track on left to remains of mine, then track on right to Horse Spring. Zero trip meter.
		GPS: N 38°31.75' W 113°15.80'
▼ 0.0		Continue into Sawmill Canyon; trail follows along Sawmill Canyon Creek.
▼ 0.5	SO	Track on left.
▼ 2.2	SO	Track on left.
▼ 2.8	SO	Communications dish on right.
▼ 2.9	SO	Start of loop around communications towers on peak.
▼ 3.0	SO	Hang gliding launch pads on left and best views from the peak.
		GPS: N 38°31.20' W 113°17.14'
▼ 3.1		End of loop. Retrace your steps back to Utah 21.
		GPS: N 38°31.19' W 113°17.11'

The launch pad for hang gliders

Frisco Ghost Town Trail

Starting Point:	Utah 21 at Frisco Historical Marker
Finishing Point:	Northern #32: Frisco Peak Trail
Total Mileage:	5.9 miles
Unpaved Mileage:	5.7 miles
Driving Time:	1 hour
Elevation Range:	5,100–6,800 feet
Usually Open:	Year-round
Difficulty Rating:	3
Scenic Rating:	8
Remoteness Rating:	+1

Special Attractions

■ Frisco ghost town, cemetery, and charcoal kilns.

History

Frisco, in its heyday, was one of the wildest and richest silver towns in Utah. Nestled in the shadow of the San Francisco Mountains, Frisco came into being in 1875 after two old prospectors, Jim Ryan and Sam Hawkes, accidentally stumbled upon a vein of nearly pure silver. According to one story, each day as the two miners left their camp, they passed by the

Mining remains in the Frisco region

same boulder. One day, Jim took a pick to it and discovered silver. They called their stake the Bonanza and almost immediately sold it for the princely sum of $25,000. The new owners found that the initial vein was the tip of the iceberg and that it contained a very high grade of silver ore. It was so soft it could be pared with a knife, and since the parings curled like an animal horn, they called their mine the Horn Silver.

It wasn't long before the silver lode changed hands again. The new owners were thrilled to receive the incredible sum of $5 million for the mine from Jay Cooke. However, Cooke didn't make out badly either, for he eventually unearthed $50 million in ore in what was perhaps the world's richest, single silver vein.

Frisco became the quintessential mining boomtown, and when Cooke managed to get a railroad into Frisco from Milford in 1880, the town really took off. At its peak in the early 1880s, Frisco had 23 saloons, a newspaper, boardinghouses, and stores—as well as brothels, gambling halls, and even opium dens—and a population of 6,000. The biggest problem was getting water to the town (which may have accounted for the number of saloons!). At times water was trucked in and sold door to door by the bucketful. The town was riotous, and murders were a daily occurrence. When a new, no-nonsense sheriff was brought in from Nevada to try to bring order to the town, he killed six people during his first night on the job—just to show he meant business!

The Horn Silver Mine was joined by other mines in the district. The Carbonate, Comet, Grand Republic, Hoodoo, and others sprang up, many with their own mills and charcoal kilns to run them. They never made as much money as the Horn Silver, but they turned a fair profit.

Frisco came to an end

Old kilns at Frisco ghost town

almost as abruptly as it began. The Horn Silver was a somewhat unconventional open pit mine, 900 feet deep, that was supported by a tangle of wooden supports; the miners had been so eager to get the silver that safety had been almost a secondary consideration. Inevitably, the mine caved in. In 1885, as the miners were changing shifts, the mine abruptly subsided. Amazingly, no one was hurt or killed, but the tons of rock crashing into the pit made the ground shake so violently that windows broke 20 miles away in Milford.

Frisco didn't last long after that. A few families stayed to pick over the mines, and a new shaft was drilled down to the silver vein. The town eventually produced another $20 million from the new shaft, but by 1920, the town was deserted. Some of the outlying mines are sporadically worked today. Frisco is one of Utah's most intact ghost towns, and it is a fascinating place to visit. Its beehive charcoal kilns are listed in the National Register of Historic Places, and a number of its faded downtown buildings still creak and whisper under the blazing sun.

Description

This trail begins with a short, 1.6-mile tour through Frisco and its mining remains. In this section, the graded dirt road is suitable for passenger cars, and the short distances between features make it ideal for a walking tour. However, some areas of Frisco are posted as private property; respect the signs and view these areas from the boundary.

The tour starts from the historical marker and picnic shelter on Utah 21, 13.5 miles west of Milford. Turn west on the graded gravel road. After 0.4 miles, the tour passes within 0.1 miles of the old overgrown cemetery, with its many iron-fenced graves and others marked only by small mounds. The numerous graves of infants and small children are testimony to the hard life and conditions in these mining camps. The trail then passes within 0.2 miles of the King David Mine. The famous Horn Silver Mine is south of the King David. This is private property; please don't go past the gate. The tour then passes by the charcoal kilns, which have been fenced. These are in generally good condition; note the slightly different shapes of each kiln and the blackened stone inside.

The trail then passes around some of the standing cabins, plus the old vault, before returning to paved Utah 21. The old railroad grade that ran through the town can be seen in several places. Hiking around some of the old ruins reveals more old mines and mining remnants. Take care, though—there are many sharp objects to catch a tire and many holes buried in the grass. Other small, and often overgrown, trails lead to some of the outlying mines on the hillsides.

Once the trail returns to Utah 21, you drive 0.2 miles before turning north along an unmarked dirt track. The trail from this point warrants a 3 rating and should only be driven by SUVs. In addition, the trails are unmarked, so follow the directions carefully; there are many dead ends and it is easy to make a wrong turn. The route winds along in the juniper and sagebrush, climbing slightly over the southern flank of San Francisco Peak, before reaching the Carbonate Mine, one of the outlying silver mines from Frisco. There are some old buildings and mining equipment here, but the area is posted against trespassers. From the Carbonate Mine, the trail is narrow and passes by the fenced Coyote Springs, and then it ends at Northern #32: Frisco Peak Trail.

Current Road Information
BLM Cedar City Field Office
176 East D.L. Sargent Drive
Cedar City, UT 84720
(435) 586-2401

Map References
BLM   Wah Wah Mountains South, Wah Wah Mountains North
USGS 1:24,000   Frisco, High Rock, Milford NW
1:100,000 Wah Wah Mountains South, Wah Wah Mountains North
Maptech CD-ROM: King Canyon/ Fillmore
Utah Atlas & Gazetteer, p. 25

Route Directions

▼ 0.0		On Utah 21, 13.5 miles west of Milford, turn west onto graded gravel road at historical marker for Frisco and zero trip meter.
1.6 ▲		Trail ends at historical marker for Frisco on paved Utah 21. Turn left for Milford.
GPS: N 38°27.17' W 113°15.54'		
▼ 0.4	TR	Straight goes 0.1 miles to cemetery.
1.2 ▲	TL	T-intersection. Track on right goes 0.1 miles to cemetery.
GPS: N 38°27.06' W 113°15.99'		
▼ 0.6	SO	Intersection. Track on left goes 0.2 miles to King David Mine. Immediately after intersection, bear right at fork.
1.0 ▲	SO	Track on right immediately before intersection. Track on right at intersection goes 0.2 miles to King David Mine.
GPS: N 38°27.20' W 113°15.99'		
▼ 0.9	SO	Intersection.
0.7 ▲	SO	Intersection.
▼ 1.0	SO	Track on right.
0.6 ▲	SO	Track on left.
▼ 1.1	SO	Track on left goes 0.1 miles to charcoal kilns.
0.5 ▲	SO	Track on right goes 0.1 miles to charcoal kilns.
▼ 1.2	TR	Intersection. Remnants of town buildings scattered around crossroads.
0.4 ▲	TL	Intersection. Remnants of town buildings scattered around crossroads.
GPS: N 38°27.61' W 113°15.55'		
▼ 1.3	SO	Intersection.
0.3 ▲	SO	Intersection.

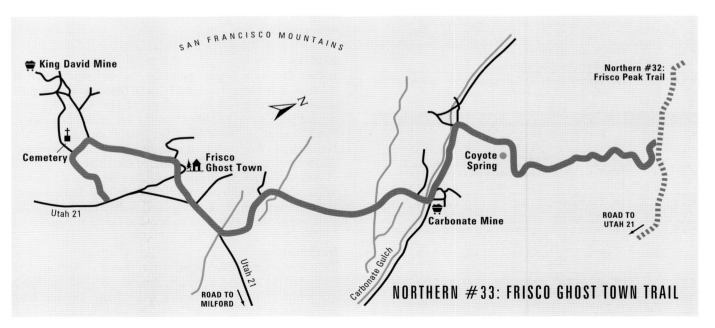

NORTHERN #33: FRISCO GHOST TOWN TRAIL

▼ 1.5		BR	Swing right toward paved road.
	0.1 ▲	SO	Track on right.
▼ 1.6		TL	Join paved Utah 21 and zero trip meter.
	0.0 ▲		Continue west on gravel track.
		GPS: N 38°27.60' W 113°15.13'	
▼ 0.0			Continue northeast on Utah 21.
	1.9 ▲	TR	Turn onto gravel track and zero trip meter.
▼ 0.2		TL	Turn onto gravel track opposite mile marker 63.
	1.7 ▲	TR	Turn onto paved Utah 21.
		GPS: N 38°27.67' W 113°14.93'	
▼ 0.4		SO	Sheds and corral on left, then track on left.
	1.5 ▲	SO	Track on right, then sheds and corral on right.
▼ 0.5		SO	Track on left.
	1.4 ▲	SO	Track on right.
▼ 0.6		SO	Cross through wash.
	1.3 ▲	SO	Cross through wash.
▼ 0.7		SO	Cross through wash.
	1.2 ▲	SO	Cross through wash.
▼ 1.0		SO	Cross through wash, then five-way junction. Go straight, heading northeast (two tracks on left, one on right).
	0.9 ▲	SO	Five-way junction. Go straight, heading southwest (two tracks on right, one on left), then cross through wash.
		GPS: N 38°28.26' W 113°14.83'	
▼ 1.1		SO	Track on left.
	0.8 ▲	SO	Track on right.
▼ 1.2		SO	Cross through wash.
	0.7 ▲	SO	Cross through wash.
▼ 1.3		BL	Faint track on right.
	0.6 ▲	BR	Faint track on left.
▼ 1.4		SO	Cross through wash.
	0.5 ▲	SO	Cross through wash.
▼ 1.5		SO	Enter wash.
	0.4 ▲	SO	Exit wash.
▼ 1.6		SO	Exit wash.
	0.3 ▲	SO	Enter wash.
▼ 1.7		SO	Cross through wash, then pass underneath powerlines. Track on left underneath powerlines.
	0.2 ▲	SO	Pass underneath powerlines. Track on right underneath powerlines, then cross through wash.
▼ 1.8		SO	Cross through wash.
	0.1 ▲	SO	Cross through wash.
▼ 1.9		TL	T-intersection at Carbonate Mine (private property). Zero trip meter.
	0.0 ▲		Continue on smaller trail.
		GPS: N 38°28.89' W 113°14.58'	
▼ 0.0			Continue on better-used trail.
	2.4 ▲	TR	Turn right opposite the Carbonate Mine and zero trip meter.
▼ 0.1		SO	Track on right to Carbonate Mine.
	2.3 ▲	SO	Track on left to Carbonate Mine (private property).
▼ 0.4		SO	Track on right.
	2.0 ▲	SO	Track on left.
▼ 0.5		TR	Track on left, then turn right on track to right, climbing away from wash.
	1.9 ▲	BL	Bear left at track on left, followed by track on right. Follow along wash.
▼ 0.6		BR	Small track on left, then bear right, followed by track on right.
	1.8 ▲	BL	Track on left, then bear left at second track.

▼ 0.9		SO	Coyote Spring on right, fenced spring and cattle tank.
	1.5 ▲	SO	Coyote Spring on left, fenced spring and cattle tank.
		GPS: N 38°29.42' W 113°14.70'	
▼ 1.7		SO	Cross through wash.
	0.7 ▲	SO	Cross through wash.
▼ 1.9		SO	Cross through wash.
	0.5 ▲	SO	Cross through wash.
▼ 2.4			Trail ends at T-intersection with Northern #32: Frisco Peak Trail. Turn left for Frisco Peak, right for Utah 21.
	0.0 ▲		On Northern #32: Frisco Peak Trail, 6.2 miles from Utah 21, turn west onto small, unsigned trail and zero trip meter.
		GPS: N 38°30.23' W 113°14.27'	

NORTHERN REGION TRAIL #34

Soldier Pass Trail

Starting Point:	Utah 21 at Milford
Finishing Point:	Utah 21 near Beaver
Total Mileage:	17.8 miles
Unpaved Mileage:	17.1 miles
Driving Time:	1 hour
Elevation Range:	4,900–7,388
Usually Open:	April to November
Difficulty Rating:	1
Scenic Rating:	8
Remoteness Rating:	+0

Special Attractions

- Easy scenic pass through the Mineral Mountains.
- Access to rockhounding areas.
- Granite Peak.

History

Soldier Pass is the highest point on the road that goes from Adamsville to Milford over the Mineral Mountains. The route was first blazed by soldiers stationed at Fort Cameron, who needed faster access to Milford on the other side of the range. Fort Cameron was positioned two miles from Beaver on the North Beaver River. The fort was one of many built to protect the citizens during the Indian Wars of the 1850s.

Adamsville, on the east side of the pass was originally called Wales, after the Welsh people who had settled it. It was known as the Beaver Iron Works for a while, before finally changing its name to Adamsville after its founder, David B. Adams.

Description

This very pretty drive connects the towns of Milford and Beaver via the 7,388-foot Soldier Pass, which winds through a gap in the Mineral Mountains, a range that is 28 miles long and averages 5 miles wide. Its major peak is Granite Peak

The start of the trail looking toward the Mineral Mountains

(9,578 feet) in the center of the range. The Mineral Mountains also contain deposits of obsidian, a dark natural glass formed from cooling lava; the Indians of southwestern Utah used obsidian as an important trade item.

The trail starts at Milford, on the southeast edge of town, and heads east. The road is graded gravel for the first part as it makes a beeline for the Mineral Mountains. At the base of the mountains, a graded road goes to a popular rockhounding spot, the Rock Corral Recreation Area.

From here, the road standard drops slightly and it becomes narrower and slightly sandy. However, in good weather and with a little care, you can easily traverse this road in a passenger vehicle. The road climbs and winds around the western side of Soldier Pass. To the south is Harkley Mountain, and to the north is Granite Peak, which you can't miss: It has prominent bare granite slabs, standing rocks and boulders, and exposed slopes. In June 1996, a massive wildfire destroyed over 600 acres of vegetation on both sides of Soldier Pass.

From the top of the pass, there are good views into the Parowan Valley to the east and over to the lower end of the Sevier Plateau and the Tushar Mountains. Looking west you can see the Escalante Desert and the Wah Wah Mountains.

The eastern side of the pass drops swiftly, following Cherry Creek to run out along the sage-covered benches into the Parowan Valley. You intersect with Northern #35: Lincoln Mine Trail, and another track leads north to the Blue Star Mine.

The trail ends on Utah 21, 4 miles west of Beaver.

Current Road Information

BLM Cedar City Field Office
176 East D.L. Sargent Drive
Cedar City, UT 84720
(435) 586-2401

Map References

BLM	Beaver, Wah Wah Mts. South
USGS	1:24,000 Milford, Ranch Canyon, Cave Canyon, Adamsville, Beaver
	1:100,000 Beaver, Wah Wah Mts. South

Maptech CD-ROM: King Canyon/Fillmore
Utah Atlas & Gazetteer, pp. 25, 26
Utah Travel Council #4

Route Directions

▼ 0.0			On Utah 21 just southeast of Milford, 0.9 miles southeast of railroad crossing, turn east on paved road at BLM sign for Rock Corral Recreation Area and zero trip meter.
	5.2 ▲		Trail ends on Utah 21, 1 mile southeast of downtown Milford. Turn right for Milford, left for Minersville.
GPS: N 38°22.79' W 113°00.10'			
▼ 0.3		SO	Cattle guard.
	4.9 ▲	SO	Cattle guard.
▼ 0.7		TR	Intersection. Road is now graded gravel.
	4.5 ▲	TL	Intersection. Road is now paved.
GPS: N 38°22.97' W 112°59.44'			
▼ 1.4		SO	Track on right.
	3.8 ▲	SO	Track on left.
▼ 1.7		SO	Tracks on right and left.
	3.5 ▲	SO	Tracks on left and right.
▼ 2.7		SO	Track on left.
	2.5 ▲	SO	Track on right.
▼ 3.2		SO	Track on left.
	2.0 ▲	SO	Track on right.
▼ 5.2		SO	Three-way junction; take middle road. Track on left goes to Rock Corral Recreation Area. Zero trip meter
	0.0 ▲		Continue straight toward Milford.
GPS: N 38°21.59' W 112°54.51'			
▼ 0.0			Trail climbs toward Soldier Pass.
	4.7 ▲	SO	Three-way junction. Continue straight. Track

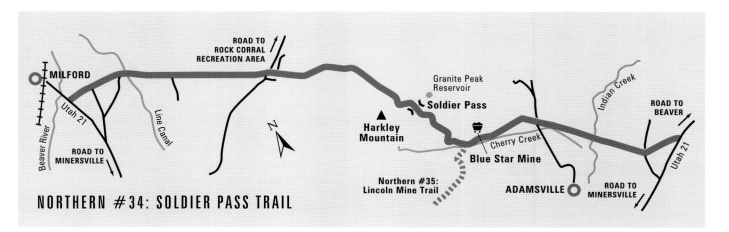

NORTHERN #34: SOLDIER PASS TRAIL

			on right goes to Rock Corral Recreation Area. Zero trip meter.
▼ 0.3		SO	Track on left.
	4.4 ▲	SO	Track on right.
▼ 0.9		SO	Track on left, then track on right.
	3.8 ▲	SO	Track on left, then track on right.
▼ 1.4		SO	Track on right, cattle guard, then second track on right.
	3.3 ▲	SO	Track on left, cattle guard, then second track on left.
▼ 2.1		SO	Track on left. Harkley Mountain on right, Granite Peak on left.
	2.6 ▲	SO	Track on right. Harkley Mountain on left, Granite Peak on right.
▼ 2.4		SO	Track on left.
	2.3 ▲	SO	Track on right.
▼ 2.6		SO	Track on right, then cross through wash.
	2.1 ▲	SO	Cross through wash, then track on left.
▼ 2.8		SO	Tracks on right and left.
	1.9 ▲	SO	Tracks on left and right.
▼ 3.5		SO	Track on left.
	1.2 ▲	SO	Track on right.
▼ 4.0		SO	Track on right.
	0.7 ▲	SO	Track on left.
▼ 4.7		SO	Cattle guard. Top of Soldier Pass. Zero trip meter.
	0.0 ▲		Trail descends from pass.

GPS: N 38°19.35′ W 112°50.73′

▼ 0.0			Trail descends from pass.
	1.9 ▲	SO	Cattle guard. Top of Soldier Pass. Zero trip meter.
▼ 0.8		SO	Track on right.
	1.1 ▲	SO	Track on left.
▼ 1.2		SO	Track on left.
	0.7 ▲	SO	Track on right.
▼ 1.6		SO	Two tracks on right.
	0.3 ▲	SO	Two tracks on left.
▼ 1.9		SO	Track on right is Northern #35: Lincoln Mine Trail. Zero trip meter.
	0.0 ▲		Continue along Cherry Creek.

GPS: N 38°18.14′ W 112°49.90′

▼ 0.0			Continue along Cherry Creek.
	1.9 ▲	SO	Track on left is Northern #35: Lincoln Mine Trail. Zero trip meter.
▼ 0.5		SO	Cross through wash. Track on left to Blue Star Mine.
	1.4 ▲	SO	Track on right to Blue Star Mine. Cross through wash.

GPS: N 38°18.10′ W 112°49.32′

▼ 0.7		SO	Cattle guard.
	1.2 ▲	SO	Cattle guard.
▼ 0.9		SO	Track on right, then track on left.
	1.0 ▲	SO	Track on right, then track on left.
▼ 1.1		SO	Tracks on left and right.
	0.8 ▲	SO	Tracks on right and left.
▼ 1.6		SO	Track on left.
	0.3 ▲	SO	Track on right.
▼ 1.9		BL	Graded dirt road on right to Adamsville. Cross cattle guard and zero trip meter.
	0.0 ▲		Continue toward Soldier Pass.

GPS: N 38°18.07′ W 112°47.78′

▼ 0.0			Continue southeast.
	4.1 ▲	SO	Cross cattle guard, then graded dirt road on left to Adamsville. Zero trip meter.
▼ 0.1		SO	Track on left.

	4.0 ▲	SO	Track on right.
▼ 1.4		SO	Tracks on left and right.
	2.7 ▲	SO	Tracks on right and left.
▼ 2.3		SO	Track on right.
	1.8 ▲	SO	Track on left.
▼ 2.6		SO	Track on right.
	1.5 ▲	SO	Track on left.
▼ 3.1		SO	Track on right, then track on left on left-hand bend.
	1.0 ▲	SO	Track on right on right-hand bend, then track on left.
▼ 3.5		SO	Track on right.
	0.6 ▲	SO	Track on left.
▼ 4.1			Cattle guard, then trail ends at Utah 21. Turn left for Beaver, right for Minersville.
	0.0 ▲		On Utah 21, 4.1 miles west of I-15 underpass at Beaver, turn west on unmarked, gravel Soldier Pass Road. Zero trip meter.

GPS: N 38°16.32′ W 112°43.72′

NORTHERN REGION TRAIL #35

Lincoln Mine Trail

Starting Point:	**Northern #34: Soldier Pass Trail**
Finishing Point:	**Utah 21, 0.2 miles east of Minersville**
Total Mileage:	**8.7 miles**
Unpaved Mileage:	**8.7 miles**
Driving Time:	**1 hour**
Elevation Range:	**5,300–7,200 feet**
Usually Open:	**May to November**
Difficulty Rating:	**5**
Scenic Rating:	**7**
Remoteness Rating:	**+0**

Special Attractions

■ The old Spanish Lincoln Mine.
■ Moderately challenging 4WD trail.

History

The Lincoln Mine is perhaps one of the oldest mines in America. It was first chiseled out by the Spanish, possibly in the 18th century, and it was later discovered in 1858 by Mormon bishop James Rollins, who found old Spanish hand tools and workings inside the ancient Mineral Mountains shaft.

At the time, the Mormons were mobilizing for a possible war with the United States—Colonel Johnston's army had camped outside Salt Lake City in 1857 under orders of President Buchanan—and they desperately needed lead to make bullets. Thinking the old Spanish vein was a lead mine, the Mormons began making bullets from the ore—only to discover that the bullets were nearly pure silver!

A small mining camp sprang up around the mines, which were named after Bishop Rollins, and the population grew to

Start of the unmaintained section of the trail during a surprise snow storm

around 500. The Mormons built smelters to process the ore, but they were inefficient. Although they succeeded in extracting some of the lead, the more profitable silver ended up in the slag heaps. Miners from the nearby settlement of Minersville built more efficient smelters and were the first to successfully extract silver.

Many gentile miners were drawn to the promising area, and they quickly outnumbered the Mormons. They voted to change the mine's name to the Lincoln Mine in honor of President Abraham Lincoln. However, in 1900, the Lincoln Mine was bought by a British company, and like the owners of the Kimberly Mine in the nearby Tushar Mountains the overseas company soon went bankrupt because of inefficiencies. Many of the smaller outlying mines flooded, and the Lincoln Mine was abandoned. However, more recently, rising silver prices have led some to try extracting the ore once again from this historic mine.

Description

This short, challenging trail connects Northern #34: Soldier Pass Trail to Utah 21 across the southern tip of the Mineral Mountains. For the most part, the trail is not maintained, but it is well used by vehicles. The fine granitic road surface gives way periodically to several large washouts—to negociate these requires good clearance and wheel articulation. Most stock SUVs will be able to handle it, though extra long vehicles or those with running boards or lower clearance may find it difficult. A short section on the northern side of the saddle can be brushy and might cause some minor scratches on your vehicle.

The trail leaves Soldier Pass Trail at an unmarked junction 1.9 miles southeast of Soldier Pass. It immediately crosses through Cherry Creek and winds up toward the saddle. From the saddle it descends, passing Dripping Spring and then fording Lincoln Gulch. After you pass the Lincoln Mine, the trail standard improves, changing to roughly graded dirt. You pass other mine workings and a pretty reed-fringed dam fed from a spring, before descending to finish on Utah 21.

Other turns around the Lincoln Mine lead to other mines, such as the Harriet and the Creole Mines and many old shafts and adits.

Current Road Information

BLM Cedar City Field Office
176 East D.L. Sargent Drive
Cedar City, UT 84720
(435) 586-2401

Map References

BLM Beaver
USGS 1:24,000 Minersville, Cave Canyon, Adamsville
1:100,000 Beaver
Maptech CD-ROM: King Canyon/Fillmore
Utah Atlas & Gazetteer, pp. 25, 26
Utah Travel Council #4 (incomplete)

Route Directions

▼ 0.0   On Northern #34: Soldier Pass Trail, 1.9 miles southeast of Soldier Pass, turn southwest on unmarked small dirt track and zero trip meter. Trail immediately crosses through Cherry Creek.

NORTHERN #35: LINCOLN MINE TRAIL

Lincoln Mine

Creole Mine

Dripping Spring

ROAD TO MILFORD

Northern #34: Soldier Pass Trail

Utah 21

MINERSVILLE

YELLOW MOUNTAIN

MINERAL MOUNTAINS

Granite Spring

5.5 ▲		Cross through Cherry Creek, then trail ends at Northern #34: Soldier Pass Trail. Turn left for Milford, right for Beaver.

GPS: N 38°18.14′ W 112°49.90′

▼ 0.1	SO	Granite Spring on left.
5.4 ▲	SO	Granite Spring on right.
▼ 0.4	SO	Small track on right on left-hand bend.
5.1 ▲	SO	Small track on left on right-hand bend.

GPS: N 38°17.90′ W 112°50.15′

▼ 1.0	SO	Track on right.
4.5 ▲	SO	Track on left.
▼ 1.5	BR	Track on left.
4.0 ▲	BL	Track on right.
▼ 1.6	SO	Track on left.
3.9 ▲	SO	Track on right.
▼ 2.1	SO	Saddle. Trail descends.
3.4 ▲	SO	Saddle. Trail descends.

GPS: N 38°17.11′ W 112°51.32′

▼ 3.1	SO	Dripping Spring on right.
2.4 ▲	SO	Dripping Spring on left.

GPS: N 38°16.55′ W 112°52.07′

▼ 4.0	BR	Old track on left; this is a washed-out creek crossing.
1.5 ▲	SO	Old track on right.
▼ 4.1	SO	Cross over wash.
1.4 ▲	SO	Cross over wash; previous crossings are washed out.

GPS: N 38°16.62′ W 112°52.90′

▼ 4.3	SO	Track on right.
1.2 ▲	BR	Track on left.

GPS: N 38°16.56′ W 112°53.00′

▼ 4.4	SO	Track on right.
1.1 ▲	SO	Track on left.
▼ 4.6	BL	Two tracks on right to Lincoln Mine. Trail is now roughly graded.
0.9 ▲	BR	Two tracks on left to Lincoln Mine. Trail is now ungraded dirt.
▼ 4.8	SO	Tracks on right and left.
0.7 ▲	SO	Tracks on right and left.
▼ 4.9	SO	Track on left.

0.6 ▲	BL	Track on right.

GPS: N 38°16.12′ W 112°53.23′

▼ 5.0	SO	Track on right.
0.5 ▲	SO	Track on left.
▼ 5.1	SO	Track on right.
0.4 ▲	SO	Track on left.
▼ 5.2	SO	Track on right.
0.3 ▲	SO	Track on left.
▼ 5.3	SO	Cross through creek.
0.2 ▲	SO	Cross through creek.
▼ 5.4	SO	Track on left before dam.
0.1 ▲	SO	Track on right.
▼ 5.5	SO	Track on left to dam, then second track on left. Zero trip meter.
0.0 ▲		Continue north.

GPS: N 38°15.82′ W 112°53.70′

▼ 0.0		Continue south.
3.2 ▲	SO	Track on right, then second track on right to dam. Zero trip meter.
▼ 0.1	BL	Track on right to mining remains, then second track on right.
3.1 ▲	SO	Track on left, then second track on left to mining remains.
▼ 0.3	SO	Tracks on right and left.
2.9 ▲	SO	Tracks on right and left.

GPS: N 38°15.55′ W 112°53.96′

▼ 1.1	SO	Track on left.
2.1 ▲	SO	Track on right.
▼ 1.9	SO	Track on left.
1.3 ▲	SO	Track on right.
▼ 3.0	SO	Track on right to gauging station.
0.2 ▲	BR	Track on left to gauging station.
▼ 3.1	SO	Tracks on right and left.
0.1 ▲	SO	Tracks on right and left.
▼ 3.2		Cattle guard, then trail ends at Utah 21, 0.2 miles east of Minersville.
0.0 ▲		On Utah 21, 0.2 miles east of Minersville, turn north onto graded dirt road, cross cattle guard, and zero trip meter.

GPS: N 38°13.16′ W 112°55.12′

The Central Region

Trails in the Central Region

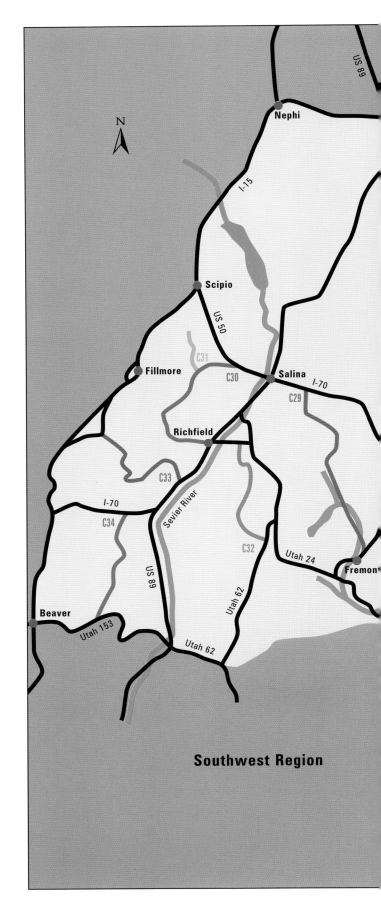

Southwest Region

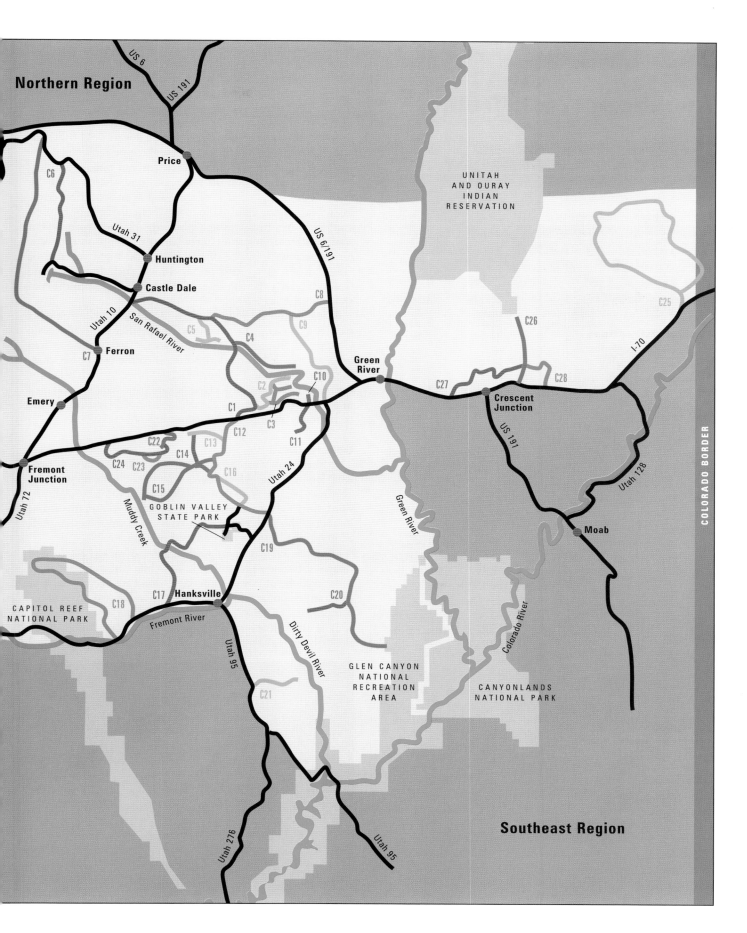

Northern Region

US 6
US 191

C6
Price

Utah 31
Huntington
Castle Dale
C8
US 6/191

UNITAH
AND OURAY
INDIAN
RESERVATION

C5
C9
C4
C25
C26
Utah 10
San Rafael River
Ferron
C7
I-70
Green River
C10
C28
C2
C27
C1
Crescent Junction
Emery
C3
US 191
C22
C12
C11
C13
C14
Fremont Junction
C24 C23
C16
Utah 24
Utah 128
C15
Utah 72
GOBLIN VALLEY STATE PARK
Muddy Creek
Moab

Green River

C19
CAPITOL REEF NATIONAL PARK
C18
C17 Hanksville
C20
Fremont River
Colorado River
GLEN CANYON NATIONAL RECREATION AREA
CANYONLANDS NATIONAL PARK
Utah 95
Dirty Devil River

C21

Utah 276
Utah 95

Southeast Region

COLORADO BORDER

Buckhorn Wash Trail

Starting Point:	I-70, exit 129
Finishing Point:	Utah 10, 1.5 miles north of Castle Dale
Total Mileage:	43 miles
Unpaved Mileage:	43 miles
Driving Time:	2 hours
Elevation Range:	5,100–6,700 feet
Usually Open:	Year-round
Difficulty Rating:	1
Scenic Rating:	8
Remoteness Rating:	+0

Special Attractions

- Panels of petroglyphs.
- Dinosaur footprint.
- Matt Warner rock inscription.
- Easy, scenic canyon road that serves as the backbone to other trails.

History

Originally, parts of the Buckhorn Wash Trail were established by the Denver and Rio Grande Western Railroad Company in an effort to build a railroad from Green River to Huntington. When the grade of the planned route exceeded early calculations, the incomplete railroad was abandoned. Many sections of the rail bed have since been washed out by floods.

In 1921, oil companies decided to expand the road by building it through Buckhorn Wash. The Civilian Conservation Corps (CCC) rebuilt the road in the 1930s and also improved the nearby road to Temple Mountain. In 1938, the CCC also constructed the Swinging Bridge across the San Rafael River.

Matt Warner's misspelled inscription

While the trail is only a little over a hundred years old, the actual path of Buckhorn Wash has a history that dates back millions of years. Originally, Buckhorn Wash was cut by an early path of the Huntington River, which has since been diverted to its present location. Inside the Navaho sandstone canyon of Buckhorn Wash, the rock walls contain evidence of ancient sand dunes, indicating the region once had a climate comparable to the Sahara Desert. Dinosaurs once roamed central Utah and many traces of their existence can still be found. Along this trail, you can see a dinosaur footprint measuring 12 by 14 inches embedded in sandstone.

About 10,000 years ago, long after that dinosaur left its mark, humans began to inhabit the area. Evidence of this early Desert Archaic culture is literally written on the canyon walls in the form of pictographs and petroglyphs. Scholars refer to this ancient rock art as Barrier Canyon style. These early peoples survived as hunters and gatherers, and it is thought that rock art may have played some role in their spiritual beliefs. Over the years, these pictures have suffered damage from people shooting at or writing on them. However, the BLM has undertaken major repairs to preserve these pictures.

A couple of miles from the rock art, you can see a different kind of inscription on the rocks: one scratched out by outlaw Matt Warner. One of the Wild West's toughest criminals, Warner was involved in many robberies both by himself and with his friend Butch Cassidy. He eventually went straight after serving three and a half years in prison and went on to become a justice of the peace and night marshal of Green River. The inscription, which includes his name (spelled "Mat") and the date, is a short distance from the trail about 30 feet up a cliff.

Cassidy himself rode through Buckhorn Draw with his partner Elza Lay while making an escape after the 1897 Castle Gate payroll robbery. As the story goes, Cassidy and Lay had long since passed through the area when the two posses chasing them met up in Buckhorn Draw. Mistaking each other for the band of outlaws, both posses opened fire. No one was killed in the exchange, but the delay allowed Cassidy and Lay to ride comfortably ahead to their hideout in Robbers Roost.

Description

The Buckhorn Wash Trail begins as a well-maintained, two-lane country road, which leaves I-70 at exit 129, and remains an easy, 1-rated trail throughout; navigation is straightforward. Initially, it parallels I-70 through the typical pinyon and juniper of this high desert country. In good weather, this graded gravel road can be traveled by a passenger car.

The trail crosses many washes, most of which are crossed by paved fords to prevent erosion. While you must negotiate some sections of powder-fine sand, none are deep enough to pose any serious problem. After 5.6 miles, you reach the turnoff for Central #2: Swasey's Leap Trail.

The trail passes by the appropriately named Bottleneck Peak about three-quarters of a mile before the San Rafael

View of Buckhorn Wash Trail south of the San Rafael River

River crossing, where it then runs along Buckhorn Wash. After the bridge, Central #4: Mexican Bend Trail branches off to the right. Cottonwoods dot the area as the wash meanders along the canyon floor. Sheer cliffs, broken by many little side canyons, rise above both sides of the trail.

While in the wash, the trail approaches a panel of Indian rock art, Matt Warner's inscription, and finally the dinosaur footprint. The footprint can be especially difficult to find; it sits about 20 feet above the road on a rock ledge off to the right. There is a small area to the left where you can park your vehicle and hike up to the ancient footprint. There is no defined trail that leads to the footprint, so it may take a bit of looking around to find it. If it seems to elude you, look under a sandstone slab. People often use a rock to cover the track in order to protect it from vandalism and weathering. After you remove the rock to see the footprint, please be sure to replace it before you leave.

As the trail continues along the wash, it intersects with Central #8: Green River Cutoff and Central #5: Wedge Overlook Trail. The latter trail overlooks what is known as Utah's "Little Grand Canyon" and offers a view a thousand feet above the wandering San Rafael River. The trail reaches Utah 10 in another 12.4 miles, the last 5 or 6 miles of which run mainly through saltbrush and shaley mounds.

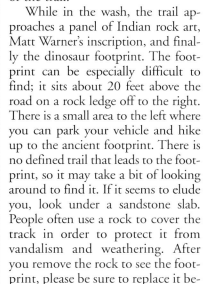

The dinosaur footprint (below) and its location on the trail (above)

Current Road Information

Emery County Road Department
120 West Highway 29
Castle Dale, UT 84513
(435) 381-2550

BLM Price Field Office
125 South 600 West
Price, UT 84501
(435) 636-3600

Map References

BLM San Rafael Desert, Huntington
USGS 1:24,000 The Wickiup, Drowned Hole Draw, Bottleneck Peak, Bob Hill Knoll, Buckhorn Reservoir, Hadden Holes
1:100,000 San Rafael Desert, Huntington
Maptech CD-ROM: Central/San Rafael
Trails Illustrated, #712
Utah Atlas & Gazetteer, pp. 39, 38
Utah Travel Council #5; #3
Other: Recreation Map of the San Rafael Swell and San Rafael Desert

Route Directions

▼ 0.0   On the north side of I-70, exit 129, zero trip meter at the intersection of the exit/entry ramps and the underpass road. Cross cattle guard and proceed along frontage road. Follow BLM sign to Buckhorn Draw, Wedge Overlook, and Buckhorn Pictograph Panel.
5.6 ▲   Turn left at signed intersection to Green River and Salina. Trail ends at I-70; turn east for Green River, west for Salina.

GPS: N 38°52.88′ W 110°39.52′

▼ 0.8   SO   Track on left.
4.8 ▲   SO   Track on right.

▼ 0.9   SO   Track on left.
4.7 ▲   SO   Track on right.

▼ 2.0   SO   Cattle guard.
3.5 ▲   SO   Cattle guard.

▼ 3.4   SO   Track on right to I-70 underpass to Jerry's Flat.
2.1 ▲   SO   Track on left.

GPS: N 38°53.98′ W 110°36.28′

▼ 5.0   SO   Fenced sinkhole on right.
0.5 ▲   SO   Fenced sinkhole on left.

▼ 5.6   SO   Track on right is Central #2: Swasey's Leap Trail. Zero trip meter.
0.0 ▲   Continue straight.

GPS: N 38°55.76′ W 110°36.03′

▼ 0.0   Continue along main road.
13.3 ▲   SO   Track on left is Central #2: Swasey's Leap Trail. Zero trip meter.

▼ 4.1   SO   Cross through wash.
9.2 ▲   SO   Cross through wash.

▼ 4.9   SO   Cross ford through wash.
8.4 ▲   SO   Cross ford through wash.

▼ 5.9   SO   Track on left reconnects with trail in 0.3 miles.
7.4 ▲   SO   Track on right.

▼ 7.2   SO   Track on left.
6.1 ▲   SO   Track on right reconnects with trail in 0.3 miles.

▼ 9.4   SO   Track on left.
3.8 ▲   SO   Track on right.

▼ 10.5   SO   Cross ford through wash.
2.7 ▲   SO   Cross ford through wash.

▼ 11.8   SO   Cross ford through wash.
1.4 ▲   SO   Cross ford through wash.

▼ 12.2   SO   Cross ford through wash.
1.1 ▲   SO   Cross ford through wash.

▼ 12.4   SO   Bottleneck Peak on left.
0.9 ▲   SO   Bottleneck Peak on right.

▼ 12.8   SO   Track on left marked "corrals." This relatively short track splits and ends at nonmotorized trails.
0.5 ▲   SO   Track on right marked "corrals." This relatively short track splits and ends at nonmotorized trails.

▼ 13.1   SO   Intersection. San Rafael Bridge Campground on right.
0.2 ▲   SO   Intersection. San Rafael Bridge Campground on left.

GPS: N 39°04.77′ W 110°40.00′

▼ 13.2   SO   Swinging bridge on left. Cross San Rafael River on contemporary bridge.
0.1 ▲   SO   Swinging bridge on right. Cross San Rafael River on contemporary bridge.

▼ 13.3   SO   Track on right is Central #4: Mexican Bend Trail. Zero trip meter and cross cattle guard.
0.0 ▲   Continue along main road.

GPS: N 39°04.98′ W 110°39.81′

CENTRAL #1: BUCKHORN WASH TRAIL

▼ 0.0			Continue along main road.
	9.4 ▲	SO	Cross cattle guard and zero trip meter. Track on left is Central #4: Mexican Bend Trail.
▼ 1.0		SO	Cross ford.
	8.3 ▲	SO	Cross ford.
▼ 1.9		SO	Cross ford.
	7.4 ▲	SO	Cross ford.
▼ 3.7		SO	Large panel of Indian art nearly 100 feet long; parking area on right.
	5.6 ▲	SO	Large panel of Indian art nearly 100 feet long; parking area on left.
		GPS: N 39°07.43' W 110°41.59'	
▼ 4.6		SO	Public toilet on right.
	4.7 ▲	SO	Public toilet on left.
▼ 4.8		SO	Cross ford.
	4.5 ▲	SO	Cross ford.
▼ 5.2		SO	Matt Warner inscription on right. Look for small unmarked pull-off area. Inscription is about 30 feet high on a rock wall to the right.
	4.2 ▲	SO	Matt Warner inscription on left. Look for small unmarked pull-off area. Inscription is about 30 feet high on a rock wall to the left.
		GPS: N 39°08.24' W 110°42.16'	
▼ 5.7		SO	Cross bridge.
	3.6 ▲	SO	Cross bridge.
▼ 6.3		SO	Cross ford.
	3.1 ▲	SO	Cross ford.

▼ 7.0		SO	Pull-off area on right and trail to pictographs. Then cross cattle guard.
	2.3 ▲	SO	Cross cattle guard. Then pull-off area on left and trail to pictographs.
		GPS: N 39°09.29' W 110°43.19'	
▼ 7.7		SO	Cross ford.
	1.7 ▲	SO	Cross ford.
▼ 7.8		SO	Pull-off area on left and trail to dinosaur footprint on right.
	1.6 ▲	SO	Pull-off area on right and trail to dinosaur footprint on left.
		GPS: N 39°09.61' W 110°43.71'	
▼ 9.0		SO	Cross bridge.
	0.4 ▲	SO	Cross bridge.
▼ 9.4		TL	T-intersection. Central #8: Green River Cutoff on right. Zero trip meter and turn left.
	0.0 ▲		Continue south.
		GPS: N 39°10.27' W 110°45.03'	
▼ 0.0			Continue northwest toward Castle Dale.
	2.3 ▲	TR	Intersection. Central #8: Green River Cutoff is straight ahead. Zero trip meter and turn right.
▼ 0.1		SO	Cross bridge.
	2.2 ▲	SO	Cross bridge.
▼ 0.3		SO	Track on left is cutoff to Central #5: Wedge Overlook Trail in 1.5 miles.
	2.0 ▲	SO	Track on left is cutoff to Central #5: Wedge Overlook Trail in 1.5 miles.

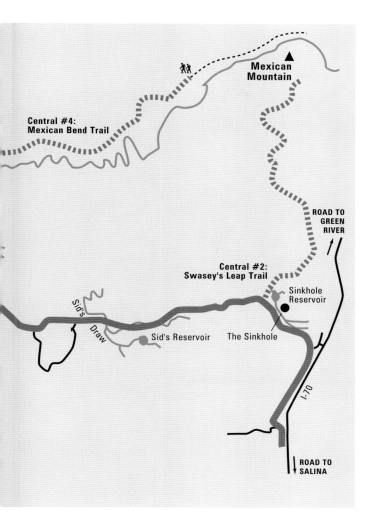

▼ 7.4		**SO**	Cross over bridge.
5.0 ▲		SO	Cross over bridge.
▼ 7.8		**SO**	Track on left.
4.6 ▲		SO	Track on right.
▼ 8.6		**SO**	Track on right to overlook on Oil Well Dome.
3.9 ▲		SO	Track on left to overlook on Oil Well Dome.
▼ 8.7		**SO**	Cattle guard.
3.8 ▲		SO	Cattle guard.
▼ 9.4		**SO**	Track on left.
3.1 ▲		SO	Track on right.
▼ 12.4			Cattle guard, then trail ends at Utah 10, 1.5 miles north of Castle Dale.
0.0 ▲			On Utah 10, 1.5 miles north of Castle Dale, turn east onto dirt road. Sign reads, "Buckhorn Draw, Wedge Overlook & Pictograph Panel." Zero trip meter and cross cattle guard. Pass corrals on right.

GPS: N 39°13.23' W 110°59.80'

CENTRAL REGION TRAIL #2

Swasey's Leap Trail

Starting Point:	**Central #1: Buckhorn Wash Trail, 5.6 miles from I-70**
Finishing Point:	**Fence line at walking trail to site of Swasey's Leap**
Total Mileage:	**12.5 miles**
Unpaved Mileage:	**12.5 miles**
Driving Time:	**1 hour**
Elevation Range:	**5,000–6,600 feet**
Usually Open:	**Year-round**
Difficulty Rating:	**3**
Scenic Rating:	**8**
Remoteness Rating:	**+0**

Special Attractions

- Scenic, seldom-used 4WD spur trail.
- The legend of Swasey's Leap.

History

In the late 1800s, the Swasey family (sometimes spelled Swazy) settled in central Utah on a homestead near Cottonwood Creek. The Swasey boys soon became known throughout the region as good-natured, hard-working cowboys. One day, while working near Black Box with his brother, Sid Swasey came upon a 14-foot-wide canyon that fell nearly 60 feet to the river below. His brother wagered him 75 head of cattle he couldn't jump across the chasm on his saddle-

A view of the old stock bridge built to straddle the span of Swasey's Leap

---

	GPS: N 39°10.08' W 110°45.27'		
▼ 2.2		**SO**	Buckhorn Well on left (small cinder-block building and tank).
0.1 ▲		SO	Buckhorn Well on right (small cinder-block building and tank).
▼ 2.3		**SO**	Buckhorn Flat Well Junction. Central #5: Wedge Overlook Trail on left; right goes to Cleveland. Zero trip meter.
0.0 ▲			Continue southeast.
	GPS: N 39°10.54' W 110°47.40'		
▼ 0.0			Continue toward Castle Dale.
12.4 ▲		SO	Buckhorn Flat Well Junction. Central #5: Wedge Overlook Trail on right; left goes to Cleveland. Zero trip meter.
▼ 0.7		**SO**	Cattle guard.
11.7 ▲		SO	Cattle guard.
▼ 2.4		**SO**	Multiple tracks on left.
10.0 ▲		SO	Multiple tracks on right.
▼ 3.9		**SO**	Track on right.
8.5 ▲		SO	Track on left.
▼ 4.4		**SO**	Track on left.
8.0 ▲		SO	Track on right.
▼ 6.4		**SO**	Cross ford through wash.
6.0 ▲		SO	Cross ford through wash.
▼ 7.2		**SO**	Track on right, then cattle guard.
5.2 ▲		SO	Cattle guard, then track on left.
	GPS: N 39°13.02' W 110°54.67'		

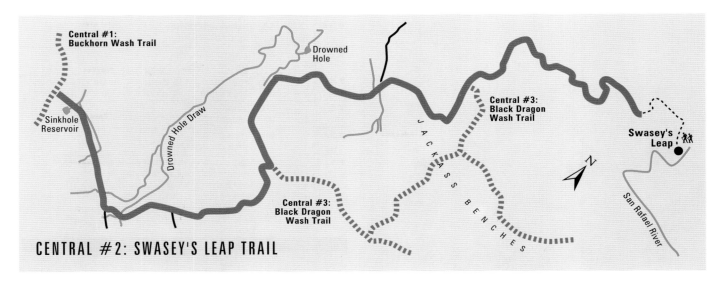

CENTRAL #2: SWASEY'S LEAP TRAIL

horse. As the story goes, Sid made the jump and won the bet.

Soon after, a bridge of cottonwood logs was constructed across the canyon to enable herds of grazing sheep to cross.

Description

As the Swasey's Leap Trail branches off of Central #1: Buckhorn Wash Trail, the road becomes noticeably less traveled and soon rates a difficulty level of 2. The spur trail crosses flat-topped mesas and grasslands of pinyon and juniper. In many places the classic terrain looks plucked from any number of Hollywood Westerns.

After 4.4 miles, you reach the intersection of Central #3: Black Dragon Wash Trail, which is a loop trail that intersects again at the 8.8-mile mark. At this point, the road deteriorates and becomes a 3-rated trail until it finishes at the boundary of the Mexican Mountain Study Area.

At the end of the driving trail, you can hike another 2 miles

A view of the San Rafael River near Swasey's Leap

along a very scenic, old 4WD trail to the area where Sid Swasey jumped his horse across the canyon. The entire area offers spectacular views of the San Rafael River and the rock formations around the edge of the canyon.

Current Road Information

Emery County Road Department
120 West Highway 29
Castle Dale, UT 84513
(435) 381-2550

BLM Price Field Office
125 South 600 West
Price, UT 84501
(435) 636-3600

Map References

BLM   San Rafael Desert
USGS   1:24,000   Drowned Hole Draw, Spotted Wolf Canyon
          1:100,000 San Rafael Desert
Maptech CD-ROM: Central/San Rafael
Trails Illustrated, #712
Utah Atlas & Gazetteer, p. 39
Utah Travel Council #5
Other: Recreation Map of the San Rafael Swell and San
       Rafael Desert

Route Directions

▼ 0.0			On Central #1: Buckhorn Wash Trail, 5.6 miles from I-70, zero trip meter and proceed east along side road.
	8.8 ▲		Trail ends at Central #1: Buckhorn Wash Trail; turn left for I-70, right for Castle Dale.
		GPS: N 38°55.76′ W 110°36.03′	
▼ 1.1		SO	Cross through wash, then cattle guard.
	7.7 ▲	SO	Cattle guard, then cross through wash.
▼ 1.5		SO	Cross through wash.
	7.3 ▲	SO	Cross through wash.
▼ 1.7		BL	Road forks. Right loops back to Buckhorn Wash Trail and to an I-70 underpass with access to Jerry's Flat.
	7.1 ▲	BR	Track on left is alternate loop to

Buckhorn Wash Trail.

	GPS: N 38°55.01' W 110°34.47'		
▼ 1.9	SO	Cross through wash.	
6.9 ▲	SO	Cross through wash.	
▼ 4.4	BL	Road forks. Straight is Central #3: Black Dragon Wash Trail.	
4.4 ▲	BR	Track on left is Central #3: Black Dragon Wash Trail.	
	GPS: N 38°56.45' W 110°32.95'		
▼ 7.2	SO	Cross through wash, then track on left.	
1.6 ▲	SO	Track on right, then cross through wash.	
	GPS: N 38°57.87' W 110°32.39'		
▼ 8.3	SO	Cross through wash.	
0.4 ▲	SO	Cross through wash.	
▼ 8.8	BL	Fork in road. Sign on left reads, "Swazys Leap and Lower Black Box." Right is Central #3: Black Dragon Wash Trail. Zero trip meter.	
0.0 ▲	BR	Proceed southwest along the main road to Central #1: Buckhorn Wash Trail. Track on left is Central #3: Black Dragon Wash. Zero trip meter.	
	GPS: N 38°58.43' W 110°31.41'		
▼ 0.0		Continue toward Swasey's Leap.	
▼ 3.5	SO	Wilderness study area boundary.	
	GPS: N 38°59.35' W 110°29.36'		
▼ 3.7		End of trail. Park and hike along old, 2-mile 4WD trail to Swasey's Leap.	
	GPS: N 38°59.29' W 110°29.17'		

CENTRAL REGION TRAIL #3

Black Dragon Wash Trail

Starting Point:	**Central #2: Swasey's Leap Trail**
Finishing Point:	**Central #2: Swasey's Leap Trail**
Total Mileage:	**12.5 miles**
Unpaved Mileage:	**12.5 miles**
Driving Time:	**1 hour**
Elevation Range:	**4,700–6,200 feet**
Usually Open:	**Year-round**
Difficulty Rating:	**5**
Scenic Rating:	**8**
Remoteness Rating:	**+1**

Special Attractions

- Provides an alternative return route from Swasey's Leap.
- Scenic views from Jackass Benches.
- Varied scenery along a moderately difficult 4WD road.
- Little-used, mostly unmapped trail in the midst of many heavily used backcountry roads.

Description

The Black Dragon Wash Trail is a loop trail off of Central #2: Swasey's Leap Trail, which connects to Central #1: Buckhorn Wash Trail. The majority of the trail does not appear on any map as it runs through some very scenic but seldom traveled

A view of the early part of the spur along Black Dragon Wash

countryside. The main attractions of this trail are its two spurs, which branch off to dead-ends.

After 1.1 miles, you reach the first spur trail, which crosses Jackass Benches and offers some spectacular views into the canyon to the north. The striking, distinct sedimentary layers of the canyon wall clearly display the geological history of the area, moving from the yellow-browns at the bottom to the vivid reds at the top. The road surface along this spur is varied; there are a few rocky patches and a couple of short sections of shelf road.

After 2.3 miles, you reach the second spur trail, which penetrates into the high-walled canyon along Black Dragon Wash. Ironically enough, while this part of the trail feels extremely remote, at times you are no more than a quarter mile from the traffic barreling down I-70. The road here becomes somewhat more difficult as it encounters a couple of narrow, off-camber sections of shelf road. A narrow ridgeline that can be quite rocky may also present you with a bit of a challenge. The road eventually connects through, in about 2 miles, to the end of Central #10: Black Dragon Pictographs Trail; however it becomes badly washed out and is more easily hiked than driven. This part of the road goes beyond the difficulty level of this book, but skilled drivers with short-wheelbase SUVs might be able to pass through.

Once you return from the second spur trail, the main trail continues another 2.2 miles to the junction with Central #2: Swasey's Leap Trail.

Current Road Information

Emery County Road Department
120 West Highway 29
Castle Dale, UT 84513
(435) 381-2550

BLM Price Field Office
125 South 600 West
Price, UT 84501
(435) 636-3600

A view of the spur trail along Black Dragon Wash

Map References

BLM San Rafael Desert (incomplete)
USGS 1:24,000 Drowned Hole Draw, Spotted Wolf
Canyon (incomplete)
1:100,000 San Rafael Desert (incomplete)
Maptech CD-ROM: Central/San Rafael
Trails Illustrated, #712
Utah Atlas & Gazetteer, p. 39
Utah Travel Council #5 (incomplete)
Other: Recreation Map of the San Rafael Swell and San
Rafael Desert

Route Directions

▼ 0.0   On Central #2: Swasey's Leap Trail, 8.8 miles from Central #1: Buckhorn Wash Trail, zero trip meter and take right fork.

GPS: N 38°58.43' W 110°31.41'

▼ 1.1   **BL**   Fork in road. Sign reads, "Sulphur Springs (6) Road ends (4)." Turn left on spur road to Sulphur Springs and Jackass Benches. Zero trip meter.

GPS: N 38°57.83' W 110°30.90'

First Leg: Jackass Benches

▼ 0.0		Head east on spur trail along Jackass Benches.
▼ 0.3	SO	Cross through wash.
▼ 1.4	SO	Cross large wash.
▼ 2.6	SO	Cross through wash

GPS: N 38°57.86' W 110°28.61'

▼ 3.5	UT	Road ends at closure fence. Wilderness study area ahead. Return to main trail and zero trip meter.

GPS: N 38°57.96' W 110°27.76'

Continuation of Main Trail

▼ 0.0	TL	Continue south.
▼ 1.2	TL	Intersection. Turn left on spur road to Black Dragon Wash. Zero trip meter.

GPS: N 38°56.84' W 110°31.08'

Second Leg: Black Dragon Wash

▼ 0.0		Continue east.
▼ 1.3	SO	Cross through wash.
▼ 2.4	SO	Stone pillar formation up on left.
▼ 4.3	SO	Cross Black Dragon Wash, then a tight squeeze against the canyon wall.

GPS: N 38°56.78' W 110°27.40'

▼ 4.5	UT	Spur trail finishes. Track is badly washed out ahead. Return to main trail and zero trip meter.

GPS: N 38°56.84' W 110°27.24'

Continuation Of Main Trail

▼ 0.0	SO	Continue west.
▼ 2.2		End at Central #2: Swasey's Leap Trail, 4.4 miles from Central #1: Buckhorn Wash Trail. Turn left for I-70, right for Swasey's Leap.

GPS: N 38°56.45' W 110°32.95'

CENTRAL #3: BLACK DRAGON WASH TRAIL

N

JACKASS BENCHES

Sulphur Springs

San Rafael River

Central #2: Swasey's Leap Trail

Black Dragon Reservoir

Black Dragon Wash

I-70

Central #10: Black Dragon Pictographs Trail

Mexican Bend Trail

Starting Point:	**Central #1: Buckhorn Wash Trail, near Swinging Bridge**
Finishing Point:	**Gate to the wilderness study area**
Total Mileage:	**13.8 miles**
Unpaved Mileage:	**13.8 miles**
Driving Time:	**1.25 hours (one-way)**
Elevation Range:	**4,700–5,500 feet**
Usually Open:	**Year-round**
Difficulty Rating:	**2**
Scenic Rating:	**8**
Remoteness Rating:	**+0**

Special Attractions
■ Numerous good camping spots beside the San Rafael River.
■ Short hike to the Black Box section of the San Rafael River; a deep, narrow sandstone canyon.

History
By the mid to late 1800s, the trail past Mexican Bend was already well known to sheepherders and early explorers. Outlaws also passed through the area on their long rides between hideouts, cattle rustling ventures, and bank robberies.

In the spring of 1897, Mexican Bend was the scene of a daylong standoff between the outlaw Joe Walker and a posse led by Sheriff Ebeneezer Tuttle. Walker was camped at Mexican Bend with three horses recently stolen from the Whitmore Ranch. The posse had been following him from Price, past Cleveland, and into the San Rafael Swell. As the lawmen came around Mexican Bend, they saw Walker cooking dinner. The lawmen immediately took cover behind large boulders, and the standoff began. As Sheriff Tuttle and two of his men tried to gain a closer position on the outlaw, they were met with a volley from Walker. The shots hit the barrel of one man's gun and struck the sheriff in the thigh. Unable to move, Tuttle had to wait until the next day for his posse to rescue him, as the men were too frightened of the dead-shot outlaw to risk leaving their cover. Walker escaped in the night, and Tuttle and his men went back to Price to lick their wounds.

Joe Walker is thought to have returned to Mexican Bend a month later. In April 1897, Butch Cassidy and Elza Lay were making their getaway from the Castle Gate payroll robbery to their hideout in Robbers Roost by way of Buckhorn Draw and Mexican Bend. Walker supposedly assisted them by cutting the telephone and telegraph lines to Price and providing them with a fresh group of horses.

Description
From Central #1: Buckhorn Wash Trail, the Mexican Bend Trail breaks off to the southeast and follows the Mexican Mountain Road. This spur trail is relatively easy, though a cou-

A view of the distinct layers of sedimentary rock vividly exposed in this area

ple of rocky sections and wash crossings warrant the 2 rating.

At the start, there are a number of buff-colored sandstone mounds, which are often used by mountain bikers. Past these, the terrain changes to iron red cliffs, which dominate the scenery on the north side for the bulk of the trail.

A drive on the Mexican Bend Trail is considerably enhanced by an exploration of its many side roads. A few lead to overlooks of the San Rafael, while others wind down to the river. There are also a number of extremely good backcountry camping spots located about a quarter mile off the main trail. Some of the most scenic can be found tucked away among the cottonwood trees that flourish on the banks of the river.

One of the area's most striking geological features is Black Box, where the San Rafael River has cut an extremely narrow canyon through the oldest exposed rock in Emery County. The lower portion is made up of 250-million-year-old Coconino sandstone. The trail intersects with a short, 500-yard hiking trail to the Upper Black Box Overlook. From here you can approach the edge and look down about 60 feet into this narrow and intimidating canyon, where the river silently makes its way through the darkness below.

The Mexican Bend Trail comes to an end at a gate marking the boundary of the Mexican Mountain Wilderness Study Area. While it was once possible to drive all the way out to the bend, today the trail is closed to vehicles before Mexican Mountain. From the gate, you can hike about 1.5 miles farther along the old 4WD trail to the start of Mexican Bend. As you continue around the bend, the valley widens, allowing easy access to the river. The hiking trail passes among many cottonwoods around Mexican Bend, and it's not hard to imagine that they once provided a shady retreat for outlaws and their horses as they passed through this otherwise rugged terrain.

A view down into the Black Box

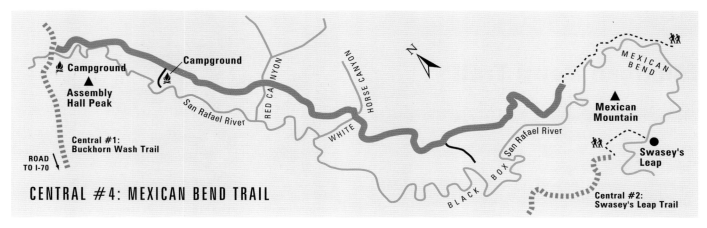

CENTRAL #4: MEXICAN BEND TRAIL

Current Road Information

Emery County Road Department
120 West Highway 29
Castle Dale, UT 84513
(435) 381-2550

BLM Price Field Office
125 South 600 West
Price, UT 84501
(435) 636-3600

Map References

BLM Huntington
USGS 1:24,000 Bottleneck Peak, Devils Hole, Mexican Mt.
1:100,000 Huntington
Maptech CD-ROM: Central/San Rafael
Trails Illustrated, #712
Utah Atlas & Gazetteer, p. 39
Utah Travel Council #3
Other: Recreation Map of the San Rafael Swell and San
Rafael Desert

Route Directions

▼ 0.0		On Central #1: Buckhorn Wash Trail, 18.9 miles from I-70 and just past the swinging bridge over the San Rafael River, zero trip meter and proceed southeast along Mexican Mountain Road. Pass message board.
GPS: N 39°04.98' W 109°39.81'		
▼ 0.5	SO	Track on right.
▼ 0.6	SO	Track on right.
▼ 0.8	SO	Track on right to river.
GPS: N 39°04.78' W 110°39.18'		
▼ 1.3	SO	Track on left to corral.
▼ 1.5	SO	Track on right.
▼ 1.6	SO	Track on left; track on right to overlook.
GPS: N 39°04.55' W 110°38.39'		
▼ 1.8	SO	Track on right, then wash; track on right.
GPS: N 39°04.41' W 110°38.28'		
▼ 2.0	SO	Track on right to river, campsites, and picnic spots among the cottonwoods.
▼ 2.2	SO	Track on right.
▼ 2.4	SO	Track on right.
GPS: N 39°04.07' W 110°37.73'		
▼ 2.7	SO	Track on right to numerous campsites along the river among the cottonwoods.

GPS: N 39°03.48' W 110°37.62'		
▼ 3.0	SO	Cross through wash.
▼ 3.9	SO	Cross through wash.
▼ 4.3	BL	Track on right to a nice river overlook.
GPS: N 39°02.97' W 110°36.36'		
▼ 4.9	SO	Track on left.
▼ 5.0	SO	Cross through Red Canyon Wash.
▼ 6.1	SO	Cross through wash.
▼ 7.1	SO	Cross through gate and close behind you.
GPS: N 39°01.93' W 110°34.07'		
▼ 7.4	SO	Cross through White Horse Canyon Wash.
▼ 8.1	SO	Upper Black Box Trail on right.
GPS: N 39°01.33' W 110°33.87'		
▼ 9.0	SO	Cross through wash.
▼ 9.6	SO	Track on right.
GPS: N 39°00.73' W 110°32.80'		
▼ 10.1	SO	Upper Black Box Trail on right.
GPS: N 39°00.79' W 110°32.26'		
▼ 11.4	SO	Cross through gate.
▼ 13.8		Trail ends at gate into wilderness study area. From here, hike down along the old 4WD trail 1.5 miles to Mexican Bend.
GPS: N 39°00.92' W 110°29.31'		

CENTRAL REGION TRAIL #5

Wedge Overlook Trail

Starting Point:	Central #1: Buckhorn Wash Trail, 2.3
	miles from junction with Central #8:
	Green River Cutoff
Finishing Point:	Wedge Overlook and rim spur trails
Total Mileage:	10.3 miles
Unpaved Mileage:	10.3 miles
Driving Time:	1 hour
Elevation Range:	5,700–6,200 feet
Usually Open:	Year-round
Difficulty Rating:	1
Scenic Rating:	9
Remoteness Rating:	+0

One of the spur trails along the north rim of the Little Grand Canyon

Special Attractions
- Many spectacular viewpoints into the Little Grand Canyon of the San Rafael River.
- Easy spur trail off of Central #1: Buckhorn Wash Trail.
- Many backcountry campsites.

Description
Initially, the Wedge Overlook Trail runs along a wide, maintained gravel road that travels through rolling brush country. After half a mile, a track on the right offers riverside access to Fuller Bottom Draw. The main trail continues toward the Wedge, and after a couple of miles the countryside turns into pleasant grassland dotted with pinyon and juniper. The trail offers numerous side roads that lead to plenty of good camping spots.

At the Wedge Overlook, take some time to admire Utah's "Little Grand Canyon." This remarkable canyon has been formed over the centuries as the San Rafael River has cut its way through the sandstone of the San Rafael Swell. It's this dramatic, stunning overlook that warrants the trail's scenic 9 rating.

From the overlook, spur trails lead in either direction along the canyon rim. At times, a large number of side trails leading to camping spots and overlooks can make navigation difficult. Just stick to the main trail as you wind through the pinyon and juniper around the rim.

Of the two rim roads, the shorter, eastern one is easier; a passenger car could easily drive it in good weather. A peninsula, jutting out above the canyon, marks the end of the eastern side trail. This is an excellent spot to view the river on either side below or to park your SUV for a dramatic photo.

The "parking spot" at the end of the

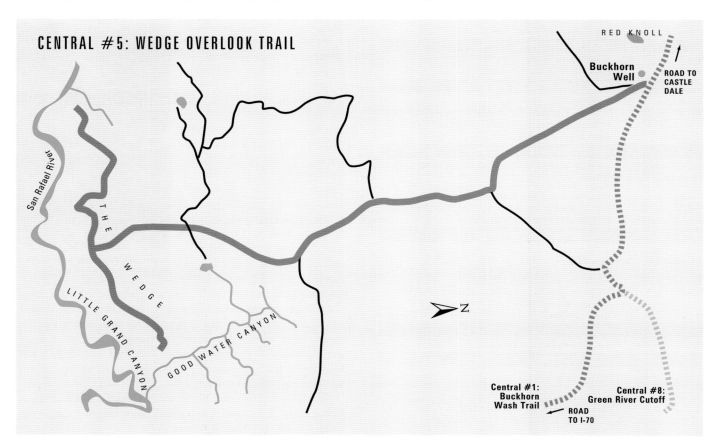

CENTRAL #5: WEDGE OVERLOOK TRAIL

Current Road Information

Emery County Road Department
120 West Highway 29
Castle Dale, UT 84513
(435) 381-2550

BLM Price Field Office
125 South 600 West
Price, UT 84501
(435) 636-3600

Map References

BLM   Huntington
USGS   1:24,000   Buckhorn Reservoir, Sids Mt., Bottleneck
Peak
1:100,000   Huntington
Maptech CD-ROM: Central/San Rafael
Trails Illustrated, #712
Utah Atlas & Gazetteer, pp. 39, 38
Utah Travel Council #3
Other: Recreation Map of the San Rafael Swell and San
Rafael Desert

Route Directions

▼ 0.0		From Central #1: Buckhorn Wash Trail, 2.3 miles from junction with Central #8: Green River Cutoff, zero trip meter and turn toward signs for Wedge Overlook.
	GPS: N 39°10.54' W 110°47.40'	
▼ 0.5	BL	Track on right to Fuller Bottom Draw.
▼ 1.0	SO	Cattle guard.
▼ 2.1	SO	Information board and track on left to Central #1: Buckhorn Wash Trail.
	GPS: N 39°09.10' W 110°46.16'	
▼ 3.2	SO	Track on right.
▼ 4.3	SO	Information board and track on left.
	GPS: N 39°07.40' W 110°45.39'	
▼ 5.4	SO	Tracks on left and right.
▼ 6.5	TR	Wedge Overlook. Spur tracks along rim to left and right. Zero trip meter and follow 4WD trail west around the rim.
	GPS: N 39°05.58' W 110°45.48'	

First Leg: Western Rim

▼ 0.0		Proceed along the western rim.
▼ 2.3		End of western rim trail. Return to main overlook and zero trip meter.
	GPS: N 39°05.43' W 110°47.12'	

Second Leg: Eastern Rim

▼ 0.0		Continue along the eastern rim.
▼ 0.7	SO	Large rock peninsula sticking out above the San Rafael Valley provides a great photo opportunity.
	GPS: N 39°05.72' W 110°44.89'	
▼ 1.5		End of the eastern rim spur.
	GPS: N 39°06.41' W 110°44.44'	

Upper Joe's Valley Trail

Starting Point:	Utah 29, 18.8 miles from Utah 10
Finishing Point:	Utah 31
Total Mileage:	20.7 miles
Unpaved Mileage:	20.2 miles
Driving Time:	2.5 hours
Elevation Range:	7,000–9,100 feet
Usually Open:	May to November
Difficulty Rating:	4
Scenic Rating:	9
Remoteness Rating:	+0

Special Attractions

- Joe's Valley Reservoir.
- Scenic Potters Ponds.

History

On June 20, 1963, the president of the Emery Water Conservancy District, O. Eugene Johansen, addressed the crowd gathered for the groundbreaking ceremony of the Joe's Valley Dam. In his speech, Johansen recalled the three Joes who make up a significant portion of the history of Joe's Valley.

As the story goes, "Indian Joe" was rescued by white settlers when they saw him being mistreated by other Indians. In return for their kindness, Joe joined up with the settlers and helped them in many ways. The second Joe was Joe Swasey, an early settler in Emery County who built many of the first fences in the region. Swasey and his family were among the first white explorers of the San Rafael Swell, and they left their names on many features in the area (such as Rods Valley, Swasey's Leap, and Swasey's Cabin). Finally, "Pete Joe," or Peter Johansen, was an early settler

A potentially muddy spot likely to be rutted even when dry

who acquired most of the local ranchlands in the early 1900s.

Any one of these Joes could be the man behind the valley's name, though no one seems to know for sure exactly how or when the valley was discovered and named. However, it must have been one of the earlier known sites in the region, since it was one of the only named features on an 1878 map created by explorer John Wesley Powell.

In 1933, Joe's Valley was the site of a Civilian Conservation Corps camp. A group of young men looking for work during the Great Depression made their way to the valley to work on a re-

Potters Ponds

forestation project. Thirty years later, the 195-foot-high, 740-foot-wide Joe's Valley Dam was completed, which also created Joe's Valley Reservoir. The reservoir is currently the largest lake in Emery County and is a favorite among fishing enthusiasts, as it holds some of the largest brown and rainbow trout in the region.

Description

Upper Joe's Valley Trail begins on Utah 29, 18.8 miles northwest of its junction with Utah 10 in Castle Dale (coming from the south, you can take a shortcut on Utah 57 to Utah 29). As the paved Utah 29 approaches Joe's Valley Reservoir, it runs through some very picturesque country. The reservoir supports quite a lot of wildlife, ranging from birds and small animals to the illusive mountain lion. The reservoir also serves as a recreational area for fishing, hiking, and camping. As well as the developed campgrounds at Joe's Valley Reservoir, there are a number of backcountry camping spots along the trail, especially from Potters Ponds to the end of the trail. During hunting season, the upper reaches of the trail near Miller Flat Reservoir are particularly popular.

Upper Joe's Valley Trail begins at FR 014, a dirt road that heads north from the reservoir off Utah 29. The maintained, two-lane country road climbs gently, passing through the mature cottonwoods along Joe's Creek.

As you enter some very scenic ranchland, the road narrows to a wide, easy single lane that's still graded and maintained. After 2.1 miles, you turn onto FR 038 and pass a number of good places to camp or picnic beside the creek. Lined with cottonwoods, aspen, and juniper, the trail makes a perfect autumn drive to view the colors, which change to a radiant gold.

After the bridge at the 4.3-mile mark, the road gets a bit more rough and warrants a 2 rating. Some points are quite rocky or rutted; be careful in wet weather as the ruts turn into deep mud holes. Some intermittent rocky sections can become considerably more difficult than the rest of the trail and rate a difficulty level of 4.

After about 8 miles from the start, there is a 2-mile stretch of very pretty ponds. The final and largest ones—known as Potters Ponds—come near the 10-mile mark and can be reached by driving a short side trail to the left.

After Potters Ponds, the trail reconnects with FR 014 and continues north 10.8 miles to end at Utah 31. From here, continue

north 4.8 miles to reach Central #7: Skyline Drive, or continue north 9.5 miles to reach Northern #14: Clear Creek Ridge Trail.

Current Road Information

Manti-La Sal National Forest
Ferron Ranger District
98 South State Street
Ferron, UT 84523
(435) 384-2372

Map References

BLM Manti, Nephi
USFS Manti-La Sal National Forest: Ferron Ranger District
USGS 1:24,000 Joes Valley Reservoir, South Tent Mt., Rilda Canyon, Candland Mt., Huntington Reservoir
1:100,000 Manti, Nephi
Maptech CD-ROM: Central/San Rafael
Utah Atlas & Gazetteer, pp. 38, 46
Utah Travel Council #3

Route Directions

▼ 0.0			On Utah 29, 18.8 miles from Utah 10 at Joe's Valley Reservoir, turn north onto FR 014 and zero trip meter.
	7.1 ▲		End at Utah 29 near Joe's Valley Reservoir; turn southeast for Utah 10.
GPS: N 39°19.21' W 111°16.53'			
▼ 0.5		SO	Cross cattle guard onto unpaved road.
	6.6 ▲	SO	Cross cattle guard onto paved road.
▼ 1.1		BR	Fork in road. FR 172 on left.
	6.0 ▲	SO	FR 172 enters on right.
▼ 1.2		SO	Cattle guard.
	5.9 ▲	SO	Cattle guard.
▼ 1.8		SO	Cattle guard.
	5.3 ▲	SO	Cattle guard.
▼ 2.1		BL	Fork in road; bear left onto FR 038. Upper Joe's Valley is straight ahead.
	5.0 ▲	BR	Road is now FR 014.
GPS: N 39°20.89' W 111°16.17'			
▼ 4.0		SO	Cross over bridge, then FR 174 on left.
	3.1 ▲	SO	FR 174 on right, then cross over bridge.
GPS: N 39°22.28' W 111°16.37'			
▼ 4.3		SO	Cross bridge.
	2.8 ▲	SO	Cross bridge.
▼ 4.9		SO	FR 2211 to Black Canyon on left.
	2.2 ▲	SO	FR 2211 to Black Canyon on right.
GPS: N 39°23.07' W 111°16.49'			
▼ 7.0		SO	Cross over creek.
	0.1 ▲	SO	Cross over creek.
▼ 7.1		SO	Cross bridge and zero trip meter.
	0.0 ▲		Continue along main trail.
GPS: N 39°24.94' W 111°16.16'			
▼ 0.0			Continue along main trail.
	2.8 ▲	SO	Cross bridge and zero trip meter.
▼ 1.6		BR	Track on left.
	1.2 ▲	BL	Track on right.
GPS: N 39°26.12' W 111°15.87'			
▼ 1.6-2.1		SO	Pass series of ponds on right.
	0.6-1.1 ▲	SO	Pass ponds on left.
▼ 2.3		SO	Cross under high-voltage transmission wires.
	0.5 ▲	SO	Cross under high-voltage transmission wires.

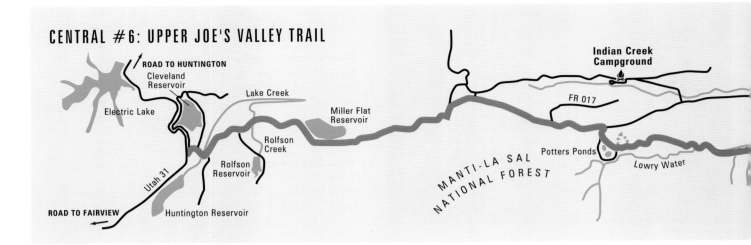

CENTRAL #6: UPPER JOE'S VALLEY TRAIL

▼ 2.3	SO	Track on left.	
0.4 ▲	SO	Track on right.	
▼ 2.8	TR	Intersection. Turn left on FR 271 to reach Potters Ponds in 0.5 miles. Zero trip meter and turn right to continue on main route.	
0.0 ▲		Continue along main route.	

GPS: N 39°26.92' W 111°15.46'

▼ 0.0		Continue along main route.	
8.4 ▲	TL	Intersection. To follow main route, turn left and zero trip meter. Straight is FR 271, which leads to Potters Ponds in 0.5 miles.	
▼ 0.1	TL	T-intersection. Turn left on FR 014 to continue on main trail. Turn right to return to Joe's Reservoir.	
8.3 ▲	TR	Turn right onto FR 038. FR 014 continues straight ahead to Joe's Reservoir.	

GPS: N 39°26.90' W 111°15.37'

▼ 1.5	SO	FR 017 on right.	
6.9 ▲	SO	FR 017 on left.	
▼ 2.2	SO	FR 020 on left.	
6.2 ▲	SO	FR 020 on right.	
▼ 3.7	SO	Track to corral on right.	
4.6 ▲	SO	Track to corral on left.	
▼ 4.0	SO	Cross over Paradise Creek.	
4.4 ▲	SO	Cross over Paradise Creek.	
▼ 4.2	BR	FR 193 on left.	
4.1 ▲	BL	FR 193 on right.	
▼ 4.9	SO	Road on right.	
3.4 ▲	BR	Road on left.	

GPS: N 39°30.69' W 111°14.91'

▼ 5.1	SO	Tracks left and right are FR 231.	
3.3 ▲	SO	Tracks left and right are FR 231.	
▼ 6.3	SO	Cross bridge.	
2.0 ▲	SO	Cross bridge.	
▼ 6.6	SO	Track on right to Miller Flat Reservoir.	
1.7 ▲	SO	Track on left to Miller Flat Reservoir.	
▼ 7.6	SO	FR 201 on right.	
0.8 ▲	SO	FR 201 on left.	
▼ 8.2	SO	Cross bridge.	
0.1 ▲	SO	Cross bridge.	
▼ 8.4	SO	On right is left fork of Huntington Creek National Recreation Trail and public toilets. Zero trip meter.	
0.0 ▲		Continue south.	

GPS: N 39°33.29' W 111°14.46'

▼ 0.0	SO	Continue north.	
2.4 ▲	SO	On left is left fork of Huntington Creek National Recreation Trail and public toilets. Zero trip meter.	
▼ 0.6	SO	Cross over Rolfson Creek.	
1.8 ▲	SO	Cross over Rolfson Creek.	
▼ 0.9	SO	FR 269 on left.	
1.5 ▲	SO	FR 269 on right.	
▼ 1.9	SO	Cross over Lake Creek.	
0.5 ▲	SO	Cross over Lake Creek.	
▼ 2.0	SO	FR 089 on right, then cross creek.	
0.4 ▲	SO	Cross creek, then FR 089 on left.	
▼ 2.1	SO	Track on right, then track on left.	
0.3 ▲	SO	Track on right, then track on left.	

GPS: N 39°34.78' W 111°14.99'

▼ 2.4		Seasonal gate, then trail ends at Utah 31; turn right for Huntington, left for Fairview.	
0.0 ▲		On Utah 31, between Huntington and Cleveland Reservoirs, zero trip meter and turn south onto FR 014.	

GPS: N 39°34.97' W 111°15.03'

CENTRAL REGION TRAIL #7

Skyline Drive Trail

Starting Point:	**Utah 31, 4.8 miles south of Northern**
	#14: Clear Creek Ridge Trail
Finishing Point:	**Ferron**
Total Mileage:	**71.8 miles**
Unpaved Mileage:	**67.6 miles**
Driving Time:	**4 hours**
Elevation Range:	**6,000–10,900 feet**
Usually Open:	**June to November**
Difficulty Rating:	**3**
Scenic Rating:	**8**
Remoteness Rating:	**+1**

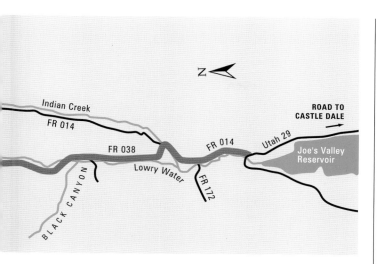

Special Attractions
- Spectacular views over miles of countryside as you cross the Wasatch Plateau, which reaches an altitude of nearly 11,000 feet.
- Varied driving conditions through a forested high-mountain setting.
- Abundant wildlife.

History
Throughout the 1930s, the Civilian Conservation Corps (CCC) made a number of improvements and restorations to Utah's many natural and historical landscapes. In 1933, the CCC came to Emery County and began work in Joe's Valley

A view along the trail as it passes North Tent Mountain

(for more on Joe's Valley, see Central #6: Upper Joe's Valley Trail). By summer 1935, CCC Company 959 had moved to Gooseberry and begun work on Skyline Drive between the Orangeville-Ephraim and Huntington-Fairview Roads. Upon the completion of the road, 5,000 people turned up for the dedication and ensuing celebration.

In autumn 1935, Company 959 moved to a year-round camp in Ferron and began construction on the road up Ferron Canyon. The route below follows a section of this road before coming to an end in Ferron.

Description
The highest road in Sanpete County, Skyline Drive runs along the dividing line between the Great Basin and the Colorado Plateau. At the start of the trail just off Utah 31, there is an overlook that provides an excellent view west into Sanpete Valley.

The trail is generally wide and allows for passing. There are some areas where water drainage has eroded the sides, making the road more narrow; but these sections are relatively short and present little if any obstacle. In the middle of the trail, a more difficult section is rough and rutted in spots, with potholes large enough to keep your speed in check.

One of the sections of the trail that can become very boggy

For most of its length, Skyline Drive travels along the treeline, initially passing a few stands of aspen before running through large groves of Engelmann spruce. Views from Skyline Drive are truly spectacular, as the landscape combines alpine meadows with distant scenery. Raptors are frequently seen along this trail riding the air currents in search of prey.

Continue along to the west of the North and South Tent Mountains, which stand at 11,230 and 11,285 feet respectively. Just before you reach Horseshoe Flat, the road improves considerably and warrants a 1 difficulty rating. For a number of sections, the road narrows along short lengths of shelf road and travels past interesting rock formations. Just after the summit, the trail runs along a mile stretch of smooth shelf road.

A mile and a half past the summit, you turn east on the maintained, gravel FR 022 to Ferron. Many side tracks split off from the main road, but none are large enough to present any navigational difficulties.

At Ferron Canyon, the trail follows a switchback down around the end and runs along the canyon floor next to the meandering Ferron Creek. After coming out of the canyon, proceed into the town of Ferron on Canyon Road; the trail ends at Utah 10 (State Street). If you are beginning the trail in Ferron, head north on Utah 10 (State Street) and follow the sign to Millsite State Park on Canyon Road.

Current Road Information
Manti-La Sal National Forest
Sanpete Ranger District
150 South Main Street
Ephraim, UT 84627
(435) 384-2372

Manti-La Sal National Forest
Ferron Ranger District
98 South State Street
Ferron, UT 84523
(435) 384-2372

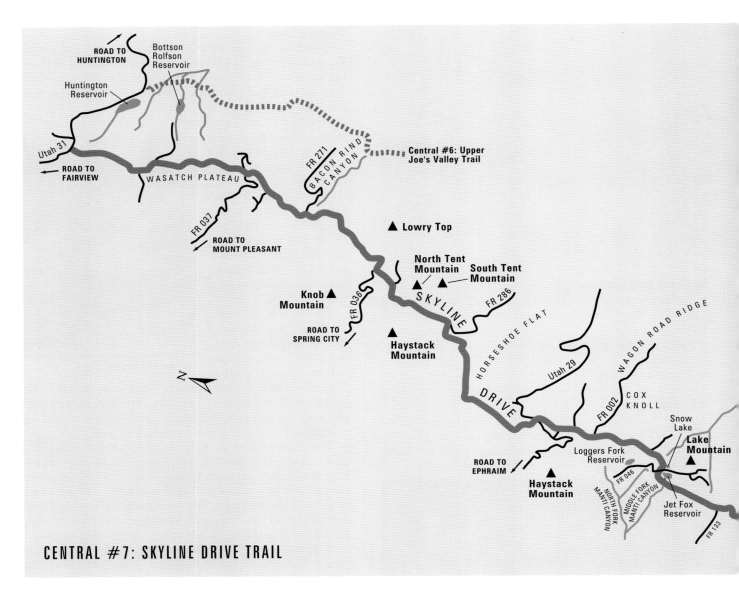

CENTRAL #7: SKYLINE DRIVE TRAIL

Map References

BLM Nephi, Manti
USFS Manti-La Sal National Forest: Sanpete and Ferron Ranger Districts
USGS 1:24,000 Huntington Reservoir, South Tent Mt., Spring City, Danish Knoll, Ferron Reservoir, Ferron Canyon, Flagstaff Peak, Ferron
1:100,000 Nephi, Manti
Maptech CD-ROM: Central/San Rafael
Utah Atlas & Gazetteer, pp. 38, 46
Utah Travel Council #3

Route Directions

▼ 0.0　　　　On Utah 31 at Sanpete Valley Overlook, zero trip meter and proceed south on FR 150. Follow signs to South Skyline Drive and Great Western Trail.
　　8.0 ▲　　Trail ends at Utah 31. Turn left for Fairview, right for Huntington.

GPS: N 39°37.03′ W 111°18.63′

▼ 0.4-0.5　　SO　Overlook of Huntington Reservoir to the east.

7.5-7.6 ▲	SO	View of Huntington Reservoir to the east.	
▼ 0.8		SO	FR 067 on right.
7.1 ▲	SO	FR 067 on left.	
▼ 1.7		SO	Track on left.
6.3 ▲	SO	Track on right.	
▼ 2.0		SO	Broad views west across valley.
6.0 ▲	SO	Broad views west across valley.	
▼ 2.5		SO	Lake Canyon Hiking Trail on left.
5.5 ▲	SO	Lake Canyon Hiking Trail on right.	
▼ 5.0		SO	Rough track on right.
3.0 ▲	SO	Rough track on left.	
▼ 6.0		SO	Cattle guard.
2.0 ▲	SO	Cattle guard.	
▼ 8.0		SO	Track on right (FR 037) to Mount Pleasant. Zero trip meter.
0.0 ▲		SO	Continue along Skyline Drive.

GPS: N 39°31.06′ W 111°18.13′

▼ 0.0			Continue along Skyline Drive.
8.5 ▲	SO	Track on left (FR 037) to Mount Pleasant. Zero trip meter.	
▼ 1.5		SO	Track on right.

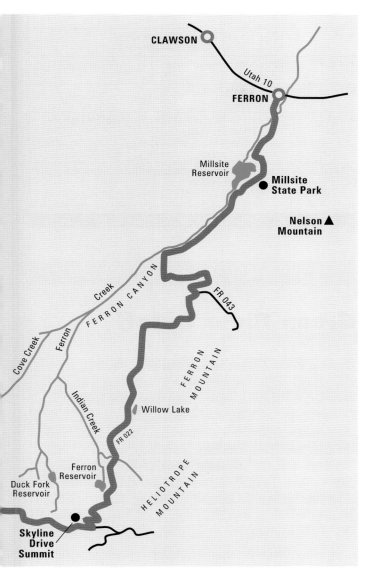

7.0 ▲	BL	Track enters on left.
▼ 1.8	SO	Pass under high-voltage wires.
6.7 ▲	SO	Pass under high-voltage wires.
▼ 3.6	SO	Track on left is FR 271 to Bacon Rind Canyon.
4.9 ▲	SO	Track on right is FR 271 to Bacon Rind Canyon.
▼ 4.8	SO	Track on left.
3.6 ▲	SO	Track on right.
▼ 6.4	BR	Track on left.
2.0 ▲	SO	Track on right.
▼ 7.4		Track on left.
1.1 ▲	SO	Track on right.
▼ 8.5	BL	Track on right is FR 036 to Spring City. Zero trip meter.
0.0 ▲		Continue north along Skyline Drive.

GPS: N 39°25.86' W 111°21.39'

▼ 0.0		Continue south along Skyline Drive.
11.5 ▲	BR	Intersection. Left is FR 036 to Spring City. Zero trip meter.
▼ 0.1	SO	Alternative entry to FR 036 on right.
11.4 ▲	SO	FR 036 on left.
▼ 0.2	SO	Track on left.

11.2 ▲	SO	Track on right.
▼ 0.9	BR	Track on left.
10.6 ▲	SO	Track on right.
▼ 2.0	SO	FR 279 on right.
9.4 ▲	SO	FR 279 on left.
▼ 3.1	SO	Track on left.
8.3 ▲	SO	Track on right.
▼ 3.3	SO	Track on left.
8.1 ▲	SO	Track on right.
▼ 3.5	SO	FR 054 on left.
8.0 ▲	SO	FR 054 on right.
▼ 4.2	SO	FR 286 on left.
7.2 ▲	SO	FR 286 on right.
▼ 7.0	SO	Tracks on left and right.
4.5 ▲	SO	Tracks on right and left.
▼ 9.4	SO	Track on right.
2.1 ▲	SO	Track on left.
▼ 10.1	SO	Track on right to radio tower.
1.4 ▲	SO	Track on left to radio tower.
▼ 11.5	BR	Intersection. Left is Utah 29 (FH8) and connects with Central #6: Upper Joe's Valley Trail. Zero trip meter.
0.0 ▲		Continue along Skyline Drive.

GPS: N 39°19.36' W 111°26.53'

▼ 0.0		Continue along Skyline Drive.
15.5 ▲	BL	Fork in road. Right is Utah 29 (FH8) and connects with Central #6: Upper Joe's Valley Trail. Zero trip meter.
▼ 0.9	BL	Road forks. Follow sign toward Manti. Right goes to Ephraim.
14.6 ▲	SO	Road to Ephraim on left.
▼ 1.4	SO	FR 346 on right through fence line. Follow sign to Snow Lake and Manti Canyon Road.
14.1 ▲	SO	FR 346 on left through fence line. Follow sign to Huntington.
▼ 1.6	SO	Road on left.
13.8 ▲	SO	Road on right.
▼ 1.9	SO	Road on left.
13.6 ▲	SO	Road on right.
▼ 2.1	SO	FR 002 on left to Wagon Road Ridge and Cox Knoll.
13.4 ▲	SO	FR 002 on right to Wagon Road Ridge and Cox Knoll.
▼ 3.9	SO	Track on right.
11.6 ▲	SO	Track on left.
▼ 4.6	BR	Track on left is FR 003 to Buck Ridge.
10.8 ▲	BL	Track on right is FR 003 to Buck Ridge.

GPS: N 39°15.50' W 111°26.68'

▼ 4.8	SO	Track on left is FR 004 to Trail Ridge.
10.7 ▲	SO	Track on right is FR 004 to Trail Ridge.
▼ 5.5	SO	Track on left to Lake Mountain.
9.9 ▲	SO	Track on right to Lake Mountain.
▼ 5.7	SO	Snow Lake on left.
9.8 ▲	SO	Snow Lake on right.
▼ 5.8	SO	Track on right.
9.7 ▲	SO	Track on left.
▼ 6.0	SO	FR 046 on right to Lowry Fork Trail, Loggers Fork Reservoir, and North Fork Manti Canyon. Road on left to Cove Lake and Cove Creek.
9.5 ▲	SO	FR 046 on left. Road to Cove Lake and Cove Creek on right.
▼ 6.2	SO	Cattle guard.
9.3 ▲	SO	Cattle guard.
▼ 6.4	SO	FR 196 and FR 197 on right.

9.0 ▲		SO	FR 196 and FR 197 on left.
▼ 7.4		SO	Cattle guard. Then FR 207 on right.
	8.1 ▲	SO	FR 207 on left. Then cattle guard.
▼ 9.1		SO	FR 045, Manti Canyon Road, on right (12 miles to Manti).
	6.4 ▲	SO	FR 045, Manti Canyon Road, on left (12 miles to Manti).
▼ 9.2		SO	Cross over drainage and FR 133 on right. Cattle guard.
	6.3 ▲	SO	Cattle guard. FR 133 on left. Cross over drainage.
▼ 9.5		SO	FR 061 on left.
	6.0 ▲	SO	FR 061 on right.
▼ 10.2		SO	Cattle guard. FR 231 on right.
	5.3 ▲	SO	FR 231 on left. Cattle guard.
▼ 11.7		BR	Road on left.
	3.7 ▲	SO	Road on right.
▼ 12.8		BR	Two roads on left.
	2.6 ▲	BL	Two roads on right.
▼ 13.9		SO	Skyline Drive summit. Elevation 10,897 feet.
	1.6 ▲	SO	Skyline Drive summit. Elevation 10,897 feet.
▼ 15.0		BR	FR 327 on left in switchback.
	0.5 ▲	BL	FR 327 on right. Continue on switchback.
▼ 15.5		UT	At intersection make a U-turn toward Ferron on FR 022. Zero trip meter.
	0.0 ▲		Continue on Skyline Drive.

GPS: N 39°08.38' W 111°29.03'

▼ 0.0			Continue toward Ferron.
	14.7 ▲	UT	At intersection U-turn to the right. Zero trip meter.
▼ 0.9		SO	Road on left (rejoins main road after a short distance).
	13.8 ▲	BL	Road on right (rejoins main road after a short distance).
▼ 1.5		SO	Road on right.
	13.1 ▲	SO	Road on left.
▼ 2.6		SO	Road on left is FR 025 to Ferron Reservoir.
	12.1 ▲	SO	Road on right is FR 025 to Ferron Reservoir.
▼ 2.7		SO	Road to reservoir on left.
	12.0 ▲	SO	Road to reservoir on right.
▼ 3.0		SO	Road to reservoir on left.
	11.7 ▲	BL	Road to reservoir on right.
▼ 3.2		BR	Duck Fork Road on left.
	11.5 ▲	BL	Duck Fork Road on right.
▼ 3.9		SO	Cattle guard and FR 070 on right.
	10.8 ▲	SO	FR 070 on left. Cattle guard.
▼ 4.3		SO	Cross over Little Horse Creek.
	10.3 ▲	SO	Cross over Little Horse Creek.
▼ 7.4		SO	Willow Lake on right.
	7.3 ▲	SO	Willow Lake on left.

GPS: N 39°08.14' W 111°22.90'

▼ 8.4		SO	FR 085 on left.
	6.2 ▲	SO	FR 085 on right.
▼ 10.5		SO	Cattle guard.
	4.2 ▲	SO	Cattle guard.
▼ 14.7		SO	Left on FR 279 leads 0.3 miles to Ferron Canyon Overlook. Then FR 043 on right to 12 Mile Flat, Horse Creek, and Wrigley Springs Reservoir. Zero trip meter.
	0.0 ▲		Continue along main road.

GPS: N 39°07.04' W 111°17.41'

▼ 0.0			Continue on main road.
	13.6 ▲	SO	FR 043 on left to 12 Mile Flat, Horse Creek, and Wrigley Springs Reservoir. Then FR 279 on right leads 0.3 miles to Ferron Canyon

			Overlook. Zero trip meter.
▼ 3.0		SO	Cross ford over Stevens Creek.
	10.6 ▲	SO	Cross ford over Stevens Creek.
▼ 4.1		SO	Cross through creek.
	9.5 ▲	SO	Cross through creek.
▼ 7.5		SO	Cattle guard.
	6.1 ▲	SO	Cattle guard.
▼ 13.4		SO	Ferron Ranger Station, Manti-La Sal National Forest, on right.
	0.2 ▲	SO	Ferron Ranger Station, Manti-La Sal National Forest, on left.
▼ 13.6			Trail ends at State Street (Utah 10) and Canyon Road in Ferron.
	0.0 ▲		On Utah 10 (State Street) in Ferron, zero trip meter and proceed west along Canyon Road.

GPS: N 39°05.30' W 111°07.85'

CENTRAL REGION TRAIL #8

Green River Cutoff

Starting Point:	**Unmarked dirt road off US 6/191, about 17 miles north of I-70**
Finishing Point:	**Central #1: Buckhorn Wash Trail**
Total Mileage:	**27.8 miles**
Unpaved Mileage:	**27.3 miles**
Driving Time:	**1.5 hours**
Elevation Range:	**4,800–6,200 feet**
Usually Open:	**Year-round**
Difficulty Rating:	**1**
Scenic Rating:	**7**
Remoteness Rating:	**+0**

Special Attractions

■ Picturesque entrance to this route through a narrow, boulder-strewn canyon.

■ Historic region includes part of the Spanish Trail and the original route of the Denver and Rio Grande Western Railroad.

■ Easy backcountry road offering alternative access to Central #1: Buckhorn Wash Trail from either Price or Green River.

History

The Green River Cutoff crosses or briefly runs along two of Utah's historic routes: The Spanish Trail and the original route of the Denver and Rio Grande Western (D&RGW) Railroad. It is often difficult to find the specific route of the Spanish Trail as it is now mostly worn away. However, it did go through much the same area as the Green River Cutoff trail. The original D&RGW railbed is a bit more defined (though still worn away) and crosses paths with the Green River Cutoff in a couple places.

Description

The start of the Green River Cutoff is unmarked; the road branches west off US 6/191 between mileposts 283 and 284.

The start of the canyon at the eastern end of the trail

The trail follows a wide, two-lane maintained country road with a gravel surface. Though a 1-rated trail, in wet weather it can become impassable. The only parts that might pose a problem in dry weather are thick sections of powder-fine dust that create huge clouds and block your vision if a car passes. Navigation is straightforward throughout, as all the side roads are much smaller.

Initially, the trail moves through rolling grasslands. It then enters a narrow, rock-strewn canyon with huge boulders on either side of the road. After 11.7 miles, you reach the intersection with Central #9: Tidwell Draw Trail. The scenery changes around the wide grasslands of Chimney Rock Flat, as the flatland spreads out around the foot of the towering Chimney Rock, which rises over 700 feet high. The road continues through grassland and varying stands of pinyon and juniper. The trail ends at Central #1: Buckhorn Wash Trail, 14.7 miles from Castle Dale.

A patch of the deep, powder-fine sand along the Green River Cutoff

Current Road Information

Emery County Road Department
120 West Highway 29
Castle Dale, UT 84513
(435) 381-2550

BLM Price Field Office
125 South 600 West
Price, UT 84501
(435) 636-3600

Map References

BLM Huntington
USGS 1:24,000 Cliff, Dry Mesa, Chimney Rock, Bob Hill Knoll
1:100,000 Huntington

Maptech CD-ROM: Central/San Rafael
Trails Illustrated, #712
Utah Atlas & Gazetteer, p. 39
Utah Travel Council #3
Other: Recreation Map of the San Rafael Swell and San Rafael Desert

Route Directions

▼ 0.0   On US 6/191 between mile markers 283 and 284, approximately 17 miles north of I-70, zero trip meter and proceed west on unmarked dirt road. Cross cattle guard. Yellow sign reads, "Roads May Be Impassable Due to Storms."

11.7 ▲   Trail ends at US 6/191; turn right for Green River, left for Price.

GPS: N 39°11.74' W 110°20.27'

▼ 0.9   **TL**   T-intersection. Turn left on old paved road.

10.8 ▲   **TR**   Turn right toward US 6/191.

GPS: N 39°12.26' W 110°21.07'

▼ 1.2   **SO**   Cross under railway overpass.

10.5 ▲   SO   Cross under railway overpass.

▼ 1.4   **TR**   Turn right onto unpaved road.

10.3 ▲   TL   Turn left onto paved road.

GPS: N 39°11.84' W 110°21.24'

▼ 2.1   **SO**   Cattle guard.

9.6 ▲   SO   Cattle guard.

▼ 3.2   **SO**   Track on left.

8.5 ▲   SO   Track on right.

▼ 5.0   **SO**   Cattle guard.

6.7 ▲   SO   Cattle guard.

▼ 5.9   **SO**   Track on right.

5.8 ▲   SO   Track on left.

▼ 6.4   **SO**   Cross over wash.

5.3 ▲   SO   Cross over wash.

▼ 7.4   **SO**   Track on right.

4.3 ▲   SO   Track on left.

GPS: N 39°10.47' W 110°25.12'

▼ 7.5   **SO**   Track on right.

4.2 ▲   SO   Track on left.

▼ 7.8   **SO**   Track on right.

3.9 ▲   SO   Track on left.

▼ 8.5   **SO**   Track on left.

3.2 ▲   SO   Track on right.

GPS: N 39°10.17' W 110°25.87'

▼ 10.5   **SO**   Cattle guard.

1.2 ▲   SO   Cattle guard.

▼ 11.0   **SO**   Track on left.

0.7 ▲   SO   Track on right.

▼ 11.7   **SO**   Track on left is Central #9: Tidwell Draw Trail to Smith's cabin. Track on right. Zero trip meter.

0.0 ▲   Continue along main road.

GPS: N 39°10.76' W 110°29.00'

▼ 0.0   Continue along main road.

8.2 ▲   SO   Track on right is Central #9: Tidwell Draw Trail to Smith's cabin. Track on left. Zero trip meter.

▼ 1.0   **SO**   Cross old railroad grade.

7.2 ▲   SO   Cross old railroad grade.

GPS: N 39°10.61' W 110°30.00'

▼ 3.5   **SO**   Chimney Rock on right, across Chimney Rock Flat.

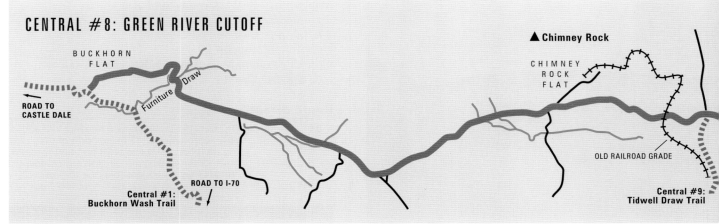

4.7 ▲	SO	Chimney Rock on left, across Chimney Rock Flat.	
▼ 3.7	SO	Track on right.	
4.5 ▲	SO	Track on left.	
▼ 4.0	SO	Two tracks on left.	
4.2 ▲	SO	Two tracks on right.	
▼ 6.2	SO	Track on left.	
2.0 ▲	SO	Track on right.	
▼ 7.5	SO	Bridge over wash.	
0.7 ▲	SO	Bridge over wash.	
▼ 8.0	SO	Track on left.	
0.2 ▲	SO	Track on right.	
▼ 8.2	SO	Track on left was portion of the Spanish Trail. Zero trip meter.	
0.0 ▲		Continue along main road.	

GPS: N 39°08.93' W 110°37.35'

▼ 0.0		Continue along main road.
7.9 ▲	SO	Track on right was portion of the Spanish Trail. Zero trip meter.
▼ 0.6	SO	Cattle guard and track on right.
7.3 ▲	SO	Track on left and cattle guard.
▼ 1.1	SO	Track on left.
6.8 ▲	SO	Track on right.
▼ 2.9	SO	Track on right and corral.
5.0 ▲	SO	Track on left and corral.
▼ 4.5	SO	Track on left.
3.4 ▲	SO	Track on right.
▼ 5.5	SO	Cross Furniture Draw. Old bridge foundation on right.
2.4 ▲	SO	Cross Furniture Draw. Old bridge foundation on left.

GPS: N 39°10.66' W 110°42.92'

▼ 5.6	SO	Cross cattle guard.
2.3 ▲	SO	Cross cattle guard.
▼ 5.8	SO	Road on right.
2.1 ▲	SO	Road on left.
▼ 6.6	SO	Descend into Buckhorn Flat.
1.3 ▲	SO	Leave Buckhorn Flat.
▼ 7.7	SO	Buckhorn corral on left.
0.2 ▲	SO	Buckhorn corral on right.
▼ 7.8	SO	Cattle guard.
0.1 ▲	SO	Cattle guard.
▼ 7.9		Sign reads: "Castle Dale straight; Buckhorn Wash Pictograph Panel and San Rafael Bridge Recreational site to the left." Then trail ends at Central #1: Buckhorn Wash Trail; turn left to

		I-70, straight to Utah 10.
0.0 ▲		On Central #1: Buckhorn Wash Trail, 14.7 miles from Utah 10, zero trip meter and proceed east into Buckhorn Flat.

GPS: N 39°10.27' W 110°45.03'

CENTRAL REGION TRAIL #9

Tidwell Draw Trail

Starting Point:	**Central #8: Green River Cutoff, 11.7 miles from US 6/191**
Finishing Point:	**I-70, exit 147**
Total Mileage:	**23.8 miles**
Unpaved Mileage:	**23.8 miles**
Driving Time:	**2.5 hours**
Elevation Range:	**4,400–5,300 feet**
Usually Open:	**Year-round**
Difficulty Rating:	**3**
Scenic Rating:	**8**
Remoteness Rating:	**+0**

Special Attractions
■ Smith's cabin.
■ Historic, varied, and under-used trail.

History
After they were married in 1933, Wayne and Betty Smith settled down to start a ranch in the San Rafael Swell. They chose a site near a spring, which would supply them with the water necessary for survival. However, artificial seismic activity in the region, caused by drilling for water, destroyed the natural spring. Wayne and Betty later moved to Green River. Today at Smith's cabin, there are several ranch buildings and corrals still standing. Though some of the cabins and cattle yards are currently in various states of decay, enough is left of this scenic ranch to give you a good feel of frontier life in the San Rafael Swell.

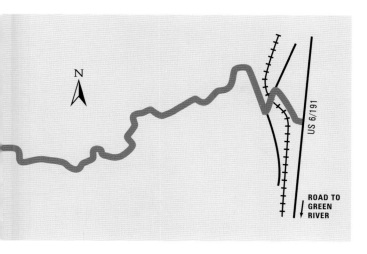

A good portion of the trail follows the original Denver and Rio Grande Western (D&RGW) railbed through Emery County. Thinking this line would become part of the shortest route across the continent, the D&RGW built this section

Cement Crossing

of railbed from Green River toward Buckhorn Flat in the early 1880s. However, the company decided to postpone plans for a transcontinental line and focus its efforts on Salt Lake City and the Wasatch Front. It wasn't until after they had spent over $200,000 on the railbed that D&RGW's senior management realized that this route through Emery County was still under construction. Realizing the mistake, they quickly abandoned the railbed and fired the project's unfortunate head surveyor.

Description
The Tidwell Draw Trail begins on Central #8: Green River Cutoff, 11.7 miles from US 6/191. The area is typical of San Rafael country, with various rock formations, canyons, and rolling grasslands dotted with sage, pinyon, and juniper.

Overall, the trail is rather easy, as it moves across a number of sandy patches. However, a couple of stream crossings, slickrock areas, and eroded sandy sections provide an added element of difficulty. After Smith's cabin, the trail evens out and the difficulty rating drops to a 1.

The trail's high scenic rating is mainly due to its history in connection with the remains of the D&RGW railroad, the Spanish Trail, and Smith's cabin. The trail more or less follows the path of the old railbed for the first 15 miles or so.

Toward the end of the trail, the few remains of an old mining district lie in Buckmaster Draw. You can still see some foundations, mines, and tailing dumps, and the ground itself remains scarred from what was most likely open mining. The trail finishes at I-70.

Current Road Information
Emery County Road Department
120 West Highway 29
Castle Dale, UT 84513
(435) 381-2550

BLM Price Field Office
125 South 600 West
Price, UT 84501
(435) 636-3600

Map References
BLM Huntington, San Rafael Desert (incomplete)
USGS 1:24,000 Dry Mesa, Mexican Mt., Desert, Jessies Twist, Spotted Wolf Canyon
1:100,000 Huntington, San Rafael Desert (incomplete)
Maptech CD-ROM: Central/San Rafael
Trails Illustrated, #712
Utah Atlas & Gazetteer, p. 39
Utah Travel Council #3; #5
Other: Recreation Map of the San Rafael Swell and San Rafael Desert

Route Directions

▼ 0.0			On Central #8: Green River Cutoff, 11.7 miles from US 6/191, turn south onto dirt track.
	4.3 ▲		Trail ends at Central #8: Green River Cutoff; turn right for US 6/191, left for Central #1: Buckhorn Wash Trail.
		GPS: N 39°10.76' W 110°29.00'	
▼ 0.1		**BR**	Fork in road.
	4.2 ▲	**BL**	Fork in road.
▼ 0.3		**SO**	Cross through sandy wash.
	4.0 ▲	**SO**	Cross through sandy wash.
▼ 1.1		**SO**	Cross through wash.
	3.2 ▲	**SO**	Cross through wash.
▼ 1.7		**SO**	Cross through wash.
	2.6 ▲	**SO**	Cross through wash.
▼ 2.1		**SO**	Structures on left include well and stock trough.

Smith's cabin and ranch outbuildings

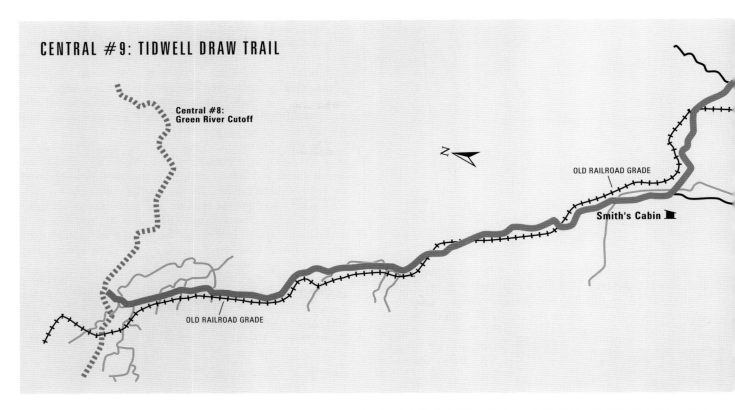

2.2 ▲	SO	Structures on right include well and stock trough.	
		GPS: N 39°09.15' W 110°28.34'	
▼ 2.3	SO	Sign on right notes this was part of the Spanish Trail.	
2.0 ▲	SO	Sign on left notes this was part of the Spanish Trail.	
▼ 2.3	BL	Fork in road. Bear left across Cement Crossing.	
1.9 ▲	BR	Cross Cement Crossing. Road on left.	
		GPS: N 39°09.03' W 110°28.44'	
▼ 2.5	SO	Track on right.	
1.8 ▲	SO	Track on left.	
▼ 2.7	SO	Cross through rocky wash.	
1.6 ▲	SO	Cross through rocky wash.	
▼ 2.8	SO	Culvert on left.	
1.4 ▲	SO	Culvert on right.	
▼ 3.2	SO	Cross through wash.	
1.1 ▲	SO	Cross through wash.	
▼ 4.3	SO	Cross through gate and close behind you. Zero trip meter.	
0.0 ▲		Continue north.	
		GPS: N 39°07.74' W 110°27.69'	
▼ 0.0		Continue south.	
7.0 ▲	SO	Cross through gate and close behind you. Zero trip meter.	
▼ 0.3	SO	Track on left.	
6.7 ▲	SO	Track on right.	
▼ 1.0	SO	Cross through wash.	
5.9 ▲	SO	Cross through wash.	
▼ 1.8	SO	Cross through large wash.	
5.1 ▲	SO	Cross through large wash.	
		GPS: N 39°06.31' W 110°26.81'	
▼ 2.7	BL	Tracks on right.	
4.3 ▲	BR	Tracks on left.	

▼ 3.0	SO	Cross through wash.	
4.0 ▲	SO	Cross through wash.	
▼ 3.6	SO	Track on right.	
3.3 ▲	SO	Track on left.	
▼ 3.7	SO	Track on right.	
3.2 ▲	SO	Track on left.	
▼ 3.9	SO	Cross through wash.	
3.1 ▲	SO	Cross through wash.	
▼ 5.4	SO	Cross through creek.	
1.6 ▲	SO	Cross through creek.	
		GPS: N 39°03.77' W 110°24.89'	
▼ 5.8	SO	Track on left.	
1.2 ▲	SO	Track on right.	
▼ 7.0	SO	Pass through gate and close behind you. Zero trip meter.	
0.0 ▲		Continue north.	
		GPS: N 39°02.82' W 110°24.04'	
▼ 0.0		Continue south.	
1.2 ▲	SO	Pass through gate and close behind you. Zero trip meter.	
▼ 0.1	SO	Track on right.	
1.1 ▲	SO	Track on left.	
▼ 1.2	TL	Pass through gate and close behind you. Then intersection. Track on right is a short side road that goes 0.2 miles to Smith's cabin and buildings. After visiting cabin, return to this intersection and zero trip meter.	
0.0 ▲		Intersection. Turn left (north) onto main trail. Pass through gate and close behind you.	
		GPS: N 39°01.89' W 110°23.64'	
▼ 0.0		Intersection. Continue straight (east) on main trail.	
4.3 ▲	TR	Intersection. Track ahead is a short side road that goes 0.2 miles to Smith's cabin and buildings. After visiting cabin, return to this intersection and zero trip meter.	

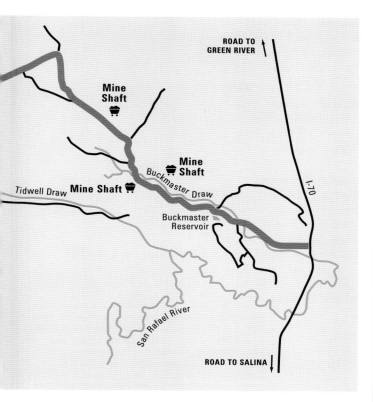

| ▼ 1.2 | SO | Pass through gate and close behind you. |
| 3.1 ▲ | SO | Pass through gate and close behind you. |

GPS: N 39°01.97' W 110°22.60'

| ▼ 2.1 | SO | Track on left. Old railroad grade crosses. |
| 2.2 ▲ | SO | Track on right. Old railroad grade crosses. |

GPS: N 39°01.88' W 110°21.64'

| ▼ 3.0 | BR | Track on left. |
| 1.2 ▲ | BL | Track on right. |

| ▼ 4.3 | TR | T-intersection. Turn right to Buckmaster Reservoir. Left goes to US 6/191. Zero trip meter. |
| 0.0 ▲ | | Continue along road. |

GPS: N 39°00.53' W 110°19.94'

| ▼ 0.0 | | Proceed toward reservoir. |
| 7.0 ▲ | TL | Intersection. Take road on left and zero trip meter. |

| ▼ 1.4 | SO | Track on right. |
| 5.6 ▲ | SO | Track on left. |

| ▼ 2.3 | TR | Intersection. |
| 4.7 ▲ | TL | Intersection. |

GPS: N 38°58.95' W 110°21.43'

| ▼ 3.0 | SO | Track on right. Then mine shaft visible on left. |
| 3.9 ▲ | BR | Mine shaft on right. Then track on left. |

| ▼ 5.1 | SO | Old corral on right. |
| 1.9 ▲ | SO | Old corral on left. |

| ▼ 6.8 | SO | Cattle guard. |
| 0.1 ▲ | SO | Cattle guard. |

| ▼ 7.0 | | Trail ends at I-70, exit 147; turn left for Green River, right for Salina. |
| 0.0 ▲ | | Take I-70, exit 147, to intersection of exit ramp and the overpass on the north side of highway; zero trip meter and proceed north. Road becomes unpaved almost immediately. |

GPS: N 38°55.48' W 110°22.60'

Black Dragon Pictographs Trail

Starting Point:	I-70, 0.3 miles westbound past mile marker 145
Finishing Point:	BLM fence near the Black Dragon pictographs
Total Mileage:	1.7 miles
Unpaved Mileage:	1.7 miles
Driving Time:	15 minutes (one-way)
Elevation Range:	4,300–4,400 feet
Usually Open:	Year-round
Difficulty Rating:	3
Scenic Rating:	9
Remoteness Rating:	+0

Special Attractions

- The famous Black Dragon pictographs.
- The scenic Black Dragon Canyon.
- Short spur trail can be combined with Central #11: Three Fingers Petroglyphs Trail.

History

In Black Dragon Canyon, you will find panels of artwork on the canyon walls in the Barrier Canyon style, which predates the Fremont Indians. While it is difficult to accurately date the paintings, they are at least 1,500 years old. There are two zoomorphs (representations of animals with human qualities or characteristics), one of which resembles a dragon and the figure to its right resembles a praying dog. At about the same height along the canyon wall to the left are three red-colored, three- to seven-foot-tall pictures that resemble humans with elongated bodies.

The Black Dragon pictographs

Description

The Black Dragon Pictographs Trail is short but interesting and can serve as a quick side trip off of I-70 if you are just passing through. As the trail does not start from a proper exit off the interstate, use caution when slowing down to pull off the road. Do not stop until you are completely off I-70. Heading westbound past mile marker 145, look for a gate about 20 yards off to the side; this marks the beginning of the trail.

Once you're through the gate, you almost immediately pass the track on the left that leads under the freeway culvert

A view of the specacular canyon you travel through to get to the Black Dragon pictographs

to Central #11: Three Fingers Petroglyphs Trail. The Black Dragon trail is easy—and accessible for any vehicle—until toward the end, when it becomes more difficult and jumps up to a difficulty level of 3. Here you need a high-clearance vehicle to traverse the rocks and washes of the canyon floor. The scenic canyon and pictographs make the trail very striking and enjoyable.

The road continues past the pictographs into the canyon and eventually connects with Central #3: Black Dragon Wash Trail after about 2 miles. However, this part of the road is badly washed out after about 1.3 miles with rough spots that have steep angles of entry and departure. The road here goes beyond the difficulty level of this book. Skilled drivers might be able to pass through this stretch of road, especially if they have short-wheelbase SUVs. Otherwise, we recommend that you park your vehicle and hike up the canyon.

Current Road Information

Emery County Road Department
120 West Highway 29
Castle Dale, UT 84513
(435) 381-2550

BLM Price Field Office
125 South 600 West
Price, UT 84501
(435) 636-3600

Map References

USGS 1:24,000 Spotted Wolf Canyon
Maptech CD-ROM: Central/San Rafael
Trails Illustrated, #712
Utah Atlas & Gazetteer, p. 39
Other: Recreation Map of the San Rafael Swell and San Rafael Desert

Route Directions

▼ 0.0		Westbound on I-70, 0.3 miles past mile marker 145, pull off highway at a wire gate with a BLM sign. Pass through gate, zero trip meter, and follow the dirt road north. Then pass a track on left that leads under the freeway culvert to Central #11: Three Fingers Petroglyphs Trail.
		GPS: N 38°55.54' W 110°24.99'
▼ 0.1	SO	Cross through wash.
▼ 0.6	SO	Track on left.
▼ 1.0	BL	Fork in road. Bear left following BLM marker for Black Dragon.
		GPS: N 38°56.21' W 110°25.06'
▼ 1.1	SO	Track on right. Tracks straight and on left both continue to the pictographs. Straight goes through wash.
▼ 1.2	SO	Track on right.
▼ 1.7		Trail ends at BLM fence and marker. The Black Dragon pictographs are inside BLM fenced area about 40 feet up, above a talus slope.
		GPS: N 38°56.32' W 110°25.36'

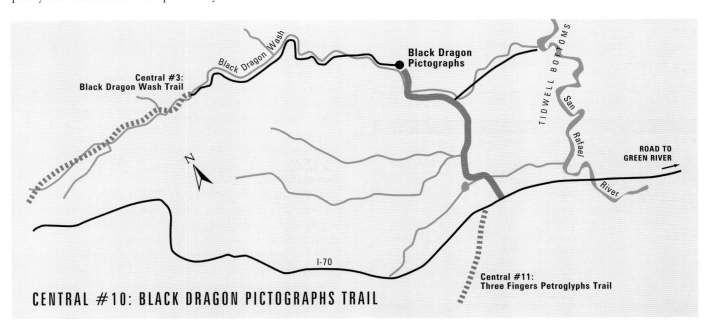

CENTRAL #10: BLACK DRAGON PICTOGRAPHS TRAIL

Three Fingers Petroglyphs Trail

Starting Point:	I-70, 0.7 miles eastbound past mile marker 144
Finishing Point:	Three Fingers petroglyphs
Total Mileage:	8 miles
Unpaved Mileage:	8 miles
Driving Time:	45 minutes (one-way)
Elevation Range:	4,300–4,600 feet
Usually Open:	Year-round
Difficulty Rating:	5
Scenic Rating:	9
Remoteness Rating:	+1

Special Attractions

■ Three Fingers petroglyphs.
■ A short, scenic spur trail that can be combined with Central #10: Black Dragon Pictographs Trail.

Description

The trail to the Three Fingers petroglyphs starts out rather easy and remains so until the more difficult final 2 miles. About 0.1 miles from the start, the trail intersects a road to the right that crosses through a culvert under the interstate and connects in 0.2 miles with Central #10: Black Dragon Pictographs Trail. The Three Fingers Trail bears to the left and proceeds along the foot of the San Rafael Reef. The first section of road is periodically graded and runs through a number of wash crossings and sandy spots. This part of the trail is relatively flat but very scenic, with a typical red mesa to the left and the windblown reef on the right.

The entrance to the canyon in the San Rafael Reef where the Three Fingers petroglyphs are located

After about 6 miles, the trail turns right and heads directly for the reef. This is where a few sections of the trail can become considerably more difficult and rate a 5. An awkward wash crossing, a couple of badly washed out narrow sections, and a short but steep descent can all pose potential difficulties. As you approach the reef, the terrain is sporadically dotted with pinyon and juniper. At the end of the trail, you must

A panel of the Three Fingers petroglyphs

hike a short distance into the facing canyon to view the petroglyphs, which are on the right-hand side. The main panel is located next to a tunnel, about ten feet up the canyon wall.

Current Road Information

Emery County Road Department
120 West Highway 29
Castle Dale, UT 84513
(435) 381-2550

BLM Price Field Office
125 South 600 West
Price, UT 84501
(435) 636-3600

Map References

BLM San Rafael Desert
USGS 1:24,000 Spotted Wolf Canyon, Greasewood Draw
  1:100,000 San Rafael Desert
Maptech CD-ROM: Central/San Rafael
Trails Illustrated, #712
Utah Atlas & Gazetteer, p. 39
Other: Recreation Map of the San Rafael Swell and San Rafael Desert

Route Directions

▼ 0.0		Eastbound on I-70, 0.7 miles past mile marker 144, look for unmarked dirt track on right. Pass through gate and close it behind you. Zero trip meter.
	GPS: N 38°55.43' W 110°25.05'	
▼ 0.1	BL	Track on right goes through culvert to Central #10: Black Dragon Pictographs Trail.
▼ 0.6	SO	Cross through wash.
▼ 0.9	SO	Cross through wash.
▼ 1.0	SO	Cross through wash.
▼ 1.1	SO	Cross through wash.
▼ 1.3	SO	Cross through wash.
▼ 1.6	SO	Cross through wash.
▼ 1.8	SO	Cross through wash.
▼ 2.1	SO	Cross through wash.
▼ 3.5	SO	Road on right.
▼ 4.9	BR	Bear right at fork in road.

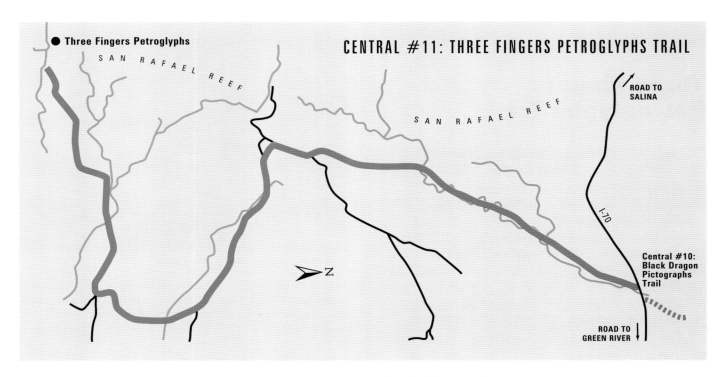

		GPS: N 38°52.34' W 110°25.38'
▼ 5.8	TR	Take small, unmaintained track on right. Zero trip meter.
		GPS: N 38°51.62' W 110°25.63'
▼ 0.0		Continue along trail. Then bear right, proceeding toward rock reef.
▼ 0.7	SO	Cross through sandy wash.
		GPS: N 38°51.76' W 110°26.31'
▼ 1.5	SO/BR	Short, steep, narrow downhill section and then bear right.
▼ 1.9	BL	Fork in road.
▼ 2.0	BL	Fork in road.
▼ 2.2		Road ends. The panels are a short walk farther on the right-hand side of a canyon in the reef wall you are facing.
		GPS: N 38°51.46' W 110°27.80'

CENTRAL REGION TRAIL #12

Temple Mountain Trail

Starting Point:	I-70, exit 129
Finishing Point:	Utah 24
Total Mileage:	28.3 miles
Unpaved Mileage:	22.0 miles
Driving Time:	1.25 hours
Elevation Range:	4,900–7,000 feet
Usually Open:	Year-round
Difficulty Rating:	2
Scenic Rating:	7
Remoteness Rating:	+0

Special Attractions

- Backbone for many other 4WD trails in the area.
- The scenic, white Temple Mountain set against the deep red of the surrounding countryside.
- Access to numerous backcountry campsites.

Description

The Temple Mountain Trail begins at I-70, exit 129, and heads south through rolling grassland. Over the course of the first 14.7 miles, you pass the turnoffs to Central #13: Swasey's

Temple Mountain

Cabin Trail, Central #15: Reds Canyon Trail, and Central #16: Temple Wash and Mining Camp Trail.

After the Reds Canyon turnoff, the canyon country becomes far more dramatic with wonderful views of Temple Mountain. The red road set against the white rock of Temple Mountain makes for a striking contrast and a very scenic drive.

Overall, the road is easy; it is a 1-rated trail through the

pinyon-and-juniper-dotted canyon. After Flat Top Mountain, there are numerous mines and backcountry camping spots, especially near the part of the trail that runs along Temple Wash to where the road is paved.

Shortly after the road becomes paved is the turnoff for Goblin Valley State Park (fee required), which has an unusual display of hundreds of sandstone, mudstone, and siltstone "goblins." These unique, rock formations have been carved out over millions of years by wind and rain and are thought by many to resemble little goblin-like creatures. This strange collection of pinnacles inhabits the floor of Goblin Valley and was first noted by the region's early cowboys and ranchers. However, the valley remained relatively unknown until the 1950s, when photographs taken by Arthur Chaffin brought widespread publicity to the area and its now-famous goblins.

The trail ends at Utah 24, approximately 24 miles south of I-70.

Current Road Information

Emery County Road Department
120 West Highway 29
Castle Dale, UT 84513
(435) 381-2550

BLM Price Field Office
125 South 600 West
Price, UT 84501
(435) 636-3600

Map References

BLM   San Rafael Desert
USGS   1:24,000 The Wickiup, Twin Knolls, San Rafael
       Knob, Horse Valley, Temple Mt., Old Woman
       1:100,000 San Rafael Desert
Maptech CD-ROM: Central/San Rafael
Trails Illustrated, #712
Utah Atlas & Gazetteer, p. 38
Utah Travel Council #5
Other: Recreation Map of the San Rafael Swell and San
       Rafael Desert

Route Directions

▼ 0.0		On I-70, take exit 129 at ranch. On south side of highway, at intersection of exit ramp and underpass, zero trip meter and proceed south. Cross cattle guard and follow road across Indian Flat.
4.9 ▲		Trail ends at I-70, exit 129; turn right for Green River, left for Salina.
GPS: N 38°52.82′ W 110°39.45′		
▼ 0.1	BR	Follow sign to Goblin Valley, Temple Mountain, and Utah 24.
4.8 ▲	BL	Follow sign to I-70.
▼ 1.2	SO	The Big Pond on left.
3.7 ▲	SO	The Big Pond on right.
▼ 1.8	SO	Cross over ditch and enter Paige Flat.
3.1 ▲	SO	Cross over ditch.
▼ 3.0	SO	Tracks on left and right. Cross cattle guard.
1.9 ▲	SO	Cross cattle guard. Tracks on left and right.

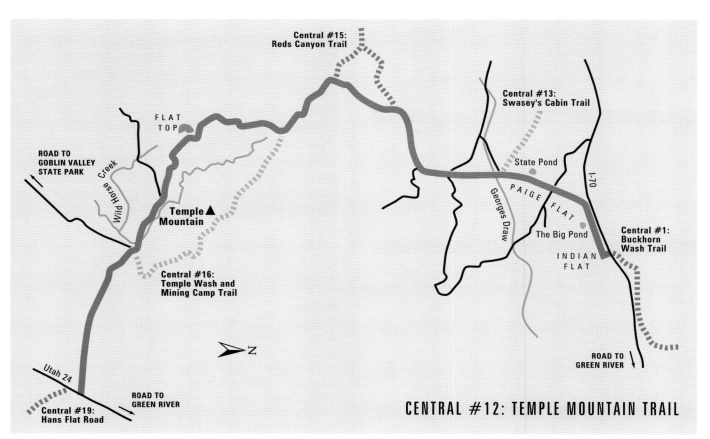

CENTRAL #12: TEMPLE MOUNTAIN TRAIL

| ▼ 3.8 | SO | Message board, then track on right goes past State Pond. |
| 1.1 ▲ | SO | Track on left goes past State Pond. |

GPS: N 38°50.61' W 110°42.28'

▼ 4.1	SO	Cross through wash.
0.8 ▲	SO	Cross through wash.
▼ 4.9	SO	Track on right is Central #13: Swasey's Cabin Trail. Zero trip meter. Follow sign to Utah 24.
0.0 ▲		Proceed straight.

GPS: N 38°49.69' W 110°42.44'

▼ 0.0		Proceed straight.
4.9 ▲	SO	Track on left is Central #13: Swasey's Cabin Trail. Zero trip meter and follow sign to I-70.
▼ 0.1	SO	Track on right.
4.8 ▲	SO	Track on left.
▼ 0.3	SO	Cross through Georges Draw.
4.6 ▲	SO	Cross through Georges Draw.
▼ 1.5	SO	Track on left.
3.4 ▲	SO	Track on right.
▼ 1.7	SO	Cross cattle guard, then track on left.
3.2 ▲	SO	Track on right, then cattle guard.
▼ 2.6	SO	Track on left to motorcycle trailhead.
2.3 ▲	SO	Track on right to motorcycle trailhead.
▼ 3.1	SO	Cross through wash.
1.8 ▲	SO	Cross through wash.
▼ 4.9	BL	Fork in road. Right is Central #15: Reds Canyon Trail. Zero trip meter.
0.0 ▲		Continue along main road.

GPS: N 38°46.63' W 110°44.73'

▼ 0.0		Continue toward Goblin Valley and Temple Mountain.
2.6 ▲	BR	Road on left is Central #15: Reds Canyon Trail. Zero trip meter.
▼ 0.7	SO	Track on left.
1.9 ▲	SO	Track on right.
▼ 0.9	SO	Track on right.
1.7 ▲	SO	Track on left.
▼ 2.6	BL	Intersection. Right is Central #15: Reds Canyon Trail. Zero trip meter.
0.0 ▲		Continue toward I-70.

GPS: N 38°44.70' W 110°45.76'

▼ 0.0		Continue toward Goblin Valley and Temple Mountain.
2.1 ▲	BR	Track on left is Central #15: Reds Canyon Trail. Zero trip meter.
▼ 1.4	SO	Track on left.
0.7 ▲	SO	Track on right.
▼ 2.1	SO	Track on left is Central #16: Temple Wash and Mining Camp Trail. Zero trip meter.
0.0 ▲		Continue toward I-70.

GPS: N 38°43.60' W 110°44.04'

▼ 0.0		Continue toward Utah 24.
8.7 ▲	SO	Track on right is Central #16: Temple Wash and Mining Camp Trail. Zero trip meter.
▼ 2.6	SO	Track on right.
6.1 ▲	SO	Track on left.
▼ 4.4	SO	Track on right.
4.3 ▲	SO	Track on left.
▼ 5.0	SO	Track on right.
3.7 ▲	SO	Track on left.
▼ 6.7	SO	Track on right to Wild Horse Creek.
2.0 ▲	SO	Track on left to Wild Horse Creek.

GPS: N 38°40.04' W 110°41.22'

▼ 7.0	SO	Track on left. Note that in this area there are numerous side trails, many to good backcountry campsites. Most have been ignored in these directions.
1.7 ▲	SO	Track on right.
▼ 7.3	SO	Track on left in wash.
1.4 ▲	SO	Track on right in wash.
▼ 7.5	SO	Road becomes paved.
1.2 ▲	SO	Road becomes unpaved.
▼ 7.7	SO	Track on left.
1.0 ▲	SO	Track on right.
▼ 8.7	SO	Intersection. Right goes to Goblin Valley State Park. Track on left is Central #16: Temple Wash and Mining Camp Trail. Zero trip meter.
0.0 ▲		Continue straight.

GPS: N 38°39.20' W 110°39.23'

▼ 0.0		Continue straight toward Utah 24.
5.1 ▲	SO	Intersection. Left goes to Goblin Valley State Park. Track on right is Central #16: Temple Wash and Mining Camp Trail. Zero trip meter.
▼ 5.1		Trail ends at Utah 24; turn left for Green River, right for Hanksville.
0.0 ▲		On Utah 24, about 24 miles south of I-70, zero trip meter and proceed west on paved road.

GPS: N 38°37.84' W 110°33.97'

CENTRAL REGION TRAIL #13

Swasey's Cabin Trail

Starting Point:	**Central #12: Temple Mountain Trail, 4.9 miles from I-70**
Finishing Point:	**Swasey's cabin**
Total Mileage:	**7.5 miles**
Unpaved Mileage:	**7.5 miles**
Driving Time:	**30 minutes (one-way)**
Elevation Range:	**6,800–7,200 feet**
Usually Open:	**Year-round**
Difficulty Rating:	**2**
Scenic Rating:	**8**
Remoteness Rating:	**+0**

Special Attractions

- Swasey's cabin and spectacular rock formations.
- Part of a network of 4WD trails.

History

Although it only dates back to the 1920s, Swasey's cabin is one of the oldest remaining structures in the desert. Tucked in a remote location, the cabin stands in front of a unique and striking rock formation. When the Swaseys lived there, they used a cool cave behind the house as a year-round meat locker. You can still see the Swaseys' "refrigerator," as it has come to be called; simply approach the rock formation behind the cabin and pass through the tight crevice to the rock's left.

Swasey's cabin watched over by a very distinctive sandstone pillar behind it

Description

Generally, the road to Swasey's cabin is fairly easy, passing along rolling grassland dotted with sagebrush, pinyon, and juniper. A high-clearance vehicle is preferred as the road suffers washouts every now and then.

After 6.7 miles, you reach the intersection with Central #14: Rods Valley Trail, and a little farther on, there are many backcountry campsites near Swasey's cabin. Though the road continues beyond the cabin, it is recommended that you turn around here, as it becomes very narrow and eroded about a half mile ahead. The track running in front of Swasey's cabin continues north around the cliff faces and leads to numerous backcountry campsites. Most of these tracks eventually make their way back to the main Swasey's Cabin Trail.

Current Road Information

Emery County Road Department
120 West Highway 29
Castle Dale, UT 84513
(435) 381-2550

BLM Price Field Office
125 South 600 West
Price, UT 84501
(435) 636-3600

Map References

BLM   San Rafael Desert
USGS 1:24,000 Twin Knolls, San Rafael Knob
        1:100,000 San Rafael Desert
Maptech CD-ROM: Central/San Rafael
Trails Illustrated, #712
Utah Atlas & Gazetteer, p. 39
Utah Travel Council #5
Other: Recreation Map of the San Rafael Swell and San
      Rafael Desert

Route Directions

▼ 0.0		On Central #12: Temple Mountain Trail, 4.9 miles from I-70, zero trip meter and turn west onto road marked "Head of Sinbad."
4.4 ▲		Trail ends at Central #12: Temple Mountain Trail; turn left for I-70, right for Utah 24.
GPS: N 38°49.70' W 110°42.44'		
▼ 0.5	SO	Cross through wash.
3.9 ▲	SO	Cross through wash.
▼ 1.0	SO	Track on right, then cross cattle guard.
3.4 ▲	SO	Cross cattle guard, then track on left.
▼ 2.0	SO	Cross through wash. Cattle guard.
2.4 ▲	SO	Cattle guard. Then cross through wash.
▼ 2.6	BR	Tracks on left.

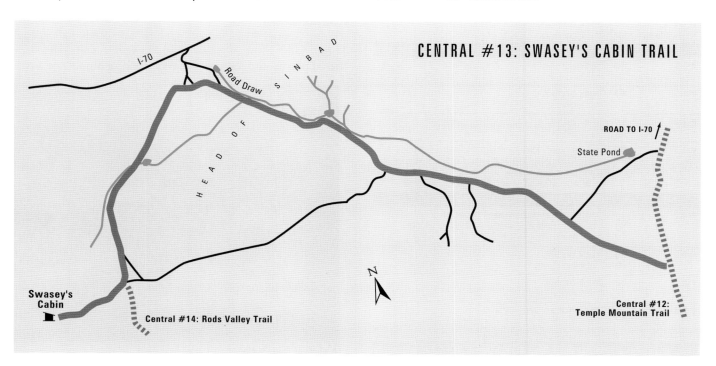

CENTRAL #13: SWASEY'S CABIN TRAIL

I-70

Road Draw

HEAD OF SINBAD

ROAD TO I-70

State Pond

Swasey's Cabin

Central #14: Rods Valley Trail

N

Central #12:
Temple Mountain Trail

Typical erosion that can make Swasey's Cabin Trail difficult

1.7 ▲		BL	Tracks on right.
			GPS: N 38°50.88' W 110°44.94'
▼ 2.7		SO	Cross through large wash.
	1.7 ▲	SO	Cross through large wash.
▼ 3.6		BR	Track on left.
	0.8 ▲	BL	Track on right.
▼ 3.7		SO	Track on left.
	0.6 ▲	SO	Track on right.
▼ 4.4		SO	Track on right to I-70. Zero trip meter.
	0.0 ▲		Continue east.
			GPS: N 38°51.71' W 110°46.45'
▼ 0.0			Continue west.
	2.3 ▲	SO	Track on left to I-70. Zero trip meter.
▼ 0.3		SO	Track on right.
	2.0 ▲	SO	Track on left.
			GPS: N 38°51.78' W 110°46.80'
▼ 0.9		SO	Track and corral on right.
	1.4 ▲	SO	Another track to corral on left.
▼ 1.0		SO	Another track to corral on right.
	1.3 ▲	SO	Track and corral on left.
▼ 1.1		SO	Cattle guard. Then track on right. Stock pond on left.
	1.2 ▲	SO	Stock pond on right. Track on left. Cross cattle guard.
▼ 1.5		SO	Track on right.
	0.8 ▲	SO	Track on left.
			GPS: N 38°51.01' W 110°47.71'
▼ 1.6		SO	Tracks on right.
	0.7 ▲	SO	Tracks on left.
▼ 1.9		SO	Track on left.
	0.4 ▲	SO	Track on right.
▼ 2.0		BL	Track on right.
	0.3 ▲	BR	Track on left.
▼ 2.3		BR	Fork in road. Proceed right toward Swasey's cabin. Track on left is Central #14: Rods Valley Trail. Zero trip meter.
	0.0 ▲		Continue along main trail.
			GPS: N 38°50.37' W 110°47.67'
▼ 0.0			Continue toward Swasey's cabin.
	0.8 ▲	SO	Track on right is Central #14: Rods Valley Trail. Zero trip meter.
▼ 0.2		SO	Track on left.
	0.6 ▲	SO	Track on right.
▼ 0.7		SO	Track on left.
	0.1 ▲	SO	Track on right.
▼ 0.8			Trail ends at Swasey's cabin.
	0.0 ▲		From Swasey's cabin, zero trip meter and return along main trail.
			GPS: N 38°50.15' W 110°48.39'

Rods Valley Trail

Starting Point:	Central #13: Swasey's Cabin Trail
Finishing Point:	Central #15: Reds Canyon Trail
Total Mileage:	5.8 miles
Unpaved Mileage:	5.8 miles
Driving Time:	30 minutes
Elevation Range:	6,700–7,200 feet
Usually Open:	Year-round
Difficulty Rating:	3
Scenic Rating:	8
Remoteness Rating:	+0

Special Attractions

- Provides an alternative route to connect through to Central #15: Reds Canyon Trail.
- Numerous backcountry camping sites.

History

As the Swasey family (sometimes spelled Swazy) was settling the region in and around the San Rafael Swell in the late 1800s, they became well liked by the local homesteaders, who considered them good-natured, skillful cowboys. Their true home was said to be the open range, and so today they are not linked to any one place, though a number of landforms in central Utah are named after the family or one of its members. Rod Swasey was said to have been so impressed with this scenic valley that he named it after himself.

Description

From Central #13: Swasey's Cabin Trail, Rods Valley Trail heads south through grassland and sagebrush with some scattered pinyon and juniper. The trail crosses a number of wash-

A view of Rods Valley

es and passes through a dense area of pinyon and juniper as an interesting mix of red- and buff-colored cliffs rise up on either side.

The 3-rated trail is not one of the more frequently used and has a number of good backcountry camping spots. Both the beginning and end of the trail are relatively easy to drive. A few wash crossings in the middle section tend to be the most difficult. Ending at Central #15: Reds Canyon Trail, Rods Valley Trail finishes as it started—in sagebrush and grassland with only occasional pinyon and juniper.

Current Road Information
Emery County Road Department
120 West Highway 29
Castle Dale, UT 84513
(435) 381-2550

BLM Price Field Office
125 South 600 West
Price, UT 84501
(435) 636-3600

Map References
BLM San Rafael Desert
USGS 1:24,000 San Rafael Knob
1:100,000 San Rafael Desert
Maptech CD-ROM: Central/San Rafael
Trails Illustrated, #712
Utah Atlas & Gazetteer, p. 39
Other: Recreation Map of the San Rafael Swell and San Rafael Desert

A rough section of Rods Valley Trail

Route Directions

▼ 0.0			On Central #13: Swasey's Cabin Trail, 6.7 miles from Central #12: Temple Mountain Trail, zero trip meter and proceed southeast.
	5.8 ▲		Trail ends at Central #13: Swasey's Cabin Trail; turn left for Swasey's cabin, right for Central #12: Temple Mountain Trail.
	GPS: N 38°50.37' W 110°47.67'		
▼ 0.1		SO	Track on right.
	5.7 ▲	SO	Track on left.
▼ 0.8		SO	Track on right.
	4.9 ▲	SO	Track on left.
▼ 1.2		BR	Fork in road through wash.
	4.6 ▲	BL	Road on right.
▼ 1.6		SO	Track on right, then cross through wash.
	4.2 ▲	SO	Cross through wash, then track on left.
	GPS: N 38°49.16' W 110°48.04'		
▼ 1.8		SO	Pass through gate and close behind you.
	3.9 ▲	SO	Pass through gate and close behind you.
▼ 2.4		SO	Cross through wash.
	3.3 ▲	SO	Cross through wash.
▼ 3.3		SO	Track on right.
	2.4 ▲	SO	Track on left.
	GPS: N 38°47.76' W 110°48.44'		
▼ 3.9		SO	Cross through wash.
	1.8 ▲	SO	Cross through wash.
▼ 5.4		SO	Pass through gate and close behind you.
	0.4 ▲	SO	Pass through gate and close behind you.
	GPS: N 38°46.22' W 110°47.83'		
▼ 5.8			Trail ends at Central #15: Reds Canyon Trail; turn left for Central #12: Temple Mountain Trail, turn right for Reds Canyon.
	0.0 ▲		On Central #15: Reds Canyon Trail, 3 miles from northern intersection with Central #12: Temple Mountain Trail, zero trip meter and proceed north. Follow sign that reads, "Rods Valley Road, Swasey Cabin 6."
	GPS: N 38°45.96' W 110°47.69'		

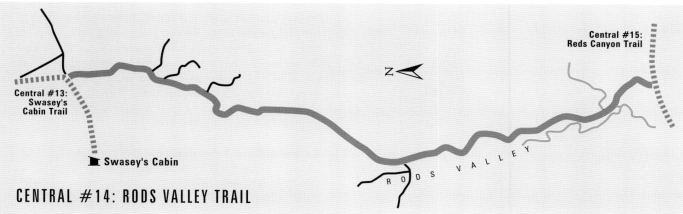

CENTRAL #14: RODS VALLEY TRAIL

Central #13: Swasey's Cabin Trail

Swasey's Cabin

N

R O D S   V A L L E Y

Central #15: Reds Canyon Trail

Reds Canyon Trail

Starting Point:	Central #12: Temple Mountain Trail
Finishing Point:	Central #12: Temple Mountain Trail
Total Mileage:	37.6 miles
Unpaved Mileage:	37.6 miles
Driving Time:	2.5 hours
Elevation Range:	5,200–7,000 feet
Usually Open:	Year-round
Difficulty Rating:	3
Scenic Rating:	10
Remoteness Rating:	+0

Special Attractions

- A moderately easy, fun, varied loop drive.
- Driving along Reds Wash through magnificent red canyon scenery.
- Hondoo Arch.
- Numerous old uranium mines.

History

In the 1950s, uranium prospectors came into Reds Canyon looking for a lucky strike. Vernon Pick, a farmer and mechanic from Minnesota with no prospecting experience, was one of them. Though most prospectors quickly abandoned the harsh landscape for easier pickings around Moab, in June 1952, Pick came upon a large deposit of the mineral and staked his claim, the Delta Mine, in this section of the San Rafael Swell.

Pick was determined to make the remote mine a success and soon was pumping out 1,500 tons of ore a month, making the Delta Mine one of the more successful uranium mines in Emery County. In 1954, a wealthy entrepreneur named Floyd Odlum liked the prospects of the Delta Mine and asked its owner to name his price. Pick reportedly asked for and was paid $9 million. Renaming it Hidden Splendor Mine, Odlum

Towering Tomsich Butte (rear) along Reds Canyon Trail

made only a fraction of his money back before the ore pinched out. The deal soon became known as Odlum's Hidden Blunder.

The Hidden Splendor Mine had one of the larger deposits in the region; other mines, such as the one on Tomsich Butte, were much smaller. Tomsich was the name of a prospector near Muddy Creek who, along with his dog, drank the poison creek water. Tomsich survived, but his ill-fated dog did not. Eventually, Tomsich and

Old mines on the south face of Tomsich Butte

his partner Hannert found uranium on the mountain. They immediately staked claims around the butte and began to mine the ore. However, once the ore tapped out, the mine and some of its machinery were abandoned.

Description

The Reds Canyon Trail is a loop trail that begins and ends on Central #12: Temple Mountain Trail. It sets off through sagebrush and rolling grasslands dotted with pinyon and juniper, where layers of deep red- and buff-colored soil stand out in sharp contrast with each other.

The road's rating of 3 is contingent upon the amount of erosion from recent rain and/or how long it has been since the road was last graded. If graded and dry, the road would rate a 2. However, if there have been recent washouts, the trail could be considerably more difficult, perhaps even impassable without some road repairs.

The road moves through the deep red canyon, traveling in the wash for about 7.5 miles. As you leave the wash, there are some excellent views of Tomsich Butte (also spelled Tomsick), which rises some 700 feet ahead to an elevation of 5,805 feet above sea level. The trail winds around the eastern side of Tomsich Butte along short sections of shelf road before eventually reaching an intersection south of the butte.

For the best view of Hondoo Arch, turn right at this intersection and head down a short, half-mile spur road toward Muddy Creek. The arch is on the left, and mines still sit to the right of the trail along the southern side of Tomsich Butte.

From the Hondoo Arch viewpoint to the end, the trail levels out and becomes a 1-rated road, passing through rolling grassland and sagebrush (used for cattle grazing). Five miles from Hondoo Arch you reach the turnoff for the Hidden Splendor Mine, and after 16.8 miles you meet back up with Central #12: Temple Mountain Trail.

Current Road Information

Emery County Road Department
120 West Highway 29
Castle Dale, UT 84513
(435) 381-2550

BLM Price Field Office
125 South 600 West
Price, UT 84501
(435) 636-3600

Map References

BLM San Rafael Desert
USGS 1:24,000 Twin Knolls, San Rafael Knob, Copper
Globe, Tomsich Butte, Horse Valley
1:100,000 San Rafael Desert
Maptech CD-ROM: Central/San Rafael
Trails Illustrated, #712
Utah Atlas & Gazetteer, pp. 38, 39
Utah Travel Council #5
Other: Recreation Map of the San Rafael Swell and San
Rafael Desert

Route Directions

▼ 0.0		On Central #12: Temple Mountain Trail, 9.8 miles from I-70, zero trip meter and proceed southeast.
3.0 ▲		Trail ends at Central #12: Temple Mountain Trail; turn left for I-70, right for Utah 24.
GPS: N 38°46.63' W 110°44.73'		
▼ 3.0	SO	Trail on right is Central #14: Rods Valley Trail. Zero trip meter.
0.0 ▲		Continue along main trail.
GPS: N 38°45.96' W 110°47.69'		
▼ 0.0		Continue along main trail.
10.7 ▲	SO	Trail on left is Central #14: Rods Valley Trail. Zero trip meter.
▼ 0.6	TR	Cross through wash, then turn right at T-intersection. Left returns to Temple Mountain Trail. Follow sign to Reds Canyon and McKay Flat.
10.1 ▲	TL	Take track on left. Then cross through wash.
GPS: N 38°45.60' W 110°48.14'		
▼ 0.7	SO	Cattle guard. Then track on right.
10.0 ▲	SO	Track on right. Then cattle guard.
▼ 1.5	SO	Track on left to McKay Flat. Continue toward Reds Canyon.
9.1 ▲	SO	Track on right to McKay Flat.
GPS: N 38°45.29' W 110°48.97'		
▼ 2.5	SO	Track on right.
8.2 ▲	SO	Track on left.
▼ 10.7	SO	Track on right. Zero trip meter
0.0 ▲		Continue northeast.
GPS: N 38°44.77' W 110°56.28'		
▼ 0.0		Continue southwest.
5.8 ▲	SO	Track on left. Zero trip meter.
▼ 5.2	BL	Roads on right.
0.6 ▲	BR	Roads on left.
GPS: N 38°41.40' W 110°59.04'		
▼ 5.7	BR	Fork in road.
0.1 ▲	SO	Road on right.
▼ 5.8	TR	T-intersection. Zero trip meter. Turn left to head down toward Muddy Creek for the best views of Hondoo Arch. Note: You will return to this point to continue along the main route.
0.0 ▲		Continue along main route.
GPS: N 38°40.98' W 110°59.21'		
▼ 0.0		Continue toward Tomsich Butte.
1.2 ▲	TL	Intersection back with the main trail.
▼ 0.2	SO	Track on right to mine.
1.0 ▲	SO	Track on left to mine.
▼ 0.3	SO	Track on right.
0.9 ▲	SO	Track on left.
▼ 0.4	BR	Track on left.
0.8 ▲	SO	Track on right.
▼ 0.6	UT	Track on right. View of Hondoo Arch to the left. Return to intersection noted above.

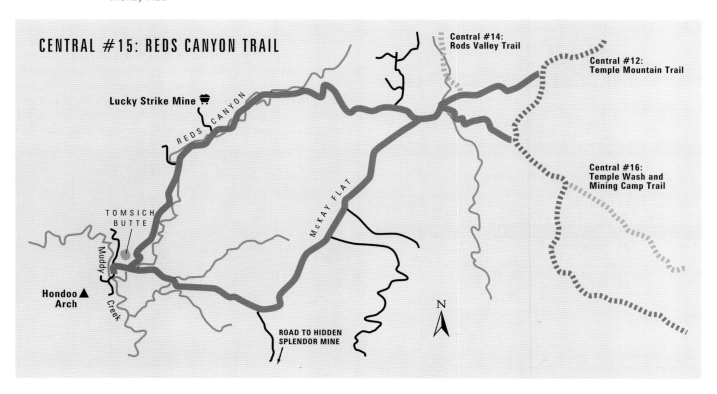

CENTRAL #15: REDS CANYON TRAIL

0.6 ▲		UT	Track on right. View of Hondoo Arch. Return to intersection noted below.

GPS: N 38°41.05' W 110°59.88'

▼ 1.2		BR	Intersection. Continue along the main trail. Zero trip meter.
	0.0 ▲		Continue along route.

GPS: N 38°40.98' W 110°59.21'

▼ 0.0			Proceed southeast along the main trail.
	5.0 ▲	BL	Bear left toward Muddy Creek and zero trip meter. This spur to the main trail will provide the best views of Hondoo Arch as you proceed toward Muddy Creek. Note: You will return to this intersection to continue along the main route.
▼ 0.1		SO/SO	Track on left. Then track on right.
	4.9 ▲	SO/BL	Track on left. Then bear left at fork in road. Follow sign to Hondoo Arch.
▼ 1.4		SO	Cross through wash.
	3.6 ▲	SO	Cross through wash.
▼ 1.6		SO	Cattle guard.
	3.4 ▲	SO	Cattle guard.

GPS: N 38°40.62' W 110°57.79'

▼ 5.0		BL	Track on right to Hidden Splendor Mine. Zero trip meter.
	0.0 ▲		Continue west.

GPS: N 38°39.77' W 110°54.37'

▼ 0.0			Continue east.
	8.3 ▲	BR	Fork in road. Left goes to Hidden Splendor Mine. Zero trip meter.
▼ 3.2		SO	Track on right.
	5.0 ▲	SO	Track on left.
▼ 3.4		SO	Track on left.
	4.9 ▲	SO	Track on right.

GPS: N 38°42.10' W 110°52.21'

▼ 4.0		SO	Track on left.
	4.2 ▲	SO	Track on right.
▼ 4.2		SO	Tracks on left.
	4.1 ▲	SO	Tracks on right.
▼ 4.4		SO	Track on right.
	3.9 ▲	SO	Track on left.
▼ 4.6		SO	Cattle guard.
	3.7 ▲	SO	Cattle guard.

GPS: N 38°43.01' W 110°51.61'

▼ 7.2		SO	Track on right.
	1.1 ▲	SO	Track on left.
▼ 8.3		TR	T-intersection. Zero trip meter.
	0.0 ▲		Continue southwest.

GPS: N 38°45.27' W 110°48.98'

▼ 0.0			Continue east.
	3.5 ▲	TL	Intersection. Follow sign to McKay Flat. Zero trip meter.
▼ 0.8		SO	Track on left. Then cattle guard.
	2.7 ▲	SO	Cattle guard. Then track on right.

GPS: N 38°45.59' W 110°48.19'

▼ 0.9		SO	Track on left.
	2.6 ▲	SO	Track on right.
▼ 1.0		SO	Cross through wash.
	2.5 ▲	SO	Cross through wash.
▼ 3.5			Trail ends at Central #12: Temple Mountain Trail; turn right for Utah 24, left for I-70.
	0.0 ▲		On Central #12: Temple Mountain Trail, 12.4 miles from I-70, zero trip meter and proceed west. Follow sign to Tan Seep and Reds Canyon.

GPS: N 38°44.70' W 110°45.75'

Temple Wash and Mining Camp Trail

Starting Point:	**Central #12: Temple Mountain Trail**
Finishing Point:	**Central #12: Temple Mountain Trail**
Total Mileage:	**9.2 miles**
Unpaved Mileage:	**9.2 miles**
Driving Time:	**1.5 hours**
Elevation Range:	**5,300–6,800 feet**
Usually Open:	**Year-round**
Difficulty Rating:	**4**
Scenic Rating:	**9**
Remoteness Rating:	**+1**

Special Attractions

- Mines and old mining camp.
- Moderately challenging alternative trail around Temple Mountain.

History

The town of Temple Mountain was first settled just before the turn of the 20th century when prospectors discovered uranium, radium, and vanadium ores at the spot. By 1910, it was a small village. Most of the valuable minerals in the area were exported to France, and it is believed that some of the radium mined in Temple Mountain ended up in the laboratory of Madame Curie and played a part in her famous discovery.

After World War I, the town folded as cheaper sources of uranium were found elsewhere, and it was not until the uranium boom of the 1950s that people returned to the area. At that point, the center of town was moved away from the mine to the mine road's junction with Utah 24. When the uranium boom died in the late 1960s, the town once again did too. In its years of operation, the Temple Mountain dis-

A building still stands at the mining camp

trict produced more than 2.5 million tons of ore. While there are still several interesting buildings standing in town, note that the mine itself remains radioactive and constitutes a health hazard.

Description

Temple Wash and Mining Camp Trail begins and ends along Central #12: Temple Mountain Trail in the region known as Sinbad Country, so-called because the area's rock formations, cliffs, and canyons bear a resemblance to the exotic scenery described in the *Arabian Nights*.

After a half mile or so, the trail follows an easy shelf road along the side of a canyon with great views straight ahead to

Temple Mountain and east over the San Rafael Desert. This 3-rated section is fairly rough and rocky and can be somewhat hard on tires. After about 4 miles, at the base of Temple Mountain, the road becomes considerably rougher as you cross back and forth through the wash. This 4-rated section of the trail also offers remarkable views of Temple Mountain and the very attractive country around it.

The section of trail that squeezes through the narrow canyon

After 5.2 miles, you reach the Temple Mountain ghost town and uranium mining operation. You can still see the remains of the old camp, open mine portals, tailings, and other assorted mine structures. Be sure not to go into any of the mine entrances as they are dangerous.

After the ghost town, the trail improves, becoming a 1-rated graded track. The trail descends through a narrow canyon that cuts through the San Rafael Reef on its way to

the edge of the San Rafael Desert. For the better part of a mile along the wash, sheer canyon walls crowd in on both sides. The trail ends at Central #12: Temple Mountain Trail at an information board opposite the paved turnoff to Goblin Valley State Park.

Current Road Information

Emery County Road Department
120 West Highway 29
Castle Dale, UT 84513
(435) 381-2550

BLM Price Field Office
125 South 600 West
Price, UT 84501
(435) 636-3600

Map References

BLM San Rafael Desert
USGS 1:24,000 Temple Mt.
　　　　1:100,000 San Rafael Desert
Maptech CD-ROM: Central/San Rafael
Trails Illustrated, #712
Utah Atlas & Gazetteer, p. 39
Utah Travel Council #5 (incomplete)
Other: Recreation Map of the San Rafael Swell and San Rafael Desert

Route Directions

▼ 0.0		On Central #12: Temple Mountain Trail, 14.5 miles from I-70, zero trip meter and turn east onto unmarked road.
5.2 ▲		Trail ends at Central #12: Temple Mountain Trail; turn right for I-70, left for Utah 24.
GPS: N 38°43.60' W 110°44.04'		
▼ 0.3	BR	Road on left.
4.9 ▲	BL	Road on right.
▼ 3.6	SO	Cross through wash.
1.5 ▲	SO	Cross through wash.
GPS: N 38°41.97' W 110°40.82'		

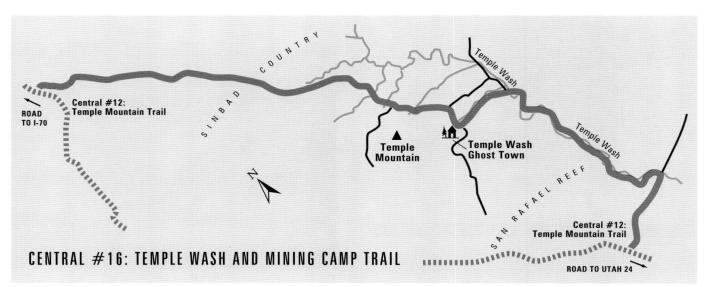

CENTRAL #16: TEMPLE WASH AND MINING CAMP TRAIL

Central #12: Temple Mountain Trail

ROAD TO I-70

SINBAD COUNTRY

Temple Mountain

Temple Wash Ghost Town

Temple Wash

Temple Wash

SAN RAFAEL REEF

Central #12: Temple Mountain Trail

ROAD TO UTAH 24

N

▼ 3.9		SO	Cross through wash.
	1.3 ▲	SO	Cross through wash.
▼ 4.0		BL	Track on right.
	1.1 ▲	BR	Track on left.
		GPS: N 38°41.72' W 110°40.65'	
▼ 4.2		BL	Cross through wash. Track on right.
	0.9 ▲	BR	Track on left. Cross through wash.
▼ 4.5		BL	Track on right.
	0.6 ▲	BR	Intersection. Follow track to the right.
		GPS: N 38°41.40' W 110°40.40'	
▼ 5.0		SO	Cross through wash.
	0.2 ▲	SO	Cross through wash.
▼ 5.1		BL	Intersection. Road on right, then cross through wash.
	0.1 ▲	BR	Cross through wash, then road on left.
		GPS: N 38°41.15' W 110°40.03'	
▼ 5.2		BL	Intersection. Right goes to mines. Then pass Temple Wash ghost town. Zero trip meter at building on left.
	0.0 ▲		Cross through wash.
		GPS: N 38°41.08' W 110°40.03'	
▼ 0.0			Proceed past track on right and continue.
	4.0 ▲	BR	Temple Wash ghost town. Zero trip meter at building on right. Straight on goes to mines.
▼ 0.6		BR	Track on left.
	3.3 ▲	BL	Track on right.
▼ 0.7		SO	Cross through wash twice.
	3.3 ▲	SO	Cross through wash twice.
▼ 0.8		SO	Cross through wash.
	3.2 ▲	SO	Cross through wash.
▼ 1.1		SO	Cross through wash.
	2.9 ▲	SO	Cross through wash.
		GPS: N 38°40.82' W 110°39.16'	
▼ 2.5		SO	Track on left.
	1.5 ▲	SO	Track on right.
▼ 2.7		BL	Track on right.
	1.2 ▲	SO	Track on left.
▼ 3.0		BR	Intersection. Road on left.
	1.0 ▲	BL	Road on right.
		GPS: N 38°39.64' W 110°38.33'	
▼ 3.2		SO	Track on right.
	0.8 ▲	SO	Track on left.
▼ 3.5		SO	Cross through wash, then tracks on right.
	0.4 ▲	SO	Tracks on left, then cross through wash.
▼ 3.6		BL	Tracks on right.
	0.4 ▲	BR	Tracks on left.
▼ 3.9		TR	Four-way intersection. Turn right toward message board.
	0.1 ▲	TL	Four-way intersection.
▼ 4.0			Trail ends at paved intersection with Central #12: Temple Mountain Trail. Go straight for Goblin Valley State Park, left for Utah 24.
	0.0 ▲		On Central #12: Temple Mountain Trail, 5.1 miles from Utah 24, zero trip meter and turn north at message board, opposite the paved turn-off to Goblin Valley State Park.
		GPS: N 38°39.20' W 110°39.23'	

Wild Horse Mesa Trail

Starting Point:	Utah 24, 9.7 miles west of Hanksville
Finishing Point:	Goblin Valley State Park
Total Mileage:	28.9 miles
Unpaved Mileage:	28.9 miles
Driving Time:	3 hours
Elevation Range:	4,500–5,000 feet
Usually Open:	Year-round
Difficulty Rating:	3
Scenic Rating:	9
Remoteness Rating:	+1

Special Attractions

- Old timber cabins and springs near Muddy Creek.
- Goblin Valley State Park.
- Desert scenery along Wild Horse Mesa, San Rafael Reef, and Wild Horse Canyon.

History

It is thought that one of the earliest European explorers in the San Rafael Swell was John C. Frémont. His artist's renditions of his travels in 1853 when scouting for a route for the railroad include drawings with striking similarities to Wild Horse Mesa.

One of the landmarks on this trail is Factory Butte, which was originally named Provo Factory by the road exploration teams of the early 1880s, as it reminded them of the Provo Woollen Mills, one of the earliest major industries in Utah.

Like many other regions around Utah, the San Rafael Swell saw its share of uranium exploration. The most famous rags-to-riches story concerns Vernon Pick and the Hidden Splendor Mine, which can be accessed from this trail; see Central #15: Reds Canyon Trail for a full description of Pick's legendary strike.

The trail looking toward Hunt Draw Gap in the San Rafael Reef

A two-story cabin along the trail

Description

This route crosses the lower parts of the San Rafael Swell and finishes at Goblin Valley State Park. It makes an interesting backcountry access to Goblin Valley and travels through a wide variety of arid desert scenery.

The trail commences on Utah 24, 9.7 miles west of Hanksville. The graded gravel road is unmarked, but the highly distinctive and isolated Factory Butte, with its high sides and sheer cliffs standing high above the Factory Benches, is hard to miss.

The trail leads toward Factory Butte and passes it on its eastern side. After 9.2 miles the trail standard drops from wide, graded gravel to a narrower dirt trail, and it is marked for high-clearance vehicles only. After another 1.4 miles, you crest a slight rise and the trail abruptly disappears! At this point, the trail meets a T-intersection and descends down an escarpment to the east. Ahead is a sheer drop to a claypan. This spot is particularly scenic; you drive over gray shale domes while admiring the tilted pink slabs of the North Caineville Reef in the distance.

The crossing of Muddy Creek is the most difficult portion of the trail. There are often alternative crossings and the creek can be soft and, not surprisingly, muddy. When the trail was surveyed, the upstream crossing was easiest, but this may change. Immediately after the creek crossing, a track on the left heads north to the Hidden Splendor Mine.

Shortly after Muddy Creek, the trail passes by a spring in a thicket of tamarisk and the remains of a two-story wooden cabin. There are animal sheds and corrals and a second cabin a little farther on, but the story behind the cabins is unknown.

From the cabins, the trail climbs onto Little Wild Horse Mesa and then drops down to enter the canyon. It travels for a couple of miles in the wash of Little Wild Horse Creek before exiting the canyon to the north and turning east to parallel the San Rafael Reef. After passing the popular hiking trail for Little Wild Horse and Bell Canyons, 10.4 miles after Muddy Creek, the trail follows a sandy track along the wide, grassy valley to finish at Goblin Valley State Park.

This trail is impassable in wet weather; the clay on the Factory Benches becomes incredibly greasy and it is impossible to get any traction at all. There is also the danger of sudden flash flooding in Little Wild Horse Canyon. There are some pretty backcountry campsites here, but camping is not advised in the canyon.

Current Road Information

BLM Price Field Office
125 South 600 West
Price, UT 84501
(435) 636-3600

Map References

BLM Hanksville, San Rafael Desert (incomplete)
USGS 1:24,000 Town Point, Factory Butte, Hunt Draw, Little Wild Horse Mesa, Goblin Valley
1:100,000 Hanksville, San Rafael Desert (incomplete)
Maptech CD-ROM: Moab/Canyonlands; Central/San Rafael
Utah Atlas & Gazetteer, pp. 28, 29
Utah Travel Council #5
Other: Recreation Map of the San Rafael Swell and San Rafael Desert (incomplete)
Recreation Map of the Henry Mountains Area (incomplete)

Route Directions

▼ 0.0			From Utah 24, 9.7 miles west of Hanksville, zero trip meter and turn north on unmarked graded gravel road toward Factory Butte.
	9.2 ▲		Trail ends at Utah 24. Turn right for Capitol Reef National Park, left for Hanksville.
GPS: N 38°22.03' W 110°53.50'			
▼ 0.7		SO	Track on left.
	8.5 ▲	SO	Track on right.
▼ 1.4		SO	Track on left.
	7.8 ▲	SO	Track on right.
▼ 1.7		SO	Cross over Neilson Wash. Factory Butte is to the left.
	7.5 ▲	SO	Cross over Neilson Wash. Factory Butte is to the right.
▼ 2.3		SO	Cross over wash.
	6.9 ▲	SO	Cross over wash.
▼ 3.6		SO	Dam on left, then track on right.
	5.6 ▲	SO	Track on left, then dam on right.
▼ 5.8		SO	Track on right.
	3.4 ▲	SO	Track on left.
▼ 6.6		SO	Track on right.
	2.6 ▲	SO	Track on left.
▼ 7.1		SO	Track on right.
	2.1 ▲	SO	Track on left.
▼ 7.8		SO	Cross through wash.
	1.4 ▲	SO	Cross through wash.
▼ 8.4		SO	Cross through Coal Mine Wash.
	0.8 ▲	SO	Cross through Coal Mine Wash.
▼ 9.2		BL	Trail becomes narrow, dirt road. Larger track on right. Zero trip meter.
	0.0 ▲		Continue on wider gravel road.
GPS: N 38°29.17' W 110°55.14'			
▼ 0.0			Continue on narrower trail.
	4.2 ▲	SO	Larger track on left. Zero trip meter.
▼ 1.4		TR	T-intersection—caution! Steep drop ahead. North Caineville Reef is ahead. Trail winds down shelf road to right.
	2.8 ▲	TL	Turn left near the top of shelf road.
▼ 2.7		SO	Descend to cross over creek.
	1.5 ▲	SO	Cross over creek and ascend short shelf road.
▼ 4.1		SO	Cross bed of Muddy Creek, multichanneled and surrounded by tamarisks.

CENTRAL #17: WILD HORSE MESA TRAIL

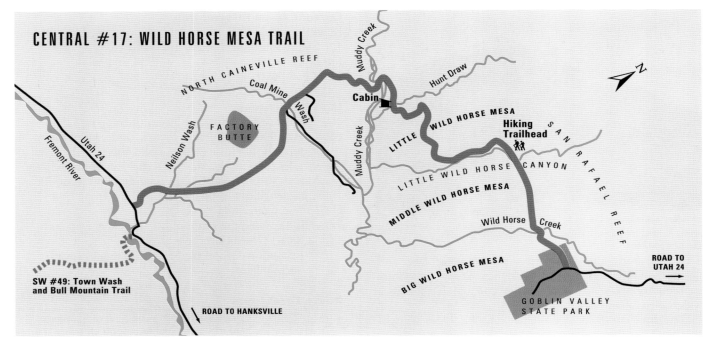

0.1 ▲	SO	Cross bed of Muddy Creek, multichanneled and surrounded by tamarisks.	
▼ 4.2	BL	Two options to ford Muddy Creek's main channel; upstream is generally easier. Both can be soft on approach and exit, but have firmer bottoms. Zero trip meter after crossing.	
0.0 ▲		Continue along trail.	

GPS: N 38°31.90' W 110°54.14'

▼ 0.0		Continue northeast alongside Muddy Creek.
10.4 ▲	SO	Two options to ford Muddy Creek's main channel; upstream crossing is generally easier. Both can be soft on approach and exit, but have firmer bottoms. Zero trip meter before crossing.
▼ 0.1	SO	Track on left to Hidden Splendor Mine, then rejoin downstream crossing.
10.3 ▲	SO	Track on left is first creek crossing, then track on right to Hidden Splendor Mine.

GPS: N 38°31.93' W 110°54.25'

▼ 0.4	SO	Cross through wash.
10.0 ▲	SO	Cross through wash.
▼ 1.2	SO	Cross through wash, then track on right goes to old two-story wooden cabin, spring, and animal yards.
9.2 ▲	SO	Track on left goes to old two-story wooden cabin, spring, and animal yards, then cross through wash.

GPS: N 38°31.95' W 110°53.17'

▼ 1.6	SO	Cross through Hunt Draw.
8.8 ▲	SO	Cross through Hunt Draw.
▼ 2.6	SO	Track on left.
7.8 ▲	SO	Track on right.
▼ 3.2	SO	Cross through wash.
7.2 ▲	SO	Cross through wash.

GPS: N 38°32.77' W 110°52.09'

▼ 3.7	SO	Cross through wash.
6.7 ▲	SO	Cross through wash.
▼ 4.3	SO	Cross through wash.
6.1 ▲	SO	Cross through wash.
▼ 4.5	SO	Cross through wash.

5.9 ▲	SO	Cross through wash.
▼ 4.6	SO	Cross through wash.
5.8 ▲	SO	Cross through wash.

GPS: N 38°32.43' W 110°50.90'

▼ 5.3	SO	Small rocky steps descend to cross a series of washes in the next 0.3 miles.
5.1 ▲	SO	End of series of washes and rocky section.

GPS: N 38°32.59' W 110°50.27'

▼ 5.5	BL	Track on right.
4.9 ▲	BR	Track on left.

GPS: N 38°32.45' W 110°50.17'

▼ 5.6	SO	End of series of washes and rocky section.
4.8 ▲	SO	Small rocky steps and a series of washes in the next 0.3 miles.
▼ 6.0	SO	Track on right to spring.
4.4 ▲	SO	Track on left to spring.

GPS: N 38°32.41' W 110°49.75'

▼ 6.4	SO	Track on left.
4.0 ▲	SO	Track on right.
▼ 6.5	SO	Track winds down into Little Wild Horse Canyon.
3.9 ▲	SO	Track leaves Little Wild Horse Canyon.
▼ 6.8	SO	Enter Little Wild Horse Canyon creek wash.
3.6 ▲	SO	Exit Little Wild Horse Canyon creek wash.

GPS: N 38°32.89' W 110°49.54'

▼ 8.6	SO	Exit narrow part of canyon.
1.8 ▲	SO	Entering narrow part of Little Wild Horse Canyon.
▼ 10.4	SO	Trail exits wash. Little Wild Horse Canyon and Bell Canyon hiking trail and parking area on left. Zero trip meter.
0.0 ▲		Continue along wash.

GPS: N 38°34.97' W 110°48.13'

▼ 0.0		Continue on graded road.
5.1 ▲	SO	Little Wild Horse Canyon and Bell Canyon hiking trail and parking area on right. Trail enters Little Wild Horse Canyon creek wash.
▼ 0.4	SO	Track on right.
4.7 ▲	SO	Track on left.

▼ 0.7		SO	Cross through wash.
	4.4 ▲	SO	Cross through wash.
▼ 1.9		SO	Track on right.
	3.2 ▲	SO	Track on left.
▼ 2.8		SO	Cross through wash.
	2.3 ▲	SO	Cross through wash.
▼ 3.1		SO	Cross through Wild Horse Canyon creek wash.
	2.0 ▲	SO	Cross through Wild Horse Canyon creek wash.
		GPS: N 38°34.57′ W 110°44.68′	
▼ 3.4		SO	Track on right.
	1.7 ▲	SO	Track on left.
▼ 3.6		SO	Cattle guard. Entering Goblin Valley State Park.
	1.5 ▲	SO	Cattle guard. Leaving Goblin Valley State Park.
		GPS: N 38°34.70′ W 110°43.98′	
▼ 5.1			Trail ends at T-intersection with paved road. Turn right to enter Goblin Valley, left for Utah 24.
	0.0 ▲		On Goblin Valley Road, 10.5 miles from Utah 24, turn west onto graded dirt road, following the sign for Muddy Creek, and zero trip meter.
		GPS: N 38°34.99′ W 110°42.56′	

A spectacular vantage point for the more intrepid backcountry travelers

CENTRAL REGION TRAIL #18

Cathedral Valley Trail

Starting Point:	**Utah 24, 2.6 miles east of Capitol Reef National Park**
Finishing Point:	**Caineville, Utah 24**
Total Mileage:	**55.1 miles**
Unpaved Mileage:	**55.1 miles**
Driving Time:	**7 hours**
Elevation Range:	**4,500–6,900 feet**
Usually Open:	**Year-round**
Difficulty Rating:	**2**
Scenic Rating:	**10**
Remoteness Rating:	**+1**

Special Attractions

- Desert viewpoints of Lower and Upper South Desert Overlooks.
- Historic Morrell cabin.
- Desert scenery in Cathedral Valley in Capitol Reef National Park.

History

Cathedral Valley was named in 1945 by Charles Kelly, the first superintendent of Capitol Reef National Park, and Frank Beckwith because they thought the valley's large monoliths looked like gothic cathedrals. John Frémont's 1853 expedition passed through the valley.

Morrell's cabin, a small log cabin in Cathedral Valley, was originally built by Paul Christensen on Thousand Lake Mountain to the west. The Christensen family lived there every summer for 20 years, working a sawmill on Lake Creek. Then in the late 1930s, Lesley Morrell bought the cabin and

moved it piece by piece to Cathedral Valley and carefully reconstructed it. Here, cowboys used the cabin during roundups and when moving cattle from summer to winter pastures. The property was incorporated into Capitol Reef National Park in 1970 and is listed on the National Register of Historic Places.

Other pioneers have given their names to features around Cathedral Valley. Hartnet Draw is named for David Hartnet, who was the first to use this route to travel from Fremont to Caineville. His rough road was used to transport freight between Caineville and the northern areas of Wayne County. The present-day Cathedral Valley Trail follows the lower reaches of this original pioneer road down Caineville Wash. Hartnet's road passed Willow Spring and Rock Water Spring before ascending Polk Creek to Thousand Lake Mountain. Pete Ackland, an early cattle rancher in the area, gave his name to springs in Hartnet Draw.

Caineville, at the end of the trail, is a one-time ghost town that now struggles to survive. It was settled in the early 1880s by Mormon pioneers, who planted a variety of crops. Sorghum was the most successful; as well as being used as a sweetener, it was boiled down to produce a potent liquor, which was sold to local cattlemen and miners or exchanged for lumber and hard goods. One project unique to Caineville was the growing of silk! Acting under the directive of the church, the pioneers imported silkworms and mulberry bushes, but

Cathedral Valley overlook with yuccas in the foreground

the attempt was never successful and was soon abandoned.

Like the neighboring ghost town of Giles, Caineville suffered frequent flooding by the Fremont River, and by 1910 the town was abandoned. Today, Caineville has a few residents, who live mainly in more modern housing. Most of the original townsite is derelict or gone.

Description

This long route travels through remote areas of Capitol Reef National Park and BLM land north of Caineville. The route is normally suitable for a 2WD high-clearance vehicle in good weather. Long stretches of sand, some minor rough sections, and the Fremont River crossing make it unsuitable for passenger vehicles.

The route commences 2.6 miles east of Capitol Reef National Park on Utah 24. There is a small sign that reads "river ford" and a gate, which may be closed but not locked. Half a

Crossing the Fremont River

mile from the start is the ford over the Fremont River. It is a long crossing at an angle; bear slightly downstream to exit on the far bank approximately 50 yards downriver. The ford itself has a firm bottom and unless the river is in flood or running high, it should be negotiable by high-clearance vehicles.

The entire trail is graded dirt road. The early sections can be sandy, especially as the trail runs along the Blue Hills and dips down to cross several washes. After 8.6 miles, the trail winds through the spectacular Bentonite Hills, whose purple hues are formed from volcanic ash. This section of the trail is impassable in wet weather.

After 13.4 miles, you reach the first of the two South Desert overlooks, with the immense Jailhouse Rock in the middle, in Capitol Reef National Park. This one is at the end of a 1.1-mile spur trail and a short walk. There used to be an old vehicle trail that continued down from this viewpoint, but unfortunately it's only for foot and pack travel these days.

About 2 miles farther, the trail enters Capitol Reef National Park and travels through the Hartnet Exclosure (established 1983) and Hartnet Draw. Camping in the park is restricted to the free primitive campground at Cathedral Valley. There are many hiking trails to overlooks and points of interest along the route. One of the best is the Upper South Desert Overlook,

where a short hike around the rim and then a scramble up to the high point yields surreal views over the South Desert far below. Just past this spot is another good viewpoint, the Cathedral Valley Overlook, which looks down on the trail and the famous monoliths. The Cathedral Campground is a quarter mile farther.

The trail then winds down some easy switchbacks into Cathedral Valley. Another short hike leads to the historic Morrell cabin, set against a backdrop of red rock buttes, and farther along other short spurs lead to the Temples of the Sun and Moon, Entrada sandstone towers rising abruptly from the valley floor. After this, the trail leaves Cathedral Valley and enters Caineville Wash. Finally, the trail follows alongside the Caineville Reef before finishing at Utah 24 at the small settlement of Caineville.

There are great views for almost the entire trail. At many points the Henry Mountains are visible to the southeast, the Waterpocket Fold to the southwest, the Caineville Mesas to the south, and Thousand Lake Mountain to the west.

Current Road Information

BLM Henry Mountain Field Station
406 South 100 West
Hanksville, UT 84734
(435) 542-3461

Capitol Reef National Park
HC-70 Box 15
Torrey, UT 84775
(435) 425-3791

Map References

BLM   Loa, Salina
USGS 1:24,000 Caineville, Fruita, Fruita NW, Cathedral
          Mt., Solomon's Temple, Caine Springs
          1:100,000 Loa, Salina
Maptech CD-ROM: Escalante/Dixie National Forest;
          Central/San Rafael
Trails Illustrated, #213
Utah Atlas & Gazetteer, p. 28
Utah Travel Council #5
Other: Capitol Reef National Park
          Recreation Map of the Henry Mountains Area
          (incomplete)

Route Directions

▼ 0.0		On Utah 24, 2.6 miles east of Capitol Reef National Park, turn northeast on graded dirt road at the sign for "river ford." Pass through gate and zero trip meter.
0.5 ▲		Pass through gate, then trail ends at Utah 24. Turn right for Capitol Reef National Park, left for Hanksville.
GPS: N 38°16.50' W 111°05.34'		
▼ 0.4	TL	Pass through gate and turn left. Track on right to corral.
0.1 ▲	TR	Turn right, then pass through gate. Track on left to corral.
▼ 0.5	BR	Ford Fremont River; bear right downstream for approximately 50 yards to exit. Zero trip meter on far bank.

0.0 ▲		Continue toward Utah 24.

GPS: N 38°16.49' W 111°04.76'

▼ 0.0		Continue away from river.
8.1 ▲	BR	Zero trip meter on bank, then ford Fremont River; bear right upstream for approximately 50 yards to exit.

▼ 0.1	SO	Track on left is old upper ford crossing (not used).
8.0 ▲	SO	Track on right is old upper ford crossing (not used).

▼ 0.2	SO	Cross through wash.
7.9 ▲	SO	Cross through wash.

▼ 2.1	SO	Track on right.
6.0 ▲	SO	Track on left.

▼ 2.2	SO	Cattle guard.
5.9 ▲	SO	Cattle guard.

▼ 2.3	SO	Cross through wash. Many wash crossings in the next 4.1 miles.
5.8 ▲	SO	Cross through wash.

▼ 2.8	SO	Track on right.
5.3 ▲	SO	Track on left.

▼ 4.8	SO	Cross through wash, then track on right.
3.3 ▲	SO	Track on left, then cross through wash.

GPS: N 38°19.29' W 111°06.09'

▼ 6.4	SO	Old drilling rig on right.
1.7 ▲	SO	Old drilling rig on left. Many wash crossings in the next 4.1 miles.

GPS: N 38°20.34' W 111°07.16'

▼ 8.1	SO	Marker post for Bentonite Hills. Zero trip meter.
0.0 ▲		Continue southeast.

GPS: N 38°21.67' W 111°07.65'

▼ 0.0		Continue northwest.
4.8 ▲	SO	Marker post for Bentonite Hills. Zero trip meter.

▼ 0.6	SO	Track on right to Guys Reservoir.
4.2 ▲	SO	Track on left to Guys Reservoir.

GPS: N 38°22.25' W 111°07.78'

▼ 1.2	BL	Track on right to Rock Water Spring.

3.6 ▲	BR	Track on left to Rock Water Spring.

GPS: N 38°22.57' W 111°08.09'

▼ 2.4	SO	Track on left.
2.4 ▲	SO	Track on right.

▼ 4.6	SO	Cross through wash.
0.2 ▲	SO	Cross through wash.

▼ 4.8	SO	Cross through wash, then track on left to Lower South Desert Overlook (1.1 miles). Zero trip meter.
0.0 ▲		Continue toward Utah 24.

GPS: N 38°24.13' W 111°11.08'

▼ 0.0		Continue toward Capitol Reef National Park.
2.2 ▲	SO	Track on right to Lower South Desert Overlook (1.1 miles). Zero trip meter, then cross through wash.

▼ 0.5	SO	Cross through wash.
1.7 ▲	SO	Cross through wash.

▼ 0.7	SO	Cattle guard.
1.5 ▲	SO	Cattle guard.

▼ 0.9	SO	Cross through wash.
1.3 ▲	SO	Cross through wash.

▼ 2.0	SO	Cross through wash.
0.2 ▲	SO	Cross through wash.

▼ 2.2	SO	Entering Capitol Reef National Park. Zero trip meter.
0.0 ▲		Continue away from Capitol Reef National Park.

GPS: N 38°25.54' W 111°11.19'

▼ 0.0		Continue into Capitol Reef National Park.
3.5 ▲	SO	Leaving Capitol Reef National Park. Zero trip meter.

▼ 0.3	SO	Exclosure on right.
3.2 ▲	SO	Exclosure on left.

▼ 1.1	SO	Hiking trail on right to Lower Cathedral Valley Overlook.
2.4 ▲	SO	Hiking trail on left to Lower Cathedral Valley Overlook.

GPS: N 38°25.82' W 111°12.28'

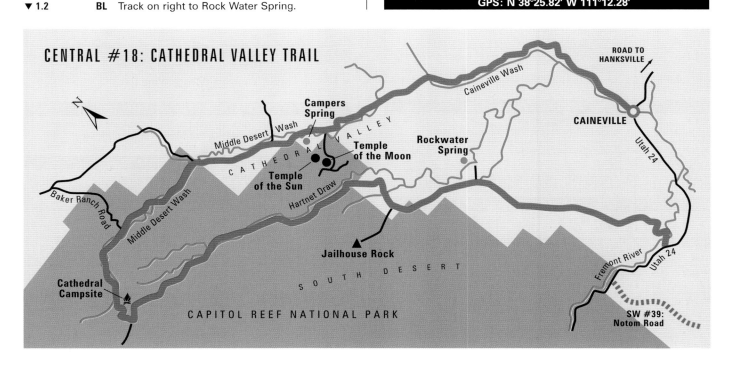

CENTRAL #18: CATHEDRAL VALLEY TRAIL

▼ 2.1		SO	Hartnet Exclosure on left.
	1.4 ▲	SO	Hartnet Exclosure on right.
▼ 2.9		SO	Cross through wash.
	0.6 ▲	SO	Cross through wash.
▼ 3.3		SO	Cross through Hartnet Draw.
	0.2 ▲	SO	Cross through Hartnet Draw.
▼ 3.4		SO	Cross through Hartnet Draw.
	0.1 ▲	SO	Cross through Hartnet Draw.
▼ 3.5		SO	Cross through Hartnet Draw. Ackland Spring immediately after wash on right. Zero trip meter.
	0.0 ▲		Continue southeast.
GPS: N 38°26.73′ W 111°14.46′			
▼ 0.0			Continue northwest. Many wash crossings in next 5 miles.
	7.3 ▲	SO	Ackland Spring on left, then cross through Hartnet Draw. Zero trip meter.
▼ 5.0		SO	Trail climbs out of canyon.
	2.3 ▲	SO	Trail enters canyon, many wash crossings in next 5 miles.
▼ 6.7		SO	Track on left to Upper South Desert Overlook.
	0.6 ▲	SO	Track on right to Upper South Desert Overlook.
GPS: N 38°28.45′ W 111°21.14′			
▼ 7.0		SO	Track on right to Cathedral Valley Overlook.
	0.3 ▲	SO	Track on left to Cathedral Valley Overlook.
GPS: N 38°28.39′ W 111°21.50′			
▼ 7.3		TR	Track ahead to Thousand Lake Mountain. Zero trip meter.
	0.0 ▲		Continue toward Cathedral Valley Overlook
GPS: N 38°28.18′ W 111°21.78′			
▼ 0.0			Continue toward Cathedral Campground.
	5.0 ▲	TL	Track on right to Thousand Lake Mountain. Zero trip meter.
▼ 0.3		SO	Cathedral Campground on left.
	4.7 ▲	SO	Cathedral Campground on right.
GPS: N 38°28.43′ W 111°21.88′			
▼ 0.4		SO	Descend into Cathedral Valley on wide shelf road.
	4.6 ▲	SO	End of shelf road.
▼ 1.3		SO	Enter Cathedral Valley.
	3.7 ▲	SO	Exit Cathedral Valley up wide shelf road.
▼ 1.7		SO	Small parking area and short hike to Morrell cabin on left.
	3.3 ▲	SO	Small parking area and short hike to Morrell cabin on right.
GPS: N 38°29.02′ W 111°21.65′			
▼ 1.8		SO	Cross through wash.
	3.2 ▲	SO	Cross through wash.
▼ 1.9		SO	Cross through wash.
	3.1 ▲	SO	Cross through wash.
▼ 2.3		SO	Cathedral Trail hiking trailhead on left.
	2.7 ▲	SO	Cathedral Trail hiking trailhead on right.
GPS: N 38°29.29′ W 111°21.16′			
▼ 2.7		SO	Enter wash.
	2.3 ▲	SO	Exit wash.
▼ 2.8		SO	Exit wash.
	2.2 ▲	SO	Enter wash.
▼ 3.3		SO	Cross through wash.
	1.7 ▲	SO	Cross through wash.
▼ 3.5		SO	Cross through wash.
	1.5 ▲	SO	Cross through wash.
▼ 3.8		SO	Cross through creek.
	1.2 ▲	SO	Cross through creek.

▼ 4.6		SO	Cross through wash, then cross through fence line.
	0.4 ▲	SO	Cross through fence line, then cross through wash.
▼ 5.0		SO	Track on left is Baker Ranch Road, which goes to I-70. Zero trip meter.
	0.0 ▲		Continue toward Cathedral Campground.
GPS: N 38°30.35′ W 111°19.00′			
▼ 0.0			Continue toward Utah 24.
	4.1 ▲	SO	Track on right is Baker Ranch Road, which goes to I-70. Zero trip meter.
▼ 0.1		BL	Track on right to Gypsum Sinkholes.
	4.0 ▲	SO	Track on left to Gypsum Sinkholes.
GPS: N 38°30.34′ W 111°18.88′			
▼ 2.2		SO	Cross through wash.
	1.9 ▲	SO	Cross through wash.
▼ 2.5		SO	Enter Middle Desert Wash.
	1.6 ▲	SO	Exit Middle Desert Wash.
▼ 2.6		SO	Exit Middle Desert Wash.
	1.5 ▲	SO	Enter Middle Desert Wash.
▼ 3.1		SO	Exclosure on left.
	1.0 ▲	SO	Exclosure on right.
▼ 3.3		SO	Cross through wash.
	0.8 ▲	SO	Cross through wash.
▼ 3.6		SO	Cross through wash.
	0.5 ▲	SO	Cross through wash.
▼ 4.0		SO	Track on left.
	0.1 ▲	SO	Track on right.
GPS: N 38°29.96′ W 111°14.87′			
▼ 4.1		SO	Leaving Capitol Reef National Park. Zero trip meter.
	0.0 ▲		Continue into Capitol Reef National Park.
GPS: N 38°29.91′ W 111°14.84′			
▼ 0.0			Continue toward Caineville.
	4.9 ▲	SO	Entering Capitol Reef National Park. Zero trip meter.
▼ 0.1		SO	Cross through wash.
	4.8 ▲	SO	Cross through wash.
▼ 0.3		SO	Cattle guard, then cross through wash.
	4.6 ▲	SO	Cross through wash, then cattle guard.
▼ 2.0		SO	Cross through wash.
	2.9 ▲	SO	Cross through wash.
▼ 3.9		SO	Cross through wash.
	1.0 ▲	SO	Cross through wash.
▼ 4.2		SO	Campers Spring on right.
	0.7 ▲	SO	Campers Spring on left.
GPS: N 38°27.94′ W 111°11.10′			
▼ 4.9		SO	Track on right to the Temple of the Sun and Temple of the Moon. Zero trip meter.
	0.0 ▲		Continue toward Capitol Reef National Park.
GPS: N 38°27.57′ W 111°10.50′			
▼ 0.0			Continue toward Caineville.
	14.7 ▲	SO	Track on left to the Temple of the Sun and Temple of the Moon. Zero trip meter.
▼ 0.6		SO	Track on left.
	14.1 ▲	SO	Track on right.
▼ 0.8		SO	Cross through wash.
	13.9 ▲	SO	Cross through wash.
▼ 2.1		SO	Track on right.
	12.6 ▲	SO	Track on left.
GPS: N 38°26.84′ W 111°08.54′			
▼ 2.2		SO	Tracks on right and left.
	12.5 ▲	SO	Tracks on right and left.
▼ 2.6		SO	Cross through wash.

12.1 ▲	SO	Cross through wash.	
▼ 3.2	SO	Cross through two washes.	
11.5 ▲	SO	Cross through two washes.	
▼ 3.6	SO	Cross over wash.	
11.1 ▲	SO	Cross over wash.	
▼ 3.7	SO	Leaving Cathedral Valley.	
11.0 ▲	SO	Entering Cathedral Valley.	

GPS: N 38°26.18' W 111°06.92'

▼ 4.5	SO	Track on left.
10.2 ▲	SO	Track on right.
▼ 4.6	SO	Cross through wash. Caineville Mesa and the Henry Mountains directly ahead.
10.1 ▲	SO	Cross through wash.
▼ 4.7	SO	Cross through Caineville Wash.
10.0 ▲	SO	Cross through Caineville Wash.
▼ 5.4	SO	Cross through wash.
9.3 ▲	SO	Cross through wash.
▼ 5.8	SO	Track on right.
8.9 ▲	SO	Track on left.

GPS: N 38°25.21' W 111°05.25'

▼ 6.0	SO	Small dam on left.
8.7 ▲	SO	Small dam on right.
▼ 6.4	SO	Cross through two washes.
8.3 ▲	SO	Cross through two washes.
▼ 6.7	SO	Cross wash.
8.0 ▲	SO	Cross wash.
▼ 6.8	SO	Small track on left.
7.9 ▲	SO	Small track on right.
▼ 7.0	SO	Salt Wash on right.
7.7 ▲	SO	Salt Wash on left.

GPS: N 38°24.68' W 111°04.17'

▼ 7.2	SO	Willow Seep on right.
7.5 ▲	SO	Willow Seep on left.

GPS: N 38°24.59' W 111°04.02'

▼ 7.4	SO	Cross through wash.
7.3 ▲	SO	Cross through wash.
▼ 8.0	SO	Cross through wash.
6.7 ▲	SO	Cross through wash.
▼ 8.3	SO	Cross through wash.
6.4 ▲	SO	Cross through wash.
▼ 8.8	SO	Track on left; views east to North and South Caineville Mesas.
5.9 ▲	SO	Track on right; views east to North and South Caineville Mesas.

GPS: N 38°24.02' W 111°01.89'

▼ 10.7	SO	Track on right.
4.0 ▲	SO	Track on left.
▼ 11.7	SO	Carl's Reservoir on left.
3.0 ▲	SO	Carl's Reservoir on right.

GPS: N 38°22.66' W 111°01.74'

▼ 11.9	SO	Cattle guard, then track on right.
2.8 ▲	SO	Track on left, then cattle guard.
▼ 12.3	SO	Cross through wash, then track on left.
2.4 ▲	SO	Track on right, then cross through wash.
▼ 14.4	SO	Track on right.
0.3 ▲	SO	Track on left.
▼ 14.7		Cross cattle guard, then trail ends at Utah 24 at Caineville. Turn right for Capitol Reef National Park, left for Hanksville.
0.0 ▲		On Utah 24 at Caineville, turn northwest on graded dirt road, following sign for Caineville Wash Road. Zero trip meter.

GPS: N 38°20.06' W 111°01.40'

Hans Flat Road

Starting Point:	Utah 24, 18 miles north of Hanksville
Finishing Point:	Hans Flat Ranger Station
Total Mileage:	42.7 miles
Unpaved Mileage:	42.7 miles
Driving Time:	3 hours
Elevation Range:	5,000–6,500 feet
Usually Open:	Year-round
Difficulty Rating:	1
Scenic Rating:	7
Remoteness Rating:	+0

Special Attractions

■ Access to Canyonlands National Park Maze District.
■ Access to historic Robbers Roost area.
■ Remote, lightly traveled route.

Description

The Hans Flat Road is the major access to the remote Maze District of Canyonlands National Park. As a whole, the Maze receives a fraction of the visitors that the more accessible Island in the Sky and Needles District do, but it is no less spectacular. This graded dirt road is open year-round, as it is the primary access for the national park rangers who live at the re-

A view of the trail with Little Flat Top in the background

mote Hans Flat Ranger Station. It may become temporarily impassable after heavy rain or snow. In dry weather it is accessible to passenger vehicles, but all trails within the Maze District, including the Flint Trail, past the ranger station require a high-clearance 4WD.

The route heads east from Utah 24 about 18 miles north of Hanksville. The first features on the trail are the aptly named mesas Little Flat Top and Big Flat Top. The sandy trail then wraps down to the south, passing by Spire Point, and ascends to run along the ridge of Texas Hill. From the hill there are 360-degree views: to the north over the San Rafael Desert, Dugout Wash, and the Sweetwater Reef; to the east all the way to the La Sal Mountains; and of course, to the southwest to the bulk of the Henry Mountains.

After 22.8 miles, a major road heads north to the Horseshoe Canyon Unit of Canyonlands National Park, which is famous for its petroglyph panels. An information board at the junction gives public land information for the unit as well as for other public lands. The trail then enters the broad Antelope Valley and crests Burr Pass, which is unmarked. Central #20: Robbers Roost Spring Trail leaves from here, and this spur trail makes a nice addition to the main route.

The trail finishes at the Hans Flat Ranger Station, which is open all year. Note that camping in the Maze District is limited to designated sites, and at peak times, typically spring and fall, you will almost certainly need advance booking. There are some reasonable sites outside the park, mainly at the Hans Flat end where there are more trees for shelter. Access to the Maze District from the ranger station is via the Flint Trail, a narrow series of switchbacks that are impassable for most of the winter, since snow builds up on the north-facing switchbacks. Alternate access to the Maze District is from Hite Crossing.

There is a good chance of seeing wildlife along this trail, especially pronghorn antelope, coyotes, and various raptors.

Current Road Information

BLM Henry Mountain Field Station
406 South 100 West
Hanksville, UT 84734
(435) 542-3461

Canyonlands National Park
Maze District
(435) 259-2652

Map References

BLM San Rafael Desert, Hanksville
USGS 1:24,000 Gilson Butte, The Flat Tops, Point of Rocks East, Whitbeck Knoll, Robbers Roost Flats, Head Spur
1:100,000 San Rafael Desert, Hanksville
Maptech CD-ROM: Central/San Rafael, Moab/Canyonlands
Trails Illustrated, # 213 (incomplete); #246 (incomplete)
Utah Atlas & Gazetteer, p. 29
Utah Travel Council #5
Other: Canyon Country Off-Road Vehicle Map-Maze Area

Route Directions

| ▼ 0.0 | | From Utah 24, 0.3 miles north of mile marker 136 and just south of turn to Goblin Valley State Park, turn southeast on graded dirt road (signed to the Maze) and cross cattle guard. Zero trip meter. |
| 9.0 ▲ | | Trail ends at Utah 24; turn right for Goblin Valley State Park and Green River, left for Hanksville. |

GPS: N 38°37.41' W 110°34.20'

| ▼ 2.4 | SO | Track on right to Utah 24, track on left. |
| 6.6 ▲ | SO | Track on left to Utah 24, track on right. |

GPS: N 38°35.30' W 110°33.34'

| ▼ 2.6 | SO | Cattle guard. |
| 6.4 ▲ | SO | Cattle guard. |

| ▼ 6.3 | TL | Corral on right. Turn left in front of small hill. |
| 2.7 ▲ | TR | Turn right. Corral on left. |

GPS: N 38°31.78' W 110°32.41'

| ▼ 7.4 | SO | Track on right. |
| 1.6 ▲ | SO | Track on left. |

| ▼ 7.6 | SO | Second entrance to track on right. |
| 1.4 ▲ | SO | Second entrance to track on left. |

| ▼ 9.0 | SO | Track on left around base of Little Flat Top. Zero trip meter directly underneath the butte at the cattle guard on slight rise between Little |

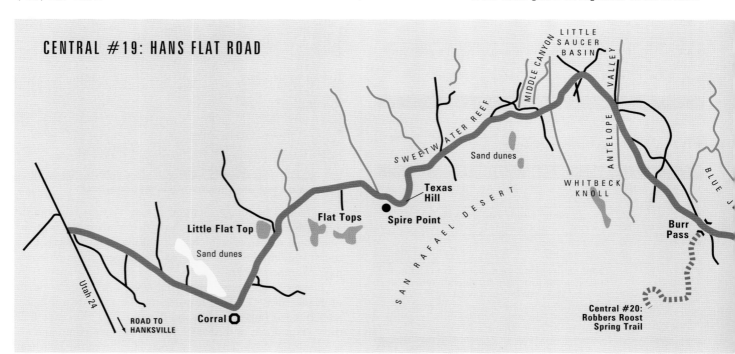

CENTRAL #19: HANS FLAT ROAD

Flat Top and Big Flat Top.

0.0 ▲ Continue toward Utah 24.

GPS: N 38°32.29' W 110°29.42'

▼ 0.0   Continue away from Little Flat Top.

5.7 ▲   SO   Zero trip meter directly underneath the butte at the cattle guard on slight rise between Little Flat Top and Big Flat Top. Track on right around base of Little Flat Top.

▼ 0.1   SO   Track on left.
5.6 ▲   SO   Track on right.

▼ 1.3   SO   Track on left.
4.4 ▲   SO   Track on right.

GPS: N 38°32.53' W 110°27.88'

▼ 3.1   SO   Track on right.
2.6 ▲   SO   Track on left.

▼ 3.4   SO   Track on right.
2.3 ▲   SO   Track on left.

▼ 4.6   SO   Track on left. Spire Point on right.
1.1 ▲   SO   Track on right. Spire Point on left.

GPS: N 38°30.60' W 110°25.42'

▼ 5.3   SO   Track on left.
0.4 ▲   SO   Track on left.

▼ 5.7   SO   Trail winds up to the top of Texas Hill. Graded dirt road on right to large shed. Zero trip meter.

0.0 ▲   Continue toward Utah 24.

GPS: N 38°29.98' W 110°24.83'

▼ 0.0   Continue south toward Hans Flat Ranger Station.

8.1 ▲   SO   Graded dirt road on left to large shed. Trail descends from Texas Hill. Zero trip meter.

▼ 0.3   SO   Track on right.
7.8 ▲   SO   Track on left.

▼ 2.2   SO   Track on left along edge of Sweetwater Reef.
5.9 ▲   SO   Track on right along edge of Sweetwater Reef.

▼ 3.9   SO   Track on right.
4.2 ▲   SO   Track on left.

▼ 6.2   SO   Track on right to corral.

1.9 ▲   SO   Track on left to corral.

GPS: N 38°28.51' W 110°18.90'

▼ 6.6   SO   Track on right.
1.5 ▲   SO   Track on left.

▼ 7.8   SO   Track on right and track on left.
0.3 ▲   SO   Track on left and track on right.

▼ 8.0   SO   Track on left.
0.1 ▲   SO   Track on right.

▼ 8.1   BR   Small track on left, then major graded road on left to Horseshoe Canyon and Green River. Information board for the Maze District and Horseshoe Canyon at the junction. Zero trip meter.

0.0 ▲   Continue toward the ridge of Texas Hill. Immediately small track on right.

GPS: N 38°28.37' W 110°16.79'

▼ 0.0   Continue into Antelope Valley.

6.7 ▲   SO   Major graded road on right to Horseshoe Canyon and Green River. Information board for the Maze District and Horseshoe Canyon at the junction. Zero trip meter.

▼ 1.6   SO   Faint track on left.
5.1 ▲   SO   Faint track on right.

▼ 3.4   SO   Cattle guard, then track on left.
3.3 ▲   SO   Track on right, then cattle guard.

GPS: N 38°25.49' W 110°17.70'

▼ 4.6   SO   Track on left and faint track on right. Main trail runs along a slight ridge with views left into the Maze and Bluejohn Canyon.

2.1 ▲   SO   Track on right and faint track on left. Main trail runs along a slight ridge with views right into the Maze and Bluejohn Canyon.

▼ 6.5   SO   Faint track on left, then cross over wash.
0.2 ▲   SO   Cross over wash, then faint track on right.

▼ 6.7   BL   Top of Burr Pass. Track on right is Central #20: Robbers Roost Spring Trail. Zero trip meter and bear left, following sign to Hans Flat Ranger Station.

0.0 ▲   Continue toward Utah 24.

GPS: N 38°22.65' W 110°18.28'

▼ 0.0   Continue toward ranger station.

13.2 ▲   SO   Top of Burr Pass. Track on left is Central #20: Robbers Roost Spring Trail. Zero trip meter.

▼ 2.5   BR   Track on left.
10.7 ▲   SO   Second entrance to track on right.

GPS: N 38°20.44' W 110°17.65'

▼ 2.6   SO   Second entrance to track on left.
10.6 ▲   SO   Track on right.

▼ 5.5   SO   Track on right.
7.7 ▲   SO   Track on left.

GPS: N 38°17.81' W 110°17.29'

▼ 6.3   SO   Track on right.
6.9 ▲   SO   Track on left.

▼ 6.5   SO   Track on right.
6.7 ▲   SO   Track on left.

GPS: N 38°16.95' W 110°16.95'

▼ 7.0   SO   Cattle guard.
6.2 ▲   SO   Cattle guard.

▼ 7.4   SO   Cross through wash.
5.8 ▲   SO   Cross through wash.

▼ 7.6   SO   Cross over wash.
5.6 ▲   SO   Cross over wash.

▼ 7.9   SO   Track on right.
5.3 ▲   SO   Track on left.

GPS: N 38°15.97' W 110°16.05'

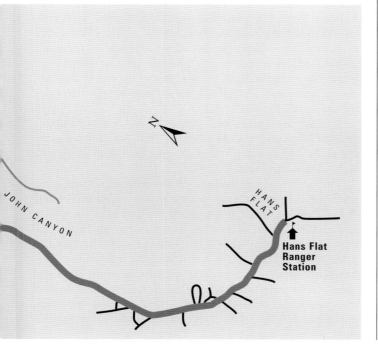

JOHN CANYON

HANS FLAT

Hans Flat Ranger Station

▼ 8.6		SO	Track on left.
	4.6 ▲	SO	Track on right.
▼ 8.9		SO	Track on right.
	4.3 ▲	SO	Track on left.
▼ 9.5		SO	Faint track on right.
	3.7 ▲	SO	Faint track on left.
▼ 10.7		SO	Track on right.
	2.5 ▲	SO	Track on left.
		GPS: N 38°15.11′ W 110°13.39′	
▼ 12.6		SO	Track on left to limited use area. Enter Hans Flat.
	0.6 ▲	SO	Track on right to limited use area. Leave Hans Flat.
		GPS: N 38°15.32′ W 110°11.41′	
▼ 12.8		SO	Track on right.
	0.4 ▲	SO	Track on left.
▼ 13.2			Trail ends at Hans Flat Ranger Station in the Maze District of Canyonlands National Park.
	0.0 ▲		Trail commences at the Hans Flat Ranger Station in the Maze District of Canyonlands National Park. Zero trip meter at the ranger station and proceed west along the graded dirt road.
		GPS: N 38°15.31′ W 110°10.73′	

CENTRAL REGION TRAIL #20

Robbers Roost Spring Trail

Starting Point:	**Burr Pass on Central #19: Hans Flat Road**
Finishing Point:	**Overlook into Robbers Roost Canyon**
Total Mileage:	**9.3 miles**
Unpaved Mileage:	**9.3 miles**
Driving Time:	**1 hour (one-way)**
Elevation Range:	**4,900–5,600 feet**
Usually Open:	**Year-round**
Difficulty Rating:	**2**
Scenic Rating:	**8**
Remoteness Rating:	**+1**

Special Attractions
- Area was historic hideout for Butch Cassidy and other outlaws.
- Viewpoint over both North and Middle Forks of Robbers Roost Canyon.
- Robbers Roost Spring and Cottrell cabin ruins.

History
The Robbers Roost area was a hideout for cattle rustlers long before Butch Cassidy gave the area its notoriety. A maze of deep canyons, Robbers Roost allowed outlaws to move through undetected and go to ground when the law closed in. Robbers Roost Spring, located in the South Fork of Robbers Roost Canyon, was used by Butch Cassidy and the Wild Bunch as one of their hiding places.

Slightly upstream from the spring are the stone remains of the Cottrell cabin, which was built in 1890 by Joe Bernard, the foreman of the 3B Ranch, as a line cabin for the hands to use when rounding up cattle. Jack Cottrell became the foreman of the 3B Ranch soon after and moved his family to the cabin. After he moved out in the mid-1890s, the cabin continued to be used as a line cabin and, increasingly, as shelter for outlaws until it burnt to the ground. Only the stone chimney remains today. Supposedly, so the story goes, it burnt down when someone tried to smoke out a rat!

Just north of the Cottrell cabin is Silvertip Spring, which was named after a horsethief who often used the Robbers Roost Spring and cabin to hide from the sheriff.

Description
This spur trail runs just over 9 miles and ends at a high viewpoint over the North and Middle Forks of Robbers Roost Canyon, but there is plenty to see before you get there! The smooth, sandy trail runs around the head of the South Fork of

At the end of the trail

Robbers Roost Canyon. After 5.7 miles, a track to the left leads down to the Robbers Roost Spring and the Cottrell cabin. A small cairn marks the turnoff, which leads 0.2 miles to a turnaround under a large cottonwood on the edge of the wash. The spring is slightly to the west of the end of the trail, down in the wash; you will see the wooden troughs that mark the spring.

To reach the remains of the Cottrell cabin, walk east up the remains of an old washed out 4WD trail for approximately 0.2 miles. To the left of the small creek in a small rocky cove is the cabin's chimney.

The main trail past the spring is less used; it can have some small gullies from washouts, but it remains graded for the next 2.3 miles to the oil drilling post. At the drill hole, there is an ambiguously placed WSA sign—it is near enough to the trail that it almost looks like it is blocking the way. The National Park Service at Hans Flat says that the track is accessible to vehicles, but that an inexperienced person placed the signs and some of them were in the wrong position. From here the trail is an ungraded two track as it runs out on the narrow point, giving glimpses into both North and Middle Forks, until it ends above the confluence.

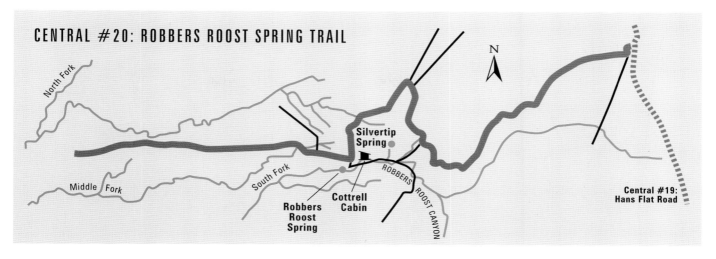

CENTRAL #20: ROBBERS ROOST SPRING TRAIL

Current Road Information
BLM Henry Mountain Field Station
406 South 100 West
Hanksville, UT 84734
(435) 542-3461

Map References
BLM Hanksville
USGS 1:24,000 Whitbeck Knoll, Robbers Roost Flats,
Angel Point
1:100,000 Hanksville
Maptech CD-ROM: Moab/Canyonlands
Utah Atlas & Gazetteer, p. 29

Route Directions

▼ 0.0		At Burr Pass on Central #19: Hans Flat Road, 29.5 miles from Utah 24, turn southwest on the graded track, following the sign for Ekker Ranch, and zero trip meter.
GPS: N 38°22.65' W 110°18.28'		
▼ 0.1	TR	Track continues straight to Ekker Ranch.
GPS: N 38°22.59' W 110°18.30'		
▼ 3.1	SO	Turnout on left with overlook of the South Fork of Robbers Roost Canyon.
▼ 3.4	SO	Two tracks on left.
▼ 4.3	SO	Faint track on right.
▼ 5.6	SO	Cross through wash.
▼ 5.7	BR	Trail forks at small cairn. The track on left goes 0.2 miles to Robbers Roost Spring and stone chimney ruins. Zero trip meter.
GPS: N 38°21.76' W 110°22.28'		
▼ 0.0		Continue toward overlook.
▼ 0.5	BR	Faint track on left.
▼ 0.6	SO	Cross through wash.
▼ 1.6	SO	View left into Middle Fork and view right into North Fork of Robbers Roost Canyon.
▼ 2.3	SO	Drill hole on left. Trail is now ungraded.
GPS: N 38°21.99' W 110°24.85'		
▼ 2.8	SO	Turnout on right with overlook of North Fork of Robbers Roost Canyon.
GPS: N 38°22.17' W 110°25.34'		
▼ 3.6		Trail ends at small turning circle and overlook of the confluence of North Fork and Middle Fork of Robbers Roost Canyon.
GPS: N 38°22.04' W 110°26.15'		

Burr Point Trail

Starting Point:	Utah 95, .6 miles south of mile marker 15
Finishing Point:	Burr Point
Total Mileage:	10 miles
Unpaved Mileage:	10 miles
Driving Time:	30 minutes (one-way)
Elevation Range:	4,900–5,400 feet
Usually Open:	Year-round
Difficulty Rating:	1
Scenic Rating:	8
Remoteness Rating:	+0

Special Attractions
- Panoramic view over Dirty Devil River Canyon.
- Access to a network of graded roads and trails to viewpoints.
- Historic Robbers Roost region.

The volcanic Henry Mountains tower above Burr Point Trail

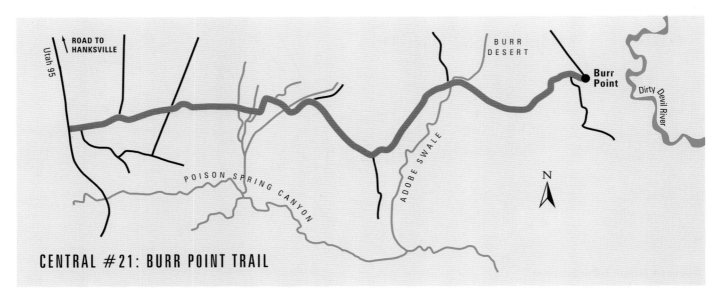

CENTRAL #21: BURR POINT TRAIL

Description

There are many trails in the Robbers Roost area, but most of them peter out before long. This trail is a graded dirt road that goes to an overlook over the Dirty Devil River Canyon. It is an easy trail that's suitable for passenger vehicles in dry weather. Short sections of the trail run in a creek wash. There are side trails that lead down to overlooks at Poison Spring Canyon and Adobe Swale.

On the return trip, there are excellent views west over the towering volcanic Henry Mountains.

Current Road Information

BLM Henry Mountain Field Station
406 South 100 West
Hanksville, UT 84734
(435) 542-3461

A view over Dirty Devil River Canyon from the near end of the trail

Map References

BLM Hanksville
USGS 1:24,000 Baking Skillet Knoll, Burr Point
1:100,000 Hanksville
Maptech CD-ROM: Moab/Canyonlands
Trails Illustrated, #213
Utah Atlas & Gazetteer, p. 29
Utah Travel Council #5
Other: Recreation Map of the Henry Mountains Area

Route Directions

▼ 0.0		On Utah 95, 0.6 miles south of mile marker 15, turn northeast on the graded dirt road at sign for Burr Point.
	GPS: N 38°09.53' W 110°37.25'	
▼ 0.1	SO	Track on right.
▼ 1.7	SO	Track on left.
	GPS: N 38°09.83' W 110°35.35'	
▼ 1.9	SO	Track on left.
▼ 2.5	SO	Cattle guard.
▼ 2.8	SO	Track on right.
▼ 3.1	SO	Enter wash.
▼ 3.2	SO	Track on right to corral.
	GPS: N 38°09.85' W 110°33.69'	
▼ 3.3	SO	Exit wash.
▼ 3.4	SO	Track on right rejoins from corral, then track on left.
▼ 3.7	SO	Cross through wash.
▼ 4.2	BR	Graded track on left to dam and tank. Zero trip meter.
	GPS: N 38°09.98' W 110°32.78'	
▼ 0.0		Continue east to Burr Point.
▼ 0.1	SO	Cross through wash.
▼ 0.3	SO	Cross through wash.
▼ 0.7	SO	Cross through wash, then track on left up wash.
▼ 1.0	SO	Cross through wash.
▼ 1.3	BL	Track on right to Adobe Swale.
	GPS: N 38°09.14' W 110°31.65'	
▼ 1.8	SO	Adobe Swale Canyon on right.
▼ 3.2	BR	Small track on right, then larger graded track on left.
	GPS: N 38°10.20' W 110°30.17'	

▼ 3.4	BR	Track on left.
▼ 3.5	SO	Cross small dam wall; dam on left.
GPS: N 38°10.21' W 110°29.88'		
▼ 4.6	SO	Track on left to drill hole.
▼ 5.6	SO	Track on right.
GPS: N 38°10.32' W 110°27.98'		
▼ 5.8		Trail ends at a drill hole on Burr Point at overlook of Dirty Devil River. Track on right and track on left at end of trail.
GPS: N 38°10.30' W 110°27.71'		

CENTRAL REGION TRAIL #22

Copper Globe Mine Trail

Starting Point:	I-70, exit 114
Finishing Point:	Copper Globe Mine near Central #24:
	Kimball Draw Trail
Total Mileage:	6.6 miles
Unpaved Mileage:	6.3 miles
Driving Time:	1 hour
Elevation Range:	6,800–7,200 feet
Usually Open:	Year-round
Difficulty Rating:	3
Scenic Rating:	10
Remoteness Rating:	+1

Special Attractions

- Many artifacts remain at the Copper Globe Mine.
- The area is home to a herd of wild mustangs.
- Varied and scenic terrain.
- The Sheepherder's End marker.

History

In the days of the Old West, Justensen Flats used to be a favorite place for local cowboys to chase wild horses. Although these untamed horses used to be a common sight in the West, today it is a rare treat to spot one. The herd around Justensen Flats is one of the largest, so keep your eyes peeled for the hors-

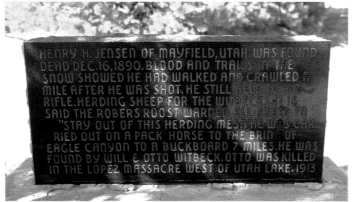

Sheepherder's End marker relates the death of Henry H. Jensen

es as you drive along to the Copper Globe Mine.

Toward the end of the trail, you come across the Sheepherder's End marker. This unusual monument relates the story of local sheepherder Henry H. Jensen, who was found dead in the snow here in December 1890. It is said that the gang at Robbers Roost warned Jensen to keep his sheep out of the area, though no one knows for sure who actually killed him. Take a moment to read the marker's story on your way to the remains of the old mine.

One of the Copper Globe Mine adits

The Copper Globe Mine was worked by Jessie Fugate and his son, Conn, between 1900 and 1905. The ore mined at Copper Globe was of a rather poor quality and was not worth hauling out by wagon. So Fugate built a smelter on the site. There is still a pile of wood about 75 feet long near the mine, which was used, along with a large bellows, to fire the ore in the smelter. Although this self-contained mining operation seemed like a good idea at first, the miners soon found they had used the wrong bricks. Built of building brick rather than refractory brick, the smelter melted before the ore inside it and soon collapsed.

While you are there, take a minute to look at the entrances to the mine shafts. There is one in particular that stands out as having an almost perfectly square opening and very smooth walls. Nearby, the remains of a man-made drainage basin, which was used to catch rainwater, sit along the cliff wall to the west. A few old cabins used by the miners round out the scene of this remote copper mine.

Description

Starting out from I-70, the trail runs through a sandy plateau with an abundance of side tracks and campsites. The yellow or buff-colored sands of Justensen Flats are the same color as the cliffs rising above them. As you drive through the thick pinyon and juniper, just past a sign for Copper Globe, you can see the San Rafael Knob about 3 miles southeast of Justensen Flats.

The periodically graded trail is narrow at first, and it is not very difficult even though it is very dusty and can be rather bumpy at times. The only real potential difficulty is passing through some of the sandier sections. There is a bit of shelf road, but none of it is dangerously narrow, and the road widens every now and then to allow for passing.

Overall, the varied terrain and mine remains make for a very scenic drive.

Current Road Information

Emery County Road Department
120 West Highway 29
Castle Dale, UT 84513
(435) 381-2550

CENTRAL #22: COPPER GLOBE MINE TRAIL

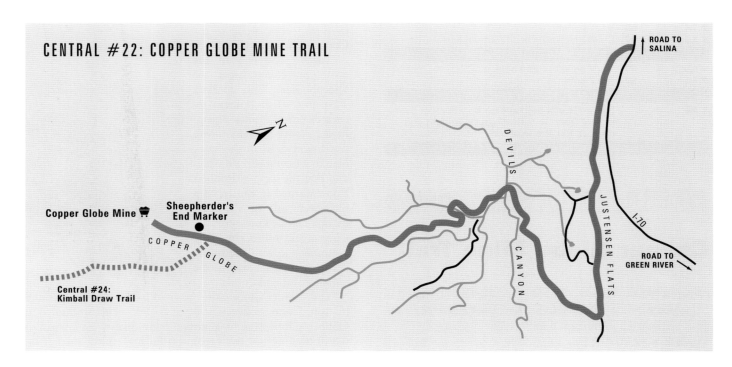

BLM Price Field Office
125 South 600 West
Price, UT 84501
(435) 636-3600

Map References

BLM   San Rafael Desert
USGS 1:24,000 Copper Globe
          1:100,000 San Rafael Desert
Maptech CD-ROM: Central/San Rafael
Trails Illustrated, #712
Utah Atlas & Gazetteer, p. 39
Utah Travel Council #5
Other: Recreation Map of the San Rafael Swell and San Rafael
      Desert

Route Directions

▼ 0.0		On the south side of I-70 at exit 114 (signed for Moore and as a "View Area"), zero trip meter at intersection of the overpass and the entry/exit ramps.
6.2 ▲		Trail ends at I-70, exit 114. Turn right for Green River, left for Salina.

An old cabin at the Copper Globe Mine

		GPS: N 38°51.28' W 110°54.55'	
▼ 0.2		SO	Cattle guard.
	5.9 ▲	SO	Cattle guard.
▼ 0.7		SO	Travel through cutting.
	5.5 ▲	SO	Travel through cutting.
▼ 1.2		SO	Travel past Justensen Flats.
	5.0 ▲	SO	Travel past Justensen Flats.
▼ 1.3		SO	Road on right signed to Justensen Flats.
	4.8 ▲	SO	Road on left signed to Justensen Flats.
▼ 1.4		SO	Road on left.
	4.8 ▲	SO	Road on right.
▼ 1.7		SO	Track on right.
	4.5 ▲	SO	Track on left.
▼ 2.2		BR	Turn right toward Copper Globe Road and Devils Canyon. San Rafael Knob (elevation 7,921 feet) is straight ahead.
	3.9 ▲	BL	Follow road to the left.
▼ 3.6		SO	Cross through large, sandy wash.
	2.6 ▲	SO	Cross through large, sandy wash.
		GPS: N 38°50.19' W 110°53.84'	
▼ 4.0		SO	Cross through wash.
	2.2 ▲	SO	Cross through wash.
▼ 6.2		BR	Bear right at fork in road. Left is Central #24: Kimball Draw Trail. Zero trip meter.
	0.0 ▲		Continue along trail.
		GPS: N 38°48.44' W 110°54.32'	
▼ 0.0			Continue along toward Copper Globe Mine.
	0.4 ▲	BL	Road on right is Central #24: Kimball Draw Trail. Zero trip meter.
▼ 0.1		SO	Sheepherder's End marker 20 yards off the road on right.
	0.3 ▲	SO	Sheepherder's End marker 20 yards off the road on left.
▼ 0.4			Trail ends at Copper Globe Mine historic site.
	0.0 ▲		At the Copper Globe Mine, zero trip meter and return along the trail.
		GPS: N 38°48.21' W 110°54.57'	

Reds Canyon Overlook Trail

Starting Point:	Central #24: Kimball Draw Trail
Finishing Point:	Central #24: Kimball Draw Trail
Total Mileage:	4.5 miles
Unpaved Mileage:	4.5 miles
Driving Time:	45 minutes
Elevation Range:	5,400–7,200 feet
Usually Open:	Year-round
Difficulty Rating:	3
Scenic Rating:	8
Remoteness Rating:	+1

Special Attractions

- Panoramic viewpoint over Reds Canyon.
- Access to backcountry campsites on Link Flats.

Description

This short loop trail includes a spur trail to an overlook high above Reds Canyon to the south. It makes an interesting side trip to Central #24: Kimball Draw Trail. The trail crosses Link Flats on an ungraded two-track before swinging around and climbing to the overlook. The trail is not difficult, but there are a couple of narrow gullies that may catch the rear of longer vehicles or those with less clearance. The climb to the overlook is a little loose, but any driver who is confident navigating the Kimball Draw Trail will have no problems on this one. Those driving wider vehicles may find that a couple of sections may be a little brushy.

At the overlook, you can see into Reds Canyon and the San Rafael Swell; vehicle trails are visible in the bottom running along the creek. To the south, you can see over the Hondoo

Old machinery abandoned beside the trail

country to the Henry Mountains. Tomsich Butte and a nearby unnamed butte are closer to the southwest, while Family Butte is east.

There are a couple of secluded backcountry campsites tucked into the juniper, some with views over Reds Canyon. Others are easy to find on the grassy Link Flats.

From the turn to the overlook, the trail continues another mile across Link Flats to finish back on the Kimball Draw Trail, 1.6 miles from the start of the loop.

Current Road Information

Emery County Road Department
120 West Highway 29
Castle Dale, UT 84513
(435) 381-2550

BLM Price Field Office
125 South 600 West
Price, UT 84501
(435) 636-3600

Map References

BLM San Rafael Desert (incomplete)
USGS 1:24,000 Copper Globe (incomplete)
 1:100,000 San Rafael Desert, (incomplete)
Maptech CD-ROM: Central/San Rafael
Trails Illustrated, #712
Utah Atlas & Gazetteer, p. 38
Other: Recreation Map of the San Rafael Swell and San Rafael Desert

Route Directions

▼ 0.0			On Central #24: Kimball Draw Trail, 15.3 miles from I-70, zero trip meter and turn south on ungraded dirt trail at sign for Link Flats.
	1.9 ▲		Trail ends at Central #24: Kimball Draw Trail; turn left for I-70, right for Central #22: Copper Globe Mine Trail.
		GPS: N 38°47.19' W 110°57.38'	
▼ 0.2		SO	Cross through small sandy wash.
	1.7 ▲	SO	Cross through small sandy wash.
▼ 0.3		SO	Cross through small sandy wash.
	1.6 ▲	SO	Cross through small sandy wash.
▼ 0.4		SO	Cross through small sandy wash.
	1.5 ▲	SO	Cross through small sandy wash.
▼ 0.5		SO	Cross through sandy wash.
	1.4 ▲	SO	Cross through sandy wash.
▼ 0.8		BL	Track on right goes partway to alternative overlook. Trail is washed out after 0.8 miles.
	1.1 ▲	BR	Track on left goes partway to alternative overlook. Trail is washed out after 0.8 miles.
		GPS: N 38°46.46' W 110°57.12'	
▼ 1.9		TR	T-intersection. Take sharp right for spur trail to overlook. Take left to loop back to Kimball Draw Trail. Zero trip meter.
	0.0 ▲		Continue the loop back to Kimball Draw Trail.
		GPS: N 38°46.24' W 110°55.86'	

Spur trail to overlook

▼ 0.0			Continue toward overlook. A large washout immediately past the turn may catch the rear

CENTRAL #23: REDS CANYON OVERLOOK TRAIL

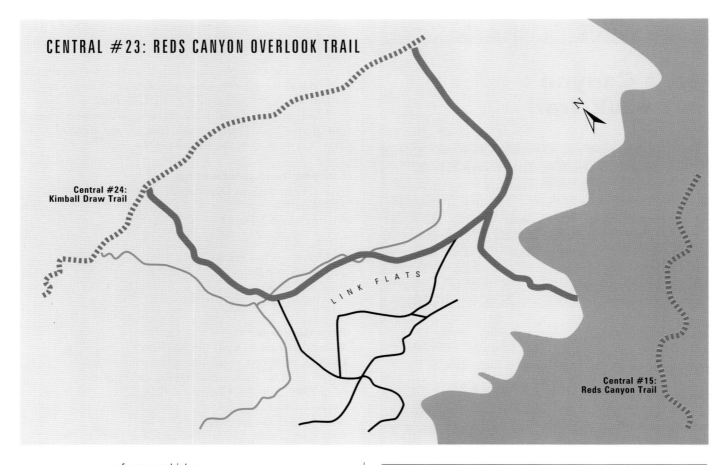

Central #24: Kimball Draw Trail

LINK FLATS

Central #15: Reds Canyon Trail

			of some vehicles.
▼ 0.5		SO	Short rocky climb to overlook.
▼ 0.8		UT	Trail reaches overlook on promontory over Reds Canyon. Return to main trail intersection, zero trip meter, and continue straight to finish loop to Kimball Draw Trail.

GPS: N 38°45.72' W 110°55.78'

Continuation of Loop

▼ 0.0			Continue straight around loop. Track immediately on right goes 0.2 miles to campsite and alternate viewpoint over Reds Canyon.
	1.0 ▲	SO	Spur trail to overlook is straight ahead. Right continues loop to Kimball Draw Trail. Zero trip meter.

GPS: N 38°46.24' W 110°55.86'

▼ 0.1		SO	Old machinery on right.
	0.9 ▲	SO	Old machinery on left.

GPS: N 38°46.30' W 110°55.79'

▼ 0.5		SO	Faint track on left.
	0.5 ▲	SO	Faint track on right.

▼ 0.7		SO	Faint track on left, then track on right.
	0.3 ▲	BR	Bear right at track on left, and then immediately bear left at track on right.

▼ 1.0			Trail ends at Central #24: Kimball Draw Trail; turn left for I-70, right for Central #22: Copper Globe Mine Trail.
	0.0 ▲		On Central #24: Kimball Draw Trail, 2.6 miles from junction with Central #22: Copper Globe Mine Trail, zero trip meter and turn south on ungraded, unmarked dirt trail.

GPS: N 38°47.04' W 110°55.66'

CENTRAL REGION TRAIL #24

Kimball Draw Trail

Starting Point:	I-70, exit 105
Finishing Point:	Central #22: Copper Globe Mine Trail
Total Mileage:	19.5 miles
Unpaved Mileage:	19.5 miles
Driving Time:	2 hours
Elevation Range:	5,400–7,100 feet
Usually Open:	Year-round
Difficulty Rating:	4
Scenic Rating:	7
Remoteness Rating:	+1

Special Attractions

■ Remote route that travels along two canyons.
■ Rockhounding for selenite in Kimball Draw.
■ Access to a network of 4WD trails.

Description

This trail loops around in the San Rafael Swell to the south of I-70. It follows the path of two canyons: the gentle Kimball Draw and the narrow, twisting Cat Canyon. The most chal-

One of the very sandy sections along Kimball Draw Trail

lenging part of the trail is the very deep, loose sand near the western end of the trail just south of I-70. This section can be several miles long and makes the trail suitable only for 4WD vehicles. It may be necessary to lower tire pressures to avoid getting stuck.

From I-70, exit 105, the trail takes CR 923 south for a few miles, running along Salt Creek, where the worst of the sand is, before turning east to follow Kimball Draw.

Once in Kimball Draw, the gravelly trail surface is firmer and smooth. The trail follows the wash, sometimes traveling along it for long stretches. One bonus for rock hounds is a section of the canyon wall where there are prolific selenite (gypsum) crystals. On sunny days they are easy to spot, as they reflect the sun's rays and can be seen from quite a distance. There are plenty of small crystals on the surface, and larger specimens can be found with a bit of hunting.

The trail climbs gradually out of Kimball Draw, crosses a ridge top with great views west over to Fishlake National Forest, and drops down along some switch-

Looking into Cat Canyon

backs into the narrower and deeper Cat Canyon. The descent is along a wide section of trail with a good surface. Once inside Cat Canyon, the trail is tighter and twists within the confines of the walls. The exit out of the canyon has some loose sandy sections, but these are shorter and generally not as difficult as the county road section.

Once out of Cat Canyon, the trail intersects with Central #23: Reds Canyon Overlook Trail, a loop trail that returns to this trail 1.6 miles farther, then it crosses the northern end of Link Flats before following the Cat Canyon wash once again. Sections in the wash could be brushy; drivers of wider vehicles risk scratching their paint. From here, the trail is rockier as it descends to cross over Cat Canyon wash before joining Cen-

tral #22: Copper Globe Mine Trail near the Sheepherder's End marker, where the trail ends.

Like most trails in the region, this trail is likely to be impassable following heavy rainfall and may wash out after heavy runoff. Snow may temporarily close parts of the trail in winter.

Current Road Information
Emery County Road Department
120 West Highway 29
Castle Dale, UT 84513
(435) 381-2550

BLM Price Field Office
125 South 600 West
Price, UT 84501
(435) 636-3600

Map References
BLM   San Rafael Desert, Salina
USGS 1:24,000 Copper Globe, Big Bend Draw
          1:100,000 San Rafael Desert, Salina
Maptech CD-ROM: Central/San Rafael
Trails Illustrated, #712
Utah Atlas & Gazetteer, p. 38
Utah Travel Council #5
Other: Recreation Map of the San Rafael Swell and San
       Rafael Desert

Route Directions

▼ 0.0			From I-70, exit 105, turn southwest on CR 923 and zero trip meter at cattle guard.
	5.0 ▲		Trail ends at I-70, exit 105. Turn right for Green River, left for Salina.
GPS: N 38°50.50' W 111°03.78'			
▼ 0.1		TR	Track on left.
	4.9 ▲	TL	Track on right.
▼ 0.4		BR	Track on left. Follow the smaller, sandy trail right. From this point the trail is extremely sandy.
	4.6 ▲	SO	Track on right. Join larger graded county road, CR 923.
GPS: N 38°50.16' W 111°03.85'			
▼ 0.7		SO	Track on left.
	4.3 ▲	SO	Track on right.
▼ 0.9		SO	Cross through sandy wash.
	4.1 ▲	SO	Cross through sandy wash.
▼ 1.1		SO	Track on left.
	3.9 ▲	SO	Track on right.
▼ 3.2		SO	Cross over wash.
	1.8 ▲	SO	Cross over wash.
▼ 3.7		SO	Cross through wash.
	1.3 ▲	SO	Cross through wash.
▼ 4.2		SO	Cross through Salt Creek.
	0.8 ▲	SO	Cross through Salt Creek.
GPS: N 38°47.90' W 111°06.01'			
▼ 4.5		SO	Cross through small wash.
	0.5 ▲	SO	Cross through small wash.
▼ 4.6		SO	Cross through small wash.
	0.4 ▲	SO	Cross through small wash.
▼ 4.7		SO	Cross through small wash.
	0.3 ▲	SO	Cross through small wash.

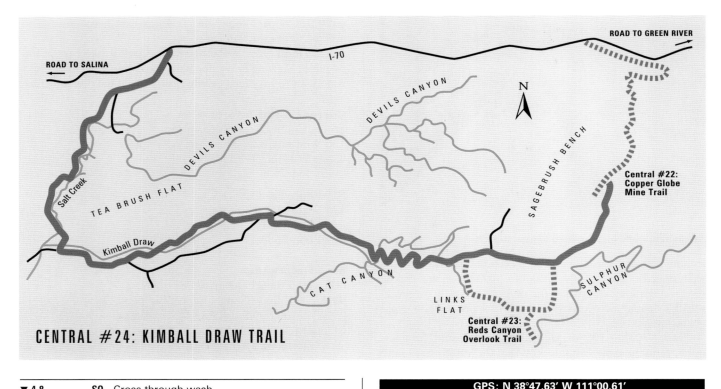

CENTRAL #24: KIMBALL DRAW TRAIL

▼ 4.8		SO	Cross through wash.
	0.2 ▲	SO	Cross through wash.
▼ 5.0		TL	T-intersection. Track on right to Muddy River. Turn left, following sign for Kimball Draw, and zero trip meter.
	0.0 ▲		Continue toward I-70. From this point the trail is extremely sandy.

GPS: N 38°47.29′ W 111°05.84′

▼ 0.0			Continue into Kimball Draw.
	4.8 ▲	BR	Track ahead to Muddy River. Zero trip meter at intersection.
▼ 0.5		SO	Two faint tracks on left. Enter wash. Trail in or alongside wash, with numerous crossings, for next 5.8 miles.
	4.3 ▲	SO	Exit wash. Two faint tracks on right.
▼ 0.6		SO	Cattle trough on left.
	4.2 ▲	SO	Cattle trough on right.
▼ 1.4		SO	Track on right.
	3.4 ▲	SO	Track on left.

GPS: N 38°47.08′ W 111°04.57′

▼ 4.0		SO	Spring in hollow on left.
	0.8 ▲	SO	Spring in hollow on right.

GPS: N 38°47.80′ W 111°02.09′

▼ 4.2		SO	Selenite crystals can be found on both sides of the trail in the canyon walls.
	0.6 ▲	SO	Selenite crystals can be found on both sides of the trail in the canyon walls.
▼ 4.8		BL	Well-used track on right. Zero trip meter.
	0.0 ▲		Continue along Kimball Draw.

GPS: N 38°47.85′ W 111°01.50′

▼ 0.0			Continue along Kimball Draw.
	5.5 ▲	SO	Well-used track on left. Zero trip meter.
▼ 0.4		SO	Faint track on left.
	5.1 ▲	SO	Faint track on right.
▼ 1.0		SO	Timber footings and pipes of oil drilling hole on left.
	4.5 ▲	SO	Timber footings and pipes of oil drilling hole on right.

GPS: N 38°47.63′ W 111°00.61′

▼ 1.5		SO	Leaving Kimball Draw across ridge top.
	4.0 ▲	SO	Trail descends into Kimball Draw and runs in or alongside wash, with numerous crossings for next 5.8 miles.
▼ 2.4		SO	Top of ridge. Views west to Fishlake National Forest. Trail descends into Cat Canyon.
	3.1 ▲	SO	Top of ridge and end of climb out of Cat Canyon. Views west to Fishlake National Forest.

GPS: N 38°47.31′ W 110°59.30′

▼ 2.8		SO	Trail follows along the bottom of Cat Canyon in wash.
	2.7 ▲	SO	Trail climbs out of Cat Canyon.

GPS: N 38°47.23′ W 110°59.11′

▼ 3.4		SO	Cross through old fence line.
	2.1 ▲	SO	Cross through old fence line.
▼ 4.5		SO	Cattle trough on left.
	1.0 ▲	SO	Cattle trough on right.
▼ 4.9		SO	Track on left.
	0.6 ▲	SO	Track on right.
▼ 5.4		SO	Exit Cat Canyon wash.
	0.1 ▲	SO	Enter Cat Canyon wash.
▼ 5.5		SO	Track on right at sign for Link Flats is western end of Central #23: Reds Canyon Overlook Trail. Zero trip meter.
	0.0 ▲		Continue into Cat Canyon.

GPS: N 38°47.19′ W 110°57.39′

▼ 0.0			Continue across the northern end of Link Flats.
	1.6 ▲	SO	Track on left at sign for Link Flats is western end of Central #23: Reds Canyon Overlook Trail. Zero trip meter.
▼ 0.4		SO	Cross through wash.
	1.2 ▲	SO	Cross through wash.
▼ 0.5		SO	Cross through wash.
	1.1 ▲	SO	Cross through wash.
▼ 0.6		SO	Faint track on left. Short brushy section along wash.
	1.0 ▲	SO	Faint track on right.

▼ 1.3	SO	Trail leaves wash.
0.3 ▲	SO	Trail enters wash. Short brushy section along wash.
▼ 1.6	SO	Track on right is eastern end of Central #23: Reds Canyon Overlook Trail. Zero trip meter.
0.0 ▲		Continue along main trail.

GPS: N 38°47.03' W 110°55.67'

▼ 0.0		Continue along main trail.
2.6 ▲	SO	Track on left is eastern end of Central #23: Reds Canyon Overlook Trail.
▼ 0.4	BR	Swing right on flat rock in front of Cat Canyon.
2.2 ▲	BL	Swing left on flat rock in front of Cat Canyon.

GPS: N 38°47.18' W 110°55.23'

| ▼ 0.6 | TL | T-intersection. Smaller track on right. |
| 2.0 ▲ | TR | Turn right on main trail; smaller track straight ahead. |

GPS: N 38°47.14' W 110°55.15'

▼ 0.8	SO	Cross through Cat Canyon wash. Old dam on left.
1.8 ▲	SO	Cross through Cat Canyon wash. Old dam on right.
▼ 1.2	SO	Track on left.
1.4 ▲	SO	Track on right.
▼ 1.7	SO	Cross through the sandy Cat Canyon wash.
0.9 ▲	SO	Cross through the sandy Cat Canyon wash.

GPS: N 38°47.70' W 110°54.46'

▼ 2.0	SO	Cross through wash.
0.6 ▲	SO	Cross through wash.
▼ 2.6		Small track on right, then trail ends at Central #22: Copper Globe Mine Trail near the Sheepherder's End marker. Turn left for Copper Globe Mine, right for I-70.
0.0 ▲		On Central #22: Copper Globe Mine Trail, near the Sheepherder's End marker, zero trip meter and turn south following the sign for Muddy River.

GPS: N 38°48.44' W 110°54.32'

CENTRAL REGION TRAIL #25

Book Cliffs Loop

Starting Point:	I-70, exit 225
Finishing Point:	I-70, exit 225
Total Mileage:	76.3 miles
Unpaved Mileage:	65.9 miles
Driving Time:	4 hours
Elevation Range:	4,700–8,400 feet
Usually Open:	May to November
Difficulty Rating:	1
Scenic Rating:	7
Remoteness Rating:	+2

Special Attractions:

■ Panoramic views from high elevations.

■ An interesting, remote trail through one of America's foremost hydrocarbon fields.

A view of the San Arroyo mining camp

History

In the early 1800s, there were only a few trails leading into the Uinta Basin. Once fur traders discovered this area of eastern Utah, they quickly began trapping in the region. One of the routes followed the Colorado River into eastern Utah and then turned toward the Roan Plateau via Westwater Creek.

It was along this route that Antoine Robidoux, who established Utah's first non-Indian settlement and business, came into the area. He left proof of his passing in the form of a French inscription written on a rock. The translation reads, "Antoine Robidoux passed here November 13, 1837, to establish a house of trade on the Green or Uinta River." However, some scholars disagree as to whether this indicates the Uinta or the White River as there are trading posts (or the remains of buildings thought to have been trading posts) at both places.

From the mid-1900s to the present, Grand and Uintah Counties have both relied heavily on their reserves of natural gas. In 1925, natural gas was discovered in the Ashley Valley Field and provided both Vernal and Ashley Valley with the valuable fuel. Reserves began to dwindle in the early 1940s, and the Public Service Commission decided to stop piping gas to Uintah County.

The inscription by Antoine Robidoux

However, in 1960, the Mountain Fuel Supply Company found other gas reserves in western Uintah County and five years later helped build a pipeline to Bonanza. Today, natural gas production in Utah continues to reach new highs, and it contributes approximately 2 percent of the national average.

Description

This is a very long and remote trail with no facilities along it. Whether you complete the loop or take one of its connecting trails, it is highly recommended that you fill up your tank with gasoline before starting.

The Book Cliffs Loop begins at I-70, exit 225, and proceeds for 8.5 miles along the old US 6, which is a paved but deteriorated road. Moving through grasslands and sagebrush, and after passing the state line into Colorado, the trail then turns northwest onto a wide, country gravel road and heads through Grande Valley toward the Book Cliffs. The elevation at the start of the trail is about 4,700 feet, and along the way you will climb about 3,700 feet higher to the top of the Roan Plateau before coming back down into the valley. The beginning of the trail crosses several well-maintained side roads used by fuel companies for extensive oil and gas exploration in the area.

Leaving the flat ranchlands, the trail begins to run through the canyons, which are filled with saltbush, pinyon, and juniper. Then the trail follows a broad shelf road and gains altitude quickly along a 3.5-mile climb, passing the main regional base for the San Arroyo natural gas operations on the way.

From the high vantage point on top of the plateau, where pinyon pines dominate the immediate landscape, there are great views of the surrounding country. A few miles farther and about halfway along, the trail intersects with Northern #29: Dragon Ghost Town Trail near some radio towers. Broad, panoramic views continue to unfold in all directions as you drive from here, and 7 miles later another intersection leads to the Northern #28: Rainbow and Watson Ghost Towns Trail.

The last leg of the Book Cliffs Loop runs down through Hay Canyon along a broad shelf road with plenty of room to allow passing. The dusty surface can sometimes become slippery, but usually it is an easy, 1-rated road. From the intersection before Hay Canyon, the trail descends sharply, dropping over 1,000 feet in 2 miles along steep canyon walls dotted with pine trees. Toward the end of the trail, a side trail leads about 75 yards to a corral, where you can see the rock with the inscription by fur trader and explorer Antoine Robidoux. However, the inscription is on private property, so don't go into the corral or cross the fence line to get a closer look.

Current Road Information

BLM Moab Field Office
82 East Dogwood
Moab, UT 84532
(435) 259-2100

Map References

BLM Westwater
USGS 1:24,000 Harley Dome, Bitter Creek Well, Bar X Wash, Bryson Canyon, San Arroyo Ridge, Jim Canyon, PR Spring, Cedar Camp Canyon, Preacher Canyon, Dry Canyon
1:100,000 Westwater
Maptech CD-ROM: High Uinta/Flaming Gorge
Utah Atlas & Gazetteer, pp. 41, 49
Utah Travel Council #5 (incomplete)

Route Directions

▼ 0.0   On I-70, take exit 225 (marked "Westwater") toward the Book Cliffs. Zero trip meter at the intersection of the entry/exit ramps and the

		underpass on the north side of the freeway.
8.5 ▲		Trail ends at I-70, exit 225; turn right for Crescent Junction, left for Colorado.
GPS: N 39°10.50' W 109°07.66'		
▼ 0.2	TR	Turn north onto Old Highway 6 (Harley Dome to State Line Road), which parallels I-70 for a while.
8.3 ▲	TL	Turn left at intersection.
▼ 2.4	SO	Intersection with other end of the Book Cliffs Loop.
6.1 ▲	SO	Track on right is the Book Cliffs Loop.
GPS: N 39°12.24' W 109°06.85'		
▼ 3.1	SO	Cross bridge.
5.4 ▲	SO	Cross bridge.
▼ 4.4	SO	Cross bridge.
4.1 ▲	SO	Cross bridge.
▼ 5.6	SO	Cross bridge.
2.9 ▲	SO	Cross bridge.
▼ 5.7	SO	State line marker; cross Utah/Colorado border.
2.8 ▲	SO	State line marker; cross Utah/Colorado border.
GPS: N 39°12.39' W 109°03.05'		
▼ 8.5	TL	Turn north on gravel road and zero trip meter.
0.0 ▲		Continue southwest.
GPS: N 39°14.13' W 109°00.89'		
▼ 0.0		Continue north.
9.8 ▲	TR	Turn southwest on Old Highway 6 and zero trip meter.
▼ 1.0	SO	Track on right.
8.7 ▲	SO	Track on left.
▼ 4.1	SO	Cross through fence line at Colorado/Utah border. Road on right.
5.7 ▲	SO	Road on left. Cross through fence line at Colorado/Utah border.
GPS: N 39°17.20' W 109°03.02'		
▼ 4.8	SO	Cross through wash.
5.0 ▲	SO	Cross through wash.
▼ 5.7	SO	Road on left.
4.0 ▲	SO	Road on right.
▼ 8.7	SO	Track on right.
1.0 ▲	SO	Track on left.
▼ 9.6	SO	Road on left.
0.1 ▲	SO	Road on right.
▼ 9.8	BR	Fork in road. Zero trip meter.
0.0 ▲		Continue along main road.
GPS: N 39°19.88' W 109°08.43'		
▼ 0.0		Continue along track.
5.7 ▲	BL	Road enters on right. Zero trip meter.
▼ 0.1	SO	Track on right.
5.6 ▲	SO	Track on left.
▼ 0.2	SO	Track on left.
5.5 ▲	SO	Track on right.
▼ 0.3	SO	Track on right.
5.3 ▲	SO	Track on left.
▼ 0.5	SO	Road on right.
5.2 ▲	SO	Road on left.
▼ 0.9	SO	Cross through Bitter Creek Wash.
4.7 ▲	SO	Cross through Bitter Creek Wash.
▼ 1.4	SO	Track on left.
4.3 ▲	SO	Track on right.
▼ 1.9	SO	Track on left.
3.8 ▲	SO	Track on right.
▼ 2.3	SO	Track on left.
3.3 ▲	SO	Track on right.
▼ 2.8	SO	Road on left.

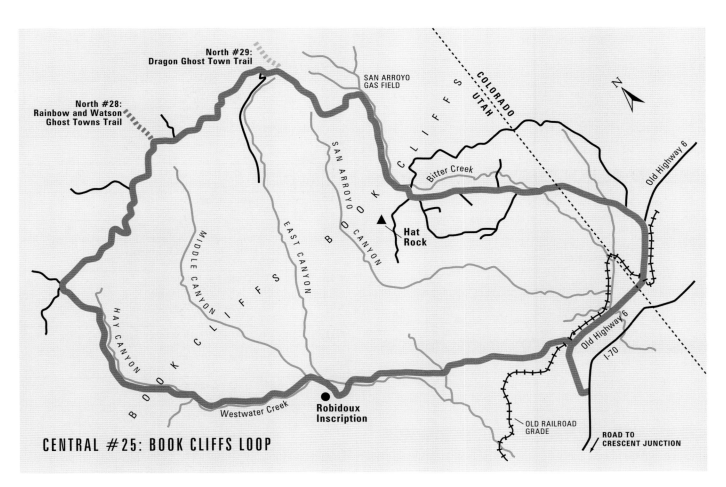

CENTRAL #25: BOOK CLIFFS LOOP

	2.9 ▲	SO	Road on right.

GPS: N 39°21.97' W 109°08.18'

▼ 3.1		SO	Track on left.
	2.6 ▲	SO	Track on right.
▼ 3.5		SO	Track on right.
	2.1 ▲	SO	Track on left.
▼ 4.3		SO	Track on right.
	1.4 ▲	SO	Track on left.

GPS: N 39°23.04' W 109°07.67'

▼ 5.0		SO	Track on right.
	0.6 ▲	SO	Track on left.
▼ 5.4		SO	Track on left.
	0.2 ▲	SO	Track on right.
▼ 5.7		BL	Fork in road. San Arroyo Gas Plant truck loading station on right. Zero trip meter.
	0.0 ▲		Continue along main trail.

GPS: N 39°24.08' W 109°07.48'

▼ 0.0			Proceed uphill.
	7.4 ▲	BR	Track enters on left. Zero trip meter.
▼ 0.3		SO	The main San Arroyo Gas Plant on left.
	7.1 ▲	SO	The main San Arroyo Gas Plant on right.
▼ 1.5		SO	Track on right to mining works.
	5.9 ▲	SO	Track on left to mining works.
▼ 2.6		UT	Intersection. U-turn right.
	4.7 ▲	UT	U-turn left.
▼ 3.3		BL	Track on right to gas well.
	4.0 ▲	BR	Track on left to gas well.
▼ 3.5		SO	Track on right. Proceed downhill.
	3.9 ▲	SO	Track on left.

GPS: N 39°24.14' W 109°08.89'

▼ 4.3		BR	Switchback past oil well facility on left.
	3.0 ▲	BL	Switchback past oil well facility on right.
▼ 4.4		SO	Road on left.
	3.0 ▲	SO	Road on right.
▼ 4.6		BR	Track on left.
	2.8 ▲	SO	Track on right.
▼ 5.3		SO	Track on left.
	2.0 ▲	SO	Track on right.

GPS: N 39°25.06' W 109°09.32'

▼ 7.2		SO	Cattle guard.
	0.2 ▲	SO	Cattle guard.
▼ 7.4		SO	Intersection. Road on right is Northern #29: Dragon Ghost Town Trail, signed to Atchee Ridge and McCook Ridge. Road on left to radio tower. Zero trip meter in the middle of intersection.
	0.0 ▲		Proceed straight across toward San Arroyo and Grand Junction.

GPS: N 39°26.59' W 109°09.84'

▼ 0.0			Proceed straight across toward PR Spring and Ouray.
	7.1 ▲	SO	Road on right to radio tower. Road on left is Northern #29: Dragon Ghost Town Trail, signed to Atchee Ridge and McCook Ridge. Zero trip meter in the middle of intersection.
▼ 0.5		SO	Intersection. Road on left to East Canyon. Proceed straight along Seep Ridge Road.
	6.6 ▲	SO	Road on right to East Canyon.

GPS: N 39°26.87' W 109°10.27'

▼ 1.4		SO	Track on right.
	5.6 ▲	SO	Track on left.
▼ 2.7		SO	Track on right.
	4.4 ▲	SO	Track on left.
▼ 3.0		SO	Track on right.
	4.0 ▲	SO	Track on left.
▼ 3.6		SO	Gas well on left.
	3.5 ▲	SO	Gas well on right.
▼ 4.4		SO	Tracks on left and right.
	2.7 ▲	SO	Tracks on right and left.
GPS: N 39°26.77' W 109°13.91'			
▼ 5.0		BR	Road and radio tower on left.
	2.0 ▲	BL	Road and radio tower on right.
▼ 5.5		SO	Cattle guard. Corral and track on right.
	1.6 ▲	SO	Corral and track on left. Cattle guard.
▼ 6.1		SO	Road on right to South Canyon and Sweetwater Canyon.
	1.0 ▲	SO	Road on left to South Canyon and Sweetwater Canyon.
▼ 6.5		SO	Track on right to Black Horse Canyon; it ends in 6 miles.
	0.5 ▲	SO	Track on left to Black Horse Canyon; it ends in 6 miles.
GPS: N 39°26.91' W 109°15.90'			
▼ 7.1		TL	Intersection. Turn left, following sign to Winter Ridge Junction, and zero trip meter. Straight is Northern #28: Rainbow and Watson Ghost Towns Trail, which also leads to Seep Ridge Road and Ouray.
	0.0 ▲		Continue along trail.
GPS: N 39°27.14' W 109°16.43'			
▼ 0.0			Continue toward Winter Ridge Junction.
	8.9 ▲	TR	Intersection. Turn right to McCook Ridge and zero trip meter. Left is Northern #28: Rainbow and Watson Ghost Towns Trail.
▼ 1.0		SO	Track on left.
	7.9 ▲	SO	Track on right.
▼ 2.6		SO	Cross cattle guard.
	6.2 ▲	SO	Cross cattle guard.
▼ 3.2		SO	Eroded track on right.
	5.6 ▲	SO	Track on left.
▼ 5.5		SO	Track on right.
	3.4 ▲	SO	Track on left.
▼ 5.8		SO	Gas well on right.
	3.1 ▲	SO	Gas well on left.
▼ 5.9		SO	Track on right.
	2.9 ▲	SO	Track on left.
▼ 6.7		SO	Track on left.
	2.1 ▲	SO	Track on right.
▼ 8.0		SO	Cross cattle guard.
	0.9 ▲	SO	Cross cattle guard.
▼ 8.5		BL	Road forks.
	0.4 ▲	SO	Road on left.
▼ 8.6		SO	Road on right.
	0.3 ▲	BR	Road forks.
▼ 8.8		BL	Road on right.
	0.1 ▲	SO	Road on left.
▼ 8.9		TL	Intersection. Straight ahead is Cedar Camp and Steer Ridge. Right to Winter Ridge and Bull Canyon. Zero trip meter.
	0.0 ▲		Proceed toward Seep Ridge.
GPS: N 39°24.98' W 109°23.90'			
▼ 0.0			Continue along trail toward Hay Canyon and I-70.
	14.4 ▲	TR	Intersection. Straight is Winter Ridge and Bull

			Canyon. Left is Cedar Camp, and Steer Ridge. Zero trip meter.
▼ 2.2		SO	Track on left.
	12.2 ▲	SO	Track on right.
▼ 5.2		SO	Track on right.
	9.2 ▲	SO	Track on left.
▼ 6.0		SO	Cross cattle guard.
	8.4 ▲	SO	Cross cattle guard.
▼ 8.0		SO	Cross through large wash.
	6.4 ▲	SO	Cross through large wash.
▼ 8.5		SO	Two tracks on right.
	5.9 ▲	SO	Two tracks on left.
▼ 9.0		SO	Cattle guard.
	5.4 ▲	SO	Cattle guard.
▼ 9.4		SO	Cross through creek. The trail crosses Westwater Creek and its tributaries many times over next 2.0 miles.
	5.0 ▲	SO	Cross through creek.
▼ 9.6		SO	Cross through creek.
	4.8 ▲	SO	Cross through creek.
▼ 10.8		SO	Cross through creek.
	3.6 ▲	SO	Cross through creek.
▼ 11.4		SO	Cross through creek.
	3.0 ▲	SO	Cross through creek. The trail crosses Westwater Creek and its tributaries many times over next 2.0 miles.
▼ 12.0		SO	Track on left.
	2.4 ▲	BL	Track on right.
▼ 13.9		TR	Intersection. Left goes to Middle Canyon
	0.5 ▲	TL	Straight goes to Middle Canyon. Continue toward Hay Canyon.
▼ 14.1		SO	Cross through creek.
	0.3 ▲	SO	Cross through creek.
▼ 14.4		SO	Cross cattle guard, then intersection; zero trip meter. Left to East Canyon. Right leads to Antoine Robidoux inscription on rock by a corral (private property) against the canyon wall.
	0.0 ▲		Continue along trail.
GPS: N 39°16.56' W 109°17.13'			
▼ 0.0			Continue along trail.
	14.5 ▲	SO	Intersection; zero trip meter. Continue straight to Hay Canyon. Right to East Canyon. Left to Antoine Robidoux inscription on rock by a corral (private property) against canyon wall.
▼ 0.7		SO	Track on right.
	13.8 ▲	SO	Track on left.
▼ 1.0		SO	Cattle guard.
	13.4 ▲	SO	Cattle guard.
▼ 1.4		SO	Cattle guard.
	13.0 ▲	SO	Cattle guard.
▼ 1.8		SO	Cross through creek.
	12.7 ▲	SO	Cross through creek.
▼ 2.2		SO	Cross through wash, then gas plant on right.
	12.2 ▲	SO	Gas plant on left, then cross through wash.
▼ 4.1		SO	Cattle guard, then cross through large wash.
	10.3 ▲	SO	Cross through large wash, then cattle guard.
▼ 4.4		SO	Road on right.
	10.1 ▲	SO	Road on left.
▼ 6.3		BL	Road on right.
	8.1 ▲	BR	Road on left.
GPS: N 39°14.04' W 109°12.30'			
▼ 6.7		BR	Road to Bryson Ridge and San Arroyo Canyon on left.
	7.8 ▲	BL	Bear left toward Hay Canyon.

▼ 10.3	SO	Dirt road on left.	
4.1 ▲	SO	Dirt road on right.	
▼ 12.1	TR	Intersection with Old Highway 6.	
2.3 ▲	TL	Turn left onto road.	

GPS: N 39°12.24' W 109°06.85'

▼ 14.3	TL	Turn left toward I-70.	
0.2 ▲	TR	Turn right onto Old Highway 6.	

GPS: N 39°10.59' W 109°07.89'

▼ 14.5		Trail ends at I-70, exit 225. Turn right for Crescent Junction, left for Colorado.
0.0 ▲		On I-70, take exit 225 (marked "Westwater") toward the Book Cliffs. Zero trip meter at the intersection of the entry/exit ramps and the underpass on the north side of freeway.

GPS: N 39°10.50' W 109°07.66'

CENTRAL REGION TRAIL #26

Sego Ghost Town Trail

Starting Point:	**I-70 at Thompson Springs, exit 185**
Finishing Point:	**Gate at Uintah and Ouray Indian**
	Reservation
Total Mileage:	**15.1 miles**
Unpaved Mileage:	**11 miles**
Driving Time:	**1.25 hours (one-way)**
Elevation Range:	**5,100–8,400 feet**
Usually Open:	**Year-round (as far as Sego ghost town)**
Difficulty Rating:	**2**
Scenic Rating:	**9**
Remoteness Rating:	**+1**

Special Attractions:

■ Rock art panels.
■ Sego ghost town and the old railroad grade.
■ Connects with Central #28: Sagers Canyon Trail and Central #27: Floy Wash Trail.
■ Panoramic views.

History

This trail starts in the small town of Thompson Springs, which sits at the mouth of Thompson Canyon near a natural spring. The land at this favorable location was originally purchased by brothers Harry and Arthur P. Ballard in the 1880s; they then laid out and promoted the town. With its water supplies and the successful coal mining operations at nearby Sego, it was for a time an important railroad stop.

A few miles north of Thompson Springs, both pictographs and petroglyphs of three Indian cultures can be found on the walls of Sego Canyon. The BLM acquired the panels in 1993 and have begun efforts to preserve them. They contain Barrier Canyon style art, which dates from 500 B.C. to A.D. 500; Fremont Indian art, which dates from A.D. 1000 to 1150; and Ute Indian pictographs from the 19th

One of the panels of pictographs along the trail

century. The Ute consider the area sacred.

Named for Utah's state flower, the sego lily, Sego was a coal mining town whose boom-and-bust history was repeated many times in Utah. After Harry Ballard discovered coal here in the early 1890s, he bought up the land and started mining operations on a small scale. Soon after, he sold his business to Salt Lake City investors who built a store, a boardinghouse, and other buildings as part of a grand plan for a long run of coal production. Sego grew to nearly 500 residents, and the Denver and Rio Grande Railroad built a subsidiary railroad from the Thompson Springs station to the mines. Although Sego's mines were productive for many years, a series of mining disasters and financial mismanagement eventually doomed the operation. Production ceased in 1947, and the property was sold at auction. Today, several original structures still stand in the ghost town of Sego.

Description

The Sego Ghost Town Trail may be short, but it makes up in beauty and historical interest what it lacks in length. This trail makes an easy side trip along I-70 if you want to take in some local scenery and don't have much time.

From I-70, exit 185, Thompson Springs is about three-quarters of a mile north. As you drive through town, you cross a railroad line with a small station and pass by many buildings

The old boardinghouse at Sego ghost town

CENTRAL #26: SEGO GHOST TOWN TRAIL

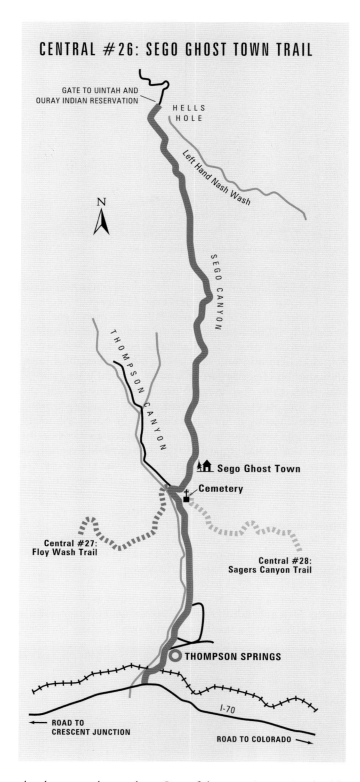

GATE TO UINTAH AND
OURAY INDIAN RESERVATION

HELLS
HOLE

Left Hand Nash Wash

N

SEGO CANYON

THOMPSON CANYON

🏠 Sego Ghost Town

✝ Cemetery

Central #27:
Floy Wash Trail

Central #28:
Sagers Canyon Trail

◯ THOMPSON SPRINGS

I-70

← ROAD TO
CRESCENT JUNCTION

ROAD TO COLORADO →

rock art on the right of the trail beside the cattle guard. As you continue along the trail through the canyon, you cross the main wash many times. About a half mile beyond the petroglyphs, you reach the intersection with Central #27: Floy Wash Trail and, a little farther, Central #28: Sagers Canyon Trail.

As you approach the ruins of Sego, you pass by a railroad cutting and an old cemetery. Sego still has a couple of buildings standing above their foundations, including the stone general store, which remains in pretty good shape. Across from it, the old saloon/boardinghouse is not holding up as well, but you can still make out its basic structure.

About 1.2 miles past the ghost town, the trail drops into the wash, traveling along it for about 2 miles up Sego Canyon.

The old general store at Sego ghost town

Navigation in the canyon is not an issue, as there are no real side trails.

Toward the end, the trail climbs easy, 1-rated switchbacks out of the canyon. The road is wide and maintained and could easily take passenger cars. At the end of the climb, the road heads west across a saddle with views south of Sego Canyon, and then it ends at a gate into the Uintah and Ouray Indian Reservation. No trespassing is allowed beyond this point.

Overall, the Sego Ghost Town Trail is a varied but easy trail. It offers impressive views of the Book Cliffs and travels through vegetation ranging from saltbush in the canyon to aspen, pinyon, and juniper in the mountains. The trail itself is rather smooth, though some rocky sections and variable levels of water in the washes (depending on the recent weather) could pose minor difficulties.

Current Road Information
BLM Moab Field Office
82 East Dogwood
Moab, UT 84532
(435) 259-2100

Map References
BLM   Moab, Westwater
USGS 1:24,000 Thompson Springs, Sego Canyon, Bogart
Canyon
1:100,000 Moab, Westwater

that have seen better days. One of the more interesting buildings in Thompson is the tiny, pink post office at the railroad crossing; it looks as if it were built in miniature.

After about 4 miles, you come to a small parking area on the left with some information boards and public toilets. From here you can walk to the panels of Indian rock art that adorn some of the surrounding canyon walls. There is also

Maptech CD-ROM: Moab/Canyonlands; High Uinta/
    Flaming Gorge
Utah Atlas & Gazetteer, p. 40
Utah Travel Council #3; #5

Route Directions

▼ 0.0		On I-70, take exit 185 and zero trip meter at intersection of the entry/exit ramps and the underpass on north side of highway. Proceed north on SSR 94 toward Thompson Springs.
	GPS: N 38°57.80′ W 109°43.30′	
▼ 0.1	BR	Intersection.
▼ 0.8	SO	Two stop signs. Cross Thompson Springs railroad tracks.
▼ 0.9	SO	Post office on left. Then bear left where the road forks.
▼ 1.2	BL	Road on right. Follow BLM sign toward Sego Canyon.
▼ 2.1	SO	Road on right.
▼ 4.1	SO	Two washes with short, unmarked track on left between them. Track leads to numerous pictographs and petroglyphs with BLM information boards.
▼ 4.2	SO	Cattle guard. Further rock art panels are down a track on right immediately prior to cattle guard.
▼ 4.3	SO	Cross wash. Note old railway bridge on right.
▼ 4.4	SO	Cross through wash.
▼ 4.5	SO	Cross through wash. Then track on right to old building and railroad cutting; track rejoins at the turnoff to Central #28: Sagers Canyon Trail.
	GPS: N 39°01.42′ W 109°42.71′	
▼ 4.6	TR	Turn right toward Sego Canyon. Left is Central #27: Floy Wash Trail.
	GPS: N 39°01.49′ W 109°42.73′	
▼ 4.7	SO	Cemetery on right.
	GPS: N 39°01.41′ W 109°42.59′	
▼ 4.8	SO	Track on right is Central #28: Sagers Canyon Trail.
	GPS: N 39°01.45′ W 109°42.51′	
▼ 5.3	SO	Cross through wash.
▼ 5.4	SO	Cross through wash. Railway bridge on right and old structures on left.
▼ 5.5	SO	Cross through wash. Railway bridge on left.
▼ 5.6	SO	Buildings on right and left are remains of Sego. Stone building on right was the company/general store. Wooden building on left was the old boardinghouse. Zero trip meter between buildings.
	GPS: N 39°02.03′ W 109°42.16′	
▼ 0.0		Continue along main trail.
▼ 0.4	SO	Cross through wash. Stone foundation on left.
▼ 0.5	SO	Track on left ends in about 100 yards from where you can see old houses and foundations in the overgrowth if you look over the edge of the hill toward the main road.
	GPS: N 39°02.40′ W 109°42.09′	
▼ 0.6	SO	Cross through wash.
▼ 0.7	SO	Cross through wash.
▼ 1.2	SO	Cattle guard.
▼ 3.3	SO	Cross through large wash.
▼ 7.7	SO	Travel along a ridgeline with views.
	GPS: N 39°07.86′ W 109°42.64′	
▼ 9.5		Sego hiking and horse trail on left (open May to November). Then trail ends at gate to the Uintah and Ouray Indian Reservation.
	GPS: N 39°08.98′ W 109°43.00′	

Floy Wash Trail

Starting Point:	**Central #26: Sego Ghost Town Trail**
Finishing Point:	**I-70, exit 173 (11 miles east of Green River)**
Total Mileage:	**23.3 miles**
Unpaved Mileage:	**23 miles**
Driving Time:	**1.75 hours**
Elevation Range:	**4,600–6,000 feet**
Usually Open:	**Year-round**
Difficulty Rating:	**2**
Scenic Rating:	**8**
Remoteness Rating:	**+0**

Special Attractions

- Spectacular views from the edge of the Book Cliffs.
- Forms a loop trail off of I-70 when combined with Central #26: Sego Ghost Town Trail.

History

During the construction of the Denver and Rio Grande Western Railroad through eastern Utah, Floy Station (also called Little Grande Station) served as a construction camp for the workers. The town is located just west of Crescent Junction on I-70, which follows the same route as the railroad.

Over the years, people have attempted to mine various minerals around Floy. A small gold discovery was made along the Floy Wash in 1929, though it did not amount to much. Manganese mining proved to be more successful; the Colorado Fuel and Iron Company ran a manganese mill and mining camp at Floy Station for many years.

Description

The Floy Wash Trail departs Central #26: Sego Ghost Town Trail at the 4.6-mile mark through sandy soil and thick juniper. The wide, single-lane, 2-rated road is periodically grad-

A view of the trail traveling along the upper reaches of the Book Cliffs

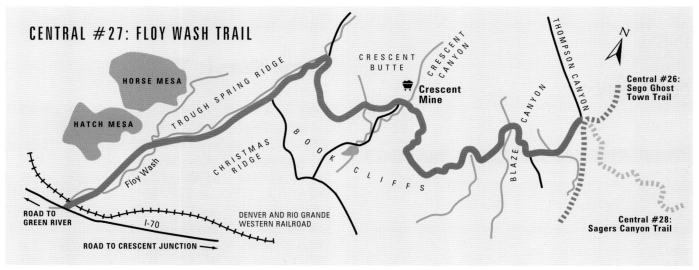

CENTRAL #27: FLOY WASH TRAIL

ed. You loop around the head of deep canyons, which cut through the edge of the Book Cliffs and offer distant views through the canyons, across Crescent Flat, and into the San Rafael Desert far below. Initially, the road follows the upper rim of the Book Cliffs, which rise over 1,000 feet above the flat country to the south.

For the last 10 to 12 miles, the trail follows a wide, well-maintained two-lane road, though there are some deep sandy sections that are potential hazards if the road is wet.

Near the end, the trail emerges from a somewhat narrow canyon into wide ranchland. After driving through the broad flatland, the canyon once again narrows before opening up into a vast expanse of flat grassland that stretches for miles.

Current Road Information
BLM Moab Field Office
82 East Dogwood
Moab, UT 84532
(435) 259-2100

Map References
BLM Westwater, Moab
USGS 1:24,000 Sego Canyon, Crescent Junction, Floy Canyon South, Hutch Mesa
1:100,000 Westwater, Moab
Maptech CD-ROM: High Uinta/Flaming Gorge; Moab/Canyonlands
Utah Atlas & Gazetteer, p. 40
Utah Travel Council #3; #5

Route Directions

▼ 0.0			On Central #26: Sego Ghost Town Trail, 4.6 miles from I-70, zero trip meter and take left trail. Note that straight goes to Thompson Canyon and right goes to Sego.
	10.6 ▲		Trail ends at Central #26: Sego Ghost Town Trail; go straight for Sego, right for I-70.
		GPS: N 39°01.49′ W 109°42.73′	
▼ 0.1		SO	Cross through wash.
	10.5 ▲	SO	Cross through wash.

▼ 0.4		SO	Cross through wash.
	10.1 ▲	SO	Cross through wash.
▼ 0.6		SO	Cross through gate and leave it as you found it.
	10.0 ▲	SO	Cross through gate and leave it as you found it.
		GPS: N 39°01.15′ W 109°42.90′	
▼ 2.1		SO	Track on left.
	8.4 ▲	SO	Track on right.
		GPS: N 39°00.30′ W 109°43.97′	
▼ 2.6		SO	Track on left.
	8.0 ▲	SO	Track on right.
▼ 2.7		SO	Cross through gate and leave it as you found it.
	7.9 ▲	SO	Cross through gate and leave it as you found it.
		GPS: N 39°00.57′ W 109°44.37′	
▼ 3.1		SO	Cross through wash.
	7.5 ▲	SO	Cross through wash.
▼ 3.3		SO	Track on right.
	7.3 ▲	SO	Track on left.
▼ 3.3		SO	Cross through wash.
	7.2 ▲	SO	Cross through wash.
▼ 3.4		SO	Old cabin on right. Cross through gate.
	7.1 ▲	SO	Cross through gate. Old cabin on left.
▼ 3.5		SO	Cross through wash.
	7.1 ▲	SO	Cross through wash.
▼ 3.7		SO	Cross through wash.
	6.9 ▲	SO	Cross through wash.
▼ 3.8		SO	Cross through gate.
	6.7 ▲	SO	Cross through gate.
▼ 4.2		SO	Cross through wash.
	6.4 ▲	SO	Cross through wash.
▼ 5.1		SO	Cross through wash.
	5.5 ▲	SO	Cross through wash.
▼ 5.4		SO	Cross through gate and leave it as you found it.
	5.2 ▲	SO	Cross through gate and leave it as you found it.
		GPS: N 38°59.83′ W 109°45.66′	
▼ 6.5		SO	Cross through wash.
	4.1 ▲	SO	Cross through wash.
▼ 7.6		SO	Cross through wash.
	3.0 ▲	SO	Cross through wash.
▼ 8.7		SO	Cross through wash.
	1.9 ▲	SO	Cross through wash.
▼ 9.3		SO	Cross through wash.
	1.3 ▲	SO	Cross through wash.
▼ 9.9		SO	Cross through wash.

	0.7 ▲	SO	Cross through wash.
▼ 10.2		SO	Track on right.
	0.3 ▲	SO	Track on left.
▼ 10.6		TR	Intersection. Zero trip meter.
	0.0 ▲		Continue along trail.

GPS: N 39°00.29' W 109°48.26'

▼ 0.0			Continue along trail.
	3.8 ▲	TL	Intersection. Zero trip meter.
▼ 0.7		SO	Cross through wash.
	3.0 ▲	SO	Cross through wash.
▼ 1.1		SO	Cross through washes.
	2.7 ▲	SO	Cross through washes.
▼ 1.3		SO	Cattle guard.
	2.4 ▲	SO	Cattle guard.
▼ 2.0		SO	Track on left.
	1.8 ▲	SO	Track on right.
▼ 3.5		SO	Cross through wash.
	0.3 ▲	SO	Cross through wash.
▼ 3.8		TL	Intersection. Zero trip meter.
	0.0 ▲		Continue along trail.

GPS: N 39°00.92' W 109°50.67'

▼ 0.0			Continue along trail.
	5.3 ▲	BR	Turn onto track on right. Zero trip meter.
▼ 0.2		SO	Cross through wash.
	5.1 ▲	SO	Cross through wash.
▼ 0.3		SO	Corral on right.
	4.9 ▲	SO	Corral on left.
▼ 0.4		SO	Cross through Floy Wash several times over next mile.
	4.8 ▲	SO	Cross through wash.
▼ 0.6		SO	Cross through wash.
	4.7 ▲	SO	Cross through wash.
▼ 0.7		SO	Cross through wash.
	4.6 ▲	SO	Cross through wash.
▼ 1.4		SO	Cross through wash.
	3.9 ▲	SO	Cross through Floy Wash several times over next mile.
▼ 2.0		BR	Road forks.
	3.3 ▲	SO	Road on right.

GPS: N 38°59.63' W 109°51.87'

▼ 4.2		SO	Cattle guard.
	1.1 ▲	SO	Cattle guard.

GPS: N 38°58.15' W 109°53.34'

▼ 5.3		BL	Cross through wash with very sandy road surface. Then left at fork in road. Zero trip meter.
	0.0 ▲		Continue along trail.

GPS: N 38°57.71' W 109°54.41'

▼ 0.0			Continue along trail.
	3.6 ▲	BR	Road on left. Cross through wash with very sandy road surface. Zero trip meter.
▼ 0.3		SO	Cross through washes.
	3.3 ▲	SO	Cross through washes.
▼ 1.6		SO	Cattle guard.
	2.0 ▲	SO	Cattle guard.
▼ 2.4		SO	Cross through wash.
	1.2 ▲	SO	Cross through wash.
▼ 2.5		SO	Track on right.
	1.1 ▲	SO	Track on left.
▼ 3.0		SO	Cross railroad tracks. Then track on left; bear right.
	0.6 ▲	SO	Track on right, then bear left across railroad tracks.

GPS: N 38°55.50' W 109°56.14'

▼ 3.3		TL	Cross through fence line. Then intersection. Turn onto paved frontage road.
	0.3 ▲	TR	Road on left. Turn onto unpaved road and follow sign to Floy Canyon.

GPS: N 38°55.34' W 109°56.38'

▼ 3.5		SO	Cattle guard.
	0.1 ▲	SO	Cattle guard.
▼ 3.6			Trail ends at I-70, exit 173; turn right for Green River, left for Crescent Junction.
	0.0 ▲		On I-70, take exit 173 and zero trip meter at intersection of exit/entry ramps and highway overpass on north side. Proceed north before turning west on frontage road.

GPS: N 38°55.31' W 109°56.09'

Sagers Canyon Trail

Starting Point:	Central #26: Sego Ghost Town Trail
Finishing Point:	I-70, exit 190
Total Mileage:	14.9 miles
Unpaved Mileage:	14 miles
Driving Time:	1.25 hours
Elevation Range:	4,800–6,000 feet
Usually Open:	Year-round
Difficulty Rating:	2
Scenic Rating:	7
Remoteness Rating:	+1

Special Attractions

■ Interesting, remote trail.
■ Combined with Central #26: Sego Ghost Town Trail, it forms a loop trail off I-70.

History

Like Floy Station, Sagers Station was a railroad camp along the Denver and Rio Grande Western Railroad's line across eastern Utah. The station was located about seven miles east of Thompson Springs but has since disappeared. There is, how-

A view of the trail as it winds around to cross Sagers Canyon

CENTRAL #28: SAGERS CANYON TRAIL

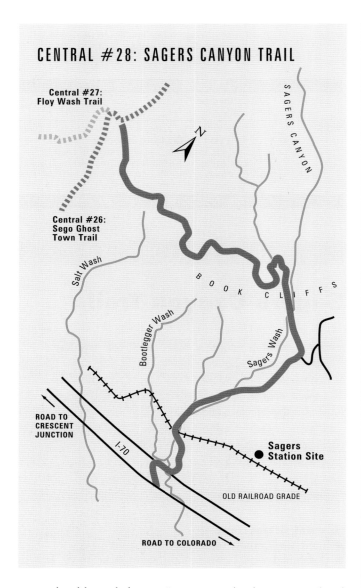

ever, a local legend about a Japanese cook who was murdered for a cache of money he was thought to have buried somewhere in the area. The money was never found, and local legend has it that it may still lie buried somewhere in the vicinity of Sagers Station or Sagers Canyon.

Description

From Central #26: Sego Ghost Town Trail at the 4.8-mile mark, the Sagers Canyon Trail runs along an occasionally graded road. If it has rained recently, you may need to carefully negotiate some rough mud holes. Also, the first part of the trail contains a number of washes—only the most conspicuous have been marked in the route directions.

After 7.2 miles, you begin a steep descent and enjoy some spectacular views as the trail switchbacks to the canyon floor. Driving along the bottom of the narrow canyons, the trail again crosses a number of washes. Carry on through the sagebrush and juniper until you reach the end of the trail at I-70, exit 190. Sagers Station was located about a mile east of where you cross under the railway line.

Current Road Information
BLM Moab Field Office
82 East Dogwood
Moab, UT 84532
(435) 259-2100

Map References

BLM   Westwater, Moab
USGS 1:24,000   Sego Canyon, Calf Canyon, Sagers Flat
          1:100,000 Westwater, Moab
Maptech CD-ROM: High Uinta/Flaming Gorge; Moab/
          Canyonlands
Utah Atlas & Gazetteer, p. 40
Utah Travel Council #3; #5

Route Directions

▼ 0.0		On Central #26: Sego Ghost Town Trail, 4.8 miles from I-70, zero trip meter and turn right on side road. Take the left fork and cross through wash.
9.8 ▲		Trail ends at Central #26: Sego Ghost Town Trail; turn right for Sego, left for I-70.
GPS: N 39°01.45′ W 109°42.51′		
▼ 0.1	SO	Cross through old fence line.
9.7 ▲	SO	Cross through old fence line.
▼ 0.2	SO	Cross through wash, then cross through gate.
9.5 ▲	SO	Cross through gate, then cross through wash.
▼ 0.6	SO	Cross through wash.
9.1 ▲	SO	Cross through wash.
▼ 0.7	SO	Cross through wash.
9.0 ▲	SO	Cross through wash.
▼ 1.1	SO	Track on right.
8.7 ▲	SO	Track on left.
▼ 2.7	SO	Cross through wash.
7.0 ▲	SO	Cross through wash.
▼ 2.8	SO	Cross through gate.
6.9 ▲	SO	Cross through gate.
GPS: N 39°00.68′ W 109°40.22′		
▼ 3.1	SO	Cross through wash.
6.6 ▲	SO	Cross through wash.
▼ 4.7	SO	Cross through Bootlegger Wash.
5.1 ▲	SO	Cross through Bootlegger Wash.
▼ 5.8	SO	Cross through fence line.
3.9 ▲	SO	Cross through fence line.
GPS: N 39°00.76′ W 109°38.04′		
▼ 7.2	SO	Steep descent into canyon.
2.5 ▲	SO	Steep descent into canyon.
▼ 8.1	SO	Track on left.
1.7 ▲	SO	Track on right.
▼ 9.8	TR	T-Intersection. Zero trip meter.
0.0 ▲		Continue along trail.
GPS: N 38°59.97′ W 109°36.05′		
▼ 0.0		Continue along trail.
5.1 ▲	BL	Track on left. Zero trip meter.
▼ 2.2	SO	Cross through Sagers Wash several times over next mile.
2.9 ▲	SO	Cross through wash.
GPS: N 38°58.39′ W 109°37.04′		
▼ 2.5	SO	Cross through wash.
2.6 ▲	SO	Cross through wash.
▼ 2.9	SO	Cross through wash.
2.2 ▲	SO	Cross through wash.

▼ 3.1	SO	Cross through wash and under railroad line.
2.0 ▲	SO	Cross under railroad line and then cross through Sagers Wash several times over next mile.
	GPS: N 38°57.67′ W 109°37.27′	
▼ 3.2	SO	Track on right. Then track on left.
1.9 ▲	SO	Track on right. Then track on left.
▼ 3.5	SO	Track on left.
1.6 ▲	BL	Track on right.
▼ 3.9	SO	Track on right
1.2 ▲	SO	Track on left.
	GPS: N 38°57.12′ W 109°36.79′	
▼ 4.2	TR	Intersection with paved frontage road.
0.9 ▲	TL	Turn onto dirt road. BLM sign reads, "Sagers Canyon 6."
	GPS: N 38°56.95′ W 109°36.70′	
▼ 4.3	SO	Cross bridge over wash.
0.8 ▲	SO	Cross bridge over wash.
▼ 4.6	UT	U-turn left.
0.5 ▲	UT	U-turn right onto frontage road.
	GPS: N 38°56.93′ W 109°37.25′	
▼ 5.1		Trail ends at I-70, exit 190; turn right for Thompson Springs, left for Colorado.
0.0 ▲		On I-70, take exit 190 and zero trip meter at intersection of the overpass and the entry/exit ramps on north side. This exit is 5.7 miles east of Thompson Springs.
	GPS: N 38°56.62′ W 109°36.85′	

CENTRAL REGION TRAIL #29

Gooseberry-Fremont Road

Starting Point:	**Utah 72, 4.8 miles northeast of Fremont**
Finishing Point:	**I-70, exit 61**
Total Mileage:	**40.2 miles**
Unpaved Mileage:	**23.2 miles**
Driving Time:	**2.5 hours**
Elevation Range:	**7,500–10,500 feet**
Usually Open:	**June to October**
Difficulty Rating:	**1**
Scenic Rating:	**7**
Remoteness Rating:	**+0**

Special Attractions

- Long, easy trail for scenic touring.
- Access to a network of 4WD, ATV, and hiking trails.
- Fishing and camping opportunities, both developed and primitive.

Description

This long trail through Fishlake National Forest is a pleasant drive, and in dry weather, it is traversable by passenger vehicles. The first 12.6 miles are paved, as are the last 4.4 miles, and the rest of the trail is a good graded gravel road. It is common to see wildlife on this trail, including mule deer at all

The bridge across Sevenmile Creek

times of day. There are also large herds of elk and a herd of moose in Fishlake Basin. Other animals to watch out for include coyotes, ground squirrels, and the less-appealing skunks and rattlesnakes.

The trail first passes the large Mill Meadow Reservoir and then follows alongside the Fremont River. Camping is restricted along this stretch. RVs and vehicles can use the paved pull-ins to park overnight. Walk-in tent camping is permitted in some of the river meadows.

At Johnson Valley Reservoir in Fishlake Basin, the road follows around the northeast shore, giving good views over the lake. Camping is permitted in developed campgrounds only, and the operation of ATVs is prohibited. Here the trail becomes a smaller graded gravel road and climbs gradually to the plateau alongside Sevenmile Creek. Dispersed camping is permitted on this part of the route after the first 1.5 miles. Once on the plateau, the trail runs mainly through open meadows interspersed with stands of aspen and pine. There are some pleasant camping areas, but they are fairly exposed.

Stands of aspens along the trail

About 6 miles from Johnson Valley Reservoir, you can see Lost Creek Reservoir to the west and Mount Terrill (11,547 feet) to the east. The Mount Terrill Guard Station is hidden in the trees, down a short track, just before the turnoff for Lost Creek Reservoir. In 2000, the forest service made the guard station available for overnight accomodation. The trail then winds down, offering wide views to the east. It passes by the trailheads for many ATV trails and some interesting 4WD roads—mainly dead-end trails or short loops. There is a wider variety of campsites on this northern end of the trail.

The trail passes the Gooseberry Guard Station, Gooseberry Youth Camp, and the Gooseberry National Forest Campground (with facilities) before leaving Fishlake National Forest. There are several seasonal closure gates on this end of the trail. The forest service uses them mainly to control vehicle access during spring runoff, when the trail can be easily damaged. Exact dates vary, but the trail is normally accessible in part by May and completely by June.

The trail ends at I-70, exit 61, 7 miles east of Salina.

Current Road Information
BLM Richfield Field Office
150 East 900 North
Richfield, UT 84701
(435) 896-1500

Fishlake National Forest
Loa Ranger District
138 South Main
Loa, UT 84747
(435) 836-2811

Map References
BLM   Loa, Salina
USFS Fishlake National Forest: Loa Ranger District
USGS 1:24,000 Lyman, Forsyth Reservoir, Fish Lake, Mt. Terrill, Gooseberry Creek, Steves Mt.
          1:100,000 Loa, Salina
Maptech CD-ROM: Escalante/Dixie National Forest;
          Central/San Rafael
Trails Illustrated, #707
Utah Atlas & Gazetteer, pp. 27, 37
Utah Travel Council #4

Route Directions

▼ 0.0			On Utah 72, 4.8 miles northeast of Fremont, zero trip meter and turn west onto paved CR 3268, following signs to Mill Meadow Reservoir.
	12.6 ▲		Trail ends at Utah 72. Turn right for Fremont.
		GPS: N 38°29.37′ W 111°32.46′	
▼ 1.3		SO	Scenic overlook on left.
	11.3 ▲	SO	Scenic overlook on right.
▼ 1.4		SO	Entrance to Mill Meadow Dam on left. Route follows east shore of Mill Meadow Dam.
	11.2 ▲	SO	Entrance to Mill Meadow Dam on right.
▼ 1.5		SO	Cattle guard.
	11.1 ▲	SO	Cattle guard.
▼ 1.6		SO	Enter Fishlake National Forest; road becomes FR 036. Many access tracks lead left to lakeshore. Camping restricted to designated areas.
	11.0 ▲	SO	Leaving Fishlake National Forest; road becomes CR 3268.
		GPS: N 38°30.02′ W 111°33.75′	
▼ 2.8		SO	Track on right.
	9.8 ▲	SO	Track on left.

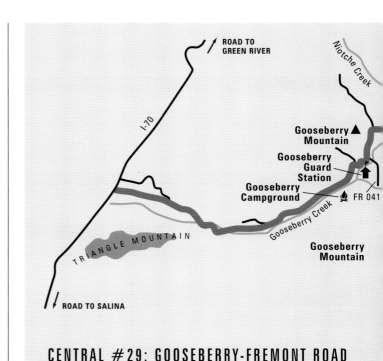

CENTRAL #29: GOOSEBERRY-FREMONT ROAD

▼ 3.2		SO	Road leaves Mill Meadow Dam.
	9.4 ▲	SO	Mill Meadow Dam on right. Many access tracks lead right to lakeshore.
▼ 3.5		SO	FR 046, Mytoge Mountain Road, on left.
	9.1 ▲	SO	FR 046, Mytoge Mountain Road, on right.
▼ 5.1		SO	Pole Canyon Trail (#117) on left.
	7.5 ▲	SO	Pole Canyon Trail (#117) on right.
		GPS: N 38°32.60′ W 111°35.05′	
▼ 5.8		SO	Ivie Canyon Trail (#366) on left; trail on right is #143.
	6.8 ▲	SO	Ivie Canyon Trail (#366) on right; trail on left is #143.
▼ 6.5		SO	Track on left.
	6.1 ▲	SO	Track on right.
▼ 6.6		SO	Cattle guard.
	6.0 ▲	SO	Cattle guard.
▼ 7.4		SO	Splatter Canyon Trail (#118) on left.
	5.2 ▲	SO	Splatter Canyon Trail (#118) on right.
▼ 8.7		SO	Track on left.
	3.9 ▲	SO	Track on right.
▼ 9.2		SO	Cattle guard.
	3.4 ▲	SO	Cattle guard.
▼ 9.7		SO	Track on left.
	2.9 ▲	SO	Track on right.
▼ 10.1		SO	Cross over Fremont River on bridge.
	2.5 ▲	SO	Cross over Fremont River on bridge.
▼ 10.4		SO	Two tracks on right, then tracks left and right.
	2.2 ▲	SO	Tracks on left and right, then two tracks on left.
▼ 10.5		SO	Gravel road on right, FR 015, to U. M. Creek and Sheep Valley.
	2.1 ▲	SO	Gravel road on left, FR 015, to U. M. Creek and Sheep Valley.
		GPS: N 38°36.43′ W 111°37.06′	
▼ 11.0		SO	Track on left. Main trail enters Fishlake Basin; camping in developed campgrounds only.

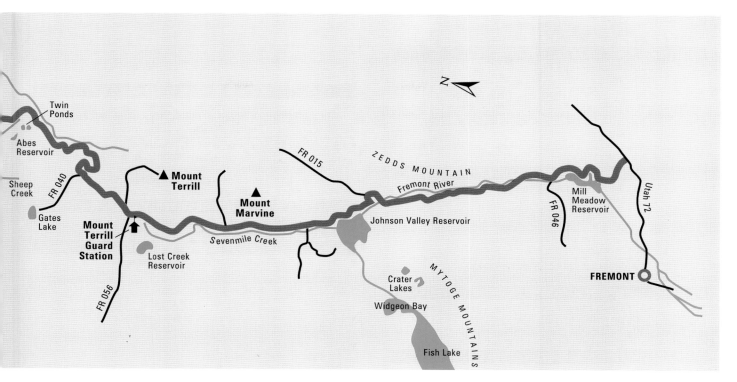

1.6 ▲	SO	Track on right.	
▼ 11.3	SO	Johnson Valley Reservoir on left.	
1.3 ▲	SO	Leaving Johnson Valley Reservoir.	
▼ 11.6	SO	Road on left to boat ramp.	
1.0 ▲	SO	Road on right to boat ramp.	
▼ 12.6	TR	Cross over Sevenmile Creek on bridge, then turn north onto graded gravel road, FR 640. Zero trip meter.	
0.0 ▲		Continue on paved road past Johnson Valley Reservoir.	

GPS: N 38°37.27' W 111°38.81'

▼ 0.0		Continue north.
6.8 ▲	TL	Johnson Valley road is directly ahead. Turn left onto paved road, FR 036, toward Fremont. Zero trip meter.
▼ 0.1	SO	Seasonal closure gate.
6.7 ▲	SO	Seasonal closure gate.
▼ 0.9	SO	Cattle guard.
5.9 ▲	SO	Cattle guard.
▼ 1.0	SO	Cross over Sevenmile Creek on narrow wooden bridge.
5.8 ▲	SO	Cross over Sevenmile Creek on narrow wooden bridge.
▼ 1.3	SO	Track on right. Entering dispersed camping area. Many tracks on right lead to campsites over next mile.
5.5 ▲	SO	Track on left, entering restricted camping area.
▼ 2.3	SO	Cattle guard. Route is now CR 2554.
4.5 ▲	SO	Cattle guard. Route is now CR 3268. Many tracks on left lead to campsites over next mile.
▼ 3.1	SO	Cattle guard.
3.7 ▲	SO	Cattle guard.
▼ 3.5	SO	Track on right is FR 942.
3.3 ▲	SO	Track on left is FR 942.
▼ 3.9	SO	Cattle guard.

2.9 ▲	SO	Cattle guard.
▼ 4.1	SO	Track on right to corral.
2.7 ▲	SO	Track on left to corral.
▼ 4.5	SO	Small track on right.
2.3 ▲	SO	Small track on left.
▼ 5.1	SO	Cattle guard.
1.7 ▲	SO	Cattle guard.
▼ 5.5	SO	Track on right, then campsite on left.
1.3 ▲	SO	Campsite on right, then track on left.
▼ 5.8	SO	Track on left to Mount Terrill Guard Station. Hilgard Mountain on right.
1.0 ▲	SO	Track on right to Mount Terrill Guard Station. Hilgard Mountain on left.

GPS: N 38°42.41' W 111°40.83'

▼ 6.4	SO	Track on left, track on right, then cattle guard. Lost Creek Reservoir on left.
0.4 ▲	SO	Cattle guard, track on left, then track on right. Lost Creek Reservoir on right.
▼ 6.8	SO	Track on left is FR 056 to Lost Creek Reservoir. Zero trip meter at intersection.
0.0 ▲		Continue south.

GPS: N 38°42.81' W 111°40.80'

▼ 0.0		Continue north.
10.6 ▲	SO	Track on right is FR 056 to Lost Creek Reservoir. Zero trip meter at intersection.
▼ 0.4	SO	Track on left.
10.2 ▲	SO	Track on right.
▼ 0.5	SO	Track on right to Mount Terrill (11,547 feet).
10.1 ▲	SO	Track on left to Mount Terrill (11,547 feet).

GPS: N 38°43.23' W 111°40.68'

▼ 0.6	SO	Track on left is FR 1242.
10.0 ▲	SO	Track on right is FR 1242.
▼ 0.9	SO	Cattle guard.
9.7 ▲	SO	Cattle guard.
▼ 1.0	SO	Track on left.
9.6 ▲	SO	Track on right.

▼ 2.4	SO	Track on left is FR 040 to Gates Lake.
8.2 ▲	SO	Track on right is FR 040 to Gates Lake.

GPS: N 38°44.73' W 111°40.05'

▼ 2.5	SO	Track on right.
8.1 ▲	SO	Track on left.
▼ 2.7	BL	FR 1240 on right, then track on right.
7.9 ▲	BR	Track on left, then FR 1240 on left.
▼ 2.8	SO	Niotche–Lost Creek Divide. Two tracks on left.
7.8 ▲	SO	Niotche–Lost Creek Divide. Two tracks on right.

GPS: N 38°45.00' W 111°39.79'

▼ 4.2	SO	Track on right to campsite, then track on left.
6.4 ▲	SO	Track on right, then track on left to campsite.
▼ 4.8	SO	Track on left.
5.8 ▲	SO	Track on right.
▼ 4.9	SO	Track on right to Niotche Creek.
5.7 ▲	SO	Track on left to Niotche Creek.

GPS: N 38°45.14' W 111°38.90'

▼ 5.7	SO	Large campsite on left, then Salina Reservoir on left.
4.9 ▲	SO	Salina Reservoir on right, then large campsite on right.

GPS: N 38°45.67' W 111°39.13'

▼ 5.8	SO	Track on left.
4.8 ▲	SO	Track on right.
▼ 6.4	SO	Track on left to Harves River.
4.2 ▲	SO	Track on right to Harves River.

GPS: N 38°46.13' W 111°39.10'

▼ 6.8	BR	Campsite on left, then track on left. Remain on gravel road.
3.8 ▲	BL	Track on right, then campsite on right. Remain on gravel road.

GPS: N 38°46.38' W 111°38.79'

▼ 6.9	SO	Track on left.
3.7 ▲	SO	Track on right.
▼ 7.5	SO	Track on left to Cold Spring. Campsite at intersection.
3.1 ▲	SO	Track on right to Cold Spring. Campsite at intersection.

GPS: N 38°46.94' W 111°38.47'

▼ 7.7	SO	Campsite on right.
2.9 ▲	SO	Campsite on left.
▼ 7.9	SO	Track on left to Twin Ponds, then corral on right.
2.7 ▲	SO	Corral on left, then track on right to Twin Ponds.

GPS: N 38°47.18' W 111°38.22'

▼ 8.0	SO	Cattle guard, then Beaver Dams Road on right to Niotche Creek.
2.6 ▲	SO	Beaver Dams Road on left to Niotche Creek, then cattle guard.

GPS: N 38°47.25' W 111°38.13'

▼ 9.3	SO	Campsites on right and left. Gooseberry Mountain is directly ahead.
1.3 ▲	SO	Campsites on right and left. Gooseberry Mountain is on left.
▼ 9.4	SO	Gravel road on right is FR 038 to Antone Hollow.
1.2 ▲	SO	Gravel road on left is FR 038 to Antone Hollow.

GPS: N 38°48.15' W 111°39.01'

▼ 10.2	SO	Track on right.
0.4 ▲	SO	Track on left.

▼ 10.5	SO	Track on left is FR 041 to Sheep Creek.
0.1 ▲	SO	Track on right is FR 041 to Sheep Creek.
▼ 10.6	SO	Track on right is Oak Ridge Road (FR 032) to Squaw Hollow. Zero trip meter.
0.0 ▲		Continue east.

GPS: N 38°47.95' W 111°40.27'

▼ 0.0		Continue west.
10.2 ▲	SO	Track on left is Oak Ridge Road (FR 032) to Squaw Hollow. Zero trip meter.
▼ 1.0	SO	Track on left to Gooseberry Guard Station and Gooseberry Youth Camp. Track on right.
9.2 ▲	SO	Track on right to Gooseberry Guard Station and Gooseberry Youth Camp. Track on left.

GPS: N 38°48.18' W 111°40.95'

▼ 1.1	SO	Seasonal closure gate.
9.1 ▲	SO	Seasonal closure gate.

GPS: N 38°48.22' W 111°41.10'

▼ 1.2	SO	Gooseberry Campground on left.
9.0 ▲	SO	Gooseberry Campground on right.
▼ 2.2	SO	Seasonal closure gate.
8.0 ▲	SO	Seasonal closure gate.
▼ 3.4	SO	Track on right at German Flat.
6.8 ▲	SO	Track on left at German Flat.
▼ 3.9	SO	Track on right.
6.3 ▲	SO	Track on left.
▼ 4.2	SO	Cross over creek on bridge, seasonal closure gate, then track on left.
6.0 ▲	SO	Track on right, seasonal closure gate, then cross over creek on bridge.
▼ 4.7	SO	Corral on left.
5.5 ▲	SO	Corral on right.
▼ 5.1	SO	Cross over Gates Creek, then track on left.
5.1 ▲	SO	Track on right, then cross over Gates Creek.
▼ 5.4	SO	Track on right.
4.8 ▲	SO	Track on left.
▼ 5.5	SO	Track on right.
4.7 ▲	SO	Track on left.
▼ 5.8	SO	Cattle guard, then corral on left. Road is now paved.
4.4 ▲	SO	Corral on right, then cattle guard. Road is now graded gravel.

GPS: N 38°51.23' W 111°44.61'

▼ 5.9	SO	Track on left.
4.3 ▲	SO	Track on right.
▼ 6.2	SO	Track on left to Salina.
4.0 ▲	SO	Track on right to Salina.

GPS: N 38°51.60' W 111°44.65'

▼ 6.3	SO	Cattle guard.
3.9 ▲	SO	Cattle guard.
▼ 7.8	SO	Track on left.
2.4 ▲	SO	Track on right.
▼ 8.3	SO	Cattle guard.
1.9 ▲	SO	Cattle guard.
▼ 8.6	SO	Track on right.
1.6 ▲	SO	Track on left.
▼ 10.1	SO	Cross frontage road, then cattle guard.
0.1 ▲	SO	Cattle guard, then cross frontage road.
▼ 10.2		Trail ends at I-70, exit 61; turn west for Salina, east for Green River.
0.0 ▲		On I-70 at exit 61, 7 miles east of Salina, turn south on paved FR 640 and zero trip meter.

GPS: N 38°54.97' W 111°44.35'

Richfield Pioneer Road

Starting Point:	US 50, 6.3 miles north of Salina
Finishing Point:	Richfield, at I-70 underpass
Total Mileage:	34.9 miles
Unpaved Mileage:	34.9 miles
Driving Time:	3.5 hours
Elevation Range:	5,300–9,700 feet
Usually Open:	Late June to October
Difficulty Rating:	2
Scenic Rating:	9
Remoteness Rating:	+0

Special Attractions

■ Long, easy route for scenic touring.
■ Access to a network of 4WD, ATV, and hiking trails.
■ Spectacular views from the Pahvant Range.

History

The town of Richfield was settled in the 1860s as a Mormon settlement. Unlike most Mormon pioneer settlements, Richfield was not settled at the direct request of Brigham Young, but by a band of pioneers acting on their own initiative and led by Albert Lewis, formerly of Manti. Attracted by the fertile valleys, reliable water source, and nearby forest, the pioneers arrived in January 1864, and by February of that year the first house was built. The new settlement was originally named Warm Springs; it was later changed to Omni (in honor of a Mormon prophet) and finally became Richfield for the richness of the farmlands.

Traditionally, the Pahvant Range and neighboring areas were used by Ute Indians, and they resented the growing intrusion on their land. When access to Ute hunting grounds became restricted, a series of small armed conflicts escalated into what became known as the Black Hawk War, though this was more a series of skirmishes than a full-scale war. A fort was built at Rich-

field in 1865 for defense, but in April 1867, the Mormon Church leaders in Salt Lake City ordered the town evacuated. A peace treaty ending the war was signed in 1868, but fighting continued sporadically for several years. However, by 1871, most settlers had returned to Richfield. The Utes had done very little damage to property.

The Richfield Pioneer Road crosses the Pahvant Range, which runs from Scipio Valley to the northeast to Clear Creek to the southwest. Pahvant is a Paiute word thought to mean "water people." Several peaks in the range exceed 10,000 feet, including White Pine Peak, Jacks Peak, and Mount Catherine.

The road was originally built by the pioneers to serve as a timber-access road. The Pahvant Range was a rich source of timber for building, fencing, and firewood. As the lower and more accessible sources of timber were used, the road across

The red colors typical of the scenery along this trail

the plateau was developed to provide access to deeper sources of timber. The Mormon settlers also established cooperatively owned herds of cattle and sheep, which grazed the meadows of the Pahvant Range. There was no management of the grazing, and the range became seriously overgrazed, causing erosion and flooding in the valley towns. Locals petitioned the government to correct the problem, and in 1899, President William McKinley established a forest reserve, which eventually became part of Fishlake National Forest.

Description

This beautiful touring route is traversable by most high-clearance vehicles in dry weather. It offers a wide variety of features and views, mainly on the eastern side of the range. It is part of the 230-mile-long Paiute ATV Trail (PATVT), a loop trail that circles Richfield. Many parts of this trail are accessible to 4WD vehicles. The route leaves from US 50, 6.3 miles north of Salina, and enters Fishlake National Forest 3 miles later. It winds up to the top of the Pahvant Plateau by way of Willow Creek. There are some lovely shady campsites along the lower sections of the creek. It is an easy grade as the trail climbs up onto the Pahvant Range. The last part of climb provides spectacular views to the east over Scipio Lake, the distinctive pyramid of Beehive Peak, and the deep canyon of Willow Creek.

After 6 miles the trail reaches the ridge top, and from the ridge, many roads and trails run down into the valleys on both sides, including Central #31: Coffee Peak Trail. The trail crosses mainly open meadows, interspersed with aspens and hardwood mahogany. As the trail descends toward Richfield, it reenters stands of sagebrush and scattered pinyon and juniper.

In wet weather, particularly during the spring runoff and the summer monsoon season, the trail can be very slippery. Much of the surface is clay, which is also highly prone to rutting. The trail is graded and maintained, but it can still be rough going.

A view of the trail as it crosses a ridgeline

Current Road Information

BLM Fillmore Field Office
35 East 500 North
Fillmore, UT 84631
(435) 743-6811

Fishlake National Forest
Fillmore Ranger District
390 South Main
Fillmore, UT 84631
(435) 743-5721

Map References

BLM Richfield
USFS Fishlake National Forest: Fillmore Ranger District
USGS 1:24,000 Beehive Peak, Mt. Catherine, White Pine
Peak, Richfield
1:100,000 Richfield
Maptech CD-ROM: King Canyon/Fillmore
Trails Illustrated, #708
Utah Atlas & Gazetteer, pp. 36, 37
Utah Travel Council #4

Route Directions

▼ 0.0

On US 50, 6.3 miles northwest of Salina, turn west onto unmarked gravel road across a cattle guard and zero trip meter.

3.5 ▲ Trail ends at US 50. Turn right for Salina, left for I-15.

GPS: N 38°58.90′ W 111°59.48′

▼ 0.7 SO Track on right.
2.8 ▲ SO Track on left.

▼ 0.8 SO Track on left.
2.7 ▲ SO Track on right.

▼ 1.4 SO Track on left.
2.1 ▲ SO Track on right.

▼ 1.6 SO Track on right, then track on left is Paiute ATV Trail #01 (PATVT#01).
1.9 ▲ SO Track on right is PATVT#01, then track on left.

GPS: N 38°59.18′ W 112°01.25′

▼ 2.5 SO Cattle guard.
1.0 ▲ SO Cattle guard.

▼ 2.6 SO Track on left.
0.9 ▲ SO Track on right.

▼ 2.7 SO Track on right.
0.8 ▲ SO Track on left.

▼ 3.5 SO Track on left, then cattle guard. Entering Fishlake National Forest. Trail is now FR 102. Zero trip meter.
0.0 ▲ Trail crosses a small section of private land.

GPS: N 38°58.89′ W 112°03.33′

▼ 0.0 Continue into Fishlake National Forest.
6.1 ▲ SO Cattle guard; zero trip meter. Leaving Fishlake National Forest, followed by track on right.

▼ 0.6 SO Campsites on right and left.
5.5 ▲ SO Campsites on right and left.

▼ 0.7 SO Cross through Willow Creek, followed by seasonal closure gate. Trail follows Willow Creek, with many campsites along creek for next 2.1 miles.
5.4 ▲ SO Seasonal closure gate, then cross through Willow Creek. Trail leaves creek.

▼ 2.8 BL PATVT#01 goes right, ATV use only.
3.3 ▲ BR PATVT#01 goes left, ATV use only. Main trail follows Willow Creek, with many campsites along creek for next 2.1 miles.

GPS: N 38°58.68′ W 112°06.01′

▼ 4.8 BR Red Canyon Hiking Trail (#015) on left to Aurora.
1.3 ▲ BL Red Canyon Hiking Trail (#015) on right to Aurora.

GPS: N 38°57.64′ W 112°05.48′

▼ 5.1 SO Track on right to campsite.
1.0 ▲ SO Track on left to campsite.

▼ 5.3 SO Track on left to exposed camping area with great view.
0.8 ▲ SO Track on right to exposed camping area with great view.

▼ 5.5 SO Track on left to corral, then cattle guard.
0.6 ▲ SO Track on right to corral, then cattle guard.

▼ 6.1 SO Track on right is Central #31: Coffee Peak Trail (FR 096). Main trail is now FR 096. Travel information board at intersection.
0.0 ▲ Descend into Willow Creek Canyon.

GPS: N 38°57.54′ W 112°06.69′

▼ 0.0 Continue along ridge top.
1.4 ▲ SO Track on left is Central #31: Coffee Peak Trail (FR 096). Travel information board at intersection. Main trail is now FR 102.

▼ 0.9 SO Valley on right is North Fork Chalk Creek.
0.5 ▲ SO Valley on left is North Fork Chalk Creek.

▼ 1.2 BL Track on right.
0.2 ▲ SO Track on left.

▼ 1.4 BL Track on right is FR 100 to Fillmore. Zero trip meter.
0.0 ▲ Continue on FR 096.

GPS: N 38°56.70′ W 112°07.80′

▼ 0.0 Continue on FR 096.
9.1 ▲ SO Track on left is FR 100 to Fillmore. Zero trip meter.

▼ 0.3 SO Chokecherry hiking trail (#024) on right, then track on right (FR 392).
8.8 ▲ SO Track on left (FR 392), then Chokecherry hiking trail (#024) on left.

GPS: N 38°56.36′ W 112°07.86′

▼ 1.0 SO Faint track on right to campsite.
8.1 ▲ SO Faint track on left to campsite.

▼ 1.1 SO Small track on left to campsite.
8.0 ▲ SO Small track on right to campsite.

▼ 1.8 SO Cattle guard.
7.3 ▲ SO Cattle guard.

▼ 3.2 SO Track on left.
5.9 ▲ SO Track on right.

▼ 3.5 SO Campsite on left.
5.6 ▲ SO Campsite on right.

▼ 4.4 SO Track on left to remains of Solitude Guard Station.
4.7 ▲ SO Track on right to remains of Solitude Guard Station.

▼ 5.0 SO Cattle guard, then small track on right.
4.1 ▲ SO Small track on left, then cattle guard.

▼ 6.6 SO Track on right, then track on left.
2.5 ▲ SO Track on right, then track on left.

GPS: N 38°52.33′ W 112°11.42′

▼ 7.7 SO Trail on left is South Cedar Ridge hiking trail (#028).
1.4 ▲ SO Trail on right is South Cedar Ridge hiking trail (#028).

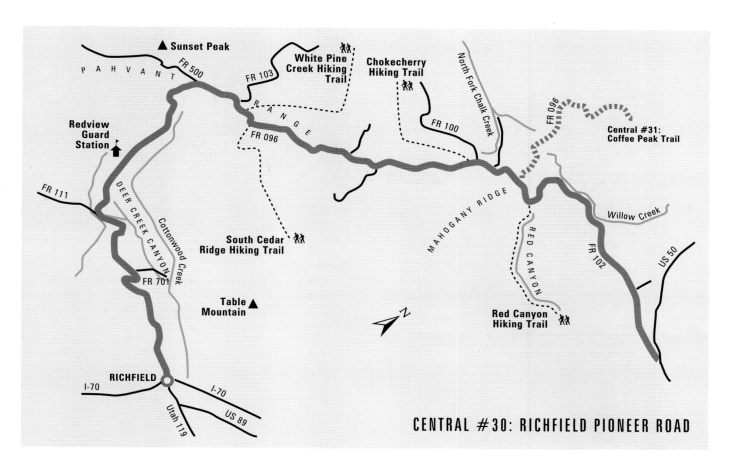

CENTRAL #30: RICHFIELD PIONEER ROAD

GPS: N 38°51.56' W 112°12.11'			
▼ 8.0	SO	Cattle guard.	
1.1 ▲	SO	Cattle guard.	
▼ 8.7	SO	White Pine Creek hiking trail (#027) on right. Vehicles can drive first 0.5 miles to an old cabin.	
0.4 ▲	SO	White Pine Creek hiking trail (#027) on left. Vehicles can drive first 0.5 miles to an old cabin.	
GPS: N 38°51.38' W 112°13.10'			
▼ 9.1	SO	Track right is FR 103 to Fillmore. Zero trip meter.	
0.0 ▲		Continue on FR 096.	
GPS: N 38°51.25' W 112°13.58'			
▼ 0.0		Continue on FR 096.	
7.4 ▲	SO	Track on left is FR 103 to Fillmore. Zero trip meter.	
▼ 0.3	SO	Cabin on left and track on left.	
7.1 ▲	SO	Cabin on right and track on right.	
▼ 1.1	SO	Meadow Creek hiking trail (#032) on right.	
6.3 ▲	SO	Meadow Creek hiking trail (#032) on left.	
GPS: N 38°50.51' W 112°14.26'			
▼ 1.6	TL	FR 500 on right to Goat Springs. Travel information board at intersection. Sunset Peak is directly ahead.	
5.8 ▲	TR	FR 500 on left to Goat Springs. Travel information board at intersection. Sunset Peak is on left.	
GPS: N 38°50.34' W 112°14.74'			
▼ 2.9	SO	Track on right is FR 508.	
4.5 ▲	SO	Track on left is FR 508.	
▼ 4.2	SO	Track on right to dam.	

3.2 ▲	SO	Track on left to dam.	
▼ 4.5	SO	Track on right to campsite.	
2.9 ▲	SO	Track on left to campsite.	
▼ 5.3	SO	Cattle guard.	
2.1 ▲	SO	Cattle guard.	
▼ 5.4	SO	Redview Guard Station on right.	
2.0 ▲	SO	Redview Guard Station on left.	
GPS: N 38°47.90' W 112°12.90'			
▼ 6.2	SO	Track on left, then cross through Deer Creek.	
1.2 ▲	SO	Cross though Deer Creek, then track on right.	
▼ 6.8	SO	Track on right is FR 506.	
0.6 ▲	SO	Track on left is FR 506. View ahead to Redview Guard Station.	
GPS: N 38°46.97' W 112°11.88'			
▼ 7.1	SO	Track on left, then track on right.	
0.3 ▲	SO	Track on left, then track on right.	
▼ 7.4	TL	T-intersection. Right is FR 111, the southern continuation of PATVT#01. Zero trip meter	
0.0 ▲		Continue on FR 096, which is now PATVT#01.	
GPS: N 38°46.53' W 112°11.65'			
▼ 0.0		Continue on FR 096, which is now Paiute ATV Side Trail #04.	
7.4 ▲	TR	Ahead is FR 111, the southern continuation of PATVT#01. Zero trip meter.	
▼ 0.2	SO	Track on right.	
7.2 ▲	SO	Track on left.	
▼ 0.6	SO	Track on left.	
6.8 ▲	SO	Track on right.	
▼ 0.7	SO	Track on left.	
6.7 ▲	SO	Track on right.	

▼ 1.1		SO	Cattle guard.
	6.3 ▲	SO	Cattle guard.
▼ 2.6		SO	Cross through wash.
	4.8 ▲	SO	Cross through wash.
▼ 2.7		SO	Track on left.
	4.7 ▲	SO	Track on right.
▼ 2.8		SO	Track on left.
	4.6 ▲	SO	Track on right.
▼ 3.0		SO	Track on left is FR 701, also track on right.
	4.4 ▲	SO	Track on right is FR 701, also track on left.

GPS: N 38°46.75' W 112°09.20'

▼ 5.3		SO	Tracks on left and right. Many tracks right and left over next 0.9 miles lead to campsites.
	2.1 ▲	SO	Tracks on left and right.
▼ 6.2		SO	Seasonal closure gate.
	1.2 ▲	SO	Seasonal closure gate. Many tracks right and left over next 0.9 miles lead to campsites.
▼ 6.3		BR	Track on left is FR 1747.
	1.1 ▲	BL	Track on right is FR 1747.

GPS: N 38°46.81' W 112°06.64'

▼ 6.6		SO	Leaving Fishlake National Forest.
	0.8 ▲	SO	Entering Fishlake National Forest.

GPS: N 38°46.69' W 112°06.43'

▼ 7.0		SO	Town water tank on left.
	0.4 ▲	SO	Town water tank on right.
▼ 7.4			Trail ends as it passes underneath I-70. Continue into Richfield. ATVs are permitted on some streets in Richfield; regulation board at end of trail.
	0.0 ▲		On US 89 in Richfield, turn west onto 300 North Street. Trail commences as it passes underneath I-70 overpass; zero trip meter. ATV regulation board at start of trail.

GPS: N 38°46.33' W 112°05.93'

CENTRAL REGION TRAIL #31

Coffee Peak Trail

Starting Point:	**Central #30: Richfield Pioneer Road (FR 102), 9.6 miles from US 50**
Finishing Point:	**Coffee Peak**
Total Mileage:	**11.2 miles**
Unpaved Mileage:	**11.2 miles**
Driving Time:	**1.5 hours (one-way)**
Elevation Range:	**8,700–9,800 feet**
Usually Open:	**July to October**
Difficulty Rating:	**3**
Scenic Rating:	**9**
Remoteness Rating:	**+0**

Special Attractions

- Spectacular ridge trail with views to the east and west.
- Mountain peaks of Jacks Peak, Willow Creek Peak, and Coffee Peak.
- Access to a number of hiking trails.

A section of the trail that affords a wonderful view across the valleys below

Description

This breathtaking spur trail leads off Central #30: Richfield Pioneer Road. For most of its length it runs across the narrow ridge tops, with sheer drops on one or both sides. The views are awesome; you can see Willow Creek Canyon, Beehive Peak, Chalk Creek Canyon, and Scipio Lake. The trail surface is rough but easily traversable in dry weather. The National Forest Service has realigned one section of the route just after the turn to Pioneer Peak. The realigned track is steep and has loose, deep bulldust, which in wet weather turns into a greasy slide downhill. Returning up this section could be difficult to impossible in adverse weather.

The trail is entirely within a restricted travel area of Fishlake National Forest. Vehicle travel, including by ATVs, is restricted to designated trails.

The trail is mainly across open meadows, with stands of aspen and a small stand of bristlecone pine just after the turn for Pioneer Peak. There are some sections of shelf road, but they are wide for a single vehicle and there are plenty of passing places. There are some quiet backcountry campsites as well as the more developed sites at Maple Grove and Maple Hollow.

The trail ends for vehicle travel immediately north of Coffee Peak; a hiking trail continues all the way to Scipio. To exit, vehicles must return to Richfield Pioneer Road.

Current Road Information

BLM Fillmore Field Office
35 East 500 North
Fillmore, UT 84631
(435) 743-6811

Fishlake National Forest
Fillmore Ranger District
390 South Main
Fillmore, UT 84631
(435) 743-5721

Map References

BLM Richfield, Delta
USFS Fishlake National Forest: Fillmore Ranger District
USGS 1:24,000 Beehive Peak, Mt. Catherine, Coffee Peak, Scipio Lake
1:100,000 Richfield, Delta

CENTRAL #31: COFFEE PEAK TRAIL

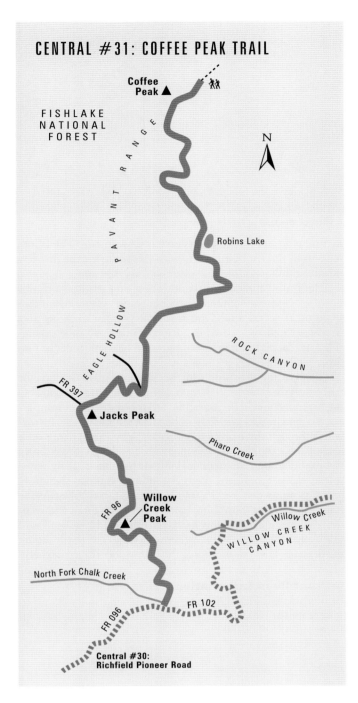

Maptech CD-ROM: King Canyon/Fillmore
Trails Illustrated, #708 (incomplete)
Utah Atlas & Gazetteer, p. 37
Utah Travel Council #4 (incomplete)

Route Directions

▼ 0.0		On Central #30: Richfield Pioneer Road (FR 102), 9.6 miles from US 50, turn north on FR 096, following sign for Coffee Peak Trail. Cross cattle guard and zero trip meter. (Note that FR 096 also continues south along the ridge).

GPS: N 38°57.54' W 112°06.69'

▼ 0.1	SO	Views left over North Fork Chalk Creek.
▼ 0.3	SO	Views right over Willow Creek Canyon.
▼ 0.7	SO	Campsite on right with view over Willow Creek Canyon.
▼ 1.7	SO	Track on left.

GPS: N 38°58.35' W 112°07.65'

▼ 2.4	SO	Willow Creek Canyon on right. FR 102 is visible below.
▼ 3.1	SO	Cattle guard.

GPS: N 38°59.23' W 112°07.83'

▼ 4.1	SO	Track on left is FR 397 to Pioneer Peak. Jacks Peak (10,072 feet) is on right; summit is marked by cairn. Zero trip meter.

GPS: N 38°59.71' W 112°08.48'

▼ 0.0		Continue on FR 096. Cross cattle guard and pass through some scattered bristlecone pines.
▼ 0.8	SO	Track on left. Main graded trail descends steeply. Surface is deep bulldust.
▼ 1.0	SO	Track on left rejoins, followed by cattle guard and second track on left to Eagle Hollow.

GPS: N 39°00.01' W 112°07.67'

▼ 1.5	SO	Track on right is viewpoint.
▼ 2.1	BR	Track on left is undesignated route FR 867 (closed to vehicle travel).

GPS: N 39°00.96' W 112°07.64'

▼ 2.5	SO	Trail #013 on right. Hiking and horse access only.

GPS: N 39°01.07' W 112°07.31'

▼ 3.1	SO	Scipio Lake is visible in valley on right.
▼ 4.0	SO	Track on left, followed by track on right. Main trail crosses the head of Robins Valley. Dry lake on right.
▼ 4.1	SO	Cattle guard, followed by track on right to sheltered campsite in grassy depression.
▼ 4.2	SO	Track on left to campsite. Hiking Trail #012 on right to Maple Grove Campground.

GPS: N 39°02.08' W 112°07.38'

▼ 6.3	SO	Hiking Trail #010 on the left to Maple Hollow Campground.

GPS: N 39°03.18' W 112°08.14'

▼ 7.1		Trail ends just north of Coffee Peak. Hiking Trail #005 continues north. Some limited camping at end of vehicle trail.

GPS: N 39°03.84' W 112°07.76'

CENTRAL REGION TRAIL #32

Cove Mountain and Magleby Pass Trail

Starting Point:	**Utah 62 at Koosharem**
Finishing Point:	**Center Street in Glenwood**
Total Mileage:	**33.7 miles**
Unpaved Mileage:	**33.7 miles**
Driving Time:	**2 hours**
Elevation Range:	**5,300–10,400 feet**
Usually Open:	**June to October**
Difficulty Rating:	**1**
Scenic Rating:	**6**
Remoteness Rating:	**+0**

Special Attractions
- Access to a number of ATV and hiking trails.
- Easy, scenic drive through a variety of forest scenery.
- Access to a number of backcountry campsites.

History
The town of Koosharem was settled in 1877. The name comes from an Indian word meaning "clover blossom"; Indians considered this plant's edible tubers a staple food. Farther up the trail, the Koosharem Guard Station, built in 1911, is the oldest National Forest Service guard station in Utah. The forest service has plans to use it as an interpretive site for the area.

Cove Mountain takes its name from Cove Fort, which is due west, just south of the Pahvant Range near the intersection of I-15 and I-70. The fort has influenced the names of many features around this general area. Located in an extremely protected site, Cove Fort was built in 1867 as a refuge for Mormon travelers during the Black Hawk War.

In 1872, a sawmill was established on Cove Mountain by Joseph Young, a prominent local Mormon. However, three years later, for unknown reasons, it was moved to Clear Creek Canyon. More recently, a TV booster station was located on Cove Mountain, but its presence was never authorized by the forest service. In 1957, the forest service was successful in its case to have it removed as "unlicensed equipment," and it was moved farther down the mountain onto private land.

Glenwood, at the north end of the trail, was settled in 1864. Mormon settlers were sent by Brigham Young to establish the community. The settlement was originally named Glens Cove, after an early pioneer, John Wilson Glenn, and the name metamorphosed into "Glencoe" before becoming Glenwood. A stone fort was built there in 1866 to protect the settlers during the Black Hawk War.

The fish hatchery at the trail's northern endpoint was completed in 1921, and at the time it was Utah's third largest trout hatchery. Today, it is double the size of the original hatchery and handles over 135,000 pounds of fish.

Description
This gentle trail links the small towns of Koosharem and Glenwood via a graded dirt forest road. The trail rises up to over 10,000 feet in elevation and mainly passes through the

Big Lake

A view of the trail at Hunters Flat

mature pine and spruce forests on Cove Mountain. The Paiute ATV Trail (PATVT) intersects with this route for the first few miles and follows along the route in some sections.

The trail commences in Koosharem and gradually climbs up the sagebrush-covered benches onto Cove Mountain Plateau. After 5.6 miles, you reach the popular camping area of Milos Kitchen. Located in a flat area in a small valley alongside Greenwich Creek, the campground has a pit toilet but no other facilities.

After passing the turnoff for Koosharem Guard Station, the trail enters the forest. Large sections of the forest are currently being harvested for timber, so public access is restricted in some areas. Logging trucks are likely to be active on the road. The trail winds through the mature forest to Magleby Pass. Hiking trails lead off from the pass to Monument Peak and Signal Peak. Since the pass is among the trees, it does not have particularly widespread views. From here, the trail continues through the forest, giving glimpses east over Plateau Valley and Grass Valley. As the trail descends past Cove Mountain, it leaves the forest and reenters the sagebrush, crossing Hunters Flat and heading toward Glenwood. There are some excellent views to the north during the descent. The trail finishes at the Glenwood Trout Hatchery.

Current Road Information
BLM Richfield Field Office
150 East 900 North
Richfield, UT 84701
(435) 896-1500

Fishlake National Forest
Richfield Ranger District
115 East 900 North
Richfield, UT 84701
(435) 896-9233

Map References
BLM   Salina
USFS Fishlake National Forest: Richfield Ranger District
USGS 1:24,000 Sigourd, Water Creek Canyon, Koosharem
          1:100,000 Salina
Maptech CD-ROM: Central/San Rafael
Trails Illustrated, #708
Utah Atlas & Gazetteer, pp. 27, 28
Utah Travel Council #4 (incomplete)

Route Directions

▼ 0.0		On Utah 62 in Koosharem, turn west on FR 076 (Koosharem Road) and zero trip meter. Cross over Koosharem Canal on bridge and continue west to the edge of town.
6.5 ▲		Cross over Koosharem Canal on bridge, then trail ends in Koosharem at Utah 62.

GPS: N 38°30.63′ W 111°52.84′

▼ 0.3	SO	Intersection. Road is also Paiute ATV Trail #01 (PATVT#01).
6.2 ▲	SO	Intersection. Continue straight into town.
▼ 0.4	BR	Track on left.
6.1 ▲	SO	Track on right.
▼ 0.6	SO	Multiple tracks on right and left. Proceed northwest on main track.
5.9 ▲	SO	Multiple tracks on left and right. Proceed southeast on main track.
▼ 1.1	SO	Tracks on right and left.
5.4 ▲	SO	Tracks on left and right.
▼ 1.6	SO	Entering Fishlake National Forest. Track on left.
4.9 ▲	SO	Leaving Fishlake National Forest. Track on right.

GPS: N 38°31.40′ W 111°54.22′

▼ 2.2	BL	Track on right is continuation of PATVT#01. Many unmarked trails on right and left, mainly to campsites, around junction.
4.3 ▲	SO	Track on left. PATVT#01 joins main trail here. Many unmarked trails on left and right, mainly to campsites, around junction.
▼ 4.1	BR	Two tracks on left.
2.4 ▲	BL	Two tracks on right.

GPS: N 38°31.53′ W 111°56.21′

▼ 5.6	SO	Milos Kitchen camping area on left. Paiute ATV Side Trail #33 (PATVST#33/Pine Canyon Trail) crosses trail; right to Hunters Flat, left to Pine Canyon.
0.9 ▲	SO	Milos Kitchen camping area on right. PATVST#33 (Pine Canyon Trail) crosses trail; left to Hunters Flat, right to Pine Canyon.

GPS: N 38°31.94′ W 111°57.11′

▼ 5.9	SO	PATVT#01 enters on right and joins main trail.
0.6 ▲	SO	PATVT#01 leaves main trail on left.
▼ 6.0	BL	Track on right is Killian–Pine Canyon Trail #4076; hiking and horses only.
0.5 ▲	BR	Track on left is Killian–Pine Canyon Trail #4076; hiking and horses only.

GPS: N 38°32.24′ W 111°57.34′

▼ 6.2	SO	Cattle guard.
0.3 ▲	SO	Cattle guard.
▼ 6.3	SO	Track on right.
0.2 ▲	SO	Track on left.
▼ 6.5	SO	Go straight; trail becomes FR 068 and PATVST#68. Zero trip meter. Track on left is FR 068 and PATVT#01.
0.0 ▲		Continue on FR 076 toward Koosharem.

GPS: N 38°32.23′ W 111°57.64′

▼ 0.0		Continue on FR 068 toward Koosharem Guard Station.
8.7 ▲	SO	Go straight; trail becomes FR 076 and PATVST#01. Zero trip meter. Track on right is FR 068 and PATVT#01.
▼ 0.1	SO	Track on right.
8.6 ▲	SO	Track on left.
▼ 0.5	SO	Track on right.
8.2 ▲	SO	Track on left.
▼ 0.8	SO	Track on left is FR 165.
7.9 ▲	SO	Track on right is FR 165.
▼ 1.7	SO	Track on left is FR 163 (PATVST#44) to Koosharem Guard Station. Cross cattle guard.
7.0 ▲	SO	Cross cattle guard, then track on right is FR 163 (PATVST#44) to Koosharem Guard Station.

GPS: N 38°33.48′ W 111°58.67′

▼ 1.8	SO	Track on right is Koosharem Canyon ATV Trail.
6.9 ▲	SO	Track on left is Koosharem Canyon ATV Trail.
▼ 2.4	SO	Small track on left.

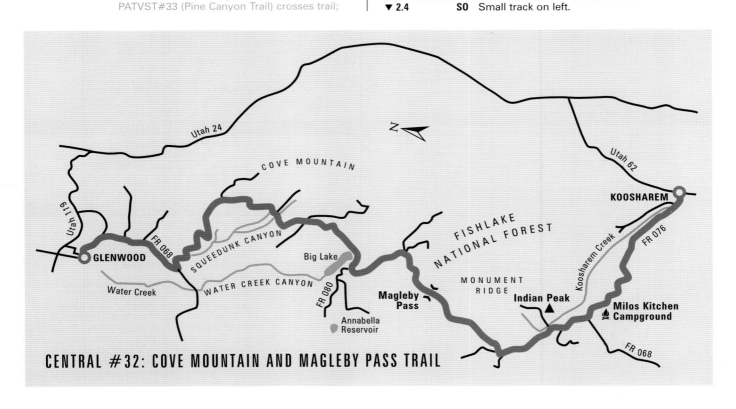

CENTRAL #32: COVE MOUNTAIN AND MAGLEBY PASS TRAIL

	6.3 ▲	SO	Small track on right.
▼ 2.7		SO	Track on right.
	6.0 ▲	SO	Track on left.
▼ 3.4		SO	Track on right, cattle guard, then track on left.
	5.3 ▲	SO	Track on right, cattle guard, then track on left.
▼ 3.5		SO	Seasonal closure gate.
	5.2 ▲	SO	Seasonal closure gate.

GPS: N 38°33.97' W 111°57.04'

▼ 4.3		SO	Track on left.
	4.4 ▲	SO	Track on right.
▼ 6.7		SO	Track on right is timber sale area—closed to public. Many such closed areas on right and left for next 2 miles.
	2.0 ▲	SO	Track on left is the end of current timber sale area.
▼ 8.5		SO	Track on right.
	0.2 ▲	SO	Track on left.
▼ 8.7		SO	Magleby Pass. Parking area and hiking trail on left. Two hiking trails on left are both #110 to Monument Peak and Signal Peak. Zero trip meter.
	0.0 ▲		Continue southwest toward Koosharem.

GPS: N 38°36.76' W 111°58.03'

▼ 0.0			Continue northeast toward Glenwood.
	4.6 ▲	SO	Magleby Pass. Parking area and hiking trail on right. Two hiking trails on right are both #110 to Monument Peak and Signal Peak. Zero trip meter. Many tracks on right and left in next 2 miles lead to timber sale areas, which are closed to public.
▼ 2.4		SO	Track on left is timber sale area.
	2.2 ▲	SO	Track on right is timber sale area.
▼ 2.7		SO	Cattle guard.
	1.9 ▲	SO	Cattle guard.
▼ 4.6		TL	Track on right is FR 176, followed by T-intersection. Turn left at T-intersection toward Glenwood. Zero trip meter.
	0.0 ▲		Continue toward Koosharem.

GPS: N 38°38.28' W 111°57.63'

▼ 0.0			Continue toward Glenwood.
	9.1 ▲	TR	Turn at signpost for Koosharem, and zero trip meter. Then continue straight past a track on left (FR 176).
▼ 0.7		BR	Track on left is FR 080 to Annabella Reservoir.
	8.4 ▲	BL	Track on right is FR 080 to Annabella Reservoir.

GPS: N 38°38.78' W 111°57.74'

▼ 1.1		SO	Track on right. Trail skirts south end of Big Lake.
	8.0 ▲	SO	Track on left. Trail skirts south end of Big Lake.
▼ 1.2		SO	Two tracks on right.
	7.9 ▲	SO	Two tracks on left.
▼ 1.4		SO	Track on left is FR 154, which skirts northwest shore of Big Lake.
	7.7 ▲	SO	Track on right is FR 154, which skirts northwest shore of Big Lake.
▼ 1.5		SO	Track on right is FR 155.
	7.6 ▲	SO	Second entrance to FR 155.
▼ 1.6		SO	Second entrance to FR 155, then cattle guard.
	7.5 ▲	SO	Cattle guard, then track on left is FR 155.
▼ 1.8		SO	Track on right.
	7.3 ▲	SO	Track on left.
▼ 2.0		SO	Track on left to large camping area.
	7.1 ▲	SO	Track on right to large camping area.
▼ 2.5		SO	Track on right.
	6.6 ▲	SO	Track on left.
▼ 3.5		SO	Track on left to campsite.

	5.6 ▲	SO	Track on right to campsite.
▼ 3.6		SO	ATV staging area on right, track on right, then cattle guard.
	5.5 ▲	SO	Cattle guard, track on left, then ATV staging area on left.

GPS: N 38°40.23' W 111°56.48'

▼ 4.2		SO	Track on left.
	4.9 ▲	SO	Track on right.
▼ 4.7		BL	Track on left is Killian Hollow Trail.
	4.4 ▲	BR	Track on right is Killian Hollow Trail.

GPS: N 38°40.94' W 111°56.46'

▼ 4.9		SO	Track on left.
	4.2 ▲	SO	Track on right.
▼ 5.0		SO	Cattle guard.
	4.1 ▲	SO	Cattle guard.
▼ 5.3		SO	Davis Hollow. Track on right and track on left (FR 1142).
	3.8 ▲	SO	Davis Hollow. Track on left and track on right (FR 1142).

GPS: N 38°41.21' W 111°56.18'

▼ 5.8		SO	Track on left.
	3.3 ▲	SO	Track on right.
▼ 6.3		BL	Two tracks on right at small dam.
	2.8 ▲	BR	Two tracks on left at small dam.
▼ 6.6		SO	Track on left.
	2.5 ▲	SO	Track on right.
▼ 6.7		BL	Track on right.
	2.4 ▲	BR	Track on left.
▼ 7.2		BL	Track on right.
	1.9 ▲	BR	Track on left.
▼ 7.3		BL	Two tracks on right.
	1.8 ▲	BR	Two tracks on left.
▼ 7.4		SO	Cattle guard.
	1.7 ▲	SO	Cattle guard.
▼ 7.5		SO	Track on right.
	1.6 ▲	SO	Track on left.

GPS: N 38°42.61' W 111°56.51'

▼ 8.0		SO	Bell Rock Ridge. Track on right.
	1.1 ▲	SO	Bell Rock Ridge. Track on left.
▼ 8.2		SO	Cattle guard.
	0.9 ▲	SO	Cattle guard.
▼ 9.1		SO	Leaving Fishlake National Forest over cattle guard. Zero trip meter.
	0.0 ▲		Continue toward Koosharem.

GPS: N 38°42.85' W 111°57.67'

▼ 0.0			Continue toward Glenwood.
	4.8 ▲	SO	Entering Fishlake National Forest over cattle guard. Road becomes FR 068. Zero trip meter.
▼ 2.0		TR	Road ahead to Annabella.
	2.8 ▲	TL	T-intersection. Road on right to Annabella.

GPS: N 38°43.29' W 111°58.96'

▼ 2.9		SO	Track on right, then cattle guard.
	1.9 ▲	SO	Cattle guard, then track on left.
▼ 3.3		SO	Track on right. Many small ATV tracks on right and left from here to end of trail.
	1.5 ▲	SO	Track on left.
▼ 4.8			Trail ends at Glenwood Fish Hatchery. Continue straight on paved road to Glenwood.
	0.0 ▲		At Glenwood Fish Hatchery, 0.7 miles southeast of Glenwood, on Center Street, zero trip meter, and continue southeast toward Cove Mountain on graded dirt road. Many small ATV trails on right and left for first 1.5 miles.

GPS: N 38°45.47' W 111°48.61'

Pahvant Range Trail

Starting Point:	Elsinore
Finishing Point:	Kanosh
Total Mileage:	31.2 miles
Unpaved Mileage:	30.1 miles
Driving Time:	3 hours
Elevation Range:	5,000–9,000 feet
Usually Open:	June to October
Difficulty Rating:	4
Scenic Rating:	7
Remoteness Rating:	+0

Special Attractions

- Albinus and Kanosh Canyons.
- Access to a network of 4WD and ATV trails.
- Excellent for viewing wildlife and fall foliage.

History

Mount Joseph, midway along this trail, is named after Joseph A. Young, the first president of the Mormon Church in Sevier County. The town of Joseph, 6 miles southwest of Elsinore, is also named after him.

The town of Kanosh takes its name from Chief Kanosh, the peacemaker. Kanosh—whose name means "willow bowl" (Kan-oush)—first came here with his mother and three brothers, and by 1850, he was the chief of a band of 500 Indians living in the Pahvant Valley. One of his brothers was the famous Chief Walker, who was active in the Black Hawk War. Kanosh was as peaceful as his brother was fierce, and after the Mormon settlement of the region, he devoted himself to keeping the peace between the Indians and white settlers.

Utah has many tales of lost Spanish treasure and mines. One such tale centers around the communities of Fillmore and Kanosh. In 1852, the Mormon leader Brigham Young paid a visit to Fillmore. A young Indian told him of a legendary Spanish silver mine in western Millard County. Brigham Young commissioned John Brown to lead a party to investigate and to "take possession of the mine." The party departed Salt Lake City in June 1852, stopped at

The trail descending the spur road to Cottonwood Creek

Fillmore for wagon repairs, and then proceeded to Corn Creek to talk to Chief Kanosh. Kanosh was unaware of the supposed Spanish mine, but he had heard rumor of another one on the Beaver River. Brown's party hired an Indian guide, and they went to search the Beaver River, but no mine was ever found.

The expedition then explored up Corn Creek before leaving the wagons behind and traveling farther over the Pahvant Range and south into the Tushar Mountains. At Pine Creek, later renamed Bullion Creek, they panned for gold and quickly decided that "there was no gold and never has been any." Forty years later, the boomtown of Kimberly was founded on the same spot, becoming one of the most successful gold camps in Utah!

Corn Creek was named by early pioneers who arrived to find corn growing there. The corn was planted by the Pahvant Utes,

Looking back down Albinus Canyon toward Elsinore

who returned to Corn Creek annually to sow their staple crop. In the early 1980s, Corn Creek was badly damaged by flooding, but it was restored by the Division of Wildlife Resources and the National Forest Service.

Description

This moderate-length trail traverses the Pahvant Range between the towns of Elsinore and Kanosh, and it alternately crosses through Fishlake National Forest and private lands. It leaves Elsinore up Albinus Canyon, a gentle gradient on a predominantly graded gravel road. Once on top of the range, the trail swings around to the southwest and the trail standard becomes harder. The trail surface up on the range can be very greasy and impassable when wet, as some large ruts made by previous travelers testify. Navigation can be a bit tricky as well; although most of the forest roads are signed, there are many unmarked tracks.

After 7 miles, you turn south on FR 111. On the Fishlake National Forest map, this route is shown as traversing private property, though it is a historical right of way. Posted warnings ask you not to trespass off the roadway, and please respect the rights and wishes of local property owners: Do not deviate from the right of way or hunt, fish, or camp on private land. There are many other trails that lead off from the main trail through private property. Access rights to the forest beyond vary; please check with the National Forest Service or the property owners before traveling on other trails.

Just after the turnoff for FR 111 is the intersection with FR 107. While the Fishlake National Forest map shows this route as being open to 4WD vehicles, once the trail passes some private property, it is used almost exclusively by ATVs traveling the Paiute ATV Trail (PATVT). This very scenic route runs parallel to FR 111 and can be driven as an alternate to that section of this trail; it offers extensive views down some of the canyons on the west side of the Pahvant Range. However, it has some extremely narrow sections of muddy shelf road that may be impassable to large vehicles.

The trail described here crosses through private property and passes across the southern flank of Mount Joseph. It trav-

DANGER
FLASH FLOOD AREA

Kanosh Canyon is subject to FLASH FLOODING due to wildfire damage. If thunderstorms occur at higher elevations of this canyon, leave the canyon. Floods can occur 1 to 7 hours following the storm event.

Flash flood warning sign along Corn Creek

els across a mix of open meadow and large stands of aspen before leaving the private property and traveling along Chokecherry Canyon. Where it rejoins the Paiute ATV Trail, the trail becomes narrower and rougher. It undulates down over a rough, loose rock surface to join the graded road along Second Creek. This descent is the hardest portion of the trail in dry weather, since it is steep with loose rocky sections and a number of washouts. However, it should cause no problems to most high-clearance SUVs.

Once on the graded road, the trail follows Second Creek and then Corn Creek as it runs down Kanosh Canyon. This exceptionally pretty canyon is also extremely prone to flash floods, as the many signs posted by the forest service warn. For this reason, camping is not recommended in the canyon except at the very scenic National Forest Service campground on Corn Creek, though this is still in the flash flood zone.

Wild turkeys were successfully introduced into Utah in the 1950s, and there is a thriving population around Corn Creek. They are often seen around the campground. Best times to see them are just after sunrise, when they fly down to feed from the roost, and around sunset. Corn Creek is also a popular trout fishing spot.

Current Road Information
BLM Fillmore Field Office
35 East 500 North
Fillmore, UT 84631
(435) 743-6811

Fishlake National Forest
Beaver Ranger District
575 South Main
Beaver, UT 84713
(435) 438-2436

Map References
BLM Richfield
USFS Fishlake National Forest: Beaver Ranger District
USGS 1:24,000 Elsinore, Joseph Peak, Sunset Peak, Kanosh
1:100,000 Richfield
Maptech CD-ROM: King Canyon/Fillmore
Trails Illustrated, #708
Utah Atlas & Gazetteer, p. 36
Utah Travel Council #4

Route Directions

▼ 0.0   In Elsinore, cross underneath I-70 and turn southwest on small paved road. Zero trip meter at cattle guard.
7.2 ▲   Trail ends in Elsinore, where the trail passes underneath I-70. Continue on to join I-70.

GPS: N 38°40.95' W 112°09.39'

▼ 0.2   SO   Cattle guard, then cross over canal. Track on right. Road is now graded dirt.
7.0 ▲   BR   Track on left; cross over canal, then cattle guard. Road is now paved.

▼ 0.5   SO   Tracks on right and left. Trail swings around into Albinus Canyon.
6.7 ▲   SO   Trail leaves Albinus Canyon. Tracks on left and right.

▼ 1.7   SO   Track on right. Enter Fishlake National Forest. Trail is now FR 105.
5.5 ▲   SO   Track on left. Leave Fishlake National Forest.

▼ 1.8   SO   Track on left.
5.4 ▲   SO   Track on right.

▼ 2.0   SO   Seasonal closure gate.
5.2 ▲   SO   Seasonal closure gate.

GPS: N 38°41.31' W 112°11.17'

▼ 3.6   SO   Tracks on right and left.
3.6 ▲   SO   Tracks on left and right.

▼ 3.8   BL   Track on right.
3.4 ▲   BR   Track on left.

▼ 4.0   SO   Two tracks on right, track on left.
3.2 ▲   SO   Track on right, two tracks on left.

GPS: N 38°42.65' W 112°11.11'

▼ 4.1   SO   Track on left. Views on right into Flat Canyon.
3.1 ▲   SO   Track on right. Views on left into Flat Canyon.

▼ 4.2   SO   Tracks on right and left.
3.0 ▲   SO   Tracks on left and right.

▼ 4.3   SO   Track on left.
2.9 ▲   SO   Track on right.

▼ 4.5   SO   Track on left.
2.7 ▲   SO   Track on right.

▼ 4.9   SO   Seasonal closure gate.
2.3 ▲   SO   Seasonal closure gate.

GPS: N 38°43.21' W 112°11.81'

▼ 5.3   SO   Track on right.
1.9 ▲   SO   Track on left.

▼ 5.4   SO   Track on right.
1.8 ▲   SO   Track on left.

▼ 5.9   SO   Track on left.
1.3 ▲   SO   Track on right.

▼ 6.2   BR   Track on left.
1.0 ▲   SO   Track on right.

▼ 6.8   SO   Cattle guard, then track on left.
0.4 ▲   SO   Track on right, then cattle guard.

▼ 7.0   TL   T-intersection; turn left on FR 111 (PATVT#01), then pass second track on left after junction.
0.2 ▲   TR   Two tracks on right; turn right on second track, FR 105 (unmarked). Paiute ATV Trail continues straight ahead.

▼ 7.2   BL   Continue on FR 111. Track on right is FR 107 (alternate route). Campsite on right. Zero trip meter.
0.0 ▲   Continue toward Albinus Canyon.

GPS: N 38°43.39' W 112°13.96'

▼ 0.0   Continue along FR 111.
4.7 ▲   SO   Track on left is FR 107 (alternate route). Campsite on left. Zero trip meter.

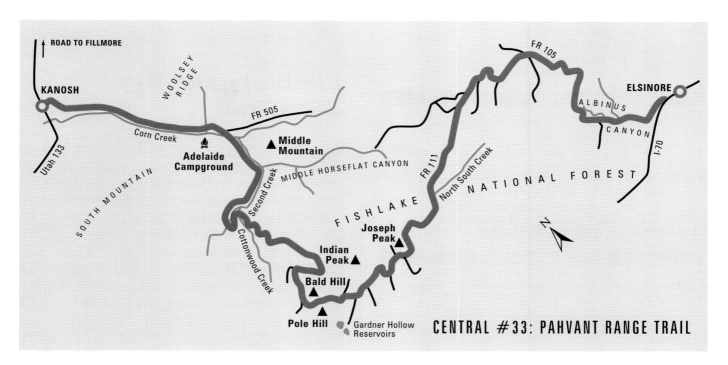

CENTRAL #33: PAHVANT RANGE TRAIL

| ▼ 0.4 | **SO** | Track on right, then leave Fishlake National Forest. Entering private property for next 3.5 miles. |
| 4.3 ▲ | **SO** | Entering Fishlake National Forest, leaving private property. Track on left. |

| ▼ 0.5 | **SO** | Cattle guard. |
| 4.2 ▲ | **SO** | Cattle guard. |

| ▼ 0.7 | **SO** | Track on right. |
| 4.0 ▲ | **SO** | Track on left. |

| ▼ 1.0 | **SO** | Cattle guard. |
| 3.7 ▲ | **SO** | Cattle guard. |

| ▼ 1.1 | **SO** | Track on left. |
| 3.6 ▲ | **SO** | Track on right. |

| ▼ 2.3 | **SO** | Log cabin on right (private). |
| 2.4 ▲ | **SO** | Log cabin on left (private). |

GPS: N 38°42.08' W 112°15.81'

| ▼ 2.9 | **SO** | Dam on left. |
| 1.8 ▲ | **SO** | Dam on right. |

| ▼ 3.2 | **SO** | Cattle guard, followed by track on left. |
| 1.5 ▲ | **SO** | Track on right, followed by cattle guard. |

| ▼ 3.7 | **BL** | Road closed on right. |
| 1.0 ▲ | **SO** | Road closed on left. |

| ▼ 3.9 | **SO** | Cattle guard; entering Fishlake National Forest. |
| 0.8 ▲ | **SO** | Cattle guard; leaving Fishlake National Forest. Enter private property for next 3.5 miles. |

GPS: N 38°41.16' W 112°16.91'

| ▼ 4.4 | **SO** | Track on left. |
| 0.3 ▲ | **SO** | Track on right. |

GPS: N 38°40.79' W 112°17.09'

| ▼ 4.7 | **TR** | Leave national forest over cattle guard; entering private property for next 4.4 miles. Zero trip meter. |
| 0.0 ▲ | | Continue northeast. |

GPS: N 38°40.76' W 112°17.40'

| ▼ 0.0 | | Continue southwest. |
| 7.4 ▲ | **TL** | Enter national forest over cattle guard; leaving private property. Zero trip meter. |

| ▼ 0.3 | **SO** | Private road on right. |
| 7.1 ▲ | **SO** | Private road on left. |

| ▼ 1.5 | **SO** | Private road on left. |
| 6.9 ▲ | **SO** | Private road on right. |

GPS: N 38°40.36' W 112°18.41'

| ▼ 1.7 | **SO** | Track on right. |
| 5.7 ▲ | **SO** | Track on left. |

| ▼ 2.3 | **SO** | Track on right is PATVST#97. |
| 5.1 ▲ | **SO** | Track on left is PATVST#97. |

GPS: N 38°40.18' W 112°19.07'

| ▼ 2.8 | **SO** | Track on right. |
| 4.6 ▲ | **SO** | Track on left. |

| ▼ 3.2 | **SO** | Crossroads. PATVT#01 goes left. |
| 4.2 ▲ | **SO** | Crossroads. PATVT#01 goes right. |

GPS: N 38°40.08' W 112°19.83'

| ▼ 3.6 | **BR** | Track on left is PATVT#01. |
| 3.8 ▲ | **SO** | Track on right is PATVT#01 |

GPS: N 38°40.01' W 112°20.17'

| ▼ 4.4 | **SO** | Leaving private property; entering Fishlake National Forest. |
| 3.0 ▲ | **SO** | Entering private property for next 4.4 miles; leaving Fishlake National Forest. |

| ▼ 4.6 | **SO** | Track on right, then track on left. |
| 2.8 ▲ | **SO** | Track on right, then track on left. |

| ▼ 4.7 | **SO** | Entering private property over cattle guard. |
| 2.7 ▲ | **SO** | Leaving private property over cattle guard. |

| ▼ 5.1 | **BR** | Track on left is private. |
| 2.3 ▲ | **SO** | Track on right is private. |

| ▼ 5.2 | **SO** | Entering National Forest over cattle guard. |
| 2.2 ▲ | **SO** | Leaving Fishlake National Forest over cattle guard. |

GPS: N 38°40.39' W 112°21.63'

| ▼ 5.6 | **SO** | Track on right. |
| 1.8 ▲ | **SO** | Track on left. |

| ▼ 6.0 | **SO** | Track on right, then track on left. |
| 1.4 ▲ | **SO** | Track on right, then track on left. |

| ▼ 6.2 | **TR** | T-intersection. Turn right; trail follows PATVT#01. |
| 1.2 ▲ | **TL** | Turn left. |

GPS: N 38°41.28' W 112°21.51'

▼ 7.0	BL	Track on right.
0.4 ▲	TR	Track on left.
▼ 7.4	TL	Turn left, trail follows PATVST#06. PATVT#01 goes right. Zero trip meter.
0.0 ▲		Continue toward Elsinore on wider trail.

GPS: N 38°41.16' W 112°20.68'

▼ 0.0		Continue toward Kanosh on narrower trail.
3.3 ▲	TR	Turn right; PATVT#01 goes left. Zero trip meter.
▼ 2.7	SO	Track on left is Cottonwood hiking trail #044.
0.6 ▲	SO	Track on right is Cottonwood hiking trail #044.
▼ 3.1	SO	Ford through small creek, then cattle guard.
0.2 ▲	SO	Cattle guard, then ford through small creek.
▼ 3.3	TR	Ford through Cottonwood Creek, then turn right on FR 106; trail follows PATVST#06. PATVT#01 goes left. Zero trip meter.
0.0 ▲		Climb away from creek on smaller trail.

GPS: N 38°43.01' W 112°22.46'

▼ 0.0		Follow along with Cottonwood Creek on right.
8.6 ▲	TL	Turn left onto unmarked smaller trail and ford Cottonwood Creek; trail follows PATVST#06. Ahead is PATVT#01. Zero trip meter.
▼ 0.1	SO	Campsite on right.
8.5 ▲	SO	Campsite on left.
▼ 1.0	SO	Track on left is FR 490 to First Creek Spring.
7.6 ▲	SO	Track on right is FR 490 to First Creek Spring.
▼ 1.6	SO	Track on right.
7.0 ▲	SO	Track on left.
▼ 2.1	SO	Track on right is Horseflat Canyon Trail.
6.5 ▲	SO	Track on left is Horseflat Canyon Trail.
▼ 2.6	SO	Cattle guard.
6.0 ▲	SO	Cattle guard.
▼ 2.7	SO	Seasonal closure gate. Trail becomes narrow graded gravel road leading down Kanosh Canyon.
5.9 ▲	SO	Seasonal closure gate.
▼ 3.1	SO	Cross over Corn Creek on bridge, then track on right is FR 505.
5.5 ▲	SO	Track on left is FR 505, then cross over Corn Creek on bridge.
▼ 3.8	SO	Adelaide National Forest Campground on left.
4.8 ▲	SO	Adelaide National Forest Campground on right.

GPS: N 38°45.24' W 112°21.93'

▼ 4.0	SO	Track on right is Leavitts Trail—vehicle use for first part only.
4.6 ▲	SO	Track on left is Leavitts Trail—vehicle use for first part only.

GPS: N 38°45.24' W 112°22.04'

▼ 6.0	SO	Seasonal closure gate and information board. Leaving Fishlake National Forest over cattle guard.
2.6 ▲	SO	Seasonal closure gate and information board. Entering Fishlake National Forest over cattle guard.
▼ 7.6	SO	Road on left.
1.0 ▲	SO	Road on right.
▼ 7.7	SO	Road is now paved.
0.9 ▲	SO	Road is now graded gravel.
▼ 8.6		Trail ends in Kanosh at the corner of Main Street and 300 South. Turn right for Utah 133 and Fillmore.
0.0 ▲		In Kanosh at corner of Main Street and 300 South, turn east following sign for FR 106. Road is paved. Zero trip meter.

GPS: N 38°47.69' W 112°26.17'

Kimberly and Big John Trail

Starting Point:	I-70, exit 17
Finishing Point:	Utah 153
Total Mileage:	29.4 miles
Unpaved Mileage:	29.4 miles
Driving Time:	4 hours
Elevation Range:	6,000–11,400 feet
Usually Open:	July to October
Difficulty Rating:	4
Scenic Rating:	10
Remoteness Rating:	+0

Special Attractions
- Panoramic mountain scenery and views.
- Moderately challenging high-mountain driving.
- Old mining remains of Kimberly and the Silver King Mine.

History
The ghost town of Kimberly, originally named Snyder City, is at the northern end of the Tushar Mountains. It was named after Peter Kimberly from Chicago, who bought the major gold mill in town in 1899, renamed it the Annie Laurie Mill, and turned the town into one of Utah's most successful gold camps. Workers earned three dollars a day in the mines, which ran seven days a week, and the town had two hotels, the Southern and Skougaard's, several saloons, a bakery, two newspapers, a dancehall, and an impregnable jail, which is now on display at Lagoon Amusement Park's Pioneer Village north of Salt Lake City. Due to the steep canyon location, the town was split into two areas: Lower Kimberly, which contained the

ATVs climbing the shelf road around Mount Belknap

mill, stores, and commercial buildings, and Upper Kimberly, the residential district, home to over 500 people.

At its height, the town earned its Wild West reputation. Butch Cassidy and his Wild Bunch were known to spend time here. Although they never touched the mine's payroll, that didn't mean the mine never lost any gold. As one story goes, the stagecoach from Kimberly was taking gold bars to the railroad at Sevier when the coach overturned and spilled the bars down a steep cliffside. Though most of the gold was recovered, the mining company never revealed its losses, and rumor has it there may still be some out there in the undergrowth.

Mine near the trail

In 1905, Peter Kimberly died and the Annie Laurie was sold to an English company that knew little about mining and less about miners. Workers, previously paid in cash, were now given paper vouchers to redeem at the company store. Many workers just up and left. The new company then ran into debt after building a new mill. The bank foreclosed in 1908, the remaining workers abandoned the mine, and Kimberly faded quickly. It didn't take many years of disuse for the mines to fall into disrepair; water flooded the shafts and caved in others.

There was a brief revival in the 1930s when a new vein was worked by 50 families, but after a few years the vein ran out and the town was once again silent.

Farther along the trail is the Silver King Mine, which was struck by Brigham Daniel Darger of Spanish Fork, Utah, in 1894. The Silver King actually mined gold, which was hauled by mule to the five arrastras on Deer Creek. There the ore was ground down before being shipped out for processing. The National Forest Service has built a quarter-mile interpretive trail that explains the mining features around the Silver King. At the start of the trail is the two-story cabin where Brigham lived with his wife, who was 14 years his junior.

Description

This fantastic trail is somewhat reminiscent of a high-altitude Colorado 4WD trail. The Kimberly and Big John Trail takes you high above the surrounding forests on narrow shelf roads, past small alpine lakes and the remains of mining ghost towns, and finishes by dropping through alpine meadows and pine forests to Big John Flat. The well-used trail is suitable for most high-clearance SUVs, and it is mainly ungraded. There are some minor rocky sections and some long sections on the north side of the saddle that could be difficult in wet weather.

The trail starts at I-70, exit 17, 22 miles south of Richfield. Take FR 113 south; it winds along Mill Creek and climbs into the Tushar Mountains. Much of the trail follows along the same route as the Paiute ATV Trail (PATVT), and you'll find ATV staging areas and clear trail markers. There are some pleasant and extremely popular campsites at the first crossing

of Mill Creek, where another trail heads up Sevier Canyon. You reach the remains of Lower Kimberly after about 7 miles; the old Annie Laurie Mill is visible on the far side of the valley, and a track leads down to more mining works.

You reach Upper Kimberly about a mile after Lower Kimberly; there are several mining remains and a log cabin standing at a trail junction. If you explore the area on foot, you can find other old cabins and forgotten relics. Just past this is a more modern artifact, a Snowtel Data Site, which measures precipitation to forecast water supplies.

The trail continues to climb along a wide shelf road to Winkler Point, which has panoramic views north. Winkler Point was named after Ernest Winkler, a former supervisor of Fishlake National Forest. The extensive remains of the Silver King Mine are 1.7 miles farther. The National Forest Service has built a short interpretive trail around the points of interest at the mine.

After Marysvale Road, the trail climbs to its highest point. The shelf road around Beaver Creek is long and rough. It is an adequate width for a full-size vehicle, with sufficient passing

A view of the trail winding down to Mud Lake

places, but drivers should be prepared to reverse up to a passing place if an oncoming vehicle is encountered. At the upper end of the shelf road, the trail comes out of the trees and runs across the bare slopes and scree around Mount Belknap. This is the narrowest part of the shelf road and the most spectacular. Far below are the upper reaches of Beaver Creek and Big Meadow. The elevation at the saddle, the highest part of the trail, between Mount Belknap and Delano Peak is over 11,400 feet, and the area contains a krummholz or elfenwood forest: the stunted trees are shaped by the prevailing winter winds and only have branches on the downwind side. There is a magnificent viewpoint here with a sweeping panorama of Mount Baldy, Mount Belknap, Gold Mountain, and Copper Belt Peak to the north and Shelly Baldy Peak, Mount Delano, and Mount Holly to the south.

From the saddle, the trail switchbacks down to Mud Lake. From here, the trail is an easy gradient as it runs south to Big John Flat. This is an extremely popular camping area, with several pit toilets and many primitive campsites. However, the forest service restricts vehicle travel across the flat itself to reduce environmental impact, so if you are vehicle camping, pick one of the many other camps or hike across the flat to your campsite.

The trail is graded and smoother after Big John Flat, and passenger vehicles can even access Big John Flat from the south in dry weather. The trail finishes on the paved Utah 153, 2.4 miles west of Elk Meadows Ski area.

Current Road Information

BLM Fillmore Field Office
35 East 500 North
Fillmore, UT 84631
(435) 743-6811

Fishlake National Forest
Beaver Ranger District
575 South Main
Beaver, UT 84713
(435) 438-2436

Map References

BLM Richfield, Beaver (incomplete)
USFS Fishlake National Forest: Beaver Ranger District
USGS 1:24,000 Marysvale Canyon, Trail Mt., Mt. Belknap, Mt. Brigham, Shelly Baldy Peak
1:100,000 Richfield, Beaver, (incomplete)
Maptech CD-ROM: King Canyon/Fillmore
Utah Atlas & Gazetteer, p. 26
Utah Travel Council #4

Route Directions

▼ 0.0   On I-70 at exit 17, turn southwest on the graded gravel FR 113, which is on the north side of the freeway, and zero trip meter. This is also Paiute ATV Side Trail #13 (PATVST#13).

8.0 ▲   Trail ends at I-70, exit 171; go east for Richfield, west for I-15.

	GPS: N 38°34.26' W 112°21.06'

▼ 0.3   SO   Cattle guard.

7.7 ▲	SO	Cattle guard.
▼ 0.8	SO	Track on left to ATV staging area.
7.2 ▲	SO	Track on right to ATV staging area.
▼ 1.1	SO	Track on right.
6.9 ▲	SO	Track on left.
▼ 1.3	SO	Cattle guard, then track on right to corral; also track on left.
6.7 ▲	SO	Track on left to corral, then cattle guard; also track on right.
▼ 1.6	SO	Track on right. Trail runs along Mill Creek.
6.4 ▲	SO	Track on left.
▼ 2.0	SO	Cross through small creek on concrete ford.
6.0 ▲	SO	Cross through small creek on concrete ford.
▼ 2.4	SO	Pass underneath I-70, then cattle guard.
5.6 ▲	SO	Cattle guard, then pass underneath I-70.
▼ 2.5	SO	Track on right is FR 115 (PATVST#5).
5.5 ▲	SO	Track on left is FR 115 (PATVST#5).

	GPS: N 38°32.83' W 112°22.90'

▼ 2.8	SO	Track on right is FR 116 to Sevier Canyon. Continue straight on main trail and cross through Mill Creek. Many campsites in this area.
5.2 ▲	SO	Cross through Mill Creek, then track on left is FR 116 to Sevier Canyon. Many campsites in this area.

	GPS: N 38°32.68' W 112°23.11'

▼ 3.7	SO	Cattle guard, entering Middle Canyon.
4.3 ▲	SO	Cattle guard, leaving Middle Canyon.
▼ 4.5	BL	Track on right, then cross over Mill Creek.
3.5 ▲	SO	Cross over Mill Creek, then track on left.

	GPS: N 38°31.26' W 112°23.57'

▼ 5.1	SO	Track on left.
2.9 ▲	SO	Track on right.
▼ 6.1	SO	Track on left.
1.9 ▲	SO	Track on right.
▼ 6.2	SO	Track on left.
1.8 ▲	SO	Track on right.
▼ 6.7	SO	Track on right to denuded old mine area. Track on left.
1.3 ▲	SO	Track on left to denuded old mine area. Track on right.
▼ 7.0	SO	Annie Laurie Mill is visible on far side of valley.

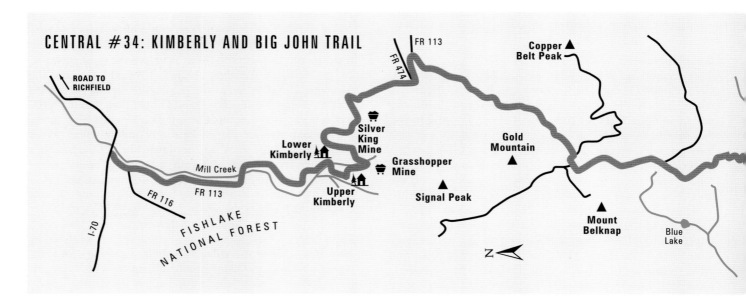

CENTRAL #34: KIMBERLY AND BIG JOHN TRAIL

1.0 ▲	SO	Annie Laurie Mill is visible on far side of valley.

GPS: N 38°29.73' W 112°23.52'

▼ 7.1	SO	Track on left.
0.9 ▲	SO	Track on right.
▼ 7.2	SO	Track on right to Lower Kimberly.
0.8 ▲	SO	Track on left to Lower Kimberly.

GPS: N 38°29.50' W 112°23.41'

▼ 7.5	SO	Track on left to old mining works and stone foundations.
0.5 ▲	SO	Track on right to old mining works and stone foundations.
▼ 7.8	SO	Mining ruins on right.
0.2 ▲	SO	Mining ruins on left.

GPS: N 38°29.18' W 112°23.73'

▼ 8.0	BL	Track on right at old cabin. This is the area of Upper Kimberly. Zero trip meter.
0.0 ▲		Continue northeast.

GPS: N 38°29.12' W 112°23.80'

▼ 0.0		Continue east.
3.4 ▲	BR	Track on left at old cabin. This is the area of Upper Kimberly. Zero trip meter.
▼ 0.1	SO	Track on right to remains of old cabin, then tracks right and left to campsites.
3.3 ▲	SO	Tracks right and left to campsites, then track on left to remains of old cabin.

GPS: N 38°29.12' W 112°23.67'

▼ 0.3	SO	Track on left to Snowtel Data Site.
3.1 ▲	SO	Track on right to Snowtel Data Site.
▼ 0.6	BL	Track on right, then small creek crossing.
2.8 ▲	SO	Small creek crossing, then track on left.
▼ 0.9	SO	Track on right. Start of shelf road.
2.5 ▲	BR	Track on left. Shelf road ends.
▼ 1.7	BR	Winkler Point. Views to the north. End of shelf road.
1.7 ▲	BL	Winkler Point. Views to the north. Start of shelf road.

GPS: N 38°29.59' W 112°22.85'

▼ 2.5	SO	Track on right.
0.9 ▲	SO	Track on left.
▼ 3.0	SO	Track on left is FR 475. PATVT#01 enters here and follows main trail.
0.4 ▲	SO	Track on left is FR 475 (continuation of PATVT#01).

GPS: N 38°29.08' W 112°21.96'

▼ 3.3	SO	ATV trail on right.
0.1 ▲	SO	ATV trail on left.
▼ 3.4	SO	Track on right is parking area for Silver King Mine interpretive trail. Zero trip meter.
0.0 ▲		Continue to climb.

GPS: N 38°28.90' W 112°22.20'

▼ 0.0		Continue descent into Spring Gulch.
2.6 ▲	SO	Track on left is parking area for Silver King Mine interpretive trail. Zero trip meter.
▼ 0.5	BL	Track on right.
2.1 ▲	SO	Track on left.
▼ 0.9	SO	Track on left.
1.7 ▲	SO	Track on right.
▼ 1.1	SO	Track on right.
1.5 ▲	SO	Track on left.
▼ 1.3	SO	Track on left is Deer Creek Trail (FR 474/PATVST#84) to US 89. Cross over Deer Creek; start of shelf road.
1.3 ▲	SO	End of shelf road; cross over Deer Creek. Track on right is Deer Creek Trail (FR 474/PATVST#84) to US 89.

GPS: N 38°28.03' W 112°21.82'

▼ 2.3	SO	Track on left; end of shelf road.
0.3 ▲	SO	Track on right; start of shelf road.

GPS: N 38°28.24' W 112°20.73'

▼ 2.6	TR	T-intersection. Turn right on FR 123 (PATVT#01) toward Big John Flat, and zero trip meter. Track on left is FR 113 (PATVST#02) to Marysvale. Seasonal closure gate; entering vehicle restricted area (remain on designated roads). Start of shelf road; Beaver Creek is below.
0.0 ▲		Continue northeast.

GPS: N 38°28.02' W 112°20.92'

▼ 0.0		Continue southwest.
8.7 ▲	TL	Seasonal closure gate; leaving vehicle restricted area. Shelf road ends. Turn left on FR 113; right is FR 113 (PATVST#02) to Marysvale. Zero trip meter. Beaver Creek is below.
▼ 2.8	SO	Track on left. Gold Mountain on right.
5.9 ▲	SO	Track on right. Gold Mountain on left.

GPS: N 38°26.20' W 112°22.54'

▼ 3.6	SO	Track on right.
5.1 ▲	SO	Track on left.

GPS: N 38°25.80' W 112°23.12'

▼ 3.8	SO	Track on left.
4.9 ▲	SO	Track on right.

GPS: N 38°25.65' W 112°23.18'

▼ 4.5	SO	Track on right, then second track on right.
4.2 ▲	SO	Track on left, then second track on left.
▼ 4.8	SO	Track on right, then trail crosses scree slope under summit of Mount Belknap.
3.9 ▲	BR	Trail crosses scree slope under summit of Mount Belknap, then track on left.
▼ 6.2	BR	Miners Park Trail #074 on left-hiking and pack use only.
2.5 ▲	BL	Miners Park Trail #074 on right-hiking and pack use only.

GPS: N 38°24.24' W 112°23.72'

▼ 6.3	SO	Track on right.
2.4 ▲	SO	Track on left.
▼ 6.8	SO	Passing through elfenwood forest. Track on right to panoramic viewpoint.
1.9 ▲	SO	Passing through elfenwood forest. Track on left to panoramic viewpoint.

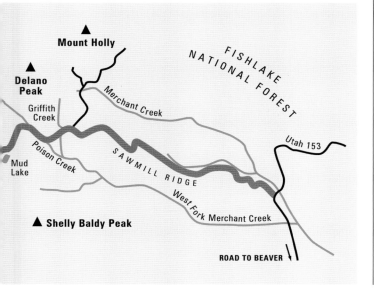

GPS: N 38°23.75' W 112°24.16'			
▼ 7.1		SO	Cross saddle between Mount Belknap and Mount Delano.
	1.6 ▲	SO	Cross saddle between Mount Belknap and Mount Delano.
GPS: N 38°23.52' W 112°23.98'			
▼ 7.7		SO	High point of trail.
	1.0 ▲	SO	High point of trail.
GPS: N 38°23.13' W 112°23.83'			
▼ 8.2		SO	Track on left to telecommunications tower.
	0.5 ▲	SO	Track on right to telecommunications tower.
GPS: N 38°22.98' W 112°23.78'			
▼ 8.7		SO	Mud Lake on right. Zero trip meter. Trail on right is Fishlake Trail #172—hiking and pack use only.
	0.0 ▲		Continue north.
GPS: N 38°22.77' W 112°24.01'			
▼ 0.0			Continue south.
	6.7 ▲	SO	Mud Lake on left. Zero trip meter. Trail on left is Fishlake Trail #172—hiking and pack use only.
▼ 0.4		SO	Cross through small creek.
	6.3 ▲	SO	Cross through small creek.
▼ 1.0		SO	Track on right.
	5.7 ▲	SO	Track on left.
GPS: N 38°22.31' W 112°23.51'			
▼ 1.1		SO	Seasonal closure gate, then cross through Poison Creek.
	5.6 ▲	SO	Cross through Poison Creek, then seasonal closure gate.
▼ 2.0		BL	Cross through Griffith Creek, then tracks right and left to campsites.
	4.7 ▲	BR	Tracks right and left to campsites, then cross through Griffith Creek.
GPS: N 38°21.70' W 112°23.60'			
▼ 2.2		SO	Skyline National Recreation Trail (hikers, horses, and bicycles only). Trail on left to Big Flat, on right to Blue Lake. Small hut, pit toilet, and forest information board at trailhead.
	4.5 ▲	SO	Skyline National Recreation Trail (hikers, horses, and bicycles only). Trail on right to Big Flat, on left to Blue Lake. Small hut, pit toilet, and forest information board at trailhead.

GPS: N 38°21.60' W 112°23.57'			
▼ 2.7		SO	Track on right.
	4.0 ▲	SO	Track on left.
▼ 2.8		SO	Pit toilet on right and many campsites on right and left.
	3.9 ▲	SO	Pit toilet on left and many campsites on left and right.
▼ 3.3		SO	Seasonal closure gate and cattle guard. Big John Flat, with many scattered campsites, on right. End of vehicle restricted area. Trail standard improves to graded road.
	3.4 ▲	SO	Big John Flat, with many scattered campsites, on left. Road becomes ungraded smaller trail. Start of vehicle restricted area (on designated roads only). Seasonal closure gate and cattle guard.
GPS: N 38°20.69' W 112°23.93'			
▼ 3.5		SO	Track on right. PATVT#01 on right; no ATVs allowed on main trail from this point.
	3.2 ▲	SO	Track on left. PATVT#01 on left; ATVs allowed on main trail from this point.
GPS: N 38°20.61' W 112°24.01'			
▼ 4.4		SO	Track on left to Hamilton Flat.
	2.3 ▲	SO	Track on right to Hamilton Flat.
▼ 5.5		SO	Track on left is PATVST#26.
	1.2 ▲	SO	Track on right is PATVST#26.
GPS: N 38°19.16' W 112°24.48'			
▼ 6.0		SO	Seasonal closure gate.
	0.7 ▲	SO	Seasonal closure gate.
▼ 6.1		SO	PATVT#01 (ATV use only) crosses main trail.
	0.6 ▲	SO	PATVT#01 (ATV use only) crosses main trail.
GPS: N 38°18.84' W 112°24.89'			
▼ 6.5		SO	Track on left is FR 128 to Sawmill Fork.
	0.2 ▲	SO	Track on right is FR 128 to Sawmill Fork.
▼ 6.7			Trail ends at paved Utah 153. Turn left for Elk Meadows ski resort and Junction (through-route in summer only), turn right for Beaver.
	0.0 ▲		On paved Utah 153, 2.4 miles west of Elk Meadows ski resort and 16 miles east of Beaver, turn north onto FR 123 and zero trip meter.
GPS: N 38°18.33' W 112°25.10'			

Selected
Further Reading

Massey, Peter, and Jeanne Wilson. *4WD Adventures: Colorado.* Castle Rock, Colo.: Swagman Publishing Inc., 1999.

—. *Backcountry Adventures: Arizona.* Castle Rock, Colo.: Swagman Publishing Inc., 2001

—. *4WD Trails: North-Central Colorado.* Castle Rock, Colo.: Swagman Publishing Inc., 1999.

—. *4WD Trails: South-Central Colorado.* Castle Rock, Colo.: Swagman Publishing Inc., 1999.

—. *4WD Trails: Southwest Colorado.* Castle Rock, Colo.: Swagman Publishing Inc., 1999.

—. *4WD Trails: Northern Utah.* Castle Rock, Colo.: Swagman Publishing Inc., 2001.

—. *4WD Trails: Southwest Utah.* Castle Rock, Colo.: Swagman Publishing Inc., 2001.

—. *4WD Trails: Central Utah.* Castle Rock, Colo.: Swagman Publishing Inc., 2001.

—. *4WD Trails: Southeast Utah.* Castle Rock, Colo.: Swagman Publishing Inc., 2001.

Akens, Jean. *High Desert Treasures: The State Parks of Southeastern Utah.* Moab, Utah: Four Corners Publications, Inc., 1990.

Akens, John. "Utah Rails." *Canyon Legacy: Planes, Trains and Automobiles: A Regional History 8.* Moab, Utah: The Southeastern Utah Society of Arts and Sciences, Winter 1990.

Alden, Peter, and Peter Friederici. *National Audubon Society Field Guide to the Southwestern States.* New York: Alfred A. Knopf, 1999.

Alexander, Thomas G. *Utah, the Right Place.* Salt Lake City: Gibbs M. Smith, Inc., 1996.

Allen, Diane, and Larry Frederick. *In Pictures: Arches and Canyonlands the Continuing Story.* Las Vegas: KC Publications, 1993.

Allen, Steve. *Canyoneering the San Rafael Swell.* Salt Lake City, Utah: University of Utah Press, 1992.

American Park Network, Utah's National Parks. San Francisco: American Park Network, 1998.

Athearn, Robert. *The Denver and Rio Grande Western Railroad.* Lincoln, Nebr.: University of Nebraska Press, 1962.

Arizona. Salt Lake City: Gibbs M. Smith, Inc., 1983.

Baars, Donald L. *The Colorado Plateau, A Geologic History.* Albequerque, N.Mex.: University of New Mexico Press, 1972.

Baker, Pearl. *The Wild Bunch at Robbers Roost.* Lincoln, Nebr.: University of Nebraska Press. 1989.

Barnes, F. A. *Canyonlands National Park: Early History and First Descriptions*, vol. 16. Moab, Utah: Canyon Country Publications, 1988.

—. *Canyon Country Explorer 2.* N.p: Canyon Country Publications, 1996.

—. *Canyon County: Off-Road Vehicle Trails—Arches and La Sals Areas.* Moab, Utah: Canyon Country Publications, 1989.

—. *Canyon County: Off-Road Vehicle Trails—Canyon Rims & Needles Areas.* Moab, Utah: Canyon Country Publications, 1990.

—. *Canyon Country: Off-Road Vehicle Trails—Canyon Rims Recreation Area.* Moab, Utah: Canyon Country Publications, 1991.

—. *Canyon Country: Off-Road Vehicle Trails—Island Area.* Moab, Utah: Canyon Country Publications, 1988.

—. *Canyon Country Camping.* Salt Lake City: Wasatch Publishers, 1991.

Barnes, Fran, and Terby Barnes. *Canyon Country Historic Remnants: Bits and Pieces of the Past.* Moab, Utah: Canyon Country Publications, 1996.

Behler, John. *National Audubon Society Field Guide to North American Reptiles and Amphibians.* New York: Alfred A. Knopf, Inc., 1996.

Bender, Henry E. *Uintah Railway: The Gilsonite Route.* New York: Heimburger House, 1970.

Bennett, Cynthia Larsen. *Roadside History of Utah.* Missoula, Mont.: Mountain Press Publishing Company, 1999.

Benson, Joe. *Scenic Driving Utah.* Helena, Mont.: Falcon Publishing, Inc., 1996.

Best, Gerald M. *Promontory's Locomotives.* San Marino, Calif.: Golden West Books, 1980.

Best Western: Utah Fun Tours. N.p, n.d.

Bickers, Jack. *Canyon Country: Off-Road Vehicle Trails—Maze Area.* Edited by F. A. Barnes. Moab, Utah: Canyon Country Publications, 1988.

Boren, Kerry Ross, and Lisa Lee Boren. *The Gold of Carre-Shinob.* Salt Lake City: Bonneville Books, 1998.

Burt, William H., and Richard P. Grossenheider. *Peterson Field Guides: Mammals.* New York: Houghton Mifflin, 1980.

Buchanan, Hayle. *Wildflowers of Southwestern Utah.* Hong Kong: Bryce Canyon Natural History Association, Inc., 1992.

Campbell, Todd. *Above and Beyond Slickrock*, rev. ed. Salt Lake City: Wasatch Publishers, 1995.

Canyon Legacy: *A Journal of the Dan O'Laurie Museum— Moab, Utah*. No. 8, 9, 10, 18, 22.

Carr, Stephen L. *The Historical Guide to Utah Ghost Towns*. Salt Lake City: Western Epics, 1972.

Carr, Stephen L., and Robert W. Edwards. *Utah Ghost Rails*. Salt Lake City: Western Epics, 1989.

Castle Country Chapter of the League of Utah Writers and Guest Writers of Carbon and Emery Counties. *Legends of Carbon and Emery Counties*. N.p., 1996.

Chronic, Halka. *Roadside Geology of Utah*. Missoula, Mont.: Mountain Press Publishing Co., 1990.

Clark, Carol. *Explorers of the West*. Salt Lake City: Great Mountain West Supply, 1997.

Colclazer, Suasan. *In Pictures-Bryce Canyon: The Continuing Story*. Las Vegas: KC Publications, 1989.

Cole, Jim. *Utah Wildlife Viewing Guide*. Helena, Mont.: Falcon Press Publishing Co., Inc., 1990.

Colwell, Joseph I. *Boulder Mountain, Throne of the Colorado Plateau*. Salt Lake City: Dixie Interpretive Association, 1992.

Combs, Barry B. *Westward to Promontory*. New York: Crown Publishers, Inc., 1969.

Cox, Douglas C., and Wilma W. Tanner. *Snakes of Utah*. Provo, Utah: Brigham Young University, 1995.

Crampton, C. Gregory. *Standing Up Country: The Canyon Lands of Utah and Arizona*. Salt Lake City: Peregrine Smith Books, 1983.

DeCourten, Frank. *Dinosaurs of Utah*. Salt Lake City: University of Utah Press, 1998.

DeJournette, Dick, and Dawn Dejournette. *One Hundred Years of Brown's Park and Diamond Mountain*. Vernal, Utah: DeJournette Enterprises, 1994.

Dixie National Forest...Land of Many Uses!. Blackner Card and Souvenir Co, n.d.

Egan, Ferol. *Frémont: Explorer for a Restless Nation*. Reno, Neva.: University of Nevada Press, 1985.

Elmore, Francis H. *Shrubs and Trees of the Southwest Uplands*. Tucson, Ariz.: Southwest Parks and Monuments Association, 1976.

Fagan, Damian. *Canyon Country Wildflowers*. Helena, Mont.: Falcon Publishing, 1998.

Fife, Carolyn Perry, and Wallace Dean Fife, eds. *Travelers' Choice: A Guide to the Best of Utah's National Parks, Monuments, and Recreation Areas*. Salt Lake City: D and C Publishing, 1998.

Fisher, Chris C. *Birds of the Rocky Mountains*. Edmonton, Canada: Lone Pine Publishing, 1997.

Foster, Mike. *The Life of Ferdinand Vandeveer Hayden*. Niwot, Colo.: Roberts Rinehart Publishers, 1994.

Godfrey, Andrew E. *A Guide to the Paiute ATV Trail*. N.p.: Fishlake Discovery Association, n.d.

Golden Spike National Historic Site. Trans-Continental, vol. 1, no. 9, 1999 edition.

Gray, Mary Taylor. *Watchable Birds*. Missoula, Mont.: Mountain Press Publishing Co., 1992.

Griggs, Jack. *All the Birds of North America*. New York: Harper Perennial, 1997.

Guild, Thelma S., and Harvey L. Carter. *Kit Carson: A Pattern for Heroes*. London: University of Nebraska Press, 1984.

Hammerson, Geoffrey A., *Amphibians and Reptiles in Colorado*. N.p.: Colorado Division of Wildlife, 1986.

Harris, Edward D. *John Charles Frémont and the Great Western Reconnaissance*. New York: Chelsea House Publishers, 1990.

Heck, Larry E. *The Adventures of Pass Patrol. Vol. 1, In Search of the Outlaw Trail*. Aurora, Colo.: Outback Publications, Inc., 1996.

—. *The Adventures of Pass Patrol. Vol. 2, 4-Wheel Drive Trails and Outlaw Hideouts of Utah*. Aurora, Colo.: Outback Publications, Inc., 1999.

—. *The Adventures of Pass Patrol. Vol. 6, 4-Wheel Drive Roads to Hole in the Rock*. Aurora, Colo.: Outback Publications, Inc., 1998.

Hemingway, Donald W. *Utah and the Mormons*. Salt Lake City: Great Mountain West Supply, 1994.

Hinton, Wayne K. *Utah: Unusual Beginning to Unique Present*. New York: Windsor Publications, Inc., 1988.

How to Identify Trees on the Ashley National Forest. N.P.: United States Department of Agriculture Forest Service, n.d.

Huegel, Tony. *Utah Byways: Backcountry Drives for the Whole Family*. Idaho Falls, Idaho: Post Company, 1996.

Johnson, David W. *Canyonlands: The Story Behind the Scenery*. N.p.: KC Publication, 1990.

Kelly, Charles. *The Outlaw Trail: A History of Butch Cassidy and His Wild Bunch*. Lincoln, Nebr.: University of Nebraska Press, 1996.

Kelsey, Michael R. *Hiking, Biking and Exploring in Canyonlands National Park and Vicinity*. Provo, Utah: Kelsey Publishing, 1992.

—. *Hiking, Climbing and Exploring Western Utah's Jack Watson's Ibex Country*. Provo, Utah: Kelsey Publishing, 1997.

—. *Canyon Hiking Guide to the Colorado Plateau*, 4th ed. Provo, Utah: Kelsey Publishing, 1999.

—. *Hiking and Exploring the Paria River*, 3rd ed. Provo, Utah: Kelsey Publishing, 1998.

—. *Hiking and Exploring Utah's Henry Mountains and Robbers Roost*, rev. ed. Provo, Utah: Kelsey Publishing, 1990.

Korns, J. Roderic, and Dale L. Morgan, eds. *West from Fort Bridger: The Pioneering of Immigrant Trails across Utah, 1846-1850*. Logan, Utah: Utah State University Press, 1994.

Kouris, Diane Allen. *The Romantic and Notorious History of Brown's Park*. Basin, Wyo.: Wolverine Gallery, 1988.

Lamb, Susan. *The Smithsonian Guides to Natural America: The Southern Rockies*. Washington, D.C.: Smithsonian Books, 1995.

Liddiard, Mary, and Jim Liddiard. *A Guide to Rock Art in Nine Mile Canyon.* N.p.: Arrowhead Enerprises Inc., 1993.

Little, Elbert L. *National Audubon Society Field Guide to North American Trees: Western Region.* New York: Alfred A. Knopf, 1996.

Madsen, Brigham D. *The Shoshoni Frontier and the Bear River Massacre.* Salt Lake City: University of Utah Press, 1985.

May, Dean L. *Utah: A People's History.* Salt Lake City: University of Utah Press, 1987.

McClenahan, Owen. *Utah's Scenic San Rafael Swell.* Castle Dale, Utah: McClenahan, 1993.

McGlashan, C.F. *History of the Donner Party.* Stanford, Calif.: Stanford University Press, 1947.

McGrath, Roger D. *Gunfighters, Highwaymen and Vigilantes.* Los Angeles: University of California Press, 1984.

McIvor, D. E. *Birding Utah.* Helena, Mont.: Falcon Publishing, 1998.

Morgan, Dale L. *Jedediah Smith and the Opening of the West.* Lincoln, Nebr.: University of Nebraska, 1953.

Mitchell, Patricia B. *Dining Cars and Depots.* N.p.: Historic Sims-Mitchell House, n.d.

Miller, David E. *Hole in the Rock.* N.p.: University of Utah Press, 1998.

Nabhan, Gary Paul, and Caroline Wilson. *Canyons of Color: Utah's Slickrock Wildlands.* Del Mar, Calif.: Tehabi Books, 1995.

National Geographic Society. *Field Guide to the Birds of North America.* Washington, DC: National Geographic Society, 1999.

National Geographic Society. *Wild Animals of North America.* Washington, DC: Book Division National Geographic Society, 1998.

Notarianni, Philip F., ed. *Carbon County: Eastern Utah's Industrialized Island,* 1st ed. Salt Lake City: Utah State Historical Society, 1981.

The Outlaw Trail Journal, 1992-1999.

Patterson, Richard. *Historical Atlas of the Outlaw West.* Boulder, Colo.: Johnson Publishing Co., 1997

Peterson, Charles S. *Utah: A Bicentennial History.* New York: W. W. Norton and Co., Inc., 1977.

Pettit, Jan. *Utes: The Mountain People.* Boulder, Colo.: Johnson Books, 1990.

Poll, Richard D., ed. *Utah's History.* Logan, Utah: Utah State University Press, 1989.

Powell, Allan Kent. *The Utah Guide.* Golden, Colo.: Fulcrum Publishing, 1995.

——. *The Utah History Encyclopedia.* Salt Lake City: University of Utah Press, 1994.

Raymond, Anan S., and Richard E. Fike, *Rails East to Promontory: The Utah Stations,* no. 8 of Cultural Resource Series. N.p.: Bureau of Land Management Utah, 1981; N.p.: Pioneer Enterprises, 1997.

Reyher, Ken. *Antoine Robidoux and Fort Uncompahgre.* Ouray,
Colo.: Western Reflections, Inc., 1998.

Rutter, Michael. *Utah: Off the Beaten Path.* Guilford, Conn.: The Globe Pequot Press, 1999.

Schneider, Bill. *Exploring Canyonlands and Arches National Parks.* Helena, Mont.: Falcon Publishing, 1997.

Schussman, Brenda, and Walters, Bob, eds. *Bald Eagle (Haliaeetus leucocephalus),* No. 3 of Wildlife Notebook Series. Salt Lake City: Utah Division of Wildlife Resources, n.d.

Shaw, Richard J. *Utah Wildflowers.* Logan, Utah: Utah State University Press, 1995.

Stebbins, Robert C. *A Field Guide to Western Reptiles and Amphibians.* Boston, Mass.: Houghton Mifflin Company, 1966.

Stuckey, Maggie, and George Palmer. *Western Trees: A Field Guide.* Helena, Mont.: Falcon Publishing, 1998.

Spellenberg, Richard. *National Audubon Society Field Guide to North American Wildflowers: Western Region.* New York: Alfred A. Knopf, 1998.

Thompson, George A. *Some Dreams Die: Utah's Ghost Towns and Lost Treasures.* Salt Lake City: Dream Garden Press, 1999.

Thrapp, Dan L. *Encyclopedia of Frontier Biography.* 3 vols. London: University of Nebraska Press, 1988.

Trenholm, Virginia Cole, and Maurine Carley. *The Shoshonis: Sentinels of the Rockies.* Norman, Okla.: University of Oklahoma Press, 1964.

Tweit, Susan J. *The Great Southwest Nature Factbook.* Anchorage, Alaska: Alaska Northwest Books, 1992.

Utah's Amphibians and Reptiles. Salt Lake City: Nongame Management Section, n.d.

Utah Historical Quarterly. Spring 2000, vol. 68, no. 2.

Utah State Historical Society. Utah History Suite CD-ROM. Provo, Utah: Historical Views, 1998-99.

Van Cott, John W. *Utah Place Names.* Salt Lake City: University of Utah Press, 1990.

Wassink, Jan L. *Mammals of the Central Rockies.* Missoula, Mont.: Mountain Press, 1993.

Weibel, Michael R. *Utah Travel Smart.* Santa Fe, N.Mex.: John Muir Publications, 1999.

——. *Utah: Travel Smart.* Santa Fe, N.Mex.: John Muir Publications, 1999.

Wells, Charles A. *Guide to Moab, UT Backroads and 4-Wheel Drive Trails.* Colorado Springs, Colo.: FunTreks, Inc., 2000.

Wharton, Gayen, and Tom Wharton. *It Happened in Utah.* Helena, Mont.: Falcon Publishing, 1998.

——. *Utah.* Oakland, Cali.: Fodor's Travel Publications, 1995.

——. *Utah.* Oakland, Cali.: Compass American Guides, 1950.

Whitney, Stephen. *The National Audubon Society Nature Guides: Western Forests.* New York: Alfred A. Knopf, 1997.

Zim, Herbert S., Ph.D., Sc.D., and Hobart M. Smith, Ph.D. *Reptiles and Amphibians* (A Golden Guide). Racine, Wisc.: Western, 1987.

Index

Hell Hole Pass Trail, 238-239
Hell Roaring Canyon Rim Trail, 121-123
Hells Backbone Trail, 286-289
Helper, 35, 405
Henderson. *See* Osiris
Henderson, William J., 39
Hendrickson, Andrew, 69
Henry Mountains, 340-341, 345
Henry, Joseph, 341
heron, great blue, 92
Herring, Johnny, 40
Hidden Canyon Rim Escape Trail, 129-130
Hidden Canyon Rim Trail, 127-129
Hidden Canyon Wash Trail, 125-127
Hidden Splendor Mine, 472, 476
Hinckley, Ira Nathaniel, 30
Hog Canyon Trail, 256-258
Hole-in-the-Rock, 26, 50-51, 282-283, 323
Hole-in-the-Rock Trail, 282-286
hollyhock, wild, 95
Holt, Nancy, 37
Holt, W. F., 39, 50
Hondoo Arch, 472
Honeymoon Trail, 244, 245-246
Horn Silver Mine, 32, 432
Horn, Tom, 66-67
Horsehoof Arch, 175
Houston. *See* Widstoe
Howarth, Jane, 48
Hudson, Spud, 167
Hudson's Bay Company, 58
hummingbird, 92
Hurrah Pass Trail, 210-212
Hurricane Cliffs Trail, 245-247

I

Ibapah, 381
Ibex, 35, 427
ibis, white-faced, 94
Idaho Loop, 367-369
Ignatio. *See* White River
"Indian Joe," 452
Indian Spring Trail, 234-236
Indiana Jones and the Last Crusade, 38
Inspiration Point Trail, 369-371

J

Jackass Benches, 447
jacking, to recover a vehicle, 19
jackrabbit, 86
Jackson, William Henry, 57, 62
Jarvie, John, 51, 62-63, 65, 408
jay, pinyon, 93
Jensen, Henry H., 489
Johansen, O. Eugene, 452
Johansen, Peter, 452
John R Flat Trail, 258-261
Johns Canyon Overlook Trail, 191-193
Johns Canyon Trail, 193-194
Johnson, 35-36, 258
Johnson, Ferg, 371
Johnson, Neils (or Nels), 32-33
Johnston, Albert Sidney, 28, 63, 80
Joshua Tree Loop, 241-243
Joshua trees, 99, 234, 241
Jug Handle Arch, 118
juniper, Rocky Mountain, 100
juniper, Utah, 99

K

Kanab, 36, 255, 258
Kane, Thomas, 63, 80
Kanosh, 517
Kanosh, Chief, 517
Kelly, Charles, 479
Kelton, 36, 377-378
Kemple, John, 43

kestrel, american, 91
Ketchum, Black Jack, 67
Kid Curry. *See* Logan, Harvey
Kimball Draw Trail, 492-495
Kimberly, 36-37, 520-521
Kimberly, Peter, 36-37, 520-521
Kimberly and Big John Trail, 520-524
King David Mine, 432-433
King, Clarence, 58
King, Samuel, 162
Kings Ferry, 162
kiva, 206
Klingensmith, Phillip, 25
Klondike Bluffs Trail, 135-137
Knight, Jesse, 44
Kodachrome Basin, 265
Kokopelli Trail, 162, 164
Koosharem, 514

L

Lake Bonneville, 27, 80-81, 371, 375, 423
Lake Powell, 276
larkspur, 96
Lane, Frank, 427
Lassie, 36
Lathrop Canyon Trail, 114-115
Lathrop, Howard, 114
Latuda, 37
Latuda, Frank, 37
Lay, Elza, 28, 51, 66-68
Lee, John D., 44, 63-64, 246, 258, 261
Lee's Ferry, 64, 258
Left Hand Fork Canyon Trail, 359-360
Levi Well Trail, 140-142
Lewis, Albert, 509
Liberty. *See* Latuda
Lick Skillet. *See* Tonaquint
lights, driving, 22
Lincoln Mine, 436-437
Lincoln Mine Trail, 436-438
Little Eva Mines, 146, 150
"Little Grand Canyon," 451
lizard, horned, 90
lizard, yellow-headed collard, 91
Logan, 37
Logan, Ephraim, 37
Logan, Harvey "Kid Curry," 68
Long Canyon Trail, 118-120
Longabaugh, Harry "The Sundance Kid," 42, 51-52, 66-69
Looking Glass Rock, 169
Lost Josephine Mine, 32
Lucin, 37, 372, 377
Lucin Cutoff, 37, 55, 372, 377
lupine, 96
Lyman, Joseph, 26
Lyman, Walter C., 26
Lynch, Patrick, 412

M

MacDonald, Graham Duncan, 25
Mack, Colorado, 416, 420
Mackenna's Gold, 255, 258, 269
Macomb, John, 58
magpie, black-billed, 91
map references, 13
maps
    Bureau of Land Management, 13
    Maptech CD-ROMs, 13
    Trails Illustrated ® maps, 13
    U.S. Forest Service maps, 13
    Utah Atlas & Gazetteer, 13
    Utah Travel Council maps, 13
Maptech CD-ROM maps, 13
marigold, marsh, 96

marmot, 86
Masterson, Bat, 53
Maxwell, C. L. "Gunplay," 69
McCarty, Tom, 69
McCartys, 412
McGath Lake Trail, 289-290
McGinnis, William, 67
McKee, James, 410
McKinley, President William, 509
Mexican Bend Trail, 449-450
Mi Vida Mine, 65, 146
Milford, 430, 432
milk snake, 90
milkweed, 96
Mill Canyon Dinosaur Trail, 133
Millville, 357
Millville Canyon Trail, 356-359
Miners Basin, 38, 226
Miners Basin Trail, 226-227
Mineral Point Trail, 120-121
Minersville, 437
mining, 82, 217-218, 226, 345, 375
    coal, 392
    copper, 33, 132, 136, 489
    gilsonite, 31, 416, 420
    gold, 33, 345, 521
    manganese, 501
    potash, 108
    silver, 430, 432
    uranium, 62-63, 108, 145-146, 221, 321, 335, 472, 474
Moab, 38, 115, 132, 154, 210, 224
Moab Jeep Safari, 129, 156, 171
Monitor and Merrimac Trail, 132-135
monkeyflower, yellow, 97
monkshood, western, 97
Montezuma, 207, 258
Montezuma Canyon Trail, 206-210
Monticello, 38, 186
Moonflower Canyon, 210
Moorehouse, Charles, 430
moose, 86
Moquith Mountains Trail, 255-256
Moran, Thomas, 57
Morgan, Rose, 69
Mormon immigration, 76-77
Mormon Pioneer Trail, 200
Mormon tea bush, 100
Morrell, Lesley, 479
Moses and Zeus Rocks, 115
moss campion, 96
mountain goat, 86-87
mountain lion, 84
Mountain Meadows Massacre, 40, 62-64
movies
    Arabian Nights, The, 36, 255
    Buffalo Bill, 36, 258
    Butch Cassidy and the Sundance Kid, 34, 249
    Cattle Drive, 269
    City Slickers II, 38
    Covered Wagon, The, 430
    Deadwood Coach, 36
    Greatest Story Ever Told, The, 271
    Indiana Jones and the Last Crusade, 38
    Mackenna's Gold, 255, 258, 269
    One Little Indian, 255
    Perfect Getaway, The, 210
    Planet of the Apes, 271
    Pony Express, 258
    Rainmaker, The, 36
    Rio Grande, 210
    Sergeants Three, 269
    Spacehunter-Adventures in the Forbidden Zone, 210
    Sundown, 47
    Thelma and Louise, 38, 47, 108
    Wagon Master, 38
mule deer, 87
Munsee, Eugene, 372

Murdock, A.M., 31
Murphy, Tom, 110
Musselman Arch, 110
Musselman, Ross A., 110
Mutual, 38
Mutual Coal Company, 38
Myton, 38-39, 399-400
Myton, H.P., 39

N

Navajo, 68, 70
Neslin. *See* Sego
Neslin, Richard, 43
Never Sweat. *See* Tonaquint
Newberry, John, 58
Newhouse, 39, 430
Newhouse, Samuel, 39, 426, 430
Nickell, Willie, 67
Nicollet, Joseph, 423
Nine Mile Canyon, 35, 49, 74,
Nine Mile Canyon Trail, 387-391
Nipple Creek and Tibbet Canyon Trail, 277-280
North and South Elk Ridge Trail, 183-185
North Long Point Trail, 181-183
Northern Shoshone, 70
Notom, 39, 321
Notom Road, 320-323
Nutter, Preston, 35, 64, 388

O

oak, gambel, 99
Odlum, Floyd, 472
Ogden, Peter, 58
Old Ephraim, 78, 364
Old Ephraim Trail, 364-365
Oliver, John, 193
Oliver, William, 79
Omni. *See* Richfield
One Little Indian, 255
Onion Creek and Thompson Canyon Trail, 222-224
Osiris, 39
Ott, Nancy Ferguson, 31
Outlaw Trail, 51-53, 407, 411, 413, 486
Overholt, Aaron, 61
Overland Stage route, 381
Overland Telegraph, 78
owl, great horned, 92

P

Pacheco, Bernardo Miera y, 76
Pahreah. *See* Paria
Pahvant Range, 509, 517
Pahvant Range Trail, 517-520
paintbrush, 96
Paiute, 57, 70, 72, 79, 251, 261
Palmer, Jimmy, 193
Palmer, William Jackson, 53
Panther. *See* Heiner
Panther Coal Mine, 35, 42
Parco Mines, 146, 150
Paria, 39-40, 265-266, 269
Paria River Valley Trail, 269-270
Parker, Maximilian, 66
Parker, Robert LeRoy. *See* Cassidy, Butch
Parowan, 77
parry primrose, 96
Pats Hole, 413
Peek-a-boo Rock, 328
Peerless, 40
Peerless Coal Company, 40
Pennell Creek Bench Trail, 339-340
Perfect Getaway, The, 210
permits, 15
Peter Sinks Trail, 366-367
petroleum, 495
phalarope, wilson's, 94-95
phlox, 96

Pick, Vernon, 472
Pierce, President Franklin, 60
pika, 85
pines
    bristlecone, 98
    limber, 100
    lodgepole, 100
    pinyon, 100
    ponderosa, 101
    red, 99
Pinto, 40
Place, Etta, 69
Planet of the Apes, 271
Pleasant Creek (Pleasant Dale). *See* Notom
Poison Strip, 145-146, 149-150
Polar Mesa Trail, 220-222
Pony Express, 258
Pony Express, 26, 28, 32, 78-79, 381
Pony Express Trail, 380-385
porcupine, 87-88
Posey Lake Road, 292-295
Posey War, 26, 79, 189-190
Potato Valley. *See* Escalante
Powell Point Trail, 314-316
Powell, John Wesley, 40, 43, 58-59, 247, 251, 324, 341, 387, 452
prairie dog, 89
Pratt, Teancum, 35
Pratt's Landing. *See* Helper
preparation of vehicle, 14
Price, 40-41
Price, William, 40
prickly pear, 101
Promontory, 41, 54-55, 377
pronghorn antelope, 88
Provost, Etienne, 58
puma, 84
Purple and Blue Lakes Trail, 302-304

R

rabbit, cottontail, 84
rabbit brush, 101
raccoon, 88
railroads
    Atchison, Topeka & Santa Fe, 53
    Carbon County Railway, 392
    Central Pacific Railroad, 54-55
    Denver & Rio Grande Western (D&RGW), 53-54
    Lucin Cutoff, 55
    Rio Grande Western Railway, 35, 53-54, 132, 385, 404, 442, 458, 461, 501
    Transcontinental Railroad, 54-55, 377, 407
    Uintah Railway, 31, 41, 48-49, 55, 416, 420
    Union Pacific Railroad, 53-55
    Utah and Pleasant Valley Railway, 53
Rainbow, 41, 416
Rainbow and Island Park Trail, 410-412
Rainbow and Watson Ghost Towns Trail, 416-419
Rainbow Rocks Trail, 138-140
Rainmaker, The, 36
Rains, 41
Rains, L. F., 41
Rampton, Calvin L., 85
Rash, Matt, 66
Rasmussen's Cave, 388
rattlesnake, 90-91
Reds Canyon Overlook Trail, 491-492
Reds Canyon Trail, 472-474
Reed, James, 76
Reed, William, 59
remoteness ratings, 12
reptiles, 90-91
Reservation Ridge Trail, 401-403
Rich, Charles C., 42
Richards, Willard, 369
Richfield, 49, 509

Richfield Pioneer Road, 509-512
Riddle, Issac, 49
Ringtail Mine, 150
Rio Grande, 210
Rio Grande Western Railway, 54
Rishel, W. D., 371
river otter, 88
road information, 12
Road Draw Road, 291-292
Robbers Roost Spring Trail, 486-487
Robbers Roost, 51-52, 66, 486
Robidoux, Antoine, 59, 495
rock art, 71, 73, 210, 387-388, 442, 499
    petroglyphs, 193, 410, 412, 465
    pictographs, 174, 395, 463
rockhounding, 423, 427, 435
    geodes, 382
Rocklands Ranch, 169
Rockville, 41-42, 247
Rockwell, Orrin Porter, 64
Rocky Mountain Fur Company, 56, 60-61
Rods Valley Trail, 470-471
Rolapp. *See* Royal
Rolapp, Henry, 42
Rollins, James, 436-438
roof racks, 22
Roughing It, 381
Round Valley, 42, 361
Roundy, Lorenzo Wesley, 25
Roundys Station. *See* Alton
route directions, 12-13
route planning, 11
Royal, 42
Rozel, 377
Ruple, Hank, 410-411
Ruple, May, 410-411
Ryan, Jim, 432

S

sagebrush, 101
Sagers Canyon Trail, 503-505
Sagers Station, 503-504
salsify, 97
"salt cedar," 102
Salt Lake Cutoff, 53
Salt Valley Road, 152-154
Salt Wash Overlook Trail, 154-155
saltbush, 101
Sand Flats Road, 224-226
Sand Wash, 42
Sand Wash ferry, 399
Sandy Ranch, 298, 321
Sawtooth Mountain Trail, 423-426
Scarecrow Peak Trail, 236-238
scenic ratings, 12
Scorup, Al, 171, 174
Seely, Orange, 28
Sego, 43, 499
Sego Ghost Town Trail, 499-501
sego lily, 97
Sergeants Three, 269
Sevier Lake, 423
Shafer Trail, 108-110
Shafer, Frank, 108
Shafer, John, 108
sheep, desert bighorn, 85
Sheepherder's End marker, 469
Shirts, Peter, 40, 265, 269
Shootaring Mill, 335
Shootering Canyon Trail, 334-337
shooting star, 97
Shoshone, 70, 73, 357
shrubs, 98-102
Shunes, Chief, 43, 251
Shunesburg, 43, 251
Sieber, Al, 67
Silver Island Mountains Loop, 374-377

About the Authors

Peter Massey grew up in the outback of Australia, where he acquired a life-long love of the backcountry. After retiring from a career in investment banking in 1986 at the age of thirty-five, he served as a director of a number of companies in the United States, the United Kingdom, and Australia. He moved to Colorado in 1993.

Jeanne Wilson was born and grew up in Maryland. After moving to New York City in 1980, she worked in advertising and public relations before moving to Colorado in 1993.

After traveling extensively in Australia, Europe, Asia, and Africa, the authors covered more than 80,000 miles touring the United States and the Australian outback between 1993 and 1997. Since then they have traveled more than 25,000 miles doing research for their two guidebook series: *Backcountry Adventures* and *4WD Trails.*

Photograph Credits

Unless otherwise indicated in the following list of acknowledgments (which is organized by section and page number), all color photographs were taken by Peter Massey and are copyrighted by Swagman Publishing Inc., or by Peter Massey.

26-55 Utah State Historical Society; **56** (upper left) Utah State Historical Society; (middle left) Denver Public Library Western History Collection; (right) Utah State Historical Society; **57** (upper & lower left) Denver Public Library Western History Collection; (lower right) Utah State Historical Society; **58-69** Utah State Historical Society; **70** Maggie Pinder and Donald McGann; **71** (left) Maggie Pinder and Donald McGann; (right) Denver Public Library Western History Collection; **72** (left) Denver Public Library Western History Collection; (right) Utah State Historical Society; **73** (both) Denver Public Library Western History Collection; **75** Joe Tucciarone, Interstell; **77-81** Utah State Historical Society; **82** (left) Utah State Historical Society; (upper & lower right) PhotoDisc; **83-86** PhotoDisc; **87** (upper left) PhotoDisc; (lower left) Robert McCaw; (right) PhotoDisc; **88** PhotoDisc; **89** (left) Denver Public Library; (upper right) Utah's Hogle Zoo; (lower right) PhotoDisc; **90** (upper left) Bushducks; (middle & lower left) Lauren J. Livo and Steve Wilcox; (upper right) Don Baccus Photography; (middle & lower right) Lauren J. Livo and Steve Wilcox; **91** (upper left) Lauren J. Livo and Steve Wilcox; (middle left) Maggie Pinder and Donald McGann; (lower left) Cornell Lab of Ornithology; (upper right) PhotoDisc; (middle right) Cornell Lab of Ornithology; (lower right) PhotoDisc; **92** (upper left) Don Baccus Photography; (upper middle left) PhotoDisc; (lower middle left) Don Baccus Photography; (lower left) PhotoDisc; (upper, middle & lower right) PhotoDisc; **93** (upper left) Don Baccus Photography; (upper middle left) Cornell Lab of Ornithology; (lower middle & lower left) Don Baccus Photography; (upper right) Cornell Lab of Ornithology (upper middle right) Don Baccus Photography; (lower middle right) Cornell Lab of Ornithology; (lower right) PhotoDisc; **94** (upper left) PhotoDisc; (lower left) Don Baccus Photography; (upper & middle right) Cornell Lab of Ornithology; (lower right) Don Baccus Photography; **95** (upper left) Don Baccus Photography; (upper middle & lower middle left) Helen Fowler Library, Denver Botanic Gardens; (lower left) PhotoDisc; (right - all) Helen Fowler Library, Denver Botanic Gardens; **96** (upper left) Helen Fowler Library, Denver Botanic Gardens; (upper middle left) Lauren J. Livo and Steve Wilcox (lower middle & lower left) Helen Fowler Library, Denver Botanic Gardens; (right - all) Helen Fowler Library, Denver Botanic Gardens; **97** (all) Helen Fowler Library, Denver Botanic Gardens; **98** (upper left) PhotoDisc; (upper middle left) Maggie Pinder and Donald McGann; (lower middle right) Maggie Pinder and Donald McGann; **99** (upper left) Doug Von Gausig, naturesongs; (lower left) Denver Botanic Gardens; (upper right) Doug Von Gausig; (middle right) Maggie Pinder and Donald McGann; **100** (upper & upper middle left) Denver Botanic Gardens; (upper middle right) Maggie Pinder and Donald McGann; (lower middle and lower right) Denver Botanic Gardens; **101** (lower middle left) Maggie Pinder and Donald McGann; (lower left) Denver Botanic Gardens; (upper right) PhotoDisc; (lower right) Doug Von Gausig; **102** (middle and lower left) Lauren J. Livo & Steve Wilcox; (upper right) Denver Botanic Gardens; (lower right) Doug Von Gausig; **108-348** Maggie Pinder and Donald McGann; **423-437** Maggie Pinder and Donald McGann; **445** Utah State Historical Society; **476-488** Maggie Pinder and Donald McGann; **491-493** Maggie Pinder and Donald McGann; **505-521** Maggie Pinder and Donald McGann.

Front cover photography: (inset) Maggie Pinder and Donald McGann

Rear cover photography: (Sego lily) Helen Fowler Library, Denver Botanic Gardens; (Cougar) PhotoDisc; (View from Northern #27: Echo Park and Yampa Bench Trail) Peter Massey; (Harvey "Kid Curry" Logan) Utah State Historical Society

ABOUT THE SERIES OF
swagman guides

The Adventures series of backcountry guidebooks are the ultimate for both adventurous four-wheelers and scenic sightseers. Each volume in the Adventures series covers an entire state or a distinct region. In addition to meticulously detailed route directions and trail maps, these full-color guides include extensive information on the history of towns, ghost towns, and regions passed along the way, as well as a history of the American Indian tribes who lived in the area prior to Euro-American settlement. The guides also provide wildlife information and photographs to help readers identify the great variety of native birds, plants, and animals they are likely to see. All you need is your SUV and your Adventures book to confidently explore all the best sites in each state's backcountry.

71 TRAILS
232 PAGES
209 PHOTOGRAPHS
PRICE $29.95
ISBN: 0-9665675-5-2

4WD Adventures: Colorado gets you safely to the banks of the beautiful Crystal River or over America's highest pass road, Mosquito Pass. This book guides you to the numerous lost ghost towns that speckle Colorado's mountains. In addition to the enormously detailed trail information, there are hundreds of photos of historic mining operations, old railroad routes, wildflowers, and native animals. Trail history is brought to life through the accounts of sheriffs and gunslingers like Bat Masterson and Doc Holliday; millionaires like Horace Tabor and Thomas Walsh; and American Indian warriors like Chiefs Ouray and Antero.

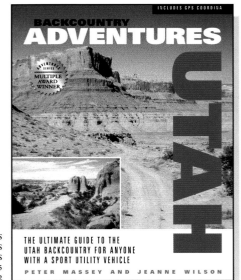

Backcountry Adventures: Utah navigates you along 3,721 miles through the spectacular Canyonlands region of Utah, to the top of the Uinta Range, across vast salt flats, and along trails unchanged since the late 19th century when riders of the Pony Express sped from station to station and daring young outlaws wreaked havoc on newly established stage lines, railroads, and frontier towns. In addition to enormously detailed trail information, there are hundreds of photos of frontier towns, historic mining operations, old rail-

175 TRAILS
544 PAGES
544 PHOTOGRAPHS
PRICE $34.95
ISBN: 1-930193-12-2

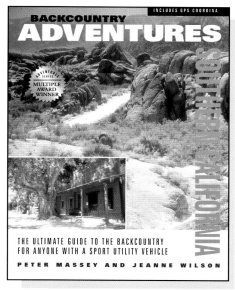

153 TRAILS
640 PAGES
645 PHOTOGRAPHS
PRICE $34.95
ISBN: 1-930193-04-1

157 TRAILS
576 PAGES
524 PHOTOGRAPHS
PRICE $34.95
ISBN: 0-9665675-0-1

road routes, wildflowers, and native animals. Trail history is brought to life through the accounts of outlaws like Butch Cassidy and his Wild Bunch; explorers and mountain men like Jim Bridger; and early Mormon settlers led by Brigham Young.

Backcountry Adventures: Arizona guides you along the back roads of the state's most remote and scenic regions, from the lowlands of the Yuma Desert to the high plains of the Kaibab Plateau. In addition to the enormously detailed trail information, there are hundreds of photos of frontier towns, historic mining operations, old railroad routes, wildflowers, and native animals. Trail history is brought to life through the accounts of Indian warriors like Cochise and Geronimo; trailblazers like Edward F. Beale; and the famous lawman Wyatt Earp, a survivor of the Shoot-out at the O.K. Corral in Tombstone.

Backcountry Adventures: Southern California takes you from the beautiful mountain regions of Big Sur, through the arid Mojave Desert, and straight into the heart of the aptly named Death Valley. In addition to the enormously detailed trail information, there are hundreds of photos of frontier towns, historic mining operations, old railroad routes, wildflowers, and native animals. Trail history is brought to life through the accounts of Spanish missionaries who first settled the coastal regions of Southern California; eager prospectors looking to cash in during California's gold rush; and legends of lost mines still hidden in the state's expansive backcountry.

Additional titles in the series will cover other states with four-wheel driving opportunities. Northern California is scheduled for release during 2002. Information on all upcoming books, including special pre-publication discount offers, can be found on the Internet at www.4WDbooks.com.

order
our award-winning guides

to order

phone	800-660-5107
internet	www.4WDbooks.com
fax	fax this order form to 303-688-4388
mail	mail this order form to Swagman Publishing, Inc. PO Box 519, Castle Rock, CO 80104

NORTHERN CALIFORNIA COMING MID-2002

Backcountry Adventure Series

copies				
_____ copies	4WD Adventures: Colorado	(ISBN: 0-9665675-5-2)	Retail: $29.95	$_____
_____ copies	Backcountry Adventures: Utah	(ISBN: 1-930193-12-2)	Retail: $34.95	$_____
_____ copies	Backcountry Adventures: Arizona	(ISBN: 0-9665675-0-1)	Retail: $34.95	$_____
_____ copies	Backcountry Adventures: S. California	(ISBN: 1-930193-04-1)	Retail: $34.95	$_____

4WD Trails Series

copies				
_____ copies	4WD Trails: South-Central Colorado	(ISBN: 0-9665675-2-8)	Retail: $14.95	$_____
_____ copies	4WD Trails: North-Central Colorado	(ISBN: 0-9665675-3-6)	Retail: $14.95	$_____
_____ copies	4WD Trails: Southwest Colorado	(ISBN: 0-9665675-4-4)	Retail: $14.95	$_____
_____ copies	4WD Trails: Northern Utah	(ISBN: 0-9665675-7-9)	Retail: $14.95	$_____
_____ copies	4WD Trails: Southwest Utah	(ISBN: 0-9665675-8-7)	Retail: $16.95	$_____
_____ copies	4WD Trails: Central Utah	(ISBN: 0-9665675-9-5)	Retail: $14.95	$_____
_____ copies	4WD Trails: Southeast Utah	(ISBN: 0-9665675-6-0)	Retail: $16.95	$_____

TOTAL PAYMENT DUE $_____
(sales tax and shipping costs will be added)

I understand that I may return any book for a full refund—for any reason, no questions asked

NAME (PLEASE PRINT) _____

COMPANY _____

STREET ADDRESS _____

CITY / STATE / ZIP _____

PHONE _____

Method of payment ❏ CHECK OR MONEY ORDER ❏ VISA ❏ MASTERCARD ❏ AMERICAN EXPRESS

CARD NUMBER _____

EXPIRATION DATE _____

CARDHOLDER'S SIGNATURE _____

call toll free and order now

order
our award-winning guides

to order

phone 800-660-5107
internet www.4wdbooks.com
fax fax this order form to 303-688-4388
mail mail this order form to Swagman Publishing, Inc.
PO Box 519, Castle Rock, CO 80104

NORTHERN CALIFORNIA COMING MID-2002

Backcountry Adventure Series

_____ copies	4WD Adventures: Colorado	(ISBN: 0-9665675-5-2)	Retail: $29.95	$_____
_____ copies	Backcountry Adventures: Utah	(ISBN: 1-930193-12-2)	Retail: $34.95	$_____
_____ copies	Backcountry Adventures: Arizona	(ISBN: 0-9665675-0-1)	Retail: $34.95	$_____
_____ copies	Backcountry Adventures: S. California	(ISBN: 1-930193-04-1)	Retail: $34.95	$_____

4WD Trails Series

_____ copies	4WD Trails: South-Central Colorado	(ISBN: 0-9665675-2-8)	Retail: $14.95	$_____
_____ copies	4WD Trails: North-Central Colorado	(ISBN: 0-9665675-3-6)	Retail: $14.95	$_____
_____ copies	4WD Trails: Southwest Colorado	(ISBN: 0-9665675-4-4)	Retail: $14.95	$_____
_____ copies	4WD Trails: Northern Utah	(ISBN: 0-9665675-7-9)	Retail: $14.95	$_____
_____ copies	4WD Trails: Southwest Utah	(ISBN: 0-9665675-8-7)	Retail: $16.95	$_____
_____ copies	4WD Trails: Central Utah	(ISBN: 0-9665675-9-5)	Retail: $14.95	$_____
_____ copies	4WD Trails: Southeast Utah	(ISBN: 0-9665675-6-0)	Retail: $16.95	$_____

TOTAL PAYMENT DUE $_____
(sales tax and shipping costs will be added)

I understand that I may return any book for a full refund—for any reason, no questions asked

NAME (PLEASE PRINT) _____

COMPANY _____

STREET ADDRESS _____

CITY / STATE / ZIP _____

PHONE _____

Method of payment ❏ CHECK OR MONEY ORDER ❏ VISA ❏ MASTERCARD ❏ AMERICAN EXPRESS

CARD NUMBER _____

EXPIRATION DATE _____

CARDHOLDER'S SIGNATURE _____

call toll free and order now

backcountry adventures series

WINNER OF FOUR PRESTIGIOUS BOOK AWARDS

"The 540-page tome is an incredible resource for getting to, and returning from, almost anywhere in Utah. Concise maps, backed with GPS, make getting lost something you'd have to do on purpose...To borrow a line from a well-known company: Don't leave home without it."

— Truck Trend

"Based on our initial experience, we expect our review copy of *Backcountry Adventures: Arizona* to be well used in the coming months... To say we'd strongly recommend this book is an understatement."

— Auto Week

"*4WD Adventures*...serves as a regional travel guide, complete with glossaries and color photos of wildflowers, animals, famous towns, and natural wonders."

— Four Wheeler Magazine

"Tired of being cooped up in your house because of the weather? This book, designed for owners of SUVs will get you out of the suburbs, off the highways, out of the cities, and into the backcountry..."

— Salt Lake Magazine

"The authors have compiled information that every SUV owner will find handy...Whether you want to know more about four-wheel driving techniques or if you are a snowmobiler or SUV owner looking for places to explore, *4WD Adventures* is the ultimate book...[They] bring the history of these trails to life through their accounts of the pioneers who built them to open up the territory to mining, ranching, and commerce in the 1800s."

— The Denver Post

"[The book]...is a massive undertaking, a textbook-size guide that seems well worth its price. Using this book, SUV owners should be able to explore areas they never knew existed, plus identify plants, animals, ghost towns and Indian history they'll see along the way."

— The Arizona Republic

"Similar to any good history book, once you get started, it's hard to put it down. Not only will it help flesh out your adventures off road, it will also broaden your appreciation of this beautiful country...The wealth of information is second to none, and the presentation makes it a pleasure to read."

— 4 Wheel Drive & Sport Utility Magazine

"This comprehensive book provides over 500 pages of photographs, maps, and detailed information about the trails and sights that make for fun 'wheeling in the Beehive State."

— Peterson's 4Wheel & Off-Road Magazine

"This book is a 10. It contains, in one volume, every kind of information I would want on a 4WD excursion."

— Awards Judge